# THE
# FINANCIAL
# CRISIS
## INQUIRY REPORT

This printing includes all corrections contained in the errata sheet issued
by the Commission as found on the FCIC website as of February 25, 2011.

# THE
# FINANCIAL
# CRISIS
## INQUIRY REPORT

FINAL REPORT OF THE NATIONAL COMMISSION
ON THE CAUSES OF THE FINANCIAL AND
ECONOMIC CRISIS IN THE UNITED STATES

Submitted by
THE FINANCIAL CRISIS INQUIRY COMMISSION
Pursuant to Public Law 111-21
January 2011

OFFICIAL GOVERNMENT EDITION

For sale by the Superintendent of Documents, U.S. Government Printing Office
Internet: bookstore.gpo.gov   Phone: toll free (866) 512-1800;   DC area (202) 512-1800
Fax: (202) 512-2104 Mail: Stop IDCC, Washington, DC 20402-0001

ISBN 978-0-16-087983-8

# CONTENTS

## PART IV: THE UNRAVELING

## PART V: THE AFTERSHOCKS

## DISSENTING VIEWS

*Index available online at www.publicaffairsbooks.com/fcicindex.pdf*

## MEMBERS OF
## THE FINANCIAL CRISIS INQUIRY COMMISSION

### Phil Angelides
*Chairman*

### Hon. Bill Thomas
*Vice Chairman*

**Brooksley Born**
*Commissioner*

**Douglas Holtz-Eakin**
*Commissioner*

**Byron Georgiou**
*Commissioner*

**Heather H. Murren, CFA**
*Commissioner*

**Senator Bob Graham**
*Commissioner*

**John W. Thompson**
*Commissioner*

**Keith Hennessey**
*Commissioner*

**Peter J. Wallison**
*Commissioner*

# COMMISSION STAFF

Wendy Edelberg, *Executive Director*
Gary J. Cohen, *General Counsel*
Chris Seefer, *Director of Investigations*
Greg Feldberg, *Director of Research*

Shaista I. Ahmed
Hilary J. Allen
Jonathan E. Armstrong
Rob Bachmann
Barton Baker
Susan Baltake
Bradley J. Bondi
Sylvia Boone
Tom Borgers
Ron Borzekowski
Mike Bryan
Ryan Bubb
Troy A. Burrus
R. Richard Cheng
Jennifer Vaughn Collins
Matthew Cooper
Alberto Crego
Victor J. Cunicelli
Jobe G. Danganan
Sam Davidson
Elizabeth A. Del Real
Kirstin Downey
Karen Dubas
Desi Duncker
Bartly A. Dzivi
Michael E. Easterly
Alice Falk
Megan L. Fasules

Michael Flagg
Sean J. Flynn, Jr.
Scott C. Ganz
Thomas Greene
Maryann Haggerty
Robert C. Hinkley
Anthony C. Ingoglia
Ben Jacobs
Peter Adrian Kavounas
Michael Keegan
Thomas J. Keegan
Brook L. Kellerman
Sarah Knaus
Thomas L. Krebs
Jay N. Lerner
Jane E. Lewin
Susan Mandel
Julie A. Marcacci
Alexander Maasry
Courtney Mayo
Carl McCarden
Bruce G. McWilliams
Menjie L. Medina
Joel Miller
Steven L. Mintz
Clara Morain
Girija Natarajan
Gretchen Kinney Newsom

Dixie Noonan
Donna K. Norman
Adam M. Paul
Jane D. Poulin
Andrew C. Robinson
Steve Sanderford
Ryan Thomas Schulte
Lorretto J. Scott
Skipper Seabold
Kim Leslie Shafer
Gordon Shemin
Stuart C. P. Shroff
Alexis Simendinger
Mina Simhai
Jeffrey Smith
Thomas H. Stanton
Landon W. Stroebel
Brian P. Sylvester
Shirley Tang
Fereshteh Z. Vahdati
Antonio A. Vargas Cornejo
Melana Zyla Vickers
George Wahl
Tucker Warren
Cassidy D. Waskowicz
Arthur E. Wilmarth, Jr.
Sarah Zuckerman

# PREFACE

The Financial Crisis Inquiry Commission was created to "examine the causes of the current financial and economic crisis in the United States." In this report, the Commission presents to the President, the Congress, and the American people the results of its examination and its conclusions as to the causes of the crisis.

More than two years after the worst of the financial crisis, our economy, as well as communities and families across the country, continues to experience the aftershocks. Millions of Americans have lost their jobs and their homes, and the economy is still struggling to rebound. This report is intended to provide a historical accounting of what brought our financial system and economy to a precipice and to help policy makers and the public better understand how this calamity came to be.

The Commission was established as part of the Fraud Enforcement and Recovery Act (Public Law 111-21) passed by Congress and signed by the President in May 2009. This independent, 10-member panel was composed of private citizens with experience in areas such as housing, economics, finance, market regulation, banking, and consumer protection. Six members of the Commission were appointed by the Democratic leadership of Congress and four members by the Republican leadership.

The Commission's statutory instructions set out 22 specific topics for inquiry and called for the examination of the collapse of major financial institutions that failed or would have failed if not for exceptional assistance from the government. This report fulfills these mandates. In addition, the Commission was instructed to refer to the attorney general of the United States and any appropriate state attorney general any person that the Commission found may have violated the laws of the United States in relation to the crisis. Where the Commission found such potential violations, it referred those matters to the appropriate authorities. The Commission used the authority it was given to issue subpoenas to compel testimony and the production of documents, but in the vast majority of instances, companies and individuals voluntarily cooperated with this inquiry.

In the course of its research and investigation, the Commission reviewed millions of pages of documents, interviewed more than 700 witnesses, and held 19 days of public hearings in New York, Washington, D.C., and communities across the country

that were hard hit by the crisis. The Commission also drew from a large body of existing work about the crisis developed by congressional committees, government agencies, academics, journalists, legal investigators, and many others.

We have tried in this report to explain in clear, understandable terms how our complex financial system worked, how the pieces fit together, and how the crisis occurred. Doing so required research into broad and sometimes arcane subjects, such as mortgage lending and securitization, derivatives, corporate governance, and risk management. To bring these subjects out of the realm of the abstract, we conducted case study investigations of specific financial firms—and in many cases specific facets of these institutions—that played pivotal roles. Those institutions included American International Group (AIG), Bear Stearns, Citigroup, Countrywide Financial, Fannie Mae, Goldman Sachs, Lehman Brothers, Merrill Lynch, Moody's, and Wachovia. We looked more generally at the roles and actions of scores of other companies.

We also studied relevant policies put in place by successive Congresses and administrations. And importantly, we examined the roles of policy makers and regulators, including at the Federal Deposit Insurance Corporation, the Federal Reserve Board, the Federal Reserve Bank of New York, the Department of Housing and Urban Development, the Office of the Comptroller of the Currency, the Office of Federal Housing Enterprise Oversight (and its successor, the Federal Housing Finance Agency), the Office of Thrift Supervision, the Securities and Exchange Commission, and the Treasury Department.

Of course, there is much work the Commission did not undertake. Congress did not ask the Commission to offer policy recommendations, but required it to delve into what caused the crisis. In that sense, the Commission has functioned somewhat like the National Transportation Safety Board, which investigates aviation and other transportation accidents so that knowledge of the probable causes can help avoid future accidents. Nor were we tasked with evaluating the federal law (the Troubled Asset Relief Program, known as TARP) that provided financial assistance to major financial institutions. That duty was assigned to the Congressional Oversight Panel and the Special Inspector General for TARP.

This report is not the sole repository of what the panel found. A website—www.fcic.gov—will host a wealth of information beyond what could be presented here. It will contain a stockpile of materials—including documents and emails, video of the Commission's public hearings, testimony, and supporting research—that can be studied for years to come. Much of what is footnoted in this report can be found on the website. In addition, more materials that cannot be released yet for various reasons will eventually be made public through the National Archives and Records Administration.

Our work reflects the extraordinary commitment and knowledge of the members of the Commission who were accorded the honor of this public service. We also benefited immensely from the perspectives shared with commissioners by thousands of concerned Americans through their letters and emails. And we are grateful to the hundreds of individuals and organizations that offered expertise, information, and personal accounts in extensive interviews, testimony, and discussions with the Commission.

We want to thank the Commission staff, and in particular, Wendy Edelberg, our executive director, for the professionalism, passion, and long hours they brought to this mission in service of their country. This report would not have been possible without their extraordinary dedication.

With this report and our website, the Commission's work comes to a close. We present what we have found in the hope that readers can use this report to reach their own conclusions, even as the comprehensive historical record of this crisis continues to be written.

# CONCLUSIONS OF THE
# FINANCIAL CRISIS INQUIRY COMMISSION

The Financial Crisis Inquiry Commission has been called upon to examine the financial and economic crisis that has gripped our country and explain its causes to the American people. We are keenly aware of the significance of our charge, given the economic damage that America has suffered in the wake of the greatest financial crisis since the Great Depression.

Our task was first to determine what happened and how it happened so that we could understand why it happened. Here we present our conclusions. We encourage the American people to join us in making their own assessments based on the evidence gathered in our inquiry. If we do not learn from history, we are unlikely to fully recover from it. Some on Wall Street and in Washington with a stake in the status quo may be tempted to wipe from memory the events of this crisis, or to suggest that no one could have foreseen or prevented them. This report endeavors to expose the facts, identify responsibility, unravel myths, and help us understand how the crisis could have been avoided. It is an attempt to record history, not to rewrite it, nor allow it to be rewritten.

To help our fellow citizens better understand this crisis and its causes, we also present specific conclusions at the end of chapters in Parts III, IV, and V of this report.

The subject of this report is of no small consequence to this nation. The profound events of 2007 and 2008 were neither bumps in the road nor an accentuated dip in the financial and business cycles we have come to expect in a free market economic system. This was a fundamental disruption—a financial upheaval, if you will—that wreaked havoc in communities and neighborhoods across this country.

As this report goes to print, there are more than 26 million Americans who are out of work, cannot find full-time work, or have given up looking for work. About four million families have lost their homes to foreclosure and another four and a half million have slipped into the foreclosure process or are seriously behind on their mortgage payments. Nearly $11 trillion in household wealth has vanished, with retirement accounts and life savings swept away. Businesses, large and small, have felt

the sting of a deep recession. There is much anger about what has transpired, and justifiably so. Many people who abided by all the rules now find themselves out of work and uncertain about their future prospects. The collateral damage of this crisis has been real people and real communities. The impacts of this crisis are likely to be felt for a generation. And the nation faces no easy path to renewed economic strength.

Like so many Americans, we began our exploration with our own views and some preliminary knowledge about how the world's strongest financial system came to the brink of collapse. Even at the time of our appointment to this independent panel, much had already been written and said about the crisis. Yet all of us have been deeply affected by what we have learned in the course of our inquiry. We have been at various times fascinated, surprised, and even shocked by what we saw, heard, and read. Ours has been a journey of revelation.

Much attention over the past two years has been focused on the decisions by the federal government to provide massive financial assistance to stabilize the financial system and rescue large financial institutions that were deemed too systemically important to fail. Those decisions—and the deep emotions surrounding them—will be debated long into the future. But our mission was to ask and answer this central question: *how did it come to pass that in 2008 our nation was forced to choose between two stark and painful alternatives*—either risk the total collapse of our financial system and economy or inject trillions of taxpayer dollars into the financial system and an array of companies, as millions of Americans still lost their jobs, their savings, and their homes?

In this report, we detail the events of the crisis. But a simple summary, as we see it, is useful at the outset. While the vulnerabilities that created the potential for crisis were years in the making, it was the collapse of the housing bubble—fueled by low interest rates, easy and available credit, scant regulation, and toxic mortgages—that was the spark that ignited a string of events, which led to a full-blown crisis in the fall of 2008. Trillions of dollars in risky mortgages had become embedded throughout the financial system, as mortgage-related securities were packaged, repackaged, and sold to investors around the world. When the bubble burst, hundreds of billions of dollars in losses in mortgages and mortgage-related securities shook markets as well as financial institutions that had significant exposures to those mortgages and had borrowed heavily against them. This happened not just in the United States but around the world. The losses were magnified by derivatives such as synthetic securities.

The crisis reached seismic proportions in September 2008 with the failure of Lehman Brothers and the impending collapse of the insurance giant American International Group (AIG). Panic fanned by a lack of transparency of the balance sheets of major financial institutions, coupled with a tangle of interconnections among institutions perceived to be "too big to fail," caused the credit markets to seize up. Trading ground to a halt. The stock market plummeted. The economy plunged into a deep recession.

The financial system we examined bears little resemblance to that of our parents' generation. The changes in the past three decades alone have been remarkable. The

financial markets have become increasingly globalized. Technology has transformed the efficiency, speed, and complexity of financial instruments and transactions. There is broader access to and lower costs of financing than ever before. And the financial sector itself has become a much more dominant force in our economy.

From 1978 to 2007, the amount of debt held by the financial sector soared from $3 trillion to $36 trillion, more than doubling as a share of gross domestic product. The very nature of many Wall Street firms changed—from relatively staid private partnerships to publicly traded corporations taking greater and more diverse kinds of risks. By 2005, the 10 largest U.S. commercial banks held 55% of the industry's assets, more than double the level held in 1990. On the eve of the crisis in 2006, financial sector profits constituted 27% of all corporate profits in the United States, up from 15% in 1980. Understanding this transformation has been critical to the Commission's analysis.

Now to our major findings and conclusions, which are based on the facts contained in this report: they are offered with the hope that lessons may be learned to help avoid future catastrophe.

- **We conclude this financial crisis was avoidable.** The crisis was the result of human action and inaction, not of Mother Nature or computer models gone haywire. The captains of finance and the public stewards of our financial system ignored warnings and failed to question, understand, and manage evolving risks within a system essential to the well-being of the American public. Theirs was a big miss, not a stumble. While the business cycle cannot be repealed, a crisis of this magnitude need not have occurred. To paraphrase Shakespeare, the fault lies not in the stars, but in us.

Despite the expressed view of many on Wall Street and in Washington that the crisis could not have been foreseen or avoided, there were warning signs. The tragedy was that they were ignored or discounted. There was an explosion in risky subprime lending and securitization, an unsustainable rise in housing prices, widespread reports of egregious and predatory lending practices, dramatic increases in household mortgage debt, and exponential growth in financial firms' trading activities, unregulated derivatives, and short-term "repo" lending markets, among many other red flags. Yet there was pervasive permissiveness; little meaningful action was taken to quell the threats in a timely manner.

The prime example is the Federal Reserve's pivotal failure to stem the flow of toxic mortgages, which it could have done by setting prudent mortgage-lending standards. The Federal Reserve was the one entity empowered to do so and it did not. The record of our examination is replete with evidence of other failures: financial institutions made, bought, and sold mortgage securities they never examined, did not care to examine, or knew to be defective; firms depended on tens of billions of dollars of borrowing that had to be renewed each and every night, secured by subprime mortgage securities; and major firms and investors blindly relied on credit rating agencies as their arbiters of risk. What else could one expect on a highway where there were neither speed limits nor neatly painted lines?

• **We conclude widespread failures in financial regulation and supervision proved devastating to the stability of the nation's financial markets.** The sentries were not at their posts, in no small part due to the widely accepted faith in the self-correcting nature of the markets and the ability of financial institutions to effectively police themselves. More than 30 years of deregulation and reliance on self-regulation by financial institutions, championed by former Federal Reserve chairman Alan Greenspan and others, supported by successive administrations and Congresses, and actively pushed by the powerful financial industry at every turn, had stripped away key safeguards, which could have helped avoid catastrophe. This approach had opened up gaps in oversight of critical areas with trillions of dollars at risk, such as the shadow banking system and over-the-counter derivatives markets. In addition, the government permitted financial firms to pick their preferred regulators in what became a race to the weakest supervisor.

Yet we do not accept the view that regulators lacked the power to protect the financial system. They had ample power in many arenas and they chose not to use it. To give just three examples: the Securities and Exchange Commission could have required more capital and halted risky practices at the big investment banks. It did not. The Federal Reserve Bank of New York and other regulators could have clamped down on Citigroup's excesses in the run-up to the crisis. They did not. Policy makers and regulators could have stopped the runaway mortgage securitization train. They did not. In case after case after case, regulators continued to rate the institutions they oversaw as safe and sound even in the face of mounting troubles, often downgrading them just before their collapse. And where regulators lacked authority, they could have sought it. Too often, they lacked the political will—in a political and ideological environment that constrained it—as well as the fortitude to critically challenge the institutions and the entire system they were entrusted to oversee.

Changes in the regulatory system occurred in many instances as financial markets evolved. But as the report will show, the financial industry itself played a key role in weakening regulatory constraints on institutions, markets, and products. It did not surprise the Commission that an industry of such wealth and power would exert pressure on policy makers and regulators. From 1999 to 2008, the financial sector expended $2.7 billion in reported federal lobbying expenses; individuals and political action committees in the sector made more than $1 billion in campaign contributions. What troubled us was the extent to which the nation was deprived of the necessary strength and independence of the oversight necessary to safeguard financial stability.

• **We conclude dramatic failures of corporate governance and risk management at many systemically important financial institutions were a key cause of this crisis.** There was a view that instincts for self-preservation inside major financial firms would shield them from fatal risk-taking without the need for a steady regulatory hand, which, the firms argued, would stifle innovation. Too many of these institutions acted recklessly, taking on too much risk, with too little capital, and with too much dependence on short-term funding. In many respects, this reflected a funda-

mental change in these institutions, particularly the large investment banks and bank holding companies, which focused their activities increasingly on risky trading activities that produced hefty profits. They took on enormous exposures in acquiring and supporting subprime lenders and creating, packaging, repackaging, and selling trillions of dollars in mortgage-related securities, including synthetic financial products. Like Icarus, they never feared flying ever closer to the sun.

Many of these institutions grew aggressively through poorly executed acquisition and integration strategies that made effective management more challenging. The CEO of Citigroup told the Commission that a $40 billion position in highly rated mortgage securities would "not in any way have excited my attention," and the co-head of Citigroup's investment bank said he spent "a small fraction of 1%" of his time on those securities. In this instance, too big to fail meant too big to manage.

Financial institutions and credit rating agencies embraced mathematical models as reliable predictors of risks, replacing judgment in too many instances. Too often, risk management became risk justification.

Compensation systems—designed in an environment of cheap money, intense competition, and light regulation—too often rewarded the quick deal, the short-term gain—without proper consideration of long-term consequences. Often, those systems encouraged the big bet—where the payoff on the upside could be huge and the downside limited. This was the case up and down the line—from the corporate boardroom to the mortgage broker on the street.

Our examination revealed stunning instances of governance breakdowns and irresponsibility. You will read, among other things, about AIG senior management's ignorance of the terms and risks of the company's $79 billion derivatives exposure to mortgage-related securities; Fannie Mae's quest for bigger market share, profits, and bonuses, which led it to ramp up its exposure to risky loans and securities as the housing market was peaking; and the costly surprise when Merrill Lynch's top management realized that the company held $55 billion in "super-senior" and supposedly "super-safe" mortgage-related securities that resulted in billions of dollars in losses.

- **We conclude a combination of excessive borrowing, risky investments, and lack of transparency put the financial system on a collision course with crisis.** Clearly, this vulnerability was related to failures of corporate governance and regulation, but it is significant enough by itself to warrant our attention here.

In the years leading up to the crisis, too many financial institutions, as well as too many households, borrowed to the hilt, leaving them vulnerable to financial distress or ruin if the value of their investments declined even modestly. For example, as of 2007, the five major investment banks—Bear Stearns, Goldman Sachs, Lehman Brothers, Merrill Lynch, and Morgan Stanley—were operating with extraordinarily thin capital. By one measure, their leverage ratios were as high as 40 to 1, meaning for every $40 in assets, there was only $1 in capital to cover losses. Less than a 3% drop in asset values could wipe out a firm. To make matters worse, much of their borrowing was short-term, in the overnight market—meaning the borrowing had to be renewed each and every day. For example, at the end of 2007, Bear Stearns had $11.8 billion in

equity and $383.6 billion in liabilities and was borrowing as much as $70 billion in the overnight market. It was the equivalent of a small business with $50,000 in equity borrowing $1.6 million, with $296,750 of that due each and every day. One can't really ask "What were they thinking?" when it seems that too many of them were thinking alike.

And the leverage was often hidden—in derivatives positions, in off-balance-sheet entities, and through "window dressing" of financial reports available to the investing public.

The kings of leverage were Fannie Mae and Freddie Mac, the two behemoth government-sponsored enterprises (GSEs). For example, by the end of 2007, Fannie's and Freddie's combined leverage ratio, including loans they owned and guaranteed, stood at 75 to 1.

But financial firms were not alone in the borrowing spree: from 2001 to 2007, national mortgage debt almost doubled, and the amount of mortgage debt per household rose more than 63% from $91,500 to $149,500, even while wages were essentially stagnant. When the housing downturn hit, heavily indebted financial firms and families alike were walloped.

The heavy debt taken on by some financial institutions was exacerbated by the risky assets they were acquiring with that debt. As the mortgage and real estate markets churned out riskier and riskier loans and securities, many financial institutions loaded up on them. By the end of 2007, Lehman had amassed $111 billion in commercial and residential real estate holdings and securities, which was almost twice what it held just two years before, and more than four times its total equity. And again, the risk wasn't being taken on just by the big financial firms, but by families, too. Nearly one in 10 mortgage borrowers in 2005 and 2006 took out "option ARM" loans, which meant they could choose to make payments so low that their mortgage balances rose every month.

Within the financial system, the dangers of this debt were magnified because transparency was not required or desired. Massive, short-term borrowing, combined with obligations unseen by others in the market, heightened the chances the system could rapidly unravel. In the early part of the 20th century, we erected a series of protections—the Federal Reserve as a lender of last resort, federal deposit insurance, ample regulations—to provide a bulwark against the panics that had regularly plagued America's banking system in the 19th century. Yet, over the past 30-plus years, we permitted the growth of a shadow banking system—opaque and laden with short-term debt—that rivaled the size of the traditional banking system. Key components of the market—for example, the multitrillion-dollar repo lending market, off-balance-sheet entities, and the use of over-the-counter derivatives—were hidden from view, without the protections we had constructed to prevent financial meltdowns. We had a 21st-century financial system with 19th-century safeguards.

When the housing and mortgage markets cratered, the lack of transparency, the extraordinary debt loads, the short-term loans, and the risky assets all came home to roost. What resulted was panic. We had reaped what we had sown.

- **We conclude the government was ill prepared for the crisis, and its inconsistent response added to the uncertainty and panic in the financial markets.** As part of our charge, it was appropriate to review government actions taken in response to the developing crisis, not just those policies or actions that preceded it, to determine if any of those responses contributed to or exacerbated the crisis.

As our report shows, key policy makers—the Treasury Department, the Federal Reserve Board, and the Federal Reserve Bank of New York—who were best positioned to watch over our markets were ill prepared for the events of 2007 and 2008. Other agencies were also behind the curve. They were hampered because they did not have a clear grasp of the financial system they were charged with overseeing, particularly as it had evolved in the years leading up to the crisis. This was in no small measure due to the lack of transparency in key markets. They thought risk had been diversified when, in fact, it had been concentrated. Time and again, from the spring of 2007 on, policy makers and regulators were caught off guard as the contagion spread, responding on an ad hoc basis with specific programs to put fingers in the dike. There was no comprehensive and strategic plan for containment, because they lacked a full understanding of the risks and interconnections in the financial markets. Some regulators have conceded this error. We had allowed the system to race ahead of our ability to protect it.

While there was some awareness of, or at least a debate about, the housing bubble, the record reflects that senior public officials did not recognize that a bursting of the bubble could threaten the entire financial system. Throughout the summer of 2007, both Federal Reserve Chairman Ben Bernanke and Treasury Secretary Henry Paulson offered public assurances that the turmoil in the subprime mortgage markets would be contained. When Bear Stearns's hedge funds, which were heavily invested in mortgage-related securities, imploded in June 2007, the Federal Reserve discussed the implications of the collapse. Despite the fact that so many other funds were exposed to the same risks as those hedge funds, the Bear Stearns funds were thought to be "relatively unique." Days before the collapse of Bear Stearns in March 2008, SEC Chairman Christopher Cox expressed "comfort about the capital cushions" at the big investment banks. It was not until August 2008, just weeks before the government takeover of Fannie Mae and Freddie Mac, that the Treasury Department understood the full measure of the dire financial conditions of those two institutions. And just a month before Lehman's collapse, the Federal Reserve Bank of New York was still seeking information on the exposures created by Lehman's more than 900,000 derivatives contracts.

In addition, the government's inconsistent handling of major financial institutions during the crisis—the decision to rescue Bear Stearns and then to place Fannie Mae and Freddie Mac into conservatorship, followed by its decision not to save Lehman Brothers and then to save AIG—increased uncertainty and panic in the market.

In making these observations, we deeply respect and appreciate the efforts made by Secretary Paulson, Chairman Bernanke, and Timothy Geithner, formerly president of the Federal Reserve Bank of New York and now treasury secretary, and so

many others who labored to stabilize our financial system and our economy in the most chaotic and challenging of circumstances.

- **We conclude there was a systemic breakdown in accountability and ethics.** The integrity of our financial markets and the public's trust in those markets are essential to the economic well-being of our nation. The soundness and the sustained prosperity of the financial system and our economy rely on the notions of fair dealing, responsibility, and transparency. In our economy, we expect businesses and individuals to pursue profits, at the same time that they produce products and services of quality and conduct themselves well.

Unfortunately—as has been the case in past speculative booms and busts—we witnessed an erosion of standards of responsibility and ethics that exacerbated the financial crisis. This was not universal, but these breaches stretched from the ground level to the corporate suites. They resulted not only in significant financial consequences but also in damage to the trust of investors, businesses, and the public in the financial system.

For example, our examination found, according to one measure, that the percentage of borrowers who defaulted on their mortgages within just a matter of months after taking a loan nearly doubled from the summer of 2006 to late 2007. This data indicates they likely took out mortgages that they never had the capacity or intention to pay. You will read about mortgage brokers who were paid "yield spread premiums" by lenders to put borrowers into higher-cost loans so they would get bigger fees, often never disclosed to borrowers. The report catalogues the rising incidence of mortgage fraud, which flourished in an environment of collapsing lending standards and lax regulation. The number of suspicious activity reports—reports of possible financial crimes filed by depository banks and their affiliates—related to mortgage fraud grew 20-fold between 1996 and 2005 and then more than doubled again between 2005 and 2009. One study places the losses resulting from fraud on mortgage loans made between 2005 and 2007 at $112 billion.

Lenders made loans that they knew borrowers could not afford and that could cause massive losses to investors in mortgage securities. As early as September 2004, Countrywide executives recognized that many of the loans they were originating could result in "catastrophic consequences." Less than a year later, they noted that certain high-risk loans they were making could result not only in foreclosures but also in "financial and reputational catastrophe" for the firm. But they did not stop.

And the report documents that major financial institutions ineffectively sampled loans they were purchasing to package and sell to investors. They knew a significant percentage of the sampled loans did not meet their own underwriting standards or those of the originators. Nonetheless, they sold those securities to investors. The Commission's review of many prospectuses provided to investors found that this critical information was not disclosed.

THESE CONCLUSIONS must be viewed in the context of human nature and individual and societal responsibility. First, to pin this crisis on mortal flaws like greed and

hubris would be simplistic. It was the failure to account for human weakness that is relevant to this crisis.

Second, we clearly believe the crisis was a result of human mistakes, misjudgments, and misdeeds that resulted in systemic failures for which our nation has paid dearly. As you read this report, you will see that specific firms and individuals acted irresponsibly. Yet a crisis of this magnitude cannot be the work of a few bad actors, and such was not the case here. At the same time, the breadth of this crisis does not mean that "everyone is at fault"; many firms and individuals did not participate in the excesses that spawned disaster.

We do place special responsibility with the public leaders charged with protecting our financial system, those entrusted to run our regulatory agencies, and the chief executives of companies whose failures drove us to crisis. These individuals sought and accepted positions of significant responsibility and obligation. Tone at the top does matter and, in this instance, we were let down. No one said "no."

But as a nation, we must also accept responsibility for what we permitted to occur. Collectively, but certainly not unanimously, we acquiesced to or embraced a system, a set of policies and actions, that gave rise to our present predicament.

<p style="text-align:center">* * *</p>

THIS REPORT DESCRIBES THE EVENTS and the system that propelled our nation toward crisis. The complex machinery of our financial markets has many essential gears—some of which played a critical role as the crisis developed and deepened. Here we render our conclusions about specific components of the system that we believe contributed significantly to the financial meltdown.

- **We conclude collapsing mortgage-lending standards and the mortgage securitization pipeline lit and spread the flame of contagion and crisis.** When housing prices fell and mortgage borrowers defaulted, the lights began to dim on Wall Street. This report catalogues the corrosion of mortgage-lending standards and the securitization pipeline that transported toxic mortgages from neighborhoods across America to investors around the globe.

Many mortgage lenders set the bar so low that lenders simply took eager borrowers' qualifications on faith, often with a willful disregard for a borrower's ability to pay. Nearly one-quarter of all mortgages made in the first half of 2005 were interest-only loans. During the same year, 68% of "option ARM" loans originated by Countrywide and Washington Mutual had low- or no-documentation requirements.

These trends were not secret. As irresponsible lending, including predatory and fraudulent practices, became more prevalent, the Federal Reserve and other regulators and authorities heard warnings from many quarters. Yet the Federal Reserve neglected its mission "to ensure the safety and soundness of the nation's banking and financial system and to protect the credit rights of consumers." It failed to build the retaining wall before it was too late. And the Office of the Comptroller of the Currency and the Office of Thrift Supervision, caught up in turf wars, preempted state regulators from reining in abuses.

While many of these mortgages were kept on banks' books, the bigger money came from global investors who clamored to put their cash into newly created mortgage-related securities. It appeared to financial institutions, investors, and regulators alike that risk had been conquered: the investors held highly rated securities they thought were sure to perform; the banks thought they had taken the riskiest loans off their books; and regulators saw firms making profits and borrowing costs reduced. But each step in the mortgage securitization pipeline depended on the next step to keep demand going. From the speculators who flipped houses to the mortgage brokers who scouted the loans, to the lenders who issued the mortgages, to the financial firms that created the mortgage-backed securities, collateralized debt obligations (CDOs), CDOs squared, and synthetic CDOs: no one in this pipeline of toxic mortgages had enough skin in the game. They all believed they could off-load their risks on a moment's notice to the next person in line. They were wrong. When borrowers stopped making mortgage payments, the losses—amplified by derivatives—rushed through the pipeline. As it turned out, these losses were concentrated in a set of systemically important financial institutions.

In the end, the system that created millions of mortgages so efficiently has proven to be difficult to unwind. Its complexity has erected barriers to modifying mortgages so families can stay in their homes and has created further uncertainty about the health of the housing market and financial institutions.

- **We conclude over-the-counter derivatives contributed significantly to this crisis.** The enactment of legislation in 2000 to ban the regulation by both the federal and state governments of over-the-counter (OTC) derivatives was a key turning point in the march toward the financial crisis.

From financial firms to corporations, to farmers, and to investors, derivatives have been used to hedge against, or speculate on, changes in prices, rates, or indices or even on events such as the potential defaults on debts. Yet, without any oversight, OTC derivatives rapidly spiraled out of control and out of sight, growing to $673 trillion in notional amount. This report explains the uncontrolled leverage; lack of transparency, capital, and collateral requirements; speculation; interconnections among firms; and concentrations of risk in this market.

OTC derivatives contributed to the crisis in three significant ways. First, one type of derivative—credit default swaps (CDS)—fueled the mortgage securitization pipeline. CDS were sold to investors to protect against the default or decline in value of mortgage-related securities backed by risky loans. Companies sold protection—to the tune of $79 billion, in AIG's case—to investors in these newfangled mortgage securities, helping to launch and expand the market and, in turn, to further fuel the housing bubble.

Second, CDS were essential to the creation of synthetic CDOs. These synthetic CDOs were merely bets on the performance of real mortgage-related securities. They amplified the losses from the collapse of the housing bubble by allowing multiple bets on the same securities and helped spread them throughout the financial system. Goldman Sachs alone packaged and sold $73 billion in synthetic CDOs from July 1,

2004, to May 31, 2007. Synthetic CDOs created by Goldman referenced more than 3,400 mortgage securities, and 610 of them were referenced at least twice. This is apart from how many times these securities may have been referenced in synthetic CDOs created by other firms.

Finally, when the housing bubble popped and crisis followed, derivatives were in the center of the storm. AIG, which had not been required to put aside capital reserves as a cushion for the protection it was selling, was bailed out when it could not meet its obligations. The government ultimately committed more than $180 billion because of concerns that AIG's collapse would trigger cascading losses throughout the global financial system. In addition, the existence of millions of derivatives contracts of all types between systemically important financial institutions—unseen and unknown in this unregulated market—added to uncertainty and escalated panic, helping to precipitate government assistance to those institutions.

• **We conclude the failures of credit rating agencies were essential cogs in the wheel of financial destruction.** The three credit rating agencies were key enablers of the financial meltdown. The mortgage-related securities at the heart of the crisis could not have been marketed and sold without their seal of approval. Investors relied on them, often blindly. In some cases, they were obligated to use them, or regulatory capital standards were hinged on them. This crisis could not have happened without the rating agencies. Their ratings helped the market soar and their downgrades through 2007 and 2008 wreaked havoc across markets and firms.

In our report, you will read about the breakdowns at Moody's, examined by the Commission as a case study. From 2000 to 2007, Moody's rated nearly 45,000 mortgage-related securities as triple-A. This compares with six private-sector companies in the United States that carried this coveted rating in early 2010. In 2006 alone, Moody's put its triple-A stamp of approval on 30 mortgage-related securities every working day. The results were disastrous: 83% of the mortgage securities rated triple-A that year ultimately were downgraded.

You will also read about the forces at work behind the breakdowns at Moody's, including the flawed computer models, the pressure from financial firms that paid for the ratings, the relentless drive for market share, the lack of resources to do the job despite record profits, and the absence of meaningful public oversight. And you will see that without the active participation of the rating agencies, the market for mortgage-related securities could not have been what it became.

\* \* \*

THERE ARE MANY COMPETING VIEWS as to the causes of this crisis. In this regard, the Commission has endeavored to address key questions posed to us. Here we discuss three: capital availability and excess liquidity, the role of Fannie Mae and Freddie Mac (the GSEs), and government housing policy.

First, as to the matter of excess liquidity: in our report, we outline monetary policies and capital flows during the years leading up to the crisis. Low interest rates, widely available capital, and international investors seeking to put their money in real

estate assets in the United States were prerequisites for the creation of a credit bubble. Those conditions created increased risks, which should have been recognized by market participants, policy makers, and regulators. However, it is the Commission's conclusion that excess liquidity did not need to cause a crisis. It was the failures outlined above—including the failure to effectively rein in excesses in the mortgage and financial markets—that were the principal causes of this crisis. Indeed, the availability of well-priced capital—both foreign and domestic—is an opportunity for economic expansion and growth if encouraged to flow in productive directions.

Second, we examined the role of the GSEs, with Fannie Mae serving as the Commission's case study in this area. These government-sponsored enterprises had a deeply flawed business model as publicly traded corporations with the implicit backing of and subsidies from the federal government and with a public mission. Their $5 trillion mortgage exposure and market position were significant. In 2005 and 2006, they decided to ramp up their purchase and guarantee of risky mortgages, just as the housing market was peaking. They used their political power for decades to ward off effective regulation and oversight—spending $164 million on lobbying from 1999 to 2008. They suffered from many of the same failures of corporate governance and risk management as the Commission discovered in other financial firms. Through the third quarter of 2010, the Treasury Department had provided $151 billion in financial support to keep them afloat.

We conclude that these two entities contributed to the crisis, but were not a primary cause. Importantly, GSE mortgage securities essentially maintained their value throughout the crisis and did not contribute to the significant financial firm losses that were central to the financial crisis.

The GSEs participated in the expansion of subprime and other risky mortgages, but they followed rather than led Wall Street and other lenders in the rush for fool's gold. They purchased the highest rated non-GSE mortgage-backed securities and their participation in this market added helium to the housing balloon, but their purchases never represented a majority of the market. Those purchases represented 10.5% of non-GSE subprime mortgage-backed securities in 2001, with the share rising to 40% in 2004, and falling back to 28% by 2008. They relaxed their underwriting standards to purchase or guarantee riskier loans and related securities in order to meet stock market analysts' and investors' expectations for growth, to regain market share, and to ensure generous compensation for their executives and employees—justifying their activities on the broad and sustained public policy support for homeownership.

The Commission also probed the performance of the loans purchased or guaranteed by Fannie and Freddie. While they generated substantial losses, delinquency rates for GSE loans were substantially lower than loans securitized by other financial firms. For example, data compiled by the Commission for a subset of borrowers with similar credit scores—scores below 660—show that by the end of 2008, GSE mortgages were far less likely to be seriously delinquent than were non-GSE securitized mortgages: 6.2% versus 28.3%.

We also studied at length how the Department of Housing and Urban Development's (HUD's) affordable housing goals for the GSEs affected their investment in

risky mortgages. Based on the evidence and interviews with dozens of individuals involved in this subject area, we determined these goals only contributed marginally to Fannie's and Freddie's participation in those mortgages.

Finally, as to the matter of whether government housing policies were a primary cause of the crisis: for decades, government policy has encouraged homeownership through a set of incentives, assistance programs, and mandates. These policies were put in place and promoted by several administrations and Congresses—indeed, both Presidents Bill Clinton and George W. Bush set aggressive goals to increase homeownership.

In conducting our inquiry, we took a careful look at HUD's affordable housing goals, as noted above, and the Community Reinvestment Act (CRA). The CRA was enacted in 1977 to combat "redlining" by banks—the practice of denying credit to individuals and businesses in certain neighborhoods without regard to their creditworthiness. The CRA requires banks and savings and loans to lend, invest, and provide services to the communities from which they take deposits, consistent with bank safety and soundness.

The Commission concludes the CRA was not a significant factor in subprime lending or the crisis. Many subprime lenders were not subject to the CRA. Research indicates only 6% of high-cost loans—a proxy for subprime loans—had any connection to the law. Loans made by CRA-regulated lenders in the neighborhoods in which they were required to lend were half as likely to default as similar loans made in the same neighborhoods by independent mortgage originators not subject to the law.

Nonetheless, we make the following observation about government housing policies—they failed in this respect: As a nation, we set aggressive homeownership goals with the desire to extend credit to families previously denied access to the financial markets. Yet the government failed to ensure that the philosophy of opportunity was being matched by the practical realities on the ground. Witness again the failure of the Federal Reserve and other regulators to rein in irresponsible lending. Homeownership peaked in the spring of 2004 and then began to decline. From that point on, the talk of opportunity was tragically at odds with the reality of a financial disaster in the making.

\* \* \*

When this Commission began its work 18 months ago, some imagined that the events of 2008 and their consequences would be well behind us by the time we issued this report. Yet more than two years after the federal government intervened in an unprecedented manner in our financial markets, our country finds itself still grappling with the aftereffects of the calamity. Our financial system is, in many respects, still unchanged from what existed on the eve of the crisis. Indeed, in the wake of the crisis, the U.S. financial sector is now more concentrated than ever in the hands of a few large, systemically significant institutions.

While we have not been charged with making policy recommendations, the very purpose of our report has been to take stock of what happened so we can plot a new course. In our inquiry, we found dramatic breakdowns of corporate governance,

profound lapses in regulatory oversight, and near fatal flaws in our financial system. We also found that a series of choices and actions led us toward a catastrophe for which we were ill prepared. These are serious matters that must be addressed and resolved to restore faith in our financial markets, to avoid the next crisis, and to re-build a system of capital that provides the foundation for a new era of broadly shared prosperity.

The greatest tragedy would be to accept the refrain that no one could have seen this coming and thus nothing could have been done. If we accept this notion, it will happen again.

This report should not be viewed as the end of the nation's examination of this crisis. There is still much to learn, much to investigate, and much to fix.

This is our collective responsibility. It falls to us to make different choices if we want different results.

# PART I

## Crisis on the Horizon

# 1

## BEFORE OUR VERY EYES

In examining the worst financial meltdown since the Great Depression, the Financial Crisis Inquiry Commission reviewed millions of pages of documents and questioned hundreds of individuals—financial executives, business leaders, policy makers, regulators, community leaders, people from all walks of life—to find out how and why it happened.

In public hearings and interviews, many financial industry executives and top public officials testified that they had been blindsided by the crisis, describing it as a dramatic and mystifying turn of events. Even among those who worried that the housing bubble might burst, few—if any—foresaw the magnitude of the crisis that would ensue.

Charles Prince, the former chairman and chief executive officer of Citigroup Inc., called the collapse in housing prices "wholly unanticipated."[1] Warren Buffett, the chairman and chief executive officer of Berkshire Hathaway Inc., which until 2009 was the largest single shareholder of Moody's Corporation, told the Commission that "very, very few people could appreciate the bubble," which he called a "mass delusion" shared by "300 million Americans."[2] Lloyd Blankfein, the chairman and chief executive officer of Goldman Sachs Group, Inc., likened the financial crisis to a hurricane.[3]

Regulators echoed a similar refrain. Ben Bernanke, the chairman of the Federal Reserve Board since 2006, told the Commission a "perfect storm" had occurred that regulators could not have anticipated; but when asked about whether the Fed's lack of aggressiveness in regulating the mortgage market during the housing boom was a failure, Bernanke responded, "It was, indeed. I think it was the most severe failure of the Fed in this particular episode."[4] Alan Greenspan, the Fed chairman during the two decades leading up to the crash, told the Commission that it was beyond the ability of regulators to ever foresee such a sharp decline. "History tells us [regulators] cannot identify the timing of a crisis, or anticipate exactly where it will be located or how large the losses and spillovers will be."[5]

In fact, there were warning signs. In the decade preceding the collapse, there were many signs that house prices were inflated, that lending practices had spun out of control, that too many homeowners were taking on mortgages and debt they could ill afford, and that risks to the financial system were growing unchecked. Alarm bells

were clanging inside financial institutions, regulatory offices, consumer service organizations, state law enforcement agencies, and corporations throughout America, as well as in neighborhoods across the country. Many knowledgeable executives saw trouble and managed to avoid the train wreck. While countless Americans joined in the financial euphoria that seized the nation, many others were shouting to government officials in Washington and within state legislatures, pointing to what would become a human disaster, not just an economic debacle.

"Everybody in the whole world knew that the mortgage bubble was there," said Richard Breeden, the former chairman of the Securities and Exchange Commission appointed by President George H. W. Bush. "I mean, it wasn't hidden. . . . You cannot look at any of this and say that the regulators did their job. This was not some hidden problem. It wasn't out on Mars or Pluto or somewhere. It was right here. . . . You can't make trillions of dollars' worth of mortgages and not have people notice."[6]

Paul McCulley, a managing director at PIMCO, one of the nation's largest money management firms, told the Commission that he and his colleagues began to get worried about "serious signs of bubbles" in 2005; they therefore sent out credit analysts to 20 cities to do what he called "old-fashioned shoe-leather research," talking to real estate brokers, mortgage brokers, and local investors about the housing and mortgage markets. They witnessed what he called "the outright degradation of underwriting standards," McCulley asserted, and they shared what they had learned when they got back home to the company's Newport Beach, California, headquarters. "And when our group came back, they reported what they saw, and we adjusted our risk accordingly," McCulley told the Commission. The company "severely limited" its participation in risky mortgage securities.[7]

Veteran bankers, particularly those who remembered the savings and loan crisis, knew that age-old rules of prudent lending had been cast aside. Arnold Cattani, the chairman of Bakersfield, California–based Mission Bank, told the Commission that he grew uncomfortable with the "pure lunacy" he saw in the local home-building market, fueled by "voracious" Wall Street investment banks; he thus opted out of certain kinds of investments by 2005.[8]

William Martin, the vice chairman and chief executive officer of Service 1st Bank of Nevada, told the FCIC that the desire for a "high and quick return" blinded people to fiscal realities. "You may recall Tommy Lee Jones in *Men in Black*, where he holds a device in the air, and with a bright flash wipes clean the memories of everyone who has witnessed an alien event," he said.[9]

Unlike so many other bubbles—tulip bulbs in Holland in the 1600s, South Sea stocks in the 1700s, Internet stocks in the late 1990s—this one involved not just another commodity but a building block of community and social life and a cornerstone of the economy: the family home. Homes are the foundation upon which many of our social, personal, governmental, and economic structures rest. Children usually go to schools linked to their home addresses; local governments decide how much money they can spend on roads, firehouses, and public safety based on how much property tax revenue they have; house prices are tied to consumer spending. Downturns in the housing industry can cause ripple effects almost everywhere.

When the Federal Reserve cut interest rates early in the new century and mortgage rates fell, home refinancing surged, climbing from $460 billion in 2000 to $2.8 trillion in 2003,[10] allowing people to withdraw equity built up over previous decades and to consume more, despite stagnant wages. Home sales volume started to increase, and average home prices nationwide climbed, rising 67% in eight years by one measure and hitting a national high of $227,100 in early 2006.[11] Home prices in many areas skyrocketed: prices increased nearly two and one-half times in Sacramento, for example, in just five years,[12] and shot up by about the same percentage in Bakersfield, Miami, and Key West. Prices about doubled in more than 110 metropolitan areas, including Phoenix, Atlantic City, Baltimore, Ft. Lauderdale, Los Angeles, Poughkeepsie, San Diego, and West Palm Beach.[13] Housing starts nationwide climbed 53%, from 1.4 million in 1995 to more than 2 million in 2005. Encouraged by government policies, homeownership reached a record 69.2% in the spring of 2004, although it wouldn't rise an inch further even as the mortgage machine kept churning for another three years. By refinancing their homes, Americans extracted $2.0 trillion in home equity between 2000 and 2007, including $334 billion in 2006 alone, more than seven times the amount they took out in 1996.[14] Real estate speculators and potential homeowners stood in line outside new subdivisions for a chance to buy houses before the ground had even been broken. By the first half of 2005, more than one out of every ten home sales was to an investor, speculator, or someone buying a second home.[15] Bigger was better, and even the structures themselves ballooned in size; the floor area of an average new home grew by 15%, to 2,277 square feet, in the decade from 1997 to 2007.

Money washed through the economy like water rushing through a broken dam. Low interest rates and then foreign capital helped fuel the boom. Construction workers, landscape architects, real estate agents, loan brokers, and appraisers profited on Main Street, while investment bankers and traders on Wall Street moved even higher on the American earnings pyramid and the share prices of the most aggressive financial service firms reached all-time highs.[16] Homeowners pulled cash out of their homes to send their kids to college, pay medical bills, install designer kitchens with granite counters, take vacations, or launch new businesses. They also paid off credit cards, even as personal debt rose nationally. Survey evidence shows that about 5% of homeowners pulled out cash to buy a vehicle and over 40% spent the cash on a catch-all category including tax payments, clothing, gifts, and living expenses.[17] Renters used new forms of loans to buy homes and to move to suburban subdivisions, erecting swing sets in their backyards and enrolling their children in local schools.

In an interview with the Commission, Angelo Mozilo, the longtime CEO of Countrywide Financial—a lender brought down by its risky mortgages—said that a "gold rush" mentality overtook the country during these years, and that he was swept up in it as well: "Housing prices were rising so rapidly—at a rate that I'd never seen in my 55 years in the business—that people, regular people, average people got caught up in the mania of buying a house, and flipping it, making money. It was happening. They buy a house, make $50,000 . . . and talk at a cocktail party about it. . . . Housing suddenly went from being part of the American dream to house my family to settle

down—it became a commodity. That was a change in the culture. . . . It was sudden, unexpected."[18]

On the surface, it looked like prosperity. After all, the basic mechanisms making the real estate machine hum—the mortgage-lending instruments and the financing techniques that turned mortgages into investments called securities, which kept cash flowing from Wall Street into the U.S. housing market—were tools that had worked well for many years.

But underneath, something was going wrong. Like a science fiction movie in which ordinary household objects turn hostile, familiar market mechanisms were being transformed. The time-tested 30-year fixed-rate mortgage, with a 20% down payment, went out of style. There was a burgeoning global demand for residential mortgage–backed securities that offered seemingly solid and secure returns. Investors around the world clamored to purchase securities built on American real estate, seemingly one of the safest bets in the world.

Wall Street labored mightily to meet that demand. Bond salesmen earned multi-million-dollar bonuses packaging and selling new kinds of loans, offered by new kinds of lenders, into new kinds of investment products that were deemed safe but possessed complex and hidden risks. Federal officials praised the changes—these financial innovations, they said, had lowered borrowing costs for consumers and moved risks away from the biggest and most systemically important financial institutions. But the nation's financial system had become vulnerable and interconnected in ways that were not understood by either the captains of finance or the system's public stewards. In fact, some of the largest institutions had taken on what would prove to be debilitating risks. Trillions of dollars had been wagered on the belief that housing prices would always rise and that borrowers would seldom default on mortgages, even as their debt grew. Shaky loans had been bundled into investment products in ways that seemed to give investors the best of both worlds—high-yield, risk-free—but instead, in many cases, would prove to be high-risk and yield-free.

All this financial creativity was a lot "like cheap sangria," said Michael Mayo, a managing director and financial services analyst at Calyon Securities (USA) Inc. "A lot of cheap ingredients repackaged to sell at a premium," he told the Commission. "It might taste good for a while, but then you get headaches later and you have no idea what's really inside."[19]

The securitization machine began to guzzle these once-rare mortgage products with their strange-sounding names: Alt-A, subprime, I-O (interest-only), low-doc, no-doc, or ninja (no income, no job, no assets) loans; 2–28s and 3–27s; liar loans; piggyback second mortgages; payment-option or pick-a-pay adjustable rate mortgages. New variants on adjustable-rate mortgages, called "exploding" ARMs, featured low monthly costs at first, but payments could suddenly double or triple, if borrowers were unable to refinance. Loans with negative amortization would eat away the borrower's equity. Soon there were a multitude of different kinds of mortgages available on the market, confounding consumers who didn't examine the fine print, baffling

conscientious borrowers who tried to puzzle out their implications, and opening the door for those who wanted in on the action.

Many people chose poorly. Some people wanted to live beyond their means, and by mid-2005, nearly one-quarter of all borrowers nationwide were taking out interest-only loans that allowed them to defer the payment of principal.[20] Some borrowers opted for nontraditional mortgages because that was the only way they could get a foothold in areas such as the sky-high California housing market.[21] Some speculators saw the chance to snatch up investment properties and flip them for profit—and Florida and Georgia became a particular target for investors who used these loans to acquire real estate.[22] Some were misled by salespeople who came to their homes and persuaded them to sign loan documents on their kitchen tables. Some borrowers naively trusted mortgage brokers who earned more money placing them in risky loans than in safe ones.[23] With these loans, buyers were able to bid up the prices of houses even if they didn't have enough income to qualify for traditional loans.

Some of these exotic loans had existed in the past, used by high-income, financially secure people as a cash-management tool. Some had been targeted to borrowers with impaired credit, offering them the opportunity to build a stronger payment history before they refinanced. But the instruments began to deluge the larger market in 2004 and 2005. The changed occurred "almost overnight," Faith Schwartz, then an executive at the subprime lender Option One and later the executive director of Hope Now, a lending-industry foreclosure relief group, told the Federal Reserve's Consumer Advisory Council. "I would suggest most every lender in the country is in it, one way or another."[24]

At first not a lot of people really understood the potential hazards of these new loans. They were new, they were different, and the consequences were uncertain. But it soon became apparent that what had looked like newfound wealth was a mirage based on borrowed money. Overall mortgage indebtedness in the United States climbed from $5.3 trillion in 2001 to $10.5 trillion in 2007. The mortgage debt of American households rose almost as much in the six years from 2001 to 2007 as it had over the course of the country's more than 200-year history. The amount of mortgage debt per household rose from $91,500 in 2001 to $149,500 in 2007.[25] With a simple flourish of a pen on paper, millions of Americans traded away decades of equity tucked away in their homes.

Under the radar, the lending and the financial services industry had mutated. In the past, lenders had avoided making unsound loans because they would be stuck with them in their loan portfolios. But because of the growth of securitization, it wasn't even clear anymore who the lender was. The mortgages would be packaged, sliced, repackaged, insured, and sold as incomprehensibly complicated debt securities to an assortment of hungry investors. Now even the worst loans could find a buyer.

More loan sales meant higher profits for everyone in the chain. Business boomed for Christopher Cruise, a Maryland-based corporate educator who trained loan officers for companies that were expanding mortgage originations. He crisscrossed the nation, coaching about 10,000 loan originators a year in auditoriums and classrooms.

His clients included many of the largest lenders—Countrywide, Ameriquest, and Ditech among them. Most of their new hires were young, with no mortgage experience, fresh out of school and with previous jobs "flipping burgers," he told the FCIC. Given the right training, however, the best of them could "easily" earn millions.[26]

"I was a sales and marketing trainer in terms of helping people to know how to sell these products to, in some cases, frankly unsophisticated and unsuspecting borrowers," he said. He taught them the new playbook: "You had no incentive whatsoever to be concerned about the quality of the loan, whether it was suitable for the borrower or whether the loan performed. In fact, you were in a way encouraged not to worry about those macro issues." He added, "I knew that the risk was being shunted off. I knew that we could be writing crap. But in the end it was like a game of musical chairs. Volume might go down but we were not going to be hurt."[27]

On Wall Street, where many of these loans were packaged into securities and sold to investors around the globe, a new term was coined: IBGYBG, "I'll be gone, you'll be gone."[28] It referred to deals that brought in big fees up front while risking much larger losses in the future. And, for a long time, IBGYBG worked at every level.

Most home loans entered the pipeline soon after borrowers signed the documents and picked up their keys. Loans were put into packages and sold off in bulk to securitization firms—including investment banks such as Merrill Lynch, Bear Stearns, and Lehman Brothers, and commercial banks and thrifts such as Citibank, Wells Fargo, and Washington Mutual. The firms would package the loans into residential mortgage–backed securities that would mostly be stamped with triple-A ratings by the credit rating agencies, and sold to investors. In many cases, the securities were repackaged again into collateralized debt obligations (CDOs)—often composed of the riskier portions of these securities—which would then be sold to other investors. Most of these securities would also receive the coveted triple-A ratings that investors believed attested to their quality and safety. Some investors would buy an invention from the 1990s called a credit default swap (CDS) to protect against the securities' defaulting. For every buyer of a credit default swap, there was a seller: as these investors made opposing bets, the layers of entanglement in the securities market increased.

The instruments grew more and more complex; CDOs were constructed out of CDOs, creating CDOs squared. When firms ran out of real product, they started generating cheaper-to-produce synthetic CDOs—composed not of real mortgage securities but just of bets on other mortgage products. Each new permutation created an opportunity to extract more fees and trading profits. And each new layer brought in more investors wagering on the mortgage market—even well after the market had started to turn. So by the time the process was complete, a mortgage on a home in south Florida might become part of dozens of securities owned by hundreds of investors—or parts of bets being made by hundreds more. Treasury Secretary Timothy Geithner, the president of the New York Federal Reserve Bank during the crisis, described the resulting product as "cooked spaghetti" that became hard to "untangle."[29]

Ralph Cioffi spent several years creating CDOs for Bear Stearns and a couple of more years on the repurchase or "repo" desk, which was responsible for borrowing

money every night to finance Bear Stearns's broader securities portfolio. In September 2003, Cioffi created a hedge fund within Bear Stearns with a minimum investment of $1 million. As was common, he used borrowed money—up to $9 borrowed for every $1 from investors—to buy CDOs. Cioffi's first fund was extremely successful; it earned 17% for investors in 2004 and 10% in 2005—after the annual management fee and the 20% slice of the profit for Cioffi and his Bear Stearns team—and grew to almost $9 billion by the end of 2005. In the fall of 2006, he created another, more aggressive fund. This one would shoot for leverage of up to 12 to 1. By the end of 2006, the two hedge funds had $18 billion invested, half in securities issued by CDOs centered on housing. As a CDO manager, Cioffi also managed another $18 billion of mortgage-related CDOs for other investors.

Cioffi's investors and others like them wanted high-yielding mortgage securities. That, in turn, required high-yielding mortgages. An advertising barrage bombarded potential borrowers, urging them to buy or refinance homes. Direct-mail solicitations flooded people's mailboxes.[30] Dancing figures, depicting happy homeowners, boogied on computer monitors. Telephones began ringing off the hook with calls from loan officers offering the latest loan products: One percent loan! (But only for the first year.) No money down! (Leaving no equity if home prices fell.) No income documentation needed! (Mortgages soon dubbed "liar loans" by the industry itself.) Borrowers answered the call, many believing that with ever-rising prices, housing was the investment that couldn't lose.

In Washington, four intermingled issues came into play that made it difficult to acknowledge the looming threats. First, efforts to boost homeownership had broad political support—from Presidents Bill Clinton and George W. Bush and successive Congresses—even though in reality the homeownership rate had peaked in the spring of 2004. Second, the real estate boom was generating a lot of cash on Wall Street and creating a lot of jobs in the housing industry at a time when performance in other sectors of the economy was dreary. Third, many top officials and regulators were reluctant to challenge the profitable and powerful financial industry. And finally, policy makers believed that even if the housing market tanked, the broader financial system and economy would hold up.

As the mortgage market began its transformation in the late 1990s, consumer advocates and front-line local government officials were among the first to spot the changes: homeowners began streaming into their offices to seek help in dealing with mortgages they could not afford to pay. They began raising the issue with the Federal Reserve and other banking regulators.[31] Bob Gnaizda, the general counsel and policy director of the Greenlining Institute, a California-based nonprofit housing group, told the Commission that he began meeting with Greenspan at least once a year starting in 1999, each time highlighting to him the growth of predatory lending practices and discussing with him the social and economic problems they were creating.[32]

One of the first places to see the bad lending practices envelop an entire market was Cleveland, Ohio. From 1989 to 1999, home prices in Cleveland rose 66%, climbing from a median of $75,200 to $125,100, while home prices nationally rose about 49% in those same years; at the same time, the city's unemployment rate, ranging

from 5.8% in 1990 to 4.2% in 1999, more or less tracked the broader U.S. pattern. James Rokakis, the longtime county treasurer of Cuyahoga County, where Cleveland is located, told the Commission that the region's housing market was juiced by "flipping on mega-steroids," with rings of real estate agents, appraisers, and loan originators earning fees on each transaction and feeding the securitized loans to Wall Street. City officials began to hear reports that these activities were being propelled by new kinds of nontraditional loans that enabled investors to buy properties with little or no money down and gave homeowners the ability to refinance their houses, regardless of whether they could afford to repay the loans. Foreclosures shot up in Cuyahoga County from 3,500 a year in 1995 to 7,000 a year in 2000.[33] Rokakis and other public officials watched as families who had lived for years in modest residences lost their homes. After they were gone, many homes were ultimately abandoned, vandalized, and then stripped bare, as scavengers ripped away their copper pipes and aluminum siding to sell for scrap.

"Securitization was one of the most brilliant financial innovations of the 20th century," Rokakis told the Commission. "It freed up a lot of capital. If it had been done responsibly, it would have been a wondrous thing because nothing is more stable, there's nothing safer, than the American mortgage market. . . . It worked for years. But then people realized they could scam it."[34]

Officials in Cleveland and other Ohio cities reached out to the federal government for help. They asked the Federal Reserve, the one entity with the authority to regulate risky lending practices by all mortgage lenders, to use the power it had been granted in 1994 under the Home Ownership and Equity Protection Act (HOEPA) to issue new mortgage lending rules. In March 2001, Fed Governor Edward Gramlich, an advocate for expanding access to credit but only with safeguards in place, attended a conference on the topic in Cleveland. He spoke about the Fed's power under HOEPA, declared some of the lending practices to be "clearly illegal," and said they could be "combated with legal enforcement measures."[35]

Looking back, Rokakis remarked to the Commission, "I naively believed they'd go back and tell Mr. Greenspan and presto, we'd have some new rules. . . . I thought it would result in action being taken. It was kind of quaint."[36]

In 2000, when Cleveland was looking for help from the federal government, other cities around the country were doing the same. John Taylor, the president of the National Community Reinvestment Coalition, with the support of community leaders from Nevada, Michigan, Maryland, Delaware, Chicago, Vermont, North Carolina, New Jersey, and Ohio, went to the Office of Thrift Supervision (OTS), which regulated savings and loan institutions, asking the agency to crack down on what they called "exploitative" practices they believed were putting both borrowers and lenders at risk.[37]

The California Reinvestment Coalition, a nonprofit housing group based in Northern California, also begged regulators to act, CRC officials told the Commission. The nonprofit group had reviewed the loans of 125 borrowers and discovered that many individuals were being placed into high-cost loans when they qualified for better mortgages and that many had been misled about the terms of their loans.[38]

There were government reports, too. The Department of Housing and Urban Development and the Treasury Department issued a joint report on predatory lending in June 2000 that made a number of recommendations for reducing the risks to borrowers.[39] In December 2001, the Federal Reserve Board used the HOEPA law to amend some regulations; among the changes were new rules aimed at limiting high-interest lending and preventing multiple refinancings over a short period of time, if they were not in the borrower's best interest.[40] As it would turn out, those rules covered only 1% of subprime loans. FDIC Chairman Sheila C. Bair, then an assistant treasury secretary in the administration of President George W. Bush, characterized the action to the FCIC as addressing only a "narrow range of predatory lending issues."[41] In 2002, Gramlich noted again the "increasing reports of abusive, unethical and in some cases, illegal, lending practices."[42]

Bair told the Commission that this was when "really poorly underwritten loans, the payment shock loans" were beginning to proliferate, placing "pressure" on traditional banks to follow suit.[43] She said that she and Gramlich considered seeking rules to rein in the growth of these kinds of loans, but Gramlich told her that he thought the Fed, despite its broad powers in this area, would not support the effort. Instead, they sought voluntary rules for lenders, but that effort fell by the wayside as well.[44]

In an environment of minimal government restrictions, the number of nontraditional loans surged and lending standards declined. The companies issuing these loans made profits that attracted envious eyes. New lenders entered the field. Investors clamored for mortgage-related securities and borrowers wanted mortgages. The volume of subprime and nontraditional lending rose sharply. In 2000, the top 25 nonprime lenders originated $105 billion in loans. Their volume rose to $188 billion in 2002, and then $310 billion in 2003.[45]

California, with its high housing costs, was a particular hotbed for this kind of lending. In 2001, nearly $52 billion, or 25% of all nontraditional loans nationwide, were made in that state; California's share rose to 35% by 2003, with these kinds of loans growing to $95 billion or by 84% in California in just two years.[46] In those years, "subprime and option ARM loans saturated California communities," Kevin Stein, the associate director of the California Reinvestment Coalition, testified to the Commission. "We estimated at that time that the average subprime borrower in California was paying over $600 more per month on their mortgage payment as a result of having received the subprime loan."[47]

Gail Burks, president and CEO of Nevada Fair Housing, Inc., a Las Vegas–based housing clinic, told the Commission she and other groups took their concerns directly to Greenspan at this time, describing to him in person what she called the "metamorphosis" in the lending industry. She told him that besides predatory lending practices such as flipping loans or misinforming seniors about reverse mortgages, she also witnessed examples of growing sloppiness in paperwork: not crediting payments appropriately or miscalculating accounts.[48]

Lisa Madigan, the attorney general in Illinois, also spotted the emergence of a troubling trend. She joined state attorneys general from Minnesota, California, Washington, Arizona, Florida, New York, and Massachusetts in pursuing allegations

about First Alliance Mortgage Company, a California-based mortgage lender. Consumers complained that they had been deceived into taking out loans with hefty fees. The company was then packaging the loans and selling them as securities to Lehman Brothers, Madigan said. The case was settled in 2002, and borrowers received $50 million. First Alliance went out of business. But other firms stepped into the void.[49]

State officials from around the country joined together again in 2003 to investigate another fast-growing lender, California-based Ameriquest. It became the nation's largest subprime lender, originating $39 billion in subprime loans in 2003—mostly refinances that let borrowers take cash out of their homes, but with hefty fees that ate away at their equity.[50] Madigan testified to the FCIC, "Our multistate investigation of Ameriquest revealed that the company engaged in the kinds of fraudulent practices that other predatory lenders subsequently emulated on a wide scale: inflating home appraisals; increasing the interest rates on borrowers' loans or switching their loans from fixed to adjustable interest rates at closing; and promising borrowers that they could refinance their costly loans into loans with better terms in just a few months or a year, even when borrowers had no equity to absorb another refinance."[51]

Ed Parker, the former head of Ameriquest's Mortgage Fraud Investigations Department, told the Commission that he detected fraud at the company within one month of starting his job there in January 2003, but senior management did nothing with the reports he sent. He heard that other departments were complaining he "looked too much" into the loans. In November 2005, he was downgraded from "manager" to "supervisor," and was laid off in May 2006.[52]

In late 2003, Prentiss Cox, then a Minnesota assistant attorney general, asked Ameriquest to produce information about its loans. He received about 10 boxes of documents. He pulled one file at random, and stared at it. He pulled out another and another. He noted file after file where the borrowers were described as "antiques dealers"—in his view, a blatant misrepresentation of employment. In another loan file, he recalled in an interview with the FCIC, a disabled borrower in his 80s who used a walker was described in the loan application as being employed in "light construction."[53]

"It didn't take Sherlock Holmes to figure out this was bogus," Cox told the Commission. As he tried to figure out why Ameriquest would make such obviously fraudulent loans, a friend suggested that he "look upstream." Cox suddenly realized that the lenders were simply generating product to ship to Wall Street to sell to investors. "I got that it had shifted," Cox recalled. "The lending pattern had shifted."[54]

Ultimately, 49 states and the District of Columbia joined in the lawsuit against Ameriquest, on behalf of "more than 240,000 borrowers." The result was a $325 million settlement. But during the years when the investigation was under way, between 2002 and 2005, Ameriquest originated another $217.9 billion in loans,[55] which then flowed to Wall Street for securitization.

Although the federal government played no role in the Ameriquest investigation, some federal officials said they had followed the case. At the Department of Housing and Urban Development, "we began to get rumors" that other firms were "running

wild, taking applications over the Internet, not verifying peoples' income or their ability to have a job," recalled Alphonso Jackson, the HUD secretary from 2004 to 2008, in an interview with the Commission. "Everybody was making a great deal of money . . . and there wasn't a great deal of oversight going on." Although he was the nation's top housing official at the time, he placed much of the blame on Congress.[56]

Cox, the former Minnesota prosecutor, and Madigan, the Illinois attorney general, told the Commission that one of the single biggest obstacles to effective state regulation of unfair lending came from the federal government, particularly the Office of the Comptroller of the Currency (OCC), which regulated nationally chartered banks—including Bank of America, Citibank, and Wachovia—and the OTS, which regulated nationally chartered thrifts. The OCC and OTS issued rules preempting states from enforcing rules against national banks and thrifts.[57] Cox recalled that in 2001, Julie Williams, the chief counsel of the OCC, had delivered what he called a "lecture" to the states' attorneys general, in a meeting in Washington, warning them that the OCC would "quash" them if they persisted in attempting to control the consumer practices of nationally regulated institutions.[58]

Two former OCC comptrollers, John Hawke and John Dugan, told the Commission that they were defending the agency's constitutional obligation to block state efforts to impinge on federally created entities. Because state-chartered lenders had more lending problems, they said, the states should have been focusing there rather than looking to involve themselves in federally chartered institutions, an arena where they had no jurisdiction.[59] However, Madigan told the Commission that national banks funded 21 of the 25 largest subprime loan issuers operating with state charters, and that those banks were the end market for abusive loans originated by the state-chartered firms. She noted that the OCC was "particularly zealous in its efforts to thwart state authority over national lenders, and lax in its efforts to protect consumers from the coming crisis."[60]

Many states nevertheless pushed ahead in enforcing their own lending regulations, as did some cities. In 2003, Charlotte, North Carolina–based Wachovia Bank told state regulators that it would not abide by state laws, because it was a national bank and fell under the supervision of the OCC. Michigan protested Wachovia's announcement, and Wachovia sued Michigan. The OCC, the American Bankers Association, and the Mortgage Bankers Association entered the fray on Wachovia's side; the other 49 states, Puerto Rico, and the District of Columbia aligned themselves with Michigan. The legal battle lasted four years. The Supreme Court ruled 5–3 in Wachovia's favor on April 17, 2007, leaving the OCC its sole regulator for mortgage lending. Cox criticized the federal government: "Not only were they negligent, they were aggressive players attempting to stop any enforcement action[s]. . . . Those guys should have been on our side."[61]

Nonprime lending surged to $730 billion in 2004 and then $1.0 trillion in 2005, and its impact began to be felt in more and more places.[62] Many of those loans were funneled into the pipeline by mortgage brokers—the link between borrowers and the lenders who financed the mortgages—who prepared the paperwork for loans and earned fees from lenders for doing it. More than 200,000 new mortgage brokers

began their jobs during the boom, and some were less than honorable in their dealings with borrowers.[63] According to an investigative news report published in 2008, between 2000 and 2007, at least 10,500 people with criminal records entered the field in Florida, for example, including 4,065 who had previously been convicted of such crimes as fraud, bank robbery, racketeering, and extortion.[64] J. Thomas Cardwell, the commissioner of the Florida Office of Financial Regulation, told the Commission that "lax lending standards" and a "lack of accountability . . . created a condition in which fraud flourished."[65] Marc S. Savitt, a past president of the National Association of Mortgage Brokers, told the Commission that while most mortgage brokers looked out for borrowers' best interests and steered them away from risky loans, about 50,000 of the newcomers to the field nationwide were willing to do whatever it took to maximize the number of loans they made. He added that some loan origination firms, such as Ameriquest, were "absolutely" corrupt.[66]

In Bakersfield, California, where home starts doubled and home values grew even faster between 2001 and 2006, the real estate appraiser Gary Crabtree initially felt pride that his birthplace, 110 miles north of Los Angeles, "had finally been discovered" by other Californians. The city, a farming and oil industry center in the San Joaquin Valley, was drawing national attention for the pace of its development. Wide-open farm fields were plowed under and divided into thousands of building lots. Home prices jumped 11% in Bakersfield in 2002, 17% in 2003, 32% in 2004, and 29% more in 2005.

Crabtree, an appraiser for 48 years, started in 2003 and 2004 to think that things were not making sense. People were paying inflated prices for their homes, and they didn't seem to have enough income to pay for what they had bought. Within a few years, when he passed some of these same houses, he saw that they were vacant. "For sale" signs appeared on the front lawns. And when he passed again, the yards were untended and the grass was turning brown. Next, the houses went into foreclosure, and that's when he noticed that the empty houses were being vandalized, which pulled down values for the new suburban subdivisions.

The Cleveland phenomenon had come to Bakersfield, a place far from the Rust Belt. Crabtree watched as foreclosures spread like an infectious disease through the community. Houses fell into disrepair and neighborhoods disintegrated.

Crabtree began studying the market. In 2006, he ended up identifying what he believed were 214 fraudulent transactions in Bakersfield; some, for instance, were allowing insiders to siphon cash from each property transfer. The transactions involved many of the nation's largest lenders. One house, for example, was listed for sale for $565,000, and was recorded as selling for $605,000 with 100% financing, though the real estate agent told Crabtree that it actually sold for $535,000. Crabtree realized that the gap between the sales price and loan amount allowed these insiders to pocket $70,000. The terms of the loan required the buyer to occupy the house, but it was never occupied. The house went into foreclosure and was sold in a distress sale for $322,000.[67]

Crabtree began calling lenders to tell them what he had found; but to his shock, they did not seem to care. He finally reached one quality assurance officer at Fremont

Investment & Loan, the nation's eighth-largest subprime lender. "Don't put your nose where it doesn't belong," he was told.[68]

Crabtree took his story to state law enforcement officials and to the Federal Bureau of Investigation. "I was screaming at the top of my lungs," he said. He grew infuriated at the slow pace of enforcement and at prosecutors' lack of response to a problem that was wreaking economic havoc in Bakersfield.[69]

At the Washington, D.C., headquarters of the FBI, Chris Swecker, an assistant director, was also trying to get people to pay attention to mortgage fraud. "It has the potential to be an epidemic," he said at a news conference in Washington in 2004. "We think we can prevent a problem that could have as much impact as the S&L crisis."[70]

Swecker called another news conference in December 2005 to say the same thing, this time adding that mortgage fraud was a "pervasive problem" that was "on the rise." He was joined by officials from HUD, the U.S. Postal Service, and the Internal Revenue Service. The officials told reporters that real estate and banking executives were not doing enough to root out mortgage fraud and that lenders needed to do more to "police their own organizations."[71]

Meanwhile, the number of cases of reported mortgage fraud continued to swell. Suspicious activity reports, also known as SARs, are reports filed by banks to the Financial Crimes Enforcement Network (FinCEN), a bureau within the Treasury Department. In November 2006, the network published an analysis that found a 20-fold increase in mortgage fraud reports between 1996 and 2005. According to FinCEN, the figures likely represented a substantial underreporting, because two-thirds of all the loans being created were originated by mortgage brokers who were not subject to any federal standard or oversight.[72] In addition, many lenders who were required to submit reports did not in fact do so.[73]

"The claim that no one could have foreseen the crisis is false," said William K. Black, an expert on white-collar crime and a former staff director of the National Commission on Financial Institution Reform, Recovery and Enforcement, created by Congress in 1990 as the savings and loan crisis was unfolding.[74]

Former attorney general Alberto Gonzales, who served from February 2005 to 2007, told the FCIC he could not remember the press conferences or news reports about mortgage fraud. Both Gonzales and his successor Michael Mukasey, who served as attorney general in 2007 and 2008, told the FCIC that mortgage fraud had never been communicated to them as a top priority. "National security . . . was an overriding" concern, Mukasey said.[75]

To community activists and local officials, however, the lending practices were a matter of national economic concern. Ruhi Maker, a lawyer who worked on foreclosure cases at the Empire Justice Center in Rochester, New York, told Fed Governors Bernanke, Susan Bies, and Roger Ferguson in October 2004 that she suspected that some investment banks—she specified Bear Stearns and Lehman Brothers—were producing such bad loans that the very survival of the firms was put in question. "We repeatedly see false appraisals and false income," she told the Fed officials, who were gathered at the public hearing period of a Consumer Advisory Council meeting. She urged the Fed to prod the Securities and Exchange Commission to examine the

quality of the firms' due diligence; otherwise, she said, serious questions could arise about whether they could be forced to buy back bad loans that they had made or securitized.[76]

Maker told the board that she feared an "enormous economic impact" could result from a confluence of financial events: flat or declining incomes, a housing bubble, and fraudulent loans with overstated values.[77]

In an interview with the FCIC, Maker said that Fed officials seemed impervious to what the consumer advocates were saying. The Fed governors politely listened and said little, she recalled. "They had their economic models, and their economic models did not see this coming," she said. "We kept getting back, 'This is all anecdotal.'"[78]

Soon nontraditional mortgages were crowding other kinds of products out of the market in many parts of the country. More mortgage borrowers nationwide took out interest-only loans, and the trend was far more pronounced on the West and East Coasts.[79] Because of their easy credit terms, nontraditional loans enabled borrowers to buy more expensive homes and ratchet up the prices in bidding wars. The loans were also riskier, however, and a pattern of higher foreclosure rates frequently appeared soon after.

As home prices shot up in much of the country, many observers began to wonder if the country was witnessing a housing bubble. On June 18, 2005, the *Economist* magazine's cover story posited that the day of reckoning was at hand, with the headline "House Prices: After the Fall." The illustration depicted a brick plummeting out of the sky. "It is not going to be pretty," the article declared. "How the current housing boom ends could decide the course of the entire world economy over the next few years."[80]

That same month, Fed Chairman Greenspan acknowledged the issue, telling the Joint Economic Committee of the U.S. Congress that "the apparent froth in housing markets may have spilled over into the mortgage markets."[81] For years, he had warned that Fannie Mae and Freddie Mac, bolstered by investors' belief that these institutions had the backing of the U.S. government, were growing so large, with so little oversight, that they were creating systemic risks for the financial system. Still, he reassured legislators that the U.S. economy was on a "reasonably firm footing" and that the financial system would be resilient if the housing market turned sour.

"The dramatic increase in the prevalence of interest-only loans, as well as the introduction of other relatively exotic forms of adjustable rate mortgages, are developments of particular concern," he testified in June.

> To be sure, these financing vehicles have their appropriate uses. But to the extent that some households may be employing these instruments to purchase a home that would otherwise be unaffordable, their use is beginning to add to the pressures in the marketplace. . . .
>
>   Although we certainly cannot rule out home price declines, especially in some local markets, these declines, were they to occur, likely would not have substantial macroeconomic implications. Nationwide banking and widespread securitization of mortgages makes it less likely

that financial intermediation would be impaired than was the case in prior episodes of regional house price corrections.[82]

Indeed, Greenspan would not be the only one confident that a housing downturn would leave the broader financial system largely unscathed. As late as March 2007, after housing prices had been declining for a year, Bernanke testified to Congress that "the problems in the subprime market were likely to be contained"—that is, he expected little spillover to the broader economy.[83]

Some were less sanguine. For example, the consumer lawyer Sheila Canavan, of Moab, Utah, informed the Fed's Consumer Advisory Council in October 2005 that 61% of recently originated loans in California were interest-only, a proportion that was more than twice the national average. "That's insanity," she told the Fed governors. "That means we're facing something down the road that we haven't faced before and we are going to be looking at a safety and soundness crisis."[84]

On another front, some academics offered pointed analyses as they raised alarms. For example, in August 2005, the Yale professor Robert Shiller, who along with Karl Case developed the Case-Shiller Index, charted home prices to illustrate how precipitously they had climbed and how distorted the market appeared in historical terms. Shiller warned that the housing bubble would likely burst.[85]

In that same month, a conclave of economists gathered at Jackson Lake Lodge in Wyoming, in a conference center nestled in Grand Teton National Park. It was a "who's who of central bankers," recalled Raghuram Rajan, who was then on leave from the University of Chicago's business school while serving as the chief economist of the International Monetary Fund. Greenspan was there, and so was Bernanke. Jean-Claude Trichet, the president of the European Central Bank, and Mervyn King, the governor of the Bank of England, were among the other dignitaries.[86]

Rajan presented a paper with a provocative title: "Has Financial Development Made the World Riskier?" He posited that executives were being overcompensated for short-term gains but let off the hook for any eventual losses—the IBGYBG syndrome. Rajan added that investment strategies such as credit default swaps could have disastrous consequences if the system became unstable, and that regulatory institutions might be unable to deal with the fallout.[87]

He recalled to the FCIC that he was treated with scorn. Lawrence Summers, a former U.S. treasury secretary who was then president of Harvard University, called Rajan a "Luddite," implying that he was simply opposed to technological change.[88] "I felt like an early Christian who had wandered into a convention of half-starved lions," Rajan wrote later.[89]

Susan M. Wachter, a professor of real estate and finance at the University of Pennsylvania's Wharton School, prepared a research paper in 2003 suggesting that the United States could have a real estate crisis similar to that suffered in Asia in the 1990s. When she discussed her work at another Jackson Hole gathering two years later, it received a chilly reception, she told the Commission. "It was universally panned," she said, and an economist from the Mortgage Bankers Association called it "absurd."[90]

In 2005, news reports were beginning to highlight indications that the real estate market was weakening. Home sales began to drop, and Fitch Ratings reported signs that mortgage delinquencies were rising. That year, the hedge fund manager Mark Klipsch of Orix Credit Corp. told participants at the American Securitization Forum, a securities trade group, that investors had become "over optimistic" about the market. "I see a lot of irrationality," he added. He said he was unnerved because people were saying, "It's different this time"—a rationale commonly heard before previous collapses.[91]

Some real estate appraisers had also been expressing concerns for years. From 2000 to 2007, a coalition of appraisal organizations circulated and ultimately delivered to Washington officials a public petition; signed by 11,000 appraisers and including the name and address of each, it charged that lenders were pressuring appraisers to place artificially high prices on properties. According to the petition, lenders were "blacklisting honest appraisers" and instead assigning business only to appraisers who would hit the desired price targets. "The powers that be cannot claim ignorance," the appraiser Dennis J. Black of Port Charlotte, Florida, testified to the Commission.[92]

The appraiser Karen Mann of Discovery Bay, California, another industry veteran, told the Commission that lenders had opened subsidiaries to perform appraisals, allowing them to extract extra fees from "unknowing" consumers and making it easier to inflate home values. The steep hike in home prices and the unmerited and inflated appraisals she was seeing in Northern California convinced her that the housing industry was headed for a cataclysmic downturn. In 2005, she laid off some of her staff in order to cut her overhead expenses, in anticipation of the coming storm; two years later, she shut down her office and began working out of her home.[93]

Despite all the signs that the housing market was slowing, Wall Street just kept going and going—ordering up loans, packaging them into securities, taking profits, earning bonuses. By the third quarter of 2006, home prices were falling and mortgage delinquencies were rising, a combination that spelled trouble for mortgage-backed securities. But from the third quarter of 2006 on, banks created and sold some $1.3 trillion in mortgage-backed securities and more than $350 billion in mortgage-related CDOs.[94]

Not everyone on Wall Street kept applauding, however. Some executives were urging caution, as corporate governance and risk management were breaking down. Reflecting on the causes of the crisis, Jamie Dimon, CEO of JP Morgan testified to the FCIC, "I blame the management teams 100% and . . . no one else."[95]

At too many financial firms, management brushed aside the growing risks to their firms. At Lehman Brothers, for example, Michael Gelband, the head of fixed income, and his colleague Madelyn Antoncic warned against taking on too much risk in the face of growing pressure to compete aggressively against other investment banks. Antoncic, who was the firm's chief risk officer from 2004 to 2007, was shunted aside: "At the senior level, they were trying to push so hard that the wheels started to come off," she told the Commission. She was reassigned to a policy position working with gov-

ernment regulators.[96] Gelband left; Lehman officials blamed Gelband's departure on "philosophical differences."[97]

At Citigroup, meanwhile, Richard Bowen, a veteran banker in the consumer lending group, received a promotion in early 2006 when he was named business chief underwriter. He would go on to oversee loan quality for over $90 billion a year of mortgages underwritten and purchased by CitiFinancial. These mortgages were sold to Fannie Mae, Freddie Mac, and others. In June 2006, Bowen discovered that as much as 60% of the loans that Citi was buying were defective. They did not meet Citigroup's loan guidelines and thus endangered the company—if the borrowers were to default on their loans, the investors could force Citi to buy them back. Bowen told the Commission that he tried to alert top managers at the firm by "email, weekly reports, committee presentations, and discussions"; but though they expressed concern, it "never translated into any action." Instead, he said, "there was a considerable push to build volumes, to increase market share." Indeed, Bowen recalled, Citi began to loosen its own standards during these years up to 2005: specifically, it started to purchase stated-income loans. "So we joined the other lemmings headed for the cliff," he said in an interview with the FCIC.[98]

He finally took his warnings to the highest level he could reach—Robert Rubin, the chairman of the Executive Committee of the Board of Directors and a former U.S. treasury secretary in the Clinton administration, and three other bank officials. He sent Rubin and the others a memo with the words "URGENT—READ IMMEDI-ATELY" in the subject line. Sharing his concerns, he stressed to top managers that Citi faced billions of dollars in losses if investors were to demand that Citi repurchase the defective loans.[99]

Rubin told the Commission in a public hearing in April 2010 that Citibank handled the Bowen matter promptly and effectively. "I do recollect this and that either I or somebody else, and I truly do not remember who, but either I or somebody else sent it to the appropriate people, and I do know factually that that was acted on promptly and actions were taken in response to it."[100] According to Citigroup, the bank undertook an investigation in response to Bowen's claims and the system of underwriting reviews was revised.[101]

Bowen told the Commission that after he alerted management by sending emails, he went from supervising 220 people to supervising only 2, his bonus was reduced, and he was downgraded in his performance review.[102]

Some industry veterans took their concerns directly to government officials. J. Kyle Bass, a Dallas-based hedge fund manager and a former Bear Stearns executive, testified to the FCIC that he told the Federal Reserve that he believed the housing securitization market to be on a shaky foundation. "Their answer at the time was, and this was also the thought that was—that was homogeneous throughout Wall Street's analysts—was home prices always track income growth and jobs growth. And they showed me income growth on one chart and jobs growth on another, and said, 'We don't see what you're talking about because incomes are still growing and jobs are still growing.' And I said, well, you obviously don't realize where the dog is and where the tail is, and what's moving what."[103]

Even those who had profited from the growth of nontraditional lending practices said they became disturbed by what was happening. Herb Sandler, the co-founder of the mortgage lender Golden West Financial Corporation, which was heavily loaded with option ARM loans, wrote a letter to officials at the Federal Reserve, the FDIC, the OTS, and the OCC warning that regulators were "too dependent" on ratings agencies and "there is a high potential for gaming when virtually any asset can be churned through securitization and transformed into a AAA-rated asset, and when a multi-billion dollar industry is all too eager to facilitate this alchemy."[104]

Similarly, Lewis Ranieri, a mortgage finance veteran who helped engineer the Wall Street mortgage securitization machine in the 1980s, said he didn't like what he called "the madness" that had descended on the real estate market. Ranieri told the Commission, "I was not the only guy. I'm not telling you I was John the Baptist. There were enough of us, analysts and others, wandering around going 'look at this stuff,' that it would be hard to miss it."[105] Ranieri's own Houston-based Franklin Bank Corporation would itself collapse under the weight of the financial crisis in November 2008.

Other industry veterans inside the business also acknowledged that the rules of the game were being changed. "Poison" was the word famously used by Countrywide's Mozilo to describe one of the loan products his firm was originating.[106] "In all my years in the business I have never seen a more toxic [product]," he wrote in an internal email.[107] Others at the bank argued in response that they were offering products "pervasively offered in the marketplace by virtually every relevant competitor of ours."[108] Still, Mozilo was nervous. "There was a time when savings and loans were doing things because their competitors were doing it," he told the other executives. "They all went broke."[109]

In late 2005, regulators decided to take a look at the changing mortgage market. Sabeth Siddique, the assistant director for credit risk in the Division of Banking Supervision and Regulation at the Federal Reserve Board, was charged with investigating how broadly loan patterns were changing. He took the questions directly to large banks in 2005 and asked them how many of which kinds of loans they were making. Siddique found the information he received "very alarming," he told the Commission.[110] In fact, nontraditional loans made up 59% percent of originations at Countrywide, 58% percent at Wells Fargo, 51% at National City, 31% at Washington Mutual, 26.5% at CitiFinancial, and 18.3% at Bank of America. Moreover, the banks expected that their originations of nontraditional loans would rise by 17% in 2005, to $608.5 billion. The review also noted the "slowly deteriorating quality of loans due to loosening underwriting standards." In addition, it found that two-thirds of the nontraditional loans made by the banks in 2003 had been of the stated-income, minimal documentation variety known as liar loans, which had a particularly great likelihood of going sour.[111]

The reaction to Siddique's briefing was mixed. Federal Reserve Governor Bies recalled the response by the Fed governors and regional board directors as divided from the beginning. "Some people on the board and regional presidents . . . just wanted to come to a different answer. So they did ignore it, or the full thrust of it," she told the Commission.[112]

The OCC was also pondering the situation. Former comptroller of the currency John C. Dugan told the Commission that the push had come from below, from bank examiners who had become concerned about what they were seeing in the field.[113]

The agency began to consider issuing "guidance," a kind of nonbinding official warning to banks, that nontraditional loans could jeopardize safety and soundness and would invite scrutiny by bank examiners. Siddique said the OCC led the effort, which became a multiagency initiative.[114]

Bies said that deliberations over the potential guidance also stirred debate within the Fed, because some critics feared it both would stifle the financial innovation that was bringing record profits to Wall Street and the banks and would make homes less affordable. Moreover, all the agencies—the Fed, the OCC, the OTS, the FDIC, and the National Credit Union Administration—would need to work together on it, or it would unfairly block one group of lenders from issuing types of loans that were available from other lenders. The American Bankers Association and Mortgage Bankers Association opposed it as regulatory overreach.

"The bankers pushed back," Bies told the Commission. "The members of Congress pushed back. Some of our internal people at the Fed pushed back."[115]

The Mortgage Insurance Companies of America, which represents mortgage insurance companies, weighed in on the other side. "We are deeply concerned about the contagion effect from poorly underwritten or unsuitable mortgages and home equity loans," the trade association wrote to regulators in 2006. "The most recent market trends show alarming signs of undue risk-taking that puts both lenders and consumers at risk."[116]

In congressional testimony about a month later, William A. Simpson, the group's vice president, pointedly referred to past real estate downturns. "We take a conservative position on risk because of our first loss position," Simpson informed the Senate Subcommittee on Housing, Transportation and Community Development and the Senate Subcommittee on Economic Policy. "However, we also have a historical perspective. We were there when the mortgage markets turned sharply down during the mid-1980s especially in the oil patch and the early 1990s in California and the Northeast."[117]

Within the Fed, the debate grew heated and emotional, Siddique recalled. "It got very personal," he told the Commission. The ideological turf war lasted more than a year, while the number of nontraditional loans kept growing and growing.[118]

Consumer advocates kept up the heat. In a Fed Consumer Advisory Council meeting in March 2006, Fed Governors Bernanke, Mark Olson, and Kevin Warsh were specifically and publicly warned of dangers that nontraditional loans posed to the economy. Stella Adams, the executive director of the North Carolina Fair Housing Center, raised concerns that nontraditional lending "may precipitate a downward spiral that starts on the coast and then creates panic in the east that could have implications on our total economy as well."[119]

At the next meeting of the Fed's Consumer Advisory Council, held in June 2006 and attended by Bernanke, Bies, Olson, and Warsh, several consumer advocates described to the Fed governors alarming incidents that were now occurring all over the

country. Edward Sivak, the director of policy and evaluation at the Enterprise Corp. of the Delta, in Jackson, Mississippi, spoke of being told by mortgage brokers that property values were being inflated to maximize profit for real estate appraisers and loan originators. Alan White, the supervising attorney at Community Legal Services in Philadelphia, reported a "huge surge in foreclosures," noting that up to half of the borrowers he was seeing with troubled loans had been overcharged and given high-interest rate mortgages when their credit had qualified them for lower-cost loans. Hattie B. Dorsey, the president and chief executive officer of Atlanta Neighborhood Development, said she worried that houses were being flipped back and forth so much that the result would be neighborhood "decay." Carolyn Carter of the National Consumer Law Center in Massachusetts urged the Fed to use its regulatory authority to "prohibit abuses in the mortgage market."[120]

The balance was tipping. According to Siddique, before Greenspan left his post as Fed chairman in January 2006, he had indicated his willingness to accept the guidance. Ferguson worked with the Fed board and the regional Fed presidents to get it done. Bies supported it, and Bernanke did as well.[121]

More than a year after the OCC had began discussing the guidance, and after the housing market had peaked, it was issued in September 2006 as an interagency warning that affected banks, thrifts, and credit unions nationwide. Dozens of states followed, directing their versions of the guidance to tens of thousands of state-chartered lenders and mortgage brokers.

Then, in July 2008, long after the risky, nontraditional mortgage market had disappeared and the Wall Street mortgage securitization machine had ground to a halt, the Federal Reserve finally adopted new rules under HOEPA to curb the abuses about which consumer groups had raised red flags for years—including a requirement that borrowers have the ability to repay loans made to them.

By that time, however, the damage had been done. The total value of mortgage-backed securities issued between 2001 and 2006 reached $13.4 trillion.[122] There was a mountain of problematic securities, debt, and derivatives resting on real estate assets that were far less secure than they were thought to have been.

Just as Bernanke thought the spillovers from a housing market crash would be contained, so too policymakers, regulators, and financial executives did not understand how dangerously exposed major firms and markets had become to the potential contagion from these risky financial instruments. As the housing market began to turn, they scrambled to understand the rapid deterioration in the financial system and respond as losses in one part of that system would ricochet to others.

By the end of 2007, most of the subprime lenders had failed or been acquired, including New Century Financial, Ameriquest, and American Home Mortgage. In January 2008, Bank of America announced it would acquire the ailing lender Countrywide. It soon became clear that risk—rather than being diversified across the financial system, as had been thought—was concentrated at the largest financial firms. Bear Stearns, laden with risky mortgage assets and dependent on fickle short-term lending, was bought by JP Morgan with government assistance in the spring.

Before the summer was over, Fannie Mae and Freddie Mac would be put into conservatorship. Then, in September, Lehman Brothers failed and the remaining investment banks, Merrill Lynch, Goldman Sachs, and Morgan Stanley, struggled as they lost the market's confidence. AIG, with its massive credit default swap portfolio and exposure to the subprime mortgage market, was rescued by the government. Finally, many commercial banks and thrifts, which had their own exposures to declining mortgage assets and their own exposures to short-term credit markets, teetered. IndyMac had already failed over the summer; in September, Washington Mutual became the largest bank failure in U.S. history. In October, Wachovia struck a deal to be acquired by Wells Fargo. Citigroup and Bank of America fought to stay afloat. Before it was over, taxpayers had committed trillions of dollars through more than two dozen extraordinary programs to stabilize the financial system and to prop up the nation's largest financial institutions.

The crisis that befell the country in 2008 had been years in the making. In testimony to the Commission, former Fed chairman Greenspan defended his record and said most of his judgments had been correct. "I was right 70% of the time but I was wrong 30% of the time," he told the Commission.[123] Yet the consequences of what went wrong in the run-up to the crisis would be enormous.

The economic impact of the crisis has been devastating. And the human devastation is continuing. The officially reported unemployment rate hovered at almost 10% in November 2010, but the underemployment rate, which includes those who have given up looking for work and part-time workers who would prefer to be working full-time, was above 17%. And the share of unemployed workers who have been out of work for more than six months was just above 40%. Of large metropolitan areas, Las Vegas, Nevada, and Riverside–San Bernardino, California, had the highest unemployment—their rates were above 14%.

The loans were as lethal as many had predicted, and it has been estimated that ultimately as many as 13 million households in the United States may lose their homes to foreclosure. As of 2010, foreclosure rates were highest in Florida and Nevada; in Florida, nearly 14% of loans were in foreclosure, and Nevada was not very far behind.[124] Nearly one-quarter of American mortgage borrowers owed more on their mortgages than their home was worth. In Nevada, the percentage was nearly 70%.[125] Households have lost $11 trillion in wealth since 2006.

As Mark Zandi, the chief economist of Moody's Economy.com, testified to the Commission, "The financial crisis has dealt a very serious blow to the U.S. economy. The immediate impact was the Great Recession: the longest, broadest and most severe downturn since the Great Depression of the 1930s. . . . The longer-term fallout from the economic crisis is also very substantial. . . . It will take years for employment to regain its pre-crisis level."[126]

Looking back on the years before the crisis, the economist Dean Baker said: "So much of this was absolute public knowledge in the sense that we knew the number of loans that were being issued with zero down. Now, do we suddenly think we have that many more people—who are capable of taking on a loan with zero down who we

think are going to be able to pay that off—than was true 10, 15, 20 years ago? I mean, what's changed in the world? There were a lot of things that didn't require any investigation at all; these were totally available in the data."[127]

Warren Peterson, a home builder in Bakersfield, felt that he could pinpoint when the world changed to the day. Peterson built homes in an upscale neighborhood, and each Monday morning, he would arrive at the office to find a bevy of real estate agents, sales contracts in hand, vying to be the ones chosen to purchase the new homes he was building. The stream of traffic was constant. On one Saturday in November 2005, he was at the sales office and noticed that not a single purchaser had entered the building.

He called a friend, also in the home-building business, who said he had noticed the same thing, and asked him what he thought about it.

"It's over," his friend told Peterson.[128]

# PART II

## Setting the Stage

# 2

## SHADOW BANKING

---

### CONTENTS

The financial crisis of 2007 and 2008 was not a single event but a series of crises that rippled through the financial system and, ultimately, the economy. Distress in one area of the financial markets led to failures in other areas by way of interconnections and vulnerabilities that bankers, government officials, and others had missed or dismissed. When subprime and other risky mortgages—issued during a housing bubble that many experts failed to identify, and whose consequences were not understood— began to default at unexpected rates, a once-obscure market for complex investment securities backed by those mortgages abruptly failed. When the contagion spread, investors panicked—and the danger inherent in the whole system became manifest. Financial markets teetered on the edge, and brand-name financial institutions were left bankrupt or dependent on the taxpayers for survival.

Federal Reserve Chairman Ben Bernanke now acknowledges that he missed the systemic risks. "Prospective subprime losses were clearly not large enough on their own to account for the magnitude of the crisis," Bernanke told the Commission. "Rather, the system's vulnerabilities, together with gaps in the government's crisis-response toolkit, were the principal explanations of why the crisis was so severe and had such devastating effects on the broader economy."[1]

This part of our report explores the origins of risks as they developed in the financial system over recent decades. It is a fascinating story with profound consequences—a complex history that could yield its own report. Instead, we focus on four key developments that helped shape the events that shook our financial markets and economy. Detailed books could be written about each of them; we stick to the essentials for understanding our specific concern, which is the recent crisis.

First, we describe the phenomenal growth of the shadow banking system—the investment banks, most prominently, but also other financial institutions—that freely operated in capital markets beyond the reach of the regulatory apparatus that had been put in place in the wake of the crash of 1929 and the Great Depression.

This new system threatened the once-dominant traditional commercial banks, and they took their grievances to their regulators and to Congress, which slowly but steadily removed long-standing restrictions and helped banks break out of their traditional mold and join the feverish growth. As a result, two parallel financial systems of enormous scale emerged. This new competition not only benefited Wall Street but also seemed to help all Americans, lowering the costs of their mortgages and boosting the returns on their 401(k)s. Shadow banks and commercial banks were codependent competitors. Their new activities were very profitable—and, it turned out, very risky.

Second, we look at the evolution of financial regulation. To the Federal Reserve and other regulators, the new dual system that granted greater license to market participants appeared to provide a safer and more dynamic alternative to the era of traditional banking. More and more, regulators looked to financial institutions to police themselves—"deregulation" was the label. Former Fed chairman Alan Greenspan put it this way: "The market-stabilizing private regulatory forces should gradually displace many cumbersome, increasingly ineffective government structures."[2] In the Fed's view, if problems emerged in the shadow banking system, the large commercial banks—which were believed to be well-run, well-capitalized, and well-regulated despite the loosening of their restraints—could provide vital support. And if problems outstripped the market's ability to right itself, the Federal Reserve would take on the responsibility to restore financial stability. It did so again and again in the decades leading up to the recent crisis. And, understandably, much of the country came to assume that the Fed could always and would always save the day.

Third, we follow the profound changes in the mortgage industry, from the sleepy days when local lenders took full responsibility for making and servicing 30-year loans to a new era in which the idea was to sell the loans off as soon as possible, so that they could be packaged and sold to investors around the world. New mortgage products proliferated, and so did new borrowers. Inevitably, this became a market in which the participants—mortgage brokers, lenders, and Wall Street firms—had a greater stake in the quantity of mortgages signed up and sold than in their quality. We also trace the history of Fannie Mae and Freddie Mac, publicly traded corporations established by Congress that became dominant forces in providing financing to support the mortgage market while also seeking to maximize returns for investors.

Fourth, we introduce some of the most arcane subjects in our report: securitization, structured finance, and derivatives—words that entered the national vocabulary as the financial markets unraveled through 2007 and 2008. Put simply and most pertinently, structured finance was the mechanism by which subprime and other mortgages were turned into complex investments often accorded triple-A ratings by credit rating agencies whose own motives were conflicted. This entire market depended on finely honed computer models—which turned out to be divorced from reality—and on ever-rising housing prices. When that bubble burst, the complexity bubble also burst: the securities almost no one understood, backed by mortgages no lender would have signed 20 years earlier, were the first dominoes to fall in the financial sector.

A basic understanding of these four developments will bring the reader up to speed in grasping where matters stood for the financial system in the year 2000, at the dawn of a decade of promise and peril.

## COMMERCIAL PAPER AND REPOS:
## "UNFETTERED MARKETS"

For most of the 20th century, banks and thrifts accepted deposits and loaned that money to home buyers or businesses. Before the Depression, these institutions were vulnerable to runs, when reports or merely rumors that a bank was in trouble spurred depositors to demand their cash. If the run was widespread, the bank might not have enough cash on hand to meet depositors' demands: runs were common before the Civil War and then occurred in 1873, 1884, 1890, 1893, 1896, and 1907.[3] To stabilize financial markets, Congress created the Federal Reserve System in 1913, which acted as the lender of last resort to banks.

But the creation of the Fed was not enough to avert bank runs and sharp contractions in the financial markets in the 1920s and 1930s. So in 1933 Congress passed the Glass-Steagall Act, which, among other changes, established the Federal Deposit Insurance Corporation. The FDIC insured bank deposits up to $2,500—an amount that covered the vast majority of deposits at the time; that limit would climb to $100,000 by 1980, where it stayed until it was raised to $250,000 during the crisis in October 2008. Depositors no longer needed to worry about being first in line at a troubled bank's door. And if banks were short of cash, they could now borrow from the Federal Reserve, even when they could borrow nowhere else. The Fed, acting as lender of last resort, would ensure that banks would not fail simply from a lack of liquidity.

With these backstops in place, Congress restricted banks' activities to discourage them from taking excessive risks, another move intended to help prevent bank failures, with taxpayer dollars now at risk. Furthermore, Congress let the Federal Reserve cap interest rates that banks and thrifts—also known as savings and loans, or S&Ls—could pay depositors. This rule, known as Regulation Q, was also intended to keep institutions safe by ensuring that competition for deposits did not get out of hand.[4]

The system was stable as long as interest rates remained relatively steady, which they did during the first two decades after World War II. Beginning in the late-1960s, however, inflation started to increase, pushing up interest rates. For example, the rates that banks paid other banks for overnight loans had rarely exceeded 6% in the decades before 1980, when it reached 20%. However, thanks to Regulation Q, banks and thrifts were stuck offering roughly less than 6% on most deposits. Clearly, this was an untenable bind for the depository institutions, which could not compete on the most basic level of the interest rate offered on a deposit.

Compete with whom? In the 1970s, Merrill Lynch, Fidelity, Vanguard, and others persuaded consumers and businesses to abandon banks and thrifts for higher returns. These firms—eager to find new businesses, particularly after the Securities and Exchange Commission (SEC) abolished fixed commissions on stock trades in 1975—created money market mutual funds that invested these depositors' money in

short-term, safe securities such as Treasury bonds and highly rated corporate debt, and the funds paid higher interest rates than banks and thrifts were allowed to pay. The funds functioned like bank accounts, although with a different mechanism: customers bought shares redeemable daily at a stable value. In 1977, Merrill Lynch introduced something even more like a bank account: "cash management accounts" allowed customers to write checks. Other money market mutual funds quickly followed.[5]

These funds differed from bank and thrift deposits in one important respect: they were not protected by FDIC deposit insurance. Nevertheless, consumers liked the higher interest rates, and the stature of the funds' sponsors reassured them. The fund sponsors implicitly promised to maintain the full $1 net asset value of a share. The funds would not "break the buck," in Wall Street terms. Even without FDIC insurance, then, depositors considered these funds almost as safe as deposits in a bank or thrift. Business boomed, and so was born a key player in the shadow banking industry, the less-regulated market for capital that was growing up beside the traditional banking system. Assets in money market mutual funds jumped from $3 billion in 1977 to more than $740 billion in 1995 and $1.8 trillion by 2000.[6]

To maintain their edge over the insured banks and thrifts, the money market funds needed safe, high-quality assets to invest in, and they quickly developed an appetite for two booming markets: the "commercial paper" and "repo" markets. Through these instruments, Merrill Lynch, Morgan Stanley, and other Wall Street investment banks could broker and provide (for a fee) short-term financing to large corporations. Commercial paper was unsecured corporate debt—meaning that it was backed not by a pledge of collateral but only by the corporation's promise to pay. These loans were cheaper because they were short-term—for less than nine months, sometimes as short as two weeks and, eventually, as short as one day; the borrowers usually "rolled them over" when the loan came due, and then again and again. Because only financially stable corporations were able to issue commercial paper, it was considered a very safe investment; companies such as General Electric and IBM, investors believed, would always be good for the money. Corporations had been issuing commercial paper to raise money since the beginning of the century, but the practice grew much more popular in the 1960s.

This market, though, underwent a crisis that demonstrated that capital markets, too, were vulnerable to runs. Yet that crisis actually strengthened the market. In 1970, the Penn Central Transportation Company, the sixth-largest nonfinancial corporation in the U.S., filed for bankruptcy with $200 million in commercial paper outstanding. The railroad's default caused investors to worry about the broader commercial paper market; holders of that paper—the lenders—refused to roll over their loans to other corporate borrowers. The commercial paper market virtually shut down. In response, the Federal Reserve supported the commercial banks with almost $600 million in emergency loans and with interest rate cuts.[7] The Fed's actions enabled the banks, in turn, to lend to corporations so that they could pay off their commercial paper. After the Penn Central crisis, the issuers of commercial paper—the borrowers—typically set up standby lines of credit with major banks to en-

able them to pay off their debts should there be another shock. These moves reassured investors that commercial paper was a safe investment.

In the 1960s, the commercial paper market jumped more than sevenfold. Then in the 1970s, it grew almost fourfold. Among the largest buyers of commercial paper were the money market mutual funds. It seemed a win-win-win deal: the mutual funds could earn a solid return, stable companies could borrow more cheaply, and Wall Street firms could earn fees for putting the deals together. By 2000, commercial paper had risen to $1.6 trillion from less than $125 billion in 1980.[8]

The second major shadow banking market that grew significantly was the market for repos, or repurchase agreements. Like commercial paper, repos have a long history, but they proliferated quickly in the 1970s. Wall Street securities dealers often sold Treasury bonds with their relatively low returns to banks and other conservative investors, while then investing the cash proceeds of these sales in securities that paid higher interest rates. The dealers agreed to repurchase the Treasuries—often within a day—at a slightly higher price than that for which they sold them. This repo transaction—in essence a loan—made it inexpensive and convenient for Wall Street firms to borrow. Because these deals were essentially collateralized loans, the securities dealers borrowed nearly the full value of the collateral, minus a small "haircut." Like commercial paper, repos were renewed, or "rolled over," frequently. For that reason, both forms of borrowing could be considered "hot money"—because lenders could quickly move in and out of these investments in search of the highest returns, they could be a risky source of funding.

The repo market, too, had vulnerabilities, but it, too, had emerged from an early crisis stronger than ever. In 1982, two major borrowers, the securities firms Drysdale and Lombard-Wall, defaulted on their repo obligations, creating large losses for lenders. In the ensuing fallout, the Federal Reserve acted as lender of last resort to support a shadow banking market. The Fed loosened the terms on which it lent Treasuries to securities firms, leading to a 10-fold increase in its securities lending. Following this episode, most repo participants switched to a tri-party arrangement in which a large clearing bank acted as intermediary between borrower and lender, essentially protecting the collateral and the funds by putting them in escrow.[9] This mechanism would have severe consequences in 2007 and 2008. In the 1980s, however, these new procedures stabilized the repo market.

The new parallel banking system—with commercial paper and repo providing cheaper financing, and money market funds providing better returns for consumers and institutional investors—had a crucial catch: its popularity came at the expense of the banks and thrifts. Some regulators viewed this development with growing alarm. According to Alan Blinder, the vice chairman of the Federal Reserve from 1994 to 1996, "We were concerned as bank regulators with the eroding competitive position of banks, which of course would threaten ultimately their safety and soundness, due to the competition they were getting from a variety of nonbanks—and these were mainly Wall Street firms, that were taking deposits from them, and getting into the loan business to some extent. So, yeah, it was a concern; you could see a downward trend in the share of banking assets to financial assets."[10]

## Traditional and Shadow Banking Systems

*The funding available through the shadow banking system grew sharply in the 2000s, exceeding the traditional banking system in the years before the crisis.*

IN TRILLIONS OF DOLLARS

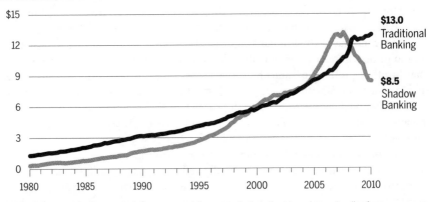

NOTE: Shadow banking funding includes commercial paper and other short-term borrowing (bankers acceptances), repo, net securities loaned, liabilities of asset-backed securities issuers, and money market mutual fund assets.

SOURCE: Federal Reserve Flow of Funds Report

*Figure 2.1*

Figure 2.1 shows that during the 1990s the shadow banking system steadily gained ground on the traditional banking sector—and actually surpassed the banking sector for a brief time after 2000.

Banks argued that their problems stemmed from the Glass-Steagall Act. Glass-Steagall strictly limited commercial banks' participation in the securities markets, in part to end the practices of the 1920s, when banks sold highly speculative securities to depositors. In 1956, Congress also imposed new regulatory requirements on banks owned by holding companies, in order to prevent a holding company from endangering any of its deposit-taking banks.

Bank supervisors monitored banks' leverage—their assets relative to equity—because excessive leverage endangered a bank. Leverage, used by nearly every financial institution, amplifies returns. For example, if an investor uses $100 of his own money to purchase a security that increases in value by 10%, he earns $10. However, if he borrows another $900 and invests 10 times as much ($1,000), the same 10% increase in value yields a profit of $100, double his out-of-pocket investment. If the investment sours, though, leverage magnifies the loss just as much. A decline of 10% costs the unleveraged investor $10, leaving him with $90, but wipes out the leveraged investor's $100. An investor buying assets worth 10 times his capital has a leverage

ratio of 10:1, with the numbers representing the total money invested compared to the money the investor has committed to the deal.

In 1981, bank supervisors established the first formal minimum capital standards, which mandated that capital—the amount by which assets exceed debt and other liabilities—should be at least 5% of assets for most banks. Capital, in general, reflects the value of shareholders' investment in the bank, which bears the first risk of any potential losses.

By comparison, Wall Street investment banks could employ far greater leverage, unhindered by oversight of their safety and soundness or by capital requirements outside of their broker-dealer subsidiaries, which were subject to a net capital rule. The main shadow banking participants—the money market funds and the investment banks that sponsored many of them—were not subject to the same supervision as banks and thrifts. The money in the shadow banking markets came not from federally insured depositors but principally from investors (in the case of money market funds) or commercial paper and repo markets (in the case of investment banks). Both money market funds and securities firms were regulated by the Securities and Exchange Commission. But the SEC, created in 1934, was supposed to supervise the securities markets to protect investors. It was charged with ensuring that issuers of securities disclosed sufficient information for investors, and it required firms that bought, sold, and brokered transactions in securities to comply with procedural restrictions such as keeping customers' funds in separate accounts. Historically, the SEC did not focus on the safety and soundness of securities firms, although it did impose capital requirements on broker-dealers designed to protect their clients.

Meanwhile, since deposit insurance did not cover such instruments as money market mutual funds, the government was not on the hook. There was little concern about a run. In theory, the investors had knowingly risked their money. If an investment lost value, it lost value. If a firm failed, it failed. As a result, money market funds had no capital or leverage standards. "There was no regulation," former Fed chairman Paul Volcker told the Financial Crisis Inquiry Commission. "It was kind of a free ride."[11] The funds had to follow only regulations restricting the type of securities in which they could invest, the duration of those securities, and the diversification of their portfolios. These requirements were supposed to ensure that investors' shares would not diminish in value and would be available anytime—important reassurances, but not the same as FDIC insurance. The only protection against losses was the implicit guarantee of sponsors like Merrill Lynch with reputations to protect.

Increasingly, the traditional world of banks and thrifts was ill-equipped to keep up with the parallel world of the Wall Street firms. The new shadow banks had few constraints on raising and investing money. Commercial banks were at a disadvantage and in danger of losing their dominant position. Their bind was labeled "disintermediation," and many critics of the financial regulatory system concluded that policy makers, all the way back to the Depression, had trapped depository institutions in this unprofitable straitjacket not only by capping the interest rates they could pay depositors and imposing capital requirements but also by preventing the institutions from competing against the investment banks (and their money market mutual

funds). Moreover, critics argued, the regulatory constraints on industries across the entire economy discouraged competition and restricted innovation, and the financial sector was a prime example of such a hampered industry.

Years later, Fed Chairman Greenspan described the argument for deregulation: "Those of us who support market capitalism in its more competitive forms might argue that unfettered markets create a degree of wealth that fosters a more civilized existence. I have always found that insight compelling."[12]

## THE SAVINGS AND LOAN CRISIS:
### "THEY PUT A LOT OF PRESSURE ON THEIR REGULATORS"

Traditional financial institutions continued to chafe against the regulations still in place. The playing field wasn't level, which "put a lot of pressure on institutions to get higher-rate performing assets," former SEC Chairman Richard Breeden told the FCIC. "And they put a lot of pressure on their regulators to allow this to happen."[13]

The banks and the S&Ls went to Congress for help. In 1980, the Depository Institutions Deregulation and Monetary Control Act repealed the limits on the interest rates that depository institutions could offer on their deposits. Although this law removed a significant regulatory constraint on banks and thrifts, it could not restore their competitive advantage. Depositors wanted a higher rate of return, which banks and thrifts were now free to pay. But the interest banks and thrifts could earn off of mortgages and other long-term loans was largely fixed and could not match their new costs. While their deposit base increased, they now faced an interest rate squeeze. In 1979, the difference in interest earned on the banks' and thrifts' safest investments (one-year Treasury notes) over interest paid on deposits was almost 5.5 percentage points; by 1994, it was only 2.6 percentage points. The institutions lost almost 3 percentage points of the advantage they had enjoyed when the rates were capped.[14] The 1980 legislation had not done enough to reduce the competitive pressures facing the banks and thrifts.

That legislation was followed in 1982 by the Garn-St. Germain Act, which significantly broadened the types of loans and investments that thrifts could make. The act also gave banks and thrifts broader scope in the mortgage market. Traditionally, they had relied on 30-year, fixed-rate mortgages. But the interest on fixed-rate mortgages on their books fell short as inflation surged in the mid-1970s and early 1980s and banks and thrifts found it increasingly difficult to cover the rising costs of their short-term deposits. In the Garn-St. Germain Act, Congress sought to relieve this interest rate mismatch by permitting banks and thrifts to issue interest-only, balloon-payment, and adjustable-rate mortgages (ARMs), even in states where state laws forbade these loans. For consumers, interest-only and balloon mortgages made homeownership more affordable, but only in the short term. Borrowers with ARMs enjoyed lower mortgage rates when interest rates decreased, but their rates would rise when interest rates rose. For banks and thrifts, ARMs offered an interest rate that floated in relationship to the rates they were paying to attract money from depositors. The floating mortgage rate protected banks and S&Ls from the interest rate

squeeze caused by inflation, but it effectively transferred the risk of rising interest rates to borrowers.

Then, beginning in 1987, the Federal Reserve accommodated a series of requests from the banks to undertake activities forbidden under Glass-Steagall and its modifications. The new rules permitted nonbank subsidiaries of bank holding companies to engage in "bank-ineligible" activities, including selling or holding certain kinds of securities that were not permissible for national banks to invest in or underwrite. At first, the Fed strictly limited these bank-ineligible securities activities to no more than 5% of the assets or revenue of any subsidiary. Over time, however, the Fed relaxed these restrictions. By 1997, bank-ineligible securities could represent up to 25% of assets or revenues of a securities subsidiary, and the Fed also weakened or eliminated other firewalls between traditional banking subsidiaries and the new securities subsidiaries of bank holding companies.[15]

Meanwhile, the OCC, the regulator of banks with national charters, was expanding the permissible activities of national banks to include those that were "functionally equivalent to, or a logical outgrowth of, a recognized bank power."[16] Among these new activities were underwriting as well as trading bets and hedges, known as derivatives, on the prices of certain assets. Between 1983 and 1994, the OCC broadened the derivatives in which banks might deal to include those related to debt securities (1983), interest and currency exchange rates (1988), stock indices (1988), precious metals such as gold and silver (1991), and equity stocks (1994).

Fed Chairman Greenspan and many other regulators and legislators supported and encouraged this shift toward deregulated financial markets. They argued that financial institutions had strong incentives to protect their shareholders and would therefore regulate themselves through improved risk management. Likewise, financial markets would exert strong and effective discipline through analysts, credit rating agencies, and investors. Greenspan argued that the urgent question about government regulation was whether it strengthened or weakened private regulation. Testifying before Congress in 1997, he framed the issue this way: financial "modernization" was needed to "remove outdated restrictions that serve no useful purpose, that decrease economic efficiency, and that . . . limit choices and options for the consumer of financial services." Removing the barriers "would permit banking organizations to compete more effectively in their natural markets. The result would be a more efficient financial system providing better services to the public."[17]

During the 1980s and early 1990s, banks and thrifts expanded into higher-risk loans with higher interest payments. They made loans to oil and gas producers, financed leveraged buyouts of corporations, and funded developers of residential and commercial real estate. The largest commercial banks advanced money to companies and governments in "emerging markets," such as countries in Asia and Latin America. Those markets offered potentially higher profits, but were much riskier than the banks' traditional lending. The consequences appeared almost immediately—especially in the real estate markets, with a bubble and massive overbuilding in residential and commercial sectors in certain regions. For example, house prices rose 7% per year in Texas from 1980 to 1985.[18] In California, prices rose 13% annually from 1985

to 1990.[19] The bubble burst first in Texas in 1985 and 1986, but the trouble rapidly spread across the Southeast to the mid-Atlantic states and New England, then swept back across the country to California and Arizona. Before the crisis ended, house prices had declined nationally by 2.5% from July 1990 to February 1992[20]—the first such fall since the Depression—driven by steep drops in regional markets.[21] In the 1980s, with the mortgages in their portfolios paying considerably less than current interest rates, spiraling defaults on the thrifts' residential and commercial real estate loans, and losses on energy-related, leveraged-buyout, and overseas loans, the industry was shattered.[22]

Almost 3,000 commercial banks and thrifts failed in what became known as the S&L crisis of the 1980s and early 1990s. By comparison, only 243 banks had failed between 1934 and 1980. By 1994, one-sixth of federally insured depository institutions had either closed or required financial assistance, affecting 20% of the banking system's assets.[23] More than 1,000 bank and S&L executives were convicted of felonies.[24] By the time the government cleanup was complete, the ultimate cost of the crisis was $160 billion.[25]

Despite new laws passed by Congress in 1989 and 1991 in response to the S&L crisis that toughened supervision of thrifts, the impulse toward deregulation continued. The deregulatory movement focused in part on continuing to dismantle regulations that limited depository institutions' activities in the capital markets. In 1991, the Treasury Department issued an extensive study calling for the elimination of the old regulatory framework for banks, including removal of all geographic restrictions on banking and repeal of the Glass-Steagall Act. The study urged Congress to abolish these restrictions in the belief that large nationwide banks closely tied to the capital markets would be more profitable and more competitive with the largest banks from the United Kingdom, Europe, and Japan. The report contended that its proposals would let banks embrace innovation and produce a "stronger, more diversified financial system that will provide important benefits to the consumer and important protections to the taxpayer."[26]

The biggest banks pushed Congress to adopt Treasury's recommendations. Opposed were insurance agents, real estate brokers, and smaller banks, who felt threatened by the possibility that the largest banks and their huge pools of deposits would be unleashed to compete without restraint. The House of Representatives rejected Treasury's proposal in 1991, but similar proposals were adopted by Congress later in the 1990s.

In dealing with the banking and thrift crisis of the 1980s and early 1990s, Congress was greatly concerned by a spate of high-profile bank bailouts. In 1984, federal regulators rescued Continental Illinois, the nation's 7th-largest bank; in 1988, First Republic, number 14; in 1989, MCorp, number 36; in 1991, Bank of New England, number 33. These banks had relied heavily on uninsured short-term financing to aggressively expand into high-risk lending, leaving them vulnerable to abrupt withdrawals once confidence in their solvency evaporated. Deposits covered by the FDIC were protected from loss, but regulators felt obliged to protect the uninsured depositors—those whose balances exceeded the statutorily protected limits—to prevent po-

tential runs on even larger banks that reportedly may have lacked sufficient assets to satisfy their obligations, such as First Chicago, Bank of America, and Manufacturers Hanover.[27]

During a hearing on the rescue of Continental Illinois, Comptroller of the Currency C. Todd Conover stated that federal regulators would not allow the 11 largest "money center banks" to fail.[28] This was a new regulatory principle, and within moments it had a catchy name. Representative Stewart McKinney of Connecticut responded, "We have a new kind of bank. It is called 'too big to fail'—TBTF—and it is a wonderful bank."[29]

In 1990, during this era of federal rescues of large commercial banks, Drexel Burnham Lambert—once the country's fifth-largest investment bank—failed. Crippled by legal troubles and losses in its junk bond portfolio, the firm was forced into the largest bankruptcy in the securities industry to date when lenders shunned it in the commercial paper and repo markets. While creditors, including other investment banks, were rattled and absorbed heavy losses, the government did not step in, and Drexel's failure did not cause a crisis. So far, it seemed that among financial firms, only commercial banks were deemed too big to fail.

In 1991, Congress tried to limit this "too big to fail" principle, passing the Federal Deposit Insurance Corporation Improvement Act (FDICIA), which sought to curb the use of taxpayer funds to rescue failing depository institutions. FDICIA mandated that federal regulators must intervene early when a bank or thrift got into trouble. In addition, if an institution did fail, the FDIC had to resolve the failed institution in a manner that produced the least cost to the FDIC's deposit insurance fund. However, the legislation contained two important loopholes. One exempted the FDIC from the least-cost constraints if it, the Treasury, and the Federal Reserve determined that the failure of an institution posed a "systemic risk" to markets. The other loophole addressed a concern raised by some Wall Street investment banks, Goldman Sachs in particular: the reluctance of commercial banks to help securities firms during previous market disruptions, such as Drexel's failure. Wall Street firms successfully lobbied for an amendment to FDICIA to authorize the Fed to act as lender of last resort to investment banks by extending loans collateralized by the investment banks' securities.[30]

In the end, the 1991 legislation sent financial institutions a mixed message: you are *not* too big to fail—until and unless you *are* too big to fail. So the possibility of bailouts for the biggest, most centrally placed institutions—in the commercial and shadow banking industries—remained an open question until the next crisis, 16 years later.

# 3

# SECURITIZATION AND DERIVATIVES

<hr>

## CONTENTS

## FANNIE MAE AND FREDDIE MAC:
## "THE WHOLE ARMY OF LOBBYISTS"

The crisis in the thrift industry created an opening for Fannie Mae and Freddie Mac, the two massive government-sponsored enterprises (GSEs) created by Congress to support the mortgage market.

Fannie Mae (officially, the Federal National Mortgage Association) was chartered by the Reconstruction Finance Corporation during the Great Depression in 1938 to buy mortgages insured by the Federal Housing Administration (FHA). The new government agency was authorized to purchase mortgages that adhered to the FHA's underwriting standards, thereby virtually guaranteeing the supply of mortgage credit that banks and thrifts could extend to homebuyers. Fannie Mae either held the mortgages in its portfolio or, less often, resold them to thrifts, insurance companies, or other investors. After World War II, Fannie Mae got authority to buy home loans guaranteed by the Veterans Administration (VA) as well.

This system worked well, but it had a weakness: Fannie Mae bought mortgages by borrowing. By 1968, Fannie's mortgage portfolio had grown to $7.2 billion and its debt weighed on the federal government.[1] To get Fannie's debt off of the government's balance sheet, the Johnson administration and Congress reorganized it as a publicly traded corporation and created a new government entity, Ginnie Mae (officially, the Government National Mortgage Association) to take over Fannie's subsidized mortgage programs and loan portfolio. Ginnie also began guaranteeing pools of FHA and VA mortgages. The new Fannie still purchased federally insured mortgages, but it was now a hybrid, a "government-sponsored enterprise."

Two years later, in 1970, the thrifts persuaded Congress to charter a second GSE, Freddie Mac (officially, the Federal Home Loan Mortgage Corporation), to help the

thrifts sell their mortgages. The legislation also authorized Fannie and Freddie to buy "conventional" fixed-rate mortgages, which were not backed by the FHA or the VA. Conventional mortgages were stiff competition to FHA mortgages because borrowers could get them more quickly and with lower fees. Still, the conventional mortgages did have to conform to the GSEs' loan size limits and underwriting guidelines, such as debt-to-income and loan-to-value ratios. The GSEs purchased only these "conforming" mortgages.

Before 1968, Fannie Mae generally held the mortgages it purchased, profiting from the difference—or spread—between its cost of funds and the interest paid on these mortgages. The 1968 and 1970 laws gave Ginnie, Fannie, and Freddie another option: securitization. Ginnie was the first to securitize mortgages, in 1970. A lender would assemble a pool of mortgages and issue securities backed by the mortgage pool. Those securities would be sold to investors, with Ginnie guaranteeing timely payment of principal and interest. Ginnie charged a fee to issuers for this guarantee. In 1971, Freddie got into the business of buying mortgages, pooling them, and then selling mortgage-backed securities. Freddie collected fees from lenders for guaranteeing timely payment of principal and interest. In 1981, after a spike in interest rates caused large losses on Fannie's portfolio of mortgages, Fannie followed. During the 1980s and 1990s, the conventional mortgage market expanded, the GSEs grew in importance, and the market share of the FHA and VA declined.

Fannie and Freddie had dual missions, both public and private: support the mortgage market and maximize returns for shareholders. They did not originate mortgages; they purchased them—from banks, thrifts, and mortgage companies—and either held them in their portfolios or securitized and guaranteed them. Congress granted both enterprises special privileges, such as exemptions from state and local taxes and a $2.25 billion line of credit each from the Treasury. The Federal Reserve provided services such as electronically clearing payments for GSE debt and securities as if they were Treasury bonds. So Fannie and Freddie could borrow at rates almost as low as the Treasury paid. Federal laws allowed banks, thrifts, and investment funds to invest in GSE securities with relatively favorable capital requirements and without limits. By contrast, laws and regulations strictly limited the amount of loans banks could make to a single borrower and restricted their investments in the debt obligations of other firms. In addition, unlike banks and thrifts, the GSEs were required to hold very little capital to protect against losses: only 0.45% to back their guarantees of mortgage-backed securities and 2.5% to back the mortgages in their portfolios. This compared to bank and thrift capital requirements of at least 4% of mortgages assets under capital standards. Such privileges led investors and creditors to believe that the government implicitly guaranteed the GSEs' mortgage-backed securities and debt and that GSE securities were therefore almost as safe as Treasury bills. As a result, investors accepted very low returns on GSE-guaranteed mortgage-backed securities and GSE debt obligations.

Mortgages are long-term assets often funded by short-term borrowings. For example, thrifts generally used customer deposits to fund their mortgages. Fannie

bought its mortgage portfolio by borrowing short- and medium-term. In 1979, when the Fed increased short-term interest rates to quell inflation, Fannie, like the thrifts, found that its cost of funding rose while income from mortgages did not. By the 1980s, the Department of Housing and Urban Development (HUD) estimated Fannie had a negative net worth of $10 billion.[2] Freddie emerged unscathed because unlike Fannie then, its primary business was guaranteeing mortgage-backed securities, not holding mortgages in its portfolio. In guaranteeing mortgage-backed securities, Freddie Mac avoided taking the interest rate risk that hit Fannie's portfolio.

In 1982, Congress provided tax relief and HUD relaxed Fannie's capital requirements to help the company avert failure. These efforts were consistent with lawmakers' repeated proclamations that a vibrant market for home mortgages served the best interests of the country, but the moves also reinforced the impression that the government would never abandon Fannie and Freddie. Fannie and Freddie would soon buy and either hold or securitize mortgages worth hundreds of billions, then trillions, of dollars. Among the investors were U.S. banks, thrifts, investment funds, and pension funds, as well as central banks and investment funds around the world. Fannie and Freddie had become too big to fail.

While the government continued to favor Fannie and Freddie, they toughened regulation of the thrifts following the savings and loan crisis. Thrifts had previously dominated the mortgage business as large holders of mortgages. In the Financial Institutions Reform, Recovery, and Enforcement Act of 1989 (FIRREA), Congress imposed tougher, bank-style capital requirements and regulations on thrifts. By contrast, in the Federal Housing Enterprises Financial Safety and Soundness Act of 1992, Congress created a supervisor for the GSEs, the Office of Federal Housing Enterprise Oversight (OFHEO), without legal powers comparable to those of bank and thrift supervisors in enforcement, capital requirements, funding, and receivership. Cracking down on thrifts while not on the GSEs was no accident. The GSEs had shown their immense political power during the drafting of the 1992 law.[3] "OFHEO was structurally weak and almost designed to fail," said Armando Falcon Jr., a former director of the agency, to the FCIC.[4]

All this added up to a generous federal subsidy. One 2005 study put the value of that subsidy at $122 billion or more and estimated that more than half of these benefits accrued to shareholders, not to homebuyers.[5]

Given these circumstances, regulatory arbitrage worked as it always does: the markets shifted to the lowest-cost, least-regulated havens. After Congress imposed stricter capital requirements on thrifts, it became increasingly profitable for them to securitize with or sell loans to Fannie and Freddie rather than hold on to the loans. The stampede was on. Fannie's and Freddie's debt obligations and outstanding mortgage-backed securities grew from $759 billion in 1990 to $1.4 trillion in 1995 and $2.4 trillion in 2000.[6]

The legislation that transformed Fannie in 1968 also authorized HUD to prescribe affordable housing goals for Fannie: to "require that a reasonable portion of the corporation's mortgage purchases be related to the national goal of providing adequate

housing for low and moderate income families, but with reasonable economic return to the corporation."[7] In 1978, HUD tried to implement the law and, after a barrage of criticism from the GSEs and the mortgage and real estate industries, issued a weak regulation encouraging affordable housing.[8] In the 1992 Federal Housing Enterprises Financial Safety and Soundness Act, Congress extended HUD's authority to set affordable housing goals for Fannie and Freddie. Congress also changed the language to say that in the pursuit of affordable housing, "a reasonable economic return . . . may be less than the return earned on other activities." The law required HUD to consider "the need to maintain the sound financial condition of the enterprises." The act now ordered HUD to set goals for Fannie and Freddie to buy loans for low- and moderate-income housing, special affordable housing, and housing in central cities, rural areas, and other underserved areas. Congress instructed HUD to periodically set a goal for each category as a percentage of the GSEs' mortgage purchases.

In 1995, President Bill Clinton announced an initiative to boost homeownership from 65.1% to 67.5% of families by 2000, and one component raised the affordable housing goals at the GSEs. Between 1993 and 1995, almost 2.8 million households entered the ranks of homeowners, nearly twice as many as in the previous two years. "But we have to do a lot better," Clinton said. "This is the new way home for the American middle class. We have got to raise incomes in this country. We have got to increase security for people who are doing the right thing, and we have got to make people believe that they can have some permanence and stability in their lives even as they deal with all the changing forces that are out there in this global economy."[9] The push to expand homeownership continued under President George W. Bush, who, for example, introduced a "Zero Down Payment Initiative" that under certain circumstances could remove the 3% down payment rule for first-time home buyers with FHA-insured mortgages.[10]

In describing the GSEs' affordable housing loans, Andrew Cuomo, secretary of Housing and Urban Development from 1997 to 2001 and now governor of New York, told the FCIC, "Affordability means many things. There were moderate income loans. These were teachers, these were firefighters, these were municipal employees, these were people with jobs who paid mortgages. These were not subprime, predatory loans at all."[11]

Fannie and Freddie were now crucial to the housing market, but their dual missions—promoting mortgage lending while maximizing returns to shareholders—were problematic. Former Fannie CEO Daniel Mudd told the FCIC that "the GSE structure required the companies to maintain a fine balance between financial goals and what we call the mission goals . . . the root cause of the GSEs' troubles lies with their business model."[12] Former Freddie CEO Richard Syron concurred: "I don't think it's a good business model."[13]

Fannie and Freddie accumulated political clout because they depended on federal subsidies and an implicit government guarantee, and because they had to deal with regulators, affordable housing goals, and capital standards imposed by Congress and HUD. From 1999 to 2008, the two reported spending more than $164 million on lobbying, and their employees and political action committees contributed $15 million

to federal election campaigns.[14] The "Fannie and Freddie political machine resisted any meaningful regulation using highly improper tactics," Falcon, who regulated them from 1999 to 2005, testified. "OFHEO was constantly subjected to malicious political attacks and efforts of intimidation."[15] James Lockhart, the director of OFHEO and its successor, the Federal Housing Finance Agency, from 2006 through 2009, testified that he argued for reform from the moment he became director and that the companies were "allowed to be . . . so politically strong that for many years they resisted the very legislation that might have saved them."[16] Former HUD secretary Mel Martinez described to the FCIC "the whole army of lobbyists that continually paraded in a bipartisan fashion through my offices. . . . It's pretty amazing the number of people that were in their employ."[17]

In 1995, that army helped secure new regulations allowing the GSEs to count toward their affordable housing goals not just their whole loans but mortgage-related securities issued by other companies, which the GSEs wanted to purchase as investments. Still, Congressional Budget Office Director June O'Neill declared in 1998 that "the goals are not difficult to achieve, and it is not clear how much they have affected the enterprises' actions. In fact . . . depository institutions as well as the Federal Housing Administration devote a larger proportion of their mortgage lending to targeted borrowers and areas than do the enterprises."[18]

Something else was clear: Fannie and Freddie, with their low borrowing costs and lax capital requirements, were immensely profitable throughout the 1990s. In 2000, Fannie had a return on equity of 26%; Freddie, 39%. That year, Fannie and Freddie held or guaranteed more than $2 trillion of mortgages, backed by only $35.7 billion of shareholder equity.[19]

## STRUCTURED FINANCE:
### "IT WASN'T REDUCING THE RISK"

While Fannie and Freddie enjoyed a near-monopoly on securitizing fixed-rate mortgages that were within their permitted loan limits, in the 1980s the markets began to securitize many other types of loans, including adjustable-rate mortgages (ARMs) and other mortgages the GSEs were not eligible or willing to buy. The mechanism worked the same: an investment bank, such as Lehman Brothers or Morgan Stanley (or a securities affiliate of a bank), bundled loans from a bank or other lender into securities and sold them to investors, who received investment returns funded by the principal and interest payments from the loans. Investors held or traded these securities, which were often more complicated than the GSEs' basic mortgage-backed securities; the assets were not just mortgages but equipment leases, credit card debt, auto loans, and manufactured housing loans. Over time, banks and securities firms used securitization to mimic banking activities outside the regulatory framework for banks. For example, where banks traditionally took money from deposits to make loans and held them until maturity, banks now used money from the capital markets—often from money market mutual funds—to make loans, packaging them into securities to sell to investors.

For commercial banks, the benefits were large. By moving loans off their books, the banks reduced the amount of capital they were required to hold as protection against losses, thereby improving their earnings. Securitization also let banks rely less on deposits for funding, because selling securities generated cash that could be used to make loans. Banks could also keep parts of the securities on their books as collateral for borrowing, and fees from securitization became an important source of revenues.

Lawrence Lindsey, a former Federal Reserve governor and the director of the National Economic Council under President George W. Bush, told the FCIC that previous housing downturns made regulators worry about banks' holding whole loans on their books. "If you had a regional . . . real estate downturn it took down the banks in that region along with it, which exacerbated the downturn," Lindsey said. "So we said to ourselves, 'How on earth do we get around this problem?' And the answer was, 'Let's have a national securities market so we don't have regional concentration.' . . . It was intentional."[20]

Private securitizations, or structured finance securities, had two key benefits to investors: *pooling* and *tranching*. If many loans were pooled into one security, a few defaults would have minimal impact. Structured finance securities could also be sliced up and sold in portions—known as tranches—which let buyers customize their payments. Risk-averse investors would buy tranches that paid off first in the event of default, but had lower yields. Return-oriented investors bought riskier tranches with higher yields. Bankers often compared it to a waterfall; the holders of the senior tranches—at the top of the waterfall—were paid before the more junior tranches. And if payments came in below expectations, those at the bottom would be the first to be left high and dry.

Securitization was designed to benefit lenders, investment bankers, and investors. Lenders earned fees for originating and selling loans. Investment banks earned fees for issuing mortgage-backed securities. These securities fetched a higher price than if the underlying loans were sold individually, because the securities were customized to investors' needs, were more diversified, and could be easily traded. Purchasers of the safer tranches got a higher rate of return than ultra-safe Treasury notes without much extra risk—at least in theory. However, the financial engineering behind these investments made them harder to understand and to price than individual loans. To determine likely returns, investors had to calculate the statistical probabilities that certain kinds of mortgages might default, and to estimate the revenues that would be lost because of those defaults. Then investors had to determine the effect of the losses on the payments to different tranches.

This complexity transformed the three leading credit rating agencies—Moody's, Standard & Poor's (S&P), and Fitch—into key players in the process, positioned between the issuers and the investors of securities. Before securitization became common, the credit rating agencies had mainly helped investors evaluate the safety of municipal and corporate bonds and commercial paper. Although evaluating probabilities was their stock-in-trade, they found that rating these securities required a new type of analysis.

Participants in the securitization industry realized that they needed to secure favorable credit ratings in order to sell structured products to investors. Investment banks therefore paid handsome fees to the rating agencies to obtain the desired ratings. "The rating agencies were important tools to do that because you know the people that we were selling these bonds to had never really had any history in the mortgage business.... They were looking for an independent party to develop an opinion," Jim Callahan told the FCIC; Callahan is CEO of PentAlpha, which services the securitization industry, and years ago he worked on some of the earliest securitizations.[21]

With these pieces in place—banks that wanted to shed assets and transfer risk, investors ready to put their money to work, securities firms poised to earn fees, rating agencies ready to expand, and information technology capable of handling the job— the securitization market exploded. By 1999, when the market was 16 years old, about $900 billion worth of securitizations, beyond those done by Fannie, Freddie, and Ginnie, were outstanding (see figure 3.1). That included $114 billion of automobile loans and over $250 billion of credit card debt; nearly $150 billion worth of securities were mortgages ineligible for securitization by Fannie and Freddie. Many were subprime.[22]

Securitization was not just a boon for commercial banks; it was also a lucrative new line of business for the Wall Street investment banks, with which the commercial banks worked to create the new securities. Wall Street firms such as Salomon Brothers and Morgan Stanley became major players in these complex markets and relied increasingly on quantitative analysts, called "quants." As early as the 1970s, Wall Street executives had hired quants—analysts adept in advanced mathematical theory and computers—to develop models to predict how markets or securities might change. Securitization increased the importance of this expertise. Scott Patterson, author of *The Quants,* told the FCIC that using models dramatically changed finance. "Wall Street is essentially floating on a sea of mathematics and computer power," Patterson said.[23]

The increasing dependence on mathematics let the quants create more complex products and let their managers say, and maybe even believe, that they could better manage those products' risk. JP Morgan developed the first "Value at Risk" model (VaR), and the industry soon adopted different versions. These models purported to predict with at least 95% certainty how much a firm could lose if market prices changed.[24] But models relied on assumptions based on limited historical data; for mortgage-backed securities, the models would turn out to be woefully inadequate. And modeling human behavior was different from the problems the quants had addressed in graduate school. "It's not like trying to shoot a rocket to the moon where you know the law of gravity," Emanuel Derman, a Columbia University finance professor who worked at Goldman Sachs for 17 years, told the Commission. "The way people feel about gravity on a given day isn't going to affect the way the rocket behaves."[25]

Paul Volcker, Fed chairman from 1979 to 1987, told the Commission that regulators were concerned as early as the late 1980s that once banks began selling instead of holding the loans they were making, they would care less about loan quality. Yet as

## Asset-Backed Securities Outstanding

*In the 1990s, many kinds of loans were packaged into asset-backed securities.*

IN BILLIONS OF DOLLARS

NOTE: Residential loans do not include loans securitized by government-sponsored enterprises.
SOURCE: Securities Industry and Financial Markets Association

*Figure 3.1*

these instruments became increasingly complex, regulators increasingly relied on the banks to police their own risks. "It was all tied up in the hubris of financial engineers, but the greater hubris let markets take care of themselves," Volcker said.[26] Vincent Reinhart, a former director of the Fed's Division of Monetary Affairs, told the Commission that he and other regulators failed to appreciate the complexity of the new financial instruments and the difficulties that complexity posed in assessing risk.[27]

Securitization "was diversifying the risk," said Lindsey, the former Fed governor. "But it wasn't reducing the risk. . . . You as an individual can diversify your risk. The system as a whole, though, cannot reduce the risk. And that's where the confusion lies."[28]

### THE GROWTH OF DERIVATIVES: "BY FAR THE MOST SIGNIFICANT EVENT IN FINANCE DURING THE PAST DECADE"

During the financial crisis, leverage and complexity became closely identified with one element of the story: derivatives. Derivatives are financial contracts whose prices are determined by, or "derived" from, the value of some underlying asset, rate, index,

or event. They are not used for capital formation or investment, as are securities; rather, they are instruments for hedging business risk or for speculating on changes in prices, interest rates, and the like. Derivatives come in many forms; the most common are over-the-counter-swaps and exchange-traded futures and options.[29] They may be based on commodities (including agricultural products, metals, and energy products), interest rates, currency rates, stocks and indexes, and credit risk. They can even be tied to events such as hurricanes or announcements of government figures.

Many financial and commercial firms use such derivatives. A firm may hedge its price risk by entering into a derivatives contract that offsets the effect of price movements. Losses suffered because of price movements can be recouped through gains on the derivatives contract. Institutional investors that are risk-averse sometimes use interest rate swaps to reduce the risk to their investment portfolios of inflation and rising interest rates by trading fixed interest payments for floating payments with risk-taking entities, such as hedge funds. Hedge funds may use these swaps for the purpose of speculating, in hopes of profiting on the rise or fall of a price or interest rate.

The derivatives markets are organized as exchanges or as over-the-counter (OTC) markets, although some recent electronic trading facilities blur the distinctions. The oldest U.S. exchange is the Chicago Board of Trade, where futures and options are traded. Such exchanges are regulated by federal law and play a useful role in price discovery—that is, in revealing the market's view on prices of commodities or rates underlying futures and options. OTC derivatives are traded by large financial institutions—traditionally, bank holding companies and investment banks—which act as derivatives dealers, buying and selling contracts with customers. Unlike the futures and options exchanges, the OTC market is neither centralized nor regulated. Nor is it transparent, and thus price discovery is limited. No matter the measurement—trading volume, dollar volume, risk exposure—derivatives represent a very significant sector of the U.S. financial system.

The principal legislation governing these markets is the Commodity Exchange Act of 1936, which originally applied only to derivatives on domestic agricultural products. In 1974, Congress amended the act to require that futures and options contracts on virtually all commodities, including financial instruments, be traded on a regulated exchange, and created a new federal independent agency, the Commodity Futures Trading Commission (CFTC), to regulate and supervise the market.[30]

Outside of this regulated market, an over-the-counter market began to develop and grow rapidly in the 1980s. The large financial institutions acting as OTC derivatives dealers worried that the Commodity Exchange Act's requirement that trading occur on a regulated exchange might be applied to the products they were buying and selling. In 1993, the CFTC sought to address these concerns by exempting certain nonstandardized OTC derivatives from that requirement and from certain other provisions of the Commodity Exchange Act, except for prohibitions against fraud and manipulation.[31]

As the OTC market grew following the CFTC's exemption, a wave of significant losses and scandals hit the market. Among many examples, in 1994 Procter & Gamble,

a leading consumer products company, reported a pretax loss of $157 million, the largest derivatives loss by a nonfinancial firm, stemming from OTC interest and foreign exchange rate derivatives sold to it by Bankers Trust. Procter & Gamble sued Bankers Trust for fraud—a suit settled when Bankers Trust forgave most of the money that Procter & Gamble owed it. That year, the CFTC and the Securities and Exchange Commission (SEC) fined Bankers Trust $10 million for misleading Gibson Greeting Cards on interest rate swaps resulting in a mark-to-market loss of $23 million, larger than Gibson's prior-year profits. In late 1994, Orange County, California, announced it had lost $1.5 billion speculating in OTC derivatives. The county filed for bankruptcy—the largest by a municipality in U.S. history. Its derivatives dealer, Merrill Lynch, paid $400 million to settle claims.[32] In response, the U.S. General Accounting Office issued a report on financial derivatives that found dangers in the concentration of OTC derivatives activity among 15 major dealers, concluding that "the sudden failure or abrupt withdrawal from trading of any one of these large dealers could cause liquidity problems in the markets and could also pose risks to the others, including federally insured banks and the financial system as a whole."[33] While Congress then held hearings on the OTC derivatives market, the adoption of regulatory legislation failed amid intense lobbying by the OTC derivatives dealers and opposition by Fed Chairman Greenspan.

In 1996, Japan's Sumitomo Corporation lost $2.6 billion on copper derivatives traded on a London exchange. The CFTC charged the company with using derivatives to manipulate copper prices, including using OTC derivatives contracts to disguise the speculation and to finance the scheme. Sumitomo settled for $150 million in penalties and restitution. The CFTC also charged Merrill Lynch with knowingly and intentionally aiding, abetting, and assisting the manipulation of copper prices; it settled for a fine of $15 million.[34]

Debate intensified in 1998. In May, the CFTC under Chairperson Brooksley Born said the agency would reexamine the way it regulated the OTC derivatives market, given the market's rapid evolution and the string of major losses since 1993. The CFTC requested comments. It got them.

Some came from other regulators, who took the unusual step of publicly criticizing the CFTC. On the day that the CFTC issued a concept release, Treasury Secretary Robert Rubin, Greenspan, and SEC Chairman Arthur Levitt issued a joint statement denouncing the CFTC's move: "We have grave concerns about this action and its possible consequences. . . . We are very concerned about reports that the CFTC's action may increase the legal uncertainty concerning certain types of OTC derivatives."[35] They proposed a moratorium on the CFTC's ability to regulate OTC derivatives.

For months, Rubin, Greenspan, Levitt, and Deputy Treasury Secretary Lawrence Summers opposed the CFTC's efforts in testimony to Congress and in other public pronouncements. As Alan Greenspan said: "Aside from safety and soundness regulation of derivatives dealers under the banking and securities laws, regulation of derivatives transactions that are privately negotiated by professionals is unnecessary."[36]

In September, the Federal Reserve Bank of New York orchestrated a $3.6 billion recapitalization of Long-Term Capital Management (LTCM) by 14 major OTC

derivatives dealers. An enormous hedge fund, LTCM had amassed more than $1 trillion in notional amount of OTC derivatives and $125 billion of securities on $4.8 billion of capital without the knowledge of its major derivatives counterparties or federal regulators.[37] Greenspan testified to Congress that in the New York Fed's judgment, LTCM's failure would potentially have had systemic effects: a default by LTCM "would not only have a significant distorting impact on market prices but also in the process could produce large losses, or worse, for a number of creditors and counterparties, and for other market participants who were not directly involved with LTCM."[38]

Nonetheless, just weeks later, in October 1998, Congress passed the requested moratorium.

Greenspan continued to champion derivatives and advocate deregulation of the OTC market and the exchange-traded market. "By far the most significant event in finance during the past decade has been the extraordinary development and expansion of financial derivatives," Greenspan said at a Futures Industry Association conference in March 1999. "The fact that the OTC markets function quite effectively without the benefits of [CFTC regulation] provides a strong argument for development of a less burdensome regime for exchange-traded financial derivatives."[39]

The following year—after Born's resignation—the President's Working Group on Financial Markets, a committee of the heads of the Treasury, Federal Reserve, SEC, and Commodity Futures Trading Commission charged with tracking the financial system and chaired by then Treasury Secretary Larry Summers, essentially adopted Greenspan's view. The group issued a report urging Congress to deregulate OTC derivatives broadly and to reduce CFTC regulation of exchange-traded derivatives as well.[40]

In December 2000, in response, Congress passed and President Clinton signed the Commodity Futures Modernization Act of 2000 (CFMA), which in essence deregulated the OTC derivatives market and eliminated oversight by both the CFTC and the SEC. The law also preempted application of state laws on gaming and on bucket shops (illegal brokerage operations) that otherwise could have made OTC derivatives transactions illegal. The SEC did retain antifraud authority over securities-based OTC derivatives such as stock options. In addition, the regulatory powers of the CFTC relating to exchange-traded derivatives were weakened but not eliminated.

The CFMA effectively shielded OTC derivatives from virtually all regulation or oversight. Subsequently, other laws enabled the expansion of the market. For example, under a 2005 amendment to the bankruptcy laws, derivatives counterparties were given the advantage over other creditors of being able to immediately terminate their contracts and seize collateral at the time of bankruptcy.

The OTC derivatives market boomed. At year-end 2000, when the CFMA was passed, the notional amount of OTC derivatives outstanding globally was $95.2 trillion, and the gross market value was $3.2 trillion.[41] In the seven and a half years from then until June 2008, when the market peaked, outstanding OTC derivatives increased more than sevenfold to a notional amount of $672.6 trillion; their gross market value was $20.3 trillion.[42]

Greenspan testified to the FCIC that credit default swaps—a small part of the

market when Congress discussed regulating derivatives in the 1990s—"did create problems" during the financial crisis.[43] Rubin testified that when the CFMA passed he was "not opposed to the regulation of derivatives" and had personally agreed with Born's views, but that "very strongly held views in the financial services industry in opposition to regulation" were insurmountable.[44] Summers told the FCIC that while risks could not necessarily have been foreseen years ago, "by 2008 our regulatory framework with respect to derivatives was manifestly inadequate," and that "the derivatives that proved to be by far the most serious, those associated with credit default swaps, increased 100 fold between 2000 and 2008."[45]

One reason for the rapid growth of the derivatives market was the capital requirements advantage that many financial institutions could obtain through hedging with derivatives. As discussed above, financial firms may use derivatives to hedge their risks. Such use of derivatives can lower a firm's Value at Risk as determined by computer models. In addition to gaining this advantage in risk management, such hedges can lower the amount of capital that banks are required to hold, thanks to a 1996 amendment to the regulatory regime known as the Basel International Capital Accord, or "Basel I."

Meeting in Basel, Switzerland, in 1988, the world's central banks and bank supervisors adopted principles for banks' capital standards, and U.S. banking regulators made adjustments to implement them. Among the most important was the requirement that banks hold more capital against riskier assets. Fatefully, the Basel rules made capital requirements for mortgages and mortgage-backed securities looser than for all other assets related to corporate and consumer loans.[46] Indeed, capital requirements for banks' holdings of Fannie's and Freddie's securities were less than for all other assets except those explicitly backed by the U.S. government.[47]

These international capital standards accommodated the shift to increased leverage. In 1996, large banks sought more favorable capital treatment for their trading, and the Basel Committee on Banking Supervision adopted the Market Risk Amendment to Basel I. This provided that if banks hedged their credit or market risks using derivatives, they could hold less capital against their exposures from trading and other activities.[48]

OTC derivatives let derivatives traders—including the large banks and investment banks—increase their leverage. For example, entering into an equity swap that mimicked the returns of someone who owned the actual stock may have had some upfront costs, but the amount of collateral posted was much smaller than the upfront cost of purchasing the stock directly. Often no collateral was required at all. Traders could use derivatives to receive the same gains—or losses—as if they had bought the actual security, and with only a fraction of a buyer's initial financial outlay.[49] Warren Buffett, the chairman and chief executive officer of Berkshire Hathaway Inc., testified to the FCIC about the unique characteristics of the derivatives market, saying, "they accentuated enormously, in my view, the leverage in the system." He went on to call derivatives "very dangerous stuff," difficult for market participants, regulators, auditors, and investors to understand—indeed, he concluded, "I don't think I could manage" a complex derivatives book.[50]

A key OTC derivative in the financial crisis was the credit default swap (CDS), which offered the seller a little potential upside at the relatively small risk of a potentially large downside. The purchaser of a CDS transferred to the seller the default risk of an underlying debt. The debt security could be any bond or loan obligation. The CDS buyer made periodic payments to the seller during the life of the swap. In return, the seller offered protection against default or specified "credit events" such as a partial default. If a credit event such as a default occurred, the CDS seller would typically pay the buyer the face value of the debt.

Credit default swaps were often compared to insurance: the seller was described as insuring against a default in the underlying asset. However, while similar to insurance, CDS escaped regulation by state insurance supervisors because they were treated as deregulated OTC derivatives. This made CDS very different from insurance in at least two important respects. First, only a person with an insurable interest can obtain an insurance policy. A car owner can insure only the car she owns—not her neighbor's. But a CDS purchaser can use it to speculate on the default of a loan the purchaser does not own. These are often called "naked credit default swaps" and can inflate potential losses and corresponding gains on the default of a loan or institution.

Before the CFMA was passed, there was uncertainty about whether or not state insurance regulators had authority over credit default swaps. In June 2000, in response to a letter from the law firm of Skadden, Arps, Slate, Meagher & Flom, LLP, the New York State Insurance Department determined that "naked" credit default swaps did not count as insurance and were therefore not subject to regulation.[51]

In addition, when an insurance company sells a policy, insurance regulators require that it put aside reserves in case of a loss. In the housing boom, CDS were sold by firms that failed to put up any reserves or initial collateral or to hedge their exposure. In the run-up to the crisis, AIG, the largest U.S. insurance company, would accumulate a one-half trillion dollar position in credit risk through the OTC market without being required to post one dollar's worth of initial collateral or making any other provision for loss.[52] AIG was not alone. The value of the underlying assets for CDS outstanding worldwide grew from $6.4 trillion at the end of 2004 to a peak of $58.2 trillion at the end of 2007.[53] A significant portion was apparently speculative or naked credit default swaps.[54]

Much of the risk of CDS and other derivatives was concentrated in a few of the very largest banks, investment banks, and others—such as AIG Financial Products, a unit of AIG[55]—that dominated dealing in OTC derivatives. Among U.S. bank holding companies, 97% of the notional amount of OTC derivatives, millions of contracts, were traded by just five large institutions (in 2008, JPMorgan Chase, Citigroup, Bank of America, Wachovia, and HSBC)—many of the same firms that would find themselves in trouble during the financial crisis.[56] The country's five largest investment banks were also among the world's largest OTC derivatives dealers.

While financial institutions surveyed by the FCIC said they do not track revenues and profits generated by their derivatives operations, some firms did provide estimates. For example, Goldman Sachs estimated that between 25% and 35% of its revenues from 2006 through 2009 were generated by derivatives, including 70% to

75% of the firm's commodities business, and half or more of its interest rate and currencies business. From May 2007 through November 2008, $133 billion, or 86%, of the $155 billion of trades made by Goldman's mortgage department were derivative transactions.[57]

When the nation's biggest financial institutions were teetering on the edge of failure in 2008, everyone watched the derivatives markets. What were the institutions' holdings? Who were the counterparties? How would they fare? Market participants and regulators would find themselves straining to understand an unknown battlefield shaped by unseen exposures and interconnections as they fought to keep the financial system from collapsing.

# 4

# DEREGULATION REDUX

## CONTENTS

## EXPANSION OF BANKING ACTIVITIES:
### "SHATTERER OF GLASS-STEAGALL"

By the mid-1990s, the parallel banking system was booming, some of the largest commercial banks appeared increasingly like the large investment banks, and all of them were becoming larger, more complex, and more active in securitization. Some academics and industry analysts argued that advances in data processing, telecommunications, and information services created economies of scale and scope in finance and thereby justified ever-larger financial institutions. Bigger would be safer, the argument went, and more diversified, innovative, efficient, and better able to serve the needs of an expanding economy. Others contended that the largest banks were not necessarily more efficient but grew because of their commanding market positions and creditors' perception they were too big to fail. As they grew, the large banks pressed regulators, state legislatures, and Congress to remove almost all remaining barriers to growth and competition. They had much success. In 1994 Congress authorized nationwide banking with the Riegle-Neal Interstate Banking and Branching Efficiency Act. This let bank holding companies acquire banks in every state, and removed most restrictions on opening branches in more than one state. It preempted any state law that restricted the ability of out-of-state banks to compete within the state's borders.[1]

Removing barriers helped consolidate the banking industry. Between 1990 and 2005, 74 "megamergers" occurred involving banks with assets of more than $10 billion each. Meanwhile the 10 largest jumped from owning 25% of the industry's assets

to 55%. From 1998 to 2007, the combined assets of the five largest U.S. banks—Bank of America, Citigroup, JP Morgan, Wachovia, and Wells Fargo—more than tripled, from $2.2 trillion to $6.8 trillion.[2] And investment banks were growing bigger, too. Smith Barney acquired Shearson in 1993 and Salomon Brothers in 1997, while Paine Webber purchased Kidder, Peabody in 1995. Two years later, Morgan Stanley merged with Dean Witter, and Bankers Trust purchased Alex. Brown & Sons. The assets of the five largest investment banks—Goldman Sachs, Morgan Stanley, Merrill Lynch, Lehman Brothers, and Bear Stearns—quadrupled, from $1 trillion in 1998 to $4 trillion in 2007.[3]

In 1996, the Economic Growth and Regulatory Paperwork Reduction Act required federal regulators to review their rules every decade and solicit comments on "outdated, unnecessary, or unduly burdensome" rules.[4] Some agencies responded with gusto. In 2003, the Federal Deposit Insurance Corporation's annual report included a photograph of the vice chairman, John Reich; the director of the Office of Thrift Supervision (OTS), James Gilleran; and three banking industry representatives using a chainsaw and pruning shears to cut the "red tape" binding a large stack of documents representing regulations.

Less enthusiastic agencies felt heat. Former Securities and Exchange Commission chairman Arthur Levitt told the FCIC that once word of a proposed regulation got out, industry lobbyists would rush to complain to members of the congressional committee with jurisdiction over the financial activity at issue. According to Levitt, these members would then "harass" the SEC with frequent letters demanding answers to complex questions and appearances of officials before Congress. These requests consumed much of the agency's time and discouraged it from making regulations. Levitt described it as "kind of a blood sport to make the particular agency look stupid or inept or venal."[5]

However, others said interference—at least from the executive branch—was modest. John Hawke, a former comptroller of the currency, told the FCIC he found the Treasury Department "exceedingly sensitive" to his agency's independence. His successor, John Dugan, said "statutory firewalls" prevented interference from the executive branch.[6]

Deregulation went beyond dismantling regulations; its supporters were also disinclined to adopt new regulations or challenge industry on the risks of innovations. Federal Reserve officials argued that financial institutions, with strong incentives to protect shareholders, would regulate themselves by carefully managing their own risks. In a 2003 speech, Fed Vice Chairman Roger Ferguson praised "the truly impressive improvement in methods of risk measurement and management and the growing adoption of these technologies by mostly large banks and other financial intermediaries."[7] Likewise, Fed and other officials believed that markets would self-regulate through the activities of analysts and investors. "It is critically important to recognize that no market is ever truly unregulated," said Fed Chairman Alan Greenspan in 1997. "The self-interest of market participants generates private market regulation. Thus, the real question is not whether a market should be regulated.

Rather, the real question is whether government intervention strengthens or weakens private regulation."[8]

Richard Spillenkothen, the Fed's director of Banking Supervision and Regulation from 1991 to 2006, discussed banking supervision in a memorandum submitted to the FCIC: "Supervisors understood that forceful and proactive supervision, especially early intervention before management weaknesses were reflected in poor financial performance, might be viewed as i) overly-intrusive, burdensome, and heavy-handed, ii) an undesirable constraint on credit availability, or iii) inconsistent with the Fed's public posture."[9]

To create checks and balances and keep any agency from becoming arbitrary or inflexible, senior policy makers pushed to keep multiple regulators.[10] In 1994, Greenspan testified against proposals to consolidate bank regulation: "The current structure provides banks with a method . . . of shifting their regulator, an effective test that provides a limit on the arbitrary position or excessively rigid posture of any one regulator. The pressure of a potential loss of institutions has inhibited excessive regulation and acted as a countervailing force to the bias of a regulatory agency to overregulate."[11] Further, some regulators, including the OTS and Office of the Comptroller of the Currency (OCC), were funded largely by assessments from the institutions they regulated. As a result, the larger the number of institutions that chose these regulators, the greater their budget.

Emboldened by success and the tenor of the times, the largest banks and their regulators continued to oppose limits on banks' activities or growth. The barriers separating commercial banks and investment banks had been crumbling, little by little, and now seemed the time to remove the last remnants of the restrictions that separated banks, securities firms, and insurance companies.

In the spring of 1996, after years of opposing repeal of Glass-Steagall, the Securities Industry Association—the trade organization of Wall Street firms such as Goldman Sachs and Merrill Lynch—changed course. Because restrictions on banks had been slowly removed during the previous decade, banks already had beachheads in securities and insurance. Despite numerous lawsuits against the Fed and the OCC, securities firms and insurance companies could not stop this piecemeal process of deregulation through agency rulings.[12] Edward Yingling, the CEO of the American Bankers Association (a lobbying organization), said, "Because we had knocked so many holes in the walls separating commercial and investment banking and insurance, we were able to aggressively enter their businesses—in some cases more aggressively than they could enter ours. So first the securities industry, then the insurance companies, and finally the agents came over and said let's negotiate a deal and work together."[13]

In 1998, Citicorp forced the issue by seeking a merger with the insurance giant Travelers to form Citigroup. The Fed approved it, citing a technical exemption to the Bank Holding Company Act,[14] but Citigroup would have to divest itself of many Travelers assets within five years unless the laws were changed. Congress had to make a decision: Was it prepared to break up the nation's largest financial firm? Was it time to repeal the Glass-Steagall Act, once and for all?

As Congress began fashioning legislation, the banks were close at hand. In 1999, the financial sector spent $187 million lobbying at the federal level, and individuals and political action committees (PACs) in the sector donated $202 million to federal election campaigns in the 2000 election cycle. From 1999 through 2008, federal lobbying by the financial sector reached $2.7 billion; campaign donations from individuals and PACs topped $1 billion.[15]

In November 1999, Congress passed and President Clinton signed the Gramm-Leach-Bliley Act (GLBA), which lifted most of the remaining Glass-Steagall-era restrictions. The new law embodied many of the measures Treasury had previously advocated.[16] The *New York Times* reported that Citigroup CEO Sandy Weill hung in his office "a hunk of wood—at least 4 feet wide—etched with his portrait and the words 'The Shatterer of Glass-Steagall.'"[17]

Now, as long as bank holding companies satisfied certain safety and soundness conditions, they could underwrite and sell banking, securities, and insurance products and services. Their securities affiliates were no longer bound by the Fed's 25% limit—their primary regulator, the SEC, set their only boundaries. Supporters of the legislation argued that the new holding companies would be more profitable (due to economies of scale and scope), safer (through a broader diversification of risks), more useful to consumers (thanks to the convenience of one-stop shopping for financial services), and more competitive with large foreign banks, which already offered loans, securities, and insurance products. The legislation's opponents warned that allowing banks to combine with securities firms would promote excessive speculation and could trigger a crisis like the crash of 1929. John Reed, former co-CEO of Citigroup, acknowledged to the FCIC that, in hindsight, "the compartmentalization that was created by Glass-Steagall would be a positive factor," making less likely a "catastrophic failure" of the financial system.[18]

To win the securities industry's support, the new law left in place two exceptions that let securities firms own thrifts and industrial loan companies, a type of depository institution with stricter limits on its activities. Through them, securities firms could access FDIC-insured deposits without supervision by the Fed. Some securities firms immediately expanded their industrial loan company and thrift subsidiaries. Merrill's industrial loan company grew from less than $1 billion in assets in 1998 to $4 billion in 1999, and to $78 billion in 2007. Lehman's thrift grew from $88 million in 1998 to $3 billion in 1999, and its assets rose as high as $24 billion in 2005.[19]

For institutions regulated by the Fed, the new law also established a hybrid regulatory structure known colloquially as "Fed-Lite." The Fed supervised financial holding companies as a whole, looking only for risks that cut across the various subsidiaries owned by the holding company. To avoid duplicating other regulators' work, the Fed was required to rely "to the fullest extent possible" on examinations and reports of those agencies regarding subsidiaries of the holding company, including banks, securities firms, and insurance companies. The expressed intent of Fed-Lite was to eliminate excessive or duplicative regulation.[20] However, Fed Chairman Ben Bernanke told the FCIC that Fed-Lite "made it difficult for any single regulator to reliably see the whole picture of activities and risks of large, complex banking institutions."[21]

Indeed, the regulators, including the Fed, would fail to identify excessive risks and unsound practices building up in nonbank subsidiaries of financial holding companies such as Citigroup and Wachovia.[22]

The convergence of banks and securities firms also undermined the supportive relationship between banking and securities markets that Fed Chairman Greenspan had considered a source of stability. He compared it to a "spare tire": if large commercial banks ran into trouble, their large customers could borrow from investment banks and others in the capital markets; if those markets froze, banks could lend using their deposits. After 1990, securitized mortgage lending provided another source of credit to home buyers and other borrowers that softened a steep decline in lending by thrifts and banks. The system's resilience following the crisis in Asian financial markets in the late 1990s further proved his point, Greenspan said.[23]

The new regime encouraged growth and consolidation within and across banking, securities, and insurance. The bank-centered financial holding companies such as Citigroup, JP Morgan, and Bank of America could compete directly with the "big five" investment banks—Goldman Sachs, Morgan Stanley, Merrill Lynch, Lehman Brothers, and Bear Stearns—in securitization, stock and bond underwriting, loan syndication, and trading in over-the-counter (OTC) derivatives. The biggest bank holding companies became major players in investment banking. The strategies of the largest commercial banks and their holding companies came to more closely resemble the strategies of investment banks. Each had advantages: commercial banks enjoyed greater access to insured deposits, and the investment banks enjoyed less regulation. Both prospered from the late 1990s until the outbreak of the financial crisis in 2007. However, Greenspan's "spare tire" that had helped make the system less vulnerable would be gone when the financial crisis emerged—all the wheels of the system would be spinning on the same axle.

## LONG-TERM CAPITAL MANAGEMENT:
## "THAT'S WHAT HISTORY HAD PROVED TO THEM"

In August 1998, Russia defaulted on part of its national debt, panicking markets. Russia announced it would restructure its debt and postpone some payments. In the aftermath, investors dumped higher-risk securities, including those having nothing to do with Russia, and fled to the safety of U.S. Treasury bills and FDIC-insured deposits. In response, the Federal Reserve cut short-term interest rates three times in seven weeks.[24] With the commercial paper market in turmoil, it was up to the commercial banks to take up the slack by lending to corporations that could not roll over their short-term paper. Banks loaned $30 billion in September and October of 1998—about 2.5 times the usual amount[25]—and helped prevent a serious disruption from becoming much worse. The economy avoided a slump.

Not so for Long-Term Capital Management, a large U.S. hedge fund. LTCM had devastating losses on its $125 billion portfolio of high-risk debt securities, including the junk bonds and emerging market debt that investors were dumping.[26] To buy these securities, the firm had borrowed $24 for every $1 of investors' equity;[27] lenders

included Merrill Lynch, JP Morgan, Morgan Stanley, Lehman Brothers, Goldman Sachs, and Chase Manhattan. The previous four years, LTCM's leveraging strategy had produced magnificent returns: 19.9%, 42.8%, 40.8%, and 17.1%, while the S&P 500 yielded an average 21%.[28]

But leverage works both ways, and in just one month after Russia's partial default, the fund lost more than $4 billion—or more than 80% of its nearly $5 billion in capital. Its debt was about $120 billion. The firm faced insolvency.[29]

If it were only a matter of less than $5 billion, LTCM's failure might have been manageable. But the firm had further leveraged itself by entering into derivatives contracts with more than $1 trillion in notional amount—mostly interest rate and equity derivatives.[30] With very little capital in reserve, it threatened to default on its obligations to its derivatives counterparties—including many of the largest commercial and investment banks. Because LTCM had negotiated its derivatives transactions in the opaque over-the-counter market, the markets did not know the size of its positions or the fact that it had posted very little collateral against those positions. As the Fed noted then, if all the fund's counterparties had tried to liquidate their positions simultaneously, asset prices across the market might have plummeted, which would have created "exaggerated" losses. This was a classic setup for a run: losses were likely, but nobody knew who would get burned. The Fed worried that with financial markets already fragile, these losses would spill over to investors with no relationship to LTCM, and credit and derivatives markets might "cease to function for a period of one or more days and maybe longer."[31]

To avert such a disaster, the Fed called an emergency meeting of major banks and securities firms with large exposures to LTCM.[32] On September 23, after considerable urging, 14 institutions agreed to organize a consortium to inject $3.6 billion into LTCM in return for 90% of its stock.[33] The firms contributed between $100 million and $300 million each, although Bear Stearns declined to participate.[34] An orderly liquidation of LTCM's securities and derivatives followed.

William McDonough, then president of the New York Fed, insisted "no Federal Reserve official pressured anyone, and no promises were made."[35] The rescue involved no government funds. Nevertheless, the Fed's orchestration raised a question: how far would it go to forestall what it saw as a systemic crisis?

The Fed's aggressive response had precedents in the previous two decades. In 1970, the Fed had supported the commercial paper market; in 1980, dealers in silver futures; in 1982, the repo market; in 1987, the stock market after the Dow Jones Industrial Average fell by 26% percent in three days. All provided a template for future interventions. Each time, the Fed cut short-term interest rates and encouraged financial firms in the parallel banking and traditional banking sectors to help ailing markets. And sometimes it organized a consortium of financial institutions to rescue firms.[36]

During the same period, federal regulators also rescued several large banks that they viewed as "too big to fail" and protected creditors of those banks, including uninsured depositors. Their rationale was that major banks were crucial to the financial markets and the economy, and regulators could not allow the collapse of one

large bank to trigger a panic among uninsured depositors that might lead to more bank failures.

But it was a completely different proposition to argue that a hedge fund could be considered too big to fail because its collapse might destabilize capital markets. Did LTCM's rescue indicate that the Fed was prepared to protect creditors of any type of firm if its collapse might threaten the capital markets? Harvey Miller, the bankruptcy counsel for Lehman Brothers when it failed in 2008, told the FCIC that "they [hedge funds] expected the Fed to save Lehman, based on the Fed's involvement in LTCM's rescue. That's what history had proved to them."[37]

For Stanley O'Neal, Merrill's CFO during the LTCM rescue, the experience was "indelible." He told the FCIC, "The lesson I took away from it though was that had the market seizure and panic and lack of liquidity lasted longer, there would have been a lot of firms across the Street that were irreparably harmed, and Merrill would have been one of those."[38]

Greenspan argued that the events of 1998 had confirmed the spare tire theory. He said in a 1999 speech that the successful resolution of the 1998 crisis showed that "diversity within the financial sector provides insurance against a financial problem turning into economy-wide distress."[39] The President's Working Group on Financial Markets came to a less definite conclusion. In a 1999 report, the group noted that LTCM and its counterparties had "underestimated the likelihood that liquidity, credit, and volatility spreads would move in a similar fashion in markets across the world at the same time."[40] Many financial firms would make essentially the same mistake a decade later. For the Working Group, this miscalculation raised an important issue: "As new technology has fostered a major expansion in the volume and, in some cases, the leverage of transactions, some existing risk models have underestimated the probability of severe losses. This shows the need for insuring that decisions about the appropriate level of capital for risky positions become an issue that is explicitly considered."[41]

The need for risk management grew in the following decade. The Working Group was already concerned that neither the markets nor their regulators were prepared for tail risk—an unanticipated event causing catastrophic damage to financial institutions and the economy. Nevertheless, it cautioned that overreacting to threats such as LTCM would diminish the dynamism of the financial sector and the real economy: "Policy initiatives that are aimed at simply reducing default likelihoods to extremely low levels might be counterproductive if they unnecessarily disrupt trading activity and the intermediation of risks that support the financing of real economic activity."[42]

Following the Working Group's findings, the SEC five years later would issue a rule expanding the number of hedge fund advisors—to include most advisors—that needed to register with the SEC. The rule would be struck down in 2006 by the United States Court of Appeals for the District of Columbia after the SEC was sued by an investment advisor and hedge fund.[43]

Markets were relatively calm after 1998, Glass-Steagall would be deemed unnecessary, OTC derivatives would be deregulated, and the stock market and the economy would continue to prosper for some time. Like all the others (with the exception

of the Great Depression), this crisis soon faded into memory. But not before, in February 1999, *Time* magazine featured Robert Rubin, Larry Summers, and Alan Greenspan on its cover as "The Committee to Save the World." Federal Reserve Chairman Greenspan became a cult hero—the "Maestro"—who had handled every emergency since the 1987 stock market crash.[44]

## DOT-COM CRASH: "LAY ON MORE RISK"

The late 1990s was a good time for investment banking. Annual public underwritings and private placements of corporate securities in U.S. markets almost quadrupled, from $600 billion in 1994 to $2.2 trillion in 2001. Annual initial public offerings of stocks (IPOs) soared from $28 billion in 1994 to $76 billion in 2000 as banks and securities firms sponsored IPOs for new Internet and telecommunications companies—the dot-coms and telecoms.[45] A stock market boom ensued comparable to the great bull market of the 1920s. The value of publicly traded stocks rose from $5.8 trillion in December 1994 to $17.8 trillion in March 2000.[46] The boom was particularly striking in recent dot-com and telecom issues on the NASDAQ exchange. Over this period, the NASDAQ skyrocketed from 752 to 5,048.

In the spring of 2000, the tech bubble burst. The "new economy" dot-coms and telecoms had failed to match the lofty expectations of investors, who had relied on bullish—and, as it turned out, sometimes deceptive—research reports issued by the same banks and securities firms that had underwritten the tech companies' initial public offerings. Between March 2000 and March 2001, the NASDAQ fell by almost two-thirds. This slump accelerated after the terrorist attacks on September 11 as the nation slipped into recession. Investors were further shaken by revelations of accounting frauds and other scandals at prominent firms such as Enron and Worldcom. Some leading commercial and investment banks settled with regulators over improper practices in the allocation of IPO shares during the bubble—for spinning (doling out shares in "hot" IPOs in return for reciprocal business) and laddering (doling out shares to investors who agreed to buy more later at higher prices).[47] The regulators also found that public research reports prepared by investment banks' analysts were tainted by conflicts of interest. The SEC, New York's attorney general, the National Association of Securities Dealers (now FINRA), and state regulators settled enforcement actions against 10 firms for $875 million, forbade certain practices, and instituted reforms.[48]

The sudden collapses of Enron and WorldCom were shocking; with assets of $63 billion and $104 billion, respectively, they were the largest corporate bankruptcies before the default of Lehman Brothers in 2008.

Following legal proceedings and investigations, Citigroup, JP Morgan, Merrill Lynch, and other Wall Street banks paid billions of dollars—although admitted no wrongdoing—for helping Enron hide its debt until just before its collapse. Enron and its bankers had created entities to do complex transactions generating fictitious earnings, disguised debt as sales and derivative transactions, and understated the firm's leverage. Executives at the banks had pressured their analysts to write glowing

evaluations of Enron. The scandal cost Citigroup, JP Morgan, CIBC, Merrill Lynch, and other financial institutions more than $400 million in settlements with the SEC; Citigroup, JP Morgan, CIBC, Lehman Brothers, and Bank of America paid another $6.9 billion to investors to settle class action lawsuits.[49] In response, the Sarbanes-Oxley Act of 2002 required the personal certification of financial reports by CEOs and CFOs; independent audit committees; longer jail sentences and larger fines for executives who misstate financial results; and protections for whistleblowers.

Some firms that lent to companies that failed during the stock market bust were successfully hedged, having earlier purchased credit default swaps on these firms. Regulators seemed to draw comfort from the fact that major banks had succeeded in transferring losses from those relationships to investors through these and other hedging transactions. In November 2002, Fed Chairman Greenspan said credit derivatives "appear to have effectively spread losses" from defaults by Enron and other large corporations. Although he conceded the market was "still too new to have been tested" thoroughly, he observed that "to date, it appears to have functioned well."[50] The following year, Fed Vice Chairman Roger Ferguson noted that "the most remarkable fact regarding the banking industry during this period is its resilience and retention of fundamental strength."[51]

This resilience led many executives and regulators to presume the financial system had achieved unprecedented stability and strong risk management. The Wall Street banks' pivotal role in the Enron debacle did not seem to trouble senior Fed officials. In a memorandum to the FCIC, Richard Spillenkothen described a presentation to the Board of Governors in which some Fed governors received details of the banks' complicity "coolly" and were "clearly unimpressed" by analysts' findings. "The message to some supervisory staff was neither ambiguous nor subtle," Spillenkothen wrote. Earlier in the decade, he remembered, senior economists at the Fed had called Enron an example of a derivatives market participant successfully regulated by market discipline without government oversight.[52]

The Fed cut interest rates aggressively in order to contain damage from the dot-com and telecom bust, the terrorist attacks, and the financial market scandals. In January 2001, the federal funds rate, the overnight bank-to-bank lending rate, was 6.5%. By mid-2003, the Fed had cut that rate to just 1%, the lowest in half a century, where it stayed for another year. In addition, to offset the market disruptions following the 9/11 attacks, the Fed flooded the financial markets with money by purchasing more than $150 billion in government securities and lending $45 billion to banks. It also suspended restrictions on bank holding companies so the banks could make large loans to their securities affiliates. With these actions the Fed prevented a protracted liquidity crunch in the financial markets during the fall of 2001, just as it had done during the 1987 stock market crash and the 1998 Russian crisis.

Why wouldn't the markets assume the central bank would act again—and again save the day? Two weeks before the Fed cut short-term rates in January 2001, the *Economist* anticipated it: "the 'Greenspan put' is once again the talk of Wall Street. . . . The idea is that the Federal Reserve can be relied upon in times of crisis to come to

the rescue, cutting interest rates and pumping in liquidity, thus providing a floor for equity prices."[53] The "Greenspan put" was analysts' shorthand for investors' faith that the Fed would keep the capital markets functioning no matter what. The Fed's policy was clear: to restrain growth of an asset bubble, it would take only small steps, such as warning investors some asset prices might fall; but after a bubble burst, it would use all the tools available to stabilize the markets. Greenspan argued that intentionally bursting a bubble would heavily damage the economy. "Instead of trying to contain a putative bubble by drastic actions with largely unpredictable consequences," he said in 2004, when housing prices were ballooning, "we chose . . . to focus on policies 'to mitigate the fallout when it occurs and, hopefully, ease the transition to the next expansion.'"[54]

This asymmetric policy—allowing unrestrained growth, then working hard to cushion the impact of a bust—raised the question of "moral hazard": did the policy encourage investors and financial institutions to gamble because their upside was unlimited while the full power and influence of the Fed protected their downside (at least against catastrophic losses)? Greenspan himself warned about this in a 2005 speech, noting that higher asset prices were "in part the indirect result of investors accepting lower compensation for risk" and cautioning that "newly abundant liquidity can readily disappear."[55] Yet the only real action would be an upward march of the federal funds rate that had begun in the summer of 2004, although, as he pointed out in the same 2005 speech, this had little effect.

And the markets were undeterred. "We had convinced ourselves that we were in a less risky world," former Federal Reserve governor and National Economic Council director under President George W. Bush Lawrence Lindsey told the Commission. "And how should any rational investor respond to a less risky world? They should lay on more risk."[56]

## THE WAGES OF FINANCE:
## "WELL, THIS ONE'S DOING IT, SO HOW CAN I NOT DO IT?"

As figure 4.1 demonstrates, for almost half a century after the Great Depression, pay inside the financial industry and out was roughly equal. Beginning in 1980, they diverged. By 2007, financial sector compensation was more than 80% greater than in other businesses—a considerably larger gap than before the Great Depression.

Until 1970, the New York Stock Exchange, a private self-regulatory organization, required members to operate as partnerships.[57] Peter J. Solomon, a former Lehman Brothers partner, testified before the FCIC that this profoundly affected the investment bank's culture. Before the change, he and the other partners had sat in a single room at headquarters, not to socialize but to "overhear, interact, and monitor" each other. They were all on the hook together. "Since they were personally liable as partners, they took risk very seriously," Solomon said.[58] Brian Leach, formerly an executive at Morgan Stanley, described to FCIC staff Morgan Stanley's compensation practices before it issued stock and became a public corporation: "When I first

## Compensation in Financial and Nonfinancial Sectors

*Compensation in the financial sector outstripped pay elsewhere,*
*a pattern not seen since the years before the Great Depression.*

ANNUAL AVERAGE, IN 2009 DOLLARS

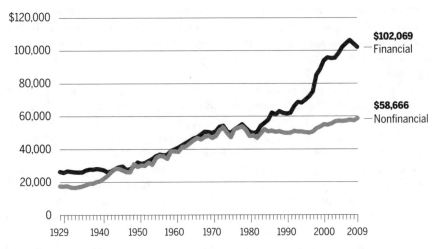

NOTE: Average compensation includes wages, salaries, commissions, tips, bonuses, and payments for
government insurance and pension programs. Nonfinancial sector is all domestic employees except those in
finance and insurance.
SOURCES: Bureau of Economic Analysis, Bureau of Labor Statistics, CPI-Urban, FCIC calculations

*Figure 4.1*

started at Morgan Stanley, it was a private company. When you're a private company,
you don't get paid until you retire. I mean, you get a good, you know, year-to-year
compensation." But the big payout was "when you retire."[59]

When the investment banks went public in the 1980s and 1990s, the close rela-
tionship between bankers' decisions and their compensation broke down. They were
now trading with shareholders' money. Talented traders and managers once tethered
to their firms were now free agents who could play companies against each other for
more money. To keep them from leaving, firms began providing aggressive incen-
tives, often tied to the price of their shares and often with accelerated payouts. To
keep up, commercial banks did the same. Some included "clawback" provisions that
would require the return of compensation under narrow circumstances, but those
proved too limited to restrain the behavior of traders and managers.

Studies have found that the real value of executive pay, adjusted for inflation, grew

only 0.8% a year during the 30 years after World War II, lagging companies' increasing size.[60] But the rate picked up during the 1970s and rose faster each decade, reaching 10% a year from 1995 to 1999.[61] Much of the change reflected higher earnings in the financial sector, where by 2005 executives' pay averaged $3.4 million annually, the highest of any industry. Though base salaries differed relatively little across sectors, banking and finance paid much higher bonuses and awarded more stock. And brokers and dealers did by far the best, averaging more than $7 million in compensation.[62]

Both before and after going public, investment banks typically paid out half their revenues in compensation. For example, Goldman Sachs spent between 44% and 49% a year between 2005 and 2008, when Morgan Stanley allotted between 46% and 59%. Merrill paid out similar percentages in 2005 and 2006, but gave 141% in 2007—a year it suffered dramatic losses.[63]

As the scale, revenue, and profitability of the firms grew, compensation packages soared for senior executives and other key employees. John Gutfreund, reported to be the highest-paid executive on Wall Street in the late 1980s, received $3.2 million in 1986 as CEO of Salomon Brothers.[64] Stanley O'Neal's package was worth more than $91 million in 2006, the last full year he was CEO of Merrill Lynch.[65] In 2007, Lloyd Blankfein, CEO at Goldman Sachs, received $68.5 million;[66] Richard Fuld, CEO of Lehman Brothers, and Jamie Dimon, CEO of JPMorgan Chase, received about $34 million and $28 million, respectively.[67] That year Wall Street paid workers in New York roughly $33 billion in year-end bonuses alone.[68] Total compensation for the major U.S. banks and securities firms was estimated at $137 billion.[69]

Stock options became a popular form of compensation, allowing employees to buy the company's stock in the future at some predetermined price, and thus to reap rewards when the stock price was higher than that predetermined price. In fact, the option would have no value if the stock price was below that price. Encouraging the awarding of stock options was 1993 legislation making compensation in excess of $1 million taxable to the corporation unless performance-based. Stock options had potentially unlimited upside, while the downside was simply to receive nothing if the stock didn't rise to the predetermined price. The same applied to plans that tied pay to return on equity: they meant that executives could win more than they could lose. These pay structures had the unintended consequence of creating incentives to increase both risk and leverage, which could lead to larger jumps in a company's stock price.

As these options motivated financial firms to take more risk and use more leverage, the evolution of the system provided the means. Shadow banking institutions faced few regulatory constraints on leverage; changes in regulations loosened the constraints on commercial banks. OTC derivatives allowing for enormous leverage proliferated. And risk management, thought to be keeping ahead of these developments, would fail to rein in the increasing risks.

The dangers of the new pay structures were clear, but senior executives believed they were powerless to change it. Former Citigroup CEO Sandy Weill told the Commission, "I think if you look at the results of what happened on Wall Street, it became,

'Well, this one's doing it, so how can I not do it, if I don't do it, then the people are going to leave my place and go someplace else.'" Managing risk "became less of an important function in a broad base of companies, I would guess."[70]

And regulatory entities, one source of checks on excessive risk taking, had challenges recruiting financial experts who could otherwise work in the private sector. Lord Adair Turner, chairman of the U.K. Financial Services Authority, told the Commission, "It's not easy. This is like a continual process of, you know, high-skilled people versus high-skilled people, and the poachers are better paid than the gamekeepers."[71] Bernanke said the same at an FCIC hearing: "It's just simply never going to be the case that the government can pay what Wall Street can pay."[72]

Tying compensation to earnings also, in some cases, created the temptation to manipulate the numbers. Former Fannie Mae regulator Armando Falcon Jr. told the FCIC, "Fannie began the last decade with an ambitious goal—double earnings in 5 years to $6.46 [per share]. A large part of the executives' compensation was tied to meeting that goal." Achieving it brought CEO Franklin Raines $52 million of his $90 million pay from 1998 to 2003. However, Falcon said, the goal "turned out to be unachievable without breaking rules and hiding risks. Fannie and Freddie executives worked hard to persuade investors that mortgage-related assets were a riskless investment, while at the same time covering up the volatility and risks of their own mortgage portfolios and balance sheets." Fannie's estimate of how many mortgage holders would pay off was off by $400 million at year-end 1998, which meant no bonuses. So Fannie counted only half the $400 million on its books, enabling Raines and other executives to meet the earnings target and receive 100% of their bonuses.[73]

Compensation structures were skewed all along the mortgage securitization chain, from people who originated mortgages to people on Wall Street who packaged them into securities. Regarding mortgage brokers, often the first link in the process, FDIC Chairman Sheila Bair told the FCIC that their "standard compensation practice . . . was based on the volume of loans originated rather than the performance and quality of the loans made." She concluded, "The crisis has shown that most financial-institution compensation systems were not properly linked to risk management. Formula-driven compensation allows high short-term profits to be translated into generous bonus payments, without regard to any longer-term risks."[74] SEC Chairman Mary Schapiro told the FCIC, "Many major financial institutions created asymmetric compensation packages that paid employees enormous sums for short-term success, even if these same decisions result in significant long-term losses or failure for investors and taxpayers."[75]

## FINANCIAL SECTOR GROWTH:
### "I THINK WE OVERDID FINANCE VERSUS THE REAL ECONOMY"

For about two decades, beginning in the early 1980s, the financial sector grew faster than the rest of the economy—rising from about 5% of gross domestic product (GDP) to about 8% in the early 21st century. In 1980, financial sector profits were about 15% of corporate profits. In 2003, they hit a high of 33% but fell back to 27%

in 2006, on the eve of the financial crisis. The largest firms became considerably larger. JP Morgan's assets increased from $667 billion in 1999 to $2.2 trillion in 2008, a compound annual growth rate of 16%. Bank of America and Citigroup grew by 14% and 12% a year, respectively, with Citigroup reaching $1.9 trillion in assets in 2008 (down from $2.2 trillion in 2007) and Bank of America $1.8 trillion. The investment banks also grew significantly from 2000 to 2007, often much faster than commercial banks. Goldman's assets grew from $250 billion in 1999 to $1.1 trillion by 2007, an annual growth rate of 21%. At Lehman, assets rose from $192 billion to $691 billion, or 17%.[76]

Fannie and Freddie grew quickly, too. Fannie's assets and guaranteed mortgages increased from $1.4 trillion in 2000 to $3.2 trillion in 2008, or 11% annually. At Freddie, they increased from $1 trillion to $2.2 trillion, or 10% a year.[77]

As they grew, many financial firms added lots of leverage. That meant potentially higher returns for shareholders, and more money for compensation. Increasing leverage also meant less capital to absorb losses.

Fannie and Freddie were the most leveraged. The law set the government-sponsored enterprises' minimum capital requirement at 2.5% of assets plus 0.45% of the mortgage-backed securities they guaranteed. So they could borrow more than $200 for each dollar of capital used to guarantee mortgage-backed securities. If they wanted to own the securities, they could borrow $40 for each dollar of capital. Combined, Fannie and Freddie owned or guaranteed $5.3 trillion of mortgage-related assets at the end of 2007 against just $70.7 billion of capital, a ratio of 75:1.

From 2000 to 2007, large banks and thrifts generally had $16 to $22 in assets for each dollar of capital, for leverage ratios between 16:1 and 22:1. For some banks, leverage remained roughly constant. JP Morgan's reported leverage was between 20:1 and 22:1. Wells Fargo's generally ranged between 16:1 and 17:1. Other banks upped their leverage. Bank of America's rose from 18:1 in 2000 to 27:1 in 2007. Citigroup's increased from 18:1 to 22:1, then shot up to 32:1 by the end of 2007, when Citi brought off-balance sheet assets onto the balance sheet. More than other banks, Citigroup held assets off of its balance sheet, in part to hold down capital requirements. In 2007, even after bringing $80 billion worth of assets on balance sheet, substantial assets remained off. If those had been included, leverage in 2007 would have been 48:1, or about 53% higher. In comparison, at Wells Fargo and Bank of America, including off-balance-sheet assets would have raised the 2007 leverage ratios 17% and 28%, respectively.[78]

Because investment banks were not subject to the same capital requirements as commercial and retail banks, they were given greater latitude to rely on their internal risk models in determining capital requirements, and they reported higher leverage. At Goldman Sachs, leverage increased from 17:1 in 2000 to 32:1 in 2007. Morgan Stanley and Lehman increased about 67% and 22%, respectively, and both reached 40:1 by the end of 2007.[79] Several investment banks artificially lowered leverage ratios by selling assets right before the reporting period and subsequently buying them back.

As the investment banks grew, their business models changed. Traditionally, investment banks advised and underwrote equity and debt for corporations, financial

institutions, investment funds, governments, and individuals. An increasing amount of the investment banks' revenues and earnings was generated by trading and investments, including securitization and derivatives activities. At Goldman, revenues from trading and principal investments increased from 39% of the total in 1997 to 68% in 2007. At Merrill Lynch, they generated 55% of revenue in 2006, up from 42% in 1997. At Lehman, similar activities generated up to 80% of pretax earnings in 2006, up from 32% in 1997. At Bear Stearns, they accounted for more than 100% of pretax earnings in some years after 2002 because of pretax losses in other businesses.[80]

Between 1978 and 2007, debt held by financial companies grew from $3 trillion to $36 trillion, more than doubling from 130% to 270% of GDP. Former Treasury Secretary John Snow told the FCIC that while the financial sector must play a "critical" role in allocating capital to the most productive uses, it was reasonable to ask whether over the last 20 or 30 years it had become too large. Financial firms had grown mainly by simply lending to each other, he said, not by creating opportunities for investment.[81] In 1978, financial companies borrowed $13 in the credit markets for every $100 borrowed by nonfinancial companies. By 2007, financial companies were borrowing $51 for every $100. "We have a lot more debt than we used to have, which means we have a much bigger financial sector," said Snow. "I think we overdid finance versus the real economy and got it a little lopsided as a result."[82]

# 5

# SUBPRIME LENDING

## CONTENTS

In the early 1980s, subprime lenders such as Household Finance Corp. and thrifts such as Long Beach Savings and Loan made home equity loans, often second mortgages, to borrowers who had yet to establish credit histories or had troubled financial histories, sometimes reflecting setbacks such as unemployment, divorce, medical emergencies, and the like. Banks might have been unwilling to lend to these borrowers, but a subprime lender would if the borrower paid a higher interest rate to offset the extra risk. "No one can debate the need for legitimate non-prime (subprime) lending products," Gail Burks, president of the Nevada Fair Housing Center, Inc., testified to the FCIC.[1]

Interest rates on subprime mortgages, with substantial collateral—the house—weren't as high as those for car loans, and were much less than credit cards. The advantages of a mortgage over other forms of debt were solidified in 1986 with the Tax Reform Act, which barred deducting interest payments on consumer loans but kept the deduction for mortgage interest payments.

In the 1980s and into the early 1990s, before computerized "credit scoring"—a statistical technique used to measure a borrower's creditworthiness—automated the assessment of risk, mortgage lenders (including subprime lenders) relied on other factors when underwriting mortgages. As Tom Putnam, a Sacramento-based mortgage banker, told the Commission, they traditionally lent based on the four C's: credit (quantity, quality, and duration of the borrower's credit obligations), capacity (amount and stability of income), capital (sufficient liquid funds to cover down payments, closing costs, and reserves), and collateral (value and condition of the property).[2] Their decisions depended on judgments about how strength in one area, such as collateral, might offset weaknesses in others, such as credit. They underwrote borrowers one at a time, out of local offices.

In a few cases, such as CitiFinancial, subprime lending firms were part of a bank holding company, but most—including Household, Beneficial Finance, The Money Store, and Champion Mortgage—were independent consumer finance companies. Without access to deposits, they generally funded themselves with short-term lines of credit, or "warehouse lines," from commercial or investment banks. In many cases, the finance companies did not keep the mortgages. Some sold the loans to the same banks extending the warehouse lines. The banks would securitize and sell the loans to investors or keep them on their balance sheets. In other cases, the finance company itself packaged and sold the loans—often partnering with the banks extending the warehouse lines. Meanwhile, the S&Ls that originated subprime loans generally financed their own mortgage operations and kept the loans on their balance sheets.

## MORTGAGE SECURITIZATION: "THIS STUFF IS SO COMPLICATED HOW IS ANYBODY GOING TO KNOW?"

Debt outstanding in U.S. credit markets tripled during the 1980s, reaching $13.8 trillion in 1990; 11% was securitized mortgages and GSE debt. Later, mortgage securities made up 18% of the debt markets, overtaking government Treasuries as the single largest component—a position they maintained through the financial crisis.[3]

In the 1990s mortgage companies, banks, and Wall Street securities firms began securitizing mortgages (see figure 5.1). And more of them were subprime. Salomon Brothers, Merrill Lynch, and other Wall Street firms started packaging and selling "non-agency" mortgages—that is, loans that did not conform to Fannie's and Freddie's standards. Selling these required investors to adjust expectations. With securitizations handled by Fannie and Freddie, the question was not "will you get the money back" but "when," former Salomon Brothers trader and CEO of PentAlpha Jim Callahan told the FCIC.[4] With these new non-agency securities, investors had to worry about getting paid back, and that created an opportunity for S&P and Moody's. As Lewis Ranieri, a pioneer in the market, told the Commission, when he presented the concept of non-agency securitization to policy makers, they asked, "'This stuff is so complicated how is anybody going to know? How are the buyers going to buy?'" Ranieri said, "One of the solutions was, it had to have a rating. And that put the rating services in the business."[5]

Non-agency securitizations were only a few years old when they received a powerful stimulus from an unlikely source: the federal government. The savings and loan crisis had left Uncle Sam with $402 billion in loans and real estate from failed thrifts and banks. Congress established the Resolution Trust Corporation (RTC) in 1989 to offload mortgages and real estate, and sometimes the failed thrifts themselves, now owned by the government. While the RTC was able to sell $6.1 billion of these mortgages to Fannie and Freddie, most did not meet the GSEs' standards. Some were what might be called subprime today, but others had outright documentation errors or servicing problems, not unlike the low-documentation loans that later became popular.[6]

# Funding for Mortgages

*The sources of funds for mortgages changed over the decades.*

IN PERCENT, BY SOURCE

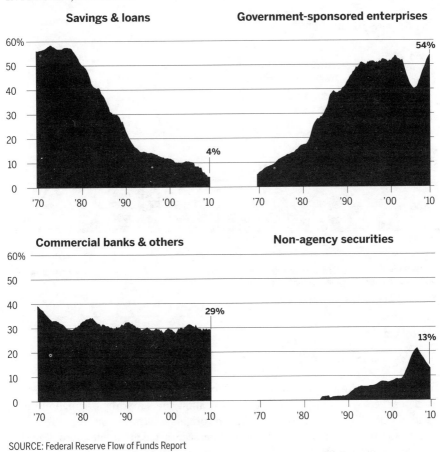

**Savings & loans**

**Government-sponsored enterprises**

54%

4%

**Commercial banks & others**

**Non-agency securities**

29%

13%

SOURCE: Federal Reserve Flow of Funds Report

*Figure 5.1*

RTC officials soon concluded that they had neither the time nor the resources to sell off the assets in their portfolio one by one and thrift by thrift. They turned to the private sector, contracting with real estate and financial professionals to securitize some of the assets. By the time the RTC concluded its work, it had securitized $25 billion in residential mortgages.[7] The RTC in effect helped expand the securitization of mortgages ineligible for GSE guarantees.[8] In the early 1990s, as investors became

## Subprime Mortgage Originations

*In 2006, $600 billion of subprime loans were originated, most of which were securitized. That year, subprime lending accounted for 23.5% of all mortgage originations.*

IN BILLIONS OF DOLLARS

NOTE: Percent securitized is defined as subprime securities issued divided by originations in a given year. In 2007, securities issued exceeded originations.

SOURCE: Inside Mortgage Finance

*Figure 5.2*

more familiar with the securitization of these assets, mortgage specialists and Wall Street bankers got in on the action. Securitization and subprime originations grew hand in hand. As figure 5.2 shows, subprime originations increased from $70 billion in 1996 to $100 billion in 2000. The proportion securitized in the late 1990s peaked at 56%, and subprime mortgage originations' share of all originations hovered around 10%.

Securitizations by the RTC and by Wall Street were similar to the Fannie and Freddie securitizations. The first step was to get principal and interest payments from a group of mortgages to flow into a single pool. But in "private-label" securities (that is, securitizations not done by Fannie or Freddie), the payments were then "tranched" in a way to protect some investors from losses. Investors in the tranches received different streams of principal and interest in different orders.

Most of the earliest private-label deals, in the late 1980s and early 1990s, used a rudimentary form of tranching. There were typically two tranches in each deal. The

less risky tranche received principal and interest payments first and was usually guaranteed by an insurance company. The more risky tranche received payments second, was not guaranteed, and was usually kept by the company that originated the mortgages.

Within a decade, securitizations had become much more complex: they had more tranches, each with different payment streams and different risks, which were tailored to meet investors' demands. The entire private-label mortgage securitization market—those who created, sold, and bought the investments—would become highly dependent on this slice-and-dice process, and regulators and market participants alike took for granted that it efficiently allocated risk to those best able and willing to bear that risk.

To demonstrate how this process worked, we'll describe a typical deal, named CMLTI 2006-NC2, involving $947 million in mortgage-backed bonds.[9] In 2006, New Century Financial, a California-based lender, originated and sold 4,499 subprime mortgages to Citigroup, which sold them to a separate legal entity that Citigroup sponsored that would own the mortgages and issue the tranches. The entity purchased the loans with cash it had raised by selling the securities these loans would back. The entity had been created as a separate legal structure so that the assets would sit off Citigroup's balance sheet, an arrangement with tax and regulatory benefits.

The 4,499 mortgages carried the rights to the borrowers' monthly payments, which the Citigroup entity divided into 19 tranches of mortgage-backed securities; each tranche gave investors a different priority claim on the flow of payments from the borrowers, and a different interest rate and repayment schedule. The credit rating agencies assigned ratings to most of these tranches for investors, who—as securitization became increasingly complicated—came to rely more heavily on these ratings. Tranches were assigned letter ratings by the rating agencies based on their riskiness. In this report, ratings are generally presented in S&P's classification system, which assigns ratings such as "AAA" (the highest rating for the safest investments, referred to here as triple-A), "AA" (less safe than AAA), "A," "BBB," and "BB," and further distinguishes ratings with "+" and "−." Anything rated below "BBB-" is considered "junk." Moody's uses a similar system in which "Aaa" is highest, followed by "Aa," "A," "Baa," "Ba," and so forth. For example, an S&P rating of BBB would correspond to a Moody's rating of Baa. In this Citigroup deal, the four senior tranches—the safest— were rated triple-A by the agencies.

Below the senior tranches and next in line for payments were eleven "mezzanine" tranches—so named because they sat between the riskiest and the safest tranches. These were riskier than the senior tranches and, because they paid off more slowly, carried a higher risk that an increase in interest rates would make the locked-in interest payments less valuable. As a result, they paid a correspondingly higher interest rate. Three of these tranches in the Citigroup deal were rated AA, three were A, three were BBB (the lowest investment-grade rating), and two were BB, or junk.

The last to be paid was the most junior tranche, called the "equity," "residual," or "first-loss" tranche, set up to receive whatever cash flow was left over after all the other investors had been paid. This tranche would suffer the first losses from any

defaults of the mortgages in the pool. Commensurate with this high risk, it provided the highest yields (see figure 5.3). In the Citigroup deal, as was common, this piece of the deal was not rated at all. Citigroup and a hedge fund each held half the equity tranche.[10]

While investors in the lower-rated tranches received higher interest rates because they knew there was a risk of loss, investors in the triple-A tranches did not expect payments from the mortgages to stop. This expectation of safety was important, so the firms structuring securities focused on achieving high ratings. In the structure of this Citigroup deal, which was typical, $737 million, or 78%, was rated triple-A.

## GREATER ACCESS TO LENDING:
## "A BUSINESS WHERE WE CAN MAKE SOME MONEY"

As private-label securitization began to take hold, new computer and modeling technologies were reshaping the mortgage market. In the mid-1990s, standardized data with loan-level information on mortgage performance became more widely available. Lenders underwrote mortgages using credit scores, such as the FICO score, developed by Fair Isaac Corporation. In 1994, Freddie Mac rolled out Loan Prospector, an automated system for mortgage underwriting for use by lenders, and Fannie Mae released its own system, Desktop Underwriter, two months later. The days of laborious, slow, and manual underwriting of individual mortgage applicants were over, lowering cost and broadening access to mortgages.

This new process was based on quantitative expectations: Given the borrower, the home, and the mortgage characteristics, what was the probability payments would be on time? What was the probability that borrowers would prepay their loans, either because they sold their homes or refinanced at lower interest rates?

In the 1990s, technology also affected implementation of the Community Reinvestment Act (CRA). Congress enacted the CRA in 1977 to ensure that banks and thrifts served their communities, in response to concerns that banks and thrifts were refusing to lend in certain neighborhoods without regard to the creditworthiness of individuals and businesses in those neighborhoods (a practice known as redlining).[11]

The CRA called on banks and thrifts to invest, lend, and service areas where they took in deposits, so long as these activities didn't impair their own financial safety and soundness. It directed regulators to consider CRA performance whenever a bank or thrift applied for regulatory approval for mergers, to open new branches, or to engage in new businesses.[12]

The CRA encouraged banks to lend to borrowers to whom they may have previously denied credit. While these borrowers often had lower-than-average income, a 1997 study indicated that loans made under the CRA performed consistently with the rest of the banks' portfolios, suggesting CRA lending was not riskier than the banks' other lending.[13] "There is little or no evidence that banks' safety and soundness have been compromised by such lending, and bankers often report sound business opportunities," Federal Reserve Chairman Alan Greenspan said of CRA lending in 1998.[14]

# Residential Mortgage-Backed Securities

*Financial institutions packaged subprime, Alt-A and other mortgages into securities. As long as the housing market continued to boom, these securities would perform. But when the economy faltered and the mortgages defaulted, lower-rated tranches were left worthless.*

## 1 Originate

Lenders extend mortgages, including subprime and Alt-A loans.

## 2 Pool

Securities firms purchase these loans and pool them.

## 3 Tranche

Residential mortgage-backed securities are sold to investors, giving them the right to the principal and interest from the mortgages. These securities are sold in tranches, or slices. The flow of cash determines the rating of the securities, with AAA tranches getting the first cut of principal and interest payments, then AA, then A, and so on.

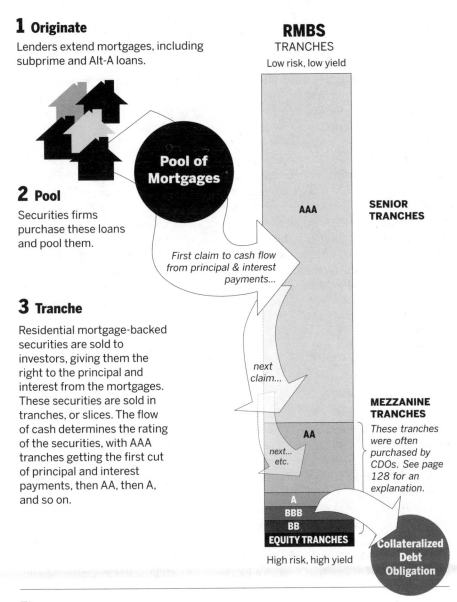

**RMBS**
TRANCHES
Low risk, low yield

Pool of Mortgages

AAA — **SENIOR TRANCHES**

*First claim to cash flow from principal & interest payments...*

*next claim...*

AA — **MEZZANINE TRANCHES**
*These tranches were often purchased by CDOs. See page 128 for an explanation.*

*next... etc.*

A
BBB
BB
EQUITY TRANCHES

High risk, high yield

Collateralized Debt Obligation

*Figure 5.3*

In 1993, President Bill Clinton asked regulators to improve banks' CRA perform-ance while responding to industry complaints that the regulatory review process for compliance was too burdensome and too subjective. In 1995, the Fed, Office of Thrift Supervision (OTS), Office of the Comptroller of the Currency (OCC), and Federal Deposit Insurance Corporation (FDIC) issued regulations that shifted the regulatory focus from the efforts that banks made to comply with the CRA to their actual re-sults. Regulators and community advocates could now point to objective, observable numbers that measured banks' compliance with the law.

Former comptroller John Dugan told FCIC staff that the impact of the CRA had been lasting, because it encouraged banks to lend to people who in the past might not have had access to credit. He said, "There is a tremendous amount of investment that goes on in inner cities and other places to build things that are quite impressive. . . . And the bankers conversely say, 'This is proven to be a business where we can make some money; not a lot, but when you factor that in plus the good will that we get from it, it kind of works.'"[15]

Lawrence Lindsey, a former Fed governor who was responsible for the Fed's Divi-sion of Consumer and Community Affairs, which oversees CRA enforcement, told the FCIC that improved enforcement had given the banks an incentive to invest in technology that would make lending to lower-income borrowers profitable by such means as creating credit scoring models customized to the market. Shadow banks not covered by the CRA would use these same credit scoring models, which could draw on now more substantial historical lending data for their estimates, to under-write loans. "We basically got a cycle going which particularly the shadow banking industry could, using recent historic data, show the default rates on this type of lend-ing were very, very low," he said.[16] Indeed, default rates were low during the prosper-ous 1990s, and regulators, bankers, and lenders in the shadow banking system took note of this success.

## SUBPRIME LENDERS IN TURMOIL: "ADVERSE MARKET CONDITIONS"

Among nonbank mortgage originators, the late 1990s were a turning point. During the market disruption caused by the Russian debt crisis and the Long-Term Capital Management collapse, the markets saw a "flight to quality"—that is, a steep fall in de-mand among investors for risky assets, including subprime securitizations. The rate of subprime mortgage securitization dropped from 55.1% in 1998 to 37.4% in 1999. Meanwhile, subprime originators saw the interest rate at which they could borrow in credit markets skyrocket. They were caught in a squeeze: borrowing costs increased at the very moment that their revenue stream dried up.[17] And some were caught holding tranches of subprime securities that turned out to be worth far less than the value they had been assigned.

Mortgage lenders that depended on liquidity and short-term funding had imme-diate problems. For example, Southern Pacific Funding (SFC), an Oregon-based sub-prime lender that securitized its loans, reported relatively positive second-quarter

results in August 1998. Then, in September, SFC notified investors about "recent adverse market conditions" in the securities markets and expressed concern about "the continued viability of securitization in the foreseeable future."[18] A week later, SFC filed for bankruptcy protection. Several other nonbank subprime lenders that were also dependent on short-term financing from the capital markets also filed for bankruptcy in 1998 and 1999. In the two years following the Russian default crisis, 8 of the top 10 subprime lenders declared bankruptcy, ceased operations, or sold out to stronger firms.[19]

When these firms were sold, their buyers would frequently absorb large losses. First Union, a large regional bank headquartered in North Carolina, incurred charges of almost $1.7 billion after it bought The Money Store. First Union eventually shut down or sold off most of The Money Store's operations.

Conseco, a leading insurance company, purchased Green Tree Financial, another subprime lender. Disruptions in the securitization markets, as well as unexpected mortgage defaults, eventually drove Conseco into bankruptcy in December 2002. At the time, this was the third-largest bankruptcy in U.S. history (after WorldCom and Enron).

Accounting misrepresentations would also bring down subprime lenders. Keystone, a small national bank in West Virginia that made and securitized subprime mortgage loans, failed in 1999. In the securitization process—as was common practice in the 1990s—Keystone retained the riskiest "first-loss" residual tranches for its own account. These holdings far exceeded the bank's capital. But Keystone assigned them grossly inflated values. The OCC closed the bank in September 1999, after discovering "fraud committed by the bank management," as executives had overstated the value of the residual tranches and other bank assets.[20] Perhaps the most significant failure occurred at Superior Bank, one of the most aggressive subprime mortgage lenders. Like Keystone, it too failed after having kept and overvalued the first-loss tranches on its balance sheet.

Many of the lenders that survived or were bought in the 1990s reemerged in other forms. Long Beach was the ancestor of Ameriquest and Long Beach Mortgage (which was in turn purchased by Washington Mutual), two of the more aggressive lenders during the first decade of the new century. Associates First was sold to Citigroup, and Household bought Beneficial Mortgage before it was itself acquired by HSBC in 2003.

With the subprime market disrupted, subprime originations totaled $100 billion in 2000, down from $135 billion two years earlier.[21] Over the next few years, however, subprime lending and securitization would more than rebound.

## THE REGULATORS: "OH, I SEE"

During the 1990s, various federal agencies had taken increasing notice of abusive subprime lending practices. But the regulatory system was not well equipped to respond consistently—and on a national basis—to protect borrowers. State regulators, as well as either the Fed or the FDIC, supervised the mortgage practices of state

banks. The OCC supervised the national banks. The OTS or state regulators were responsible for the thrifts. Some state regulators also licensed mortgage brokers, a growing portion of the market, but did not supervise them.[22]

Despite this diffusion of authority, one entity was unquestionably authorized by Congress to write strong and consistent rules regulating mortgages for all types of lenders: the Federal Reserve, through the Truth in Lending Act of 1968. In 1969, the Fed adopted Regulation Z for the purpose of implementing the act. But while Regulation Z applied to all lenders, its enforcement was divided among America's many financial regulators.

One sticking point was the supervision of nonbank subsidiaries such as subprime lenders. The Fed had the legal mandate to supervise bank holding companies, including the authority to supervise their nonbank subsidiaries. The Federal Trade Commission was given explicit authority by Congress to enforce the consumer protections embodied in the Truth in Lending Act with respect to these nonbank lenders. Although the FTC brought some enforcement actions against mortgage companies, Henry Cisneros, a former secretary of the Department of Housing and Urban Development (HUD), worried that its budget and staff were not commensurate with its mandate to supervise these lenders. "We could have had the FTC oversee mortgage contracts," Cisneros told the Commission. "But the FTC is up to their neck in work today with what they've got. They don't have the staff to go out and search out mortgage problems."[23]

Glenn Loney, deputy director of the Fed's Consumer and Community Affairs Division from 1998 to 2010, told the FCIC that ever since he joined the agency in 1975, Fed officials had been debating whether they—in addition to the FTC—should enforce rules for nonbank lenders. But they worried about whether the Fed would be stepping on congressional prerogatives by assuming enforcement responsibilities that legislation had delegated to the FTC. "A number of governors came in and said, 'You mean to say we don't look at these?'" Loney said. "And then we tried to explain it to them, and they'd say, 'Oh, I see.'"[24] The Federal Reserve would not exert its authority in this area, nor others that came under its purview in 1994, with any real force until after the housing bubble burst.

The 1994 legislation that gave the Fed new responsibilities was the Home Ownership and Equity Protection Act (HOEPA), passed by Congress and signed by President Clinton to address growing concerns about abusive and predatory mortgage lending practices that especially affected low-income borrowers. HOEPA specifically noted that certain communities were "being victimized . . . by second mortgage lenders, home improvement contractors, and finance companies who peddle high-rate, high-fee home equity loans to cash-poor homeowners."[25] For example, a Senate report highlighted the case of a 72-year-old homeowner, who testified at a hearing that she paid more than $23,000 in upfront finance charges on a $150,000 second mortgage. In addition, the monthly payments on the mortgage exceeded her income.[26]

HOEPA prohibited abusive practices relating to certain high-cost refinance mortgage loans, including prepayment penalties, negative amortization, and balloon pay-

ments with a term of less than five years. The legislation also prohibited lenders from making high-cost refinance loans based on the collateral value of the property alone and "without regard to the consumers' repayment ability, including the consumers' current and expected income, current obligations, and employment."[27] However, only a small percentage of mortgages were initially subject to the HOEPA restrictions, because the interest rate and fee levels for triggering HOEPA's coverage were set too high to catch most subprime loans.[28] Even so, HOEPA specifically directed the Fed to act more broadly to "prohibit acts or practices in connection with [mortgage loans] that [the Board] finds to be unfair, deceptive or designed to evade the provisions of this [act]."[29]

In June 1997, two years after HOEPA took effect, the Fed held the first set of public hearings required under the act. The venues were Los Angeles, Atlanta, and Washington, D.C. Consumer advocates reported abuses by home equity lenders. A report summarizing the hearings, jointly issued with the Department of Housing and Urban Development and released in July 1998, said that mortgage lenders acknowledged that some abuses existed, blamed some of these on mortgage brokers, and suggested that the increasing securitization of subprime mortgages was likely to limit the opportunity for widespread abuses. The report stated, "Creditors that package and securitize their home equity loans must comply with a series of representations and warranties. These include creditors' representations that they have complied with strict underwriting guidelines concerning the borrower's ability to repay the loan."[30] But in the years to come, these representations and warranties would prove to be inaccurate.

Still, the Fed continued not to press its prerogatives. In January 1998, it formalized its long-standing policy of "not routinely conducting consumer compliance examinations of nonbank subsidiaries of bank holding companies,"[31] a decision that would be criticized by a November 1999 General Accounting Office report for creating a "lack of regulatory oversight."[32] The July 1998 report also made recommendations on mortgage reform.[33] While preparing draft recommendations for the report, Fed staff wrote to the Fed's Committee on Consumer and Community Affairs that "given the Board's traditional reluctance to support substantive limitations on market behavior, the draft report discusses various options but does not advocate any particular approach to addressing these problems."[34]

In the end, although the two agencies did not agree on the full set of recommendations addressing predatory lending, both the Fed and HUD supported legislative bans on balloon payments and advance collection of lump-sum insurance premiums, stronger enforcement of current laws, and nonregulatory strategies such as community outreach efforts and consumer education and counseling. But Congress did not act on these recommendations.

The Fed-Lite provisions under the Gramm-Leach-Bliley Act affirmed the Fed's hands-off approach to the regulation of mortgage lending. Even so, the shakeup in the subprime industry in the late 1990s had drawn regulators' attention to at least some of the risks associated with this lending. For that reason, the Federal Reserve, FDIC, OCC, and OTS jointly issued subprime lending guidance on March 1, 1999.

This guidance applied only to regulated banks and thrifts, and even for them it would not be binding but merely laid out the criteria underlying regulators' bank examinations. It explained that "recent turmoil in the equity and asset-backed securities market has caused some non-bank subprime specialists to exit the market, thus creating increased opportunities for financial institutions to enter, or expand their participation in, the subprime lending business."[35]

The agencies then identified key features of subprime lending programs and the need for increased capital, risk management, and board and senior management oversight. They further noted concerns about various accounting issues, notably the valuation of any residual tranches held by the securitizing firm. The guidance went on to warn, "Institutions that originate or purchase subprime loans must take special care to avoid violating fair lending and consumer protection laws and regulations. Higher fees and interest rates combined with compensation incentives can foster predatory pricing. . . . An adequate compliance management program must identify, monitor and control the consumer protection hazards associated with subprime lending."[36]

In spring 2000, in response to growing complaints about lending practices, and at the urging of members of Congress, HUD Secretary Andrew Cuomo and Treasury Secretary Lawrence Summers convened the joint National Predatory Lending Task Force. It included members of consumer advocacy groups; industry trade associations representing mortgage lenders, brokers, and appraisers; local and state officials; and academics. As the Fed had done three years earlier, this new entity took to the field, conducting hearings in Atlanta, Los Angeles, New York, Baltimore, and Chicago. The task force found "patterns" of abusive practices, reporting "substantial evidence of too-frequent abuses in the subprime lending market." Questionable practices included loan flipping (repeated refinancing of borrowers' loans in a short time), high fees and prepayment penalties that resulted in borrowers' losing the equity in their homes, and outright fraud and abuse involving deceptive or high-pressure sales tactics. The report cited testimony regarding incidents of forged signatures, falsification of incomes and appraisals, illegitimate fees, and bait-and-switch tactics. The investigation confirmed that subprime lenders often preyed on the elderly, minorities, and borrowers with lower incomes and less education, frequently targeting individuals who had "limited access to the mainstream financial sector"—meaning the banks, thrifts, and credit unions, which it viewed as subject to more extensive government oversight.[37]

Consumer protection groups took the same message to public officials. In interviews with and testimony to the FCIC, representatives of the National Consumer Law Center (NCLC), Nevada Fair Housing Center, Inc., and California Reinvestment Coalition each said they had contacted Congress and the four bank regulatory agencies multiple times about their concerns over unfair and deceptive lending practices.[38] "It was apparent on the ground as early as '96 or '98 . . . that the market for low-income consumers was being flooded with inappropriate products," Diane Thompson of the NCLC told the Commission.[39]

The HUD-Treasury task force recommended a set of reforms aimed at protecting

borrowers from the most egregious practices in the mortgage market, including bet-
ter disclosure, improved financial literacy, strengthened enforcement, and new leg-
islative protections. However, the report also recognized the downside of restricting
the lending practices that offered many borrowers with less-than-prime credit a
chance at homeownership. It was a dilemma. Gary Gensler, who worked on the re-
port as a senior Treasury official and is currently the chairman of the Commodity Fu-
tures Trading Commission, told the FCIC that the report's recommendations "lasted
on Capitol Hill a very short time. . . . There wasn't much appetite or mood to take
these recommendations."[40]

But problems persisted, and others would take up the cause. Through the early
years of the new decade, "the really poorly underwritten loans, the payment shock
loans" continued to proliferate outside the traditional banking sector, said FDIC
Chairman Sheila Bair, who served at Treasury as the assistant secretary for financial
institutions from 2001 to 2002. In testimony to the Commission, she observed that
these poor-quality loans pulled market share from traditional banks and "created
negative competitive pressure for the banks and thrifts to start following suit." She
added,

> [Subprime lending] was started and the lion's share of it occurred in the
> nonbank sector, but it clearly created competitive pressures on
> banks. . . . I think nipping this in the bud in 2000 and 2001 with some
> strong consumer rules applying across the board that just simply said
> you've got to document a customer's income to make sure they can re-
> pay the loan, you've got to make sure the income is sufficient to pay the
> loans when the interest rate resets, just simple rules like that . . . could
> have done a lot to stop this.[41]

After Bair was nominated to her position at Treasury, and when she was making
the rounds on Capitol Hill, Senator Paul Sarbanes, chairman of the Committee on
Banking, Housing, and Urban Affairs, told her about lending problems in Baltimore,
where foreclosures were on the rise. He asked Bair to read the HUD-Treasury report
on predatory lending, and she became interested in the issue. Sarbanes introduced
legislation to remedy the problem, but it faced significant resistance from the mort-
gage industry and within Congress, Bair told the Commission. Bair decided to try to
get the industry to adopt a set of "best practices" that would include a voluntary ban
on mortgages that strip borrowers of their equity, and would offer borrowers the op-
portunity to avoid prepayment penalties by agreeing instead to pay a higher interest
rate. She reached out to Edward Gramlich, a governor at the Fed who shared her con-
cerns, to enlist his help in getting companies to abide by these rules. Bair said that
Gramlich didn't talk out of school but made it clear to her that the Fed avenue wasn't
going to happen.[42] Similarly, Sandra Braunstein, the director of the Division of Con-
sumer and Community Affairs at the Fed, said that Gramlich told the staff that
Greenspan was not interested in increased regulation.[43]

When Bair and Gramlich approached a number of lenders about the voluntary

program, Bair said some originators appeared willing to participate. But the Wall Street firms that securitized the loans resisted, saying that they were concerned about possible liability if they did not adhere to the proposed best practices, she recalled. The effort died.[44]

Of course, even as these initiatives went nowhere, the market did not stand still. Subprime mortgages were proliferating rapidly, becoming mainstream products. Originations were increasing, and products were changing. By 1999, three of every four subprime mortgages was a first mortgage, and of those 82% were used for refinancing rather than a home purchase. Fifty-nine percent of those refinancings were cash-outs,[45] helping to fuel consumer spending while whittling away homeowners' equity.

# PART III

## The Boom and Bust

# 6

# CREDIT EXPANSION

## CONTENTS

By the end of 2000, the economy had grown 39 straight quarters. Federal Reserve Chairman Alan Greenspan argued the financial system had achieved unprecedented resilience. Large financial companies were—or at least to many observers at the time, appeared to be—profitable, diversified, and, executives and regulators agreed, protected from catastrophe by sophisticated new techniques of managing risk.

The housing market was also strong. Between 1995 and 2000, prices rose at an annual rate of 5.2%; over the next five years, the rate would hit 11.5%.[1] Lower interest rates for mortgage borrowers were partly the reason, as was greater access to mortgage credit for households who had traditionally been left out—including subprime borrowers. Lower interest rates and broader access to credit were available for other types of borrowing, too, such as credit cards and auto loans.

Increased access to credit meant a more stable, secure life for those who managed their finances prudently. It meant families could borrow during temporary income drops, pay for unexpected expenses, or buy major appliances and cars. It allowed other families to borrow and spend beyond their means. Most of all, it meant a shot at homeownership, with all its benefits; and for some, an opportunity to speculate in the real estate market.

As home prices rose, homeowners with greater equity felt more financially secure and, partly as a result, saved less and less. Many others went one step further, borrowing against the equity. The effect was unprecedented debt: between 2001 and 2007, mortgage debt nationally nearly doubled. Household debt rose from 80% of disposable personal income in 1993 to almost 130% by mid-2006. More than three-quarters

of this increase was mortgage debt. Part of the increase was from new home purchases, part from new debt on older homes.

Mortgage credit became more available when subprime lending started to grow again after many of the major subprime lenders failed or were purchased in 1998 and 1999. Afterward, the biggest banks moved in. In 2000, Citigroup, with $800 billion in assets, paid $31 billion for Associates First Capital, the second-biggest subprime lender. Still, subprime lending remained only a niche, just 9.5% of new mortgages in 2000.[2]

Subprime lending risks and questionable practices remained a concern. Yet the Federal Reserve did not aggressively employ the unique authority granted it by the Home Ownership and Equity Protection Act (HOEPA). Although in 2004 the Fed fined Citigroup $70 million for lending violations, it only minimally revised the rules for a narrow set of high-cost mortgages.[3] Following losses by several banks in subprime securitization, the Fed and other regulators revised capital standards.

## HOUSING: "A POWERFUL STABILIZING FORCE"

By the beginning of 2001, the economy was slowing, even though unemployment remained at a 30-year low of 4%. To stimulate borrowing and spending, the Federal Reserve's Federal Open Market Committee lowered short-term interest rates aggressively. On January 3, 2001, in a rare conference call between scheduled meetings, it cut the benchmark federal funds rate—at which banks lend to each other overnight—by a half percentage point, rather than the more typical quarter point. Later that month, the committee cut the rate another half point, and it continued cutting throughout the year—11 times in all—to 1.75%, the lowest in 40 years.

In the end, the recession of 2001 was relatively mild, lasting only eight months, from March to November, and gross domestic product, or GDP—the most common gauge of the economy—dropped by only 0.3%. Some policy makers concluded that perhaps, with effective monetary policy, the economy had reached the so-called end of the business cycle, which some economists had been predicting since before the tech crash. "Recessions have become less frequent and less severe," said Ben Bernanke, then a Fed governor, in a speech early in 2004. "Whether the dominant cause of the Great Moderation is structural change, improved monetary policy, or simply good luck is an important question about which no consensus has yet formed."[4]

With the recession over and mortgage rates at 40-year lows, housing kicked into high gear—again. The nation would lose more than 340,000 nonfarm jobs in 2002 but make small gains in construction. In states where bubbles soon appeared, construction picked up quickly. California ended 2002 with a total of only 2,300 more jobs, but with 21,100 new construction jobs. In Florida, 14% of net job growth was in construction. In 2003, builders started more than 1.8 million single-family dwellings, a rate unseen since the late 1970s. From 2002 to 2005, residential construction contributed three times more to the economy than it had contributed on average since 1990.

But elsewhere the economy remained sluggish, and employment gains were frustratingly small. Experts began talking about a "jobless recovery"—more production without a corresponding increase in employment. For those with jobs, wages stagnated. Between 2002 and 2005, weekly private nonfarm, nonsupervisory wages actually fell by 1% after adjusting for inflation. Faced with these challenges, the Fed shifted perspective, now considering the possibility that consumer prices could *fall*, an event that had worsened the Great Depression seven decades earlier. While concerned, the Fed believed deflation would be avoided. In a widely quoted 2002 speech, Bernanke said the chances of deflation were "extremely small" for two reasons. First, the economy's natural resilience: "Despite the adverse shocks of the past year, our banking system remains healthy and well-regulated, and firm and household balance sheets are for the most part in good shape." Second, the Fed would not allow it. "I am confident that the Fed would take whatever means necessary to prevent significant deflation in the United States. . . . [T]he U.S. government has a technology, called a printing press (or, today, its electronic equivalent), that allows it to produce as many U.S. dollars as it wishes at essentially no cost."[5]

The Fed's monetary policy kept short-term interest rates low. During 2003, the strongest U.S. companies could borrow for 90 days in the commercial paper market at an average 1.1%, compared with 6.3% just three years earlier; rates on three-month Treasury bills dropped below 1% in mid-2003 from 6% in 2000.[6]

Low rates cut the cost of homeownership: interest rates for the typical 30-year fixed-rate mortgage traditionally moved with the overnight fed funds rate, and from 2000 to 2003, this relationship held (see figure 6.1). By 2003, creditworthy home buyers could get fixed-rate mortgages for 5.2%, 3 percentage points lower than three years earlier. The savings were immediate and large. For a home bought at the median price of $180,000, with a 20% down payment, the monthly mortgage payment would be $286 less than in 2000. Or to turn the perspective around—as many people did—for the same monthly payment of $1,077, a homeowner could move up from a $180,000 home to a $245,000 one.[7]

An adjustable-rate mortgage (ARM) gave buyers even lower initial payments or made a larger house affordable—unless interest rates rose. In 2001, just 4% of prime borrowers with new mortgages chose ARMs; in 2003, 10% did. In 2004, the proportion rose to 21%.[8] Among subprime borrowers, already heavy users of ARMs, it rose from around 60% to 76%.[9]

As people jumped into the housing market, prices rose, and in hot markets they really took off (see figure 6.2). In Florida, average home prices gained 4.1% annually from 1995 to 2000 and then 11.1% annually from 2000 to 2003. In California, those numbers were even higher: 6.1% and 13.6%. In California, a house bought for $200,000 in 1995 was worth $454,428 nine years later. However, soaring prices were not necessarily the norm. In Washington State, prices continued to appreciate, but more slowly: 5.9% annually from 1995 to 2000, 5.5% annually from 2000 to 2003. In Ohio, the numbers were 4.3% and 3.6%.[10] Nationwide, home prices rose 9.8% annually from 2000 to 2003—historically high, but well under the fastest-growing markets.

## Bank Borrowing and Mortgage Interest Rates

*Rates for both banks and homeowners have been low in recent years.*

IN PERCENT

SOURCE: Federal Reserve Bank of St. Louis, Federal Reserve Economic Database

*Figure 6.1*

Homeownership increased steadily, peaking at 69.2% of households in 2004.[11] Because so many families were benefiting from higher home values, household wealth rose to nearly six times income, up from five times a few years earlier. The top 10% of households by net worth, of whom 96% owned their homes, saw the value of their primary residences rise between 2001 and 2004 from $372,800 to $450,000 (adjusted for inflation), an increase of more than $77,000. Median net worth for all households in the top 10%, after accounting for other housing value and assets, as well as all liabilities, was $1.4 million in 2004. Homeownership rates for the bottom 25% of households ticked up from 14% to 15% between 2001 and 2004; the median value of their primary residences rose from $52,700 to $65,000, an increase of more than $12,000. Median net worth for households in the bottom 25% was $1,700 in 2004.[12]

Historically, every $1,000 increase in housing wealth boosted consumer spending by an estimated $50 a year.[13] But economists debated whether the wealth increases would affect spending more than in past years, because so many homeowners at so many levels of wealth saw increases and because it was easier and cheaper to tap home equity.

Higher home prices and low mortgage rates brought a wave of refinancing to the prime mortgage market. In 2003 alone, lenders refinanced over 15 million mortgages, more than one in four—an unprecedented level.[14] Many homeowners took out cash while cutting their interest rates. From 2001 through 2003, cash-out refinanc-

## U.S. Home Prices

INDEX VALUE: JANUARY 2000 = 100

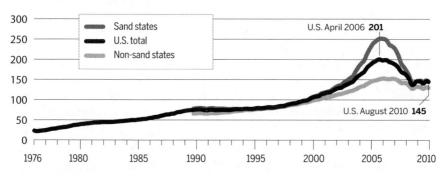

NOTE: Sand states are Arizona, California, Florida, and Nevada.
SOURCE: CoreLogic and U.S. Census Bureau: 2007 American Community Survey, FCIC calculations

*Figure 6.2*

ings netted these households an estimated $427 billion; homeowners accessed an-
other $430 billion via home equity loans.[15] Some were typical second liens; others
were a newer invention, the home equity line of credit. These operated much like a
credit card, letting the borrower borrow and repay as needed, often with the conven-
ience of an actual plastic card.

According to the Fed's 2004 Survey of Consumer Finances, 45.0% of homeowners
who tapped their equity used that money for expenses such as medical bills, taxes, elec-
tronics, and vacations, or to consolidate debt; another 31.0% used it for home improve-
ments; and the rest purchased more real estate, cars, investments, clothing, or jewelry.

A Congressional Budget Office paper from 2007 reported on the recent history:
"As housing prices surged in the late 1990s and early 2000s, consumers boosted their
spending faster than their income rose. That was reflected in a sharp drop in the per-
sonal savings rate."[16] Between 1998 and 2005, increased consumer spending ac-
counted for between 67% and 168% of GDP growth in any year—rising above 100%
in years when spending growth offset declines elsewhere in the economy. Meanwhile,
the personal saving rate dropped from 5.2% to 1.4%. Some components of spending
grew remarkably fast: home furnishings and other household durables, recreational
goods and vehicles, spending at restaurants, and health care. Overall consumer
spending grew faster than the economy, and in some years it grew faster than real
disposable income.

Nonetheless, the economy looked stable. By 2003, it had weathered the brief re-
cession of 2001 and the dot-com bust, which had caused the largest loss of wealth in

decades. With new financial products like the home equity line of credit, households could borrow against their homes to compensate for investment losses or unemployment. Deflation, against which the Fed had struck preemptively, did not materialize.

At a congressional hearing in November 2002, Greenspan acknowledged—at least implicitly—that after the dot-com bubble burst, the Fed cut interest rates in part to promote housing. Greenspan argued that the Fed's low-interest-rate policy had stimulated the economy by encouraging home sales and housing starts with "mortgage interest rates that are at lows not seen in decades." As Greenspan explained, "Mortgage markets have also been a powerful stabilizing force over the past two years of economic distress by facilitating the extraction of some of the equity that homeowners had built up."[17] In February 2004, he reiterated his point, referring to "a large extraction of cash from home equity."[18]

## SUBPRIME LOANS: "BUYERS WILL PAY A HIGH PREMIUM"

The subprime market roared back from its shakeout in the late 1990s. The value of subprime loans originated almost doubled from 2001 through 2003, to $310 billion. In 2000, 52% of these were securitized; in 2003, 63%.[19] Low interest rates spurred this boom, which would have long-term repercussions, but so did increasingly widespread computerized credit scores, the growing statistical history on subprime borrowers, and the scale of the firms entering the market.

Subprime was dominated by a narrowing field of ever-larger firms; the marginal players from the past decade had merged or vanished. By 2003, the top 25 subprime lenders made 93% of all subprime loans, up from 47% in 1996.[20]

There were now three main kinds of companies in the subprime origination and securitization business: commercial banks and thrifts, Wall Street investment banks, and independent mortgage lenders. Some of the biggest banks and thrifts—Citigroup, National City Bank, HSBC, and Washington Mutual—spent billions on boosting subprime lending by creating new units, acquiring firms, or offering financing to other mortgage originators. Almost always, these operations were sequestered in nonbank subsidiaries, leaving them in a regulatory no-man's-land.

When it came to subprime lending, now it was Wall Street investment banks that worried about competition posed by the largest commercial banks and thrifts. Former Lehman president Bart McDade told the FCIC that the banks had gained their own securitization skills and didn't need the investment banks to structure and distribute.[21] So the investment banks moved into mortgage origination to guarantee a supply of loans they could securitize and sell to the growing legions of investors. For example, Lehman Brothers, the fourth-largest investment bank, purchased six different domestic lenders between 1998 and 2004, including BNC and Aurora.[22] Bear Stearns, the fifth-largest, ramped up its subprime lending arm and eventually acquired three subprime originators in the United States, including Encore. In 2006, Merrill Lynch acquired First Franklin, and Morgan Stanley bought Saxon Capital; in 2007, Goldman Sachs upped its stake in Senderra Funding, a small subprime lender.

Meanwhile, several independent mortgage companies took steps to boost growth.

New Century and Ameriquest were especially aggressive. New Century's "Focus 2000" plan concentrated on "originating loans with characteristics for which whole loan buyers will pay a high premium."[23] Those "whole loan buyers" were the firms on Wall Street that purchased loans and, most often, bundled them into mortgage-backed securities. They were eager customers. In 2003, New Century sold $20.8 billion in whole loans, up from $3.1 billion three years before,[24] launching the firm from tenth to second place among subprime originators. Three-quarters went to two securitizing firms—Morgan Stanley and Credit Suisse—but New Century reassured its investors that there were "many more prospective buyers."[25]

Ameriquest, in particular, pursued volume. According to the company's public statements, it paid its account executives less per mortgage than the competition, but it encouraged them to make up the difference by underwriting more loans. "Our people make more volume per employee than the rest of the industry," Aseem Mital, CEO of Ameriquest, said in 2005. The company cut costs elsewhere in the origination process, too. The back office for the firm's retail division operated in assembly-line fashion, Mital told a reporter for *American Banker;* the work was divided into specialized tasks, including data entry, underwriting, customer service, account management, and funding. Ameriquest used its savings to undercut by as much as 0.55% what competing originators charged securitizing firms, according to an industry analyst's estimate. Between 2000 and 2003, Ameriquest loan origination rose from an estimated $4 billion to $39 billion annually. That vaulted the firm from eleventh to first place among subprime originators. "They are clearly the aggressor," Countrywide CEO Angelo Mozilo told his investors in 2005.[26] By 2005, Countrywide was third on the list.

The subprime players followed diverse strategies. Lehman and Countrywide pursued a "vertically integrated" model, involving them in every link of the mortgage chain: originating and funding the loans, packaging them into securities, and finally selling the securities to investors. Others concentrated on niches: New Century, for example, mainly originated mortgages for immediate sale to other firms in the chain.

When originators made loans to hold through maturity—an approach known as *originate-to-hold*—they had a clear incentive to underwrite carefully and consider the risks. However, when they originated mortgages to sell, for securitization or otherwise—known as *originate-to-distribute*—they no longer risked losses if the loan defaulted. As long as they made accurate representations and warranties, the only risk was to their reputations if a lot of their loans went bad—but during the boom, loans were not going bad. In total, this originate-to-distribute pipeline carried more than half of all mortgages before the crisis, and a much larger piece of subprime mortgages.

For decades, a version of the originate-to-distribute model produced safe mortgages. Fannie and Freddie had been buying prime, conforming mortgages since the 1970s, protected by strict underwriting standards. But some saw that the model now had problems. "If you look at how many people are playing, from the real estate agent all the way through to the guy who is issuing the security and the underwriter and the underwriting group and blah, blah, blah, then nobody in this entire chain is responsible to anybody," Lewis Ranieri, an early leader in securitization, told the FCIC,

not the outcome he and other investment bankers had expected. "None of us wrote and said, 'Oh, by the way, you have to be responsible for your actions,'" Ranieri said. "It was pretty self-evident."[27]

The starting point for many mortgages was a mortgage broker. These independent brokers, with access to a variety of lenders, worked with borrowers to complete the application process. Using brokers allowed more rapid expansion, with no need to build branches; lowered costs, with no need for full-time salespeople; and extended geographic reach.

For brokers, compensation generally came as up-front fees—from the borrower, from the lender, or both—so the loan's performance mattered little. These fees were often paid without the borrower's knowledge. Indeed, many borrowers mistakenly believed the mortgage brokers acted in borrowers' best interest.[28] One common fee paid by the lender to the broker was the "yield spread premium": on higher-interest loans, the lending bank would pay the broker a higher premium, giving the incentive to sign the borrower to the highest possible rate. "If the broker decides he's going to try and make more money on the loan, then he's going to raise the rate," said Jay Jeffries, a former sales manager for Fremont Investment & Loan, to the Commission. "We've got a higher rate loan, we're paying the broker for that yield spread premium."[29]

In theory, borrowers are the first defense against abusive lending. By shopping around, they should realize, for example, if a broker is trying to sell them a higher-priced loan or to place them in a subprime loan when they would qualify for a less-expensive prime loan. But many borrowers do not understand the most basic aspects of their mortgage. A study by two Federal Reserve economists estimated at least 38% of borrowers with adjustable-rate mortgages did not understand how much their interest rates could reset at one time, and more than half underestimated how high their rates could reach over the years.[30] The same lack of awareness extended to other terms of the loan—for example, the level of documentation provided to the lender. "Most borrowers didn't even realize that they were getting a no-doc loan," said Michael Calhoun, president of the Center for Responsible Lending. "They'd come in with their W-2 and end up with a no-doc loan simply because the broker was getting paid more and the lender was getting paid more and there was extra yield left over for Wall Street because the loan carried a higher interest rate."[31]

And borrowers with less access to credit are particularly ill equipped to challenge the more experienced person across the desk. "While many [consumers] believe they are pretty good at dealing with day-to-day financial matters, in actuality they engage in financial behaviors that generate expenses and fees: overdrawing checking accounts, making late credit card payments, or exceeding limits on credit card charges," Annamaria Lusardi, a professor of economics at Dartmouth College, told the FCIC. "Comparing terms of financial contracts and shopping around before making financial decisions are not at all common among the population."[32]

Recall our case study securitization deal discussed earlier—in which New Century sold 4,499 mortgages to Citigroup, which then sold them to the securitization trust, which then bundled them into 19 tranches for sale to investors. Out of those 4,499 mortgages, brokers originated 3,466 on behalf of New Century. For each, the

brokers received an average fee from the borrowers of $3,756, or 1.81% of the loan amount. On top of that, the brokers also received yield spread premiums from New Century for 1,744 of these loans, averaging $2,585 each. In total, the brokers received more than $17.5 million in fees for the 3,466 loans.[33]

Critics argued that with this much money at stake, mortgage brokers had every incentive to seek "the highest combination of fees and mortgage interest rates the market will bear."[34] Herb Sandler, the founder and CEO of the thrift Golden West Financial Corporation, told the FCIC that brokers were the "whores of the world."[35] As the housing and mortgage market boomed, so did the brokers. Wholesale Access, which tracks the mortgage industry, reported that from 2000 to 2003, the number of brokerage firms rose from about 30,000 to 50,000. In 2000, brokers originated 55% of loans; in 2003, they peaked at 68%.[36] JP Morgan CEO Jamie Dimon testified to the FCIC that his firm eventually ended its broker-originated business in 2009 after discovering the loans had more than twice the losses of the loans that JP Morgan itself originated.[37]

As the housing market expanded, another problem emerged, in subprime and prime mortgages alike: inflated appraisals. For the lender, inflated appraisals meant greater losses if a borrower defaulted. But for the borrower or for the broker or loan officer who hired the appraiser, an inflated value could make the difference between closing and losing the deal. Imagine a home selling for $200,000 that an appraiser says is actually worth only $175,000. In this case, a bank won't lend a borrower, say, $180,000 to buy the home. The deal dies. Sure enough, appraisers began feeling pressure. One 2003 survey found that 55% of the appraisers had felt pressed to inflate the value of homes; by 2006, this had climbed to 90%. The pressure came most frequently from the mortgage brokers, but appraisers reported it from real estate agents, lenders, and in many cases borrowers themselves. Most often, refusal to raise the appraisal meant losing the client.[38] Dennis J. Black, president of the Florida appraisal and brokerage services firm D. J. Black & Co. and an appraiser with 24 years' experience, held continuing education sessions all over the country for the National Association of Independent Fee Appraisers. He heard complaints from the appraisers that they had been pressured to ignore missing kitchens, damaged walls, and inoperable mechanical systems. Black told the FCIC, "The story I have heard most often is the client saying he could not use the appraisal because the value was [not] what they needed."[39] The client would hire somebody else.

Changes in regulations reinforced the trend toward laxer appraisal standards, as Karen Mann, a Sacramento appraiser with 30 years' experience, explained in testimony to the FCIC. In 1994, the Federal Reserve, Office of the Comptroller of the Currency, Office of Thrift Supervision, and Federal Deposit Insurance Corporation loosened the appraisal requirements for the lenders they regulated by raising from $100,000 to $250,000 the minimum home value at which an appraisal from a licensed professional was required. In addition, Mann cited the lack of oversight of appraisers, noting, "We had a vast increase of licensed appraisers in [California] in spite of the lack of qualified/experienced trainers."[40] The Bakersfield appraiser Gary Crabtree told the FCIC that California's Office of Real Estate Appraisers had eight investigators to supervise 21,000 appraisers.[41]

In 2005, the four bank regulators issued new guidance to strengthen appraisals. They recommended that an originator's loan production staff not select appraisers. That led Washington Mutual to use an "appraisal management company," First American Corporation, to choose appraisers. Nevertheless, in 2007 the New York State attorney general sued First American: relying on internal company documents, the complaint alleged the corporation improperly let Washington Mutual's loan production staff "hand-pick appraisers who bring in appraisal values high enough to permit WaMu's loans to close, and improperly permit[ted] WaMu to pressure . . . appraisers to change appraisal values that are too low to permit loans to close."[42]

## CITIGROUP: "INVITED REGULATORY SCRUTINY"

As subprime originations grew, Citigroup decided to expand, with troubling consequences. Barely a year after the Gramm-Leach-Bliley Act validated its 1998 merger with Travelers, Citigroup made its next big move. In September 2000, it paid $31 billion for Associates First, then the second-largest subprime lender in the country (after Household Finance.). Such a merger would usually have required approval from the Federal Reserve and the other bank regulators, because Associates First owned three small banks (in Utah, Delaware, and South Dakota). But because these banks were specialized, a provision tucked away in Gramm-Leach-Bliley kept the Fed out of the mix. The OCC, FDIC, and New York State banking regulators reviewed the deal. Consumer groups fought it, citing a long record of alleged lending abuses by Associates First, including high prepayment penalties, excessive fees, and other opaque charges in loan documents—all targeting unsophisticated borrowers who typically could not evaluate the forms. "It's simply unacceptable to have the largest bank in America take over the icon of predatory lending," said Martin Eakes, founder of a nonprofit community lender in North Carolina.[43]

Advocates for the merger argued that a large bank under a rigorous regulator could reform the company, and Citigroup promised to take strong actions. Regulators approved the merger in November 2000, and by the next summer Citigroup had started suspending mortgage purchases from close to two-thirds of the brokers and half the banks that had sold loans to Associates First. "We were aware that brokers were at the heart of that public discussion and were at the heart of a lot of the [controversial] cases," said Pam Flaherty, a Citigroup senior vice president for community relations and outreach.[44]

The merger exposed Citigroup to enhanced regulatory scrutiny. In 2001, the Federal Trade Commission, which regulates independent mortgage companies' compliance with consumer protection laws, launched an investigation into Associates First's premerger business and found that the company had pressured borrowers to refinance into expensive mortgages and to buy expensive mortgage insurance. In 2002, Citigroup reached a record $215 million civil settlement with the FTC over Associates' "systematic and widespread deceptive and abusive lending practices."[45]

In 2001, the New York Fed used the occasion of Citigroup's next proposed acquisition—European American Bank on Long Island, New York—to launch its own in-

vestigation of CitiFinancial, which now contained Associates First. "The manner in which [Citigroup] approached that transaction invited regulatory scrutiny," former Fed Governor Mark Olson told the FCIC. "They bought a passel of problems for themselves and it was at least a two-year [issue]."[46] The Fed eventually accused Citi-Financial of converting unsecured personal loans (usually for borrowers in financial trouble) into home equity loans without properly assessing the borrower's ability to repay. Reviewing lending practices from 2000 and 2001, the Fed also accused the unit of selling credit insurance to borrowers without checking if they would qualify for a mortgage without it. For these violations and for impeding its investigation, the Fed in 2004 assessed $70 million in penalties. The company said it expected to pay another $30 million in restitution to borrowers.[47]

## FEDERAL RULES:
## "INTENDED TO CURB UNFAIR OR ABUSIVE LENDING"

As Citigroup was buying Associates First in 2000, the Federal Reserve revisited the rules protecting borrowers from predatory conduct. It conducted its second round of hearings on the Home Ownership and Equity Protection Act (HOEPA), and subsequently the staff offered two reform proposals. The first would have effectively barred lenders from granting any mortgage—not just the limited set of high-cost loans defined by HOEPA—solely on the value of the collateral and without regard to the borrower's ability to repay. For high-cost loans, the lender would have to verify and document the borrower's income and debt; for other loans, the documentation standard was weaker, as the lender could rely on the borrower's payment history and the like. The staff memo explained this would mainly "affect lenders who make no-documentation loans." The second proposal addressed practices such as deceptive advertisements, misrepresenting loan terms, and having consumers sign blank documents—acts that involve fraud, deception, or misrepresentations.[48]

Despite evidence of predatory tactics from their own hearings and from the recently released HUD-Treasury report, Fed officials remained divided on how aggressively to strengthen borrower protections. They grappled with the same trade-off that the HUD-Treasury report had recently noted. "We want to encourage the growth in the subprime lending market," Fed Governor Edward Gramlich remarked at the Financial Services Roundtable in early 2004. "But we also don't want to encourage the abuses; indeed, we want to do what we can to stop these abuses."[49] Fed General Counsel Scott Alvarez told the FCIC, "There was concern that if you put out a broad rule, you would stop things that were not unfair and deceptive because you were trying to get at the bad practices and you just couldn't think of all of the details you would need. And if you did think of all of the details, you'd end up writing a rule that people could get around very easily."[50]

Greenspan, too, later said that to prohibit certain products might be harmful. "These and other kinds of loan products, when made to borrowers meeting appropriate underwriting standards, should not necessarily be regarded as improper," he said, "and on the contrary facilitated the national policy of making homeownership

more broadly available."[51] Instead, at least for certain violations of consumer protection laws, he suggested another approach: "If there is egregious fraud, if there is egregious practice, one doesn't need supervision and regulation, what one needs is law enforcement."[52] But the Federal Reserve would not use the legal system to rein in predatory lenders. From 2000 to the end of Greenspan's tenure in 2006, the Fed referred to the Justice Department only three institutions for fair lending violations related to mortgages: First American Bank, in Carpentersville, Illinois; Desert Community Bank, in Victorville, California; and the New York branch of Société Générale, a large French bank.

Fed officials rejected the staff proposals. After some wrangling, in December 2001 the Fed did modify HOEPA, but only at the margins. Explaining its actions, the board highlighted compromise: "The final rule is intended to curb unfair or abusive lending practices without unduly interfering with the flow of credit, creating unnecessary creditor burden, or narrowing consumers' options in legitimate transactions." The status quo would change little. Fed economists had estimated the percentage of subprime loans covered by HOEPA would increase from 9% to as much as 38% under the new regulations.[53] But lenders changed the terms of mortgages to avoid the new rules' revised interest rate and fee triggers. By late 2005, it was clear that the new regulations would end up covering only about 1% of subprime loans.[54] Nevertheless, reflecting on the Federal Reserve's efforts, Greenspan contended in an FCIC interview that the Fed had developed a set of rules that have held up to this day.[55]

This was a missed opportunity, says FDIC Chairman Sheila Bair, who described the "one bullet" that might have prevented the financial crisis: "I absolutely would have been over at the Fed writing rules, prescribing mortgage lending standards across the board for everybody, bank and nonbank, that you cannot make a mortgage unless you have documented income that the borrower can repay the loan."[56]

The Fed held back on enforcement and supervision, too. While discussing HOEPA rule changes in 2000, the staff of the Fed's Division of Consumer and Community Affairs also proposed a pilot program to examine lending practices at bank holding companies' nonbank subsidiaries,[57] such as CitiFinancial and HSBC Finance, whose influence in the subprime market was growing. The nonbank subsidiaries were subject to enforcement actions by the Federal Trade Commission, while the banks and thrifts were overseen by their primary regulators. As the holding company regulator, the Fed had the authority to examine nonbank subsidiaries for "compliance with the [Bank Holding Company Act] or any other Federal law that the Board has specific jurisdiction to enforce"; however, the consumer protection laws did not explicitly give the Fed enforcement authority in this area.[58]

The Fed resisted routine examinations of these companies, and despite the support of Fed Governor Gramlich, the initiative stalled. Sandra Braunstein, then a staff member in the Fed's Consumer and Community Affairs Division and now its director, told the FCIC that Greenspan and other officials were concerned that routinely examining the nonbank subsidiaries could create an uneven playing field because the subsidiaries had to compete with the independent mortgage companies, over which

the Fed had no supervisory authority (although the Fed's HOEPA rules applied to all lenders).[59] In an interview with the FCIC, Greenspan went further, arguing that with or without a mandate, the Fed lacked sufficient resources to examine the nonbank subsidiaries. Worse, the former chairman said, inadequate regulation sends a misleading message to the firms and the market; if you examine an organization incompletely, it tends to put a sign in their window that it was examined by the Fed, and partial supervision is dangerous because it creates a Good Housekeeping stamp.[60]

But if resources were the issue, the Fed chairman could have argued for more. The Fed draws income from interest on the Treasury bonds it owns, so it did not have to ask Congress for appropriations. It was always mindful, however, that it could be subject to a government audit of its finances.

In the same FCIC interview, Greenspan recalled that he sat in countless meetings on consumer protection, but that he couldn't pretend to have the kind of expertise on this subject that the staff had.[61]

Gramlich, who chaired the Fed's consumer subcommittee, favored tighter supervision of all subprime lenders—including units of banks, thrifts, bank holding companies, and state-chartered mortgage companies. He acknowledged that because such oversight would extend Fed authority to firms (such as independent mortgage companies) whose lending practices were not subject to routine supervision, the change would require congressional legislation "and might antagonize the states." But without such oversight, the mortgage business was "like a city with a murder law, but no cops on the beat."[62] In an interview in 2007, Gramlich told the *Wall Street Journal* that he privately urged Greenspan to clamp down on predatory lending. Greenspan demurred and, lacking support on the board, Gramlich backed away. Gramlich told the *Journal*, "He was opposed to it, so I did not really pursue it."[63] (Gramlich died in 2008 of leukemia, at age 68.)

The Fed's failure to stop predatory practices infuriated consumer advocates and some members of Congress. Critics charged that accounts of abuses were brushed off as anecdotal. Patricia McCoy, a law professor at the University of Connecticut who served on the Fed's Consumer Advisory Council between 2002 and 2004, was familiar with the Fed's reaction to stories of individual consumers. "That is classic Fed mindset," said McCoy. "If you cannot prove that it is a broad-based problem that threatens systemic consequences, then you will be dismissed." It frustrated Margot Saunders of the National Consumer Law Center: "I stood up at a Fed meeting in 2005 and said, 'How many anecdotes makes it real? . . . How many tens [of] thousands of anecdotes will it take to convince you that this is a trend?'"[64]

The Fed's reluctance to take action trumped the 2000 HUD-Treasury report and reports issued by the General Accounting Office in 1999 and 2004.[65] The Fed did not begin routinely examining subprime subsidiaries until a pilot program in July 2007, under new chairman Ben Bernanke.[66] The Fed did not issue new rules under HOEPA until July 2008, a year after the subprime market had shut down. These rules banned deceptive practices in a much broader category of "higher-priced mortgage loans"; moreover, they prohibited making those loans without regard to the borrower's ability

to pay, and required companies to verify income and assets.[67] The rules would not take effect until October 1, 2009, which was too little, too late.

Looking back, Fed General Counsel Alvarez said his institution succumbed to the climate of the times. He told the FCIC, "The mind-set was that there should be no regulation; the market should take care of policing, unless there already is an identified problem. . . . We were in the reactive mode because that's what the mind-set was of the '90s and the early 2000s." The strong housing market also reassured people. Alvarez noted the long history of low mortgage default rates and the desire to help people who traditionally had few dealings with banks become homeowners.[68]

## STATES: "LONG-STANDING POSITION"

As the Fed balked, many states proceeded on their own, enacting "mini-HOEPA" laws and undertaking vigorous enforcement. They would face opposition from two federal regulators, the OCC and the OTS.

In 1999, North Carolina led the way, establishing a fee trigger of 5%: that is, for the most part any mortgage with points and fees at origination of more than 5% of the loan qualified as "high-cost mortgage" subject to state regulations. This was considerably lower than the 8% set by the Fed's 2001 HOEPA regulations. Other provisions addressed an even broader class of loans, banning prepayment penalties for mortgage loans under $150,000 and prohibiting repeated refinancing, known as loan "flipping."[69]

These rules did not apply to federally chartered thrifts. In 1996, the Office of Thrift Supervision reasserted its "long-standing position" that its regulations "occupy the entire field of lending regulation for federal savings associations, leaving no room for state regulation." Exempting states from "a hodgepodge of conflicting and overlapping state lending requirements," the OTS said, would let thrifts deliver "low-cost credit to the public free from undue regulatory duplication and burden." Meanwhile, "the elaborate network of federal borrower-protection statutes" would protect consumers.[70]

Nevertheless, other states copied North Carolina's tactic. State attorneys general launched thousands of enforcement actions, including more than 3,000 in 2006 alone.[71] By 2007, 29 states and the District of Columbia would pass some form of anti-predatory lending legislation. In some cases, two or more states teamed up to produce large settlements: in 2002, for example, a suit by Illinois, Massachusetts, and Minnesota recovered more than $50 million from First Alliance Mortgage Company, even though the firm had filed for bankruptcy. Also that year, Household Finance—later acquired by HSBC—was ordered to pay $484 million in penalties and restitution to consumers. In 2006, a coalition of 49 states and the District of Columbia settled with Ameriquest for $325 million and required the company to follow restrictions on its lending practices.

As we will see, however, these efforts would be severely hindered with respect to national banks when the OCC in 2004 officially joined the OTS in constraining states

from taking such actions. "The federal regulators' refusal to reform [predatory] practices and products served as an implicit endorsement of their legality," Illinois Attorney General Lisa Madigan testified to the Commission.[72]

## COMMUNITY-LENDING PLEDGES:
## "WHAT WE DO IS REAFFIRM OUR INTENTION"

While consumer groups unsuccessfully lobbied the Fed for more protection against
predatory lenders, they also lobbied the banks to invest in and loan to low- and moderate-income communities. The resulting promises were sometimes called "CRA
commitments" or "community development" commitments. These pledges were not
required under law, including the Community Reinvestment Act of 1977; in fact,
they were often outside the scope of the CRA. For example, they frequently involved
lending to individuals whose incomes exceeded those covered by the CRA, lending
in geographic areas not covered by the CRA, or lending to minorities, on which the
CRA is silent. The banks would either sign agreements with community groups or
else unilaterally pledge to lend to and invest in specific communities or populations.

Banks often made these commitments when courting public opinion during the
merger mania at the turn of the 21st century. One of the most notable promises was
made by Citigroup soon after its merger with Travelers in 1998: a $115 billion lending
and investment commitment, some of which would include mortgages. Later, Citigroup made a $120 billion commitment when it acquired California Federal Bank in
2002. When merging with FleetBoston Financial Corporation in 2004, Bank of America announced its largest commitment to date: $750 billion over 10 years. Chase announced commitments of $18.1 billion and $800 billion, respectively, in its mergers
with Chemical Bank and Bank One. The National Community Reinvestment Coalition, an advocacy group, eventually tallied more than $4.5 trillion in commitments
from 1977 to 2007; mortgage lending made up a significant portion of them.[73]

Although banks touted these commitments in press releases, the NCRC says it
and other community groups could not verify this lending happened.[74] The FCIC
sent a series of requests to Bank of America, JP Morgan, Citigroup, and Wells Fargo,
the nation's four largest banks, regarding their "CRA and community lending commitments." In response, the banks indicated they had fulfilled most promises. According to the documents provided, the value of commitments to community groups
was much smaller than the larger unilateral pledges by the banks. Further, the
pledges generally covered broader categories than did the CRA, including mortgages
to minority borrowers and to borrowers with up-to-median income. For example,
only 22% of the mortgages made under JP Morgan's $800 billion "community development initiative" would have fallen under the CRA.[75] Bank of America, which
would count all low- and moderate-income and minority lending as satisfying its
pledges, stated that just over half were likely to meet CRA requirements.

Many of these loans were not very risky. This is not surprising, because such broad
definitions necessarily included loans to borrowers with strong credit histories—low

income and weak or subprime credit are not the same. In fact, Citigroup's 2002 pledge of $80 billion in mortgage lending "consisted of entirely prime loans" to low- and moderate-income households, low- and moderate-income neighborhoods, and minority borrowers. These loans performed well.[76] JP Morgan's largest commitment to a community group was to the Chicago CRA Coalition: $12 billion in loans over 11 years. Of loans issued between 2004 and 2006, fewer than 5% have been 90-or-more-days delinquent, even as of late 2010.[77] Wachovia made $12 billion in mortgage loans between 2004 and 2006 under its $100 billion in unilateral pledges: only about 7.3% were ever more than 90 days delinquent over the life of the loan, compared with an estimated national average of 14%.[78] The better performance was partly the result of Wachovia's lending concentration in the relatively stable Southeast, and partly a reflection of the credit profile of many of these borrowers.

During the early years of the CRA, the Federal Reserve Board, when considering whether to approve mergers, gave some weight to commitments made to regulators. This changed in February 1989, when the board denied Continental Bank's application to merge with Grand Canyon State Bank, saying the bank's commitment to improve community service could not offset its poor lending record.[79] In April 1989, the FDIC, OCC, and Federal Home Loan Bank Board (the precursor of the OTS) joined the Fed in announcing that commitments to regulators about lending would be considered only when addressing "specific problems in an otherwise satisfactory record."[80]

Internal documents, and its public statements, show the Fed never considered pledges to community groups in evaluating mergers and acquisitions, nor did it enforce them. As Glenn Loney, a former Fed official, told Commission staff, "At the very beginning, [we] said we're not going to be in a posture where the Fed's going to be sort of coercing banks into making deals with . . . community groups so that they can get their applications through."[81]

In fact, the rules implementing the 1995 changes to the CRA made it clear that the Federal Reserve would not consider promises to third parties or enforce prior agreements with those parties. The rules state "an institution's record of fulfilling these types of agreements [with third parties] is not an appropriate CRA performance criterion."[82] Still, the banks highlighted past acts and assurances for the future. In 1998, for example, when NationsBank said it was merging with BankAmerica, it also announced a 10-year, $350 billion initiative that included pledges of $115 billion for affordable housing, $30 billion for consumer lending, $180 billion for small businesses, and $25 and $10 billion for economic and community development, respectively.

This merger was perhaps the most controversial of its time because of the size of the two banks. The Fed held four public hearings and received more than 1,600 comments. Supporters touted the community investment commitment, while opponents decried its lack of specificity. The Fed's internal staff memorandum recommending approval repeated the Fed's insistence on not considering these promises: "The Board considers CRA agreements to be agreements between private parties and has not facilitated, monitored, judged, required, or enforced agreements or specific portions of agreements. . . . NationsBank remains obligated to meet the credit needs of its entire

community, including [low- and moderate-income] areas, with or without private agreements."[83]

In its public order approving the merger, the Federal Reserve mentioned the commitment but then went on to state that "an applicant must demonstrate a satisfactory record of performance under the CRA without reliance on plans or commitments for future action. . . . The Board believes that the CRA plan—whether made as a plan or as an enforceable commitment—has no relevance in this case without the demonstrated record of performance of the companies involved."[84]

So were these commitments a meaningful step, or only a gesture? Lloyd Brown, a managing director at Citigroup, told the FCIC that most of the commitments would have been fulfilled in the normal course of business.[85] Speaking of the 2007 merger with Countrywide, Andrew Plepler, head of Global Corporate Social Responsibility at Bank of America, told the FCIC: "At a time of mergers, there is a lot of concern, sometimes, that one plus one will not equal two in the eyes of communities where the acquired bank has been investing. . . . So, what we do is reaffirm our intention to continue to lend and invest so that the communities where we live and work will continue to economically thrive." He explained further that the pledge amount was arrived at by working "closely with our business partners" who project current levels of business activity that qualifies toward community lending goals into the future to assure the community that past lending and investing practices will continue.[86]

In essence, banks promised to keep doing what they had been doing, and community groups had the assurance that they would.

## BANK CAPITAL STANDARDS: "ARBITRAGE"

Although the Federal Reserve had decided against stronger protections for consumers, it internalized the lessons of 1998 and 1999, when the first generation of subprime lenders put themselves at serious risk; some, such as Keystone Bank and Superior Bank, collapsed when the values of the subprime securitized assets they held proved to be inflated. In response, the Federal Reserve and other regulators reworked the capital requirements on securitization by banks and thrifts.

In October 2001, they introduced the "Recourse Rule" governing how much capital a bank needed to hold against securitized assets. If a bank retained an interest in a residual tranche of a mortgage security, as Keystone, Superior, and others had done, it would have to keep a dollar in capital for every dollar of residual interest. That seemed to make sense, since the bank, in this instance, would be the first to take losses on the loans in the pool. Under the old rules, banks held only 8% in capital to protect against losses on residual interests and any other exposures they retained in securitizations; Keystone and others had been allowed to seriously understate their risks and to not hold sufficient capital. Ironically, because the new rule made the capital charge on residual interests 100%, it increased banks' incentive to sell the residual interests in securitizations—so that they were no longer the first to lose when the loans went bad.

The Recourse Rule also imposed a new framework for asset-backed securities. The capital requirement would be directly linked to the rating agencies' assessment of the tranches. Holding securities rated AAA or AA required far less capital than holding lower-rated investments. For example, $100 invested in AAA or AA mortgage-backed securities required holding only $1.60 in capital (the same as for securities backed by government-sponsored enterprises). But the same amount invested in anything with a BB rating required $16 in capital, or 10 times more.

Banks could reduce the capital they were required to hold for a pool of mortgages simply by securitizing them, rather than holding them on their books as whole loans. If a bank kept $100 in mortgages on its books, it might have to set aside about $5, including $4 in capital against unexpected losses and $1 in reserves against expected losses. But if the bank created a $100 mortgage-backed security, sold that security in tranches, and then bought all the tranches, the capital requirement would be about $4.10.[87] "Regulatory capital arbitrage does play a role in bank decision making," said David Jones, a Fed economist who wrote an article about the subject in 2000, in an FCIC interview. But "it is not the only thing that matters."[88]

And a final comparison: under bank regulatory capital standards, a $100 triple-A corporate bond required $8 in capital—five times as much as the triple-A mortgage-backed security. Unlike the corporate bond, it was ultimately backed by real estate.

The new requirements put the rating agencies in the driver's seat. How much capital a bank held depended in part on the ratings of the securities it held. Tying capital standards to the views of rating agencies would come in for criticism after the crisis began. It was "a dangerous crutch," former Treasury Secretary Henry Paulson testified to the Commission.[89] However, the Fed's Jones noted it was better than the alternative—"to let the banks rate their own exposures." That alternative "would be terrible," he said, noting that banks had been coming to the Fed and arguing for lower capital requirements on the grounds that the rating agencies were too conservative.[90]

Meanwhile, banks and regulators were not prepared for significant losses on triple-A mortgage-backed securities, which were, after all, supposed to be among the safest investments. Nor were they prepared for ratings downgrades due to expected losses, which would require banks to post more capital. And were downgrades to occur at the moment the banks wanted to sell their securities to raise capital, there would be no buyers. All these things would occur within a few years.

## COMMISSION CONCLUSIONS ON CHAPTER 6

The Commission concludes that there was untrammeled growth in risky mortgages. Unsustainable, toxic loans polluted the financial system and fueled the housing bubble.

Subprime lending was supported in significant ways by major financial institutions. Some firms, such as Citigroup, Lehman Brothers, and Morgan Stanley, acquired subprime lenders. In addition, major financial institutions facilitated the growth in subprime mortgage–lending companies with lines of credit, securitization, purchase guarantees and other mechanisms.

Regulators failed to rein in risky home mortgage lending. In particular, the Federal Reserve failed to meet its statutory obligation to establish and maintain prudent mortgage lending standards and to protect against predatory lending.

# 7

# THE MORTGAGE MACHINE

## CONTENTS

In 2004, commercial banks, thrifts, and investment banks caught up with Fannie Mae and Freddie Mac in securitizing home loans. By 2005, they had taken the lead. The two government-sponsored enterprises maintained their monopoly on securitizing prime mortgages below their loan limits, but the wave of home refinancing by prime borrowers spurred by very low, steady interest rates petered out. Meanwhile, Wall Street focused on the higher-yield loans that the GSEs could not purchase and securitize—loans too large, called jumbo loans, and nonprime loans that didn't meet the GSEs' standards. The nonprime loans soon became the biggest part of the market—"subprime" loans for borrowers with weak credit and "Alt-A" loans, with characteristics riskier than prime loans, to borrowers with strong credit.[1]

By 2005 and 2006, Wall Street was securitizing one-third more loans than Fannie and Freddie. In just two years, private-label mortgage-backed securities had grown more than 30%, reaching $1.15 trillion in 2006; 71% were subprime or Alt-A.[2]

Many investors preferred securities highly rated by the rating agencies—or were encouraged or restricted by regulations to buy them. And with yields low on other highly rated assets, investors hungered for Wall Street mortgage securities backed by higher-yield mortgages—those loans made to subprime borrowers, those with nontraditional features, those with limited or no documentation ("no-doc loans"), or those that failed in some other way to meet strong underwriting standards.

"Securitization could be seen as a factory line," former Citigroup CEO Charles Prince told the FCIC. "As more and more and more of these subprime mortgages were created as raw material for the securitization process, not surprisingly in hindsight, more and more of it was of lower and lower quality. And at the end of that

process, the raw material going into it was actually bad quality, it was toxic quality, and that is what ended up coming out the other end of the pipeline. Wall Street obviously participated in that flow of activity."[3]

The origination and securitization of these mortgages also relied on short-term financing from the shadow banking system. Unlike banks and thrifts with access to deposits, investment banks relied more on money market funds and other investors for cash; commercial paper and repo loans were the main sources. With house prices already up 91% from 1995 to 2003, this flood of money and the securitization apparatus helped boost home prices another 36% from the beginning of 2004 until the peak in April 2006—even as homeownership was falling. The biggest gains over this period were in the "sand states": places like the Los Angeles suburbs (54%), Las Vegas (36%), and Orlando (72%).

## FOREIGN INVESTORS:
## "AN IRRESISTIBLE PROFIT OPPORTUNITY"

From June 2003 through June 2004, the Federal Reserve kept the federal funds rate low at 1% to stimulate the economy following the 2001 recession. Over the next two years, as deflation fears waned, the Fed gradually raised rates to 5.25% in 17 quarter-point increases.

In the view of some, the Fed simply kept rates too low too long. John Taylor, a Stanford economist and former under secretary of treasury for international affairs, blamed the crisis primarily on this action. If the Fed had followed its usual pattern, he told the FCIC, short-term interest rates would have been much higher, discouraging excessive investment in mortgages. "The boom in housing construction starts would have been much more mild, might not even call it a boom, and the bust as well would have been mild," Taylor said.[4] Others were more blunt: "Greenspan bailed out the world's largest equity bubble with the world's largest real estate bubble," wrote William A. Fleckenstein, the president of a Seattle-based money management firm.[5]

Ben Bernanke and Alan Greenspan disagree. Both the current and former Fed chairman argue that deciding to purchase a home depends on long-term interest rates on mortgages, not the short-term rates controlled by the Fed, and that short-term and long-term rates had become de-linked. "Between 1971 and 2002, the fed funds rate and the mortgage rate moved in lock-step," Greenspan said.[6] When the Fed started to raise rates in 2004, officials expected mortgage rates to rise, too, slowing growth. Instead, mortgage rates continued to fall for another year. The construction industry continued to build houses, peaking at an annualized rate of 2.27 million starts in January 2006—more than a 30-year high.

As Greenspan told Congress in 2005, this was a "conundrum."[7] One theory pointed to foreign money. Developing countries were booming and—vulnerable to financial problems in the past—encouraged strong saving. Investors in these countries placed their savings in apparently safe and high-yield securities in the United States. Fed Chairman Bernanke called it a "global savings glut."[8]

As the United States ran a large current account deficit, flows into the country were unprecedented. Over six years from 2000 to 2006, U.S. Treasury debt held by foreign official public entities rose from $0.6 trillion to $1.43 trillion; as a percentage of U.S. debt held by the public, these holdings increased from 18.2% to 28.8%. Foreigners also bought securities backed by Fannie and Freddie, which, with their implicit government guarantee, seemed nearly as safe as Treasuries. As the Asian financial crisis ended in 1998, foreign holdings of GSE securities held steady at the level of almost 10 years earlier, about $186 billion. By 2000—just two years later—foreigners owned $348 billion in GSE securities; by 2004, $875 billion. "You had a huge inflow of liquidity. A very unique kind of situation where poor countries like China were shipping money to advanced countries because their financial systems were so weak that they [were] better off shipping [money] to countries like the United States rather than keeping it in their own countries," former Fed governor Frederic Mishkin told the FCIC. "The system was awash with liquidity, which helped lower long-term interest rates."[9]

Foreign investors sought other high-grade debt almost as safe as Treasuries and GSE securities but with a slightly higher return. They found the triple-A assets pouring from the Wall Street mortgage securitization machine. As overseas demand drove up prices for securitized debt, it "created an irresistible profit opportunity for the U.S. financial system: to engineer 'quasi' safe debt instruments by bundling riskier assets and selling the senior tranches," Pierre-Olivier Gourinchas, an economist at the University of California, Berkeley, told the FCIC.[10]

Paul Krugman, an economist at Princeton University, told the FCIC, "It's hard to envisage us having had this crisis without considering international monetary capital movements. The U.S. housing bubble was financed by large capital inflows. So were Spanish and Irish and Baltic bubbles. It's a combination of, in the narrow sense, of a less regulated financial system and a world that was increasingly wide open for big international capital movements."[11]

It was an ocean of money.

## MORTGAGES: "A GOOD LOAN"

The refinancing boom was over, but originators still needed mortgages to sell to the Street. They needed new products that, as prices kept rising, could make expensive homes more affordable to still-eager borrowers. The solution was riskier, more aggressive, mortgage products that brought higher yields for investors but correspondingly greater risks for borrowers. "Holding a subprime loan has become something of a high-stakes wager," the Center for Responsible Lending warned in 2006.[12]

Subprime mortgages rose from 8% of mortgage originations in 2003 to 20% in 2005.[13] About 70% of subprime borrowers used hybrid adjustable-rate mortgages (ARMs) such as 2/28s and 3/27s—mortgages whose low "teaser" rate lasts for the first two or three years, and then adjusts periodically thereafter.[14] Prime borrowers also used more alternative mortgages. The dollar volume of Alt-A securitization rose almost 350% from 2003 to 2005.[15] In general, these loans made borrowers' monthly

mortgage payments on ever more expensive homes affordable—at least initially. Popular Alt-A products included interest-only mortgages and payment-option ARMs. Option ARMs let borrowers pick their payment each month, including payments that actually increased the principal—any shortfall on the interest payment was added to the principal, something called negative amortization. If the balance got large enough, the loan would convert to a fixed-rate mortgage, increasing the monthly payment—perhaps dramatically. Option ARMs rose from 2% of mortgages in 2003 to 9% in 2006. [16]

Simultaneously, underwriting standards for nonprime and prime mortgages weakened. Combined loan-to-value ratios—reflecting first, second, and even third mortgages—rose. Debt-to-income ratios climbed, as did loans made for non-owner-occupied properties. Fannie Mae and Freddie Mac's market share shrank from 57% of all mortgages purchased in 2003 to 42% in 2004, and down to 37% by 2006.[17] Taking their place were private-label securitizations—meaning those not issued and guaranteed by the GSEs.

In this new market, originators competed fiercely; Countrywide Financial Corporation took the crown.[18] It was the biggest mortgage originator from 2004 until the market collapsed in 2007. Even after Countrywide nearly failed, buckling under a mortgage portfolio with loans that its co-founder and CEO Angelo Mozilo once called "toxic," Mozilo would describe his 40-year-old company to the Commission as having helped 25 million people buy homes and prevented social unrest by extending loans to minorities, historically the victims of discrimination: "Countrywide was one of the greatest companies in the history of this country and probably made more difference to society, to the integrity of our society, than any company in the history of America."[19] Lending to home buyers was only part of the business. Countrywide's President and COO David Sambol told the Commission, as long as a loan did not harm the company from a financial or reputation standpoint, Countrywide was "a seller of securities to Wall Street." Countrywide's essential business strategy was "originating what was salable in the secondary market."[20] The company sold or securitized 87% of the $1.5 trillion in mortgages it originated between 2002 and 2005.

In 2004, Mozilo announced a very aggressive goal of gaining "market dominance" by capturing 30% of the origination market.[21] His share at the time was 12%. But Countrywide was not unique: Ameriquest, New Century, Washington Mutual, and others all pursued loans as aggressively. They competed by originating types of mortgages created years before as niche products, but now transformed into riskier, mass-market versions. "The definition of a good loan changed from 'one that pays' to 'one that could be sold,'" Patricia Lindsay, formerly a fraud specialist at New Century, told the FCIC.[22]

## 2/28s and 3/27s: "Adjust for the affordability"

Historically, 2/28s or 3/27s, also known as *hybrid ARMs*, let credit-impaired borrowers repair their credit. During the first two or three years, a lower interest rate meant a manageable payment schedule and enabled borrowers to demonstrate they could make timely payments. Eventually the interest rates would rise sharply, and payments

could double or even triple, leaving borrowers with few alternatives: if they had established their creditworthiness, they could refinance into a similar mortgage or one with a better interest rate, often with the same lender;[23] if unable to refinance, the borrower was unlikely to be able to afford the new higher payments and would have to sell the home and repay the mortgage. If they could not sell or make the higher payments, they would have to default.

But as house prices rose after 2000, the 2/28s and 3/27s acquired a new role: helping to get people into homes or to move up to bigger homes. "As homes got less and less affordable, you would adjust for the affordability in the mortgage because you couldn't really adjust people's income," Andrew Davidson, the president of Andrew Davidson & Co. and a veteran of the mortgage markets, told the FCIC.[24] Lenders qualified borrowers at low teaser rates, with little thought to what might happen when rates reset. Hybrid ARMs became the workhorses of the subprime securitization market.

Consumer protection groups such as the Leadership Conference on Civil Rights railed against 2/28s and 3/27s, which, they said, neither rehabilitated credit nor turned renters into owners. David Berenbaum from the National Community Reinvestment Coalition testified to Congress in the summer of 2007: "The industry has flooded the market with exotic mortgage lending such as 2/28 and 3/27 ARMs. These exotic subprime mortgages overwhelm borrowers when interest rates shoot up after an introductory time period."[25] To their critics, they were simply a way for lenders to strip equity from low-income borrowers. The loans came with big fees that got rolled into the mortgage, increasing the chances that the mortgage could be larger than the home's value at the reset date. If the borrower could not refinance, the lender would foreclose—and then own the home in a rising real estate market.

## Option ARMs: "Our most profitable mortgage loan"

When they were originally introduced in the 1980s, option ARMs were niche products, too, but by 2004 they too became loans of choice because their payments were lower than more traditional mortgages. During the housing boom, many borrowers repeatedly made only the minimum payments required, adding to the principal balance of their loan every month.

An early seller of option ARMs was Golden West Savings, an Oakland, California–based thrift founded in 1929 and acquired in 1963 by Marion and Herbert Sandler. In 1975, the Sandlers merged Golden West with World Savings; Golden West Financial Corp., the parent company, operated branches under the name World Savings Bank. The thrift issued about $274 billion in option ARMs between 1981 and 2005.[26] Unlike other mortgage companies, Golden West held onto them.

Sandler told the FCIC that Golden West's option ARMs—marketed as "Pick-a-Pay" loans—had the lowest losses in the industry for that product. Even in 2005—the last year prior to its acquisition by Wachovia—when its portfolio was almost entirely in option ARMs, Golden West's losses were low by industry standards. Sandler attributed Golden West's performance to its diligence in running simulations about what

would happen to its loans under various scenarios—for example, if interest rates went up or down or if house prices dropped 5%, even 10%. "For a quarter of a century, it worked exactly as the simulations showed that it would," Sandler said. "And we have never been able to identify a single loan that was delinquent because of the structure of the loan, much less a loss or foreclosure."[27] But after Wachovia acquired Golden West in 2006 and the housing market soured, charge-offs on the Pick-a-Pay portfolio would suddenly jump from 0.04% to 2.69% by September 2008. And foreclosures would climb.

Early in the decade, banks and thrifts such as Countrywide and Washington Mutual increased their origination of option ARM loans, changing the product in ways that made payment shocks more likely. At Golden West, after 10 years, or if the principal balance grew to 125% of its original size, the Pick-a-Pay mortgage would recast into a new fixed-rate mortgage. At Countrywide and Washington Mutual, the new loans would recast in as little as five years, or when the balance hit just 110% of the original size. They also offered lower teaser rates—as low as 1%—and loan-to-value ratios as high as 100%. All of these features raised the chances that the borrower's required payment could rise more sharply, more quickly, and with less cushion.

In 2002, Washington Mutual was the second-largest mortgage originator, just ahead of Countrywide. It had offered the option ARM since 1986, and in 2003, as cited by the Senate Permanent Subcommittee on Investigations, the originator conducted a study "to explore what Washington Mutual could do to increase sales of Option ARMs, our most profitable mortgage loan."[28] A focus group made clear that few customers were requesting option ARMs and that "this is not a product that sells itself."[29] The study found "the best selling point for the Option Arm" was to show consumers "how much lower their monthly payment would be by choosing the Option Arm versus a fixed-rate loan."[30] The study also revealed that many WaMu brokers "felt these loans were 'bad' for customers."[31] One member of the focus group remarked, "A lot of (Loan) Consultants don't believe in it . . . and don't think [it's] good for the customer. You're going to have to change the mindset."[32]

Despite these challenges, option ARM originations soared at Washington Mutual from $30 billion in 2003 to $68 billion in 2004, when they were more than half of WaMu's originations and had become the thrift's signature adjustable-rate home loan product.[33] The average FICO score was around 700, well into the range considered "prime," and about two-thirds were jumbo loans—mortgage loans exceeding the maximum Fannie Mae and Freddie Mac were allowed to purchase or guarantee.[34] More than half were in California.[35]

Countrywide's option ARM business peaked at $14.5 billion in originations in the second quarter of 2005, about 25% of all its loans originated that quarter.[36] But it had to relax underwriting standards to get there. In July 2004, Countrywide decided it would lend up to 90% of a home's appraised value, up from 80%, and reduced the minimum credit score to as low as 620.[37] In early 2005, Countrywide eased standards again, increasing the allowable combined loan-to-value ratio (including second liens) to 95%.[38]

The risk in these loans was growing. From 2003 to 2005, the average loan-to-value ratio rose about 4%, the combined loan-to-value ratio rose about 6%, and debt-to-income ratios had risen from 34% to 38%: borrowers were pledging more of their income to their mortgage payments. Moreover, 68% of these two originators' option ARMs had low documentation in 2005.[39] The percentage of these loans made to investors and speculators—that is, borrowers with no plans to use the home as their primary residence—also rose.

These changes worried the lenders even as they continued to make the loans. In September 2004 and August 2005, Mozilo emailed to senior management that these loans could bring "financial and reputational catastrophe."[40] Countrywide should not market them to investors, he insisted. "Pay option loans being used by investors is a pure commercial spec[ulation] loan and not the traditional home loan that we have successfully managed throughout our history," Mozilo wrote to Carlos Garcia, CEO of Countrywide Bank. Speculative investors "should go to Chase or Wells not us. It is also important for you and your team to understand from my point of view that there is nothing intrinsically wrong with pay options loans themselves, the problem is the quality of borrowers who are being offered the product and the abuse by third party originators. . . . [I]f you are unable to find sufficient product then slow down the growth of the Bank for the time being."[41]

However, Countrywide's growth did not slow. Nor did the volume of option ARMs retained on its balance sheet, increasing from $5 billion in 2004 to $26 billion in 2005 and peaking in 2006 at $33 billion.[42] Finding these loans very profitable, through 2006, WaMu also retained option ARMs—more than $60 billion with the bulk from California, followed by Florida.[43] But in the end, these loans would cause significant losses during the crisis.

Mentioning Countrywide and WaMu as tough, "in our face" competitors, John Stumpf, the CEO, chairman, and president of Wells Fargo, recalled Wells's decision not to write option ARMs, even as it originated many other high-risk mortgages. These were "hard decisions to make at the time," he said, noting "we did lose revenue, and we did lose volume."[44]

Across the market, the volume of option ARMs had risen nearly fourfold from 2003 to 2006, from approximately $65 billion to $255 billion. By then, WaMu and Countrywide had plenty of evidence that more borrowers were making only the minimum payments and that their mortgages were negatively amortizing—which meant their equity was being eaten away. The percentage of Countrywide's option ARMs that were negatively amortizing grew from just 1% in 2004 to 53% in 2005 and then to more than 90% by 2007.[45] At WaMu, it was 2% in 2003, 28% in 2004, and 82% in 2007.[46] Declines in house prices added to borrowers' problems: any equity remaining after the negative amortization would simply be eroded. Increasingly, borrowers would owe more on their mortgages than their homes were worth on the market, giving them an incentive to walk away from both home and mortgage.

Kevin Stein, from the California Reinvestment Coalition, testified to the FCIC that option ARMs were sold inappropriately: "Nowhere was this dynamic more clearly on display than in the summer of 2006 when the Federal Reserve convened

HOEPA (Home Ownership and Equity Protection Act) hearings in San Francisco. At the hearing, consumers testified to being sold option ARM loans in their primary non-English language, only to be pressured to sign English-only documents with significantly worse terms. Some consumers testified to being unable to make even their initial payments because they had been lied to so completely by their brokers."[47] Mona Tawatao, a regional counsel with Legal Services of Northern California, described the borrowers she was assisting as "people who got steered or defrauded into entering option ARMs with teaser rates or pick-a-pay loans forcing them to pay into—pay loans that they could never pay off. Prevalent among these clients are seniors, people of color, people with disabilities, and limited English speakers and seniors who are African American and Latino."[48]

### Underwriting standards: "We're going to have to hold our nose"

Another shift would have serious consequences. For decades, the down payment for a prime mortgage had been 20% (in other words, the loan-to-value ratio (LTV) had been 80%). As prices continued to rise, finding the cash to put 20% down became harder, and from 2000 on, lenders began accepting smaller down payments.

There had always been a place for borrowers with down payments below 20%. Typically, lenders required such borrower to purchase private mortgage insurance for a monthly fee. If a mortgage ended in foreclosure, the mortgage insurance company would make the lender whole. Worried about defaults, the GSEs would not buy or guarantee mortgages with down payments below 20% unless the borrower bought the insurance. Unluckily for many homeowners, for the housing industry, and for the financial system, lenders devised a way to get rid of these monthly fees that had added to the cost of homeownership: lower down payments that did not require insurance.

Lenders had latitude in setting down payments. In 1991, Congress ordered federal regulators to prescribe standards for real estate lending that would apply to banks and thrifts. The goal was to "curtail abusive real estate lending practices in order to reduce risk to the deposit insurance funds and enhance the safety and soundness of insured depository institutions."[49] Congress had debated including explicit LTV standards, but chose not to, leaving that to the regulators. In the end, regulators declined to introduce standards for LTV ratios or for documentation for home mortgages.[50] The agencies explained: "A significant number of commenters expressed concern that rigid application of a regulation implementing LTV ratios would constrict credit, impose additional lending costs, reduce lending flexibility, impede economic growth, and cause other undesirable consequences."[51]

In 1999, regulators revisited the issue, as high LTV lending was increasing. They tightened reporting requirements and limited a bank's total holdings of loans with LTVs above 90% that lacked mortgage insurance or some other protection; they also reminded the banks and thrifts that they should establish internal guidelines to manage the risk of these loans.[52]

High LTV lending soon became even more common, thanks to the so-called

piggyback mortgage. The lender offered a first mortgage for perhaps 80% of the home's value and a second mortgage for another 10% or even 20%. Borrowers liked these because their monthly payments were often cheaper than a traditional mortgage plus the required mortgage insurance, and the interest payments were tax deductible. Lenders liked them because the smaller first mortgage—even without mortgage insurance—could potentially be sold to the GSEs.

At the same time, the piggybacks added risks. A borrower with a higher combined LTV had less equity in the home. In a rising market, should payments become unmanageable, the borrower could always sell the home and come out ahead. However, should the payments become unmanageable in a falling market, the borrower might owe more than the home was worth. Piggyback loans—which often required nothing down—guaranteed that many borrowers would end up with negative equity if house prices fell, especially if the appraisal had overstated the initial value.

But piggyback lending helped address a significant challenge for companies like New Century, which were big players in the market for mortgages. Meeting investor demand required finding new borrowers, and homebuyers without down payments were a relatively untapped source. Yet among borrowers with mortgages originated in 2004, by September 2005 those with piggybacks were four times as likely as other mortgage holders to be 60 or more days delinquent. When senior management at New Century heard these numbers, the head of the Secondary Marketing Department asked for "thoughts on what to do with this . . . pretty compelling" information. Nonetheless, New Century increased mortgages with piggybacks to 35% of loan production by the end of 2005, up from only 9% in 2003.[53] They were not alone. Across securitized subprime mortgages, the average combined LTV rose from 79% to 86% between 2001 and 2006.[54]

Another way to get people into mortgages—and quickly—was to require less information of the borrower. "Stated income" or "low-documentation" (or sometimes "no-documentation") loans had emerged years earlier for people with fluctuating or hard-to-verify incomes, such as the self-employed, or to serve longtime customers with strong credit. Or lenders might waive information requirements if the loan looked safe in other respects. "If I'm making a 65%, 75%, 70% loan-to-value, I'm not going to get all of the documentation," Sandler of Golden West told the FCIC. The process was too cumbersome and unnecessary. He already had a good idea how much money teachers, accountants, and engineers made—and if he didn't, he could easily find out. All he needed was to verify that his borrowers worked where they said they did. If he guessed wrong, the loan-to-value ratio still protected his investment.[55]

Around 2005, however, low- and no-documentation loans took on an entirely different character. Nonprime lenders now boasted they could offer borrowers the convenience of quicker decisions and not having to provide tons of paperwork. In return, they charged a higher interest rate. The idea caught on: from 2000 to 2007, low- and no-doc loans skyrocketed from less than 2% to roughly 9% of all outstanding loans.[56] Among Alt-A securitizations, 80% of loans issued in 2006 had limited or no documentation.[57] As William Black, a former banking regulator, testified before the FCIC, the mortgage industry's own fraud specialists described stated income

loans as "an open 'invitation to fraud' that justified the industry term 'liar's loans.'"[58] Speaking of lending up to 2005 at Citigroup, Richard Bowen, a veteran banker in the consumer lending group, told the FCIC, "A decision was made that 'We're going to have to hold our nose and start buying the stated product if we want to stay in business.'"[59] Jamie Dimon, the CEO of JP Morgan, told the Commission, "In mortgage underwriting, somehow we just missed, you know, that home prices don't go up forever and that it's not sufficient to have stated income."[60]

In the end, companies in subprime and Alt-A mortgages had, in essence, placed all their chips on black: they were betting that home prices would never stop rising. This was the only scenario that would keep the mortgage machine humming. The evidence is present in our case study mortgage-backed security, CMLTI 2006-NC2, whose loans have many of the characteristics just described.

The 4,499 loans bundled in this deal were adjustable-rate and fixed-rate residential mortgages originated by New Century. They had an average principal balance of $210,536—just under the median home price of $221,900 in 2006.[61] The vast majority had a 30-year maturity, and more than 90% were originated in May, June, and July 2006, just after national home prices had peaked. More than 90% were reportedly for primary residences, with 43% for home purchases and 48% for cash-out refinancings. The loans were from all 50 states and the District of Columbia, but more than a fifth came from California and more than a tenth from Florida.[62]

About 80% of the loans were ARMs, and most of these were 2/28s or 3/27s. In a twist, many of these hybrid ARMs had other "affordability features" as well. For example, more than 20% of the ARMs were interest-only—during the first two or three years, not only would borrowers pay a lower fixed rate, they would not have to pay any principal. In addition, more than 40% of the ARMs were "2/28 hybrid balloon" loans, in which the principal would amortize over 40 years—lowering the monthly payments even further, but as a result leaving the borrower with a final principal payment at the end of the 30-year term.

The great majority of the pool was secured by first mortgages; of these, 33% had a piggyback mortgage on the same property. As a result, more than one-third of the mortgages in this deal had a combined loan-to-value ratio between 95% and 100%. Raising the risk a bit more, 42% of the mortgages were no-doc loans. The rest were "full-doc," although their documentation was fuller in some cases than in others.[63] In sum, the loans bundled in this deal mirrored the market: complex products with high LTVs and little documentation. And even as many warned of this toxic mix, the regulators were not on the same page.

## FEDERAL REGULATORS: "IMMUNITY FROM MANY STATE LAWS IS A SIGNIFICANT BENEFIT"

For years, some states had tried to regulate the mortgage business, especially to clamp down on the predatory mortgages proliferating in the subprime market. The national thrifts and banks and their federal regulators—the Office of Thrift Supervision (OTS) and the Office of the Comptroller of the Currency (OCC), respectively—resisted the

states' efforts to regulate those national banks and thrifts. The companies claimed that without one uniform set of rules, they could not easily do business across the country, and the regulators agreed. In August 2003, as the market for riskier subprime and Alt-A loans grew, and as lenders piled on more risk with smaller down payments, reduced documentation requirements, interest-only loans, and payment-option loans, the OCC fired a salvo. The OCC proposed strong preemption rules for national banks, nearly identical to earlier OTS rules that empowered nationally chartered thrifts to disregard state consumer laws.[64]

Back in 1996 the OTS had issued rules saying federal law preempted state predatory lending laws for federally regulated thrifts.[65] In 2003, the OTS referred to these rules in issuing four opinion letters declaring that laws in Georgia, New York, New Jersey, and New Mexico did not apply to national thrifts. In the New Mexico opinion, the regulator pronounced invalid New Mexico's bans on balloon payments, negative amortization, prepayment penalties, loan flipping, and lending without regard to the borrower's ability to repay.

The Comptroller of the Currency took the same line on the national banks that it regulated, offering preemption as an inducement to use a national bank charter. In a 2002 speech, before the final OCC rules were passed, Comptroller John D. Hawke Jr. pointed to "national banks' immunity from many state laws" as "a significant benefit of the national charter—a benefit that the OCC has fought hard over the years to preserve."[66] In an interview that year, Hawke explained that the potential loss of regulatory market share for the OCC "was a matter of concern."[67]

In August 2003 the OCC issued its first preemptive order, aimed at Georgia's mini-HOEPA statute, and in January 2004 the OCC adopted a sweeping preemption rule applying to all state laws that interfered with or placed conditions on national banks' ability to lend. Shortly afterward, three large banks with combined assets of more than $1 trillion said they would convert from state charters to national charters, which increased OCC's annual budget 15%.[68]

State-chartered operating subsidiaries were another point of contention in the preemption battle. In 2001 the OCC had adopted a regulation preempting state law regarding state-chartered operating subsidiaries of national banks. In response, several large national banks moved their mortgage-lending operations into subsidiaries and asserted that the subsidiaries were exempt from state mortgage lending laws. Four states challenged the regulation, but the Supreme Court ruled against them in 2007.[69]

Once OCC and OTS preemption was in place, the two federal agencies were the only regulators with the power to prohibit abusive lending practices by national banks and thrifts and their direct subsidiaries. Comptroller John Dugan, who succeeded Hawke, defended preemption, noting that "72% of all nonprime mortgages were made by lenders that were subject to state law. Well over half were made by mortgage lenders that were exclusively subject to state law."[70] Lisa Madigan, the attorney general of Illinois, flipped the argument around, noting that national banks and thrifts, and their subsidiaries, were heavily involved in subprime lending. Using different data, she contended: "National banks and federal thrifts and . . . their sub-

sidiaries . . . were responsible for almost 32 percent of subprime mortgage loans, 40.1 percent of the Alt-A loans, and 51 percent of the pay-option and interest-only ARMs that were sold." Madigan told the FCIC:

> Even as the Fed was doing little to protect consumers and our financial system from the effects of predatory lending, the OCC and OTS were actively engaged in a campaign to thwart state efforts to avert the coming crisis. . . . In the wake of the federal regulators' push to curtail state authority, many of the largest mortgage-lenders shed their state licenses and sought shelter behind the shield of a national charter. And I think that it is no coincidence that the era of expanded federal preemption gave rise to the worst lending abuses in our nation's history.[71]

Comptroller Hawke offered the FCIC a different interpretation: "While some critics have suggested that the OCC's actions on preemption have been a grab for power, the fact is that the agency has simply responded to increasingly aggressive initiatives at the state level to control the banking activities of federally chartered institutions."[72]

## MORTGAGE SECURITIES PLAYERS: "WALL STREET WAS VERY HUNGRY FOR OUR PRODUCT"

Subprime and Alt-A mortgage–backed securities depended on a complex supply chain, largely funded through short-term lending in the commercial paper and repo market—which would become critical as the financial crisis began to unfold in 2007. These loans were increasingly collateralized not by Treasuries and GSE securities but by highly rated mortgage securities backed by increasingly risky loans. Independent mortgage originators such as Ameriquest and New Century—without access to deposits—typically relied on financing to originate mortgages from warehouse lines of credit extended by banks, from their own commercial paper programs, or from money borrowed in the repo market.

For commercial banks such as Citigroup, warehouse lending was a multibillion-dollar business. From 2000 to 2010, Citigroup made available at any one time as much as $7 billion in warehouse lines of credit to mortgage originators, including $950 million to New Century and more than $3.5 billion to Ameriquest.[73] Citigroup CEO Chuck Prince told the FCIC he would not have approved, had he known. "I found out at the end of my tenure, I did not know it before, that we had some warehouse lines out to some originators. And I think getting that close to the origination function—being that involved in the origination of some of these products—is something that I wasn't comfortable with and that I did not view as consistent with the prescription I had laid down for the company not to be involved in originating these products."[74]

As early as 1998, Moody's called the new asset-backed commercial paper (ABCP) programs "a whole new ball game."[75] As asset-backed commercial paper became a popular method to fund the mortgage business, it grew from about one-quarter to about one-half of commercial paper sold between 1997 and 2001.

In 2001, only five mortgage companies borrowed a total of $4 billion through asset-backed commercial paper; in 2006, 19 entities borrowed $43 billion.[76] For instance, Countrywide launched the commercial paper programs Park Granada in 2003 and Park Sienna in 2004.[77] By May 2007, it was borrowing $13 billion through Park Granada and $5.3 billion through Park Sienna. These programs would house subprime and other mortgages until they were sold.[78]

Commercial banks used commercial paper, in part, for regulatory arbitrage. When banks kept mortgages on their balance sheets, regulators required them to hold 4% in capital to protect against loss. When banks put mortgages into off-balance-sheet entities such as commercial paper programs, there was no capital charge (in 2004, a small charge was imposed). But to make the deals work for investors, banks had to provide liquidity support to these programs, for which they earned a fee. This liquidity support meant that the bank would purchase, at a previously set price, any commercial paper that investors were unwilling to buy when it came up for renewal. During the financial crisis these promises had to be kept, eventually putting substantial pressure on banks' balance sheets.

When the Financial Accounting Standards Board, the private group that establishes standards for financial reports, responded to the Enron scandal by making it harder for companies to get off-balance-sheet treatment for these programs, the favorable capital rules were in jeopardy. The asset-backed commercial paper market stalled. Banks protested that their programs differed from the practices at Enron and should be excluded from the new standards. In 2003, bank regulators responded by proposing to let banks remove these assets from their balance sheets when calculating regulatory capital. The proposal would have also introduced for the first time a capital charge amounting to at most 1.6% of the liquidity support banks provided to the ABCP programs. However, after strong pushback—the American Securitization Forum, an industry association, called that charge "arbitrary," and State Street Bank complained it was "too conservative"[79]—regulators in 2004 announced a final rule setting the charge at up to 0.8%, or half the amount of the first proposal. Growth in this market resumed.

Regulatory changes—in this case, changes in the bankruptcy laws—also boosted growth in the repo market by transforming the types of repo collateral. Prior to 2005, repo lenders had clear and immediate rights to their collateral following the borrower's bankruptcy only if that collateral was Treasury or GSE securities. In the Bankruptcy Abuse Prevention and Consumer Protection Act of 2005, Congress expanded that provision to include many other assets, including mortgage loans, mortgage-backed securities, collateralized debt obligations, and certain derivatives. The result was a short-term repo market increasingly reliant on highly rated non-agency mortgage-backed securities; but beginning in mid-2007, when banks and investors became skittish about the mortgage market, they would prove to be an unstable funding source (see figure 7.1). Once the crisis hit, these "illiquid, hard-to-value securities made up a greater share of the tri-party repo market than most people would have wanted," Darryll Hendricks, a UBS executive and chair of a New York Fed task force examining the repo market after the crisis, told the Commission.[80]

## Repo Borrowing

*Broker-dealers' use of repo borrowing rose sharply before the crisis.*

IN BILLIONS OF DOLLARS

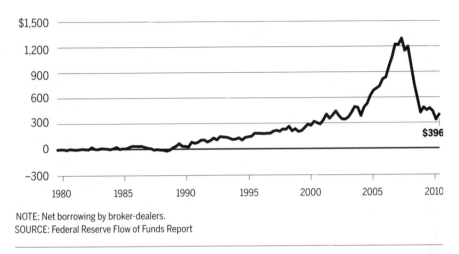

NOTE: Net borrowing by broker-dealers.
SOURCE: Federal Reserve Flow of Funds Report

*Figure 7.1*

Our sample deal, CMLTI 2006-NC2, shows how these funding and securitization markets worked in practice. Eight banks and securities firms provided most of the money New Century needed to make the 4,499 mortgages it would sell to Citigroup. Most of the funds came through repo agreements from a set of banks—including Morgan Stanley ($424 million); Barclays Capital, a division of a U.K.-based bank ($221 million); Bank of America ($147 million); and Bear Stearns ($64 million).[81] The financing was provided when New Century originated these mortgages; so for about two months, New Century owed these banks approximately $940 million secured by the mortgages. Another $12 million in funding came from New Century itself, including $3 million through its own commercial paper program. On August 29, 2006, Citigroup paid New Century $979 million for the mortgages (and accrued interest), and New Century repaid the repo lenders after keeping a $24 million (2.5%) premium.[82]

### The investors in the deal

Investors for mortgage-backed securities came from all over the globe; what made securitization work were the customized tranches catering to every one of them. CMLTI 2006-NC2 had 19 tranches, whose investors are shown in figure 7.2. Fannie Mae bought the entire $155 million triple-A-rated A1 tranche, which paid a better return than super-safe U.S. Treasuries.[83] The other triple-A-rated tranches, worth

# Selected Investors in CMLTI 2006-NC2

*A wide variety of investors throughout the world purchased the securities in this deal, including Fannie Mae, many international banks, SIVs and many CDOs.*

| | Tranche | Original Balance (MILLIONS) | Original Rating[1] | Spread[2] | Selected Investors |
|---|---|---|---|---|---|
| **SENIOR** 78% | A1 | $154.6 | AAA | 0.14% | Fannie Mae |
| | A2-A | $281.7 | AAA | 0.04% | Chase Security Lendings Asset Management; 1 investment fund in China; 6 investment funds |
| | A2-B | $282.4 | AAA | 0.06% | Federal Home Loan Bank of Chicago; 3 banks in Germany, Italy and France; 11 investment funds; 3 retail investors |
| | A2-C | $18.3 | AAA | 0.24% | 2 banks in the U.S. and Germany |
| **MEZZANINE** 21% | M-1 | $39.3 | AA+ | 0.29% | 1 investment fund and 2 banks in Italy; Cheyne Finance Limited; 3 asset managers |
| | M-2 | $44 .0 | AA | 0.31% | Parvest ABS Euribor; 4 asset managers; 1 bank in China; 1 CDO |
| | M-3 | $14.2 | AA- | 0.34% | 2 CDOs; 1 asset manager |
| | M-4 | $16.1 | A+ | 0.39% | 1 CDO; 1 hedge fund |
| | M-5 | $16.6 | A | 0.40% | 2 CDOs |
| | M-6 | $10.9 | A- | 0.46% | 3 CDOs |
| | M-7 | $9.9 | BBB+ | 0.70% | 3 CDOs |
| | M-8 | $8.5 | BBB | 0.80% | 2 CDOs; 1 bank |
| | M-9 | $11.8 | BBB- | 1.50% | 5 CDOs; 2 asset managers |
| | M-10 | $13.7 | BB+ | 2.50% | 3 CDOs; 1 asset manager |
| | M-11 | $10.9 | BB | 2.50% | NA |
| **EQUITY** 1% | CE | $13.3 | NR | | Citi and Capmark Fin Grp |

P, R, Rx: Additional tranches entitled to specific payments

[1] Standard & Poor's.
[2] The yield is the rate on the one-month London Interbank Offered Rate (LIBOR), an interbank lending interest rate, plus the spread listed. For example, when the deal was issued, Fannie Mae would have received the LIBOR rate of 5.32% plus 0.14% to give a total yield of 5.46%.

SOURCES: Citigroup; Standard & Poor's; FCIC calculations

*Figure 7.2*

$582 million, went to more than 20 institutional investors around the world, spreading the risk globally.[84] These triple-A tranches represented 78% of the deal. Among the buyers were foreign banks and funds in China, Italy, France, and Germany; the Federal Home Loan Bank of Chicago; the Kentucky Retirement Systems; a hospital; and JP Morgan, which purchased part of the tranche using cash from its securities-lending operation.[85] (In other words, JP Morgan lent securities held by its clients to other financial institutions in exchange for cash collateral, and then put that cash to work investing in this deal. Securities lending was a large, but ultimately unstable, source of cash that flowed into this market.)

The middle, mezzanine tranches in this deal constituted about 21% of the total value of the security. If losses rose above 1% to 3% (by design the threshold would increase over time), investors in the residual tranches would be wiped out, and the mezzanine investors would start to lose money. Creators of collateralized debt obligations, or CDOs—discussed in the next chapter—bought most of the mezzanine tranches rated below triple-A and nearly all those rated below AA. Only a few of the highest-rated mezzanine tranches were not put into CDOs. For example, Cheyne Finance Limited purchased $7 million of the top mezzanine tranche. Cheyne—a structured investment vehicle (SIV)—would be one of the first casualties of the crisis, sparking panic during the summer of 2007. Parvest ABS Euribor, which purchased $20 million of the second mezzanine tranche,[86] would be one of the BNP Paribas funds which helped ignite the financial crisis that summer.[87]

Typically, investors seeking high returns, such as hedge funds, would buy the equity tranches of mortgage-backed securities; they would be the first to lose if there were problems. These investors anticipated returns of 15%, 20%, or even 30%. Citigroup retained part of the residual or "first-loss" tranches, sharing the rest with Capmark Financial Group.[88]

## "Compensated very well"

The business of structuring, selling, and distributing this deal, and the thousands like it, was lucrative for the banks. The mortgage originators profited when they sold loans for securitization.[89] Some of this profit flowed down to employees—particularly those generating mortgage volume.

Part of the $24 million premium received by New Century for the deal we analyzed went to pay the many employees who participated. "The originators, the loan officers, account executives, basically the salespeople [who] were the reason our loans came in . . . were compensated very well," New Century's Patricia Lindsay told the FCIC. And volume mattered more than quality. She noted, "Wall Street was very hungry for our product. We had our loans sold three months in advance, before they were even made at one point."[90]

Similar incentives were at work at Long Beach Mortgage, the subprime division of Washington Mutual, which organized its 2004 Incentive Plan by volume. As WaMu showed in a 2007 plan, "Home Loans Product Strategy," the goals were also product-specific: to drive "growth in higher margin products (Option ARM, Alt A, Home Equity,

Subprime)," "recruit and leverage seasoned Option ARM sales force," and "maintain a compensation structure that supports the high margin product strategy."[91]

After structuring a security, an underwriter, often an investment bank, marketed and sold it to investors. The bank collected a percentage of the sale (generally between 0.2% and 1.5%) as discounts, concessions, or commissions.[92] For a $1 billion deal like CMLTI 2006-NC2, a 1% fee would earn Citigroup $10 million. In this case, though, Citigroup instead kept parts of the residual tranches. Doing so could yield large profits as long as the deal performed as expected.

Options Group, which compiles compensation figures for investment banks, examined the mortgage-backed securities sales and trading desks at 11 commercial and investment banks from 2005 to 2007.[93] It found that associates had average annual base salaries of $65,000 to $90,000 from 2005 through 2007, but received bonuses that could well exceed their salaries. On the next rung, vice presidents averaged base salaries and bonuses from $200,000 to $1,150,000. Directors averaged $625,000 to $1,625,000.[94] At the top was the head of the unit. For example, in 2006, Dow Kim, the head of Merrill's Global Markets and Investment Banking segment, received a base salary of $350,000 plus a $35 million bonus, a package second only to Merrill Lynch's CEO.[95]

## MOODY'S: "GIVEN A BLANK CHECK"

The rating agencies were essential to the smooth functioning of the mortgage-backed securities market. Issuers needed them to approve the structure of their deals; banks needed their ratings to determine the amount of capital to hold; repo markets needed their ratings to determine loan terms; some investors could buy only securities with a triple-A rating; and the rating agencies' judgment was baked into collateral agreements and other financial contracts. To examine the rating process, the Commission focused on Moody's Investors Service, the largest and oldest of the three rating agencies.

The rating of structured finance products such as mortgage-backed securities made up close to half of Moody's rating revenues in 2005, 2006, and 2007.[96] From 2000 to 2007, revenues from rating such financial instruments increased more than fourfold.[97] But the rating process involved many conflicts, which would come into focus during the crisis.

To do its work, Moody's rated mortgage-backed securities using models based, in part, on periods of relatively strong credit performance. Moody's did not sufficiently account for the deterioration in underwriting standards or a dramatic decline in home prices. And Moody's did not even develop a model specifically to take into account the layered risks of subprime securities until late 2006, after it had already rated nearly 19,000 subprime securities.[98]

### "In the business forevermore"

Credit ratings have been linked to government regulations for three-quarters of a century.[99] In 1931, the Office of the Comptroller of the Currency let banks report publicly traded bonds with a rating of BBB or better at book value (that is, the price

they paid for the bonds); lower-rated bonds had to be reported at current market prices, which might be lower. In 1951, the National Association of Insurance Commissioners adopted higher capital requirements on lower-rated bonds held by insurers.[100] But the watershed event in federal regulation occurred in 1975, when the Securities and Exchange Commission modified its minimum capital requirements for broker-dealers to base them on credit ratings by a "nationally recognized statistical rating organization" (NRSRO); at the time, that was Moody's, S&P, or Fitch. Ratings are also built into banking capital regulations under the Recourse Rule, which, since 2001, has permitted banks to hold less capital for higher-rated securities. For example, BBB rated securities require five times as much capital as AAA and AA rated securities, and BB securities require ten times more capital. Banks in some countries were subject to similar requirements under the Basel II international capital agreement, signed in June 2004, although U.S. banks had not fully implemented the advanced approaches allowed under those rules.

Credit ratings also determined whether investors could buy certain investments at all. The SEC restricts money market funds to purchasing "securities that have received credit ratings from any two NRSROs . . . in one of the two highest short-term rating categories or comparable unrated securities."[101] The Department of Labor restricts pension fund investments to securities rated A or higher. Credit ratings affect even private transactions: contracts may contain triggers that require the posting of collateral or immediate repayment, should a security or entity be downgraded. Triggers played an important role in the financial crisis and helped cripple AIG.

Importantly for the mortgage market, the Secondary Mortgage Market Enhancement Act of 1984 permitted federal- and state-chartered financial institutions to invest in mortgage-related securities if the securities had high ratings from at least one rating agency. "Look at the language of the original bill," Lewis Ranieri told the FCIC. "It requires a rating. . . . It put them in the business forevermore. It became one of the biggest, if not the biggest, business."[102] As Eric Kolchinsky, a former Moody's managing director, would summarize the situation, "the rating agencies were given a blank check."[103]

The agencies themselves were able to avoid regulation for decades. Beginning in 1975, the SEC had to approve a company's application to become an NRSRO—but if approved, a company faced no further regulation. More than 30 years later, the SEC got limited authority to oversee NRSROs in the Credit Rating Agency Reform Act of 2006. That law, taking effect in June 2007, focused on mandatory disclosure of the rating agencies' methodologies; however, the law barred the SEC from regulating "the substance of the credit ratings or the procedures and methodologies."[104]

Many investors, such as some pension funds and university endowments, relied on credit ratings because they had neither access to the same data as the rating agencies nor the capacity or analytical ability to assess the securities they were purchasing. As Moody's former managing director Jerome Fons has acknowledged, "Subprime [residential mortgage–backed securities] and their offshoots offer little transparency around composition and characteristics of the loan collateral. . . . Loan-by-loan data, the highest level of detail, is generally not available to investors."[105] Others, even large

financial institutions, relied on the ratings. Still, some investors who did their home-work were skeptical of these products despite their ratings. Arnold Cattani, chairman of Mission Bank in Bakersfield, California, described deciding to sell the bank's hold-ings of mortgage-backed securities and CDOs:

> At one meeting, when things started getting difficult, maybe in 2006, I asked the CFO what the mechanical steps were in . . . mortgage-backed securities, if a borrower in Des Moines, Iowa, defaulted. I know what it is if a borrower in Bakersfield defaults, and somebody has that mort-gage. But as a package security, what happens? And he couldn't answer the question. And I told him to sell them, sell all of them, then, because we didn't understand it, and I don't know that we had the capability to understand the financial complexities; didn't want any part of it.[106]

Notably, rating agencies were not liable for misstatements in securities registra-tions because courts ruled that their ratings were opinions, protected by the First Amendment. Moody's standard disclaimer reads "The ratings . . . are, and must be construed solely as, statements of opinion and not statements of fact or recommen-dations to purchase, sell, or hold any securities." Gary Witt, a former team managing director at Moody's, told the FCIC, "People expect too much from ratings . . . invest-ment decisions should always be based on much more than just a rating."[107]

## "Everything but the elephant sitting on the table"

The ratings were intended to provide a means of comparing risks across asset classes and time. In other words, the risk of a triple-A rated mortgage security was supposed to be similar to the risk of a triple-A rated corporate bond.

Since the mid-1990s, Moody's has rated tranches of mortgage-backed securities using three models. The first, developed in 1996, rated residential mortgage–backed securities. In 2003, Moody's created a new model, M3 Prime, to rate prime, jumbo, and Alt-A deals. Only in the fall of 2006, when the housing market had already peaked, did it develop its model for rating subprime deals, called M3 Subprime.[108]

The models incorporated firm- and security-specific factors, market factors, regu-latory and legal factors, and macroeconomic trends. The M3 Prime model let Moody's automate more of the process. Although Moody's did not sample or review individual loans, the company used loan-level information from the issuer. Relying on loan-to-value ratios, borrower credit scores, originator quality, and loan terms and other information, the model simulated the performance of each loan in 1,250 scenarios, including variations in interest rates and state-level unemployment as well as home price changes. On average, across the scenarios, home prices trended up-ward at approximately 4% per year.[109] The model put little weight on the possibility prices would fall sharply nationwide. Jay Siegel, a former Moody's team managing di-rector involved in developing the model, told the FCIC, "There may have been [state-level] components of this real estate drop that the statistics would have covered, but

the 38% national drop, staying down over this short but multiple-year period, is more stressful than the statistics call for." Even as housing prices rose to unprecedented levels, Moody's never adjusted the scenarios to put greater weight on the possibility of a decline. According to Siegel, in 2005, "Moody's position was that there was not a . . . national housing bubble."[110]

When the initial quantitative analysis was complete, the lead analyst on the deal convened a rating committee of other analysts and managers to assess it and determine the overall ratings for the securities.[111] Siegel told the FCIC that qualitative analysis was also integral: "One common misperception is that Moody's credit ratings are derived solely from the application of a mathematical process or model. This is not the case. . . . The credit rating process involves much more—most importantly, the exercise of independent judgment by members of the rating committee. Ultimately, ratings are subjective opinions that reflect the majority view of the committee's members."[112] As Roger Stein, a Moody's managing director, noted, "Overall, the model has to contemplate events for which there is no data."[113]

After rating subprime deals with the 1996 model for years, in 2006 Moody's introduced a parallel model for rating subprime mortgage–backed securities. Like M3 Prime, the subprime model ran the mortgages through 1,250 scenarios.[114] Moody's officials told the FCIC they recognized that stress scenarios were not sufficiently severe, so they applied additional weight to the most stressful scenario, which reduced the portion of each deal rated triple-A. Stein, who helped develop the subprime model, said the output was manually "calibrated" to be more conservative to ensure predicted losses were consistent with analysts' "expert views." Stein also noted Moody's concern about a suitably negative stress scenario; for example, as one step, analysts took the "single worst case" from the M3 Subprime model simulations and multiplied it by a factor in order to add deterioration.[115]

Moody's did not, however, sufficiently account for the deteriorating quality of the loans being securitized. Fons described this problem to the FCIC: "I sat on this high-level Structured Credit committee, which you'd think would be dealing with such issues [of declining mortgage-underwriting standards], and never once was it raised to this group or put on our agenda that the decline in quality that was going into pools, the impact possibly on ratings, other things. . . . We talked about everything but, you know, the elephant sitting on the table."[116]

To rate CMLTI 2006-NC2, our sample deal, Moody's first used its model to simulate losses in the mortgage pool. Those estimates, in turn, determined how big the junior tranches of the deal would have to be in order to protect the senior tranches from losses. In analyzing the deal, the lead analyst noted it was similar to another Citigroup deal of New Century loans that Moody's had rated earlier and recommended the same amount.[117] Then the deal was tweaked to account for certain riskier types of loans, including interest-only mortgages.[118] For its efforts, Moody's was paid an estimated $208,000.[119] (S&P also rated this deal and received $135,000.)[120]

As we will describe later, three tranches of this deal would be downgraded less than a year after issuance—part of Moody's mass downgrade on July 10, 2007, when housing prices had declined by only 4%. In October 2007, the M4–M11 tranches

were downgraded and by 2008, all the tranches had been downgraded. Of all mortgage-backed securities it had rated triple-A in 2006, Moody's downgraded 73% to junk.[121] The consequences would reverberate throughout the financial system.

## FANNIE MAE AND FREDDIE MAC:
## "LESS COMPETITIVE IN THE MARKETPLACE"

In 2004, Fannie and Freddie faced problems on multiple fronts. They had violated accounting rules and now faced corrections and fines.[122] They were losing market share to Wall Street, which was beginning to dominate the securitization market. Struggling to remain dominant, they loosened their underwriting standards, purchasing and guaranteeing riskier loans, and increasing their securities purchases.[123] Yet their regulator, the Office of Federal Housing Enterprise Oversight (OFHEO), focused more on accounting and other operational issues than on Fannie's and Freddie's increasing investments in risky mortgages and securities.

In 2002, Freddie changed accounting firms. The company had been using Arthur Andersen for many years, but when Andersen got into trouble in the Enron debacle (which put both Enron and its accountant out of business), Freddie switched to PricewaterhouseCoopers. The new accountant found the company had understated its earnings by $5 billion from 2000 through the third quarter of 2002, in an effort to smooth reported earnings and promote itself as "Steady Freddie," a company of strong and steady growth. Bonuses were tied to the reported earnings, and OFHEO found that this arrangement contributed to the accounting manipulations. Freddie's board ousted most top managers, including Chairman and CEO Leland Brendsel, President and COO David Glenn, and CFO Vaughn Clarke.[124] In December 2003, Freddie agreed with OFHEO to pay a $125 million penalty and correct governance, internal controls, accounting, and risk management. In January 2004, OFHEO directed Freddie to maintain 30% more than its minimum capital requirement until it reduced operational risk and could produce timely, certified financial statements. Freddie Mac would settle shareholder lawsuits for $410 million and pay $50 million in penalties to the SEC.

Fannie was next. In September 2004, OFHEO discovered violations of accounting rules that called into question previous filings. In 2006, OFHEO reported that Fannie had overstated earnings from 1998 through 2002 by $11 billion and that it, too, had manipulated accounting in ways influenced by compensation plans.[125] OFHEO made Fannie improve accounting controls, maintain the same 30% capital surplus imposed on Freddie, and improve governance and internal controls. Fannie's board ousted CEO Franklin Raines and others, and the SEC required Fannie to restate its results for 2001 through mid-2004. Fannie settled SEC and OFHEO enforcement actions for $400 million in penalties. Donald Bisenius, an executive vice president at Freddie Mac, told the FCIC that the accounting issues distracted management from the mortgage business, taking "a tremendous amount of management's time and attention and probably led to us being less aggressive or less competitive in the marketplace [than] we otherwise might have been."[126]

As the scandals unfolded, subprime private label mortgage–backed securities (PLS) issued by Wall Street increased from $87 billion in 2001 to $465 billion in 2005 (shown in figure 7.3); the value of Alt-A mortgage–backed securities increased from $11 billion to $332 billion. Starting in 2001 for Freddie and 2002 for Fannie, the GSEs—particularly Freddie—became buyers in this market. While private investors always bought the most, the GSEs purchased 10.5% of the private-issued subprime mortgage–backed securities in 2001. The share peaked at 40% in 2004 and then fell back to 28% in 2008. The share for Alt-A mortgage–backed securities was always lower.[127] The GSEs almost always bought the safest, triple-A-rated tranches. From 2005 through 2008, the GSEs' purchases declined, both in dollar amount and as a percentage.

These investments were profitable at first, but as delinquencies increased in 2007 and 2008, both GSEs began to take significant losses on their private-label mortgage–backed securities—disproportionately from their purchases of Alt-A securities. By the third quarter of 2010, total impairments on securities totaled $46 billion at the two companies—enough to wipe out nearly 60% of their pre-crisis capital.[128]

OFHEO knew about the GSEs' purchases of subprime and Alt-A mortgage–backed securities. In its 2004 examination, the regulator noted Freddie's purchases of these securities. It also noted that Freddie was purchasing whole mortgages with "higher risk attributes which exceeded the Enterprise's modeling and costing capabilities," including "No Income/No Asset loans" that introduced "considerable risk." OFHEO reported that mortgage insurers were already seeing abuses with these loans.[129] But the regulator concluded that the purchases of mortgage-backed securities and riskier mortgages were not a "significant supervisory concern," and the examination focused more on Freddie's efforts to address accounting and internal deficiencies.[130] OFHEO included nothing in Fannie's report about its purchases of subprime and Alt-A mortgage–backed securities, and its credit risk management was deemed satisfactory.[131]

The reasons for the GSEs' purchases of subprime and Alt-A mortgage–backed securities have been debated. Some observers, including Alan Greenspan, have linked the GSEs' purchases of private mortgage–backed securities to their push to fulfill their higher goals for affordable housing. The former Fed chairman wrote in a working paper submitted as part of his testimony to the FCIC that when the GSEs were pressed to "expand 'affordable housing commitments,' they chose to meet them by investing heavily in subprime securities."[132] Using data provided by Fannie Mae and Freddie Mac, the FCIC examined how single-family, multifamily, and securities purchases contributed to meeting the affordable housing goals. In 2003 and 2004, Fannie Mae's single- and multifamily purchases alone met each of the goals; in other words, the enterprise would have met its obligations without buying subprime or Alt-A mortgage–backed securities. In fact, none of Fannie Mae's 2004 purchases of subprime or Alt-A securities were ever submitted to HUD to be counted toward the goals.

Before 2005, 50% or less of the GSEs' loan purchases had to satisfy the affordable housing goals. In 2005 the goals were increased above 50%; but even then, single- and multifamily purchases alone met the overall goals.[133] Securities purchases did, in

## Buyers of Non-GSE Mortgage-Backed Securities

*The GSEs purchased subprime and Alt-A nonagency securities during the 2000s. These purchases peaked in 2004.*

IN BILLIONS OF DOLLARS

SOURCES: Inside Mortgage Finance, Fannie Mae, Freddie Mac

*Figure 7.3*

several cases, help Fannie meet its subgoals—specific targets requiring the GSEs to purchase or guarantee loans to purchase homes. In 2005, Fannie missed one of these subgoals and would have missed a second without the securities purchases; in 2006, the securities purchases helped Fannie meet those two subgoals.

The pattern is the same at Freddie Mac, a larger purchaser of non-agency mortgage–backed securities.[134] Estimates by the FCIC show that from 2003 through 2006, Freddie would have met the affordable housing goals without any purchases of Alt-A or subprime securities, but used the securities to help meet subgoals.[135]

Robert Levin, the former chief business officer of Fannie Mae, told the FCIC that buying private-label mortgage–backed securities "was a moneymaking activity—it was all positive economics. . . . [T]here was no trade-off [between making money and hitting goals], it was a very broad-brushed effort" that could be characterized as "win-win-win: money, goals, and share."[136] Mark Winer, the head of Fannie's Business, Analysis, and Decisions Group, stated that the purchase of triple-A tranches of mortgage-backed securities backed by subprime loans was viewed as an attractive opportunity with good returns. He said that the mortgage-backed securities satisfied

housing goals, and that the goals became a factor in the decision to increase purchases of private label securities. [137]

Overall, while the mortgages behind the subprime mortgage–backed securities were often issued to borrowers that could help Fannie and Freddie fulfill their goals, the mortgages behind the Alt-A securities were not. Alt-A mortgages were not generally extended to lower-income borrowers, and the regulations prohibited mortgages to borrowers with unstated income levels—a hallmark of Alt-A loans—from counting toward affordability goals.[138] Levin told the FCIC that they believed that the purchase of Alt-A securities "did not have a net positive effect on Fannie Mae's housing goals."[139] Instead, they had to be offset with more mortgages for low- and moderate-income borrowers to meet the goals.

Fannie and Freddie continued to purchase subprime and Alt-A mortgage–backed securities from 2005 to 2008 and also bought and securitized greater numbers of riskier mortgages. The results would be disastrous for the companies, their shareholders, and American taxpayers.

---

### COMMISSION CONCLUSIONS ON CHAPTER 7

The Commission concludes that the monetary policy of the Federal Reserve, along with capital flows from abroad, created conditions in which a housing bubble could develop. However, these conditions need not have led to a crisis. The Federal Reserve and other regulators did not take actions necessary to constrain the credit bubble. In addition, the Federal Reserve's policies and pronouncements encouraged rather than inhibited the growth of mortgage debt and the housing bubble.

Lending standards collapsed, and there was a significant failure of accountability and responsibility throughout each level of the lending system. This included borrowers, mortgage brokers, appraisers, originators, securitizers, credit rating agencies, and investors, and ranged from corporate boardrooms to individuals. Loans were often premised on ever-rising home prices and were made regardless of ability to pay.

The nonprime mortgage securitization process created a pipeline through which risky mortgages were conveyed and sold throughout the financial system. This pipeline was essential to the origination of the burgeoning numbers of high-risk mortgages. The originate-to-distribute model undermined responsibility and accountability for the long-term viability of mortgages and mortgage-related securities and contributed to the poor quality of mortgage loans.

*(continues)*

*(continued)*

Federal and state rules required or encouraged financial firms and some institutional investors to make investments based on the ratings of credit rating agencies, leading to undue reliance on those ratings. However, the rating agencies were not adequately regulated by the Securities and Exchange Commission or any other regulator to ensure the quality and accuracy of their ratings. Moody's, the Commission's case study in this area, relied on flawed and outdated models to issue erroneous ratings on mortgage-related securities, failed to perform meaningful due diligence on the assets underlying the securities, and continued to rely on those models even after it became obvious that the models were wrong.

Not only did the federal banking supervisors fail to rein in risky mortgage-lending practices, but the Office of the Comptroller of the Currency and the Office of Thrift Supervision preempted the applicability of state laws and regulatory efforts to national banks and thrifts, thus preventing adequate protection for borrowers and weakening constraints on this segment of the mortgage market.

# 8

# THE CDO MACHINE

## CONTENTS

In the first decade of the 21st century, a previously obscure financial product called the collateralized debt obligation, or CDO, transformed the mortgage market by creating a new source of demand for the lower-rated tranches of mortgage-backed securities.*

Despite their relatively high returns, tranches rated other than triple-A could be hard to sell. If borrowers were delinquent or defaulted, investors in these tranches were out of luck because of where they sat in the payments waterfall.

Wall Street came up with a solution: in the words of one banker, they "created the investor."[1] That is, they built new securities that would buy the tranches that had become harder to sell. Bankers would take those low investment-grade tranches, largely rated BBB or A, from many mortgage-backed securities and repackage them into the new securities—CDOs. Approximately 80% of these CDO tranches would be rated triple-A despite the fact that they generally comprised the lower-rated tranches of mortgage-backed securities. CDO securities would be sold with their own waterfalls, with the risk-averse investors, again, paid first and the risk-seeking investors paid last. As they did in the case of mortgage-backed securities, the rating agencies gave their highest, triple-A ratings to the securities at the top (see figure 8.1).

Still, it was not obvious that a pool of mortgage-backed securities rated BBB could be transformed into a new security that is mostly rated triple-A. But math made it so.

---

*Throughout this book, unless otherwise noted, we use the term "CDOs" to refer to cash CDOs backed by asset-backed securities (such as mortgage-backed securities), also known as ABS CDOs.

## Collateralized Debt Obligations

*Collateralized debt obligations (CDOs) are structured financial instruments that purchase and pool financial assets such as the riskier tranches of various mortgage-backed securities.*

### 1. Purchase

The CDO manager and securities firm select and purchase assets, such as some of the lower-rated tranches of mortgage-backed securities.

### 3. CDO tranches

Similar to mortgage-backed securities, the CDO issues securities in tranches that vary based on their place in the cash flow waterfall.

Low risk, low yield

First claim to cash flow from principal & interest payments...

New pool of RMBS and other securities

AAA

next claim...

### 2. Pool

The CDO manager and securities firm pool various assets in an attempt to get diversification benefits.

AA

next... etc.

High risk, high yield

*Figure 8.1*

The securities firms argued—and the rating agencies agreed—that if they pooled many BBB-rated mortgage-backed securities, they would create additional diversification benefits. The rating agencies believed that those diversification benefits were significant—that if one security went bad, the second had only a very small chance of going bad at the same time. And as long as losses were limited, only those investors at the bottom would lose money. They would absorb the blow, and the other investors would continue to get paid.

Relying on that logic, the CDO machine gobbled up the BBB and other lower-rated

tranches of mortgage-backed securities, growing from a bit player to a multi-hundred-billion-dollar industry. Between 2003 and 2007, as house prices rose 27% nationally and $4 trillion in mortgage-backed securities were created, Wall Street issued nearly $700 billion in CDOs that included mortgage-backed securities as collateral.[2] With ready buyers for their own product, mortgage securitizers continued to demand loans for their pools, and hundreds of billions of dollars flooded the mortgage world. In effect, the CDO became the engine that powered the mortgage supply chain. "There is a machine going," Scott Eichel, a senior managing director at Bear Stearns, told a financial journalist in May 2005. "There is a lot of brain power to keep this going."[3]

Everyone involved in keeping this machine humming—the CDO managers and underwriters who packaged and sold the securities, the rating agencies that gave most of them sterling ratings, and the guarantors who wrote protection against their defaulting—collected fees based on the dollar volume of securities sold. For the bankers who had put these deals together, as for the executives of their companies, volume equaled fees equaled bonuses. And those fees were in the billions of dollars across the market.

But when the housing market went south, the models on which CDOs were based proved tragically wrong. The mortgage-backed securities turned out to be highly correlated—meaning they performed similarly. Across the country, in regions where subprime and Alt-A mortgages were heavily concentrated, borrowers would default in large numbers. This was not how it was supposed to work. Losses in one region were supposed to be offset by successful loans in another region. In the end, CDOs turned out to be some of the most ill-fated assets in the financial crisis. The greatest losses would be experienced by big CDO arrangers such as Citigroup, Merrill Lynch, and UBS, and by financial guarantors such as AIG, Ambac, and MBIA. These players had believed their own models and retained exposure to what were understood to be the least risky tranches of the CDOs: those rated triple-A or even "super-senior," which were assumed to be safer than triple-A-rated tranches.

"The whole concept of ABS CDOs had been an abomination," Patrick Parkinson, currently the head of banking supervision and regulation at the Federal Reserve Board, told the FCIC.[4]

## CDOs: "WE CREATED THE INVESTOR"

Michael Milken's Drexel Burnham Lambert assembled the first rated collateralized debt obligation in 1987 out of different companies' junk bonds. The strategy made sense—pooling many bonds reduced investors' exposure to the failure of any one bond, and putting the securities into tranches enabled investors to pick their preferred level of risk and return.

For the managers who created CDOs, the key to profitability of the CDO was the fee and the spread—the difference between the interest that the CDO received on the bonds or loans that it held and the interest that the CDO paid to investors. Throughout the 1990s, CDO managers generally purchased corporate and emerging market bonds and bank loans. When the liquidity crisis of 1998 drove up returns on asset-backed

securities, Prudential Securities saw an opportunity and launched a series of CDOs that combined different kinds of asset-backed securities into one CDO. These "multisector" or "ABS" securities were backed by mortgages, mobile home loans, aircraft leases, mutual fund fees, and other asset classes with predictable income streams. The diversity was supposed to provide yet another layer of safety for investors.

Multisector CDOs went through a tough patch when some of the asset-backed securities in which they invested started to perform poorly in 2002—particularly those backed by mobile home loans (after borrowers defaulted in large numbers), aircraft leases (after 9/11), and mutual fund fees (after the dot-com bust).[5] The accepted wisdom among many investment banks, investors, and rating agencies was that the wide range of assets had actually contributed to the problem; according to this view, the asset managers who selected the portfolios could not be experts in sectors as diverse as aircraft leases and mutual funds.

So the CDO industry turned to nonprime mortgage–backed securities, which CDO managers believed they understood, which seemed to have a record of good performance, and which paid relatively high returns for what was considered a safe investment. "Everyone looked at the sector and said, the CDO construct works, but we just need to find more stable collateral," said Wing Chau, who ran two firms, Maxim Group and Harding Advisory, that managed CDOs mostly underwritten by Merrill Lynch. "And the industry looked at residential mortgage–backed securities, Alt-A, subprime, and non-agency mortgages, and saw the relative stability."[6]

CDOs quickly became ubiquitous in the mortgage business.[7] Investors liked the combination of apparent safety and strong returns, and investment bankers liked having a new source of demand for the lower tranches of mortgage-backed securities and other asset-backed securities that they created. "We told you these [BBB-rated securities] were a great deal, and priced at great spreads, but nobody stepped up," the Credit Suisse banker Joe Donovan told a Phoenix conference of securitization bankers in February 2002. "So we created the investor."[8]

By 2004, creators of CDOs were the dominant buyers of the BBB-rated tranches of mortgage-backed securities, and their bids significantly influenced prices in the market for these securities. By 2005, they were buying "virtually all" of the BBB tranches.[9] Just as mortgage-backed securities provided the cash to originate mortgages, now CDOs would provide the cash to fund mortgage-backed securities. Also by 2004, mortgage-backed securities accounted for more than half of the collateral in CDOs, up from 35% in 2002.[10] Sales of these CDOs more than doubled every year, jumping from $30 billion in 2003 to $225 billion in 2006.[11] Filling this pipeline would require hundreds of billions of dollars of subprime and Alt-A mortgages.

### "It was a lot of effort"

Five key types of players were involved in the construction of CDOs: securities firms, CDO managers, rating agencies, investors, and financial guarantors. Each took varying degrees of risk and, for a time, profited handsomely.

Securities firms underwrote the CDOs: that is, they approved the selection of col-

lateral, structured the notes into tranches, and were responsible for selling them to investors. Three firms—Merrill Lynch, Goldman Sachs, and the securities arm of Citigroup—accounted for more than 30% of CDOs structured from 2004 to 2007. Deutsche Bank and UBS were also major participants.[12] "We had sales representatives in all those [global] locations, and their jobs were to sell structured products," Nestor Dominguez, the co-head of Citigroup's CDO desk, told the FCIC. "We spent a lot of effort to have people in place to educate, to pitch structured products. So, it was a lot of effort, about 100 people. And I presume our competitors did the same."[13]

The underwriters' focus was on generating fees and structuring deals that they could sell. Underwriting did entail risks, however. The securities firm had to hold the assets, such as the BBB-rated tranches of mortgage-backed securities, during the ramp-up period—six to nine months when the firm was accumulating the mortgage-backed securities for the CDOs. Typically, during that period, the securities firm took the risk that the assets might lose value. "Our business was to make new issue fees, [and to] make sure that if the market did have a downturn, we were somehow hedged," Michael Lamont, the former co-head for CDOs at Deutsche Bank, told the FCIC.[14] Chris Ricciardi, formerly head of the CDO desk at Merrill Lynch, likewise told the FCIC that he did not track the performance of CDOs after underwriting them.[15] Moreover, Lamont said it was not his job to decide whether the rating agencies' models had the correct underlying assumptions. That "was not what we brought to the table," he said.[16] In many cases, though, underwriters helped CDO managers select collateral, leading to potential conflicts (more on that later).

The role of the CDO manager was to select the collateral, such as mortgage-backed securities, and in some cases manage the portfolio on an ongoing basis. Managers ranged from independent investment firms such as Chau's to units of large asset management companies such as PIMCO and Blackrock.

CDO managers received periodic fees based on the dollar amount of assets in the CDO and in some cases on performance. On a percentage basis, these may have looked small—sometimes measured in tenths of a percentage point—but the amounts were far from trivial. For CDOs that focused on the relatively senior tranches of mortgage-backed securities, annual manager fees tended to be in the range of $600,000 to a million dollars per year for a $1 billion dollar deal. For CDOs that focused on the more junior tranches, which were often smaller, fees would be $750,000 to $1.5 million per year for a $500 million deal.[17] As managers did more deals, they generated more fees without much additional cost. "You'd hear statements like, 'Everybody and his uncle now wants to be a CDO manager,'" Mark Adelson, then a structured finance analyst at Nomura Securities and currently chief credit officer at S&P, told the FCIC. "That was an observation voiced repeatedly at several of the industry conferences around those times—the enormous proliferation of CDO managers— . . . because it was very lucrative."[18] CDO managers industry-wide earned at least $1.5 billion in management fees between 2003 and 2007.[19]

The role of the rating agencies was to provide basic guidelines on the collateral and the structure of the CDOs—that is, the sizes and returns of the various tranches—in close consultation with the underwriters. For many investors, the

triple-A rating made those products appropriate investments. Rating agency fees were typically between $250,000 and $500,000 for CDOs.[20] For most deals, at least two rating agencies would provide ratings and receive those fees—although the views tended to be in sync.

The CDO investors, like investors in mortgage-backed securities, focused on different tranches based on their preference for risk and return. CDO underwriters such as Citigroup, Merrill Lynch, and UBS often retained the super-senior triple-A tranches for reasons we will see later. They also sold them to commercial paper programs that invested in CDOs and other highly rated assets. Hedge funds often bought the equity tranches.[21]

Eventually, other CDOs became the most important class of investor for the mezzanine tranches of CDOs. By 2005, CDO underwriters were selling most of the mezzanine tranches—including those rated A—and, especially, those rated BBB, the lowest and riskiest investment-grade rating—to other CDO managers, to be packaged into other CDOs.[22] It was common for CDOs to be structured with 5% or 15% of their cash invested in other CDOs; CDOs with as much as 80% to 100% of their cash invested in other CDOs were typically known as "CDOs squared."

Finally, the issuers of over-the-counter derivatives called credit default swaps, most notably AIG, played a central role by issuing swaps to investors in CDO tranches, promising to reimburse them for any losses on the tranches in exchange for a stream of premium-like payments. This credit default swap protection made the CDOs much more attractive to potential investors because they appeared to be virtually risk free, but it created huge exposures for the credit default swap issuers if significant losses did occur.

Profit from the creation of CDOs, as is customary on Wall Street, was reflected in employee bonuses. And, as demand for all types of financial products soared during the liquidity boom at the beginning of the 21st century, pretax profit for the five largest investment banks doubled between 2003 and 2006, from $20 billion to $43 billion; total compensation at these investment banks for their employees across the world rose from $34 billion to $61 billion.[23] A part of the growth could be credited to mortgage-backed securities, CDOs, and various derivatives, and thus employees in those areas could be expected to be compensated accordingly. "Credit derivatives traders as well as mortgage and asset-backed securities salespeople should especially enjoy bonus season," a firm that compiles compensation figures for investment banks reported in 2005.[24]

To see in more detail how the CDO pipeline worked, we revisit our illustrative Citigroup mortgage-backed security, CMLTI 2006-NC2. Earlier, we described how most of the below-triple-A bonds issued in this deal went into CDOs. One such CDO was Kleros Real Estate Funding III, which was underwritten by UBS, a Swiss bank.[25] The CDO manager was Strategos Capital Management, a subsidiary of Cohen & Company; that investment company was headed by Chris Ricciardi, who had earlier built Merrill's CDO business.[26] Kleros III, launched in 2006, purchased and held $9.6 million in securities from the A-rated M5 tranche of Citigroup's security, along with 187 junior tranches of other mortgage-backed securities. In total, it owned $975 mil-

lion of mortgage-related securities, of which 45% were rated BBB or lower, 16% A, and the rest higher than A. To fund those purchases, Kleros III issued $1 billion of bonds to investors. As was typical for this type of CDO at the time, roughly 88% of the Kleros III bonds were triple-A-rated. At least half of the below-triple-A tranches issued by Kleros III went into other CDOs.[27]

## *"Mother's milk to the . . . market"*

The growth of CDOs had important impacts on the mortgage market itself. CDO managers who were eager to expand the assets that they were managing—on which their income was based—were willing to pay high prices to accumulate BBB-rated tranches of mortgage-backed securities. This "CDO bid" pushed up market prices on those tranches, pricing out of the market traditional investors in mortgage-backed securities.

Informed institutional investors such as insurance companies had purchased the private-label mortgage–backed securities issued in the 1990s. These securities were typically protected from losses by bond insurers, who had analyzed the deals as well. Beginning in the late 1990s, mortgage-backed securities that were structured with six or more tranches and other features to protect the triple-A investors became more common, replacing the earlier structures that had relied on bond insurance to protect investors. By 2004, the earlier forms of mortgage-backed securities had essentially vanished, leaving the market increasingly to the multitranche structures and their CDO investors.

This was a critical development, given that the focus of CDO managers differed from that of traditional investors. "The CDO manager and the CDO investor are not the same kind of folks [as the monoline bond insurers], who just backed away," Adelson said. "They're mostly not mortgage professionals, not real estate professionals. They are derivatives folks."[28]

Indeed, Chau, the CDO manager, portrayed his job as creating structures that rating agencies would approve and investors would buy, and making sure the mortgage-backed securities that he bought "met industry standards." He said that he relied on the rating agencies. "Unfortunately, what lulled a lot of investors, and I'm in that camp as well, what lulled us into that sense of comfort was that the rating stability was so solid and that it was so consistent. I mean, the rating agencies did a very good job of making everything consistent."[29] CDO production was effectively on autopilot. "Mortgage traders speak lovingly of 'the CDO bid.' It is mother's milk to the . . . market," James Grant, a market commentator, wrote in 2006. "Without it, fewer asset-backed structures could be built, and those that were would have to meet a much more conservative standard of design. The resulting pangs of credit withdrawal would certainly be felt in the residential real-estate market."[30]

UBS's Global CDO Group agreed, noting that CDOs "have now become bullies in their respective collateral markets." By promoting an increase in both the volume and the price of mortgage-backed securities, bids from CDOs had "an impact on the overall U.S. economy that goes well beyond the CDO market."[31] Without the demand for mortgage-backed securities from CDOs, lenders would have been able to sell

fewer mortgages, and thus they would have had less reason to push so hard to make the loans in the first place.

## *"Leverage is inherent in CDOs"*

The mortgage pipeline also introduced leverage at every step. Most financial institutions thrive on leverage—that is, on investing borrowed money. Leverage increases profits in good times, but also increases losses in bad times. The mortgage itself creates leverage—particularly when the loan is of the low down payment, high loan-to-value ratio variety. Mortgage-backed securities and CDOs created further leverage because they were financed with debt. And the CDOs were often purchased as collateral by those creating other CDOs with yet another round of debt. Synthetic CDOs consisting of credit default swaps, described below, amplified the leverage. The CDO, backed by securities that were themselves backed by mortgages, created leverage on leverage, as Dan Sparks, mortgage department head at Goldman Sachs, explained to the FCIC.[32] "People were looking for other forms of leverage. . . . You could either take leverage individually, as an institution, or you could take leverage within the structure," Citigroup's Dominguez told the FCIC.[33]

Even the investor that bought the CDOs could use leverage. Structured investment vehicles—a type of commercial paper program that invested mostly in triple-A-rated securities—were leveraged an average of just under 14-to-1: in other words, these SIVs would hold $14 in assets for every dollar of capital.[34] The assets would be financed with debt. Hedge funds, which were common purchasers, were also often highly leveraged in the repo market, as we will see. But it would become clear during the crisis that some of the highest leverage was created by companies such as Merrill, Citigroup, and AIG when they retained or purchased the triple-A and super-senior tranches of CDOs with little or no capital backing.

Thus, in 2004, when the homeownership rate was peaking, and when new mortgages were increasingly being driven by serial refinancings, by investors and speculators, and by second home purchases, the value of trillions of dollars of securities rested on just two things: the ability of millions of homeowners to make the payments on their subprime and Alt-A mortgages and the stability of the market value of homes whose mortgages were the basis of the securities. Those dangers were understood all along by some market participants. "Leverage is inherent in [asset-backed securities] CDOs," Mark Klipsch, a banker with Orix Capital Markets, an asset management firm, told a Boca Raton conference of securitization bankers in October 2004. While it was good for short-term profits, losses could be large later on. Klipsch said, "We'll see some problems down the road."[35]

## BEAR STEARNS'S HEDGE FUNDS: "IT FUNCTIONED FINE UP UNTIL ONE DAY IT JUST DIDN'T FUNCTION"

Bear Stearns, the smallest of the five large investment banks, started its asset management business in 1985 when it established Bear Stearns Asset Management (BSAM).

Asset management brought in steady fee income, allowed banks to offer new products to customers and required little capital.

BSAM played a prominent role in the CDO business as both a CDO manager and a hedge fund that invested in mortgage-backed securities and CDOs. At BSAM, by the end of 2006 Ralph Cioffi was managing 11 CDOs with $18.3 billion in assets and 2 hedge funds with $18 billion in assets.[36] Although Bear Stearns owned BSAM, Bear's management exercised little supervision over its business.[37] The eventual failure of Cioffi's two large mortgage-focused hedge funds would be an important event in 2007, early in the financial crisis.

In 2003, Cioffi launched his first fund at BSAM, the High-Grade Structured Credit Strategies Fund, and in 2006 he added the High-Grade Structured Credit Strategies Enhanced Leverage Fund. The funds purchased mostly mortgage-backed securities or CDOs, and used leverage to enhance their returns. The target was for 90% of assets to be rated either AAA or AA. As Cioffi told the FCIC, "The thesis behind the fund was that the structured credit markets offered yield over and above what their ratings suggested they should offer."[38] Cioffi targeted a leverage ratio of 10 to 1 for the first High-Grade fund. For Enhanced Leverage, Cioffi upped the ante, touting the Enhanced Leverage fund as "a levered version of the [High Grade] fund" that targeted leverage of 12 to 1.[39] At the end of 2006, the High-Grade fund contained $8.6 billion in assets (using $0.9 billion of his hedge fund investors' money and $7.7 billion in borrowed money). The Enhanced Leverage Fund had $9.4 billion (using $0.9 billion from investors and $8.5 billion in borrowed money).[40]

BSAM financed these asset purchases by borrowing in the repo markets, which was typical for hedge funds. A survey conducted by the FCIC identified at least $275 billion of repo borrowing as of June 2008 by the approximately 170 hedge funds that responded. The respondents invested at least $45 billion in mortgage-backed securities or CDOs as of June 2007.[41] The ability to borrow using the AAA and AA tranches of CDOs as repo collateral facilitated demand for those securities.

But repo borrowing carried risks: it created significant leverage and it had to be renewed frequently. For example, an investor buying a stock on margin—meaning with borrowed money—might have to put up 50 cents on the dollar, with the other 50 cents loaned by his or her stockbroker, for a leverage ratio of 2 to 1. A homeowner buying a house might make a 10% down payment and take out a mortgage for the rest, a leverage ratio of 10 to 1. By contrast, repo lending allowed an investor to buy a security for much less out of pocket—in the case of a Treasury security, an investor may have to put in only 0.25%, borrowing 99.75% from a securities firm (400 to 1). In the case of a mortgage-backed security, an investor might pay 5% (20 to 1).[42]

With this amount of leverage, a 5% change in the value of that mortgage-backed security can double the investor's money—or lose all of the initial investment.

Another inherent fallacy in the structure was the assumption that the underlying collateral could be sold easily. But when it came to selling them in times of distress, private-label mortgage-backed securities would prove to be very different from U.S. Treasuries.

The short-term nature of repo money also makes it inherently risky and unreliable: funding that is offered at certain terms today could be gone tomorrow. Cioffi's funds, for example, took the risk that its repo lenders would decide not to extend, or "roll," the repo lines on any given day. Yet more and more, repo lenders were loaning money to funds like Cioffi's, rolling the debt nightly, and not worrying very much about the real quality of the collateral.

The firms loaning money to Cioffi's hedge funds were often also selling them mortgage-related securities, and the hedge funds pledged those same securities to secure the loans.[43] If the market value of the collateral fell, the repo lenders could and would demand more collateral from the hedge fund to back the repo loan. This dynamic would play a pivotal role in the fate of many hedge funds in 2007—most spectacularly in the case of Cioffi's funds. "The repo market, I mean it functioned fine up until one day it just didn't function," Cioffi told the FCIC. Up to that point, his hedge funds could buy billions of dollars of CDOs on borrowed money because of the market's bullishness about mortgage assets, he said. "It became . . . a more and more acceptable asset class, [with] more traders, more repo lenders, more investors obviously. [It had a] much broader footprint domestically as well as internationally. So the market just really exploded."[44]

BSAM touted its CDO holdings to investors, telling them that CDOs were a market opportunity because they were complex and therefore undervalued in the general marketplace. In 2003, this was a promising market with seemingly manageable risks. Cioffi and his team not only bought CDOs, they also created and managed other CDOs. Cioffi would purchase mortgage-backed securities, CDOs, and other securities for his hedge funds. When he had reached his firm's internal investment limits, he would repackage those securities and sell CDO securities to other customers. With the proceeds, Cioffi would pay off his repo lenders, and at the same time he would acquire the equity tranche of a new CDO.[45]

Because Cioffi managed these newly created CDOs that selected collateral from his own hedge funds,[46] he was positioned on both sides of the transaction. The structure created a conflict of interest between Cioffi's obligation to his hedge fund investors and his obligation to his CDO investors; this was not unique on Wall Street, and BSAM disclosed the structure, and the conflict of interest, to potential investors.[47] For example, a critical question was at what price the CDO should purchase assets from the hedge fund: if the CDO paid above-market prices for a security, that would advantage the hedge fund investors and disadvantage the CDO investors.

BSAM's flagship CDOs—dubbed Klio I, II, and III—were created in rapid succession over 2004 and 2005, with Citigroup as their underwriter. All three deals were mainly composed of mortgage- and asset-backed securities that BSAM already owned, and BSAM retained the equity position in all three; all three were primarily funded with asset-backed commercial paper.[48] Typical for the industry at the time, the expected return for the CDO manager, who was managing assets and holding the equity tranche, was between 15% and 23% annually, assuming no defaults on the underlying collateral.[49] Thanks to the combination of mortgage-backed securities,

CDOs, and leverage, Cioffi's funds earned healthy returns for a time: the High-Grade fund had returns of 17% in 2004, 10% in 2005, and 9% in 2006 after fees.[50] Cioffi and Tannin made millions before the hedge funds collapsed in 2007. Cioffi was rewarded with total compensation worth more than $41 million from 2005 to 2007. In 2007, the year the two hedge funds filed for bankruptcy, Cioffi made more than $17.6 million in total compensation. Matt Tannin, his lead manager, was awarded compensation of more than $5.6 million from 2005 to 2007.[51] Both managers invested some of their own money in the funds, and used this as a selling point when pitching the funds to others.[52]

But when house prices fell and investors started to question the value of mortgage-backed securities in 2007, the same short-term leverage that had inflated Cioffi's returns would amplify losses and quickly put his two hedge funds out of business.

## CITIGROUP'S LIQUIDITY PUTS:
## "A POTENTIAL CONFLICT OF INTEREST"

By the middle of the decade, Citigroup was a market leader in selling CDOs, often using its depositor-based commercial bank to provide liquidity support. For much of this period, the company was in various types of trouble with its regulators, and then-CEO Charles Prince told the FCIC that dealing with those troubles took up more than half his time.[53] After paying the $70 million fine related to subprime mortgage lending, Citigroup again got into trouble, charged with helping Enron—before that company filed for bankruptcy in 2001—use structured finance transactions to manipulate its financial statements. In July 2003, Citigroup agreed to pay the SEC $120 million to settle these allegations and also agreed, under formal enforcement actions by the Federal Reserve and Office of the Comptroller of the Currency, to overhaul its risk management practices.[54]

By March 2005, the Fed had seen enough: it banned Citigroup from making any more major acquisitions until it improved its governance and legal compliance. According to Prince, he had already decided to turn "the company's focus from an acquisition-driven strategy to more of a balanced strategy involving organic growth."[55] Robert Rubin, a former treasury secretary and former Goldman Sachs co-CEO who was at that time chairman of the Executive Committee of Citigroup's board of directors, recommended that Citigroup increase its risk taking—assuming, he told the FCIC, that the firm managed those risks properly.[56]

Citigroup's investment bank subsidiary was a natural area for growth after the Fed and then Congress had done away with restrictions on activities that could be pursued by investment banks affiliated with commercial banks. One opportunity among many was the CDO business, which was just then taking off amid the booming mortgage market.

In 2003, Citi's CDO desk was a tiny unit in the company's investment banking arm, "eight guys and a Bloomberg" terminal, in the words of Nestor Dominguez, then co-head of the desk.[57] Nevertheless, this tiny operation under the command of

Thomas Maheras, co-CEO of the investment bank, had become a leader in the nascent market for CDOs, creating more than $18 billion in 2003 and 2004—close to one-fifth of the market in those years.

The eight guys had picked up on a novel structure pioneered by Goldman Sachs and WestLB, a German bank. Instead of issuing the triple-A tranches of the CDOs as long-term debt, Citigroup structured them as short-term asset-backed commercial paper.[58] Of course, using commercial paper introduced liquidity risk (not present when the tranches were sold as long-term debt), because the CDO would have to reissue the paper to investors regularly—usually within days or weeks—for the life of the CDO. But asset-backed commercial paper was a cheap form of funding at the time, and it had a large base of potential investors, particularly among money market mutual funds. To mitigate the liquidity risk and to ensure that the rating agencies would give it their top ratings, Citibank (Citigroup's national bank subsidiary) provided assurances to investors, in the form of liquidity puts. In selling the liquidity put, for an ongoing fee the bank would be on the hook to step in and buy the commercial paper if there were no buyers when it matured or if the cost of funding rose by a predetermined amount.[59]

The CDO team at Citigroup had jumped into the market in July 2003 with a $1.5 billion CDO named Grenadier Funding that included a $1.3 billion tranche backed by a liquidity put from Citibank.[60] Over the next three years, Citi would write liquidity puts on $25 billion of commercial paper issued by CDOs,[61] more than any other company. BSAM's three Klio CDOs, which Citigroup had underwritten, accounted for just over $10 billion of this total,[62] a large number that would not bode well for the bank. But initially, this "strategic initiative," as Dominguez called it, was very profitable for Citigroup. The CDO desk earned roughly 1% of the total deal value in structuring fees for Citigroup's investment banking arm, or about $10 million for a $1 billion deal. In addition, Citigroup would generally charge buyers 0.10% to 0.20% in premiums annually for the liquidity puts.[63] In other words, for a typical $1 billion deal, Citibank would receive $1 to $2 million annually on the liquidity puts alone—practically free money, it seemed, because the trading desk believed that these puts would never be triggered.[64]

In effect, the liquidity put was yet another highly leveraged bet: a contingent liability that would be triggered in some circumstances. Prior to the 2004 change in the capital rules regarding liquidity puts (discussed earlier), Citigroup did not have to hold any capital against such contingencies. Rather, it was permitted to use its own risk models to determine the appropriate capital charge. But Citigroup's financial models estimated only a remote possibility that the puts would be triggered. Following the 2004 rule change, Citibank was required to hold 0.16% in capital against the amount of commercial paper supported by the liquidity put, or $1.6 million for a $1 billion liquidity put. Given a $1 to $2 million annual fee for the put, the annual return on that capital could still exceed 100%. No doubt about it, Dominguez told the FCIC, the triple-A or similar ratings, the multiple fees, and the low capital requirements made the liquidity puts "a much better trade" for Citi's balance sheet.[65] The events of 2007 would reveal the fallacy of those assumptions and catapult the entire $25 billion

in commercial paper straight onto the bank's balance sheet, requiring it to come up with $25 billion in cash as well as more capital to satisfy bank regulators.

The liquidity puts were approved by Citigroup's Capital Markets Approval Committee, which was charged with reviewing all new financial products.[66] Deeming them to be low risk, the company based its opinions on the credit risk of the underlying collateral, but failed to consider the liquidity risk posed by a general market disruption.[67] The OCC, the supervisor of Citigroup's largest commercial bank subsidiary, was aware that the bank had issued the liquidity puts.[68] However, the terms of the OCC's post-Enron enforcement action focused only on whether Citibank had a process in place to review the product, and not on the risks of the puts to Citibank's balance sheet.[69]

Besides Citigroup, only a few large financial institutions, such as AIG Financial Products, BNP, WestLB of Germany, and Société Générale of France, wrote significant amounts of liquidity puts on commercial paper issued by CDOs.[70] Bank of America, the biggest commercial bank in the United States, wrote small deals through 2006 but did $6 billion worth in 2007, just before the market crashed.[71] When asked why other market participants were not writing liquidity puts, Dominguez stated that Société Générale and BNP were big players in that market. "You needed to be a bank with a strong balance sheet, access to collateral, and existing relationships with collateral managers," he said.[72]

The CDO desk stopped writing liquidity puts in early 2006,[73] when it reached its internal limits. Citibank's treasury function had set a $23 billion cap on liquidity puts;[74] it granted one final exception, bringing the total to $25 billion.[75] Risk management had also set a $25 billion risk limit on top-rated asset-backed securities, which included the liquidity puts. Later, in an October 2006 memo, Citigroup's Financial Control Group criticized the firm's pricing of the puts, which failed to consider the risk that investors would not buy the commercial paper protected by the liquidity puts when it came due, thereby creating a $25 billion cash demand on Citibank.[76] An undated and unattributed internal document (believed to have been drafted in 2006) also questioned one of the practices of Citigroup's investment bank, which paid traders on its CDO desk for generating the deals without regard to later losses: "There is a potential conflict of interest in pricing the liquidity put cheep [sic] so that more CDO equities can be sold and more structuring fee to be generated."[77] The result would be losses so severe that they would help bring the huge financial conglomerate to the brink of failure, as we will see.

## AIG: "GOLDEN GOOSE FOR THE ENTIRE STREET"

In 2004, American International Group was the largest insurance company in the world as measured by stock market value: a massive conglomerate with $850 billion in assets, 116,000 employees in 130 countries, and 223 subsidiaries.

But to Wall Street, AIG's most valuable asset was its credit rating: that it was awarded the highest possible rating—Aaa by Moody's since 1986, AAA by S&P since

1983—was crucial, because these sterling ratings let it borrow cheaply and deploy the money in lucrative investments. Only six private-sector companies in the United States in early 2010 carried those ratings.[78]

Starting in 1998, AIG Financial Products, a Connecticut-based unit with major operations in London, figured out a new way to make money from those ratings. Relying on the guarantee of its parent, AIG, AIG Financial Products became a major over-the-counter derivatives dealer, eventually having a portfolio of $2.7 trillion in notional amount. Among other derivatives activities, the unit issued credit default swaps guaranteeing debt obligations held by financial institutions and other investors. In exchange for a stream of premium-like payments, AIG Financial Products agreed to reimburse the investor in such a debt obligation in the event of any default. The credit default swap (CDS) is often compared to insurance, but when an insurance company sells a policy, regulations require that it set aside a reserve in case of a loss. Because credit default swaps were not regulated insurance contracts, no such requirement was applicable. In this case, the unit predicted with 99.85% confidence that there would be no realized economic loss on the supposedly safest portions of the CDOs on which they wrote CDS protection, and failed to make any provisions whatsoever for declines in value—or unrealized losses—a decision that would prove fatal to AIG in 2008.[79]

AIG Financial Products had a huge business selling CDS to European banks on a variety of financial assets, including bonds, mortgage-backed securities, CDOs, and other debt securities. For AIG, the fee for selling protection via the swap appeared well worth the risk. For the banks purchasing protection, the swap enabled them to neutralize the credit risk and thereby hold less capital against its assets. Purchasing credit default swaps from AIG could reduce the amount of regulatory capital that the bank needed to hold against an asset from 8% to 1.6%.[80] By 2005, AIG had written $107 billion in CDS for such regulatory capital benefits; most were with European banks for a variety of asset types. That total would rise to $379 billion by 2007.[81]

The same advantages could be enjoyed by banks in the United States, where regulators had introduced similar capital standards for banks' holdings of mortgage-backed securities and other investments under the Recourse Rule in 2001. So a credit default swap with AIG could also lower American banks' capital requirements.

In 2004 and 2005, AIG sold protection on super-senior CDO tranches valued at $54 billion, up from just $2 billion in 2003.[82] In an interview with the FCIC, one AIG executive described AIG Financial Products' principal swap salesman, Alan Frost, as "the golden goose for the entire Street."[83]

AIG's biggest customer in this business was always Goldman Sachs, consistently a leading CDO underwriter. AIG also wrote billions of dollars of protection for Merrill Lynch, Société Générale, and other firms. AIG "looked like the perfect customer for this," Craig Broderick, Goldman's chief risk officer, told the FCIC. "They really ticked all the boxes. They were among the highest-rated [corporations] around. They had what appeared to be unquestioned expertise. They had tremendous financial strength. They had huge, appropriate interest in this space, backed by a long history of trading in it."[84]

AIG also bestowed the imprimatur of its pristine credit rating on commercial paper programs by providing liquidity puts, similar to the ones that Citigroup's bank wrote for many of its own deals, guaranteeing it would buy commercial paper if no one else wanted it. It entered this business in 2002; by 2005, it had written more than $6 billion of liquidity puts on commercial paper issued by CDOs. AIG also wrote more than $7 billion in CDS to protect Société Générale against the risks on liquidity puts that the French bank itself wrote on commercial paper issued by CDOs.[85] "What we would always try to do is to structure a transaction where the transaction was virtually riskless, and get paid a small premium," Gene Park, who was a managing director at AIG Financial Products, told the FCIC. "And we're one of the few guys who can do that. Because if you think about it, no one wants to buy disaster protection from someone who is not going to be around. . . . That was AIGFP's sales pitch to the Street or to banks."[86]

AIG's business of offering credit protection on assets of many sorts, including mortgage-backed securities and CDOs, grew from $20 billion in 2002 to $211 billion in 2005 and $533 billion in 2007.[87] This business was a small part of the AIG Financial Services business unit, which included AIG Financial Products; AIG Financial Services generated operating income of $4.4 billion in 2005, or 29% of AIG's total.

AIG did not post any collateral when it wrote these contracts; but unlike monoline insurers, AIG Financial Products agreed to post collateral if the value of the underlying securities dropped, or if the rating agencies downgraded AIG's long-term debt ratings. Its competitors, the monoline financial guarantors—insurance companies such as MBIA and Ambac that focused on guaranteeing financial contracts— were forbidden under insurance regulations from paying out until actual losses occurred. The collateral posting terms in AIG's credit default swap contracts would have an enormous impact on the crisis about to unfold.

But during the boom, these terms didn't matter. The investors got their triple-A-rated protection, AIG got its fees for providing that insurance—about 0.12% of the notional amount of the swap per year[88]—and the managers got their bonuses. In the case of the London subsidiary that ran the operation, the bonus pool was 30% of new earnings.[89] Financial Products CEO Joseph J. Cassano made the allocations at the end of the year.[90] Between 2002 and 2007, the least amount Cassano paid himself in a year was $38 million. In the later years, his compensation was sometimes double that of the parent company's CEO.[91]

In the spring of 2005, disaster struck: AIG lost its triple-A rating when auditors discovered that it had manipulated earnings. By November 2005, the company had reduced its reported earnings over the five-year period by $3.9 billion.[92] The board forced out Maurice "Hank" Greenberg, who had been CEO for 38 years. New York Attorney General Eliot Spitzer prepared to bring fraud charges against him.

Greenberg told the FCIC, "When the AAA credit rating disappeared in spring 2005, it would have been logical for AIG to have exited or reduced its business of writing credit default swaps."[93] But that didn't happen. Instead, AIG Financial Products wrote another $36 billion in credit default swaps on super-senior tranches of

CDOs in 2005.[94] The company wouldn't make the decision to stop writing these contracts until 2006.[95]

## GOLDMAN SACHS: "MULTIPLIED THE EFFECTS OF THE COLLAPSE IN SUBPRIME"

Henry Paulson, the CEO of Goldman Sachs from 1999 until he became secretary of the Treasury in 2006, testified to the FCIC that by the time he became secretary many bad loans already had been issued—"most of the toothpaste was out of the tube"— and that "there really wasn't the proper regulatory apparatus to deal with it."[96] Paulson provided examples: "Subprime mortgages went from accounting for 5 percent of total mortgages in 1994 to 20 percent by 2006. . . . Securitization separated originators from the risk of the products they originated." The result, Paulson observed, "was a housing bubble that eventually burst in far more spectacular fashion than most previous bubbles."[97]

Under Paulson's leadership, Goldman Sachs had played a central role in the creation and sale of mortgage securities. From 2004 through 2006, the company provided billions of dollars in loans to mortgage lenders; most went to the subprime lenders Ameriquest, Long Beach, Fremont, New Century, and Countrywide through warehouse lines of credit, often in the form of repos.[98] During the same period, Goldman acquired $53 billion of loans from these and other subprime loan originators, which it securitized and sold to investors.[99] From 2004 to 2006, Goldman issued 318 mortgage securitizations totaling $184 billion (about a quarter were subprime), and 63 CDOs totaling $32 billion; Goldman also issued 22 synthetic or hybrid CDOs with a face value of $35 billion between 2004 and June 2006.[100]

Synthetic CDOs were complex paper transactions involving credit default swaps. Unlike the traditional cash CDO, synthetic CDOs contained no actual tranches of mortgage-backed securities, or even tranches of other CDOs. Instead, they simply referenced these mortgage securities and thus were bets on whether borrowers would pay their mortgages. In the place of real mortgage assets, these CDOs contained credit default swaps and did not finance a single home purchase. Investors in these CDOs included "funded" long investors, who paid cash to purchase actual securities issued by the CDO; "unfunded" long investors, who entered into swaps with the CDO, making money if the reference securities performed; and "short" investors, who bought credit default swaps on the reference securities, making money if the securities failed. While funded investors received interest if the reference securities performed, they could lose all of their investment if the reference securities defaulted. Unfunded investors, which were highest in the payment waterfall, received premium-like payments from the CDO as long as the reference securities performed but would have to pay if the reference securities deteriorated beyond a certain point and if the CDO did not have sufficient funds to pay the short investors. Short investors, often hedge funds, bought the credit default swaps from the CDOs and paid those premiums. Hybrid CDOs were a combination of traditional and synthetic CDOs.

Firms like Goldman found synthetic CDOs cheaper and easier to create than tra-

ditional CDOs at the same time as the supply of mortgages was beginning to dry up. Because there were no mortgage assets to collect and finance, creating synthetic CDOs took a fraction of the time. They also were easier to customize, because CDO managers and underwriters could reference any mortgage-backed security—they were not limited to the universe of securities available for them to buy. Figure 8.2 provides an example of how such a deal worked.

In 2004, Goldman launched its first major synthetic CDO, Abacus 2004-1—a deal worth $2 billion. About one-third of the swaps referenced residential mortgage-backed securities, another third referenced existing CDOs, and the rest, commercial mortgage–backed securities (made up of bundled commercial real estate loans) and other securities.

Goldman was the short investor for the entire $2 billion deal: it purchased credit default swap protection on these reference securities from the CDO. The funded investors—IKB (a German bank), the TCW Group, and Wachovia—put up a total of $195 million to purchase mezzanine tranches of the deal.[101] These investors would receive scheduled principal and interest payments if the referenced assets performed. If the referenced assets did not perform, Goldman, as the short investor, would receive the $195 million.[102] In this sense, IKB, TCW, and Wachovia were "long" investors, betting that the referenced assets would perform well, and Goldman was a "short" investor, betting that they would fail.

The unfunded investors—TCW and GSC Partners (asset management firms that managed both hedge funds and CDOs)—did not put up any money up front; they received annual premiums from the CDO in return for the promise that they would pay the CDO if the reference securities failed and the CDO did not have enough funds to pay the short investors.[103]

Goldman was the largest unfunded investor at the time that the deal was originated, retaining the $1.8 billion super-senior tranche. Goldman's $2 billion short position more than offset that exposure; about one year later, it transferred the unfunded long position by buying credit protection from AIG, in return for an annual payment of $2.2 million.[104] As a result, by 2005, AIG was effectively the largest unfunded investor in the super-senior tranches of the Abacus deal.

All told, long investors in Abacus 2004-1 stood to receive millions of dollars if the reference securities performed (just as a bond investor makes money when a bond performs). On the other hand, Goldman stood to gain nearly $2 billion if the assets failed.

In the end, Goldman, the short investor in the Abacus 2004-1 CDO, has received about $930 million while the long investors have lost just about all of their investments. In April 2008, GSC paid Goldman $7.3 million as a result of CDS protection sold by GSC to Goldman on the first and second loss tranches. In June 2009, Goldman received $806 million from AIG Financial Products as a result of the CDS protection it had purchased against the super-senior tranche. The same month it received $23 million from TCW as a result of the CDS purchased against the junior mezzanine tranches, and $30 million from IKB because of the CDS it purchased against the C tranche. In April 2010, IKB paid Goldman another $40 million as a result of the CDS against the B tranche.

# Synthetic CDO

*Synthetic CDOs, such as Goldman Sachs's Abacus 2004-1 deal, were complex paper transactions involving credit default swaps.*

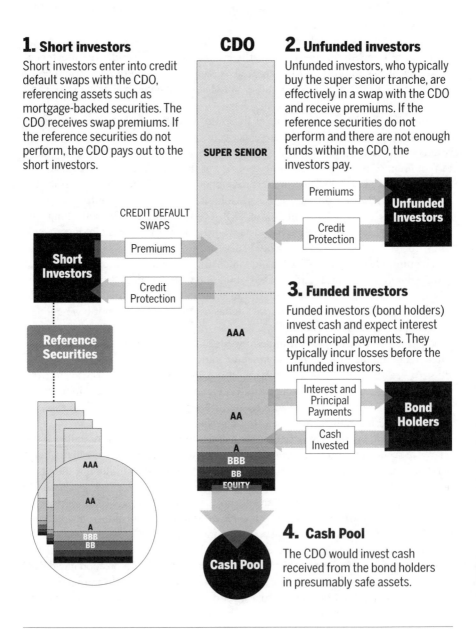

### 1. Short investors

Short investors enter into credit default swaps with the CDO, referencing assets such as mortgage-backed securities. The CDO receives swap premiums. If the reference securities do not perform, the CDO pays out to the short investors.

### 2. Unfunded investors

Unfunded investors, who typically buy the super senior tranche, are effectively in a swap with the CDO and receive premiums. If the reference securities do not perform and there are not enough funds within the CDO, the investors pay.

### 3. Funded investors

Funded investors (bond holders) invest cash and expect interest and principal payments. They typically incur losses before the unfunded investors.

### 4. Cash Pool

The CDO would invest cash received from the bond holders in presumably safe assets.

*Figure 8.2*

Through May 2010, Goldman received $24 million from IKB, Wachovia, and TCW as a result of the credit default swaps against the A tranche. As was common, some of the tranches of Abacus 2004-1 found their way into other funds and CDOs; for example, TCW put tranches of Abacus 2004-1 into three of its own CDOs.

In total, between July 1, 2004, and May 31, 2007, Goldman packaged and sold 47 synthetic CDOs, with an aggregate face value of $66 billion.[105] Its underwriting fee was 0.50% to 1.50% of the deal totals, Dan Sparks, the former head of Goldman's mortgage desk, told the FCIC.[106] Goldman would earn profits from shorting many of these deals; on others, it would profit by facilitating the transaction between the buyer and the seller of credit default swap protection.

As we will see, these new instruments would yield substantial profits for investors that held a short position in the synthetic CDOs—that is, investors betting that the housing boom was a bubble about to burst. They also would multiply losses when housing prices collapsed. When borrowers defaulted on their mortgages, the investors expecting cash from the mortgage payments lost. And investors betting on these mortgage-backed securities via synthetic CDOs also lost (while those betting against the mortgages would gain).[107] As a result, the losses from the housing collapse were multiplied exponentially.

To see this play out, we can return to our illustrative Citigroup mortgage-backed securities deal, CMLTI 2006-NC2. Credit default swaps made it possible for new market participants to bet for or against the performance of these securities. Synthetic CDOs significantly increased the demand for such bets. For example, there were about $12 million worth of bonds in the M9 (BBB-rated) tranche—one of the mezzanine tranches of the security. Synthetic CDOs such as Auriga, Volans, and Neptune CDO IV all contained credit default swaps in which the M9 tranche was referenced. As long as the M9 bonds performed, investors betting that the tranche would fail (short investors) would make regular payments into the CDO, which would be paid out to other investors banking on it to succeed (long investors). If the M9 bonds defaulted, then the long investors would make large payments to the short investors. That is the bet—and there were more than $50 million in such bets in early 2007 on the M9 tranche of this deal. Thus, on the basis of the performance of $12 million in bonds, more than $60 million could potentially change hands. Goldman's Sparks put it succinctly to the FCIC: if there's a problem with a product, synthetics increase the impact.[108]

The amplification of the M9 tranche was not unique. A $15 million tranche of the Glacier Funding CDO 2006-4A, rated A, was referenced in $85 million worth of synthetic CDOs. A $28 million tranche of the Soundview Home Equity Loan Trust 2006-EQ1, also rated A, was referenced in $79 million worth of synthetic CDOs. A $13 million tranche of the Soundview Home Equity Loan Trust 2006-EQ1, rated BBB, was referenced in $49 million worth of synthetic CDOs.[109]

In total, synthetic CDOs created by Goldman referenced 3,408 mortgage securities, some of them multiple times. For example, 610 securities were referenced twice. Indeed, one single mortgage-backed security was referenced in nine different synthetic

CDOs created by Goldman Sachs.[110] Because of such deals, when the housing bubble burst, billions of dollars changed hands.

Although Goldman executives agreed that synthetic CDOs were "bets" that magnified overall risk, they also maintained that their creation had "social utility" because it added liquidity to the market and enabled investors to customize the exposures they wanted in their portfolios.[111] In testimony before the Commission, Goldman's President and Chief Operating Officer Gary Cohn argued: "This is no different than the tens of thousands of swaps written every day on the U.S. dollar versus another currency. Or, more importantly, on U.S. Treasuries . . . This is the way that the financial markets work."[112]

Others, however, criticized these deals. Patrick Parkinson, the current director of the Division of Banking Supervision and Regulation at the Federal Reserve Board, noted that synthetic CDOs "multiplied the effects of the collapse in subprime."[113] Other observers were even harsher in their assessment. "I don't think they have social value," Michael Greenberger, a professor at the University of Maryland School of Law and former director of the Division of Trading and Markets at the Commodity Futures Trading Commission, told the FCIC. He characterized the credit default swap market as a "casino." And he testified that "the concept of lawful betting of billions of dollars on the question of whether a homeowner would default on a mortgage that was not owned by either party, has had a profound effect on the American public and taxpayers."[114]

## MOODY'S: "ACHIEVED THROUGH SOME ALCHEMY"

The machine churning out CDOs would not have worked without the stamp of approval given to these deals by the three leading rating agencies: Moody's, S&P, and Fitch. Investors often relied on the rating agencies' views rather than conduct their own credit analysis. Moody's was paid according to the size of each deal, with caps set at a half-million dollars for a "standard" CDO in 2006 and 2007 and as much as $850,000 for a "complex" CDO.[115]

In rating both synthetic and cash CDOs, Moody's faced two key challenges: first, estimating the probability of default for the mortgage-backed securities purchased by the CDO (or its synthetic equivalent) and, second, gauging the correlation between those defaults—that is, the likelihood that the securities would default at the same time.[116] Imagine flipping a coin to see how many times it comes up heads. Each flip is unrelated to the others; that is, the flips are uncorrelated. Now, imagine a loaf of sliced bread. When there is one moldy slice, there are likely other moldy slices. The freshness of each slice is highly correlated with that of the other slices. As investors now understand, the mortgage-backed securities in CDOs were less like coins than like slices of bread.

To estimate the probability of default, Moody's relied almost exclusively on its own ratings of the mortgage-backed securities purchased by the CDOs.[117] At no time did the agencies "look through" the securities to the underlying subprime mortgages. "We took the rating that had already been assigned by the [mortgage-backed securi-

ties] group," Gary Witt, formerly one of Moody's team managing directors for the CDO unit, told the FCIC. This approach would lead to problems for Moody's—and for investors. Witt testified that the underlying collateral "just completely disintegrated below us and we didn't react and we should have. . . . We had to be looking for a problem. And we weren't looking."[118]

To determine the likelihood that any given security in the CDO would default, Moody's plugged in assumptions based on those original ratings. This was no simple task. Meanwhile, if the initial ratings turned out—owing to poor underwriting, fraud, or any other cause—to poorly reflect the quality of the mortgages in the bonds, the error was blindly compounded when mortgage-backed securities were packaged into CDOs.

Even more difficult was the estimation of the default correlation between the securities in the portfolio—always tricky, but particularly so in the case of CDOs consisting of subprime and Alt-A mortgage-backed securities that had only a short performance history. So the firm explicitly relied on the judgment of its analysts. "In the absence of meaningful default data, it is impossible to develop empirical default correlation measures based on actual observations of defaults," Moody's acknowledged in one early explanation of its process.[119]

In plainer English, Witt said, Moody's didn't have a good model on which to estimate correlations between mortgage-backed securities—so they "made them up." He recalled, "They went to the analyst in each of the groups and they said, 'Well, you know, how related do you think these types of [mortgage-backed securities] are?'"[120] This problem would become more serious with the rise of CDOs in the middle of the decade. Witt felt strongly that Moody's needed to update its CDO rating model to explicitly address the increasing concentration of risky mortgage-related securities in the collateral underlying CDOs.[121] He undertook two initiatives to address this issue. First, in mid-2004, he developed a new rating methodology that directly incorporated correlation into the model. However, the technique he devised was not applied to CDO ratings for another year.[122] Second, he proposed a research initiative in early 2005 to "look through" a few CDO deals at the level of the underlying mortgage-backed securities and to see if "the assumptions that we're making for AAA CDOs are consistent . . . with the correlation assumptions that we're making for AAA [mortgage-backed securities]." Although Witt received approval from his superiors for this investigation, contractual disagreements prevented him from buying the software he needed to conduct the look-through analysis.[123]

In June 2005, Moody's updated its approach for estimating default correlation, but it based the new model on trends from the previous 20 years, a period when housing prices were rising and mortgage delinquencies were very low—and a period in which nontraditional mortgage products had been a very small niche. Then, Moody's modified this optimistic set of "empirical" assumptions with ad hoc adjustments based on factors such as region, year of origination, and servicer. For example, if two mortgage-backed securities were issued in the same region—say, Southern California— Moody's boosted the correlation; if they shared a common mortgage servicer, Moody's boosted it further. But at the same time, it would make other technical

choices that lowered the estimated correlation of default, which would improve the ratings for these securities. Using these methods, Moody's estimated that two mortgage-backed securities would be less closely correlated than two securities backed by other consumer credit assets, such as credit card or auto loans.[124]

The other major rating agencies followed a similar approach.[125] Academics, including some who worked at regulatory agencies, cautioned investors that assumption-heavy CDO credit ratings could be dangerous. "The complexity of structured finance transactions may lead to situations where investors tend to rely more heavily on ratings than for other types of rated securities. On this basis, the transformation of risk involved in structured finance gives rise to a number of questions with important potential implications. One such question is whether tranched instruments might result in unanticipated concentrations of risk in institutions' portfolios," a report from the Bank for International Settlements, an international financial organization sponsored by the world's regulators and central banks, warned in June 2005.[126]

CDO managers and underwriters relied on the ratings to promote the bonds. For each new CDO, they created marketing material, including a pitch book that investors used to decide whether to subscribe to a new CDO. Each book described the types of assets that would make up the portfolio without providing details.[127] Without exception, every pitch book examined by the FCIC staff cited an analysis from either Moody's or S&P that contrasted the historical "stability" of these new products' ratings with the stability of corporate bonds. Statistics that made this case included the fact that between 1983 and 2006, 92% of these new products did not experience any rating changes over a twelve-month period while only 78% of corporate bonds maintained their ratings. Over a longer time period, however, structured finance ratings were not so stable. Between 1983 and 2006, only 56% of triple-A-rated structured finance securities retained their original rating after five years.[128] Underwriters continued to sell CDOs using these statistics in their pitch books during 2006 and 2007, after mortgage defaults had started to rise but before the rating agencies had downgraded large numbers of mortgage-backed securities. Of course, each pitch book did include the disclaimer that "past performance is not a guarantee of future performance" and encouraged investors to perform their own due diligence.

As Kyle Bass of Dallas-based Hayman Capital Advisors testified before the House Financial Services Committee, CDOs that purchased lower-rated tranches of mortgage-backed securities "are arcane structured finance products that were designed specifically to make dangerous, lowly rated tranches of subprime debt deceptively attractive to investors. This was achieved through some alchemy and some negligence in adapting unrealistic correlation assumptions on behalf of the ratings agencies. They convinced investors that 80% of a collection of toxic subprime tranches were the ratings equivalent of U.S. Government bonds."[129]

When housing prices started to fall nationwide and defaults increased, it turned out that the mortgage-backed securities were in fact much more highly correlated than the rating agencies had estimated—that is, they stopped performing at roughly the same time. These losses led to massive downgrades in the ratings of the CDOs. In 2007, 20% of U.S. CDO securities would be downgraded. In 2008, 91% would.[130]

In late 2008, Moody's would throw out its key CDO assumptions and replace them with an asset correlation assumption two to three times higher than used before the crisis.[131]

In retrospect, it is clear that the agencies' CDO models made two key mistakes. First, they assumed that securitizers could create safer financial products by diversifying among many mortgage-backed securities, when in fact these securities weren't that different to begin with. "There were a lot of things [the credit rating agencies] did wrong," Federal Reserve Chairman Ben Bernanke told the FCIC. "They did not take into account the appropriate correlation between [and] across the categories of mortgages."[132]

Second, the agencies based their CDO ratings on ratings they themselves had assigned on the underlying collateral. "The danger with CDOs is when they are based on structured finance ratings," Ann Rutledge, a structured finance expert, told the FCIC. "Ratings are not predictive of future defaults; they only describe a ratings management process, and a mean and static expectation of security loss."[133]

Of course, rating CDOs was a profitable business for the rating agencies. Including all types of CDOs—not just those that were mortgage-related—Moody's rated 220 deals in 2004, 363 in 2005, 749 in 2006, and 717 in 2007; the value of those deals rose from $90 billion in 2004 to $162 billion in 2005, $337 billion in 2006, and $326 billion in 2007.[134] The reported revenues of Moody's Investors Service from structured products—which included mortgage-backed securities and CDOs—grew from $199 million in 2000, or 33% of Moody's Corporation's revenues, to $887 million in 2006 or 44% of overall corporate revenue. The rating of asset-backed CDOs alone contributed more than 10% of the revenue from structured finance.[135] The boom years of structured finance coincided with a company-wide surge in revenue and profits. From 2000 to 2006, the corporation's revenues surged from $602 million to $2 billion and its profit margin climbed from 26% to 37%.

Yet the increase in the CDO group's workload and revenue was not paralleled by a staffing increase. "We were under-resourced, you know, we were always playing catch-up," Witt said.[136] Moody's "penny-pinching" and "stingy" management was reluctant to pay up for experienced employees. "The problem of recruiting and retaining good staff was insoluble. Investment banks often hired away our best people. As far as I can remember, we were never allocated funds to make counter offers," Witt said. "We had almost no ability to do meaningful research."[137] Eric Kolchinsky, a former team managing director at Moody's, told the FCIC that from 2004 to 2006, the increase in the number of deals rated was "huge . . . but our personnel did not go up accordingly." By 2006, Kolchinsky recalled, "My role as a team leader was crisis management. Each deal was a crisis."[138] When personnel worked to create a new methodology, Witt said, "We had to kind of do it in our spare time."[139]

The agencies worked closely with CDO underwriters and managers as each new CDO was devised. And the rating agencies now relied for a substantial amount of their revenues on a small number of players. Citigroup and Merrill alone accounted for more than $140 billion of CDO deals between 2005 and 2007.[140]

The ratings agencies' correlation assumptions had a direct and critical impact on

how CDOs were structured: assumptions of a lower correlation made possible larger easy-to-sell triple-A tranches and smaller harder-to-sell BBB tranches. Thus, as is discussed later, underwriters crafted the structure to earn more favorable ratings from the agencies—for example, by increasing the size of the senior tranches. Moreover, because issuers could choose which rating agencies to do business with, and because the agencies depended on the issuers for their revenues, rating agencies felt pressured to give favorable ratings so that they might remain competitive.

The pressure on rating agency employees was also intense as a result of the high turnover—a revolving door that often left raters dealing with their old colleagues, this time as clients. In her interview with FCIC staff, Yuri Yoshizawa, a Moody's team managing director for U.S. derivatives in 2005, was presented with an organization chart from July 2005. She identified 13 out of 51 analysts—about 25% of the staff—who had left Moody's to work for investment or commercial banks.[141]

Brian Clarkson, who oversaw the structured finance group before becoming the president of Moody's Investors Service, explained to FCIC investigators that retaining employees was always a challenge, for the simple reason that the banks paid more. As a precaution, Moody's employees were prohibited from rating deals by a bank or issuer while they were interviewing for a job with that particular institution, but the responsibility for notifying management of the interview rested on the employee. After leaving Moody's, former employees were barred from interacting with Moody's on the same series of deals they had rated while in its employ, but there were no bans against working on other deals with Moody's.[142]

## SEC: "IT'S GOING TO BE AN AWFULLY BIG MESS"

The five major U.S. investment banks expanded their involvement in the mortgage and mortgage securities industries in the early 21st century with little formal government regulation beyond their broker-dealer subsidiaries. In 2002, the European Union told U.S. financial firms that to continue to do business in Europe, they would need a "consolidated" supervisor by 2004—that is, one regulator that had responsibility for the holding company. The U.S. commercial banks already met that criterion—their consolidated supervisor was the Federal Reserve—and the Office of Thrift Supervision's oversight of AIG would later also satisfy the Europeans. The five investment banks, however, did not meet the standard: the SEC was supervising their securities arms, but no one supervisor kept track of these companies on a consolidated basis. Thus all five faced an important decision: what agency would they prefer as their regulator?

By 2004, the combined assets at the five firms totaled $2.5 trillion, more than half of the $4.7 trillion of assets held by the five largest U.S. bank holding companies. In the next three years the investment banks' assets would grow to $4.3 trillion. Goldman Sachs was the largest, followed by Morgan Stanley and Merrill, then Lehman and Bear. These large, diverse international firms had transformed their business models over the years. For their revenues they relied increasingly on trading and OTC derivatives

dealing, investments, securitization, and similar activities on top of their traditional investment banking functions. Recall that at Bear Stearns, trading and investments accounted for more than 100% of pretax earnings in some years after 2002.

The investment banks also owned depository institutions through which they could provide FDIC-insured accounts to their brokerage customers; the deposits provided cheap but limited funding. These depositories took the form of a thrift (supervised by the OTS) or an industrial loan company (supervised by the Federal Deposit Insurance Corporation and a state supervisor). Merrill and Lehman, which had among the largest of these subsidiaries, used them to finance their mortgage origination activities.

The investment banks' possession of depository subsidiaries suggested two obvious choices when they found themselves in need of a consolidated supervisor. If a firm chartered its depository as a commercial bank, the Fed would be its holding company supervisor; if as a thrift, the OTS would do the job. But the investment banks came up with a third option. They lobbied the SEC to devise a system of regulation that would satisfy the terms of the European directive and keep them from European oversight[143]—and the SEC was willing to step in, although its historical focus was on investor protection.

In November 2003, almost a year after the Europeans made their announcement, the SEC suggested the creation of the Consolidated Supervised Entity (CSE) program to oversee the holding companies of investment banks and all their subsidiaries. The CSE program was open only to investment banks that had large U.S. broker-dealer subsidiaries already subject to SEC regulation. However, this was the SEC's first foray into supervising firms for safety and soundness. The SEC did not have express legislative authority to require the investment banks to submit to consolidated regulation, so it proposed that the CSE program be voluntary; the SEC crafted the new program out of its authority to make rules for the broker-dealer subsidiaries of investment banks. The program would apply to broker-dealers that volunteered to be subject to consolidated supervision under the CSE program, or those that already were subject to supervision by the Fed at the holding company level, such as JP Morgan and Citigroup. The CSE program would introduce a limited form of supervision by SEC examiners. CSE firms were allowed to use a new methodology to calculate the regulatory capital that they were holding against their securities portfolios—a methodology based on the volatility of market prices. This methodology, referred to as the "alternative net capital rule," would be similar to the standards—based on the 1996 Market Risk Amendment to the Basel rules—that large commercial banks and bank holding companies used for their securities portfolios.

The traditional net capital rule that had governed broker-dealers since 1975 had required straightforward calculations based on asset classes and credit ratings, a bright-line approach that gave firms little discretion in calculating their capital. The new rules would allow the investment banks to create their own proprietary Value at Risk (VaR) models to calculate their regulatory capital—that is, the capital each firm would have to hold to protect its customers' assets should it experience losses on its

securities and derivatives. All in all, the SEC estimated that the proposed new re-liance on proprietary VaR models would allow broker-dealers to reduce average cap-ital charges by 40%. The firms would be required to give the SEC an early-warning notice if their tentative net capital (net capital minus hard-to-sell assets) fell below $5 billion at any time.

Meanwhile, the OTS was already supervising the thrifts owned by several securi-ties firms and argued that it therefore was the natural supervisor of their holding companies. In a letter to the SEC, the OTS was harshly critical of the agency's pro-posal, which it said had "the potential to duplicate or conflict with OTS's supervisory responsibilities" over savings and loan holding companies that would also be CSEs. The OTS argued that the SEC was interfering with the intentions of Congress, which, in the Gramm-Leach-Bliley Act, "carefully kept the responsibility for supervision of the holding company itself with the OTS or the Federal Reserve Board, depending upon whether the holding company was a [thrift holding company] or a bank hold-ing company. This was in recognition of the expertise developed over the years by these regulators in evaluating the risks posed to depository institutions and the fed-eral deposit insurance funds by depository institution holding companies and their affiliates." The OTS declared: "We believe that the SEC's proposed assertion of au-thority over [savings and loan holding companies] is unfounded and could pose sig-nificant risks to these entities, their insured deposit institution subsidiaries and the federal deposit insurance funds."[144]

In contrast, the response from the financial services industry to the SEC proposal was overwhelmingly positive, particularly with regard to the alternative net capital computation. Lehman Brothers, for example, wrote that it "applauds and supports the Commission." JP Morgan was supportive of what it saw as an improvement over the old net capital rule that still governed securities subsidiaries of the commercial banks: "The existing capital rule overstates the amount of capital a broker-dealer needs," the company wrote. Deutsche Bank found it to be "a great stride towards con-sistency with modern comprehensive risk management practices."[145] In FCIC inter-views, SEC officials and executives at the investment banks stated that the firms preferred the SEC because it was more familiar with their core securities-related businesses.

In an April 2004 meeting, SEC commissioners voted to adopt the CSE program and the new net capital calculations that went along with it. Over the following year and a half, the five largest investment banks volunteered for this supervision, al-though Merrill's and Lehman's thrifts continued to be supervised by the OTS. Several firms delayed entry to the program in order to develop systems that could measure their exposures to market price movements.

Harvey Goldschmid, SEC commissioner from 2002 to 2005, told FCIC staff that before the CSE program was created, SEC staff members were concerned about how little authority they had over the Wall Street firms, including their hedge funds and overseas subsidiaries. Once the CSE program was in place, the SEC had "the author-ity to look at everything."[146] SEC commissioners discussed at the time the risks they were taking by allowing firms to reduce their capital. "If anything goes wrong it's go-

ing to be an awfully big mess," Goldschmid said at a 2004 meeting. "Do we feel secure if these drops in capital and other things [occur] we really will have investor protection?" In response, Annette Nazareth, the SEC official who would be in charge of the program, assured the commissioners that her division was up to the challenge.[147]

The new program was housed primarily in the SEC's Office of Prudential Supervision and Risk Analysis, an office with a staff of 10 to 12 within the Division of Market Regulation.[148] In the beginning, it was supported by the SEC's much larger examination staff; by 2008 the staff dedicated to the CSE program had grown to 24.[149] Still, only 10 "monitors" were responsible for the five investment banks; 3 monitors were assigned to each firm, with some overlap.[150]

The CSE program was based on the bank supervision model, but the SEC did not try to do exactly what bank examiners did.[151] For one thing, unlike supervisors of large banks, the SEC never assigned on-site examiners under the CSE program; by comparison, the OCC alone assigned more than 60 examiners full-time at Citibank. According to Erik Sirri, the SEC's former director of trading and markets, the CSE program was intended to focus mainly on liquidity because, unlike a commercial bank, a securities firm traditionally had no access to a lender of last resort.[152] (Of course, that would change during the crisis.) The investment banks were subject to annual examinations, during which staff reviewed the firms' systems and records and verified that the firms had instituted control processes.

The CSE program was troubled from the start. The SEC conducted an exam for each investment bank when it entered the program. The result of Bear Stearns's entrance exam, in 2005, showed several deficiencies. For example, examiners were concerned that there were no firmwide VaR limits and that contingency funding plans relied on overly optimistic stress scenarios.[153] In addition, the SEC was aware of the firm's concentration of mortgage securities and its high leverage. Nonetheless, the SEC did not ask Bear to change its asset balance, decrease its leverage, or increase its cash liquidity pool—all actions well within its prerogative, according to SEC officials.[154] Then, because the CSE program was preoccupied with its own staff reorganization, Bear did not have its next annual exam, during which the SEC was supposed to be on-site. The SEC did meet monthly with all CSE firms, including Bear,[155] and it did conduct occasional targeted examinations across firms. In 2006, the SEC worried that Bear was too reliant on unsecured commercial paper funding, and Bear reduced its exposure to unsecured commercial paper and increased its reliance on secured repo lending.[156] Unfortunately, tens of billions of dollars of that repo lending was overnight funding that could disappear with no warning. Ironically, in the second week of March 2008, when the firm went into its four-day death spiral, the SEC was on-site conducting its first CSE exam since Bear's entrance exam more than two years earlier.[157]

Leverage at the investment banks increased from 2004 to 2007, growth that some critics have blamed on the SEC's change in the net capital rules. Goldschmid told the FCIC that the increase was owed to "a wild capital time and the firms being irresponsible."[158] In fact, leverage had been higher at the five investment banks in the late 1990s, then dropped before increasing over the life of the CSE program—a history

that suggests that the program was not solely responsible for the changes.[159] In 2009, Sirri noted that under the CSE program the investment banks' net capital levels "remained relatively stable . . . and, in some cases, increased significantly" over the program.[160] Still, Goldschmid, who left the SEC in 2005, argued that the SEC had the power to do more to rein in the investment banks. He insisted, "There was much more than enough moral suasion and kind of practical power that was involved. . . . The SEC has the practical ability to do a lot if it uses its power."[161]

Overall, the CSE program was widely viewed as a failure. From 2004 until the financial crisis, all five investment banks continued their spectacular growth, relying heavily on short-term funding. Former SEC chairman Christopher Cox called the CSE supervisory program "fundamentally flawed from the beginning."[162] Mary Schapiro, the current SEC chairman, concluded that the program "was not successful in providing prudential supervision."[163] And, as we will see in the chapters ahead, the SEC's inspector general would be quite critical, too. In September 2008, in the midst of the financial crisis, the CSE program was discontinued after all five of the largest independent investment banks had either closed down (Lehman Brothers), merged into other entities (Bear Stearns and Merrill Lynch), or converted to bank holding companies to be supervised by the Federal Reserve (Goldman Sachs and Morgan Stanley).

For the Fed, there would be a certain irony in that last development concerning Goldman and Morgan Stanley. Fed officials had seen their agency's regulatory purview shrinking over the course of the decade, as JP Morgan switched the charter of its banking subsidiary to the OCC[164] and as the OTS and SEC promoted their alternatives for consolidated supervision. "The OTS and SEC were very aggressive in trying to promote themselves as a regulator in that environment and wanted to be the consolidated supervisor . . . to meet the requirements in Europe for a consolidated supervisor," said Mark Olson, a Fed governor from 2001 to 2006. "There was a lot of competitiveness among the regulators."[165] In January 2008, Fed staff had prepared an internal study to find out why none of the investment banks had chosen the Fed as its consolidated supervisor. The staff interviewed five firms that already were supervised by the Fed and four that had chosen the SEC. According to the report, the biggest reason firms opted not to be supervised by the Fed was the "comprehensiveness" of the Fed's supervisory approach, "particularly when compared to alternatives such as Office of Thrift Supervision (OTS) or Securities & Exchange Commission (SEC) holding company supervision."[166]

## COMMISSION CONCLUSIONS ON CHAPTER 8

The Commission concludes declining demand for riskier portions (or tranches) of mortgage-related securities led to the creation of an enormous volume of collateralized debt obligations (CDOs). These CDOs—composed of the riskier tranches—fueled demand for nonprime mortgage securitization and contributed to the housing bubble. Certain products also played an important role in doing so, including CDOs squared, credit default swaps, synthetic CDOs, and asset-backed commercial paper programs that invested in mortgage-backed securities and CDOs. Many of these risky assets ended up on the balance sheets of systemically important institutions and contributed to their failure or near failure in the financial crisis.

Credit default swaps, sold to provide protection against default to purchasers of the top-rated tranches of CDOs, facilitated the sale of those tranches by convincing investors of their low risk, but greatly increased the exposure of the sellers of the credit default swap protection to the housing bubble's collapse.

Synthetic CDOs, which consisted in whole or in part of credit default swaps, enabled securitization to continue and expand even as the mortgage market dried up and provided speculators with a means of betting on the housing market. By layering on correlated risk, they spread and amplified exposure to losses when the housing market collapsed.

The high ratings erroneously given CDOs by credit rating agencies encouraged investors and financial institutions to purchase them and enabled the continuing securitization of nonprime mortgages. There was a clear failure of corporate governance at Moody's, which did not ensure the quality of its ratings on tens of thousands of mortgage-backed securities and CDOs.

The Securities and Exchange Commission's poor oversight of the five largest investment banks failed to restrict their risky activities and did not require them to hold adequate capital and liquidity for their activities, contributing to the failure or need for government bailouts of all five of the supervised investment banks during the financial crisis.

# 9

# ALL IN

## CONTENTS

In 2003, the Bakersfield, California, homebuilder Warren Peterson was paying as little as $35,000 for a 10,000-square-foot lot, about the size of three tennis courts. The next year the cost more than tripled to $120,000, as real estate boomed. Over the previous quarter century, Peterson had built between 3 and 10 custom and semi-custom homes a year. For a while, he was building as many as 30. And then came the crash.

"I have built exactly one new home since late 2005," he told the FCIC five years later.[1]

In 2003, the average price was $155,000 for a new house in Bakersfield, at the southern end of California's agricultural center, the San Joaquin Valley. That jumped to almost $300,000 by June 2006.[2] "By 2004, money seemed to be coming in very fast and from everywhere," said Lloyd Plank, a Bakersfield real estate broker. "They would purchase a house in Bakersfield, keep it for a short period and resell it. Sometimes they would flip the house while it was still in escrow, and would still make 20% to 30%."[3]

Nationally, housing prices jumped 152% between 1997 and their peak in 2006,[4] more than in any decade since at least 1920.[5] It would be catastrophically downhill from there—yet the mortgage machine kept churning well into 2007, apparently indifferent to the fact that housing prices were starting to fall and lending standards to deteriorate. Newspaper stories highlighted the weakness in the housing market—even suggesting this was a bubble that could burst anytime. Checks were in place, but

they were failing. Loan purchasers and securitizers ignored their own due diligence on what they were buying. The Federal Reserve and the other regulators increasingly recognized the impending troubles in housing but thought their impact would be contained. Increased securitization, lower underwriting standards, and easier access to credit were common in other markets, too. For example, credit was flowing into commercial real estate and corporate loans. How to react to what increasingly appeared to be a credit bubble? Many enterprises, such as Lehman Brothers and Fannie Mae, pushed deeper.

All along the assembly line, from the origination of the mortgages to the creation and marketing of the mortgage-backed securities and collateralized debt obligations (CDOs), many understood and the regulators at least suspected that every cog was reliant on the mortgages themselves, which would not perform as advertised.

## THE BUBBLE: "A CREDIT-INDUCED BOOM"

Irvine, California–based New Century—once the nation's second-largest subprime lender—ignored early warnings that its own loan quality was deteriorating and stripped power from two risk-control departments that had noted the evidence. In a June 2004 presentation, the Quality Assurance staff reported they had found severe underwriting errors, including evidence of predatory lending, legal and state violations, and credit issues, in 25% of the loans they audited in November and December 2003. In 2004, Chief Operating Officer and later CEO Brad Morrice recommended these results be removed from the statistical tools used to track loan performance, and in 2005, the department was dissolved and its personnel terminated. The same year, the Internal Audit department identified numerous deficiencies in loan files; out of nine reviews it conducted in 2005, it gave the company's loan production department "unsatisfactory" ratings seven times. Patrick Flanagan, president of New Century's mortgage-originating subsidiary, cut the department's budget, saying in a memo that the "group was out of control and tries to dictate business practices instead of audit."[6]

This happened as the company struggled with increasing requests that it buy back soured loans from investors. By December 2006, almost 17% of its loans were going into default within the first three months after origination. "New Century had a brazen obsession with increasing loan originations, without due regard to the risks associated with that business strategy," New Century's bankruptcy examiner reported.[7]

In September 2005—seven months before the housing market peaked—thousands of originators, securitizers, and investors met at the ABS East 2005 conference in Boca Raton, Florida, to play golf, do deals, and talk about the market. The asset-backed security business was still good, but even the most optimistic could read the signs. Panelists had three concerns: Were housing prices overheated, or just driven by "fundamentals" such as increased demand? Would rising interest rates halt the

market? And was the CDO, because of its ratings-driven investors, distorting the mortgage market?[8]

The numbers were stark. Nationwide, house prices had never risen so far, so fast. And national indices masked important variations. House prices in the four sand states, especially California, had dramatically larger spikes—and subsequent declines—than did the nation. If there was a bubble, perhaps, as Fed Chairman Alan Greenspan said, it was only in certain regions. He told a congressional committee in June 2005 that growth in nonprime mortgages was helping to push home prices in some markets to unsustainable levels, "although a 'bubble' in home prices for the nation as a whole does not appear likely."[9]

Globally, prices jumped in many countries around the world during the 2000s. As Christopher Mayer, an economist from Columbia Business School, noted to the Commission, "What really sticks out is how unremarkable the United States house price experience is relative to our European peers."[10] From 1997 to 2007, price increases in the United Kingdom and Spain were above those in the United States, while price increases in Ireland and France were just below. In an International Monetary Fund study from 2009, more than one half of the 21 developed countries analyzed had greater home price appreciation than the United States from late 2001 through the third quarter of 2006, and yet some of these countries did not suffer sharp price declines.[11] Notably, Canada had strong home price increases followed by a modest and temporary decline in 2009. Researchers at the Federal Reserve Bank of Cleveland attributed Canada's experience to tighter lending standards than in the United States as well as regulatory and structural differences in the financial system.[12] Other countries, such as the United Kingdom, Ireland, and Spain, saw steep house price declines.

American economists and policy makers struggled to explain the house price increases. The good news was the economy was growing and unemployment was low. But, a Federal Reserve study in May 2005 presented evidence that the cost of owning rather than renting was much higher than had been the case historically: home prices had risen from 20 times the annual cost of renting to 25 times.[13] In some cities, the change was particularly dramatic. From 1997 to 2006, the ratio of house prices to rents rose in Los Angeles, Miami, and New York City by 147%, 121%, and 98%, respectively.[14] In 2006, the National Association of Realtors' affordability index—which measures whether a typical family could qualify for a mortgage on a typical home—had reached a record low.[15] But that was based on the cost of a traditional mortgage with a 20% down payment,[16] which was no longer required. Perhaps such measures were no longer relevant, when Americans could make lower down payments and obtain loans such as payment-option adjustable-rate mortgages and interest-only mortgages, with reduced initial mortgage payments. Or perhaps buying a home continued to make financial sense, given homeowners' expectations of further price gains.

During a June meeting, the Federal Open Market Committee (FOMC), composed of Federal Reserve governors, four regional Federal Reserve Bank presidents, and the Federal Reserve Bank of New York president, heard five presentations on

mortgage risks and the housing market. Members and staff had difficulty developing a consensus on whether housing prices were overvalued and "it was hard for many FOMC participants . . . to ascribe substantial conviction to the proposition that overvaluation in the housing market posed the major systemic risks that we now know it did," according to a letter from Fed Chairman Ben Bernanke to the FCIC. "The national mortgage system might bend but will likely not break," and "neither borrowers nor lenders appeared particularly shaky," one presentation argued, according to the letter. In discussions about nontraditional mortgage products, the argument was made that "interest-only mortgages are not an especially sinister development," and their risks "could be cushioned by large down payments." The presentation also noted that while loan-to-value ratios were rising on a portion of interest-only loans, the ratios for most remained around 80%. Another presentation suggested that housing market activity could be the result of "solid fundamentals." Yet another presentation concluded that the impact of changes in household wealth on spending would be "perhaps only half as large as that of the 1990s stock bubble." Most FOMC participants agreed "the probability of spillovers to financial institutions seemed moderate."[17]

As one recent study argues, many economists were "agnostics" on housing, unwilling to risk their reputations or spook markets by alleging a bubble without finding support in economic theory.[18] Fed Vice Chairman Donald Kohn was one. "Identification [of a bubble] is a tricky proposition because not all the fundamental factors driving asset prices are directly observable," Kohn said in a 2006 speech, citing research by the European Central Bank. "For this reason, any judgment by a central bank that stocks or homes are overpriced is inherently highly uncertain."[19]

But not all economists hesitated to sound a louder alarm. "The situation is beginning to look like a credit-induced boom in housing that could very well result in a systemic bust if credit conditions or economic conditions should deteriorate," Federal Deposit Insurance Corporation Chief Economist Richard Brown wrote in a March 2005 report. "During the past five years, the average U.S. home has risen in value by 50%, while homes in the fastest-growing markets have approximately doubled in value." While this increase might have been explained by strong market fundamentals, "the dramatic broadening of the housing boom in 2004 strongly suggests the influence of systemic factors, including the low cost and wide availability of mortgage credit."[20]

A couple of months later, Fed economists in an internal memo acknowledged the possibility that housing prices were overvalued, but downplayed the potential impacts of a downturn. Even in the face of a large price decline, they argued, defaults would not be widespread, given the large equity that many borrowers still had in their homes. Structural changes in the mortgage market made a crisis less likely, and the financial system seemed well capitalized. "Even historically large declines in house prices would be small relative to the recent decline in household wealth owing to the stock market," the economists concluded. "From a wealth-effects perspective, this seems unlikely to create substantial macroeconomic problems."[21]

## MORTGAGE FRAUD:
## "CRIME-FACILITATIVE ENVIRONMENTS"

New Century—where 40% of the mortgages were loans with little or no documentation[22]—was not the only company that ignored concerns about poor loan quality. Across the mortgage industry, with the bubble at its peak, standards had declined, documentation was no longer verified, and warnings from internal audit departments and concerned employees were ignored. These conditions created an environment ripe for fraud. William Black, a former banking regulator who analyzed criminal patterns during the savings and loan crisis, told the Commission that by one estimate, in the mid-2000s, at least 1.5 million loans annually contained "some sort of fraud," in part because of the large percentage of no-doc loans originated then.[23]

Fraud for housing can entail a borrower's lying or intentionally omitting information on a loan application. Fraud for profit typically involves a deception to gain financially from the sale of a house. Illinois Attorney General Lisa Madigan defines fraud more broadly to include lenders' "sale of unaffordable or structurally unfair mortgage products to borrowers."[24]

In 80% of cases, according to the FBI, fraud involves industry insiders.[25] For example, property flipping can involve buyers, real estate agents, appraisers, and complicit closing agents. In a "silent second," the buyer, with the collusion of a loan officer and without the knowledge of the first mortgage lender, disguises the existence of a second mortgage to hide the fact that no down payment has been made. "Straw buyers" allow their names and credit scores to be used, for a fee, by buyers who want to conceal their ownership.[26]

In one instance, two women in South Florida were indicted in 2010 for placing ads between 2004 and 2007 in Haitian community newspapers offering assistance with immigration problems; they were accused of then stealing the identities of hundreds of people who came for help and using the information to buy properties, take title in their names, and resell at a profit. U.S. Attorney Wilfredo A. Ferrer told the Commission it was "one of the cruelest schemes" he had seen.[27]

Estimates vary on the extent of fraud, as it is seldom investigated unless properties go into foreclosure. Ann Fulmer, vice president of business relations at Interthinx, a fraud detection service, told the FCIC that her firm analyzed a large sample of all loans from 2005 to 2007 and found 13% contained lies or omissions significant enough to rescind the loan or demand a buyback if it had been securitized. The firm's analysis indicated that about $1 trillion of the loans made during the period were fraudulent. Fulmer further estimated $160 billion worth of fraudulent loans from 2005 to 2007 resulted in foreclosures, leading to losses of $112 billion for the holders. According to Fulmer, experts in the field—lenders' quality assurance officers, attorneys who specialize in loan loss mitigation, and white-collar criminologists—say the percentage of transactions involving less significant forms of fraud, such as relatively minor misrepresentations of fact, could reach 60% of originations.[28] Such loans could stay comfortably under the radar, because many borrowers made payments on time.

Ed Parker, the head of mortgage fraud investigation at Ameriquest, the largest subprime lender in 2003, 2004, and 2005, told the FCIC that fraudulent loans were very common at the company. "No one was watching. The volume was up and now you see the fallout behind the loan origination process," he told the FCIC.[29] David Gussmann, the former vice president of Enterprise Management Capital Markets at Fannie Mae, told the Commission that in one package of 50 securitized loans his analysts found one purchaser who had bought 19 properties, falsely identifying himself each time as the owner of only one property, while another had bought five properties.[30] Fannie Mae's detection of fraud increased steadily during the housing bubble and accelerated in late 2006, according to William Brewster, the current director of the company's mortgage fraud program. He said that, seeing evidence of fraud, Fannie demanded that lenders such as Bank of America, Countrywide, Citigroup, and JP Morgan Chase repurchase about $550 million in mortgages in 2008 and $650 million in 2009.[31] "Lax or practically non-existent government oversight created what criminologists have labeled 'crime-facilitative environments,' where crime could thrive," said Henry N. Pontell, a professor of criminology at the University of California, Irvine, in testimony to the Commission.[32]

The responsibility to investigate and prosecute mortgage fraud violations falls to local, state and federal law enforcement officials. On the federal level, the Federal Bureau of Investigation investigates and refers cases for prosecution to U.S. Attorneys, who are part of the Department of Justice. Cases may also involve other agencies, including the U.S. Postal Inspection Service, the Department of Housing and Urban Development, and the Internal Revenue Service. The FBI, which has the broadest jurisdiction of any federal law enforcement agency, was aware of the extent of the fraudulent mortgage problem.[33] FBI Assistant Director Chris Swecker began noticing a rise in mortgage fraud while he was the special agent in charge of the Charlotte, North Carolina, office from 1999 to 2004. In 2002, that office investigated First Beneficial Mortgage for selling fraudulent loans to Fannie Mae, leading to the successful criminal prosecution of the company's owner, James Edward McLean Jr., and others. First Beneficial repurchased the mortgages after Fannie discovered evidence of fraud, but then—without any interference from Fannie—resold them to Ginnie Mae.[34] For not alerting Ginnie, Fannie paid $7.5 million of restitution to the government. McLean came to the attention of the FBI after buying a luxury yacht for $800,000 in cash.[35] Soon after Swecker was promoted to assistant FBI director for investigations in 2004, he turned a spotlight on mortgage fraud. "The potential impact of mortgage fraud is clear," Swecker told a congressional committee in 2004. "If fraudulent practices become systemic within the mortgage industry and mortgage fraud is allowed to become unrestrained, it will ultimately place financial institutions at risk and have adverse effects on the stock market."[36]

In that testimony, Swecker pointed out the inadequacies of data regarding fraud and recommended that Congress mandate a reporting system and other remedies and require all lenders to participate, whether federally regulated or not. For example, suspicious activity reports, also known as SARs, are reports filed by FDIC-insured banks and their affiliates to the Financial Crimes Enforcement Network

(FinCEN), a bureau within the Treasury Department that administers money-laundering laws and works closely with law enforcement to combat financial crimes. SARs are filed by financial institutions when they suspect criminal activity in a financial transaction. But many mortgage originators, such as Ameriquest, New Century, and Option One, were outside FinCEN's jurisdiction—and thus the loans they generated, which were then placed into securitized pools by larger lenders or investment banks, were not subject to FinCEN review. William Black testified to the Commission that an estimated 80% of nonprime mortgage loans were made by noninsured lenders not required to file SARs. And as for those institutions required to do so, he believed he saw evidence of underreporting in that, he said, only about 10% of federally insured mortgage lenders filed even a single criminal referral for alleged mortgage fraud in the first half of 2009.[37]

Countrywide, the nation's largest mortgage lender at the time, had about 5,000 internal referrals of potentially fraudulent activity in its mortgage business in 2005, 10,000 in 2006, and 20,000 in 2007, according to Francisco San Pedro, the former senior vice president of special investigations at the company.[38] But it filed only 855 SARs in 2005, 2,895 in 2006, and 2,621 in 2007.[39]

Similarly, in examining Bank of America in 2007, its lead bank regulator, the Office of the Comptroller of the Currency (OCC), sampled 50 mortgages and found 16 with "quality assurance referrals" for suspicious activity for which no report had been filed with FinCEN. All 16 met the legal requirement for a filing. The OCC consequently required management to refine its processes to ensure that SARs were consistently filed.[40]

Darcy Parmer, a former quality assurance and fraud analyst at Wells Fargo, the second largest mortgage lender from 2004 through 2007 and the largest in 2008, told the Commission that "hundreds and hundreds and hundreds of fraud cases" that she knew were identified within Wells Fargo's home equity loan division were not reported to FinCEN. And, she added, at least half the loans she flagged for fraud were nevertheless funded, over her objections.[41]

Despite the underreporting, the jump in mortgage fraud drew attention. FinCEN in November 2006 reported a 20-fold increase in SARs related to mortgage fraud between 1996 and 2005. It noted that two-thirds of the loans being created were originated by mortgage brokers who were not subject to any federal standard or oversight.[42] Swecker unsuccessfully asked legislators to compel all lenders to forward information about criminal fraud to regulators and law enforcement agencies.[43]

Swecker attempted to gain more funding to combat mortgage fraud but was resisted. Swecker told the FCIC his funding requests were cut at either the director level at the FBI, at the Justice Department, or at the Office of Management and Budget. He called his struggle for more resources an "uphill slog."[44]

In 2005, 25,988 SARs related to mortgage fraud were filed; in 2006 there were 37,457. The number kept climbing, to 52,862 in 2007, 65,004 in 2008, and 67,507 in 2009.[45] At the same time, top FBI officials, focusing on terrorist threats, reduced the agents assigned to white-collar crime from 2,342 in the 2004 fiscal year to fewer than 2,000 by 2007. That year, its mortgage fraud program had only 120 agents at any one

time to review more than 50,000 SARs filed with FinCEN. In response to inquiries from the FCIC, the FBI said that to compensate for a lack of manpower, it had developed "new and innovative methods to detect and combat mortgage fraud," such as a computer application, created in 2006, to detect property flipping.[46]

Robert Mueller, the FBI's director since 2001, said mortgage fraud needed to be considered "in context of other priorities," such as terrorism. He told the Commission that he hired additional resources to fight fraud, but that "we didn't get what we had requested" during the budget process. He also said that the FBI allocated additional resources to reflect the growth in mortgage fraud, but acknowledged that those resources may have been insufficient. "I am not going to tell you that that is adequate for what is out there," he said. In the wake of the crisis, the FBI is continuing to investigate fraud, and Mueller suggested that some prosecutions may be still to come.[47]

Alberto Gonzales, the nation's attorney general from February 2005 to September 2007, told the Commission that while he might have done more on mortgage fraud, in hindsight he believed that other issues were more pressing: "I don't think anyone can credibly argue that [mortgage fraud] is more important than the war on terror. Mortgage fraud doesn't involve taking loss of life so it doesn't rank above the priority of protecting neighborhoods from dangerous gangs or predators attacking our children."[48]

In 2008, the Office of Federal Housing Enterprise Oversight, the regulator of the GSEs, released a report showing a "significant rise in the incidence of fraud in mortgage lending in 2006 and the first half of 2007." OFHEO stated it had been working closely with law enforcement and was an active member of the Department of Justice Mortgage Fraud Working Group.[49] "The concern about mortgage fraud and fraud in general was an issue," Richard Spillenkothen, head of banking supervision and regulation at the Fed from 1991 to 2006, told the FCIC. "And we understood there was an increasing incidence of [mortgage fraud]."[50]

Michael B. Mukasey, who served as U.S. attorney general from November 2007 to the end of 2008, told the Commission that he recalled "receiving reports of mortgage failures and of there being fraudulent activity in connection with flipping houses, overvaluation, and the like. . . . I have a dim recollection of outside people commenting that additional resources should be devoted, and there being speculation about whether resources that were being diverted to national security investigations, and in particular the terrorism investigations were somehow impeding fraud investigations, which I thought was a bogus issue." He said that the department had other pressing priorities, such as terrorism, gang violence, and southwestern border issues.[51]

In letters to the FCIC, the Department of Justice outlined actions it undertook along with the FBI to combat mortgage fraud. For example, in 2004, the FBI launched Operation Continued Action, targeting a variety of financial crimes, including mortgage fraud. In that same year, the agency started to publish an annual mortgage fraud report. The following year, the FBI and other federal agencies announced a joint effort combating mortgage fraud. From July to October 2005, this program, Operation Quick Flip, produced 156 indictments, 81 arrests, and 89

convictions for mortgage fraud. In 2007, the FBI started specifically tracking mortgage fraud cases and increased personnel dedicated to those efforts. And in 2008, Operation Malicious Mortgage resulted in 144 mortgage fraud cases in which 406 defendants were charged by U.S. Attorneys offices throughout the country.[52]

William Black told the Commission that Washington essentially ignored the issue and allowed it to worsen. "The FBI did have severe limits," because of the need to respond to the 9/11 attacks, Black said, and the problem was compounded by the lack of cooperation: "The terrible thing that happened was that the FBI got virtually no assistance from the regulators, the banking regulators and the thrift regulators."[53] Swecker, the former FBI official, told the Commission he had no contact with banking regulators during his tenure.[54]

As mortgage fraud grew, state agencies took action. In Florida, Ellen Wilcox, a special agent with the state Department of Law Enforcement, teamed with the Tampa police department and Hillsborough County Consumer Protection Agency to bring down a criminal ring scamming homeowners in the Tampa area. Its key member was Orson Benn, a New York–based vice president of Argent Mortgage Company, a unit of Ameriquest. Beginning in 2004, 10 investigators and two prosecutors worked for years to unravel a network of alliances between real estate brokers, appraisers, home repair contractors, title companies, notaries, and a convicted felon in a case that involved some 130 loans.[55]

According to charging documents in the case, the perpetrators would walk through neighborhoods, looking for elderly homeowners they thought were likely to have substantial equity in their homes. They would suggest repairs or improvements to the homes. The homeowners would fill out paperwork, and insiders would use the information to apply for loans in their names. Members of the ring would prepare fraudulent loan documents, including false W-2 forms, filled with information about invented employment and falsified salaries, and take out home equity loans in the homeowners' names. Each person involved in the transaction would receive a fee for his or her role; Benn, at Argent, received a $3,000 kickback for each loan he helped secure. When the loan was funded, the checks were frequently made out to the bogus home construction company that had proposed the work, which would then disappear with the proceeds. Some of the homeowners never received a penny from the refinancing on their homes. Hillsborough County officials learned of the scam when homeowners approached them to say that scheduled repairs had never been made to their homes, and then sometimes learned that they had lost years' worth of equity as well. Sixteen of 18 defendants, including Benn, have been convicted or have pled guilty.[56]

Wilcox told the Commission that the "cost and length of these investigations make them less attractive to most investigative agencies and prosecutors trying to justify their budgets based on investigative statistics."[57] She said it has been hard to follow up on other cases because so many of the subprime lenders have gone out of business, making it difficult to track down perpetrators and witnesses. Ameriquest, for example, collapsed in 2007, although Argent, and the company's loan-servicing arm, were bought by Citigroup that same year.

## DISCLOSURE AND DUE DILIGENCE:
## "A QUALITY CONTROL ISSUE IN THE FACTORY"

In addition to the rising fraud and egregious lending practices, lending standards deteriorated in the final years of the bubble. After growing for years, Alt-A lending increased another 5% from 2005 to 2006. In particular, option ARMs grew 7% during that period, interest-only mortgages grew 9%, and no-documentation or low-documentation loans (measured for borrowers with fixed-rate mortgages) grew 14%. Overall, by 2006 no-doc or low-doc loans made up 27% of all mortgages originated. Many of these products would perform only if prices continued to rise and the borrower could refinance at a low rate.[58]

In theory, every participant along the securitization pipeline should have had an interest in the quality of every underlying mortgage. In practice, their interests were often not aligned. Two New York Fed economists have pointed out the "seven deadly frictions" in mortgage securitization—places along the pipeline where one party knew more than the other, creating opportunities to take advantage.[59] For example, the lender who originated the mortgage for sale, earning a commission, knew a great deal about the loan and the borrower but had no long-term stake in whether the mortgage was paid, beyond the lender's own business reputation. The securitizer who packaged mortgages into mortgage-backed securities, similarly, was less likely to retain a stake in those securities.

In theory, the rating agencies were important watchdogs over the securitization process. They described their role as being "an umpire in the market."[60] But they did not review the quality of individual mortgages in a mortgage-backed security, nor did they check to see that the mortgages were what the securitizers said they were.

So the integrity of the market depended on two critical checks. First, firms purchasing and securitizing the mortgages would conduct due diligence reviews of the mortgage pools, either using third-party firms or doing the reviews in-house. Second, following Securities and Exchange Commission rules, parties in the securitization process were expected to disclose what they were selling to investors. Neither of these checks performed as they should have.

### Due diligence firms: "Waived in"

As subprime mortgage securitization took off, securitizers undertook due diligence on their own or through third parties on the mortgage pools that originators were selling them. The originator and the securitizer negotiated the extent of the due diligence investigation. While the percentage of the pool examined could be as high as 30%, it was often much lower; according to some observers, as the market grew and originators became more concentrated, they had more bargaining power over the mortgage purchasers, and samples were sometimes as low as 2% to 3%.[61] Some securitizers requested that the due diligence firm analyze a random sample of mortgages from the pool; others asked for a sampling of those most likely to be deficient in some way, in an effort to efficiently detect more of the problem loans.

Clayton Holdings, a Connecticut-based firm, was a major provider of third-party due diligence services. [62] As Clayton Vice President Vicki Beal explained to the FCIC, firms like hers were "not retained by [their] clients to provide an opinion as to whether a loan is a good loan or a bad loan." Rather, they were hired to identify, among other things, whether the loans met the originator's stated underwriting guidelines and, in some measure, to enable clients to negotiate better prices on pools of loans.[63]

The review fell into three general areas: credit, compliance, and valuation. Did the loans meet the underwriting guidelines (generally the originator's standards, sometimes with overlays or additional guidelines provided by the financial institutions purchasing the loans)? Did the loans comply with federal and state laws, notably predatory-lending laws and truth-in-lending requirements? Were the reported property values accurate?[64] And, critically: to the degree that a loan was deficient, did it have any "compensating factors" that offset these deficiencies? For example, if a loan had a higher loan-to-value ratio than guidelines called for, did another characteristic such as the borrower's higher income mitigate that weakness? The due diligence firm would then grade the loan sample and forward the data to its client. Report in hand, the securitizer would negotiate a price for the pool and could "kick out" loans that did not meet the stated guidelines.

Because of the volume of loans examined by Clayton during the housing boom, the firm had a unique inside view of the underwriting standards that originators were actually applying—and that securitizers were willing to accept. Loans were classified into three groups: loans that met guidelines (a Grade 1 Event), those that failed to meet guidelines but were approved because of compensating factors (a Grade 2 Event), and those that failed to meet guidelines and were not approved (a Grade 3 Event). Overall, for the 18 months that ended June 30, 2007, Clayton rated 54% of the 911,039 loans it analyzed as Grade 1, and another 18% as Grade 2—for a total of 72% that met the guidelines outright or with compensating factors. The remaining 28% of the loans were Grade 3.[65] In theory, the banks could have refused to buy a loan pool, or, indeed, they could have used the findings of the due diligence firm to probe the loans' quality more deeply. Over the 18-month period, 39% of the loans that Clayton found to be deficient—Grade 3—were "waived in" by the banks. Thus 11% of the loans sampled by Clayton were accepted even though the company had found a basis for rejecting them (see figure 9.1).

Referring to the data, Keith Johnson, the president of Clayton from May 2006 to May 2009, told the Commission, "That 54% to me says there [was] a quality control issue in the factory" for mortgage-backed securities.[66] Johnson concluded that his clients often waived in loans to preserve their business relationship with the loan originator—a high number of rejections might lead the originator to sell the loans to a competitor. Simply put, it was a sellers' market. "Probably the seller had more power than the Wall Street issuer," Johnson told the FCIC.[67]

The high rate of waivers following rejections may not itself be evidence of something wrong in the process, Beal testified. She said that as originators' lending guidelines were declining, she saw the securitizing firms introduce additional credit

# Rejected Loans Waived in by Selected Banks

*From January 2006 through June 2007, Clayton rejected 28% of the mortgages it reviewed. Of these, 39% were waived in anyway.*

| | **A**<br>ACCEPTED LOANS<br>*(Event 1 & 2)/*<br>*Total pool of loans* | **B**<br>REJECTED LOANS<br>*(Event 3)/*<br>*Total pool of loans* | **C**<br>REJECTED LOANS<br>WAIVED IN BY<br>FINANCIAL<br>INSTITUTIONS | **D**<br>REJECTED LOANS AFTER WAIVERS<br>*(B–C)* | **E**<br>FINANCIAL INSTITUTION WAIVER RATE<br>*(C/B)* |
|---|---|---|---|---|---|
| **Financial Institution** | | | | | |
| Citigroup | 58% | 42% | 13% | 29% | 31% |
| Credit Suisse | 68 | 32 | 11 | 21 | 33 |
| Deutsche | 65 | 35 | 17 | 17 | 50 |
| Goldman | 77 | 23 | 7 | 16 | 29 |
| JP Morgan | 73 | 27 | 14 | 13 | 51 |
| Lehman | 74 | 26 | 10 | 16 | 37 |
| Merrill | 77 | 23 | 7 | 16 | 32 |
| UBS | 80 | 20 | 6 | 13 | 33 |
| WaMu | 73 | 27 | 8 | 19 | 29 |
| **Total Bank Sample** | **72%** | **28%** | **11%** | **17%** | **39%** |

NOTES: From Clayton Trending Reports. Numbers may not add due to rounding.
SOURCE: Clayton Holdings

*Figure 9.1*

guidelines. "As you know, there was stated income, they were telling us look for reasonableness of that income, things like that."[68] With stricter guidelines, one would expect more rejections, and, after the securitizer looks more closely at the rejected loans, possibly more waivers. As Moody's Investors Service explained in a letter to the FCIC, "A high rate of waivers from an institution with extremely tight underwriting standards could result in a pool that is less risky than a pool with no waivers from an institution with extremely loose underwriting standards."[69] Nonetheless, many prospectuses indicated that the loans in the pools either met guidelines outright or had compensating factors, even though Clayton's records show that only a portion of the loans were sampled, and that of those that were sampled, a substantial percentage of Grade 3 Event loans were waived in.

Johnson said he approached the rating agencies in 2006 and 2007 to gauge their interest in the exception-tracking product that Clayton was developing. He said he shared some of their company's results, attempting to convince the agencies that the data would benefit the ratings process. "We went to the rating agencies and said, 'Wouldn't this information be great for you to have as you assign tranche levels of

risk?'" Johnson recalled. The agencies thought the due diligence firm's data were "great," but they did not want the information, Johnson said, because it would presumably produce lower ratings for the securitizations and cost the agency business—even in 2007, as the private securitization market was winding down.[70]

When securitizers did kick loans out of the pools, some originators simply put them into new pools, presumably in hopes that those loans would not be captured in the next pool's sampling. The examiner's report for New Century Financial's bankruptcy describes such a practice.[71] Similarly, Fremont Investment & Loan had a policy of putting loans into subsequent pools until they were kicked out three times, the company's former regulatory compliance and risk manager, Roger Ehrnman, told the FCIC. As Johnson described the practice to the FCIC, this was the "three strikes, you're out rule."[72]

Some mortgage securitizers did their own due diligence, but seemed to devote only limited resources to it. At Morgan Stanley, the head of due diligence was based not in New York but rather in Boca Raton, Florida. He had, at any one time, two to five individuals reporting to him directly—and they were actually employees of a personnel consultant, Equinox.[73] Deutsche Bank and JP Morgan likewise also had only small due diligence teams.[74]

Banks did not necessarily have better processes for monitoring the mortgages that they purchased. At an FCIC hearing on the mortgage business, Richard Bowen, a whistleblower who had been a senior vice president at CitiFinancial Mortgage in charge of a staff of 200-plus professional underwriters, testified that his team conducted quality assurance checks on the loans bought by Citigroup from a network of lenders, including both subprime mortgages that Citigroup intended to hold and prime mortgages that it intended to sell to Fannie Mae and Freddie Mac.

For subprime purchases, Bowen's team would review the physical credit file of the loans they were purchasing. "During 2006 and 2007, I witnessed many changes to the way the credit risk was being evaluated for these pools during the purchase processes," Bowen said. For example, he said, the chief risk officer in Citigroup's Consumer Lending business reversed large numbers of underwriting decisions from "turn down" to "approved."[75]

Another part of Bowen's charge was to supervise the purchase of roughly $50 billion annually in prime loan pools, a high percentage of which were sold to Fannie Mae and Freddie Mac for securitization. The sampling provided to Bowen's staff for quality control was supposed to include at least 5% of the loan pool for a given securitization, but "this corporate mandate was usually ignored." Samples of 2% were more likely, and the loan samples that Bowen's group did examine showed extremely high rates of noncompliance. "At the time that I became involved, which was early to mid-2006, we identified that 40 to 60 percent of the files either had a 'disagree' decision, or they were missing critical documents."[76]

Bowen repeatedly expressed concerns to his direct supervisor and company executives about the quality and underwriting of mortgages that CitiMortgage purchased and then sold to the GSEs. As discussed in a later chapter, the GSEs would later re-

quire Citigroup to buy back $1.5 billion in loans as of November 2010, finding that the loans Citigroup had sold them did not conform to GSE standards.

## SEC: "The elephant in the room is that we didn't review the prospectus supplements"

By the time the financial crisis hit, investors held more than $2 trillion of non-GSE mortgage-backed securities and close to $700 billion of CDOs that held mortgage-backed securities.[77] These securities were issued with practically no SEC oversight. And only a minority were subject to the SEC's ongoing public reporting requirements. The SEC's mandate is to protect investors—generally not by reviewing the quality of securities, but simply by ensuring adequate disclosures so that investors can make up their own minds. In the case of initial public offerings of a company's shares, the work has historically involved a lengthy review of the issuer's prospectus and other "offering materials" prior to sale.[78]

However, with the advent of "shelf registration," a method of registering securities on an ongoing basis, the process became much quicker for mortgage-backed securities ranked in the highest grades by the rating agencies. The process allowed issuers to file a base prospectus with the SEC, giving investors notice that the issuer intended to offer securities in the future. The issuer then filed a supplemental prospectus describing each offering's terms. "The elephant in the room is that we didn't review the prospectus supplements," the SEC's deputy director for disclosure in corporation finance, Shelley Parratt, told the FCIC.[79] To improve disclosures pertaining to mortgage-backed securities and other asset-backed securities, the SEC issued Regulation AB in late 2004. The regulation required that every prospectus include "a description of the solicitation, credit-granting or underwriting criteria used to originate or purchase the pool assets, including, to the extent known, any changes in such criteria and the extent to which such policies and criteria are or could be overridden."[80]

With essentially no review or oversight, how good were disclosures about mortgage-backed securities? Prospectuses usually included disclaimers to the effect that not all mortgages would comply with the lending policies of the originator: "On a case-by-case basis [the originator] may determine that, based upon compensating factors, a prospective mortgage not strictly qualifying under the underwriting risk category or other guidelines described below warrants an underwriting exception."[81] The disclosure typically had a sentence stating that "a substantial number" or perhaps "a substantial portion of the Mortgage Loans will represent these exceptions."[82] Citigroup's Bowen criticized the extent of information provided on loan pools: "There was no disclosure made to the investors with regard to the quality of the files they were purchasing."[83]

Such disclosures were insufficient for investors to know what criteria the mortgages they were buying actually did meet. Only a small portion—as little as 2% to 3%—of the loans in any deal were sampled, and evidence from Clayton shows that a significant number did not meet stated guidelines or have compensating factors.[84] On

the loans in the remainder of the mortgage pool that were not sampled (as much as 97%), Clayton and the securitizers had no information, but one could reasonably expect them to have many of the same deficiencies, and at the same rate, as the sampled loans. Prospectuses for the ultimate investors in the mortgage-backed securities did not contain this information, or information on how few loans were reviewed, raising the question of whether the disclosures were materially misleading, in violation of the securities laws.

CDOs were issued under a different regulatory framework from the one that applied to many mortgage-backed securities, and were not subject even to the minimal shelf registration rules. Underwriters typically issued CDOs under the SEC's Rule 144A, which allows the unregistered resale of certain securities to so-called qualified institutional buyers (QIBs); these included investors as diverse as insurance companies like MetLife, pension funds like the California State Teachers' Retirement System, and investment banks like Goldman Sachs.[85]

The SEC created Rule 144A in 1990, making securities markets more attractive to borrowers and U.S. investment banks more competitive with their foreign counterparts; at the time, market participants viewed U.S. disclosure requirements as more onerous than those in other countries. The new rule significantly expanded the market for these securities by declaring that distributions which complied with the rule would no longer be considered "public offerings" and therefore would not be subject to the SEC's registration requirements. In 1996, Congress reinforced this exemption with the National Securities Markets Improvements Act, legislation that Denise Voigt Crawford, a commissioner on the Texas Securities Board, characterized to the Commission "as prohibit[ing] the states from taking preventative actions in areas that we now know have been substantial contributing factors to the current crisis."[86] Under this legislation, state securities regulators were preempted from overseeing private placements such as CDOs. In the absence of registration requirements, a new debt market developed quickly under Rule 144A. This market was liquid, since qualified investors could freely trade Rule 144A debt securities. But debt securities when Rule 144A was enacted were mostly corporate bonds, very different from the CDOs that dominated the private placement market more than a decade later.[87]

After the crisis unfolded, investors, arguing that disclosure hadn't been adequate, filed numerous lawsuits under federal and state securities laws. As we will see, some have already resulted in substantial settlements.

## REGULATORS: "MARKETS WILL ALWAYS SELF-CORRECT"

Where were the regulators? Declining underwriting standards and new mortgage products had been on regulators' radar screens in the years before the crisis, but disagreements among the agencies and their traditional preference for minimal interference delayed action.

Supervisors had, since the 1990s, followed a "risk-focused" approach that relied extensively on banks' own internal risk management systems.[88] "As internal systems improve, the basic thrust of the examination process should shift from largely dupli-

cating many activities already conducted within the bank to providing constructive feedback that the bank can use to enhance further the quality of its risk-management systems," Chairman Greenspan had said in 1999.[89] Across agencies, there was a "historic vision, historic approach, that a lighter hand at regulation was the appropriate way to regulate," Eugene Ludwig, comptroller of the currency from 1993 to 1998, told the FCIC, referring to the Gramm-Leach-Bliley Act in 1999.[90] The New York Fed, in a "lessons-learned" analysis after the crisis, pointed to the mistaken belief that "markets will always self-correct." "A deference to the self-correcting property of markets inhibited supervisors from imposing prescriptive views on banks," the report concluded.[91]

The reliance on banks' own risk management would extend to capital standards. Banks had complained for years that the original 1988 Basel standards did not allow them sufficient latitude to base their capital on the riskiness of particular assets. After years of negotiations, international regulators, with strong support from the Fed, introduced the Basel II capital regime in June 2004, which would allow banks to lower their capital charges if they could show they had sophisticated internal models for estimating the riskiness of their assets. While no U.S. bank fully implemented the more sophisticated approaches that it allowed, Basel II reflected and reinforced the supervisors' risk-focused approach. Spillenkothen said that one of the regulators' biggest mistakes was their "acceptance of Basel II premises," which he described as displaying "an excessive faith in internal bank risk models, an infatuation with the specious accuracy of complex quantitative risk measurement techniques, and a willingness (at least in the early days of Basel II) to tolerate a reduction in regulatory capital in return for the prospect of better risk management and greater risk-sensitivity."[92]

Regulators had been taking notice of the mortgage market for several years before the crisis. As early as 2004, they recognized that mortgage products and borrowers had changed during and following the refinancing boom of the previous year, and they began work on providing guidance to banks and thrifts. But too little was done, and too late, because of interagency discord, industry pushback, and a widely held view that market participants had the situation well in hand.

"Within the board, people understood that many of these loan types had gotten to an extreme," Susan Bies, then a Fed governor and chair of the Federal Reserve Board's subcommittees on both safety and soundness supervision and consumer protection supervision, told the FCIC. "So the main debate within the board was how tightly [should we] rein in the abuses that we were seeing. So it was more of 'to a degree.'"[93]

Indeed, in the same June 2005 Federal Open Market Committee meeting described earlier, one FOMC member noted that "some of the newer, more intricate and untested credit default instruments had caused some market turmoil." Another participant was concerned "that subprime lending was an accident waiting to happen." A third participant noted the risks in mortgage securities, the rapid growth of subprime lending, and the fact that many lenders had "inadequate information on borrowers," adding, however, that record profits and high capital levels allayed those concerns. A fourth participant said that "we could be seeing the final gasps of house price appreciation." The participant expressed concern about "creative financing" and was "worried that piggybacks and other non-traditional loans," whose risk of default

could be higher than suggested by the securities they backed, "could be making the books of GSEs look better than they really were." Fed staff replied that the GSEs were not large purchasers of private label securities.[94]

In the spring of 2006, the FOMC would again discuss risks in the housing and mortgage markets and express nervousness about the growing "ingenuity" of the mortgage sector. One participant noted that negative amortization loans had the pernicious effect of stripping equity and wealth from homeowners and raised concerns about nontraditional lending practices that seemed based on the presumption of continued increases in home prices.

John Snow, then treasury secretary, told the FCIC that he called a meeting in late 2004 or early 2005 to urge regulators to address the proliferation of poor lending practices. He said he was struck that regulators tended not to see a problem at their own institutions. "Nobody had a full 360-degree view. The basic reaction from financial regulators was, 'Well, there may be a problem. But it's not in my field of view,'" Snow told the FCIC. Regulators responded to Snow's questions by saying, "Our default rates are very low. Our institutions are very well capitalized. Our institutions [have] very low delinquencies. So we don't see any real big problem."[95]

In May 2005, the banking agencies did issue guidance on the risks of home equity lines of credit and home equity loans. It cautioned financial institutions about credit risk management practices, pointing to interest-only features, low- or no-documentation loans, high loan-to-value and debt-to-income ratios, lower credit scores, greater use of automated valuation models, and the increase in transactions generated through a loan broker or other third party. While this guidance identified many of the problematic lending practices engaged in by bank lenders, it was limited to home equity loans. It did not apply to first mortgages.[96]

In 2005, examiners from the Fed and other agencies conducted a confidential "peer group" study of mortgage practices at six companies that together had originated $1.3 trillion in mortgages in 2005, almost half the national total. In the group were five banks whose holding companies were under the Fed's supervisory purview—Bank of America, Citigroup, Countrywide, National City, and Wells Fargo—as well as the largest thrift, Washington Mutual.[97] The study "showed a very rapid increase in the volume of these irresponsible loans, very risky loans," Sabeth Siddique, then head of credit risk at the Federal Reserve Board's Division of Banking Supervision and Regulation, told the FCIC.[98] A large percentage of their loans issued were subprime and Alt-A mortgages, and the underwriting standards for these products had deteriorated.[99]

Once the Fed and other supervisors had identified the mortgage problems, they agreed to express those concerns to the industry in the form of nonbinding guidance. "There was among the Board of Governors folks, you know, some who felt that if we just put out guidance, the banks would get the message," Bies said.[100]

The federal agencies therefore drafted guidance on nontraditional mortgages such as option ARMs, issuing it for public comment in late 2005. The draft guidance directed lenders to consider a borrower's ability to make the loan payment when rates

adjusted, rather than just the lower starting rate. It warned lenders that low-documentation loans should be "used with caution."[101]

Immediately, the industry was up in arms. The American Bankers Association said the guidance "overstate[d] the risk of non-traditional mortgages."[102] Other market participants complained that the guidance required them to assume "a worst case scenario," that is, the scenario in which borrowers would have to make the full payment when rates adjusted.[103] They disputed the warning on low-documentation loans, maintaining that "almost any form of documentation can be appropriate."[104] They denied that better disclosures were required to protect borrowers from the risks of nontraditional mortgages, arguing that they were "not aware of any empirical evidence that supports the need for further consumer protection standards."[105]

The need for guidance was controversial within the agencies, too. "We got tremendous pushback from the industry as well as Congress as well as, you know, internally," the Fed's Siddique told the FCIC. "Because it was stifling innovation, potentially, and it was denying the American dream to many people."[106]

The pressures to weaken and delay the guidance were strong and came from many sources. Opposition by the Office of Thrift Supervision helped delay the mortgage guidance for almost a year.[107] Bies said, "There was some real concern about if the Fed tightened down on [the banks it regulated], whether that would create an unlevel playing field . . . [for] stand-alone mortgage lenders whom the [Fed] did not regulate." Another challenge to regulating the mortgage market was Congress. She recalled an occasion when she testified about a proposed rule and "members of Congress [said] that we were going to deny the dream of homeownership to Americans if we put this new stronger standard in place."[108]

When guidance was put in place in 2006, regulators policed their guidance through bank examinations and informal measures such as "voluntary agreements" with supervised institutions.

It also appeared some institutions switched regulators in search of more lenient treatment. In December 2006, Countrywide applied to switch regulators from the Fed and OCC to the OTS. Countrywide's move came after several months of evaluation within the company about the benefits of OTS regulation, many of which were promoted by the OTS itself over the course of an "outreach effort" initiated in mid-2005 after John Reich became director of the agency. Publicly, Countrywide stated that the decision to switch to the OTS was driven by the desire to have one, housing-focused regulator, rather than separate regulators for the bank and the holding company.[109]

However, other factors came into play as well. The OCC's top Countrywide examiner told the FCIC that Countrywide CEO Angelo Mozilo and President and COO David Sambol thought the OCC's position on property appraisals would be "killing the business."[110] An internal July 2006 Countrywide briefing paper noted, "The OTS regulation of holding companies is not as intrusive as that of the Federal Reserve. In particular, the OTS rarely conducts extensive onsite examinations and when they do conduct an onsite examination they are generally not considered intrusive to the holding company." The briefing paper also noted, "The OTS generally is considered a

less sophisticated regulator than the Federal Reserve."[111] In August 2006, Mozilo wrote to members of his executive team, "It appears that the Fed is now troubled by pay options while the OTS is not. Since pay options are a major component of both our volumes and profitability the Fed may force us into a decision faster than we would like." Countrywide Chief Risk Officer John McMurray responded that "based on my meetings with the FRB and OTS, the OTS appears to be both more familiar and more comfortable with Option ARMs."[112]

The OTS approved Countrywide's application for a thrift charter on March 5, 2007.

## LEVERAGED LOANS AND COMMERCIAL REAL ESTATE: "YOU'VE GOT TO GET UP AND DANCE"

The credit bubble was not confined to the residential mortgage market. The markets for commercial real estate and leveraged loans (typically loans to below-investment-grade companies to aid their business or to finance buyouts) also experienced similar bubble-and-bust dynamics, although the effects were not as large and damaging as in residential real estate. From 2000 to 2007, these other two markets grew tremendously, spurred by structured finance products—commercial mortgage–backed securities and collateralized loan obligations (CLOs), respectively—which were in many ways similar to residential mortgage-backed securities and CDOs. And just as in the residential mortgage market, underwriting standards loosened, even as the cost of borrowing decreased,[113] and trading in these securities was bolstered by the development of new credit derivatives products.[114]

Historically, leveraged loans had been made by commercial banks; but a market for institutional investors developed and grew in the mid- to late 1990s.[115] An "agent" bank would originate a package of loans to only one company and then sell or syndicate the loans in the package to other banks and large nonbank investors. The package generally included loans with different maturities. Some were short-term lines of credit, which would be syndicated to banks; the rest were longer-term loans syndicated to nonbank, institutional investors. Leveraged loan issuance more than doubled from 2000 to 2007, but the rapid growth was in the longer-term institutional loans rather than in short-term lending. By 2007, the longer-term leveraged loans rose to $387 billion, up from $46 billion in 2000.[116]

Starting in 1998, the longer-term leveraged loans were packaged in CLOs, which were rated according to methodologies similar to those the rating agencies used for CDOs. Like CDOs, CLOs had tranches, underwriters, and collateral managers. The market was less than $5 billion annually from 1998 to 2002, but then it started growing dramatically. Annual issuance exceeded $40 billion in 2005 and peaked above $80 billion in 2007. From 2000 through the third quarter of 2007, more than 60% of leveraged loans were packaged into CLOs.[117]

As the market for leveraged loans grew, credit became looser and leverage increased as well. The deals became larger and costs of borrowing declined. Loans that in 2003 had paid interest of 4 percentage points over an interbank lending rate were

refinanced in early 2007 into loans paying just 2 percentage points over that same rate. During the peak of the recent leveraged buyout boom, leveraged loans were frequently issued with interest-only, "payment-in-kind," and "covenant-lite" terms.[118] Payment-in-kind loans allowed borrowers to defer paying interest by issuing new debt to cover accrued interest. Covenant-lite loans exempted borrowers from standard loan covenants that usually require corporate firms to limit their other debts and to maintain minimum levels of cash. Private equity firms, those that specialized in investing directly in companies, found it easier and cheaper to finance their leveraged buyouts. Just as home prices rose, so too did the prices of the target companies.

One of the largest deals ever made involving leveraged loans was announced on April 2, 2007, by KKR, a private equity firm. KKR said it intended to purchase First Data Corporation, a processor of electronic data including credit and debit card payments, for about $29 billion. As part of this transaction, KKR would issue $8 billion in junk bonds and take out another $15 billion in leveraged loans from a consortium of banks including Citigroup, Deutsche Bank, Goldman Sachs, HSBC Securities, Lehman Brothers, and Merrill Lynch.[119]

As late as July 2007, Citigroup and others were still increasing their leveraged loan business.[120] Citigroup CEO Charles Prince then said of the business, "When the music stops, in terms of liquidity, things will be complicated. But as long as the music is playing, you've got to get up and dance. We're still dancing." Prince later explained to the FCIC, "At that point in time, because interest rates had been so low for so long, the private equity firms were driving very hard bargains with the banks. And at that point in time the banks individually had no credibility to stop participating in this lending business. It was not credible for one institution to unilaterally back away from this leveraged lending business. It was in that context that I suggested that all of us, we were all regulated entities, that the regulators had an interest in tightening up lending standards in the leveraged lending area."[121]

The CLO market would seize up in the summer of 2007 during the financial crisis, just as the much-larger mortgage-related CDO market seized. At the time this would be roughly $300 billion in outstanding commitments for new loans; as demand in the secondary market dried up, these loans ended up on the banks' balance sheets.[122]

Commercial real estate—multifamily apartment buildings, office buildings, hotels, retail establishments, and industrial properties—went through a bubble similar to that in the housing market. Investment banks created commercial mortgage–backed securities and even CDOs out of commercial real estate loans, just as they did with residential mortgages. And, just as houses appreciated from 2000 on, so too did commercial real estate values. Office prices rose by nearly 60% between 2003 and 2008 in the central business districts of the 32 markets for which data are available. The increase was 193% in Phoenix, 153% in Tampa, 147% in Manhattan, and 146% in Los Angeles.[123]

Issuance of commercial mortgage–backed securities rose from $47 billion in 2000 to $169 billion in 2005, reaching $230 billion in 2007. When securitization markets contracted, issuance fell to $12 billion in 2008 and $3 billion in 2009. When about

one-fourth of commercial real estate mortgages were securitized in 2007, securitizers issued $41 billion of commercial mortgage CDOs, a number that again dropped precipitously in 2008.[124]

Leveraged loans and the commercial real estate sector came together on July 3, 2007, when the Blackstone Group announced its plan to buy Hilton—a hotel chain with 2,900 properties—for $26 billion, a 40% premium over the share price. A year later, one author described this deal as "the apogee of the early-millennial megabuyout frenzy, where cheap and readily available credit, coupled with a relentless one-upmanship, spurred private equity firms to buy out companies at often absurd overvaluations, saddle them with massive debt, and then pay themselves hefty fees for the trouble."[125] Twenty billion dollars in financing came from the top five investment banks and large commercial banks such as Bank of America and Deutsche Bank.[126]

Bear Stearns was increasingly active in these markets. While Bear topped the 2006 market in residential securitizations, it ranked in the bottom half in commercial securitizations.[127] But it was racing to catch up, and in a 2007 presentation boasted: "In 2006, we firmly established Bear Stearns as a global presence in commercial real estate finance." The firm's commercial real estate mortgage originations more than doubled between 2004 and 2006.[128]

And then the market came crashing to a halt. Although the commercial real estate mortgage market was much smaller than the residential real estate market—in 2008, commercial real estate debt was less than $4 trillion, compared to $12 trillion for residential mortgages[129]—it declined even more steeply. From its peak, commercial real estate fell roughly 45% in value, and prices have remained close to their lows. Losses on commercial real estate would be an issue across Wall Street, particularly for Lehman and Bear. And potentially for the taxpayer. When the Federal Reserve would assume $30 billion of Bear's illiquid assets in 2008, that would include roughly $4 billion in loans from the unsold portion of the Hilton financing package.[130] And the commercial real estate market would continue to decline long after the housing market had begun to stabilize.

## LEHMAN: FROM "MOVING" TO "STORAGE"

Even as the market was nearing its peak, Lehman took on more risk.

On October 5, 2007, when commercial real estate already made up 6.3% of its assets, Lehman Brothers acquired a major stake in Archstone Smith, a publicly traded real estate investment trust, for $5.4 billion. Archstone owned more than 88,000 apartments, including units still under construction, in over 340 communities in the United States. It was the bank's largest commercial real estate investment.[131]

Lehman initially projected that Archstone would generate more than $1.3 billion in profits over 10 years—projections based on optimistic assumptions, given the state of the market at that point. Both Lehman and Archstone were highly leveraged: Archstone had little cushion if its rent receipts should go down, and Lehman had little cushion if investments such as Archstone should lose value.[132] Although the firm

had proclaimed that "Risk Management is at the very core of Lehman's business model," the Executive Committee simply left its risk officer, Madelyn Antoncic, out of the loop when it made this investment.[133]

Since the late 1990s, Lehman had also built a large mortgage origination arm, a formidable securities issuance business, and a powerful underwriting division as well. Then, in its March 2006 "Global Strategy Offsite," CEO Richard Fuld and other executives explained to their colleagues a new move toward an aggressive growth strategy, including greater risk and more leverage. They described the change as a shift from a "moving" or securitization business to a "storage" business, in which Lehman would make and hold longer-term investments.[134]

By summer 2006, the housing market faced ballooning inventories, sharply reduced sales volumes, and wavering prices. Senior management regularly disregarded the firm's risk policies and limits—and warnings from risk managers—and pursued its "countercyclical growth strategy." It had worked well during prior market dislocations, and Lehman's management assumed that it would work again.[135] Lehman's Aurora unit continued to originate Alt-A loans after the housing market had begun to show signs of weakening.[136] Lehman also continued to securitize mortgage assets for sale but was now holding more of them as investments. Across both the commercial and residential real estate sectors, the mortgage-related assets on Lehman's books increased from $67 billion in 2006 to $111 billion in 2007. This increase would be part of Lehman's undoing a year later.

Lehman's regulators did not restrain its rapid growth. The SEC, Lehman's main regulator, knew of the firm's disregard of risk management. The SEC knew that Lehman continued to increase its holding of mortgage securities, and that it had increased and exceeded risk limits—facts noted almost monthly in official SEC reports obtained by the FCIC.[137] Nonetheless, Erik Sirri, who led the SEC's supervision program, told the FCIC that it would not have mattered if the agency had fully recognized the risks associated with commercial real estate. To avoid serious losses, Sirri maintained, Lehman would have had to start selling real estate assets in 2006.[138] Instead, it kept buying, well into the first quarter of 2008.

In addition, according to the bankruptcy examiner, Lehman understated its leverage through "Repo 105" transactions—an accounting maneuver to temporarily remove assets from the balance sheet before each reporting period. Martin Kelly, Lehman's global financial controller, stated that the transactions had "no substance"—their "only purpose or motive . . . was reduction in the balance sheet." Other Lehman executives described Repo 105 transactions as an "accounting gimmick" and a "lazy way of managing the balance sheet as opposed to legitimately meeting balance sheet targets at quarter-end." Bart McDade, who became Lehman's president and chief operating officer in June 2008, in an email called Repo 105 transactions "another drug we R on."[139]

Ernst & Young (E&Y), Lehman's auditor, was aware of the Repo 105 practice but did not question Lehman's failure to publicly disclose it, despite being informed in May 2008 by Lehman Senior Vice President Matthew Lee that the practice was improper. The Lehman bankruptcy examiner concluded that E&Y took "virtually no

action to investigate the Repo 105 allegations, . . . took no steps to question or challenge the non-disclosure by Lehman," and that "colorable claims exist that E&Y did not meet professional standards, both in investigating Lee's allegations and in connection with its audit and review of Lehman's financial statements."[140] New York Attorney General Andrew Cuomo sued E&Y in December 2010, accusing the firm of facilitating a "massive accounting fraud" by helping Lehman to deceive the public about its financial condition.[141]

The Office of Thrift Supervision had also regulated Lehman since 1999 through its jurisdiction over Lehman's thrift subsidiary. Although "the SEC was regarded as the primary regulator," the OTS examiner told the FCIC, "we in no way just assumed that [the SEC] would do the right thing, so we regulated and supervised the holding company."[142] Still, not until July 2008—just a few months before Lehman failed—would the OTS issue a report warning that Lehman had made an "outsized bet" on commercial real estate—larger than that by its peer firms, despite Lehman's smaller size; that Lehman was "materially overexposed" to the commercial real estate sector; and that Lehman had "major failings in its risk management process."[143]

## FANNIE MAE AND FREDDIE MAC: "TWO STARK CHOICES"

In 2005, while Countrywide, Citigroup, Lehman, and many others in the mortgage and CDO businesses were going into overdrive, executives at the two behemoth GSEs, Fannie and Freddie, worried they were being left behind. One sign of the times: Fannie's biggest source of mortgages, Countrywide, expanded—that is, loosened—its underwriting criteria, and Fannie would not buy the new mortgages, Countrywide President and COO Sambol told the FCIC.[144] Typical of the market as a whole, Countrywide sold 72% of its loans to Fannie in 2003 but only 45% in 2004 and 32% in 2005.[145]

"The risk in the environment has accelerated dramatically," Thomas Lund, Fannie's head of single-family lending, told fellow senior officers at a strategic planning meeting on June 27, 2005. In a bulleted list, he ticked off changes in the market: the "proliferation of higher risk alternative mortgage products, growing concern about housing bubbles, growing concerns about borrowers taking on increased risks and higher debt, [and] aggressive risk layering."[146]

"We face two stark choices: stay the course [or] meet the market where the market is," Lund said. If Fannie Mae stayed the course, it would maintain its credit discipline, protect the quality of its book, preserve capital, and intensify the company's public voice on concerns. However, it would also face lower volumes and revenues, continued declines in market share, lower earnings, and a weakening of key customer relationships.[147] It was simply a matter of relevance, former CEO Dan Mudd told the FCIC: "If you're not relevant, you're unprofitable, and you're not serving the mission. And there was danger to profitability. I'm speaking more long term than in any given quarter or any given year. So this was a real strategic rethinking."[148]

Lund saw significant obstacles to meeting the market. He noted Fannie's lack of capability and infrastructure to structure the types of riskier mortgage-backed secu-

rities offered by Wall Street, its unfamiliarity with the new credit risks, worries that the price of the mortgages wouldn't be worth the risk, and regulatory concerns surrounding certain products.[149] At this and other meetings, Lund recommended studying whether the current market changes were cyclical or more permanent, but he also recommended that Fannie "dedicate significant resources to develop capabilities to compete in any mortgage environment."[150] Citibank executives also made a presentation to Fannie's board in July 2005, warning that Fannie was increasingly at risk of being marginalized, and that "stay the course" was not an option. Citibank proposed that Fannie expand its guarantee business to cover nontraditional products such as Alt-A and subprime mortgages.[151] Of course, as the second-largest seller of mortgages to Fannie, Citibank would benefit from such a move. Over the next two years, Citibank would increase its sales to Fannie by more than a quarter, to $56 billion in the 2007 fiscal year, while more than tripling its sales of interest-only mortgages, to $4 billion.[152]

Lund told the FCIC that in 2005, the board would adopt his recommendation: for the time being, Fannie would "stay the course," while developing capabilities to compete with Wall Street in nonprime mortgages.[153] In fact, however, internal reports show that by September 2005, the company had already begun to increase its acquisitions of riskier loans. By the end of 2005, its Alt-A loans were $181 billion, up from $147 billion in 2004 and $138 billion in 2003; its loans without full documentation were $278 billion, up from $200 billion in 2003; and its interest-only mortgages were $75 billion in 2005, up from $12 billion in 2003. (Note that these categories can overlap. For example, Alt-A loans may also lack full documentation.) To cover potential losses from all of its business activities, Fannie had a total of $40 billion in capital at the end of 2005. "Plans to meet market share targets resulted in strategies to increase purchases of higher risk products, creating a conflict between prudent credit risk management and corporate business objectives," the Federal Housing Finance Agency (the successor to the Office of Federal Housing Enterprise Oversight) would write in September 2008 on the eve of the government takeover of Fannie Mae. "Since 2005, Fannie Mae has grown its Alt-A portfolio and other higher risk products rapidly without adequate controls in place."[154]

In its financial statements, Fannie Mae's disclosures about key loan characteristics changed over time, making it difficult to discern the company's exposure to subprime and Alt-A mortgages. For example, from 2005 until 2007, the company's definition of a "subprime" loan was one originated by a company or a part of a company that specialized in subprime loans. Using that definition, Fannie Mae stated that subprime loans accounted for less than 1% of its business volume during those years even while it reported that 5% of its conventional, single-family loans in 2005, 2006 and 2007 loans were to borrowers with FICO scores less than 620.[155]

Similarly, Freddie had enlarged its portfolios quickly with limited capital.[156] In 2005, CEO Richard Syron fired David Andrukonis, Freddie's longtime chief risk officer. Syron said one of the reasons that Andrukonis was fired was that Andrukonis was concerned about relaxing underwriting standards to meet mission goals. He told the FCIC, "I had a legitimate difference of opinion on how dangerous it was. Now, as

it turns out . . . he was able to foresee the market better than a lot of the rest of us could."[157] The new risk officer, Anurag Saksena, recounted to the FCIC staff that he repeatedly made the case for increasing capital to compensate for the increasing risk,[158] although Donald Bisenius, Freddie's executive vice president for single-family housing, told FCIC staff that he did not recall such discussions.[159] Syron never made Saksena part of the senior management team.[160]

OFHEO, the GSEs' regulator, noted their increasing purchases of riskier loans and securities in every examination report. But OFHEO never told the GSEs to stop. Rather, year after year, the regulator said that both companies had adequate capital, strong asset quality, prudent credit risk management, and qualified and active officers and directors.

In May 2006, at the same time as it paid a $400 million penalty related to deficiencies in its accounting practices, Fannie agreed to limit its on-balance-sheet mortgage portfolio to $728 billion, the level on December 31, 2005.[161] Two months later, Freddie agreed to limit the growth of its portfolio to 2% per year.[162] In examination reports for the year 2005, issued to both companies in May 2006, OFHEO noted the growth in purchases of risky loans and non-GSE securities but concluded that each GSE had "strong" asset quality and was adequately capitalized. OFHEO reported that management at Freddie was committed to resolving weaknesses and its Board was "qualified and active." The 2005 examination of Fannie was limited in scope—focusing primarily on the company's efforts to fix accounting and internal control deficiencies—because of the extensive resources needed to complete a three-year special examination initiated in the wake of Fannie's accounting scandal.[163]

In that special examination, OFHEO pinned many of the GSEs' problems on their corporate cultures. Its May 2006 special examination report on Fannie Mae detailed the "arrogant and unethical corporate culture where Fannie Mae employees manipulated accounting and earnings to trigger bonuses for senior executives from 1998 to 2004."[164] OFHEO Director James Lockhart (who had assumed that position the month the report was issued) recalled discovering during the special examination an email from Mudd, then Fannie's chief operating officer, to CEO Franklin Raines. Mudd wrote, "The old political reality [at Fannie] was that we always won, we took no prisoners . . . we used to . . . be able to write, or have written rules that worked for us."[165]

Soon after his arrival, Lockhart began advocating for reform. "The need for legislation was obvious as OFHEO was regulating two of the largest and most systematically important US financial institutions," he told the FCIC.[166] But no reform legislation would be passed until July 30, 2008, and by then it would be too late.

## 2006: "Increase our penetration into subprime"

After several years during which Fannie Mae purchased riskier loans and securities, then-Chief Financial Officer Robert Levin proposed a strategic initiative to "increase our penetration into subprime" at Fannie's January 2006 board meeting.[167] In the next month the board gave its approval.[168] Fannie would become more and more aggressive in its purchases. During a summer retreat for Fannie's senior officers, as

Stephen Ashley, the chairman of the board, introduced Fannie's new chief risk officer, Enrico Dallavecchia, he declared that the new CRO would not stand in the way of risk taking: "We have to think differently and creatively about risk, about compliance, and about controls. Historically these have not been strong suits of Fannie Mae. . . . Today's thinking requires that these areas become active partners with the business units and be viewed as tools that enable us to develop product and address market needs. Enrico Dallavecchia was not brought on-board to be a business dampener."[169]

In 2006, Fannie acquired $516 billion of loans; of those (including some overlap), $65 billion, or about 13%, had combined loan-to-value ratios above 95%; 15% were interest-only; and 28% did not have full documentation.[170] Fannie also purchased $36 billion of subprime and $12 billion of Alt-A non-GSE mortgage-backed securities.[171] The total amount of riskier loans represented larger multiples of capital than before.

At least initially, while house prices were still increasing, the strategic plan to increase risk and market share appeared to be successful. Fannie reported net income of $6 billion in 2005 and then $4 billion in 2006. In those two years, CEO Mudd's compensation totaled $24.4 million and Levin, who was interim CFO and then chief business officer, received $15.5 million.[172]

In 2006, Freddie Mac also continued to increase risk, "expand[ing] the purchase and guarantee of higher-risk mortgages . . . to increase market share, meet mission goals, stay competitive, and be responsive to sellers' needs."[173] It lowered its underwriting standards, increasing the use of credit policy waivers and exceptions. Newer alternative products, offered to a broader range of customers than ever before, accounted for about 24% of that year's purchases. Freddie Mac's plan also seemed to be successful. The company increased risk and market share while maintaining the same net income for 2005 and 2006, $2 billion.[174] CEO Richard Syron's compensation totaled $23.2 million for 2005 and 2006 combined,[175] while Chief Operating Officer Eugene McQuade received $13.4 million.[176]

Again, OFHEO was aware of these developments. Its March 2007 report noted that Fannie's new initiative to purchase higher-risk products included a plan to capture 20% of the subprime market by 2011. And OFHEO reported that credit risk increased "slightly" because of growth in subprime and other nontraditional products. But overall asset quality in its single-family business was found to be "strong," and the board members were "qualified and active." And, of course, Fannie was "adequately capitalized."[177]

Similarly, OFHEO told Freddie in 2007 that it had weaknesses that raised some possibility of failure, but that overall, Freddie's strength and financial capacity made failure unlikely.[178] Freddie did remain a "significant supervisory concern,"[179] and OFHEO noted the significant shift toward higher-risk mortgages.[180] But again, as in previous years, the regulator concluded that Freddie had "adequate capital," and its asset quality and credit risk management were "strong."[181]

The GSEs charged a fee for guaranteeing payments on GSE mortgage–backed securities, and OFHEO was silent about Fannie's practice of charging less to guarantee securities than their models indicated was appropriate. Mark Winer, the head of Fannie's Business, Analysis and Decisions Group since May 2006 and the person responsible for

modeling pricing fees, raised concerns that Fannie Mae was not charging fees for Alt-A mortgages that adequately compensated for the risk. Winer recalled that Levin was critical of his models, asking, "Can you show me why you think you're right and everyone else is wrong?"[182] Undercharging for the guarantee fees was intended to increase market share, according to Todd Hempstead, the senior vice president at Fannie in charge of the western region.[183] Mudd acknowledged the difference between the model fee and the fee actually charged and also told the FCIC that the scarcity of historical data for many loans caused the model fee to be unreliable.[184]

In the September 6, 2008, memo that would recommend that Fannie be placed into conservatorship, OFHEO would expressly cite this practice as unsafe and unsound: "During 2006 and 2007, modeled loan fees were higher than actual fees charged, due to an emphasis on growing market share and competing with Wall Street and the other GSE."[185]

### 2007: "Moving deeper into the credit pool"

By the time housing prices had peaked in the second quarter of 2006, delinquencies had started to rise. During the board meeting held in April 2007, Lund said that dislocation in the housing market was an opportunity for Fannie to reclaim market share. At the same time, Fannie would support the housing market by increasing liquidity.[186] At the next month's meeting, Lund reported that Fannie's market share could increase to 60% from about 37% in 2006.[187] Indeed, in 2007 Fannie Mae forged ahead, purchasing more high-risk loans.[188] Fannie also purchased $16 billion of subprime non-GSE securities, and $5 billion of Alt-A.[189]

In June, Fannie prepared its 2007 five-year strategic plan, titled "Deepen Segments—Develop Breadth." The plan, which mentioned Fannie's "tough new challenges—a weakening housing market" and "slower-growing mortgage debt market"—included taking and managing "more mortgage credit risk, moving deeper into the credit pool to serve a large and growing part of the mortgage market." Overall, revenues and earnings were projected to increase in each of the following five years.[190]

Management told the board that Fannie's risk management function had all the necessary means and budget to act on the plan. Chief Risk Officer Dallavecchia did not agree, especially in light of a planned 16% cut in his budget. In a July 16, 2007, email to CEO Mudd, Dallavecchia wrote that he was very upset that he had to hear at the board meeting that Fannie had the "will and the money to change our culture and support taking more credit risk," given the proposed budget cut for his department in 2008 after a 25% reduction in headcount in 2007.[191] In an earlier email, Dallavecchia had written to Chief Operating Officer Michael Williams that Fannie had "one of the weakest control processes" that he "ever witnessed in [his] career, . . . was not even close to having proper control processes for credit, market and operational risk," and was "already back to the old days of scraping on controls . . . to reduce expenses." These deficiencies indicated that "people don't care about the [risk] function or they don't get it."[192]

Mudd responded, "My experience is that email is not a very good venue for conversation, venting or negotiating." If Dallavecchia felt that he had been dealt with in bad faith, he should "address it man to man," unless he wanted Mudd "to be the one to carry messages for you to your peers." Mudd concluded, "Please come and see me today face to face."[193] Dallavecchia told the FCIC that when he wrote this email he was tired and upset, and that the view it expressed was more extreme than what he thought at the time.[194] Fannie, after continuing to purchase and guarantee higher-risk mortgages in 2007, would report a $2.1 billion net loss for the year, caused by credit losses. In 2007, Mudd's compensation totaled $11.6 million and Levin's totaled $7 million.

In 2007, Freddie Mac also persisted in increasing purchases of riskier loans. A strategic plan from March highlighted "pressure on the franchise" and the "risk of falling below our return aspirations."[195] The company would try to improve earnings by entering adjacent markets: "Freddie Mac has competitive advantages over non-GSE participants in nonprime," the strategy document explained. "We have an opportunity to expand into markets we have missed—Subprime and Alt-A."[196] It took that opportunity. As OFHEO would note in its 2007 examination report, Freddie purchased and guaranteed loans originated in 2006 and 2007 with higher-risk characteristics, including interest-only loans, loans with FICO scores less than 620, loans with higher loan-to-value ratios, loans with high debt-to-income ratios, and loans without full documentation. Financial results in 2007 were poor: a $3.1 billion net loss driven by credit losses. The value of the $152 billion subprime and Alt-A private-label securities book suffered a $13 billion decline in market value.[197] In 2007, Syron's compensation totaled $18.3 million and McQuade's totaled $3.8 million.

### Affordable housing goals: "GSEs cried bloody murder forever"

As discussed earlier, beginning in 1978, the Department of Housing and Urban Development (HUD) periodically set goals for the GSEs related to increasing homeownership among low- and moderate-income borrowers and borrowers in underserved areas. Until 2005, these goals were based on the fraction of the total mortgage market made up of low- and moderate-income families. The goals were intended to be only a modest reach beyond the mortgages that the GSEs would normally purchase.[198]

From 1997 to 2000, 42% of GSE purchases were required to meet goals for low- and moderate-income borrowers. In 2001, the goal was raised to 50%.[199] Mudd said that as long as the goals remained below half of the GSEs' lending, loans made in the normal course of business would satisfy the goals: "What comes in the door through the natural course of business will tend to match the market, and therefore will tend to meet the goals."[200] Levin told the FCIC that "there was a great deal of business that came through normal channels that met goals" and that most of the loans that satisfied the goals "would have been made anyway."[201]

In 2004 HUD announced that starting in 2005, 52% of the GSEs' purchases would need to satisfy the low- and moderate-income goals. The targets would reach 55% in 2007 and 56% in 2008.[202] Given the dramatic growth in the number of riskier loans

originated in the market, the new goals were closer to where the market really was. But, as Mudd noted, "When 50% became 57[%] ultimately, then you have to work harder, pay more attention, and create a preference for those loans."[203] Targeted goals loans (loans made specifically to meet the targets), while always a small share of the GSEs' purchases, rose in importance.

Mudd testified that by 2008, when the housing market was in turmoil, Fannie Mae could no longer balance its obligations to shareholders with its affordable housing goals and other mission-related demands: "There may have been no way to satisfy 100% of the myriad demands for Fannie Mae to support all manner of projects [or] housing goals which were set above the origination levels in the marketplace."[204] As the combined size of the GSEs rose steadily from $3.6 trillion in 2003 to $4.9 trillion in 2007,[205] the number of mortgage borrowers that the GSEs needed to serve in order to fulfill the affordable housing goals also rose. By 2005, Fannie and Freddie were stretching to meet the higher goals, according to a number of GSE executives, OFHEO officials, and market observers.

Yet all but two of the dozens of current and former Fannie Mae employees and regulators interviewed on the subject told the FCIC that reaching the goals was not the primary driver of the GSEs' purchases of riskier mortgages and of subprime and Alt-A non-GSE mortgage–backed securities. Executives from Fannie, including Mudd, pointed to a "mix" of reasons for the purchases, such as reversing the declines in market share, responding to originators' demands, and responding to shareholder demands to increase market share and profits, in addition to fulfilling the mission of meeting affordable housing goals and providing liquidity to the market.

For example, Levin told the FCIC that while Fannie, to meet its housing goals, did purchase some subprime mortgages and mortgage-backed securities it would otherwise have passed up, Fannie was driven to "meet the market" and to reverse declining market share. On the other hand, he said that most Alt-A loans were high-income-oriented and would not have counted toward the goals, so those were purchased solely to increase profits.[206] Similarly, Lund told the FCIC that the desire for market share was the main driver behind Fannie's strategy in 2006. Housing goals had been a factor, but not the primary one.[207] And Dallavecchia likewise told the FCIC that Fannie increased its purchases of Alt-A loans to regain relevance in the market and meet customer needs.[208]

Hempstead, Fannie's principal contact with Countrywide, told the FCIC that while housing goals were one reason for Fannie's strategy, the main reason Fannie entered the riskier mortgage market was that those were the types of loans being originated in the primary market.[209] If Fannie wanted to continue purchasing large quantities of loans, the company would need to buy riskier loans. Kenneth Bacon, Fannie's executive vice president of multifamily lending, said much the same thing, and added that shareholders also wanted to see market share and returns rise.[210] Former Fannie chairman Stephen Ashley told the FCIC that the change in strategy in 2005 and 2006 was owed to a "mix of reasons," including the desire to regain market share and the need to respond to pressures from originators as well as to pressures from real estate industry advocates to be more engaged in the marketplace.[211]

To ensure an adequate supply of mortgages in case the goals were not met in the normal course of business, Fannie and Freddie instituted outreach programs in underserved geographic areas and conducted educational programs for originators and brokers.[212] In addition, as explained by Mike Quinn, the Fannie executive responsible for the goals, Fannie set lower fees on loans that met the goals, although it would not purchase mortgages that fell outside its predetermined risk targets.[213] Ashley also maintained that Fannie did not shift eligibility or underwriting standards to meet goals but instead directed its resources to marketing and promotional efforts, housing fairs, and outreach programs run by the company's partnership offices. "The effort was really in the outreach as opposed to reduced or diminished or loosened standards," Ashley told the FCIC.[214]

Former OFHEO Director Armando Falcon Jr. testified that the GSEs invested in subprime and Alt-A mortgages in order to increase profits and regain market share and that any impact on meeting affordable housing goals was simply a by-product of this activity.[215] Lockhart, a subsequent OFHEO director, attributed the GSEs' change in strategy to their drive for profit and market share, as well as the need to meet housing goals. Noting that the affordable housing goals increased markedly in 2005,[216] he said in an FCIC interview that the "goals were just one reason, certainly not the exclusive reason" for the change.[217] These views were corroborated by numerous other officials from the agency.[218]

The former HUD official Mike Price told the FCIC that while the "GSEs cried bloody murder forever" when it came to the goals, they touted their contribution to increasing homeownership. In addition, Price and other HUD officials told the FCIC that the GSEs never claimed that meeting the goals would leave them in an unsafe or unsound condition.[219]

Indeed, the law allowed both Fannie Mae and Freddie Mac to fall short of meeting housing goals that were "infeasible" or that would affect the companies' safety and soundness.[220] And while the GSEs often exceeded the goals, in some cases those targets were adjusted downward by HUD or, in rare cases, were simply missed by the GSEs.[221] For example, on December 12, 2007, Mudd wrote to HUD: "Fannie Mae believes that the low- and moderate-income and special affordable subgoals are infeasible for 2007."[222] Fannie Mae's 2007 strategic plan had already anticipated such a communication, stating, "In the event we reach a viewpoint that achieving the goals this year is 'infeasible,' we will determine how best to address the matter with HUD and will continue to keep the Board apprised accordingly."[223] In fact, both Fannie and Freddie appealed to HUD to lower two components of the goals for affordable housing. HUD complied and allowed the GSEs to fall short without any consequences.[224]

## The impact of the goals

At least until HUD set new affordable housing goals for 2005, the GSEs only supplemented their routine purchases with a small volume of loans and non-GSE mortgage-backed securities needed to meet their requirements. The GSEs knew that they might not earn as much on these targeted goal loans as they would earn on both

goal-qualifying and non-goal-qualifying loans purchased in the usual course of business; on some of these loans, they might even lose money. The organizations also had administrative and other costs related to the housing goals.

In June 2009 Freddie Mac staff made a presentation to the Business and Risk Committee of the Board of Directors on the costs of meeting its goals. From 2000 to 2003, the cost of the targeted goal loans was effectively zero, as the goals were reached through "profitable expansion" of the company's multifamily business. During the refinance boom, the goals became more challenging and cost Freddie money in the multifamily business; thus, only after 2004 did meeting the multifamily and single-family goals cost the GSE money. Still, only about 4% of all loans purchased by Freddie between 2005 and 2008 were bought "specifically because they contribute to the goals"—loans it labeled as "targeted affordable." These loans did have higher than average expected default rates, although Freddie also charged a higher fee to guarantee them. From 2003 through 2008, Freddie's costs of complying with the housing goals averaged $200 million annually. The costs of complying with these goals took into account three components: expected revenues, expected defaults, and foregone revenues (based on an assumption of what they might have earned elsewhere). These costs were only computed on the narrow set of loans specifically purchased to achieve the goals, as opposed to goal-qualifying loans purchased in the normal course of business.[225] For comparison, the company's net earnings averaged just under $3 billion per year from 2003 to 2006.[226]

In 2004, Fannie Mae retained McKinsey and Citigroup to determine whether it would be worthwhile to give up the company's charter as a GSE, which—while affording the company enormous benefits—imposed regulations and put constraints on business practices, including its mission goals. The final report to Fannie Mae's top management, called Project Phineas, found that the explicit cost of compliance with the goals from 2000 to 2003 was close to zero: "it is hard to discern a fundamental marginal cost to meeting the housing goals on the single family business side."[227] The report came to this conclusion despite the slightly greater difficulty of meeting the goals in the 2003 refinancing boom: the large numbers of homeowners refinancing, in particular those who were middle and upper income, necessarily reduced the percentage of the pool that would qualify for the goals.

In calculating these costs, the consultants computed the difference between fees charged on goal-qualifying loans and the higher fees suggested by Fannie's own models. But this cost was not unique to goal qualifying loans. Across its portfolio, Fannie charged lower fees than its models computed for goals loans as well as for non-goals loans. As a result, goals loans, even targeted goals loans, were not solely responsible for this cost. In fact, Fannie's discount was actually smaller for many goal-qualifying loans than for the others from 2000 to 2004.

Facing more aggressive goals in 2006 and 2007, Fannie Mae expanded initiatives to purchase targeted goals loans. These included mortgages acquired under the My Community Mortgage program, mortgages underwritten with looser standards, and manufactured housing loans. For these loans, Fannie explicitly calculated the opportunity cost (foregone revenues based on an assumption of what they might have

earned elsewhere) along with the so-called cash flow cost, or the difference between their expected losses and expected revenue on these loans. For 2006, as the market was peaking, Fannie Mae estimated the cash flow cost of the loans to be $115 million and the opportunity cost of the targeted goals loans $390 million, compared to net income that year to Fannie of $4.1 billion—a figure that includes returns on the goal-qualifying loans made during the normal course of business.[228] The targeted goals loans amounted to $18 billion, or 3.4%, of Fannie Mae's $524 billion of single-family mortgage purchases in 2006.[229] As the markets tightened in the middle of 2007, the opportunity cost for that year was forecast to be roughly $1 billion.[230]

Looking back at how the targeted affordable portfolio performed in comparison with overall losses, the 2009 presentation at Freddie Mac took the analysis of the goals' costs one step further. While the outstanding $60 billion of these targeted affordable loans was only 4% of the total portfolio, these were relatively high-risk loans and were expected to account for 19% of total projected losses. In fact, as of late 2008, they had accounted for only 8% of losses—meaning that they had performed better than expected in relation to the whole portfolio. The company's major losses came from loans acquired in the normal course of business. The presentation noted that many of these defaulted loans were Alt-A.[231]

---

### COMMISSION CONCLUSIONS ON CHAPTER 9

The Commission concludes that firms securitizing mortgages failed to perform adequate due diligence on the mortgages they purchased and at times knowingly waived compliance with underwriting standards. Potential investors were not fully informed or were misled about the poor quality of the mortgages contained in some mortgage-related securities. These problems appear to have been significant. The Securities and Exchange Commission failed to adequately enforce its disclosure requirements governing mortgage securities, exempted some sales of such securities from its review, and preempted states from applying state law to them, thereby failing in its core mission to protect investors.

The Federal Reserve failed to recognize the cataclysmic danger posed by the housing bubble to the financial system and refused to take timely action to constrain its growth, believing that it could contain the damage from the bubble's collapse.

Lax mortgage regulation and collapsing mortgage-lending standards and practices created conditions that were ripe for mortgage fraud.

# 10

# THE MADNESS

## CONTENTS

The collateralized debt obligation machine could have sputtered to a natural end by the spring of 2006. Housing prices peaked, and AIG started to slow down its business of insuring subprime-mortgage CDOs. But it turned out that Wall Street didn't need its golden goose any more. Securities firms were starting to take on a significant share of the risks from their own deals, without AIG as the ultimate bearer of the risk of losses on super-senior CDO tranches. The machine kept humming throughout 2006 and into 2007. "That just seemed kind of odd, given everything we had seen and what we had concluded," Gary Gorton, a Yale finance professor who had designed AIG's model for analyzing its CDO positions, told the FCIC.[1]

The CDO machine had become self-fueling. Senior executives—particularly at three of the leading promoters of CDOs, Citigroup, Merrill Lynch, and UBS—apparently did not accept or perhaps even understand the risks inherent in the products they were creating. More and more, the senior tranches were retained by the arranging securities firms, the mezzanine tranches were bought by other CDOs, and the equity tranches were bought by hedge funds that were often engaged in complex trading strategies: they made money when the CDOs performed, but could also make money if the market crashed. These factors helped keep the mortgage market going long after house prices had begun to fall and created massive exposures on the books of large financial institutions—exposures that would ultimately bring many of them to the brink of failure.

The subprime mortgage securitization pioneer Lewis Ranieri called the willing suspension of prudent standards "the madness." He told the FCIC, "You had the

breakdown of the standards, . . . because you break down the checks and balances that normally would have stopped them."[2]

Synthetic CDOs boomed. They provided easier opportunities for bullish and bearish investors to bet for and against the housing boom and the securities that depended on it. Synthetic CDOs also made it easier for investment banks and CDO managers to create CDOs more quickly. But synthetic CDO issuers and managers had two sets of customers, each with different interests. And managers sometimes had help from customers in selecting the collateral—including those who were betting against the collateral, as a high-profile case launched by the Securities and Exchange Commission against Goldman Sachs would eventually illustrate.[3]

Regulators reacted weakly. As early as 2005, supervisors recognized that CDOs and credit default swaps (CDS) could actually concentrate rather than diversify risk, but they concluded that Wall Street knew what it was doing. Supervisors issued guidance in late 2006 warning banks of the risks of complex structured finance transactions—but excluded mortgage-backed securities and CDOs, because they saw the risks of those products as relatively straightforward and well understood.[4]

Disaster was fast approaching.

## CDO MANAGERS: "WE ARE NOT A RENT-A-MANAGER"

During the "madness," when everyone wanted a piece of the action, CDO managers faced growing competitive pressures. Managers' compensation declined, as demand for mortgage-backed securities drove up prices, squeezing the profit they made on CDOs. At the same time, new CDO managers were entering the arena. Wing Chau, a CDO manager who frequently worked with Merrill Lynch, said the fees fell by half for mezzanine CDOs over time.[5] And overall compensation could be maintained by creating and managing more new product.

More than had been the case three or four years earlier, in picking the collateral the managers were influenced by the underwriters—the securities firms that created and marketed the deals. An FCIC survey of 40 CDO managers confirmed this point.[6] Sometimes managers were given a portfolio constructed by the securities firm; the managers would then choose the mortgage assets from that portfolio. The equity investors—who often initiated the deal in the first place—also influenced the selection of assets in many instances. Still, some managers said that they acted independently. "We are not a rent-a-manager, we actually select our collateral," said Lloyd Fass, the general counsel at Vertical Capital.[7] As we will see, securities firms often had particular CDO managers with whom they preferred to work. Merrill, the market leader, had a constellation of managers; CDOs underwritten by Merrill frequently bought tranches of other Merrill CDOs.

According to market participants, CDOs stimulated greater demand for mortgage-backed securities, particularly those with high yields, and the greater demand in turn affected the standards for originating mortgages underlying those securities.[8] As standards fell, at least one firm opted out: PIMCO, one of the largest investment

funds in the country, whose CDO management unit was one of the nation's largest in 2004. Early in 2005, it announced that it would not manage any new deals, in part because of the deterioration in the credit quality of mortgage-backed securities. "There is an awful lot of moral hazard in the sector," Scott Simon, a managing director at PIMCO, told the audience at an industry conference in 2005. "You either take the high road or you don't—we're not going to hurt accounts or damage our reputation for fees." Simon said the rating agencies' methodologies were not sufficiently stringent, particularly because they were being applied to new types of subprime and Alt-A loans with little or no historical performance data.[9] Not everyone agreed with this viewpoint. "Managers who are sticking in this business are doing it right," Armand Pastine, the chief operating officer at Maxim Group, responded at that same conference. "To suggest that CDO managers would pull out of an economically viable deal for moral reasons—that's a cop-out."[10] As was typical for the industry during the crisis, two of Maxim's eight mortgage-backed CDOs, Maxim High Grade CDO I and Maxim High Grade CDO II, would default on interest payments to investors—including investors holding bonds that had originally been rated triple-A—and the other six would be downgraded to junk status, including all of those originally rated triple-A.[11]

Another development also changed the CDOs: in 2005 and 2006, CDO managers were less likely to put their own money into their deals. Early in the decade, investors had taken the managers' investment in the equity tranche of their own CDOs to be an assurance of quality, believing that if the managers were sharing the risk of loss, they would have an incentive to pick collateral wisely. But this fail-safe lost force as the amount of managers' investment per transaction declined over time. ACA Management, a unit of the financial guarantor ACA Capital, provides a good illustration of this trend. ACA held 100% of the equity in the CDOs it originated in 2002 and 2003, 52% and 61% of two deals it originated in 2004, between 10% and 25% of deals in 2005, and between 0% and 11% of deals in 2006.[12]

And synthetic CDOs, as we will see, had no fail-safe at all with regard to the managers' incentives. By the very nature of the credit default swaps bundled into these synthetics, customers on the short side of the deal were betting that the assets would fail.

## CREDIT DEFAULT SWAPS: "DUMB QUESTION"

In June 2005, derivatives dealers introduced the "pay-as-you-go" credit default swap, a complex instrument that mimicked the timing of the cash flows of real mortgage-backed securities.[13] Because of this feature, the synthetic CDOs into which these new swaps were bundled were much easier to issue and sell.

The pay-as-you-go swap also enabled a second major development, introduced in January 2006: the first index based on the prices of credit default swaps on mortgage-backed securities. Known as the ABX.HE, it was really a series of indices, meant to act as a sort of Dow Jones Industrial Average for the nonprime mortgage market, and it became a popular way to bet on the performance of the market. Every six months, a

consortium of securities firms would select 20 credit default swaps on mortgage-backed securities in each of five ratings-based tranches: AAA, AA, A, BBB, and BBB-. Investors who believed that the bonds in any given category would fall behind in their payments could buy protection through credit default swaps. As demand for protection rose, the index would fall. The index was therefore a barometer recording the confidence of the market.

Synthetic CDOs proliferated, in part because it was much quicker and easier for managers to assemble a synthetic portfolio out of pay-as-you-go credit default swaps than to assemble a regular cash CDO out of mortgage-backed securities. "The beauty in a way of the synthetic deals is you can look at the entire universe, you don't have to go and buy the cash bonds," said Laura Schwartz of ACA Capital.[14] There were also no warehousing costs or associated risks. And they tended to offer the potential for higher returns on the equity tranches: one analyst estimated that the equity tranche on a synthetic CDO could typically yield about 21%, while the equity tranche of a typical cash CDO could pay 13%.[15]

An important driver in the growth of synthetic CDOs was the demand for credit default swaps on mortgage-backed securities. Greg Lippmann, a Deutsche Bank mortgage trader, told the FCIC that he often brokered these deals, matching the "shorts" with the "longs" and minimizing any risk for his own bank. Lippmann said that between 2006 and 2007 he brokered deals for at least 50 and maybe as many as 100 hedge funds that wanted to short the mezzanine tranches of mortgage-backed securities. Meanwhile, on the long side, "Most of our CDS purchases were from UBS, Merrill, and Citibank, because they were the most aggressive underwriters of [synthetic] CDOs."[16] In many cases, they were buying those positions from Lippmann to put them into synthetic CDOs; as it would turn out, the banks would retain much of the risk of those synthetic CDOs by keeping the super-senior and triple-A tranches, selling below-triple-A tranches largely to other CDOs, and selling equity tranches to hedge funds.

Issuance of synthetic CDOs jumped from $15 billion in 2005 to $61 billion just one year later. (We include all CDOs with 50% or more synthetic collateral; again, unless otherwise noted, our data refers to CDOs that include mortgage-backed securities.) Even CDOs that were labeled as "cash CDOs" increasingly held some credit derivatives. A total of $225 billion in CDOs were issued in 2006, including those labeled as cash, "hybrid," or synthetic; the FCIC estimates that 27% of the collateral was derivatives, compared with 9% in 2005 and 7% in 2004.[17]

The advent of synthetic CDOs changed the incentives of CDO managers and hedge fund investors. Once short investors were involved, the CDO had two types of investors with opposing interests: those who would benefit if the assets performed, and those who would benefit if the mortgage borrowers stopped making payments and the assets failed to perform.

Even the incentives of long investors became conflicted. Synthetic CDOs enabled sophisticated investors to place bets against the housing market or pursue more complex trading strategies. Investors, usually hedge funds, often used credit default swaps to take offsetting positions in different tranches of the same CDO security; that way,

they could make some money as long as the CDOs performed, but they stood to make more money if the entire market crashed. An FCIC survey of more than 170 hedge funds encompassing over $1.1 trillion in assets as of early 2010 found this to be a common strategy among medium-size hedge funds: of all the CDOs issued in the second half of 2006, more than half of the equity tranches were purchased by hedge funds that also shorted other tranches.[18] The same approach was being used in the mortgage-backed securities market as well. The FCIC's survey found that by June 2007, the largest hedge funds held $25 billion in equity and other lower-rated tranches of mortgage-backed securities. These were more than offset by $45 billion in short positions.[19]

These types of trades changed the structured finance market. Investors in the equity and most junior tranches of CDOs and mortgage-backed securities traditionally had the greatest incentive to monitor the credit risk of an underlying portfolio. With the advent of credit default swaps, it was no longer clear who—if anyone—had that incentive.

For one example, consider Merrill Lynch's $1.5 billion Norma CDO, issued in 2007. The equity investor, Magnetar Capital, a hedge fund, was executing a common strategy known as the correlation trade—it bought the equity tranche while shorting other tranches in Norma and other CDOs. According to court documents, Magnetar was also involved in selecting assets for Norma.[20] Magnetar received $4.5 million related to this transaction and NIR Capital Management, the CDO manager, was paid a fee of $75,000 plus additional fees.[21] Magnetar's counsel told the FCIC that the $4.5 million was a discount in the form of a rebate on the price of the equity tranche and other long positions purchased by Magnetar and not a payment received in return for good or services.[22] Court documents indicate that Magnetar was involved in selecting collateral, and that NIR abdicated its asset selection duties to Magnetar with Merrill's knowledge. In addition, they show that when one Merrill employee learned that Magnetar had executed approximately $600 million in trades for Norma without NIR's apparent involvement or knowledge, she emailed colleagues, "Dumb question. Is Magnetar allowed to trade for NIR?"[23] Merrill failed to disclose that Magnetar was paid $4.5 million or that Magnetar was selecting collateral when it also had a short position that would benefit from losses.[24]

The counsel for Merrill's new owner, Bank of America, explained to the FCIC that it was a common industry practice for "the equity investor in a CDO, which had the riskiest investment, to have input during the collateral selection process[;] . . . however, the collateral manager made the ultimate decisions regarding portfolio composition."[25] The letter did not specifically mention the Norma CDO. Bank of America failed to produce documents related to this issue requested by the FCIC.

Federal regulators have identified abuses that involved short investors influencing the choice of the instruments inside synthetic CDOs. In April 2010, the SEC charged Goldman Sachs with fraud for telling investors that an independent CDO manager, ACA Management, had picked the underlying assets in a CDO when in fact a short investor, the Paulson & Co. hedge fund, had played a "significant role" in the selection. The SEC alleged that those misrepresentations were in Goldman's marketing materials for Abacus 2007-AC1, one of Goldman's 24 Abacus deals.[26]

Ira Wagner, the head of Bear Stearns's CDO Group in 2007, told the FCIC that he rejected the deal when approached by Paulson representatives. When asked about Goldman's contention that Paulson's picking the collateral was immaterial because the collateral was disclosed and because Paulson was not well-known at that time, Wagner called the argument "ridiculous." He said that the structure encouraged Paulson to pick the worst assets. While acknowledging the point that every synthetic deal necessarily had long and short investors, Wagner saw having the short investors select the referenced collateral as a serious conflict and for that reason declined to participate.[27]

ACA executives told the FCIC they were not initially aware that the short investor was involved in choosing the collateral. CEO Alan Roseman said that he first heard of Paulson's role when he reviewed the SEC's complaint.[28] Laura Schwartz, who was responsible for the deal at ACA, said she believed that Paulson's firm was the investor taking the equity tranche and would therefore have an interest in the deal performing well. She said she would not have been surprised that Paulson would also have had a short position, because the correlation trade was common in the market, but added, "To be honest, [at that time,] until the SEC testimony I did not even know that Paulson was only short."[29] Paulson told the FCIC that any synthetic CDO would have to invest in "a pool that both a buyer and seller of protection could agree on." He didn't understand the objections: "Every [synthetic] CDO has a buyer and seller of protection. So for anyone to say that they didn't want to structure a CDO because someone was buying protection in that CDO, then you wouldn't do any CDOs."[30]

In July 2010, Goldman Sachs settled the case, paying a record $550 million fine. Goldman "acknowledge[d] that the marketing materials for the ABACUS 2007-AC1 transaction contained incomplete information. In particular, it was a mistake for the Goldman marketing materials to state that the reference portfolio was 'selected by' ACA Management LLC without disclosing the role of Paulson & Co. Inc. in the portfolio selection process and that Paulson's economic interests were adverse to CDO investors."[31]

The new derivatives provided a golden opportunity for bearish investors to bet against the housing boom. Home prices in the hottest markets in California and Florida had blasted into the stratosphere; it was hard for skeptics to believe that their upward trajectory could continue. And if it did not, the landing would not be a soft one. Some spoke out publicly. Others bet the bubble would burst. Betting against CDOs was also, in some cases, a bet against the rating agencies and their models. Jamie Mai and Ben Hockett, principals at the small investment firm Cornwall Capital, told the FCIC that they had warned the SEC in 2007 that the agencies were dangerously overoptimistic in their assessment of mortgage-backed CDOs. Mai and Hockett saw the rating agencies as "the root of the mess," because their ratings removed the need for buyers to study prices and perform due diligence, even as "there was a massive amount of gaming going on."[32]

Shorting CDOs was "pretty attractive" because the rating agencies had given too much credit for diversification, Sihan Shu of Paulson & Co. told the FCIC. Paulson established a fund in June 2006 that initially focused only on shorting BBB-rated tranches. By the end of 2007, Paulson & Co.'s Credit Opportunities fund, set up less

than a year earlier to bet exclusively against the subprime housing market, was up 590%. "Each MBS tranche typically would be 30% mortgages in California, 10% in Florida, 10% in New York, and when you aggregate 100 MBS positions you still have the same geographic diversification. To us, there was not much diversification in CDOs." Shu's research convinced him that if home prices were to stop appreciating, BBB-rated mortgage-backed securities would be at risk for downgrades. Should prices drop 5%, CDO losses would increase 20-fold.[33]

And if a relatively small number of the underlying loans were to go into fore-closure, the losses would render virtually all of the riskier BBB-rated tranches worthless. "The whole system worked fine as long as everyone could refinance," Steve Eisman, the founder of a fund within FrontPoint Partners, told the FCIC. The minute refinancing stopped, "losses would explode. . . . By 2006, about half [the mortgages sold] were no-doc or low-doc. You were at max underwriting weakness at max housing prices. And so the system imploded. Everyone was so levered there was no ability to take any pain."[34] On October 6, 2006, James Grant wrote in his newsletter about the "mysterious alchemical processes" in which "Wall Street transforms BBB-minus-rated mortgages into AAA-rated tranches of mortgage securities" by creating CDOs. He estimated that even the triple-A tranches of CDOs would experience some losses if national home prices were to fall just 4% or less within two years; and if prices were to fall 10%, investors of tranches rated AA- or below would be completely wiped out.[35]

In 2005, Eisman and others were already looking for the best way to bet on this disaster by shorting all these shaky mortgage-related securities. Buying credit default swaps was efficient. Eisman realized that he could pick what he considered the most vulnerable tranches of the mortgage-backed bonds and bet millions of dollars against them, relatively cheaply and with considerable leverage. And that's what he did.

By the end of 2007, Eisman had put millions of dollars into short positions on credit default swaps. It was, he was sure, just a matter of time. "Everyone really did believe that things were going to be okay," Eisman said. "[I] thought they were certifiable lunatics."[36]

Michael Burry, another short who became well-known after the crisis hit, was a doctor-turned-investor whose hedge fund, Scion Capital, in Northern California's Silicon Valley, bet big against mortgage-backed securities—reflecting a change of heart, because he had invested in homebuilder stocks in 2002. But the closer he looked, the more he wondered about the financing that supported this booming market. Burry decided that some of the newfangled adjustable rate mortgages were "the most toxic mortgages" created. He told the FCIC, "I watched those with interest as they migrated down the credit spectrum to the subprime market. As [home] prices had increased on the back of virtually no accompanying rise in wages and incomes, I came to the judgment that in two years there will be a final judgment on housing when those two-year [adjustable rate mortgages] seek refinancing."[37] By the middle of 2005, Burry had bought credit default swaps on billions of dollars of mortgage-backed securities and the bonds of financial companies in the housing market, including Fannie Mae, Freddie Mac, and AIG.

Eisman, Cornwall, Paulson, and Burry were not alone in shorting the housing mar-

ket. In fact, on one side of tens of billions of dollars worth of synthetic CDOs were investors taking short positions. The purchasers of credit default swaps illustrate the impact of derivatives in introducing new risks and leverage into the system. Although these investors profited spectacularly from the housing crisis, they never made a single subprime loan or bought an actual mortgage. In other words, they were not purchasing insurance against anything they owned. Instead, they merely made side bets on the risks undertaken by others. Paulson told the FCIC that his research indicated that if home prices remained flat, losses would wipe out the BBB-rated tranches; meanwhile, at the time he could purchase default swap protection on them very cheaply.[38]

On the other side of the zero-sum game were often the major U.S. financial institutions that would eventually be battered. Burry acknowledged to the FCIC, "There is an argument to be made that you shouldn't allow what I did." But the problem, he said, was not the short positions he was taking; it was the risks that others were accepting. "When I did the shorts, the whole time I was putting on the positions . . . there were people on the other side that were just eating them up. I think it's a catastrophe and I think it was preventable."[39]

Credit default swaps greased the CDO machine in several ways. First, they allowed CDO managers to create synthetic and hybrid CDOs more quickly than they could create cash CDOs. Second, they enabled investors in the CDOs (including the originating banks, such as Citigroup and Merrill) to transfer the risk of default to the issuer of the credit default swap (such as AIG and other insurance companies). Third, they made correlation trading possible. As the FCIC survey revealed, most hedge fund purchases of equity and other junior tranches of mortgage-backed securities and CDOs were done as part of complex trading strategies.[40] As a result, credit default swaps were critical to facilitate demand from hedge funds for the equity or other junior tranches of mortgage-backed securities and CDOs. Finally, they allowed speculators to make bets for or against the housing market without putting up much cash.

On the other hand, it can be argued that credit default swaps helped end the housing and mortgage-backed securities bubble. Because CDO arrangers could more easily buy mortgage exposure for their CDOs through credit default swaps than through actual mortgage-backed securities, demand for credit default swaps may in fact have reduced the need to originate high-yield mortgages. In addition, some market participants have contended that without the ability to short the housing market via credit default swaps, the bubble would have lasted longer. As we will see, the declines in the ABX index in late 2006 would be one of the first harbingers of market turmoil. "Once [pessimists] can, in effect, sell short via the CDS, prices must reflect their views and not just the views of the leveraged optimists," John Geanakoplos, a Yale economics professor and a partner in the hedge fund Ellington Capital Management, which both invested in and managed CDOs, told the FCIC.[41]

## CITIGROUP: "I DO NOT BELIEVE WE WERE POWERLESS"

While the hedge funds were betting against the housing market in 2005 and 2006, Citigroup's CDO desk was pushing more money to the center of the table.

But after writing $25 billion in liquidity puts—protecting investors who bought commercial paper issued by Citigroup's CDOs—the bank's treasury department had put a stop to the practice. To keep doing deals, the CDO desk had to find another market for the super-senior tranches of the CDOs it was underwriting—or it had to find a way to get the company to support the CDO production line. The CDO desk accumulated another $18 billion in super-senior exposures, most between early 2006 and August 2007, which it otherwise would have been able to sell into the market only for a loss.[42] It was also increasingly financing securities that it was holding in its CDO warehouse—that is, securities that were waiting to be put into new CDOs.

Historically, owning securities was not what securities firms did. The adage "We are in the moving business, not the storage business" suggests that they were structuring and selling securities, not buying or retaining them.

However, as the biggest commercial banks and investment banks competed in the securities business in the late 1990s and on into the new century, they often touted the "balance sheet" that they could make available to support the sale of new securities. In this regard, Citigroup broke new ground in the CDO market. Citigroup retained significant exposure to potential losses on its CDO business, particularly within Citibank, the $1 trillion commercial bank whose deposits were insured by the FDIC. While its competitors did the same, few did so as aggressively or, ultimately, with such losses.

In 2006, Citigroup retained the super-senior and triple-A tranches of most of the CDOs it created. In many cases Citigroup would hedge the associated credit risk from these tranches by obtaining credit protection from a monoline insurance company such as Ambac. Because these hedges were in place, Citigroup presumed that the risk associated with the retained tranches had been neutralized.

Citigroup reported these tranches at values for which they could not be sold, raising questions about their accuracy and, therefore, the accuracy of reported earnings. "As everybody in any business knows, if inventory is growing, that means you're not pricing it correctly," Richard Bookstaber, who had been head of risk management at Citigroup in the late 1990s, told the FCIC. But keeping the tranches on the books at these prices improved the finances for creating the deal. "It was a hidden subsidy of the CDO business by mispricing," Bookstaber said.[43] The company would not begin writing the securities down toward the market's real valuations until the fall of 2007.

Part of the reason for retaining exposures to super-senior positions in CDOs was their favorable capital treatment. As we saw in an earlier chapter, under the 2001 Recourse Rule, one of the attractions of triple-A-rated securities was that banks were required to hold relatively less capital against them than against lower-rated securities. And if the bank held those assets in their trading account (as opposed to holding them as a long-term investment), it could get even better capital treatment under the 1996 Market Risk Amendment. That rule allowed banks to use their own models to determine how much capital to hold, an amount that varied according to how much market prices moved. Citigroup judged that the capital requirement for the super-senior tranches of synthetic CDOs it held for trading purposes was effectively zero, be-

cause the prices didn't move much. As a result, Citigroup held little regulatory capital against the super-senior tranches.

Citibank also held "unfunded" positions in super-senior tranches of some synthetic CDOs; that is, it sold protection to the CDO. If the referenced mortgage collateral underperformed, the short investors would begin to get paid. Money to pay them would come first from wiping out long investors who had bought tranches that were below triple-A. Then, if the short investors were still owed money, Citibank would have to pay. For taking on this risk, Citi typically received about 0.20% to 0.40% in annual fees on the super-senior protection; on a billion-dollar transaction, it would earn an annual fee of $2 million to $4 million.

Citigroup also had exposure to the mortgage-backed and other securities that went into CDOs during the ramp-up period, which could be as long as six or nine months, before it packaged and sold the CDO. Typically, Citigroup's securities unit would set up a warehouse funding line for the CDO manager. During the ramp-up period, the collateral securities would pay interest; depending on the terms of the agreement, that interest would either go exclusively to Citigroup or be split with the manager. For the CDO desk, this frequently represented a substantial income stream. The securities sitting in the warehouse facility had relatively attractive yields—often 1.0% to 2.5% more than the typical bank borrowing rate—and it was not uncommon for the CDO desk to earn $10 to $15 million in interest on a single transaction.[44] Traders on the desk would get credit for those revenues at bonus time. But Citigroup would also be on the hook for any losses incurred on assets stuck in the warehouse. When the financial crisis deepened, many CDO transactions could not be completed; Citigroup and other investment banks were forced to write down the value of securities held in their warehouses. The result would be substantial losses across Wall Street. In many cases, to offload assets underwriters placed collateral from CDO warehouses into other CDOs.

A factor that made firm-wide hedging complicated was that different units of Citigroup could have various and offsetting exposures to the same CDO. It was possible, even likely, that the CDO desk would structure a given CDO, a different division would buy protection for the underlying collateral, and yet another division would buy the unfunded super-senior tranche. If the collateral in this CDO ran into trouble, the CDO immediately would have to pay the division that bought credit protection on the underlying collateral; if the CDO ran out of money to pay, it would have to draw on the division that bought the unfunded tranche. In November 2007, after Citigroup had reported substantial losses on its CDO portfolio, regulators would note that the company did not have a good understanding of its firmwide CDO exposures: "The nature, origin, and size of CDO exposure were surprising to many in senior management and the board. The liquidity put exposure was not well known. In particular, management did not consider or effectively manage the credit risk inherent in CDO positions."[45]

Citigroup's willingness to use its balance sheet to support the CDO business had the desired effect. Its CDO desk created $11 billion in CDOs that included mortgage-

backed securities in their collateral in 2005 and $22 billion in 2006. Among CDO underwriters, including all types of CDOs, Citigroup rose from fourteenth place in 2003 to second place in 2007, according to FCIC analysis of Moody's data.[46]

What was good for Citigroup's investment bank was also lucrative for its investment bankers. Thomas Maheras, the co-CEO of the investment bank who said he spent less than 1% of his time thinking about CDOs, was a highly paid Citigroup executive, earning more than $34 million in salary and bonus compensation in 2006. Co-head of Global Fixed Income Randolph Barker made about $21 million in that same year. Citigroup's chief risk officer made $7.4 million.[47] Others were also well rewarded. The co-heads of the global CDO business, Nestor Dominguez and Janice Warne, each made about $6 million in total compensation in 2006.[48]

Citi did have "clawback" provisions: under narrowly specified circumstances, compensation would have to be returned to the firm. But despite Citigroup's eventual large losses, no compensation was ever clawed back under this policy. The Corporate Library, which rates firms' corporate governance, gave Citigroup a C. In early 2007, the Corporate Library would downgrade Citigroup to a D, "reflecting a high degree of governance risk." Among the issues cited: executive compensation practices that were poorly aligned with shareholder interests.[49]

Where were Citigroup's regulators while the company piled up tens of billions of dollars of risk in the CDO business? Citigroup had a complex corporate structure and, as a result, faced an array of supervisors. The Federal Reserve supervised the holding company but, as the Gramm-Leach-Bliley legislation directed, relied on others to monitor the most important subsidiaries: the Office of the Comptroller of the Currency (OCC) supervised the largest bank subsidiary, Citibank, and the SEC supervised the securities firm, Citigroup Global Markets. Moreover, Citigroup did not really align its various businesses with the legal entities. An individual working on the CDO desk on an intricate transaction could interact with various components of the firm in complicated ways.

The SEC regularly examined the securities arm on a three-year examination cycle, although it would also sometimes conduct other examinations to target specific concerns. Unlike the Fed and OCC, which had risk management and safety and soundness rules, the SEC used these exams to look for general weaknesses in risk management. Unlike safety and soundness regulators, who concentrated on preventing firms from failing, the SEC always kept its focus on protecting investors. Its most recent review of Citigroup's securities arm preceding the crisis was in 2005, and the examiners completed their report in June 2006. In that exam, they told the FCIC, they saw nothing "earth shattering," but they did note key weaknesses in risk management practices that would prove relevant—weaknesses in internal pricing and valuation controls, for example, and a willingness to allow traders to exceed their risk limits.[50]

Unlike the SEC, the Fed and OCC did maintain a continuous on-site presence. During the years that CDOs boomed, the OCC team regularly criticized the company for its weaknesses in risk management, including specific problems in the CDO

business. "Earnings and profitability growth have taken precedence over risk management and internal control," the OCC told the company in January 2005.[51] Another document from that year stated, "The findings of this examination are disappointing, in that the business grew far in excess of management's underlying infrastructure and control processes."[52] In May 2005, a review undertaken by peers at the other Federal Reserve banks was critical of the New York Fed—then headed by the current treasury secretary, Timothy Geithner—for its oversight of Citigroup. The review concluded that the Fed's on-site Citigroup team appeared to have "insufficient resources to conduct continuous supervisory activities in a consistent manner. At Citi, much of the limited team's energy is absorbed by topical supervisory issues that detract from the team's continuous supervision objectives . . . the level of the staffing within the Citi team has not kept pace with the magnitude of supervisory issues that the institution has realized."[53] That the Fed's 2005 examination of Citigroup did not raise the concerns expressed that same year by the OCC may illustrate these problems. Four years later, the next peer review would again find substantial weaknesses in the New York Fed's oversight of Citigroup.[54]

In April 2006, the Fed raised the holding company's supervisory rating from the previous year's "fair" to "satisfactory."[55] It lifted the ban on new mergers imposed the previous year in response to Citigroup's many regulatory problems.[56] The Fed and OCC examiners concurred that the company had made "substantial progress" in implementing CEO Charles Prince's plan to overhaul risk management. The Fed declared: "The company has . . . completed improvements necessary to bring the company into substantial compliance with two existing Federal Reserve enforcement actions related to the execution of highly structured transactions and controls."[57] The following year, Citigroup's board would allude to Prince's successful resolution of its regulatory compliance problems in justifying his 20% compensation increase.[58]

The OCC noted in retrospect that the lifting of supervisory constraints in 2006 had been a key turning point. "After regulatory restraints against significant acquisitions were lifted, Citigroup embarked on an aggressive acquisition program," the OCC wrote to Vikram Pandit, Prince's replacement, in early 2008. "Additionally, with the removal of formal and informal agreements, the previous focus on risk and compliance gave way to business expansion and profits." Meanwhile, risk managers granted exceptions to limits, and increased exposure limits, instead of keeping business units in check as they had told the regulators.[59] Well after Citigroup sustained large losses on its CDOs, the Fed would criticize the firm for using its commercial bank to support its investment banking activities. "Senior management allowed business lines largely unchallenged access to the balance sheet to pursue revenue growth," the Fed wrote in an April 2008 letter to Pandit. "Citigroup attained significant market share across numerous products, including leveraged finance and structured credit trading, utilizing balance sheet for its 'originate to distribute' strategy. Senior management did not appropriately consider the potential balance sheet implications of this strategy in the case of market disruptions. Further, they did not adequately access the potential negative impact of earnings volatility of these businesses on the firm's capital position."[60]

Geithner told the Commission that he and others in leadership positions could have done more to prevent the crisis, testifying, "I do not believe we were powerless."[61]

## AIG: "I'M NOT GETTING PAID ENOUGH
## TO STAND ON THESE TRACKS"

Unlike their peers at Citigroup, some senior executives at AIG's Financial Products subsidiary had figured out that the company was taking on too much risk. Nonetheless, they did not do enough about it. Doubts about all the credit default swaps that they were originating emerged in 2005 among AIG Financial Products executives, including Andrew Forster and Gene Park. Park told the FCIC that he witnessed Financial Products CEO Joseph Cassano berating a salesman over the large volume of credit default swaps being written by AIG Financial Products, suggesting there was already some high-level uneasiness with these deals. Told by a consultant, Gary Gorton, that the "multisector" CDOs on which AIG was selling credit default swaps consisted mainly of mortgage-backed securities with less than 10% subprime and Alt-A mortgages, Park asked Adam Budnick, another AIG employee, for verification. Budnick double checked and returned to say, according to Park, "'I can't believe it. You know, it's like 80 or 90%.'" Reviewing the portfolio—and thinking about a friend who had received 100% financing for his new home after losing his job—Park said, "This is horrendous business. We should get out of it."[62]

In July 2005, Park's colleague Andrew Forster sent an email both to Alan Frost, the AIG salesman primarily responsible for the company's booming credit default swap business, and to Gorton, who had engineered the formula to determine how much risk AIG was taking on each CDS it wrote. "We are taking on a huge amount of sub prime mortgage exposure here," Forster wrote. "Everyone we have talked to says they are worried about deals with huge amounts [of high-risk mortgage] exposure yet I regularly see deals with 80% [high-risk mortgage] concentrations currently. Are these really the same risk as other deals?"[63]

Park and others studied the issue for weeks, talked to bank analysts and other experts, and considered whether it made sense for AIG to continue to write protection on the subprime and Alt-A mortgage markets. The general view of others was that some of the underlying mortgages "were structured to fail, [but] that all the borrowers would basically be bailed out as long as real estate prices went up."[64]

The AIG consultant Gorton recalled a meeting that he and others from AIG had with one Bear Stearns analyst. The analyst was so optimistic about the housing market that they thought he was "out of his mind" and "must be on drugs or something."[65] Speaking of a potential decline in the housing market, Park related to the FCIC the risks as he and some of his colleagues saw them, saying, "We weren't getting paid enough money to take that risk. . . . I'm not going to opine on whether there's a train on its way. I just know that I'm not getting paid enough to stand on these tracks."[66]

By February 2006, Park and others persuaded Cassano and Frost to stop writing

CDS protection on subprime mortgage–backed securities. In an email to Cassano on February 28, Park wrote:

> Joe,
>
> Below summarizes the message we plan on delivering to dealers later this week with regard to our approach to the CDO of ABS super senior business going forward. We feel that the CDO of ABS market has increasingly become less diverse over the last year or so and is currently at a state where deals are almost totally reliant on subprime/non prime residential mortgage collateral. Given current trends in the housing market, our perception of deteriorating underwriting standards, and the potential for higher rates we are no longer as comfortable taking such concentrated exposure to certain parts of the non prime mortgage securitizations. On the deals that we participate on we would like to see significant change in the composition of these deals going forward—i.e. more diversification into the non-correlated asset classes.
>
> As a result of our ongoing due diligence we are not as comfortable with the mezzanine layers (namely BBB and single A tranches) of this asset class. . . . We realize that this is likely to take us out of the CDO of ABS market for the time being given the arbitrage in subprime collateral. However, we remain committed to working with underwriters and managers in developing the CDO of ABS market to hopefully become more diversified from a collateral perspective. With that in mind, we will be open to including new asset classes to these structures or increasing allocations to others such as [collateralized loan obligations] and [emerging market] CDOs.[67]

AIG's counterparties responded with indifference. "The day that you [AIG] drop out, we're going to have 10 other people who are going to replace you," Park says he was told by an investment banker at another firm.[68] In any event, counterparties had some time to find new takers, because AIG Financial Products continued to write the credit default swaps. While the bearish executives were researching the issue from the summer of 2005 onward, the team continued to work on deals that were in the pipeline, even after February 2006. Overall, they completed 37 deals between September 2005 and July 2006—one of them on a CDO backed by 93% subprime assets.[69]

By June 2007, AIG had written swaps on $79 billion in multisector CDOs, five times the $18 billion held at the end of 2005.[70] Park asserted that neither he nor most others at AIG knew at the time that the swaps entailed collateral calls on AIG if the market value of the referenced securities declined.[71] Park said their concern was simply that AIG would be on the hook if subprime and Alt-A borrowers defaulted in large numbers. Cassano, however, told the FCIC that he did know about the possible

calls,[72] but AIG's SEC filings to investors for 2005 mentioned the risk of collateral calls only if AIG were downgraded.

Still, AIG never hedged more than $150 million of its total subprime exposure.[73] Some of AIG's counterparties not only used AIG's swaps to hedge other positions but also hedged AIG's ability to make good on its contracts. As we will see later, Goldman Sachs hedged aggressively by buying CDS protection on AIG and by shorting other securities and indexes to counterbalance the risk that AIG would fail to pay up on its swaps or that a collapsing subprime market would pull down the value of mortgage-backed securities.

## MERRILL: "WHATEVER IT TAKES"

When Dow Kim became co-president of Merrill Lynch's Global Markets and Investment Banking Group in July 2003, he was instructed to boost revenue, especially in businesses in which Merrill lagged behind its competitors.[74] Kim focused on the CDO business; clients saw CDOs as an integral part of their trading strategy, CEO Stanley O'Neal told the FCIC.[75] Kim hired Chris Ricciardi from Credit Suisse, where Ricciardi's group had sold more CDOs than anyone else.[76]

Ricciardi came through, lifting Merrill's CDO business from fifteenth place in 2002 to second place behind only Citigroup in 2004 and Goldman in 2005.[77] Then, in February 2006, he left the bank to become CEO of Cohen & Company, an asset management business; at Cohen he would manage several CDOs, often deals underwritten by Merrill.

After Ricciardi left, Kim instructed the rest of the team to do "whatever it takes" not just to maintain market share but also to take over the number one ranking, former employees said in a complaint filed against Merrill Lynch.[78] Kim told FCIC staff that he couldn't recall specific conversations but that after Ricciardi left, Merrill was still trying to expand the CDO business globally and that he, Kim, wanted people to know that Merrill was willing to commit its people, resources, and balance sheet to achieve that goal.[79]

It was indeed willing. Despite the loss of its rainmaker, Merrill swamped the competition, originating a total $38.9 billion in mortgage-related CDOs in 2006, while the second-ranked firm, Morgan Stanley, did only $21.3 billion, and earning another first-place ranking in 2007,[80] on the strength of the CDO machine Ricciardi had built—a machine that brought in more than $1 billion in fees between 2003 and 2006.[81]

To keep its CDO business going, Merrill pursued three strategies, all of which involved repackaging riskier mortgages more attractively or buying its own products when no one else would. Like Citigroup, Merrill increasingly retained for its own portfolio substantial portions of the CDOs it was creating, mainly the super-senior tranches, and it increasingly repackaged the hard-to-sell BBB-rated and other low-rated tranches of its CDOs into its other CDOs; it used the cash sitting in its synthetic CDOs to purchase other CDO tranches.

It had long been standard practice for CDO underwriters to sell some mezzanine tranches to other CDO managers. Even in the early days of ABS CDOs, these assets often contained a small percentage of mezzanine tranches of other CDOs; the rating agencies signed off on this practice when rating each deal. But reliance on them became heavier as the demand from traditional investors waned, as it had for the riskier tranches of mortgage-backed securities. The market came to call traditional investors the "real money," to distinguish them from CDO managers who were buying tranches just to put them into their CDOs. Between 2005 and 2007, the typical amount a CDO could include of the tranches of other CDOs and still maintain its ratings grew from 5% to 30%, according to the CDO manager Wing Chau.[82] According to data compiled by the FCIC, tranches from CDOs rose from an average of 7% of the collateral in mortgage-backed CDOs in 2003 to 14% by 2007. CDO-squared deals—those engineered primarily from the tranches of other CDOs—grew from 36 marketwide in 2005 to 48 in 2006 and 41 in 2007. Merrill created and sold 11 of them.[83]

Still, there are clear signs that few "real money" investors remained in the CDO market by late 2006. Consider Merrill: for the 44 ABS CDOs that Merrill created and sold from the fourth quarter of 2006 through August 2007, nearly 80% of the mezzanine tranches were purchased by CDO managers.[84] The pattern was similar for Chau: an FCIC analysis determined that 88% of the mezzanine tranches sold by the 13 CDOs managed by Chau were sold for inclusion into other CDOs.[85] An estimated 10 different CDO managers purchased tranches in Merrill's Norma CDO. In the most extreme case found by the FCIC, CDO managers were the only purchasers of Merrill's Neo CDO.[86]

Marketwide, in 2003 CDOs took in about 13% of the A tranches, 23% of the Aa tranches, and 43% of the Baa tranches issued by other CDOs, as rated by Moody's. (Moody's rating of Aaa is equivalent to S&P's AAA, Aa to AA, Baa to BBB, and Ba to BB). In 2007, those numbers were 87%, 81%, and 89%, respectively.[87] Merrill and other investment banks simply created demand for CDOs by manufacturing new ones to buy the harder-to-sell portions of the old ones.

As SEC attorneys told the FCIC, heading into 2007 there was a Streetwide gentleman's agreement: you buy my BBB tranche and I'll buy yours.[88]

Merrill and its CDO managers were the biggest buyers of their own products. Merrill created and sold 142 CDOs from 2003 to 2007. All but 8 of these—134 CDOs—sold at least one tranche into another Merrill CDO. In Merrill's deals, on average, 10% of the collateral packed into the CDOs consisted of tranches of other CDOs that Merrill itself had created and sold. This was a relatively high percentage, but not the highest: for Citigroup, another big player in this market, the figure was 13%. For UBS, it was just 3%.[89]

Managers defended the practice. Chau, who managed 13 CDOs created and sold by Merrill at Maxim Group and later Harding Advisory and had worked with Ricciardi at Prudential Securities in the early days of multisector CDOs, told the FCIC that plain mortgage-backed securities had become expensive in relation to their returns, even as the real estate market sagged. Because CDOs paid better returns than did

similarly rated mortgage-backed securities, they were in demand, and that is why CDO managers packed their securities with other CDOs.[90]

And Merrill continued to push its CDO business despite signals that the market was weakening. As late as the spring of 2006, when AIG stopped insuring even the very safest, super-senior CDO tranches for Merrill and others, it did not reconsider its strategy. Cut off from AIG, which had already insured $9.9 billion of its CDO bonds[91]—Merrill was AIG's third-largest counterparty, after Goldman and Société Générale—Merrill switched to the monoline insurance companies for protection. In the summer of 2006, Merrill management noticed that Citigroup, its biggest competitor in underwriting CDOs, was taking more super-senior tranches of CDOs onto its own balance sheet at razor-thin margins, and thus in effect subsidizing returns for investors in the BBB-rated and equity tranches. In response, Merrill continued to ramp up its CDO warehouses and inventory; and in an effort to compete and get deals done, it increasingly took on super-senior positions without insurance from AIG or the monolines.[92]

This would not be the end of Merrill's all-in wager on the mortgage and CDO businesses. Even though it did grab the first-place trophy in the mortgage-related CDO business in 2006, it had come late to the "vertical integration" mortgage model that Lehman Brothers and Bear Stearns had pioneered, which required having a stake in every step of the mortgage business—originating mortgages, bundling these loans into securities, bundling these securities into other securities, and selling all of them on Wall Street. In September 2006, months after the housing bubble had started to deflate and delinquencies had begun to rise, Merrill announced it would acquire a subprime lender, First Franklin Financial Corp., from National City Corp. for $1.3 billion. As a finance reporter later noted, this move "puzzled analysts because the market for subprime loans was souring in a hurry."[93] And Merrill already had a $100 million ownership position in Ownit Mortgage Solutions Inc., for which it provided a warehouse line of credit; it also provided a line of credit to Mortgage Lenders Network.[94] Both of those companies would cease operations soon after the First Franklin purchase.[95]

Nor did Merrill cut back in September 2006, when one of its own analysts issued a report warning that this subprime exposure could lead to a sudden cut in earnings, because demand for these mortgages assets could dry up quickly.[96] That assessment was not in line with the corporate strategy, and Merrill did nothing. Finally, at the end of 2006, Kim instructed his people to reduce credit risk across the board.[97] As it would turn out, they were too late. The pipeline was too large.

## REGULATORS: "ARE UNDUE CONCENTRATIONS OF RISK DEVELOPING?"

As had happened when they faced the question of guidance on nontraditional mortgages, in dealing with the rapidly changing structured finance market the regulators failed to take timely action. They missed a crucial opportunity. On January 2, 2003, one year after the collapse of Enron, the U.S. Senate Permanent Subcommittee on In-

vestigations called on the Fed, OCC, and SEC "to immediately initiate a one-time, joint review of banks and securities firms participating in complex structured finance products with U.S. public companies to identify those structured finance products, transactions, or practices which facilitate a U.S. company's use of deceptive accounting in its financial statements or reports." The subcommittee recommended the agencies issue joint guidance on "acceptable and unacceptable structured finance products, transactions and practices" by June 2003.[98] Four years later, the banking agencies and the SEC issued their "Interagency Statement on Sound Practices Concerning Elevated Risk Complex Structured Finance Activities," a document that was all of nine pages long.[99]

In the intervening years, from 2003 to 2007, the banking agencies and SEC issued two draft statements for public comment. The 2004 draft, issued the year after the OCC, Fed, and SEC had brought enforcement actions against Citigroup and JP Morgan for helping Enron to manipulate its financial statements, focused on the policies and procedures that financial institutions should have for managing the structured finance business.[100] The aim was to avoid another Enron—and for that reason, the statement encouraged financial institutions to look out for customers that, like Enron, were trying to use structured transactions to circumvent regulatory or financial reporting requirements, evade tax liabilities, or engage in other illegal or improper behavior.

Industry groups criticized the draft guidance as too broad, prescriptive, and burdensome. Several said it would cover many structured finance products that did not pose significant legal or reputational risks. Another said that it "would disrupt the market for legitimate structured finance products and place U.S. financial institutions at a competitive disadvantage in the market for [complex structured finance transactions] in the United States and abroad."[101]

Two years later, in May 2006, the agencies issued an abbreviated draft that reflected a more "principles-based" approach, and again requested comments. Most of the requirements were very similar to those that the OCC and Fed had imposed on Citigroup and JP Morgan in the 2003 enforcement actions.[102]

When the regulators issued the final guidance in January 2007, the industry was more supportive. One reason was that mortgage-backed securities and CDOs were specifically excluded: "Most structured finance transactions, such as standard public mortgage-backed securities and hedging-type transactions involving 'plain vanilla' derivatives or collateralized debt obligations, are familiar to participants in the financial markets, have well-established track records, and typically would not be considered [complex structured finance transactions] for purposes of the Final Statement."[103] Those exclusions had been added after the regulators received comments on the 2004 draft.

Regulators did take note of the potential risks of CDOs and credit default swaps. In 2005, the Basel Committee on Banking Supervision's Joint Forum, which includes banking, securities, and insurance regulators from around the world, issued a comprehensive report on these products. The report focused on whether banks and other firms involved in the CDO and credit default swap business understood the credit

risk they were taking. It advised them to make sure that they understood the nature of the rating agencies' models, especially for CDOs. And it further advised them to make sure that counterparties from whom they bought credit protection—such as AIG and the financial guarantors—would be good for that protection if it was needed.[104]

The regulators also said they had researched in some depth, for the CDO and derivatives market, the question "Are undue concentrations of risk developing?" Their answer: probably not. The credit risk was "quite modest," the regulators concluded, and the monoline financial guarantors appeared to know what they were doing.[105]

> The [Joint Forum's Working Group on Risk Assessment and Capital] has not found evidence of 'hidden concentrations' of credit risk. There are some non-bank firms whose primary business model focuses on taking on credit risk. Most important among these firms are the monoline financial guarantors. Other market participants seem to be fully aware of the nature of these firms. In the case of the monolines, credit risk has always been a primary business activity and they have invested heavily in obtaining the relevant expertise. While obviously this does not rule out the potential for one of these firms to experience unanticipated problems or to misjudge the risks, their risks are primarily at the catastrophic or macroeconomic level. It is also clear that such firms are subjected to regulatory, rating agency, and market scrutiny.[106]

The regulators noted that industry participants appeared to have learned from earlier flare-ups in the CDO sector: "The Working Group believes that it is important for investors in CDOs to seek to develop a sound understanding of the credit risks involved and not to rely solely on rating agency assessments. In many respects, the losses and downgrades experienced on some of the early generation of CDOs have probably been salutary in highlighting the potential risks involved."[107]

## MOODY'S: "IT WAS ALL ABOUT REVENUE"

Like other market participants, Moody's Investors Service, one of the three dominant rating agencies, was swept up in the frenzy of the structured products market. The tranching structure of mortgage-backed securities and CDOs was standardized according to guidelines set by the agencies; without their models and their generous allotment of triple-A ratings, there would have been little investor interest and few deals. Between 2002 and 2006, the volume of Moody's business devoted to rating residential mortgage–backed securities more than doubled; the dollar value of that business increased from $62 million to $169 million; the number of staff rating these deals doubled. But over the same period, while the volume of CDOs to be rated increased sevenfold, staffing increased only 24%. From 2003 to 2006, annual revenue tied to CDOs grew from $12 million to $91 million.[108]

When Moody's Corporation went public in 2000, the investor Warren Buffett's

Berkshire Hathaway held 15% of the company. After share repurchases by Moody's Corporation, Berkshire Hathaway's holdings of outstanding shares increased to over 20% by 2008. As of 2010, Berkshire Hathaway and three other investors owned a combined 50.5% of Moody's. When asked whether he was satisfied with the internal controls at Moody's, Buffett responded to the FCIC that he knew nothing about the management of Moody's. "I had no idea. I'd never been at Moody's, I don't know where they are located."[109] Buffett said that he invested in the company because the rating agency business was "a natural duopoly," which gave it "incredible" pricing power—and "the single-most important decision in evaluating a business is pricing power."[110]

Many former employees said that after the public listing, the company culture changed—it went "from [a culture] resembling a university academic department to one which values revenues at all costs," according to Eric Kolchinsky, a former managing director.[111] Employees also identified a new focus on market share directed by former president of Moody's Investors Service Brian Clarkson. Clarkson had joined Moody's in 1991 as a senior analyst in the residential mortgage group, and after successive promotions he became co-chief operating officer of the rating agency in 2004, and then president in August 2007.[112] Gary Witt, a former team managing director covering U.S. derivatives, described the cultural transformation under Clarkson: "My kind of working hypothesis was that [former chairman and CEO] John Rutherford was thinking, 'I want to remake the culture of this company to increase profitability dramatically [after Moody's became an independent corporation],' and that he made personnel decisions to make that happen, and he was successful in that regard. And that was why Brian Clarkson's rise was so meteoric: . . . he was the enforcer who could change the culture to have more focus on market share."[113] The former managing director Jerome Fons, who was responsible for assembling an internal history of Moody's, agreed: "The main problem was . . . that the firm became so focused, particularly the structured area, on revenues, on market share, and the ambitions of Brian Clarkson, that they willingly looked the other way, traded the firm's reputation for short-term profits."[114]

Moody's Corporation Chairman and CEO Raymond McDaniel did not agree with this assessment, telling the FCIC that he didn't see "any particular difference in culture" after the spin-off.[115] Clarkson also disputed this version of events, explaining that market share was important to Moody's well before it was an independent company. "[The idea that before Moody's] was spun off from Dun & Bradstreet, it was a sort of sleepy, academic kind of company that was in an ivory tower . . . isn't the case, you know," he explained. "I think [the ivory tower] was really a misnomer. I think that Moody's has always been focused on business."[116]

Clarkson and McDaniel also adamantly disagreed with the perception that concerns about market share trumped ratings quality. Clarkson told the FCIC that it was fine for Moody's to lose transactions if it was for the "right reasons": "If it was an analytical reason or it was a credit reason, there's not a lot you can do about that. But if you're losing a deal because you're not communicating, you're not being transparent, you're not picking up the phone, that could be problematic."[117] McDaniel cited unforeseen market conditions as the reason that the models did not accurately predict the credit

quality.[118] He testified to the FCIC, "We believed that our ratings were our best opinion at the time that we assigned them. As we obtained new information and were able to update our judgments based on the new information and the trends we were seeing in the housing market, we made what I think are appropriate changes to our ratings."[119]

Nonetheless, Moody's president did not seem to have the same enthusiasm for compliance as he did for market share and profit, according to those who worked with him. Scott McCleskey, a former chief compliance officer at Moody's, recounted a story to the FCIC about an evening when he and Clarkson were dining with the board of directors after the company had announced strong earnings, particularly in the business of rating mortgage-backed securities and CDOs. "So Brian Clarkson comes up to me, in front of everybody at the table, including board members, and says literally, 'How much revenue did Compliance bring in this quarter? Nothing. Nothing.' . . . For him to say that in front of the board, that's just so telling of how he felt that he was bulletproof. . . . For him, it was all about revenue."[120] Clarkson told the FCIC that he didn't remember this conversation transpiring and said, "From my perspective, compliance is a very important function."[121]

According to some former Moody's employees, Clarkson's management style left little room for discussion or dissent. Witt referred to Clarkson as the "dictator" of Moody's and said that if he asked an employee to do something, "either you comply with his request or you start looking for another job."[122] "When I joined Moody's in late 1997, an analyst's worst fear was that we would contribute to the assignment of a rating that was wrong," Mark Froeba, former senior vice president, testified to the FCIC. "When I left Moody's, an analyst's worst fear was that he would do something, or she, that would allow him or her to be singled out for jeopardizing Moody's market share."[123] Clarkson denied having a "forceful" management style, and his supervisor, Raymond McDaniel, told the FCIC that Clarkson was a "good manager."[124]

Former team managing director Gary Witt recalled that he received a monthly email from Clarkson "that outlined basically my market share in the areas that I was in charge of. . . . I believe it listed the deals that we did, and then it would list the deals like S&P and/or Fitch did that we didn't do that was in my area. And at times, I would have to comment on that verbally or even write a written report about—you know, look into what was it about that deal, why did we not rate it. So, you know, it was clear that market share was important to him." Witt acknowledged the pressures that he felt as a manager: "When I was an analyst, I just thought about getting the deals right. . . . Once I [was promoted to managing director and] had a budget to meet, I had salaries to pay, I started thinking bigger picture. I started realizing, yes, we do have shareholders and, yes, they deserved to make some money. We need to get the ratings right first, that's the most important thing; but you do have to think about market share."[125]

Even as far back as 2001, a strong emphasis on market share was evident in employee performance evaluations. In July 2001, Clarkson circulated a spreadsheet to subordinates that listed 49 analysts and the number and dollar volume of deals each had "rated" or "NOT rated." Clarkson's instructions: "You should be using this in PE's

[performance evaluations] and to give people a heads up on where they stand relative to their peers."[126] Team managing directors, who oversaw the analysts rating the deals, received a base salary, cash bonus, and stock options. Their performance goals generally fell into the categories of market coverage, revenue, market outreach (such as speeches and publications), ratings quality, and development of analytical tools, only one of which was impossible to measure in real time as compensation was being awarded: ratings quality. It might take years for the poor quality of a rating to become clear as the rated asset failed to perform as expected.

In January 2006, a derivatives manager listed his most important achievements in a 2005 performance evaluation. At the top of the list: "Protected our market share in the CDO corporate cash flow sector. . . . To my knowledge we missed only one CLO [collateralized loan obligation] from BofA and that CLO was unratable by us because of it's [sic] bizarre structure."[127]

More evidence of Moody's emphasis on market share was provided by an email that circulated in the fall of 2007, in the midst of significant downgrades in the structured finance market. Group Managing Director of U.S. Derivatives Yuri Yoshizawa asked her team's managing directors to explain a market share decrease from 98% to 94%.[128]

Despite this apparent emphasis on market share, Clarkson told the FCIC that "the most important goal for any managing director would be credibility . . . and performance [of] the ratings."[129] McDaniel, the chairman and CEO of Moody's Corporation, elaborated: "I disagree that there was a drive for market share. We pay attention to our position in the market. . . . But ratings quality, getting the ratings to the best possible predictive content, predictive status, is paramount."[130]

Whatever McDaniel's or Clarkson's intended message, some employees continued to see an emphasis on Moody's market share. Former team managing director Witt recalled that the "smoking gun" moment of his employment at Moody's occurred during a "town hall" meeting in the third quarter of 2007 with Moody's management and its managing directors, after Moody's had already announced mass downgrades on mortgage-related securities.[131] After McDaniel made a presentation about Moody's financial outlook for the year ahead, one managing director responded: "I was interested, Ray, to hear your belief that the first thing in the minds of people in this room is the financial outlook for the remainder of the year. . . . [M]y thinking is there's a much greater concern about the franchise." He added, "I think that the greater anxiety being felt by the people in this room and . . . by the analysts is what's going on with the ratings and what the outlook is[,] . . . specifically the severe ratings transitions we're dealing with . . . and uncertainty about what's ahead on that, the ratings accuracy."[132] Witt recalled, "Moody's reputation was just being absolutely lacerated; and that these people are standing here, and they're not even addressing—they're acting like it's not even happening, even now that it's already happened. . . . [T]hat just made it so clear to me . . . that the balance was far too much on the side of short-term profitability."[133]

In an internal memorandum from October 2007 sent to McDaniel, in a section titled "Conflict of Interest: Market Share," Chief Credit Officer Andrew Kimball

explained that "Moody's has erected safeguards to keep teams from too easily solving the market share problem by lowering standards." But he observed that these protections were far from fail-safe, as he detailed in two area. First, "Ratings are assigned by committee, not individuals. (However, entire committees, entire departments, are susceptible to market share objectives)." Second, "Methodologies & criteria are published and thus put boundaries on rating committee discretion. (However, there is usually plenty of latitude within those boundaries to register market influence.)"[134]

Moreover, the pressure for market share, combined with complacency, may have deterred Moody's from creating new models or updating its assumptions, as Kimball wrote: "Organizations often interpret past successes as evidencing their competence and the adequacy of their procedures rather than a run of good luck. . . . [O]ur 24 years of success rating RMBS [residential mortgage–backed securities] may have induced managers to merely fine-tune the existing system—to make it more efficient, more profitable, cheaper, more versatile. Fine-tuning rarely raises the probability of success; in fact, it often makes success less certain."[135]

If an issuer didn't like a Moody's rating on a particular deal, it might get a better rating from another ratings agency. The agencies were compensated only for rated deals—in effect, only for the deals for which their ratings were accepted by the issuer. So the pressure came from two directions: in-house insistence on increasing market share and direct demands from the issuers and investment bankers, who pushed for better ratings with fewer conditions.[136]

Richard Michalek, a former Moody's vice president and senior credit officer, testified to the FCIC, "The threat of losing business to a competitor, even if not realized, absolutely tilted the balance away from an independent arbiter of risk towards a captive facilitator of risk transfer."[137] Witt agreed. When asked if the investment banks frequently threatened to withdraw their business if they didn't get their desired rating, Witt replied, "Oh God, are you kidding? All the time. I mean, that's routine. I mean, they would threaten you all of the time. . . . It's like, 'Well, next time, we're just going to go with Fitch and S&P.'"[138] Clarkson affirmed that "it wouldn't surprise me to hear people say that" about issuer pressure on Moody's employees.[139]

Former managing director Fons suggested that Moody's was complaisant when it should have been principled: "[Moody's] knew that they were being bullied into caving in to bank pressure from the investment banks and originators of these things. . . . Moody's allow[ed] itself to be bullied. And, you know, they willingly played the game. . . . They could have stood up and said, 'I'm sorry, this is not—we're not going to sign off on this. We're going to protect investors. We're going to stop—you know, we're going to try to protect our reputation. We're not going to rate these CDOs, we're not going to rate these subprime RMBS.'"[140]

Kimball elaborated further in his October 2007 memorandum:

> Ideally, competition would be primarily on the basis of ratings quality, with a second component of price and a third component of service.

Unfortunately, of the three competitive factors, rating quality is proving the least powerful given the long tail in measuring performance. . . . The real problem is not that the market does underweights [sic] ratings quality but rather that, in some sectors, it actually penalizes quality by awarding rating mandates based on the lowest credit enhancement needed for the highest rating. Unchecked, competition on this basis can place the entire financial system at risk. It turns out that ratings quality has surprisingly few friends: issuers want high ratings; investors don't want rating downgrades; and bankers game the rating agencies for a few extra basis points on execution.[141]

Moody's employees told the FCIC that one tactic used by the investment bankers to apply subtle pressure was to submit a deal for a rating within a very tight time frame. Kolchinsky, who oversaw ratings on CDOs, recalled the case of a particular CDO: "What the trouble on this deal was, and this is crucial about the market share, was that the banker gave us hardly any notice and any documents and any time to analyze this deal. . . . Because bankers knew that we could not say no to a deal, could not walk away from the deal because of a market share, they took advantage of that."[142] For this CDO deal, the bankers allowed only three or four days for review and final judgment. Kolchinsky emailed Yoshizawa that the transactions had "egregiously pushed our time limits (and analysts)."[143] Before the frothy days of the peak of the housing boom, an agency took six weeks or even two months to rate a CDO.[144] By 2006, Kolchinsky described a very different environment in the CDO group: "Bankers were pushing more aggressively, so that it became from a quiet little group to more of a machine."[145] In 2006, Moody's gave triple-A ratings to an average of more than 30 mortgage securities each and every working day.[146]

Such pressure can be seen in an April 2006 email to Yoshizawa from a managing director in synthetic CDO trading at Credit Suisse, who explained, "I'm going to have a major political problem if we can't make this [deal rating] short and sweet because, even though I always explain to investors that closing is subject to Moody's timelines, they often choose not to hear it."[147]

The external pressure was summed up in Kimball's October 2007 memorandum: "Analysts and [managing directors] are continually 'pitched' by bankers, issuers, investors—all with reasonable arguments—whose views can color credit judgment, sometimes improving it, other times degrading it (we 'drink the kool-aid'). Coupled with strong internal emphasis on market share & margin focus, this does constitute a 'risk' to ratings quality."[148]

The SEC investigated the rating agencies' ratings of mortgage-backed securities and CDOs in 2007, reporting its findings to Moody's in July 2008. The SEC criticized Moody's for, among other things, failing to verify the accuracy of mortgage information, leaving that work to due diligence firms and other parties; failing to retain documentation about how most deals were rated; allowing ratings quality to be compromised by the complexity of CDO deals; not hiring sufficient staff to rate

CDOs; pushing ratings out the door with insufficient review; failing to adequately disclose its rating process for mortgage-backed securities and CDOs; and allowing conflicts of interest to affect rating decisions.[149]

So matters stood in 2007, when the machine that had been humming so smoothly and so lucratively slipped a gear, and then another, and another—and then seized up entirely.

---

## COMMISSION CONCLUSIONS ON CHAPTER 10

The Commission concludes that the credit rating agencies abysmally failed in their central mission to provide quality ratings on securities for the benefit of investors. They did not heed many warning signs indicating significant problems in the housing and mortgage sector. Moody's, the Commission's case study in this area, continued issuing ratings on mortgage-related securities, using its outdated analytical models, rather than making the necessary adjustments. The business model under which firms issuing securities paid for their ratings seriously undermined the quality and integrity of those ratings; the rating agencies placed market share and profit considerations above the quality and integrity of their ratings.

Despite the leveling off and subsequent decline of the housing market beginning in 2006, securitization of collateralized debt obligations (CDOs), CDOs squared, and synthetic CDOs continued unabated, greatly expanding the exposure to losses when the housing market collapsed and exacerbating the impact of the collapse on the financial system and the economy.

During this period, speculators fueled the market for synthetic CDOs to bet on the future of the housing market. CDO managers of these synthetic products had potential conflicts in trying to serve the interests of customers who were betting mortgage borrowers would continue to make their payments and of customers who were betting the housing market would collapse.

There were also potential conflicts for underwriters of mortgage-related securities to the extent they shorted the products for their own accounts outside of their roles as market makers.

# 11

## THE BUST

### CONTENTS

What happens when a bubble bursts? In early 2007, it became obvious that home prices were falling in regions that had once boomed, that mortgage originators were floundering, and that more and more families, especially those with subprime and Alt-A loans, would be unable to make their mortgage payments.

What was not immediately clear was how the housing crisis would affect the financial system that had helped inflate the bubble. Were all those mortgage-backed securities and collateralized debt obligations ticking time bombs on the balance sheets of the world's largest financial institutions? "The concerns were just that if people . . . couldn't value the assets, then that created . . . questions about the solvency of the firms," William C. Dudley, now president of the Federal Reserve Bank of New York, told the FCIC.[1]

In theory, securitization, over-the-counter derivatives and the many byways of the shadow banking system were supposed to distribute risk efficiently among investors. The theory would prove to be wrong. Much of the risk from mortgage-backed securities had actually been taken by a small group of systemically important companies with outsized holdings of, or exposure to, the super-senior and triple-A tranches of CDOs. These companies would ultimately bear great losses, even though those investments were supposed to be super-safe.

As 2007 went on, increasing mortgage delinquencies and defaults compelled the ratings agencies to downgrade first mortgage-backed securities, then CDOs. Alarmed investors sent prices plummeting. Hedge funds faced with margin calls from their repo lenders were forced to sell at distressed prices; many would shut down. Banks wrote down the value of their holdings by tens of billions of dollars.

The summer of 2007 also saw a near halt in many securitization markets, including the market for non-agency mortgage securitizations. For example, a total of $75 billion in subprime securitizations were issued in the second quarter of 2007 (already down from prior quarters). That figure dropped precipitously to $27 billion in the third quarter and to only $12 billion in the fourth quarter of 2007. Alt-A issuance topped $100 billion in the second quarter, but fell to $13 billion in the fourth quarter of 2007. Once-booming markets were now gone—only $4 billion in subprime or Alt-A mortgage-backed securities were issued in the first half of 2008, and almost none after that.[2]

CDOs followed suit. From a high of more than $90 billion in the first quarter of 2007, worldwide issuance of CDOs with mortgage-backed securities as collateral plummeted to $29 billion in the third quarter of 2007 and only $5 billion in the fourth quarter. And as the CDO market ground to a halt, investors no longer trusted other structured products.[3] Over $80 billion of collateralized loan obligations (CLOs), or securitized leveraged loans, were issued in 2007; only $10 billion were issued in 2008. The issuance of commercial real estate mortgage–backed securities plummeted from $232 billion in 2007 to $12 billion in 2008.[4]

Those securitization markets that held up during the turmoil in 2007 eventually suffered in 2008 as the crisis deepened. Securitization of auto loans, credit cards, small business loans, and equipment leases all nearly ceased in the third and fourth quarters of 2008.

## DELINQUENCIES: "THE TURN OF THE HOUSING MARKET"

Home prices rose 15% nationally in 2005, their third year of double-digit growth. But by the spring of 2006, as the sales pace slowed, the number of months it would take to sell off all the homes on the market rose to its highest level in 10 years. Nationwide, home prices peaked in April 2006.

Members of the Federal Reserve's Federal Open Market Committee (FOMC) discussed housing prices in the spring of 2006. Chairman Ben Bernanke and other members predicted a decline in home prices but were uncertain whether the decline would be slow or fast. Bernanke believed some correction in the housing market would be healthy and that the goal of the FOMC should be to ensure the correction did not overly affect the growth of the rest of the economy.[5]

In October 2006, with the housing market downturn under way, Moody's Economy.com, a business unit separate from Moody's Investors Service, issued a report authored by Chief Economist Mark Zandi titled "Housing at the Tipping Point: The Outlook for the U.S. Residential Real Estate Market." He came to the following conclusion:

> Nearly 20 of the nation's metro areas will experience a crash in house prices; a double-digit peak-to-trough decline in house prices. . . . These sharp declines in house prices are expected along the Southwest coast of Florida, in the metro areas of Arizona and Nevada, in a number of Cali-

fornia areas, throughout the broad Washington, D.C. area, and in and around Detroit. Many more metro areas are expected to experience only house-price corrections in which peak-to-trough price declines remain in the single digits. . . . It is important to note that price declines in various markets are expected to extend into 2008 and even 2009.

With over 100 metro areas representing nearly one-half of the nation's housing stock experiencing or about to experience price declines, national house prices are also set to decline. Indeed, odds are high that national house prices will decline in 2007.[6]

For 2007, the National Association of Realtors announced that the number of sales of existing homes had experienced the sharpest fall in 25 years. That year, home prices declined 9%. In 2008, they would drop a stunning 17%. Overall, by the end of 2009, prices would drop 28% from their peak in 2006.[7] Some cities saw a particularly large drop: in Las Vegas, as of August 2010, home prices were down 55% from their peak. And areas that never saw huge price gains have experienced losses as well: home prices in Denver have fallen 18% since their peak.

In some areas, home prices started to fall as early as late 2005. For example, in Ocean City, New Jersey, where many properties are vacation homes, home prices had risen 144% since 2001; they topped out in December 2005 and fell 4% in the first half of 2006. By mid-2010, they would be 22% below their peak. Prices topped out in Sacramento in October 2005 and are today down nearly 50%. In most places, prices rose for a bit longer. For instance, in Tucson, Arizona, prices kept increasing for much of 2006, climbing 95% from 2001 to their high point in August 2006, and then fell only 3% by the end of the year.[8]

One of the first signs of the housing crash was an upswing in early payment defaults—usually defined as borrowers' being 60 or more days delinquent within the first year. Figures provided to the FCIC show that by the summer of 2006, 1.5% of loans less than a year old were in default. The figure would peak in late 2007 at 2.5%, well above the 1.0% peak in the 2000 recession. Even more stunning, first payment defaults—that is, mortgages taken out by borrowers who never made a single payment—went above 1.5% of loans in early 2007.[9] Responding to questions about that data, CoreLogic Chief Economist Mark Fleming told the FCIC that the early payment default rate "certainly correlates with the increase in the Alt-A and subprime shares and the turn of the housing market and the sensitivity of those loan products."[10]

Mortgages in serious delinquency, defined as those 90 or more days past due or in foreclosure, had hovered around 1% during the early part of the decade, jumped in 2006, and kept climbing. By the end of 2009, 9.7% of mortgage loans were seriously delinquent. By comparison, serious delinquencies peaked at 2.4% in 2002 following the previous recession.[11]

Serious delinquency was highest in areas of the country that had experienced the biggest housing booms. In the "sand states"—California, Arizona, Nevada, and Florida—serious delinquency rose to 3% in mid-2007 and 15% by late 2009, double the rate in other areas of the country (see figure 11.1).[12]

## Mortgage Delinquencies by Region

*Arizona, California, Florida, and Nevada—the "sand states"—had the most problem loans.*

IN PERCENT, BY REGION

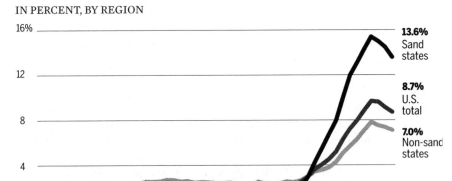

NOTE: Serious delinquencies include mortgages 90 days or more past due and those in foreclosure.
SOURCE: Mortgage Bankers Association National Delinquency Survey

*Figure 11.1*

Serious delinquency also varied by type of loan (see figure 11.2). Subprime adjustable-rate mortgages began to show increases in serious delinquency in early 2006, even as house prices were peaking; the rate rose rapidly to 20% in 2007. By late 2009, the delinquency rate for subprime ARMs was 40%. Prime ARMs did not weaken until 2007, at about the same time as subprime fixed-rate mortgages. Prime fixed-rate mortgages, which have historically been the least risky, showed a slow increase in serious delinquency that coincided with the increasing severity of the recession and of unemployment in 2008.

The FCIC undertook an extensive examination of the relative performance of mortgages purchased or guaranteed by the GSEs, those securitized in the private market, and those insured by the Federal Housing Administration or Veterans Administration (see figure 11.3). The analysis was conducted using roughly 25 million mortgages outstanding at the end of each year from 2006 through 2009.[13] The data contained mortgages in four groups—loans that were sold into private label securitizations labeled subprime by issuers (labeled SUB), loans sold into private label Alt-A securitizations (ALT), loans either purchased or guaranteed by the GSEs (GSE), and loans guaranteed by the Federal Housing Administration or Veterans Administration (FHA).[14] The GSE group, in addition to the more traditional conforming GSE loans,

## Mortgage Delinquencies by Loan Type

*Serious delinquencies started earlier and were substantially higher among subprime adjustable-rate loans, compared with other loan types.*

IN PERCENT, BY TYPE

NOTE: Serious delinquencies include mortgages 90 days or more past due and those in foreclosure.
SOURCE: Mortgage Bankers Association National Delinquency Survey

*Figure 11.2*

also includes mortgages that the GSEs identified as subprime and Alt-A loans owing to their higher-risk characteristics, as discussed in earlier chapters.

Within each of the four groups, the FCIC created subgroups based on characteristics that could affect loan performance: FICO credit scores, loan-to-value ratios (LTVs), and mortgage size. For example, one subgroup would be GSE loans with a balance below $417,000 (conforming to GSE loan size limits), a FICO score between 640 and 659 (a borrower with below-average credit history), and LTV between 80% and 100%. Another group would be Alt-A loans with the same characteristics. In each year, the loans were broken into 576 different subgroups—144 each for GSE, SUB, ALT, and FHA.[15]

Figure 11.3 graphically demonstrates the results of the examination. The various bars show the range of average delinquencies for each of the four groups examined, based on the distribution of delinquency rates within the 144 subgroups for each loan category. The black portion of each bar represents the middle 50% (25% on either side of the median) of the distribution of average delinquency rates. The full bar, including both dark and light shading, represents the middle 90% of the distribution of average delinquency rates. The bars exclude the 5% at the extremes of each end of the distribution. For example, at the end of 2008, the black portion of the GSE bar

## Loan Performance in Various Mortgage-Market Segments

*Bars shows distribution of average rate of serious delinquency.*

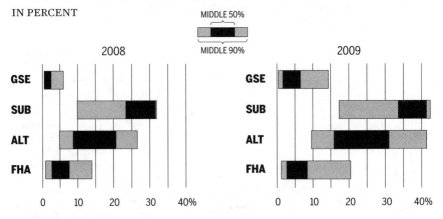

NOTE: Serious delinquencies include mortgages 90 days or more past due and those in foreclosure.
SOURCE: FCIC calculations, based on CoreLogic and Loan Processing Service Inc.

*Figure 11.3*

spans a 0.6% average delinquency rate on the low end and a 2.4% average delinquency rate on the high end. The full bar for the GSEs spans average delinquency rates from 0.1% to 6.0%. That means that only 5% of GSE loans were in subgroups with average delinquency rates above 6.0%. In sharp contrast, the black bar for private-label subprime securitizations (SUB) spans average delinquency rates between 24.0% on the low end and 31.0% on the high end, and the full bar spans average delinquency rates between 10.0% and 32.0%. That means that only 5% of SUB loans were in subgroups with average delinquency rates below 10%. The worst-performing 5% of GSE loans are in subgroups with rates of serious delinquency similar to the best-performing 5% of SUB loans.[16]

By the end of 2009, performance within all segments of the market had weakened. The median delinquency rate—the midpoints of the black bars—rose from 1% in 2008 to 2.5% for GSE loans, from 29% to 39% for SUB loans, from 12% to 21% for Alt-A loans, and remained at roughly 6% for FHA loans.

The data illustrate that in 2008 and 2009, GSE loans performed significantly better than privately securitized, or non-GSE, subprime and Alt-A loans. That holds true even when comparing loans in GSE pools that share the same key characteristics with the loans in privately securitized mortgages, such as low FICO scores. For example, among loans to borrowers with FICO scores below 660, a privately securitized mortgage was more than four times as likely to be seriously delinquent as a GSE.

In 2008, the respective average delinquency rates for the non-GSE and GSE loans were 28.3% and 6.2%. These patterns are most likely driven by differences in under-writing standards as well as by some differences not captured in these mortgages.[17] For instance, in the GSE pool, borrowers tended to make bigger down payments. The FCIC's data show that 58% of GSE loans with FICO scores below 660 had an original loan-to-value ratio below 80%, indicating that the borrower made a down payment of at least 20% of the sales price. This relatively large down payment would help offset the effect of the lower FICO score. In contrast, only 31% of loans with FICO scores below 660 in non-GSE subprime securitizations had an LTV under 80%. The data il-lustrate that non-agency securitized loans were much more likely to have more than one risk factor and thereby exhibit so-called risk layering, such as low FICO scores on top of small down payments.

GSE mortgages with Alt-A characteristics also performed significantly better than mortgages packaged into non-GSE Alt-A securities. For example, in 2008 among loans with an LTV above 90%, the GSE pools have an average rate of serious delin-quency of 5.7%, versus a rate of 15.5% for loans in private Alt-A securities.[18] These results are also, in large part, driven by differences in risk layering.

Others frame the situation differently. According to Ed Pinto, a mortgage finance industry consultant who was the chief credit officer at Fannie Mae in the 1980s, GSEs dominated the market for risky loans. In written analyses reviewed by the FCIC staff and sent to Commissioners as well as in a number of interviews, Pinto has argued that the GSE loans that had FICO scores below 660, a combined loan-to-value ratio greater than 90%, or other mortgage characteristics such as interest-only payments were essentially equivalent to those mortgages in securitizations labeled subprime and Alt-A by issuers.

Using strict cutoffs on FICO score and loan-to-value ratios that ignore risk layer-ing and thus are only partly related to mortgage performance (as well as relying on a number of other assumptions), Pinto estimates that as of June 30, 2008, 49% of all mortgages in the country—26.7 million of them—were risky mortgages that he de-fines as subprime or Alt-A. Of these, Pinto counts 11.9 million, or 45%, that were purchased or guaranteed by the GSEs.[19] In contrast, the GSEs categorize fewer than 3 million of their loans as subprime or Alt-A.[20]

Importantly, as the FCIC review shows, the GSE loans classified as subprime or Alt-A in Pinto's analysis did not perform nearly as poorly as loans in non-agency sub-prime or Alt-A securities. These differences suggest that grouping all of these loans together is misleading. In direct contrast to Pinto's claim, GSE mortgages with some riskier characteristics such as high loan-to-value ratios are not at all equivalent to those mortgages in securitizations labeled subprime and Alt-A by issuers. The per-formance data assembled and analyzed by the FCIC show that non-GSE securitized loans experienced much higher rates of delinquency than did the GSE loans with similar characteristics.

In addition to examining loans owned and guaranteed by the GSEs, Pinto also com-mented on the role of the Community Reinvestment Act (CRA) in causing the crisis, declaring, "The pain and hardship that CRA has likely spawned are immeasurable."[21]

Contrary to this view, two Fed economists determined that lenders actually made few subprime loans to meet their CRA requirements. Analyzing a database of nearly 14 million loans originated in 2006, they found that only a small percentage of all higher-cost loans as defined by the Home Mortgage Disclosure Act had any connection to the CRA. These higher-cost loans serve as a rough proxy for subprime mortgages. Specifically, the study found that only 6% of such higher-cost loans were made to low- or moderate-income borrowers or in low- or moderate-income neighborhoods by banks and thrifts (and their subsidiaries and affiliates) covered by the CRA. The other 94% of higher-cost loans either were made by CRA-covered institutions that did not receive CRA credit for these loans or were made by lenders not covered by the CRA. Using other data sources, these economists also found that CRA-related subprime loans appeared to perform better than other subprime loans. "Taken together, the available evidence seems to run counter to the contention that the CRA contributed in any substantive way to the current crisis," they wrote.[22]

Subsequent research has come to similar conclusions. For example, two economists at the San Francisco Fed, using a different methodology and analyzing data on the California mortgage market, found that only 16% of loans made by CRA-covered lenders were located in low- and moderate-income census tracts versus over 20% for independent mortgage companies not covered by the CRA. Further, fewer than 30% of the loans made by CRA lenders in low-income communities were higher priced, even at the peak of the market. In contrast, about one-half of the loans originated by independent mortgage companies in these communities were higher priced. And after accounting for characteristics of the loans and the borrowers, such as income and credit score, the authors found that loans made by CRA-covered lenders in the low- and moderate-income areas they serve were half as likely to default as similar loans made by independent mortgage companies, which are not subject to CRA and are subject to less regulatory oversight in general. "While certainly not conclusive, this suggests that the CRA, and particularly its emphasis on loans made within a lender's assessment area, helped to ensure responsible lending, even during a period of overall declines in underwriting standards," they concluded.[23]

Overall, in 2004, 2005, and 2006, CRA-covered banks and thrifts accounted for at least 60% of all mortgage lending but only between 36% and 41% of higher-priced mortgages. Independent mortgage companies originated less than one-third of all mortgages but about one-half of all higher-priced mortgages.[24] Finally, lending by nonbank affiliates of CRA-covered depository institutions is counted toward CRA performance at the discretion of the bank or thrift. These affiliates accounted for another roughly 10% of mortgage lending but about 12% of high-price lending.

Bank of America provided the FCIC with performance data on its CRA-qualifying portfolio, which represented only 7% of the bank's mortgage portfolio.[25] In the end of the first quarter of 2010, 8% of the bank's $212 billion portfolio of residential mortgages was nonperforming: 21% of the $15 billion CRA-qualifying portfolio was nonperforming at that date.

John Reed, a former CEO of Citigroup, when asked whether he thought government policies such as the CRA played a role in the crisis, said that he didn't believe

banks would originate "a bad mortgage because they thought the government policy allowed it" unless the bank could sell off the mortgage to Fannie or Freddie, which had their own obligations in this arena. He said, "It's hard for me to answer. If the reason the regulators didn't jump up and down and yell at the low-doc, no-doc subprime mortgage was because they felt that they, Congress had sort of pushed in that direction, then I would say yes."[26]

"You know, CRA could be a pain in the neck," the banker Lewis Ranieri told the FCIC. "But you know what? It always, in my view, it always did much more good than it did anything. You know, we did a lot. CRA made a big difference in communities. . . . You were really putting money in the communities in ways that really stabilized the communities and made a difference." But lenders including Countrywide used pro-homeownership policies as a "smokescreen" to do away with underwriting standards such as requiring down payments, he said. "The danger is that it gives air cover to all of this kind of madness that had nothing to do with the housing goal."[27]

## RATING DOWNGRADES: "NEVER BEFORE"

Prior to 2004, the ratings of mortgage-backed securities at Moody's were monitored by the same analysts who had rated them in the first place. In 2004, Nicolas Weill, Moody's chief credit officer and team managing director, was charged with creating an independent surveillance team to monitor previously rated deals.[28]

In November 2006, the surveillance team began to see a rise in early payment defaults in mortgages originated by Fremont Investment & Loan,[29] and downgraded several securities with underlying Fremont loans or put them on watch for future downgrades. "This was a very unusual situation as never before had we put on watch deals rated in the same calendar year," Weill later wrote to Raymond McDaniel, the chairman and CEO of Moody's Corporation, and Brian Clarkson, the president of Moody's Investors Service.[30]

In early 2007, a Moody's special report, overseen by Weill, about the sharp increases in early payment defaults stated that the foreclosures were concentrated in subprime mortgage pools. In addition, more than 2.75% of the subprime mortgages securitized in the second quarter of 2006 were 60 days delinquent within six months, more than double the rate a year earlier (1.25%). The exact cause of the trouble was still unclear to the ratings agency, though. "Moody's is currently assessing whether this represents an overall worsening of collateral credit quality or merely a shifting forward of eventual defaults which may not significantly impact a pool's overall expected loss."[31]

For the next few months, the company published regular updates about the subprime mortgage market. Over the next three months, Moody's took negative rating actions on 4.5% of the outstanding subprime mortgage securities rated Baa. Then, on July 10, 2007, in an unprecedented move, Moody's downgraded 399 subprime mortgage-backed securities that had been issued in 2006 and put an additional 32 securities on watch. The $5.2 billion of securities that were affected, all rated Baa and lower, made up 19% of the subprime securities that Moody's rated Baa in 2006. For the time

being, there were no downgrades on higher-rated tranches. Moody's attributed the downgrades to "aggressive underwriting combined with prolonged, slowing home price appreciation" and noted that about 60% of the securities affected contained mortgages from one of four originators: Fremont Investment & Loan, Long Beach Mortgage Company, New Century Mortgage Corporation, and WMC Mortgage Corp.[32]

Weill later told the FCIC staff that Moody's issued a mass announcement, rather than downgrading a few securities at a time, to avoid creating confusion in the market.[33] A few days later, Standard & Poor's downgraded 498 similar tranches. These initial downgrades were remarkable not only because of the number of securities involved but also because of the sharp rating cuts—an average of four notches per security, when one or two notches was more routine (for example, a single notch would be a downgrade from AA to AA-). Among the tranches downgraded in July 2007 were the bottom three mezzanine tranches (M9, M10, and M11) of the Citigroup deal that we have been examining, CMLTI 2006-NC2. By that point, nearly 12% of the original loan pool had prepaid but another 11% were 90 or more days past due or in foreclosure.[34]

Investors across the world were assessing their own exposure, and guessing at that of others, however indirect, to these assets. A report from Bear Stearns Asset Management detailed its exposure. One of its CDOs, Tall Ships, had direct exposure to our sample deal, owning $8 million of the M7 and M8 tranches. BSAM's High-Grade hedge fund also had exposure through a $10 million credit default swap position with Lehman referencing the M8 tranche. And BSAM's Enhanced Leverage hedge fund owned parts of the equity in Independence CDO, which in turn owned the M9 tranche of our sample deal. In addition, these funds had exposure through their holdings of other CDOs that in turn owned tranches of the Citigroup deal.[35]

Then, on October 11, Moody's downgraded another 2,506 tranches ($33.4 billion) of subprime mortgage–backed securities and placed 577 tranches ($23.8 billion) on watch for potential downgrade. Now the total of securities downgraded and put on watch represented 13.4% of the original dollar volume of all 2006 subprime mortgage–backed securities that Moody's had rated. Of the securities placed on watch in October, 48 tranches ($6.9 billion) were originally Aaa-rated and 529 ($16.9 billion) were Aa-rated. All told, in the first 10 months of 2007, 92% of the mortgage-backed security deals issued in 2006 had at least one tranche downgraded or put on watch.[36]

By this point in October, 13% of the loans in our case study deal CMLTI 2006-NC2 were seriously delinquent and some homes had already been repossessed. The M4 through M8 tranches were downgraded as part of the second wave of mass downgrades. Five additional tranches would eventually be downgraded in April 2008.[37]

Before it was over, Moody's would downgrade 83% of all the 2006 Aaa mortgage-backed securities tranches and all of the Baa tranches. For those securities issued in the second half of 2007, nearly all Aaa and Baa tranches were downgraded. Of all

tranches initially rated investment grade—that is, rated Baa3 or higher—76% of those issued in 2006 were downgraded to junk, as were 89% of those from 2007.[38]

## CDOs: "CLIMBING THE WALL OF SUBPRIME WORRY"

In March 2007, Moody's reported that CDOs with high concentrations of subprime mortgage–backed securities could incur "severe" downgrades.[39] In an internal email sent five days after the report, Group Managing Director of U.S. Derivatives Yuri Yoshizawa explained to Moody's Chairman McDaniel and to Executive Vice President Noel Kirnon that one managing director at Credit Suisse First Boston "sees banks like Merrill, Citi, and UBS still furiously doing transactions to clear out their warehouses. . . . He believes that they are creating and pricing the CDOs in order to remove the assets from the warehouses, but that they are holding on to the CDOs . . . in hopes that they will be able to sell them later."[40] Several months later, in a review of the CDO market titled "Climbing the Wall of Subprime Worry," Moody's noted, "Some of the first quarter's activity [in 2007] was the result of some arrangers feverishly working to clear inventory and reduce their balance sheet exposure to the subprime class."[41] Even though Moody's was aware that the investment banks were dumping collateral out of the warehouses and into CDOs—possibly regardless of quality—the firm continued to rate new CDOs using existing assumptions.

Former Moody's executive Richard Michalek testified to the FCIC, "It was a case of, with respect to why didn't we stop and change our methodology, there is a very conservative culture at Moody's, at least while I was there, that suggested that the only thing worse than quickly getting a new methodology in place is quickly getting the wrong methodology in place and having to unwind that and to fail to consider the unintended consequences."[42]

In July, McDaniel gave a presentation to the board on the company's 2007 strategic plan. His slides had such bleak titles as "Spotlight on Mortgages: Quality Continues to Erode," "House Prices Are Falling . . . ," "Mortgage Payment Resets Are Mounting," and "1.3 MM Mortgage Defaults Forecast 2007–08."[43] Despite all the evidence that the quality of the underlying mortgages was declining, Moody's did not make any significant adjustments to its CDO ratings assumptions until late September.[44] Out of $51 billion in CDOs that Moody's rated after its mass downgrade of subprime mortgage–backed securities on July 10, 2007, 88% were rated Aaa.[45]

Moody's had hoped that rating downgrades could be staved off by mortgage modifications—if their monthly payments became more affordable, borrowers might stay current. However, in mid-September, Eric Kolchinsky, a team managing director for CDOs, learned that a survey of servicers indicated that very few troubled mortgages were being modified.[46] Worried that continuing to rate CDOs without adjusting for known deterioration in the underlying securities could expose Moody's to liability, Kolchinsky advised Yoshizawa that the company should stop rating CDOs until the securities downgrades were completed. Kolchinsky told the FCIC that Yoshizawa "admonished" him for making the suggestion.[47]

By the end of 2008, more than 90% of all tranches of CDOs had been down-graded. Moody's downgraded nearly all of the 2006 Aaa and all of the Baa CDO tranches. And, again, the downgrades were large—more than 80% of Aaa CDO bonds and more than 90% of Baa CDO bonds were eventually downgraded to junk.[48]

## LEGAL REMEDIES: "ON THE BASIS OF THE INFORMATION"

The housing bust exposed the flaws in the mortgages that had been made and securitized. After the crisis unfolded, those with exposure to mortgages and structured products—including investors, financial firms, and private mortgage insurance firms—closely examined the representations and warranties made by mortgage originators and securities issuers. When mortgages were securitized, sold, or insured, certain representations and warranties were made to assure investors and insurers that the mortgages met stated guidelines. As mortgage securities lost value, investors found significant deficiencies in securitizers' due diligence on the mortgage pools underlying the mortgage-backed securities as well as in their disclosure about the characteristics of those deals. As private mortgage insurance companies found similar deficiencies in the loans they insured, they have denied claims to an unprecedented extent.

Fannie and Freddie acquired or guaranteed millions of loans each year. They delegated underwriting authority to originators subject to a legal agreement—representations and warranties—that the loans meet specified criteria. They then checked samples of the loans to ensure that these representations and warranties were not breached. If there was a breach and the loans were "ineligible" for purchase, the GSE had the right to require the seller to buy back the loan—assuming, of course, that the seller had not gone bankrupt.

As a result of such sampling, during the three years and eight months ending August 31, 2010, Freddie and Fannie required sellers to repurchase 167,000 loans totaling $34.8 billion. So far, Freddie has received $9.1 billion from sellers, and Fannie has received $11.8 billion—a total of $20.9 billion.[49] The amount put back is notable in that it represents 21% of $163 billion in credit-related expenses recorded by the GSEs since the beginning of 2008 through September 2010.[50]

In testing to ensure compliance with its standards, Freddie reviews a small percentage of performing loans and a high percentage of foreclosed loans (including well over 90% of all loans that default in the first two years). In total, Freddie reviewed $76.8 billion of loans (out of $1.51 trillion in loans acquired or guaranteed) and found $21.7 billion to be ineligible, meaning they did not meet representations and warranties.[51]

Among the performing loans that were sampled, over time an increasing percentage were found to be ineligible, rising from 10% for mortgages originated in 2005 to 23% in 2008. Still, Freddie put back very few of these performing loans to the originators. Among mortgages originated from 2005 to 2008, it found that 17% of the delinquent loans were ineligible, as were 27% of the loans in foreclosure.[52] Most of these were put back to originators—again, in cases in which the originators were still in op-

eration. Sometimes, if the reasons for ineligibility were sufficiently minor, the loans were not put back.

Overall, of the delinquent loans and loans in foreclosure sampled by Freddie, 20% were put back. In 2009 and 2010, Freddie put back significant loan volumes to the following lenders: Countrywide, $1.9 billion; Wells Fargo, $1.2 billion; Chase Home Financial, $1.1 billion; Bank of America, $476 million; and Ally Financial, $453 million.[53]

Using a method similar to Freddie's to test for loan eligibility, Fannie reviewed between 2% and 5% of the mortgages originated since 2005—sampling at the higher rates for delinquent loans. From 2007 through 2010, Fannie put back loans to the following large lenders: Bank of America, $6.9 billion; Wells Fargo, $2.3 billion; JP Morgan Chase, $2.2 billion; Citigroup, $1.5 billion; SunTrust Bank, $898 million; and Ally Financial, $838 million.[54] In early January 2011, Bank of America reached a deal with Fannie and Freddie, settling the GSEs' claims with a payment of more than $2.5 billion. [55]

Like Fannie and Freddie, private mortgage insurance (PMI) companies have been finding significant deficiencies in mortgages. They are refusing to pay claims on some insured mortgages that have gone into default. This insurance protects the holder of the mortgage if a homeowner defaults on a loan, even though the responsibility for the premiums generally lies with the homeowner. By the end of 2006, PMI companies had insured a total of $668 billion in potential mortgage losses.[56]

As defaults and losses on the insured mortgages have been increasing, the PMI companies have seen a spike in claims. As of October 2010, the seven largest PMI companies, which share 98% of the market, had rejected about 25% of the claims (or $6 billion of $24 billion) brought to them, because of violations of origination guidelines, improper employment and income reporting, and issues with property valuation.[57]

Separate from their purchase and guarantee of mortgages, over the course of the housing boom the GSEs purchased $690 billion of subprime and Alt-A private-label securities.[58] The GSEs have recorded $46 billion in charges on securities from January 1, 2008 to September 30, 2010.[59] Frustrated with the lack of information from the securities' servicers and trustees, in many cases large banks, on July 12, 2010, the GSEs through their regulator, the Federal Housing Finance Agency, issued 64 subpoenas to various trustees and servicers in transactions in which the GSEs lost money.[60] Where they find that the nonperforming loans in the pools have violations, the GSEs intend to demand that the trustees recognize their rights (including any rights to put loans back to the originator or wholesaler).[61]

While this strategy being followed by the GSEs is based in contract law, other investors are relying on securities law to file lawsuits, claiming that they were misled by inaccurate or incomplete prospectuses; and, in a number of cases, they are winning.

As of mid-2010, court actions embroiled almost all major loan originators and underwriters—there were more than 400 lawsuits related to breaches of representations and warranties, by one estimate.[62] These lawsuits filed in the wake of the financial crisis include those alleging "untrue statements of material fact" or "material

misrepresentations" in the registration statements and prospectuses provided to investors who purchased securities. They generally allege violations of the Securities Exchange Act of 1934 and the Securities Act of 1933.

Both private and government entities have gone to court. For example, the investment brokerage Charles Schwab has sued units of Bank of America, Wells Fargo, and UBS Securities.[63] The Massachusetts attorney general's office settled charges against Morgan Stanley and Goldman Sachs, after accusing the firms of inadequate disclosure relating to their sales of mortgage-backed securities. Morgan Stanley agreed to pay $102 million and Goldman Sachs agreed to pay $60 million.[64]

To take another example, the Federal Home Loan Bank of Chicago has sued several defendants, including Bank of America, Credit Suisse Securities, Citigroup, and Goldman Sachs, over its $3.3 billion investment in private mortgage-backed securities, claiming they failed to provide accurate information about the securities. Similarly, Cambridge Place Investment Management has sued units of Morgan Stanley, Citigroup, HSBC, Goldman Sachs, Barclays, and Bank of America, among others, "on the basis of the information contained in the applicable registration statement, prospectus, and prospective supplements."[65]

## LOSSES: "WHO OWNS RESIDENTIAL CREDIT RISK?"

Through 2007 and into 2008, as the rating agencies downgraded mortgage-backed securities and CDOs, and investors began to panic, market prices for these securities plunged. Both the direct losses as well as the marketwide contagion and panic that ensued would lead to the failure or near failure of many large financial firms across the system. The drop in market prices for mortgage-related securities reflected the higher probability that the underlying mortgages would actually default (meaning that less cash would flow to the investors) as well as the more generalized fear among investors that this market had become illiquid. Investors valued liquidity because they wanted the assurance that they could sell securities quickly to raise cash if necessary. Potential investors worried they might get stuck holding these securities as market participants looked to limit their exposure to the collapsing mortgage market.

As market prices dropped, "mark-to-market" accounting rules required firms to write down their holdings to reflect the lower market prices. In the first quarter of 2007, the largest banks and investment banks began complying with a new accounting rule and for the first time reported their assets in one of three valuation categories: "Level 1 assets," which had observable market prices, like stocks on the stock exchange; "Level 2 assets," which were not as easily priced because they were not actively traded; and "Level 3 assets," which were illiquid and had no discernible market prices or other inputs. To determine the value of Level 3 and in some cases Level 2 assets where market prices were unavailable, firms used models that relied on assumptions. Many financial institutions reported Level 3 assets that substantially exceeded their capital. For example, for the first quarter of 2007, Bear Stearns reported about $19 billion in Level 3 assets, compared to $13 billion in capital; Morgan Stanley re-

ported about $60 billion in Level 3 assets, against capital of $38 billion; and Goldman reported about $48 billion, and capital of $37 billion.

Mark-to-market write-downs were required on many securities even if there were no actual realized losses and in some cases even if the firms did not intend to sell the securities. The charges reflecting unrealized losses were based, in part, on credit rating agencies' and investors' expectations that the mortgages would default. But only when those defaults came to pass would holders of the securities actually have realized losses. Determining the market value of securities that did not trade was difficult, was subjective, and became a contentious issue during the crisis. Why? Because the write-downs reduced earnings and capital, and triggered collateral calls.

These mark-to-market accounting rules received a good deal of criticism in recent years, as firms argued that the lower market prices did not reflect market values but rather fire-sale prices driven by forced sales. Joseph Grundfest, when he was a member of the SEC's Committee on Improvements to Financial Reporting, noted that at times, marking securities at market prices "creates situations where you have to go out and raise physical capital in order to cover losses that as a practical matter were never really there."[66] But not valuing assets based on market prices could mean that firms were not recording losses required by the accounting rules and therefore were overstating earnings and capital.

As the mortgage market was crashing, some economists and analysts estimated that actual losses, also known as realized losses, on subprime and Alt-A mortgages would total $200 to $300 billion;[67] so far, by 2010, the figure has turned out not to be much more than that. As of year-end 2009, the dollar value of all impaired Alt-A and subprime mortgage–backed securities total about $300 billion.[68] Securities are impaired when they have suffered realized losses or are expected to suffer realized losses imminently. While those numbers are small in relation to the $14 trillion U.S. economy, the losses had a disproportionate impact. "Subprime mortgages themselves are a pretty small asset class," Fed Chairman Ben Bernanke told the FCIC, explaining how in 2007 he and Treasury Secretary Henry Paulson had underestimated the repercussions of the emerging housing crisis. "You know, the stock market goes up and down every day more than the entire value of the subprime mortgages in the country. But what created the contagion, or one of the things that created the contagion, was that the subprime mortgages were entangled in these huge securitized pools."[69]

The large drop in market prices of the mortgage securities had large spillover effects to the financial sector, for a number of reasons. For example, as just discussed, when the prices of mortgage-backed securities and CDOs fell, many of the holders of those securities marked down the value of their holdings—before they had experienced any actual losses.

In addition, rather than spreading the risks of losses among many investors, the securitization market had concentrated them. "Who owns residential credit risk?" two Lehman analysts asked in a September 2007 report. The answer: three-quarters of subprime and Alt-A mortgages had been securitized—and "much of the risk in

these securitizations is in the investment-grade securities and has been almost entirely transferred to AAA collateralized debt obligation (CDO) holders."[70] A set of large, systemically important firms with significant holdings or exposure to these securities would be found to be holding very little capital to protect against potential losses. And most of those companies would turn out to be considered by the authorities too big to fail in the midst of a financial crisis.

The International Monetary Fund's Global Financial Stability Report published in October 2008 examined where the declining assets were held and estimated how severe the write-downs would be. All told, the IMF calculated that roughly $10 trillion in mortgage assets were held throughout the financial system. Of these, $3.8 trillion were GSE mortgage–backed securities; the IMF expected losses of $80 billion, but investors holding these securities would lose no money, because of the GSEs' guarantee. Another $4.7 trillion in mortgage assets were estimated to be prime and nonprime mortgages held largely by the banks and the GSEs. These were expected to suffer as much as $170 billion in write-downs due to declines in market value. The remaining $1.5 trillion in assets were estimated to be mortgage-backed securities and CDOs. Write-downs on those assets were expected to be $500 billion. And, even more troubling, more than one-half of these losses were expected to be borne by the investment banks, commercial banks, and thrifts. The rest of the write-downs from non-agency mortgage–backed securities were shared among institutions such as insurance companies, pension funds, the GSEs, and hedge funds. The October report also expected another $655 billion in write-downs on commercial mortgage–backed securities, CLOs, leveraged loans, and other loans and securities—with more than half coming from commercial mortgage–backed securities. Again, the commercial banks and thrifts and investment banks were expected to bear much of the brunt.[71]

Furthermore, when the crisis began, uncertainty (suggested by the sizable revisions in the IMF estimates) and leverage would promote contagion. Investors would realize they did not know as much as they wanted to know about the mortgage assets that banks, investment banks, and other firms held or to which they were exposed. To an extent not understood by many before the crisis, financial institutions had leveraged themselves with commercial paper, with derivatives, and in the short-term repo markets, in part by using mortgage-backed securities and CDOs as collateral. Lenders would question the value of the assets that those companies had posted as collateral at the same time that they were questioning the value of those companies' balance sheets.

Even the highest-rated tranches of mortgage-backed securities were downgraded, and large write-downs were recorded on financial institutions' balance sheets based on declines in market value. However, although this could not be known in 2007, at the end of 2010 most of the triple-A tranches of mortgage-backed securities have avoided actual losses in cash flow through 2010 and may avoid significant realized losses going forward.

Overall, for 2005 to 2007 vintage tranches of mortgage-backed securities originally rated triple-A, despite the mass downgrades, only about 10% of Alt-A and 4% of subprime securities had been "materially impaired"—meaning that losses were im-

# Impaired Securities

*Impairment of 2005-2007 vintage mortgage-backed securities (MBS) and CDOs as of year-end 2009, by initial rating. A security is impaired when it is downgraded to C or Ca, or when it suffers a principal loss.*

IN BILLIONS OF DOLLARS

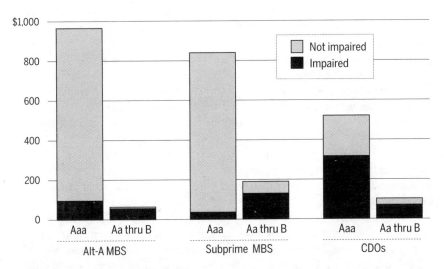

SOURCE: Moody's Investors Service, "Special Comment: Default & Loss Rates of Structured Finance Securities: 1993-2009"; Moody's SFDRS.

*Figure 11.4*

minent or had already been suffered—by the end of 2009 (see figure 11.4). For the lower-rated Baa tranches, 96.5% of Alt-A and 95.5% of subprime securities were impaired. In all, by the end of 2009, $320 billion worth of subprime and Alt-A tranches had been materially impaired—including $132.6 billion originally rated triple-A. The outcome would be far worse for CDO investors, whose fate largely depended on the performance of lower-rated mortgage-backed securities. More than 90% of Baa CDO bonds and 71.3% of Aaa CDO bonds were ultimately impaired.[72]

The housing bust would not be the end of the story. As Chairman Bernanke testified to the FCIC: "What I did not recognize was the extent to which the system had flaws and weaknesses in it that were going to amplify the initial shock from subprime and make it into a much bigger crisis."[73]

## COMMISSION CONCLUSIONS ON CHAPTER 11

The Commission concludes that the collapse of the housing bubble began the chain of events that led to the financial crisis.

High leverage, inadequate capital, and short-term funding made many financial institutions extraordinarily vulnerable to the downturn in the market in 2007. The investment banks had leverage ratios, by one measure, of up to 40 to 1. This means that for every $40 of assets, they held only $1 of capital. Fannie Mae and Freddie Mac (the GSEs) had even greater leverage—with a combined 75 to 1 ratio. Leverage or capital inadequacy at many institutions was even greater than reported when one takes into account "window dressing," off-balance-sheet exposures such as those of Citigroup, and derivatives positions such as those of AIG.

The GSEs contributed to, but were not a primary cause of, the financial crisis. Their $5 trillion mortgage exposure and market position were significant, and they were without question dramatic failures. They participated in the expansion of risky mortgage lending and declining mortgage standards, adding significant demand for less-than-prime loans. However, they followed, rather than led, the Wall Street firms. The delinquency rates on the loans that they purchased or guaranteed were significantly lower than those purchased and securitized by other financial institutions.

The Community Reinvestment Act (CRA)—which requires regulated banks and thrifts to lend, invest, and provide services consistent with safety and soundness to the areas where they take deposits—was not a significant factor in subprime lending. However, community lending commitments not required by the CRA were clearly used by lending institutions for public relations purposes.

# PART IV

## The Unraveling

# 12

## EARLY 2007:
## SPREADING SUBPRIME WORRIES

### CONTENTS

Over the course of 2007, the collapse of the housing bubble and the abrupt shutdown of subprime lending led to losses for many financial institutions, runs on money market funds, tighter credit, and higher interest rates. Unemployment remained relatively steady, hovering just below 4.5% until the end of the year, and oil prices rose dramatically. By the middle of 2007, home prices had declined almost 4% from their peak in 2006. Early evidence of the coming storm was the 1.5% drop in November 2006 of the ABX Index—a Dow Jones–like index for credit default swaps on BBB-tranches of mortgage-backed securities issued in the first half of 2006.[1]

That drop came after Moody's and S&P put on negative watch selected tranches in one deal backed by mortgages from one originator: Fremont Investment & Loan.[2] In December, the same index fell another 3% after the mortgage companies Ownit Mortgage Solutions and Sebring Capital ceased operations. Senior risk officers of the five largest investment banks told the Securities and Exchange Commission that they expected to see further subprime lender failures in 2007. "There is a broad recognition that, with the refinancing and real estate booms over, the business model of many of the smaller subprime originators is no longer viable," SEC analysts told Director Erik Sirri in a January 4, 2007, memorandum.[3]

That became more and more evident. In January, Mortgage Lenders Network announced it had stopped funding mortgages and accepting applications. In February, New Century reported bigger-than-expected mortgage credit losses and HSBC, the largest subprime lender in the United States, announced a $1.8 billion increase in its quarterly provision for losses. In March, Fremont stopped originating subprime loans after receiving a cease and desist order from the Federal Deposit Insurance Corporation. In April, New Century filed for bankruptcy.

These institutions had relied for their operating cash on short-term funding through commercial paper and the repo market. But commercial paper buyers and banks became unwilling to continue funding them, and repo lenders became less and less willing to accept subprime and Alt-A mortgages or mortgage-backed securities as collateral. They also insisted on ever-shorter maturities, eventually of just one day—an inherently destabilizing demand, because it gave them the option of withholding funding on short notice if they lost confidence in the borrower.

Another sign of problems in the market came when financial companies began to report more detail about their assets under the new mark-to-market accounting rule, particularly about mortgage-related securities that were becoming illiquid and hard to value. The sum of more illiquid Level 2 and 3 assets at these firms was "eye-popping in terms of the amount of leverage the banks and investment banks had," according to Jim Chanos, a New York hedge fund manager. Chanos said that the new disclosures also revealed for the first time that many firms retained large exposures from securitizations. "You clearly didn't get the magnitude, and the market didn't grasp the magnitude until spring of '07, when the figures began to be published, and then it was as if someone rang a bell, because almost immediately upon the publication of these numbers, journalists began writing about it, and hedge funds began talking about it, and people began speaking about it in the marketplace."[4]

In late 2006 and early 2007, some banks moved to reduce their subprime exposures by selling assets and buying protection through credit default swaps. Some, such as Citigroup and Merrill Lynch, reduced mortgage exposure in some areas of the firm but increased it in others. Banks that had been busy for nearly four years creating and selling subprime-backed collateralized debt obligations (CDOs) scrambled in about that many months to sell or hedge whatever they could. They now dumped these products into some of the most ill-fated CDOs ever engineered. Citigroup, Merrill Lynch, and UBS, particularly, were forced to retain larger and larger quantities of the "super-senior" tranches of these CDOs. The bankers could always hope—and many apparently even believed—that all would turn out well with these super seniors, which were, in theory, the safest of all.

With such uncertainty about the market value of mortgage assets, trades became scarce and setting prices for these instruments became difficult.

Although government officials knew about the deterioration in the subprime markets, they misjudged the risks posed to the financial system. In January 2007, SEC officials noted that investment banks had credit exposure to struggling subprime lenders but argued that "none of these exposures are material."[5] The Treasury and Fed insisted throughout the spring and early summer that the damage would be limited. "The impact on the broader economy and financial markets of the problems in the subprime market seems likely to be contained,"[6] Fed Chairman Ben Bernanke testified before the Joint Economic Committee of Congress on March 28. That same day, Treasury Secretary Henry Paulson told a House Appropriations subcommittee: "From the standpoint of the overall economy, my bottom line is we're watching it closely but it appears to be contained."[7]

## GOLDMAN: "LET'S BE AGGRESSIVE DISTRIBUTING THINGS"

In December 2006, following the initial decline in ABX BBB indices and after 10 consecutive days of trading losses on its mortgage desk, executives at Goldman Sachs decided to reduce the firm's subprime exposure. Goldman marked down the value of its mortgage-related products to reflect the lower ABX prices, and began posting daily losses for this inventory.[8]

Responding to the volatility in the subprime market, Goldman analysts delivered an internal report on December 13, 2006, regarding "the major risk in the Mortgage business" to Chief Financial Officer David Viniar and Chief Risk Officer Craig Broderick.[9] The next day, executives determined that they would get "closer to home," meaning that they wanted to reduce their mortgage exposure: sell what could be sold as is, repackage and sell everything else.[10] Kevin Gasvoda, the managing director for Goldman's Fixed Income, Currency, and Commodities business line, instructed the sales team to sell asset-backed security and CDO positions, even at a loss: "Pls refocus on retained new issue bond positions and move them out. There will be big opportunities the next several months and we don't want to be hamstrung based on old inventory. Refocus efforts and move stuff out even if you have to take a small loss."[11] In a December 15 email, Viniar described the strategy to Tom Montag, the co-head of global securities: "On ABX, the position is reasonably sensible but is just too big. Might have to spend a little to size it appropriately. On everything else my basic message was let's be aggressive distributing things because there will be very good opportunities as the market goes into what is likely to be even greater distress and we want to be in position to take advantage of them."[12]

Subsequent emails suggest that the "everything else" meant mortgage-related assets. On December 20, in an internal email with broad distribution, Goldman's Stacy Bash-Polley, a partner and the co-head of fixed income sales, noted that the firm, unlike others, had been able to find buyers for the super-senior and equity tranches of CDOs, but the mezzanine tranches remained a challenge. The "best target," she said, would be to put them in other CDOs: "We have been thinking collectively as a group about how to help move some of the risk. While we have made great progress moving the tail risks—[super-senior] and equity—we think it is critical to focus on the mezz risk that has been built up over the past few months. . . . Given some of the feedback we have received so far [from investors,] it seems that cdo's maybe the best target for moving some of this risk but clearly in limited size (and timing right now not ideal)."[13]

It was becoming harder to find buyers for these securities. Back in October, Goldman Sachs traders had complained that they were being asked to "distribute junk that nobody was dumb enough to take first time around."[14] Despite the first of Goldman's business principles—that "our clients' interests always come first"—documents indicate that the firm targeted less-sophisticated customers in its efforts to reduce subprime exposure. In a December 28 email discussing a list of customers to target for the year, Goldman's Fabrice Tourre, then a vice president on the structured product correlation trading desk, said to "focus efforts" on "buy and hold rating-based buyers"

rather than "sophisticated hedge funds" that "will be on the same side of the trade as we will."[15] The "same of side of the trade" as Goldman was the selling or shorting side—those who expected the mortgage market to continue to decline. In January, Daniel Sparks, the head of Goldman's mortgage department, extolled Goldman's success in reducing its subprime inventory, writing that the team had "structured like mad and traveled the world, and worked their tails off to make some lemonade from some big old lemons."[16] Tourre acknowledged that there was "more and more leverage in the system," and—writing of himself in the third person—said he was "standing in middle of all these complex, highly levered, exotic trades he created without necessarily understanding all the implications of those monstrosities."[17]

On February 11, Goldman CEO Lloyd Blankfein questioned Montag about the $20 million in losses on residual positions from old deals, asking, "Could/should we have cleaned up these books before and are we doing enough right now to sell off cats and dogs in other books throughout the division?"[18]

The numbers suggest that the answer was yes, they had cleaned up pretty well, even given a $20 million write-off and billions of dollars of subprime exposure still retained. In the first quarter of 2007, its mortgage business earned a record $266 million, driven primarily by short positions, including a $10 billion short position on the bellwether ABX BBB index, whose drop the previous November had been the red flag that got Goldman's attention.

In the following months, Goldman reduced its own mortgage risk while continuing to create and sell mortgage-related products to its clients. From December 2006 through August 2007, it created and sold approximately $25.4 billion of CDOs—including $17.6 billion of synthetic CDOs. The firm used the cash CDOs to unload much of its own remaining inventory of other CDO securities and mortgage-backed securities.[19]

Goldman has been criticized—and sued—for selling its subprime mortgage securities to clients while simultaneously betting against those securities. Sylvain Raynes, a structured finance expert at R&R Consulting in New York, reportedly called Goldman's practice "the most cynical use of credit information that I have ever seen," and compared it to "buying fire insurance on someone else's house and then committing arson."[20]

During a FCIC hearing, Goldman CEO Lloyd Blankfein was asked if he believed it was a proper, legal, or ethical practice for Goldman to sell clients mortgage securities that Goldman believed would default, while simultaneously shorting them. Blankfein responded, "I do think that the behavior is improper and we regret the result—the consequence [is] that people have lost money"[21] The next day, Goldman issued a press release declaring Blankfein did not state that Goldman's "practices with respect to the sale of mortgage-related securities were improper. . . . Blankfein was responding to a lengthy series of statements followed by a question that was predicated on the assumption that a firm was selling a product that it thought was going to default. Mr. Blankfein agreed that, if such an assumption was true, the practice would be improper. Mr. Blankfein does not believe, nor did he say, that Goldman Sachs had behaved improperly in any way."[22]

In addition, Goldman President and Chief Operating Officer Gary Cohn testified: "During the two years of the financial crisis, Goldman Sachs lost $1.2 billion in its residential mortgage–related business. . . . We did not bet against our clients, and these numbers underscore that fact."[23]

Indeed, Goldman's short position was not the whole story. The daily mortgage "Value at Risk" measure, or VaR, which tracked potential losses if the market moved unexpectedly, increased in the three months through February. By February, Goldman's company-wide VaR reached an all-time high, according to SEC reports. The dominant driver of the increase was the one-sided bet on the mortgage market's continuing to decline. Preferring to be relatively neutral, between March and May, the mortgage securities desk reduced its short position on the ABX Index;[24] between June and August, it again reversed course, increasing its short position by purchasing protection on mortgage-related assets.

The Basis Yield Alpha Fund, a hedge fund and Goldman client that claims to have invested $11.25 million in Goldman's Timberwolf CDO, sued Goldman for fraud in 2010. The Timberwolf deal was heavily criticized by Senator Carl Levin and other members of the Permanent Subcommittee on Investigations during an April 2010 hearing. The Basis Yield Alpha Fund alleged that Goldman designed Timberwolf to quickly fail so that Goldman could offload low-quality assets and profit from betting against the CDO. Within two weeks of the fund's investment, Goldman began making margin calls on the deal. By the end of July 2007, it had demanded more than $35 million.[25] According to the hedge fund, Goldman's demands forced it into bankruptcy in August 2007—Goldman received about $40 million from the liquidation. Goldman denies Basis Yield Alpha Fund's claims, and CEO Blankfein dismissed the notion that Goldman misled investors. "I will tell you, we only dealt with people who knew what they were buying. And of course when you look after the fact, someone's going to come along and say they really didn't know," he told the FCIC.[26]

In addition to selling its subprime securities to customers, the firm took short positions using credit default swaps; it also took short positions on the ABX indices and on some of the financial firms with which it did business. Like every market participant, Goldman "marked," or valued, its securities after considering both actual market trades and surveys of how other institutions valued the assets. As the crisis unfolded, Goldman marked mortgage-related securities at prices that were significantly lower than those of other companies. Goldman knew that those lower marks might hurt those other companies—including some clients—because they could require marking down those assets and similar assets. In addition, Goldman's marks would get picked up by competitors in dealer surveys. As a result, Goldman's marks could contribute to other companies recording "mark-to-market" losses: that is, the reported value of their assets could fall and their earnings would decline.

The markdowns of these assets could also require that companies reduce their repo borrowings or post additional collateral to counterparties to whom they had sold credit default swap protection. In a May 11 email, Craig Broderick, who as Goldman's chief risk officer was responsible for tracking how much of the company's money was at risk,[27] noted to colleagues that the mortgage group was "in the process

of considering making significant downward adjustments to the marks on their mortgage portfolio [especially] CDOs and CDO squared. This will potentially have a big [profit and loss] impact on us, but also to our clients due to the marks and associated margin calls on repos, derivatives, and other products. We need to survey our clients and take a shot at determining the most vulnerable clients, knock on implications, etc. This is getting lots of 30th floor attention right now."[28]

Broderick was right about the impact of Goldman's marks on clients and counterparties. The first significant dispute about these marks began in May 2007: it concerned the two high-flying, mortgage-focused hedge funds run by Bear Stearns Asset Management (BSAM).

## BEAR STEARNS'S HEDGE FUNDS: "LOOKS PRETTY DAMN UGLY"

In 2003, Ralph Cioffi and Matthew Tannin, who had structured CDOs at Bear Stearns, were busy managing BSAM's High-Grade Structured Credit Strategies Fund. When they added the higher-leveraged, higher-risk Enhanced Fund in 2006 they became even busier.

By April 2007, internal BSAM risk exposure reports showed about 60% of the High-Grade fund's collateral to be subprime mortgage–backed CDOs, assets that were beginning to lose market value.[29] In a diary kept in his personal email account because he "didn't want to use [his] work email anymore," Tannin recounted that in 2006 "a wave of fear set over [him]" when he realized that the Enhanced Fund "was going to subject investors to 'blow up risk'" and "we could not run the leverage as high as I had thought we could."[30]

This "blow up risk," coupled with bad timing, proved fatal for the Enhanced Fund. Shortly after the fund opened, the ABX BBB- index started to falter, falling 4% in the last three months of 2006; then another 8% in January and 25% in February. The market's confidence fell with the ABX. Investors began to bail out of both Enhanced and High-Grade. Cioffi and Tannin stepped up their marketing. On March 7, 2007, Tannin said in an email to investors, "we see an opportunity here—not crazy opportunity—but prudent opportunity—I am putting in additional capital—I think you should as well."[31] On a March 12 conference call, Tannin and Cioffi assured investors that both funds "have plenty of liquidity," and they continued to use the investment of their own money as evidence of their confidence.[32] Tannin even said he was increasing his personal investment, although, according to the SEC, he never did.[33]

Despite their avowals of confidence, Cioffi and Tannin were in full red-alert mode. In April, Cioffi redeemed $2 million of his own $6.1 million investment in Enhanced Leverage and transferred the funds to a third hedge fund he managed.[34] They tried to sell the toxic CDO securities held by the hedge funds. They had little success selling them directly on the market,[35] but there was another way.

In late May, BSAM put together a CDO-squared deal that would take $4 billion of CDO assets off the hedge funds' books. The senior-most tranches, worth $3.2 billion,

were sold as commercial paper to short-term investors such as money market mutual funds.[36]

Critically, Bank of America guaranteed those deals with a liquidity put—for a fee. Later, commercial paper investors would refuse to roll over this particular paper; Bank of America ultimately lost more than $4 billion on this arrangement.[37]

## "19% is doomsday"

Nearly all hedge funds provide their investors with market value reports, at least monthly, based on computed mark-to-market prices for the fund's various investments. Industry standards generally called for valuing readily traded assets, such as stocks, at the current trading price, while assets in very slow markets were marked by surveying price quotes from other dealers, factoring in other pricing information, and then arriving at a final net asset value. For mortgage-backed investments, marking assets was an extremely important exercise, because the market values were used to inform investors and to calculate the hedge fund's total fund value for internal risk management purposes, and because these assets were held as collateral for repo and other lenders. Crucially, if the value of a hedge fund's portfolio declined, repo and other lenders might require more collateral. In April, JP Morgan told Alan Schwartz, Bear Stearns's co-president, that the bank would be asking the BSAM hedge funds to post additional collateral to support its repo borrowing.[38]

Dealer marks were slow to keep up with movements in the ABX indices. Even as the ABX BBB- index recovered some in March, rebounding 6%, marks by broker-dealers finally started to reflect the lower values. On April 2, 2007, Goldman sent BSAM marks ranging from 65 cents to 100 cents on the dollar—meaning that some securities were worth as little as 65% of their initial value.[39] On Thursday, April 19, in preparation for an investor call the following week, BSAM analysts informed Cioffi and Tannin that in their view, the value of the funds' portfolios had declined sharply.[40] On Sunday, Tannin sent an email from his personal account to Cioffi's personal account arguing that both hedge funds should be closed and liquidated: "Looks pretty damn ugly. . . . If we believe the runs [the analyst] has been doing are ANYWHERE CLOSE to accurate, I think we should close the Funds now. . . . If [the runs] are correct then the entire sub-prime market is toast."[41] But by the following Wednesday, Cioffi and Tannin were back on the same upbeat page. At the beginning of the conference call, Tannin told investors, "The key sort of big picture point for us at this point is our confidence that the structured credit market and the sub-prime market in particular, has not systemically broken down; . . . we're very comfortable with exactly where we are." Cioffi also assured investors that the funds would likely finish the year with positive returns.[42] On May 1, 2007, the two hedge funds had attracted more than $60 million in new funds, but more than $28 million was redeemed by investors.[43]

That same day, Goldman sent BSAM marks ranging from 55 cents to 100 cents on the dollar.[44] Cioffi disputed Goldman's marks as well as marks from Lehman, Citigroup,

and JP Morgan.[45] On May 16, in a preliminary estimate, Cioffi told investors that the net asset value of the Enhanced Leverage Fund was down 6.6% in April.[46] In computing the final numbers later that month, he requested that BSAM's Pricing Committee instead use fair value marks based on his team's modeling, which implied losses that were $25 to $50 million less than losses using Goldman's marks.[47] On June 4, although Goldman's marks were considered low, the Pricing Committee decided to continue to average dealer marks rather than to use fair value. The committee also noted that the decline in net asset value would be greater than the 6.6% estimate, because "many of the positions that were marked down received dealer marks after release of the estimate."[48] The decline was revised from 6.6% to 19%. According to Cioffi, a number of factors contributed to the April revision, and Goldman's marks were one factor.[49] After these meetings, Cioffi emailed one committee member: "There is no market . . . its [sic] all academic anyway—19% [value] is doomsday."[50] On June 7, BSAM announced the 19% drop and froze redemptions.

### *"Canary in the mine shaft"*

When JP Morgan contacted Bear's co-president Alan Schwartz in April about its upcoming margin call, Schwartz convened an executive committee meeting to discuss how repo lenders were marking down positions and making margin calls on the basis of those new marks.[51] In early June, Bear met with BSAM's repo lenders to explain that BSAM lacked cash to meet margin calls and to negotiate a 60-day reprieve. Some of these very same firms had sold Enhanced and High-Grade some of the same CDOs and other securities that were turning out to be such bad assets.[52] Now all 10 refused Schwartz's appeal; instead, they made margin calls.[53] As a direct result, the two funds had to sell collateral at distressed prices to raise cash.[54] Selling the bonds led to a complete loss of confidence by the investors, whose requests for redemptions accelerated.

Shortly after BSAM froze redemptions, Merrill Lynch seized more than $850 million of its collateral posted by Bear for its outstanding repo loans. Merrill was able to sell just $181 million of the seized collateral at auction by July 5—and at discounts to its face value.[55] Other repo lenders were increasing their collateral requirements or refusing to roll over their loans.[56] This run on both hedge funds left both BSAM and Bear Stearns with limited options. Although it owned the asset management business, Bear's equity positions in the two BSAM hedge funds were relatively small. On April 26, Bear's co-president Warren Spector approved a $25 million investment into the Enhanced Leverage Fund.[57] Bear Stearns had no legal obligation to rescue either the funds or their repo lenders. However, those lenders were the same large investment banks that Bear Stearns dealt with every day.[58] Moreover, any failure of entities related to Bear Stearns could raise investors' concerns about the firm itself.

Thomas Marano, the head of the mortgage trading desk, told FCIC staff that the constant barrage of margin calls had created chaos at Bear. In late June, Bear Stearns dispatched him to engineer a solution with Richard Marin, BSAM's CEO. Marano now worked to understand the portfolio, including what it might be worth in a worst-

case scenario in which significant amounts of assets had to be sold.[59] Bear Stearns's conclusion: High-Grade still had positive value, but Enhanced Leverage did not.

On the basis of that analysis, Bear Stearns committed up to $3.2 billion—and ultimately loaned $1.6 billion—to take out the High-Grade Fund repo lenders and become the sole repo lender to the fund; Enhanced Leverage was on its own.

During a June Federal Open Market Committee (FOMC) meeting, members were informed about the subprime market and the BSAM hedge funds. The staff reported that the subprime market was "very unsettled and reflected deteriorating fundamentals in the housing market." The liquidation of subprime securities at the two BSAM hedge funds was compared to the troubles faced by Long-Term Capital Management in 1998. Chairman Bernanke noted that the problems the hedge funds experienced were a good example of how leverage can increase liquidity risk, especially in situations in which counterparties were not willing to give them time to liquidate and possibly realize whatever value might be in the positions. But it was also noted that the BSAM hedge funds appeared to be "relatively unique" among sponsored funds in their concentration in subprime mortgages.[60]

Some members were concerned about the lack of transparency around hedge funds, the consequent lack of market discipline on valuations of hedge fund holdings, and the fact that the Federal Reserve could not systematically collect information from hedge funds because they were outside its jurisdiction. These facts caused members to be concerned about whether they understood the scope of the problem.

During the same meeting, FOMC members noted that the size of the credit derivatives market, its lack of transparency and activities related to subprime debt could be a gathering cloud in the background of policy.

Meanwhile, Bear Stearns executives who supported the High-Grade bailout did not expect to lose money. However, that support was not universal—CEO James Cayne and Earl Hedin, the former senior managing director of Bear Stearns and BSAM, were opposed, because they did not want to increase shareholders' potential losses.[61] Their fears proved accurate. By July, the two hedge funds had shrunk to almost nothing: High-Grade Fund was down 91%; Enhanced Leverage Fund, 100%.[62] On July 31, both filed for bankruptcy. Cioffi and Tannin would be criminally charged with fraud in their communications with investors, but they were acquitted of all charges in November 2009. Civil charges brought by the SEC were still pending as of the date of this report.

Looking back, Marano told the FCIC, "We caught a lot of flak for allowing the funds to fail, but we had no option."[63] In an internal email in June, Bill Jamison of Federated Investors, one of the largest of all mutual fund companies, referred to the Bear Stearns hedge funds as the "canary in the mine shaft" and predicted more market turmoil.[64] As the two funds were collapsing, repo lending tightened across the board. Many repo lenders sharpened their focus on the valuation of any collateral with potential subprime exposure, and on the relative exposures of different financial institutions. They required increased margins on loans to institutions that appeared to be exposed to the mortgage market; they often required Treasury securities as collateral; in many cases, they demanded shorter lending terms.[65] Clearly, the triple-A-rated

mortgage-backed securities and CDOs were not considered the "super-safe" invest-ments in which investors—and some dealers—had only recently believed.

Cayne called Spector into the office and asked him to resign. On Sunday, August 5, Spector submitted his resignation to the board.

## RATING AGENCIES: "IT CAN'T BE . . . ALL OF A SUDDEN"

While BSAM was wrestling with its two ailing flagship hedge funds, the major credit rating agencies finally admitted that subprime mortgage–backed securities would not perform as advertised. On July 10, 2007, they issued comprehensive rating down-grades and credit watch warnings on an array of residential mortgage–backed securi-ties. These announcements foreshadowed the actual losses to come.

S&P announced that it had placed 612 tranches backed by U.S. subprime collat-eral, or some $7.35 billion in securities, on negative watch. S&P promised to review every deal in its ratings database for adverse effects. In the afternoon, Moody's down-graded 399 mortgage-backed securities issued in 2006 backed by U.S. subprime col-lateral and put an additional 32 tranches on watch. These Moody's downgrades affected about $5.2 billion in securities. The following day, Moody's placed 184 tranches of CDOs, with original face value of about $5 billion, on watch for possible downgrade. Two days after its original announcement, S&P downgraded 498 of the 612 tranches it had placed on negative watch. Fitch Ratings, the smallest of the three major credit rating agencies, announced similar downgrades.[66]

These actions were meaningful for all who understood their implications. While the specific securities downgraded were only a small fraction of the universe (less than 2% of mortgage-backed securities issued in 2006), investors knew that more downgrades might come. Many investors were critical of the rating agencies, lam-basting them for their belated reactions. By July 2007, by one measure, housing prices had already fallen about 4% nationally from their peak at the spring of 2006.[67]

On a July 10 conference call with S&P, the hedge fund manager Steve Eisman ques-tioned Tom Warrack, the managing director of S&P's residential mortgage–backed se-curities group. Eisman asked, "I'd like to know why now. I mean, the news has been out on subprime now for many, many months. The delinquencies have been a disaster now for many, many months. (Your) ratings have been called into question now for many, many months. I'd like to understand why you're making this move today when you—and why didn't you do this many, many months ago. . . . I mean, it can't be that all of a sudden, the performance has reached a level where you've woken up." Warrack responded that S&P "took action as soon as possible given the information at hand."[68]

The ratings agencies' downgrades, in tandem with the problems at Bear Stearns's hedge funds, had a further chilling effect on the markets. The ABX BBB- index fell another 33% in July, confirming and guaranteeing even more problems for holders of mortgage securities. Enacting the same inexorable dynamic that had taken down the Bear Stearns funds, repo lenders increasingly required other borrowers that had put up mortgage-backed securities as collateral to put up more, because their value was unclear or depressed. Many of these borrowers sold assets to meet these margin calls,

and each sale had the potential to further depress prices. If at all possible, the borrowers sold other assets in more liquid markets, for which prices were readily available, pushing prices downward in those markets, too.

## AIG: "WELL BIGGER THAN WE EVER PLANNED FOR"

Of all the possible losers in the looming rout, AIG should have been among the most concerned. After several years of aggressive growth, AIG's Financial Products subsidiary had written $79 billion in over-the-counter credit default swap (CDS) protection on super-senior tranches of multisector CDOs backed mostly by subprime mortgages.

In a phone call made July 11, the day after the downgrades, Andrew Forster, the head of credit trading at AIG Financial Products, told Alan Frost, the executive vice president of Financial Product's Marketing Group, that he had to analyze exposures because "every f***ing . . . rating agency we've spoken to . . . [came] out with more downgrades" and that he was increasingly concerned: "About a month ago I was like, you know, suicidal. . . . The problem that we're going to face is that we're going to have just enormous downgrades on the stuff that we've got. . . . Everyone tells me that it's trading and it's two points lower and all the rest of it and how come you can't mark your book. So it's definitely going to give it renewed focus. I mean we can't . . . we have to mark it. It's, it's, uh, we're [unintelligible] f***ed basically."[69]

Forster was likely worried that most of AIG's credit default swap contracts required that collateral be posted to the purchasers, should the market value of the referenced securities decline by a certain amount, or should rating agencies downgrade AIG's long-term debt. That is, collateral calls could be triggered even if there were no actual cash losses in, for example, the super-senior tranches of CDOs upon which the protection had been written. Remarkably, top AIG executives—including CEO Martin Sullivan, CFO Steven Bensinger, Chief Risk Officer Robert Lewis, Chief Credit Officer Kevin McGinn, and Financial Services Division CFO Elias Habayeb—told FCIC investigators that they did not even know about these terms of the swaps until the collateral calls started rolling in during July.[70] Office of Thrift Supervision regulators who supervised AIG on a consolidated basis didn't know either.[71] Frost, who was the chief credit default swap salesman at AIG Financial Products, did know about the terms, and he said he believed they were standard for the industry.[72] Joseph Cassano, the division's CEO, also knew about the terms.[73]

And the counterparties knew, of course. On the evening of July 26, Goldman Sachs, which held $21 billion of AIG's super-senior credit default swaps,[74] sent news of the first collateral call in the form of an email from Goldman's salesman Andrew Davilman to Frost:

DAVILMAN: Sorry to bother you on vacation. Margin call coming your way. Want to give you a heads up.
FROST, *18 minutes later:* On what?
DAVILMAN, *one minute later:* 20bb [$20 billion] of supersenior.[75]

The next day, Goldman made the collateral call official by forwarding an invoice requesting $1.8 billion.[76] On the same day, Goldman purchased $100 million of five-year protection—in the form of credit default swaps—against the possibility that AIG might default on its obligations.[77]

Frost never responded to Davilman's email. And when he returned from vacation, he was instructed to not have any involvement in the issue, because Cassano wanted Forster to take the lead on resolving the dispute.[78] AIG's models showed there would be no defaults on any of the bond payments that AIG's swaps insured. The Goldman executives considered those models irrelevant, because the contracts required collateral to be posted if market value declined, irrespective of any long-term cash losses.[79] Goldman estimated that the average decline in the market value of the bonds was 15%.[80]

So, first Bear Stearns's hedge funds and now AIG was getting hit by Goldman's marks on mortgage-backed securities. Like Cioffi and his colleagues at Bear Stearns, Frost and his colleagues at AIG disputed Goldman's marks. On July 30, Forster was told by another AIG trader that "[AIG] would be in fine shape if Goldman wasn't hanging its head out there." The margin call was "something that hit out of the blue and it's a f***ing number that's well bigger than we ever planned for." He acknowledged that dealers might say the marks "could be anything from 80 to sort of, you know, 95" because of the lack of trading but said Goldman's marks were "ridiculous."[81]

In testimony to the FCIC, Viniar said Goldman had stood ready to sell mortgage-backed securities to AIG at Goldman's own marks.[82] AIG's Forster stated that he would not buy the bonds at even 90 cents on the dollar, because values might drop further. Additionally, AIG would be required to value its own portfolio of similar assets at the same price. Forster said, "In the current environment I still wouldn't buy them . . . because they could probably go low . . . we can't mark any of our positions, and obviously that's what saves us having this enormous mark to market. If we start buying the physical bonds back then any accountant is going to turn around and say, well, John, you know you traded at 90, you must be able to mark your bonds then."[83]

Tough, lengthy negotiations followed. Goldman "was not budging" on its collateral demands, according to Tom Athan, a managing director at AIG Financial Products, describing a conference call with Goldman executives on August 1. "I played almost every card I had, legal wording, market practice, intent of the language, meaning of the [contract], and also stressed the potential damage to the relationship and GS said that this has gone to the 'highest levels' at GS and they feel that . . . this is a 'test case.'"[84]

Goldman Sachs and AIG would continue to argue about Goldman's marks, even as AIG would continue to post collateral that would fall short of Goldman's demands and Goldman would continue to purchase CDS contracts against the possibility of AIG's default. Over the next 14 months, more such disputes would cost AIG tens of billions of dollars and help lead to one of the biggest government bailouts in American history.

## COMMISSION CONCLUSIONS ON CHAPTER 12

The Commission concludes that entities such as Bear Stearns's hedge funds and AIG Financial Products that had significant subprime exposure were affected by the collapse of the housing bubble first, creating financial pressures on their parent companies. The commercial paper and repo markets—two key components of the shadow banking lending markets—quickly reflected the impact of the housing bubble collapse because of the decline in collateral asset values and concern about financial firms' subprime exposure.

# 13

## SUMMER 2007:
## DISRUPTIONS IN FUNDING

---

### CONTENTS

In the summer of 2007, as the prices of some highly rated mortgage securities crashed and Bear's hedge funds imploded, broader repercussions from the declining housing market were still not clear. "I don't think [the subprime mess] poses any threat to the overall economy," Treasury Secretary Henry Paulson told Bloomberg on July 26.[1] Meanwhile, nervous market participants were looking under every rock for any sign of hidden or latent subprime exposure. In late July, they found it in the market for asset-backed commercial paper (ABCP), a crucial, usually boring backwater of the financial sector.

This kind of financing allowed companies to raise money by borrowing against high-quality, short-term assets. By mid-2007, hundreds of billions out of the $1.2 trillion U.S. ABCP market were backed by mortgage-related assets, including some with subprime exposure.[2]

As noted, the rating agencies had given all of these ABCP programs their top investment-grade ratings, often because of liquidity puts from commercial banks. When the mortgage securities market dried up and money market mutual funds became skittish about broad categories of ABCP, the banks would be required under these liquidity puts to stand behind the paper and bring the assets onto their balance sheets, transferring losses back into the commercial banking system. In some cases, to protect relationships with investors, banks would support programs they had sponsored even when they had made no prior commitment to do so.

### IKB OF GERMANY: "REAL MONEY INVESTORS"

The first big casualty of the run on asset-backed commercial paper was a German

bank, IKB Deutsche Industriebank AG. Since its foundation in 1924, IKB had focused on lending to midsize German businesses, but in the past decade, management diversified. In 2002, IKB created an off-balance-sheet commercial paper program, called Rhineland, to purchase a portfolio of structured finance securities backed by credit card receivables, business loans, auto loans, and mortgages. It made money by using less expensive short-term commercial paper to purchase higher-yielding long-term securities, a strategy known as "securities arbitrage." By the end of June, Rhineland owned €14 billion ($18.9 billion) of assets, 95% of which were CDOs and CLOs (collateralized loan obligations—that is, securitized leveraged loans). And at least €8 billion ($10.8 billion) of that was protected by IKB through liquidity puts.[3] Importantly, German regulators at the time did not require IKB to hold any capital to offset potential Rhineland losses.[4]

As late as June 2007, when so many were bailing out of the structured products market, IKB was still planning to expand its off-balance-sheet holdings and was willing to take long positions in mortgage-related derivatives such as synthetic CDOs.[5] This attitude made IKB a favorite of the investment banks and hedge funds that were desperate to take the short side of the deal.

In early 2007, when Goldman was looking for buyers for Abacus 2007-AC1, the synthetic CDO mentioned in part III, it looked to IKB. An employee of Paulson & Co., the hedge fund that was taking the short side of the deal, bluntly said that "real money" investors such as IKB were outgunned. "The market is not pricing the subprime [residential mortgage–backed securities] wipeout scenario," the Paulson employee wrote in an email. "In my opinion this situation is due to the fact that rating agencies, CDO managers and underwriters have all the incentives to keep the game going, while 'real money' investors have neither the analytical tools nor the institutional framework to take action before the losses that one could anticipate based [on] the 'news' available everywhere are actually realized."[6] IKB subsequently purchased $150 million of the A1 and A2 tranches of the Abacus CDO and placed them in Rhineland.[7] It would lose 100% of that investment.

In mid-2007, Rhineland's asset-backed commercial paper was held by a number of American investors, including the Montana Board of Investments, the city of Oakland, California, and the Robbinsdale Area School District in suburban Minneapolis. On July 20, IKB reassured its investors that ratings downgrades of mortgage-backed securities would have only a limited impact on its business.[8] However, within days, Goldman Sachs, which regularly helped Rhineland raise money in the commercial paper market, told IKB that it would not sell any more Rhineland paper to its clients. On Friday, July 27, Deutsche Bank, recognizing that the ABCP markets would soon abandon Rhineland and that IKB would have to provide substantial support to the program, decided that doing business with IKB was too risky and cut off its credit lines. These were necessary for IKB to continue running its business. Deutsche Bank also alerted the German bank regulator to IKB's critical state. With the regulator's encouragement, IKB's largest shareholder, KfW Bankengruppe, announced on July 30 that it would bail out IKB. On August 7, Rhineland exercised its liquidity puts with

IKB. Rhineland's commercial paper investors were able to get rid of the paper, and KfW took the hit instead—with its losses expected to eventually reach 95%.[9]

The IKB episode served notice that exposures to toxic mortgage assets were lurking in the portfolios of even risk-averse investors. Soon, panic seized the short-term funding markets—even those that were not exposed to risky mortgages. "There was a recognition, I'd say an acute recognition, that potentially some of the asset-backed commercial paper conduits could have exposure to those areas. As a result, investors in general—without even looking into the underlying assets—decided 'I don't want to be in any asset-backed commercial paper, I don't want to invest in a fund that may have those positions,'" Steven Meier, global cash investment officer at State Street Global Advisors, testified to the FCIC.[10]

From its peak of $1.2 billion on August 8, the asset-backed commercial paper market would decline by almost $400 billion by the end of 2007.

## COUNTRYWIDE: "THAT'S OUR 9/11"

On August 2, three days after the IKB rescue, Countrywide CEO Angelo Mozilo realized that his company was unable to roll its commercial paper or borrow on the repo market. "When we talk about [August 2] at Countrywide, that's our 9/11," he said. "We worked seven days a week trying to figure this thing out and trying to work with the banks. . . . Our repurchase lines were coming due billions and billions of dollars."[11]

Mozilo emailed Lyle Gramley, a former Fed governor and a former Countrywide director, "Fear in the credit markets is now tending towards panic. There is little to no liquidity in the mortgage market with the exception of Fannie and Freddie. . . . Any mortgage product that is not deemed to be conforming either cannot be sold into the secondary markets or are subject to egregious discounts."[12]

On August 2, despite the internal turmoil at Countrywide, CFO Eric Sieracki told investors that Countrywide had "significant short-term funding liquidity cushions" and "ample liquidity sources of our bank. . . . It is important to note that the company has experienced no disruption in financing its ongoing daily operations, including placement of commercial paper."[13] Moody's reaffirmed its A3 ratings and stable outlook on the company.

The ratings agencies and the company itself would quickly reverse their positions. On August 6, Mozilo reported to the board during a specially convened meeting that, as the meeting minutes recorded, "the secondary market for virtually all classes of mortgage securities (both prime and non-prime) had unexpectedly and with almost no warning seized up and . . . the Company was unable to sell high-quality mortgage[-]backed securities." President and COO David Sambol told the board, "Management can only plan on a week by week basis due to the tenuous nature of the situation." Mozilo reported that although he continued to negotiate with banks for alternative sources of liquidity, the "unprecedented and unanticipated" absence of a secondary market could force the company to draw down on its backup credit lines.[14]

Shortly after the Countrywide board meeting, the Fed's Federal Open Market

Committee members discussed the "considerable financial turbulence" in the sub-prime mortgage market and that some firms, including Countrywide, were showing some strain. They noted that the data did not indicate a collapse of the housing market was imminent and that, if the more optimistic scenarios proved to be accurate, they might look back and be surprised that the financial events did not have a stronger impact on the real economy. But the FOMC members also expressed concern that the effects of subprime developments could spread to other sectors and noted that they had been repeatedly surprised by the depth and duration of the deterioration of these markets. One participant, in a paraphrase of a quote he attributed to Winston Churchill, said that no amount of rewriting of history would exonerate those present if they did not prepare for the more dire scenarios discussed in the staff presentations.[15]

Several days later, on August 14, Countrywide released its July 2007 operational results, reporting that foreclosures and delinquencies were up and that loan production had fallen by 14% during the preceding month. A company spokesman said layoffs would be considered. On the same day, Fed staff, who had supervised Countrywide's holding company until the bank switched to a thrift charter in March 2007, sent a confidential memo to the Fed's Board of Governors warning about the company's condition:

> The company is heavily reliant on an originate-to-distribute model, and, given current market conditions, the firm is unable to securitize or sell any of its non-conforming mortgages. . . . Countrywide's short-term funding strategy relied heavily on commercial paper (CP) and, especially, on ABCP. In current market conditions, the viability of that strategy is questionable. . . . The ability of the company to use [mortgage] securities as collateral in [repo transactions] is consequently uncertain in the current market environment. . . . As a result, it could face severe liquidity pressures. Those liquidity pressures conceivably could lead eventually to possible insolvency.[16]

Countrywide asked its regulator, the Office of Thrift Supervision, if the Fed could provide assistance, perhaps by waiving a Fed rule and allowing Countrywide's thrift subsidiary to support its holding company by raising money from insured depositors, or perhaps through discount-window lending, which would require the Fed to accept risky mortgage-backed securities as collateral, something it never had done and would not do—until the following spring. The Fed did not intervene: "Substantial statutory requirements would have to be met before the Board could authorize lending to the holding company or mortgage subsidiary," staff wrote. "The Federal Reserve had not lent to a nonbank in many decades; and . . . such lending in the current circumstances seemed highly improbable."[17]

The following day, lacking any other funding, Mozilo recommended to his board that the company notify lenders of its intention to draw down $11.5 billion on backup lines of credit.[18] Mozilo and his team knew that the decision could lead to ratings

downgrades. "The only option we had was to pull down those lines," he told the FCIC. "We had a pipeline of loans and we either had to say to the borrowers, the customers, 'we're out of business, we're not going to fund'—and there's great risk to that, litigation risk, we had committed to fund. . . . When it's between your ass and your image, you hold on to your ass."[19]

On the same day that Countrywide's board approved the $11.5 billion drawdown—but before the company announced it publicly—the Merrill Lynch analyst Kenneth Bruce, who had reissued his "buy" rating on the company's stock two days earlier, switched to "sell" with a "negative" outlook because of Countrywide's funding pressures, adding, "if the market loses confidence in its ability to function properly, then the model can break. . . . If liquidations occur in a weak market, then it is possible for [Countrywide] to go bankrupt."[20]

The next day, as news of Bruce's call spread, Countrywide informed markets about the drawdown. Moody's downgraded its senior unsecured debt rating to the lowest tier of investment grade. Countrywide shares fell 11%, closing at $18.95; for the year, the company's stock was down 50%. The bad news led to an old-fashioned bank run. Mozilo singled out an August 16 *Los Angeles Times* article covering Bruce's report, which, he said, "caused a run on our bank of $8 billion on Monday." The article spurred customers to withdraw their funds by noting specific addresses of Countrywide branches in southern California, Mozilo told the FCIC. A reporter "came out with a photographer and, you know, interviewed the people in line, and he created—it was just horrible. Horrible for the people, horrible for us. Totally unnecessary," Mozilo said.[21]

Six days later, on August 22, Bank of America announced it would invest $2 billion for a 16% stake in Countrywide. Both companies denied rumors that the nation's biggest bank would soon acquire the mortgage lender. Mozilo told the press, "There was never a question about our survival"; he said the investment reinforced Countrywide's position as one of the "strongest and best-run companies in the country."[22]

In October, Countrywide reported a net loss of $1.2 billion, its first quarterly loss in 25 years. As charge-offs on its mortgage portfolio grew, Countrywide raised provisions for loan losses to $934 million from only $38 million one year earlier. On January 11, 2008, Bank of America issued a press release announcing a "definitive agreement" to purchase Countrywide for approximately $4 billion. It said the combined entity would stop originating subprime loans and would expand programs to help distressed borrowers.

## BNP PARIBAS: "THE RINGING OF THE BELL"

Meanwhile, problems in U.S. financial markets hit the largest French bank. On August 9, BNP Paribas SA suspended redemptions from three investment funds that had plunged 20% in less than two weeks. Total assets in those funds were $2.2 billion, with a third of that amount in subprime securities rated AA or higher.[23] The bank said it would also stop calculating a fair market value for the funds because "the complete evaporation of liquidity in certain market segments of the US securitization

# Asset-Backed Commercial Paper Outstanding

*At the onset of the crisis in summer 2007, asset-backed commercial paper outstanding dropped as concerns about asset quality quickly spread. By the end of 2007, the amount outstanding had dropped nearly $400 billion.*

IN BILLIONS OF DOLLARS

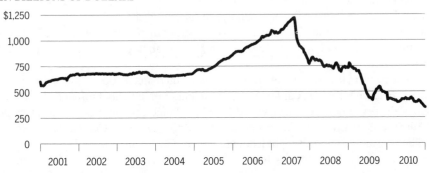

NOTE: Seasonally adjusted
SOURCE: Federal Reserve Board of Governors

*Figure 13.1*

market has made it impossible to value certain assets fairly regardless of their quality or credit rating."[24]

In retrospect, many investors regarded the suspension of the French funds as the beginning of the 2007 liquidity crisis. August 9 "was the ringing of the bell" for short-term funding markets, Paul McCulley, a managing director at PIMCO, told the FCIC. "The buyers went on a buyer strike and simply weren't rolling."[25] That is, they stopped rolling over their commercial paper and instead demanded payment on their loans. On August 9, the interest rates for overnight lending of A-1 rated asset-backed commercial paper rose from 5.39% to 5.75%—the highest level since January 2001. It would continue rising unevenly, hitting 6.14% in August 10, 2007. Figure 13.1 shows how, in response, lending declined.

In August alone, the asset-backed commercial paper market shrank by $190 billion, or 20%. On August 6, subprime lender American Home Mortgage's asset-backed commercial paper program invoked its privilege of postponing repayment, trapping lenders' money for several months. Lenders quickly withdrew from programs with similar provisions, which shrank that market from $35 billion to $4 billion between May and August.[26]

The paper that did sell had significantly shorter maturities, reflecting creditors' desire to reassess their counterparties' creditworthiness as frequently as possible. The average maturity of all asset-backed commercial paper in the United States fell from

about 31 days in late July to about 23 days by mid-September, though the over-whelming majority was issued for just 1 to 4 days.[27]

Disruptions quickly spread to other parts of the money market. In a flight to qual-ity, investors dumped their repo and commercial paper holdings and increased their holdings in seemingly safer money market funds and Treasury bonds. Market partici-pants, unsure of each other's potential subprime exposures, scrambled to amass funds for their own liquidity. Banks became less willing to lend to each other. A closely watched indicator of interbank lending rates, called the one-month LIBOR-OIS spread, increased, signifying that banks were concerned about the credit risk involved in lending to each other. On August 9, it rose sharply, increasing three-to fourfold over historical values, and by September 7, it climbed by another 150%. In 2008, it would peak much higher.

The panic in the repo, commercial paper, and interbank markets was met by imme-diate government action. On August 10, the day after BNP Paribas suspended redemp-tions, the Fed announced that it would "provid[e] liquidity as necessary to facilitate the orderly functioning of financial markets,"[28] and the European Central Bank infused billions of Euros into overnight lending markets. On August 17, the Fed cut the dis-count rate by 50 basis points—from 6.25% to 5.75%. This would be the first of many such cuts aimed at increasing liquidity. The Fed also extended the term of discount-window lending to 30 days (from the usual overnight or very short-term period) to of-fer banks a more stable source of funds. On the same day, the Fed's FOMC released a statement acknowledging the continued market deterioration and promising that it was "prepared to act as needed to mitigate the adverse effects on the economy."[29]

## SIVs: "AN OASIS OF CALM"

In August, the turmoil in asset-backed commercial paper markets hit the market for structured investment vehicles, or SIVs, even though most of these programs had lit-tle subprime mortgage exposure. SIVs had a stable history since their introduction in 1988. These investments had weathered a number of credit crises—even through early summer of 2007, as noted in a Moody's report issued on July 20, 2007, titled "SIVs: An Oasis of Calm in the Sub-prime Maelstrom."[30]

Unlike typical asset-backed commercial paper programs, SIVs were funded pri-marily through medium-term notes—bonds maturing in one to five years. SIVs held significant amounts of highly liquid assets and marked those assets to market prices daily or weekly, which allowed them to operate without explicit liquidity support from their sponsors.

The SIV sector tripled in assets between 2004 and 2007. On the eve of the crisis, there were 36 SIVs with almost $400 billion in assets.[31] About one-quarter of that money was invested in mortgage-backed securities or in CDOs, but only 6% was in-vested in subprime mortgage–backed securities and CDOs holding mortgage-backed securities.

Not surprisingly, the first SIVs to fail were concentrated in subprime mortgage–

backed securities, mortgage-related CDOs, or both. These included Cheyne Finance (managed by London-based Cheyne Capital Management), Rhinebridge (another IKB program), Golden Key, and Mainsail II (both structured by Barclays Capital). Between August and October, each of these four was forced to restructure or liquidate.

Investors soon ran from even the safer SIVs. "The media was quite happy to sensationalize the collapse of the next 'leaking SIV' or the next 'SIV-positive' institution," then-Moody's managing director Henry Tabe told the FCIC.[32] The situation was complicated by the SIVs' lack of transparency. "In a context of opacity about where risk resides, . . . a general distrust has contaminated many asset classes. What had once been liquid is now illiquid. Good collateral cannot be sold or financed at anything approaching its true value," Moody's wrote on September 5.[33]

Even high-quality assets that had nothing to do with the mortgage market were declining in value. One SIV marked down a CDO to seven cents on the dollar while it was still rated triple-A.[34] To raise cash, managers sold assets. But selling high-quality assets into a declining market depressed the prices of these unimpaired securities and pushed down the market values of other SIV portfolios.

By the end of November, SIVs still in operation had liquidated 23% of their portfolios, on average.[35] Sponsors rescued some SIVs. Other SIVs restructured or liquidated; some investors had to wait a year or more to receive payments and, even then, recouped only some of their money. In the case of Rhinebridge, investors lost 45% and only gradually received their payments over the next year.[36] Investors in one SIV, Sigma, lost more than 95%.[37] As of fall 2010, not a single SIV remained in its original form. The subprime crisis had brought to its knees a historically resilient market in which losses due to subprime mortgage defaults had been, if anything, modest and localized.

## MONEY FUNDS AND OTHER INVESTORS: "DRINK[ING] FROM A FIRE HOSE"

The next dominoes were the money market funds and other funds. Most were sponsored by investment banks, bank holding companies, or "mutual fund complexes" such as Fidelity, Vanguard, and Federated. Under SEC regulations, money market funds that serve retail investors must keep two sets of accounting books, one reflecting the price they paid for securities and the other the fund's mark-to-market value (the "shadow price," in market parlance). However, funds do not have to disclose the shadow price unless the fund's net asset value (NAV) has fallen by 0.5% below $1 (to $0.995) per share. Such a decline in market value is known as "breaking the buck" and generally leads to a fund's collapse. It can happen, for example, if just 5% of a fund's portfolio is in an investment that loses just 10% of its value. So a fund manager cannot afford big risks.

But SIVs were considered very safe investments—they always had been—and were widely held by money market funds. In fall 2007, dozens of money market funds faced losses on SIVs and other asset-backed commercial paper. To prevent their funds from breaking the buck, at least 44 sponsors, including large banks such

as Bank of America, US Bancorp, and SunTrust, purchased SIV assets from their money market funds.[38]

Similar dramas played out in the less-regulated realm of the money market sector known as enhanced cash funds. These funds serve not retail investors but rather "qualified purchasers," which may include wealthy investors who invest $25 million or more. Enhanced cash funds fall outside most SEC regulations and disclosure requirements. Because they have much higher investment thresholds than retail funds, and because they face less regulation, investors expect somewhat riskier investing and higher returns. Nonetheless, these funds also aim to maintain a $1 net asset value.

As the market turned, some of these funds did break the buck, while the sponsors of others stepped in to support their value. The $5 billion GE Asset Management Trust Enhanced Cash Trust, a GE-sponsored fund that managed GE's own pension and employee benefit assets, ran aground in the summer; it had 50% of its assets in mortgage-backed securities. When the fund reportedly lost $200 million and closed in November 2007, investors redeemed their interests at $0.96.[39] Bank of America supported its Strategic Cash Portfolio—the nation's largest enhanced cash fund, with $40 billion in assets at its peak—after one of that fund's largest investors withdrew $20 billion in November 2007.[40]

An interesting case study is provided by the meteoric rise and decline of the Credit Suisse Institutional Money Market Prime Fund. The fund sought to attract investors through Internet-based trading platforms called "portals," which supplied an estimated $300 billion to money market funds and other funds. Investors used these portals to quickly move their cash to the highest-yielding fund. Posting a higher return could attract significant funds: one money market fund manager later compared the use of portal money to "drink[ing] from a fire hose."[41] But the money could vanish just as quickly. The Credit Suisse fund posted the highest returns in the industry during the 12 months before the liquidity crisis, and increased its assets from about $5 billion in the summer of 2006 to more than $25 billion in the summer of 2007. To deliver those high returns and attract investors, though, it focused on structured finance products, including CDOs and SIVs such as Cheyne. When investors became concerned about such assets, they yanked about $10 billion out of the fund in August 2007 alone. Credit Suisse, the Swiss bank that sponsored the fund, was forced to bail it out, purchasing $5.7 billion of assets in August.[42] The episode highlights the risks of money market funds' relying on "hot money"—that is, institutional investors who move quickly in and out of funds in search of the highest returns.

The losses on SIVs and other mortgage-tainted investments also battered local government investment pools across the country, some of which held billions of dollars in these securities. Pooling provides municipalities, school districts, and other government agencies with economies of scale, investment diversification, and liquidity. In some cases, participation is mandatory.

With $27 billion in assets, Florida's local government investment pool was the largest in the country, and "intended to operate like a highly liquid, low-risk money market fund, with securities like cash, certificates of deposit, . . . U.S. Treasury bills,

and bonds issued by other U.S. government agencies," as an investigation by the state legislature noted.[43] But by November 2007, because of ratings downgrades, the fund held at least $1.5 billion in securities that no longer met the state's requirements. It had more than $2 billion in SIVs and other distressed securities, of which about $725 million had already defaulted. And it held $650 million in Countrywide certificates of deposit with maturities that stretched out as far as June 2008.[44] In early November, following a series of news reports, the fund suffered a run. Local governments withdrew $8 billion in just two weeks. Orange and Pinellas counties pulled out their entire investments. On November 29, the fund's managers stopped all withdrawals. Florida's was the hardest hit, but other state investment pools also took significant losses on SIVs and other mortgage-related holdings.

## COMMISSION CONCLUSIONS ON CHAPTER 13

The Commission concludes that the shadow banking system was permitted to grow to rival the commercial banking system with inadequate supervision and regulation. That system was very fragile due to high leverage, short-term funding, risky assets, inadequate liquidity, and the lack of a federal backstop. When the mortgage market collapsed and financial firms began to abandon the commercial paper and repo lending markets, some institutions depending on them for funding their operations failed or, later in the crisis, had to be rescued. These markets and other interconnections created contagion, as the crisis spread even to markets and firms that had little or no direct exposure to the mortgage market.

In addition, regulation and supervision of traditional banking had been weakened significantly, allowing commercial banks and thrifts to operate with fewer constraints and to engage in a wider range of financial activities, including activities in the shadow banking system.

The financial sector, which grew enormously in the years leading up to the financial crisis, wielded great political power to weaken institutional supervision and market regulation of both the shadow banking system and the traditional banking system. This deregulation made the financial system especially vulnerable to the financial crisis and exacerbated its effects.

# 14

# LATE 2007 TO EARLY 2008: BILLIONS IN SUBPRIME LOSSES

## CONTENTS

While a handful of banks were bailing out their money market funds and commercial paper programs in the fall of 2007, the financial sector faced a larger problem: billions of dollars in mortgage-related losses on loans, securities, and derivatives, with no end in sight. Among U.S. firms, Citigroup and Merrill Lynch reported the most spectacular losses, largely because of their extensive collateralized debt obligation (CDO) businesses, writing down a total of $23.8 billion and $24.7 billion, respectively, by the end of the year. Billions more in losses were reported by large financial institutions such as Bank of America ($9.7 billion), Morgan Stanley ($10.3 billion), JP Morgan ($5.3 billion), and Bear Stearns ($2.6 billion).[1] Insurance companies, hedge funds, and other financial institutions collectively had taken additional mortgage-related losses of about $100 billion.[2]

The large write-downs strained these firms' capital and cash reserves. Further, market participants began discriminating between firms perceived to be relatively healthy and others about which they were not so sure. Bear Stearns and Lehman Brothers were at the top of the "suspect" list; by year-end 2007 the cost of five-year protection against default on their obligations in the credit default swap market stood at, respectively, $176,000 and $119,000 annually for every $10 million, while the cost for the relatively stronger Goldman Sachs stood at $68,000.[3]

Meanwhile, the economy was beginning to show signs of stress. Facing turmoil in financial markets, declining home prices, and oil prices above $75 a barrel, consumer spending was slowing. The Federal Reserve lowered the overnight bank borrowing rate from 5.25% earlier in the year to 4.75% in September, 4.5% in October, and then 4.25% in December.

## MERRILL LYNCH: "DAWNING AWARENESS
## OVER THE COURSE OF THE SUMMER"

On October 24, Merrill Lynch stunned investors when it announced that third-quarter earnings would include a $6.9 billion loss on CDOs and $1 billion on subprime mortgages—$7.9 billion in total, the largest Wall Street write-down to that point, and nearly twice the $4.5 billion loss that the company had warned investors to expect just three weeks earlier. Six days later, the embattled CEO Stanley O'Neal, a 21-year Merrill veteran, resigned.

Much of this write-down came from the firm's holdings of the super-senior tranches of mortgage-related CDOs that Merrill had previously thought to be extremely safe. As late as fall 2006, its management had been "bullish on growth" and "bullish on [the subprime] asset class."[4] But later that year, the signs of trouble were becoming difficult even for Merrill to ignore. Two mortgage originators to which the firm had extended credit lines failed: Ownit, in which Merrill also had a small equity stake, and Mortgage Lenders Network. Merrill seized the collateral backing those loans: $1.5 billion from Mortgage Lenders, $1.2 billion from Ownit.

Merrill, like many of its competitors, started to ramp up its sales efforts, packaging its inventory of mortgage loans and securities into CDOs with new vigor. Its goal was to reduce the firm's risk by getting those loans and securities off its balance sheet. Yet it found that it could not sell the super-senior tranches of those CDOs at acceptable prices; it therefore had to "take down senior tranches into inventory in order to execute deals"[5]—leading to the accumulation of tens of billions of dollars of those tranches on Merrill's books. Dow Kim, then the co-president of Merrill's investment banking segment, told FCIC staff that the buildup of the retained super-senior tranches in the CDO positions was actually part of a strategy begun in late 2006 to reduce the firm's inventory of subprime and Alt-A mortgages. Sell the lower-rated CDO tranches, retain the super-senior tranches: those had been his instructions to his managers at the end of 2006, Kim recalled. He believed that this strategy would reduce overall credit risk. After all, the super-senior tranches were theoretically the safest pieces of those investments.[6] To some degree, however, the strategy was involuntary: his people were having trouble selling these investments, and some were even sold at a loss.[7]

Initially, the strategy seemed to work. By May, the amount of mortgage loans and securities to be packaged into CDOs had declined to $3.5 billion from $12.8 billion in March.[8] According to a September 2007 internal Merrill presentation, the net amount in retained super-senior CDO tranches had increased from $9.3 billion in September 2006 to $25.4 billion by March 2007 and $28.9 billion by May.[9] But as the mortgage market came under increasing pressure and as the market value of even super-senior tranches crumbled, the strategy would come back to haunt the firm.

Merrill's first-quarter earnings for 2007—net revenues of $9.9 billion—were its second-highest quarterly results ever, including a record for the Fixed Income, Currencies and Commodities business, which housed the retained CDO positions. These

results were announced during a conference call with analysts—an event that investors and analysts rely on to obtain important information about the company and that, like other public statements, is subject to federal securities laws.

Merrill's then-CFO Jeffrey Edwards indicated that the company's results would not be hurt by the dislocation in the subprime market, because "revenues from subprime mortgage-related activities comprise[d] less than 1% of our net revenues" over the past five quarters, and because Merrill's "risk management capabilities are better than ever, and crucial to our success in navigating turbulent markets." Providing further assurances, he stated, "We believe the issues in this narrow slice of the market remain contained and have not negatively impacted other sectors."[10]

However, Edwards did not disclose the large increase in retained super-senior CDO tranches or the difficulty of selling those tranches, even at a loss—though specific questions on the subject were raised.

In July, Merrill followed its strong first-quarter report with another for the second quarter that "enabled the company to achieve record net revenues, net earnings and net earnings per diluted share for the first half of 2007."[11] During the conference call announcing the results, the analyst Glenn Schorr of UBS, a large Swiss bank, asked the CFO to provide some "color around myth versus reality" on Merrill's exposure to retained CDO positions. As he had three months earlier, Edwards stressed Merrill's risk management and the fact that the CDO business was a small part of Merrill's overall business. He said that there had been significant reductions in Merrill's retained exposures to lower-rated segments of the market, although he did not disclose that the total amount of Merrill's retained CDOs had reached $30.4 billion by June. Edwards declined to provide details about the company's exposure to subprime mortgage CDOs and any inventory of mortgage-backed securities to be packaged into CDOs. "We don't disclose our capital allocations against any specific or even broader group," Edwards said.[12]

On July 22, after the super-senior tranches had been accumulating for many months, Merrill executives first officially informed its board about the buildup. At a presentation to the board's Finance Committee, Dale Lattanzio, co-head of the American branch of the Fixed Income, Currencies and Commodities business, reported a "net" exposure of $32 billion in CDO-related assets, essentially all of them rated triple-A, with exposure to the lower-rated asset class significantly reduced.[13] This net exposure was the amount of CDO positions left after the subtraction of the hedges—guarantees in one form or another—that Merrill had purchased to pass along its ultimate risk to third parties willing to provide that protection and take that risk for a fee. AIG and the small club of monoline insurers were significant suppliers of these guarantees, commonly done as credit default swaps. In July 2007, Merrill had begun to increase the amount of CDS protection to offset the retained CDO positions.

Lattanzio told the committee, "[Management] decided in the beginning of this year to significantly reduce exposure to lower-rated assets in the sub-prime asset class and instead migrate exposure to senior and super senior tranches."[14] Edwards did not see any problems. As Kim insisted, "Everyone at the firm and most people in the industry felt that super-senior was super safe."[15]

Former CEO O'Neal told FCIC investigators he had not known that the company was retaining the super-senior tranches of the CDOs until Lattanzio's presentation to the Finance Committee. He was startled, if only because he had been under the impression that Merrill's mortgage-backed-assets business had been driven by demand: he had assumed that if there were no new customers, there would be no new offerings. If customers demanded the CDOs, why would Merrill have to retain CDO tranches on the balance sheet? O'Neal said he was surprised about the retained positions but stated that the presentation, analysis, and estimation of potential losses were not sufficient to sound "alarm bells."[16] Lattanzio's report in July indicated that the retained positions had experienced only $73 million in losses.[17] Over the next three months, the market value of the super-senior tranches plummeted and losses ballooned; O'Neal told the FCIC: "It was a dawning awareness over the course of the summer and through September as the size of the losses were being estimated."[18]

On October 21, Merrill executives gave its board a detailed account of how the firm found itself with what was by that time $15.2 billion in net exposure to the super-senior tranches—down from a peak in July of $32.2 billion because the firm had increasingly hedged, written off, and sold its exposure. On October 24, Merrill announced its third-quarter earnings: a stunning $7.9 billion mortgage-related write-down contributing to a net loss of $2.3 billion. Merrill also reported—for the first time—its $15.2 billion net exposure to retained CDO positions. Still, in their conference call with analysts, O'Neal and Edwards refused to disclose the gross exposures, excluding the hedges from the monolines and AIG. "I just don't want to get into the details behind that," Edwards said. "Let me just say that what we have provided again we think is an extraordinarily high level of disclosure and it should be sufficient."[19] According to the Securities and Exchange Commission, by September 2007, Merrill had accumulated $55 billion of "gross" retained CDO positions, almost four times the $15.2 billion of "net" CDO positions reported during the October 24 conference call.[20]

On October 30, when O'Neal resigned, he left with a severance package worth $161.5 million[21]—on top of the $91.4 million in total compensation he earned in 2006, when his company was still expanding its mortgage banking operations. Kim, who oversaw the strategy that left Merrill with billions in losses, had left in May 2007 after being paid $40 million for his work in 2006, which was a profitable year for Merrill as a firm.[22]

By late 2007, the viability of the monoline insurers from which Merrill had purchased almost $100 billion in hedges had come into question, and the rating agencies were downgrading them, as we will see in more detail shortly. The SEC had told Merrill that it would impose a punitive capital charge on the firm if it purchased additional credit default protection from the financially troubled monolines. Recognizing that the monolines might not be good for all the protection purchased, Merrill began to put aside loss allowances, starting with $2.6 billion on January 17, 2008. By the end of 2008, Merrill would put aside a total of $13 billion related to monolines and had recorded total write-downs on nearly $44 billion of other mortgage-related exposures.

## CITIGROUP: "THAT WOULD NOT IN ANY WAY
## HAVE EXCITED MY ATTENTION"

Five days after O'Neal's October 30 departure from Merrill Lynch, Citigroup announced that its total subprime exposure was $55 billion, which was $42 billion more than it had told investors just three weeks earlier. Citigroup also announced it would be taking an $8 to $11 billion loss on its subprime mortgage–related holdings and that Chuck Prince was resigning as its CEO. Like O'Neal, Prince had learned late of his company's subprime-related CDO exposures. Prince and Robert Rubin, chairman of the Executive Committee of the board, told the FCIC that before September 2007, they had not known that Citigroup's investment banking division had sold some CDOs with liquidity puts and retained the super-senior tranches of others.[23]

Prince told the FCIC that even in hindsight it was difficult for him to criticize any of his team's decisions. "If someone had elevated to my level that we were putting on a $2 trillion balance sheet, $40 billion of triple-A-rated, zero-risk paper, that would not in any way have excited my attention," Prince said. "It wouldn't have been useful for someone to come to me and say, 'Now, we have got $2 trillion on the balance sheet of assets. I want to point out to you there is a one in a billion chance that this $40 billion could go south.' That would not have been useful information. There is nothing I can do with that, because there is that level of chance on everything."[24] In fact, the odds were much higher than that. Even before the mass downgrades of CDOs in late 2007, a triple-A tranche of a CDO had a 1 in 10 chance of being downgraded within 5 years of its original rating.[25]

Certainly, Citigroup was a large and complex organization. That $2 trillion balance sheet—and $1.2 trillion off-balance sheet—was spread among more than 2,000 operating subsidiaries in 2007. Prince insisted that Citigroup was not "too big to manage."[26] But it was an organization in which one unit would decide to reduce mortgage risk while another unit increased it. And it was an organization in which senior management would not be notified of $43 billion in concentrated exposure— 2% of the company's balance sheet and more than a third of its capital—because it was perceived to be "zero-risk paper."[27]

Significantly, Citigroup's Financial Control Group had argued in 2006 that the liquidity puts that Citigroup had written on its CDOs had been priced for investors too cheaply in light of the risks.[28] Also, in early 2006, Susan Mills, a managing director in the securitization unit—which bought mortgages from other companies and bundled them for sale to investors—took note of rising delinquencies in the subprime market and created a surveillance group to track loans that her unit purchased.[29] By mid-2006, her group saw a deterioration in loan quality and an increase in early payment defaults—that is, more borrowers were defaulting within a few months of getting a loan. From 2005 to 2007, Mills recalled before the FCIC, the early payment default rates nearly tripled from 2% to 5% or 6%.[30] In response, the securitization unit slowed down its purchase of loans, demanded higher-quality mortgages, and conducted more extensive due diligence on what it bought. However, neither Mills nor other members of the unit shared any of this information with other divisions in Citi-

group, including the CDO desk.[31] Around March or April 2007, in contrast with the securitization desk, Citigroup's CDO desk increased its purchases of mortgage-backed securities because it saw the distressed market as a buying opportunity.[32]

"Effective communication across businesses was lacking," the company's regulators later observed. "Management acknowledged that, in looking back, it should have made the mortgage deterioration known earlier throughout the firm. The Global Consumer Group saw signs of sub-prime issues and avoided losses, as did mortgage backed securities traders, but CDO structures business did so belatedly—[there was] no dialogue across businesses."[33]

Co-head of the CDO desk Janice Warne told the FCIC that she first saw weaknesses in the underlying market in early 2007. In February, when the ABX.HE.BBB- 06-2 fell to 37% below par, the CDO desk decided to slow down on the financing of mortgage securities for inventory to produce CDOs.[34] Shortly thereafter, however, the same ABX index started to rally, rising to 26% below par in March and holding around that level through May. So, the CDO desk reversed course and accelerated its purchases of inventory in April, according to Nestor Dominguez, Warne's co-head on the CDO desk.[35] Dominguez said he didn't see the market weakening until the summer, when the index fell to less than 60% below par.[36]

Murray Barnes, the Citigroup risk officer assigned to the CDO business, approved the CDO desk's request to temporarily increase its limits on purchasing collateral. Barnes observed, in hindsight, that rather than looking at the widening spreads as an opportunity, Citigroup should have reassessed its assumptions and examined whether the decline in the ABX was a sign of strain in the mortgage market. He admitted "complacency" about the desk's ability to manage its risk.[37]

The risk management division also increased the CDO desk's limits for retaining the most senior tranches from $30 billion to $35 billion in the first half of 2007. As at Merrill, traders and risk managers at Citigroup believed that the super-senior tranches carried little risk.[38] Citigroup's regulators later wrote, "An acknowledgement of the risk in its Super Senior AAA CDO exposure was perhaps Citigroup's 'biggest miss.' . . . As management felt comfortable with the credit risk of these tranches, it began to retain large positions on the balance sheet. . . . As the sub-prime market began to deteriorate, the risk perceived in these tranches increased, causing large write-downs."[39] Ultimately, losses at Citigroup from mortgages, Alt-A mortgage–backed securities, and mortgage-related CDOs would total about $58 billion, nearly half of Citigroup's capital at the end of 2006. About $8 billion of that loss related to protection purchased from the monoline insurers.[40]

Barnes's decision to increase the CDO risk limits was approved by his superior, Ellen Duke. Barnes and Duke reported to David Bushnell, the chief risk officer. Bushnell—whom Prince called "the best risk manager on Wall Street"—told the FCIC that he did not remember specifically approving the increase but that, in general, the risk management function did approve higher risk limits when a business line was growing.[41] He described a "firm-wide initiative" to increase Citigroup's structured products business.[42]

Perhaps what is most remarkable about the conflicting strategies employed by the

securitization and CDO desks is that their respective risk officers attended the same weekly independent risk meetings. Duke reflected that she was not overly concerned when the issue came up, saying she and her risk team were "seduced by structuring and failed to look at the underlying collateral."[43] According to Barnes, the CDO desk didn't look at the CDOs' underlying collateral because it lacked the "ability" to see loan performance data, such as delinquencies and early payment defaults.[44] Yet the surveillance unit in Citigroup's securitization desk might have been able to provide some insights based on its own data.[45] Barnes told the FCIC that Citigroup's risk management tended to be managed along business lines, noting that he was only two offices away from his colleague who covered the securitization business and yet didn't understand the nuances of what was happening to the underlying loans. He regretted not reaching out to the consumer bank to "get the pulse" of mortgage origination.[46]

## *"That has never happened since the Depression"*

Prince and Rubin appeared to believe up until the fall of 2007 that any downside risk in the CDO business was minuscule. "I don't think anybody focused on the CDOs. This was one business in a vast enterprise, and until the trouble developed, it wasn't one that had any particular profile," Rubin—in Prince's words, a "very important member of [the] board"[47]—told the FCIC. "You know, Tom Maheras was in charge of trading. Tom was an extremely well regarded trading figure on the street. . . . And this is what traders do, they handle these kinds of problems."[48] Maheras, the co-head of Citigroup's investment bank, told the FCIC that he spent "a small fraction of 1%" of his time thinking about or dealing with the CDO business.[49]

Citigroup's risk management function was simply not very concerned about housing market risks. According to Prince, Bushnell and others told him, in effect, "'Gosh, housing prices would have to go down 30% nationwide for us to have, not a problem with [mortgage-backed securities] CDOs, but for us to have problems,' and that has never happened since the Depression."[50] Housing prices would be down much less than 30% when Citigroup began having problems because of write-downs and the liquidity puts it had written.

By June 2007, national house prices had fallen 4.5%, and about 16% of subprime adjustable-rate mortgages were delinquent. Yet Citigroup still did not expect that the liquidity puts could be triggered, and it remained unconcerned about the value of its retained super-senior tranches of CDOs. On June 4, 2007, Citigroup made a presentation to the SEC about subprime exposure in its CDO business. The presentation noted that Citigroup did not factor two positions into this exposure: $14.6 billion in super-senior tranches and $23.2 billion in liquidity puts. The presentation explained that the liquidity puts were not a concern: "The risk of default is extremely unlikely . . . [and] certain market events must also occur for us to be required to fund. Therefore, we view these positions to be even less risky than the Super Senior Book."[51]

Just a few weeks later, the July 2007 failure of the two Bear Stearns hedge funds spelled trouble. Commercial paper written against three Citigroup-underwritten CDOs for which Bear Stearns Asset Management was the asset manager and on

which Citigroup had issued liquidity puts began losing value, and their interest rates began rising. The liquidity puts would be triggered if interest rates on the asset-backed commercial paper rose above a certain level.

The Office of the Comptroller of the Currency, the regulator of Citigroup's national bank subsidiary, had expressed no apprehensions about the liquidity puts in 2003. But by the summer of 2007, OCC Examiner-in-Charge John Lyons told the FCIC, the OCC became concerned. Buying the commercial paper would drain $25 billion of the company's cash and expose it to possible balance-sheet losses at a time when markets were increasingly in distress. But given the rising rates, Lyons also said Citigroup did not have the option to wait. Over the next six months, Citigroup purchased all $25 billion of the paper that had been subject to its liquidity puts.[52]

On a July 20 conference call, CFO Gary Crittenden told analysts and investors that the company's subprime exposures had fallen from $24 billion at the end of 2006 to $13 billion on June 30. But he made no mention of the super-senior exposures and liquidity puts. "I think our risk team did a nice job of anticipating that this was going to be a difficult environment, and so set about in a pretty concentrated effort to reduce our exposure over the last six months,"[53] he said. A week later, on a July 27 call, Crittenden reiterated that subprime exposure had been cut: "So I think we've had good risk management that has been anticipating some market dislocation here."[54]

By August, as market conditions worsened, Citigroup's CDO desk was revaluing its super-senior tranches, though it had no effective model for assigning value. However, as the market congealed, then froze, the paucity of actual market prices for these tranches demanded a model. The New York Fed later noted that "the model for Super Senior CDOs, based on fundamental economic factors, could not be fully validated by Citigroup's current validation methodologies yet it was relied upon for reporting exposures."[55]

Barnes, the CDO risk officer, told the FCIC that sometime that summer he met with the co-heads of the CDO desk to express his concerns about possible losses on both the unsold CDO inventory and the retained super-senior tranches. The message got through. Nestor Dominguez told the FCIC, "We began extensive discussions about the implications of the . . . dramatic decline of the underlying subprime markets, and how that would feed into the super-senior positions."[56] Also at this time— for the first time—such concerns reached Maheras. He justified his lack of prior knowledge of the billions of dollars in inventory and super-senior tranches by pointing out "that the business was appropriately supervised by experienced and highly competent managers and by an independent risk group and that I was properly apprised of the general nature of our work in this area and its attendant risks."[57]

The exact dates are not certain, but according to Bushnell, he remembers a discussion at a "Business Heads" meeting about the growing mark-to-market volatility on those super-senior tranches in late August or early September, well after Citigroup started to buy the commercial paper backing the super-senior tranches of the CDOs that BSAM managed.[58] This was also when Chairman and CEO Prince first heard about the possible amount of "open positions" on the super-senior CDO tranches that Citigroup held: "It wasn't presented at the time in a startling fashion . . . [but]

then it got bigger and bigger and bigger, obviously, over the next 30 days."[59] In late August, Citigroup's valuation models suggested that losses on the super-senior tranches might range from $15 million to $2 billion. This number was recalculated as $300 to $500 million in mid-September, as the valuation methodology was refined.[60] In the weeks ahead, those numbers would skyrocket.

## "DEFCON calls"

To get a handle on potential losses from the CDOs and liquidity puts, starting on September 9 Prince convened a series of meetings—and later, nightly "DEFCON calls"—with members of his senior management team; they included Rubin, Maheras, Crittenden, and Bushnell, as well as Lou Kaden, the chief administrative officer.[61] Rubin was in Korea during the first meeting but Kaden kept him informed.[62] Rubin later emailed Prince: "According to Lou, Tom [Maheras] never did provide a clear and direct answer on the super seniors. If that is so, and the meeting did not bring that to a head, isn't that deeply troubling not as to what happened—that is a different question that is also troubling—but as to providing full and clear information and analysis now." Prince disagreed, writing, "I thought, for first mtg, it was good. We weren't trying to get to final answers."[63]

A second meeting was held September 12, after Rubin was back in the country. This meeting marked the first time Rubin recalled hearing of the super-senior and liquidity put exposure. He later commented, "As far as I was concerned they were all one thing, because if there was a put back to Citi under any circumstance, however remote that circumstance might be, you hadn't fully disposed of the risk."[64] And, of course, the circumstance was not remote, since billions of dollars in subprime mortgage assets had already come back onto Citigroup's books.

Prince told the FCIC that Maheras had assured him throughout the meetings and the DEFCON calls that the super seniors posed no risk to Citigroup, even as the market deteriorated; he added that he became increasingly uneasy with Maheras's assessment. "Tom had said and said till his last day at work [October 11]: 'We are never going to lose a penny on these super seniors. We are never going to lose a penny on these super seniors. . . . ' And as we went along and I was more and more uncomfortable with this and more and more uncomfortable with Tom's conclusions on ultimate valuations, that is when I really began to have some very serious concerns about what was going to happen."[65]

Despite Prince's concerns, Citigroup remained publicly silent about the additional subprime exposure from the super-senior positions and liquidity puts, even as it pre-announced some details of its third-quarter earnings on October 1, 2007.

On October 11, the rating agencies announced the first in a series of downgrades on thousands of securities. In Prince's view, these downgrades were "the precipitating event in the financial crisis."[66] On the same day, Prince restructured the investment bank, a move that led to the resignation of Maheras.

Four days later, the question of the super-senior CDOs and liquidity puts was specifically raised at the board of directors' Corporate Audit and Risk Management

Committee meeting and brought up to the full board. A presentation concluded that "total sub-prime exposure in [the investment bank] was $13bn with an additional $16bn in Direct Super Senior and $27bn in Liquidity and Par Puts."[67] Citigroup's total subprime exposure was $56 billion, nearly half of its capital. The calculation was straightforward, but during an analysts' conference call that day Crittenden omitted any mention of the super-senior- and liquidity-put-related exposure as he told participants that Citigroup had under $13 billion in subprime exposure.[68]

A week later, on Saturday, October 27, Prince learned from Crittenden that the company would have to report subprime-related losses of $8 to $11 billion; on Monday he tendered his resignation to the board. He later reflected, "When I drove home and Gary called me and told me it wasn't going to be two or 300 million but it was going to be eight billion—I will never forget that call. I continued driving, and I got home, I walked in the door, I told my wife, I said here's what I just heard and if this turns out to be true, I am resigning."[69]

On November 4, Citigroup revealed the accurate subprime exposure—now estimated at $55 billion—and it disclosed the subprime-related losses. Though Prince had resigned, he remained on Citigroup's payroll until the end of the year, and the board of directors gave him a generous parting compensation package: $11.9 million in cash and $24 million in stock, bringing his total compensation to $79 million from 2004 to 2007.[70] The SEC later sued Citigroup for its delayed disclosures. To resolve the charges, the bank paid $75 million. The New York Fed would later conclude, "There was little communications on the extensive level of subprime exposure posed by Super Senior CDO. . . . Senior management, as well as the independent Risk Management function charged with monitoring responsibilities, did not properly identify and analyze these risks in a timely fashion."[71]

Prince's replacements as chairman and CEO—Richard Parsons and Vikram Pandit—were announced in December. Rubin would stay until January 2009, having been paid more than $115 million from 2000 to 2009[72] during his tenure at the company, including his role as chairman of the Executive Committee, a position that carried "no operational responsibilities," Rubin told the FCIC. "My agreement with Citi provided that I'd have no management of personnel or operations."[73]

John Reed, former co-CEO of Citigroup, attributed the firm's failures in part to a culture change that occurred when the bank took on Salomon Brothers as part of the 1998 Travelers merger. He said that Salomon executives "were used to taking big risks" and "had a history . . . [of] making a lot of money . . . but then getting into trouble."[74]

## AIG'S DISPUTE WITH GOLDMAN: "THERE COULD NEVER BE LOSSES"

Beginning on July 26, 2007, when Goldman's Davilman sent the email that disrupted the vacation of AIG's Alan Frost, the dispute between Goldman and AIG over the need for collateral to back credit default swaps captured the attention of the senior management of both companies. For 14 months, Goldman pressed its case and sent AIG a formal demand letter every single business day. It would pursue AIG relentlessly with

demands for collateral based on marks that were initially well below those of other firms—while AIG and its management struggled to come to grips with the burgeoning crisis.

The initial collateral call was a shock to AIG's senior executives, most of whom had not even known that the credit default swaps with Goldman contained collateral call provisions.

They had known there were enormous exposures—$79 billion, backed in large part by subprime and Alt-A loans, in 2007,[75] compared with the parent company's total reported capital of $95.8 billion—but executives said they had never been concerned. "The mantra at [AIG Financial Products] had always been (in my experience) that there could never be losses," Vice President of Accounting Policy Joseph St. Denis said.[76]

Then came that first collateral call. St. Denis told FCIC staff that he was so "stunned" when he got the news that he "had to sit down."[77] The collateral provisions surprised even Gene Park, the executive who had insisted 18 months earlier that AIG stop writing the swaps. He told the FCIC that "rule Number 1 at AIG FP" was to never post collateral. This was particularly important in the credit default swap business, he said, because it was the only unhedged business that AIG ran.[78]

But Jake Sun, the general counsel of the Financial Products subsidiary, who reviewed the swap contracts before they were executed, told the FCIC that the provisions were standard both at AIG and in the industry.[79] Frost, who was the first to learn of the collateral call, agreed and said that other financial institutions also commonly did deals with collateral posting provisions.[80] Pierre Micottis, the Paris-based head of the AIG Financial Products' Enterprise Risk Management department, told the FCIC that collateral provisions were indeed common in derivatives contracts—but surprising in the super-senior CDS contracts, which were considered safe.[81] Insurance supervisors did not permit regulated insurance companies like MBIA and Ambac to pay out except when the insured entity suffered an actual loss, and therefore those companies were forbidden to post collateral for a decline in market value or unrealized losses. Because AIG Financial Products was not regulated as an insurance company, it was not subject to this prohibition.

As disturbing as the senior AIG executives' surprise at the collateral provisions was their firm's inability to assess the validity of Goldman's numbers. AIG Financial Products did not have its own model or otherwise try to value the CDO portfolio that it guaranteed through credit default swaps, nor did it hedge its exposure. Gene Park explained that hedging was seen as unnecessary in part because of the mistaken belief that AIG would have to pay counterparties only if holders of the super-senior tranches incurred actual losses. He also said that purchasing a hedge from UBS, the Swiss bank, was considered, but that Andrew Forster, the head of credit trading at AIG Financial Products, rejected the idea because it would cost more than the fees that AIG Financial Products was receiving to write the CDS protection. "We're not going to pay a dime for this," Forster told Park.[82]

Therefore, AIG Financial Products relied on an actuarial model that did not provide a tool for monitoring the CDOs' market value. The model was developed by

Gary Gorton, then a finance professor at the University of Pennsylvania's Wharton School, who began working as a consultant to AIG Financial Products in 1996 and was close to its CEO, Joe Cassano. The Gorton model had determined with 99.85% confidence that the owners of the super-senior tranches of the CDOs insured by AIG Financial Products would never suffer real economic losses, even in an economy as troubled as the worst post–World War II recession. The company's auditors, PricewaterhouseCoopers (PwC), who were apparently also not aware of the collateral requirements, concluded that "the risk of default on [AIG's] portfolio has been effectively removed and as a result from a risk management perspective, there are no substantive economic risks in the portfolio and as a result the fair value of the liability stream on these positions from a risk management perspective could reasonably be considered to be zero."[83]

In speaking with the FCIC, Cassano was adamant that the "CDS book" was effectively hedged. He said that AIG could never suffer losses on the swaps, because the CDS contracts were written only on the super-senior tranches of top-rated securities with high "attachment points"—that is, many securities in the CDOs would have to default in order for losses to reach the super-senior tranches—and because the bulk of the exposure came from loans made before 2006, when he thought underwriting standards had begun to deteriorate.[84] Indeed, according to Gene Park, Cassano put a halt to a $150 million hedge, in which AIG had taken a short position in the ABX index. As Park explained, "Joe stopped that because after we put on the first 150 . . . the market moved against us . . . we were losing money on the 150 million. . . . Joe said, 'You know, I don't think the world is going to blow up . . . I don't want to spend that money. Stop it.'"[85]

Despite the limited market transparency in the summer of 2007, Goldman used what information there was, including information from ABX and other indices, to estimate what it considered to be realistic prices. Goldman also spoke with other companies to see what values they assigned to the securities. Finally, Goldman looked to its own experience: in most cases, when the bank bought credit protection on an investment, it turned around and sold credit protection on the same investment to other counterparties. These deals yielded more price information.[86]

Until the dispute with Goldman, AIG relied on the Gorton model, which did not estimate the market value of underlying securities. So Goldman's marks caught AIG by surprise. When AIG pushed back, Goldman almost immediately reduced its July 27 collateral demand from $1.8 billion to $1.2 billion, a move that underscored the difficulty of finding reliable market prices. The new demand was still too high, in AIG's view, which was corroborated by third-party marks. Goldman valued the CDOs between 80 and 97 cents on the dollar, while Merrill Lynch, for example, valued the same securities between 95 and 100 cents.[87]

On August 7, Cassano told PwC that there was "little or no price transparency" and that it was "difficult to determine whether [collateral calls] were indicative of true market levels moving."[88] AIG managers did call other dealers holding similar bonds to check their marks in order to help its case with Goldman, but those marks were not "actionable"—that is, the dealers would not actually execute transactions at the

quoted prices. "The above estimated values . . . do not represent actual bids or offers by Merrill Lynch" was the disclaimer in a listing of estimated market values provided by Merrill to AIG.[89] Goldman Sachs disputed the reliability of such estimates.

## "Without being flippant"

On August 9, for the first time, AIG executives publicly disclosed the $79 billion in credit default swaps on the super-senior tranches of CDOs during the company's second-quarter earnings call. They acknowledged that the great majority of the underlying bonds thus insured—$64 billion—were backed by subprime mortgages. Of this amount, $19 billion was written on CDOs predominantly backed by risky BBB-rated collateral. On the call, Cassano maintained that the exposures were no problem: "It is hard for us, without being flippant, to even see a scenario within any kind of realm or reason that would see us losing $1 in any of those transactions." He concluded: "We see no issues at all emerging. We see no dollar of loss associated with any of [the CDO] business. Any reasonable scenario that anyone can draw, and when I say reasonable, I mean a severe recession scenario that you can draw out for the life of the securities." Senior Vice President and Chief Risk Officer Robert Lewis seconded that reassurance: "We believe that it would take declines in housing values to reach depression proportions, along with default frequencies never experienced, before our AAA and AA investments would be impaired."[90]

These assurances focused on the risk that actual mortgage defaults would create real economic losses on the company's credit default swap positions.[91] But more important at the time were the other tremendous risks that AIG executives had already discussed internally. No one on the conference call mentioned Goldman's demand for $1.2 billion in collateral; the clear possibility that future, much-larger collateral calls could jeopardize AIG's liquidity; or the risk that AIG would be forced to take an "enormous mark" on its existing book, the concern Forster had noted.

The day after the conference call, AIG posted $450 million in cash to Goldman, its first collateral posting since Goldman had requested the $1.2 billion. As Frost wrote to Forster in an August 16, 2007, email, the idea was "to get everyone to chill out."[92] For one thing, some AIG executives, including Cassano, had late-summer vacations planned. Cassano signed off on the $450 million "good faith deposit" before leaving for a cycling trip through Germany and Austria.[93] The parties executed a side letter making clear that both disputed the amount. For the time being, two companies that had been doing business together for decades agreed to disagree.

On August 14, Frost went to Goldman's offices to "start the dialog," which had stalled while Cassano and other key executives were on vacation. Two days later, Frost wrote to Forster: "Trust me. This is not the last margin call we are going to debate."[94] He was right. By September 11, Société Générale—known more commonly as Soc-Gen—had demanded $40 million in collateral on CDS it had purchased from AIG Financial Products, UBS had demanded $67 million, and Goldman had upped its demand by $300 million. The SocGen demand was based on an 82.5 bid price provided by Goldman, which AIG disputed. Tom Athan, managing director at AIG Fi-

nancial Products, told Forster that SocGen "received marks from GS on positions that would result in big collateral calls but SG disputed them with GS."[95] Several weeks later, Cassano told AIG Financial Services CFO Elias Habayeb that he believed the SocGen margin call had been "spurred by Goldman," and that AIG "disputed the call and [had] not heard from SocGen again on that specific call."[96] In the second week of October, the rating agencies announced hundreds of additional downgrades affecting tens of billions of dollars of subprime mortgage–backed securities and CDOs. By November 2, Goldman's demand had almost doubled, to $2.8 billion. On November 6, Bensinger, the CFO, informed AIG's Audit Committee that Financial Products had received margin calls from five counterparties and was disputing every single one.[97]

This stance was rooted in the company's continuing belief that Goldman had set values too low. AIG's position was corroborated, at least in part, by the wide disparity in marks from other counterparties. At one point, Merrill Lynch and Goldman made collateral demands on the very same CDS positions, but Goldman's marks were almost 35% lower than Merrill's.[98] Goldman insisted that its marks represented the "constantly evolving additional information from our market making activities, including trades that we had executed, market activity we observed, price changes in comparable securities and derivatives and the current prices of relevant liquid . . . indices."[99] Trading in the ABX would fall from over 400 trades per week through the end of September 2007 to less than 250 per week in the fourth quarter of 2007; trading in the TABX, which focuses on lower-rated tranches, dropped from roughly 50 trades per week through mid-July to almost zero by mid-August.[100]

But Cassano believed that the quick reduction in Goldman's first collateral demand (from $1.8 billion on July 27 to $1.2 billion on August 2) and the interim agreement on the $450 million deposit confirmed that Goldman was not as certain of its marks as it later insisted. According to Cassano, Michael Sherwood, co-CEO of Goldman Sachs International, told him that Goldman "didn't cover ourselves in glory during this period" but that "the market's starting to come our [Goldman's] way"; Cassano took those comments as an implicit admission that Goldman's initial marks had been aggressive.[101]

### *"More love notes"*

In mid-August, Forster told Frost in an email that Goldman was pursuing a strategy of aggressively marking down assets to "cause maximum pain to their competitors."[102] PricewaterhouseCoopers, which served as auditor for both AIG and Goldman during this period, knew full well that AIG had never before marked these positions to market. In the third quarter of 2007, with the collateral demands piling up, PwC prompted AIG to begin developing a model of its own. Prior to the Goldman margin call, PwC had concluded that "compensating controls" made up for AIG's not having a model. Among those was notice from counterparties that collateral was due.[103] In other words, one of AIG's risk management tools was to learn of its own problems from counterparties who did have the ability to mark their own positions to market prices and then demand collateral from AIG.

The decision to develop a valuation model was not unanimous. In mid-September, Cassano and Forster met with Habayeb and others to discuss marking the positions down and actually recording valuation losses in AIG's financial statements. Cassano still thought the valuation process unnecessary because the possibility of defaults was "remote."[104] He sent Forster and others emails describing requests from Habayeb as "more love notes . . . [asking us to go through] the same drill of drafting answers."[105] Nevertheless, by October, and in consultation with PwC, AIG started to evaluate the pricing model for subprime instruments developed and used by Moody's. Cassano considered the Moody's model only a "gut check" until it was fully validated internally.[106] AIG coupled this model with generic CDO tranche data sold by JP Morgan that were considered to be relatively representative of the market. Of course, by this time—and for several preceding months—there was no active market for many of these tranches. Everyone understood that this was not a perfect solution, but AIG and its auditors thought it could serve as an interim step. The makeshift model was up and running in the third quarter.

### "Confident in our marks"

On November 7, when AIG reported its third-quarter earnings, it disclosed that it was taking a $352 million charge "related to its super senior credit default swap portfolio" and "a further unrealized market valuation loss through October 2007 of approximately $550 million before tax [on that] portfolio." On a conference call, CEO Sullivan assured investors that the insurance company had "active and strong risk management." He said, "AIG continues to believe that it is highly unlikely that AIGFP will be required to make payments with respect to these derivatives." Cassano added that AIG had "more than enough resources to meet any of the collateral calls that might come in."[107] While the company remained adamant that there would be no realized economic losses from the credit default swaps, it used the newly adopted—and adapted—Moody's model to estimate the $352 million charge. In fact, PwC had questioned the relevance of the model: it hadn't been validated in advance of the earnings release, it didn't take into account important structural information about the swap contracts, and there were questions about the quality of the data.[108] AIG didn't mention those caveats on the call.

Two weeks later, on November 23, Goldman demanded an additional $3 billion in cash. AIG protested, but paid $1.55 billion, bringing the total posted to $2 billion.[109] Four days later, Cassano circulated a memo from Forster listing the pertinent marks for the securities from Goldman Sachs, Merrill Lynch, Calyon, Bank of Montreal, and SocGen.[110] The marks varied widely, from as little as 55% of the bonds' original value to virtually full value. Goldman's estimated values were much lower than those of other dealers. For example, Goldman valued one CDO, the Dunhill CDO, at 75% of par, whereas Merrill valued it at 95% of par; the Orient Point CDO was valued at 60% of par by Goldman but at 95% of par by Merrill. Forster suggested that the marks validated AIG's long-standing contention that "there is no one dealer with more knowledge than the others or with a better deal flow of trades and all admit to

'guesstimating' pricing."[111] Cassano agreed. "No one seems to know how to discern a market valuation price from the current opaque market environment," Cassano wrote to a colleague. "This information is limited due to the lack of participants [willing] to even give indications on these obligations."[112]

One week later, Cassano called Sherwood in Goldman's London office and demanded reimbursement of $1.4 billion. He told both AIG and Goldman executives that independent third-party pricing for 70% of the 3,500 securities underlying the CDOs on which AIG FP had written CDS and AIG's own valuation for the other 30% indicated that Goldman's demand was unsupported—therefore Goldman should return the money.[113] Goldman refused, and instead demanded more.[114]

By late November, there was relative agreement within AIG and with its auditor that the Moody's model incorporated into AIG's valuation system was inadequate for valuing the super-senior book.[115] But there was no consensus on how that book should be valued. Inputting generic CDO collateral data into the Moody's model would result in a $1.5 billion valuation loss; using Goldman's marks would result in a $5 billion valuation loss, which would wipe out the quarter's profits.[116] On November 29, PwC auditors met with senior executives from AIG and the Financial Products subsidiary to discuss the whole situation. According to PwC meeting notes, AIG reported that disagreements with Goldman continued, and AIG did not have data to dispute Goldman's marks. Forster recalled that Sullivan said that he was going to have a heart attack when he learned that using Goldman's marks would eliminate the quarter's profits.[117] Sullivan told FCIC staff that he did not remember this part of the meeting.[118]

AIG adjusted the number, and in doing so it chose not to rely on dealer quotes. James Bridgewater, the Financial Products executive vice president in charge of models, came up with a solution. Convinced that there was a calculable difference between the value of the underlying bonds and the value of the swap protection AIG had written on those bonds, Bridgewater suggested using a "negative basis adjustment," which would reduce the unrealized loss estimate from $5.1 billion (Goldman's figure) to about $1.5 billion. With their auditor's knowledge, Cassano and others agreed that the negative basis adjustment was the way to go.

Several documents given to the FCIC by PwC, AIG, and Cassano reflect discussions during and after the November 29 meeting. During a second meeting at which only the auditor and parent company executives were present (Financial Products executives, including Cassano and Forster, did not attend), PwC expressed significant concerns about risk management, specifically related to the valuation of the credit default swap portfolio, as well as to the company's procedures in posting collateral. AIG Financial Products had paid out $2 billion without active involvement from the parent company's Enterprise Risk Management group. Another issue was "the way in which AIGFP [had] been 'managing' the SS [super senior] valuation process—saying PwC will not get any more information until after the investor day presentation."[119]

The auditors laid out their concerns about conflicting strategies pursued by AIG subsidiaries. Notably, the securities-lending subsidiary had been purchasing mortgage-backed securities, using cash raised by lending securities that AIG held on

behalf of its insurance subsidiaries. From the end of 2006 through September 2007, its holdings rose from $69 billion to $88 billion. Meanwhile, Financial Products, acting on its own analysis, had decided in 2006 to begin pulling back on writing credit default swaps on CDOs. In PwC's view, in allowing one subsidiary to increase exposure to subprime while another subsidiary worked to exit the market entirely, the parent company's risk management failed. PwC also said that the company's second quarter of 2007 financial disclosures would have been changed if the exposure of the securities-lending business had been known. The auditors concluded that "these items together raised control concerns around risk management which could be a material weakness."[120] Kevin McGinn, AIG's chief credit officer, shared these concerns about the conflicting strategies. In a November 20, 2007, email, McGinn wrote: "All units were apprised regularly of our concerns about the housing market. Some listened and responded; others simply chose not to listen and then, to add insult to injury, not to spot the manifest signs." He concluded that this was akin to "Nero playing the fiddle while Rome burns."[121] On the opposite side, Sullivan insisted to the FCIC that the conflicting strategies in the securities-lending business and at AIG Financial Products simply revealed that the two subsidiaries adopted different business models, and did not constitute a risk management failure.[122]

On December 5, six days after receiving PwC's warnings, Sullivan boasted on another conference call about AIG's risk management systems and the company's oversight of the subprime exposure: "The risk we have taken in the U.S. residential housing sector is supported by sound analysis and a risk management structure. . . . we believe the probability that it will sustain an economic loss is close to zero. . . . We are confident in our marks and the reasonableness of our valuation methods." Charlie Gates, an analyst at Credit Suisse, a Swiss bank, asked directly about valuation and collateral disputes with counterparties to which AIG had alluded in its third-quarter financial results. Cassano replied, "We have from time to time gotten collateral calls from people and then we say to them, well we don't agree with your numbers. And they go, oh, and they go away. And you say well what was that? It's like a drive-by in a way. And the other times they sat down with us, and none of this is hostile or anything, it's all very cordial, and we sit down and we try and find the middle ground and compare where we are."[123]

Cassano did not reveal the $2 billion collateral posted to Goldman, the several hundred million dollars posted to other counterparties, and the daily demands from Goldman and the others for additional cash. The analysts and investors on the call were not informed about the "negative basis adjustment" used to derive the announced $1.5 billion maximum potential exposure. Investors therefore did not know that AIG's earnings were overstated by $3.6 billion—and they would not learn that information until February 11, 2008.

## "Material weakness"

By January 2008, AIG still did not have a reliable way to determine the market price of the securities on which it had written credit protection. Nevertheless, on January

16, Cassano sent an email to Michael Sherwood and CFO David Viniar at Goldman demanding that they return $1.1 billion of the $2 billion posted.[124] He attached a spreadsheet showing that AIG valued many securities at par, as if there had been no decline in their value. That was simply not credible, Goldman executives told the FCIC.[125] Meanwhile, Goldman had by then built up $1.45 billion in protection by purchasing credit default swaps on AIG to cover the difference between the amount of collateral they had demanded and the amount that AIG had paid.[126]

On February 6, 2008, PwC auditors met with Robert Willumstad, the chairman of AIG's board of directors. They informed him that the "negative basis adjustment" used to reach the $1.5 billion estimate disclosed on the December 5 investor call had been improper and unsupported, and was a sign that "controls over the AIG Financial Products super senior credit default swap portfolio valuation process and oversight thereof were not effective." PwC concluded that "this deficiency was a material weakness as of December 31, 2007."[127] In other words, PwC would have to announce that the numbers AIG had already publicly reported were wrong. Why the auditors waited so long to make this pronouncement is unclear, particularly given that PwC had known about the adjustment in November.

In the meeting with Willumstad, the auditors were broadly critical of Sullivan; Bensinger, whom they deemed unable to compensate for Sullivan's weaknesses; and Lewis, who might not have "the skill sets" to run an enterprise-wide risk management department. The auditors concluded that "a lack of leadership, unwillingness to make difficult decisions regarding [Financial Products] in the past and inexperience in dealing with these complex matters" had contributed to the problems.[128] Despite PwC's findings, Sullivan received $107 million over four years in compensation from AIG, including a severance package of $18 million. When asked about these figures at a FCIC hearing, he said, "I have no knowledge or recollection of those numbers whatsoever, sir. . . . I certainly don't recall earning that amount of money, sir."[129]

The following day, PwC met with the entire AIG Audit Committee and repeated the analysis presented to Willumstad. The auditors said they could complete AIG's audit, but only if Cassano "did not interfere in the process." Retaining Cassano was a "management judgment, but the culture needed to change at FP."[130] On February 11, AIG disclosed in an SEC filing that its auditor had identified the material weakness, acknowledging that it had reduced its December valuation loss estimates by $3.6 billion—that is, the difference between the estimates of $5.1 billion and $1.5 billion—because of the unsupportable negative basis adjustment.

The rating agencies responded immediately. Moody's and S&P announced downgrades, and Fitch placed AIG on "Ratings Watch Negative," suggesting that a future downgrade was possible. AIG's stock declined 12% for the day, closing at $44.74.

At the end of February, Goldman held $2 billion in cash collateral, was demanding an additional $2.5 billion, and had upped to $2.15 billion its CDS protection against an AIG failure. On February 28, AIG disappointed Wall Street again—this time with dismal fourth-quarter and fiscal year 2007 earnings. The company reported a net loss of $5.29 billion, largely due to $11.12 billion in valuation losses related to the super-senior CDO credit default swap exposure and more than $2.6

billion in losses relating to the securities-lending business's mortgage-backed purchases. Along with the losses, Sullivan announced Cassano's retirement, but the news wasn't all bad for the former Financial Products chief: He made more than $300 million from the time he joined AIG Financial Products in January of 1987 until his retirement in 2008, including a $1 million-a-month consulting agreement after his retirement.[131]

In March, the Office of Thrift Supervision, the federal regulator in charge of regulating AIG and its subsidiaries, downgraded the company's composite rating from a 2, signifying that AIG was "fundamentally sound," to a 3, indicating moderate to severe supervisory concern. The OTS still judged the threat to overall viability as remote.[132] It did not schedule a follow-up review of the company's financial condition for another six months.

By then, it would be too late.

## FEDERAL RESERVE:
## "THE DISCOUNT WINDOW WASN'T WORKING"

Over the course of the fall, the announcements by Citigroup, Merrill, and others made it clear that financial institutions were going to take serious losses from their exposures to the mortgage market. Stocks of financial firms fell sharply; by the end of November, the S&P Financials Index had lost more than 16% for the year. Between July and November, asset-backed commercial paper declined about 30%, which meant that those assets had to be sold or funded by other means. Investment banks and other financial institutions faced tighter funding markets and increasing cash pressures. As a result, the Federal Reserve decided that its interest rate cuts and other measures since August had not been sufficient to provide liquidity and stability to financial markets. The Fed's discount window hadn't attracted much bank borrowing because of the stigma attached to it. "The problem with the discount window is that people don't like to use it because they view it as a risk that they will be viewed as weak," William Dudley, then head of the capital markets group at the New York Fed and currently its president, told the FCIC.[133]

Banks and thrifts preferred to draw on other sources of liquidity; in particular, during the second half of 2007, the Federal Home Loan Banks—which are government-sponsored entities that lend to banks and thrifts, accepting mortgages as collateral—boosted their lending by $235 billion to $875 billion (a 37% increase) when the securitization market froze. Between the end of March and the end of December 2007, Washington Mutual, the largest thrift, increased its borrowing from the Federal Home Loan Banks from $28 billion to $73 billion; Countrywide increased its borrowing from $27 billion to $48 billion; Bank of America increased its borrowing from $38 billion to $56 billion. The Federal Home Loan Banks could thus be seen as the lender of next to last resort for commercial banks and thrifts—the Fed being the last resort.[134]

In addition, the loss of liquidity in the financial sector was making it more diffi-

cult for businesses and consumers to get credit, raising the Fed's concerns. From July to October, the percentage of loan officers reporting tightening standards on prime mortgages increased from 15% to about 40%. Over that time, the percentage of loan officers reporting tightening standards on loans to large and midsize companies increased from 8% to 19%, its highest level since 2003.[135] "The Federal Reserve pursued a whole slew of nonconventional policies . . . very creative measures when the discount window wasn't working as hoped," Frederic Mishkin, a Fed governor from 2006 to 2008, told the FCIC. "These actions were very aggressive, [and] they were extremely controversial."[136] The first of these measures, announced on December 12, was the creation of the Term Auction Facility (TAF). The idea was to reduce the discount window stigma by making the money available to all banks at once through a regular auction. The program had some success, with banks borrowing $40 billion by the end of the year. Over time, the Fed would continue to tweak the TAF auctions, offering more credit and longer maturities.

Another Fed concern was that banks and others who did have cash would hoard it. Hoarding meant foreign banks had difficulty borrowing in dollars and were therefore under pressure to sell dollar-denominated assets such as mortgage-backed securities. Those sales and fears of more sales to come weighed on the market prices of U.S. securities. In response, the Fed and other central banks around the world announced (also on December 12) new "currency swap lines" to help foreign banks borrow dollars. Under this mechanism, foreign central banks swapped currencies with the Federal Reserve—local currency for U.S. dollars—and lent these dollars to foreign banks. "During the crisis, the U.S. banks were very reluctant to extend liquidity to European banks," Dudley said.[137] Central banks had used similar arrangements in the aftermath of the 9/11 attacks to bolster the global financial markets. In late 2001, the swap lines totaled $88 billion. During the financial crisis seven years later, they would reach $580 billion.

The Fed hoped the TAF and the swap lines would reduce strains in short-term money markets, easing some of the funding pressure on other struggling participants such as investment banks. Importantly, it wasn't just the commercial banks and thrifts but the "broader financial system" that concerned the Fed, Dudley said. "Historically, the Federal Reserve has always tended to supply liquidity to the banks with the idea that liquidity provided to the banking system can be [lent on] to solvent institutions in the nonbank sector. What we saw in this crisis was that didn't always take place to the extent that it had in the past. . . . I don't think people going in really had a full understanding of the complexity of the shadow banking system, the role of [structured investment vehicles] and conduits, the backstops that banks were providing SIV conduits either explicitly or implicitly."[138]

Burdened with capital losses and desperate to cover their own funding commitments, the banks were not stable enough to fill the void, even after the Fed lowered interest rates and began the TAF auctions. In January 2008, the Fed cut rates again—and then again, twice within two weeks, a highly unusual move that brought the federal funds rate from 4.25% to 3.0%.

The Fed also started plans for a new program that would use its emergency authority, the Term Securities Lending Facility, though it wasn't launched until March. "The TLSF was more a view that the liquidity that we were providing to the banks through the TAF was not leading to a significant diminishment of financing pressures elsewhere," Dudley told the FCIC. "So maybe we should think about bypassing the banking system and [try] to come up with a vehicle to provide liquidity support to the primary dealer community more directly."[139]

On March 7, the Fed increased the total available in each of the biweekly TAF auctions from $30 billion to $50 billion, and guaranteed at least that amount for six months. The Fed also liberalized its standard for collateral. Primary dealers—mainly the investment banks and the broker-dealer affiliates of large commercial banks—could post debt of government-sponsored enterprises, including GSE mortgage-backed securities, as collateral. The Fed expected to have $100 billion in such loans outstanding at any given time.

Also at this time, the U.S. central bank began contemplating a step that was revolutionary: a program that would allow investment banks—institutions over which the Fed had no supervisory or regulatory responsibility—to borrow from the discount window on terms similar to those available to commercial banks.

## MONOLINE INSURERS: "WE NEVER EXPECTED LOSSES"

Meanwhile, the rating agencies continued to downgrade mortgage-backed securities and CDOs through 2007. By January 2008, as a result of the stress in the mortgage market, S&P had downgraded 3,389 tranches of residential mortgage–backed securities and 1,383 tranches from 420 CDOs. MBIA and Ambac, the two largest monoline insurers, had taken on a combined $265 billion of guarantees on mortgage securities and other structured products. Downgrades on the products that they insured brought the financial strength of these companies into question. After conducting stress analysis, S&P estimated in February 2008 that Ambac would need up to $400 million in capital to cover potential losses on structured products.[140] Such charges would affect the monolines' own credit ratings, which in turn could lead to more downgrades of the products they had guaranteed.

Like many of the monolines, ACA, the smallest of them, kept razor-thin capital—less than $700 million—against its obligations that included $69 billion in credit default swaps on CDOs. In late 2007, ACA reported a net loss of $1.7 billion, almost entirely due to credit default swaps.

This was news. The notion of "zero-loss tolerance" was central to the viability of the monoline business model, and they and various stakeholders—the rating agencies, investors, and monoline creditors—had traditionally assumed that the monolines never would have to take a loss. As Alan Roseman, CEO of ACA, told FCIC staff: "We never expected losses. . . . We were providing hedges on market volatility to institutional counterparties. . . . We were positioned, we believed, to take the volatility because we didn't have to post collateral against the changes in market value to our counterparty, number one. Number two, we were told by the rating agencies that

rated us that that mark-to-market variation was not important to our rating, from a financial strength point of view at the insurance company."[141]

In early November, the SEC called the growing concern about Merrill's use of the monolines for hedging "a concern that we also share."[142] The large Wall Street firms attempted to minimize their exposure to the monolines, particularly ACA. On December 19, S&P downgraded ACA to junk status, rating the company CCC, which was fatal for a company whose CEO said that its "rating is the franchise."[143] Firms like Merrill Lynch would get virtually nothing for the guarantees they had purchased from ACA.

Despite the stresses in the market, the SEC saw the monoline problems as largely confined to ACA. A January 2008 internal SEC document said, "While there is a clear sentiment that capital raising will need to continue, the fact that the guarantors (with the exception of ACA) are relatively insulated from liquidity driven failures provides hope that event[s] in this sector will unfold in a manageable manner."[144]

Still, the rating agencies told the monolines that if they wanted to retain their stellar ratings, they would have to raise capital. MBIA and Ambac ultimately did raise $1.65 billion and $1.5 billion, respectively. Nonetheless, S&P downgraded both to AA in June 2008. As the crisis unfolded, most of the monolines stopped writing new coverage.

The subprime contagion spread through the monolines and into a previously unimpaired market: municipal bonds. The path of these falling dominoes is easy to follow: in anticipation of the monoline downgrades, investors devalued the protection the monolines provided for other securities—even those that had nothing to do with the mortgage-backed markets, including a set of investments known as auction rate securities, or ARS. An ARS is a long-term bond whose interest rate is reset at regularly scheduled auctions held every one to seven weeks.[145] Existing investors can choose to rebid for the bonds and new investors can come in. The debt is frequently municipal bonds. As of December 13, 2007, state and local governments had issued $165 billion in ARS, accounting for half of the $330 billion market. The other half were primarily bundles of student loans and debt of nonprofits such as museums and hospitals.

The key point: these entities wanted to borrow long-term but get the benefit of lower short-term rates, and investors wanted to get the safety of investing in these securities without tying up their money for a long time. Unlike commercial paper, this market had no explicit liquidity backstop from a bank, but there was an implicit backstop: often, if there were not enough new buyers to replace the previous investors, the dealers running these auctions, including firms like UBS, Citigroup, and Merrill Lynch, would step in and pick up the shortfall. Because of these interventions, there were only 13 failures between 1984 and early 2007 in more than 100,000 auctions. Dealers highlighted those minuscule failure rates to convince clients that ARS were very liquid, short-term instruments, even in times of stress.[146]

However, if an auction did fail, the previous ARS investors would be obligated to retain their investments. In compensation, the interest rates on the debt would reset, often much higher, but investors' funds would be trapped until new investors or the

dealer stepped up or the borrower paid off the loan. ARS investors were typically very risk averse and valued liquidity, and so they were willing to pay a premium for guarantees on the ARS investments from monolines. It necessarily followed that the monolines' growing problems in the latter half of 2007 affected the ARS market. Fearing that the monolines would not be able to perform on their guarantees, investors fled. The dealers' interventions were all that kept the market going, but the stress became too great. With their own problems to contend with, the dealers were unable to step in and ensure successful auctions. In February, en masse, they pulled up stakes. The market collapsed almost instantaneously. On February 14, in one of the starkest market dislocations of the financial crisis, 80% of the ARS auctions failed; the following week, 67% failed.

Hundreds of billions of dollars were trapped by ARS instruments as investors were obligated to retain their investments. And retail investors—individuals investing less than $1 million, small businesses, and charities—constituted more than $110 billion of this $330 billion market.[147] Moreover, investors who chose to remain in the market demanded a premium to take on the risk. Between investor demands and interest rate resets, countless governments, infrastructure projects, and nonprofits on tight budgets were slammed with interest rates of 10% or higher. Problems in the ARS market cost Georgetown University, a borrower, $6 million.[148] New York State was stuck with interest rates that soared from about 3.5% to more than 14% on $4 billion of its debt. The Port Authority of New York and New Jersey saw the interest rate on its debt jump from 4.3% to 20% in a single week in February.[149]

In 2008 alone, the SEC received more than 1,000 investor complaints regarding the failed ARS auctions. Investors argued that brokers had led them to believe that ARS were safe and liquid, essentially the equivalent of money market accounts but with the potential for a slightly higher interest rate. Investors also reported that the frozen market blocked their access to money for short-term needs such as medical expenses, college tuition, and, for some small businesses and charities, payroll. By 2009, the SEC had settled with financial institutions including Bank of America, RBC Capital Markets, and Deutsche Bank to resolve charges that the firms misled investors. As a result, these and other banks made more than $50 billion available to pay off tens of thousands of ARS investors.[150]

## COMMISSION CONCLUSIONS ON CHAPTER 14

The Commission concludes that some large investment banks, bank holding companies, and insurance companies, including Merrill Lynch, Citigroup, and AIG, experienced massive losses related to the subprime mortgage market because of significant failures of corporate governance, including risk management. Executive and employee compensation systems at these institutions disproportionally rewarded short-term risk taking.

The regulators—the Securities and Exchange Commission for the large investment banks and the banking supervisors for the bank holding companies and AIG—failed to adequately supervise their safety and soundness, allowing them to take inordinate risk in activities such as nonprime mortgage securitization and over-the-counter (OTC) derivatives dealing and to hold inadequate capital and liquidity.

# 15

## MARCH 2008:
## THE FALL OF BEAR STEARNS

### CONTENTS

After its hedge funds failed in July 2007, Bear Stearns faced more challenges in the second half of the year. Taking out the repo lenders to the High-Grade Fund brought nearly $1.6 billion in subprime assets onto Bear's books, contributing to a $1.9 billion write-down on mortgage-related assets in November. That prompted investors to scrutinize Bear Stearns's finances. Over the fall, Bear's repo lenders—mostly money market mutual funds—increasingly required Bear to post more collateral and pay higher interest rates. Then, in just one week in March 2008, a run by these lenders, hedge fund customers, and derivatives counterparties led to Bear's having to be taken over in a government-backed rescue.

Mortgage securitization was the biggest piece of Bear Stearns's most-profitable division, its fixed-income business, which generated 45% of the firm's total revenues. Growing fast was the Global Client Services division, which included Bear's prime brokerage operation. Bear Stearns was the second-biggest prime broker in the country, with a 21% market share in 2006, trailing Morgan Stanley's 23%.[1] This business would figure prominently in the crisis.

In mortgage securitization, Bear followed a vertically integrated model that made money at every step, from loan origination through securitization and sale. It both acquired and created its own captive originators to generate mortgages that Bear bundled, turned into securities, and sold to investors.[2] The smallest of the five large investment banks, it was still a top-three underwriter of private-label mortgage–backed securities from 2000 to 2007.[3] In 2006, it underwrote $36 billion in collateralized debt obligations of all kinds, more than double its 2005 figure of $14.5 billion.

The total included $6.3 billion in CDOs that included mortgage-backed securities, putting it in the top 12 in that business.[4] As was typical on Wall Street, the company's view was that Bear was in the moving business, not the storage business—that is, it sought to provide services to clients rather than take on long-term exposures of its own.[5]

Bear expanded its mortgage business despite evidence that the market was beginning to falter, as did other firms such as Citigroup and Merrill. As early as May 2006, Bear had lost $3 million relating to defaults[6] on mortgages which occurred within 90 days of origination, which had been rare in the decade. But Bear persisted, assuming the setback would be temporary. In February 2007, Bear even acquired Encore Credit, its third captive mortgage originator in the United States, doubling its capacity. The purchase was consistent with Bear's contrarian business model—buying into distressed markets and waiting for them to turn around.[7]

Only a month after the purchase of Encore, the Securities and Exchange Commission wrote in an internal report, "Bear's mortgage business incurred significant market risk losses" on its Alt-A mortgage assets.[8] The losses were small, but the SEC reported that "risk managers note[d] that these events reflect a more rapid and severe deterioration in collateral performance than anticipated in ex ante models of stress events."[9]

## "I REQUESTED SOME FORBEARANCE"

Vacationing on Nantucket Island when the two Bear-sponsored hedge funds declared bankruptcy on July 31, 2007, former Bear treasurer Robert Upton anticipated that the rating agencies would downgrade the company, raising borrowing costs. Bear funded much of its operations borrowing short-term in the repo market; it borrowed between $50 and $70 billion overnight.[10] Even a threat of a downgrade by a rating agency would make financing more expensive, starting the next morning.

Investors, analysts, and the credit rating agencies closely scrutinized leverage ratios, available at the end of each quarter. By November 2007, Bear's leverage ratio had reached nearly 38 to 1. By the end of 2007, Bear's Level 3 assets—illiquid assets difficult to value and to sell—were 269% of its tangible common equity; thus, writing down these illiquid assets by 37% would wipe out tangible common equity.

At the end of each quarter, Bear would lower its leverage ratio by selling assets, only to buy them back at the beginning of the next quarter. Bear and other firms booked these transactions as sales—even though the assets didn't stay off the balance sheet for long—in order to reduce the amount of the company's assets and lower its leverage ratio. Bear's former treasurer Upton called the move "window dressing" and said it ensured that creditors and rating agencies were happy.[11] Bear's public filings reflected this, to some degree: for example, its 2007 annual report said the balance sheet was approximately 12% lower than the average month-end balance over the previous twelve months.[12]

To forestall a downgrade, Upton spoke with the three main rating agencies, Moody's, Standard & Poor's, and Fitch, in early August.[13] Several times in 2007—

including April 9 and June 22—S&P had confirmed Bear's strong ratings, noting in April that "Bear's risk profile is relatively conservative" and "strong senior management oversight and a strong culture throughout the firm are the foundation of Bear's risk management process." On June 22, Moody's had also confirmed its A1 rating, and Fitch had confirmed its "stable" outlook.

Now, in early August, Upton provided them information about Bear and argued that management had learned its lesson about governance and risk management from the failure of the two hedge funds and was going to rely less on short-term unsecured funding and more on the repo market. Bear and other market participants did not foresee that Bear's own repo lenders might refuse to lend against risky mortgage assets and eventually not even against Treasuries.

"I requested some forbearance" from S&P, Upton told the FCIC.[14] He did not get it. On August 3, just three days after the two Bear Stearns hedge funds declared bankruptcy, S&P highlighted the funds, Bear's mortgage-related investments, and its relatively small capital base as it placed Bear on a "negative outlook."[15]

Asked how he felt about the rating agency's actions, Jimmy Cayne, Bear's CEO until 2008, said, "A negative outlook can touch a number of parts of your businesses. . . . It was like having a beautiful child and they have a disease of some sort that you never expect to happen and it did. How did I feel? Lousy."[16]

To reassure investors that no more shoes would drop, Bear invited them on a conference call that same day. The call did not go well. By the end of the day, Bear's stock slid 6%, to $108.35, 36% below its all-time high of $169.61, reached earlier in 2007.

## "WE WERE SUITABLY SKEPTICAL"

On Sunday, August 5, two days after the conference call, Bear had another opportunity to make its case: this time, with the SEC. The two SEC supervisors who visited the company that Sunday were Michael Macchiaroli and Matthew Eichner, respectively, associate director and assistant director of the division of market regulation. The regulators reviewed Bear's exposures to the mortgage market, including the $13 billion in adjustable-rate mortgages on the firm's books that were waiting to be securitized. Bear executives gave assurances that inventory would shrink once investors returned in September from their retreats in the Hamptons. "Obviously, regulators are not supposed to listen to happy talk and go away smiling," Eichner told the FCIC. "Thirteen billion in ARMs is no joke." Still, Eichner did not believe the Bear executives were being disingenuous. He thought they were just emphasizing the upside.[17]

Alan Schwartz, the co-president who later succeeded Jimmy Cayne as CEO, and Thomas Marano, head of Global Mortgages and Asset Backed Securities, seemed unconcerned. But other executives were leery. Wendy de Monchaux, the head of proprietary trading, urged Marano to trim the mortgage portfolio, as did Steven Meyer, the co-head of stock sales and trading.[18] According to Chief Risk Officer Michael Alix, former chairman Alan Greenberg would say, "the best hedge is a sale."[19] Bear finally reduced the portfolio from $56 billion in the third quarter of 2007 to $46.1 billion in the fourth quarter, but it was too little too late.

That summer, the SEC felt Bear's liquidity was adequate for the immediate future, but supervisors "were suitably skeptical," Eichner insisted. After the August 5 meeting, the SEC required that Bear Stearns report daily on Bear's liquidity. However, Eichner admitted that he and his agency had grossly underestimated the possibility of a liquidity crisis down the road.[20]

Every weeknight Upton updated the SEC on Bear's $400 billion balance sheet, with specifics on repo and commercial paper. On September 27, Bear Stearns raised approximately $2.5 billion in unsecured 10-year bonds. The reports slowed to once a week.[21] The SEC's inspector general later criticized the regulators, writing that they did not push Bear to reduce leverage or "make any efforts to limit Bear Stearns' mortgage securities concentration," despite "aware[ness] that risk management of mortgages at Bear Stearns had numerous shortcomings, including lack of expertise by risk managers in mortgage backed securities" and "persistent understaffing; a proximity of risk managers to traders suggesting a lack of independence; turnover of key personnel during times of crisis; and the inability or unwillingness to update models to reflect changing circumstances."[22]

Michael Halloran, a senior adviser to SEC Chairman Christopher Cox, told the FCIC the SEC had ample information and authority to require Bear Stearns to decrease leverage and sell mortgage-backed securities, as other financial institutions were doing. Halloran said that as early as the first quarter of 2007, he had asked Erik Sirri, in charge of the SEC's Consolidated Supervised Entities program, about Bear Stearns (and Lehman Brothers), "Why can't we make them reduce risk?" According to Halloran, Sirri said the SEC's job was not to tell the banks how to run their companies but to protect their customers' assets.[23]

## "TURN INTO A DEATH SPIRAL"

In August, after the rating agencies revised their outlook on Bear, Cayne tried to obtain lines of credit from Citigroup and JP Morgan. Both banks acknowledged Bear had always been a very good customer and maintained they were interested in helping.[24] "We wanted to try to be belts-and-suspenders," said CFO Samuel Molinaro, as Bear attempted both to obtain lines of credit with banks and to reinforce traditional sources of short-term liquidity such as money market funds. But, Cayne told the FCIC, nothing happened. "Why the [large] banks were not more willing to participate and provide lines during that period of time, I can't tell you," Molinaro said.[25]

A major money market fund manager, Federated Investors, had decided on October 1 to drop Bear Stearns from its list of approved counterparties for unsecured commercial paper,[26] illustrating why unsecured commercial paper was traditionally seen as a riskier lifeline than repo. Throughout 2007, Bear Stearns reduced its unsecured commercial paper (from $20.7 billion at the end of 2006 to only $3.9 billion at the end of 2007) and replaced it with secured repo borrowing (which rose from $69 billion to $102 billion). But Bear Stearns's growing dependence on overnight repo would create a different set of problems.

The tri-party repo market used two clearing banks, JP Morgan and BNY Mellon.

During every business day, these clearing banks return cash to lenders; take possession of borrowers' collateral, essentially keeping it in escrow; and then lend their own cash to borrowers during the day. This is referred to as "unwinding" the repo transaction; it allows borrowers to change the assets posted as collateral every day. The transaction is then "rewound" at the end of the day, when the lenders post cash to the clearing banks in return for the new collateral.

The little-regulated tri-party repo market had grown from $800 billion in average daily volume in 2002 to $1.7 trillion in 2005, $2.4 trillion in 2007, and $2.8 trillion by early 2008.[27] It had become a very deep and liquid market. Even though most borrowers rolled repo overnight, it was also considered a very safe market, because transactions were overcollateralized (loans were made for less than the collateral was worth). That was the general view before the onset of the financial crisis.

As Bear increased its tri-party repo borrowing, it became more dependent on JP Morgan, the clearing bank. A risk that was little appreciated before 2007 was that JP Morgan and BNY Mellon could face large losses if a counterparty such as Bear defaulted during the day. Essentially, JP Morgan served as Bear's daytime repo lender.

Even long-term repo loans have to be unwound every day by the clearing bank, if not by the lender. Seth Carpenter, an officer at the Federal Reserve Board, compared it to a mortgage that has to be refinanced every week: "Imagine that your mortgage is only a week. Instead of a 30-year mortgage, you've got a one-week mortgage. If everything's going fine, you get to the end of the week, you go out and you refinance that mortgage because you don't have enough cash on hand to pay off the whole mortgage. And then you get to the end of another week and you refinance that mortgage. And that's, for all intents and purposes, what repos are like for many institutions."[28]

During the fall, Federated Investors, which had taken Bear Stearns off its list of approved commercial paper counterparties, continued to provide secured repo loans.[29] Fidelity Investments, another major lender, limited its overall exposure to Bear, and shortened the maturities.[30] In October, State Street Global Advisors refused any repo lending to Bear other than overnight.[31]

Often, backing Bear's borrowing were mortgage-related securities and of these, $17.2 billion—more than Bear's equity—were Level 3 assets.

In the fourth quarter of 2007, Bear Stearns reported its first quarterly loss, $379 million. Still, the SEC saw "no evidence of any deterioration in the firm's liquidity position following the release and related negative press coverage." The SEC concluded, "Bear Stearns' liquidity pool remains stable."[32]

In the fall of 2007, Bear's board had commissioned the consultant Oliver Wyman to review the firm's risk management. The report, "Risk Governance Diagnostic: Recommendations and Case for Economic Capital Development," was presented on February 5, 2008, to the management committee. Among its conclusions: risk assessment was "infrequent and ad hoc" and "hampered by insufficient and poorly aligned resources," "risk managers [were] not effectively positioned to challenge front office decisions," and risk management was "understaffed" and considered a "low priority." Schwartz told the FCIC the findings did not indicate substantial deficiencies. He wasn't looking for positive feedback from the consultants, because the Wyman re-

port was meant to provide a road map of what "the gold standard" in risk manage-ment would be.[33]

In January 2008, before the report was completed, Cayne resigned as CEO, after receiving $93.6 million in compensation from 2004 through 2007.[34] He remained as non-executive chairman of the board. Some senior executives sharply criticized him and the board. Thomas Marano told the FCIC that Cayne played a lot of golf and bridge.[35] Speaking of the board, Paul Friedman, a former senior managing director at Bear Stearns, said, "I guess because I'd never worked at a firm with a real board, it never dawned on me that at some point somebody would have or should have gotten the board involved in all of this," although he told the FCIC that he made these com-ments in anger and frustration in the wake of Bear's failure.[36] In its final report on Bear, the Corporate Library, which researches and rates firms for corporate gover-nance, gave the company a "D," reflecting "a high degree of governance risk" resulting from "high levels of concern related to the board and compensation."[37] When asked if he had made mistakes while at Bear Stearns, Cayne told the FCIC, "I take responsi-bility for what happened. I'm not going to walk away from the responsibility."[38]

At Bear, compensation was based largely on the return on equity in a given year. For senior executives, about half of each bonus was paid in cash, and about half in re-stricted stock that vested over three years and had to be held for five.[39] The formula for the size of each year's compensation pool was determined by a subcommittee of the board. Stockholders approved the performance compensation plan and capital accu-mulation plan for senior managing directors. Cayne told the FCIC he set his own compensation and the compensation for all five members of the Executive Commit-tee. According to Cayne, no one, including the board, questioned his decisions.[40]

For 2007, even with its losses, Bear Stearns paid out 58% of revenues in compensa-tion. Alix, who sat on the Compensation Committee, told FCIC staff the firm typically paid 50% but that the percentage increased in 2007 because revenues fell—if manage-ment had lowered compensation proportionately, he said, many employees might have quit.[41] Base salaries for senior managers were capped at $250,000, with the re-mainder of compensation a discretionary mix of cash, restricted stock, and options.[42]

From 2000 through 2008, the top five executives at Bear Stearns took home over $326.5 million in cash and over $1.1 billion from stock sales, for more than a total of $1.4 billion. This exceeded the annual budget for the SEC.[43] Alan Schwartz, who took over as CEO after Cayne and had been a leading proponent of investing in the mort-gage sector, earned more than $87 million from 2004 to 2007. Warren Spector, the co-president responsible for overseeing the two hedge funds that had failed, received more than $98 million during the same period. Although Spector was asked to re-sign, Bear never asked him to return any money. In 2006, Cayne, Schwartz, and Spec-tor each earned more than 10 times as much as Alix, the chief risk officer.[44]

Cayne was out, Schwartz was in, and Bear Stearns continued hanging on in early 2008. Bear was still able to fund its balance sheet through repo loans, though the interest rates the firm had to pay had increased.[45] Marano said he worried this in-creased cost would signal to the market that Bear was distressed, which could "make our problems turn into a death spiral."[46]

## "DUTY TO PROTECT THEIR INVESTORS"

On Wednesday, January 30, 2008, Treasurer Upton reported an internal accounting error that showed Bear Stearns to have less than $5 billion in liquidity—triggering a report to the SEC. While the company identified the error, the SEC reinstituted daily reporting by the company of its liquidity.[47]

Lenders and customers were more and more reluctant to do business with the company. On February 15, Bear Stearns had $36.7 billion in mortgages, mortgage-backed securities, and asset-backed securities on its balance sheet, down almost $10 billion from November. Nearly $26 billion were subprime or Alt-A mortgage–backed securities and CDOs.

The hedge funds that were clients of Bear's prime brokerage services were particularly concerned that Bear would be unable to return their cash and securities. Lou Lebedin, the head of Bear's prime brokerage, told the FCIC that hedge fund clients occasionally inquired about the bank's financial condition in the latter half of 2007, but that such inquiries picked up at the beginning of 2008, particularly as the cost increased of purchasing credit default swap protection on Bear. The inquiries became withdrawals—hedge funds started taking their business elsewhere. "They felt there were too many concerns about us and felt that this was a short-term move," Lebedin said. "Often they would tell us they'd be happy to bring the business back, but that they had the duty to protect their investors." Renaissance Technologies, one of Bear's biggest prime brokerage clients, pulled out all of its business. By April, Lebedin's prime brokerage operation would be holding $90 billion in assets under management, down more than 40% from $160 billion in January.[48]

Nonetheless, during the week of March 3, when SEC staff inspected Bear's liquidity pool, they identified "no significant issues." The SEC found Bear's liquidity pool ranged from $18 billion to $20 billion.[49]

Bear opened for business on Monday, March 10, with approximately $18 billion in cash reserves. The same day, Moody's downgraded 15 mortgage-backed securities issued by Bear Stearns Alt-A Trust, a special purpose entity. News reports on the downgrades carried abbreviated headlines stating, "Moody's Downgrades Bear Stearns," Upton said.[50] Rumors flew and counterparties panicked.[51] Bear's liquidity pool began to dry up, and the SEC was now concerned that Bear was being squeezed from all directions.[52] While "everything rolled" during the day—that is, Bear's repo lenders renewed their commitments—SEC officials worried that this would "probably not continue."[53]

On Tuesday, the Fed announced it would lend to investment banks and other "primary dealers." The Term Securities Lending Facility (TSLF) would make available up to $200 billion in Treasury securities, accepting as collateral GSE mortgage-backed securities and non-GSE mortgage–backed securities rated triple-A. The hope was that lenders would lend to investment banks if the collateral was Treasuries rather than other highly rated but now suspect assets such as mortgage-backed securities. The Fed also announced it would extend loans from overnight to 28 days, giv-

ing investment banks an added breather from the relentless need to unwind repos every morning.

With the TSLF, the Fed would be setting a new precedent by extending emergency credit to institutions other than commercial banks. To do so, the Federal Reserve Board was required under section 13(3) of the Federal Reserve Act to determine that there were "unusual and exigent circumstances." The Fed had not invoked its section 13(3) authority since the Great Depression; it was the Fed's first use of the authority since Congress had expanded the language of the act in 1991 to allow the Fed to lend to investment banks.[54] The Fed was taking the unusual step of declaring its willingness to soon open its checkbook to institutions it did not regulate and whose financial condition it had never examined.

But the Fed would not launch the TSLF until March 27, more than two weeks later—and it was not clear that Bear could last that long. The following day, Jim Embersit of the Federal Reserve Board checked on Bear's liquidity with the SEC. The SEC said Bear had $12.5 billion in cash—down from about $18 billion at the start of the week—and was able to finance all its bank loans and most of its equity securities through the repo market. He summarized, "The SEC indicates that no notable losses have been sustained and that the capital position of the firm is 'fine.'"[55]

Derivatives counterparties were increasingly reluctant to be exposed to Bear. In some cases they unwound trades in which they faced Bear, and in others they made margin or collateral calls.[56] In Bear's last few years as an independent company, it had substantially increased its exposure to derivatives. At the end of fiscal year 2007, Bear had $13.4 trillion in notional exposure on derivatives contracts, compared with $8.7 trillion at 2006 fiscal year-end and $5.5 trillion at the end of 2005.

Derivatives counterparties who worried about Bear's ability to make good on their payments could get out of their derivative positions with Bear through assignments or novations. Assignments allow counterparties to assign their positions to someone else: if firm $X$ has a derivatives contract with firm $Y$, then firm $X$ can assign its position to firm $Z$, so that $Z$ now is the one that has a derivatives contract with $Y$. Novations also allow counterparties to get out of their exposure to each other, but by bringing in a third party: instead of $X$ facing $Y$, $X$ faces $Z$ and $Z$ faces $Y$. Both assignments and novations are routine transactions on Wall Street. But on Tuesday, Brian Peters of the New York Fed advised Eichner at the SEC that the New York Fed was "seeing some HFs [hedge funds] wishing to assign trades the clients had done with Bear to other CPs [counterparties] so that Bear 'steps out.'"[57] Counterparties did not want to have Bear Stearns as a derivatives counterparty any more.

Bear Stearns also encountered difficulties stepping into trades. Hayman Capital Partners, a hedge fund in Texas wanting to decrease its exposure to subprime mortgages, had decided to close out a relatively small $5 million subprime derivative position with Goldman Sachs. Bear Stearns offered the best bid, so Hayman expected to assign its position to Bear, which would then become Goldman's counterparty in the derivative. Hayman notified Goldman by a routine email on Tuesday, March 11, at 4:06 P.M. The reply 41 minutes later was unexpected: "GS does not consent to this trade."[58]

That startled Kyle Bass, Hayman's managing partner. He told the FCIC he could not recall any counterparty rejecting a routine novation.[59] Pressed for an explanation, Goldman the next morning offered no details: "Our trading desk would prefer to stay facing Hayman. We do not want to face Bear."[60] Adding to the mystery, 16 minutes later Goldman agreed to accept Bear Sterns as the counterparty after all.[61] But the damage was done. The news hit the street that Goldman had refused a routine transaction with one of the other big five investment banks. The message: don't rely on Bear Stearns.

CEO Alan Schwartz hoped an appearance on CNBC would reassure markets. Questioned about this incident, Schwartz said he had no knowledge of such a refusal and rhetorically asked, "Why do rumors start?"[62] SEC Chairman Cox told reporters his agency was monitoring capital levels at Bear Stearns and other securities firms "on a constant basis" and has "a good deal of comfort about the capital cushions at these firms at the moment."[63]

Still, the run on Bear accelerated. Many investors believed the Fed's announcement about its new loan program was directed at Bear Stearns, and they worried about the facility's not being available for several weeks. On Wednesday, March 12, the SEC noted that Bear paid another $1.1 billion for margin calls from 142 nervous derivatives counterparties.[64]

Repo lenders who had already tightened the terms for their contracts over the preceding four or five months shortened the leash again, demanding more collateral from Bear Stearns.[65] Worries about a default quickly mounted.[66]

By that evening, Bear's ability to borrow in the repo market was drying up. The SEC noted that some large and important money funds, including Fidelity and Mellon, had told Bear after the close of business Wednesday they "might be hesitant to roll some funding tomorrow." The SEC said that though they believed the amounts were "very manageable (between $1 and $2 billion)," the withdrawals would not send a helpful signal to the market.[67] But the issue was almost moot. Schwartz called New York Fed President Timothy Geithner that night to discuss possible Fed flexibility in the event that some repo lenders did pull away.[68]

Upton, the treasurer, said that before that week, he had never worried about the disappearance of repo lending. By Thursday, he believed the end was near.[69] Bear executives informed the board that the rumors were dissuading counterparties from doing business with Bear, that Bear was receiving and meeting significant margin calls, that $14 billion in repo was not going to roll over, and that "there was a reasonable chance that there would not be enough cash to meet [Bear's] needs."[70] Some repo lenders were already so averse to Bear that they stopped lending to the company at all, not even against Treasury collateral, Upton told the FCIC.[71] Derivatives counterparties continued to run from Bear. By that night, liquidity had dwindled to a mere $2 billion (see figure 15.1).

Bear had run out of cash in one week. Executives and regulators continued to believe the firm was solvent, however. Former SEC Chairman Cox testified before the FCIC, "At all times during the week of March 10 to 17, up to and including the time of its agreement to be acquired by JP Morgan, Bear Stearns had a capital cushion well above what is required."[72]

## Bear Stearns Liquidity

*In the four days before Bear Stearns collapsed, the company's liquidity dropped by $16 billion.*

IN BILLIONS OF DOLLARS, DAILY

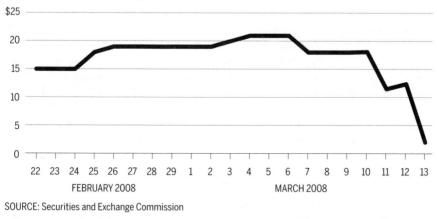

FEBRUARY 2008             MARCH 2008

SOURCE: Securities and Exchange Commission

*Figure 15.1*

### "THE GOVERNMENT
### WOULD NOT PERMIT A HIGHER NUMBER"

On Thursday evening, March 13, Bear Stearns informed the SEC that it would be "unable to operate normally on Friday."[73] CEO Alan Schwartz called JP Morgan CEO Jamie Dimon to request a $30 billion credit line. Dimon turned him down,[74] citing, according to Schwartz, JP Morgan's own significant exposure to the mortgage market. Because Bear also had a large, illiquid portfolio of mortgage assets, JP Morgan would not render assistance without government support. Schwartz spoke with Geithner again. Schwartz insisted Bear's problem was liquidity, not insufficient capital. A series of calls between Schwartz, Dimon, Geithner, and Treasury Secretary Henry Paulson followed.[75] To address Bear's liquidity needs, the New York Fed made a $12.9 billion loan to Bear Stearns through JP Morgan on the morning of Friday, March 14. Standard & Poor's lowered Bear's rating three levels to BBB. Moody's and Fitch also downgraded the company. By the end of the day, Bear was out of cash. Its stock plummeted 47%, closing below $30.

The markets evidently viewed the loan as a sign of terminal weakness. After markets closed on Friday, Paulson and Geithner informed Bear CEO Schwartz that the Fed loan to JP Morgan would not be available after the weekend. Without that loan, Bear could not conduct business. In fact, Bear Stearns had to find a buyer before the Asian markets opened Sunday night or the game would be over.[76] Schwartz,

Molinaro, Alix, and others spent the weekend in due diligence meetings with JP Morgan and other potential buyers, including the private equity firm J.C. Flowers and Co. According to Schwartz, the participants determined JP Morgan was the only candidate with the size and stature to make a credible offer within 48 hours.[77] As Bear Stearns's clearing bank for repo trades, JP Morgan held much of Bear Stearns's assets as collateral and had been assessing their value daily.[78] This knowledge let JP Morgan move more quickly.

On Sunday, March 16, JP Morgan informed the New York Fed and the Treasury that it was interested in a deal if it included financial support from the Fed.[79] The Federal Reserve Board, again finding "unusual and exigent circumstances" as required under section 13(3) of the Federal Reserve Act, agreed to purchase $29.97 billion of Bear's assets to get them off the firm's books through a new entity called Maiden Lane LLC (named for a street alongside the New York Fed). Those assets—mostly mortgage-related securities, other assets, and hedges from Bear's mortgage trading desk—would be under New York Fed management. To finance the purchases, JP Morgan made a $1.15 billion subordinated loan and the New York Fed lent $28.82 billion. Because of its loan, JP Morgan bore the risk of the first $1.15 billion of losses; the Fed would bear any further losses up to $28.82 billion.[80] The Fed's loan would be repaid as Maiden Lane sold the collateral.

On Sunday night, with Maiden Lane in place, JP Morgan publicly announced a deal to buy Bear Stearns for $2 a share. Minutes of Bear's board meeting indicate that JP Morgan had considered $4 but cut it to $2 "because the government would not permit a higher number. . . . The Fed and the Treasury Department would not support a transaction where [Bear Stearns] equity holders received any significant consideration because of the 'moral hazard' of the federal government using taxpayer money to 'bail out' the investment bank's stockholders."[81]

Eight days later, on March 24, Bear Stearns and JP Morgan agreed to increase the price to $10. John Chrin, co-head of the financial institutions mergers and acquisitions group at JP Morgan, told the FCIC they increased the price to make Bear shareholders' approval more likely.[82] Bear CEO Schwartz told the FCIC the increase let Bear preserve the company's value "to the greatest extent possible under the circumstances for our shareholders, our 14,000 employees, and our creditors."[83]

## "IT WAS HEADING TO A BLACK HOLE"

The SEC regulators Macchiaroli and Eichner were as stunned as everyone else by the speed of Bear's collapse. Macchiaroli had had doubts as far back as August, he told the FCIC, but he and his colleagues expected Bear would be able to fund itself through the repo market, albeit at higher margins.[84]

Fed Chairman Ben Bernanke later called the Bear Stearns decision the toughest of the financial crisis. The $2.8 trillion tri-party repo market had "really [begun] to break down," Bernanke said. "As the fear increased," short-term lenders began demanding more collateral, "which was making it more and more difficult for the financial firms to finance themselves and creating more and more liquidity pressure on

them. And, it was heading sort of to a black hole." He saw the collapse of Bear Stearns as threatening to freeze the tri-party repo market, leaving the short-term lenders with collateral they would try to "dump on the market. You would have a big crunch in asset prices."[85]

"Bear Stearns, which is not that big a firm, our view on why it was important to save it—you may disagree—but our view was that because it was so essentially involved in this critical repo financing market, that its failure would have brought down that market, which would have had implications for other firms," Bernanke told the FCIC.[86]

Geithner explained the need for government support for Bear's acquisition by JP Morgan as follows: "The sudden discovery by Bear's derivative counterparties that important financial positions they had put in place to protect themselves from financial risk were no longer operative would have triggered substantial further dislocation in markets. This would have precipitated a rush by Bear's counterparties to liquidate the collateral they held against those positions and to attempt to replicate those positions in already very fragile markets."[87]

Paulson told the FCIC that Bear had both a liquidity problem and a capital problem. "Could you just imagine the mess we would have had? If Bear had gone there were hundreds, maybe thousands of counterparties that all would have grabbed their collateral, would have started trying to sell their collateral, drove down prices, create even bigger losses. There was huge fear about the investment banking model at that time." Paulson believed that if Bear had filed for bankruptcy, "you would have had Lehman going . . . almost immediately if Bear had gone, and just the whole process would have just started earlier."[88]

---

## COMMISSION CONCLUSIONS ON CHAPTER 15

The Commission concludes the failure of Bear Stearns and its resulting government-assisted rescue were caused by its exposure to risky mortgage assets, its reliance on short-term funding, and its high leverage. These were a result of weak corporate governance and risk management. Its executive and employee compensation system was based largely on return on equity, creating incentives to use excessive leverage and to focus on short-term gains such as annual growth goals.

Bear experienced runs by repo lenders, hedge fund customers, and derivatives counterparties and was rescued by a government-assisted purchase by JP Morgan because the government considered it too interconnected to fail. Bear's failure was in part a result of inadequate supervision by the Securities and Exchange Commission, which did not restrict its risky activities and which allowed undue leverage and insufficient liquidity.

# 16

# MARCH TO AUGUST 2008:
# SYSTEMIC RISK CONCERNS

## CONTENTS

JP Morgan's federally assisted acquisition of Bear Stearns averted catastrophe—for the time being. The Federal Reserve had found new ways to lend cash to the financial system, and some investors and lenders believed the Bear episode had set a precedent for extraordinary government intervention. Investors began to worry less about a recession and more about inflation, as the price of oil continued to rise (hitting almost $144 per barrel in July). At the beginning of 2008, the stock market had fallen almost 15% from its peak in the fall of 2007. Then, in May 2008, the Dow Jones climbed to 13,058, within 8% of the record 14,164 set in October 2007. The cost of protecting against the risk of default by financial institutions—reflected in the prices of credit default swaps—declined from the highs of March and April. "In hindsight, the markets were surprisingly stable and almost seemed to be neutral a month after Bear Stearns, leading all the way up to September," said David Wong, Morgan Stanley's treasurer.[1] Taking advantage of the brief respite in investor concern, the top ten American banks and the four remaining big investment banks, anticipating losses, raised just under $100 billion and $40 billion, respectively, in new equity by the end of June.

Despite this good news, bankers and their regulators were haunted by the speed of Bear Stearns's demise. And they knew that the other investment banks shared Bear's weaknesses: leverage, reliance on overnight funding, dependence on securitization markets, and concentrations in illiquid mortgage securities and other troubled assets. In particular, the run on Bear had exposed the dangers of tri-party repo agreements and the counterparty risk caused by derivatives contracts.

And the word on the street—despite the assurances of Lehman CEO Dick Fuld at

an April shareholder meeting that "the worst is behind us"[2]—was that Bear would not be the only failure.

## THE FEDERAL RESERVE: "WHEN PEOPLE GOT SCARED"

The most pressing danger was the potential failure of the repo market—a market that "grew very, very quickly with no single regulator having a purview of it," former Treasury Secretary Henry Paulson would tell the FCIC.[3] Market participants believed that the tri-party repo market was a relatively safe and durable source of collateralized short-term financing. It was on precisely this understanding that Bear had shifted approximately $30 billion of its unsecured funding into repos in 2007. But now it was clear that repo funding could be just as vulnerable to runs as were other forms of short-term financing.

The repo runs of 2007, which had devastated hedge funds such as the two Bear Stearns Asset Management funds and mortgage originators such as Countrywide, had seized the attention of the financial community, and the run on Bear Stearns was similarly eye-opening. Market participants and regulators now better appreciated how the quality of repo collateral had shifted over time from Treasury notes and securities issued by Fannie Mae and Freddie Mac to highly rated non-GSE mortgage-backed securities and collateralized debt obligations (CDOs).[4] At its peak before the crisis, this riskier collateral accounted for as much as 30% of the total posted.[5] In April 2005, the Bankruptcy Abuse Prevention and Consumer Protection Act of 2005 had dramatically expanded protections for repo lenders holding collateral, such as mortgage-related securities, that was riskier than government or highly rated corporate debt. These protections gave lenders confidence that they had clear, immediate rights to collateral if a borrower should declare bankruptcy. Nonetheless, Jamie Dimon, the CEO of JP Morgan, told the FCIC, "When people got scared, they wouldn't finance the nonstandard stuff at all."[6]

To the surprise of both borrowers and regulators, high-quality collateral was not enough to ensure access to the repo market. Repo lenders cared just as much about the financial health of the borrower as about the quality of the collateral. In fact, even for the same collateral, repo lenders demanded different haircuts from different borrowers.[7] Despite the bankruptcy provisions in the 2005 act, lenders were reluctant to risk the hassle of seizing collateral, even good collateral, from a bankrupt borrower. Steven Meier of State Street testified to the FCIC: "I would say the counterparties are a first line of defense, and we don't want to go through that uncomfortable process of having to liquidate collateral."[8] William Dudley of the New York Fed told the FCIC, "At the first sign of trouble, these investors in tri-party repo tend to run rather than take the collateral that they've lent against. . . . So high-quality collateral itself is not sufficient when and if an institution gets in trouble."[9]

Moreover, if a borrower in the repo market defaults, money market funds—frequent lenders in this market—may have to seize collateral that they cannot legally own. For example, a money market fund cannot hold long-term securities, such as

agency mortgage–backed securities. Typically, if a fund takes possession of such collateral, it liquidates the securities immediately, even—as was the case during the crisis—into a declining market. As a result, funds simply avoided lending against mortgage-related securities. In the crisis, investors didn't consider secured funding to be much better than unsecured, according to Darryll Hendricks, a managing director and global head of risk methodology at UBS, as well as the head of a private-sector task force on the repo market organized by the New York Fed.[10]

As noted, the Fed had announced a new program, the Term Securities Lending Facility (TSLF), on the Tuesday before Bear's collapse, but it would not be available until March 27. The TSLF would lend a total of up to $200 billion of Treasury securities at any one time to the investment banks and other primary dealers—the securities affiliates of the large commercial banks and investment banks that trade with the New York Fed, such as Citigroup, Morgan Stanley, or Merrill Lynch—for up to 28 days. The borrowers would trade highly rated securities, including debt in government-sponsored enterprises, in return for Treasuries. The primary dealers could then use those Treasuries as collateral to borrow cash in the repo market. Like the Term Auction Facility for commercial banks, described earlier, the TSLF would run as a regular auction to reduce the stigma of borrowing from the Fed. However, after Bear's collapse, Fed officials recognized that the situation called for a program that could be up and running right away. And they concluded that the TSLF alone would not be enough.

So, the Fed would create another program first. On the Sunday of Bear's collapse, the Fed announced the new Primary Dealer Credit Facility—again invoking its authority under 13(3) of the Federal Reserve Act—to provide cash, not Treasuries, to investment banks and other primary dealers on terms close to those that depository institutions—banks and thrifts—received through the Fed's discount window. The move came "just about 45 minutes" too late for Bear, Jimmy Cayne, its former CEO, told the FCIC.[11]

Unlike the TSLF, which would offer Treasuries for 28 days, the PDCF offered overnight cash loans in exchange for collateral. In effect, this program could serve as an alternative to the overnight tri-party repo lenders, potentially providing hundreds of billions of dollars of credit. "So the idea of the PDCF then was . . . anything that the dealer couldn't finance—the securities that were acceptable under the discount window—if they couldn't get financing in the market, they could get financing from the Federal Reserve," said Seth Carpenter, deputy associate director in the Division of Monetary Affairs at the Federal Reserve Board. "And that way, you don't have to worry. And by providing that support, other lenders know that they're going to be able to get their money back the next day."[12]

By charging the Federal Reserve's discount rate and adding additional fees for regular use, the Federal Reserve encouraged dealers to use the PDCF only as a last resort. In its first week of operation, this program immediately provided over $340 billion in cash to Bear Stearns (as bridge financing until the JP Morgan deal officially closed), Lehman Brothers, and the securities affiliate of Citigroup, among others. However, as the immediate post-Bear concerns subsided, use of the facility declined

after April and ceased completely by late July.[13] Because the dealers feared that markets would see reliance on the PDCF as an indication of severe distress, the facility carried a stigma similar to the Fed's discount window. "Paradoxically, while the PDCF was created to mitigate the liquidity flight caused by the loss of confidence in an investment bank, use of the PDCF was seen both within Lehman, and possibly by the broader market, as an event that could trigger a loss of confidence," noted the Lehman bankruptcy examiner.[14]

On May 2, the Fed broadened the kinds of collateral allowed in the TSLF to include other triple-A-rated asset-backed securities, such as auto and credit card loans. In June, the Fed's Dudley urged in an internal email that both programs be extended at least through the end of the year. "PDCF remains critical to the stability of some of the [investment banks]," he wrote. "Amounts don't matter here, it is the fact that the PDCF underpins the tri-party repo system."[15] On July 30, the Fed extended both programs through January 30, 2009.

## JP MORGAN: "REFUSING TO UNWIND . . . WOULD BE UNFORGIVABLE"

The repo run on Bear also alerted the two repo clearing banks—JP Morgan, the main clearing bank for Lehman and Merrill Lynch, as it had been for Bear Stearns, and BNY Mellon, the main clearing bank for Goldman Sachs and Morgan Stanley—to the risks they were taking.

Before Bear's collapse, the market had not really understood the colossal exposures that the tri-party repo market created for these clearing banks. As explained earlier, the "unwind/rewind" mechanism could leave JP Morgan and BNY Mellon with an enormous "intraday" exposure—an interim exposure, but no less real for its brevity. In an interview with the FCIC, Dimon said that he had not become fully aware of the risks stemming from his bank's tri-party repo clearing business until the Bear crisis in 2008.[16] A clearing bank had two concerns: First, if repo lenders abandoned an investment bank, it could be pressured into taking over the role of the lenders. Second, and worse—if the investment bank defaulted, it could be stuck with unwanted securities. "If they defaulted intraday, we own the securities and we have to liquidate them. That's a huge risk to us," Dimon explained.[17]

To address those risks in 2008, for the first time both JP Morgan and BNY Mellon started to demand that intraday loans to tri-party repo borrowers—mostly the large investment banks—be overcollateralized.

The Fed increasingly focused on the systemic risk posed by the two repo clearing banks. In the chain-reaction scenario that it envisioned, if either JP Morgan or BNY Mellon chose not to unwind its trades one morning, the money funds and other repo lenders could be stuck with billions of dollars in repo collateral. Those lenders would then be in the difficult position of having to sell off large amounts of collateral in order to meet their own cash needs, an action that in turn might lead to widespread fire sales of repo collateral and runs by lenders.[18]

The PDCF provided overnight funding, in case money market funds and other

repo lenders refused to lend as they had in the case of Bear Stearns, but it did not pro-
tect against clearing banks' refusing exposure to an investment bank during the day.

On July 11, Fed officials circulated a plan, ultimately never implemented, that ad-
dressed the possibility that one of the two clearing banks would become unwilling or
unable to unwind its trades.[19] The plan would allow the Fed to provide troubled in-
vestment banks, such as Lehman Brothers, with $200 billion in tri-party repo financ-
ing during the day—essentially covering for JP Morgan or BNY Mellon if the two
clearing banks would not or could not provide that level of financing.[20] Fed officials
made a case for the proposal in an internal memo: "Should a dealer lose the confi-
dence of its investors or clearing bank, their efforts to pull away from providing
credit could be disastrous for the firm and also cast widespread doubt about the in-
strument as a nearly risk free, liquid overnight investment."[21]

But the New York Fed's new plan shouldn't be necessary as long as the PDCF was
there to back up the overnight lenders, argued Patrick Parkinson, then deputy direc-
tor of the Federal Reserve Board's Division of Research and Statistics. "We should tell
[JP Morgan] that with the PDCF in place refusing to unwind is unnecessary and
would be unforgiveable," he emailed Dudley and others.[22]

A week later, on July 20, Parkinson wrote to Fed Governor Kevin Warsh and Fed
General Counsel Scott Alvarez that JP Morgan, because of its clearing role, was
"likely to be the first to realize that the money funds and other investors that provide
tri-party financing to [Lehman Brothers] are pulling back significantly." Parkinson
described the chain-reaction scenario, in which a clearing bank's refusal to unwind
would lead to a widespread fire sale and market panic. "Fear of these consequences is,
of course, why we facilitated Bear's acquisition by JPMC," he said.[23]

Still, it was possible that the PDCF could prove insufficient to dissuade JP Morgan
from refusing to unwind Lehman's repos, Parkinson said. Because a large portion of
Lehman's collateral was ineligible to be funded by the PDCF, and because Lehman
could fail during the day (before the repos were settled), JP Morgan still faced signifi-
cant risks. Parkinson noted that even if the Fed lent as much as $200 billion to
Lehman, the sum might not be enough to ensure the firm's survival in the absence of
an acquirer: if the stigma associated with PDCF borrowing caused other funding
counterparties to stop providing funding to Lehman, the company would fail.[24]

## THE FED AND THE SEC: "WEAK LIQUIDITY POSITION"

Among the four remaining investment banks, one key measure of liquidity risk was
the portion of total liabilities that the firms funded through the repo market: 15% to
20% for Lehman and Merrill Lynch, 10% to 15% for Morgan Stanley, and about 10%
for Goldman Sachs.[25] Another metric was the reliance on overnight repo (which ma-
ture in one day) or open repo (which can be terminated at any time). Despite efforts
among the investment banks to reduce the portion of their repo financing that was
overnight or open, the ratio of overnight and open repo funding to total repo fund-
ing still exceeded 40% for all but Goldman Sachs. Comparing the period between
March and May to the period between July and August, Lehman's percentage fell

from 45% to 40%, Merrill Lynch's fell from 46% to 43%, Morgan Stanley's fell from 70% to 55%, and Goldman's fell from 18% to 10%.[26] Another measure of risk was the haircuts on repo loans—that is, the amount of excess collateral that lenders demanded for a given loan. Fed officials kept tabs on the haircuts demanded of investment banks, hedge funds, and other repo borrowers. As Fed analysts later noted, "With lenders worrying that they could lose money on the securities they held as collateral, haircuts increased—doubling for some agency mortgage securities and increasing significantly even for borrowers with high credit ratings and on relatively safe collateral such as Treasury securities."[27]

On the day of Bear's demise, in an effort to get a better understanding of the investment banks, the New York Fed and the SEC sent teams to work on-site at Lehman Brothers, Merrill Lynch, Goldman Sachs, and Morgan Stanley. According to Erik Sirri, director of the SEC's Division of Trading and Markets, the initial rounds of meetings covered the quality of assets, funding, and capital.[28]

Fed Chairman Ben Bernanke would testify before a House committee that the Fed's primary role at the investment banks in 2008 was not as a regulator but as a lender through the new emergency lending facilities.[29] Two questions guided the Fed's analyses: First, was each investment bank liquid—did it have access to the cash needed to meet its commitments? Second, was it solvent—was its net equity (the value of assets minus the value of liabilities) sufficient to cover probable losses?[30]

The U.S. Treasury also dispatched so-called SWAT teams to the investment banks in the spring of 2008. The arrival of officials from the Treasury and the Fed created a full-time on-site presence—something the SEC had never had. Historically, the SEC's primary concern with the investment banks had been liquidity risk, because these firms were entirely dependent on the credit markets for funding.[31] The SEC already required these firms to implement so-called liquidity models, designed to ensure that they had sufficient cash available to sustain themselves on a stand-alone basis for a minimum of one year without access to unsecured funding and without having to sell a substantial amount of assets. Before the run on Bear in the repo market, the SEC's liquidity stress scenarios—also known as stress tests—had not taken account of the possibility that a firm would lose access to secured funding. According to the SEC's Sirri, the SEC never thought that a situation would arise where an investment bank couldn't enter into a repo transaction backed by high-quality collateral including Treasuries. He told the FCIC that as the financial crisis worsened, the SEC began to see liquidity and funding risks as the most critical for the investment banks, and the SEC encouraged a reduction in reliance on unsecured commercial paper and an extension of the maturities of repo loans.[32]

The Fed and the SEC collaborated in developing two new stress tests to determine the investment banks' ability to withstand a potential run or a systemwide disruption in the repo market. The stress scenarios, called "Bear Stearns" and "Bear Stearns Light," were developed jointly with the remaining investment banks. In May, Lehman, for example, would be $84 billion short of cash in the more stringent Bear Stearns scenario and $15 billion short under Bear Stearns Light.[33]

The Fed conducted another liquidity stress analysis in June. While each firm ran

different scenarios that matched its risk profile, the supervisors tried to maintain comparability between the tests. The tests assumed that each firm would lose 100% of unsecured funding and a fraction of repo funding that would vary with the quality of its collateral. The stress tests, under just one estimated scenario, concluded that Goldman Sachs and Morgan Stanley were relatively sound. Merrill Lynch and Lehman Brothers failed: the two banks came out $22 billion and $15 billion short of cash, respectively; each had only 78% of the liquidity it would need under the stress scenario.[34]

The Fed's internal report on the stress tests criticized Merrill's "significant amount of illiquid fixed income assets" and noted that "Merrill's liquidity pool is low, a fact [the company] does not acknowledge." As for Lehman Brothers, the Fed concluded that "Lehman's weak liquidity position is driven by its relatively large exposure to overnight [commercial paper], combined with significant overnight secured [repo] funding of less liquid assets."[35] These "less liquid assets" included mortgage-related securities—now devalued. Meanwhile, Lehman ran stress tests of its own and passed with billions in "excess cash."[36]

Although the SEC and the Fed worked together on the liquidity stress tests, with equal access to the data, each agency has said that for months during the crisis, the other did not share its analyses and conclusions. For example, following Lehman's failure in September, the Fed told the bankruptcy examiner that the SEC had declined to share two horizontal (cross-firm) reviews of the banks' liquidity positions and exposures to commercial real estate. The SEC's response was that the documents were in "draft" form and had not been reviewed or finalized. Adding to the tension, the Fed's on-site personnel believed that the SEC on-site personnel did not have the background or expertise to adequately evaluate the data.[37] This lack of communication was remedied only by a formal memorandum of understanding (MOU) to govern information sharing. According to former SEC Chairman Christopher Cox, "One reason the MOU was needed was that the Fed was reluctant to share supervisory information with the SEC, out of concern that the investment banks would not be forthcoming with information if they thought they would be referred to the SEC for enforcement."[38] The MOU was not executed until July 2008, more than three months after the collapse of Bear Stearns.

## DERIVATIVES: "EARLY STAGES OF ASSESSING THE POTENTIAL SYSTEMIC RISK"

The Fed's Parkinson advised colleagues in an internal August 8 email that the systemic risks of the repo and derivatives markets demanded attention: "We have given considerable thought to what might be done to avoid a fire sale of tri-party repo collateral. (That said, the options under existing authority are not very attractive—lots of risk to Fed/taxpayer, lots of moral hazard.) We still are at the early stages of assessing the potential systemic risk from close-out of OTC derivatives transactions by an investment bank's counterparties and identifying potential mitigants."[39]

The repo market was huge, but as discussed in earlier chapters, it was dwarfed by

## Notional Amount and Gross Market Value of OTC Derivatives Outstanding

IN TRILLIONS OF DOLLARS, SEMIANNUAL

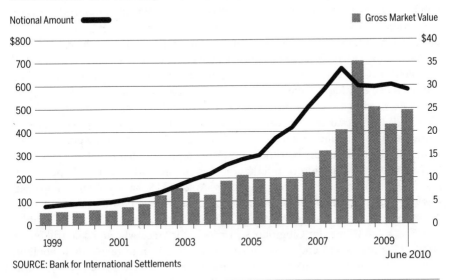

SOURCE: Bank for International Settlements

*Figure 16.1*

the global derivatives market. At the end of June 2008, the notional amount of the over-the-counter derivatives market was $673 trillion and the gross market value was $20 trillion (see figure 16.1). Adequate information about the risks in this market was not available to market participants or government regulators like the Federal Reserve. Because the market had been deregulated by statute in 2000, market participants were not subject to reporting or disclosure requirements and no government agency had oversight responsibility. While the Office of the Comptroller of the Currency did report information on derivatives positions from commercial banks and bank holding companies, it did not collect such information from the large investment banks and insurance companies like AIG, which were also major OTC derivatives dealers. During the crisis the lack of such basic information created heightened uncertainty.

At this point in the crisis, regulators also worried about the interlocking relationships that derivatives created among the small number of large financial firms that act as dealers in the OTC derivatives business. A derivatives contract creates a credit relationship between parties, such that one party may have to make large and unexpected payments to the other based on sudden price or rate changes or loan defaults. If a party is unable to make those payments when they become due, that failure may

cause significant financial harm to its counterparty, which may have offsetting obligations to third parties and depend on prompt payment. Indeed, most OTC derivatives dealers hedge their contracts with offsetting contracts; thus, if they are owed payments on one contract, they most likely owe similar amounts on an offsetting contract, creating the potential for a series of losses or defaults. Since these contracts numbered in the millions and allowed a party to have virtually unlimited leverage, the possibility of sudden large and devastating losses in this market could pose a significant danger to market participants and the financial system as a whole.

The Counterparty Risk Management Policy Group, led by former New York Fed President E. Gerald Corrigan and consisting of the major securities firms, had warned that a backlog in paperwork confirming derivatives trades and master agreements exposed firms to risk should corporate defaults occur.[40] With urging from New York Fed President Timothy Geithner, by September 2006, 14 major market participants had significantly reduced the backlog and had ended the practice of assigning trades to third parties without the prior consent of their counterparties.[41]

Large derivatives positions, and the resulting counterparty credit and operational risks, were concentrated in a very few firms. Among U.S. bank holding companies, the following institutions held enormous OTC derivatives positions as of June 30, 2008: $94.5 trillion in notional amount for JP Morgan, $37.7 trillion for Bank of America, $35.8 trillion for Citigroup, $4.1 trillion for Wachovia, and $3.9 trillion for HSBC. Goldman Sachs and Morgan Stanley, which began to report their holdings only after they became bank holding companies in 2008, held $45.9 and $37.0 trillion, respectively, in notional amount of OTC derivatives in the first quarter of 2009.[42] In 2008, the current and potential exposure to derivatives at the top five U.S. bank holding companies was on average three times greater than the capital they had on hand to meet regulatory requirements. The risk was even higher at the investment banks. Goldman Sachs, just after it changed its charter, had derivatives exposure more than 10 times capital. These concentrations of positions in the hands of the largest bank holding companies and investment banks posed risks for the financial system because of their interconnections with other financial institutions.

Broad classes of OTC derivatives markets showed stress in 2008. By the summer of 2008, outstanding amounts of some types of derivatives had begun to decline sharply. As we will see, over the course of the second half of 2008, the OTC derivatives market would undergo an unprecedented contraction, creating serious problems for hedging and price discovery.

The Fed was uneasy in part because derivatives counterparties had played an important role in the run on Bear Stearns. The novations by derivatives counterparties to assign their positions away from Bear—and the rumored refusal by Goldman to accept Bear as a derivatives counterparty—were still a fresh memory across Wall Street. Chris Mewbourne, a portfolio manager at PIMCO, told the FCIC that the ability to novate ceased to exist and this was a key event in the demise of Bear Stearns.[43]

Credit derivatives in particular were a serious source of worry. Of greatest interest were the sellers of credit default swaps: the monoline insurers and AIG, which back-

stopped the market in CDOs. In addition, the credit rating agencies' decision to issue a negative outlook on the monoline insurers had jolted everyone, because they guaranteed hundreds of billions of dollars in structured products. As we have seen, when their credit ratings were downgraded, the value of all the assets they guaranteed, including municipal bonds and other securities, necessarily lost some value in the market, a drop that affected the conservative institutional investors in those markets. In the vernacular of Wall Street, this outcome is the knock-on effect; in the vernacular of Main Street, the domino effect; in the vernacular of the Fed, systemic risk.

## BANKS: "THE MARKETS WERE REALLY, REALLY DICEY"

By the fall of 2007, signs of strain were beginning to emerge among the commercial banks. In the fourth quarter of 2007, commercial banks' earnings declined to a 16-year low, driven by write-downs on mortgage-backed securities and CDOs and by record provisions for future loan losses, as borrowers had increasing difficulty meeting their mortgage payments—and even greater difficulty was anticipated. The net charge-off rate—the ratio of failed loans to total loans—rose to its highest level since 2002, when the economy was coming out of the post-9/11 recession. Earnings continued to decline in 2008—at first, more for big banks than small banks, in part because of write-downs related to their investment banking–type activities, including the packaging of mortgage-backed securities, CDOs, and collateralized loan obligations. Declines in market values required banks to write down the value of their holdings of these securities. As previously noted, several of the largest banks had also provided support to off-balance-sheet activities, such as money market funds and commercial paper programs, bringing additional assets onto their balance sheets— assets that were losing value fast. Supervisors had begun to downgrade the ratings of many smaller banks in response to their high exposures in residential real estate construction, an industry that virtually went out of business as financing dried up in mid-2007. By the end of 2007, the FDIC had 76 banks, mainly smaller ones, on its "problem list"; their combined assets totaled $22.2 billion.[44] (When large banks started to be downgraded, in early 2008, they stayed off the FDIC's problem list, as supervisors rarely give the largest institutions the lowest ratings.)[45]

The market for nonconforming mortgage securitizations (those backed by mortgages that did not meet Fannie Mae's or Freddie Mac's underwriting or mortgage size guidelines) had also vanished in the fourth quarter of 2007. Not only did these nonconforming loans prove harder to sell, but they also proved less attractive to keep on balance sheet, as house price forecasts looked increasingly grim. Already, house prices had fallen about 7% for the year, depending on the measure. In the first quarter of 2008, real estate loans in the banking sector showed the smallest quarterly increase since 2003.[46] IndyMac reported a 21% decline in loan production for that quarter from a year earlier, because it had stopped making nonconforming loans. Washington Mutual, the largest thrift, discontinued all remaining lending through its subprime mortgage channel in April 2008.

But those actions could not reduce the subprime and Alt-A exposure that these

large banks and thrifts already had. And on these assets, the markdowns continued in 2008. Regulators began to focus on solvency, urging the banks to raise new capital. In January 2008, Citigroup secured a total of $14 billion in capital from Kuwait, Singapore, Saudi Prince Alwaleed bin Talal, and others. In April, Washington Mutual raised $7 billion from an investor group led by the buyout firm TPG Capital. Wachovia raised $6 billion in capital at the turn of the year and then an additional $8 billion in April 2008. Despite the capital raises, though, the downgrades by banking regulators continued.

"The markets were really, really dicey during a significant part of this period, starting with August 2007," Roger Cole, then-director of the Division of Banking Supervision and Regulation at the Federal Reserve Board, told the FCIC.[47] The same was true for the thrifts. Michael Solomon, a managing director in risk management manager in the Office of Thrift Supervision (OTS), told the FCIC, "It was hard for businesses, particularly small, midsized thrifts—to keep up with [how quickly the ratings downgrades occurred during the crisis] and change their business models and not get stuck without the chair when the music stopped . . . They got caught. The rating downgrades started and by the time the thrift was able to do something about it, it was too late . . . Business models . . . can't keep up with what we saw in 2008."[48]

As the commercial banks' health worsened in 2008, examiners downgraded even large institutions that had maintained favorable ratings and required several to fix their risk management processes. These ratings downgrades and enforcement actions came late in the day—often just as firms were on the verge of failure. In cases that the FCIC investigated, regulators either did not identify the problems early enough or did not act forcefully enough to compel the necessary changes.

### Citigroup: "Time to come up with a new playbook"

For Citigroup, supervisors at the New York Fed, who examined the bank holding company, and at the Office of the Comptroller of the Currency, who oversaw the national bank subsidiary, finally downgraded the company and its main bank to "less than satisfactory" in April 2008—five months after the firm's announcement in November 2007 of billions of dollars in write-downs related to its mortgage-related holdings. The supervisors put the company under new enforcement actions in May and June. Only a year earlier, both the Fed and the OCC had upgraded the company, after lifting all remaining restrictions and enforcement actions related to complex transactions that it had structured for Enron and to the actions of its subprime subsidiary CitiFinancial, discussed in an earlier chapter. "The risk management assessment for 2006 is reflective of a control environment where the risks facing Citigroup continue to be managed in a satisfactory manner," the New York Fed's rating upgrade, delivered in its annual inspection report on April 9, 2007, had noted. "During 2006, all formal restrictions and enforcement actions between the Federal Reserve and Citigroup were lifted. Board and senior management remain actively engaged in improving relevant processes."[49]

But the market disruption had jolted Citigroup's supervisors. In November 2007,

the New York Fed led a team of international supervisors, the Senior Supervisors Group, in evaluating 11 of the largest firms to assess lessons learned from the financial crisis up to that point. Much of the toughest language was reserved for Citigroup. "The firm did not have an adequate, firm-wide consolidated understanding of its risk factor sensitivities," the supervisors wrote in an internal November 19 memo describing meetings with Citigroup management. "Stress tests were not designed for this type of extreme market event. . . . Management had believed that CDOs and leveraged loans would be syndicated, and that the credit risk in super senior AAA CDOs was negligible."[50]

In retrospect, Citigroup had two key problems: a lack of effective enterprise-wide management to monitor and control risks and a lack of proper infrastructure and internal controls with respect to the creation of CDOs. The OCC appears to have identified some of these issues as early as 2005 but did not effectively act to rectify them. In particular, the OCC assessed both the liquidity puts and the super-senior tranches as part of its reviews of the bank's compliance with the post-Enron enforcement action, but it did not examine the risks of these exposures. As for the issues it did spot, the OCC failed to take forceful steps to require mandatory corrective action, and it relied on management's assurances in 2006 that the executives would strive to meet the OCC's goals for improving risk management.

In contrast, documents obtained by the FCIC from the New York Fed give no indication that its examination staff had any independent knowledge of those two core problems. An evaluation of the New York Fed's supervision of Citigroup, conducted by examiners from other Reserve Banks (the December 2009 Operations Review of the New York Fed, which covered the previous four years), concluded:

> The supervision program for Citigroup has been less than effective. Although the dedicated supervisory team is well qualified and generally has sound knowledge of the organization, there have been significant weaknesses in the execution of the supervisory program. The team has not been proactive in making changes to the regulatory ratings of the firm, as evidenced by the double downgrades in the firm's financial component and related subcomponents at year-end 2007. Additionally, the supervisory program has lacked the appropriate level of focus on the firm's risk oversight and internal audit functions. As a result, there is currently significant work to be done in both of these areas. Moreover, the team has lacked a disciplined and proactive approach in assessing and validating actions taken by the firm to address supervisory issues.[51]

Timothy Geithner, secretary of the Treasury and former president of the Federal Reserve Bank of New York, reflected on the Fed's oversight of Citigroup, telling the Commission, "I do not think we did enough as an institution with the authority we had to help contain the risks that ultimately emerged in that institution."[52]

In January 2008, an OCC review of the breakdown in the CDO business noted that the risk in the unit had grown rapidly since 2006, after the OCC's and Fed's

lifting of supervisory agreements associated with various control problems at Citigroup. In April 2008, the Fed and OCC downgraded their overall ratings of the company and its largest bank subsidiary from 2 (satisfactory) to 3 (less than satisfactory), reflecting weaknesses in risk management that were now apparent to the supervisors.

Both Fed and OCC officials cited the Gramm-Leach-Bliley Act of 1999 as an obstacle that prevented each from obtaining a complete understanding of the risks assumed by large financial firms such as Citigroup. The act made it more difficult— though not impossible—for regulators to look beyond the legal entities under their direct purview into other areas of a large firm. Citigroup, for example, had many regulators across the world; even the securitization businesses were dispersed across subsidiaries with different supervisors—including those from the Fed, OCC, SEC, OTS, and state agencies.

In May and June 2008, Citigroup entered into memoranda of understanding with both the New York Fed and OCC to resolve the risk management weaknesses that the events of 2007 had laid bare. In the ensuing months, Fed and OCC officials said, they were satisfied with Citigroup's compliance with their recommendations. Indeed, in speaking to the FCIC, Steve Manzari, the senior relationship manager for Citigroup at the New York Fed from April to September 2008, complimented Citigroup on its assertiveness in executing its regulators' requests: aggressively replacing management, raising capital from investors in late 2007, and putting in place a number of much needed "internal fixes." However, Manzari went on, "Citi was trapped in what was a pretty vicious . . . systemic event," and for regulators "it was time to come up with a new playbook."[53]

### Wachovia: "The Golden West acquisition was a mistake"

At Wachovia, which was supervised by the OCC as well as the OTS and the Federal Reserve, a 2007 end-of-year report showed that credit losses in its subsidiary Golden West's portfolio of "Pick-a-Pay" adjustable-rate mortgages, or option ARMs, were expected to rise to about 1% of the portfolio for 2008; in 2006, losses in this portfolio had been less than 0.1%. It would soon become clear that the higher estimate for 2008 was not high enough. The company would hike its estimate of the eventual losses on the portfolio to 9% by June and to 22% by September.

Facing these and other growing concerns, Wachovia raised additional capital. Then, in April, Wachovia announced a loss of $350 million for the first three months of the year. Depositors withdrew about $15 billion in the following weeks, and lenders reduced their exposure to the bank, shortening terms, increasing rates, and reducing loan amounts.[54] By June, according to Angus McBryde, then Wachovia's senior vice president for Treasury and Balance Sheet Management, management had launched a liquidity crisis management plan in anticipation of an even more adverse market reaction to second-quarter losses that would be announced in July.[55]

On June 2, Wachovia's board ousted CEO Ken Thompson after he had spent 32 years at the bank, 8 of them at its helm.[56] At the end of the month, the bank announced that it would stop originating Golden West's Pick-a-Pay products and would

waive all fees and prepayment penalties associated with them. On July 22, Wachovia reported an $8.9 billion second-quarter loss. The new CEO, Robert Steel, most recently an undersecretary of the treasury, announced a plan to improve the bank's financial condition: raise capital, cut the stock dividend, and lay off 10% to 12% of the staff.

The rating agencies and supervisors ignored those reassurances. On the same day as the announcement, S&P downgraded the bank, and the Fed, after years of "satisfactory" ratings, downgraded Wachovia to 3, or "less than satisfactory." The Fed noted that 2008 projections showed losses that could wipe out the recently raised capital: 2008 losses alone could exceed $3 billion, an amount that could cause a further ratings downgrade.[57] The Fed directed Wachovia to reevaluate and update its capital plans and its liquidity management. Despite having consistently rated Wachovia as "satisfactory" right up to the summer meltdown, the Fed now declared that many of Wachovia's problems were "long-term in nature and result[ed] from delayed investment decisions and a desire to have business lines operate autonomously."[58]

The Fed bluntly criticized the board and senior management for "an environment with inconsistent and inadequate identification, escalation and coverage of all risk-taking activities, including deficiencies in stress testing" and "little accountability for errors." Wachovia management had not completely understood the level of risk across the company, particularly in certain nonbank investments, and management had delayed fixing these known deficiencies. In addition, the company's board had not sufficiently questioned investment decisions.[59] Nonetheless, the Fed concluded that Wachovia's liquidity was currently adequate and that throughout the market disruption, management had minimized exposure to overnight funding markets.

On August 4, the OCC downgraded Wachovia Bank and assessed its overall risk profile as "high." The OCC noted many of the same issues as the Fed, and added particularly strong remarks about the acquisition of Golden West, identifying that mortgage portfolio and associated real estate foreclosures as the heart of Wachovia's problem. The OCC noted that the board had "acknowledged that the Golden West acquisition was a mistake."[60]

The OCC wrote that the market was focused on the company's weakened condition and that some large fund providers had already limited their exposure to Wachovia. Like the Fed, however, the OCC concluded that the bank's liquidity was adequate, unless events undermined market confidence.[61] And, like the Fed, the OCC approved of the new management and a new, more hands-on oversight role for the board of directors.

Yet Wachovia's problems would continue, and in the fall regulators would scramble to find a buyer for the troubled bank.

## Washington Mutual: "Management's persistent lack of progress"

Washington Mutual, often called WaMu, was the largest thrift in the country, with over $300 billion in assets at the end of 2007. At the time, $59 billion of the home loans on its balance sheet were option ARMs, two times its capital and reserves, with

concentrated exposure in California. The reason WaMu liked option ARMs was simple: in 2005, in combination with other nontraditional mortgages such as subprime loans, they had generated returns up to 8 times those on GSE mortgage–backed securities.[62] But that was then. WaMu was forced to write off $1.9 billion for the fourth quarter of 2007 and another $1.1 billion in the first quarter of 2008, mostly related to its portfolio of option ARMs.

In response to these losses, the Office of Thrift Supervision, WaMu's regulator, requested that the thrift address concerns about asset quality, earnings, and liquidity— issues that the OTS had raised in the past but that had not been reflected in supervisory ratings. "It has been hard for us to justify doing much more than constantly nagging (okay, 'chastising') through ROE [Reports of Examination] and meetings, since they have not really been adversely impacted in terms of losses,"[63] the OTS's lead examiner at the company had commented in a 2005 email. Indeed, the nontraditional mortgage portfolio had been performing very well through 2005 and 2006.

But with WaMu now taking losses, the OTS determined on February 27, 2008, that its condition required a downgrade in its rating from a 2 to a 3, or "less than satisfactory."[64] In March, the OTS advised that WaMu undertake "strategic initiatives"— that is, either find a buyer or raise new capital. In April, WaMu secured a $7 billion investment from a consortium led by the Texas Pacific Group, a private equity firm.[65]

But bad news continued for thrifts. On July 14, the OTS closed IndyMac Bank in Pasadena, California, making that company the largest-ever thrift to fail. On July 22, 2008, WaMu reported a $3.3 billion loss in the second quarter. WaMu's depositors withdrew $10 billion over the next two weeks.[66] And the Federal Home Loan Bank of San Francisco—which, as noted, had historically served with the other 11 Federal Home Loan Banks as an important source of funds for WaMu and others—began to limit WaMu's borrowing capacity. The OTS issued more downgrades in various assessment categories, while maintaining the overall rating at 3.

As the insurer of many of WaMu's deposits, the FDIC had a stake in WaMu's condition, and it was not as generous as the OTS in its assessment. It had already dropped WaMu's rating significantly in March 2008, indicating a "high level of concern."[67]

The FDIC expressly disagreed with the OTS's decision to maintain the 3 overall rating, recommending a 4 instead.[68] Ordinarily, 4 would have triggered a formal enforcement action, but none was forthcoming. In an August 2008 interview, William Isaac, who was chairman of the FDIC from 1981 until 1985, noted that the OTS and FDIC had competing interests. OTS, as primary regulator, "tends to want to see if they can rehabilitate the bank and doesn't want to act precipitously as a rule." On the other hand, "The FDIC's job is to handle the failures, and it—generally speaking— would rather be tougher . . . on the theory that the sooner the problems are resolved, the less expensive the cleanup will be."[69]

FDIC Chairman Sheila Bair underscored this tension, telling the FCIC that "our examiners, much earlier, were very concerned about the underwriting quality of WaMu's mortgage portfolio, and we were actively opposed by the OTS in terms of going in and letting our [FDIC] examiners do loan-level analysis."[70]

The Treasury's inspector general would later criticize OTS's supervision of Washington Mutual: "We concluded that OTS should have lowered WaMu's composite rating sooner and taken stronger enforcement action sooner to force WaMu's management to correct the problems identified by OTS. Specifically, given WaMu management's persistent lack of progress in correcting OTS-identified weaknesses, we believe OTS should have followed its own policies and taken formal enforcement action rather than informal enforcement action."[71]

## Regulators: "A lot of that pushback"

In these examples and others that the Commission studied, regulators either failed or were late to identify the mistakes and problems of commercial banks and thrifts or did not react strongly enough when they were identified. In part, this failure reflects the nature of bank examinations conducted during periods of apparent financial calm when institutions were reporting profits. In addition to their role as enforcers of regulation, regulators acted something like consultants, working with banks to assess the adequacy of their systems. This function was, to a degree, a reflection of the supervisors' "risk-focused" approach. The OCC *Large Bank Supervision Handbook* published in January 2010 explains, "Under this approach, examiners do not attempt to restrict risk-taking but rather determine whether banks identify, understand, and control the risks they assume."[72] As the crisis developed, bank regulators were slow to shift gears.

Senior supervisors told the FCIC it was difficult to express their concerns forcefully when financial institutions were generating record-level profits. The Fed's Roger Cole told the FCIC that supervisors did discuss issues such as whether banks were growing too fast and taking too much risk, but ran into pushback. "Frankly a lot of that pushback was given credence on the part of the firms by the fact that—like a Citigroup was earning $4 to $5 billion a quarter. And that is really hard for a supervisor to successfully challenge. When that kind of money is flowing out quarter after quarter after quarter, and their capital ratios are way above the minimums, it's very hard to challenge."[73]

Supervisors also told the FCIC that they feared aggravating a bank's already-existing problems. For the large banks, the issuance of a formal, public supervisory action taken under the federal banking statutes marked a severe regulatory assessment of the bank's risk practices, and it was rarely employed for banks that were determined to be going concerns. Richard Spillenkothen, the Fed's head of supervision until early 2006, attributed supervisory reluctance to "a belief that the traditional, nonpublic (behind-the-scenes) approach to supervision was less confrontational and more likely to induce bank management to cooperate; a desire not to inject an element of contentiousness into what was felt to be a constructive or equable relationship with management; and a fear that financial markets would overreact to public actions, possibly causing a run." Spillenkothen argued that these concerns were relevant but that "at times they can impede effective supervision and delay the implementation of needed corrective action. One of the lessons of this crisis . . . is that the working presumption should be earlier and stronger supervisory follow up."[74]

Douglas Roeder, the OCC's senior deputy comptroller for Large Bank Supervision from 2001 to 2010, said that the regulators were hampered by inadequate information from the banks but acknowledged that regulators did not do a good job of intervening at key points in the run-up to the crisis. He said that regulators, market participants, and others should have balanced their concerns about safety and soundness with the need to let markets work, noting, "We underestimated what systemic risk would be in the marketplace."[75]

Regulators also blame the complexity of the supervisory system in the United States. The patchwork quilt of regulators created opportunities for banks to shop for the most lenient regulator, and the presence of more than one supervisor at an organization. For example, a large firm like Citigroup could have the Fed supervising the bank holding company, the OCC supervising the national bank subsidiary, the SEC supervising the securities firm, and the OTS supervising the thrift subsidiary—creating the potential for both gaps in coverage and problematic overlap. Successive Treasury secretaries and Congressional leaders have proposed consolidation of the supervisors to simplify this system over the years. Notably, Secretary Henry Paulson released the "Blueprint for a Modernized Financial Regulatory Structure" on March 31, 2008, two weeks after the Bear rescue, in which he proposed getting rid of the thrift charter, creating a federal charter for insurance companies (now regulated only by the states), and merging the SEC and CFTC. The proposals did not move forward in 2008.[76]

---

## COMMISSION CONCLUSIONS ON CHAPTER 16

The Commission concludes that the banking supervisors failed to adequately and proactively identify and police the weaknesses of the banks and thrifts or their poor corporate governance and risk management, often maintaining satisfactory ratings on institutions until just before their collapse. This failure was caused by many factors, including beliefs that regulation was unduly burdensome, that financial institutions were capable of self-regulation, and that regulators should not interfere with activities reported as profitable.

Large commercial banks and thrifts, such as Wachovia and IndyMac, that had significant exposure to risky mortgage assets were subject to runs by creditors and depositors.

The Federal Reserve realized far too late the systemic danger inherent in the interconnections of the unregulated over-the-counter (OTC) derivatives market and did not have the information needed to act.

# 17

# SEPTEMBER 2008: THE TAKEOVER
# OF FANNIE MAE AND FREDDIE MAC

## CONTENTS

From the fall of 2007 until Fannie Mae and Freddie Mac were placed into conservatorship on September 7, 2008, government officials struggled to strike the right balance between the safety and soundness of the two government-sponsored enterprises and their mission to support the mortgage market. The task was critical because the mortgage market was quickly weakening—home prices were declining, loan delinquencies were rising, and, as a result, the values of mortgage securities were plummeting. Lenders were more willing to refinance borrowers into affordable mortgages if these government-sponsored enterprises (GSEs) would purchase the new loans. If the GSEs bought more loans, that would stabilize the market, but it would also leave the GSEs with more risk on their already-strained balance sheets.

The GSEs were highly leveraged—owning and guaranteeing $5.3 trillion of mortgages with capital of less than 2%. When interviewed by the FCIC, former Treasury Secretary Henry Paulson acknowledged that after he was briefed on the GSEs upon taking office in June 2006, he believed that they were "a disaster waiting to happen" and that one key problem was the legal definition of capital, which their regulator lacked discretion to adjust; indeed, he said that some people referred to it as "bullsh*t capital."[1] Still, the GSEs kept buying more of the riskier mortgage loans and securities, which by fall 2007 constituted multiples of their reported capital. The GSEs

reported billions of dollars of net losses on these loans and securities, beginning in the third quarter of 2007.

But many in Treasury believed the country needed the GSEs to provide liquidity to the mortgage market by purchasing and guaranteeing loans and securities at a time when no one else would. Paulson told the FCIC that after the housing market dried up in the summer of 2007, the key to getting through the crisis was to limit the decline in housing, prevent foreclosures, and ensure continued mortgage funding, all of which required that the GSEs remain viable.[2] However, there were constraints on how many loans the GSEs could fund; they and their regulators had agreed to portfolio caps—limits on the loans and securities they could hold on their books—and a 30% capital surplus requirement.

So, even as each company reported billions of dollars in losses in 2007 and 2008, their regulator, the Office of Federal Housing Enterprise Oversight (OFHEO), loosened those constraints. "From the fall of 2007, to the conservatorships, it was a tightrope with no safety net," former OFHEO Director James Lockhart testified to the FCIC.[3] Unfortunately, the balancing act ultimately failed and both companies were placed into conservatorship, costing the U.S. taxpayers $151 billion—so far.

## "A GOOD TIME TO BUY"

In an August 1, 2007, letter to Lockhart, Fannie Mae CEO Daniel Mudd sought immediate relief from the portfolio caps required by the consent agreement executed in May 2006 following Fannie's accounting scandal. "We have witnessed growing evidence of turmoil in virtually all sectors of the housing finance market," Mudd wrote, and "the immediate crisis in subprime is indicative of a serious liquidity event impacting the entire credit market, not just subprime."[4] As demand for purchasing loans dried up, large lenders like Countrywide kept loans that they normally securitized, and smaller lenders went under. A number of firms told Fannie that they would stop making loans if Fannie would not buy them.

Mudd argued that a relaxed cap would let his company provide that liquidity. "A moderate, 10 percent increase in the Fannie Mae portfolio cap would provide us with flexibility . . . and send a strong signal to the market that the GSEs are able to address liquidity events before they become crises." He maintained that the consent agreement allowed OFHEO to lift the cap to address "market liquidity issues." Moreover, the company had largely corrected its accounting and internal control deficiencies—the primary condition for removing the cap. Finally, he stressed that the GSEs' charter required Fannie to provide liquidity and stability to the market. "Ultimately," Mudd concluded, "this request is about restoring market confidence that the GSEs can fulfill their stabilizing role in housing."[5]

Fannie Mae executives also saw an opportunity to make money. Because there was less competition, the GSEs could charge higher fees for guaranteeing securities and pay less for loans and securities they wanted to own, enabling them (in theory) to increase returns.[6] Tom Lund, a longtime Fannie Mae executive who led the firm's single-family business, told the FCIC that the market moved in Fannie Mae's favor af-

ter August 2007 as competitors dropped out and prices of loans and securities fell. Lund told FCIC staff that after the 2007 liquidity shock, Fannie had "more comfort that the relationship between risk and price was correct."[7] Robert Levin, the company's chief business officer, recalled, "It was a good time to buy."[8]

On August 10, OFHEO's Lockhart notified Fannie that increasing the portfolio cap would be "premature" but the regulator would keep the request under "active consideration." Lockhart wrote that he would not authorize changes, because Fannie could still guarantee mortgages even if it couldn't buy them and because Fannie remained a "significant supervisory concern." In addition, Lockhart noted that Fannie could not prudently address the problems in the subprime and Alt-A mortgage market, and the company's charter did not permit it to address problems in the market for jumbo loans (mortgages larger than the GSEs' loan limit).[9] Although there had been progress in dealing with the accounting and internal control deficiencies, he observed, much work remained. Fannie still had not filed financial statements for 2006 or 2007, "a particularly troubling issue in unsettled markets."[10]

As Lockhart testified to the FCIC, "It became clear by August 2007 that the turmoil was too big for the Enterprises [the GSEs] to solve in a safe and sound manner." He was worried that fewer controls would mean more losses. "They were fulfilling their mission," Lockhart told the FCIC, "but they had no power to do more in a safe and sound manner. If their mission is to provide stability and lessen market turmoil, there was nothing in their capital structure" that would allow them to do so.[11]

Lockhart had worried about the financial stability of the two GSEs and about OFHEO's ability to regulate the behemoths from the day he became director in May 2006, and he advocated for more regulatory powers for his largely toothless agency. Lockhart pushed for the power to increase capital requirements and to limit growth, and he sought authority over mission goals set by the Department of Housing and Urban Development, as well as litigation authority independent of the Department of Justice. His shopping list also included the authority to put Fannie and Freddie into receivership, a power held by bank regulators over banks, and to liquidate the GSEs if necessary. As it stood, OFHEO had the authority to place the GSEs in conservatorship—in effect, to force a government takeover—but because it lacked funding to operate the GSEs as conservator, that authority was impracticable. The GSEs would deteriorate even further before Lockhart secured the powers he sought.[12]

## "THE ONLY GAME IN TOWN"

But Fannie and Freddie were "the only game in town" once the housing market dried up in the summer of 2007, Paulson told the FCIC. And by the spring of 2008, "[the GSEs,] more than anyone, were the engine we needed to get through the problem."[13]

Few doubted Fannie and Freddie were needed to support the struggling housing market. The question was how to do so safely.[14] Purchasing and guaranteeing risky mortgage-backed securities helped make money available for borrowers, but it could also result in further losses for the two huge companies later on. "There's a real trade-off," Lockhart said in late 2007—a trade-off made all the more difficult by the state of

the GSEs' balance sheets.[15] The value of risky loans and securities was swamping their reported capital. By the end of 2007, guaranteed and portfolio mortgages with FICO scores less than 660 exceeded reported capital at Fannie Mae by more than seven to one; Alt-A loans and securities, by more than six to one. Loans for which borrowers did not provide full documentation amounted to more than ten times reported capital.[16]

In mid-September, OFHEO relented and marginally loosened the GSEs' portfolio cap, from about $728 billion to $735 billion. It allowed Fannie to increase the amount of mortgage loans and securities it owned by 2% per year—a power that Freddie already had under its agreement with OFHEO. OFHEO ruled out more dramatic increases "because the remediation process is not yet finished, many safety and soundness issues are not yet resolved, and the criteria in the Fannie Mae consent agreement and Freddie Mac's voluntary agreement have not been met."[17]

As the year progressed, Fannie and Freddie became increasingly important to the mortgage market. By the fourth quarter of 2007, they were purchasing 75% of new mortgages, nearly twice the 2006 level. With $5 trillion in mortgages resting on razor-thin capital, the GSEs were doomed if the market did not stabilize. According to Lockhart, "a withdrawal by Freddie Mac and Fannie Mae or even a drop in confidence in the Enterprises would have created a self-fulfilling credit crisis."[18]

In early October, Senator Charles Schumer and Representative Barney Frank introduced similar bills to temporarily lift portfolio limits on the GSEs by 10 percent, or approximately $150 billion, most of which would be designated for refinancing subprime loans. The measures, which Federal Reserve Chairman Ben Bernanke called "ill advised," were not enacted.[19]

In November, Fannie and Freddie reported third-quarter losses of $1.5 billion and $2 billion, respectively. At the end of December 2007, Fannie reported that it had $44 billion of capital to absorb potential losses on $879 billion of assets and $2.2 trillion of guarantees on mortgage-backed securities; if losses exceeded 1.45%, it would be insolvent. Freddie would be insolvent if losses exceeded 1.7%. Moreover, there were serious questions about the validity of their "reported" capital.

## "IT'S A TIME GAME . . . BE COOL"

In the first quarter, real gross domestic product fell 0.7% at an annual rate, reflecting in part the first decline in consumer spending since the early 1990s. The unemployment rate averaged 5% in the first three months of 2008, up from a low of 4.4% in spring of 2007. As the Fed continued to cut interest rates, the economy was sinking further into recession. In February, Congress passed the Economic Stimulus Act, which raised the limits on the size of mortgages that Fannie and Freddie could purchase, among other measures.

The push to get OFHEO to loosen requirements on the GSEs also continued. Schumer pressed OFHEO to justify or lower the 30% capital surcharge; such a stringent requirement, he wrote Lockhart on February 25, hampered Fannie's ability to provide financing to homeowners.[20]

Two days later, Fannie CEO Mudd reported losses in the fourth quarter of 2007, acknowledging that Fannie was "working through the toughest housing and mortgage markets in a generation."[21] The company had issued $7.8 billion of preferred stock, had completed all 81 requirements of the consent agreement with OFHEO, and was discussing with OFHEO the possibility of reducing the 30% capital surplus requirement. The next day, Freddie also reported losses and said the company had raised $6 billion of preferred stock.

As both companies had filed current financial statements by this time, fulfilling a condition of lifting the restrictions imposed by the consent agreements, Lockhart announced that OFHEO would remove the portfolio caps on March 1, 2008. He also said OFHEO would consider gradually lowering the 30% capital surplus requirement, because both companies had made progress in satisfying their consent agreements and had recently raised capital through preferred stock offerings. Mudd told the FCIC that he sought relief from the capital surplus requirement because he did not want to face further regulatory discipline if Fannie fell short of required capital levels.[22]

On February 28, 2008, the day after OFHEO lifted the growth limits, a New York Fed analyst noted to Treasury that the 30% capital surcharge was a constraint that prevented the GSEs from providing additional liquidity to the secondary mortgage market.[23]

Calls to ease the surcharge also came from the marketplace. Mike Farrell, the CEO of Annaly Capital Management, warned Treasury Undersecretary Robert Steel that a crisis loomed in the credit markets that only the GSEs could solve. "We believe that we are nearing a tipping point; . . . lack of transparency on pricing for virtually every asset class" and "a dearth of buyers" foreshadowed worse news, Farrell wrote. Removing the capital surcharge and passing legislation to overhaul the GSEs would make it possible for them to provide more stability, he said. Farrell recognized that the GSEs might believe their return on capital would be insufficient, but contended that "they will have to get past that and focus on fulfilling their charters," because "the big picture is that right now whatever is best for the economy and the financial security of America trumps the ROI [return on investment] for Fannie and Freddie shareholders."[24]

Days before Bear Stearns collapsed, Steel reported to Mudd that he had "encouraging" conversations with Senator Richard Shelby, the ranking member of the Senate Committee on Banking, Housing, and Urban Affairs, and Representative Frank, chairman of the House Financial Services Committee, about the possibility of GSE reform legislation and capital relief for the GSEs. He intended to speak with Senate Banking Committee Chairman Christopher Dodd. Confident that the government desperately needed the GSEs to back up the mortgage market, Mudd proposed an "easier trade." If regulators would eliminate the surcharge, Fannie Mae would agree to raise new capital.[25] In a March 7 email to Fannie chief business officer Levin, Mudd suggested that the 30% capital surplus requirement might be reduced without any trade: "It's a time game . . . whether they need us more . . . or if we hit the capital wall first. Be cool."[26]

On the next day, March 8, Treasury and White House officials received additional information about Fannie's condition. The White House economist Jason Thomas sent Steel an email enclosing an alarming analysis: it claimed that in reporting its 2007 financial results, Fannie was masking its insolvency through fraudulent accounting practices. The analysis, which resembled one offered in a March 10 *Barron's* article, stated:

> Any realistic assessment of Fannie Mae's capital position would show the company is currently insolvent. Accounting fraud has resulted in several asset categories (non-agency securities, deferred tax assets, low-income partnership investment) being overstated, while the guarantee obligation liability is understated. These accounting shenanigans add up to tens of billions of exaggerated net worth.
>
> Yet, the impact of a tsunami of mortgage defaults has yet to run through Fannie's income statement and further annihilate its capital. Such grim results are a logical consequence of Fannie's dual mandate to serve the housing market while maximizing shareholder returns. In trying to do both, Fannie has done neither well. With shareholder capital depleted, a government seizure of the company is inevitable.[27]

Given the turmoil of the Bear Stearns crisis, Paulson said he wanted to increase confidence in the mortgage market by having Fannie and Freddie raise capital. Steel told him that Treasury, OFHEO, and the Fed were preparing plans to relax the GSEs' capital surcharges in exchange for assurances that the companies would raise capital.

On March 16, 2008, Steel also reported to his Treasury colleagues that William Dudley, then executive vice president of the New York Fed, wanted to "harden" the implicit government guarantee of Freddie and Fannie. Steel wrote that Dudley "leaned on me hard" to make the guarantee explicit in conjunction with dialing back the surcharge and attempting to raise new capital, and Steel worried about how this might affect the federal government's balance sheet: "I do not like that and it has not been part of my conversation with anyone else. I view that as a very significant move, way above my pay grade to double the size of the U.S. debt in one fell swoop."[28]

## "THE IDEA STRIKES ME AS PERVERSE"

Regulators at OFHEO and the Treasury huddled with GSE executives to discuss lowering capital requirements if the GSEs would raise more capital. "The entire mortgage market was at risk," Lockhart told the FCIC.[29] The pushing and tugging continued. Paulson told the FCIC that personal commitments from Mudd and Freddie Mac CEO Richard Syron to raise capital cinched the deal.[30] Just days earlier, on March 13, Syron had announced in a quarterly call to investors that his company would not raise new capital. Fannie and Freddie executives prepared a draft press release before a discussion with Lockhart and Steel. It announced a reduction in the capital surcharge from 30% to 20%. Lockhart was not pleased; the draft lacked a com-

mitment to raise additional capital, stating instead that the GSEs planned to raise it "over time as needed."[31] It looked as if the GSEs were making the deal with their fingers crossed. In an email to Steel and the CEOs of both entities, Lockhart wrote: "The idea strikes me as perverse, and I assume it would seem perverse to the markets that a regulator would agree to allow a regulatee to increase its very high mortgage credit risk leverage (not to mention increasing interest rate risk) without any new capital." The initial negotiations had the GSEs raising $2 of capital for each $1 of reduction in the surplus. Lockhart wrote in frustration, "We seem to have gone from 2 to 1 right through 1 to 1 to now 0 to 1."[32]

Despite Lockhart's reservations, OFHEO announced the deal, unaltered in any material way, on March 19. OFHEO agreed to ease the capital restraint from 30% to 20%; Fannie and Freddie pledged to "begin the process to raise significant capital," giving no concrete commitment.[33] Paulson told the FCIC that the agreement, which included a promise to raise capital, was "a no-brainer," and that he had no memory of Lockhart ever having called it "perverse."[34]

The market analyst Joshua Rosner panned the deal. "We view any reduction [in capital] as a comment not only on the GSEs but on the burgeoning panic in Washington," he wrote. "If this action results in the destabilizing of the GSEs, OFHEO will go from being the only regulator that prevented its charges from getting into trouble, to a textbook example of why regulators should be shielded from outside political pressure."[35]

Fannie would keep its promise by raising $7.4 billion in preferred stock. Freddie reneged. Executive Vice President Donald Bisenius offered two reasons why, in hindsight, Fannie Mae did not raise additional capital. First was protecting the assets of existing shareholders. "I'm sure [Fannie's] investors are not very happy," Bisenius told the FCIC. "Part two is . . . if you actually fundamentally believe you have enough capital to withstand even a fairly significant downturn in house prices, you wouldn't raise capital."[36]

Similarly, CEO Syron spoke of the downside of raising capital on August 6, 2008: "Raising a lot more capital at these kinds of prices could be quite dilutive to our shareholders, so we have to balance the interest of our shareholders."[37] But Lockhart saw it differently; in his view, Syron's public comments put "a good face on Freddie's inability to raise capital." He speculated that Syron was masking a different concern: lawsuits. "[Syron] was getting advice from his attorneys about the high risk of raising capital before releasing [quarterly earnings] . . . and our lawyers could not disagree because we know about their accounting issues," Lockhart told the FCIC.[38]

## "IT WILL INCREASE CONFIDENCE"

In May, the two companies announced further losses in the first quarter. Even as the situation deteriorated, on June 9 OFHEO rewarded Fannie Mae for raising $7.4 billion in new capital by further lowering the capital surcharge, from 20% to 15%. In June, Fannie's stock fell 28%; Freddie's, 34%. The price of protection on $10 million in Fannie's debt through credit default swaps jumped to $66,000 in June, up from

$47,700 in May; between 2004 and 2006, it had typically been about $13,000. In August, they both reported more losses for the second quarter.

Even after both Fannie and Freddie became public companies owned by shareholders, they had continued to possess an asset that is hard to quantify: the implicit full faith and credit of the U.S. government. The government worried that it could not let the $5.3 trillion GSEs fail, because they were the only source of liquidity in the mortgage market and because their failure would cause losses to owners of their debt and their guaranteed mortgage securities. Uncle Sam had rescued GSEs before. It bailed out Fannie when double-digit inflation wrecked its balance sheet in the early 1980s, and it came through in the mid-1980s for another GSE in duress, the Farm Credit System. In the mid-1990s, even a GSE-type organization, the Financing Corporation, was given a helping hand.

As the market grappled with the fundamental question of whether Fannie and Freddie would be backed by the government, the yield on the GSEs' long-term bonds rose. The difference between the rate that the GSEs paid on their debt and rates on Treasuries—a premium that reflects investors' assessment of risk—widened in 2007 to one-half a percentage point. That was low compared with the same figure for other publicly traded companies, but high for the ultra-safe GSEs. By June 2008, the spread had risen 65% over the 2007 level; by September 5, just before regulators parachuted in, the spread had nearly doubled from its 2007 level to just under 1%, making it more difficult and costly for the GSEs to fund their operations. On the other hand, the prices of Fannie Mae mortgage–backed securities actually increased slightly over this time period, while the prices of private-label mortgage–backed securities dramatically declined. For example, the price of the FNCI7 index—an index of Fannie mortgage–backed securities with an average coupon of 7%—increased from 102 in January 2007 to 103 on September 5, 2008, two days prior to the conservatorship. As another example, the price of the FNCI5 index—Fannie securities with an average coupon of 5%—increased from 95 to 96 during the same time period.

In July and August 2008, Fannie suffered a liquidity squeeze, because it was unable to borrow against its own securities to raise sufficient cash in the repo market. Its stock price dove to less than $7 a share. Fannie asked the Fed for help.[39] A senior adviser in the Federal Reserve Board's Division of Banking Supervision and Regulation gave the FCIC a bleak account of the situation at the two GSEs and noted that "liquidity was just becoming so essential, so the Federal Reserve agreed to help provide it."[40]

On July 13, the Federal Reserve Board in Washington authorized the New York Fed to extend emergency loans to the GSEs "should such lending prove necessary . . . to promote the availability of home mortgage credit during a period of stress in financial markets."[41] Fannie and Freddie would never tap the Fed for that funding.[42]

Also on July 13, Treasury laid out a three-part legislative plan to strengthen the GSEs by temporarily increasing their lines of credit with the Treasury, authorizing Treasury to inject capital into the GSEs, and replacing OFHEO with the new Federal Housing Finance Agency (FHFA), with the power to place the GSEs into receivership. Paulson told the Senate that regulators needed "a bazooka" at their disposal.

"You are not likely to take it out," Paulson told legislators. "I just say that by having something that is unspecified, it will increase confidence. And by increasing confidence it will greatly reduce the likelihood it will ever be used."[43] Fannie's Mudd and Freddie's Syron praised the plan.[44]

At the end of July, Congress passed the Housing and Economic Recovery Act (HERA) of 2008, giving Paulson his bazooka—the ability to extend secured lines of credit to the GSEs, to purchase their mortgage securities, and to inject capital. The 261-page bill also strengthened regulation of the GSEs by creating FHFA, an independent federal agency, as their primary regulator, with expanded authority over Fannie's and Freddie's portfolios, capital levels, and compensation. In addition, the bill raised the federal debt ceiling by $800 billion to $10.6 trillion, providing funds to operate the GSEs if they were placed into conservatorship.

After the Federal Reserve Board consented in mid-July to furnish emergency loans, Fed staff and representatives of the Office of the Comptroller of the Currency (OCC), along with Morgan Stanley, which acted as an adviser to Treasury, initiated a review of the GSEs. Timothy Clark, who oversaw the weeklong review for the Fed, told the FCIC that it was the first time they ever had access to information from the GSEs. He said that previously, "The GSEs [saw] the Fed as public enemy number one. . . . There was a battle between us and them." Clark added, "We would deal with OFHEO, which was also very guarded. So we did not have access to info until they wanted funding from us."[45] Although Fed and OCC personnel were at the GSEs and conferring with executives, Mudd told the FCIC that he did not know of the agencies' involvement until their enterprises were both in conservatorship.[46]

The Fed and the OCC discovered that the problems were worse than their suspicions and reports from FHFA had led them to believe. According to Clark, the Fed found that the GSEs were significantly "underreserved," with huge potential losses, and their operations were "unsafe and unsound."[47] The OCC rejected the forecasting methodologies on which Fannie and Freddie relied. Using its own metrics, it found insufficient reserves for future losses and identified significant problems in credit and risk management. Kevin Bailey, the OCC deputy comptroller for regulatory policy, told the FCIC that Fannie's loan loss forecasting was problematic, and that its loan losses therefore were understated. He added that Fannie had overvalued its deferred tax assets—because without future profits, deferred tax assets had no value.[48]

Loss projections calculated by Morgan Stanley substantiated the Fed's and OCC's findings. Morgan Stanley concluded that Fannie's loss projection methodology was flawed, and resulted in the company substantially understating losses. Nearly all of the loss projections calculated by Morgan Stanley showed that Fannie would fall below its regulatory capital requirement. Fannie's projections did not.

All told, the litany of understatements and shortfalls led the OCC's Bailey to a firm conclusion. If the GSEs were not insolvent at the time, they were "almost there," he told the FCIC.[49] Regulators also learned that Fannie was not charging off loans until they were delinquent for two years, a head-in-the-sand approach. Banks are required to charge off loans once they are 180 days delinquent. For these and numerous other errors and flawed methodologies, Fannie and Freddie earned rebukes. "Given

the role of the GSEs and their market dominance," the OCC report said, "they should be industry leaders with respect to effective and proactive risk management, produc- tive analysis, and comprehensive reporting. Instead they appear to significantly lag the industry in all respects."[50]

## "CRITICAL UNSAFE AND UNSOUND PRACTICES"

Paulson told the FCIC that although he learned of the Fed and OCC findings by August 15, it took him three weeks to convince Lockhart and FHFA that there was a capital shortfall, that the GSEs were not viable, and that they should be placed under government control.[51] On August 22, FHFA informed both Mudd and Syron that their firms were "adequately capitalized" under the regulations, a judgment based on financial information that was "certified and represented as true and correct by [GSE] management." But FHFA also emphasized that it was "seriously concerned about the current level of Fannie Mae's capital" if the housing market decline continued.[52]

Fannie's prospects for increasing capital grew gloomier. Fannie informed Treasury on August 25—and repeatedly told FHFA—that raising capital was infeasible and that the company was expecting additional losses. Even Fannie's "base-case earnings forecast" pointed to substantial pressure on solvency, and a "stressed" forecast indicated that "capital resources will continue to decline."[53]

By September 4, Lockhart and FHFA agreed with Treasury that the GSEs needed to be placed into conservatorship. That day, Syron and Mudd received blistering midyear reviews from FHFA. The opening paragraph of each letter informed the CEOs that their companies had been downgraded to "critical concerns," and that "the critical unsafe and unsound practices and conditions that gave rise to the Enterprise's existing condition, the deterioration in overall asset quality and significant earnings losses experienced through June 2008, as well as forecasted future losses, likely require recapitalization of the Enterprise."[54] A bad situation was expected to worsen.

The 21-page report sent to Fannie identified sweeping concerns, including failures by the board and senior management, a significant drop in the quality of mortgages and securities owned or guaranteed by the GSE, insufficient reserves, the almost exclusive reliance on short-term funding, and the inability to raise additional capital. FHFA admonished management and the board for their "imprudent decisions" to "purchase or guarantee higher risk mortgage products." The letter faulted Fannie for purchasing high-risk loans to "increase market share, raise revenue and meet housing goals," and for attempting to increase market share by competing with Wall Street firms that purchased lower-quality securities. FHFA, noting "a conflict between prudent credit risk management and corporate business objectives," found that these purchases of higher-risk loans were predicated on the relaxing of underwriting and eligibility standards. Using models that underestimated this risk, the GSE then charged fees even lower than what its own deficient models suggested were appropriate. FHFA determined that these lower fees were charged because "focus was improperly placed on market share and competing with Wall Street and [Freddie Mac]."[55]

Even after internal reports pointed to market problems, Fannie kept buying and guaranteeing riskier loan products, FHFA said. "Despite signs in the latter half of 2006 and 2007 of emerging problems, management continued activity in risky programs, and maintained its higher eligibility program for Alt-A loans without establishing limits."[56] The company also bought private-label securities backed by Alt-A and subprime loans.[57] Losses were likely to be higher than the GSEs had estimated, FHFA found.

FHFA also noted "increasing questions and concerns" regarding Fannie's accounting. The models it used to forecast losses had not been independently validated or updated for several years. FHFA judged that in an up-to-date model, estimated losses would likely show a "material increase." In addition, Fannie had overvalued its deferred tax assets. Applying more reasonable projections of future performance, FHFA found this benefit to be significantly overstated.[58]

The 22-page report delivered to Freddie included similarly harsh assessments of that GSE's safety and soundness, but more severe criticisms of its management and board. In particular, the report noted a significant lack of market confidence, which had "eliminated the ability to raise capital." FHFA, for its part, "lost confidence in the Board of Directors and the executive management team," holding them accountable for losses stemming from "a series of ill-advised and poorly executed decisions and other serious misjudgments." According to the regulator, they therefore could not be relied on, particularly in light of their widespread failures to resolve regulatory issues and address criticisms. In addition, FHFA said that Freddie's failure to raise capital despite its assurances "invite[d]" the conclusion that the board and CEO had not negotiated "in good faith" about the capital surcharge reduction.[59]

As in its assessment of Fannie, FHFA found that Freddie's unsafe and unsound practices included the purchase and guarantee of higher-risk loan products in 2006 and 2007 in a declining market. Even after being told by the regulator in 2006 that its purchases of subprime private-label securities had outpaced its risk management abilities, Freddie bought $22 billion of subprime securities in each subsequent quarter.

FHFA also found that "aggressive" accounting cast doubt on Freddie's reported earnings and capital. Despite "clear signals" that losses on mortgage assets were likely, Freddie waited to record write-downs until the regulator threatened to issue a cease and desist order. Even then, one write-down was reversed "just prior to the issuance of the second quarter financial statements." The regulator concluded that rising delinquencies and credit losses would "result in a substantial dissipation of earnings and capital."[60]

## "THEY WENT FROM ZERO
## TO THREE WITH NO WARNING IN BETWEEN"

Mudd told the FCIC that its regulator had never before communicated the kind of criticisms leveled in the September 4 letter. He said the regulator's "chronicling of the situation" then was "inconsistent with what you would consider better regulatory practice to be—like, first warning: fix it; second warning: fix it; third warning: you're

out of here. Instead, they went from zero to three with no warning in between."[61] A review of the examination reports and other documents provided by FHFA to the FCIC largely supports Mudd's view on this specific point. While OFHEO's examination reports noted concerns about increasing credit risk and slow remediation of deficiencies required by the May 2006 consent agreement, they do not include the sweeping criticisms contained in the September 4 letter.

Two days after their two companies were designated "critical concerns," Mudd at Fannie and Syron at Freddie faced a government takeover. On September 6, FHFA Acting Deputy Director Chris Dickerson sent separate memos to Lockhart recommending that FHFA be appointed conservator for each GSE.[62]

Still, conservatorship was not a foregone conclusion. Paulson, Lockhart, and Bernanke met with Mudd, Syron, and their boards to persuade them to cede control.[63] Essentially the GSEs faced a Hobson's choice: take the horse offered or none at all. "They had to voluntarily agree to a consent agreement," Lockhart told the FCIC. The alternative, a hostile action, invited trouble and "nasty lawsuits," he noted. "So we made a . . . very strong case so the board of directors did not have a choice."[64] Paulson reminded the GSEs that he had authority to inject capital, but he would not do so unless they were in conservatorship.[65]

Mudd was "stunned and angry," according to Paulson.[66] Tom Lund, who ran Fannie Mae's single-family business, told the FCIC that conservatorship came as a surprise to everyone.[67] Levin told the FCIC that he never saw a government seizure coming. He never imagined, he said, that Fannie Mae was or might become insolvent.[68] Interviewed in 2010, Mudd told the FCIC: "I did not think in any way it was fair for the government to have been in a position of being in the chorus for the company to add capital, and then to inject itself in the capital structure."[69] The conservatorship memoranda reiterated all the damning evidence presented in the letters two days earlier. Losses at Fannie Mae for the year were estimated to be between $18 billion and $50 billion.[70] Freddie Mac's memorandum differed only in the details. Its losses, recorded at $1 billion in the first six months of 2008, were projected to end up between $11 and $32 billion by the end of the year.[71]

Although the boards had a choice, the only realistic option was assent. "We were going to agree to go in a conservatorship anyway," Syron told the FCIC. "There was a very clear message that the [September 4] letter was there as a mechanism to bring about a result."[72] Mudd agreed, observing that "the purpose of the letter was really to force conservatorship."[73] The boards of both companies voted to accept conservatorship.

Both CEOs were ousted, but the fundamental problems persisted. As promised, the Treasury was prepared to take two direct steps to support solvency. First, it would buy up to $200 billion of senior preferred stock from the GSEs and extend them short-term secured loans. In addition, it pledged to buy GSE mortgage–backed securities from Wall Street firms and others until the end of 2009. Up front, Treasury bought from each GSE $1 billion in preferred stock with a 10% dividend. Each GSE also gave Treasury warrants to purchase common stock representing 79.9% of shares outstanding. Existing common and preferred shareholders were effectively wiped out. The decline in value of the preferred stock caused losses at many banks that held

these securities, contributing to the failure of 10 institutions and to the downgrading of 35 to less than "well capitalized" by their regulators.[74]

Paulson told the FCIC that he was "naive" enough to believe that the action would halt the crisis because it "would put a floor under the housing market decline, and provide confidence to the market." He realized he was wrong on the next day, when, as he told the FCIC, "Lehman started to go."[75] Former Treasury Assistant Secretary Neel Kashkari agreed. "We thought that after we stabilized Fannie and Freddie that we bought ourselves some time. Maybe a month, maybe three months. But they were such profound interventions, stabilizing such a huge part of the financial markets, that would buy us some time. We were surprised that Lehman then happened a week later, that Lehman had to be taken over or it would go into bankruptcy."[76]

The firms' failure was a huge event and increased the magnitude of the crisis, according to Fed Governor Kevin Warsh and New York Fed General Counsel Tom Baxter.[77] Warsh also told the FCIC that the events surrounding the GSE takeover led to "a massive, underreported, underappreciated jolt to the system." Then, according to Warsh, when the market grasped that it had misunderstood the risks associated with the GSEs, and that the government could have conceivably let them fail, it "caused investors to panic about the value of every asset, to reassess every portfolio."[78]

FHFA Director Lockhart described the decision to put the GSEs into conservatorship in the context of Lehman's failure. Given that the investment bank's balance sheet was about one-fifth the size of Fannie Mae's, he felt that the fallout from Lehman's bankruptcy would have paled in comparison to a GSE failure. He said, "What happened after Lehman would have been very small compared to these $5.5 trillion institutions failing."[79] Major holders of GSE securities included the Chinese and Russian central banks, which, between them, owned more than half a trillion dollars of these securities, and U.S. financial firms and investment funds had even more extensive holdings. A 2005 Fed study concluded that U.S. banks owned more than $1 trillion in GSE debt and securities—more than 150% of the banks' Tier 1 capital and 11% of their total assets at the time.[80]

Testifying before the FCIC, Mudd claimed that failure was all but inevitable. "In 2008, the companies had no refuge from the twin shocks of a housing crisis followed by a financial crisis," he said. "A monoline GSE structure asked to perform multiple tasks cannot withstand a multiyear 30% home price decline on a national scale, even without the accompanying global financial turmoil. The model allowed a balance of business and mission when home prices were rising. When prices crashed far beyond the realm of historical experience, it became 'The Pit and the Pendulum,' a choice between horrible alternatives."[81]

## "THE WORST-RUN FINANCIAL INSTITUTION"

When interviewed by the FCIC, FHFA officials were very critical of Fannie's management. John Kerr, the FHFA examiner (and an OCC veteran) in charge of Fannie examinations, minced no words. He labeled Fannie "the worst-run financial institution" he had seen in his 30 years as a bank regulator. Scott Smith, who became

associate director at FHFA after that agency replaced OFHEO, concurred; in his view, Fannie's forecasting capabilities were not particularly well thought out, and lacked a variety of stress scenarios. Both officials noted Fannie's weak forecasting models, which included hundreds of market simulations but scarcely any that contemplated declines in house prices. To Austin Kelly, an OFHEO examination specialist, there was no relying on Fannie's numbers, because their "processes were a bowl of spaghetti." Kerr and a colleague said that that they were struck that Fannie Mae, a multitrillion-dollar company, employed unsophisticated technology: it was less tech-savvy than the average community bank.[82]

Nonetheless, OFHEO's communications with Fannie prior to September 4 did not fully reflect these criticisms. FHFA officials conceded that they had made mistakes in their oversight of Fannie and Freddie. They paid too much attention to fixing operational problems and did not react to Fannie's increasing credit risk. Lockhart told the FCIC that more resources should have been dedicated to assessing credit risk of their mortgage assets and guarantees.[83] Current FHFA Acting Director Edward DeMarco told the FCIC that it would not pass the "reasonable person test" to deny that OFHEO took its eye off the ball by not paying sufficient attention to credit risk and instead focused on operational risk, accounting and lack of audited results.[84]

To Mudd and others, OFHEO's mistakes were not surprising. Mudd told the FCIC that the regulators' skill levels were "developing but below average."[85] Henry Cisneros, a former housing and urban development secretary, expressed a similar view. "OFHEO," Cisneros told the FCIC, "was puny compared to what Fannie Mae and Freddie Mac could muster in their intelligence, their Ivy League educations, their rocket scientists in their place, their lobbyists, their ability to work the Hill."[86]

The costs of the bailouts have been enormous and are expected to increase. From January 1, 2008, through the third quarter of 2010, the two companies lost $229 billion, wiping out $71 billion of combined capital that they had reported at the end of 2007 and the $7 billion of capital raised by Fannie in 2008. Treasury narrowed the gap with $151 billion in support. FHFA has estimated that costs through 2013 will range from $221 billion to $363 billion. The Congressional Budget Office has projected that the economic cost of the GSEs' downfall, including the total financial cost of government support as well as actual dollar outlays, could reach $389 billion by 2019.

## "WASN'T DONE AT MY PAY GRADE"

Fannie's two most senior executives were asked at an FCIC hearing how their charter could have been changed to make the company more sound, and to avoid the multi-billion-dollar bailout. Mudd, who made approximately $65 million from 2000 to 2008, testified that "the thing that would have made the institution more sound or have produced a different outcome would have been for it to have become over time a more normal financial institution able to diversify, able to allocate capital, able to be

long or short in the market, able to operate internationally. And if the trade for that would have been, you know, a cut in the so-called implicit ties with the government, I think that would have—that would have been a better solution."[87] Chief Business Officer Levin, who received approximately $45 million from 2000 to 2008, answered only that making such decisions "wasn't done at my pay grade."[88]

---

## COMMISSION CONCLUSIONS ON CHAPTER 17

The Commission concludes that the business model of Fannie Mae and Freddie Mac (the GSEs), as private-sector, publicly traded, profit-making companies with implicit government backing and a public mission, was fundamentally flawed. We find that the risky practices of Fannie Mae—the Commission's case study in this area—particularly from 2005 on, led to its fall: practices undertaken to meet Wall Street's expectations for growth, to regain market share, and to ensure generous compensation for its employees. Affordable housing goals imposed by the Department of Housing and Urban Development (HUD) did contribute marginally to these practices. The GSEs justified their activities, in part, on the broad and sustained public policy support for homeownership. Risky lending and securitization resulted in significant losses at Fannie Mae, which, combined with its excessive leverage permitted by law, led to the company's failure.

Corporate governance, including risk management, failed at the GSEs in part because of skewed compensation methodologies. The Office of Federal Housing Enterprise Oversight (OFHEO) lacked the authority and capacity to adequately regulate the GSEs. The GSEs exercised considerable political power and were successfully able to resist legislation and regulatory actions that would have strengthened oversight of them and restricted their risk-taking activities.

In early 2008, the decision by the federal government and the GSEs to increase the GSEs' mortgage activities and risk to support the collapsing mortgage market was made despite the unsound financial condition of the institutions. While these actions provided support to the mortgage market, they led to increased losses at the GSEs, which were ultimately borne by taxpayers, and reflected the conflicted nature of the GSEs' dual mandate.

GSE mortgage securities essentially maintained their value throughout the crisis and did not contribute to the significant financial firm losses that were central to the financial crisis.

# 18

## SEPTEMBER 2008:
## THE BANKRUPTCY OF LEHMAN

### CONTENTS

Solvency should be a simple financial concept: if your assets are worth more than your liabilities, you are solvent; if not, you are in danger of bankruptcy. But on the afternoon of Friday, September 12, 2008, experts from the country's biggest commercial and investment banks met at the Wall Street offices of the Federal Reserve to ponder the fate of Lehman Brothers, and could not agree whether or not the 157-year-old firm was solvent.

Only two days earlier, Lehman had reported shareholder equity—the measure of solvency—of $28 billion at the end of August. Over the previous nine months, the bank had lost $6 billion but raised more than $10 billion in new capital, leaving it with more reported equity than it had a year earlier.

But this arithmetic reassured hardly anyone outside the investment bank. Fed officials had been discussing Lehman's solvency for months, and the stakes were very high. To resolve the question, the Fed would not rely on Lehman's $28 billion figure, given questions about whether Lehman was reporting assets at market value. As one New York Fed official wrote to colleagues in July, "Balance-sheet capital isn't too relevant if you're suffering a massive run."[1] If there is a run, and a firm can only get fire-sale prices for assets, even large amounts of capital can disappear almost overnight.

The bankers thought Lehman's real estate assets were overvalued. In light of

Lehman's unreliable valuation methods, the bankers had good reason for their doubts. None of the bankers at the New York Fed that weekend believed the $54 billion in real estate assets (excluding real estate held for sale) on Lehman's books was an accurate figure. If the assets were worth only half that amount (a likely scenario, given market conditions), then Lehman's $28 billion in equity would be gone. In a fire sale, some might sell for even less than half their stated value.

"What does solvent mean?" JP Morgan CEO Jamie Dimon responded when the FCIC asked if Lehman had been solvent. "The answer is, I don't know. I still could not answer that question."[2] JP Morgan's Chief Risk Officer Barry Zubrow testified before the FCIC that "from a pure accounting standpoint, it was solvent," although "it obviously was financing its assets on a very leveraged basis with a lot of short-term financing."[3]

Testifying before the FCIC, former Lehman Brothers CEO Richard Fuld insisted his firm had been solvent: "There was no capital hole at Lehman Brothers. At the end of Lehman's third quarter, we had $28.4 billion of equity capital."[4] Fed Chairman Ben Bernanke disagreed: "I believe it had a capital hole." He emphasized that New York Federal Reserve Bank President Timothy Geithner, Treasury Secretary Henry Paulson, and SEC Chairman Christopher Cox agreed it was "just way too big a hole. And my own view is it's very likely that the company was insolvent, even, not just illiquid."[5] Others, such as Bank of America CEO Ken Lewis, who that week considered acquiring Lehman with government support, had no doubts either. He told the FCIC that Lehman's real estate and other assets had been overvalued by $60 to $70 billion—a message he had delivered to Paulson a few days before Lehman declared bankruptcy.[6]

It had been quite a week; it would be quite a weekend. The debate will continue over the largest bankruptcy in American history, but nothing will change the basic facts: a consortium of banks would fail to agree on a rescue, two last-minute deals would fall through, and the government would decide not to rescue this investment bank—for financial reasons, for political reasons, for practical reasons, for philosophical reasons, and because, as Bernanke told the FCIC, if the government had lent money, "the firm would fail, and not only would we be unsuccessful but we would have saddled the taxpayer with tens of billions of dollars of losses."[7]

## "GET MORE CONSERVATIVELY FUNDED"

After the demise of Bear Stearns in March 2008, most observers—including Bernanke, Paulson, Geithner, and Cox[8]—viewed Lehman Brothers as the next big worry among the four remaining large investment banks. Geithner said he was "consumed" with finding a way that Lehman might "get more conservatively funded."[9] Fed Vice Chairman Donald Kohn told Bernanke that in the wake of Bear's collapse, some institutional investors believed it was a matter not of *whether* Lehman would fail, but *when*.[10] One set of numbers in particular reinforced their doubts: on March 18, the day after JP Morgan announced its acquisition of Bear Stearns, the market

(through credit default swaps on Lehman's debt) put the cost of insuring $10 million of Lehman's five-year senior debt at $310,000 annually; for Merrill Lynch, the cost was $241,000; and for Goldman Sachs, $165,000.

The chief concerns were Lehman's real estate–related investments and its reliance on short-term funding sources, including $7.8 billion of commercial paper and $197 billion of repos at the end of the first quarter of 2008. There were also concerns about the firm's more than 900,000 derivative contracts with a myriad of counterparties.[11]

As they did for all investments banks, the Fed and SEC asked: Did Lehman have enough capital—real capital, after possible asset write-downs? And did it have sufficient liquidity—cash—to withstand the kind of run that had taken down Bear Stearns? Solvency and liquidity were essential and related. If money market funds, hedge funds, and investment banks believed Lehman's assets were worth less than Lehman's valuations, they would withdraw funds, demand more collateral, and curtail lending. That could force Lehman to sell its assets at fire-sale prices, wiping out capital and liquidity virtually overnight. Bear proved it could happen.

"The SEC traditionally took the view that liquidity was paramount in large securities firms, but the Fed, as a consequence of its banking mandate, had more of an emphasis on capital raising," Erik Sirri, head of the SEC's Division of Trading and Markets, told the FCIC. "Because the Fed had become the de facto primary regulator because of its balance sheet, its view prevailed. The SEC wanted to be collaborative, and so came to accept the Fed's focus on capital. However, as time progressed, both saw the importance of liquidity with respect to the problems at the large investment banks."[12]

In fact, both problems had to be resolved. Bear's demise had precipitated Lehman's "first real financing difficulties" since the liquidity crisis began in 2007, Lehman Treasurer Paolo Tonucci told the FCIC.[13] Over the two weeks following Bear's collapse, Lehman borrowed from the Fed's new lending facility, the Primary Dealer Credit Facility (PDCF),[14] but had to be careful to avoid seeming overreliant on the PDCF for cash, which would signal funding problems.

Lehman built up its liquidity to $45 billion at the end of May, but it and Merrill performed the worst among the four investment banks in the regulators' liquidity stress tests in the spring and summer of 2008.

Meanwhile, the company was also working to improve its capital position. First, it reduced real estate exposures (again, excluding real estate held for sale) from $90 billion to $71 billion at the end of May and to $54 billion at the end of the summer. Second, it raised new capital and longer-term debt—a total of $15.5 billion of preferred stock and senior and subordinated debt from April through June 2008.

Treasury Undersecretary Robert Steel praised Lehman's efforts, publicly stating that it was "addressing the issues."[15] But other difficulties loomed. Fuld would later describe Lehman's main problem as one of market confidence, and he suggested that the company's image was damaged by investors taking "naked short" positions (short selling Lehman's securities without first borrowing them), hoping Lehman would fail, and potentially even helping it fail by eroding confidence. "Bear went down on rumors and a liquidity crisis of confidence," Fuld told the FCIC. "Immediately there-

after, the rumors and the naked short sellers came after us."[16] The company pressed the SEC to clamp down on the naked short selling.[17] The SEC's Division of Risk, Strategy and Financial Innovation shared with the FCIC a study it did concerning short selling. As Chairman Mary Schapiro explained to the Commission, "We do not have information at this time that manipulative short selling was the cause of the collapse of Bear and Lehman or of the difficulties faced by other investment banks during the fall of 2008." The SEC to date has not brought short selling charges related to the failure of these investment banks.[18]

On March 18, Lehman reported better-than-expected earnings of $489 million for the first quarter of 2008. Its stock jumped nearly 50%, to $46.49. But investors and analysts quickly raised questions, especially concerning the reported value of Lehman's real estate assets. Portfolio.com called Lehman's write-downs "suspiciously minuscule."[19] In a speech in May, David Einhorn of Greenlight Capital, which was then shorting Lehman's stock, noted the bank's large portfolio of commercial real estate loans and said, "There is good reason to question Lehman's fair value calculations. . . . I suspect that greater transparency on these valuations would not inspire market confidence."[20]

Nell Minow, editor and co-founder of the Corporate Library, which researches and rates firms on corporate governance, raised other reasons that observers might have been skeptical of management at Lehman. "On Lehman Brothers' [board], . . . they had an actress, a theatrical producer, and an admiral, and not one person who understood financial derivatives."[21] The Corporate Library gave Lehman a D rating in June 2004, a grade it downgraded to F in September 2008.[22] On June 9, Lehman announced a preliminary $2.8 billion loss for its second quarter—the first loss since it became a public company in 1994. The share price fell to $30. Three days later Lehman announced it was replacing Chief Operating Officer Joseph Gregory and Chief Financial Officer Erin Callan. The stock slumped again, to $22.70.

## "THIS IS NOT SOUNDING GOOD AT ALL"

After Lehman reported its final second-quarter results on June 12, the New York Fed's on-site monitor at Lehman, Kirsten Harlow, reported that there had been "no adverse information on liquidity, novations, terminations or ability to fund either secured or unsecured [funds]."[23] The announced liquidity numbers were better that quarter, as were the capital numbers.

Nevertheless, Lehman's lenders and supervisors were worried. The next morning, William Dudley, then head of the New York Fed's Markets Group (and its current president), emailed Bernanke, Geithner, Kohn, and others that the PDCF should be extended because it "remains critical to the stability" of some of the investment banks—particularly Lehman. "I think without the PDCF, Lehman might have experienced a full blown liquidity crisis," he wrote.[24]

Just one week after the earnings release, Harlow reported that Lehman was indeed having funding difficulties. Four financial institutions had "trading issues" with Lehman and had reduced their exposure to the firm, including Natixis, a

French investment bank that had already eliminated all activity with Lehman. JP Morgan reported that large pension funds and some smaller Asian central banks were reducing their exposures to Lehman, as well as to Merrill Lynch. And Citigroup requested a $3 to $5 billion "comfort deposit" to cover its exposure to Lehman, settling later for $2 billion.[25] In an internal memo, Thomas Fontana, the head of risk management in Citigroup's global financial institutions group, wrote that "loss of confidence [in Lehman] is huge at the moment."[26] Timothy Clark, senior adviser in the Federal Reserve's banking supervision and regulation division, was short and direct: "This is not sounding good at all."[27]

On June 25, results from the regulators' most recent stress test showed that Lehman would need $15 billion more than the $54 billion in its liquidity pool to survive a loss of all unsecured borrowings and varying amounts of secured borrowings.[28] Lehman's borrowings in the overnight commercial paper market were increasing, however, from $3 billion at the end of November 2007 to $8 billion at the end of May 2008. And it was reliant on repo funding, particularly the portions that matured overnight and were collateralized by illiquid assets.[29] As of mid-June, 62% of Lehman's liquidity was dependent on borrowing against nontraditional securities, such as illiquid mortgage-related securities—which could not be financed with the PDCF and of which investors were becoming increasingly wary.[30]

On July 10, Federated Investors—a large money market fund and one of Lehman's largest tri-party repo lenders—notified JP Morgan, Lehman's clearing bank, that Federated would "no longer pursue additional business with Lehman," because JP Morgan was "unwilling to negotiate in good faith" and had "become increasingly uncooperative" on repo terms.[31] Dreyfus, another large money market fund and a Lehman tri-party repo lender, also pulled its repo line from the firm.[32]

### "SPOOK THE MARKET"

As the Fed considered the risks of the tri-party repo market, it also mulled over more specific measures to help Lehman. The New York Fed and FDIC both rejected the company's proposal to convert to a bank holding company, a proposal which Geithner told Fuld was "gimmicky" and "[could not] solve a liquidity/capital problem."[33] A proposal by the Fed's Dudley followed the Bear Stearns model: $60 billion of Lehman's assets would be held by a new special-purpose vehicle, financed by $5 billion of Lehman's equity and a $55 billion loan from the Fed. This proposal would remove the illiquid assets from the market and potentially avert a fire sale that could render Lehman insolvent.[34] It didn't go anywhere.

But when that idea was floated in July, the need for such action was still somewhat speculative. Not so by August. In an August 8 email to colleagues at the Federal Reserve and Treasury, Patrick Parkinson, then the deputy director of the Federal Reserve Board's Division of Research and Statistics, described a "game plan" that would (1) identify activities of Lehman that could significantly harm financial markets and the economy if it filed for chapter 11 bankruptcy protection, (2) gather information

to more accurately assess the potential effects of its failure, and (3) identify risk mitigation actions for areas of serious potential harm.[35]

As they now realized, regulators did not know nearly enough about over-the-counter derivatives activities at Lehman and other investment banks, which were major OTC derivatives dealers. Investment banks disclosed the total number of OTC derivative contracts they had, the total exposures of the contracts, and their estimated market value, but they did not publicly report the terms of the contracts or the counterparties. Thus, there was no way to know who would be owed how much and when payments would have to be made—information that would be critically important to analyze the possible impact of a Lehman bankruptcy on derivatives counterparties and the financial markets.

Parkinson reviewed a standing recommendation to form a "default management group" of senior executives of major market participants to work with regulators to anticipate issues if a major counterparty should default. The recommendation was from the private-sector Counterparty Risk Management Policy Group, the same group that had alerted the Fed to the backlog problem in the OTC derivatives market earlier in the decade. Parkinson suggested accelerating the formation of this group while being careful not to signal concerns about any one market participant.[36] On August 15, Parkinson emailed New York Fed officials that he was worried that no sensible game plan could be formulated without more information.[37] He was informed that New York Fed officials had just met with Lehman two days earlier to obtain derivative-related information, that they still needed more information, and that the meeting had "caused a stir," which in turn required assurances that requests for information would not be limited to Lehman.[38]

New York Fed officials were also "very reluctant" to request copies of the master agreements that would shed light on the Lehman's derivatives counterparties, because such a request would send a "huge negative signal."[39] The formation of the industry group seemed "less provocative," wrote a New York Fed official, but could still "spook the market."[40] Parkinson believed that the information was important, but attempting to collect it was "not without risks."[41] He also recognized the difficulties in unraveling the complex dependencies among the many Lehman subsidiaries and their counterparties, which would keep lawyers and accountants busy for a long time.[42]

On August 28, Treasury's Steve Shafran informed Parkinson that Secretary Paulson agreed on the need to collect information on OTC derivatives.[43] It just had to be done in a way that minimized disruptions. On September 5, Parkinson circulated a draft letter requesting the information from Lehman CEO Fuld.[44] Geithner would ask E. Gerald Corrigan, the Goldman Sachs executive and former New York Fed president who had co-chaired the Counterparty Risk Management Policy Group report, to form an industry group to advise on information needed from a troubled investment bank. Parkinson, Shafran, and others would also create a "playbook" for an investment bank failure at Secretary Paulson's request. Events over the following week would render these efforts moot.

On September 4, executives from Lehman Brothers apprised executives at JP Morgan, Lehman's tri-party repo clearing bank, of the third-quarter results that it would announce two weeks later. A $3.9 billion loss would reflect "significant asset write-downs." The firm was also considering several steps to bolster capital, including an investment by Korea Development Bank or others, the sale of Lehman's investment management division (Neuberger Berman), the sale of real estate assets, and the division of the company into a "good bank" and "bad bank" with private equity sponsors.[45] The executives also discussed JP Morgan's concerns about Lehman's repo collateral.

On Monday, September 8, more than 20 New York Fed officials were notified of a meeting the next morning "to continue the discussion of near-term options for dealing with a failing nonbank." They received a list documenting Lehman's tri-party repo exposure at roughly $200 billion. Before its collapse, Bear Stearns's exposure had been only $50 to $80 billion. The documentation further noted that 10 counterparties provided 80% of Lehman's repo financing, and that intraday liquidity provided by Lehman's clearing banks could become a problem. Indeed, JP Morgan, Citigroup, and Bank of America had all demanded more collateral from Lehman, with the threat they might "cut off Lehman if they don't receive it."[46]

On Tuesday morning, September 9, news there would be no investment from Korea Development Bank shook the market. Lehman's stock plunged 55% from the day before, closing at $7.79. To prepare for an afternoon call with Bernanke, Geithner directed his staff to "put together a quick 'what's different? what's the same?' list about [Lehman] vs [Bear Stearns], as well as about mid-March (then) vs. early Sept (now)."[47] The Fed's Parkinson emailed Treasury's Shafran about his concerns that Lehman would announce further losses the next week, that it might not be able to raise equity, and that even though its liquidity position was better than Bear Stearns's had been, Lehman remained vulnerable to a loss of confidence.[48]

At 5:00 P.M., Paulson convened a call with Cox, Geithner, Bernanke, and Treasury staff "to deal with a possible Lehman bankruptcy."[49] At 5:20 P.M., Treasury Chief of Staff Jim Wilkinson emailed Michelle Davis, the assistant secretary for public affairs at Treasury, to express his distaste for government assistance: "We need to talk. . . . I just can't stomach us bailing out lehman. . . . Will be horrible in the press don't u think."[50]

That same day, Fuld agreed to post an additional $3.6 billion of collateral to JP Morgan. Lehman's bankruptcy estate would later claim that Lehman did so because of JP Morgan's improper threat to withhold repo funding. Zubrow said JP Morgan requested the collateral because of its growing exposure as a derivatives trading counterparty to Lehman.[51] Steven Black, JP Morgan's president, said he requested $5 billion from Lehman, which agreed to post $3.6 billion.[52] He did not believe the request put undue pressure on Lehman. On Tuesday night, executives of Lehman and JP Morgan met again at Lehman's request to discuss options for raising capital. The JP Morgan group was not impressed. "[Lehman] sent the Junior Varsity," JP Morgan executives reported to Black. "They have no proposal and are looking to us for ideas/credit line to bridge them to the first quarter when they intend to split into good bank/bad bank." Black responded, "Let's give them an order for the same drugs

they have apparently been taking to think we would do something like that."[53] The Lehman bankruptcy estate has a different view. It alleges Black agreed to send a due diligence team, following Dimon's suggestion that his firm might be willing to purchase Lehman preferred stock, but instead sent over senior risk managers to probe Lehman's confidential records and plans.[54]

The bankruptcy estate alleges that later that night, JP Morgan demanded that Lehman execute amended agreements to its tri-party repo services before preannouncing its third-quarter earnings at 7:30 the next morning. The amendments required Lehman to provide additional guarantees, increased Lehman's potential liability, and gave JP Morgan additional control over Lehman bank accounts.[55] Again, the Lehman bankruptcy estate argues that Lehman executed the agreements because JP Morgan executives led Lehman to believe its bank would refuse to extend intraday credit if Lehman did not do so. JP Morgan denies this. Black told the FCIC, "JPMC never told Lehman that it would stop extending credit and clearing if the September Agreements were not executed before the markets opened on [Wednesday,] September 10, 2008."[56]

Before the market opened on Wednesday, Lehman announced its $3.9 billion third-quarter loss, including a $5.6 billion write-down. Four hours later, Matthew Rutherford, an adviser to Treasury, emailed colleagues that several large money funds had reduced their exposure to Lehman, although there was not yet "a wholesale pull back of [repo] lines."[57]

"Importantly, Fidelity, the largest fund complex, stressed that while they hadn't made any significant shifts yet today, they were still in the process of making decisions and wanted to update me later in the day," Rutherford wrote. By Friday, Fidelity would have reduced its tri-party repo lending to Lehman to less than $2 billion from over $12 billion the previous Friday; according to Fidelity's response to an FCIC survey of market participants, in the week prior to Bear's demise in March, Fidelity had pulled its entire $9.6 billion repo line to that company.

## "IMAGINATION HAT"

At the Federal Reserve, working groups were directed to "spend the next few hours fleshing out how a Fed-assisted BofA acquisition transaction might look, how a private consortium of preferred equity investors transaction might look, and how a Fed takeout of tri-party repo lenders would look."[58] That day, New York Fed Senior Vice President Patricia Mosser circulated her opinion on Dudley's request for "thoughts on how to resolve Lehman." She laid out three options: (1) find a buyer at any price, (2) wind down Lehman's affairs, or (3) force it into bankruptcy. Regarding option 1, Mosser said it "should be done in a way that requires minimal temporary support. . . . No more Maiden Lane LLCs and no equity position by [the] Fed. Moral hazard and reputation cost is too high. If the Fed agrees to another equity investment, it signals that everything [the Fed] did in March in terms of temporary liquidity backstops is useless. Horrible precedent; in the long run MUCH worse than option 3." Option 3, bankruptcy, would be "[a] mess on every level, but fixes the moral hazard problem."[59]

On Wednesday night, a New York Fed official circulated a "Liquidation Consortium" game plan to colleagues.[60] The plan was to convene in one room senior-level representatives of Lehman's counterparties in the tri-party repo, credit default swap, and over-the-counter derivatives markets—everyone who would suffer most if Lehman failed—and have them explore joint funding mechanisms to avert a failure. According to the proposed game plan, Secretary Paulson would tell the participants they had until the opening of business in Asia the following Monday morning (Sunday night, New York time) to devise a credible plan. The game plan stated that "we should have in mind a maximum number of how much we are willing to finance before the meeting starts, but not divulge our willingness to do so to the consortium."[61] Indeed, Paulson would tell the consortium when it met two days later that the government was willing to let Lehman fail.[62]

Former Bank of America CEO Ken Lewis told the FCIC that Treasury Secretary Paulson had called him on Wednesday, September 10, and asked him to take another look at acquiring Lehman, assuring him that Fuld was ready to deal. Paulson and Geithner had arranged for Fuld and Lewis to discuss an acquisition in July, but Fuld had not been interested in selling the entire firm at that time. Because of this history, Lewis expressed his concerns to Paulson that Fuld would not want to sell the entire company or would not be willing to sell at a realistic price. Still, a team of Bank of America executives began reviewing Lehman's books, and on the next day, Fuld sounded optimistic about a deal. But Bank of America determined that Lehman's assets were overvalued, and Lewis told Paulson there would be no deal without government assistance. Undeterred, Paulson told Lewis—as Lewis informed the FCIC—to put on his "imagination hat" and figure out a deal. His insistence kept the Bank of America executives working, but on Friday, September 12, Lewis called Paulson to repeat his assessment—no government support, no deal. Apparently Fuld had been kept out of the loop, and began to call Lewis at home. Lewis's wife told Fuld that Lewis would not come to the phone and to stop calling.[63]

On Thursday September 11, an email time-stamped 8:26 A.M. from Susan McCabe, a Goldman Sachs executive, to Dudley and others set the tone for the day: "It is not pretty, This is getting pretty scary and ugly again. . . . They [Lehman] have much bigger counter-party risk than Bear did, especially in Derivatives market, so [t]he market is getting very spooked, nervous. Also have Aig, Wamu concerns. This is just spinning out of control again. Just fyi, this is shaping up as going to be a rough day."[64] Bernanke was informed that if Lehman failed, "it would be a much more complex proposition to unwind their positions than it would have been to unwind the positions held by Bear Stearns," because Lehman was "nearly twice the size of Bear Stearns."[65]

Some believed government action was required. At 10:46 A.M., Hayley Boesky, a senior New York Fed official, forwarded to her colleagues an email from the hedge fund manager Louis Bacon suggesting the New York Fed could "attempt to stabilize or support the LEH situation" but noting that "none of the above will fix the fundamental problem, which is too many bad assets that need to get off too many balance sheets."[66]

At 1:40 P.M., Fed officials circulated the outline of a plan to create a "Lehman De-fault Management Group," a group of Lehman counterparties and creditors who would make plans to cope with a Lehman bankruptcy. They would agree to hold off on fully exercising their rights to close out their trades with Lehman; instead, they would establish a process to "net down"—that is, reduce—all exposures using a com-mon valuation method.[67] A little before midnight on Thursday, Boesky notified col-leagues that panicked hedge funds had called to say they were "expecting [a] full blown recession" and that there was a "full expectation that Leh goes, wamu and then ML [Merrill Lynch]." They were "ALL begging, pleading for a large scale solution which spans beyond just LEH." Boesky compared the level of panic to the failure of Bear Stearns—"On a scale of 1 to 10, where 10 is Bear-Stearns-week-panic, I would put sentiment today at a 12."[68]

At almost the same time, JP Morgan demanded that Lehman post another $5 bil-lion in cash "by the opening of business tomorrow in New York"; if it didn't, JP Mor-gan would "exercise our right to decline to extend credit to you."[69] JP Morgan CEO Dimon, President Black, and CRO Zubrow had first made the demand in a phone call earlier that evening to Lehman CEO Fuld, CFO Ian Lowitt, and Treasurer Paolo Tonucci.[70] Tonucci told the JP Morgan executives on the call that Lehman could not meet the demand. Dimon said Lehman's difficulties in coming up with the money were not JP Morgan's problem, Tonucci told the FCIC. "They just wanted the cash. We made the point that it's too much cash to mobilize. There was no give on that. Again, they said 'that's not our problem, we just want the cash.'"[71] When Tonucci asked what would keep JP Morgan from asking for $10 billion tomorrow, Dimon replied, "Nothing, maybe we will."[72]

Under normal circumstances, Tonucci would not have tolerated this treatment, but circumstances were far from normal. "JPM as 'clearing bank' continues to ask for more cash collateral. If we don't provide the cash, they refuse to clear, we fail," was the message circulated in an email to Lehman executives on Friday, September 12. So Lehman "delivered the $5 billion in cash only by pulling virtually every unencum-bered asset it could deliver."[73]

JP Morgan's Zubrow saw it differently. He told the FCIC that the previously posted $3.6 billion of collateral by Lehman was "inappropriate" because it was "illiq-uid" and "could not be reasonably valued." Moreover, Zubrow said the potential col-lateral shortfall was greater than $5 billion.[74] Lehman's former CEO, Fuld, told the FCIC that he agreed to post the $5 billion because JP Morgan said it would be re-turned to Lehman at the close of business the following day.[75] The Lehman bank-ruptcy estate made the same allegation. This dispute is now the subject of litigation; the Lehman bankruptcy estate is suing JP Morgan to retrieve the $5 billion—and the original $3.6 billion.[76]

## "HEADS OF FAMILY"

Should Lehman be allowed to go bankrupt? Within the government, sentiments var-ied. On Friday morning, as Secretary Paulson headed to New York to "sort through

this Lehman mess," Wilkinson wrote that he still "[couldn't] imagine a scenario where we put in [government] money . . . we shall see."[77] That afternoon, Fed Governor Warsh wrote, in response to a colleague's hope the Fed would not have to protect some of Lehman's debt holders, "I hope we don[']t protect anything!"[78] But on Friday, Fed Chairman Bernanke was taking no chances. He stayed behind in Washington, in case he had to convene the Fed's board to exercise its emergency lending powers.[79]

Early Friday evening, Treasury Secretary Paulson summoned the "heads of family"—the phrase used by Harvey Miller, Lehman's bankruptcy counsel, to describe the CEOs of the big Wall Street firms[80]—to the New York Fed's headquarters. Paulson told them that a private-sector solution was the only option to prevent a Lehman bankruptcy. The people in the room needed to come up with a realistic set of options to help limit damage to the system. A sudden and disorderly wind-down could harm the capital markets and pose the significant risk of a precipitous drop in asset prices, resulting in collateral calls and reduced liquidity: that is, systemic risk. He could not offer the prospect of containing the damage if the executives were unable to fashion an orderly resolution of the situation, as had been done in 1998 for Long-Term Capital Management. Paulson did offer the Fed's help through regulatory approvals and access to lending facilities, but emphasized that the Fed would not provide "any form of extraordinary credit support."[81] As New York Fed General Counsel Tom Baxter told the FCIC, Paulson made it clear there would be no government assistance, "not a penny."[82]

H. Rodgin Cohen, a veteran Wall Street lawyer who has represented most of the major banks, including Lehman, told the FCIC that the government's "not a penny" posture was a calculated strategy: "I don't know exactly what the government was thinking, but my impression was they were playing a game of chicken or poker or whatever. It was said on more than one occasion that it would be very politically difficult to rescue Lehman. There had been a lot of blowback after Bear Stearns. I believe the government thought that it could, with respect to a game of chicken, persuade the private sector to take a big chunk" of Lehman's liabilities.[83]

The Fed's internal liquidation consortium game plan would seem to confirm Cohen's view, given that it contemplated a financial commitment, even though that was not to be divulged.[84] Moreover, notwithstanding Paulson's "not a penny" statement, the United Kingdom's chancellor of the exchequer, Alistair Darling, said that Paulson told him that "the FRBNY might be prepared to provide Barclays with regulatory assistance to support a transaction if it was required."[85]

At that consortium meeting on Friday night, Citigroup CEO Vikram Pandit asked if the group was also going to talk about AIG. Timothy Geithner said simply: "Let's focus on Lehman."[86]

## "TELL THOSE SONS OF BITCHES TO UNWIND"

What would happen if JP Morgan refused to provide intraday credit for Lehman in the tri-party repo market on Monday, September 15? The Fed had been considering this possibility since the summer. As Parkinson noted, the fundamental problem was that even if Lehman filed for bankruptcy, the SEC would want Lehman's broker-

dealer to live on and would not want the Fed in its position as lender to grab tri-party collateral.[87] Parkinson told the FCIC staff that Zubrow informed him over the weekend that JP Morgan would not unwind Lehman's repos on Monday if the Fed did not expand the types of collateral that could be financed through the PDCF lending facility. Earlier in the year, Parkinson had said that JP Morgan's refusal to unwind would be unforgiveable. Now he told Geithner to "tell those sons of bitches . . . to unwind."[88]

Merrill CEO John Thain told the FCIC that by Saturday morning, the group of executives reviewing Lehman's assets had estimated that they were overvalued by anywhere from $15 to $25 billion. Thain thought that was more than the assembled executives would be willing to finance and, therefore, Thain believed Lehman would fail.[89] If Lehman failed, Thain believed, Merrill would be next. So he had called Ken Lewis, the CEO of Bank of America, and they met later that day at Bank of America's New York corporate apartment. By Sunday, the two agreed that Bank of America would acquire Merrill for $29 per share, payable in Bank of America stock.

On Saturday afternoon, Lehman's counsel provided the Fed with a document describing how Lehman's default on its obligations would "trigger a cascade of defaults through to the [subsidiaries] which have large OTC [derivatives] books."[90] Bernanke, Fed Governor Kohn, Geithner, and other senior Fed officials subsequently participated in a conference call to discuss the possibility of going "to Congress to ask for other authorities," something Geithner planned to "pitch."[91] However, Fed General Counsel Scott Alvarez cautioned others not to mention the plan to JP Morgan, because he did not want to "suggest Fed willingness to give JPMC cover to screw [Lehman] or anyone else."[92]

By Saturday night, however, it appeared that the parade of horrors that would result from a Lehman bankruptcy had been avoided. An agreement apparently had been reached. Barclays would purchase Lehman, excluding $40 to $50 billion of assets financed by the private consortium (even though the bankers in the consortium had estimated those assets to be significantly overvalued). Michael Klein, an adviser to Barclays, had told Lehman President Bart McDade that Barclays was willing to purchase Lehman, given the private consortium agreement to assist the deal.[93] It seemed a deal would be completed.[94]

### "THIS DOESN'T SEEM LIKE IT IS GOING TO END PRETTY"

But on Sunday, things went terribly wrong. At 8:00 A.M., Barclays CEO John Varley and President Robert Diamond told Paulson, Geithner, and Cox that the Financial Services Authority (FSA) had declined to approve the deal.[95] The issue boiled down to a guarantee—the New York Fed required Barclays to guarantee Lehman's obligations from the sale until the transaction closed, much as JP Morgan had done for Bear Stearns in March.[96] Under U.K. law, the guarantee required a Barclays shareholder vote, which could take 30 to 60 days. Though it could waive that requirement, the FSA asserted that such a waiver would be unprecedented, that it had not heard about this guarantee until Saturday night, and that Barclays did not really want to take on that obligation anyway.

Geithner pleaded with FSA Chairman Callum McCarthy to waive the shareholder vote, but McCarthy wanted the New York Fed to provide the guarantee instead of Barclays.[97] Otherwise, according to the FSA, "Barclays would have had to provide a (possibly unlimited) guarantee, for an undefined period of time, covering prior and future exposures and liabilities of Lehman that would continue to apply including in respect of all transactions entered into prior to the purchase, even in the event the transaction ultimately failed."[98]

For Paulson, such a guarantee by the Fed was unequivocally out of the question.[99] The guarantee could have put the Fed on the hook for tens of billions of dollars. If the run on Lehman had continued despite the guarantee, Barclays' shareholders could reject the acquisition, and the Fed would be in possession of an insolvent bank.

Baxter told the FCIC that Barclays had known all along that the guarantee was required, because JP Morgan had to provide the same type of guarantee when it acquired Bear Stearns. Indeed, Baxter said he was "stunned" at this development. He believed that the real reason Barclays said it could not guarantee Lehman's obligations was the U.K. government's discomfort with the transaction.[100]

On Sunday morning, Treasury's Wilkinson emailed JP Morgan Investment Bank CEO Jes Staley that he was in a meeting with Paulson and Geithner and that things did not look good. He concluded, "This doesn't seem like it is going to end pretty."[101] In another note a little more than an hour later, he added that there would be no government assistance: "No way [government] money is coming in. . . . I'm here writing the usg coms [United States government communications] plan for orderly unwind . . . also just did a call with the WH [White House] and usg is united behind no money. No way in hell Paulson could blink now . . . we will know more after this [CEO meeting] this morning but I think we are headed for winddown unless barclays deal gets untangled."[102]

It did not. Paulson made a last-ditch pitch to his U.K. counterpart, Darling, without success.[103] Two years later, Darling admitted that he had vetoed the transaction: "Yeah I did. Imagine if I had said yes to a British bank buying a very large American bank which . . . collapsed the following week." He would have found himself telling a British audience, "Everybody sitting in this room and your children and your grandchildren and their grandchildren would be paying for years to come." That Bank of America had taken itself out of the picture may have played a role in Darling's decision: "My first reaction was 'If this is such a good deal how come no American bank is going to go near it?'" So Darling concluded that for Barclays to accept the guarantee, which could have a grave impact on the British economy, was simply out of the question: "I spoke to Hank Paulson and said 'Look, there's no way we could allow a British bank to take over the liability of an American bank,' which in effect meant the British taxpayer was underwriting an American bank."[104]

Following that decision in London, Lehman Brothers was, for all practical purposes, dead. Cohen, Lehman's counsel at the time, told the FCIC, "When Secretary Paulson came out of the meeting with Geithner and Cox, they called Lehman's presi-

dent and me over and said, 'We have the consortium, but the British government won't do it. Darling said he did not want the U.S. cancer to spread to the U.K.'"[105]

At around 1:00 P.M., Lehman's team—President Bart McDade, CFO Ian Lowitt, Head of Principal Investing Alex Kirk, and others—reconvened at Lehman's offices to "digest what obviously was stark news." Upon arriving, they heard that the New York Fed would provide more flexible terms for the PDCF lending facility, which would include expanding the types of collateral borrowers could use.[106] McDade, Kirk, Lowitt, and Miller returned to the New York Fed building and met with the Fed's Baxter and Dudley, the SEC's Sirri, and others to discuss the expanded PDCF program. According to McDade and Kirk, the government officials—led by Baxter—made it plain they would not permit Lehman to borrow against the expanded types of collateral, as other firms could. The sentiment was clear but the reasons were vague, McDade told the FCIC. He said the refusal to allow Lehman to provide the expanded types of collateral made the difference in Lehman's being able to obtain the funding needed to open for business on Monday.[107]

Baxter explained to the FCIC, however, that Lehman's broker-dealer affiliate—not the holding company—could borrow against the expanded types of collateral.[108] A New York Fed email written at 2:15 P.M. on that Sunday, September 14, stated that Lehman's counsel was informed of the expansion of PDCF-eligible collateral but that such collateral would not be available to the broker-dealer if it filed for bankruptcy.[109] The minutes of Lehman's September 14 board meeting show that the Fed rejected Lehman's request for an even broader range of collateral to be eligible for PDCF financing and preferred that Lehman's holding company—but not the broker-dealer—file for bankruptcy and that the broker-dealer "be wound down in an orderly fashion."[110] In a letter dated September 14, the New York Fed informed Lehman Senior Vice President Robert Guglielmo that the broker-dealer could finance expanded types of collateral with the PDCF, but that letter was not sent until 2:24 A.M. on September 15—after Lehman had filed for bankruptcy.[111] The Lehman broker-dealer borrowed $20 to $28 billion from the PDCF each day over the next three days.[112]

As Kirk recounted to the FCIC, during that Sunday meeting at the New York Fed, government officials stepped out for an hour and came back to ask: "Are you planning on filing bankruptcy tonight?"[113] A surprised Miller replied that "no one in the room was authorized to file the company, only the Board could . . . and the Board had to be called to a meeting and have a vote. . . . There would be some lag in terms of having to put all the papers together to actually file it. There was a practical issue that you couldn't . . . get it done quickly."[114] Unmoved, government officials explained that directors of Lehman's U.K. subsidiary—LBIE—would be personally liable if they did not file for bankruptcy by the opening of business Monday. As Kirk recalled, "They then told us 'we would like you to file tonight. . . . It's the right thing to do, because there's something else which we can't tell you that will happen this evening. We would like both events to happen tonight before the opening of trading Monday morning.'"[115] The second event would turn out to be the announcement of Bank of America's acquisition of Merrill Lynch.

## "THE ONLY ALTERNATIVE WAS THAT LEHMAN HAD TO FAIL"

Miller insisted that there had to be an alternative, because filing for bankruptcy would be "Armageddon."[116] Lehman had prepared a presentation arguing that a Lehman bankruptcy would be catastrophic. It would take at least five years to resolve, cost $8 to $10 billion, and cause major disruptions in the United States and abroad.[117]

Baxter told the FCIC, "I knew that the consequences were going to be bad; that wasn't an issue. Lehman was in denial at that point in time. There was no way they believed that this story ends with a Lehman bankruptcy . . . they kept thinking that they were going to be bailed out by the taxpayer of the United States. And I'm not trying to convince you that that belief was a crazy belief because they had seen that happen in the Bear case." Baxter's mission, however, was to "try to get them to understand that they weren't going to be rescued, and then focus on what their real options were, which were drift into Monday morning with nothing done and then have chaos break out, or alternatively file." He concluded, "From my point of view, first thing was to convince Harvey that it was far better to file than to go into Monday and have complete pandemonium break out. And then he had to have discussions with the Lehman Board because they had a fiduciary duty to resolve what was in the best interests of the company and its shareholders and other stakeholders."[118]

"The only alternative was that Lehman had to fail," Miller testified to the FCIC.[119] He stated that Baxter provided no further details on the government's plan for the fallout from bankruptcy, but assured him that the situation was under control. Then, Miller told the FCIC, Baxter told the Lehman delegation to leave the Fed offices. "They basically threw us out," Miller said. Miller remembered telling his colleagues as they left the building, "'I don't think they like us.'"

Miller continued:

> We went back to the headquarters, and it was pandemonium up there—
> it was like a scene from [the 1946 film] *It's a Wonderful Life* with the run
> on the savings and loan crisis. . . . [A]ll of paparazzi running around.
> There was a guy there . . . in a sort of a Norse god uniform with a helmet
> and a picket sign saying "Down with Wall Street." . . . There were hun-
> dreds of employees going in and out. . . . Bart McDade was reporting to
> the board what had happened. Most of the board members were
> stunned. Henry Kaufman, in particular, was asking "How could this
> happen in America?"[120]

The group informed the board that the Barclays deal had fallen apart. The government had instructed the board to file for bankruptcy. SEC's Cox called. With Tom Baxter also on the line, Cox told the board that the situation was serious and required action. The board asked Cox if he was directing them to file for bankruptcy. Cox and Baxter conferred for a few minutes, and then answered that the decision was the board's to make. The board again asked if Cox and Baxter were telling them to file for bankruptcy. Cox and Baxter conferred again, then replied that they believed the gov-

ernment's position had been made perfectly clear at the meeting at the Fed earlier in the day.[121]

Following that call, McDade advised the board that Lehman would be unable to obtain funding without government assistance. The board voted to file for bankruptcy. The company filed at 1:45 A.M. on Monday morning.[122]

## "A CALAMITY"

Fed Chairman Bernanke told the FCIC that government officials understood a Lehman bankruptcy would be catastrophic:

> We never had any doubt about that. It was going to have huge impacts on funding markets. It would create a huge loss of confidence in other financial firms. It would create pressure on Merrill and Morgan Stanley, if not Goldman, which it eventually did. It would probably bring the short-term money markets into crisis, which we didn't fully anticipate; but, of course, in the end it did bring the commercial paper market and the money market mutual funds under pressure. So there was never any doubt in our minds that it would be a calamity, catastrophe, and that, you know, we should do everything we could to save it.[123]

"What's the connection between Lehman Brothers and General Motors?" he asked rhetorically. "Lehman Brothers' failure meant that commercial paper that they used to finance went bad." Bernanke noted that money market funds, in particular one named the Reserve Primary Fund, held Lehman's paper and suffered losses. He explained that this "meant there was a run in the money market mutual funds, which meant the commercial paper market spiked, which [created] problems for General Motors."[124]

"As the financial industry came under stress," Paulson told the FCIC, "investors pulled back from the market, and when Lehman collapsed, even major industrial corporations found it difficult to sell their paper. The resulting liquidity crunch showed that firms had overly relied on this short term funding and had failed to anticipate how restricted the commercial paper market could become in times of stress."[125]

Harvey Miller testified to the FCIC that "the bankruptcy of Lehman was a catalyst for systemic consequences throughout the world. It fostered a negative reaction that endangered the viability of the financial system. As a result of failed expectations of the financial markets and others, a major loss of confidence in the financial system occurred."[126]

On the day that Lehman filed for bankruptcy, the Dow plummeted more than 500 points; $700 billion in value from retirement plans, government pension funds, and other investment portfolios disappeared.[127]

As for Lehman itself, the bankruptcy affected about 8,000 subsidiaries and affiliates with $600 billion in assets and liabilities, the firm's more than 100,000 creditors, and about 26,000 employees. Its failure triggered default clauses in derivatives contracts,

allowing its counterparties to have the option of seizing its collateral and terminating the contracts. After the parent company filed, about 80 insolvency proceedings of its subsidiaries in 18 foreign countries followed. In the main bankruptcy proceeding, about 66,000 claims—exceeding $873 billion—have been filed against Lehman as of September 2010. Miller told the FCIC that Lehman's bankruptcy "represents the largest, most complex, multi-faceted and far-reaching bankruptcy case ever filed in the United States." The costs of the bankruptcy administration are approaching $1 billion; as of this writing, the proceeding is expected to last at least another two years.[128]

In his testimony before the FCIC, Bernanke admitted that the considerations behind the government's decision to allow Lehman to fail were both legal and practical. From a legal standpoint, Bernanke explained, "We are not allowed to lend without a reasonable expectation of repayment. The loan has to be secured to the satisfaction of the Reserve Bank. Remember, this was before TARP. We had no ability to inject capital or to make guarantees."[129] A Sunday afternoon email from Bernanke to Fed Governor Warsh indicated that more than $12 billion in capital assistance would have been needed to prevent Lehman's failure. "In case I am asked: How much capital injection would have been needed to keep LEH alive as a going concern? I gather $12B or so from the private guys together with Fed liquidity support was not enough."[130]

In March, the Fed had provided a loan to facilitate JP Morgan's purchase of Bear Stearns, invoking its authority under section 13(3) of the Federal Reserve Act. But, even with this authority, practical considerations were in play. Bernanke explained that Lehman had insufficient collateral and the Fed, had it acted, would have lent into a run: "On Sunday night of that weekend, what was told to me was that—and I have every reason to believe—was that there was a run proceeding on Lehman, that is people were essentially demanding liquidity from Lehman; that Lehman did not have enough collateral to allow the Fed to lend it enough to meet that run." Thus, "If we lent the money to Lehman, all that would happen would be that the run [on Lehman] would succeed, because it wouldn't be able to meet the demands, the firm would fail, and not only would we be unsuccessful but we would [have] saddled the [t]axpayer with tens of billions of dollars of losses."[131] The Fed had no choice but to stand by as Lehman went under, Bernanke insisted.

As Bernanke acknowledged to the FCIC, however, his explanation for not providing assistance to Lehman was not the explanation he offered days after the bankruptcy—at that time, he said that he believed the market was prepared for the event.[132] On September 23, 2008, he testified: "The failure of Lehman posed risks. But the troubles at Lehman had been well known for some time, and investors clearly recognized—as evidenced, for example, by the high cost of insuring Lehman's debt in the market for credit default swaps—that the failure of the firm was a significant possibility. Thus, we judged that investors and counterparties had had time to take precautionary measures."[133] In addition, though the Federal Reserve subsequently asserted that it did not have the legal ability to save Lehman because the firm did not have sufficient collateral to secure a loan from the Fed under section 13(3), the authority to lend under that provision is very broad. It requires not that loans be fully secured but rather that they be "secured to the satisfaction of the Federal Reserve

bank."[134] Indeed, in March 2009, Federal Reserve General Counsel Scott Alvarez concluded that requiring loans under 13(3) to be fully secured would "undermine the very purpose of section 13(3), which was to make credit available in unusual and exigent circumstances to help restore economic activity."[135]

To CEO Fuld and others, the Fed's emergency lending powers under section 13(3) provided a permissible vehicle to obtain government support. Although Fed officials discussed and dismissed many ideas in the chaotic days leading up to the bankruptcy, the Fed did not furnish to the FCIC any written analysis to illustrate that Lehman lacked sufficient collateral to secure a loan under 13(3). Fuld asserted to the FCIC that in fact, "Lehman had adequate financeable collateral. . . . [O]n September 12, the Friday night preceding Lehman's bankruptcy filing, Lehman financed itself and did not need access to the Fed's discount window. . . . What Lehman needed on that Sunday night was a liquidity bridge. We had the capital. Along with its excess available collateral, Lehman also could have used whole businesses as collateral—such as its Neuberger Berman subsidiary—as did AIG some two days later." Fuld also rejected assertions about Lehman's capital hole. He told the FCIC, "As of August 31, 2008, two weeks prior to the bankruptcy filing, Lehman had . . . $26.7 billion in equity capital. Positive equity of $26.7 billion is very different from the negative $30 or $60 billion 'holes' claimed by some." Moreover, Fuld maintained that Lehman would have been saved if it had been granted bank holding company status—as were Goldman Sachs and Morgan Stanley the week after Lehman's bankruptcy.[136]

The Fed chairman denied any bias against Lehman Brothers. In his view, the only real resolution short of bankruptcy had been to find a buyer. Bernanke said: "When the potential buyers were unable to carry through—in the case of Bank of America, because they changed their minds and decided they wanted to buy Merrill instead; in the case of Barclays, [because they withdrew] . . . we essentially had no choice and had to let it fail."[137]

During the September 16, 2008, meeting of the Fed's Federal Open Market Committee, some members stated that the government should not have prevented Lehman's failure because doing so would only strengthen the perception that some firms were "too big to fail" and erode market discipline. They noted that letting Lehman fail was the only way to provide credibility to the assertion that no firm was "too big to fail" and one member stated that the market was beginning to "play" the Treasury and Federal Reserve. Other meeting participants believed that the disorderly failure of a key firm could have a broad and disruptive effect on financial markets and the economy, but that the appropriate solution was capital injections, a power the Federal Reserve did not have. Bernanke's view was that only a fiscal and perhaps regulatory response could address the potential for wide-scale failure of financial institutions.[138]

Merrill's Thain made it through the Lehman weekend by negotiating a lifesaving acquisition by Bank of America, formerly Lehman's potential suitor. Thain blamed the failure to bail out Lehman on politicians and regulators who feared the political consequences of rescuing the firm. "There was a tremendous amount of criticism of what was done with Bear Stearns so that JP Morgan would buy them," Thain told

the FCIC. "There was a criticism of bailing out Wall Street. It was a combination of political unwillingness to bail out Wall Street and a belief that there needed to be a reinforcement of moral hazard. There was never a discussion about the legal ability of the Fed to do this." He noted, "There was never discussion to the best of my recollection that they couldn't [bail out Lehman]. It was only that they wouldn't."[139]

Thain also told the FCIC that in his opinion, "allowing Lehman to go bankrupt was the single biggest mistake of the whole financial crisis." He wished that he and the other Wall Street executives had tried harder to convince Paulson and Geithner to prevent Lehman's failure: "As I think about what I would do differently after that weekend . . . is try to grab them and shake them that they can't let this happen. . . . They were not very much in the mood to listen. They were not willing to listen to the idea that there had to be government support. . . . The group of us should have just grabbed them and shaken them and said, 'Look, you guys could not do this.' But we didn't, and they were not willing to entertain that discussion."[140]

FCIC staff asked Thain if he and the other executives explicitly said to Paulson, Geithner, or anyone else, "You can't let this happen." Thain replied, "We didn't do it strongly enough. We said to them, 'Look, this is going to be bad.' But it wasn't like, 'No . . . you have to help.'"[141]

Another prominent member of that select group, JP Morgan's Dimon, had a different view. He told the FCIC, "I didn't think it was so bad. I hate to say that. . . . But I [thought] it was almost the same if on Monday morning the government had saved Lehman. . . . You still would have terrible things happen. . . . AIG was going to have their problems that had nothing to do with Lehman. You were still going to have the runs on the other banks and you were going to have absolute fear and panic in the global markets. Whether Lehman itself got saved or not . . . the crisis would have unfolded along a different path, but it probably would have unfolded."[142]

Fed General Counsel Alvarez and New York Fed General Counsel Baxter told the FCIC that there would have been questions either way. As Baxter put it, "I think that if the Federal Reserve had lent to Lehman that Monday in a way that some people think—without adequate collateral and without other security to ensure repayment—this hearing and other hearings would have only been about how we wasted the taxpayers' money."[143]

## COMMISSION CONCLUSIONS ON CHAPTER 18

The Commission concludes the financial crisis reached cataclysmic proportions with the collapse of Lehman Brothers.

Lehman's collapse demonstrated weaknesses that also contributed to the failures or near failures of the other four large investment banks: inadequate regulatory oversight, risky trading activities (including securitization and over-the-counter (OTC) derivatives dealing), enormous leverage, and reliance on short-term funding. While investment banks tended to be initially more vulnerable, commercial banks suffered from many of the same weaknesses, including their involvement in the shadow banking system, and ultimately many suffered major losses, requiring government rescue.

Lehman, like other large OTC derivatives dealers, experienced runs on its derivatives operations that played a role in its failure. Its massive derivatives positions greatly complicated its bankruptcy, and the impact of its bankruptcy through interconnections with derivatives counterparties and other financial institutions contributed significantly to the severity and depth of the financial crisis.

Lehman's failure resulted in part from significant problems in its corporate governance, including risk management, exacerbated by compensation to its executives and traders that was based predominantly on short-term profits.

Federal government officials decided not to rescue Lehman for a variety of reasons, including the lack of a private firm willing and able to acquire it, uncertainty about Lehman's potential losses, concerns about moral hazard and political reaction, and erroneous assumptions that Lehman's failure would have a manageable impact on the financial system because market participants had anticipated it. After the fact, they justified their decision by stating that the Federal Reserve did not have legal authority to rescue Lehman.

The inconsistency of federal government decisions in not rescuing Lehman after having rescued Bear Stearns and the GSEs, and immediately before rescuing AIG, added to uncertainty and panic in the financial markets.

# 19

## SEPTEMBER 2008:
## THE BAILOUT OF AIG

---

### CONTENTS

Nine billion dollars is a lot of money, but as AIG executives and the board examined their balance sheet and pondered the markets in the second week of September 2008, they were almost certain $9 billion in cash could not keep the company alive through the next week.[1] The AIG corporate empire held more than $1 trillion in assets, but most of the liquid assets, including cash, were held by regulated insurance subsidiaries whose regulators did not allow the cash to flow freely up to the holding company, much less out to troubled subsidiaries such as AIG Financial Products.[2] The company's liabilities, especially those due in the near future, were much larger than the $9 billion on hand.

On Friday, September 12, 2008, AIG was facing challenges on a number of fronts. It had to fund $1.4 billion of its own commercial paper on that day[3] because traditional investors—for example, money market funds—no longer wanted even short-term unsecured exposure to AIG; and the company had another $3.2 billion coming due the following week.[4] On another front, the repo lenders—who had the comfort of holding collateral for their loans to AIG ($9.7 billion in mostly overnight funding)[5]—were nonetheless becoming skittish about the perceived weakness of the company and the low quality of most of its collateral: mortgage-related securities.[6]

On a third front, AIG had already put up billions of dollars in collateral to its credit default swap counterparties. By June of 2008, counterparties were demanding $15.7 billion, and AIG had posted $13.2 billion. By September 12, the calls had soared to $23.4 billion, and AIG had paid $18.9 billion—$7.6 billion to Goldman alone—and it looked very likely that AIG would need to post billions more in the near future.[7] That day, S&P and Moody's both warned of potential coming downgrades to AIG's credit rating, which, if they happened, would lead to an estimated $10 billion in new collateral calls.[8] A downgrade would also trigger liquidity puts that

AIG had written on commercial paper, requiring AIG to come up with another $4 to $5 billion.[9]

Finally, AIG was increasingly strained by its securities lending business. As a lender of securities, AIG received cash from borrowers, typically equal to between 100% and 102% of the market value of the securities they lent. As borrowers began questioning AIG's stability, the company had to accept below-market terms—sometimes accepting cash equal to only 90% of the value of the securities.[10] Furthermore, AIG had invested this cash in mortgage-related assets, whose value had fallen. Since September 2007, state regulators had worked with AIG to reduce exposures of the securities lending program to mortgage-related assets, according to testimony by Eric Dinallo, the former superintendent of the New York State Insurance Department (NYSID).[11] Still, by the end of June 2008, AIG had invested $75 billion in cash in mortgage-related securities, which had declined in value to $59.5 billion. By late August 2008, the parent company had to provide $3.3 billion to its struggling securities lending subsidiary, and counterparties were demanding $24 billion to offset the shortfall between the cash collateral provided and the diminished value of the securities.[12] According to Dinallo, the collateral call disputes between AIG and its credit default swap counterparties hindered an orderly wind down of the securities lending business, and in fact accelerated demands from securities lending counterparties.[13]

That Friday, AIG's board dispatched a team led by Vice Chairman Jacob Frenkel to meet with top officials at the Federal Reserve Bank of New York.[14] Elsewhere in the building, Treasury Secretary Henry Paulson and New York Fed President Timothy Geithner were telling Wall Street bankers that they had the weekend to devise a solution to prevent Lehman's bankruptcy without government assistance. Now came this emergency meeting regarding another beleaguered American institution. "Bottom line," the New York Fed later reported of that meeting, "[AIG's] Treasurer estimates that parent and [Financial Products] have 5–10 days before they are out of liquidity."[15]

AIG posed a simple question: how could it obtain an emergency loan under the Federal Reserve's 13(3) authority? Without a solution, there was no way this conglomerate, despite more than $1 trillion in assets, would survive another week.

## "CURRENT LIQUIDITY POSITION IS PRECARIOUS"

AIG's visit to the New York Fed may have been an emergency, but it should not have been a surprise. With the Primary Dealer Credit Facility (PDCF), the Fed had effectively opened its discount window—traditionally available only to depository institutions—to investment banks that qualified as primary dealers; AIG did not qualify. But over the summer, New York Fed officials had begun to consider providing emergency collateralized funding to even more large institutions that were systemically important. That led the regulators to look closely at two trillion-dollar holding companies, AIG and GE Capital. Both were large participants in the commercial paper market: AIG with $20 billion in outstanding paper, GE Capital with $90 billion.[16] In

August, the New York Fed set up a team to study the two companies' funding and liquidity risk.

On August 11, New York Fed officials met with Office of Thrift Supervision (OTS) regulators to discuss AIG.[17] The OTS said that it was "generally comfortable with [the] firm's current liquidity . . . [and] confident that the firm could access the capital markets with no problem if it had to."[18] The New York Fed did not agree. On August 14, 2008, Kevin Coffey, an analyst from the Financial Sector Policy and Analysis unit, wrote that despite raising $20 billion earlier in the year, "AIG is under increasing capital and liquidity pressure" and "appears to need to raise substantial longer term funds to address the impact of deteriorating asset values on its capital and available liquidity as well as to address certain asset/liability funding mismatches."[19]

Coffey listed six concerns: (1) AIG's significant losses on investments, primarily because of securities lending activities; (2) $26.5 billion in mark-to-market losses on AIG Financial Products' credit default swap book and related margin calls, for which AIG had posted $16.5 billion in collateral by mid-August; (3) significant near-term liabilities; (4) commitments to purchase collateralized debt obligations due to outstanding liquidity puts; (5) ratings-based triggers in derivative contracts that could cause significant additional collateral calls if AIG were downgraded; and (6) limited standby credit facilities to manage sudden cash needs. He noted Moody's and S&P had highlighted worries about earnings, capital, and liquidity following AIG's 2008 second-quarter earnings. The agencies warned they would downgrade AIG if it did not address these issues.[20]

Four days later, Goldman Sachs issued a report to clients that echoed much of Coffey's internal analysis. The report, "Don't Buy AIG: Potential Downgrades, Capital Raise on the Horizon," warned that "we foresee $9–$20 billion in economic losses from [AIG's credit default swap] book, which could result in larger cash outlays . . . resulting in a significant shift in the risk quality of AIG's assets. . . . Put simply, we have seen this credit overhang story before with another stock in our coverage universe, and foresee outcomes similar in nature but on a much larger scale."[21] Goldman appeared to be referring to Bear Stearns. Ira Selig, a manager at the New York Fed, emailed the Goldman report to Coffey and others. "The bottom line: large scale cash outflows and posting of collateral could substantially weaken AIG's balance sheet," the manager wrote.[22]

On September 2, the New York Fed's Danielle Vicente noted the situation had worsened: "AIG's current liquidity position is precarious and asset liability management appears inadequate given the substantial off balance sheet liquidity needs." Liquidating an $835 billion securities portfolio to cover liabilities would mean substantial losses and "potentially" affect prices, she wrote. Borrowing against AIG's securities through the Fed's PDCF might allow AIG to unwind its positions calmly while satisfying immediate cash needs, but Vicente questioned whether the PDCF was "necessary for the survival of the firm."[23] Arguably, however, AIG's volatile funding sources made the firm vulnerable to runs. Off-balance-sheet commitments—including collateral calls, contract terminations, and liquidity puts—could be as high as

$33 billion if AIG was downgraded. Yet AIG had only $4 billion of revolving credit facilities in addition to the $12 to $13 billion of cash it had on hand at the time.[24]

The rating agencies waited to see how AIG would address its liquidity and capital needs. Analysts worried about the losses in AIG's credit default swaps and investment portfolios, about rating agency actions, and about subsequent impacts on capital. Indeed, Goldman's August 18 report on AIG concluded that the firm itself and the rating agencies were in denial about impending losses.[25]

By early September, management was no longer in denial. At the Friday, September 12, meeting at the New York Fed, AIG executives reported that the company was "facing serious liquidity issues that threaten[ed] its survival viability" and that a downgrade, possibly after a rating agency meeting September 15, would trigger billions of dollars in collateral calls, liquidity puts, and other liquidity needs.[26] AIG's stock had fallen significantly (shares hit an intraday low of $11.49 Friday, down from a $17.55 close the day before) and credit default swap spreads had reached 14% during the day,[27] indicating that protection on $10 million of AIG debt would cost approximately $1.4 million per year. AIG reported it was having problems with its commercial paper, able to roll only $1.1 billion of the $2.5 billion that matured on September 12.[28] In addition, some banks were pulling away and even refusing to provide repo funding.[29] Assets were illiquid, their values had declined, borrowing was restricted, and raising capital was not viable.

## "SPILLOVER EFFECT"

The New York Fed knew that a failure of AIG would have dramatic, far-reaching consequences. By the evening of September 12, after the meeting with AIG executives, that possibility looked increasingly realistic. Hayley Boesky of the New York Fed emailed William Dudley and others. "More panic from [hedge funds]. Now focus is on AIG," she wrote. "I am hearing worse than LEH. Every bank and dealer has exposure to them."[30]

Shortly before midnight, New York Fed Assistant Vice President Alejandro LaTorre emailed Geithner, Dudley, and other senior officials about AIG: "The key takeaway is that they are potentially facing a severe run on their liquidity over the course of the next several (approx. 10) days if they are downgraded. . . . Their risk exposures are concentrated among the 12 largest international banks (both U.S. and European) across a wide array of product types (bank lines, derivatives, securities lending, etc.) meaning [there] could be significant counterparty losses to those firms in the event of AIG's failure."[31]

New York Fed officials met on Saturday morning, and gathered additional information about AIG's financial condition, but according to New York Fed General Counsel Tom Baxter, it "seemed clear that the private sector solution would materialize for AIG."[32] Indeed, Christopher Flowers, head of J. C. Flowers & Co., a private equity firm, had spoken to AIG CEO Robert Willumstad the prior Thursday, and the two had called Warren Buffett to discuss a possible deal. Willumstad told the FCIC

that he was in contact with about a dozen private equity firms over the weekend.[33] AIG executives also worked with then-Superintendent Eric Dinallo to help craft a deal that would have allowed AIG's regulated subsidiaries to essentially lend money to the parent company. Fed officials reported to AIG executives during a conference call on Saturday that "they should not be particularly optimistic [about financial assistance], given the hurtles [*sic*] and history of [the Fed's] 13-3 lending [authority]."[34] And by the end of the day on Saturday, AIG appeared to the Fed to be pursuing private-sector leads. "It was clear from the conversation that Flowers [is] actively involved in working with everything (AIG, regulators, bankers, etc) in putting together both the 'term sheet' with AIG, and providing analysis to NYSID on liquidity profile of the parent company," Patricia Mosser, a senior vice president at the New York Fed, wrote to LaTorre and others.[35]

On Sunday morning, September 14, Adam Ashcraft of the New York Fed circulated a memo, "Comment on Possible 13-3 Lending to AIG," discussing the effect of a fire sale by AIG on asset markets.[36] In an accompanying email, Ashcraft wrote that the "threat" by AIG to sell assets was "a clear attempt to scare policymakers into giving [AIG] access to the discount window, and avoid making otherwise hard but viable options: sell or hedge the CDO risk (little to no impact on capital), sell subsidiaries, or raise capital."[37]

Before a 2:30 P.M. meeting, LaTorre sent an analysis, "Pros and cons of lending to AIG," to colleagues. The pros included avoiding a messy collapse and dislocations in markets such as commercial paper. If AIG collapsed, it could have a "spillover effect on other firms involved in similar activities (e.g. GE Finance)" and would "lead to $18B increase in European bank capital requirements." In other words, European banks that had lowered credit risk—and, as a result, lowered capital requirements—by buying credit default swaps from AIG would lose that protection if AIG failed. AIG's bankruptcy would also affect other companies because of its "non-trivial exotic derivatives book," a $2.7 trillion over-the-counter derivatives portfolio of which $1 trillion was concentrated in 12 large counterparties. The memo also noted that an AIG failure "could cause dislocations in CDS market [that] . . . could leave dealer books significantly unbalanced."[38]

The cons of a bailout included a "chilling effect" on private-sector solutions thought to be under way; the possibility that a Fed loan would be insufficient to keep AIG afloat, "undermining efficacy of 13-3 lending as a policy tool"; an increase in moral hazard; the perception that it would be "incoherent" to lend to AIG and not Lehman; the possibility of assets being insufficient to cover the potential liquidity hole. LaTorre concluded, "Without punitive terms, lending [to AIG] could reward poor risk management," which included AIG's unwillingness to sell or hedge some of its CDO risk.[39]

The private-sector solutions LaTorre referred to had hit a wall, however. By Sunday afternoon, Flowers had been "summarily dismissed" by AIG's board. Flowers told the FCIC that under his proposal, his firm and Allianz, the giant insurance company, would have each invested $5 billion in exchange for the stock of AIG subsidiaries. With

approval from the NYSID, the subsidiaries would "upstream" $20 billion to the parent company, and the parent company would get access to bridge financing from the Fed. Then, Allianz would take control of AIG almost immediately. Flowers said that he was surprised by AIG's unwillingness to negotiate. "I'm not saying it would have worked or that it was perfect as written, but it was astounding to me that given what happened, nobody bothered to check this [deal] out," he said.[40] Willumstad referred to the Flowers deal as a "so-called offer"—he did not consider it to be a "serious effort," and so it was "dismissed immediately." With respect to the other potential investors AIG spoke with over the weekend, Willumstad said that negotiations were unsuccessful because every potential deal would have required government assistance—something Willumstad had been assured by the "highest levels" would not be forthcoming.[41]

On Monday morning—after Lehman had declared bankruptcy, and with no private-sector solution on the horizon—the Fed initiated an effort to have JP Morgan and Goldman Sachs assemble a syndicate of banks to lend about $75 billion to keep AIG afloat.[42] In the afternoon, the rating agencies announced their assessments, which were even worse than expected. All three rating agencies announced downgrades of AIG: S&P by three notches to A-, and Moody's and Fitch by two notches to A2 and A, respectively. The downgrades triggered an additional $13 billion in cash collateral calls on AIG Financial Products' credit default swaps. Goldman Sachs alone requested $2.1 billion.[43] Demands hit $32 billion, and AIG's payouts increased to $19.5 billion.[44] The company's stock plummeted 61% to $4.76 from the closing price of $12.14 the previous Friday—a fraction of its all-time high of $145.84.

The syndicate of banks did not agree on a deal, despite the expectations of Fed officials. "Once Lehman filed [for bankruptcy] on the morning of the 15th, everyone decided that, 'we've got to protect our own balance sheet,' and the banks that were going to provide the $75 billion decided that they were not going to," Baxter told the FCIC.[45] Sarah Dahlgren, a senior New York Fed official, agreed with Baxter. Lehman's bankruptcy "was the end of the private-sector solution," she told the Commission.[46]

After the markets closed, AIG informed the New York Fed it was unable to access the short-term commercial paper market.[47] Regulators spent the next several hours preparing for a late-night teleconference with Geithner. The "Lead point," according to an email circulated to the Fed's AIG monitoring group, was that "the size, name, franchise and market presence (wholesale and retail) [of AIG] raise questions about potential worldwide contagion, should this franchise become impaired."[48] Late that night, for the second time since the beginning of the crisis, the Federal Reserve Board invoked section 13(3) of the Federal Reserve Act to bail out a company. As it had done for Bear Stearns, the New York Fed, with the support of the Treasury, would rescue a brand-name financial institution.

The Federal Open Market Committee was briefed about AIG. Members were told that AIG faced a liquidity crisis but that it was unclear if there were also solvency issues. In addition, the staff noted that money market funds had even broader exposure to AIG than to Lehman and that the parent company could run out of money quite soon, even within days.[49]

On Tuesday morning, the Fed put a number on the table: it would loan $85 billion so that AIG could meet its immediate obligations. The collateral would be the assets of the parent company and its primary nonregulated subsidiaries, plus the stock of almost all the regulated insurance subsidiaries. The Fed stated that "a disorderly failure of AIG could add to already significant levels of financial market fragility and lead to substantially higher borrowing costs, reduced household wealth, and materially weaker economic performance."[50] By Wednesday, a share of AIG sold for as little as $1.99. The previous eight years' profits of $66 billion would be dwarfed by the $99.3 billion loss for this one year, 2008.

But $85 billion would soon prove insufficient. Treasury added $49.1 billion under its Troubled Asset Relief Program (TARP).[51] Ultimately, according to the Congressional Oversight Panel, taxpayer funds committed to AIG reached $182 billion. The panel faulted the government for deciding to bail out AIG too hastily: "With AIG, the Federal Reserve and Treasury broke new ground. They put the U.S. taxpayer on the line for the full cost and full risk of rescuing a failing company."[52] The Treasury Department defended its decision, saying that the panel report "overlooks the basic fact that the global economy was on the brink of collapse and there were only hours in which to make critical decisions."[53]

## "LIKE A GNAT ON AN ELEPHANT"

The Office of Thrift Supervision has acknowledged failures in its oversight of AIG. In a March 18, 2009, congressional hearing, Acting Director Scott Polakoff testified that supervisors failed to recognize the extent of liquidity risk of the Financial Products subsidiary's credit default swap portfolio.[54] John Reich, a former OTS director, told the FCIC that as late as September 2008, he had "no clue—no idea—what [AIG's] CDS liability was."[55]

According to Mike Finn, the director for the OTS's northeast region, the OTS's authority to regulate holding companies was intended to ensure the safety and soundness of the FDIC-insured subsidiary of AIG and not to focus on the potential impact on AIG of an uninsured subsidiary like AIG Financial Products.[56] Finn ignored the OTS's responsibilities under the European Union's Financial Conglomerates Directive (FCD)—responsibilities the OTS had actively sought. The directive required foreign companies doing business in Europe to have the equivalent of a "consolidated supervisor" in their home country. Starting in 2004, the OTS worked to persuade the European Union that it was capable of serving as AIG's "home country consolidated supervisor."[57] In 2005 the agency wrote: "AIG and its subsidiaries are subject to consolidated supervision by OTS. . . . As part of its supervision, OTS will conduct continuous on-site reviews of AIG and its subsidiaries."[58] Yet even Reich told FCIC staff that he did not understand his agency's responsibilities under the FCD. The former director said he was never sure what authority the OTS had over AIG Financial Products, which he said had slipped through a regulatory gap.[59]

Further undermining the OTS's claim that it lacked authority over AIG Financial Products are its own actions: the OTS did in fact examine the subsidiary, albeit much too late to matter. OTS examiners argued they got little cooperation from Joseph Cassano, the head of the subsidiary. Joseph Gonzales, the examiner in charge from April 2004 to November 2006, told FCIC staff, "I overheard one employee saying that Joe Cassano felt that [the OTS was] overreaching our scope by going into FP."[60]

The OTS did not look carefully at the credit default swap portfolio guaranteed by the parent company—even though AIG did describe the nature of its super-senior portfolio in its annual reports at that time, including the dollar amount of total credit default swaps that it had written. Gonzales said that the OTS did not know about the CDS during the 2004–05 period.[61] After a limited review in July 2007—conducted a week before Goldman sent AIG Financial Products its first demand for collateral—the OTS concluded that the risk in the CDS book was too small to be measured and decided to put off a more detailed review until 2008.[62] The agency's stated reason was its limited time and staff resources.[63]

In February 2008, AIG reported billions of dollars in losses and material weaknesses in the way it valued credit default swap positions. Yet the OTS did not initiate an in-depth review of the credit default swaps until September 2008—ten days before AIG went to the Fed seeking a rescue—completing the review on October 17, more than a month after AIG failed. It was, former OTS director of Conglomerate Operations Brad Waring admitted, "in hindsight, a bad choice."[64]

Reich told the FCIC that before 2008, AIG had not been a great concern. He also acknowledged that the OTS had never fully understood the Financial Products unit, and thus couldn't regulate it. "At the simplest level, . . . an organization like OTS cannot supervise AIG, GE, Merrill Lynch, and entities that have worldwide offices. . . . I would be the first to say that for an organization like OTS to pretend that it has total responsibility over AIG and all of its subsidiaries . . . it's like a gnat on an elephant—there's no way." Reich said that for the OTS to think it could regulate AIG was "totally impractical and unrealistic. . . . I think we thought we could grow into that responsibility. . . . But I think that was sort of pie in the sky dreaming."[65]

Geithner agreed, and told Reich so bluntly. Reich told the FCIC about a phone call from Geithner after the rescue. "About all I can remember is the foul language that I heard on the other end of the line," Reich said. He recalled Geithner telling him. "'You guys have handed me a bag of sh*t.' I just listened."[66]

## COMMISSION CONCLUSIONS ON CHAPTER 19

The Commission concludes AIG failed and was rescued by the government primarily because its enormous sales of credit default swaps were made without putting up initial collateral, setting aside capital reserves, or hedging its exposure—a profound failure in corporate governance, particularly its risk management practices.

AIG's failure was possible because of the sweeping deregulation of over-the-counter (OTC) derivatives, including credit default swaps, which effectively eliminated federal and state regulation of these products, including capital and margin requirements that would have lessened the likelihood of AIG's failure. The OTC derivatives market's lack of transparency and of effective price discovery exacerbated the collateral disputes of AIG and Goldman Sachs and similar disputes between other derivatives counterparties. AIG engaged in regulatory arbitrage by setting up a major business in this unregulated product, locating much of the business in London, and selecting a weak federal regulator, the Office of Thrift Supervision (OTS).

The OTS failed to effectively exercise its authority over AIG and its affiliates: it lacked the capability to supervise an institution of the size and complexity of AIG, did not recognize the risks inherent in AIG's sales of credit default swaps, and did not understand its responsibility to oversee the entire company, including AIG Financial Products. Furthermore, because of the deregulation of OTC derivatives, state insurance supervisors were barred from regulating AIG's sale of credit default swaps even though they were similar in effect to insurance contracts. If they had been regulated as insurance contracts, AIG would have been required to maintain adequate capital reserves, would not have been able to enter into contracts requiring the posting of collateral, and would not have been able to provide default protection to speculators; thus AIG would have been prevented from acting in such a risky manner.

AIG was so interconnected with many large commercial banks, investment banks, and other financial institutions through counterparty credit relationships on credit default swaps and other activities such as securities lending that its potential failure created systemic risk. The government concluded AIG was too big to fail and committed more than $180 billion to its rescue. Without the bailout, AIG's default and collapse could have brought down its counterparties, causing cascading losses and collapses throughout the financial system.

# 20

## CRISIS AND PANIC

<hr>

### CONTENTS

September 15, 2008—the date of the bankruptcy of Lehman Brothers and the takeover of Merrill Lynch, followed within 24 hours by the rescue of AIG—marked the beginning of the worst market disruption in postwar American history and an extraordinary rush to the safest possible investments. Creditors and investors suspected that many other large financial institutions were on the edge of failure, and the Lehman bankruptcy seemed to prove that at least some of them would not have access to the federal government's safety net.

John Mack, CEO of Morgan Stanley during the crisis, told the FCIC, "In the immediate wake of Lehman's failure on September 15, Morgan Stanley and similar institutions experienced a classic 'run on the bank,' as investors lost confidence in financial institutions and the entire investment banking business model came under siege."[1]

"The markets were very bad, the volatility, the illiquidity, some things couldn't trade at all, I mean completely locked, the markets were in terrible shape," JP Morgan CEO Jamie Dimon recalled to the FCIC. He thought the country could face 20% unemployment. "We could have survived it in my opinion, but it would have been terrible. I would have stopped lending, marketing, investing . . . and probably laid off 20,000 people. And I would have done it in three weeks. You get companies starting to take actions like that, that's what a Great Depression is."[2]

Treasury Secretary Timothy Geithner told the FCIC, "You had people starting to take their deposits out of very, very strong banks, long way removed in distance and

risk and business from the guys on Wall Street that were at the epicenter of the problem. And that is a good measure, classic measure of incipient panic."[3] In an interview in December 2009, Geithner said that "none of [the biggest banks] would have survived a situation in which we had let that fire try to burn itself out."[4]

Fed Chairman Ben Bernanke told the FCIC, "As a scholar of the Great Depression, I honestly believe that September and October of 2008 was the worst financial crisis in global history, including the Great Depression. If you look at the firms that came under pressure in that period . . . only one . . . was not at serious risk of failure. . . . So out of maybe the 13, 13 of the most important financial institutions in the United States, 12 were at risk of failure within a period of a week or two."[5]

As it had on the weekend of Bear's demise, the Federal Reserve announced new measures on Sunday, September 14, to make more cash available to investment banks and other firms. Yet again, it lowered its standards regarding the quality of the collateral that investment banks and other primary dealers could use while borrowing under the two programs to support repo lending, the Primary Dealer Credit Facility (PDCF) and the Term Securities Lending Facility (TSLF).[6] And, providing a temporary exception to its rules, it allowed the investment banks and other financial companies to borrow cash from their insured depository affiliates. The investment banks drew liberally on the Fed's lending programs. By the end of September, Morgan Stanley was getting by on $96.1 billion of Fed-provided life support; Goldman was receiving $31.5 billion.[7]

But the new measures did not quell the market panic. Among the first to be directly affected were the money market funds and other institutions that held Lehman's $4 billion in unsecured commercial paper and made loans to the company through the tri-party repo market. Investors pulled out of funds with known exposure to that jeopardy, including the Reserve Management Company's Reserve Primary Fund and Wachovia's Evergreen Investments.

Other parties with direct connections to Lehman included the hedge funds, investment banks, and investors who were on the other side of Lehman's more than 900,000 over-the-counter derivatives contracts. For example, Deutsche Bank, JP Morgan, and UBS together had more than 150,000 outstanding trades with Lehman as of May 2008. The Lehman bankruptcy caused immediate problems for these OTC derivatives counterparties. They had the right under U.S. bankruptcy law to terminate their derivatives contracts with Lehman upon its bankruptcy, and to the extent that Lehman owed them money on the contracts they could seize any Lehman collateral that they held. However, any additional amount owed to them had to be claimed in the bankruptcy proceeding. If they had posted collateral with Lehman, they would have to make a claim for the return of that collateral, and disputes over valuation of the contracts would still have to be resolved. These proceedings would delay payment and most likely result in losses. Moreover, any hedges that rested on these contracts were now gone, increasing risk.[8]

Investors also pulled out of funds that did not have direct Lehman exposure. The managers of these funds, in turn, pulled $165 billion out of the commercial paper market in September and shifted billions of dollars of repo loans to safer collateral, putting further pressure on investment banks and other finance companies that de-

# Cost of Interbank Lending

As concerns about the health of bank counterparties spread, lending banks demanded higher interest rates to compensate for the risk. The one-month LIBOR-OIS spread measures the part of the interest rates banks paid other banks that is due to this credit risk. Strains in the interbank lending markets appeared just after the crisis began in 2007 and then peaked during the fall of 2008.

IN PERCENT, DAILY

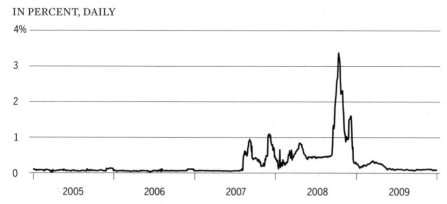

NOTE: Chart shows the spread between the one-month London Interbank Offered Rate (LIBOR) and the overnight index swap rate (OIS), both closely watched interest rates.
SOURCE: Bloomberg

*Figure 20.1*

pended on those markets.[9] "When the commercial paper market died, the biggest corporations in America thought they were finished," Harvey Miller, the bankruptcy attorney for the Lehman estate, told the FCIC.[10]

Investors and uninsured depositors yanked tens of billions of dollars out of banks whose real estate exposures might be debilitating (Washington Mutual, Wachovia) in favor of those whose real estate exposures appeared manageable (Wells Fargo, JP Morgan). Hedge funds withdrew tens of billions of dollars of assets held in custody at the remaining investment banks (Goldman Sachs, Morgan Stanley, and even Merrill Lynch, as the just-announced Bank of America acquisition wouldn't close for another three and a half months) in favor of large commercial banks with prime brokerage businesses (JP Morgan, Credit Suisse, Deutsche Bank), because the commercial banks had more diverse sources of liquidity than the investment banks as well as large bases of insured deposits. JP Morgan and BNY Mellon, the tri-party repo clearing banks, clamped down on their intraday exposures, demanding more collateral than ever from the remaining investment banks and other primary dealers. Many banks refused to lend to one another; the cost of interbank lending rose to unprecedented levels (see figure 20.1).

On Monday, September 15, the Dow Jones Industrial Average fell more than 500 points, or 4%, the largest single-day point drop since the 9/11 terrorist attacks. These drops would be exceeded on September 29—the day that the House of Representatives initially voted against the $700 billion Troubled Asset Relief Program (TARP) proposal to provide extraordinary support to financial markets and firms— when the Dow Jones fell 7% and financial stocks fell 16%. For the month, the S&P 500 would lose $889 billion of its value, a decline of 9%—the worst month since September 2002.

And specific institutions would take direct hits.

## MONEY MARKET FUNDS:
## "DEALERS WEREN'T EVEN PICKING UP THEIR PHONES"

When Lehman declared bankruptcy, the Reserve Primary Fund had $785 million invested in Lehman's commercial paper. The Primary Fund was the world's first money market mutual fund, established in 1971 by Reserve Management Company. The fund had traditionally invested in conservative assets such as government securities and bank certificates of deposit and had for years enjoyed Moody's and S&P's highest ratings for safety and liquidity.

In March 2006, the fund had advised investors that it had "slightly underperformed" its rivals, owing to a "more conservative and risk averse manner" of investing—"for example, the Reserve Funds do not invest in commercial paper."[11] But immediately after publishing this statement, it quietly but dramatically changed that strategy. Within 18 months, commercial paper grew from zero to one-half of Reserve Primary's assets. The higher yields attracted new investors and the Reserve Primary Fund was the fastest-growing money market fund complex in the United States in 2006, 2007, and 2008—doubling in the first eight months of 2008 alone.[12]

Earlier in 2008, Primary Fund's managers had loaned Bear Stearns money in the repo market up to two days before Bear's near-collapse, pulling its money only after Bear CEO Alan Schwartz appeared on CNBC in the company's final days, Primary Fund Portfolio Manager Michael Luciano told the FCIC. But after the government-assisted rescue of Bear, Luciano, like many other professional investors, said he assumed that the federal government would similarly save the day if Lehman or one of the other investment banks, which were much larger and posed greater apparent systemic risks, ran into trouble. These firms, Luciano said, were too big to fail.[13]

On September 15, when Lehman declared bankruptcy, the Primary Fund's Lehman holdings amounted to 1.2% of the fund's total assets of $62.4 billion. That morning, the fund was flooded with redemption requests totaling $10.8 billion. State Street, the fund's custodian bank, initially helped the fund meet those requests, largely through an existing overdraft facility, but stopped doing so at 10:10 A.M. With no means to borrow, Primary Fund representatives reportedly described State Street's action as "the kiss of death" for the Primary Fund.[14] Despite public assurances from the fund's investment advisors, Bruce Bent Sr. and Bruce Bent II, that the fund was

committed to maintaining a $1.00 net asset value, investors requested an additional $29 billion later on Monday and Tuesday, September 16.[15]

Meanwhile, on Monday, the fund's board had determined that the Lehman paper was worth 80 cents on the dollar. That appraisal had quickly proved optimistic. After the market closed Tuesday, Reserve Management publicly announced that the value of its Lehman paper was zero, "effective 4:00PM New York time today." As a result, the fund broke the buck.[16] Four days later, the fund sought SEC permission to officially suspend redemptions.

Other funds suffering similar losses were propped up by their sponsors. On Monday, Wachovia's asset management unit, Evergreen Investments, announced that it would support three Evergreen mutual funds that held about $540 million in Lehman paper. On Wednesday, BNY Mellon announced support for various funds that held Lehman paper, including the $22 billion Institutional Cash Reserves fund and four of its trademark Dreyfus funds. BNY Mellon would take an after-tax charge of $425 million because of this decision. Over the next two years, 62 money market funds—36 based in the United States, 26 in Europe[17]—would receive such assistance to keep their funds from breaking the buck.

After the Primary Fund broke the buck, the run took an ominous turn: it even slammed money market funds with no direct Lehman exposure. This lack of exposure was generally known, since the SEC requires these funds to report details on their investments at least quarterly. Investors pulled out simply because they feared that their fellow investors would run first. "It was overwhelmingly clear that we were staring into the abyss—that there wasn't a bottom to this—as the outflows picked up steam on Wednesday and Thursday," Fed economist Patrick McCabe told the FCIC. "The overwhelming sense was that this was a catastrophe that we were watching unfold."[18]

"We were really cognizant of the fact that there weren't backstops in the system that were resilient at that time," the Fed's Michael Palumbo said. "Liquidity crises, by their nature, invoke rapid, emergent episodes—that's what they are. By their nature, they spread very quickly."[19]

An early and significant casualty was Putnam Investments' $12 billion Prime Money Market Fund, which was hit on Wednesday with a wave of redemption requests. The fund, unable to liquidate assets quickly enough, halted redemptions. One week later, it was sold to Federated Investors.

Within a week, investors in prime money market funds—funds that invested in highly rated securities—withdrew $349 billion; within three weeks, they withdrew another $85 billion. That money was mostly headed for other funds that bought only Treasuries and agency securities; indeed, it was more money than those funds could invest, and they had to turn people away[20] (see figure 20.2). As a result of the unprecedented demand for Treasuries, the yield on four-week Treasuries fell close to 0%, levels not seen since World War II.

Money market mutual funds needing cash to honor redemptions sold their now illiquid investments. Unfortunately, there was little market to speak of. "We heard

## Investments in Money Market Funds

*In a flight to safety, investors shifted from prime money market funds to money market funds investing in Treasury and agency securities.*

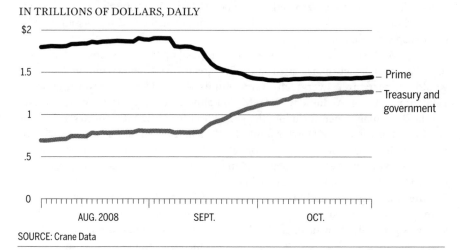

IN TRILLIONS OF DOLLARS, DAILY

SOURCE: Crane Data

*Figure 20.2*

anecdotally that the dealers weren't even picking up their phones. The funds had to get rid of their paper; they didn't have anyone to give it to," McCabe said.[21]

And holding unsecured commercial paper from any large financial institution was now simply out of the question: fund managers wanted no part of the next Lehman. An FCIC survey of the largest money market funds found that many were unwilling to purchase commercial paper from financial firms during the week after Lehman. Of the respondents, the five with the most drastic reduction in financial commercial paper cut their holdings by half, from $58 billion to $29 billion.[22] This led to unprecedented increases in the rates on commercial paper, creating problems for borrowers, particularly for financial companies, such as GE Capital, CIT, and American Express, as well as for nonfinancial corporations that used commercial paper to pay their immediate expenses such as payroll and inventories. The cost of commercial paper borrowing spiked in mid-September, dramatically surpassing the previous highs in 2007 (see figure 20.3).

"You had a broad-based run on commercial paper markets," Geithner told the FCIC. "And so you faced the prospect of some of the largest companies in the world and the United States losing the capacity to fund and access those commercial paper markets."[23] Three decades of easy borrowing for those with top-rated credit in a very liquid market had disappeared almost overnight. The panic threatened to disrupt the payments system through which financial institutions transfer trillions of dollars in

# Cost of Short-Term Borrowing

*During the crisis, the cost of borrowing for lower-rated nonfinancial firms spiked.*

IN PERCENT, DAILY

NOTE: Shown is the spread between the rate paid by second-tier rated nonfinancial companies (A2/P2) that borrowed by issuing 30-day commercial paper and the rate paid on similar paper by the best-rated companies.
SOURCE: Federal Reserve Board of Governors

*Figure 20.3*

cash and assets every day and upon which consumers rely—for example, to use their credit cards and debit cards. "At that point, you don't need to map out which particular mechanism—it's not relevant anymore—it's become systemic and endemic and it needs to be stopped," Palumbo said.[24]

The government responded with two new lending programs on Friday, September 19. Treasury would guarantee the $1 net asset value of eligible money market funds, for a fee paid by the funds.[25] And the Fed would provide loans to banks to purchase high-quality-asset-backed commercial paper from money market funds.[26] In its first two weeks, this program loaned banks $150 billion, although usage declined over the ensuing months. The two programs immediately slowed the run on money market funds.

With the financial sector in disarray, the SEC imposed a temporary ban on short-selling on the stocks of about 800 banks, insurance companies, and securities firms. This action, taken on September 18, followed an earlier temporary ban put in place over the summer on naked short-selling—that is, shorting a stock without arranging to deliver it to the buyer—of 19 financial stocks in order to protect them from "unlawful manipulation."

Meanwhile, Treasury Secretary Henry Paulson and other senior officials had decided they needed a more systematic approach to dealing with troubled firms and troubled markets. Paulson started seeking authority from Congress for TARP. "One

thing that was constant about the crisis is that we were always behind. It was always morphing and manifesting itself in ways we didn't expect," Neel Kashkari, then assistant secretary of the treasury, told the FCIC. "So we knew we'd get one shot at this authority and it was important that we provided ourselves maximum firepower and maximum flexibility. We specifically designed the authority to allow us basically to do whatever we needed to do." Kashkari "spent the next two weeks basically living on Capitol Hill."[27] As discussed below, the program was a tough sell.

## MORGAN STANLEY: "NOW WE'RE THE NEXT IN LINE"

Investors scrutinized the two remaining large, independent investment banks after the failure of Lehman and the announced acquisition of Merrill. Especially Morgan Stanley. On Monday, September 15, the annual cost of protecting $10 million in Morgan Stanley debt through credit default swaps jumped to $682,000—from $363,000 on Friday—about double the cost for Goldman. "As soon as we come in on Monday, we're in the eye of the storm with Merrill gone and Lehman gone," John Mack, then Morgan Stanley's CEO, said to the FCIC. He later added, "Now we're the next in line."[28]

Morgan Stanley officials had some reason for confidence. On the previous Friday, the company's liquidity pool was more than $130 billion—Goldman's was $120 billion[29]—and, like Goldman, it had passed the regulators' liquidity stress tests months earlier. But the early market indicators were mixed. David Wong, Morgan Stanley's treasurer, heard early from his London office that several European banks were not accepting Morgan Stanley as a counterparty on derivatives trades.[30] He called those banks and they agreed to keep their trades with Morgan Stanley, at least for the time being. But Wong well knew that rumors about derivatives counterparties fleeing through novations had contributed to the demise of Bear and Lehman. Repo lenders, primarily money market funds, likewise did not panic immediately. On Monday, only a few of them requested slightly more collateral.[31]

But the relative stability was fleeting. Morgan Stanley immediately became the target of a hedge fund run. Before the financial crisis, it had typically been prime brokers like Morgan Stanley who were worried about their exposures to hedge fund clients. Now the roles were reversed. The Lehman episode had revealed that because prime brokers were able to reuse clients' assets to raise cash for their own activities, clients' assets could be frozen or lost in bankruptcy proceedings.[32]

To protect themselves, hedge funds pulled billions of dollars in cash and other assets out of Morgan Stanley, Merrill, and Goldman in favor of prime brokers in bank holding companies, such as JP Morgan; big foreign banks, such as Deutsche Bank and Credit Suisse; and custodian banks, such as BNY Mellon and Northern Trust, which they believed were safer and more transparent. Fund managers told the FCIC that some prime brokers took aggressive measures to prevent hedge fund customers from demanding their assets. For example, "Most [hedge funds] request cash movement from [prime brokers] primarily through a fax," the hedge fund manager Jonathan Wood told the FCIC. "What tends to happen in very stressful times is those

faxes tend to get lost. I'm not sure that's just coincidental . . . that was collateral for whatever lending [prime brokers] had against you and they didn't want to give it [away]."[33]

Soon, hedge funds would suffer unprecedented runs by their own investors. According to an FCIC survey of hedge funds that survived, investor redemption requests averaged 20% of client funds in the fourth quarter of 2008.[34] This pummeled the markets. Money invested in hedge funds totaled $2.2 trillion, globally, at the end of 2007,[35] but because of leverage, their market impact was several times larger. Widespread redemptions forced hedge funds to sell extraordinary amounts of assets, further depressing market prices. Many hedge funds would halt redemptions or collapse.

On Monday, hedge funds requested about $10 billion from Morgan Stanley.[36] Then, on Tuesday morning, Morgan Stanley announced a profit of $1.4 billion for the three months ended August 31, 2008, about the same as that period a year earlier. Mack had decided to release the good news a day early, but this move had backfired. "One hedge fund manager said to me after the fact . . . that he thought preannouncing earnings a day early was a sign of weakness. So I guess it was, because people certainly continued to short our stock or sell our stock—I don't know if they were shorting it but they were certainly selling it," Mack told the FCIC.[37] Wong said, "We were managing our funding . . . but really there were other things that were happening as a result of the Lehman bankruptcy that were beginning to affect, really ripple through and affect some of our clients, our more sophisticated clients."[38]

The hedge fund run became a $32 billion torrent on Wednesday,[39] the day after AIG was bailed out and the day that "many of our sophisticated clients started to liquefy," as Wong put it.[40] Many of the hedge funds now sought to exercise their contractual capability to borrow more from Morgan Stanley's prime brokerage without needing to post collateral. Morgan Stanley borrowed $13 billion from the Fed's PDCF on Tuesday, $27 billion on Wednesday, and $35.3 billion on Friday.

These developments triggered the event that Fed policymakers had worried about over the summer: an increase in collateral calls by the two tri-party repo clearing banks, JP Morgan and BNY Mellon. As had happened during the Bear episode, the two clearing banks became concerned about their intraday exposures to Morgan Stanley, Merrill, and Goldman. On Sunday of the Lehman weekend, the Fed had lowered the bar on the collateral that it would take for overnight lending through the PDCF. But the PDCF was not designed to take the place of the intraday funding provided by JP Morgan and BNY Mellon, and neither of them wanted to accept for their intraday loans the lower-quality collateral that the Fed was accepting for its overnight loans. They would not make those loans to the three investment banks without requiring bigger haircuts, which translated into requests for more collateral.

"Big intraday issues at the clearing banks," the SEC's Matt Eichner informed New York Fed colleagues in an early Wednesday email. "They don't want exposure and are asking for cash/securities. . . . Lots of desk level noise around [Morgan Stanley] and [Merrill Lynch] and taking the name. Not pretty."[41]

"Taking the name" is Wall Street parlance for accepting a counterparty on a trade. On Thursday, BNY Mellon requested $3 billion in collateral from Morgan Stanley.

And New York Fed officials reported that JP Morgan was "thinking" about requesting $2.8 billion on top of a $2.2 billion on deposit.[42] According to a Fed examiner at Citigroup, a banker from that firm had said that "Morgan [Stanley] is the 'deer in the headlights' and having significant stress in Europe. It's looking like Lehman did a few weeks ago."[43]

Commercial paper markets also seized up for Morgan Stanley. From Friday, September 12, to the end of September, the amount of the firm's outstanding commercial paper had fallen nearly 40%, and it had rolled over only $20 million. By comparison, on average Morgan Stanley rolled over about $240 million every day in the last two weeks of August.[44]

On Saturday, Morgan Stanley executives briefed the New York Fed on the situation. By this time, the firm had a total of $35.3 billion in PDCF funding and $32.5 billion in TSLF funding from the Fed.[45] Morgan Stanley's liquidity pool had dropped from $130 billion to $55 billion in one week. Repo lenders had pulled out $31 billion and hedge funds had taken $86 billion out of Morgan Stanley's prime brokerage. That run had vastly exceeded the company's most severe scenario in stress tests administered only one month earlier.[46]

During the week, Goldman Sachs had encountered a similar run. Its liquidity pool had fallen from about $120 billion on the previous Friday to $57 billion on Thursday. At the end of the week, its Fed borrowing totaled $5 billion from the PDCF and $13.5 billion from the TSLF. Lloyd Blankfein, Goldman's CEO, told the FCIC,

> We had tremendous liquidity through the period. But there were systemic events going on, and we were very nervous. If you are asking me what would have happened but for the considerable government intervention, I would say we were in—it was a more nervous position than we would have wanted [to be] in. We never anticipated the government help. We weren't relying on those mechanisms. . . . I felt good about it, but we were going to bed every night with more risk than any responsible manager should want to have, either for our business or for the system as a whole—risk, not certainty.[47]

Bernanke told the FCIC that the Fed believed the run on Goldman that week could lead to its failure: "[Like JP Morgan,] Goldman Sachs I would say also protected themselves quite well on the whole. They had a lot of capital, a lot of liquidity. But being in the investment banking category rather than the commercial banking category, when that huge funding crisis hit all the investment banks, even Goldman Sachs, we thought there was a real chance that they would go under."[48] Although it did not keep pace with Morgan Stanley's use of the Fed's facilities, Goldman Sachs would continue to access the Fed's facilities, increasing its PDCF borrowing to a high of $24 billion in October and its TSLF borrowing to a high of $43.5 billion in December.

On Sunday, September 21, both Morgan Stanley and Goldman Sachs applied to the Fed to become bank holding companies. "In my 30-year history, [Goldman and

Morgan Stanley] had consistently opposed Federal Reserve supervision—[but after Lehman,] those franchises saw that they were next unless they did something drastic. That drastic thing was to become bank holding companies," Tom Baxter, the New York Fed's general counsel, told the FCIC.[49] The Fed, in tandem with the Department of Justice, approved the two applications with extraordinary speed, waiving the standard five-day antitrust waiting period.[50] Morgan Stanley instantly converted its $39 billion industrial loan company into a national bank, subject to supervision by the Office of the Comptroller of the Currency (OCC), and Goldman converted its $26 billion industrial loan company into a state-chartered bank that was a member of the Federal Reserve System, subject to supervision by the Fed and New York State. The Fed would begin to supervise the two new bank holding companies.

The two companies gained the immediate benefit of emergency access to the discount window for terms of up to 90 days.[51] But, more important, "I think the biggest benefit is it would show you that you're important to the system and the Fed would not make you a holding company if they thought in a very short period of time you'd be out of business," Mack told the FCIC. "It sends a signal that these two firms are going to survive."[52]

In a show of confidence, Warren Buffett invested $5 billion in Goldman Sachs, and Mitsubishi UFJ invested $9 billion in Morgan Stanley. Mack said he had been waiting all weekend for confirmation of Mitsubishi's investment when, late Sunday afternoon, he received a call from Bernanke, Geithner, and Paulson. "Basically they said they wanted me to sell the firm," Mack told the FCIC. Less than an hour later, Mitsubishi called to confirm its investment and the regulators backed off.[53]

Despite the weekend announcements, however, the run on Morgan Stanley continued. "Over the course of a week, a decreasing number of people [were] willing to do new repos," Wong said. "They just couldn't lend anymore."[54]

By the end of September, Morgan Stanley's liquidity pool would be $55 billion.[55] But Morgan Stanley's liquidity depended critically on borrowing from two Fed programs, $60 billion from the PDCF and $36 billion from the TSLF. Goldman Sachs's liquidity pool had recovered to about $80 billion, backed by $16.5 billion from the PDCF and $15 billion from the TSLF.

## OVER-THE-COUNTER DERIVATIVES: "A GRINDING HALT"

Trading in the over-the-counter derivatives markets had been declining as investors grew more concerned about counterparty risk and as hedge funds and other market participants reduced their positions or exited. Activity in many of these markets slowed to a crawl; in some cases, there was no market at all—no trades whatsoever. A sharp and unprecedented contraction of the market occurred.[56]

"The OTC derivatives markets came to a grinding halt, jeopardizing the viability of every participant regardless of their direct exposure to subprime mortgage-backed securities," the hedge fund manager Michael Masters told the FCIC.[57] "Furthermore, when the OTC derivatives markets collapsed, participants reacted by liquidating their positions in other assets those swaps were designed to hedge." This market was

unregulated and largely opaque, with no public reporting requirements and little or no price discovery. With the Lehman bankruptcy, participants in the market became concerned about the exposures and creditworthiness of their counterparties and the value of their contracts. That uncertainly caused an abrupt retreat from the market.

Badly hit was the market for derivatives based on nonprime mortgages. Firms had come to rely on the prices of derivatives contracts reflected in the ABX indices to value their nonprime mortgage assets. The ABX.HE.BBB- 06-2, whose decline in 2007 had been an early bellwether for the market crisis, had been trading around 5 cents on the dollar since May. But trading on this index had become so thin, falling from an average of about 70 transactions per week from January 2007 to September 2008 to fewer than 3 transactions per week in October 2008, that index values weren't informative.[58] So, what was a valid price for these assets? Price discovery was a guessing game, even more than it had been under normal market conditions.

The contraction of the OTC derivatives market had implications beyond the valuation of mortgage securities. Derivatives had been used to manage all manner of risk—the risk that currency exchange rates would fluctuate, the risk that interest rates would change, the risk that asset prices would move. Efficiently managing these risks in derivatives markets required liquidity so that positions could be adjusted daily and at little cost. But in the fall of 2008, everyone wanted to reduce exposure to everyone else. There was a rush for the exits as participants worked to get out of existing trades. And because everyone was worried about the risk inherent in the next trade, there often was no next trade—and volume fell further. The result was a vicious circle of justifiable caution and inaction.

Meanwhile, in the absence of a liquid derivatives market and efficient price discovery, every firm's risk management became more expensive and difficult. The usual hedging mechanisms were impaired. An investor that wanted to trade at a loss to get out of a losing position might not find a buyer, and those that needed hedges would find them more expensive or unavailable.

Several measures revealed the lack of liquidity in derivatives markets. First, the number of outstanding contracts in a broad range of OTC derivatives sharply declined. Since its deregulation by federal statute in December 2000, this market had increased more than sevenfold. From June 30, 2008 to the end of the year, however, outstanding notional amounts of OTC derivatives fell by more than 10%. This decline defied historical precedent. It was the first significant contraction in the market over a six-month period since the Bank for International Settlements began keeping statistics in 1998.[59] Moreover, it occurred during a period of great volatility in the financial markets. At such a time, firms usually turn to the derivatives market to hedge their increased risks—but now they fled the market.

The lack of liquidity in derivatives markets was also signaled by the higher prices charged by OTC derivatives dealers to enter into contracts. Dealers bear additional risks when markets are illiquid, and they pass the cost of those risks on to market participants. The cost is evident in the increased "bid-ask spread"—the difference between the price at which dealers were willing to buy contracts (the bid price) and the price at which they were willing to sell them (the ask price). As markets became less

liquid during the crisis, dealers worried that they might be saddled with unwanted exposure. As a result, they began charging more to sell contracts (raising their ask price), and the spread rose. In addition, they offered less to buy contracts (lowered their bid price), because they feared involvement with uncreditworthy counterparties. The increase in the spread in these contracts meant that the cost to a firm of hedging its exposure to the potential default of a loan or of another firm also increased. The cost of risk management rose just when the risks themselves had risen.

Meanwhile, outstanding credit derivatives contracted by 48% between December 2007, when they reached their height of $58.2 trillion in notional amount, and the latest figures as of June 2010, when they had fallen to $30.3 trillion.[60]

In sum, the sharp contraction in the OTC derivatives market in the fall of 2008 greatly diminished the ability of institutions to enter or unwind their contracts or to effectively hedge their business risks at a time when uncertainty in the financial system made risk management a top priority.

## WASHINGTON MUTUAL: "IT'S YOURS"

In the eight days after Lehman's bankruptcy, depositors pulled $16.7 billion out of Washington Mutual, which now faced imminent collapse. WaMu had been the subject of concern for some time because of its poor mortgage-underwriting standards and its exposures to payment-option adjustable-rate mortgages (ARMs). Moody's had downgraded WaMu's senior unsecured debt to Baa3, the lowest-tier investment-grade rating, in July, and then to junk status on September 11, citing "WAMU's reduced financial flexibility, deteriorating asset quality, and expected franchise erosion."[61]

The Office of Thrift Supervision (OTS) determined that the thrift likely could not "pay its obligations and meet its operating liquidity needs."[62] The government seized the bank on Thursday, September 25, 2008, appointing the Federal Deposit Insurance Corporation as receiver; many unsecured creditors suffered losses. With assets of $307 billion as of June 30, 2008, WaMu thus became the largest insured depository institution in U.S. history to fail—bigger than IndyMac, bigger than any bank or thrift failure in the 1980s and 1990s. JP Morgan paid $1.9 billion to acquire WaMu's banking operations from the FDIC on the same day; on the next day, WaMu's parent company (now minus the thrift) filed for Chapter 11 bankruptcy protection.

FDIC officials told the FCIC that they had known in advance of WaMu's troubles and thus had time to arrange the transaction with JP Morgan. JP Morgan CEO Jamie Dimon said that his bank was already examining WaMu's assets for purchase when FDIC Chairman Sheila Bair called him and asked, "Would you be prepared to bid on WaMu?" "I said yes we would," Dimon told the FCIC. "She called me up literally the next day and said—'It's yours.' . . . I thought there was another bidder, by the way, the whole time, otherwise I would have bid a dollar—not [$1.9 billion], but we wanted to win."[63]

The FDIC insurance fund came out of the WaMu bankruptcy whole. So did the uninsured depositors, and (of course) the insured depositors. But the FDIC never contemplated using FDIC funds to protect unsecured creditors, which it could have done by invoking the "systemic risk exception" under the FDIC Improvement Act of

1991. (Recall that FDICIA required that failing banks be dismantled at the least cost to the FDIC unless the FDIC, the Fed, and Treasury agree that a particular company's collapse poses a risk to the entire financial system; it had not been tested in 17 years.) Losses among those creditors created panic among the unsecured creditors of other struggling banks, particularly Wachovia—with serious consequences. Nevertheless, FDIC Chairman Bair stood behind the decision. "I absolutely do think that was the right decision," she told the FCIC. "WaMu was not a well-run institution." She characterized the resolution of WaMu as "successful."[64]

The FDIC's decision would be hotly debated. Fed General Counsel Scott Alvarez told the FCIC that he agreed with Bair that "there should not have been intervention in WaMu."[65] But Treasury officials felt differently: "We were saying that's great, we can all be tough, and we can be so tough that we plunge the financial system into the Great Depression," Treasury's Neel Kashkari told the FCIC. "And so, I think, in my judgment that was a mistake. . . . [A]t that time, the economy was in such a perilous state, it was like playing with fire."[66]

## WACHOVIA: "AT THE FRONT END OF
## THE DOMINOES AS OTHER DOMINOES FELL"

Wachovia, having bought Golden West, was the largest holder of payment-option ARMs, the same product that had helped bring down WaMu and Countrywide. Concerns about Wachovia—then the fourth-largest bank holding company—had also been escalating for some time. On September 9, the Merrill analyst Ed Najarian downgraded the company's stock to "underperform," pointing to weakness in its option ARM and commercial loan portfolios. On September 11, Wachovia executives met Fed officials to ask for an exemption from rules that limited holding companies' use of insured deposits to meet their liquidity needs. The Fed did not accede; staff believed that Wachovia's cash position was strong and that the requested relief was a "want" rather than a "need."[67]

But they changed their minds after the Lehman bankruptcy, immediately launching daily conference calls to discuss liquidity with Wachovia management. Depositor outflows increased. On September 19, the Fed supported the company's request to use insured deposits to provide liquidity to the holding company. On September 20, a Saturday, Wells Fargo Chairman Richard M. Kovacevich told Robert Steel, Wachovia's CEO and recently a Treasury undersecretary, that Wells might be interested in acquiring the besieged bank, and the two agreed to speak later in the week. The same day, Fed Governor Kevin Warsh suggested that Steel also talk to Goldman. As a former vice chairman of Goldman, Steel could easily approach the firm, but the ensuing conversations were short; Goldman was not interested.[68]

Throughout the following week, it became increasingly clear that Wachovia needed to merge with a stronger financial institution. Then, WaMu's failure on September 25 "raised creditor concern about the health of Wachovia," the Fed's Alvarez told the FCIC. "The day after the failure of WaMu, Wachovia Bank depositors accelerated the withdrawal of significant amounts from their accounts," Alvarez said. "In ad-

dition, wholesale funds providers withdrew liquidity support from Wachovia. It appeared likely that Wachovia would soon become unable to fund its operations."[69] Steel said, "As the day progressed, some liquidity pressure intensified as financial institutions began declining to conduct normal financing transactions with Wachovia."[70]

David Wilson, the Office of the Comptroller of the Currency's lead examiner at Wachovia, agreed. "The whole world changed" for Wachovia after WaMu's failure, he said.[71] The FDIC's Bair had a slightly different view. WaMu's failure "was practically a nonevent," she told the FCIC. "It was below the fold if it was even on the front page . . . barely a blip given everything else that was going on."[72]

The run on Wachovia Bank, the country's fourth-largest commercial bank, was a "silent run" by uninsured depositors and unsecured creditors sitting in front of their computers, rather than by depositors standing in lines outside bank doors.[73] By noon on Friday, September 26, creditors were refusing to roll over the bank's short-term funding, including commercial paper and brokered certificates of deposit.[74] The FDIC's John Corston testified that Wachovia lost $5.7 billion of deposits and $1.1 billion of commercial paper and repos that day.[75]

By the end of the day on Friday, Wachovia told the Fed that worried creditors had asked it to repay roughly half of its long-term debt—$50 billion to $60 billion.[76] Wachovia "did not have to pay all these funds from a contractual basis (they had not matured), but would have difficulty [borrowing from these lenders] going forward given the reluctance to repay early," Richard Westerkamp, the Richmond Fed's lead examiner at Wachovia, told the FCIC.[77]

In one day, the value of Wachovia's 10-year bonds fell from 73 cents to 29 cents on the dollar, and the cost of buying protection on $10 million of Wachovia debt jumped from $571,000 to almost $1,400,000 annually. Wachovia's stock fell 27%, wiping out $8 billion in market value. Comptroller of the Currency John Dugan, whose agency regulated Wachovia's commercial bank subsidiary, sent FDIC Chairman Bair a short and alarming email stating that Wachovia's liquidity was unstable.[78] "Wachovia was at the front end of the dominoes as other dominoes fell," Steel told the FCIC.[79]

Government officials were not prepared to let Wachovia open for business on Monday, September 29, without a deal in place.[80] "Markets were already under considerable strain after the events involving Lehman Brothers, AIG, and WaMu," the Fed's Alvarez told the FCIC. "There were fears that the failure of Wachovia would lead investors to doubt the financial strength of other organizations in similar situations, making it harder for those institutions to raise capital."[81]

Wells Fargo had already expressed interest in buying Wachovia; by Friday, Citigroup had as well. Wachovia entered into confidentiality agreements with both companies on Friday and the two suitors immediately began their due diligence investigations.[82]

The key question was whether the FDIC would provide assistance in an acquisition. Though Citigroup never considered making a bid that did not presuppose such assistance, Wells Fargo was initially interested in purchasing all of Wachovia without it.[83] FDIC assistance would require the first-ever application of the systemic risk exception under FDICIA. Over the weekend, federal officials hurriedly considered the

systemic risks if the FDIC did not intervene and if creditors and uninsured depositors suffered losses.

The signs for the bank were discouraging. Given the recent withdrawals, the FDIC and OCC predicted in an internal analysis that Wachovia could face up to $115 billion of additional cash outflows the following week—including, most prominently, $42 billion of further deposit outflows, as well as $12 billion from corporate deposit accounts and $30 billion from retail brokerage customers. Yet Wachovia had only $17 billion in cash and cash equivalents. While the FDIC and OCC estimated that the company could use its collateral to raise another $86 billion through the Fed's discount window, the repo market, and the Federal Home Loan Banks, even those efforts would bring the amount on hand to only $103 billion to cover the potential $115 billion outflow.[84]

During the weekend, the Fed argued that Wachovia should be saved, with FDIC assistance if necessary. Its analysis focused on the firm's counterparties and other "interdependencies" with large market participants, and stated that asset sales by mutual funds could cause short-term funding markets to "virtually shut down."[85] According to supporting analysis by the Richmond Fed, mutual funds held $66 billion of Wachovia debt, which Richmond Fed staff concluded represented "significant systemic consequences"; and investment banks, "already weak and exposed to low levels of confidence," owned $39 billion of Wachovia's $191 billion debt and deposits. These firms were in danger of becoming "even more reliant on Federal Reserve support programs, such as PDCF, to support operations in the event of a Wachovia[-led] disruption."[86]

In addition, Fed staff argued that a Wachovia failure would cause banks to "become even less willing to lend to businesses and households. . . . [T]hese effects would contribute to weaker economic performance, higher unemployment, and reduced wealth."[87] Secretary Paulson had recused himself from the decision because of his ties to Steel, but other members of Treasury had "vigorously advocated" saving Wachovia.[88] White House Chief of Staff Josh Bolten called Bair on Sunday to express support for the systemic risk exception.[89]

At about 6:00 P.M. on Sunday, September 28, Wells's Kovacevich told Steel that he wanted more time to review Wachovia's assets, particularly its commercial real estate holdings, and could not make a bid before Monday if there were to be no FDIC assistance. So Wells and Citigroup came to the table with proposals predicated on such assistance. Wells offered to cover the first $2 billion of losses on a pool of $127 billion worth of assets as well as 80% of subsequent losses, if they grew large enough, capping the FDIC's losses at $20 billion. Citigroup wanted the FDIC to cover losses on a different, and larger, pool of $312 billion worth of assets, but proposed to cover the first $30 billion of losses and an additional $4 billion a year for three years, while giving the FDIC $12 billion in Wachovia preferred stock and stock warrants (rights to buy stock at a predetermined price) as compensation; the FDIC would cover any additional losses above $42 billion.[90]

FDIC staff expected Wachovia's losses to be between $35 billion and $52 billion. On the basis of that analysis and the particulars of the offers, they estimated that the

Wells proposal would cost the FDIC between $5.6 billion and $7.2 billion, whereas the Citigroup proposal would cost the FDIC nothing. Late Sunday, Wachovia submitted its own proposal, under which the FDIC would provide assistance directly to the bank so that it could survive as a stand-alone entity.[91]

But the FDIC still hadn't decided to support the systemic risk exception. Its board—which included the heads of the OCC and OTS—met at 6:00 A.M. on Monday, September 29, to decide Wachovia's fate before the markets opened.[92] FDIC Associate Director Miguel Browne hewed closely to the analysis prepared by the Richmond Fed: Wachovia's failure carried the risk of knocking down too many dominoes in lines stretching in too many directions whose fall would hurt too many people, including American taxpayers. He also raised concerns about potential global implications and reduced confidence in the dollar. Bair remained reluctant to intervene in private financial markets but ultimately agreed. "Well, I think this is, you know . . . one option of a lot of not-very-good options," she said at the meeting. "I have acquiesced in that decision based on the input of my colleagues, and the fact the statute gives multiple decision makers a say in this process. I'm not completely comfortable with it but we need to move forward with something, clearly, because this institution is in a tenuous situation."[93]

To win the approval of Bair and John Reich (the OTS director who served on the FDIC board), Treasury ultimately agreed to take the unusual step of funding all government losses from the proposed transaction.[94] Without this express commitment from Treasury, the FDIC would have been the first to bear losses out of its Deposit Insurance Fund, which then held about $34.6 billion; normally, help would have come from Treasury only after that fund was depleted.[95] According to the minutes of the meeting, Bair thought it was "especially important" that Treasury agree to fund losses, given that "it has vigorously advocated the transaction."[96]

After just 30 minutes, the FDIC board voted to support government assistance. The resolution also identified the winning bidder: Citigroup. "It was the fog of war," Bair told the FCIC. "The system was highly unstable. Who was going to take the chance that Wachovia would have a depository run on Monday?"[97]

Wachovia's board quickly voted to accept Citigroup's bid. Wachovia, Citigroup, and the FDIC signed an agreement in principle and Wachovia and Citigroup executed an exclusivity agreement that prohibited Wachovia from, among other things, negotiating with other potential acquirers.[98]

In the midst of the market turmoil, the Federal Open Market Committee met at the end of September 2008, at about the time of the announced Citigroup acquisition of Wachovia and the invocation of the systemic risk exception. "The planned merger of two very large institutions led to some concern among FOMC participants that bigger and bigger firms were being created that would be 'too big to fail,'" according a letter from Chairman Bernanke to the FCIC. He added that he "shared this concern, and voiced my hope that TARP would create options other than mergers for managing problems at large institutions and that subsequently, through the process of regulatory reform, we might develop good resolution mechanisms and decisively address the issues of financial concentration and too big to fail."[99]

Citigroup and Wachovia immediately began working on the deal—even as Wachovia's stock fell 81.6% to $1.84 on September 29, the day that TARP was initially rejected by lawmakers. They faced tremendous pressure from the regulators and the markets to conclude the transaction before the following Monday, but the deal was complicated: Citigroup was not acquiring the holding company, just the bank, and Citigroup wanted to change some of the original terms. Then came a surprise: on Thursday morning, October 2, Wells Fargo returned to the table and made a competing bid to buy all of Wachovia for $7 a share—seven times Citigroup's bid, with no government assistance.

There was a great deal of speculation over the timing of Wells Fargo's new proposal, particularly given IRS Notice 2008-83. This administrative ruling, issued just two days earlier, allowed an acquiring company to write off the losses of an acquired company immediately, rather than spreading them over time. Wells told the SEC that the IRS ruling permitted the bank to reduce taxable income by $3 billion in the first year following the acquisition rather than by $1 billion per year for three years. However, Wells said this "was itself not a major factor" in its decision to bid for Wachovia without direct government assistance.[100] Former Wells chairman Kovacevich told the FCIC that Wells's revised bid reflected additional due diligence, the point he had made to Wachovia CEO Steel at the time.[101] But the FDIC's Bair said Kovacevich told her at the time that the tax change had been a factor leading to Wells's revised bid.[102]

On Thursday, October 2, three days after accepting Citigroup's federally assisted offer, Wachovia's board convened an emergency 11:00 P.M. session to discuss Wells's revised bid. The Wachovia board voted unanimously in favor.

At about 3:00 A.M. Friday, Wachovia's Steel, its General Counsel Jane Sherburne, and FDIC Chairman Bair called Citigroup CEO Vikram Pandit to inform him that Wachovia had signed a definitive merger agreement with Wells. Steel read from prepared notes. Pandit was stunned. "He was disappointed. That's an understatement," Steel told the FCIC.[103] Pandit thought Citigroup and Wachovia already had a deal. After Steel and Sherburne dropped off the phone call, Pandit asked Bair if Citigroup could keep its original loss-sharing agreement to purchase Wachovia if it matched Wells's offer of $7 a share. Bair said no, reasoning that the FDIC was not going to stand in the way of a private deal. Nor was it the role of the agency to help Citigroup in a bidding war. She also told the FCIC that she had concerns about Citigroup's own viability if it acquired Wachovia for that price. "In reality, we didn't know how unstable Citigroup was at that point," Chairman Bair said. "Here we were selling a troubled institution . . . with a troubled mortgage portfolio to another troubled institution. . . . I think if that deal had gone through, Citigroup would have had to have been bailed out again."[104]

Later Friday morning, Wachovia announced the deal with Wells with the blessing of the FDIC. "This agreement won't require even a penny from the FDIC," Kovacevich said in the press release. Steel added that the "deal enables us to keep Wachovia intact and preserve the value of an integrated company, without government support."[105]

On Monday, October 6, Citigroup filed suit to enjoin Wells Fargo's acquisition of

Wachovia, but without success. The Wells Fargo deal would close at midnight on December 31, for $7 per share.

IRS Notice 2008-83 was repealed in 2009. The Treasury's inspector general, who later conducted an investigation of the circumstances of its issuance, reported that the purpose of the notice was to encourage strong banks to acquire weak banks by removing limitations on the use of tax losses. The inspector general concluded that there was a legitimate argument that the notice may have been an improper change of the tax code by Treasury; the Constitution allows Congress alone to change the tax code. A congressional report estimated that repealing the notice saved about $7 billion of tax revenues over 10 years.[106] However, the Wells controller, Richard Levy, told the FCIC that to date Wells has not recognized any benefits from the notice, because it has not yet had taxable income to offset.[107]

## TARP: "COMPREHENSIVE APPROACH"

Ten days after the Lehman bankruptcy, the Fed had provided nearly $300 billion to investment banks and commercial banks through the PDCF and TSLF lending facilities, in an attempt to quell the storms in the repo markets, and the Fed and Treasury had announced unprecedented programs to support money market funds. By the end of September, the Fed's balance sheet had grown 67% to $1.5 trillion.

But the Fed was running out of options. In the end, it could only make collateralized loans to provide liquidity support. It could not replenish financial institutions' capital, which was quickly dissolving. Uncertainty about future losses on bad assets made it difficult for investors to determine which institutions could survive, even with all the Fed's new backstops. In short, the financial system was slipping away from its lender of last resort.

On Thursday, September 18, the Fed and Treasury proposed what Secretary Paulson called a "comprehensive approach" to stem the mounting crisis in the financial system by purchasing the toxic mortgage-related assets that were weighing down many banks' balance sheets.[108] In the early hours of Saturday, September 20, as Goldman Sachs and Morgan Stanley were preparing to become bank holding companies, Treasury sent Congress a draft proposal of the legislation for TARP. The modest length of that document—just three pages—belied its historical significance. It would give Treasury the authority to spend as much as $700 billion to purchase toxic assets from financial institutions.

The initial reaction was not promising. For example, Senate Banking Committee Chairman Christopher Dodd said on Tuesday, "This proposal is stunning and unprecedented in its scope—and lack of detail, I might add." "There are very few details in this legislation," Ranking Member Richard Shelby said. "Rather than establishing a comprehensive, workable plan for resolving this crisis, I believe this legislation merely codifies Treasury's ad hoc approach."[109]

Paulson told a Senate committee on Tuesday, "Of course, we all believe that the very best thing we can do is make sure that the capital markets are open and that

lenders are continuing to lend. And so that is what this overall program does, it deals with that."[110] Bernanke told the Joint Economic Committee Wednesday: "I think that this is the most significant financial crisis in the post-War period for the United States, and it has in fact a global reach. . . . I think it is extraordinarily important to understand that, as we have seen in many previous examples of different countries and different times, choking up of credit is like taking the lifeblood away from the economy."[111] He told the House Financial Services Committee on the same day, "People are saying, 'Wall Street, what does it have to do with me?' That is the way they are thinking about it. Unfortunately, it has a lot to do with them. It will affect their company, it will affect their job, it will affect their economy. That affects their own lives, affects their ability to borrow and to save and to save for retirement and so on."[112] By the evening of Sunday, September 28, as bankers and regulators hammered out Wachovia's rescue, congressional negotiators had agreed on the outlines of a deal.

Senator Mel Martinez, a former HUD secretary and then a member of the Banking Committee, told the FCIC about a meeting with Paulson and Bernanke that Sunday:

> I just remember thinking, you know, Armageddon. The thing that was the most frightening about it is that even with them asking for extraordinary powers, that they were not at all assured that they could prevent the kind of financial disaster that I think really was greater than the Great Depression. . . . And obviously to a person like myself I think you think, "Wow, if these guys that are in the middle of it and hold the titles that they hold believe this to be as dark as they're painting it, it must be pretty darned dark."[113]

Nevertheless, on Monday, September 29, just hours after Citigroup had announced its proposed government-assisted acquisition of Wachovia, the House rejected TARP by a vote of 228 to 205. The markets' response was immediate: the Dow Jones Industrial Average quickly plunged 778 points, or almost 7%.

To broaden the bill's appeal, TARP's supporters made changes, including a temporary increase in the cap on FDIC's deposit insurance coverage from $100,000 to $250,000 per customer account.[114] On Wednesday evening, the Senate voted in favor by a margin of 74 to 25. On Friday, October 3, the House agreed, 263 to 171, and President George W. Bush signed the law, which had grown to 169 pages. TARP's stated goal was to restore liquidity and confidence in financial markets by providing "authority for the Federal Government to purchase and insure certain types of troubled assets for the purposes of providing stability to and preventing disruption in the economy and financial system and protecting taxpayers."[115] To provide oversight for the $700 billion program, the legislation established the Congressional Oversight Panel and the Office of the Special Inspector General for the Troubled Asset Relief Program (SIGTARP).

But the markets continued to deteriorate. On Monday, October 6, the Dow closed below 10,000 for the first time in four years; by the end of the week it was down al-

most 1,900 points, or 18%, below its peak in October 2007. The spread between the interest rate at which banks lend to one another and interest rates on Treasuries—a closely watched indicator of market confidence—hit an all-time high. And the dollar value of outstanding commercial paper issued by both financial and nonfinancial companies had fallen by $264 billion in the month between Lehman's failure and TARP's enactment. Even firms that had survived the previous disruptions in the commercial paper markets were now feeling the strain. In response, on October 7, the Fed created yet another emergency program, the Commercial Paper Funding Facility, to purchase secured and unsecured commercial paper directly from eligible issuers.[116] This program, which allowed firms to roll over their debt, would be widely used by financial and nonfinancial firms. The three financial firms that made the greatest use of the program were foreign institutions: UBS (which borrowed a cumulative $72 billion over time), Dexia ($53 billion), and Barclays ($38 billion). Other financial firms included GE Capital ($16 billion), Prudential Funding ($2.4 billion), and Toyota Motor Credit Corporation ($3.6 billion). Nonfinancial firms that participated included Verizon ($1.5 billion), Harley-Davidson ($2.3 billion), McDonald's, ($203 million) and Georgia Transmission ($109 million).[117]

Treasury was already rethinking TARP. The best way to structure the program was not obvious. Which toxic assets would qualify? How would the government determine fair prices in an illiquid market? Would firms holding these assets agree to sell them at a fair price if doing so would require them to realize losses? How could the government avoid overpaying? Such problems would take time to solve, and Treasury wanted to bring stability to the deteriorating markets as quickly as possible.

The key concern for markets and regulators was that they weren't sure they understood the extent of toxic assets on the balance sheets of financial institutions—so they couldn't be sure which banks were really solvent. The quickest reassurance, then, would be to simply recapitalize the financial sector. The change was allowed under the TARP legislation, which stated that Treasury, in consultation with the Fed, could purchase financial instruments, including stock, if they deemed such purchases necessary to promote financial market stability. However, the new proposal would pose a host of new problems. By injecting capital in these firms, the government would become a major shareholder in the private financial sector.

On Sunday, October 12, after agreeing to the terms of the capital injections, Paulson, Bernanke, Bair, Dugan, and Geithner selected a small group of major financial institutions to which they would immediately offer capital: the four largest commercial bank holding companies (Bank of America, Citigroup, JP Morgan, and Wells), the three remaining large investment banks (Goldman and Morgan Stanley, which were now bank holding companies, and Merrill, which Bank of America had agreed to acquire), and two important clearing and settlement banks (BNY Mellon and State Street). Together, these nine institutions held more than $11 trillion in assets, or about 75% of all assets in U.S. banks.

Paulson summoned the firms' chief executives to Washington on Columbus Day, October 13.[118] Along with Bernanke, Bair, Dugan, and Geithner, Paulson explained that Treasury had set aside $250 billion from TARP to purchase equity in financial

institutions under the newly formed Capital Purchase Program (CPP). Specifically, Treasury would purchase senior preferred stock that would pay a 5% dividend for the first five years; the rate would rise to 9% thereafter to encourage the companies to pay the government back. Firms would also have to issue stock warrants to Treasury and agree to abide by certain standards for executive compensation and corporate governance.

The regulators had already decided to allocate half of these funds to the nine firms assembled that day: $25 billion each to Citigroup, JP Morgan, and Wells; $15 billion to Bank of America; $10 billion each to Merrill, Morgan Stanley, and Goldman; $3 billion to BNY Mellon; and $2 billion to State Street.

"We didn't want it to look or be like a nationalization" of the banking sector, Paulson told the FCIC. For that reason, the capital injections took the form of nonvoting stock, and the terms were intended to be attractive.[119] Paulson emphasized the importance of the banks' participation to provide confidence to the system. He told the CEOs: "If you don't take [the capital] and sometime later your regulator tells you that you are undercapitalized . . . you may not like the terms if you have to come back to me."[120] All nine firms took the deal. "They made a coherent, I thought, a cogent argument about responding to this crisis, which, remember, was getting dramatically worse. It wasn't leading to a run on some of the banks but it was getting worse in the marketplace," JP Morgan's Dimon told the FCIC.[121]

To further reassure markets that it would not allow the largest financial institutions to fail, the government also announced two new FDIC programs the next day. The first temporarily guaranteed certain senior debt for all FDIC-insured institutions and some holding companies. This program was used broadly. For example, Goldman Sachs had $26 billion in debt backed by the FDIC outstanding in January 2009, and $21 billion at the end of 2009, according to public filings; Morgan Stanley had $16 billion at the end of 2008 and $24 billion at the end of 2009. GE Capital, one of the heaviest users of the program, had $35 billion of FDIC-backed debt outstanding at the end of 2008 and $60 billion at the end of 2009. Citigroup had $32 billion of FDIC guaranteed debt outstanding at the end of 2008 and $65 billion at the end of 2009; JPMorgan Chase had $21 billion outstanding at the end of 2008 and $41 billion at the end of 2009.

The second provided deposit insurance to certain non-interest-bearing deposits, like checking accounts, at all insured depository institution.[122] Because of the risk to taxpayers, the measures required the Fed, the FDIC, and Treasury to declare a systemic risk exception under FDICIA, as they had done two weeks earlier to facilitate Citigroup's bid for Wachovia.

Later in the week, Treasury opened TARP to qualifying "healthy" and "viable" banks, thrifts, and holding companies, under the same terms that the first nine firms had received.[123] The appropriate federal regulator—the Fed, FDIC, OCC, or OTS— would review applications and pass them to Treasury for final approval. The program was intended not only to restore confidence in the banking system but also to provide banks with sufficient capital to fulfill their "responsibilities in the areas of lending, dividend and compensation policies, and foreclosure mitigation."[124]

"The whole reason for designing the program was so many banks would take it, would have the capital, and that would lead to lending. That was the whole purpose," Paulson told the FCIC. However, there were no specific requirements for those banks to make loans to businesses and households. "Right after we announced it we had critics start saying, 'You've got to force them to lend,'" Paulson said. Although he said he couldn't see how to do this, he did concede that the program could have been more effective in this regard.[125] The enabling legislation did have provisions affecting the compensation of senior executives and participating firms' ability to pay dividends to shareholders. Over time, these provisions would become more stringent, and the following year, in compliance with another measure in the act that created TARP, Treasury would create the Office of the Special Master for TARP Executive Compensation to review the appropriateness of compensation packages among TARP recipients.

Treasury invested about $188 billion in financial institutions under TARP's Capital Purchase Program by the end of 2008; ultimately, it would invest $205 billion in 707 financial institutions.[126]

In the ensuing months, Treasury would provide much of TARP's remaining $450 billion to specific financial institutions, including AIG ($40 billion plus a $30 billion lending facility), Citigroup ($20 billion plus loss guarantees), and Bank of America ($20 billion). On December 19, it established the Automotive Industry Financing Program, under which it ultimately invested $81 billion of TARP funds to make investments in and loans to automobile manufacturers and auto finance companies, specifically General Motors, GMAC, Chrysler, and Chrysler Financial.[127] On January 12, 2009, President Bush notified Congress that he intended not to access the second half of the $700 billion in TARP funds, so that he might "'ensure that such funds are available early' for the new administration."[128]

As of September 2010—two years after TARP's creation—Treasury had allocated $395 billion of the $700 billion authorized. Of that amount, $204 billion had been repaid, $185 billion remained outstanding, and $3.9 billion in losses had been incurred.[129] About $55 billion of the outstanding funds were in the Capital Purchase Program. Treasury still held large stakes in GM (61% of common stock), Ally Financial (formerly known as GMAC; 56%), and Chrysler (9%). Moreover, $47.5 billion of TARP funds remained invested in AIG in addition to $49.7 billion of loans from the New York Fed and a $26 billion non-TARP equity investment by the New York Fed in two of AIG's foreign insurance companies.[130] By December 2010, all nine companies invited to the initial Columbus Day meeting had fully repaid the government.[131]

Of course, TARP was only one of more than two dozen emergency programs totaling trillions of dollars put in place during the crisis to stabilize the financial system and to rescue specific firms. Indeed, TARP was not even the largest.[132] Many of these programs are discussed in this and previous chapters. For just some examples: The Fed's TSLF and PDCF programs peaked at $483 billion and $156 billion, respectively. Its money market funding peaked at $350 billion in January 2009, and its Commercial Paper Funding Facility peaked at $365 billion, also in January 2009.[133] When it was introduced, the FDIC's program to guarantee senior debt for all FDIC-insured

institutions stood ready to backstop as much as $939 billion in bank debt. The Fed's largest program, announced in November 2008, purchased $1.25 trillion in agency mortgage–backed securities.[134]

## AIG: "WE NEEDED TO STOP
## THE SUCKING CHEST WOUND IN THIS PATIENT"

AIG would be the first TARP recipient that was not part of the Capital Purchase Program. It still had two big holes to fill, despite the $85 billion loan from the New York Fed. Its securities-lending business was underwater despite payments in September and October of $24 billion that the Fed loan had enabled; and it still needed $27 billion to pay credit default swap (CDS) counterparties, despite earlier payments of $35 billion.

On November 10, the government announced that it was restructuring the New York Fed loan and, in the process, Treasury would purchase $40 billion in AIG preferred stock. As was done in the Capital Purchase Program, in return for the equity provided, Treasury received stock warrants from AIG and imposed restrictions on dividends and executive compensation.

That day, the New York Fed created two off-balance-sheet entities to hold AIG's bad assets associated with securities lending (Maiden Lane II) and CDS (Maiden Lane III). Over the next month, the New York Fed loaned Maiden Lane II $19.8 billion so that it could purchase mortgage-backed securities from AIG's life insurance company subsidiaries. This enabled those subsidiaries to pay back their securities-lending counterparties, bringing to $43.7 billion the total payments AIG would make with government help. These payments are listed in figure 20.4.[135]

Maiden Lane III was created with a $24.3 billion loan from the New York Fed and an AIG investment of $5 billion, supported by the Treasury investment. That money went to buy CDOs from 16 of AIG Financial Products' CDS counterparties. The CDOs had a face value of $62.1 billion, which AIG Financial Products had guaranteed through its CDS.[136] Because AIG had already posted $35 billion in collateral to its counterparties, Maiden Lane III paid $27.1 billion to those counterparties, providing them with the full face amount of the CDOs in return for the cancellation of their rights under the CDS.[137] A condition of this transaction was that AIG waive its legal claims against those counterparties. These payments are listed in figure 20.4.

Goldman Sachs received $14 billion in payments from Maiden Lane III related to the CDS it had purchased from AIG. During the FCIC's January 13, 2010, hearing, Goldman CEO Lloyd Blankfein testified that Goldman Sachs would not have lost any money if AIG had failed, because his firm had purchased credit protection to cover the difference between the amount of collateral it demanded from AIG and the amount of collateral paid by AIG.[138] Documents submitted to the FCIC by Goldman after the hearing do show that the firm owned $2.4 billion of credit protection in the form of CDS on AIG, although much of that protection came from financially unstable companies, including Citibank ($402.3 million), which itself had to be propped up by the government, and Lehman ($174.8 million), which was bankrupt by the

# Payments to AIG Counterparties

| Payments to AIG Securities Lending Counterparties | |
|---|---|
| IN BILLIONS OF DOLLARS | |
| Sept. 18 to Dec. 12, 2008 | |
| Barclays | $7.0 |
| Deutsche Bank | 6.4 |
| BNP Paribas | 4.9 |
| Goldman Sachs | 4.8 |
| Bank of America | 4.5 |
| HSBC | 3.3 |
| Citigroup | 2.3 |
| Dresdner Kleinwort | 2.2 |
| Merrill Lynch | 1.9 |
| UBS | 1.7 |
| ING | 1.5 |
| Morgan Stanley | 1.0 |
| Société Générale | 0.9 |
| AIG International | 0.6 |
| Credit Suisse | 0.4 |
| Paloma Securities | 0.2 |
| Citadel | 0.2 |
| **TOTAL** | **$43.7** |

Of this total, $19.5 billion came from Maiden Lane II, $17.2 billion came from the Federal Reserve Bank of New York, and $7 billion came from AIG.

| Payments to AIG Credit Default Swap Counterparties | | |
|---|---|---|
| IN BILLIONS OF DOLLARS | | |
| As of Nov. 17, 2008 | | |
| | Maiden Lane III payment | Collateral payments from AIG |
| Société Générale | $6.9 | $9.6 |
| Goldman Sachs | 5.6 | 8.4 |
| Merrill Lynch | 3.1 | 3.1 |
| Deutsche Bank | 2.8 | 5.7 |
| UBS | 2.5 | 1.3 |
| Calyon | 1.2 | 3.1 |
| Deutsche Zentral-Genossenschaftsbank | 1.0 | 0.8 |
| Bank of Montreal | 0.9 | 0.5 |
| Wachovia | 0.8 | 0.2 |
| Barclays | 0.6 | 0.9 |
| Bank of America | 0.5 | 0.3 |
| Royal Bank of Scotland | 0.5 | 0.6 |
| Dresdner Bank AG | 0.4 | 0.0 |
| Rabobank | 0.3 | 0.3 |
| Landesbank Baden-Wuerttemberg | 0.1 | 0.0 |
| HSBC Bank USA | 0.0 | 0.2 |
| **TOTAL** | **$27.1** | **$35.0** |

NOTE: Amounts may not add due to rounding.
SOURCE: Special Inspector General for TARP

*Figure 20.4*

time AIG was rescued.[139] In an FCIC hearing, Goldman CFO David Viniar said that those counterparties had posted collateral.[140]

Goldman also argued that the $14 billion of CDS protection that it purchased from AIG was part of Goldman's "matched book," meaning that Goldman sold $14 billion in offsetting protection to its own clients; it provided information to the FCIC indicating that the $14 billion received from Maiden Lane III was entirely paid to its clients.[141] Without the federal assistance, Goldman would have had to find the $14 billion some other way.

Goldman also produced documents to the FCIC that showed it received $3.4 billion from AIG related to credit default swaps on CDOs that were not part of Maiden Lane III. Of that $3.4 billion, $1.9 billion was received after, and thus made possible by, the federal bailout of AIG. And most—$2.9 billion—of the total was for proprietary trades (that is, trades made solely for Goldman's benefit rather than on behalf of a client) largely relating to Goldman's Abacus CDOs. Thus, unlike the $14 billion received from AIG on trades in which Goldman owed the money to its own counterparties, this $2.9 billion was retained by Goldman.[142]

That AIG's counterparties did not incur any losses on their investments—because AIG, once it was backed by the government, paid claims to CDS counterparties at 100% of face value—has been widely criticized. In November 2009, SIGTARP faulted the New York Fed for failing to obtain concessions. The inspector general said that seven of the top eight counterparties had insisted on 100% coverage and that the New York Fed had agreed because efforts to obtain concessions from all counterparties had little hope of success.[143]

SIGTARP was highly critical of the New York Fed's negotiations. From the outset, it found, the New York Fed was poorly prepared to assist AIG. To prevent AIG's failure, the New York Fed had hastily agreed to the $85 billion bailout on substantially the same terms that a private-sector group had contemplated.[144] SIGTARP blamed the Fed's own negotiating strategy for the outcome, which it described as the transfer of "billions of dollars of cash from the Government to AIG's counterparties, even though senior policy makers contend that assistance to AIG's counterparties was not a relevant consideration."[145]

In June 2010, TARP's Congressional Oversight Panel criticized the AIG bailout for having a "poisonous" effect on capital markets. The report said the government's failure to require "shared sacrifice" among AIG's creditors effectively altered the relationship between the government and the markets, signaling an implicit "too big to fail" guarantee for certain firms. The report said the New York Fed should have insisted on concessions from counterparties.[146]

Treasury and Fed officials countered that concessions would have led to an instant ratings downgrade and precipitated a run on AIG.[147] New York Fed officials told the FCIC that they had very little bargaining power with counterparties who were protected by the terms of their CDS contracts. And, after providing a $85 billion loan, the government could not let AIG fail. "Counterparties said 'we got the collateral, the contractual rights, you've been rescued by the Fed, Uncle Sam's behind you, why would we let you out of a contract you agreed to?" New York Fed General Counsel Tom Baxter told the FCIC. "And then the question was, should we use our regulatory power to leverage counterparties. From my view, that would have been completely inappropriate, an abuse of power, and not something we were willing to even contemplate."[148]

Sarah Dahlgren, who was in charge of the Maiden Lane III transaction at the New York Fed, said the government could not have threatened bankruptcy. "There was a financial meltdown," she told the FCIC. "The credibility of the United States government was on the line."[149] SIGTARP acknowledged that the New York Fed "felt ethi-

cally restrained from threatening an AIG bankruptcy because it had no actual plans to carry out such a threat" and that it was "uncomfortable interfering with the sanctity of the counterparties' contractual rights with AIG," which were "certainly valid concerns."[150]

Geithner has said he was confident that full reimbursement was "absolutely" the right decision. "We did it in a way that I believe was not just least cost to the taxpayer, best deal for the taxpayer, but helped avoid much, much more damage than would have happened without that."[151]

New York Fed officials told the FCIC that threats to AIG's survival continued after the $85 billion loan on September 16.[152] "If you don't fix the [securities] lending or the CDOs, [AIG would] blow through the $85 billion. So we needed to stop the sucking chest wound in this patient," Dahlgren said. "It wasn't just AIG—it was the financial markets. . . . It kept getting worse and worse and worse."[153]

Baxter told the FCIC that Maiden Lane III stopped the "hemorrhage" from AIG Financial Products, which was paying collateral to counterparties by drawing on the $85 billion government loan. In addition, because Maiden Lane III received the CDOs underlying the CDS, "as value comes back in those CDOs, that's value that is going to be first used to pay off the Fed loan; . . . the likely outcome of Maiden Lane III is that we're going to be paid in full," he said.[154]

In total, the Fed and Treasury had made available over $180 billion in assistance to AIG to prevent its failure.[155] As of September 30, 2010, the total outstanding assistance has been reduced to $124.8 billion, primarily through the sale of AIG business units.[156]

## CITIGROUP: "LET THE WORLD KNOW
## THAT WE WILL NOT PULL A LEHMAN"

The failed bid for Wachovia reflected badly on Citigroup. Its stock fell 18% on October 3, 2008, the day Wachovia announced that it preferred Wells's offer, and another 43% within a week. "Having agreed to do the deal was a recognition on our part that we needed it," Edward "Ned" Kelly III, vice chairman of Citigroup, told the FCIC. "And if we needed it and didn't get it, what did that imply for the strength of the firm going forward?"[157]

Roger Cole, then head of banking supervision at the Federal Reserve Board, saw the failed acquisition as a turning point, the moment "when Citi really came under the microscope." "It was regarded [by the market] as an indication of bad management at Citi that they lost the deal, and had it taken away from them by a smarter, more astute Wells Fargo team," Cole told the FCIC. "And then here's an organization that doesn't have the core funding [insured deposits] that we were assuming that they would get by that deal."[158]

Citigroup's stock rose 18% the day after the Columbus Day announcement that it would receive government capital, but the optimism did not last. Two days later, Citigroup announced a $2.8 billion net loss for the third quarter, concentrated in subprime and Alt-A mortgages, commercial real estate investments, and structured

investment vehicle (SIV) write-downs. The bank's stock fell 17% in the following week and, by November 12, hit single digits for the first time since 1996.

The market's unease was heightened by press speculation that the company's board had lost confidence in senior management, Kelly said.[159] On November 19, the company announced that the value of the SIVs had fallen by $1.1 billion in the month since it had released third-quarter earnings. Citigroup was therefore going to bring the remaining $17.4 billion in off-balance-sheet SIV assets onto its books. Investors clipped almost another 24% off the value of the stock, its largest single-day drop since the October 1987 stock market crash. Two days later, the stock closed at $3.77. Credit defaults swaps on Citigroup reached a steep $500,000 annually to protect $10 million in Citigroup debt against default.[160] According to Kelly, these developments threatened to make perceptions become a reality for the bank: "[Investors] look at those spreads and say, 'Is this some place I really want to put my money?' And that's not just in terms of wholesale funding, that's people who also have deposits with us at various points."[161]

The firm's various regulators watched the stock price, the daily liquidity, and the CDS spreads with alarm. On Friday, November 21, the United Kingdom's Financial Services Authority (FSA) imposed a $6.4 billion cash "lockup" to protect Citigroup's London-based broker-dealer. FDIC examiners knew that this action would be "very damaging" to the bank's liquidity and worried that the FSA or other foreign regulators might impose additional cash requirements in the following week.[162] By the close of business Friday, there was widespread concern that if the U.S. government failed to act, Citigroup might not survive; its liquidity problems had reached "crisis proportions." Among regulators at the FDIC and the Fed, there was no debate.[163] Fed Chairman Bernanke told the FCIC, "We were looking at this firm [in the fall of 2008] and saying, 'Citigroup is not a very strong firm, but it's only one firm and the others are okay,' but not recognizing that that's sort of like saying, 'Well, four out of your five heart ventricles are fine, and the fifth one is lousy.' They're all interconnected, they all connect to each other; and, therefore, the failure of one brings the others down."[164]

The FDIC's Arthur Murton emailed his colleague Michael Krimminger on November 22: "Given that the immediate risk is liquidity, the way to address that is by letting counterparties know that they will be protected both at the bank and holding company level. . . . [T]he main point is to let the world know that we will not pull a Lehman." Krimminger, special adviser to the FDIC chairman, agreed: "At this stage, it is probably appropriate to be clear and direct that the US government will not allow Citi to fail to meet its obligations."[165]

Citigroup's own calculations suggested that a drop in deposits of just 7.2% would wipe out its cash surplus. If the trend of recent withdrawals continued, the company could expect a 2% outflow of deposits per day. Unless Citigroup received a large and immediate injection of funds, its coffers would be empty before the weekend. Meanwhile, Citigroup executives remained convinced that the company was sound and that the market was simply panicking. CEO Pandit argued, "This was not a fundamental situation, it was not about the capital we had, not about the funding we had at that time, but with the stock price where it was . . . perception becomes reality."[166] All

that was needed, Citigroup contended, was for the government to expand access to existing liquidity facilities. "People were questioning what everything was worth at the time. . . . [T]here was a flight not just to quality and safety, but almost a flight to certainty," Kelly, then Pandit's adviser, told the FCIC.[167]

The FDIC dismissed Citigroup's request that the government simply expand its access to existing liquidity programs, concluding that any "incremental liquidity" could be quickly eliminated as depositors rushed out the door. Officials also believed the company did not have sufficient high-quality collateral to borrow more under the Fed's mostly collateral-based liquidity programs. In addition to the $25 billion from TARP, Citigroup was already getting by on substantial government support. As of November 21, it had $24.3 billion outstanding under the Fed's collateralized liquidity programs and $200 million under the Fed's Commercial Paper Funding Facility. And it had borrowed $84 billion from the Federal Home Loan Banks. In December, Citigroup would have a total of $32 billion in senior debt guaranteed by the FDIC under the debt guarantee program.

On Sunday, November 23, FDIC staff recommended to its board that a third systemic risk exception be made under FDICIA.[168] As they had done previously, regulators decided that a proposed resolution had to be announced over the weekend to buttress investor confidence before markets opened Monday. The failure of Citigroup "would significantly undermine business and household confidence," according to FDIC staff.[169] Regulators were also concerned that the economic effects of a Citigroup failure would undermine the impact of the recently implemented Capital Purchase Program under TARP.[170]

Treasury agreed to provide Citigroup with an additional $20 billion in TARP funds in exchange for preferred stock with an 8% dividend.[171] This injection of cash brought the company's TARP tab to $45 billion. The bank also received $19.5 billion in capital benefits related to its issuance of preferred stock and the government's guarantee of certain assets.[172] Under the guarantee, Citigroup and the government would identify a $306 billion pool of assets around which a protective "ring fence" would be placed. In effect, this was a loss-sharing agreement between Citigroup and the federal government. "There was not a huge amount of science in coming to that [$306 billion] number," Citigroup's Kelly told the FCIC. He said the deal was structured to "give the market comfort that the catastrophic risk has been taken off the table."[173] When its terms were finalized in January 2009, the guaranteed pool, which contained mainly loans and residential and commercial mortgage–backed securities, was adjusted downward to $301 billion.

Citigroup assumed responsibility for the first $39.5 billion in losses on the ring-fenced assets. The federal government would assume responsibility for 90% of all losses above that amount. Should these losses actually materialize, Treasury would absorb the first $5 billion using TARP funds, the FDIC would absorb the next $10 billion from the Deposit Insurance Fund (for which it had needed to approve the systemic risk exception), and the Fed would absorb the balance. In return, Citigroup agreed to grant the government $7 billion in preferred stock, as well as warrants that gave the government the option to purchase additional shares.[174] After analyzing the

quality of the protected assets, FDIC staff projected that the Deposit Insurance Fund would not incur any losses.[175]

Once again, the FDIC Board met late on a Sunday to determine the fate of a struggling institution. Brief dissent on the 10 P.M. conference call came from OTS Director John Reich, who questioned why similar relief had not been extended to OTS-supervised thrifts that failed earlier. "There isn't any doubt in my mind that this is a systemic situation," he said. But he added,

> In hindsight, I think there have been some systemic situations prior to this one that were not classified as such. The failure of IndyMac pointed the focus to the next weakest institution, which was WaMu, and its failure pointed to Wachovia, and now we're looking at Citi and I wonder who's next. I hope that all of the regulators, all of us, including Treasury and the Fed, are looking at these situations in a balanced manner, and I fear there has been some selective creativity exercised in the determination of what is systemic and what's not and what's possible for the government to do and what's not.[176]

The FDIC Board approved the proposal unanimously. The announcement beat the opening bell, and the markets responded positively: Citigroup's stock price soared almost 58%, closing at $5.95. The ring fence would stay in place until December 2009, at which time Citigroup terminated the government guarantee in tandem with repaying $20 billion in TARP funds. In December 2010, Treasury announced the sale of its final shares of Citigroup's common stock.[177]

## BANK OF AMERICA: "A SHOTGUN WEDDING"

With Citigroup stabilized, the markets would quickly shift focus to the next domino: Bank of America, which had swallowed Countrywide earlier in the year and, on September 15, had announced it was going to take on Merrill Lynch as well. The merger would create the world's largest brokerage and reinforce Bank of America's position as the country's largest depository institution. Given the share prices of the two companies at the time, the transaction was valued at $50 billion.

But the deal was not set to close until the first quarter of the following year. In the interim, the companies continued to operate as independent entities, pending shareholder and regulatory approval. For that reason, Merrill CEO John Thain and Bank of America CEO Ken Lewis had represented their companies separately at the Columbus Day meeting at Treasury. Treasury would invest the full $25 billion in Bank of America only after the Merrill acquisition was complete.

In October, Merrill Lynch reported a net loss for the third quarter of $5.1 billion. In its October 16 earnings press release, Merrill Lynch described write-downs related to its CDO positions and other real estate–related securities and assets affected by the "severe market dislocations." Thain told investors on the conference call that Merrill's strategy was to clean house. It now held less than $1 billion in asset-backed-security

CDOs and no Alt-A positions at all. "We're down to $295 million in subprime on our trading books," Thain said. "We cut our non-U.S. mortgage business positions in half."[178]

The Fed approved the merger on November 26, noting that both Bank of America and Merrill were well capitalized and would remain so after the merger, and that Bank of America "has sufficient financial resources to effect the proposal."[179] Shareholders of both companies approved the acquisition on December 5.

But then Bank of America executives began to have second thoughts, Lewis told the FCIC. In mid-November, Merrill Lynch's after-tax losses for the fourth quarter had been projected to reach about $5 billion; the projection grew to about $7 billion by December 3, $9 billion by December 9, and $12 billion by December 14.[180] Lewis said he learned only on December 14 that Merrill's losses had "accelerated pretty dramatically."[181] Lewis attributed the losses to a "much, much, higher deterioration of the assets we identified than we had expected going into the fourth quarter."[182]

In a January conference call, Lewis and CFO Joe Price told investors that the bank had not been aware of the extent of Merrill's fourth-quarter losses at the time of the shareholder vote. "It wasn't an issue of not identifying the assets," Ken Lewis said. "It was that we did not expect the significant deterioration, which happened in mid- to late December that we saw."[183] Merrill's Thain contests that version of events. He told the FCIC that Merrill provided daily profit and loss reports to Bank of America and that bank executives should have known about losses as they occurred.[184] The SEC later brought an enforcement action against Bank of America, charging the company with failing to disclose about $9.5 billion of known and expected Merrill Lynch losses before the December 5 shareholder vote. According to the SEC's complaint, these insufficient disclosures deprived shareholders of material information that was critical to their ability to fairly evaluate the merger. In February 2010, Bank of America would pay $150 million to settle the SEC's action.[185]

On December 17, Lewis called Treasury Secretary Paulson to inform him that Bank of America was considering invoking the material adverse change (MAC) clause of the merger agreement, which would allow the company to exit or renegotiate the terms of the acquisition. "The severity of the losses were high enough that we should at least consider a MAC," Lewis told the FCIC. "The acceleration, we thought, was beyond what should be happening. And then secondly, you had a major hole being created in the capital base with the losses—that dramatically reduced [Merrill Lynch's] equity."[186]

That afternoon, Lewis flew from North Carolina to Washington to meet at the Fed with Paulson and Fed Chairman Bernanke. The two asked Lewis to "stand down" on invoking the clause while they considered the situation.[187]

Paulson and Bernanke concluded that an attempt by Bank of America to invoke the MAC clause "was not a legally reasonable option." They believed that Bank of America would be ultimately unsuccessful in the legal action, and that the attendant litigation would likely result in Bank of America still being contractually bound to acquire a considerably weaker Merrill Lynch. Moreover, Bernanke thought the market would lose faith in Bank of America's management, given that review, preparation,

and due diligence had been ongoing for "3 months." The two officials also believed that invoking the clause would lead to a broader systemic crisis that would result in further deterioration at the two companies.[188]

Neither Merrill nor its CEO, John Thain, was informed of these deliberations at Bank of America. Lewis told the FCIC that he didn't contact Merrill Lynch about the situation because he didn't want to create an "adversarial relationship" if it could be avoided.[189] When Thain later found out that Bank of America had contemplated putting the MAC clause into effect, he was skeptical about its chances of success: "One of the things we negotiated very heavily was the Material Adverse Change clause. [It] specifically excluded market moves . . . [and] pretty much nothing happened to Merrill in the fourth quarter other than the market move."[190]

On Sunday, December 21, Paulson informed Lewis that invoking the clause would demonstrate a "colossal loss of judgment" by the company. Paulson reminded Lewis that the Fed, as its regulator, had the legal authority to replace Bank of America's management and board if they embarked on a "destructive" strategy that had "no reasonable legal basis."[191] Bernanke later told his general counsel: "Though we did not order Lewis to go forward, we did indicate that we believed that going forward [with the clause] would be detrimental to the health (safety and soundness) of his company." Congressman Edolphus Towns of New York would later refer to the Bank of America and Merrill Lynch merger as "a shotgun wedding."[192]

Regulators began to discuss a rescue package similar to the one for Citigroup, including preferred shares and an asset pool similar to Citigroup's ring fence. The staff's analysis was essentially the same as it had been for Citigroup. Meanwhile, Lewis decided to "deescalate" the situation, explaining that when the secretary of the treasury and the chairman of the Fed say that invoking the MAC would cause systemic risk, "then it obviously gives you pause."[193] At a board meeting on December 22, Lewis told his board that the Fed and Treasury believed that a failed acquisition would pose systemic risk and would lead to removal of management and the board at the insistence of the government, and that the government would provide assistance "to protect [Bank of America] against the adverse impact of certain Merrill Lynch assets," although such assistance could not be provided in time for the merger's close on January 1, 2009.[194]

The board decided not to exercise the MAC and to proceed as planned, with the understanding that the government's assistance would be "fully documented" by the time fourth-quarter earnings were announced in mid-January.[195] "Obviously if [the MAC clause] actually would cause systemic risk to the financial system, then that's not good for Bank of America," Lewis told the FCIC. "Which is finally the conclusion that I came to and the board came to."[196]

The merger was completed on January 1, 2009, with no hint of government assistance. By the time the acquisition became official, the purchase price of $50 billion announced in September had fallen to $19 billion, thanks to the decline in the stock prices of the two companies over the preceding three months. On January 9, Bank of America received the $10 billion in capital from TARP that had been allocated to Merrill Lynch, adding to the $15 billion it had received in October.[197]

In addition to those TARP investments, at the end of 2008 Bank of America and Merrill Lynch had borrowed $88 billion under the Fed's collateralized programs ($60 billion through the Term Auction Facility and $28 billion through the PDCF and TSLF) and $15 billion under the Fed's Commercial Paper Funding Facility. (During the previous fall, Bank of America's legacy securities arm had borrowed as much as $17 billion under TSLF and as much as $11 billion under PDCF.) Also at the end of 2008, the bank had issued $31.7 billion in senior debt guaranteed by the FDIC under the debt guarantee program.[198] And it had borrowed $92 billion from the Federal Home Loan Banks. Yet despite Bank of America's recourse to these many supports, the regulators worried that it would experience liquidity problems if the fourth-quarter earnings were weak.[199]

The regulators wanted to be ready to announce the details of government support in conjunction with Bank of America's disclosure of its fourth-quarter performance. They had been working on the details of that assistance since late December,[200] and had reason to be cautious: for example, 67% of Bank of America's repo and securities-lending funding, a total of $384 billion, was rolled over every night, and Merrill "legacy" businesses also funded $144 billion overnight. A one-notch downgrade in the new Bank of America's credit rating would contractually obligate the posting of $10 billion in additional collateral; a two-notch downgrade would require another $3 billion. Although the company remained adequately capitalized from a regulatory standpoint, its tangible common equity was low and, given the stressed market conditions, was likely to fall under 2%.[201] Low levels of tangible common equity—the most basic measure of capital—worried the market, which seemed to think that in the midst of the crisis, regulatory measures of capital were not informative.

On January 15, the Federal Reserve and the FDIC, after "intense" discussions, agreed on the terms:[202] Treasury would use TARP funds to purchase $20 billion of Bank of America preferred stock with an 8% dividend. The bank and the three pertinent government agencies—Treasury, the Fed, and the FDIC—designated an asset pool of $118 billion, primarily from the former Merrill Lynch portfolio, whose losses the four entities would share. The pool was analogous to Citigroup's ring fence. In this case, Bank of America would be responsible for the first $10 billion in losses on the pool, and the government would cover 90% of any additional losses. Should the government losses materialize, Treasury would cover 75%, up to a limit of $7.5 billion, and the FDIC 25%, up to a limit of $2.5 billion. Ninety percent of any additional losses would be covered by the Fed.[203]

The FDIC Board had a conference call at 10 P.M. on Thursday, January 15, and voted for the fourth time, unanimously, to approve a systemic risk exception under FDICIA.[204]

The next morning, January 16, Bank of America disclosed that Merrill Lynch had recorded a $15.3 billion net loss on real estate-related write-downs and charges. It also announced the $20 billion TARP capital investment and $118 billion ring fence that the government had provided. Despite the government's support, Bank of America's stock closed down almost 14% from the day before.

Over the next several months Bank of America worked with its regulators to identify the assets that would be included in the asset pool. Then, on May 6, Bank of America asked to exit the ring fence deal, explaining that the company had determined that losses would not exceed the $10 billion that Bank of America was required to cover in its first-loss position. Although the company was eventually allowed to terminate the deal, it was compelled to compensate the government for the benefits it had received from the market's perception that the government would insure its assets. On September 21, Bank of America agreed to pay a $425 million termination fee: $276 million to Treasury, $57 million to the Fed, and $92 million to the FDIC.

---

## COMMISSION CONCLUSIONS ON CHAPTER 20

The Commission concludes that, as massive losses spread throughout the financial system in the fall of 2008, many institutions failed, or would have failed but for government bailouts. As panic gripped the market, credit markets seized up, trading ground to a halt, and the stock market plunged. Lack of transparency contributed greatly to the crisis: the exposures of financial institutions to risky mortgage assets and other potential losses were unknown to market participants, and indeed many firms did not know their own exposures.

The scale and nature of the over-the-counter (OTC) derivatives market created significant systemic risk throughout the financial system and helped fuel the panic in the fall of 2008: millions of contracts in this opaque and deregulated market created interconnections among a vast web of financial institutions through counterparty credit risk, thus exposing the system to a contagion of spreading losses and defaults. Enormous positions concentrated in the hands of systemically significant institutions that were major OTC derivatives dealers added to uncertainty in the market. The "bank runs" on these institutions included runs on their derivatives operations through novations, collateral demands, and refusals to act as counterparties.

A series of actions, inactions, and misjudgments left the country with stark and painful alternatives—either risk the total collapse of our financial system or spend trillions of taxpayer dollars to stabilize the system and prevent catastrophic damage to the economy. In the process, the government rescued a number of financial institutions deemed "too big to fail"—so large and interconnected with other financial institutions or so important in one or more financial markets that their failure would have caused losses and failures to spread to other institutions. The government also provided substantial financial assistance to nonfinancial corporations. As a result of the rescues and consolidation of financial institutions through failures and mergers during the crisis, the U.S. financial sector is now more concentrated than ever in the hands of a few very large, systemically significant institutions. This concentration places greater responsibility on regulators for effective oversight of these institutions.

# PART V

## The Aftershocks

# 21

## THE ECONOMIC FALLOUT

### CONTENTS

Panic and uncertainty in the financial system plunged the nation into the longest and deepest recession in generations. The credit squeeze in financial markets cascaded throughout the economy. In testifying to the Commission, Bank of America CEO Brian Moynihan described the impact of the financial crisis on the economy: "Over the course of the crisis, we, as an industry, caused a lot of damage. Never has it been clearer how poor business judgments we have made have affected Main Street."[1] Indeed, Main Street felt the tremors as the upheaval in the financial system rumbled through the U.S. economy. Seventeen trillion dollars in household wealth evaporated within 21 months, and reported unemployment hit 10.1% at its peak in October 2009.

As the housing bubble deflated, families that had counted on rising housing values for cash and retirement security became anchored to mortgages that exceeded the declining value of their homes. They ratcheted back on spending, cumulatively putting the brakes on economic growth—the classic "paradox of thrift," described almost a century ago by John Maynard Keynes.

In the aftermath of the panic, when credit was severely tightened, if not frozen, for financial institutions, companies found that cheap and easy credit was gone for them, too. It was tougher to borrow to meet payrolls and to expand inventories; businesses that had neither credit nor customers trimmed costs and laid off employees. Still today, credit availability is tighter than it was before the crisis.

Without jobs, people could no longer afford their house payments. Yet even if moving could improve their job prospects, they were stuck with houses they could not sell. Millions of families entered foreclosure and millions more fell behind on their mortgage payments. Others simply walked away from their devalued properties, returning the keys to the banks—an action that would destroy families' credit for

years. The surge in foreclosed and abandoned properties dragged home prices down still more, depressing the value of surrounding real estate in neighborhoods across the country. Even those who stayed current on their mortgages found themselves whirled into the storm.

Towns that over several years had come to expect and rely on the housing boom now saw jobs and tax revenue vanish. As their resources dwindled, these communities found themselves saddled with the municipal costs they had taken on in part to expand services for a growing population. Sinking housing prices upended local budgets that relied on property taxes. Problems associated with abandoned homes required more police and fire protection.

At FCIC hearings around the country, regional experts testified that the local impact of the crisis has been severe. From 2007 to 2009, for example, banks in Sacramento had stopped lending and potential borrowers retreated, said Clarence Williams, president of the California Capital Financial Development Corporation. Bankers still complain to him not only that demand from borrowers has fallen off but also that they may be subject to increased regulatory scrutiny if they do make new loans. In September 2010, when the FCIC held its Sacramento hearing, that region's once-robust construction industry was still languishing. "Unless we begin to turn around demand, unless we begin to turn around the business situation, the employment is not going to increase here in the Sacramento area, and housing is critical to it. It is a vicious circle," Williams testified.[2]

The effects of the financial crisis have been felt in individual U.S. households and businesses, big and small, and around the world. Policy makers on the state, national, and global levels are still grappling with the aftermath, as are the homeowners and lenders now dealing with the complications that entangle the foreclosure process.

## HOUSEHOLDS: "I'M NOT EATING. I'M NOT SLEEPING"

The recession officially began in December 2007. By many measures, its effects on the job market were the worst on record, as reflected in the speed and breadth of the falloff in jobs, the rise of the ranks of underemployed workers, and the long stretches of time that millions of Americans were and still are surviving without work. The economy shed 3.6 million jobs in 2008—the largest annual plunge since record keeping began in 1940. By December 2009, the United States had lost another 4.7 million jobs. Through November 2010, the economy had regained nearly 1 million jobs, putting only a small dent in the declines.

The underemployment rate—the total of unemployed workers who are actively looking for jobs, those with part-time work who would prefer full-time jobs, and those who need jobs but say they are too discouraged to search—increased from 8.8% in December 2007 to 13.7% in December 2008, reaching 17.4% in October 2009. This was the highest level since calculations for that labor category were first made in 1994. As of November 2010, the underemployment rate stood at 17%. The average length of time individuals spent unemployed spiked from 9.4 weeks in June 2008 to 18.2 weeks in June 2009, and 25.5 weeks in June 2010. Fifty-nine percent of

all job seekers, according to the most recent government statistics, searched for work for at least 15 weeks.

The labor market is daunting across the board, but it is especially grim among African American workers, whose jobless rate is 16.0%, about 6 percentage points above the national average; workers between the ages of 16 and 19 years old, at 24.6%; and Hispanics, at 13.2%. And the impact has been especially severe in certain professions: unemployment in construction, for instance, climbed to an average of 19.1% in 2009, and averaged 20.6% during the first 11 months of 2010.

Real gross domestic product, the nation's measure of economic output adjusted for inflation, fell at an annual rate of 4% in the third quarter of 2008 and 6.8% in the fourth quarter. After falling again in the first half of 2009 and then modestly growing in the second half, average GDP for the year was 2.6% lower than in 2008, the biggest drop since 1946.

Looking at the labor market, Edward Lazear, chairman of President George W. Bush's Council of Economic Advisers during the crisis, told the Commission that the financial crisis was linked with today's economic problems: "I think most of it had to do with investment. . . . Panic in financial markets and tightness in financial markets that persisted through 2009 prevented firms from investing in the way that they otherwise would, and I think that slows the rehiring of workers and still continues to be a problem in labor markets."[3]

In June 2009, the nation officially emerged out of the recession that had begun 18 months earlier. The good news still had not reached many of the 26.2 million Americans who were out of work, who could not find full-time work, or who had stopped looking for work as of November 2010. Jeannie McDermott of Bakersfield told the FCIC she started a business refilling printer ink cartridges, but in a tight economy, she didn't earn enough to make a living. She said she had been searching for a full-time job since 2008.[4]

Households suffered the impact of the financial crisis not only in the job market but also in their net worth and their access to credit. Of the $17 trillion lost from 2007 to the first quarter of 2009 in household net wealth—the difference between what households own and what they owe—about $5.6 trillion was due to declining house prices, with much of the remainder due to the declining value of financial assets. As a point of reference, GDP in 2008 was $14.4 trillion. And, as a separate point, the amount of wealth lost in the dot-com crash early in the decade was $6.5 trillion, with far fewer repercussions for the economy as a whole. The painful drop in real estate and financial asset values followed a $6.8 trillion run-up in household debt from 2000 to 2007. Aided by the gains in home prices and, to a lesser degree, stock prices, households' net wealth had reached a peak of $66 trillion in the second quarter of 2007. The collapse of the housing and stock markets erased much of the gains from the run-up—while household debt remained near historic highs, exceeding even the levels of 2006. As of the third quarter of 2010, despite firmer stock and housing prices and a decline in household borrowing, household net worth totaled $54.9 trillion, a 16.5% drop-off from its pinnacle just three years earlier (see figure 21.1).

Nationwide, home prices dropped 32% from their peak in 2006 to their low point

## Household Net Worth

*The crisis wiped out much more wealth than other recent events such as the bursting of the dot-com bubble in 2000.*

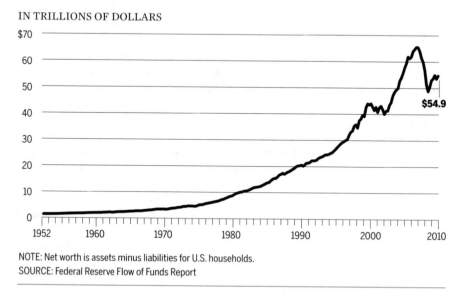

IN TRILLIONS OF DOLLARS

NOTE: Net worth is assets minus liabilities for U.S. households.
SOURCE: Federal Reserve Flow of Funds Report

*Figure 21.1*

early in 2009. The homeownership rate declined from its peak of 69.2% in 2004 to 66.9% as of the fall of 2010. Because so many American households own homes, and because for most homeowners their housing represents their single most important asset, these declines have been especially debilitating. Borrowing via home equity loans or cash-out refinancing has fallen sharply.

At an FCIC hearing in Bakersfield, California, Marie Vasile explained how her family had relocated 40 miles into the mountains to a rental house to help her husband's fragile health.[5] Their old home was put up for sale and languished on the market, losing value. Eventually, she and her husband found buyers willing to take their house in a "short sale"—that is, a sale at a price less than the balance of the mortgage. But because the lender was acting slowly to approve that deal, they risked losing the sale and then going into foreclosure. "To top this all off," Vasile told commissioners, "my husband is in the position of possibly losing his job. . . . So not only do I have a house that I don't know what's happening to, I don't know if he's going to have a job come December. This is more than I can handle. I'm not eating. I'm not sleeping."

Serious mortgage delinquencies—payments that are late 90 days or more or homes in the foreclosure process—have spread since the crisis. Among regions, the

eastern states in the Midwest (Ohio, Indiana, Illinois, Wisconsin, and Michigan) had the highest delinquency rate, topping 5% in 2007.[6] By fall 2010, this rate had risen to 9.2%. Other regions also endured high rates—especially the so-called sand states, where the housing crisis was the worst. The third quarter 2010 serious delinquency rate for Florida was 19.5%; Nevada, 17.8%; Arizona, 10.8%; and California, 10.3%.

The data company CoreLogic identified the 25 housing markets with the worst records of "distressed" sales, which include short sales and sales of foreclosed properties. Las Vegas led the list in mid-2010, with distressed sales accounting for more than 60% of all home sales.[7] "The state was overbuilt and some 100,000 jobs were predicated on a level of growth and consumer spending that seemed to evaporate almost overnight," Jeremy Aguero, an economic and marketing analyst who follows the Nevada economy, testified to the Commission.[8]

The performance of the stock market in the wake of the crisis also reduced wealth. The Standard and Poor's 500 Index fell by a third in 2008—the largest single-year decline since 1974—as big institutional investors moved to Treasury securities and other investments that they perceived as safe. Individuals felt these effects not only in their current budgets but also in their prospects for retirement. By one calculation, assets in retirement accounts such as 401(k)s lost $2.8 trillion, or about a third of their value, between September 2007 and December 2008.[9] While the stock market has recovered somewhat, the S&P 500 as of December 31, 2010, was still about 13% below where it was at the start of 2008. Similarly, stock prices worldwide plummeted more than 40% in 2008 but rebounded by 24% in 2009, according to the MSCI World Index stock fund (which represents a collection of 1,500 global stocks).

The financial market fallout jeopardized some public pension plans—many of which were already troubled before the crisis. In Colorado, state budget officials warned that losses of $11 billion, unaddressed, could cause the Public Employees Retirement Association plan—which covers 450,000 public workers and teachers—to go bust in two decades. The state cut retiree benefits to adjust for the losses.[10] Montana's public pension funds lost $2 billion, or a fourth of their value, in the six months following the 2008 downturn, in part because of investments in complex Wall Street securities.[11]

Even before the fall of 2008, consumer confidence had been on a downward slope for months. The Conference Board reported in May 2008 that its measure of consumer confidence fell to the lowest point since late 1992.[12] By early 2009, confidence had plummeted to a new low; it has recovered somewhat since then but has remained stubbornly bleak.[13]

"[We find] nobody willing to make a decision. . . . nobody willing to take a chance, because of the uncertainty in the economic environment, and that goes for both the state and the federal level," the commercial real estate developer and appraiser Gregory Bynum testified at the FCIC's Bakersfield hearing.[14]

Influenced by the dramatic loss in wealth and by job insecurity, households have cut back on debt. Total credit card debt expanded every year for two decades until it peaked at $989 billion at the end of 2008. Almost two years later, that total had fallen 19%, to $802 billion. The actions of banks have also played an important role: since

2008, they have tightened lending standards, reduced lines of credit on credit cards, and increased fees and interest rates. In the third quarter of 2008, 67% of banks imposed standards on credit cards that were tighter than those in place in the previous quarter. In the fourth quarter, 59% did so, meaning that many banks tightened again. In fact, a significant number of banks tightened credit card standards quarter after quarter until the summer of 2009. Only in the latest surveys have even a small numbers of banks begun to loosen them.[15] Faced with financial difficulties, over 1.4 million households declared bankruptcy in 2009, up from approximately 1.1 million in 2008.[16]

Together, the decline in households' financial resources, banks' tightening of lending standards, and consumers' lack of confidence have led to large cuts in spending. Consumer spending, which in the United States makes up more than two-thirds of GDP, fell at an annual rate of roughly 3.5% in the second half of 2008 and then fell again in the first half of 2009. Gains since then have been modest. Spending on cars and trucks fell by an extraordinary 40% between the end of 2007 and the spring of 2009, in part because consumer financing was less available as well as because of job and wage losses.

## BUSINESSES: "SQUIRRELS STORING NUTS"

When the financial panic hit in September 2008, business financing dried up. Firms that could roll over their commercial paper faced higher interest rates and shorter terms. Those that could not roll over their paper relied on old-fashioned financing—bank loans—or used their own cash reserves. Large firms, one analyst said at the time, turned to their cash balances like "squirrels storing nuts." Jeff Agosta, an executive at Devon Energy Corporation, told the FCIC that had the government not supported the commercial paper market, "We would have been eating grasshoppers and living in tents. Things could have been that bad."[17] While his expression was hyperbolic, the fear was very real. The lack of credit and the sharp drop in demand took its toll on businesses. In 2006, just under 20,000 U.S. companies filed for bankruptcy protection. That figure more than tripled to nearly 61,000 in 2009.[18] Firms' long-term plans suddenly had to be reevaluated—the effects of those decisions persist, even though credit markets have recovered somewhat.

As for the banks, by mid-2007 they had begun to restrict access to credit even for large and medium-size businesses.[19] The Federal Open Market Committee noted this tightening when it announced on September 18, 2007, that it was cutting the federal funds rate. After the Lehman bankruptcy, companies such as Gannett Corporation, FairPoint Communications, and Duke Energy drew down their existing lines of credit because they were worried about getting shut out of credit markets.[20]

Without access to credit, with cash reserves dwindling, and with uncertainty about the economy high, corporations laid off workers or cut their investments, inhibiting growth and reducing their potential for improving productivity. A survey of chief financial officers found that 57% of U.S. companies were somewhat or very affected by credit constraints, leading to decisions to make cuts in capital investment,

technology, and elsewhere.[21] News headlines chronicled the problems: scarce capital forced midsize firms to pare back investments and shutter offices, while industrial companies including Caterpillar, Corning, and John Deere; pharmaceutical companies such as Merck and Wyeth; and tech companies alike laid off employees as the recession took hold. Some businesses struggled to cover payrolls and the financing of inventory.

The introduction in October 2008 of the Commercial Paper Funding Facility, under which the Federal Reserve loaned money to nonfinancial entities, enabled the commercial paper market to resume functioning at more normal rates and terms. But even with the central bank's help, nearly 70% of banks tightened credit standards and lending in the fourth quarter of 2008.[22] And small businesses particularly felt the squeeze. Because they employ nearly 40% of the country's private-sector workforce, "loans to small businesses are especially vital to our economy," Federal Reserve Board Governor Elizabeth Duke told Congress early in 2010.[23] Unlike the larger firms, which had come to rely on capital markets for borrowing, these companies had generally obtained their credit from traditional banks, other financial institutions, nonfinancial companies, or personal borrowing by owners. The financial crisis disrupted all these sources, making credit more scarce and more expensive.

In a survey of small businesses by the National Federation of Independent Business in 2009, 14% of respondents called credit "harder to get." That figure compares with 9% in 2008 and a previous peak, at around 11%, during the credit crunch of 1991.[24]

Fed Chairman Ben Bernanke said in a July 2010 speech that getting a small business loan was still "very difficult." He also noted that banks' loans to small businesses had dropped from more than $710 billion in the second quarter of 2008 to less than $670 billion in the first quarter of 2010.[25]

Another factor—hesitancy to take on more debt in an anemic economy—is certainly behind some of the statistics tracking lending to small businesses. Speaking on behalf of the Independent Community Bankers of America, C. R. Cloutier, president and CEO of Midsouth Bank in Lafayette, Louisiana, told the FCIC, "Community banks are willing to lend. That's how banks generate a return and survive. However, quality loan demand is down. . . . I can tell you from my own bank's experience, customers are scared about the economic climate and are not borrowing. . . . Credit is available, but businesses are not demanding it."[26]

Still, creditworthy borrowers seeking loans face tighter credit from banks than they did before the crisis, surveys and anecdotal evidence suggest. Historically, banks charged a 2 percentage point premium over their funding costs on business loans, but that premium had hit 3 points by year-end 2008 and had continued to rise in 2009, raising the costs of borrowing.[27]

Small businesses' access to credit also declined when the housing market collapsed. During the boom, many business owners had tapped the rising equity in their homes, taking out low-interest home equity loans. Seventeen percent of small employers with a mortgage refinanced it specifically to capitalize their businesses.[28] As housing prices declined, their ability to use this option was reduced or blocked altogether by the lenders. Jerry Jost told the FCIC he borrowed against his home to help

his daughter start a bridal dress business in Bakersfield several years ago. When the economy collapsed, Jost lost his once-profitable construction business, and his daughter's business languished. The Jost family has exhausted its life savings while struggling to find steady work and reliable incomes.[29]

The standards for credit card loans, another source of financing for small businesses, also became more stringent. In the Fed's April 2010 Senior Loan Officer Survey, a majority of banks indicated that their standards for approving credit card accounts for small businesses were tighter than "the longer-run average level that prevailed before the crisis." Banks had continued to tighten their terms on business credit card loans to small businesses, for both new and existing accounts, since the end of 2009.[30] But the July 2010 update of the Fed survey showed the first positive signs since the end of 2006 that banks were easing up on underwriting standards for small businesses.[31]

In an effort to assist small business lenders, the Federal Reserve in March 2009 created the Term Asset-Backed Securities Loan Facility (TALF), a program to aid securitization of loans, including auto loans, student loans, and small business loans. Another federal effort aimed at improving small businesses' access to credit was guidance in February 2010 from the Federal Reserve and other regulators, advising banks to try to meet the credit needs of "creditworthy small business borrowers" with the assurances that government supervisors would not hinder those efforts.

Yet the prevailing headwinds have been difficult to overcome. Without access to credit, many small businesses that had depleted their cash reserves had trouble paying bills, and bankruptcies and loan defaults rose. Defaults on small business loans increased to 12% in 2008, from 8% in 2007.[32] Overall, the current state of the small business sector is a critical factor in the struggling labor market: ailing small businesses have laid people off in large numbers, and stronger small businesses are not hiring additional workers.

Independent finance companies, which had often funded themselves by issuing commercial paper, were constrained as well. The business finance company CIT Group Inc. was one such firm. Even $2.3 billion in additional capital support from the federal Troubled Asset Relief Program (TARP) program did not save CIT from filing for bankruptcy protection in November 2009. Still, some active lenders to smaller businesses, such as GE Capital, a commercial lender with a focus on middle-market customers, were able to continue to offer financing. GE Capital's commercial paper borrowing fared better than others'.[33]

Nonetheless, the terms of the company's borrowing did worsen. In 2008, it registered to borrow up to $98 billion in commercial paper through one government program and issued $13.4 billion in long-term debt and $21.8 billion in commercial paper under another program.[34] That GE Capital had trimmed commercial paper before the crisis to less than 10% of its total debt, or about $46 billion, also softened the effects of the crisis on the company. "A decision was made that it would be prudent for us to reduce our reliance on the commercial paper market, and we did," Mark Barber, the deputy treasurer of GE Company and GE Capital, told the Commission.

The firm put more than $60 billion in cash on its balance sheet, with $52 billion in back-up bank lines of credit, if needed.[35]

The decline in global trade also hurt the U.S. economy as well as economies across the world. As the financial crisis peaked in Europe and the United States, exports collapsed in nearly every major trading country.[36] The decline in exports shaved more than 3 percentage points off GDP growth in the third and fourth quarters of 2008. Recently, exports have begun to recover, and as of the fall of 2010 they are back near precrisis levels.[37]

## COMMERCIAL REAL ESTATE: "NOTHING'S MOVING"

Commercial real estate—offices, stores, warehouses—also took a pounding, an indicator both of the sector's reliance on the lending markets, which were impaired by the crisis, and of its role as a barometer of business activity. Companies do not need more space if they go out of business, lay off workers, or decide not to expand. Weak demand, in turn, lowers rents and forces landlords to give their big tenants incentives to stay put. One example: two huge real estate brokerages with headquarters in New York City received nine months' free rent for signing leases in 2008 and 2009.[38]

In fall 2010, commercial vacancy rates were still sky-high, with 20% of all office space unoccupied. And the actual rate is probably much higher because layoffs create "shadow vacancies"—a couple of desks here, part of a floor there—that tenants must fill before demand picks back up. In the absence of demand, banks remain unwilling to lend to all but the safest projects involving the most creditworthy developers that have precommitted tenants. "Banks are neither financing, nor are they dumping their bad properties, creating a log jam," one developer told a National Association of Realtors survey. "Nothing's moving."[39]

In Nevada, where tourism and construction once fed the labor force, commercial property took a huge hit. Office vacancies in Las Vegas are now hovering around 24%, compared with their low of 8% midway through 2005. Vacancies in retail commercial space in Las Vegas top 10%, compared with historical vacancy rates of 3% to 4%. The economic downturn tugged national-brand retailers into bankruptcy, emptying out the anchor retail space in Nevada's malls and shopping centers. As demand for vacant property fell, land values in and around Las Vegas plummeted.[40]

Because lenders were still reluctant, few developers nationally could afford to build or buy, right into the fall of 2010. Lehman's bankruptcy meant that Monday Properties came up short in its efforts to build a $300 million, 35-story glass office tower in Arlington, Virginia, across the river from Washington, D.C. Potential tenants wanted to know if the developer had financing; potential lenders wanted to know if it had tenants. "It's a bit of a cart-and-horse situation," said CEO Anthony Westreich, who in October 2010 took the big risk of starting construction on the building without signed tenants or permanent financing.[41] The collapse of teetering financial institutions put commercial real estate developers and commercial landlords in binds when overextended banks suddenly pulled out of commercial construction loans. And when banks

failed and were taken over by the Federal Deposit Insurance Commission, the com-
mercial landlords overnight lost major bank tenants and the long-term leases that
went with them.[42] In California, at least 35 banks have failed since 2003.[43]

Almost half of commercial real estate loans were underwater as of February 2010,
meaning the loans were larger than the market value of the property. Commercial real
estate loans are especially concentrated among the holdings of community and re-
gional banks.[44] Some commercial mortgages were also securitized, and by August
2010, the delinquency rate on these packaged mortgages neared 9%—the highest in
the history of the industry and an ominous sign for real estate a full two years after the
height of the financial storm.[45] At the end of 2008, the default rate had been 1.6%.[46]

Near the end of 2010, it was not at all clear when or even if the commercial real
estate market had hit bottom. Green Street Advisors of Newport Beach, California,
which tracks real estate investment trusts, believed that it reached its nadir in mid-
2009. About half of the decline between 2007 and 2009 has been recovered, accord-
ing to Mike Kirby, Green Street's director of research. "Nevertheless," Kirby added,
"values remain roughly 20% shy of their peak."[47] That's one perspective. On the other
side, Moody's Investors Service, whose REAL Commercial Property Price Index
tracks sales of commercial buildings, says it is too early to make a call. Moody's de-
tected some signs of a pickup in the spring and fall of 2010, and Managing Director
Nick Levidy said, "We expect commercial real estate prices to remain choppy until
transaction volumes pick up."[48] The largest commercial real estate loan losses are pro-
jected for 2011 and beyond, according to a report issued by the Congressional Over-
sight Panel.[49] And, looking forward, nearly $700 billion in commercial real estate
debt will come due from 2011 through 2013.[50]

## GOVERNMENT: "STATES STRUGGLED TO CLOSE SHORTFALLS"

### State and local government finances

The recession devastated not only many companies and their workers but also state
and local governments that saw their tax revenue fall—just when people who had lost
their jobs, or were in bankruptcy or foreclosure proceedings, were demanding more
services. Those services included Medicaid, unemployment compensation, and wel-
fare, in addition to local assistance for mental health care, for children, and for the
homeless. "At least 46 states struggled to close shortfalls when adopting budgets for
the current fiscal year," recently reported the Center on Budget and Policy Priorities,
a Washington think tank.[51]

"A critical aspect of our situation in Sacramento and . . . throughout the state is
that these increased demands for services are occurring at a time that resources . . .
are being dramatically reduced," Bruce Wagstaff, the agency administrator with
Sacramento's Countywide Services Agency, explained to the Commission.[52]

Unlike the federal government, almost every state is constitutionally required to
produce a balanced budget, so running a deficit is not an option. Sujit CanagaRetna,
a senior fiscal analyst with the Council of State Governments, told the FCIC that the

budget shortfalls facing the states "are staggering numbers. It's not just the big states; it's almost all states." He said the "great transformation" occurring in state finances means states are forced to "reorient their whole stance vis a vis the kind of programs and services they offer their citizens."[53] In the 2011 fiscal year alone, which started July 2010, states must come up with $130 billion in savings or new revenue to balance their budgets, one study estimated.[54] By the fall of 2010, there was some good news: revenue from some taxes and fees in some states had started to pick up, or at least slowed their rate of decline.[55]

In a September 2010 report, the National Conference of State Legislatures declared that the states "are waiting to see if the economy will sustain this nascent revenue growth. . . . And despite recent revenue improvements, more gaps loom as states confront the phase out of federal stimulus funds, expiring tax increases and growing spending pressures."[56]

Some states were hit harder than others, either because they were particularly affected by the crisis or because they came into the crisis with structural budget problems. In 2010, New Jersey Governor Chris Christie proposed chopping $11 billion—or a quarter—of the state budget to eliminate a deficit. California officials struggled through the summer and fall to close a $19 billion shortfall, an amount larger than the entire budgets of some states. Nonetheless, the state's independent budget analysis office said in November that the deficit had instead grown to $25 billion—$6 billion in the $87 billion budget for this year and $19 billion in the fiscal year commencing in June 2011.[57] As people lost jobs, many also lost their health insurance, helping to drive 3.8 million Americans into the Medicaid program in 2009 alone, an 8% increase—the largest in a single year since the early days of this government health insurance plan, according to the Kaiser Family Foundation, a nonprofit organization focusing on health care research. Every state showed an enrollment increase: in nine states it was greater than 15%; in Nevada and Wisconsin, greater than 20%.[58]

States share the cost of Medicaid with the federal government. Congress included $87 billion in the stimulus package to help them with this expense, and it has extended the assistance through June 2011 at a reduced level. If the economy has not improved by then, Kaiser predicts, paying for this program will be another huge potential source of trouble for the states.[59]

The National League of Cities recently said that U.S. cities are in their worst fiscal shape in at least a quarter of a century and probably have not yet hit bottom—even after four straight years of falling revenue.[60] Because property taxes are one of the main source of revenue for most local governments, and because some local assessors are only now recording lower property values, their revenue is likely to continue to decline for at least several more years.[61]

"The effects of a depressed real estate market, low levels of consumer confidence, and high levels of unemployment will likely play out in cities through 2010, 2011 and beyond," the survey of 338 cities reported. The authors of the survey projected that revenue would fall 3% in 2010, and cities' budgets would shrink another 2%, the largest cutbacks in the 25 years for which the group has published the report.[62]

Investors now look askance at once-solid state and local bonds, raising borrowing costs for many states and making their task of balancing the budget even harder. Municipalities in Florida, the state with the third-highest rate of home foreclosures, saw borrowing costs rise when they sold $442 million in bonds in September 2010.

## Impact at the federal level

The federal government's response to the financial crisis and the ensuing recession "included some of the most aggressive fiscal and monetary policies in history," said the economists Mark Zandi and Alan Blinder. "Yet almost every one of these policy initiatives remain controversial to this day, with critics calling them misguided, ineffective or both."[63]

The government's fiscal initiatives began soon after the recession started: the Economic Stimulus Act of 2008, signed into law in February, provided roughly $170 billion in tax rebates for households and tax incentives for businesses. In October 2008, at the height of the crisis, the $700 billion TARP was enacted; and in early 2009, the American Recovery and Reinvestment Act of 2009 was enacted to stimulate the weakening economy, costing another $787 billion in tax cuts and government spending.

Beginning with the rate cuts in mid-2007 through the implementation of the TALF in early 2009, the Federal Reserve provided support to the economy throughout the crisis. Aside from its emergency lending programs put in place during the financial crisis, the Fed put about $1.7 trillion into the economy from September 2008 to October 2010—primarily by buying financial assets such as mortgages-backed securities and Treasury bonds, a process known as "quantitative easing."[64] And in November 2010, officials announced another $600 billion in easing, designed to keep long-term and short-term interest rates down.

In October 2010, the Treasury Department reported that the TARP program would cost far less than the $700 billion that Congress had appropriated in the fall of 2008, because banks had begun to repay the Treasury in 2009. In fact, Treasury said, TARP would wind up costing about $29 billion, mostly owing to the bailout of the automakers General Motors and Chrysler and the mortgage modification program.[65] The latest estimates from the Congressional Budget Office (CBO) put its cost at $25 billion.[66] As reported earlier, the CBO projects that the economic cost of the GSEs' downfall, including the financial cost of government support and actual dollar outlays, could reach $389 billion by 2019.

Overall, as spending increased and revenues declined during the recession, the federal deficit grew from $459 billion in 2008 to $1.4 trillion in 2009. And it is estimated to have risen to $1.6 trillion in 2010.[67]

### THE FINANCIAL SECTOR:
#### "ALMOST TRIPLE THE LEVEL OF THREE YEARS EARLIER"

While the overall economy has struggled, the story for the financial sector is somewhat different. Like other sectors of the economy, the financial industry has cut

jobs. After growing steadily for years, employment in the financial sector fell by 128,000 in 2007, 273,000 in 2008, and another 310,000 in 2009. Areas dependent on the financial industry, such as Charlotte, North Carolina, have been hit hard. The unemployment rate in the Charlotte area rose from 4.8% in 2006 to a recent peak of 12.8% in February 2010.

Between January 2009 and December 2010, 297 banks have failed; most were small and medium-size banks.[68] The number of small banks on the FDIC's list of troubled institutions rose from 829 in the second quarter of 2010 to 860 in the third quarter, the largest number since March 1993.[69] Though a number of large financial institutions failed or nearly failed during the crisis, on the whole they have done better since the fall of 2008. Total financial sector profits peaked at $428 billion in 2006 and then fell to $128 billion in 2008, the lowest level since the early 1990s. They have since rebounded in 2009 and 2010, boosted by low interest rates and access to low-cost government borrowing. Financial sector profits were $242 billion in 2009 and reached an annual rate of $369 billion in the fall of 2010.

Within the financial sector, commercial bank profits rose from $7.6 billion in the first quarter of 2009 to $18.0 billion in the first quarter of 2010. The gains were concentrated among the larger banks.[70] For banks with assets greater than $1 billion, profits more than doubled, from $6.3 billion to $14.5 billion, from the first quarter of 2009 to the first quarter of 2010.[71] For commercial banks with less than $1 billion in assets, profits rose only 26%, from less than $1 billion to $1.2 billion.[72]

The securities industry has reported record profits and is once again distributing large bonuses. Just for those who work in New York City, bonuses at Wall Street securities firms in 2009 were $20.3 billion, up 17% from the year before, with "average compensation [rising] by 27 percent to more than $340,000."[73] After reporting $54 billion of losses during 2007 and 2008, the New York State Comptroller reported that in 2009, "industry profits reached a record $61.4 billion—almost triple the level of three years earlier."[74]

# 22

# THE FORECLOSURE CRISIS

## CONTENTS

## FORECLOSURES ON THE RISE:
## "HARD TO TALK ABOUT ANY RECOVERY"

Since the housing bubble burst, about four million families have lost their homes to foreclosure[1] and another four and a half million[2] have slipped into the foreclosure process or are seriously behind on their mortgage payments. When the economic damage finally abates, foreclosures may total between 8 million and more than 13 million, according to various estimates.[3] The foreclosure epidemic has hurt families and undermined home values in entire zip codes, strained school systems as well as community support services, and depleted state coffers. Even if the economy began suddenly booming the country would need years to recover.

Prior to 2007, the foreclosure rate was historically less than 1%. But the trend since the housing market collapsed has been dramatic: In 2009, 2.2% of all houses, or 1 out of 45, received at least one foreclosure filing.[4] In the fall of 2010, 1 in every 11 outstanding residential mortgage loans in the United States was at least one payment past due but not yet in foreclosure—an ominous warning that this wave may not have crested.[5] Distressed sales account for the majority of home sales in cities around the country, including Las Vegas, Phoenix, Sacramento, and Riverside, California.[6]

Returning to the 4,499 borrowers whose loans were pooled into CMLTI 2006-NC2: by September 2010, many had moved or refinanced their mortgages; by that point, 1,917 had entered foreclosure (mostly in Florida and California), and 729 had started loan modifications. Of the 1,715 still active loans then, 579 were seriously past due in their payments or currently in foreclosure. [7]

The causes of foreclosures have been analyzed by many academics and government agencies. Two events are typically necessary for a mortgage default. First, monthly payments become unaffordable owing to unemployment or other financial

hardship, or because mortgage payments increase. And second (in the opinion of many, now the more important factor), the home's value becomes less than the debt owed—in other words, the borrower has negative equity.

"The evidence is irrefutable," Laurie Goodman, a senior managing director with Amherst Securities, told Congress in 2009: "Negative equity is the most important predictor of default. When the borrower has negative equity, unemployment acts as one of many possible catalysts, increasing the probability of default."[8]

After falling 32% from their peak in 2006 to the spring of 2009, home prices have rebounded somewhat, but improvements are uneven across regions.[9] Nationwide, 10.8 million households, or 22.5% of those with mortgages, owe more on their mortgages than the market value of their house (see figure 22.1). In Nevada, 67% of homes with mortgages are under water, the highest rate in the country; in California, the rate is 32%.[10]

Given the extraordinary prevalence and extent of negative equity, the phenomenon of "strategic defaults" has also been on the rise: homeowners purposefully walk away from mortgage obligations when they perceive that their homes are worth less than what they owe and they believe that the value will not be going up anytime soon.

By the fall of 2010, three states particularly hard hit by foreclosures—California, Florida, and Nevada—reported some recent improvement in the initiation of foreclosures, but in November Nevada's rate was still five times higher than the national average. Foreclosure starts climbed in 33 states from their levels a year earlier, with the largest increases in Washington State (which has 9.2% unemployment), Indiana (9.8% unemployment), and South Carolina (10.6% unemployment), according to the Mortgage Bankers Association.

In Ohio, the city of Cleveland and surrounding Cuyahoga County are bulldozing blocks of abandoned houses down to the dirt with the aim of creating a northeastern Ohio "bank" of land preserved for the future. To do this, authorities seize blighted properties for unpaid taxes, and they take donations of homes from the Department of Housing and Urban Development, Fannie Mae, and some private lenders.[11] Now, the county finds itself under increasing duress, having endured 14,000 foreclosures in 2009.[12] After years of high unemployment and a fragile economy, the financial crisis took vulnerable residents and "shoved them over the edge of the cliff," Jim Rokakis, Cuyahoga's treasurer, told the Commission.[13]

In a spring 2010 survey, 85% of the responding mayors ranked the prevalence of nonprime or subprime mortgages as either first or second on a list of factors causing foreclosures in their cities. Almost all the mayors, 92%, said they expected the foreclosure problems to stay the same or worsen in their cities over the next year.[14]

"There has been no meaningful decline in the inventory of distressed properties found in the housing market," Guy Cecala, the chief executive and publisher of Inside Mortgage Finance Publications, told a congressional panel overseeing the Troubled Asset Relief Program in October 2010. "It is hard to talk about any recovery of the housing market when the share of distressed property transactions remains close to 50 percent."[15]

## "Underwater" Mortgages

*Many mortgage holders find themselves underwater; that is, owing more than their homes are worth. This is particularly true in Arizona, California, Florida, Michigan, and Nevada.*

SHARE OF LOANS WITH NEGATIVE EQUITY, THIRD QUARTER 2010

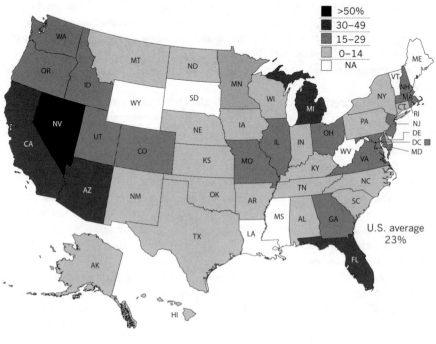

SOURCE: CoreLogic

*Figure 22.1*

"There was a fundamental change in our financial services sector that really is the reason we're in this crisis, this economic crisis, and is the reason we're seeing and will see in total probably before we're done, between 15 and 16 million foreclosure filings in this country," John Taylor, the president and CEO of the National Community Reinvestment Coalition, explained to the FCIC. "And by the way, a few hundred thousand people, even a million people going into foreclosure, you can kind of blame and say, 'Well they should have known better.' But 15 [or] 16 million American families can't all be wrong. They can't all be greedy and they can't all be stupid."[16]

## INITIATIVES TO STEM FORECLOSURES:
## "PERSISTENTLY DISREGARD"

The same system that was so efficient at creating millions of mortgage loans over the past decade has been ineffective at resolving problems in the housing market, including the efforts of homeowners to modify their mortgages. As mortgage problems mounted, the federal and state governments responded with financial incentives to encourage banks to adjust interest rates, spread loan payments over longer terms, or simply write down mortgage debts. But to date, federal auditors and independent consumer watchdogs have given the federal government's and the banks' mortgage modification programs poor grades.

The Home Affordable Modification Program (HAMP) is falling short of the 3 to 4 million families targeted for help by the end of 2012. (The program's resources come from the federal TARP funds.) As of December 2010, HAMP has resulted in the permanent modification of only 520,000 mortgages.[17] Meanwhile, the banks report that they have independently approved 3.4 million loan alterations of various kinds, although many of these modifications simply roll missed payments into a new mortgage and thus result in higher monthly payments.[18]

The effectiveness of state mortgage modification and foreclosure assistance programs is unclear. Some are just getting started. New Jersey, for instance, will begin a $112 million "HomeKeeper Program" in 2011, to offer some residents who face foreclosure because of unemployment or "substantial underemployment" a deferred-payment, no-interest loan so that they can continue making payments on their mortgages.[19]

During a series of hearings in communities around the country affected by the housing crisis, the Commission heard from many witnesses about the extraordinary difficulties they had encountered in seeking to modify their mortgages and stay in their homes. Borrowers who have been paying down mortgages for years and have built up substantial equity are especially susceptible to being turned down for loan modifications, because the lender would prefer that they simply sell their homes. Kirsten Keefe, a senior staff attorney with the Empire Justice Center in Albany, New York, brought this issue to regulators' attention in March 2010. Speaking to the Federal Reserve Board's Consumer Advisory Council in Washington, Keefe identified trends among borrowers in New York who tried to qualify for the government's HAMP program. "We are also routinely hearing that folks who have a lot of equity are . . . being denied HAMP modifications," she said.[20] Diane Thompson, from the National Consumer Law Center, testified to the United States Senate Committee on Banking, Housing, and Urban Affairs in November 2010 about the challenges of the program. She stated, "Only a very few of the potentially eligible borrowers have been able to obtain permanent modifications. Advocates continue to report that borrowers are denied improperly for HAMP . . . and that some servicers persistently disregard HAMP applications."[21]

Competing incentives may encourage banks to view foreclosure as quicker, cleaner, and often cheaper than modifying the terms of existing mortgages.[22]

For them, foreclosure is a prudent response to default because, the data suggest, many borrowers who receive temporary or permanent forgiveness on their terms will slide into default again.[23] Also, servicers may receive substantial fees for guiding a mortgage through the foreclosure process, creating an incentive to deny a modification.[24]

Frequently, there's another complication to attempting a foreclosure or modification: the second mortgages that were layered onto first mortgages. The first mortgages were commonly sold by banks into the securitization machine. The second mortgages were often retained by the same lenders who typically service the mortgage: that is, they process the monthly payments and provide customer service to borrowers. If a first mortgage is modified or foreclosed on, the entire value of the second mortgage may be wiped out. Under these circumstances, the lender holding that second lien has an incentive to delay a modification into a new loan that would make the mortgage payments more affordable to the borrower.[25]

The country's leading banks now hold on their books more than $400 billion in second mortgages.[26] To the extent the banks have reported these loans as performing, the loans have not been marked down on their books. The actual value of these second mortgages could be much less than their $400 billion-plus reported value.[27] The danger of future losses is self-evident. Some frustrated first-lien investors have sued servicers, asserting they are not protecting investors' financial interests. Instead, they claim that because the servicer is holding the second lien, the servicers are looking after their own balance sheets by encouraging borrowers to keep up the payments on their second mortgage when they cannot afford to make payments on both obligations. According to Laurie Goodman, for mortgage modifications to work, the holders of the second mortgages will have to accept some losses—a potentially expensive proposition.[28]

A number of other obstacles have made modifications difficult. For example, there are competing interests among various investors in a mortgage-backed security. Proceeds from a foreclosure may be enough to pay off the investors holding the highest-rated tranches of securities, while the holders of the lower tranches would likely be wiped out. As a result, the holders of the lower-rated tranches might prefer a modification, if it produced more cash flow than a foreclosure.

Other efforts in the private and public sectors to address the foreclosure crisis have focused on encouraging short sales. In theory, short sales should help borrowers, neighborhoods, and lenders. Borrowers avoid foreclosure; neighborhoods avoid vacant, dilapidated homes that encourage crime; and lenders avoid some of the costs of foreclosure. Nonetheless, such deals frequently stall because the process is cumbersome, demands coordination, and eats up resources. For example, lenders can be reluctant to sign off on the buyer's bid because they are not sure that the home is being sold at the highest possible price. In addition, when there are two mortgages, the holders of the first and second mortgages must both agree to the resolution.

## FLAWS IN THE PROCESS:
## "SPECULATION AND WORST-CASE SCENARIOS"

In 2010, additional issues have come to the fore, as problems with individual foreclosures have revealed systemic flaws in how lenders documented and processed mortgages for securitization. Legal experts and consumer advocates told the Commission that procedural and documentation problems with foreclosure have been laid out in court cases and academic studies for years, but were ignored until the number of foreclosures rose so dramatically.

All 50 of the nation's state attorneys general banded together in the fall of 2010 to investigate foreclosure irregularities, identify possible solutions, and explore potential redress for borrowers who were harmed by improper foreclosures. For example, lenders have relied on "robo-signers" who substituted speed for accuracy by signing, and sometimes backdating, hundreds of affidavits claiming personal knowledge of facts about mortgages that they did not actually know to be true. One such "robo-signer," Jeffrey Stephan of GMAC, said that he signed 10,000 affidavits in a month—roughly 1 per minute, in a 40-hour workweek—making it highly unlikely that he verified payment histories in each individual case of foreclosure.[29] In addition, a number of court cases have been filed alleging invalid notarizations, forged signatures, backdated mortgage paperwork, and failure to demonstrate having legal standing to foreclose—that is, being the entity with the right to repossess a home.[30]

The problem of legal standing arose because the rapid growth of mortgage securitization outpaced the ability of the legal and financial system to accurately record who owns the mortgage. During the securitization process, loans were sold multiple times. To speed up processing, the financial industry created Mortgage Electronic Registration Systems, Inc. (MERS), an organization made up of 3,000 mortgage lenders. It tracks changes in servicing rights and ownership interests in mortgage loans. MERS is designated as the "mortgagee of record" on behalf of its members, a status that is meant to give it the legal right to foreclose if the borrower fails to pay the loan. MERS has registered 66 million mortgages since launching in 1995 and had 33 million loans outstanding as of November 2010.[31]

The standing of MERS or its designees to foreclose has been called into question by courts and academics, however.[32] In a hearing before the House Judiciary Committee on the foreclosure crisis, New York State Supreme Court Justice F. Dana Winslow testified that "standing has become such a pervasive issue that I frequently use the term 'presumptive mortgagee in foreclosure'" to describe MERS. Because of "multiple unrecorded transfers of the legal ownership of the [m]ortgage," it is unclear whether MERS continued to be the mortgagee after subsequent sales of the loan, according to Winslow.[33] Moreover, courts have held that MERS does not own the underlying note and therefore cannot transfer the note or the deed of trust, or foreclose upon the property.[34]

Winslow also highlighted other deficiencies in MERS' standing, many involving sloppy paperwork: the failure to produce the correct promissory notes in court during

foreclosure proceedings; gaps in the chain of title, including printouts of the title that have differed substantially from information provided previously; retroactive assignments of notes and mortgages in an effort to clean up the paperwork problems from earlier years; questionable signatures on assignments and affidavits attesting to the ownership of the note and mortgage; and questionable notary stamps on assignments.[35]

On November 16, 2010, a bankruptcy court ruled that the Bank of New York could not foreclose on a loan it had purchased from Countrywide, because MERS had failed to endorse or deliver the note to the Bank of New York as required by the pooling and servicing agreement. This ruling could have further implications, because it was customary for Countrywide to maintain possession of the note and related loan documents when loans were securitized.[36]

Across the market, some mortgage securities holders have sued the issuers of those securities, demanding that the issuers rescind their purchases.[37] If the legal challenges succeed, investors that own mortgage-backed securities could force the issuers to buy them back at the original price—possibly with interest. The issuers would then be the owners of the securities and would bear the risk of loss.[38]

The Congressional Oversight Panel, in a report issued in November 2010, said it is on the lookout for such risks: "If documentation problems prove to be pervasive and, more importantly, throw into doubt the ownership of not only foreclosed properties but also pooled mortgages, the consequences could be severe."[39] This sentiment was echoed by University of Iowa law professor Katherine Porter who has studied foreclosures and the law: "It is lack of knowledge of how widespread the problems may be that is turning the allegations into a crisis. Lack of knowledge feeds speculation and worst-case scenarios."[40] Adam Levitin, a Georgetown University associate professor of law, has estimated that the claims could be in the trillions of dollars, rendering major U.S. banks insolvent.[41]

## NEIGHBORHOOD EFFECTS: "I'M NOT LEAVING"

For the millions of Americans who paid their bills, never flipped a house, and had never heard of a CDO, the financial crisis has been long, bewildering, and painful. A crisis that started with a housing boom that became a bubble has come back full circle to forests of "for sale" signs—but this time attracting few buyers. Stores have shuttered; employers have cut jobs; hopes have fled. Too many Americans today find themselves in suburban ghost towns or urban wastelands, where properties are vacant and construction cranes do not lift a thing for months.

Renters, who never bought into the madness, are also among the victims as lenders seize property after landlords default on loans. Renters can lose the roof over their heads as well as their security deposits. In Minneapolis, as many as 60% of buildings with foreclosures in 2006 and 2007 were renter-occupied, according to statistics cited in testimony by Deputy Assistant Secretary Erika Poethig from the U.S. Department of Housing and Urban Development to the House of Representatives Subcommittee on Housing and Community Opportunity.[42]

For children, a repossessed house—whether rented or bought—is destabilizing. The impact of foreclosures on children around the country has been enormous. One-third of the children who experienced homelessness after the financial crisis did so because of foreclosures of the housing that their parents owned or were renting, according to a recent study.[43] One school official in Nevada told the Commission about the significant challenges to the educational system created by the economic crisis.[44]

All around, the demand from people who need help is outstripping community resources. Coast to coast, communities are trying to stretch housing aid budgets to help people displaced by foreclosures. In Nevada, for example, Clark County, which contains 1.9 million people living in and around Las Vegas, was forced to cut its Financial Housing Assistance program, despite the clear needs in the community. Gail Burks, the president and chief executive of the Nevada Fair Housing Center, told the Commission that her group finds that many they counsel through the foreclosure process are in despair. "It's very stressful. There are times that the couples we are helping end up divorcing, sometimes before the process is over. . . . We've also seen threats of suicide."[45]

And the stories continue. Karen Mann, the appraiser from Discovery Bay, California, testified to the Commission about her family's circumstances. Her daughter and son-in-law refinanced their mortgage into an adjustable-rate mortgage. When the time came for the rate to adjust upward, new financial troubles made the payments more than the family could afford. Because the market value of the home was nearly equal to their mortgage debt, the family's attempts to get the mortgage modified were fruitless. They lined up a buyer for a short sale, but the deal was nixed. Then, when medical problems created yet another challenge, the couple and their four children moved in with Mann. "The children were relocated to new schools, and the adults dealt with the pain and emotional suffering while they were trying to rebuild their lives," Mann said. The couple filed for bankruptcy. Two months after the bankruptcy was completed, the lender asked them if they wanted to modify their mortgage.[46]

In Cape Coral, Florida, Dawn Hunt and her husband, a mailman, and their two children live in an attractive ranch-style home they bought for about $100,000 more than a decade ago. It was a quiet, 20-year-old subdivision where most of the residents were homeowners. In 2005 and 2006, builders rushed to the area and threw up dozens of new homes on empty lots. Homebuilder Comfort Homes of Florida LLC broke ground for a house across the street from the Hunts, but did not complete it. This fall, the house sat vacant, an empty shell. No stucco was ever applied to the concrete block exterior, and the house had no interior walls. A wasp nest decorated the electrical box near the front door. The untended grass had grown four feet high. Sharp sand spurs in the brush made it difficult to approach the property. Two doors down from the Hunts, another house was also vacant, left empty when a family split up and moved a year earlier. They abandoned a car in the garage. The roof leaked, and a blue plastic tarp put in place to keep the rain out now flaps in the breeze. The Hunts called the police after vandals broke into the house one night; intruders have been back twice more in the daylight.[47]

Now 44% of the homes in the Hunts' neighborhood are in default, are in the foreclosure process, or have been taken back by the bank.[48] Most of the other houses in the community are occupied by renters whose absentee landlords bought the houses when the homeowners lost their homes to their banks. The Hunts' house has lost two-thirds of its value from the peak of the market. Nonetheless, even though the neighborhood is not as lovely as it used to be, Dawn Hunt told the FCIC, "I'm not leaving."[49]

---

### COMMISSION CONCLUSIONS ON CHAPTER 22

The Commission concludes the unchecked increase in the complexity of mortgages and securitization has made it more difficult to solve problems in the mortgage market. This complexity has created powerful competing interests, including those of the holders of first and second mortgages and of mortgage servicers; has reduced transparency for policy makers, regulators, financial institutions, and homeowners; and has impeded mortgage modifications. The resulting disputes and inaction have caused pain largely borne by individual homeowners and created further uncertainty about the health of the housing market and financial institutions.

# Dissenting Statement of

Commissioner

## KEITH HENNESSEY

Commissioner

## DOUGLAS HOLTZ-EAKIN

Vice Chairman

## BILL THOMAS

# CAUSES OF THE
# FINANCIAL AND ECONOMIC CRISIS

## CONTENTS

## INTRODUCTION

We have identified ten causes that are essential to explaining the crisis. In this dissenting view:

- We explain how our approach differs from others';
- We briefly describe the stages of the crisis;
- We list the ten essential causes of the crisis; and
- We walk through each cause in a bit more detail.

We find areas of agreement with the majority's conclusions, but unfortunately the areas of disagreement are significant enough that we dissent and present our views in this report.

We wish to compliment the Commission staff for their investigative work. In many ways it helped shape our thinking and conclusions.

Due to a length limitation recently imposed upon us by six members of the Commission,[1] this report focuses only on the causes *essential* to explaining the crisis. We regret that the limitation means that several important topics that deserve a much fuller discussion get only a brief mention here.

## HOW OUR APPROACH DIFFERS FROM OTHERS'

During the course of the Commission's hearings and investigations, we heard frequent arguments that there was a single cause of the crisis. For some it was international capital flows or monetary policy; for others, housing policy; and for still others, it was insufficient regulation of an ambiguously defined shadow banking sector, or unregulated over-the-counter derivatives, or the greed of those in the financial sector and the political influence they had in Washington.

In each case, these arguments, when used as single-cause explanations, are too simplistic because they are incomplete. While some of these factors were essential contributors to the crisis, each is insufficient as a standalone explanation.

The majority's approach to explaining the crisis suffers from the opposite problem–it is too broad. Not everything that went wrong during the financial crisis caused the crisis, and while some causes were essential, others had only a minor impact. Not every regulatory change related to housing or the financial system prior to the crisis was a cause. The majority's almost 550-page report is more an account of bad events than a focused explanation of what happened and why. When everything is important, nothing is.

As an example, non-credit derivatives did not in any meaningful way cause or contribute to the financial crisis. Neither the Community Reinvestment Act nor removal of the Glass-Steagall firewall was a significant cause. The crisis can be explained without resorting to these factors.

We also reject as too simplistic the hypothesis that too little regulation caused the crisis, as well as its opposite, that too much regulation caused the crisis. We question this metric for determining the effectiveness of regulation. The *amount* of financial regulation should reflect the need to address particular failures in the financial system. For example, high-risk, nontraditional mortgage lending by nonbank lenders flourished in the 2000s and did tremendous damage in an ineffectively regulated environment, contributing to the financial crisis. Poorly designed government housing policies distorted market outcomes and contributed to the creation of unsound mortgages as well. Countrywide's irresponsible lending and AIG's failure were in part attributable to ineffective regulation and supervision, while Fannie Mae and Freddie Mac's failures were the result of policymakers using the power of government to blend public purpose with private gains and then socializing the losses. Both the "too little government" and "too much government" approaches are too broad-brush to explain the crisis.

The majority says the crisis was avoidable if only the United States had adopted across-the-board more restrictive regulations, in conjunction with more aggressive regulators and supervisors. This conclusion by the majority largely ignores the global nature of the crisis. For example:

- A credit bubble appeared in both the United States and Europe. This tells us that our primary explanation for the credit bubble should focus on factors common to both regions.

# House Price Appreciation in Selected Countries, 2002-2008

*The United States was one of many countries to experience rapid house price growth*

2002 INDEX = 100

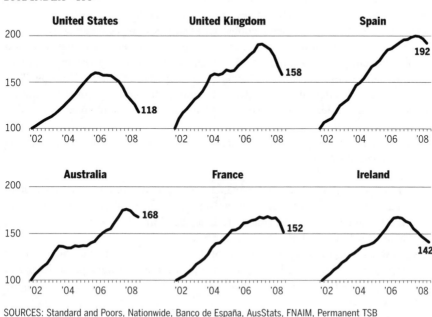

SOURCES: Standard and Poors, Nationwide, Banco de España, AusStats, FNAIM, Permanent TSB

- The report largely ignores the credit bubble beyond housing. Credit spreads declined not just for housing, but also for other asset classes like commercial real estate. This tells us to look to the credit bubble as an essential cause of the U.S. housing bubble. It also tells us that problems with U.S. housing policy or markets do not by themselves explain the U.S. housing bubble.
- There were housing bubbles in the United Kingdom, Spain, Australia, France and Ireland, some more pronounced than in the United States. Some nations with housing bubbles relied little on American-style mortgage securitization. A good explanation of the U.S. housing bubble should also take into account its parallels in other nations. This leads us to explanations broader than just U.S. housing policy, regulation, or supervision. It also tells us that while failures in U.S. securitization markets may be an essential cause, we must look for other things that went wrong as well.
- Large financial firms failed in Iceland, Spain, Germany, and the United Kingdom, among others. Not all of these firms bet solely on U.S. housing assets, and

they operated in different regulatory and supervisory regimes than U.S. commercial and investment banks. In many cases these European systems have stricter regulation than the United States, and still they faced financial firm failures similar to those in the United States.

These facts tell us that our explanation for the credit bubble should focus on factors common to both the United States and Europe, that the credit bubble is likely an essential cause of the U.S. housing bubble, and that U.S. housing policy is by itself an insufficient explanation of the crisis. Furthermore, any explanation that relies too heavily on a unique element of the U.S. regulatory or supervisory system is likely to be insufficient to explain why the same thing happened in parts of Europe. This moves inadequate international capital and liquidity standards up our list of causes, and it moves the differences between the regulation of U.S. commercial and investment banks down that list.

Applying these international comparisons directly to the majority's conclusions provokes these questions:

- If the political influence of the financial sector in Washington was an essential cause of the crisis, how does that explain similar financial institution failures in the United Kingdom, Germany, Iceland, Belgium, the Netherlands, France, Spain, Switzerland, Ireland, and Denmark?
- How can the "runaway mortgage securitization train" detailed in the majority's report explain housing bubbles in Spain, Australia, and the United Kingdom, countries with mortgage finance systems vastly different than that in the United States?
- How can the corporate and regulatory structures of investment banks explain the decisions of many U.S. commercial banks, several large American university endowments, and some state public employee pension funds, not to mention a number of large and midsize German banks, to take on too much U.S. housing risk?
- How did former Fed Chairman Alan Greenspan's "deregulatory ideology" also precipitate bank regulatory failures across Europe?

Not all of these factors identified by the majority were irrelevant; they were just not essential.

**The Commission's statutory mission is "to examine the causes, domestic and global, of the current financial and economic crisis in the United States." By focusing too narrowly on U.S. regulatory policy and supervision, ignoring international parallels, emphasizing only arguments for greater regulation, failing to prioritize the causes, and failing to distinguish sufficiently between causes and effects, the majority's report is unbalanced and leads to incorrect conclusions about what caused the crisis.**

We begin our explanation by briefly describing the stages of the crisis.

## STAGES OF THE CRISIS

As of December 2010, the United States is still in an *economic slump* caused by a *financial crisis* that first manifested itself in August 2007 and ended in early 2009. The primary features of that financial crisis were a *financial shock* in September 2008 and a concomitant *financial panic*. The financial shock and panic triggered a severe contraction in lending and hiring beginning in the fourth quarter of 2008.

Some observers describe recent economic history as a recession that began in December 2007 and continued until June 2009, and from which we are only now beginning to recover. While this definition of the recession is technically accurate, it obscures a more important chronology that connects financial market developments with the broader economy. We describe recent U.S. macroeconomic history in five stages:

- A series of foreshocks beginning in August 2007, followed by an economic slowdown and then a mild recession through August 2008, as liquidity problems emerged and three large U.S. financial institutions failed;
- A severe financial shock in September 2008, in which ten large financial institutions failed, nearly failed, or changed their institutional structure; triggering
- A financial panic and the beginning of a large contraction in the real economy in the last few months of 2008; followed by
- The end of the financial shock, panic, and rescue at the beginning of 2009; followed by
- A continued and deepening contraction in the real economy and the beginning of the financial recovery and rebuilding period.

As of December 2010, the United States is still in the last stage. The financial system is still recovering and being restructured, and the U.S. economy struggles to return to sustained strong growth. The remainder of our comments focuses on the financial crisis in the first three stages by examining its ten essential causes.

## THE TEN ESSENTIAL CAUSES
## OF THE FINANCIAL AND ECONOMIC CRISIS

The following ten causes, global and domestic, are essential to explaining the financial and economic crisis.

I. **Credit bubble.** Starting in the late 1990s, China, other large developing countries, and the big oil-producing nations built up large capital surpluses. They loaned these savings to the United States and Europe, causing interest rates to fall. Credit spreads narrowed, meaning that the cost of borrowing to finance risky investments declined. A credit bubble formed in the United States and Europe, the most notable manifestation of which was increased

investment in high-risk mortgages. U.S. monetary policy may have contributed to the credit bubble but did not cause it.

II. **Housing bubble.** Beginning in the late 1990s and accelerating in the 2000s, there was a large and sustained housing bubble in the United States. The bubble was characterized both by national increases in house prices well above the historical trend and by rapid regional boom-and-bust cycles in California, Nevada, Arizona, and Florida. Many factors contributed to the housing bubble, the bursting of which created enormous losses for homeowners and investors.

III. **Nontraditional mortgages.** Tightening credit spreads, overly optimistic assumptions about U.S. housing prices, and flaws in primary and secondary mortgage markets led to poor origination practices and combined to increase the flow of credit to U.S. housing finance. Fueled by cheap credit, firms like Countrywide, Washington Mutual, Ameriquest, and HSBC Finance originated vast numbers of high-risk, nontraditional mortgages that were in some cases deceptive, in many cases confusing, and often beyond borrowers' ability to repay. At the same time, many homebuyers and homeowners did not live up to their responsibilities to understand the terms of their mortgages and to make prudent financial decisions. These factors further amplified the housing bubble.

IV. **Credit ratings and securitization.** Failures in credit rating and securitization transformed bad mortgages into toxic financial assets. Securitizers lowered the credit quality of the mortgages they securitized. Credit rating agencies erroneously rated mortgage-backed securities and their derivatives as safe investments. Buyers failed to look behind the credit ratings and do their own due diligence. These factors fueled the creation of more bad mortgages.

V. **Financial institutions concentrated correlated risk.** Managers of many large and midsize financial institutions in the United States amassed enormous concentrations of highly correlated housing risk. Some did this knowingly by betting on rising housing prices, while others paid insufficient attention to the potential risk of carrying large amounts of housing risk on their balance sheets. This enabled large but seemingly manageable mortgage losses to precipitate the collapse of large financial institutions.

VI. **Leverage and liquidity risk.** Managers of these financial firms amplified this concentrated housing risk by holding too little capital relative to the risks they were carrying on their balance sheets. Many placed their firms on a hair trigger by relying heavily on short-term financing in repo and commercial paper markets for their day-to-day liquidity. They placed solvency bets (sometimes unknowingly) that their housing investments were solid, and liquidity bets that overnight money would always be available. Both turned out to be bad bets. In several cases, failed solvency bets triggered liquidity crises, causing some of the largest financial firms to fail or nearly fail. Firms were insufficiently transparent about their housing risk, creating uncertainty in mar-

kets that made it difficult for some to access additional capital and liquidity when needed.

**VII. Risk of contagion.** The risk of contagion was an essential cause of the crisis. In some cases, the financial system was vulnerable because policymakers were afraid of a large firm's sudden and disorderly failure triggering balance-sheet losses in its counterparties. These institutions were deemed too big and interconnected to other firms through counterparty credit risk for policymakers to be willing to allow them to fail suddenly.

**VIII. Common shock.** In other cases, unrelated financial institutions failed because of a common shock: they made similar failed bets on housing. Unconnected financial firms failed for the same reason and at roughly the same time because they had the same problem: large housing losses. This common shock meant that the problem was broader than a single failed bank–key large financial institutions were undercapitalized because of this common shock.

**IX. Financial shock and panic.** In quick succession in September 2008, the failures, near-failures, and restructurings of ten firms triggered a global financial panic. Confidence and trust in the financial system began to evaporate as the health of almost every large and midsize financial institution in the United States and Europe was questioned.

**X. Financial crisis causes economic crisis.** The financial shock and panic caused a severe contraction in the real economy. The shock and panic ended in early 2009. Harm to the real economy continues through today.

We now describe these ten essential causes of the crisis in more detail.

## THE CREDIT BUBBLE: GLOBAL CAPITAL FLOWS, UNDERPRICED RISK, AND FEDERAL RESERVE POLICY

The financial and economic crisis began with a credit bubble in the United States and Europe. Credit spreads narrowed significantly, meaning that the cost of borrowing to finance risky investments declined relative to safe assets such as U.S. Treasury securities. The most notable of these risky investments were high-risk mortgages.

The U.S. housing bubble was the most visible effect of the credit bubble but not the only one. Commercial real estate, high-yield debt, and leveraged loans were all boosted by the surplus of inexpensive credit.

There are three major possible explanations for the credit bubble: global capital flows, the repricing of risk, and monetary policy.

### Global capital flows

Starting in the late 1990s, China, other large developing countries, and the big oil-producing nations consumed and invested domestically less than they earned. As

China and other Asian economies grew, their savings grew as well. In addition, boosted by high global oil prices, the largest oil-producing nations built up large capital surpluses and looked to invest in the United States and Europe. Massive amounts of inexpensive capital flowed into the United States, making borrowing inexpensive. Americans used the cheap credit to make riskier investments than in the past. The same dynamic was at work in Europe. Germany saved, and its capital flowed to Ireland, Italy, Spain and Portugal.

Fed Chairman Ben Bernanke describes the strong relationship between financial account surplus growth (the mirror of current account deficit growth) and house price appreciation: "Countries in which current accounts worsened and capital inflows rose . . . had greater house price appreciation [from 2001 to 2006] . . . The relationship is highly significant, both statistically and economically, and about 31 percent of the variability in house price appreciation across countries is explained."[2]

Global imbalances are an essential cause of the crisis and the most important macroeconomic explanation. Steady and large increases in capital inflows into the U.S. and European economies encouraged significant increases in domestic lending, especially in high-risk mortgages.

## The repricing of risk

Low-cost capital can but does not necessarily have to lead to an increase in risky investments. Increased capital flows to the United States and Europe cannot alone explain the credit bubble.

We still don't know whether the credit bubble was the result of rational or irrational behavior. Investors may have been rational—their preferences may have changed, making them willing to accept lower returns for high-risk investments. They may have collectively been irrational—they may have adopted a bubble mentality and assumed that, while they were paying a higher price for risky assets, they could resell them later for even more. Or they may have mistakenly assumed that the world had gotten safer and that the risk of bad outcomes (especially in U.S. housing markets) had declined.

For some combination of these reasons, over a period of many years leading up to the crisis, investors grew willing to pay more for risky assets. When the housing bubble burst and the financial shock hit, investors everywhere reassessed what return they would demand for a risky investment, and therefore what price they were willing to pay for a risky asset. Credit spreads for all types of risk around the world increased suddenly and sharply, and the prices of risky assets plummeted. This was most evident in but not limited to the U.S. market for financial assets backed by high-risk, nontraditional mortgages. The credit bubble burst and caused tremendous damage.

## Monetary policy

The Federal Reserve significantly affects the availability and price of capital. This leads some to argue that the Fed contributed to the increased demand for risky in-

vestments by keeping interest rates too low for too long. Critics of Fed policy argue that, beginning under Chairman Greenspan and continuing under Chairman Bernanke, the Fed kept rates too low for too long and created a bubble in housing.

Dr. John B. Taylor is a proponent of this argument. He argues that the Fed set interest rates too low in 2002–2006 and that these low rates fueled the housing bubble as measured by housing starts. He suggests that this Fed-created housing bubble was the essential cause of the financial crisis. He further argues that, had federal funds rates instead followed the path recommended by the Taylor Rule (a monetary policy formula for setting the funds rate), the housing boom and subsequent bust would have been much smaller. He also applies this analysis to European economies and concludes that similar forces were at play.

Current Fed Chairman Bernanke and former Fed Chairman Greenspan disagree with Taylor's analysis. Chairman Bernanke argues that the Taylor Rule is a descriptive rule of thumb, but that "simple policy rules" are insufficient for making monetary policy decisions.[3] He further argues that, depending on the construction of the particular Taylor Rule, the monetary policy stance of the Fed may not have diverged significantly from its historical path. Former Chairman Greenspan adds that the connection between short-term interest rates and house prices is weak—that even if the Fed's target for overnight lending between banks was too low, this has little power to explain why rates on thirty-year mortgages were also too low.

This debate intertwines several monetary policy questions:

- How heavily should the Fed weigh a policy rule in its decisions to set interest rates? Should monetary policy be mostly rule-based or mostly discretionary?
- If the Fed thinks an asset bubble is developing, should it use monetary policy to try to pop or prevent it?
- Were interest rates too low in 2002–2006?
- Did too-low federal funds rates cause or contribute to the housing bubble?

This debate is complex and thus far unresolved. Loose monetary policy does not necessarily lead to smaller credit spreads. There are open questions about the link between short-term interest rates and house price appreciation, whether housing starts are the best measure of the housing bubble, the timing of housing price increases relative to the interest rates in 2002–2006, the European comparison, and whether the magnitude of the bubble can be explained by the gap between the Taylor Rule prescription and historic rates. At the same time, many observers argue that Taylor is right that short-term interest rates were too low during this period, and therefore that his argument is at least plausible if not provable.

We conclude that global capital flows and risk repricing caused the credit bubble, and we consider them essential to explaining the crisis. U.S. monetary policy may have been an amplifying factor, but it did not by itself cause the credit bubble, nor was it essential to causing the crisis.

The Commission should have focused more time and energy on exploring these questions about global capital flows, risk repricing, and monetary policy. Instead, the

Commission focused thousands of staff hours on investigation, and not nearly enough on analyzing these critical economic questions. The investigations were in many cases productive and informative, but there should have been more balance between investigation and analysis.

*Conclusions:*

- The credit bubble was an essential cause of the financial crisis.
- Global capital flows lowered the price of capital in the United States and much of Europe.
- Over time, investors lowered the return they required for risky investments. Their preferences may have changed, they may have adopted an irrational bubble mentality, or they may have mistakenly assumed that the world had become safer. This inflated prices for risky assets.
- U.S. monetary policy may have contributed to the credit bubble but did not cause it.

## THE HOUSING BUBBLE

The housing bubble had two components: the actual homes and the mortgages that financed them. We look briefly at each component and its possible causes.

There was a *housing* bubble in the United States—the price of U.S. housing increased by more than could be explained by market developments. This included both a national housing bubble and more concentrated regional bubbles in four "Sand States": California, Nevada, Arizona, and Florida.

Conventional wisdom is that a bubble is hard to spot while you're in one, and painfully obvious after it has burst. Even after the U.S. housing bubble burst, there is no consensus on what caused it.

While we still don't know the relative importance of the possible causes of the housing bubble, we can at least identify some of the most important hypotheses:

- **Population growth.** Arizona, Florida, Nevada, and parts of California all experienced population growth that far exceeded the national average. More people fueled more demand for houses.
- **Land use restrictions.** In some areas, local zoning rules and other land use restrictions, as well as natural barriers to building, made it hard to build new houses to meet increased demand resulting from population growth. When supply is constrained and demand increases, prices go up.
- **Over-optimism.** Even absent market fundamentals driving up prices, shared expectations of future price increases can generate booms. This is the classic explanation of a bubble.
- **Easy financing.** Nontraditional (and higher risk) mortgages made it easier for potential homebuyers to borrow enough to buy more expensive homes. This doesn't mean they could afford those homes or future mortgage payments in

the long run, but only that someone was willing to provide the initial loan. Mortgage originators often had insufficient incentive to encourage borrowers to get sustainable mortgages.

Some combination of the first two factors may apply in parts of the Sand States, but these don't explain the nationwide increase in prices.

The closely related and nationwide *mortgage* bubble was the largest and most significant manifestation of a more generalized credit bubble in the United States and Europe. Mortgage rates were low relative to the risk of losses, and risky borrowers, who in the past would have been turned down, found it possible to obtain a mortgage.[4]

In addition to the credit bubble, the proliferation of nontraditional mortgage products was a key cause of this surge in mortgage lending. Use of these products increased rapidly from the early part of the decade through 2006. There was a steady deterioration in mortgage underwriting standards (enabled by securitizers that lowered the credit quality of the mortgages they would accept, and credit rating agencies that overrated the subsequent securities and derivatives). There was a contemporaneous increase in mortgages that required little to no documentation.

As house prices rose, declining affordability would normally have constrained demand, but lenders and borrowers increasingly relied on nontraditional mortgage products to paper over this affordability issue. These mortgage products included interest-only adjustable rate mortgages (ARMs), pay-option ARMs that gave borrowers flexibility on the size of early monthly payments, and negative amortization products in which the initial payment did not even cover interest costs. These exotic mortgage products would often result in significant reductions in the initial monthly payment compared with even a standard ARM. Not surprisingly, they were the mortgages of choice for many lenders and borrowers focused on minimizing initial monthly payments.

Fed Chairman Bernanke sums up the situation this way: "At some point, both lenders and borrowers became convinced that house prices would only go up. Borrowers chose, and were extended, mortgages that they could not be expected to service in the longer term. They were provided these loans on the expectation that accumulating home equity would soon allow refinancing into more sustainable mortgages. For a time, rising house prices became a self-fulfilling prophecy, but ultimately, further appreciation could not be sustained and house prices collapsed."[5]

This explanation posits a relationship between the surge in housing prices and the surge in mortgage lending. There is not yet a consensus on which was the cause and which the effect. They appear to have been mutually reinforcing.

In understanding the growth of nontraditional mortgages, it is also difficult to determine the relative importance of causal factors, but again we can at least list those that are important:

- Nonbank mortgage lenders like New Century and Ameriquest flourished under ineffective regulatory regimes, especially at the state level. Weak disclosure standards and underwriting rules made it easy for irresponsible lenders to issue

mortgages that would probably never be repaid. Federally regulated bank and thrift lenders, such as Countrywide, Wachovia, and Washington Mutual, had lenient regulatory oversight on mortgage origination as well.

- Mortgage brokers were paid for new originations but did not ultimately bear the losses on poorly performing mortgages. Mortgage brokers therefore had an incentive to ignore negative information about borrowers.

- Many borrowers neither understood the terms of their mortgage nor appreciated the risk that home values could fall significantly, while others borrowed too much and bought bigger houses than they could ever reasonably expect to afford.

- All these factors were supplemented by government policies, many of which had been in effect for decades, that subsidized homeownership but created hidden costs to taxpayers and the economy. Elected officials of both parties pushed housing subsidies too far.

The Commission heard convincing testimony of serious mortgage fraud problems. Excruciating anecdotes showed that mortgage fraud increased substantially during the housing bubble. There is no question that this fraud did tremendous harm. But while that fraud is infuriating and may have been significant in certain areas (like Florida), the Commission was unable to measure the impact of fraud relative to the overall housing bubble.

The explosion of legal but questionable lending is an easier explanation for the creation of so many bad mortgages. Lending standards were lax enough that lenders could remain within the law but still generate huge volumes of bad mortgages. It is likely that the housing bubble and the crisis would have occurred even if there had been no mortgage fraud. We therefore classify mortgage fraud not as an essential cause of the crisis but as a contributing factor and a deplorable effect of the bubble. Even if the number of fraudulent loans was not substantial enough to have a large impact on the bubble, the increase in fraudulent activity should have been a leading indicator of deeper structural problems in the market.

## Conclusions:

- Beginning in the late 1990s and accelerating in the 2000s, there was a large and sustained housing bubble in the United States. The bubble was characterized both by national increases in house prices well above the historical trend and by more rapid regional boom-and-bust cycles in California, Nevada, Arizona, and Florida.

- There was also a contemporaneous mortgage bubble, caused primarily by the broader credit bubble.

- The causes of the housing bubble are still poorly understood. Explanations include population growth, land use restrictions, bubble psychology, and easy financing.

- The causes of the mortgage bubble and its relationship to the housing bubble

are also still poorly understood. Important factors include weak disclosure standards and underwriting rules for bank and nonbank mortgage lenders alike, the way in which mortgage brokers were compensated, borrowers who bought too much house and didn't understand or ignored the terms of their mortgages, and elected officials who over years piled on layer upon layer of government housing subsidies.

- Mortgage fraud increased substantially, but the evidence gathered by the Commission does not show that it was quantitatively significant enough to conclude that it was an essential cause.

## TURNING BAD MORTGAGES INTO TOXIC FINANCIAL ASSETS

The mortgage securitization process turned mortgages into mortgage-backed securities through the government-sponsored enterprises (GSEs) Fannie Mae and Freddie Mac, as well as Countrywide and other "private label" competitors. The securitization process allows capital to flow from investors to homebuyers. Without it, mortgage lending would be limited to banks and other portfolio lenders, supported by traditional funding sources such as deposits. Securitization allows homeowners access to enormous amounts of additional funding and thereby makes homeownership more affordable. It also can diversify housing risk among different types of lenders. If everything else is working properly, these are good things. Everything else was not working properly.

Some focus their criticism on the *form* of these financial instruments. For example, financial instruments called collateralized debt obligations (CDOs) were engineered from different bundled payment streams from mortgage-backed securities. Some argue that the conversion of a bundle of simple mortgages to a mortgage-backed security, and then to a collateralized debt obligation, was a problem. They argue that complex financial derivatives caused the crisis. We conclude that the details of this engineering are incidental to understanding the essential causes of the crisis. If the system works properly, reconfiguring streams of mortgage payments has little effect. The total amount of risk in a mortgage is unchanged if the pieces are put together in a different way.

Unfortunately, the system did not work as it should have. There were several flaws in the securitization and collateralization process that made things worse.

- Fannie Mae and Freddie Mac, as well as Countrywide and other private label competitors, all lowered the credit quality standards of the mortgages they securitized.[6] A mortgage-backed security was therefore "worse" during the crisis than in preceding years because the underlying mortgages were generally of poorer quality. This turned a bad mortgage into a worse security.
- Mortgage originators took advantage of these lower credit quality securitization standards and the easy flow of credit to relax the underwriting discipline in the loans they issued. As long as they could resell a mortgage to the secondary market, they didn't care about its quality.

- The increasing complexity of housing-related assets and the many steps between the borrower and final investor increased the importance of credit rating agencies and made independent risk assessment by investors more difficult. In this respect, complexity did contribute to the problem, but the other problems listed here are more important.
- Credit rating agencies assigned overly optimistic ratings to the CDOs built from mortgage-backed securities.[7] By erroneously rating these bundles of mortgage-backed security payments too highly, the credit rating agencies substantially contributed to the creation of toxic financial assets.
- Borrowers, originators, securitizers, rating agencies, and the ultimate buyers of the securities into which the risky mortgages were packaged all failed to exercise prudence and perform due diligence in their respective transactions. In particular, CDO buyers who were, in theory, sophisticated investors relied too heavily on credit ratings.
- Many financial institutions chose to make highly concentrated bets on housing prices. While in some cases they did that with whole loans, they were able to more easily and efficiently do so with CDOs and derivative securities.
- Regulatory capital standards, both domestically and internationally, gave preferential treatment to highly rated debt, further empowering the rating agencies and increasing the desirability of mortgage-backed structured products.
- There is a way that housing bets can be magnified using a form of derivative. A *synthetic CDO* is a security whose payments mimic that of a CDO that contains real mortgages. This is a "side bet" that allows you to assume the same risk as if you held pieces of actual mortgages. To the extent that investors and financial institutions wanted to increase their bets on housing, they were able to use synthetic CDOs. The risks in these synthetic CDOs, however, are zero-sum, since for every investor making a bet that housing performance will fall there must be other investors with equal-sized bets in the opposite direction.

These are related but different problems. While many involve the word "derivative," it is a mistake to bundle them together and say, "Derivatives or CDOs caused the crisis." In each case, we assign responsibility for the failures to the people and institutions rather than to the financial instruments they used.

## Conclusions:

Rather than "derivatives and CDOs caused the financial crisis," it is more accurate to say:

- Securitizers lowered credit quality standards;
- Mortgage originators took advantage of this to create junk mortgages;
- Credit rating agencies assigned overly optimistic ratings;
- Securities investors and others failed to perform sufficient due diligence;

- International and domestic regulators encouraged arbitrage toward lower capital standards;
- Some investors used these securities to concentrate rather than diversify risk; and
- Others used synthetic CDOs to amplify their housing bets.

## The dangerous imprecision of the term "shadow banking"

Part II of the majority's report begins with an extensive discussion of the failures of the "shadow banking system," which it defines as a "financial institutions and activities that in some respects parallel banking activities but are subject to less regulation than commercial banks." The majority's report suggests that the shadow banking system was a cause of the financial crisis.

"Shadow banking" is a term used to represent a collection of different financial institutions, instruments, and issues within the financial system. Indeed, "shadow banking" can refer to any financial activity that transforms short-term borrowing into long-term lending without a government backstop. This term can therefore include financial instruments and institutions as diverse as:

- The tri-party repo market;
- Structured Investment Vehicles and other off-balance-sheet entities used to increase leverage;
- Fannie Mae and Freddie Mac;
- Credit default swaps; and
- Hedge funds, monoline insurers, commercial paper, money market mutual funds, and investment banks.

As discussed in other parts of this paper, some of these items were important causes of the crisis. No matter what their individual roles in causing or contributing to the crisis, however, they are undoubtedly different. It is a mistake to group these issues and problems together. Each should be considered on its merits, rather than painting a poorly defined swath of the financial sector with a common brush of "too little regulation."

## BIG BANK BETS AND WHY BANKS FAILED

The story so far involves significant lost housing wealth and diminished values of securities financing those homes. Yet even larger past wealth losses did not bring the global financial system to its knees. The key differences in this case were leverage and risk concentration. Highly correlated housing risk was concentrated in large and highly leveraged financial institutions in the United States and much of Europe. This leverage magnified the effect of a housing loss on a financial institution's capital reserve, and the concentration meant these losses occurred in parallel.

In effect, many of the largest financial institutions in the world, along with hundreds of smaller ones, bet the survival of their institutions on housing prices. Some did this knowingly; others not.

Many investors made three bad assumptions about U.S. housing prices. They assumed:

- A low probability that housing prices would decline significantly;
- Prices were largely uncorrelated across different regions, so that a local housing bubble bursting in Nevada would not happen at the same time as one bursting in Florida; and
- A relatively low level of *strategic defaults*, in which an underwater homeowner voluntarily defaults on a non-recourse mortgage.

When housing prices declined nationally and quite severely in certain areas, these flawed assumptions, magnified by other problems described in previous steps, created enormous financial losses for firms exposed to housing investments.

An essential cause of the financial and economic crisis was appallingly bad risk management by the leaders of some of the largest financial institutions in the United States and Europe. Each failed firm that the Commission examined failed in part because its leaders poorly managed risk.

Based on testimony from the executives of several of the largest failed firms and the Commission staff's investigative work, we can group common risk management failures into several classes:

- **Concentration of highly correlated (housing) risk.** Firm managers bet massively on one type of asset, counting on high rates of return while comforting themselves that their competitors were doing the same.
- **Insufficient capital.** Some of the failed institutions were levered 35:1 or higher. This meant that every $35 of assets was financed with $1 of equity capital and $34 of debt. This made these firms enormously profitable when things were going well, but incredibly sensitive to even a small loss, as a 3 percent decline in the market value of these assets would leave them technically insolvent. In some cases, this increased leverage was direct and transparent. In other cases, firms used Structured Investment Vehicles, asset-backed commercial paper conduits, and other off-balance-sheet entities to try to have it both ways: further increasing their leverage while appearing not to do so. Highly concentrated, highly correlated risk combined with high leverage makes a fragile financial sector and creates a financial accident waiting to happen. These firms should have had much larger capital cushions and/or mechanisms for contingent capital upon which to draw in a crisis.
- **Overdependence on short-term liquidity from repo and commercial paper markets.** Just as each lacked sufficient capital cushions, in each case the failing firm's liquidity cushion ran out within days. The failed firms appear to have based their liquidity strategies on the flawed assumption that both the firm and

these funding markets would always be healthy and functioning smoothly. By failing to provide sufficiently for disruptions in their short-term financing, management put their firm's survival on a hair trigger.

- **Poor risk management systems.** A number of firms were unable to easily aggregate their housing risks across various business lines. Once the market began to decline, those firms that understood their total exposure were able to effectively sell or hedge their risk before the market turned down too far. Those that didn't were stuck with toxic assets in a disintegrating market.

## Solvency failure versus liquidity failure

The Commission heard testimony from the former heads of Bear Stearns, Lehman, Citigroup, and AIG, among others. A common theme pervaded the testimony of these witnesses:

- We were solvent before the liquidity run started.
- Someone (unnamed) spread bad information and started an unjustified liquidity run.
- Had that unjustified liquidity run not happened, given enough time we would have recovered and returned to a position of strength.
- Therefore, the firm failed because we ran out of time, and it's not my fault.

In each case, experts and regulators contested the former CEO's "we were solvent" claim. Technical issues make it difficult to prove otherwise, especially because the answer depends on when solvency is measured. After a few days of selling assets at fire-sale prices during a liquidity run, a highly leveraged firm's balance sheet will look measurably worse. In each case, whether or not the firm was technically solvent, the evidence strongly supports the claim that those pulling back from doing business with the firm were not irrational. In each of the cases we examined, there were huge financial losses that at a minimum placed the firm's solvency in serious doubt.

Interestingly, in each case, the CEO was willing to admit that he had poorly managed his firm's liquidity risk, but unwilling to admit that his firm was insolvent or nearly so. In each case the CEO's claims were highly unpersuasive. These firm managers knew or should have known that they were risking the solvency and therefore the survival of their firms.

## Conclusions:

- Managers of many large and midsize financial institutions in the United States and Europe amassed enormous concentrations of highly correlated housing risk on their balance sheets. In doing so they turned a building housing crisis into a subsequent crisis of failing financial institutions. Some did this knowingly; others, unknowingly.
- Managers of the largest financial firms further amplified these big bad bets by

holding too little capital and having insufficiently robust access to liquidity. Many placed their firms on a hair trigger by becoming dependent upon short-term financing from commercial paper and repo markets for their day-to-day funding. They placed failed solvency bets that their housing investments were solid, and failed liquidity bets that overnight money would always be there no matter what. In several cases, failed solvency bets triggered liquidity crises, causing some of the largest financial firms to fail or nearly fail.

### *"Investment banks caused the crisis"*

A persistent debate among members of the Commission was the relative importance of a firm's legal form and regulatory regime in the failures of large financial institutions. For example, Commissioners agreed that investment bank holding companies were too lightly (barely) regulated by the SEC leading up to the crisis and that the Consolidated Supervised Entities program of voluntary regulation of these firms failed. As a result, no regulator could force these firms to strengthen their capital or liquidity buffers. There was agreement among Commissioners that this was a contributing factor to the failure of these firms. The Commission split, however, on whether the *relatively* weaker regulation of investment banks was an essential cause of the crisis.

Institutional structure and differential regulation of various types of financial institutions were less important in causing the crisis than common factors that spanned different firm structures and regulatory regimes. Investment banks failed in the United States, and so did many commercial banks, large and small, despite a stronger regulatory and supervisory regime. Wachovia, for example, was a large insured depository institution supervised by the Fed, OCC, and FDIC. Yet it experienced a liquidity run that led to its near failure and prompted the first-ever invocation of the FDIC's systemic risk exception. Insurance companies failed as well, notably AIG and the monoline bond insurers.

Banks with different structures and operating in vastly differing regulatory regimes failed or had to be rescued in the United Kingdom, Germany, Iceland, Belgium, the Netherlands, France, Spain, Switzerland, Ireland, and Denmark. Some of these nations had far stricter regulatory and supervisory regimes than the United States. The bad loans in the United Kingdom, Ireland, and Spain were financed by federally-regulated lenders–not by "shadow banks."

Rather than attributing the crisis principally to differences in the stringency of regulation of these large financial institutions, it makes more sense to look for common factors:

- Different types of financial firms in the United States and Europe made highly concentrated, highly correlated bets on housing.
- Managers of different types of financial firms in the United States and Europe poorly managed their solvency and liquidity risk.

## TWO TYPES OF SYSTEMIC FAILURE

Government policymakers were afraid of large firms' sudden and disorderly failure and chose to intervene as a result. At times, intervention itself contributed to fear and uncertainty about the stability of the financial system. These interventions responded to two types of systemic failure.

### Systemic failure type one: contagion

We begin by defining **contagion** and **too big to fail**.

If financial firm X is a large counterparty to other firms, X's sudden and disorderly bankruptcy might weaken the finances of those other firms and cause them to fail. We call this the risk of **contagion**, when, because of a direct financial link between firms, the failure of one causes the failure of another. Financial firm X is **too big to fail** if policymakers fear contagion so much that they are unwilling to allow it to go bankrupt in a sudden and disorderly fashion. Policymakers make this judgment in large part based on how much counterparty risk other firms have to the failing firm, along with a judgment about the likelihood and possible damage of contagion.

Policymakers may also act if they worry about the effects of a failed firm on a particular financial market in which that firm is a large participant.

The determination of too big to fail rests in the minds of the policymakers who must decide whether to "bail out" a failing firm. They may be more likely to act if they are uncertain about the size of counterparty credit risk or about the health of an important financial market, or if broader market or economic conditions make them more risk averse.

This logic can explain the actions of policymakers[8] in several cases in 2008:

- In March, the Fed facilitated JPMorgan's purchase of Bear Stearns by providing a bridge loan and loss protection on a pool of Bear's assets. While policymakers were concerned about the failure of Bear Stearns itself and its direct effects on other firms, their decision to act was heightened by their uncertainty about potential broader market instability and the potential impact of Bear Stearns' sudden failure on the tri-party repo market.

- In September, the Federal Housing Finance Agency (FHFA) put Fannie Mae and Freddie Mac into conservatorship. Policymakers in effect promised that "the line would be drawn between debt and equity," such that equity holders were wiped out but GSE debt would be worth 100 cents on the dollar. They made this decision because banking regulators (and others) treated Fannie and Freddie debt as equivalent to Treasuries. A bank cannot hold all of its assets in debt issued by General Electric or AT&T, but can hold it all in Fannie or Freddie debt. The same is true for many other investors in the United States and around the world–they assumed that GSE debt was perfectly safe and so they weighted it too heavily in their portfolios. Policymakers were convinced that

this counterparty risk faced by many financial institutions meant that any write-down of GSE debt would trigger a chain of failures throughout the financial system. In addition, GSE debt was used as collateral in short-term lending markets, and by extension, their failure would have led to a sudden massive contraction of credit beyond what did occur. Finally, mortgage markets depended so heavily on the GSEs for securitization that policymakers concluded that their sudden failure would effectively halt the creation of new mortgages. All three reasons led policymakers to conclude that Fannie Mae and Freddie Mac were too big to fail.

- In September, the Federal Reserve, with support from Treasury, "bailed out" AIG, preventing it from sudden disorderly failure. They took this action because AIG was a huge seller of credit default swaps to a number of large financial firms, and they were concerned that an AIG default would trigger mandatory write-downs on those firms' balance sheets, forcing counterparties to scramble to replace hedges in a distressed market and potentially triggering a cascade of failures. AIG also had important lines of business in insuring consumer and business activities that would have been threatened by a failure of AIG's financial products division and potentially led to severe shocks to business and consumer confidence. The decision to aid AIG was also influenced by the extremely stressed market conditions resulting from other institutional failures in prior days and weeks.
- In November, the Federal Reserve, FDIC, and Treasury provided assistance to Citigroup. Regulators feared that the failure of Citigroup, one of the nation's largest banks, would both undermine confidence the financial system gained after TARP and potentially lead to the failures of Citi's major counterparties.

## Conclusion:

The risk of contagion was an essential cause of the crisis. In some cases the financial system was vulnerable because policymakers were afraid of a large firm's sudden and disorderly failure triggering balance-sheet losses in its counterparties. These institutions were too big and interconnected to other firms, through counterparty credit risk, for policymakers to be willing to allow them to fail suddenly.

## Systemic failure type two: a common shock

If contagion is like the flu, then a common shock is like food poisoning. A common factor affects a number of firms in the same way, and they all get sick at the same time. In a common shock, the failure of one firm may inform us about the breadth or depth of the problem, but the failure of one firm does not cause the failure of another.

The common factor in this case was concentrated losses on housing-related assets in large and midsize financial firms in the United States and some in Europe.

These losses wiped out capital throughout the financial sector. Policymakers were not just dealing with a single insolvent firm that might transmit its failure to others. They were dealing with a scenario in which many large, midsize, and small financial institutions took large losses at roughly the same time.

## Conclusion:

Some financial institutions failed because of a common shock: they made similar failed bets on housing. Unconnected financial firms were failing for the same reason and at roughly the same time because they had the same problem of large housing losses. This common shock meant the problem was broader than a single failed bank–key large financial institutions were undercapitalized because of this common shock.

We examine two frequently debated topics about the events of September 2008.

## "The government should not have bailed out _____"

Some argue that no firm is too big to fail, and that policymakers erred when they "bailed out" Bear Stearns, Fannie and Freddie, AIG, and later Citigroup. In our view, this misses the basic arithmetic of policymaking. Policymakers were presented, for example, with the news that "AIG is about to fail" and counseled that its sudden and disorderly failure *might* trigger a chain reaction. Given the preceding failures of Fannie Mae and Freddie Mac, the Merrill Lynch merger, Lehman's bankruptcy, and the Reserve Primary Fund breaking the buck, market confidence was on a knife's edge. A chain reaction could cause a run on the global financial system. They feared not just a run on a bank, but a generalized panic that might crash the entire system–that is, the risk of an event comparable to the Great Depression.

For a policymaker, the calculus is simple: if you bail out AIG and you're wrong, you will have wasted taxpayer money and provoked public outrage. If you don't bail out AIG and you're wrong, the global financial system collapses. It should be easy to see why policymakers favored action–there was a chance of being wrong either way, and the costs of being wrong without action were far greater than the costs of being wrong with action.

## "Bernanke, Geithner, and Paulson should not have chosen to let Lehman fail"

This is probably the most frequently discussed element of the financial crisis. To make this case one must argue:

- Bernanke, Geithner, and Paulson had a legal and viable option available to them other than Lehman filing bankruptcy.
- They knew they had this option, considered it, and rejected it.

- They were wrong to do so.
- They had a reason for choosing to allow Lehman to fail.

We have yet to find someone who can make a plausible case on all four counts. We think that these three policymakers would have saved Lehman if they thought they had a legal and viable option to do so. In hindsight, we also think they were right at the time–they did not have a legal and viable option to save Lehman.

Many prominent public officials and market observers have accused these three of making a mistake. These critics usually argue that these three *should have* saved Lehman. When asked what else they could have done, the critic's usual response is, "I don't know, but surely they could have done *something*. They chose not to and caused the crisis."

Those who want to label Lehman's failure a policy mistake are obliged to suggest an alternate course of action.

The Fed's assistance for Bear Stearns, and FDIC and Treasury's assistance for Wachovia, followed a pattern. In each case, the failing firm or the government found a buyer, and the government subsidized the purchase. In the case of Bear Stearns, the government subsidized the purchase, and in the case of Wachovia, the government made clear that assistance would be available if it were needed. The specific mechanics of the subsidy differed between the two cases, but in each bailout the key condition was the presence of a willing buyer.

Lehman had no willing buyer. Bank of America bought Merrill Lynch instead, and no other American financial institution was willing or able to step up. For months, government officials had tried and failed to facilitate transactions with possible domestic and foreign purchasers. At the end of "Lehman weekend," the most viable candidate was the British bank Barclays. To make the purchase, Barclays needed either a shareholder vote, which would take several weeks to execute, or the permission of their regulator. They could get neither in the time available.

Lehman was therefore facing an imminent liquidity run without a path to success. There was no buyer. There was the possibility that Barclays might be a buyer, some weeks in the future. Bernanke, Geithner, and Paulson were then confronted with the question of whether to provide an effectively uncapped loan to Lehman to supplant its disappearing liquidity while Lehman searched for a buyer.

This loan would have to come from the Fed, since before the enactment of the TARP legislation, Treasury had no authority to provide such financing. The law limits the Fed in these cases. The Fed can only provide *secured* loans. They were able to make this work for Bear Stearns and AIG because there were sufficient unencumbered assets to serve as collateral. Fed officials argue that Lehman had insufficient unpledged assets to secure the loan it would have needed to survive. Former Lehman executives and Fed critics argue otherwise, even though private market participants were unwilling to provide credit.

Was there another option? The Fed leaders would have had to direct the staff to re-evaluate in a more optimistic way the analysis of Lehman's balance sheet to justify a secured loan. They then would have had to decide to provide liquidity support to

Lehman for an indefinite time period while Lehman searched for a buyer. That asset revaluation would later have come under intense legal scrutiny, especially given the likely large and potentially uncapped cost to the taxpayer. In the meantime, other creditors to Lehman could have cashed out at 100 cents on the dollar, leaving taxpayers holding the bag for losses.

Fed Chairman Bernanke, his general counsel Scott Alvarez, and New York Fed general counsel Thomas C. Baxter Jr. all argued in sworn testimony that this option would not have been legal. Bernanke suggested that it also would have been unwise because, in effect, the Fed would have been providing an open-ended commitment to allow Lehman to shop for a buyer. Bernanke testified that such a loan would merely waste taxpayer money for an outcome that was quite unlikely to change.

Based on their actions to deal with other failing financial institutions in 2008, we think these policymakers would have taken any available option they thought was legal and viable. This was an active team that was in all cases erring on the side of intervention to reduce the risk of catastrophic outcomes. Fed Chairman Bernanke said that he "was very, very confident that Lehman's demise was going to be a catastrophe."[9] We find it implausible to conclude that they would have broken pattern on this one case at such an obviously risky moment if they had thought they had another option.

Some find it inconceivable that policymakers could be confronted with a situation in which there was no legal and viable course of action to avoid financial catastrophe. In this case, that is what happened.

## THE SHOCK AND THE PANIC

Conventional wisdom is that the failure of Lehman Brothers triggered the financial panic. This is because Lehman's failure was unexpected and because the debate about whether government officials could have saved Lehman is so intense.

The focus on Lehman's failure is too narrow. The events of September 2008 were a chain of one firm failure after another:

- Sunday, September 7, FHFA put Fannie Mae and Freddie Mac into conservatorship.
- This was followed by "Lehman weekend at the New York Fed," which was in fact broader than just Lehman. At the end of that weekend, Bank of America had agreed to buy Merrill Lynch, Lehman was filing for bankruptcy, and AIG was on the verge of failure.
- Monday, September 15, Lehman filed for Chapter 11 bankruptcy protection.
- Tuesday, September 16, the Reserve Primary Fund, a money market mutual fund, "broke the buck" after facing an investor run. Its net asset value declined below $1, meaning that an investment in the fund had actually lost money. This is a critical psychological threshold for a money market fund. On the same day, the Fed approved an $85 billion emergency loan to AIG to prevent it from sudden failure.

- Thursday, September 18, the Bush Administration, supported by Fed Chairman Bernanke, proposed to Congressional leaders that they appropriate funds for a new Troubled Asset Relief Program (TARP) to recapitalize banks.
- Friday, September 19, the $700 billion TARP was publically announced.
- Sunday, September 21, the Fed agreed to accept Goldman Sachs and Morgan Stanley as bank holding companies, putting them under the Fed's regulatory purview. After this, there were no large standalone investment banks remaining in the United States.
- Thursday, September 25, the FDIC was appointed receiver of Washington Mutual and later sold it to JPMorgan.
- Monday, September 29, the TARP bill failed to pass the House of Representatives, and the FDIC agreed to provide assistance to facilitate a sale of Wachovia to Citigroup.
- Wednesday, October 1, the Senate passed a revised TARP bill. Two days later, the House passed it, and the President signed it into law. Wells Fargo, rather than Citigroup, bought Wachovia.
- As the month progressed, interbank lending rates soared, indicating the heightened fear and threatening a complete freeze of lending.

The financial panic was triggered and then amplified by the close succession of these events, and not just by Lehman's failure. Lehman was the most unexpected bad news in that succession, but it's a mistake to attribute the panic entirely to Lehman's failure. There was growing realization by investors that mortgage losses were concentrated in the financial system, but nobody knew precisely where they lay.

## Conclusion:

In quick succession in September 2008, the failure, near-failure, or restructuring of ten firms triggered a global financial panic. Confidence and trust in the financial system began to evaporate as the health of almost every large and midsize financial institution in the United States and Europe was questioned.

We briefly discuss two of these failures.

## The Reserve Primary Fund

The role of the Reserve Primary Fund's failure in triggering the panic is underappreciated. This money market mutual fund faced escalating redemption requests and had to take losses from its holdings of Lehman debt. On Tuesday, September 16, it broke the buck in a disorganized manner. Investors who withdrew early recouped 100 cents on the dollar, with the remaining investors bearing the losses. This spread fear among investors that other similarly situated funds might follow. By the middle of the following week, prime money market mutual fund investors had withdrawn $349 billion.

When the SEC was unable to reassure market participants that the problem was isolated, money market mutual fund managers, in anticipation of future runs, refused to

renew the commercial paper they were funding and began to convert their holdings to Treasuries and cash. Corporations that had relied on commercial paper markets for short-term financing suddenly had to draw down their backstop lines of credit. No one had expected these corporate lines of credit to be triggered simultaneously, and this "involuntary lending" meant that banks would have to pull back on other activities.

## The role of Fannie Mae and Freddie Mac in causing the crisis

The government-sponsored enterprises Fannie Mae and Freddie Mac were elements of the crisis in several ways:

- They were part of the securitization process that lowered mortgage credit quality standards.
- As large financial institutions whose failures risked contagion, they were massive and multidimensional cases of the too big to fail problem. Policymakers were unwilling to let them fail because:
  - Financial institutions around the world bore significant counterparty risk to them through holdings of GSE debt;
  - Certain funding markets depended on the value of their debt; and
  - Ongoing mortgage market operation depended on their continued existence.
- They were by far the most expensive institutional failures to the taxpayer and are an ongoing cost.

There is vigorous debate about how big a role these two firms played in securitization relative to "private label" securitizers. There is also vigorous debate about why these two firms got involved in this problem. We think both questions are less important than the multiple points of contact Fannie Mae and Freddie Mac had with the financial system.

These two firms were guarantors and securitizers, financial institutions holding enormous portfolios of housing-related assets, and the issuers of debt that was treated like government debt by the financial system. Fannie Mae and Freddie Mac did not by themselves cause the crisis, but they contributed significantly in a number of ways.

## THE SYSTEM FREEZING

Following the shock and panic, financial intermediation operated with escalating frictions. Some funding markets collapsed entirely. Others experienced a rapid blowout in spreads following the shock and stabilized slowly as the panic subsided and the government stepped in to backstop markets and firms. We highlight three funding markets here:

- **Interbank lending.** Lending dynamics changed quickly in the federal funds market where banks loan excess reserves to one another overnight. Even large

banks were unable to get overnight loans, compounding an increasingly restricted ability to raise short-term funds elsewhere.

- **Repo.** By September 2008, repo rates increased substantially, and haircuts ballooned. Nontraditional mortgages were no longer acceptable collateral.
- **Commercial paper.** The failure of Lehman and the Reserve Primary Fund breaking the buck sparked a run on prime money market mutual funds. Money market mutual funds withdrew from investing in the commercial paper market, leading to a rapid increase in funding costs for financial and nonfinancial firms that relied on commercial paper.

The inability to find funding, financial firm deleveraging, and macroeconomic weakness translated into tighter credit for consumers and businesses. Securitization markets for other kinds of debt collapsed rapidly in 2008 and still have not recovered fully, cutting off a substantial source of financing for credit cards, car loans, student loans, and small business loans.

Decreased credit availability, the collapse of the housing bubble, and additional wealth losses from a declining stock market led to a sharp contraction in consumption and output and an increase in unemployment.

Real GDP contracted at an annual rate of 4.0 percent in the third quarter of 2008, 6.8 percent in the fourth quarter, and 4.9 percent in the first quarter of 2009. The economic contraction in the fourth quarter of 2008 was the worst in nearly three decades. Firms and households that had not previously been directly affected by the financial crisis suddenly pulled back–businesses stopped hiring and halted new investments, while families put spending plans on hold. After the panic began, the rate at which the economy shed jobs jumped, going from an average of 185,000 jobs lost per month in the first three quarters of 2008, to an average of over 700,000 jobs lost per month in the fourth quarter of 2008 and the first quarter of 2009. The economy continued to lose jobs through most of 2009, with the unemployment rate peaking at 10.1 percent in October 2009 and remaining above 9.5 percent for the rest of 2009 and the first eleven months of 2010.

While the shock and panic therefore appear to have ended in early 2009, the harm to the real economy continues through today. Firms and families are still deleveraging and are uncertain about both future economic growth and the direction of future policy. The final tragedy of the financial and economic crisis is that the needed recovery is slow and looks to be so for a while longer.

## NOTES

1. A vote of the Commission on December 6, 2010, limited dissenters to nine pages each in the approximately 550-page commercially published book. No limits apply to the official version submitted to the President and the Congress.

2. Ben S. Bernanke, "Monetary Policy and the Housing Bubble," Speech at the Annual Meeting of the American Economic Association, Atlanta, Georgia, January 3, 2010 (www.federalreserve.gov/newsevents/speech/bernanke20100103a.htm).

3. Ibid.

4. "Risky borrowers" does not mean poor. While many risky borrowers were low-income, a borrower with unproven income applying for a no-documentation mortgage for a vacation home was also risky.

5. Bernanke, "Monetary Policy and the Housing Bubble."

6. The Commission vigorously debated the relative importance and the motivations of the different types of securitizers in lowering credit quality. We think that both types of securitizers were in part responsible and that these debates are less important than the existence of lower standards and how this problem fits into the broader context.

7. While bad information created by credit rating agencies was an essential cause of the crisis, it is less clear why they did this. Important hypotheses include: (1) bad analytic models that failed to account for correlated housing price declines across wide geographies, (2) an industry model that encouraged the rating agencies to skew their ratings upward to generate business, and (3) a lack of market competition due to their government-induced oligopoly.

8. In most cases during the crisis, the three key policymakers were Treasury Secretary Henry Paulson, Federal Reserve Chairman Ben Bernanke, and Federal Reserve Bank of New York President Timothy Geithner. Other officials were key in particular cases, such as FHFA Director Jim Lockhart's GSE actions and FDIC Chairman Sheila Bair's extension of temporary loan guarantees to bank borrowing in the fall of 2008. During the financial recovery and rebuilding stage that began in early 2009, the three key policymakers were Treasury Secretary Timothy Geithner, Fed Chairman Ben Bernanke, and White House National Economic Council Director Larry Summers.

9. Ben S. Bernanke, testimony before the FCIC, Hearing on Too Big to Fail: Expectations and Impact of Extraordinary Government Intervention and the Role of Systemic Risk in the Financial Crisis, session 1: The Federal Reserve, September 2, transcript, p. 78.

# FINANCIAL CRISIS
# INQUIRY COMMISSION

## DISSENTING STATEMENT

PETER J. WALLISON
ARTHUR F. BURNS
FELLOW IN FINANCIAL POLICY STUDIES
AMERICAN ENTERPRISE INSTITUTE

JANAUARY 2011

Contact: pwallison@aei.org

# INTRODUCTION

## *Why a Dissent?*

The question I have been most frequently asked about the Financial Crisis Inquiry Commission (the "FCIC" or the "Commission") is why Congress bothered to authorize it at all. Without waiting for the Commission's insights into the causes of the financial crisis, Congress passed and the President signed the Dodd-Frank Act (DFA), far reaching and highly consequential regulatory legislation. Congress and the President acted without seeking to understand the true causes of the wrenching events of 2008, perhaps following the precept of the President's chief of staff—"Never let a good crisis go to waste." Although the FCIC's work was not the full investigation to which the American people were entitled, it has served a useful purpose by focusing attention again on the financial crisis and whether—with some distance from it—we can draw a more accurate assessment than the media did with what is often called the "first draft of history."

To avoid the next financial crisis, we must understand what caused the one from which we are now slowly emerging, and take action to avoid the same mistakes in the future. If there is doubt that these lessons are important, consider the ongoing efforts to amend the Community Reinvestment Act of 1977 (CRA). Late in the last session of the 111th Congress, a group of Democratic congressmembers introduced HR 6334. This bill, which was lauded by House Financial Services Committee Chairman Barney Frank as his "top priority" in the lame duck session of that Congress, would have extended the CRA to all "U.S. nonbank financial companies," and thus would apply, to even more of the national economy, the same government social policy mandates responsible for the mortgage meltdown and the financial crisis. Fortunately, the bill was not acted upon. Because of the recent election, it is unlikely that supporters of H.R. 6334 will have the power to adopt similar legislation in the next Congress, but in the future other lawmakers with views similar to Barney Frank's may seek to mandate similar requirements. At that time, the only real bulwark against the government's use of private entities for social policy purposes will be a full understanding of how these policies were connected to the financial crisis of 2008.

Like Congress and the Administration, the Commission's majority erred in assuming that it knew the causes of the financial crisis. Instead of pursuing a thorough study, the Commission's majority used its extensive statutory investigative authority to seek only the facts that supported its initial assumptions—that the crisis was caused by "deregulation" or lax regulation, greed and recklessness on Wall Street, predatory lending in the mortgage market, unregulated derivatives and a financial system addicted to excessive risk-taking. The Commission did not seriously investigate any other cause, and did not effectively connect the factors

443

it investigated to the financial crisis. The majority's report covers in detail many elements of the economy before the financial crisis that the authors did not like, but generally failed to show how practices that had gone on for many years suddenly caused a world-wide financial crisis. In the end, the majority's report turned out to be a just so story *about* the financial crisis, rather than a report on what *caused* the financial crisis.

## What Caused the Financial Crisis?

George Santayana is often quoted for the aphorism that "Those who cannot remember the past are condemned to repeat it." Looking back on the financial crisis, we can see why the study of history is often so contentious and why revisionist histories are so easy to construct. There are always many factors that could have caused an historical event; the difficult task is to discern which, among a welter of possible causes, were the significant ones—the ones without which history would have been different. Using this standard, I believe that the *sine qua non* of the financial crisis was U.S. government housing policy, which led to the creation of 27 million subprime and other risky loans—half of all mortgages in the United States—which were ready to default as soon as the massive 1997-2007 housing bubble began to deflate. If the U.S. government had not chosen this policy path—fostering the growth of a bubble of unprecedented size and an equally unprecedented number of weak and high risk residential mortgages—the great financial crisis of 2008 would never have occurred.

Initiated by Congress in 1992 and pressed by HUD in both the Clinton and George W. Bush Administrations, the U.S. government's housing policy sought to increase home ownership in the United States through an intensive effort to reduce mortgage underwriting standards. In pursuit of this policy, HUD used (i) the affordable housing requirements imposed by Congress in 1992 on the government-sponsored enterprises (GSEs) Fannie Mae and Freddie Mac, (ii) its control over the policies of the Federal Housing Administration (FHA), and (iii) a "Best Practices Initiative" for subprime lenders and mortgage banks, to encourage greater subprime and other high risk lending. HUD's key role in the growth of subprime and other high risk mortgage lending is covered in detail in Part III.

Ultimately, all these entities, as well as insured banks covered by the CRA, were compelled to compete for mortgage borrowers who were at or below the median income in the areas in which they lived. This competition caused underwriting standards to decline, increased the numbers of weak and high risk loans far beyond what the market would produce without government influence, and contributed importantly to the growth of the 1997-2007 housing bubble.

When the bubble began to deflate in mid-2007, the low quality and high risk loans engendered by government policies failed in unprecedented numbers. The effect of these defaults was exacerbated by the fact that few if any investors—including housing market analysts—understood at the time that Fannie Mae and Freddie Mac had been acquiring large numbers of subprime and other high risk loans in order to meet HUD's affordable housing goals.

Alarmed by the unexpected delinquencies and defaults that began to appear in mid-2007, investors fled the multi-trillion dollar market for mortgage-backed

securities (MBS), dropping MBS values—and especially those MBS backed by subprime and other risky loans—to fractions of their former prices. Mark-to-market accounting then required financial institutions to write down the value of their assets—reducing their capital positions and causing great investor and creditor unease. The mechanism by which the defaults and delinquencies on subprime and other high risk mortgages were transmitted to the financial system as a whole is covered in detail in Part II.

In this environment, the government's rescue of Bear Stearns in March of 2008 temporarily calmed investor fears but created a significant moral hazard; investors and other market participants reasonably believed after the rescue of Bear that all large financial institutions would also be rescued if they encountered financial difficulties. However, when Lehman Brothers—an investment bank even larger than Bear—was allowed to fail, market participants were shocked; suddenly, they were forced to consider the financial health of their counterparties, many of which appeared weakened by losses and the capital writedowns required by mark-to-market accounting. This caused a halt to lending and a hoarding of cash—a virtually unprecedented period of market paralysis and panic that we know as the financial crisis of 2008.

## Weren't There Other Causes of the Financial Crisis?

Many other causes of the financial crisis have been cited, including some in the report of the Commission's majority, but for the reasons outlined below none of them alone—or all in combination—provides a plausible explanation of the crisis.

*Low interest rates and a flow of funds from abroad.* Claims that various policies or phenomena—such as low interest rates in the early 2000s or financial flows from abroad—were responsible for the growth of the housing bubble, do not adequately explain either the bubble or the destruction that occurred when the bubble deflated. The U.S. has had housing bubbles in the past—most recently in the late 1970s and late 1980s—but when these bubbles deflated they did not cause a financial crisis. Similarly, other developed countries experienced housing bubbles in the 2000s, some even larger than the U.S. bubble, but when their bubbles deflated the housing losses were small. Only in the U.S. did the deflation of the most recent housing bubble cause a financial meltdown and a serious financial crisis. The reason for this is that only in the U.S. did subprime and other risky loans constitute half of all outstanding mortgages when the bubble deflated. It wasn't the size of the bubble that was the key; it was its content. The 1997-2007 U.S. housing bubble was in a class by itself. Nevertheless, demand by investors for the high yields offered by subprime loans stimulated the growth of a market for securities backed by these loans. This was an important element in the financial crisis, although the number of mortgages in this market was considerably smaller than the number fostered directly by government policy. Without the huge number of defaults that arose out of U.S. housing policy, defaults among the mortgages in the private market would not have caused a financial crisis.

*Deregulation or lax regulation.* Explanations that rely on lack of regulation or deregulation as a cause of the financial crisis are also deficient. First, no significant deregulation of financial institutions occurred in the last 30 years. The repeal of a

portion of the Glass-Steagall Act, frequently cited as an example of deregulation, had no role in the financial crisis.[1] The repeal was accomplished through the Gramm-Leach-Bliley Act of 1999, which allowed banks to affiliate for the first time since the New Deal with firms engaged in underwriting or dealing in securities. There is no evidence, however, that any bank got into trouble because of a securities affiliate. The banks that suffered losses because they held low quality mortgages or MBS were engaged in activities—mortgage lending—always permitted by Glass-Steagall; the investment banks that got into trouble—Bear Stearns, Lehman and Merrill Lynch—were not affiliated with large banks, although they had small bank affiliates that do not appear to have played any role in mortgage lending or securities trading. Moreover, the Federal Deposit Insurance Corporation Improvement Act of 1991 (FDICIA) substantially *increased* the regulation of banks and savings and loan institutions (S&Ls) after the S&L debacle in the late 1980s and early 1990s, and it is noteworthy that FDICIA—the most stringent bank regulation since the adoption of deposit insurance—failed to prevent the financial crisis.

*The shadow banking business.* The large investment banks—Bear, Lehman, Merrill, Goldman Sachs and Morgan Stanley—all encountered difficulty in the financial crisis, and the Commission majority's report lays much of the blame for this at the door of the Securities and Exchange Commission (SEC) for failing adequately to supervise them. It is true that the SEC's supervisory process was weak, but many banks and S&Ls—stringently regulated under FDICIA—also failed. This casts doubt on the claim that if investment banks had been regulated like commercial banks—or had been able to offer insured deposits like commercial banks—they would not have encountered financial difficulties. The reality is that the business model of the investment banks was quite different from banking; it was to finance a short-term trading business with short-term liabilities such as repurchase agreements (often called repos). This made them especially vulnerable in the panic that occurred in 2008, but it is not evidence that the existence of investment banks, or the quality of their regulation, was a *cause* of the financial crisis.

*Failures of risk management.* Claims that there was a general failure of risk management in financial institutions or excessive leverage or risk-taking are part of what might be called a "hindsight narrative." With hindsight, it is easy to condemn managers for failing to see the dangers of the housing bubble or the underpricing of risk that now looks so clear. However, the FCIC interviewed hundreds of financial experts, including senior officials of major banks, bank regulators and investors. It is not clear that any of them—including the redoubtable Warren Buffett—were sufficiently confident about an impending crisis that they put real money behind their judgment. Human beings have a tendency to believe that things will continue to go in the direction they are going, and are good at explaining why this must be so. Blaming the crisis on the failure to foresee it is facile and of little value for policymakers, who cannot legislate prescience. The fact that virtually all participants in the financial system failed to foresee this crisis—as they failed to foresee every other crisis—does not tell us anything about why this crisis occurred or what we should do to prevent the next one.

---

[1] See, e.g., Peter J. Wallison, "Deregulation and the Financial Crisis: Another Urban Myth," *Financial Services Outlook*, American Enterprise Institute, October 2009.

*Securitization and structured products.* Securitization—often pejoratively described as the "originate to distribute process"—has also been blamed for the financial crisis. But securitization is only a means of financing. If securitization was a cause of the financial crisis, so was lending. Are we then to condemn lending? For decades, without serious incident, securitization has been used to finance car loans, credit card loans and jumbo mortgages that were not eligible for acquisition by Fannie Mae and Freddie Mac. The problem was not securitization itself, it was the weak and high risk loans that securitization financed. Under the category of securitization, it is necessary to mention the role of collateralized debt obligations, known as CDOs. These instruments were "toxic assets" because they were ultimately backed by the subprime mortgages that began to default in huge numbers when the bubble deflated, and it was difficult to determine where those losses would ultimately settle. CDOs, accordingly, for all their dramatic content, were just another example of the way in which subprime and other high risk loans were distributed throughout the world's financial system. The question still remains why so many weak loans were created, not why a system that securitized good assets could also securitize bad ones.

*Credit default swaps and other derivatives.* Despite a diligent search, the FCIC never uncovered evidence that unregulated derivatives, and particularly credit default swaps (CDS), was a significant contributor to the financial crisis through "interconnections". The only company known to have failed because of its CDS obligations was AIG, and that firm appears to have been an outlier. Blaming CDS for the financial crisis because one company did not manage its risks properly is like blaming lending generally when a bank fails. Like everything else, derivatives can be misused, but there is no evidence that the "interconnections" among financial institutions alleged to have caused the crisis were significantly enhanced by CDS or derivatives generally. For example, Lehman Brothers was a major player in the derivatives market, but the Commission found no indication that Lehman's failure to meet its CDS and other derivatives obligations caused significant losses to any other firm, including those that had written CDS on Lehman itself.

*Predatory lending.* The Commission's report also blames predatory lending for the large build-up of subprime and other high risk mortgages in the financial system. This might be a plausible explanation if there were evidence that predatory lending was so widespread as to have produced the volume of high risk loans that were actually originated. In predatory lending, unscrupulous lenders take advantage of unwitting borrowers. This undoubtedly occurred, but it also appears that many people who received high risk loans were predatory borrowers, or engaged in mortgage fraud, because they took advantage of low mortgage underwriting standards to benefit from mortgages they knew they could not pay unless rising housing prices enabled them to sell or refinance. The Commission was never able to shed any light on the extent to which predatory lending occurred. Substantial portions of the Commission majority's report describe abusive activities by some lenders and mortgage brokers, but without giving any indication of how many such loans were originated. Further, the majority's report fails to acknowledge that most of the buyers for subprime loans were government agencies or private companies complying with government affordable housing requirements.

## Why Couldn't We Reach Agreement?

After the majority's report is published, many people will lament that it was not possible to achieve a bipartisan agreement on the facts. It may be a surprise that I am asking the same question. If the Commission's investigation had been an objective and thorough investigation, many of the points I raise in this dissent would have been known to the other commissioners before reading this dissent, and perhaps would have been influential with them. Similarly, I might have found facts that changed my own view. But the Commission's investigation was not structured or carried out in a way that could ever have garnered my support or, I believe, the support of the other Republican members.

One glaring example will illustrate the Commission's lack of objectivity. In March 2010, Edward Pinto, a resident fellow at the American Enterprise Institute (AEI) who had served as chief credit officer at Fannie Mae, provided to the Commission staff a 70-page, fully sourced memorandum on the number of subprime and other high risk mortgages in the financial system immediately before the financial crisis. In that memorandum, Pinto recorded that he had found over 25 million such mortgages (his later work showed that there were approximately 27 million).[2] Since there are about 55 million mortgages in the U.S., Pinto's research indicated that, as the financial crisis began, *half* of all U.S. mortgages were of inferior quality and liable to default when housing prices were no longer rising. In August, Pinto supplemented his initial research with a paper documenting the efforts of the Department of Housing and Urban Development (HUD), over two decades and through two administrations, to increase home ownership by reducing mortgage underwriting standards.[3]

This research raised important questions about the role of government housing policy in promoting the high risk mortgages that played such a key role in both the mortgage meltdown and the financial panic that followed. Any objective investigation of the causes of the financial crisis would have looked carefully at this research, exposed it to the members of the Commission, taken Pinto's testimony, and tested the accuracy of Pinto's research. But the Commission took none of these steps. Pinto's research was never made available to the other members of the FCIC, or even to the commissioners who were members of the subcommittee charged with considering the role of housing policy in the financial crisis.

Accordingly, the Commission majority's report ignores hypotheses about the causes of the financial crisis that any objective investigation would have considered, while focusing solely on theories that have political currency but far less plausibility. This is not the way a serious and objective inquiry should have been carried out, but that is how the Commission used its resources and its mandate.

There were many other deficiencies. The scope of the Commission's work was determined by a list of public hearings that was handed to us in early December 2009. At that point the Commission members had never discussed the possible causes of the crisis, and we were never told why those particular subjects were important or were chosen as the key issues for a set of hearings that would form the backbone

---

[2] Edward Pinto, "Triggers of the Financial Crisis" (Triggers memo), http://www.aei.org/paper/100174.

[3] Edward Pinto, "Government Housing Policies in the Lead-up to the Financial Crisis: A Forensic Study," http//ww.aei.org/docLib/Government-Housing-Policies-Financial-Crisis-Pinto-102110.pdf.

of all the Commission's work. The Commission members did not get together to discuss or decide on the causes of the financial crisis until July, 2010, well after it was too late to direct the activities of the staff. The Commission interviewed hundreds of witnesses, and the majority's report is full of statements such as "Smith told the FCIC that…." However, unless the meeting was public, the commissioners were not told that an interview would occur, did not know who was being interviewed, were not encouraged to attend, and of course did not have an opportunity to question these sources or understand the contexts in which the quoted statements were made. The Commission majority's report uses these opinions as substitutes for data, which is notably lacking in their report; opinions in general are not worth much, especially in hindsight and when given without opportunity for challenge.

The Commission's authorizing statute required that the Commission report on or before December 15, 2010. The original plan was for us to start seeing drafts of the report in April. We didn't see any drafts until November. We were then given an opportunity to submit comments in writing, but never had an opportunity to go over the wording as a group or to know whether our comments were accepted. We received a complete copy of the majority's report, for the first time, on December 15. It was almost 900 double-spaced pages long. The date for approval of the report was eight days later, on December 23. That is not the way to achieve a bipartisan report, or the full agreement of any group that takes the issues seriously.

This dissenting statement is organized as follows: Part I summarizes the main points of the dissent. Part II describes how the failure of subprime and other high risk mortgages drove the growth of the bubble and weakened financial institutions around the world when these mortgages began to default. Part III outlines in detail the housing policies of the U.S. government that were primarily responsible for the fact that approximately one half of all U.S. mortgages in 2007 were subprime or otherwise of low quality. Part IV is a brief conclusion.

# SUMMARY

Although there were many contributing factors, the housing bubble of 1997-2007 would not have reached its dizzying heights or lasted as long, nor would the financial crisis of 2008 have ensued, but for the role played by the housing policies of the United States government over the course of two administrations. As a result of these policies, by the middle of 2007, there were approximately 27 million subprime and Alt-A mortgages in the U.S. financial system—half of all mortgages outstanding—with an aggregate value of over $4.5 trillion.[4] These were unprecedented numbers, far higher than at any time in the past, and the losses associated with the delinquency and default of these mortgages fully account for the weakness and disruption of the financial system that has become known as the financial crisis.

Most subprime and Alt-A mortgages are high risk loans. A subprime mortgage is a loan to a borrower who has blemished credit, usually signified by a FICO credit score lower than 660.[5] Typically, a subprime borrower has failed in

---

[4] Unless otherwise indicated, all estimates for the number of subprime and Alt-A mortgages outstanding, as well as the use of specific terms such as loan to value ratios and delinquency rates, come from research done by Edward Pinto, a resident fellow at the American Enterprise Institute. Pinto is also a consultant to the housing finance industry and a former chief credit officer of Fannie Mae. Much of this work is posted on both my and Pinto's scholar pages at AEI as follows: http://www.aei.org/docLib/Pinto-Sizing-Total-Exposure.pdf, which accounts for all 27 million high risk loans; http://www.aei.org/docLib/Pinto-Sizing-Total-Federal-Contributions.pdf, which covers the portion of these loans that were held or guaranteed by federal agencies and the four large banks that made these loans under CRA; and http://www.aei.org/docLib/Pinto-High-LTV-Subprime-Alt-A.pdf, which covers the acquisition of these loans by government agencies from the early 1990s. The information in these memoranda is fully cited to original sources. These memoranda were the data exhibits to a Pinto memorandum submitted to the FCIC in January 2010, and revised and updated in March 2010 (collectively, the "Triggers memo").

[5] One of the confusing elements of any study of the mortgage markets is the fact that the key definitions have never been fully agreed upon. For many years, Fannie Mae treated as subprime loans only those that it purchased from subprime originators. *Inside Mortgage Finance*, a common source of data on the mortgage market, treated and recorded as subprime only those loans reported as subprime by the originators or by Fannie and Freddie. Other loans were recorded as prime, even if they had credit scores that would have classified them as subprime. However, a FICO credit score of less than 660 is generally regarded as a subprime loan, no matter how originated. That is the standard, for example, used by the Office of the Comptroller of the Currency. In this statement and in Pinto's work on this issue, loans that are classified as subprime by their originators are called "self-denominated" subprime loans, and loans to borrowers with FICO scores of less than 660 are called subprime by characteristic. Fannie and Freddie reported only a very small percentage of their loans as subprime, so in effect the subprime loans acquired by Fannie and Freddie should be added to the self-denominated subprime loans originated by others in order to derive something closer to the number and principal amount of the subprime loans outstanding in the financial system at any given time. One of the important elements of Edward Pinto's work was to show that Fannie and Freddie, for many years prior to the financial crisis, were buying loans that should have been classified as subprime because of the borrowers' credit scores and not simply because they were originated by subprime lenders. Fannie and Freddie did not do this until after they were taken over by the federal government. This lack of disclosure on the part of the GSEs appears to have been a factor in the failure of many market observers to foresee the potential severity of the mortgage defaults when the housing bubble deflated in 2007.

451

the past to meet other financial obligations. Before changes in government policy in the early 1990s, most borrowers with FICO scores below 660 did not qualify as prime borrowers and had difficulty obtaining mortgage credit other than through the Federal Housing Administration (FHA), the government's original subprime lender, or through a relatively small number of specialized subprime lenders.

An Alt-A mortgage is one that is deficient by its terms. It may have an adjustable rate, lack documentation about the borrower, require payment of interest only, or be made to an investor in rental housing, not a prospective homeowner. Another key deficiency in many Alt-A mortgages is a high loan-to-value ratio—that is, a low downpayment. A low downpayment for a home may signify the borrower's lack of financial resources, and this lack of "skin in the game" often means a reduced borrower commitment to the home. Until they became subject to HUD's affordable housing requirements, beginning in the early 1990s, Fannie and Freddie seldom acquired loans with these deficiencies.

Given the likelihood that large numbers of subprime and Alt-A mortgages would default once the housing bubble began to deflate in mid- 2007—with devastating effects for the U.S. economy and financial system—the key question for the FCIC was to determine why, beginning in the early 1990s, mortgage underwriting standards began to deteriorate so significantly that it was possible to create 27 million subprime and Alt-A mortgages. The Commission never made a serious study of this question, although understanding why and how this happened must be viewed as one of the central questions of the financial crisis.

From the beginning, the Commission's investigation was limited to validating the standard narrative about the financial crisis—that it was caused by deregulation or lack of regulation, weak risk management, predatory lending, unregulated derivatives and greed on Wall Street. Other hypotheses were either never considered or were treated only superficially. In criticizing the Commission, this statement is not intended to criticize the staff, which worked diligently and effectively under difficult circumstances, and did extraordinarily fine work in the limited areas they were directed to cover. The Commission's failures were failures of management.

## 1. GOVERNMENT POLICIES RESULTED IN AN UNPRECEDENTED NUMBER OF RISKY MORTGAGES

Three specific government programs were primarily responsible for the growth of subprime and Alt-A mortgages in the U.S. economy between 1992 and 2008, and for the decline in mortgage underwriting standards that ensued.

*The GSEs' Affordable Housing Mission.* The fact that high risk mortgages formed almost half of all U.S. mortgages by the middle of 2007 was not a chance event, nor did it just happen that banks and other mortgage originators decided on their own to offer easy credit terms to potential homebuyers beginning in the 1990s.

In 1992, Congress enacted Title XIII of the Housing and Community Development Act of 1992[6] ( the GSE Act), legislation intended to give low and

---

[6] Public Law 102-550, 106 Stat. 3672, H.R. 5334, enacted October 28, 1992.

moderate income[7] borrowers better access to mortgage credit through Fannie Mae and Freddie Mac. This effort, probably stimulated by a desire to increase home ownership, ultimately became a set of regulations that required Fannie and Freddie to reduce the mortgage underwriting standards they used when acquiring loans from originators. As the Senate Committee report said at the time, "The purpose of [the affordable housing] goals is to facilitate the development in both Fannie Mae and Freddie Mac of an ongoing business effort that will be fully integrated in their products, cultures and day-to-day operations to service the mortgage finance needs of low-and-moderate-income persons, racial minorities and inner-city residents."[8] The GSE Act, and its subsequent enforcement by HUD, set in motion a series of changes in the structure of the mortgage market in the U.S. and more particularly the gradual degrading of traditional mortgage underwriting standards. Accordingly, in this dissenting statement, I will refer to the subprime and Alt-A mortgages that were acquired because of the affordable housing AH goals, as well as other subprime and Alt-A mortgages, as non-traditional mortgages, or NTMs

The GSE Act was a radical departure from the original conception of the GSEs as managers of a secondary market in prime mortgages. Fannie Mae was established as a government agency in the New Deal era to buy mortgages from banks and other loan originators, providing them with new funds with which to make additional mortgages. In 1968, it was authorized to sell shares to the public and became a government-sponsored enterprise (GSE)[9]—a shareholder-owned company with a government mission to maintain a liquid secondary market in mortgages. Freddie Mac was chartered by Congress as another GSE in 1970. Fannie and Freddie carried out this mission effectively until the early 1990s, and in the process established conservative lending standards for the mortgages they were willing to purchase, including such elements as downpayments of 10 to 20 percent, and minimum credit standards for borrowers.

The GSE Act, however, created a new "mission" for Fannie Mae and Freddie Mac—a responsibility to support affordable housing—and authorized HUD to establish and administer what was in effect a mortgage quota system in which a certain percentage of all Fannie and Freddie mortgage purchases had to be loans to low-and- moderate income (LMI) borrowers—defined as persons with income at or below the median income in a particular area or to borrowers living in certain low income communities. The AH goals put Fannie and Freddie into direct competition with the FHA, which was then and is today an agency within HUD that functions as the federal government's principal subprime lender.

---

[7] Low income is usually defined as 80 percent of area median income (AMI) and moderate income as 100 percent of AMI.

[8] Report of the Committee on Banking Housing and Urban Affairs, United States Senate to accompany S. 2733. Report 102-282, May 15, 1992, pp. 34-5.

[9] Fannie and Freddie were considered to be government sponsored enterprises because they had been chartered by Congress and were given various privileges (such as exemption from the Securities Act of 1933 and the Securities Exchange Act of 1934) and a line of credit at the Treasury that signaled a special degree of government support. As a result, the capital markets (which continued to call them "Agencies") assumed that in the event of financial difficulties the government would stand behind them. This implied government backing gave them access to funding that was lower cost than any AAA borrower and often only a few basis points over the applicable Treasury rate.

Over the next 15 years, HUD consistently enhanced and enlarged the AH goals. In the GSE Act, Congress had initially specified that 30 percent of the GSEs' mortgage purchases meet the AH goals. This was increased to 42 percent in 1995, and 50 percent in 2000. By 2008, the main LMI goal was 56 percent, and a special affordable subgoal had been added requiring that 27 percent of the loans acquired by the GSEs be made to borrowers who were at or below 80 percent of area median income (AMI). Table 10, page 510, shows that Fannie and Freddie met the goals in almost every year between 1996 and 2008.

There is very little data available concerning Fannie and Freddie's acquisitions of subprime and Alt-A loans in the early 1990s, so it is difficult to estimate the GSEs' year-by-year acquisitions of these loans immediately after the AH goals went into effect. However, Pinto estimates the total value of these purchases at approximately $4.1 trillion (see Table 7, page 504). As shown in Table 1, page 456, on June 30, 2008, immediately prior to the onset of the financial crisis, the GSEs held or had guaranteed 12 million subprime and Alt-A loans. This was 37 percent of their total mortgage exposure of 32 million loans, which in turn was approximately 58 percent of the 55 million mortgages outstanding in the U.S. on that date. Fannie and Freddie, accordingly, were by far the dominant players in the U.S. mortgage market before the financial crisis and their underwriting standards largely set the standards for the rest of the mortgage financing industry.

*The Community Reinvestment Act.* In 1995, the regulations under the Community Reinvestment Act (CRA)[10] were tightened. As initially adopted in 1977, the CRA and its associated regulations required only that insured banks and S&Ls reach out to low-income borrowers in communities they served. The new regulations, made effective in 1995, for the first time required insured banks and S&Ls to demonstrate that they were actually making loans in low-income communities and to low-income borrowers.[11] A qualifying CRA loan was one made to a borrower at or below 80 percent of the AMI, and thus was similar to the loans that Fannie and Freddie were required to buy under HUD's AH goals.

In 2007, the National Community Reinvestment Coalition (NCRC), an umbrella organization for community activist organizations, reported that between 1997 and 2007 banks that were seeking regulatory approval for mergers committed in agreements with community groups to make over $4.5 trillion in CRA loans.[12] A substantial portion of these commitments appear to have been converted into mortgage loans, and thus would have contributed substantially to the number of subprime and other high risk loans outstanding in 2008. For this reason, they deserved Commission investigation and analysis. Unfortunately, as outlined in Part III, this was not done.

Accordingly, the GSE Act put Fannie and Freddie, FHA, and the banks that were seeking CRA loans into competition for the same mortgages—loans to borrowers at or below the applicable AMI.

*HUD's Best Practices Initiative.* In 1994, HUD added another group to this list when it set up a "Best Practices Initiative," to which 117 members of the Mortgage

---

[10] Pub.L. 95-128, Title VIII of the Housing and Community Development Act of 1977, 91 Stat. 1147, 12 U.S.C. § 2901 *et seq.*

[11] http://www.fdic.gov/regulations/laws/rules/2000-6500.html.

[12] See http://www.community-wealth.org/_pdfs/articles-publications/cdfis/report-silver-brown.pdf.

Bankers Association eventually adhered. As shown later, this program was explicitly intended to encourage a reduction in underwriting standards so as to increase access by low income borrowers to mortgage credit. Countrywide was by far the largest member of this group and by the early 2000s was also competing, along with others, for the same NTMs sought by Fannie and Freddie, FHA, and the banks under the CRA .

With all these entities seeking the same loans, it was not likely that all of them would find enough borrowers who could meet the traditional mortgage lending standards that Fannie and Freddie had established. It also created ideal conditions for a decline in underwriting standards, since every one of these competing entities was seeking NTMs not for purposes of profit but in order to meet an obligation imposed by the government. The obvious way to meet this obligation was simply to reduce the underwriting standards that impeded compliance with the government's requirements.

Indeed, by the early 1990s, traditional underwriting standards had come to be seen as an obstacle to home ownership by LMI families. In a 1991 Senate Banking Committee hearing, Gail Cincotta, a highly respected supporter of low-income lending, observed that "Lenders will respond to the most conservative standards unless [Fannie Mae and Freddie Mac] are aggressive and convincing in their efforts to expand historically narrow underwriting."[13]

In this light, it appears that Congress set out deliberately in the GSE Act not only to change the culture of the GSEs, but also to set up a mechanism that would reduce traditional underwriting standards over time, so that home ownership would be more accessible to LMI borrowers. For example, the legislation directed the GSEs to study "The implications of implementing underwriting standards that—(A) establish a downpayment requirement for mortgagors of 5 percent or less;[14] (B) allow the use of cash on hand as a source of downpayments; and (C) approve borrowers who have a credit history of delinquencies if the borrower can demonstrate a satisfactory credit history for at least the 12-month period ending on the date of the application for the mortgage."[15] None of these elements was part of traditional mortgage underwriting standards as understood at the time.

I have been unable to find any studies by Fannie or Freddie in response to this congressional direction, but HUD treated these cues as a mandate to use the AH goals as a mechanism for eroding the traditional standards. HUD was very explicit about this, as shown in Part II. In the end, the goal was accomplished by gradually expanding the requirements and enlarging the AH goals over succeeding years, so that the only way Fannie and Freddie could meet the AH goals was by purchasing increasing numbers of subprime and Alt-A mortgages, and particularly mortgages with low or no downpayments. Because the GSEs were the dominant players in the mortgage market, their purchases also put competitive pressure on the other entities that were subject to government control—FHA and the banks

---

[13] Allen Fishbein, "Filling the Half-Empty Glass: The Role of Community Advocacy in Redefining the Public Responsibilities of Government-Sponsored Housing Enterprises", Chapter 7 of *Organizing Access to Capital: Advocacy and the Democratization of Financial Institutions*, 2003, Gregory Squires, editor.

[14] At that time the GSEs' minimum downpayment was 5 percent, and was accompanied by conservative underwriting. The congressional request was to break through that limitation.

[15] GSE Act, Section 1354(a).

under CRA—to reach deeper into subprime lending in order to find the mortgages they needed to comply with their own government requirements. This was also true of the mortgage banks—the largest of which was Countrywide—that were bound to promote affordable housing through HUD's Best Practices Initiative.

By 2008, the result of these government programs was an unprecedented number of subprime and other high risk mortgages in the U.S. financial system. Table 1 shows which agencies or firms were holding the credit risk of these mortgages--or had distributed it to investors through mortgage-backed securities (MBS)--immediately before the financial crisis began. As Table 1 makes clear, government agencies, or private institutions acting under government direction, either held or had guaranteed 19.2 million of the NTM loans that were outstanding at this point. By contrast, about 7.8 million NTMs had been distributed to investors through the issuance of private mortgage-backed securities, or PMBS,[16] primarily by private issuers such as Countrywide and other subprime lenders.

The fact that the credit risk of two-thirds of all the NTMs in the financial system was held by the government or by entities acting under government control demonstrates the central role of the government's policies in the development of the 1997-2007 housing bubble, the mortgage meltdown that occurred when the bubble deflated, and the financial crisis and recession that ensued. Similarly, the fact that only 7.8 million NTMs were held by investors and financial institutions in the form of PMBS shows that this group of NTMs were less important as a cause of the financial crisis than the government's role. The Commission majority's report focuses almost entirely on the 7.8 million PMBS, and is thus an example of its determination to ignore the government's role in the financial crisis.

Table 1.[17]

| Entity | No. of Subprime and Alt-A Loans | Unpaid Principal Amount |
|---|---|---|
| Fannie Mae and Freddie Mac | 12 million | $1.8 trillion |
| FHA and other Federal* | 5 million | $0.6 trillion |
| CRA and HUD Programs | 2.2 million | $0.3 trillion |
| **Total Federal Government** | **19.2 million** | **$2.7 trillion** |
| Other (including subprime and Alt-A PMBS issued by Countrywide, Wall Street and others) | 7.8 million | $1.9 trillion |
| **Total** | **27 million** | **$4.6 trillion** |

*Includes Veterans Administration, Federal Home Loan Banks and others.

To be sure, the government's efforts to increase home ownership through the AH goals succeeded. Home ownership rates in the U.S. increased from approximately 64 percent in 1994 (where it had been for 30 years) to over 69 percent in 2004.[18] Almost everyone in and out of government was pleased with this—a long term goal

---

[16] In the process known as securitization, securities backed by a pool of mortgages (mortgage-backed securities, or MBS) and issued by private sector firms were known as private label securities (distinguishing them from securities issued by the GSEs or Ginnie Mae) or private MBS (PMBS).

[17] See Edward Pinto's analysis in Exhibit 2 to the Triggers Memo, April 21, 2010, p.4. http://www.aei.org/docLib/Pinto-Sizing-Total-Federal-Contributions.pdf.

[18] Census Bureau data.

of U.S. housing policy—until the true costs became clear with the collapse of the housing bubble in 2007. Then an elaborate process of shifting the blame began.

## 2. The Great Housing Bubble and Its Effects

Figure 1 below, based on the data of Robert J. Shiller, shows the dramatic growth of the 1997-2007 housing bubble in the United States. By mid-2007, home prices in the U.S. had increased substantially for ten years. The growth in real dollar terms had been almost 90 percent, ten times greater than any other housing bubble in modern times. As discussed below, there is good reason to believe that the 1997-2007 bubble grew larger and extended longer in time than previous bubbles because of the government's housing policies, which artificially increased the demand for housing by funneling more money into the housing market than would have been available if traditional lending standards had been maintained and the government had not promoted the growth of subprime lending.

Figure 1. The Bubble According to Shiller

That the 1997-2007 bubble lasted about twice as long as the prior housing bubbles is significant in itself. Mortgage quality declines as a housing bubble grows and originators try to structure mortgages that will allow buyers to meet monthly payments for more expensive homes; the fact that the most recent bubble was so long-lived was an important element in its ultimate destructiveness when it deflated. Why did this bubble last so long? Housing bubbles deflate when delinquencies and defaults begin to appear in unusual numbers. Investors and creditors realize that the risks of a collapse are mounting. One by one, investors cash in and leave. Eventually, the bubble tops out, those who are still in the game run for the doors, and a deflation in prices sets in. Generally, in the past, this process took three or four years. In the case of the most recent bubble, it took ten. The reason for this longevity is that one

major participant in the market was not in it for profit and was not worried about the risks to itself or to those it was controlling. It was the U.S. government, pursuing a social policy—increasing homeownership by making mortgage credit available to low and moderate income borrowers—and requiring the agencies and financial institutions it controlled or could influence through regulation to keep pumping money into housing long after the bubble, left to itself, would have deflated.

Economists have been vigorously debating whether the Fed's monetary policy in the early 2000s caused the bubble by keeping interest rates too low for too long. Naturally enough, Ben Bernanke and Alan Greenspan have argued that the Fed was not at fault. On the other hand, John Taylor, author of the Taylor rule, contends that the Fed's violation of the Taylor rule was the principal cause of the bubble. Raghuram Rajan, a professor at the Chicago Booth School of Business, argues that the Fed's low interest rates caused the bubble, but that the Fed actually followed this policy in order to combat unemployment rather than deflation.[19] Other theories blame huge inflows of funds from emerging markets or from countries that were recycling the dollars they received from trade surpluses with the U.S. These debates, however, may be missing the point. It doesn't matter where the funds that built the bubble actually originated; the important question is why they were transformed into the NTMs that were prone to failure as soon as the great bubble deflated.

Figure 2 illustrates clearly that the 1997-2007 bubble was built on a foundation of 27 million subprime and Alt-A mortgages and shows the relationship between the cumulative growth in the dollar amount of NTMs and the growth of the bubble over time. It includes both GSE and CRA contributions to the number of outstanding NTMs above the normal baseline of 30 percent,[20] and estimated CRA lending under the merger-related commitments of the four large banks—Bank of America, Wells Fargo, Citibank and JPMorgan Chase—that, with their predecessors, made most of the commitments. As noted above, these commitments were made in connection with applications to federal regulators for approvals of mergers or acquisitions. The dollar amounts involved were taken from a 2007 report by the NCRC,[21] and adjusted for announced loans and likely rates of lending. The cumulative estimated CRA

---

[19] See, Bernanke testimony before the FCIC, September 2, 2010, Alan Greenspan, in "The Crisis," Second Draft: March 9, 2010, Taylor, in testimony before the FCIC on October 20, 2009, John B. Taylor, *Getting Off Track*, Hoover Institution Press, 2009; and Raghuram Rajan, *Fault Lines: How Hidden Fractures Still Threaten the World Economy*, Princeton University Press, 2010, pp. 108-110.

[20] It appears that the GSEs' normal intake of mortgages included about 30 percent that were made to borrowers who were at or below the median income in the area in which they lived and were thus eligible for AH credit. It was only when the AH goals rose above this level, beginning in 1995, that government policy required the GSEs to acquire more AH qualifying loans than they would have purchased as a matter of course. In the case of the CRA contributions, the baseline is 1992, and includes the commitments made by the four largest banks and their predecessors listed in the NCRC report, adjusted for the loans actually announced by the banks after that date.

[21] In 2007, the National Community Reinvestment Coalition published a report on principal amount of CRA loans that banks had committed to make in connection with merger applications. The report claimed that these commitments exceeded $4.5 trillion. The original report was removed from the NCRC's website, but can still be found at http://www.community-wealth.org/ pdfs/articles-publications/ cdfis/report-silver-brown.pdf. A portion of these commitments were in fact fulfilled through CRA qualifying loans. A full discussion of these commitments and the number of loans made pursuant to them is contained in Section III.

production line also includes almost $1 trillion in NTM lending by Countrywide
Financial under HUD's Best Practices Initiative.[22]

Figure 2. The Effect of Government Policies on the Growth of the Bubble

It is not true that every bubble--even a large bubble-- has the potential to
cause a financial crisis when it deflates. This is clear in Table 2 below, prepared by
Professor Dwight Jaffee of the Haas Business School at U.C. Berkley. The table shows
that in other developed countries—many of which also had large bubbles during the
1997-2007 period—the losses associated with mortgage delinquencies and defaults
when these bubbles deflated were far lower than the losses suffered in the U.S. when
the 1997-2007 deflated.

---

[22] See note 144.

Table 2.[23] Troubled Mortgages, Western Europe and the United States

|            | ≥ 3 Month Arrears % | Impaired or Doubtful % | Foreclosures | Year |
|------------|---------------------|------------------------|--------------|------|
| Belgium    | 0.46%               |                        |              | 2009 |
| Denmark    | 0.53%               |                        |              | 2009 |
| France     |                     | 0.93%                  |              | 2008 |
| Ireland    | 3.32%               |                        |              | 2009 |
| Italy      |                     | 3.00%                  |              | 2008 |
| Portugal   | 1.17%               |                        |              | 2009 |
| Spain      |                     | 3.04%                  | 0.24%        | 2009 |
| Sweden     |                     | 1.00%                  |              | 2009 |
| UK         | 2.44%               |                        | 0.19%        | 2009 |
|            |                     |                        |              |      |
| U.S. All Loans | 9.47%           |                        | 4.58%        | 2009 |
| U.S. Prime | 6.73%               |                        | 3.31%        | 2009 |
| U.S. Subprime | 25.26%           |                        | 15.58%       | 2009 |

Source: European Mortgage Federation (2010) and Mortgage Bankers Association for U.S. Data.

The underlying reasons for the outcomes in Professor Jaffee's data were provided in testimony before the Senate Banking Committee in September 2010 by Dr. Michael Lea, Director of the Corky McMillin Center for Real Estate at San Diego State University:

> The default and foreclosure experience of the U.S. market has been far worse than in other countries. Serious default rates remain less than 3 percent in all other countries and less than 1 percent in Australia and Canada. Of the countries in this survey only Ireland, Spain and the UK have seen a significant increase in mortgage default during the crisis.

> There are several factors responsible for this result. First sub-prime lending was rare or non-existent outside of the U.S. The only country with a significant subprime share was the UK (a peak of 8 percent of mortgages in 2006). Subprime accounted for 5 percent of mortgages in Canada, less than 2 percent in Australia and negligible proportions elsewhere.

> ...[T]here was far less "risk layering" or offering limited documentation loans to subprime borrowers with little or no downpayment. There was little "no doc" lending...the proportion of loans with little or no downpayment was less than the U.S. and the decline in house prices in most countries was also less...[L]oans in other developed countries are with recourse and lenders routinely go after borrowers for deficiency judgments.[24]

The fact that the destructiveness of the 1997-2007 bubble came from its composition—the number of NTMs it contained—rather than its size is also illustrated by data on foreclosure starts published by the Mortgage Bankers

---

[23] Dwight M. Jaffee, "Reforming the U.S. Mortgage Market Through Private Market Incentives," Paper prepared for presentation at "Past, Present and Future of the Government Sponsored Enterprises," Federal Reserve Bank of St. Louis, Nov 17, 2010, Table 4.

[24] Dr. Michael J. Lea, testimony before the Subcommittee on Security and International Trade and Finance of the Senate Banking Committee, September 29, 2010, p.6.

Association (MBA).[25] This data allows a comparison between the foreclosure starts that have thus far come out of the 1997-2007 bubble and the foreclosure starts in the two most recent housing bubbles (1977-1979 and 1985-1989) shown in Figure 1. After the housing bubble that ended in 1979, when almost all mortgages were prime loans of the traditional type, foreclosure starts in the ensuing downturn reached a high point of only .87 percent in 1983. After the next bubble, which ended in 1989 and in which a high proportion of the loans were the traditional type, foreclosure starts reached a high of 1.32 percent in 1994. However, after the collapse of the 1997-2007 bubble—in which half of all mortgages were NTMs—foreclosure starts reached the unprecedented level (thus far) of 5.3 percent in 2009. And this was true despite numerous government and bank efforts to prevent or delay foreclosures.

All the foregoing data is significant for a proper analysis of the role of government policy and NTMs in the financial crisis. What it suggests is that whatever effect low interest rates or money flows from abroad might have had in creating the great U.S. housing bubble, the deflation of that bubble need not have been destructive. It wasn't just the size of the bubble; it was also the content. The enormous delinquency rates in the U.S. (see Table 3 below) were not replicated elsewhere, primarily because other developed countries did not have the numbers of NTMs that were present in the U.S. financial system when the bubble deflated. As shown in later sections of this dissent, these mortgage defaults were translated into huge housing price declines and from there—through the PMBS they were holding—into actual or apparent financial weakness in the banks and other firms that held these securities.

Accordingly, if the 1997-2007 housing bubble had not been seeded with an unprecedented number of NTMs, it is likely that the financial crisis would never have occurred.

# 3. DELINQUENCY RATES ON NONTRADITIONAL MORTGAGES

NTMs are non-traditional because, for many years before the government adopted affordable housing policies, mortgages of this kind constituted only a small portion of all housing loans in the United States.[26] The traditional residential mortgage—known as a conventional mortgage—generally had a fixed rate, often for 15 or 30 years, a downpayment of 10 to 20 percent, and was made to a borrower who had a job, a steady income and a good credit record. Before the GSE Act, even subprime loans, although made to borrowers with impaired credit, often involved substantial downpayments or existing equity in homes.[27]

Table 3 shows the delinquency rates of the NTMs that were outstanding on June 30, 2008. The grayed area contains virtually all the NTMs. The contrast in quality, based on delinquency rates, between these loans and Fannie and Freddie prime loans in lines 9 and 10 is clear.

---

[25] Mortgage Bankers Association National Delinquency Survey.

[26] See Pinto, "Government Housing Policies in the Lead-Up to the Financial Crisis: A Forensic Study," November 4, 2010, p.58, http://www.aei.org/docLib/Government-Housing-Policies-Financial-Crisis-Pinto-102110.pdf.

[27] Id., p.42.

Table 3.[28] Delinquency rates on nontraditional mortgages

| Loan Type | Estimated # of Loans | Total Delinquency Rate (30+ Days and in Foreclosure) |
|---|---|---|
| 1. High Rate Subprime (including Fannie/Freddie private MBS holdings) | 6.7 million | 45.0% |
| 2. Option Arm | 1.1 million | 30.5% |
| 3. Alt-A (inc. Fannie/Freddie/FHLBs private MBS holdings) | 2.4 million† | 23.0% |
| 4. Fannie Subprime/Atl-A/Nonprime | 6.6 million | 17.3% |
| 5. Freddie Subprime/Alt-A/Nonprime | 4.1 million | 13.8% |
| 6. Government | 4.8 million | 13.5% |
| **Subtotal # of Loans** | **25.7 million** | |
| 7. Non-Agency Jumbo Prime | 9.4 million ‡ | 6.8% |
| 8. Non-Agency Conforming Prime * | | 5.6% |
| 9. Fannie Prime ** | 11.2 million | 2.6% |
| 10. Freddie Prime *** | 8.7 million | 2.0% |
| **Total # of Loans** | **55 million** | |

* Includes an estimated 1 million subprime (FICO<660) that were (i) not high rate and (ii) non-prime CRA and HUD Best Practices Initiative loans. These are included in the "CRA and HUD Programs" line in Table 1.
** Excludes Fannie subprime/Alt-A/nonprime.
*** Excludes Freddie subprime/Alt-A/nonprime.
† Excludes loans owned or securitized by Fannie and Freddie.
‡ Non-agency jumbo prime and conforming prime counted together.
Total delinquency data sources:
1, 2, 3, 6, 7 & 8: Lender Processing Services, LPS Mortgage Monitor, June 2009.
4 & 9: Based on Fannie Mae 2009 2Q Credit Supplement. Converted from a serious delinquency rate (90+ days & in foreclosure) to an estimated Total Delinquency Rate (30+ days and in foreclosure).
5 & 10: Based on Freddie Mac 2009 2Q Financial Results Supplement. Converted from a serious delinquency rate (90+ days & in foreclosure) to an estimated Total Delinquency Rate (30+ days and in foreclosure).

# 4. THE ORIGIN AND GROWTH OF SUBPRIME PMBS

It was only in 2002 that the market for subprime PMBS—that is private mortgage-backed securities backed by subprime loans or other NTMs—reached $100 billion. In that year, the top five issuers were GMAC-RFC ($11.5 billion), Lehman ($10.6 billion), CS First Boston ($10.5 billion), Bank of America ($10.4 billion) and Ameriquest ($9 billion).[29] The issuances of PMBS that year totaled $134 billion, of which $43 billion in PMBS were issued by Wall Street financial institutions. In subsequent years, as the market grew, Wall Street institutions fell behind the major subprime issuers, so that by 2005—the biggest year for subprime PMBS issuance—only Lehman was among the top five issuers and Wall Street issuers as a group were only 27 percent of the $507 billion in total PMBS issuance in that year.[30]

---

[28] Id., Figure 53.

[29] Inside Mortgage Finance, *The 2009 Mortgage Market Statistical Annual—Vol. II*, p143.

[30] Id., p.140.

One of the many myths about the financial crisis is that Wall Street banks led the way into subprime lending and the GSEs followed. The Commission majority's report adopts this idea as a way of explaining why Fannie and Freddie acquired so many NTMs. This notion simply does not align with the facts. Not only were Wall Street institutions small factors in the subprime PMBS market, but well before 2002 Fannie and Freddie were much bigger players than the entire PMBS market in the business of acquiring NTM and other subprime loans. Table 7, page 504, shows that Fannie and Freddie had already acquired at least $701 billion in NTMs by 2001. Obviously, the GSEs did not have to follow anyone into NTM or subprime lending; they were already the dominant players in that market before 2002. Table 7 also shows that in 2002, when the entire PMBS market was $134 billion, Fannie and Freddie acquired $206 billion in whole subprime mortgages and $368 billion in other NTMs, demonstrating again that the GSEs were no strangers to risky lending well before the PMBS market began to develop.

Further evidence about which firms were first into subprime or NTM lending is provided by Fannie's 2002 10-K. This disclosure document reports that 14 percent of Fannie's credit obligations (either in portfolio or guaranteed) had FICO credit scores below 660 as of December 31, 2000, 16 percent at the end of 2001 and 17 percent at the end of 2002.[31] So Fannie and Freddie were active and major buyers of subprime loans in years when the PMBS market had total issuances of only $55 billion (2000) and $94 billion (2001). In other words, it would be more accurate to say that Wall Street followed Fannie and Freddie into subprime lending rather than vice versa. At the same time, the GSEs' purchases of subprime whole loans throughout the 1990s stimulated the growth of the subprime lending industry, which ultimately became the mainstay of the subprime PMBS market in the 2000s.

2005 was the biggest year for PMBS subprime issuances, and Ameriquest ($54 billion) and Countrywide ($38 billion) were the two largest issuers in the top 25. These numbers were still small in relation to what Fannie and Freddie had been buying since data became available in 1997. The total in Table 7 for Fannie and Freddie between 1997 and 2007 is approximately $1.5 trillion for subprime loans and over $4 trillion for all NTMs as a group.

Because subprime PMBS were rich in NTM loans eligible for credit under HUD's AH goals, Fannie and Freddie were also the largest individual purchasers of subprime PMBS from 2002 to 2006, acquiring 33 percent of the total issuances, or $579 billion.[32] In Table 3 above, which organizes mortgages by delinquency rate, these purchases are included in line 1, which had the highest rate of delinquency. These were self-denominated subprime—designated as subprime by the lender when originated—and thus had low FICO scores and usually a higher interest rate than prime loans; many also had low downpayments and were subject to other deficiencies.

Ultimately, HUD's policies were responsible for both the poor quality of the subprime and Alt-A mortgages that backed the PMBS and for the enormous size to which this market grew. This was true not only because Fannie and Freddie

---

[31] 2003 10-K, Table 33, p.84 http://www.sec.gov/Archives/edgar/data/310522/000095013303001151/ w84239e10vk.htm#031.

[32] See Table 3 of "High LTV, Subprime and Alt-A Originations Over the Period 1992-2007 and Fannie, Freddie, FHA and VA's Role" found at http://www.aei.org/docLib/Pinto-High-LTV-Subprime-Alt-A.pdf.

stimulated the growth of that market through their purchases of PMBS, but also because the huge inflow of government or government-directed funds into the housing market turned what would have been a normal housing bubble into a bubble of unprecedented size and duration. This encouraged and enabled unprecedented growth in the PMBS market in two ways.

First, the gradual increase of the AH goals, the competition between the GSEs and the FHA, the effect of HUD's Best Practices Initiative, and bank lending under the CRA, assured a continuing flow of funds into weaker and weaker mortgages. This had the effect of extending the life of the housing bubble as well as increasing its size. The growth of the bubble in turn disguised the weakness of the subprime mortgages it contained; as housing prices rose, subprime borrowers who might otherwise have defaulted were able to refinance their mortgages, using the equity that had developed in their homes solely through rising home prices. Without the continuous infusion of government or government-directed funds, delinquencies and defaults would have begun showing up within a year or two, bringing the subprime PMBS market to a halt. Instead, the bubble lasted ten years, permitting that market to grow until it reached almost $2 trillion.

Second, as housing prices rose in the bubble, it was necessary for borrowers to seek riskier mortgages so they could afford the monthly payments on more expensive homes. This gave rise to new and riskier forms of mortgage debt, such as option ARMs (resulting in negative amortization) and interest-only mortgages. Mortgages of this kind could be suitable for some borrowers, but not for those who were only eligible for subprime loans. Nevertheless, subprime loans were necessary for PMBS, because they generally bore higher interest rates and thus could support the yields that investors were expecting. As subprime loans were originated, Fannie and Freddie were willing consumers of those that might meet the AH goals; moreover, because of their lower cost of funds, they were able to buy the "best of the worst," the highest quality among the NTMs on offer. These factors—the need for higher yielding loans and the ability of Fannie and Freddie to pay up for the loans they wanted—drove private sector issuers further out on the risk curve as they sought to meet the demands of investors who were seeking exposure to subprime PMBS. From the investors' perspective, as long as the bubble kept growing, PMBS were offering the high yields associated with risk but were not showing commensurate numbers of delinquencies and defaults.

## 5. WHAT WAS KNOWN ABOUT NTMS PRIOR TO THE CRISIS?

Virtually everyone who testified before the Commission agreed that the financial crisis was initiated by the mortgage meltdown that began when the housing bubble began to deflate in 2007. None of these witnesses, however, including the academics consulted by the Commission, the representatives of the rating agencies, the officers of financial institutions that were ultimately endangered by the mortgage downdraft, regulators and supervisors of financial institutions and even the renowned investor Warren Buffett,[33] seems to have understood the dimensions

---

[33] See Buffett, testimony before the FCIC, June 2, 2010.

of the NTM problem or recognized its significance before the bubble deflated. The Commission majority's report notes that "there were warning signs." There always are if one searches for them; they are most visible in hindsight, in which the Commission majority, and many of the opinions it cites for this proposition, happily engaged. However, as Michael Lewis's acclaimed book, *The Big Short*, showed so vividly, very few people in the financial world were actually willing to bet money— even at enormously favorable odds—that the bubble would burst with huge losses. Most seem to have assumed that NTMs were present in the financial system, but not in unusually large numbers.

Even today, there are few references in the media to the number of NTMs that had accumulated in the U.S. financial system before the meltdown began. Yet this is by far the most important fact about the financial crisis. None of the other factors offered by the Commission majority to explain the crisis—lack of regulation, poor regulatory and risk management foresight, Wall Street greed and compensation policies, systemic risk caused by credit default swaps, excessive liquidity and easy credit—do so as plausibly as the failure of a large percentage of the 27 million NTMs that existed in the financial system in 2007.

It appears that market participants were unprepared for the destructiveness of this bubble's collapse because of a chronic lack of information about the composition of the mortgage market. In September 2007, for example, after the deflation of the bubble had begun, and various financial firms were beginning to encounter capital and liquidity difficulties, two Lehman Brothers analysts issued a highly detailed report entitled "Who Owns Residential Credit Risk?"[34] In the tables associated with the report, they estimated the total unpaid principal balance of subprime and Alt-A mortgages outstanding at $2.4 trillion, about half the actual number at the time. Based on this assessment, when they applied a stress scenario in which housing prices declined about 30 percent, they still found that "[t]he aggregate losses in the residential mortgage market under the 'stressed' housing conditions could be about $240 billion, which is manageable, assuming it materializes over a five-to six-year horizon." In the end, of course, the losses were much larger, and were recognized under mark-to-market accounting almost immediately, rather than over a five to six year period. But the failure of these two analysts to recognize the sheer size of the subprime and Alt-A market, even as late as 2007, is the important point.

Along with most other observers, the Lehman analysts were not aware of the true composition of the mortgage market in 2007. Under the "stressed" housing conditions they applied, they projected that the GSEs would suffer aggregate losses of $9.5 billion (net of mortgage insurance coverage) and that their guarantee fee income would be more than sufficient to cover these losses. Based on known losses and projections recently made by the Federal Housing Finance Agency (FHFA), the GSEs' credit losses alone could total $350 billion—more than 35 times the Lehman analysts' September 2007 estimate. The analysts could only make such a colossal error if they did not realize that 37 percent—or $1.65 trillion—of the GSEs' credit risk portfolio consisted of subprime and Alt-A loans (see Table 1, *supra*) or that these weak loans would account for about 75% of the GSEs' default losses over 2007-

---

[34] Vikas Shilpiekandula and Olga Gorodetski, "Who Owns Residential Credit Risk?" *Lehman Brothers Fixed Income U.S. Securitized Products Research*, September 7, 2007.

2010.[35] It is also instructive to compare the Lehman analysts' estimate that the 2006 vintage of subprime loans would suffer lifetime losses of 19 percent under "stressed" conditions to other, later, more informed estimates. In early 2010, for example, Moody's made a similar estimate for the 2006 vintage and projected a 38 percent loss rate after the 30 percent decline in housing prices had actually occurred.[36]

The Lehman loss rate projection suggests that the analysts did not have an accurate estimate of the number of NTMs actually outstanding in 2006. Indeed, I have not found any studies in the period before the financial crisis in which anyone— scholar or financial analyst—actually seemed to understand how many NTMs were in the financial system at the time. It was only after the financial crisis, when my AEI colleague, Edward Pinto, began gathering this information from various unrelated and disparate sources that the total number of NTMs in the financial markets became clear. As a result, all loss projections before Pinto's work were bound to be faulty.

Much of the Commission majority's report, which criticizes firms, regulators, corporate executives, risk managers and ratings agency analysts for failure to perceive the losses that lay ahead, is sheer hindsight. It appears that information about the composition of the mortgage market was simply not known when the bubble began to deflate. The Commission never attempted a serious study of what was known about the composition of the mortgage market in 2007, apparently satisfied simply to blame market participants for failing to understand the risks that lay before them, without trying to understand what information was actually available.

The mortgage market is studied constantly by thousands of analysts, academics, regulators, traders and investors. How could all these people have missed something as important as the actual number of NTMs outstanding? Most market participants appear to have assumed in the bubble years that Fannie and Freddie continued to adhere to the same conservative underwriting policies they had previously pursued. Until Fannie and Freddie were required to meet HUD's AH goals, they rarely acquired subprime or other low quality mortgages. Indeed, the very definition of a traditional prime mortgage was a loan that Fannie and Freddie would buy. Lesser loans were rejected, and were ultimately insured by FHA or made by a relatively small group of subprime originators and investors.

Although anyone who followed HUD's AH regulations, and thought through their implications, would have realized that Fannie and Freddie must have been shifting their buying activities to low quality loans, few people had incentives to uncover the new buying pattern. Investors believed that there was no significant risk in MBS backed by Fannie and Freddie, since they were thought (correctly, as it turns out) to be implicitly backed by the federal government. In addition, the GSEs were exempted by law from having to file information with the Securities and Exchange Commission (SEC)--they agreed to file voluntarily in 2002--leaving them free from disclosure obligations and questions from analysts about the quality of their mortgages.

When Fannie voluntarily began filing reports with the SEC in 2003, it disclosed

---

[35] Fannie Mae, 2010 Second Quarter Credit Supplement, http://www.fanniemae.com/ir/pdf/sec/2010/q2credit_summary.pdf.

[36] "Moody's Projects Losses of Almost Half of Original Balance from 2007 Subprime Mortgage Securities," http://seekingalpha.com/article/182556-moodys-projects-losses-of-almost-half-of-original-balance-from-2007-subprime-mortgage-securities.

that 16 percent of its credit obligations on mortgages had FICO scores of less than 660—the common definition of a subprime loan. There are occasionally questions about whether a FICO score of 660 is the appropriate dividing line between prime and subprime loans. The federal bank regulators use 660 as the dividing line,[37] and in the credit supplement it published for the first time with its 2008 10-K, Fannie included loans with FICO scores below 660 to disclose its exposure to loans that were other than prime. As of December 31, 2008, borrowers with a FICO of less than 660 had a serious delinquency rate about four times that for borrowers with a FICO equal to or greater than 660 (6.74% compared to 1.72%).[38] Fannie did not point out in its filing that a FICO score of less than 660 was considered a subprime loan. Although at the end of 2005 Fannie was exposed to $311 billion in subprime loans it reported in its 2005 10-K (not filed with the SEC until May 2, 2007) that: "The percentage of our single-family mortgage credit book of business consisting of subprime mortgage loans or structured Fannie Mae MBS backed by subprime mortgage loans was *not material* as of December 31, 2005."[emphasis supplied][39]

Fannie was able to make this statement because it defined subprime loans as loans it purchased from subprime lenders. Thus, in its 2007 10-K report, Fannie stated: "Subprime mortgage loans are typically originated by lenders specializing in these loans or by subprime divisions of large lenders, using processes unique to subprime loans. In reporting our subprime exposure, *we have classified mortgage loans as subprime if the mortgage loans are originated by one of these specialty lenders or a subprime division of a large lender.*"[40][emphasis supplied] The credit scores on these loans, and the riskiness associated with these credit scores, were not deemed relevant. Accordingly, as late as its 2007 10-K report, Fannie was able to make the following statements, even though it is likely that at that point it held or guaranteed enough subprime loans to drive the company into insolvency if a substantial number of these loans were to default:

> Subprime mortgage loans, whether held in our portfolio or backing Fannie Mae MBS, represented *less than 1%* of our single-family business volume in each of 2007, 2006 and 2005.[41] [emphasis supplied]

> We estimate that subprime mortgage loans held in our portfolio or subprime mortgage loans backing Fannie Mae MBS, excluding re-securitized private label mortgage related securities backed by subprime mortgage loans, represented approximately *0.3% of our single-family mortgage credit book of business* as of December 31, 2007, compared with 0.2% and 0.1% as of December 31, 2006 and 2005, respectively.[42][emphasis supplied]

These statements could have lulled market participants and others—including

---

[37] Office of Comptroller of the Currency, Federal Reserve, Federal Deposit Insurance Corporation, and Office of Thrift Supervision advised in its "Expanded Guidance for Subprime Lending Programs", published in 2001, http://www.federalreserve.gov/Boarddocs/SRletters/2001/sr0104a1.pdf that "the term 'subprime' refers to the credit characteristics of individual borrowers. Subprime borrowers typically have weakened credit histories that include payment delinquencies and possibly more severe problems such as charge-offs, judgments, and bankruptcies." A FICO score of 660 or below was evidence of "relatively high default probability."

[38] Derived from Table 12.

[39] Fannie Mae, 2005 10-K report, filed May 2, 2007.

[40] Fannie Mae, 2007 Form 10K, pp. 129 and 155.

[41] Fannie Mae, 2007 Form 10K, p.129.

[42] Fannie Mae, 2007 Form 10K, p.130.

the Lehman analysts—into believing that Fannie and Freddie did not hold or had not guaranteed substantial numbers of high risk loans, and thus that there were many fewer such loans in the financial system than in fact existed.

Of course, in the early 2000s there was no generally understood definition of the term "subprime," so Fannie and Freddie could define it as they liked, and the assumption that the GSEs only made prime loans continued to be supported by their public disclosures. So when Fannie and Freddie reported their loan acquisitions to various mortgage information aggregators they did not report those mortgages as subprime or Alt-A, and the aggregators continued to follow industry practice by placing virtually all the GSEs' loans in the "prime" category. Without understanding Fannie and Freddie's peculiar and self-serving loan classification methods, the recipients of information about the GSEs' mortgage positions simply seemed to assume that all these mortgages were prime loans, as they had always been in the past, and added them to the number of prime loans outstanding. Accordingly, by 2008 there were approximately 12 million more NTMs in the financial system—and 12 million fewer prime loans—than most market participants realized.

Appendix 1 shows that the levels of delinquency and default would be 86 percent higher than expected if there were 12 million NTMs in the financial system instead of 12 million prime loans. Appendix 2 shows that the levels of delinquency would be 150 percent higher than expected if the feedback effect of mortgage delinquencies—causing lower housing prices, in a downward spiral—were taken into account. These differences in projected losses could have misled the rating agencies into believing that, even if the bubble were to deflate, the losses on mortgage failures would not be so substantial as to have a more than local effect and would not adversely affect the AAA tranches in MBS securitizations.

The Commission never looked into this issue, or attempted to determine what market participants believed to be the number of subprime and other NTMs outstanding in the system immediately before the financial crisis. Whenever possible in the Commission's public hearings, I asked analysts and other market participants how many NTMs they believed were outstanding before the financial crisis occurred. It was clear from the responses that none of the witnesses had ever considered that question, and it appeared that none suspected that the number was large enough to substantially affect losses after the collapse of the bubble.

It was only on November 10, 2008, after Fannie had been taken over by the federal government, that the company admitted in its 10-Q report for the third quarter of 2008 that it had classified as subprime or Alt-A loans only those loans that it purchased from self-denominated subprime or Alt-A originators, and not loans that were subprime or Alt-A because of their risk characteristics. Even then Fannie wasn't fully candid. After describing its classification criteria, Fannie stated, "[H]owever, we have other loans with some features that are similar to Alt-A and subprime loans that we have not classified as Alt-A or subprime because they do not meet our classification criteria."[43] This hardly described the true nature of Fannie's obligations.

On the issue of the number of NTMs outstanding before the crisis the Commission studiously averted its eyes, and the Commission majority's report

---

[43] Fannie Mae, 2008 3rd quarter 10-Q. p.115, http://www.fanniemae.com/ir/pdf/earnings/2008/q32008.pdf.

never addresses the question. HUD's role in pressing for a reduction in mortgage underwriting standards escaped the FCIC's attention entirely, the GSEs' AH goals are mentioned only in passing, CRA is defended, and neither HUD's Best Practices Initiative nor FHA's activities are mentioned at all. No reason is advanced for the accumulation of subprime loans in the bubble other than the idea—implicit in the majority's report—that it was profitable. In sum, the majority's report is Hamlet without the prince of Denmark.

Indeed, the Commission's entire investigation seemed to be directed at minimizing the role of NTMs and the role of government housing policy. In this telling, the NTMs were a "trigger" for the financial crisis, but once the collapse of the bubble had occurred the "weaknesses and vulnerabilities" of the financial system— which had been there all along—caused the crisis. These alleged deficiencies included a lack of adequate regulation of the so-called "shadow banking system" and over-the-counter derivatives, the overly generous compensation arrangements on Wall Street, and securitization (characterized as "the originate to distribute model"). Coincidentally, all these purported weaknesses and vulnerabilities then required more government regulation, although their baleful presence hadn't been noted until the unprecedented number of subprime and Alt-A loans, created largely to comply with government housing policies, defaulted.

# 6. Conclusion

What is surprising about the many views of the causes of the financial crisis that have been published since the Lehman bankruptcy, including the Commission's own inquiry, is the juxtaposition of two facts: (i) a general agreement that the bubble and the mortgage meltdown that followed its deflation were the precipitating causes—sometimes characterized as the "trigger"—of the financial crisis, and (ii) a seemingly studious effort to avoid examining how it came to be that mortgage underwriting standards declined to the point that the bubble contained so many NTMs that were ready to fail as soon as the bubble began to deflate. Instead of thinking through what would almost certainly happen when these assets virtually disappeared from balance sheets, many observers—including the Commission majority in their report—pivoted immediately to blame the "weaknesses and vulnerabilities" of the free market or the financial or regulatory system, without considering whether *any* system could have survived such a blow.

One of the most striking examples of this approach was presented by Larry Summers, the head of the White House economic council and one of the President's key advisers. In a private interview with a few of the members of the Commission (I was not informed of the interview), Summers was asked whether the mortgage meltdown was the cause of the financial crisis. His response was that the financial crisis was like a forest fire and the mortgage meltdown like a "cigarette butt" thrown into a very dry forest. Was the cigarette butt, he asked, the cause of the forest fire, or was it the tinder dry condition of the forest?[44] The Commission majority adopted the idea that it was the tinder-dry forest. Their central argument is that the mortgage meltdown as the bubble deflated triggered the financial crisis because of the "vulnerabilities" inherent in the U.S. financial system at the time—the absence

---

[44] FCIC, Summers interview, p.77.

of regulation, lax regulation, predatory lending, greed on Wall Street and among participants in the securitization system, ineffective risk management, and excessive leverage, among other factors. One of the majority's singular notions is that "30 years of deregulation" had "stripped away key safeguards" against a crisis; this ignores completely that in 1991, in the wake of the S&L crisis, Congress adopted the FDIC Improvement Act, which was by far the toughest bank regulatory law since the advent of deposit insurance and was celebrated at the time of its enactment as finally giving the regulators the power to put an end to bank crises.

The forest metaphor turns out to be an excellent way to communicate the difference between the Commission's report and this dissenting statement. What Summers characterized as a "cigarette butt" was 27 million high risk NTMs with a total value over $4.5 trillion. Let's use a little common sense here: $4.5 trillion in high risk loans was *not* a "cigarette butt;" they were more like an exploding gasoline truck in that forest. The Commission's report blames the conditions in the financial system; I blame 27 million subprime and Alt-A mortgages—half of all mortgages outstanding in the U.S. in 2008—and a number that appears to have been unknown to most if not all market participants at the time. No financial system, in my view, could have survived the failure of large numbers of high risk mortgages once the bubble began to deflate, and no market could have avoided a panic when it became clear that the number of defaults and delinquencies among these mortgages far exceeded anything that even the most sophisticated market participants expected.

This conclusion has significant policy implications. If in fact the financial crisis was caused by government housing policies, then the Dodd-Frank Act was legislative overreach and unnecessary. The appropriate policy choice was to reduce or eliminate the government's involvement in the residential mortgage markets, not to impose significant new regulation on the financial system.

\* \* \* \*

The balance of this statement will outline (i) how the high levels of delinquency and default among the NTMs were transmitted as losses to the financial system, and (ii) how the government policies summarized above caused the accumulation of an unprecedented number of NTMs in the U.S. and around the globe.

# II. HOW 27 MILLION NTMS
# PRECIPITATED A FINANCIAL CRISIS

Although the Commission never defined the financial crisis it was supposed to investigate, it is necessary to do so in order to know where to start and stop. If, for example, the financial crisis is still continuing, then the effect of government policies such as the Troubled Asset Repurchase Program (TARP) should be evaluated.

However, it seems clear that Congress wanted the Commission to concentrate on what caused the unprecedented events that occurred largely in the fall of 2008, and for this purpose Ben Bernanke's definition of the financial crisis seems most appropriate:

> The credit boom began to unravel in early 2007 when problems surfaced with subprime mortgages—mortgages offered to less-creditworthy borrowers—and house prices in parts of the country began to fall. Mortgage delinquencies and defaults rose, and the downturn in house prices intensified, trends that continue today. Investors, stunned by losses on assets they had believed to be safe, began to pull back from a wide range of credit markets, and financial institutions—reeling from severe losses on mortgages and other loans—cut back their lending. The crisis deepened [in September 2008], when the failure or near-failure of several major financial firms caused many financial and credit markets to freeze up."[45]

In other words, the financial crisis was the result of the losses suffered by financial institutions around the world when U.S. mortgages began to fail in large numbers; the crisis became more severe in September 2008, when the failure of several major financial firms—which held or were thought to hold large amounts of mortgage-related assets—caused many financial markets to freeze up. This summary encapsulates a large number of interconnected events, but it makes clear that the underlying cause of the financial crisis was a rapid decline in the value of one specific and widely held asset: U.S. residential mortgages. The next question is how, exactly, these delinquencies and losses caused the financial crisis.

The following discussion will show that it was not all mortgages and mortgage-backed securities that were the source of the crisis, but primarily NTMs— including PMBS backed by NTMs. Traditional mortgages, which were generally prime mortgages, did not suffer substantial losses at the outset of the mortgage meltdown, although as the financial crisis turned into a recession and housing prices continued to fall, losses among prime mortgages began to approach the level of prime mortgage losses that had occurred in past housing crises. However, those levels were far lower than the losses on NTMs, which reached levels of delinquency and default between 15 and 45 percent (depending on the characteristics of the loans in question) because the loans involved were weaker as a class than in any previous housing crisis. The fact that they were also far larger in number than any

---

[45] Speech at Morehouse College, April 14, 2009.

previous bubble was what caused the catastrophic housing price declines that fueled the financial crisis.

# 1. How Failures Among NTMs
# were Transmitted to the Financial System

When the housing bubble began to deflate in mid-2007, delinquency rates among NTMs began to increase substantially. Previously, although these mortgages were weak and high risk, their delinquency rates were relatively low. This was a consequence of the bubble itself, which inflated housing prices so that homes could be sold with no loss in cases where borrowers could not meet their mortgage obligations. Alternatively, rising housing prices—coupled with liberal appraisal rules—created a form of free equity in a home, allowing the home to be refinanced easily, perhaps even at a lower interest rate. However, rising housing prices eventually reached the point where even easy credit terms could no longer keep the good times rolling, and at that point the bubble flattened and weak mortgages became exposed for what they were. As Warren Buffett has said, when the tide goes out, you can see who's swimming naked.

The role of the government's housing policy is crucial at this point. As discussed earlier, if the government had not been directing money into the mortgage markets in order to foster growth in home ownership, NTMs in the bubble would have begun to default relatively soon after they were originated. The continuous inflow of government or government-backed funds, however, kept the bubble growing—not only in size but over time—and this tended to suppress the significant delinquencies and defaults that had brought previous bubbles to an end in only three or four years. That explains why PMBS based on NTMs could become so numerous and so risky without triggering the delinquencies and defaults that caused earlier bubbles to deflate within a shorter period. With losses few and time to continue originations, Countrywide and others were able to securitize subprime PMBS in increasingly large amounts from 2002 ($134 billion) to 2006 ($483 billion) without engendering the substantial increase in delinquencies that would ordinarily have alarmed investors and brought the bubble to a halt.[46]

Indeed, the absence of delinquencies had the opposite effect. As investors around the world saw housing prices rise in the U.S. without any significant losses even among subprime and other high-yielding loans, they were encouraged to buy PMBS that—although rated AAA—still offered attractive yields. In other words, as shown in Figure 2, government housing policies—AH goals imposed on the GSEs, the decline in FHA lending standards, HUD's pressure for reduced underwriting standards among mortgage bankers, and CRA requirements for insured banks—by encouraging the growth of the bubble, increased the worldwide demand for subprime PMBS. Then, in mid-2007, the bubble began to deflate, with catastrophic consequences.

---

[46] Inside Mortgage Finance, *The 2009 Mortgage Market Statistical Annual—Volume II*, MBS database.

## 2. The Defaults Begin

The best summary of how the deflation of the housing bubble led to the financial crisis was contained in the prepared testimony that FDIC chair Sheila Bair delivered to the FCIC in a September 2 hearing:

> Starting in mid 2007, global financial markets began to experience serious *liquidity challenges* related mainly to rising concerns about U.S. mortgage credit quality. As *home prices fell*, recently originated subprime and *non-traditional mortgage loans began to default at record rates*. These developments led to *growing concerns* about the value of financial positions in mortgage-backed securities and related derivative instruments held by major financial institutions in the U.S. and around the world. The *difficulty in determining the value* of mortgage-related assets and, therefore, the *balance-sheet strength* of large banks and non-bank financial institutions ultimately led these institutions to become *wary of lending* to one another, even on a short-term basis.[47] [emphasis supplied]

All the important elements of what happened are in Chairman Bair's succinct statement: (i) in mid 2007, the markets began to experience liquidity challenges because of concerns about the credit quality of NTMs; (ii) housing prices fell; NTMs began to default at record rates; (iii) it was difficult to determine the value of MBS, and thus the financial condition of the institutions that held them; and, (iv) finally, as a consequence of this uncertainty—especially after the failure of Lehman—financial institutions would not lend to one another. That phenomenon *was* the financial crisis. The following discussion will show how each of these steps operated to bring down the financial system.

### Markets Began to Experience Liquidity Challenges

To understand the transmission mechanism, it is necessary to distinguish between PMBS, on the one hand, and the MBS that were distributed by government agencies such as FHA/Ginnie Mae and the GSEs (referred to jointly as "Agencies" in this section). As shown in Table 1, by 2008, the 27 million NTMs in the U.S. financial system were held as (i) whole mortgages, (ii) MBS guaranteed by the GSEs, or insured or held by a government agency or a bank under the CRA, or (iii) as PMBS securitized by private firms such as Countrywide. The 27 million NTMs had an aggregate unpaid principal balance of more than $4.5 trillion, and the portion represented by PMBS consisted of 7.8 million mortgages with an aggregate unpaid principal balance of approximately $1.9 trillion. As mortgage delinquencies and defaults multiplied in the U.S. financial system, the losses were transmitted to financial institutions through their holdings of PMBS. How did this happen, and what role was played by government housing policy?

Both Agency MBS and PMBS pass through to investors the principal and interest received on the mortgages in a pool that backs an issue of securities; the difference between them is the way they protect investors against credit risk—i.e., the possibility of losses in the event that the mortgages in the pool begin to default. The Agencies insure or place a guarantee on all the securities issued by a pool they or some other entity creates. Because of the Agencies' real or perceived government

---

[47] Sheila C. Bair, "Systemically Important Institutions and the Issue of 'Too-Big-to-Fail,'" Testimony to the FCIC, September 2, 2010, p.3.

backing, all these securities are rated or considered to be AAA.

PMBS rely on a classification and subordination system known as "tranching" to provide some investors in the pool with a degree of assurance that they will not suffer losses because of mortgage defaults. In the tranching system, different classes of securities are issued by the pool. The rights of some classes to receive payments of principal and interest from the mortgages in the pool are subordinated to the rights of other classes, so that the superior classes are more likely to receive payment even if there are some defaults among the mortgages in the pool.

Through this mechanism, approximately 90 percent of an issue of PMBS could be rated AAA or AA, even if the underlying mortgages are NTMs that have a higher rate of delinquency than prime loans. In theory, for example, if the historic rates of loss on a pool of NTMs is, say, five percent, then those losses will be absorbed by the ten percent of the securities holders who are in the classes rated lower than AAA or AA. Of course, if the losses are greater than anticipated—exactly what happened as the recent bubble began to deflate—they will reach into the higher classes and substantially reduce their value.[48] It is not clear whether, in 2007 or 2008, mortgage delinquencies and defaults had actually caused cash losses in the AAA tranches of PMBS, but the rate at which delinquencies and defaults among NTMs were occurring throughout the financial system was so high that such losses were a distinct possibility—obviously a matter of great concern to investors.

This means that investors in PMBS and government-backed Agency MBS had different experiences when the bubble began to deflate. Those who invested in Agency MBS did not suffer losses (the U.S. government has thus far protected all investors in Agency MBS), while those who invested in PMBS were exposed to losses if the losses on the underlying mortgages were so great that they threatened to invade the AAA and AA classes. Even if no cash losses had actually been suffered, the holders of PMBS would see a sharp decline in the market value of their holdings as investors—shocked by the large number of defaults on mortgages—fled the asset-backed market. So when we look for the *direct* effect of mortgage failures on the financial condition of various financial institutions in the financial crisis we should look only to the PMBS, not the MBS issued by the Agencies.

In addition, the default and delinquency ratios on the loans underlying the PMBS were higher than similar ratios among the loans held or guaranteed by the Agencies. Many of the loans which backed the PMBS were the self-denominated subprime loans (that is, made by subprime lenders explicitly to subprime borrowers) and were classified in the worst-performing categories in Table 3. In part, the better-performing characteristics of the NTMs held or guaranteed by the Agencies was due to the fact that the Agencies were not buying for economic purposes—to make profits—but only to meet government requirements such as the AH goals. They did not want or need the higher-yielding and thus more risky mortgages that backed the PMBS, because they did not need higher yields in order to sell their MBS. In addition, because of their lower cost funding, the Agencies could pay more for the NTMs they bought and thus could acquire the "best of the worst."

---

[48] A thorough description of the tranching system, and many more details about various methods of protecting senior tranches, is contained in Gary B. Gorton, *Slapped By the Invisible Hand: The Panic of 2007*, Oxford University Press, 2010, pp. 82-113.

## PMBS are Connected to All Other NTMs Through Housing Prices

But this does not mean that only the failure of the PMBS was responsible for the financial crisis. In a sense, all mortgages are linked to one another through housing prices, and housing prices in turn are highly sensitive to delinquencies and defaults on mortgages. This is a characteristic of mortgages that is not present in other securitized assets. If a credit card holder defaults on his obligations it has little effect on other credit card holders, but if a homeowner defaults on a mortgage the resulting foreclosure has an effect on the value of all homes in the vicinity and thus on the quality of all mortgages on those homes.

Accordingly, the PMBS were intimately connected—through housing prices—to the NTMs securitized by the Agencies. Because there were so many more NTMs held or securitized by the Agencies (see Table 1), their unprecedented numbers—even in cases where they had a lower average rate of delinquency and default than the NTMs that backed the PMBS—was the major source of downward pressure on housing prices throughout the United States. Weakening housing prices, in turn, caused more mortgage defaults, among both NTMs in general and the particular NTMs that were the collateral for PMBS. In other words, the NTMs underlying the PMBS were weakened by the delinquencies and defaults among the much larger number of mortgages held or guaranteed as MBS by the Agencies.

In reality, then, the losses on the PMBS were much higher than they would have been if the government's housing policies had not brought into being 19 million other NTMs that were failing in unprecedented numbers. These failures drove down housing prices by 30 percent--an unprecedented decline—which multiplied the losses on the PMBS.

Finally, the funds that the government directed into the housing market in pursuit of its social policies enlarged the housing bubble and extended it in time. The longer housing bubbles grow, the riskier the mortgages they contain; lenders are constantly trying to find ways to keep monthly mortgage payments down while borrowers are buying more expensive houses. While the bubble was growing, the risks that were building within it were obscured. Borrowers who would otherwise have defaulted on their loans, bringing an end to the bubble, were able to use the rising home prices to refinance, sometimes at lower interest rates. With delinquency rates relatively low, investors did not have a reason to exit the mortgage markets, and the continuing flow of funds into mortgages allowed the bubble to extend for an unprecedented 10 years. This in turn enabled the PMBS market to grow to enormous size and thus to have a more calamitous effect when it finally collapsed. If the government policies that provided a continuing source of funding for the bubble had not been pursued, it is doubtful that there would have been a PMBS market remotely as large as the one that developed, or that—when the housing bubble collapsed—the losses to financial institutions would have been as great.

## PMBS, as Securities, are Vulnerable to Investor Sentiment

In addition to their link to the Agencies' NTMs through housing prices, PMBS were particularly vulnerable to changes in investor sentiment about mortgages. The fact that the mortgages underlying the PMBS were held in securitized form was an important element of the crisis. There are many reasons for the popularity

of mortgage securitization. Beginning in 2002, for example, the Basel regulations provided that mortgages held in the form of MBS—presumably because of their superior liquidity compared to whole mortgages—required a bank to hold only 1.6 percent risk-based capital, while whole mortgages required risk-based capital backing of four percent. This made all forms of MBS, including PMBS, much less expensive to hold than whole mortgages. In addition, mortgages in securitized form could be traded more easily, and used more readily as a source of liquidity through repurchase agreements.

However, some of the benefits of securitized mortgages are also detriments when certain mortgage market conditions prevail. If housing values are declining, losses on whole mortgages are recognized only slowly in bank financial statements and will be recognized even more slowly in the larger market. PMBS, however, are far more vulnerable to swings in sentiment than whole mortgages held on bank balance sheets. First, because they are more easily traded, PMBS values can be more quickly and adversely affected by negative information about the underlying mortgages than whole mortgages in the same principal amount. PMBS markets tend to be thin, because PMBS pools differ from one another. If investors believe that mortgages in general are declining in value, or they learn of a substantial and unexpected number of defaults and delinquencies, they may abandon the market for all PMBS, causing the general PMBS price level to fall precipitously.

For example, in his book *Slapped by the Invisible Hand*, Professor Gary Gorton of Yale notes that the ABX index, initially published in late 2006, for the first time gave investors a picture of how others saw the value of a selected group of PMBS pools. The index showed steeply declining values, which caused many investors to withdraw from the market. Gorton observed: "I view the ABX indices as revealing hitherto unknown information, namely, the aggregated view that subprime was worth significantly less...It is not clear whether the housing bubble was burst by the ability to short the subprime housing market or whether house prices were going down and the implications of this were aggregated and revealed by the ABX indices"[49]

Whatever the underlying reason, as shown in Figure 3, this seems to be exactly what happened in the financial crisis. The result was a crash in the MBS market as investors fled what looked like major oncoming losses.

---

[49] Gorton, *Slapped by the Invisible Hand*, note 41, pp.121-123.

Figure 3. The MBS market reacts to the bubble's deflation

**Quarterly Residential ABS, MBS & CDO Volume**

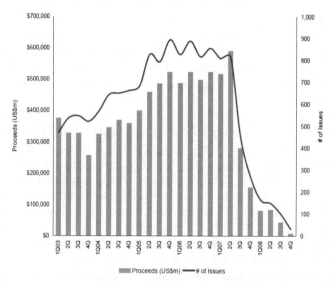

Proceeds (US$m) ——# of Issues

Source: Thompson Reuters Debt Capital Markets Review, Fourth Quarter 2008, available at http://thomsonreuters.com/products_services/financial/league_tables/debt_equity/ (accessed July 30, 2009).

The decline in housing values had a profound adverse effect on the liquidity of all financial institutions that were exposed to PMBS. As noted above, one of the benefits of holding PMBS, especially those with AAA ratings, was that they were readily marketable. As such, they were considered sound and secure investments, carried on balance sheets at par and suitable to serve as collateral for short term financing through repurchase agreements, or "repos." In a repo transaction, a borrower sells a security to a lender with an option to repurchase it at a price that provides the lender with a return appropriate for a secured loan. The lender assumes that if its counterparty defaults the collateral can be sold. Accordingly, if the collateral asset loses its reputation for high quality and liquidity, it loses much of its value for both capital and liquidity purposes, even if the collateral itself has not actually suffered losses. This is what happened to AAA-rated PMBS as housing prices first leveled off and then began to fall in 2007, and as mortgage delinquencies rolled in at rates no one had expected. As discussed more fully below, when AAA-rated PMBS became unmarketable they lost their value for liquidity purposes, making it difficult or impossible for many financial institutions to fund themselves using these assets as collateral for repos. This was the *liquidity challenge* to which Chairman Bair referred in her testimony.

The near-failure of Bear Stearns in March 2008 was an excellent example of how the unexpected collapse of the PMBS market could cause a substantial loss of liquidity by a financial institution, and ultimately its inability to survive the resulting loss in market confidence. The FCIC staff's review of the liquidity problems of Bear Stearns showed that the loss of the PMBS market was the single event that was crippling for Bear, because it eliminated a major portion of the firm's liquidity

pool—AAA-rated PMBS—as a useful source of repo financing. According to the Commission staff's Preliminary Investigative Report on Bear, prepared for hearings on May 5 and 6, 2010, 97.4 percent of Bear's short term funding was secured and only 2.6 percent unsecured. "As of January 11, 2008," the FCIC staff reported, "$45.9 billion of Bear Stearns' repo collateral was composed of agency (Fannie and Freddie) mortgage-related securities, $23.7 billion was in non-agency securitized asset backed securities [i.e., PMBS], and $19 billion was in whole loans."[50] The Agency MBS was unaffected by the collapse of the PMBS market, and could still be used for funding.

Thus, about 27 percent of Bear's readily available sources of funding consisted of PMBS that became unusable for repo financing when the PMBS market disappeared. The loss of this source of liquidity put the firm in serious jeopardy; rumors swept the market about Bear's condition, and clients began withdrawing funds. Bear's officers told the Commission that the firm was profitable in its first 2008 quarter—the quarter in which it failed; ironically they also told the Commission's staff that they had moved Bear's short term funding from commercial paper to MBS because they believed that collateral-backed funding would be more stable. In the week beginning March 10, 2008, according to the FCIC staff report, Bear had over $18 billion in cash reserves, but by March 13 the liquidity pool had fallen to $2 billion.[51] It was clear that Bear—solvent and profitable or not—could not survive a run that was fueled by fear and uncertainty about its liquidity and the possibility of its insolvency.

Parenthetically, it should be noted that the Commission's staff focused on Bear because the Commission's majority apparently believed that the business model of investment banks, which relied on relatively high leverage and repo or other short term financing, was inherently unstable. The need to rescue Bear was thought to be evidence of this fact. Clearly, the five independent investment banks—Bear, Lehman Brothers, Merrill Lynch, Morgan Stanley and Goldman Sachs—were badly damaged in the financial crisis. Only two of them remain independent firms, and those two are now regulated as bank holding companies by the Federal Reserve. Nevertheless, it is not clear that the investment banks fared any worse than the much more heavily regulated commercial banks—or Fannie and Freddie which were also regulated more stringently than the investment banks but not as stringently as banks. The investment banks did not pass the test created by the mortgage meltdown and the subsequent financial crisis, but neither did a large number of insured banks— IndyMac, Washington Mutual (WaMu) and Wachovia, to name the largest—that were much more heavily regulated and, in addition, offered insured deposits and had access to the Fed's discount window if they needed emergency funds to deal with runs. The view of the Commission majority, that investment banks—as part of the so-called "shadow banking system"—were special contributors to the financial crisis, seems misplaced for this reason. They are better classified not as contributors to the financial crisis but as victims of the panic that ensued after the housing bubble and the PMBS market collapsed.

Bear went down because the delinquencies and failures of an unprecedentedly large number of NTMs caused the collapse of the PMBS market; this destroyed the

---

[50]  FCIC, "Investigative Findings on Bear Stearns (Preliminary Draft)," April 29, 2010, p.16.

[51]  Id., p.45.

usefulness of AAA-rated PMBS as assets that Bear and others relied on for both capital and liquidity, and thus raised questions about the firm's ability to meet its obligations. Investment banks like Bear Stearns were not commercial banks; instead of using short term deposits to hold long term assets—the hallmark of a bank— their business model relied on short-term funding to carry the short term assets of a trading business. Contrary to the views of the Commission majority, there is nothing inherently wrong with that business model, but it could not survive an unprecedented financial panic as severe as that which followed the collapse in value of an asset class as large and as liquid as AAA-rated subprime PMBS.

## Mortgage Defaults at Record Rates Created Balance Sheet Losses

Chairman Bair also pointed to the relationship between the decline in the value of PMBS and "the *balance sheet strength*" of financial institutions that held these assets. Adding to liquidity-based losses, balance sheet writedowns were another major element of the loss transmission mechanism. Securitized assets held by financial institutions are subject to the rules of fair value accounting, and must be marked to market under certain circumstances. Thus, banks and other financial institutions that are holding securitized mortgages in the form of PMBS could be subject to large *accounting* losses—but not necessarily cash losses—if investor sentiment were to turn against securitized mortgages and market values decline. Accordingly, once large numbers of delinquencies and losses started showing up in the mortgage markets generally and in the mortgage pools that backed the PMBS, it was *not necessary* for all the losses to be realized before the PMBS lost substantial value. All that was necessary was that the market for these assets become seriously impaired. This is exactly what happened in the middle of 2007, leading immediately not only to severe adverse liquidity consequences for financial institutions that held PMBS but also to capital writedowns that made them appear unstable and possibly insolvent.

These mark-to-market capital losses could be greater than the actual credit losses to be anticipated. As one Federal Reserve study put it, "The financial turmoil...put downward pressure on prices of structured finance products across the whole spectrum of [asset-backed] securities, even those with only minimal ties to the riskiest underlying assets...[I]n addition to discounts from higher expected credit risk, large mark-to-market discounts are generated by uncertainty about the quality of the underlying assets, by illiquidity, and by price volatility...This illiquidity discount is the main reason why the mark-to-market discount here, and in most similar analyses, is larger than the expected credit default rates on underlying assets."[52] In other words, the illiquidity discount associated with the uncertainties in value of collateral are and can be substantially larger than the credit default spread, since the spread reflects only anticipated credit losses.

As shown so dramatically in Figure 3, the collapse of the market for PMBS was a seminal event in the history of the financial crisis. Even though delinquencies had only just begun to show up in mortgage pools, the absence of a functioning

---

[52] Daniel Beltran, Laurie Pounder and Charles Thomas, "Foreign Exposure to Asset-Backed Securities of U.S. Origin," Board of Governors of the Federal Reserve System, *International Finance Discussion Papers 939*, August 2008, pp. 11-14.

market meant that PMBS simply could not be sold at anything but distress prices. The inability of financial institutions to liquidate their PMBS assets at anything like earlier values had dire consequences, especially under mark-to-market accounting rules, and was the crux of the crisis. In effect, a whole class of assets—involving almost $2 trillion—came to be called "toxic assets" in the media, and had to be written down substantially on the balance sheets of financial institutions around the world. Although this made financial institutions look weaker than they actually were, the PMBS they held, despite being unmarketable at that point, were in many cases still flowing cash at close to expected rates. Instead of a slow decline in value— which would have occurred if whole mortgages were held on bank balance sheets and gradually deteriorated in quality—the loss of marketability of these securities caused a crash in value.

The Commission majority did not discuss the significance of mark-to-market accounting in its report. This was a serious lapse, given the views of many that accounting policies played an important role in the financial crisis. Many commentators have argued that the resulting impairment charges to balance sheets reduced the GAAP equity of financial institutions and, therefore, their capital positions, making them appear financially weaker than they actually were if viewed on the basis of the cash flows they were receiving.[53]

The investor panic that began when unanticipated and unprecedented losses started to appear among NTMs generally and in the PMBS mortgage pools now spread to financial institutions themselves; investors were no longer sure which of these institutions could survive severe mortgage-related losses. This process was succinctly described in an analysis of fair value or mark-to-market accounting in the financial crisis issued by the Institute of International Finance, an organization of the world's largest banks and financial firms:

> [O]ften-dramatic write-downs of *sound* assets required under the current implementation of fair-value accounting adversely affect market sentiment, in turn leading to further write-downs, margin calls and capital impacts in a downward spiral that may lead to large-scale fire-sales of assets, and destabilizing, pro-cyclical feedback effects These damaging feedback effects worsen liquidity problems and contribute to the conversion of liquidity problems into solvency problems.[54] [emphasis in the original]

At least one study attempted to assess the effect of this on financial institutions overall. In January 2009, Nouriel Roubini and Elisa Parisi-Capone estimated the mark-to-market losses on MBS backed by both prime loans and NTMs. Their estimate was slightly over $1 trillion, of which U.S. banks and investment banks were estimated to have lost $318 billion on a mark-to-market basis.[55]

This would be a dramatic loss if all of it were realized. In 2008, the U.S. banking system had total assets of $10 trillion; the five largest investment banks had

---

[53] FCIC Draft Staff Report, "The Role of Accounting During the Financial Crisis," p.16.

[54] Institute of International Finance, "IIF Board of Directors - Discussion Memorandum on Valuation in Illiquid Markets," April 7, 2008, p.1.

[55] Nouriel Roubini and Elisa Parisi-Carbone, "Total $3.6 Trillion Projected Loan and Securities Losses in U.S. $1.8 Trillion of Which Borneby U.S. Banks/Brokers," *RGE Monitor*, January 2009, p.8.

total assets of $4 trillion.[56] If we assume that the banks had a leverage ratio of about 15-to-1 in 2008 and the investment banks about 30-to-1, that would mean that the equity capital position of the banking industry as a whole would be about $650 billion and the same number for the investment banks would be about $130 billion, for a total of $780 billion. Under these circumstances, the collapse of the PMBS market alone reduced the capital positions of U.S. banks and investment banks by approximately 41 percent on a mark-to-market basis. This does not mean that any actual losses were suffered, only that the assets concerned might have to be written down or could not be sold for the price at which they were previously carried on the firm's balance sheet.

In addition, Roubini and Parisi-Capone estimated that U.S. commercial and investment banks suffered a further mark-to-market loss of $225 billion on unsecuritized subprime and Alt-A mortgages.[57] They also estimated that mark-to-market losses for financial institutions outside the U.S. would be about 40 percent of U.S. losses, so there was likely to be a major effect on banks and other financial institutions around the world—depending, of course, on their capital position at the time the PMBS market stopped functioning. I am not aware of any data showing the mark-to-market effect of the collapse of the PMBS market on other U.S. financial institutions, but it can be assumed that they also suffered similar losses in proportion to their holdings of PMBS.

Losses of this magnitude would certainly be enough—when combined with other losses on securities and loans not related to mortgages—to call into question the stability of a large number of banks, investment banks and other financial institutions in the U.S. and around the world. However, there was one other factor that exacerbated the adverse effect of the loss of a market for PMBS. Although accounting rules did not require all PMBS to be written down, investors and counterparties did not know which financial institutions were holding the weakest assets and how much of their assets would have to be written down over time. Whatever that amount, it would reduce their capital positions at a time when investors and counterparties were anxious about their stability. This was the *balance sheet effect* that was the third element of Chairman Bair's summary.

To summarize, then, the following are the steps through which the government's housing policies transmitted losses—through PMBS—to the largest financial institutions: (i) the 19 million NTMs acquired or guaranteed by the Agencies were major contributors to the growth of the bubble and its extension in time; (ii) the growth of the bubble suppressed the losses that would ordinarily have brought the development of NTM-backed PMBS to a halt; (ii) competition for NTMs drove subprime lenders further out the risk curve to find high-yielding mortgages to securitize, especially when these loans did not appear to be producing losses commensurate with their risk; (iv) when the bubble finally burst, the unprecedented number of delinquencies and defaults among all NTMs—the great majority of which were held or guaranteed by the Agencies—caused investors to

---

[56] Timothy F. Geithner, "Reducing Systemic Risk in a Dynamic Financial System," Remarks at the Economic Club of New York, June 9, 2008, available at http://www.ny.frb.org/newsevents/speeches/2008/tfg080609.html.

[57] Nouriel Roubini and Elisa Parisi-Carbone, "Total $3.6 Trillion Projected Loan and Securities Losses," p.7.

flee the PMBS market, reducing the liquidity of the financial institutions that held the PMBS; and (v) mark-to-market accounting required these institutions to write down the value of the PMBS they held, as well as their other mortgage-related assets, reducing their capital positions and raising further questions about their stability and solvency.

## Government Actions Create a Panic

More than any other phenomenon, the financial crisis of 2008 resembles an old-fashioned investor and creditor panic. In the classic study, *Manias, Panics and Crashes: A History of Financial Crises*, Charles Kindleberger and Robert Aliber make a distinction between a remote cause and a proximate cause of a panic: "*Causa remota* of any crisis is the expansion of credit and speculation, while *causa proxima* is some incident that saps the confidence of the system and induces investors to sell commodities, stocks, real estate, bills of exchange, or promissory notes and increase their money holdings."[58] In the great financial panic of 2008, it is reasonably clear that the remote cause was the build-up of NTMs in the financial system, primarily—as I have shown in this analysis—as a result of government housing policy. This unprecedented increase in weak and risky assets set the financial system up for a crisis of some kind. The event that turned a potential crisis into a full-fledged panic—the proximate cause of the panic—was also the government's action: the rescue of Bear Stearns in March 2008 and the subsequent failure to rescue Lehman Brothers six months later. In terms of its ultimate cost to the public, this was one of the great policy errors of all time, and the reasons for the misjudgments that led to it have not yet been fully explored.

The lesson taught by the rescue of Bear was that all large financial institutions—and especially those larger than Bear—would be rescued. The moral hazard introduced by this one act irreparably changed the position of Lehman Brothers and every other large firm in the world's financial system. From that time forward, (i) the critical need for more capital became less critical; the likelihood of a government bailout would reassure creditors, so there was no need to dilute the shareholders any further by raising additional capital; (ii) firms such as Lehman, that might have been saved through an acquisition by a larger firm or an infusion of fresh capital by a strategic investor, drove harder bargains with potential acquirers; (iii) the potential acquirers themselves waited for the U.S. government to pick up some of the cost, as it had with Bear—an offer that never came in Lehman's case; and (iv) the Reserve Fund, a money market mutual fund, apparently assuming that Lehman would be rescued, decided not to sell the heavily discounted Lehman commercial paper it held; instead, with devastating results for the money market fund industry, it waited to be bailed out on the assumption that Lehman would be saved.

But Lehman was not saved, and its creditors were not bailed out. At a time when large mark-to-market losses among U.S. financial firms raised questions about which large financial institutions were insolvent or unstable, the demise of Lehman was a major shock. It overturned all the rational expectations about government

---

[58] Charles P. Kindleberger and Robert Aliber, *Manias, Panics, and Crashes: A History of Financial Crises*, 5th edition, John Wiley & Sons, Inc., 2005, p.104.

policies that market participants had developed after the Bear rescue. With no certainty about who was strong or who was weak, there was a headlong rush to U.S. government securities. Banks—afraid that their counterparties would want a return of their investments or their corporate customers would draw on lines of credit—began to hoard cash. Banks wouldn't lend to other banks, even overnight. As Chairman Bair suggested, that *was* the financial crisis. Everything after that was simply cleaning up the mess.

This analysis lays the principal cause of the financial crisis squarely at the feet of the unprecedented number of NTMs that were brought into the U.S. financial markets by government housing policy. These weak and high risk loans helped to build the bubble, and when the bubble deflated they defaulted in unprecedented numbers. This threatened losses in the PMBS that were held by financial institutions in the U.S. and around the world, impairing both their liquidity and their apparent stability.

The accumulation of 27 million subprime and Alt-A mortgages was not a random event, or even the result of major forces such as global financial imbalances or excessively low interest rates. Instead, these loans and the bubble to which they contributed were the direct consequence of something far more mundane: U.S. government housing policy, which—led by HUD over two administrations—deliberately reduced mortgage underwriting standards so that more people could buy homes. While this process was going on, everyone was pleased. Homeownership in the U.S. actually grew to the highest level ever recorded. But the result was a financial catastrophe from which the U.S. has still not recovered.

# III. THE U.S. GOVERNMENT'S ROLE IN FOSTERING THE GROWTH OF THE NTM MARKET

The preceding section of this dissenting statement described the damage that was done to the financial system by the unprecedented number of defaults and delinquencies that occurred among the 27 million NTMs that were present there in 2008. Given the damage they caused, the most important question about the financial crisis is why so many low quality mortgages were created. Another way to state this question is to ask why mortgage standards declined so substantially before and during the 1997-2007 bubble, allowing so many NTMs to be created. This massive and unprecedented change in underwriting standards had to have a cause—some factor that was present during the 1990s and thereafter that was not present in any earlier period. Part III addresses this fundamental question.

The conventional explanation for the financial crisis is the one given by Fed Chairman Bernanke in the same speech at Morehouse College quoted at the outset of Part II:

> Saving inflows from abroad can be beneficial if the country that receives those inflows invests them well. Unfortunately, that was not always the case in the United States and some other countries. *Financial institutions reacted to the surplus of available funds by competing aggressively for borrowers, and, in the years leading up to the crisis, credit to both households and businesses became relatively cheap and easy to obtain.* One important consequence was a housing boom in the United States, a boom that was fueled in large part by a rapid expansion of mortgage lending. *Unfortunately, much of this lending was poorly done, involving, for example, little or no down payment by the borrower or insufficient consideration by the lender of the borrower's ability to make the monthly payments.* Lenders may have become careless because they, like many people at the time, expected that house prices would continue to rise--thereby allowing borrowers to build up equity in their homes--and that credit would remain easily available, so that borrowers would be able to refinance if necessary. *Regulators did not do enough to prevent poor lending, in part because many of the worst loans were made by firms subject to little or no federal regulation.* [Emphasis supplied][59]

In other words, the liquidity in the world financial market caused U.S. banks to compete for borrowers by lowering their underwriting standards for mortgages and other loans. Lenders became careless. Regulators failed. Unregulated originators made bad loans. One has to ask: is it plausible that banks would compete for borrowers by lowering their mortgage standards? Mortgage originators—whether S&Ls, commercial banks, mortgage banks or unregulated brokers—have been competing for 100 years. That competition involved offering the lowest rates and the most benefits to potential borrowers. It did not, however, generally result in

---

[59] Speech at Morehead College April 14, 2009.

or involve the weakening of underwriting standards. Those standards—what made up the traditional U.S. mortgage—were generally 15 or 30 year amortizing loans to homebuyers who could provide a downpayment of at least 10-to-20 percent and had good credit records, jobs and steady incomes. Because of its inherent quality, this loan was known as a prime mortgage.

There were subprime loans and subprime lenders, but in the early 1990s subprime lenders were generally niche players that made loans to people who could not get traditional mortgage loans; the number of loans they generated was relatively small and bore higher than normal interest rates to compensate for the risks of default. In addition, mortgage bankers and others relied on FHA insurance for loans with low downpayments, impaired credit and high debt ratios. Until the 1990s, these NTMs were never more than a fraction of the total number of mortgages outstanding. The reason that low underwriting standards were not generally used is simple. Low standards would result in large losses when these mortgages defaulted, and very few lenders wanted to hold such mortgages. In addition, Fannie and Freddie were the buyers for most middle class mortgages in the United States, and they were conservative in their approach. Unless an originator made a traditional mortgage it was unlikely that Fannie or Freddie or another secondary market buyer could be found for it.

This is common sense. If you produce an inferior product—whether it's a household cleaner, an automobile, or a loan—people soon recognize the lack of quality and you are out of business. This was not the experience with mortgages, which became weaker and riskier as the 1990s and 2000s progressed. Why did this happen?

In its report, the Commission majority seemed to assume that originators of mortgages controlled the quality of mortgages. Much is made in the majority's report of the so-called "originate to distribute" idea, where an originator is not supposed to care about the quality of the mortgages because they would eventually be sold off. The originator, it is said, has no "skin in the game." The motivation for making poor quality mortgages in this telling is to earn fees, not only on the origination but in each of the subsequent steps in the securitization process.

This theory turns the mortgage market upside down. Mortgage originators could make all the low quality mortgages they wanted, but they wouldn't earn a dime unless there was a *buyer*. The real question, then, is why there were buyers for inferior mortgages and this, as it turns out, is the same as asking why mortgage underwriting standards, beginning in the early 1990s, deteriorated so badly. As Professor Raghuram Rajan notes in *Fault Lines*, "[A]s brokers came to know that someone out there was willing to buy subprime mortgage-backed securities without asking too many questions, they rushed to originate loans without checking the borrowers' creditworthiness, and credit quality deteriorated. But for a while, the problems were hidden by growing house prices and low defaults—easy credit masked the problems caused by easy credit—until house prices stopped rising and the flood of defaults burst forth."[60]

Who were these buyers? Table 1, reporting the number of NTMs outstanding on June 30, 2008, identified government agencies and private organizations required by the government to acquire, hold or securitize NTMs as responsible for two-thirds

---

[60] Raghuram G. Rajan, *Fault Lines*, p.44.

of these mortgages, about 19 million. The table also identifies the private sector as the securitizer of the remaining one-third, about 7.8 million loans. In other words, if we are looking for the buyer of the NTMs that were being created by originators at the local level, the government's policies would seem to be the most likely culprit. The private sector certainly played a role, but it was a subordinate one. Moreover, what the private sector did was respond to demand—that's what the private sector does—but the government's role involved deliberate policy, an entirely different matter. Of its own volition, it created a demand that would not otherwise have been there.

The deterioration in mortgage standards did *not* occur—contrary to the Commission majority's apparent view—because banks and other originators suddenly started to make deficient loans; nor was it because of insufficient regulation at the originator level. The record shows unambiguously that government regulations made FHA, Fannie and Freddie, mortgage banks and insured banks of all kinds into *competing* buyers. All of them needed NTMs in order to meet various government requirements. Fannie and Freddie were subject to increasingly stringent affordable housing requirements; FHA was tasked with insuring loans to low-income borrowers that would not be made unless insured; banks and S&Ls were required by CRA to show that they were also making loans to the same group of borrowers; mortgage bankers who signed up for the HUD Best Practices Initiative and the Clinton administration's National Homeownership Strategy were required to make the same kind of loans. Profit had nothing to do with the motivations of these firms; they were responding to government direction. Under these circumstances, it should be no surprise that underwriting standards declined, as all of these organizations scrambled to acquire the same low quality mortgages.

# 1. HUD's Central Role

In testimony before the House Financial Services Committee on April 14, 2010, Shaun Donovan, Secretary of Housing and Urban Development, said in reference to the GSEs: "Seeing their market share decline [between 2004 and 2006] as a result of [a] change of demand, the GSEs made the decision to widen their focus from safer prime loans and begin chasing the non-prime market, loosening long-standing underwriting and risk management standards along the way. This would be a fateful decision that not only proved disastrous for the companies themselves –but ultimately also for the American taxpayer."

Earlier, in a "Report to Congress on the Root Causes of the Foreclosure Crisis," in January 2010, HUD declared "The serious financial troubles of the GSEs that led to their being placed into conservatorship by the Federal government provides strong testament to the fact that the GSEs were, indeed, overexposed to unduly risky mortgage investments. However, *the evidence suggests that the GSEs' decisions to purchase or guarantee non-prime loans was motivated much more by efforts to chase market share and profits than by the need to satisfy federal regulators."* [61] [emphasis supplied]

Finger-pointing in Washington is endemic when problems occur, and

---

[61] Report to Congress on the Root Causes of the Foreclosure Crisis , January 2010, p.xii, http://www. huduser.org/portal/publications/hsgfin/foreclosure_09.html.

agencies and individuals are constantly trying to find scapegoats for their own bad decisions, but HUD's effort to blame Fannie and Freddie for the decline in underwriting standards sets a new standard for running from responsibility. Contrast the 2010 statement quoted above with this statement by HUD in 2000, when it was significantly increasing Fannie and Freddie's affordable housing goals:

> Lower-income and minority families have made major gains in access to the mortgage market in the 1990s. A variety of reasons have accounted for these gains, including improved housing affordability, enhanced enforcement of the Community Reinvestment Act, *more flexible mortgage underwriting*, and stepped-up enforcement of the Fair Housing Act. *But most industry observers believe that one factor behind these gains has been the improved performance of Fannie Mae and Freddie Mac under HUD's affordable lending goals. HUD's recent increases in the goals for 2001-03 will encourage the GSEs to further step up their support for affordable lending.*[62] [emphasis supplied]

Or this statement in 2004, when HUD was again increasing the affordable housing goals for Fannie and Freddie:

> Millions of Americans with less than perfect credit or who cannot meet some of the tougher underwriting requirements of the prime market for reasons such as inadequate income documentation, limited downpayment or cash reserves, or the desire to take more cash out in a refinancing than conventional loans allow, rely on subprime lenders for access to mortgage financing. *If the GSEs reach deeper into the subprime market, more borrowers will benefit from the advantages that greater stability and standardization create.*[63] [emphasis supplied]

Or, finally, this statement in a 2005 report commissioned by HUD:

> More liberal mortgage financing has contributed to the increase in demand for housing. During the 1990s, lenders have been *encouraged by HUD and banking regulators* to increase lending to low-income and minority households. The Community Reinvestment Act (CRA), Home Mortgage Disclosure Act (HMDA), government-sponsored enterprises (GSE) housing goals and fair lending laws have strongly encouraged mortgage brokers and lenders to market to low-income and minority borrowers. *Sometimes these borrowers are higher risk, with blemished credit histories and high debt or simply little savings for a down payment. Lenders have responded with low down payment loan products and automated underwriting, which has allowed them to more carefully determine the risk of the loan.*[64] [emphasis supplied]

Despite the recent effort by HUD to deny its own role in fostering the growth of subprime and other high risk mortgage lending, there is strong—indeed irrefutable—evidence that, beginning in the early 1990s, HUD led an ultimately successful effort to lower underwriting standards in every area of the mortgage market where HUD had or could obtain influence. With support in congressional legislation, the policy was launched in the Clinton administration and extended almost to the end of the Bush administration. It involved FHA, which was under the direct control of HUD; Fannie Mae and Freddie Mac, which were subject to HUD's affordable housing regulations; and the mortgage banking industry, which—while not subject to HUD's legal jurisdiction—apparently agreed to pursue HUD's

---

[62] Issue Brief: HUD's Affordable Housing Goals for Fannie Mae and Freddie Mac, p.5.

[63] Final Rule, http://fdsys.gpo.gov/fdsys/pkg/FR-2004-11-02/pdf/04-24101.pdf.

[64] HUD PDR, May 2005, HUD Contract C-OPC-21895, Task Order CHI-T0007, "Recent House Price Trends and Homeownership Affordability", p.85.

policies out of fear that they would be brought under the Community Reinvestment Act through legislation.[65] In addition, although not subject to HUD's jurisdiction, the new tighter CRA regulations that became effective in 1995 led to a process in which community groups could obtain commitments for substantial amounts of CRA-qualifying mortgages and other loans to subprime borrowers when banks were applying for merger approvals.[66]

By 2004, HUD believed it had achieved the "revolution" it was looking for:

> Over the past ten years, there has been a 'revolution in affordable lending' that has extended homeownership opportunities to historically underserved households. Fannie Mae and Freddie Mac have been a substantial part of this 'revolution in affordable lending'. *During the mid-to-late 1990s, they added flexibility to their underwriting guidelines, introduced new low-downpayment products,* and worked to expand the use of automated underwriting in evaluating the creditworthiness of loan applicants. HMDA data suggest that the industry and GSE initiatives are increasing the flow of credit to underserved borrowers. *Between 1993 and 2003, conventional loans to low income and minority families increased at much faster rates than loans to upper-income and nonminority families.*[67][emphasis supplied]

This turned out to be an immense error of policy. By 2010, even the strongest supporters of affordable housing as enforced by HUD had recognized their error. In an interview on Larry Kudlow's CNBC television program in late August, Representative Barney Frank (D-Mass.)—the chair of the House Financial Services Committee and previously the strongest congressional advocate for affordable housing—conceded that he had erred: "I hope by next year we'll have abolished Fannie and Freddie . . . it was a great mistake to push lower-income people into housing they couldn't afford and couldn't really handle once they had it." He then added, "I had been too sanguine about Fannie and Freddie."[68]

## 2. THE DECLINE OF MORTGAGE UNDERWRITING STANDARDS

Before the enactment of the GSE Act in 1992, and HUD's adoption of a policy thereafter to reduce underwriting standards, the GSEs followed conservative underwriting practices. For example, in a random review by Fannie Mae of 25,804 loans from October 1988 to January 1992, over 78 percent had LTV ratios of 80 percent or less, while only 5.75 percent had LTV ratios of 91 to 95 percent.[69] High risk lending was confined primarily to FHA (which was controlled by HUD) and specialized subprime lenders who often sold the mortgages they originated to FHA. What caused these conservative standards to decline? The Commission majority,

---

[65] Steve Cocheo, "Fair-lending pressure builds," *ABA Banking Journal,* vol. 86, 1994, http://www.questia.com/googleScholar.qst?docId=5001707340.

[66] See NCRC, *CRA Commitments,* 2007.

[67] *Federal Register,*vol. 69, No. 211, November 2, 2004, Rules and Regulations, p.63585, http://fdsys.gpo.gov/fdsys/pkg/FR-2004-11-02/pdf/04-24101.pdf .

[68] Larry Kudlow, "Barney Frank Comes Home to the Facts," GOPUSA, August 23, 2010, available at www.gopusa.com/commentary/2010/08/kudlow-barney-frank-comes-home-to-the-facts.php#ixz z0zdCrWpCY (accessed September 20, 2010).

[69] Document in author's files.

echoing Chairman Bernanke, seems to believe that the impetus was competition among the banks, irresponsibility among originators, and the desire for profit. The majority's report offers no other explanation.

However, there is no difficulty finding the source of the reductions in mortgage underwriting standards for Fannie and Freddie, or for the originators for whom they were the buyers. HUD made clear in numerous statements that its policy—in order to make credit available to low-income borrowers—was specifically *intended* to reduce underwriting standards. The GSE Act enabled HUD to put Fannie and Freddie into competition with FHA, and vice versa, creating what became a contest to lower mortgage standards. As the Fannie Mae Foundation noted in a 2000 report, "FHA loans constituted the largest share of Countrywide's [subprime lending] activity, until Fannie Mae and Freddie Mac began accepting loans with higher LTVs [loan-to-value ratios] and greater underwriting flexibilities."[70]

Under the GSE Act, the HUD Secretary was authorized to establish affordable housing goals for Fannie and Freddie. Congress required that these goals include a low and moderate income goal and a special affordable goal (discussed below), both of which could be adjusted in the future. Among the factors the secretary was to consider in establishing the goals were national housing needs and "the ability of the enterprises [Fannie and Freddie] to lead the industry in making mortgage credit available for low-and moderate-income families." The Act also established an interim affordable housing goal of 30 percent for the two-year period beginning January 1, 1993. Under this requirement, 30 percent of the GSEs' mortgage purchases had to be affordable housing loans, defined as loans to borrowers at or below the AMI.[71]

Further, the Act established a "special affordable" goal to meet the "unaddressed needs of, and affordable to, low-income families in low-income areas and very low-income families." This category was defined as follows: "(i) 45 percent shall be mortgages of low-income families who live in census tracts in which the median income does not exceed 80 percent of the area median income; and (ii) 55 percent shall be mortgages of very low income families," which were later defined as 60 percent of AMI.[72] Although the GSE Act initially required that the GSEs spend on special affordable mortgages "not less than 1 percent of the dollar amount of the mortgage purchases by the [GSEs] for the previous year," HUD raised this requirement substantially in later years. Ultimately, it became the most difficult affordable housing AH burden for Fannie and Freddie to meet.

Finally, the GSEs were directed to: "(A) assist primary lenders to make housing credit available in areas with low-income and minority families; and (B) assist insured depository institutions to meet their obligations under the Community Reinvestment Act of 1977."[73] There will be more on the CRA and its effect on the quality of mortgages later in this section.

Congress also made clear in the act that its intention was to call into question the high quality underwriting guidelines of the time. It did so by directing Fannie and Freddie to "examine—

---

[70] Fannie Mae Foundation, "Making New Markets: Case Study of Countrywide Home Loans," 2000, http://content.knowledgeplex.org/kp2/programs/pdf/rep_newmortmkts_countrywide.pdf.

[71] GSE Act, Section 1332.

[72] Id., Section 1333.

[73] Id., Section 1335.

(1) The extent to which the underwriting guidelines prevent or inhibit the purchase or securitization of mortgages for houses in mixed-use, urban center, and predominantly minority neighborhoods and for housing for low-and moderate-income families;

(2) The standards employed by private mortgage insurers and the extent to which such standards inhibit the purchase and securitization by the enterprises of mortgages described in paragraph (1); and

(3) The implications of implementing underwriting standards that—
(A) establish a downpayment requirement for mortgagors of 5 percent or less;
(B) allow the use of cash on hand as a source of downpayments; and
(C) approve borrowers who have a credit history of delinquencies if the borrower can demonstrate a satisfactory credit history for at least the 12-month period ending on the date of the application for the mortgage."[74]

I could not find a record of reports by Fannie and Freddie required under this section of the act, but it would have been fairly clear to both companies, and to HUD, what Congress wanted in asking for these studies. Prevailing underwriting standards were inhibiting mortgage financing for low and moderate income (LMI) families, and would have to be substantially relaxed in order to meet the goals of the Act. Whatever the motivation, HUD set out to assure that downpayment requirements were substantially reduced (eventually they reached zero) and past credit history became a much less important issue when mortgages were made (permitting subprime mortgages to become far more common).

Until 1995, HUD enforced the temporary AH goals originally put in place by the GSE Act. With the exception of the special affordable requirements, which were small at this point, these goals were not burdensome. In the ordinary course of their business, the GSEs seem to have bought enough mortgages made to borrowers below the AMI to qualify for the 30 percent AH goal. In 1995, however, HUD raised the LMI goal to 40 percent, applicable to 1996, and to 42 percent for subsequent years. In terms of its effect on Fannie and Freddie, HUD's most important move at this time was to set a Special Affordable goal (low and very low income borrowers) of 12 percent, which increased to 14 percent in 1997. Efforts to find loans to low or very low income borrowers (80 percent and 60 percent of AMI, respectively) that did not involve high risks would prove difficult. As early as November 1995, even before the effect of these new and higher goals, Fannie's staff had already recognized that Fannie's Community Homebuyer Program (CHBP), which featured a 97 percent loan-to-value (LTV) ratio—i.e., 3 percent downpayment[75]—was showing significant rates of serious delinquency that exceeded Fannie's expected rates by 26percent in origination year 1992, 93 percent in 1993 and 57 percent in 1994.[76]

In 1995, continuing its efforts to erode underwriting standards in order to increase homeownership, HUD issued a policy statement entitled "The National Homeownership Strategy: Partners in the American Dream." The Strategy was prepared by HUD, "under the direction of Secretary Henry G. Cisneros, in response

---

[74] Id., Section 1354(a).

[75] Fannie Mae, "Opening Doors with Fannie Mae's Community Lending Products," 1995, p.3.

[76] Fannie Mae, Memo from Credit Policy Staff to Credit Policy Committee, "CHBP Performance," November 14, 1995, p.1.

to a request from President Clinton."[77] The first paragraph of Chapter 1 stated: "The purpose of the National Homeownership Strategy is to achieve an all-time high level of homeownership in America within the next 6 years through an unprecedented collaboration of public and private housing industry organizations."

The Strategy paper then noted that "industry representatives agreed to the formation of working groups to help develop the National Homeownership Strategy" and made clear that one of its purposes was to increase homeownership by reducing downpayments: "*Lending institutions, secondary market investors, mortgage insurers, and other members of the partnership should work collaboratively to reduce homebuyer downpayment requirements.* Mortgage financing with high loan-to-value ratios should generally be associated with enhanced homebuyer counseling and, where available, supplemental sources of downpayment assistance."[78] According to a HUD summary, the purpose of the Strategy was to make financing "more available, affordable, and flexible."[79] [emphasis supplied] It continued:

> The inability (either real or perceived) of many younger families to qualify for a mortgage is widely recognized as a very serious barrier to homeownership. The National Homeownership Strategy commits both government and the mortgage industry to a number of initiatives designed to:

> > Cut transaction costs through streamlined regulations and technological and procedural efficiencies.

> > *Reduce downpayment requirements and interest costs by making terms more flexible,* providing subsidies to low- and moderate-income families, and creating incentives to save for homeownership.

> > *Increase the availability of alternative financing products in housing markets throughout the country.*[80] [emphasis supplied]

Reductions in downpayments, the area on which HUD particularly concentrated in pursuing its AH goals and the National Homeownership Strategy, are especially important in weakening underwriting standards. Table 4, below, based on a large sample of loans from the 1990s, shows the risk relationships between downpayments and mortgage risks. It is particularly instructive to note that when low downpayments (i.e., high LTVs) are combined with low FICO scores (subprime loans) the expected delinquencies and defaults are multiplied several fold. For example, when a loan with a FICO score below 620 is combined with a downpayment of five percent, the risk of default is 4.2 times greater than it would be if the downpayment were 25 percent.

---

[77] HUD, "The National Homeownership Strategy: Partners in the American Dream," available at http://web.archive.org/web/20010106203500/www.huduser.org/publications/affhsg/homeown/chap1.html.

[78] Id., Chapter 4, Action 35.

[79] The term "flexible" has a special meaning when HUD uses it. See note 8 supra.

[80] HUD, Urban Policy Brief No.2, August 1995, available at http://www.huduser.org/publications/txt/hdbrf2.txt.

Table 4.[81] High LTVs enhance the risk of low FICO scores

|        | Column 1   | Column 2  | Column 3   | Column 4   | Column 5   | Column 6                          |
|--------|------------|-----------|------------|------------|------------|-----------------------------------|
| Row 1  | FICO Score | ≤ 70% LTV | 71-80% LTV | 81-90% LTV | 91-95% LTV | Relation of Column 5 to Column 3  |
| Row 2  | < 620      | 1.0       | 4.8        | 11         | 20         | 4.2 times                         |
| Row 3  | 620-679    | 0.5       | 2.3        | 5.3        | 9.4        | 4.1 times                         |
| Row 4  | 680-720    | 0.2       | 1.0        | 2.3        | 4.1        | 4.1 times                         |
| Row 5  | > 720      | 0.1       | 0.4        | 0.9        | 1.6        | 4 times                           |

Despite these obvious dangers, HUD saw the erosion of downpayment requirements imposed by the private sector as one of the keys to the success of its strategy to increase home ownership through the "partnership" it had established with the mortgage financing community: "The amount of borrower equity is an important factor in assessing mortgage loan quality. *However, many low-income families do not have access to sufficient funds for a downpayment. While members of the partnership have already made significant strides in reducing this barrier to home purchase, more must be done.* In 1989 only 7 percent of home mortgages were made with less than 10 percent downpayment. By August 1994, low downpayment mortgage loans had increased to 29 percent."[82] [emphasis supplied]

HUD's policy was highly successful in achieving the goals it sought. In 1989, only one in 230 homebuyers bought a home with a downpayment of 3 percent or less, but by 2003 one in seven buyers was providing a downpayment at that level, and by 2007 the number was less than one in three. The gradual increase in LTVs and CLTVs (first and second loans combined to produce a lower downpayment) under HUD's policies is shown in Figure 4. Note the date (1992) when HUD began to have some influence over the downpayments that the GSEs would accept.

That HUD's AH goals were the reason Fannie increased its high LTV (low downpayment) lending is clearly described in a Fannie presentation to HUD assistant secretary Albert Trevino on January 10, 2003: "Analyses of the market demonstrate the greatest barrier to home ownership for most renters are related to wealth—the lack of money for a downpayment...our low-downpayment lending—negligible until 1994—has grown considerably. It is a key part of our strategy to serve low-income and minority borrowers." The figure that accompanied that statement showed that Fannie's home purchase loans over 95 percent LTV had increased from one percent in 1994 to 7.9 percent in 2001.[83]

---

[81] "Deconstructing the Subprime Debacle Using New Indices of Underwriting Quality and Economic Conditions: A First Look," by Anderson, Capozza, and Van Order, found at http://www.ufanet.com/DeconstructingSubprimeJuly2008.pdf.

[82] HUD's "National Homeownership Strategy – Partners in the American Dream," http://web.archive.org/web/20010106203500/www.huduser.org/publications/affhsg/homeown/chap1.html.

[83] "Fannie Mae's Role in Affordable Housing Finance: Connecting World Capital Markets and America's Homebuyers," Presentation to HUD Assistant Secretary Albert Trevino, January 10, 2003.

Figure 4. Estimated Percentage of Home Purchase Volume with an LTV or CLTV >=97%
(Includes FHA and Conventional Loans*)
and Combined Foreclosure Start Rate for Conventional and Government Loans

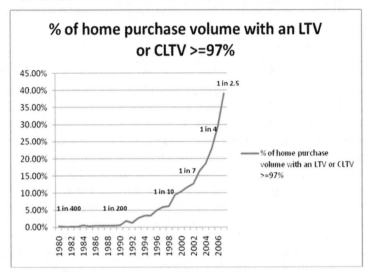

*Fannie's percentage of home purchase loans with an LTV or CLTV >=97% used as the proxy for
conventional loans.
Sources: FHA 2009 Actuarial Study, and HUD''s Office of Policy Development and Research - Profiles
of GSE Mortgage Purchases in 1999 and 2000, in 2001-2004, and in 2005-2007, and Fannie's 2007 10-K.
Compiled by Edward Pinto.

The close relationship between low downpayments and delinquencies and
defaults on mortgages is shown in Figure 5, which compares the increase in FHA 97
percent (or greater) CLTV or LTV mortgages to the increase in the foreclosure start
rate on all loans published by the Mortgage Bankers Association.

Figure 5. Relationship between low downpayments and delinquencies or defaults on mortgages

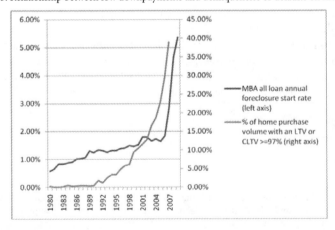

Sources: MBA National Delinquency Survey, FHA 2009 Actuarial Study, and HUD's Office of Policy
Development and Research - Profiles of GSE Mortgage Purchases in 1999 and 2000, in 2001-2004, and
in 2005-2007, SMR's "Piggyback Mortgage Lending," and Fannie's 2007 10-K. Fannie is used as the
proxy on the conventional market. Compiled by Edward Pinto.

In 1995, HUD also ruled that Fannie and Freddie could get AH credit for buying PMBS that were backed by loans to low-income borrowers.[84] This provided an opportunity for subprime lenders to create pools of subprime mortgages that were likely to be AH goals-rich. These were then sold through Wall Street underwriters to Fannie and Freddie, which became the largest buyers of these high risk PMBS between 2002 and 2005.[85] These PMBS pools were not bought for profit. As Adolfo Marzol, Fannie's Chief Credit Officer, noted to Fannie CEO Dan Mudd in a 2005 memorandum, "large 2004 private label [PMBS] volumes were necessary to achieve challenging minority lending goals and housing goals."[86] There is a strong possibility that by creating a market for PMBS backed by NTMs Fannie and Freddie enabled Wall Street—which had previously focused on securitizing prime jumbo loans—to get its start in developing an underwriting business in PMBS based on NTMs.

HUD pursued these policies throughout the balance of the Clinton administration and into the administration of George W. Bush. Ultimately, they would lead to the mortgage meltdown in 2007, as vast numbers of mortgages with low or no downpayments and other non-traditional features suffused the financial system. But in June, 1995, the dangers in HUD's policies were not recognized. As President Clinton said in a 1995 speech, "Our homeownership strategy will not cost the taxpayers one extra red cent. It will not require legislation. It will not add more federal programs or grow the Federal bureaucracy."[87] The lesson here is that the government can accomplish a lot of its goals without growing, as long as it has the power to enlist the private sector. That does not mean, however, as we have all now learned, that the taxpayers will not ultimately be faced with the costs.

The next significant move in the AH goals was made under HUD Secretary Andrew Cuomo, and it was a major step. On July 29, 1999, HUD issued a press release with the heading "Cuomo Announces Action to Provide $2.4 trillion in Mortgages for Affordable Housing for 28.1 Million Families."[88] The release began: "Housing and Urban Development Secretary Andrew Cuomo today announced a policy to require the nation's two largest housing finance companies to buy $2.4 trillion in mortgages over the next 10 years to provide affordable housing for about 28.1 million low-and moderate-income families." This was followed by a quote from President Clinton to emphasize the importance of the initiative: "During the last six and a half years, my Administration has put tremendous emphasis on promoting homeownership and making housing more affordable for all Americans...Today, the homeownership rate is at an all-time high, with more than 66 percent of all American families owning their homes. Today, we take another significant step."

The release then pointed out that the AH goals would be substantially raised and that "[u]nder the higher goals, Fannie Mae and Freddie Mac will buy an additional $488.3 billion in mortgages that will be used to provide affordable housing for 7 million more low-and moderate-income families over the next 10 years. Those new mortgages and families are over and above the $1.9 trillion in mortgages for

---

[84] http://www.washingtonpost.com/wp-dyn/content/article/2008/06/09/AR2008060902626.html.

[85] See Footnote 32.

[86] Fannie Mae, internal memo, Adolfo Marzol to Dan Mudd, "RE: Private Label Securities," March 2, 2005.

[87] William J. Clinton, Remarks on the National Homeownership Strategy, June 5, 1995.

[88] HUD Press Release, HUD No. 99-131, July 29, 1999.

21.1 million families that would have been generated if the current goals had been retained." The release also noted that "Fannie Mae Chairman Franklin D. Raines joined Cuomo at the news conference in which Cuomo announced the HUD action. Raines committed Fannie Mae to reaching HUD's increased Affordable Housing goals."

The policy behind this substantial increase in the AH goals was expressed in HUD's discussion of the rule-making: "To fulfill the intent of [the GSE Act], the GSEs should lead the industry in ensuring that access to mortgage credit is made available for very low-, low- and moderate-income families and residents of underserved areas. HUD recognizes that, to lead the mortgage industry over time, *the GSEs will have to stretch to reach certain goals and close the gap between the secondary mortgage market and the primary mortgage market. This approach is consistent with Congress' recognition that 'the enterprises will need to stretch their efforts to achieve' the goals.*"[89] [emphasis supplied]

The new AH goals announced in 1999 were not finally issued until October 2000. Their specifics were stunning and drove Fannie and Freddie into a new and far more challenging era. The basic goal, an LMI requirement of 42 percent, was raised to 50 percent, and the special affordable goal was raised from 14 percent to 20 percent. As a result, 75 percent of the increase in goals was concentrated in the low- and very-low income category—where the risks were the greatest. A HUD memo summarized the new rules:[90]

> For each year from 2001 through 2003, the goals are:
>
> • *Low- and moderate-income goal.* At least 50 percent of the dwelling units financed by each GSE's mortgage purchases should be for families with incomes no greater than area median income (AMI), defined as median income for the metropolitan area or nonmetropolitan county. The corresponding goal was 42 percent for 1997-2000.
>
> • *Special affordable goal.* At least 20 percent of the dwelling units financed by each GSE's mortgage purchases should be for very low-income families (those with incomes no greater than 60 percent of AMI) or for low-income families (those with incomes no greater than 80 percent of LMI) in low-income areas. The corresponding goal was 14 percent for 1997-2000.
>
> • *Underserved areas goal.* At least 31 percent of the dwelling units financed by each GSE's mortgage purchases should be for units located in underserved areas. Research by HUD and others has demonstrated that low-income and high-minority census tracts have high mortgage denial rates and low mortgage origination rates, and this forms the basis for HUD's definition of underserved areas. The corresponding goal was 24 percent for 1997-2000.

HUD's new and more stringent AH goal requirements immediately stimulated strong interest at the GSEs for CRA loans, substantial portions of which were likely to be goals-qualifying. This is evident in a speech by Fannie's Vice Chair, Jamie Gorelick, to an American Bankers Association conference on October 30,

---

[89] http://frwebgate.access.gpo.gov/cgi-bin/getdoc.cgi?dbname=2000_register&docid=page+65043-65092.

[90] HUD, Office of Policy Development and Research, Issue Brief No. 5, January 2001, p.3.

2000, just after HUD announced the latest increase in the AH goals for the GSEs:

> Your CRA business is very important to us. Since 1997, we have done nearly $7 billion in specially targeted CRA business—all with depositories like yours. But that is just the beginning. Before the decade is over, Fannie Mae is committed to finance over $20 billion in specially targeted CRA business and over $500 billion in CRA business altogether...
>
> We want your CRA loans because they help us meet our housing goals... We will buy them from your portfolios, or package them into securities... We will also purchase CRA mortgages you make right at the point of origination... You can originate CRA loans for our purchase with one of our CRA-friendly products, like our 3 percent down Fannie 97. Or we have special community lending products with flexible underwriting and special financing... Our approach is "CRA your way".[91]

The 50 percent level in the new HUD regulations was a turning point. Fannie and Freddie had to stretch a bit to reach the previous goal of 42 percent, but 50 percent was a significant challenge. As Dan Mudd told the Commission,

> Fannie Mae's mission regulator, HUD, imposed ever-higher housing goals that were very difficult to meet during my tenure as CEO [2005-2008]. The HUD goals greatly impacted Fannie Mae's business, as a great deal of time, resources, energy, and personnel were dedicated to finding ways to meet these goals. HUD increased the goals aggressively over time to the point where they exceeded the 50% mark, requiring Fannie Mae to place greater emphasis on purchasing loans to underserved areas. Fannie Mae had to devote a great deal of resources to running its business to satisfy HUD's goals and subgoals.[92]

Mudd's point can be illustrated with simple arithmetic. At the 50 percent level, for every mortgage acquired that was not goal-qualifying, Fannie and Freddie had to acquire a goal-qualifying loan. Although about 30 percent of prime loans were likely to be goal-qualifying in any event (because they were made to borrowers at or below the applicable AMI), most prime loans were not. Subprime and other NTM loans were goals-rich, but not every such loan was goal-qualifying. Accordingly, in order to meet a 50 percent goal, the GSEs had to purchase ever larger amounts of goals-rich NTMs in order to acquire sufficient quantities of goals-qualifying loans.

Thus, in a presentation to HUD in 2004, Fannie argued that to meet a 57 percent LMI goal (which was under consideration by HUD at the time) it would have to acquire 151.5 percent more subprime loans than the goal in order to capture enough goal-qualifying loans.[93] Moreover, with the special affordable category at 20 percent in 2004, the GSEs had to acquire large numbers of NTM loans from borrowers who were at or below 60 percent of the AMI. This requirement drove Fannie and Freddie even further into risk territory in search of loans that would meet this subgoal.

---

[91] Jamie S. Gorelick, Remarks at American Bankers Association conference, October 30, 2000. http://web.archive.org/web/20011120061407/www.fanniemae.com/news/speeches/speech_152.html.

[92] Daniel H. Mudd's Responses to the Questions Presented in the FCIC's June 3, 2010, letter, Answer to Question 6: How influential were HUD's affordable housing guidelines in Fannie Mae's purchase of subprime and Alt-A loans? Were Alt-A loans "goals-rich"? Were Alt-A loans net positive for housing goals?

[93] Fannie Mae, "Discussion of HUD's Proposed Housing Goals," Presentation to the Department of Housing and Urban development, June 9, 2004.

Most of what was going on here was under the radar, even for specialists in the housing finance field, but not everyone missed it. In a paper published in 2001,[94] financial analyst Josh Rosner recognized the deterioration in mortgage standards although he did not recognize how many loans were subject to this problem:

> Over the past decade Fannie Mae and Freddie Mac have reduced required down payments on loans that they purchase in the secondary market. Those requirements have declined from 10% to 5% to 3% and in the past few months Fannie Mae announced that it would follow Freddie Mac's recent move into the 0% down payment mortgage market. Although they are buying low down payment loans, those loans must be insured with 'private mortgage insurance' (PMI). On homes with PMI, even the closing costs can now be borrowed through unsecured loans, gifts or subsidies. This means that not only can the buyer put zero dollars down to purchase a new house but also that the mortgage can finance the closing costs....
>
> *[I]t appears a large portion of the housing sector's growth in the 1990's came from the easing of the credit underwriting process....*The virtuous cycle of increasing homeownership due to greater leverage has the potential to become a vicious cycle of lower home prices due to an accelerating rate of foreclosures.[95] [emphasis supplied]

The last increase in the AH goals occurred in 2004, when HUD raised the LMI goal to 52 percent for 2005, 53 percent for 2006, 55 percent for 2007 and 56 percent for 2008. Again, the percentage increases in the special affordable category outstripped the general LMI goal, putting added pressure on Fannie and Freddie to acquire additional risky NTMs. This category increased from 20 percent to 27 percent over the period. In the release that accompanied the increases, HUD declared:

> Millions of Americans with less than perfect credit or who cannot meet some of the tougher underwriting requirements of the prime market for reasons such as inadequate income documentation, limited downpayment or cash reserves, or the desire to take more cash out in a refinancing than conventional loans allow, rely on subprime lenders for access to mortgage financing. *If the GSEs reach deeper into the subprime market,* more borrowers will benefit from the advantages that greater stability and standardization create.[96] [emphasis supplied]

Fannie did indeed reach deeper into the subprime market, confirming in a March 2003 presentation to HUD, "Higher goals force us deeper into FHA and subprime."[97] According to HUD data, as a result of the AH goals Fannie Mae's acquisitions of goal-qualifying loans (which were primarily subprime and Alt-A) increased (i) for very low income borrowers from 5.2 percent of their acquisitions in 1993 to 12.2 percent in 2007; (ii) for special affordable borrowers from 6.4 percent in 1993 to 15.2 percent in 2007; and (iii) for less than median income borrowers (which includes the other two categories) from 29.2 percent in 1993 to 41.5 percent in 2007.[98]

---

[94] Josh Rosner, "Housing in the New Millennium: A Home Without Equity is Just a Rental With Debt," June, 2001, p.7, available at: http://papers.ssrn.com/sol3/papers.cfm?abstract_id=1162456.

[95] Id., p.29.

[96] http://fdsys.gpo.gov/fdsys/pkg/FR-2004-11-02/pdf/04-24101.pdf, p.63601.

[97] Fannie Mae, "The HUD Housing Goals", March 2003.

[98] HUD, Office of Policy Development and Research, Profiles of GSE Mortgage Purchases, 1992-2000, 2001-2004, and 2005-2007.

By 2004, Fannie and Freddie were sufficiently in need of subprime loans to meet the AH goals that their CEOs, as the following account shows, went to a meeting of mortgage bankers to ask for more subprime loan production:

> The top executives of Freddie Mac and Fannie Mae [Richard Syron and Franklin Raines] made no bones about their interest in buying loans made to borrowers formerly considered the province of nonprime and other niche lenders. ...Fannie Mae Chairman and [CEO] Franklin Raines told mortgage bankers in San Francisco that his company's lender-customers 'need to learn the best from the subprime market and bring the best from the prime market into [the subprime market].' He offered praise for nonprime lenders that, he said, 'are some of the best marketers in financial services'... *We have to push products and opportunities to people who have lesser credit quality*," he said.[99] [emphasis supplied]

Accordingly, by 2004, when HUD put new and tougher AH goals into effect, Fannie and Freddie were using every available resource to meet the goals, including subprime loans, Alt-A loans and the purchase of PMBS. Some observers, including the Commission's majority, have claimed that the GSEs bought NTM loans and PMBS for profit—that these instruments did not assist Fannie and Freddie in meeting the AH goals and therefore must have been acquired because they were profitable. However, the statement by Adolfo Marzol reported above, and the data in Table 5 furnished to the Commission by Fannie Mae shows that all three categories of NTMs—subprime loans (i.e., loans to borrowers with FICO scores less than 660), Alt-A loans and PMBS (called PLS for "Private Label Securities" in the table)—fulfilled the AH goals or subgoals for the years and in the percentages shown below. (Bolded numbers exceeded the applicable goal.) Table 5 also shows, significantly, that the gradual increase in Fannie's purchases of these NTMs closely followed the gradual increase in the goals between 1996 and 2008.

---

[99] Neil Morse, "Looking for New Customers," *Mortgage Banking*, December 1, 2004. It may be significant that the chairman of Freddie Mac at the time, Leland Brendsel, did not attend the 2000 press conference or pledge support for HUD's new goals. Raines must have forgotten his 1999 pledge to Secretary Cuomo and his speech to the mortgage bankers when he wrote in a letter to *The Wall Street Journal* on August 3, 2010: "The facts about the financial collapse of Fannie and Freddie are pretty clear and a matter of public record. The company managers, their regulator and the Treasury have all said that the losses which crippled the companies were caused by the purchase of loans with lower credit standards between 2005 and 2007. The companies explicitly changed their credit standards in order to regain market share after Wall Street began to define market credit standards in 2004."

Table 5.[100] Nontraditional Mortgages and the Affordable Housing Goals

| Year | Low & Moderate Income Base Goal | | Special Affordable Base Goal | | Underserved Base Goal | |
|------|--------|------|--------|------|--------|------|
| | Actual* | Goal | Actual* | Goal | Actual* | Goal |
| **Credit Score <660 Originations** | | | | | | |
| 1996 | 38.08% | 40 % | 12.31% | 12% | 32.10% | 21% |
| 1997 | 38.04% | 42% | 12.35% | 14% | 33.03% | 24% |
| 1998 | 37.72% | 42% | 11.76% | 14% | 29.37% | 24% |
| 1999 | 40.36% | 42% | 14.04% | 14% | 30.87% | 24% |
| 2000 | 43.69% | 42% | 17.83% | 14% | 35.79% | 24% |
| 2001 | 45.98% | 50% | 17.90% | 20% | 34.91% | 31% |
| 2002 | 49.66% | 50% | 20.09% | 20% | 37.29% | 31% |
| 2003 | 49.18% | 50% | 19.38% | 20% | 34.12% | 31% |
| 2004 | 52.71% | 50% | 22.14% | 20% | 37.54% | 31% |
| 2005 | 54.39% | 52% | 24.21% | 22% | 44.38% | 37% |
| 2006 | 56.34% | 53% | 25.85% | 23% | 46.34% | 38% |
| 2007 | 55.47% | 55% | 24.76% | 25% | 46.45% | 38% |
| 2008 | 55.24% | 56% | 25.50% | 27% | 45.39% | 39% |
| **Alt-A Originations** | | | | | | |
| 1999 | 48.83% | 42% | 24.17% | 14% | 37.41% | 24% |
| 2000 | 40.61% | 42% | 18.74% | 14% | 41.03% | 24% |
| 2001 | 39.05% | 50% | 16.41% | 20% | 40.66% | 31% |
| 2002 | 42.77% | 50% | 18.13% | 20% | 40.08% | 31% |
| 2003 | 42.42% | 50% | 16.81% | 20% | 37.34% | 31% |
| 2004 | 44.13% | 50% | 18.56% | 20% | 40.08% | 31% |
| 2005 | 43.12% | 52% | 18.57% | 22% | 45.36% | 37% |
| 2006 | 40.43% | 53% | 18.09% | 23% | 46.40% | 38% |
| 2007 | 39.02% | 55% | 17.29% | 25% | 50.29% | 38% |
| 2008 | 42.37% | 56% | 18.52% | 27% | 42.10% | 39% |
| **PLS Backed by Subprime** | | | | | | |
| 2003 | 51.43% | 50% | 19.57% | 20% | 47.09% | 31% |
| 2004 ^ | | | | | | |
| 2005 | 50.95% | 52% | 19.86% | 22% | 61.13% | 37% |
| 2006 | 60.63% | 53% | 23.51% | 23% | 60.12% | 38% |
| 2007 | 52.96% | 55% | 19.21% | 25% | 54.55% | 38% |
| 2008 | 51.42% | 56% | 17.68% | 27% | 64.45% | 39% |

*% of unit financed that qualified for base goals.
^ Not included in housing goals scoring in 2004

Table 5 also shows that ordinary subprime loans, Alt-A loans and PMBS backed by subprime loans were not always sufficient to meet the AH goals. For

---

[100] Fannie Mae, disk produced for FCIC, April 7, 2010. Throughout this analysis, I have not discussed the GSEs' compliance with the "Underserved Base Goal," which is included in this table. The Underserved Base Goal applied mostly to minorities and involved a different set of lending decisions than the LMI goal and the Special Affordable Goal.

this reason, Fannie developed special categories of loans in which the firm waived some of its regular underwriting requirements in order to supplement what they were getting from higher quality NTMs. The two principal categories were My Community Mortgage (MCM) and Expanded Approval (EA). In many cases, these two categories enabled Fannie to meet the AH goals, but at the cost of much higher delinquency rates than occurred among higher quality NTMs they acquired. As the years progressed and the AH goals increased, Fannie had to acquire increasing numbers of loans in these categories, and as shown in Table 6 these increasing numbers also exhibited increasing delinquency rates:

Table 6.[101] Higher Risk Loans Produced Higher Delinquency Rates at Fannie Mae

| Goals by Vintage | | Loan Count | Serious Delinquency Rate |
|---|---|---|---|
| 2004 & Prior | EA/MCM & Housing Goals | 115,686 | 17.59% |
| 2005 | EA/MCM & Housing Goals | 56,822 | 22.35% |
| 2006 | EA/MCM & Housing Goals | 110,539 | 25.19% |
| 2007 | EA/MCM & Housing Goals | 224, 513 | 29.70% |

Just how desperate Fannie and Freddie were to meet their AH goals is revealed by Fannie's behavior in 2004. As reported in the *American Banker* on May 13, 2005, "A House Financial Services Committee report shared with lawmakers Thursday accused Fannie Mae and Freddie Mac of engaging over several years in a series of dubious transactions to meet their affordable-housing goals…The report cited several large transactions entered into by Fannie under which sellers were allowed to repurchase loans without recourse. For example, it said that in September 2003, Fannie bought the option to buy up to $12 billion of multifamily mortgage loans from Washington Mutual, Inc., for a fee of $2 million, the report said. Under the agreement, the GSE permitted WaMu to repurchase the loans…' This was the largest multifamily transaction ever undertaken by Fannie Mae and was critical for Fannie Mae to reach the affordable-housing goals, the report said."[102]

A clearer statement of what happened here is contained in WaMu's 10-K for 2003. Freddie had engaged in a similar but larger transaction with WaMu in 2003, reported as follows in WaMu's 10-K dated December 31, 2003:

> Other noninterest income increased in 2003 compared with 2002 partially due to fees paid to the Company [WaMu] by the Federal Home Loan Mortgage Corporation ("FHLMC" or Freddie Mac"). The Company received $100 million in nonrefundable fees to induce the Company to swap approximately $6 billion of multi-family loans for 100% of the beneficial interest in those loans in the form of mortgage-backed securities issued by Freddie Mac. Since the Company has the unilateral right to collapse the securities after one year, the Company has effectively retained control over the loans. Accordingly, the assets continue to be accounted for and reported as loans. This transaction was undertaken by Freddie Mac in order to facilitate fulfilling its 2003 affordable housing goals as set by the Department of Housing and Urban Development.

Fannie and Freddie were both paying holders of mortgages to temporarily transfer to them possession of goal-qualifying loans that the GSEs could use to satisfy the AH goals for the year 2003. After the end of the year, the seller had an

---

[101] Fannie Mae, "GSE Credit Losses," presentation to House Financial Services Committee, April 16, 2010.

[102] Rob Blackwell, "Two GSEs Cut Corners to Hit Goals, Report Says," *American Banker*, May 13, 2005, p.1.

absolute right to reacquire these loans. There can be little doubt, then, that as early as 2003, Fannie and Freddie were under so much pressure to find the subprime or other loans that they needed to meet their affordable housing obligations that they were willing to pay substantial sums to window-dress their reports to HUD.

## 3. THE AFFORDABLE HOUSING GOALS WERE THE SOLE REASON THAT THE GSEs' ACQUIRED SO MANY NTMs

Up to this point, we have seen that HUD's policy was to reduce underwriting standards in order to make mortgage credit more readily available to low-income borrowers, and that Fannie and Freddie not only took the AH goals seriously but were willing to go to extraordinary lengths to make sure that they met them. Nevertheless, it seems to have become an accepted idea in some quarters—including in the Commission majority's report—that Fannie and Freddie bought large numbers of subprime and Alt-A loans between 2004 and 2007 in order to recover the market share they had lost to subprime lenders such as Countrywide or Wall Street, or to make profits. Although there is no evidence whatever for this belief—and a great deal of evidence to the contrary—it has become another urban myth, repeated so often in books, blogs and other media that it has attained a kind of reality.[103]

The formulations of the idea vary a bit. As noted earlier, HUD has claimed—absurdly, in light of its earlier efforts to reduce mortgage underwriting standards—that the GSEs were "chasing the nonprime market" or "chasing market share and profits," principally between 2004 and 2007. The inference, all too easily accepted, is that this is another example of private greed doing harm, but it is clear that HUD was simply trying to evade its own culpability for using the AH goals to degrade the GSEs' mortgage underwriting standards over the 15 year period between 1992 and 2007. The Commission majority also adopted a version of this idea in its report, blaming the GSEs' loosening of their underwriting standards on a desire to please stock market analysts and investors, as well as to increase management compensation. None of HUD's statements about its efforts to reduce underwriting standards managed to make it into the Commission majority's report, which relied entirely on the idea that the GSEs' underwriting standards were reduced by their desire to "follow Wall Street and other lenders in [the] rush for fool's gold."

These claims place the blame for Fannie and Freddie's insolvency—and the huge number of low quality mortgages in the U.S. financial system immediately prior to the financial crisis—on the firms' managements. They absolve the government, particularly HUD, from responsibility. The GSEs' managements made plenty of mistakes—and won't be defended here—but taking risks to compete for market share was not something they actually did. Because of the AH goals, Fannie and

---

[103] See, e.g., Barry Ritholtz, "Get Me ReWrite!" in *Bailout Nation, Bailouts, Credit, Real Estate, Really, Really Bad Calls*, May 13, 2010, http://www.ritholtz.com/blog/2010/05/rewriting-the-causes-of-the-credit-crisis/print/; Dean Baker, "NPR Tells Us that Republicans Believe that Fannie and Freddie Caused the Crash" *Beat the Press Blog,* Center for Economic and Policy Research http://www.cepr.net/index.php/blogs/beat-the-press/npr-tells-us-that-republicans-believe-that-fannie-and-freddie-caused-the-crash; Charles Duhigg, "Roots of the Crisis," *Frontline,* Feb 17, 2009, http://www.pbs.org/wgbh/pages/frontline/meltdown/themes/howwegothere.html.

Freddie were major buyers of NTMs well before Wall Street firms and the subprime lenders who came to dominate the business entered the subprime PMBS market in any significant way. Moreover, the GSEs did not (indeed, could not) appreciably increase their purchases of NTMs during the years 2005 and 2006, when they had lost market share to the real PMBS issuers, Countrywide and other subprime lenders.

The following discussion addresses each of the claims about the GSEs' motives in turn, and in the end will show that the only plausible motive for their actions was their effort to comply with HUD's AH goals.

## Did the GSEs acquire NTMs to "compete for market share" with Wall Street or others?

The idea that Fannie and Freddie were newcomers to the purchase of NTMs between 2004 and 2007, and reduced their underwriting standards so they could compete for market share with Wall Street or others, is wrong. As shown in Table 7, the GSEs' acquisition of subprime loans and other NTMs began in the 1990s, when they first became subject to the AH goals. Research shows that, in contravention of their earlier standards, the GSEs began to acquire high loan-to-value (LTV) mortgages in 1994, shortly after the enactment of the GSE Act and the imposition of the AH goals, and by 2001—before the PMBS market reached $100 billion in annual issuances—the GSEs had already acquired at least $700 billion in NTMs, including over $400 billion in subprime loans.[104] Far from following Wall Street or anyone else into subprime loans between 2004 and 2007, the GSEs had become the largest buyers of subprime and other NTMs many years before the PMBS market began to develop. Given these facts, it would be more accurate to say that Wall Street and the subprime lenders who later came to dominate the PMBS market followed the GSEs into subprime lending. Table 7 does not show any significant increase in the GSEs' acquisition of NTMs from 2004 to 2007, and the amount of subprime PMBS they acquired during this period actually decreased. This is consistent with the fact—outlined below—that the GSEs did not make any special effort to compete for market share during these years.

---

[104] Pinto, "Government Housing Policies in the Lead-up to the Financial Crisis: A Forensic Study," Chart 52, p.148, http://www.aei.org/docLib/Government-Housing-Policies-Financial-Crisis-Pinto-102110.pdf.

Table 7.[105] GSE Purchases of Subprime and Alt-A loans

| $ in billions | 1997 | 1998 | 1999 | 2000 | 2001 | 2002 | 2003 | 2004 | 2005 | 2006 | 2007 | 1997-2007 |
|---|---|---|---|---|---|---|---|---|---|---|---|---|
| Subprime PMBS | $3* | $18* | $18* | $11* | $16* | $38 | $82 | $180 | $169 | $110 | $62 | $707 |
| Subprime loans** | $37 | $83 | $74 | $65 | $159 | $206 | $262 | $144 | $139 | $138 | $195 | $1,502 |
| Alt-A PMBS | Unk. | Unk, | Unk. | Unk. | Unk. | $18 | $12 | $30 | $36 | $43 | $15 | $154 |
| Alt-A loans*** | Unk. | Unk, | Unk. | Unk. | Unk. | $66 | $77 | $64 | $77 | $157 | $178 | $619 |
| High LTV loans**** | $32 | $44 | $62 | $61 | $84 | $87 | $159 | $123 | $126 | $120 | $226 | $1,124 |
| Total***** | $72 | $145 | $154 | $137 | $259 | $415 | $592 | $541 | $547 | $568 | $676 | $4,106 |

*Total purchases of PMBS for 1997-2001 are known. Subprime purchases for these years were estimated based upon the percentage that subprime PMBS constituted of total PMBS purchases in 2002 (57%).
**Loans where borrower's FICO <660.
*** Fannie and Freddie used their various affordable housing programs and individual lender variance programs (many times in conjunction with their automated underwriting systems once these came into general use in the late-1990s) to approve loans with Alt-A characteristics. However, they generally did not classify these loans as Alt-A. Classification as Alt-A started in the early-1990s. There is an unknown number of additional loans that had higher debt ratios, reduced reserves, loosened credit requirements, expanded seller contributions, etc. The volume of these loans is not included.
****Loans with an original LTV or original combined LTV >90% (given industry practices, this effectively means >=95%). Data to estimate loans with CLTV.>90% is unavailable prior to 2003. Amounts for 2003-2007 are grossed up by 60% to account for the impact of loans with a CLTV >90%. These estimates are based on disclosures by Fannie and Freddie that at the end of 2007 their total exposures to loans with an LTV or CLTV >90% was 50% and 75% percent respectively higher than their exposure to loans with an LTV >90%. Fannie reports on p. 128 of its 2007 10-K that 15% of its entire book had an original combined LTV >90%. Its Original LTV percentage >90% (without counting the impact of any 2nd mortgage simultaneously negotiated) is 9.9%. Freddie reports on p60 of its Q2:2008 10 Q that 14% of its portfolio had an original combined LTV >90%. Its OLTV percentage >90% (without counting any simultaneous 2nd) is 8%. While Fannie and Freddie purchased only the first mortgage, these loans had the same or higher incidence of default as a loan with an LTV of >90%.
*****Since loans may have more than one characteristic, they may appear in more than one category. Totals are not adjusted to take this into account.

The claim that the GSEs loosened their underwriting standards in order to compete specifically with "Wall Street" can be easily dismissed—unless the Commission majority and others who have made this statement are including Countrywide (which was based in California) or other subprime lenders in the term "Wall Street." Assuming, however, that the Commission majority and other commentators have been using the term Wall Street to apply to the commercial and investment banks that operate in the financial markets of New York, the data shows that Wall Street was not a significant participant in the subprime PMBS market between 2004 and 2007 or at any time before or after those dates. The top five players in 2004 were subprime lenders Ameriquest ($55 billion) and Countrywide ($40 billion), followed by Lehman Brothers ($27 billion), GMAC RFC ($26 billion), and New Century ($22 billion). Other than Lehman, some other Wall Street firms were scattered through the list of the top 25, but were not significant players as a group.

In 2005, the biggest year for subprime issuances, the five leaders were the same, and the total for all Wall Street institutions was $137 billion, or about 27

---

[105] Id.

percent of the $508 billion issued that year.[106] In 2006, Lehman had dropped out of the top five and Countrywide had taken over the leadership among the issuers, but Wall Street's share had not significantly changed. By the middle of 2007, the PMBS market had declined to such a degree that the market share numbers were meaningless. However, in that year the GSEs' market share in NTMs increased because they had to continue buying NTMs—even though others had defaulted or left the business—in order to comply with the AH goals. Accordingly, if Fannie had ever loosened its lending standards to compete with some group, that group was not Wall Street.

The next question is whether the GSEs loosened their underwriting standards to compete with Countrywide, Ameriquest and the other subprime lenders who were the dominant players in the PMBS market between 2004 and 2007. Again, the answer seems clearly to be no. The subprime PMBS market was very small until 2002, when for the first time it exceeded $100 billion and reached $134 billion in subprime PMBS issuances.[107] Yet, Table 7 shows that in 2002 alone the GSEs bought $206 billion in subprime loans, more than the total amount securitized by all the subprime lenders and others combined in that year.

The discussion of internal documents that follows will focus almost exclusively on Fannie Mae. The Commission concentrated its investigation on Fannie and it was from Fannie that the Commission received the most complete set of internal documents.

By the early 2000s, Countrywide had succeeded in creating an integrated system of mortgage distribution that included originating, packaging, issuing and underwriting NTMs through PMBS. Other subprime lenders, as noted above, were also major issuers, but they sold their PMBS through Wall Street firms that were functioning as underwriters.

The success of Countrywide and other subprime lenders as distributors of NTMs through PMBS was troubling to Fannie for two reasons. First, Countrywide had been Fannie's largest supplier of subprime mortgages; the fact that it could now securitize mortgages it formerly sold to Fannie meant that Fannie would have more difficulty finding subprime mortgages that were AH goals-eligible. In addition, the GSEs knew that their support in Congress depended heavily on meeting the AH goals and "leading the market" in lending to low income borrowers. In 2005 and 2006, the Bush administration and a growing number of Republicans in Congress were calling for tighter regulation of Fannie and Freddie, and the GSEs needed allies in Congress to hold this off. The fact that subprime lenders were taking an increasing market share in these years—suggesting that the GSEs were no longer the most important sources of low income mortgage credit—was thus a matter of great concern to Fannie's management. Without strong support among the Democrats in Congress, there was a significant chance that the Republican Congress would enact tougher regulatory legislation. This was expressed at Fannie as concern about a loss of "relevance," and provoked wide-ranging consideration within the firm about how they could regain their leadership role in low-income lending.

Nevertheless, although Fannie had strong reasons for wanting to compete for market share with Countrywide and others, it did not have either the operational

---

[106] Inside Mortgage Finance, *The 2009 Mortgage Market Statistical Annual—Volume II*, pp. 139 and 140.

[107] Inside Mortgage Finance, *The 2009 Market Statistical Annual—Volume II*, p.143.

or financial capacity to do so. In the end, Fannie was unable to take any significant action during the key years 2005 and 2006 that would regain market share from the subprime lenders or anyone else. They reduced their underwriting standards to the degree necessary to keep pace with the increasing AH goals, but not to go significantly beyond those requirements.

In a key memo dated June 27, 2005 (the "Crossroads" memo), Tom Lund, Executive Vice President for Single Family Business, addressed the question of Fannie's loss of market share and how this share position could be regained. The date of this memo is important. It shows that even in the middle of 2005 there was still a debate going on within Fannie about *whether* to compete for market share with Countrywide and the other subprime issuers. No such competition had actually begun. Lund starts the discussion in the memo by saying "We are at a strategic crossroad...[his ellipses] We face two stark choices: 1. Stay the Course [or] 2. Meet the Market Where the Market Is". "Staying the course" meant trying to maintain the mortgage quality standards that Fannie had generally followed up to that point (except as necessary to meet HUD's AH goals). "Meeting the market" meant competing with Countrywide and others not only by acquiring substantially *more* NTMs than the AH goals required, but also by acquiring much *riskier* mortgages than Fannie—which specialized in fixed rate mortgages—had been buying up to that time.

These riskier potential acquisitions would have included much larger numbers of Option ARMs (involving negative amortization) and other loans involving multiple (or "layered") risks with which Fannie had no prior experience. Thus, Lund noted that to compete in this business Fannie lacked "capabilities and infrastructure...knowledge... willingness to compete on price..[and] a value proposition for subprime." His conclusion was as stark as the choice: *"Realistically, we are not in a position to 'Meet the Market' today."* "Therefore," Lund continued, *"we recommend that we: Pursue a 'Stay the Course' strategy and test whether market changes are cyclical vs secular."*[108] [emphasis supplied]

In the balance of the Crossroads memo, Lund notes that subprime and Alt-A loans are driving the "leakage" of "goals rich" products to PMBS issuers. He points out the severity of the loss of market share, but never suggests that this changes his view that Fannie was unequipped to compete with Countrywide and others at that time. According to an internal FCIC staff investigation, dated March 31, 2010, other senior officials—Robert Levin (Executive Vice President and Chief Business Officer), Kenneth Bacon (Executive Vice President for Housing and Community Development), and Pamela Johnson (Senior Vice President for Single Family Business)—all concurred that Fannie should follow Lund's recommendation to "stay the course."

There is no indication in any of Fannie's documents after June 2005 that Lund's "Stay the Course" recommendation was ever changed or challenged during 2005 or 2006—the period when Fannie and Freddie were supposed to have begun to acquire large numbers of NTMs (beyond what was required to meet the AH goals) in order to compete with Countrywide or (in some telling) Wall Street.

Thus, in June 2006, one year after the Lund Crossroads memo, Stephen B. Ashley, then the chairman of the board, told Fannie's senior executives: "2006 is a

---

[108] Tom Lund, "Single Family Guarantee Business: Facing Strategic Crossroads" June 27, 2005.

transition year. To be sure, there are still issues to resolve. The consent order with OFHEO [among other things, the order raised capital requirements temporarily] is demanding. And from a strategy standpoint, *it is clear that until we have eliminated operations and control weaknesses, taking on more risk or opening new lines of business will be viewed dimly by our regulators.*"[109] [emphasis supplied] So, again, we have confirmation that Fannie's top officials did not believe that the firm was in any position—in the middle of 2006—to take on the additional risk that would be necessary s to compete with Countrywide and other subprime lenders that were selling PMBS backed by subprime and other NTMs.

Moreover, there is very strong financially-based evidence that Fannie either never tried or was never financially able to compete for market share with Countrywide and other subprime lenders from 2004 to 2007. For example, set out below are Fannie's key financial data, published by OFHEO, its former regulator, in early 2008.[110]

Table 8. Fannie Mae Financial Highlights

| Earnings Performance: | 2003 | 2004 | 2005 | 2006 | 2007 |
|---|---|---|---|---|---|
| Net Income ($ billions) | 8.1 | 5.0 | 6.3 | 4.2 | -2.1 |
| Net Interest Income ($ billions) | 19.5 | 18.1 | 11.5 | 6.8 | 4.6 |
| Guarantee Fees ($ billions) | 3.4 | 3.8 | 4.0 | 4.3 | 5.1 |
| Net Interest margin (%) | 2.12 | 1.86 | 1.31 | 0.85 | 0.57 |
| Average Guarantee Fee (bps) | 21.9 | 21.8 | 22.3 | 22.2 | 23.7 |
| Return on Common Equity (%) | 27.6 | 16.6 | 19.5 | 11.3 | -8.3 |
| Dividend Payout Ratio (%) | 20.8 | 42.1 | 17.2 | 32.4 | N/M |

Table 8 shows that Fannie's average guarantee fee *increased* during the period from 2003 to 2007. To understand the significance of this, it is necessary to understand the way the mortgage business works. Most of Fannie's guarantee business—the business that competed with securitizations of PMBS by Countrywide and others—was done with wholesale sellers of mortgage pools. In these deals, the wholesaler or issuer, a Countrywide or a Wells Fargo, would assemble a pool of mortgages and look for a guaranty mechanism that would offer the best pricing. In the case of a Fannie MBS, the key issue was the GSEs' guarantee fee, because that determined how much of the profit the issuer would be able to retain. In the case of a PMBS issue, it was the amount and cost of the credit enhancement needed to attain a AAA rating for a large percentage of the securities backed by the mortgage pool.

The issuer had a choice of securitizing through Fannie, Freddie or one of the Wall Street underwriters. Thus, if Fannie wanted to compete with the private issuers for subprime and other loans there was only one way to do it—by reducing its guarantee fees (called "G-fees" at Fannie and Freddie) and in this way making itself a more attractive outlet than using a Wall Street underwriter. The fact that Fannie does not appear to have done so is strong evidence that it never tried to compete for share with Countrywide and the other subprime issuers after the date of the Crossroads memo in June 2005.

The OFHEO financial summary also shows that Fannie in reality had very

---

[109] Stephen B. Ashley Fannie Mae Chairman, remarks at senior management meeting, June 27, 2006.

[110] OFHEO, "Mortgage Markets and the Enterprises in 2007," pp. 33-34.

little flexibility to compete by lowering its G-fees. Its net income and its return on equity were all declining quickly during this period, and a cut in its G-fees would have hastened this decline.

Finally, there are Fannie's own reports about its acquisitions of subprime loans. According to Fannie's 10-K reports for 2004 (which, as restated, covered periods through 2006) and 2007, Fannie's acquisition of subprime loans barely increased from 2004 through 2007. These are the numbers:

Table 9.[111] Fannie Mae's Acquisition of Subprime Loans, 2004-2007

|  | 2004 | 2005 | 2006 | 2007 |
|---|---|---|---|---|
| FICO <620 | 5% | 5% | 6% | 6% |
| FICO 620-<660 | 11% | 11% | 11% | 12% |

These percentages are consistent with Fannie's effort to comply with the gradual increase in the AH goals during the years 2004 through 2007; they are not consistent with an effort to substantially increase its purchases of subprime mortgages in order to compete with firms like Countrywide that were growing their market share through securitizing subprime and other loans.

Finally, Fannie's 2005 10-K (which, as restated and filed in May 2007, also covered 2005 and 2006), contains a statement similar to that made in 2006, confirming that the GSE made no effort to compete for subprime loans (except as necessary to meet the AH goals), and that in fact it lost market share by declining to do so in 2004, 2005 and 2006:

> [I]n recent years, an increasing proportion of single-family mortgage loan originations has consisted of non-traditional mortgages such as interest-only mortgages, negative-amortizing mortgages and sub-prime mortgages, and demand for traditional 30-year fixed-rate mortgages has decreased. *We did not participate in large amounts of these non-traditional mortgages in 2004, 2005 and 2006* because we determined that the pricing offered for these mortgages often offered insufficient compensation for the additional credit risk associated with these mortgages. *These trends and our decision not to participate in large amounts of these non-traditional mortgages contributed to a significant loss in our share of new single-family mortgages-related securities issuances to private-label issuers during this period, with our market share decreasing from 45.0% in 2003 to 29.2% in 2004, 23.5% in 2005 and 23.7 in 2006.*[112] [emphasis supplied]

Accordingly, despite losing market share to Countrywide and others in 2004, 2005 and 2006, Fannie did not attempt to acquire unusual numbers of subprime loans in order to regain this share. Instead, it continued to acquire only the subprime and other NTM loans that were necessary to meet the AH goals. That the AH goals were Fannie's sole motive for acquiring NTMs is shown by the firm's actions after the PMBS market collapsed in 2007. At that point, Fannie's market share began to rise as Countrywide and others could not continue to issue PMBS. Nevertheless, despite the losses on subprime loans that were beginning to show up in the markets, Fannie continued to buy NTMs until they were taken over by the government in

---

[111] Fannie Mae, 2004 10-K. These totals do not include Fannie's purchases of subprime PMBS. http://www.fanniemae.com/ir/pdf/sec/2004/2004_form10K.pdf;jsessionid=N3RRJCZPD5SOVJ2FQSH SFGI, p.141 and Fannie's 2007 10-K, http://www.fanniemae.com/ir/pdf/sec/2008/form10k_022708.pdf ;jsessionid=N3RRJCZPD5SOVJ2FQSHSFGI, p.127.

[112] Fannie Mae, 2005 10-K, p.37.

September 2008. The reason for this nearly reckless behavior is obvious—they were still subject to the AH goals, which were increasing through this period. If they had only acquired these NTMs to compete with Countrywide and others for market share the competition was already over; their competitors had abandoned the field. But the fact is that Fannie did not—or could not—increase its market share between 2004 and 2006 shows without question that market share was not the reason they had acquired so many NTMs by the time they failed in September 2008.

Beleaguered by accounting problems, suffering diminished profitability, and lacking the capability to evaluate the risks of the new kinds of mortgages they would have to buy, Fannie had no option but to stay the course they had been following for 15 years. The NTMs they bought during the period from 2004 to 2007 were acquired to comply with the AH goals and not to increase their market share—as much as Fannie might have preferred to do so. Fannie's market share finally did increase in 2007, when the asset-backed market collapsed, Countrywide weakened, and neither Countrywide nor anyone else could continue to securitize mortgages. In a report to the board of directors on October 16, 2007, Mudd reported that Fannie's market share, which was 20 percent of the whole market at the beginning of 2007, had risen to 42 percent.[113]

That leaves one other possibility—that Fannie and Freddie were buying NTMs because they were profitable. That issue is addressed in the next section.

## Did Fannie acquire NTMs because these loans were profitable?

From time to time, commentators on the GSEs have suggested that the GSEs' real motive for acquiring NTMs was not that they had to comply with the AH goals, but that they were seeking the profits these risky loans produced. This could have been true in the 1990s, but after the major increase in the AH goals in 2000 Fannie began to recognize that complying with the goals was reducing the firm's profitability. By 2007, Fannie was asking for relief from the goals.

The following table, drawn from a FHFA publication, shows the applicable AH goals over the period from 1996 through 2008 and the GSEs' success in meeting them.

---

[113] Fannie Mae, Minutes of a Meeting of the Board of Directors, October 16, 2007, p.18.

Table 10.[114] GSEs' Success in Meeting Affordable Housing Goals, 1996-2007

| | 1996 | 1997 | 1998 | 1999 | 2000 | 2001 | 2002 | 2003 | 2004 | 2005 | 2006 | 2007 | 2008 |
|---|---|---|---|---|---|---|---|---|---|---|---|---|---|
| **Low & Mod Housing Goals** | **40%** | **42%** | **42%** | **42%** | **42%** | **50%** | **50%** | **50%** | **50%** | **52%** | **53%** | **55%** | **56%** |
| Fannie Actual | 45% | 45% | 44% | 46% | 50% | 51% | 52% | 52% | 53% | 55% | 57% | 56% | 54% |
| Freddie Actual | 41% | 43% | 43% | 46% | 50% | 53% | 50% | 51% | 52% | 54% | 56% | 56% | 51% |
| **Special Affordable Goal** | **12%** | **14%** | **14%** | **14%** | **14%** | **20%** | **20%** | **20%** | **20%** | **22%** | **23%** | **25%** | **27%** |
| Fannie Actual | 15% | 17% | 15% | 18% | 19% | 22% | 21% | 21% | 24% | 24% | 28% | 27% | 26% |
| Freddie Actual | 14% | 15% | 16% | 18% | 21% | 23% | 20% | 21% | 23% | 26% | 26% | 26% | 23% |
| **Underserved Goal** | **21%** | **24%** | **24%** | **24%** | **24%** | **31%** | **31%** | **31%** | **31%** | **37%** | **38%** | **38%** | **39%** |
| Fannie Actual | 25% | 29% | 27% | 27% | 31% | 33% | 33% | 32% | 32% | 41% | 43% | 43% | 39% |
| Freddie Actual | 28% | 26% | 26% | 27% | 29% | 32% | 31% | 33% | 34% | 43% | 44% | 43% | 38% |

As the table shows, Fannie and Freddie exceeded the AH goals virtually each year, but not by significant margins. They simply kept pace with the increases in the goals as these requirements came into force over the years. This alone suggests that they did not increase their purchases in order to earn profits. If that was their purpose they would have substantially exceeded the goals, since their financial advantages (low financing costs and low capital requirements) allowed them to pay more for the mortgages they wanted than any of their competitors. As HUD noted in 2000: "Because the GSEs have a funding advantage over other market participants, they have the ability to underprice their competitors and increase their market share."[115]

As early as 1999, there were clear concerns at Fannie about how the 50 percent LMI goal—which HUD had signaled as its next move—would be met. In a June 15, 1999, memorandum,[116] four Fannie staff members proposed three categories of rules changes that would enable Fannie to meet the goals more easily: (i) persuade HUD to change the goals accounting (what goes into the numerator and denominator); (ii) enter other businesses where the pickings might be goals-rich, such as manufactured housing and, significantly, Alt-A and subprime ("Efforts to expand into Alt-A and A-markets (the highest grade of subprime lending) should also yield incremental business that will have a salutary effect on our low-and moderate-income score"); and (iii) persuade HUD to adopt different methods of goals scoring.

By 2000, Fannie was effectively in competition with banks that were required to make mortgage loans under CRA to roughly the same population of low-income borrowers targeted in HUD's AH goals. Rather than selling their CRA loans to Fannie and Freddie, banks and S&Ls had begun to retain the loans in portfolio. In a presentation in November 2000, Barry Zigas, a Senior Vice President of Fannie, noted that "Our own anecdotal evidence suggests that this increase [in banks' and

---

[114] FHFA Mortgage Market Note 10-2, http://www.fhfa.gov/webfiles/15408/Housing%20Goals%201996-2009%2002-01.pdf.pdf.

[115] http://frwebgate.access.gpo.gov/cgi-bin/getdoc.cgi?dbname=2000_register&docid=page+65093-65142.

[116] Bell, Kinney, Kunde and Weech, through Zigas and Marks internal memo Frank Raines, "RE: HUD Housing Goals Options," June 15, 1999.

S&Ls' holding loans in portfolio] is due in part to below-market CRA products."[117] In other words, banks and S&Ls subject to CRA were making mortgage loans at below market interest rates, and thus could not sell them without taking losses. This was troubling for Fannie because it meant that in order to capture these loans they would have to increase what they were willing to pay for these loans. Doing so would underprice the risks they would be assuming.

It is important to recognize what was happening. Fannie, and the banks and S&Ls under CRA, were now competing for the same kinds of NTMs, and were doing so by lowering their mortgage underwriting standards and adding flexibilities and subsidies. Simply as a result of supply and demand, all of the participants in this competition were required to pay higher prices for these increasingly risky mortgages. The banks and S&Ls that acquired these loans could not sell them, without taking a loss, when market interest rates were higher than the rates on the mortgages. This is the first indication in the documents that the FCIC received from Fannie that competition for subprime loans among the GSEs, banks, S&Ls, and FHA was causing the underpricing of risk—one of the principal causes of the mortgage meltdown and thus the financial crisis.

In January 2003, Fannie began planning for how to confront HUD before the next round of increases in the AH goals, expected to occur in 2004. In an "Action Plan for the Housing Goals Rewrite," dated January 22, 2003, Fannie staff reviewed a number of options, and concluded that "Fannie should strongly oppose: goals increases and new subgoals." (Slide 35)[118]

In March 2003, as Fannie prepared for new increases in the AH goals, its staff prepared a presentation, perhaps for HUD or for policy defense in public forums. The apparent purpose was to show that the goals should not be increased significantly in 2004. Slide 5 stated:

> In 2002, Fannie Mae exceeded all our goals for the 9th straight year. But it was probably the most challenging environment we've ever faced. Meeting the goals required heroic 4th quarter efforts on the part of many across the company. Vacations were cancelled. The midnight oil burned. Moreover, the challenge freaked out the business side of the house. Especially because the tenseness around meeting the goals meant that we considered not doing deals—not fulfilling our liquidity function—*and did deals at risks and prices we would not have otherwise done.*[119] [emphasis supplied]

By September 2004, it was becoming clear that continuing increases in the AH goals were having a major adverse effect on Fannie's profitability. In a memorandum to Brian Graham (another Fannie official), Paul Weech, Director of Market Research and Policy Development, wrote: "Meeting the goals in difficult markets imposes significant costs on the Company and potentially causes market-distorting behaviors. In 1998, 2002, and 2003 especially, the Company has had to pursue certain transactions as much for housing goals attainment as for the economics of the transaction."[120]

In a June 2005 presentation entitled "Costs and Benefits of Mission

[117] Barry Zigas, "Fannie Mae and Minority Lending: Assessment and Action Plan" Presentation, November 16, 2000.

[118] Fannie Mae, "Action Plan for the Housing Goals Rewrite," January 22, 2003.

[119] Fannie Mae, "The HUD Housing Goals," March 2003.

[120] Fannie Mae internal memo, Paul Weech to Brian Graham, "RE: Mission Legislation," September 3, 2004.

Activities,"[121] the authors noted in slide 10 that AH goal costs had risen from $2,632,500 in 2000 to $13,447,500 in 2003. Slide 17 is entitled: "Meeting Future HUD Goals Appear Quite Daunting and Potentially Costly" and reports, "Based on 2003 experience where goal acquisition costs (relative to Fannie Mae model fees) cost between $65 per goals unit in the first quarter to $370 per unit in the fourth quarter, meeting the shortfall could cost the company $6.5-$36.5 million to purchase sufficient units." The presentation concludes (slide 20): "Cost of mission activities— explicit and implicit—over the 2000-2004 period likely averaged approximately $200 million per year."

Earlier, I noted the efforts of Fannie and Freddie to window-dress their records for HUD by temporarily acquiring loans that would comply with the AH goals, while giving the seller the option to reacquire the loans at a later time. In 2005, we begin to see efforts by Fannie's staff to accomplish the same window-dressing in another way--delaying acquisitions of non-goal-eligible loans so Fannie can meet the AH goals in that year; we also see the first efforts to calculate systematically the effect of goal-compliance on Fannie's profitability. In a presentation dated September 30, 2005, Barry Zigas, the key Fannie official on affordable housing, outlined a "business deferral option." Under that initiative, Fannie would ask seven major lenders to defer until 2006 sending non-goal loans to Fannie for acquisition. This would reduce the denominator of the AH goal computation and thus bring Fannie nearer to goal compliance in the 4th quarter of 2005. The cost of the deferral alone was estimated at $30-$38 million.[122]

In a presentation to HUD on October 31, 2005, entitled "Update on Fannie Mae's Housing Goals Performance,"[123] Fannie noted several "Undesirable Tradeoffs Necessary to Meet Goals." These included significant additional credit risk, and negative returns ("Deal economics are well below target returns; some deals are producing negative returns" and "G-fees may not cover expected losses"). One of the most noteworthy points was the following: "Liquidity to Questionable Products: Buying exotic product encourages continuation of risky lending; many products present with significant risk-layering; consumers are at risk of payment shock and loss of equity; potential need to waive our responsible lending policies to get goals business."

Much of the narrative about the financial crisis posits that unscrupulous and unregulated mortgage originators tricked borrowers into taking on bad mortgages. The idea that predatory lending was a major source of the NTMs in the financial system in 2008 is a significant element of the Commission majority's report, although the Commission was never able to provide any data to support this point. This Fannie slide suggests that loans later dubbed "predatory" might actually have been made to comply with the AH goals. This possibility is suggested, too, in a message sent in 2004 to Freddie's CEO, Richard Syron, by Freddie's chief risk manager, David Andrukonis, when Syron was considering whether to authorize a "Ninja" (no income/no jobs/no assets) product that he ultimately approved. Andrukonis argued against authorizing Freddie's purchase: "The potential for the perception and reality

---

[121]  Fannie Mae, "Costs and Benefits of Mission Activities, Project Phineas," June 14, 2005.

[122]  Barry Zigas, "Housing Goals and Minority Lending," September 30, 2005.

[123]  Fannie Mae, "Update on Fannie Mae's Housing Goals Performance," Presentation to the U.S. Department of Housing and Development, October 31, 2005.

of predatory lending, with this product is great."[124] But the product was approved by Freddie, probably for the reason stated by another Freddie employee: "The Alt-A [(low doc/no doc)] business makes a contribution to our HUD goals."[125]

On May 5, 2006, a Fannie staff memo to the Single Family Business Credit Committee revealed the serious credit and financial problems Fannie was facing when acquiring subprime mortgages to meet the AH goals. The memo describes the competitive landscape, in which "product enhancements from Freddie Mac, FHA, Alt-A and subprime lenders have all contributed to increased competition for goals rich loans...On the issue of seller contributions [in which the seller of the home pays cash expenses for the buyer] even FHA has expanded their guidelines by allowing 6% contributions for LTVs up to 97% that can be used toward closing, prepaid expenses, discount points and other financing concessions."[126]

The memorandum is eye-opening for what it says about the credit risks Fannie had to take in order to get the goals-rich loans it needed to meet HUD's AH requirements for 2006. Table 11 below shows the costs of NTMs in terms of the guarantee fee (G-fee) "gap." (In order to determine whether a loan contributed to a return on equity, Fannie used a G-fee pricing model that took into account credit risk as well as a number of other factors; a G-fee "gap" was the difference between the G-fees required by the pricing model for a particular loan to contribute to a return on equity and a loan that did not.) The table in this memo shows the results for three subprime products under consideration, a 30 year fixed rate mortgage (FRM), a 5 year ARM, and 35 and 40 year fixed rate mortgages. For simplicity, this analysis will discuss only the 30 year fixed rate product. The table shows that the base product, the 30 year FRM, with *a zero* downpayment should be priced according to the model at a G-fee of 106 basis points. However, the memo reports that Fannie is actually buying loans like that at a price consistent with an annual fee of 37.50 basis points, producing a gap (or loss from the model) of 68.50 basis points. The reason the gap is so large is shown in the table: the anticipated default rate on that zero-down mortgage was *34 percent*. The table then goes on to look at other possible loan alternatives, with the following results:

---

[124] Freddie Mac, internal email, Donna Cogswell on behalf of David Andrukonis to Dick Syron, "RE: No Income/No Asset (NINA) Mortgages," September 7, 2004.

[125] Freddie Mac, internal email from Mike May to Dick Syron, "FW: FINAL NINA Memo," October 6, 2004.

[126] Fannie Mae, internal memo, Single Family Business Product Management and Development to Single Family Business Credit Committee, "RE: PMD Proposal for Increasing Housing Goal Loans," May 5, 2006, p.6.

Table 11.[127] Fannie Mae Took Losses on Higher Risk Mortgages
Necessary to Meet the Affordable Housing Goals

| Individual Enhancements (cost analysis for "base" MCM enhancement-not layered) | 30 YR FRM | | |
|---|---|---|---|
| | Model Fee | Average Default % | Gap |
| Base: 100% LTV, 20% MI | 106 | 34 | -68.50 |
| Interest First (IF) | 129 | 40 | -91.50 |
| Seller Contribution (SC) | 115 | 23 | -77.50 |
| Temporary B/D (BD) | 118 | 37 | -80.50 |
| Zero Down (ZD) | 106 | 34 | -68.50 |
| Manufactured Housing (MH) | 227 | 42 | -189.50 |

From this report, it is clear that in order to meet the AH goals Fannie had to pay up for goals-rich mortgages, taking a huge credit risk along the way.

The dismal financial results that were developing at Fannie as a result of the AH goals were also described in Fannie's 10-K report for 2006, which anticipated both losses of revenue and higher credit losses as a result of acquiring the mortgages required by the AH goals:

> [W]e have made, and continue to make, significant adjustments to our mortgage loan sourcing and purchase strategies in an effort to meet HUD's increased housing goals and new subgoals. These strategies include entering into some purchase and securitization transactions with *lower expected economic returns than our typical transactions*. We have also relaxed some of our underwriting criteria to obtain goals-qualifying mortgage loans and increased our investments in higher-risk mortgage loan products that are more likely to serve the borrowers targeted by HUD's goals and subgoals, *which could increase our credit losses*. [emphasis supplied][128]

The underlying reasons for the "lower expected returns" were reported in February 2007 in a document the FCIC received from Fannie, which noted that for 2006 the "cash flow cost" of meeting the housing goals was $140 million while the "opportunity cost" was $470 million.[129] In a report to HUD on the AH goals, dated April 11, 2007, Fannie described these costs as follows: "The largest costs [of meeting the goals] are opportunity costs of foregone revenue. In 2006, opportunity cost was about $400 million, whereas the cash flow cost was about $134 million. If opportunity cost was $0, our shareholders would be indifferent to the deal. The cash flow cost is the implied out of pocket cost."[130]

By this time, "Alignment Meetings"—in which Fannie staff considered how they would meet the AH goals—were taking place almost monthly (according to the frequency with which presentations to Alignment meetings occur in the documentary record). In an Alignment Meeting on June 22, 2007, on a "Housing Goals Forecast," three plans were considered for meeting the 2007 AH goals, even

---

[127] Id., p.8.

[128] Fannie Mae, 2006 10-K, p.146.

[129] Fannie Mae, "Business Update," presentation. "Cash flow cost" equals expected revenue minus expected loss. Expected revenue is what will be received in G-fees; expected loss includes G&A and credit losses. "Opportunity cost" is the G-fee actually charged minus the model fee—the fee that Fannie's model would impose to guarantee a mortgage of the same quality in order to earn a fair market return on capital.

[130] Fannie Mae, "Housing Goals Briefing for HUD," April 11, 2007.

though half the year was already gone. One of the plans was forecast to result in opportunity costs of $767.7 million, while the other two plans resulted in opportunity costs of $817.1 million.[131] In a Forecast meeting on July 27, 2007, a "Plan to Meet Base Goals," which probably meant the topline LMI goal including all subgoals, was placed at $1.156 billion for 2007.[132]

Finally, in a December 21, 2007, letter to Brian Montgomery, Assistant Secretary of Housing, Fannie CEO Daniel Mudd asked that, in light of the financial and economic conditions then prevailing in the country—particularly the absence of a PMBS market and the increasing number of mortgage delinquencies and defaults— HUD's AH goals for 2007 be declared "infeasible." He noted that HUD also has an obligation to "consider the financial condition of the enterprise when determining the feasibility of goals." Then he continued: "Fannie Mae submits that the company took all reasonable actions to meet the subgoals that were both financially prudent and likely to contribute to the achievement of the subgoals....*In 2006, Fannie Mae relaxed certain underwriting standards and purchased some higher risk mortgage loan products in an effort to meet the housing goals.* The company continued to purchase higher risk loans into 2007, and believes these efforts to acquire goals-rich loans are partially responsible for increasing credit losses."[133] [emphasis supplied]

This statement confirms two facts that are critical on the question of why Fannie (and Freddie) acquired so many high risk loans in 2006 and earlier years: first, the companies were trying to meet the AH goals established by HUD and not because these loans were profitable. It also shows that the efforts of HUD and others— including the Commission majority in its report—to blame the managements of Fannie and Freddie for purchasing the loans that ultimately dragged them to insolvency is misplaced.

Finally, in a July 2009 report, the Federal Housing Finance Agency (FHFA, the GSEs' new regulator, replacing OFHEO), noted that Fannie and Freddie both followed the practice of cross-subsidizing the subprime and Alt-A loans that they acquired:

> Although Fannie Mae and Freddie Mac consider model-derived estimates of cost in determining the single-family guarantee fees they charge, their pricing often subsidizes their guarantees on some mortgages using higher returns they expect to earn on guarantees of other loans. In both 2007 and 2008, cross-subsidization in single-family guarantee fees charged by the Enterprises was evident across product types, credit score categories, and LTV ratio categories. In each case, there were cross-subsidies from mortgages that posed lower credit risk on average to loans that posed higher credit risk. The greatest estimated subsidies generally went to the highest-risk mortgages.[134]

The higher risk mortgages were the ones most needed by Fannie and Freddie to meet the AH goals. Needless to say, there is no need to cross-subsidize the G-fees of loans that are acquired because they are profitable.

Accordingly, both market share and profitability must be excluded as reasons that Fannie (and Freddie) acquired subprime and Alt-A loans between 2004 and

---

[131] Fannie Mae, "Housing Goals Forecast," Alignment Meeting, June 22, 2007.

[132] Fannie Mae, Forecast Meeting, July 27, 2007 slide 4.

[133] Fannie Mae letter, Daniel Mudd to Asst. Secretary Brian Montgomery, December 21, 2007, p.6.

[134] FHFA, Fannie Mae and Freddie Mac Single Family Guarantee Fees in 2007 and 2008, p.33.

2007. The only remaining motive—and the valid one—was the effect of the AH goals imposed by HUD.

In 2008, after its takeover by the government, Fannie Mae finally published a credit supplement to its 2008 10-K, which contained an accounting of its subprime and Alt-A credit exposure. The table is reproduced below in order to provide a picture of the kinds of loans Fannie acquired in order to meet the AH goals. Loans may appear in more than one category, so the table does not reveal Fannie's total net exposure to each category, nor does it include Fannie's holdings of non-Fannie MBS or PMBS, for which it did not have loan level data. Note the reference to $8.4 billion in the column for subprime loans. As noted earlier, Fannie classified as subprime only those loans that it purchased from subprime lenders. However, Fannie included loans with FICO scores of less than 660 in the table, indicating that they are not prime loans but without classifying them formally as subprime.

In a later credit supplement, filed in August 2009, Fannie eliminated the duplications among the loans in Table 12, and reported that as of June 30, 2009, it held the credit risk on NTMs with a total unpaid principal amount of $2.7 trillion. The average loan amount was $151,000, for a total of 5.73 million NTM loans.[135] This number does not include Fannie's holdings of subprime PMBS as to which it does not have loan level data.

---

[135] http://www.fanniemae.com/ir/pdf/sec/2009/q2credit summary.pdf, p.5.

Table 12. Fannie Mae Credit Profile by Key Product Features: Credit Characteristics of Single-Family Conventional Mortgage Credit Book of Business[136]

| As of Dec 31, 2008 | Overall Book | Negative-Amortizing Loans | Interest-Only Loans | Loans with FICO <620 | Loans with FICO ≥ 620 and <660 | Loans with Original LTV Ratio >90% | Loans with FICO < 620 and Original LTV Ratio > 90% | Alt-A Loans[1] | Subprime Loans[1] | Jumbo Conforming Loans[1] |
|---|---|---|---|---|---|---|---|---|---|---|
| Unpaid Principal Balance (billions)* | $2,730.9 | $17.3 | $212.9 | $123.0 | $256.1 | $278.3 | $27.3 | $292.4 | $8.4 | $19.9 |
| Share of Single-Family Conventional Credit Book[1] | 100.0% | 0.6% | 7.8% | 4.5% | 9.4% | 10.2% | 1.0% | 10.1% | 0.3% | 0.7% |
| Average Unpaid Principal Balance | $148,824 | $142,502 | $241,943 | $126,604 | $141,746 | $141,569 | $119,607 | $170,250 | $150,445 | $579,528 |
| Serious Delinquency Rate | 2.42% | 5.61% | 8.42% | 9.03% | 5.64% | 6.33% | 15.97% | 7.03% | 14.29% | 0.12% |
| Origination Years 2005-2007 | 46.5% | 62.0% | 80.9% | 56.3% | 55.0% | 58.8% | 69.8% | 72.7% | 80.7% | 1.4% |
| Weighted Average Original Loan-to-value Ratio | 71.8% | 71.1% | 75.4% | 76.7% | 77.5% | 97.3% | 98.1% | 72.6% | 77.2% | 68.4% |
| Original Loan-to-Value Ratio >90 | 10.2% | 0.3% | 9.1% | 22.2% | 21.1% | 100.0% | 100.0% | 5.3% | 6.8% | 0.0% |
| Weighted Average Mark-to Market Loan-to-Value Ratio | 70.0% | 87.2% | 93.4% | 76.3% | 77.5% | 97.6% | 97.7% | 81.0% | 87.3% | 69.9% |
| Mark-to-Mark Loan-to-Value Ratio >100 | 11.6% | 42.8% | 35.6% | 15.9% | 17.6% | 38.2% | 38.5% | 23.2% | 24.5% | 0.4% |
| Weighted Average FICO | 724 | 698 | 725 | 588 | 641 | 694 | 592 | 719 | 623 | 762 |
| FICO < 620 | 4.5% | 10.7% | 1.3% | 100.0% | 0.0% | 9.8% | 100.0% | 0.7% | 47.6% | 0.6% |
| FICO ≥ 620 and <660 | 9.4% | 10.1% | 7.7% | 0.0% | 100.0% | 19.4% | 0.0% | 8.7% | 27.8% | 0.2% |
| Fixed-rate | 90.0% | 0.1% | 39.6% | 93.6% | 92.3% | 94.2% | 96.5% | 72.3% | 73.1% | 95.2% |
| Principal Residence | 89.7% | 70.4% | 84.9% | 96.8% | 94.4% | 97.1% | 99.4% | 77.8% | 96.6% | 98.2% |
| Condo/Co-op | 9.4% | 13.5% | 16.2% | 4.9% | 6.6% | 9.8% | 5.9% | 10.8% | 4.7% | 11.5% |
| Credit Enhanced[2] | 20.9% | 76.3% | 35.0% | 35.0% | 36.3% | 92.5% | 94.1% | 38.6% | 63.4% | 11.3% |
| % of 2007 Credit Losses[3] | 100.0% | 0.9% | 15.0% | 18.8% | 21.9% | 17.4% | 6.4% | 29.2% | 1.0% | 0.0% |
| % of 2008 Q3 Credit Losses[3] | 100.0 % | 3.8% | 36.2% | 11.3% | 16.8% | 21.5% | 5.4% | 47.6% | 2.1% | 0.2% |
| % of 2008 Q4 Credit Losses[3] | 100.0% | 2.2% | 33.1% | 11.5% | 17.2% | 23.1% | 5.2% | 43.2% | 2.0% | 1.1% |
| % of 2008 Credit Losses[3] | 100.0% | 2.9% | 34.2% | 11.8% | 17.4% | 21.3% | 5.4% | 45.6% | 2.0% | 0.4% |

(1) Alt-A, Subprime, and Jumbo Conforming Loans are calculated as a percentage of the single-family mortgage credit book of business, which includes government loans. Government loans are guaranteed or insured by the U.S. Government or its agencies, such as the Department of Veterans Affairs (VA), the Federal Housing Administration (FHA) or the Rural Housing and Community Facilities Program and the Department of Agriculture.

(2) Unpaid principal balance of all loans with credit enhancement as a percentage of unpaid principal balance of single-family conventional mortgage credit book of business. Includes primary mortgage insurance, pool insurance, lender recourse and other credit enhancement.

(3) Expressed as a percentage of credit losses for the single-family mortgage credit book of business. For information on total credit losses, refer to Fannie Mae's 2008 Form 10-K.

**Freddie Mac.** As noted earlier, in its limited review of the role of the GSEs in the financial crisis, the Commission spent most of its time and staff resources on a review of Fannie Mae, and for that reason this dissent focuses primarily on documents received from Fannie. However, things were not substantially different at Freddie Mac. In a document dated June 4, 2009, entitled "Cost of Freddie Mac's Affordable Housing Mission," a report to the Business Risk Committee, of the Board of Directors,[136] several points were made that show the experience of Freddie was no different than Fannie's:

- Our housing goals compliance required little direct subsidy prior to 2003, but since then subsidies have averaged $200 million per year.

- Higher credit risk mortgages disproportionately tend to be goal-qualifying. Targeted affordable lending generally requires 'accepting' substantially higher credit risk.

- We charge more for targeted (and baseline) affordable single-family loans, but not enough to fully offset their higher incremental risk.

- Goal-qualifying single-family loans accounted for the disproportionate share of our 2008 realized losses that was predicted by our models. (slide 2)

- In 2007 Freddie Mac failed two subgoals, but compliance was subsequently deemed infeasible by the regulator due to economic conditions. In 2008 Freddie Mac failed six goals and subgoals, five of which were deemed infeasible. No enforcement action was taken regarding the sixth missed goal because of our financial condition. (slide 3)

- Goal-qualifying loans tend to be higher risk. Lower household income correlates with various risk factors such as less wealth, less employment stability, higher loan-to-value ratios, or lower credit scores. (slide 7)

- Targeted affordable loans have much higher expected default probabilities... Over one-half of targeted affordable loans have higher expected default probabilities than the highest 5% of non-goal-qualifying loans. (Slide 8)

The use of the affordable housing goals to force a reduction in the GSEs' underwriting standards was a major policy error committed by HUD in two successive administrations, and must be recognized as such if we are ever to understand what caused the financial crisis. Ultimately, the AH goals extended the housing bubble, infused it with weak and high risk NTMs, caused the insolvency of Fannie and Freddie, and—together with other elements of U.S. housing policy—was the principal cause of the financial crisis itself.

When Congress enacted the Housing and Economic Recovery Act of 2008 (HERA), it transferred the responsibility for administering the affordable housing goals from HUD to FHFA. In 2010, FHFA modified and simplified the AH goals, and eliminated one of their most troubling elements. As Fannie had noted, if the AH goals exceed the number of goals-eligible borrowers in the market, they were being forced to allocate credit, taking it from the middle class and providing it to low-income borrowers. In effect, there was a conflict between their mission to advance affordable housing and their mission to maintain a liquid secondary mortgage

---

[136] Freddie Mac, "Cost of Freddie Mac's Affordable Housing Mission," Business Risk Committee, Board of Directors, June 4, 2009.

market for most mortgages in the U.S. The new FHFA rule does not require the GSEs to purchase more qualifying loans than the percentage of the total market that these loans constitute.[137]

This does not solve all the major problems with the AH goals. In the sense that the goals enable the government to direct where a private company extends credit, they are inherently a form of government credit allocation. More significantly, the competition among the GSEs, FHA and the banks that are required under the CRA to find and acquire the same kind of loans will continue to cause the same underpricing of risk on these loans that eventually brought about the mortgage meltdown and the financial crisis. This is discussed in the next section and the section on the CRA.

## 4. COMPETITION BETWEEN THE GSEs AND FHA FOR SUBPRIME AND ALT-A MORTGAGES

One of the important facts about HUD's management of the AH goals was that it placed Fannie and Freddie in direct competition with FHA, an agency within HUD. This was already noted in some of the Fannie documents cited above. Fannie treated this as a conflict of interest at HUD, but there is a strong case that this competition is exactly what HUD and Congress wanted. It is important to recall the context in which the GSE Act was enacted in 1992. In 1990, Congress had enacted the Federal Credit Reform Act.[138] One of its purposes was to capture in the government's budget the risks to the government associated with loan guarantees, and in effect it placed a loose budgetary limit on FHA guarantees. For those in Congress and at HUD who favored increased mortgage lending to low income borrowers and underserved communities, this consequence of the FCRA may have been troubling. What had previously been a free way to extend support to groups who were not otherwise eligible for conventional mortgages—which generally required a 20 percent downpayment and the indicia of willingness and ability to pay—now appeared to be potentially restricted. Requiring the GSEs to take up the mantle of affordable housing would have looked at the time like a solution, since Fannie and Freddie had unlimited access to funds in the private markets and were off-budget entities.

Looked at from this perspective, it would make sense for Congress and HUD to place the GSEs and FHA in competition, just as it made sense to put Fannie and Freddie in competition with one another for affordable loans. With all three entities competing for the same kinds of loans, and with HUD's control of both FHA's lending standards and the GSEs' affordable housing requirements, underwriting requirements would inevitably be reduced. HUD's explicit and frequently expressed interest in reducing mortgage underwriting standards, as a means of making mortgage credit available to low income borrowers, provides ample evidence of HUD's motives for creating this competition.

---

[137] Federal Housing Finance Agency, 2010-2011 Enterprise Housing Goals; Enterprise Book-Entry Procedures; Final Rule, 12 CFR Parts 1249 and 1282, *Federal Register*, September 14, 2010, p.55892.

[138] Title V of the Congressional Budget Act of 1990. Under the FCRA, HUD must estimate the annual cost of FHA's credit subsidy for budget purposes. The credit subsidy is the net of its estimated receipts reduced by its estimated payments.

Established in 1934, now a part of HUD and administered by the Federal Housing Administrator (who is also the Assistant Secretary of Housing), FHA insures 100 percent of an eligible mortgage. It was established to provide financing to people who could not meet the standards for a bank-originated conventional loan. The loans it insured had a maximum LTV of 80 percent in 1934. This went to 95 percent in 1950, and 97 percent in 1961.[139] With its maximum LTV remaining at 97 percent, FHA maintained average FICO scores for its borrowers just below 660 from 1996 to 2006. During this period, the average FICO score for a conventional subprime borrower was somewhat lower.[140] Beginning in 1993, shortly after Fannie and Freddie were introduced as competitors, FHA began to increase its percentage of loans with low downpayments. This had the predictable effect on its delinquency rates, as shown in the figure below prepared by Edward Pinto with data from FHA, the FDIC, and the MBA:

Figure 6.

Despite its reductions in required downpayments, FHA's market share vis-a vis the GSEs began to decline. According to GAO data, in 1996, FHA's market share among lower-income borrowers was 26 percent while the GSEs' share was 23.8 percent. By 2005, FHA's share was 9.8 percent, while the GSEs' share was 31.9 percent. It appears that early on Fannie Mae deliberately targeted FHA borrowers with its Community Homebuyer Program (CHBP). In a memorandum prepared in 1993, Fannie's Credit Policy group compared Fannie's then-proposed CHBP program to FHA's requirements under its 1-to-4 family loan program (Section 203(b)) and showed that most of Fannie's requirements were competitive or better.

---

[139]  Kerry D. Vandell, "FHA Restructuring Proposals: Alternatives and Implications," *Fannie Mae Housing Policy Debate*, vol. 6, Issue 2, 1995, pp. 308-309

[140]  GAO, "Federal Housing Administration: Decline in Agency's Market Share Was Associated with Product and Process Developments of Other Mortgage Market Participants," GAO-07-645, June 2007, pp. 42 and 44.

FHA also appears to have tried to lead the GSEs. In 1999—just before the AH goals for Fannie and Freddie were to be raised—FHA almost doubled its originations of loans with LTVs equal to or greater than 97 percent, going from 22.9 percent in 1998 to 43.84 percent in 1999.[141] It also offered additional concessions on underwriting standards in order to attract subprime business. The following is from a Quicken ad in January 2000 (emphasis in the original),[142] which is likely to have been based on an FHA program as it existed in 1999:

**Borrowers can purchase with a minimum down payment.** Without FHA insurance, many families can't afford the homes they want because down payments are a major roadblock. FHA down payments range from 1.25% to 3% of the sale price and are significantly lower than the minimum that many lenders require for conventional or sub-prime loans.

**With FHA loans, borrowers need as little as 3% of the "total funds" required.** In addition to the funds needed for the down payment, borrowers also have to pay closing costs, prepaid fees for insurance and interest, as well as escrow fees which include mortgage insurance, hazard insurance, and months worth of property taxes. A FHA-insured home loan can be structured so borrowers don't pay more than 3% of the total out-of-pocket funds, including the down payment.

**The combined total of out-of-pocket funds can be a gift or loan from family members.** FHA allows homebuyers to use gifts from family members and non-profit groups to cover their down payment and additional closing costs and fees. In fact, even a 100% gift or a personal loan from a relative is acceptable.

**FHA's credit requirements are flexible.** Compared to credit requirements established by many lenders for other types of home loans, FHA focuses only on a borrower's last 12-24 month credit history. In addition, there is no minimum FICO score - mortgage bankers look at each application on a case-by-case basis. It is also perfectly acceptable for people with NO established credit to receive a loan with this program.

**FHA permits borrowers to have a higher debt-to-income ratio than most insurers typically allow.** Conventional home loans allow borrowers to have 36% of their gross income attributed to their new monthly mortgage payment combined with existing debt. FHA program allows borrowers to carry 41%, and in some circumstances, even more.

It is important to remember that 1999 is the year that HUD was planning a big step-up in the AH goals for the GSEs—from 42 percent LMI to 50 percent, with even larger percentage increases in the special affordable category that would be most competitive with FHA. The last major increase in the percent of FHA's loans with LTVs equal to or greater than 97 percent had occurred in 1991, the year before the GSE Act imposed the AH goals on Fannie and Freddie, and in effect directed them to consider downpayments of 5 percent or less. In 1991, FHA's percentage of loans

---

[141] Integrated Financial Engineering, "Actuarial Review of the Federal Housing Administration Mutual Mortgage Insurance Fund (Excluding HECMs) for Fiscal Year 2009," prepared for U.S. Department of Housing and Urban Development, November 6, 2009, p.42.

[142] Quicken press release, "Quicken Loans First To Offer FHA Home Mortgages Nationally On The Internet With HUD´s approval, Intuit expands home ownership nationwide, offering consumers widest variety of home loan options", January 20, 2000, http://web.intuit.com/about_intuit/press_releases/2000/01-20.html.

equal to or greater than 97 percent rose suddenly from 4.4 percent to 17.1 percent.[143] Again, FHA, under the control of HUD, appears to be offering competition to the GSEs that would lead them to reduce their underwriting standards. Since FHA is a government agency, its actions cannot be explained by a profit motive. Instead, it seems clear that FHA reduced its lending standards as part of a HUD policy to lead Fannie and Freddie in the same direction.

The result of Fannie's competition with FHA in high LTV lending is shown in the following figure, which compares the respective shares of FHA and Fannie in the category of loans with LTVs equal to or greater than 97 percent, including Fannie loans with a combined LTV equal to or greater than 97 percent.

Figure 7.

Whether a conscious policy of HUD or not, competition between the GSEs and FHA ensued immediately after the GSEs were given their affordable housing mission in 1992. The fact that FHA, an agency controlled by HUD, substantially increased the LTVs it would accept in 1991 (just before the GSEs were given their affordable housing mission) and again in 1999 (just before the GSEs were required to increase their affordable housing efforts) is further evidence that HUD was coordinating these policies in the interest of creating competition between FHA and the GSEs. The effect was to drive down underwriting standards, which HUD had repeatedly described as its goal.

# 5. ENLISTING MORTGAGE BANKERS AND SUBPRIME LENDERS IN AFFORDABLE HOUSING

In 1994, HUD began a program to enlist other members of the mortgage financing community in the effort to reduce underwriting standards. In that year,

---

[143] GAO, "Federal Housing Administration: Decline in Agency's Market Share Was Associated with Product and Process Developments of Other Mortgage Market Participants," GAO-07-645, June 2007, pp. 42 and 44.

the Mortgage Bankers Association (MBA)—a group of mortgage financing firms not otherwise regulated by the federal government and not subject to HUD's legal authority—agreed to join a HUD program called the "Best Practices Initiative."[144] The circumstances surrounding this agreement are somewhat obscure, but at least one contemporary account suggests that the MBA signed up to avoid an effort by HUD to cover mortgage bankers under the Community Reinvestment Act (CRA), which up to that point had only applied only to government-insured banks.

In mid-September [1994], the Mortgage Bankers Association of America-whose membership includes many bank-owned mortgage companies, signed a three-year master best-practices agreement with HUD. The agreement consisted of two parts: MBA's agreement to work on fair-lending issues in consultation with HUD and a model best-practices agreement that individual mortgage banks could use to devise their own agreements with HUD. The first such agreement, signed by Countrywide Funding Corp., the nation's largest mortgage bank, is summarized [below]. Many have seen the MBA agreement as a preemptive strike against congressional murmurings that mortgage banks should be pulled under the umbrella of the CRA.[145]

As the first member of the MBA to sign, Countrywide probably realized that there were political advantages in being seen as assisting low-income mortgage lending, and it became one of a relatively small group of subprime lenders who were to prosper enormously as Fannie and Freddie began to look for sources of the subprime loans that would enable them to meet the AH goals. By 1998, there were 117 MBA signatories to HUD's Best Practices Initiative, which was described as follows:

> The companies and associations that sign "Best Practices" Agreements not only commit to meeting the responsibilities under the Fair Housing Act, but also make a concerted effort to exceed those requirements. In general, the signatories agree to administer a review process for loan applications to ensure that all applicants have every opportunity to qualify for a mortgage. They also assent to making loans of any size so that all borrowers may be served and to provide information on all loan programs for which an applicant qualifies.... The results of the initiative are promising. As lenders discover new, untapped markets, their minority and low-income loans applications and originations have risen. Consequently, the homeownership rate for low-income and minority groups has increased throughout the nation.[146]

Countrywide was by far the most important participant in the HUD program. Under that program, it made a series of multi-billion dollar commitments, culminating in a "trillion dollar commitment" to lend to minority and low income

---

[144] HUD's Best Practices Initiative was described this way by HUD: "Since 1994, HUD has signed Fair Lending Best Practices (FLBP) Agreements with lenders across the nation that are individually tailored to public-private partnerships that are considered on the leading edge. The Agreements not only offer an opportunity to increase low-income and minority lending but they incorporate fair housing and equal opportunity principles into mortgage lending standards. These banks and mortgage lenders, as represented by Countrywide Home Loans, Inc., serve as industry leaders in their communities by demonstrating a commitment to affirmatively further fair lending." Available at: http://www.hud.gov/local/hi/working/nlwfal2001.cfm.

[145] Steve Cocheo, "Fair-Lending Pressure Builds", ABA Banking Journal, vol. 86, 1994, http://www.questia.com/googleScholar.qst?docId=5001707340.

[146] HUD, "Building Communities and New Markets for the 21st Century," FY 1998 Report , p.75, http://www.huduser.org/publications/polleg/98con/NewMarkets.pdf.

families, which in part it fulfilled by selling subprime and other NTMs to Fannie and Freddie. In a 2000 report, the Fannie Mae Foundation noted: "FHA loans constituted the largest share of Countrywide's activity, until Fannie Mae and Freddie Mac began accepting loans with higher LTVs and greater underwriting flexibilities."[147] In late 2007, a few months before its rescue by Bank of America, Countrywide reported that it had made $789 billion in mortgage loans toward its trillion dollar commitment.[148]

## 6. THE COMMUNITY REINVESTMENT ACT

The most controversial element of the vast increase in NTMs between 1993 and 2008 was the role of the CRA.[149] The act, which is applicable only to federally insured depository institutions, was originally adopted in 1977. Its purpose in part was to "require each appropriate Federal financial supervisory agency to use its authority when examining financial institutions to encourage such institutions to help meet the credit needs of the local communities in which they are chartered consistent with the safe and sound operations of such institutions." The enforcement provisions of the Act authorized the bank regulators to withhold approvals for such transactions as mergers and acquisitions and branch network expansion if the applying bank did not have a satisfactory CRA rating.

CRA did not have a substantial effect on subprime lending in the years after its enactment until the regulations under the act were tightened in 1995. The 1995 regulations required insured banks to acquire or make "flexible and innovative" mortgages that they would not otherwise have made. In this sense, the CRA and Fannie and Freddie's AH goals are cut from the same cloth.

There were two very distinct applications of the CRA. The first, and the one with the broadest applicability, is a requirement that all insured banks make CRA loans in their respective assessment areas. When the Act is defended, it is almost always discussed in terms of this category—loans in bank assessment areas. Banks (usually privately) complain that they are required by the regulators to make imprudent loans to comply with CRA. One example is the following statement by a local community bank in a report to its shareholders:

> Under the umbrella of the Community Reinvestment Act (CRA), a tremendous amount of pressure was put on banks by the regulatory authorities to make loans, especially mortgage loans, to low income borrowers and neighborhoods. The regulators were very heavy handed regarding this issue. I will not dwell on it here but they required [redacted name] to change its mortgage lending practices to meet certain CRA goals, even though we argued the changes were risky and imprudent.[150]

On the other hand, the regulators defend the act and their actions under it, and particularly any claim that the CRA had a role in the financial crisis. The most frequently cited defense is a speech by former Fed Governor Randall Kroszner on

---

[147] Fannie Mae Foundation, "Making New Markets: Case Study of Countrywide Home Loans," 2000, http://content.knowledgeplex.org/kp2/programs/pdf/rep_newmortmkts_countrywide.pdf.

[148] "Questions and Answers from Countrywide about Lending," December 11, 2007, available at http://www.realtown.com/articles/article/print/id/768.

[149] 12 U.S.C. 2901.

[150] Original letter in author's files.

December 3, 2008,[151] in which he said in pertinent part:

> Only 6 percent of all the *higher-priced loans* [those that were considered CRA loans because they bore high interest rates associated with their riskier character] were extended by *CRA-covered lenders to lower-income borrowers or neighborhoods in their assessment areas*, the local geographies that are the primary focus for CRA evaluation purposes. This result undermines the assertion by critics of the potential for a substantial role for the CRA in the subprime crisis. [emphasis supplied]

There are two points in this statement that require elaboration. First, it assumes that all CRA loans are high-priced loans. This is incorrect. Many banks, in order to be sure of obtaining the necessary number of loans to attain a satisfactory CRA rating, subsidized the loans by making them at lower interest rates than their risk characteristics would warrant. This is true, in part, because CRA loans are generally loans to low income individuals; as such, they are more likely than loans to middle income borrowers to be subprime and Alt-A loans and thus sought after by FHA, Fannie and Freddie and subprime lenders such as Countrywide; this competition is another reason why their rates are likely to be lower than their risk characteristics. Second, while bank lending under CRA in their assessment areas has probably not had a major effect on the overall presence of subprime loans in the U.S. financial system, it is not the element about CRA that raises the concerns about how CRA operated to increase the presence of NTMs in the housing bubble and in the U.S. financial system generally. There is another route through which CRA's role in the financial crisis likely to be considerably more significant.

In 1994, the Riegle-Neal Interstate Banking and Branching Efficiency Act for the first time allowed banks to merge across state lines under federal law (as distinct from interstate compacts). Under these circumstances, the enforcement provisions of the CRA, which required regulators to withhold approvals of applications for banks that did not have satisfactory CRA ratings, became particularly relevant for large banks that applied to federal bank regulators for merger approvals. In a 2007 speech, Fed Chairman Ben Bernanke stated that after the enactment of the Riegle-Neal legislation, "As public scrutiny of bank merger and acquisition activity escalated, advocacy groups increasingly used the public comment process to protest bank applications on CRA grounds. In instances of highly contested applications, the Federal Reserve Board and other agencies held public meetings to allow the public and the applicants to comment on the lending records of the banks in question. In response to these new pressures, banks began to devote more resources to their CRA programs."[152] This modest description, although accurate as far as it goes, does not fully describe the effect of the law and the application process on bank lending practices.

In 2007, the umbrella organization for many low-income or community "advocacy groups," the National Community Reinvestment Coalition, published a report entitled "CRA Commitments" which recounted the substantial success of its members in using the leverage provided by the bank application process to obtain trillions of dollars in CRA lending commitments from banks that had applied to

---

[151] Randall Kroszner, Speech at the Confronting Concentrated Poverty Forum, December 3, 2008.

[152] Ben S. Bernanke, "The Community Reinvestment Act: Its Evolution and New Challenges," March 30, 2007, p2.

federal regulators for merger approvals. The opening section of the report states (bolded language in the original):[153]

> **Since the passage of CRA in 1977, lenders and community organizations have signed over 446 CRA agreements totaling more than $4.5 trillion in reinvestment dollars flowing to minority and lower income neighborhoods.**
>
> Lenders and community groups will often sign these agreements when a lender has submitted an application to merge with another institution or expand its services. Lenders must seek the approval of federal regulators for their plans to merge or change their services. The four federal financial institution regulatory agencies will scrutinize the CRA records of lenders and will assess the likely future community reinvestment performance of lenders. *The application process, therefore, provides an incentive for lenders to sign CRA agreements with community groups that will improve their CRA performance. Recognizing the important role of collaboration between lenders and community groups, the federal agencies have established mechanisms in their application procedures that encourage dialogue and cooperation among the parties in preserving and strengthening community reinvestment.* [emphasis supplied]

A footnote to this statement reports:

> The Federal Reserve Board will grant an extension of the public comment period during its merger application process upon a joint request by a bank and community group. In its commentary to Regulation Y, the Board indicates that this procedure was added to facilitate discussions between banks and community groups regarding programs that help serve the convenience and needs of the community. In its Corporate Manual, the Office of the Comptroller of the Currency states that it will not offer the expedited application process to a lender that does not intend to honor a CRA agreement made by the institution that it is acquiring.

---

[153] See Note 12 *supra.*

In its report, the NCRC listed all 446 commitments and includes the following summary list of year-by-year commitments:

Table 13.

| Year | Annual Dollars ($ millions) | Total Dollars ($ millions) |
|------|------------------------------|-----------------------------|
| 2007 | 12, 500 | 4,566,480 |
| 2006 | 258,000 | 4,553,980 |
| 2005 | 100,276 | 4,298,980 |
| 2004 | 1,631,140 | 4,195,704 |
| 2003 | 711,669 | 2,564,564 |
| 2002 | 152,859 | 1,852,895 |
| 2001 | 414,184 | 1,700,036 |
| 2000 | 13,681 | 1,285,852 |
| 1999 | 103,036 | 1,272,171 |
| 1998 | 812,160 | 1,169,135 |
| 1997 | 221,345 | 356,975 |
| 1996 | 49,678 | 135,630 |
| 1995 | 26,590 | 85,952 |
| 1994 | 6,128 | 59,362 |
| 1993 | 10,716 | 53,234 |
| 1992 | 33,708 | 42,518 |
| 1991 | 2,443 | 8,811 |
| 1990 | 1,614 | 6,378 |
| 1989 | 2,260 | 4,764 |
| 1988 | 1,248 | 2,504 |
| 1987 | 357 | 1,256 |
| 1986 | 516 | 899 |
| 1985 | 73 | 382 |
| 1984 | 219 | 309 |
| 1983 | 1 | 90 |
| 1982 | 6 | 89 |
| 1981 | 5 | 83 |
| 1980 | 13 | 78 |
| 1979 | 15 | 65 |
| 1978 | 0 | 50 |
| 1977 | 50 | 50 |

The size of these commitments, which far outstrip the CRA loans made in assessment areas, suggests the potential significance of the CRA as a cause of the financial crisis. It is noteworthy that the Commission majority was not willing even to consider the significance of the NCRC's numbers. In connection with its only hearing on the housing issue, and before any research had been done on the NCRC statements, the Commission published a report absolving CRA of any responsibility for the financial crisis.[154]

---

[154] FCIC, "The Community Reinvestment Act and the Mortgage Crisis." *Preliminary Staff Report*, http://www.fcic.gov/reports/pdfs/2010-0407-Preliminary_Staff_Report_-_CRA_and_the_Mortgage_Crisis.pdf.

To understand CRA's role in the financial crisis, the relevant statistic is the $4.5 trillion in bank CRA lending commitments that the NCRC cited in its 2007 report. (This document and others that are relevant to this discussion were removed from the NCRC website, www.ncrc.org, after they received publicity but can still be found on the web[155]). One important question is whether the bank regulators cooperated with community groups by withholding approvals of applications for mergers and acquisitions until an agreement or commitment for CRA lending satisfactory to the community groups had been arranged. It is not difficult to imagine that the regulators did not want the severe criticism from Congress that would have followed their failure to assist community groups in reaching agreements with and getting commitments from banks that had applied for these approvals. In statements in connection with mergers it has approved the Fed has said that commitments by the bank participants about future CRA lending have no influence on the approval process. A Fed official also told the Commission's staff that the Fed did not consider these commitments in connection with merger applications. The Commission did not attempt to verify this statement, but accepted it at face value from a Fed staff official. Nevertheless, there remains no explanation for why banks have been making these enormous commitments in connection with mergers, but not otherwise.

The largest of the commitments, in terms of dollars, were made by four banks or their predecessors—Bank of America, JPMorgan Chase, Citibank, and Wells Fargo—in connection with mergers or acquisitions as shown in Table 14 below.

---

[155] http://www.community-wealth.org/_pdfs/articles-publications/cdfis/report-silver-brown.pdf.

Table 14. Announced CRA Commitments in Connection
with a Merger or Acquisition by Four Largest Banks and Their Predecessors

| Final bank | Acquired or merged bank/entity with a corresponding announcement of a CRA commitment | CRA commitment (year announced and dollar amount) |
|---|---|---|
| Wells Fargo | First Union acquired by Wachovia | 2001 ($35 b.) |
| | SouthTrust acquired by Wachovia | 2004 ($75 b.) |
| JPMorgan Chase | Chemical merges with Manufacturers Hanover | 1991 ($72.5 m.) |
| | NBD acquired by First Chicago | 1995 ($2 b.) |
| | Home Savings acquired by Washington Mutual | 1998 ($120 b.) |
| | Dime acquired by Washington Mutual | 2001 ($375 b.) |
| | Bank One acquired by JPMorgan Chase | 2004 ($800 b.) |
| Bank of America | Continental acquired by Bank of America | 1994 ($1 b.) |
| | Bank of America (acquired by NationsBank, which kept the Bank of America name). | 1998 ($350 b.) |
| | Bank of Boston acquired by Fleet | 1999 ($14.6 b.) |
| | Fleet | 2004 ($750 b.) |
| Citibank | Travelers | 1998 ($115 b.) 1998 ($115 b.) |
| | Cal Fed | 2002 ($120 b.) |

Compiled by Edward Pinto from the NCRC 2007 report CRA Commitments, found at http://www.community-wealth.org/_pdfs/articles-publications/cdfis/report-silver-brown.pdf , NCRC testimony regarding Bank of America's $1.5 trillion in CRA agreements and commitments in conjunction with its 2008 acquisition of Countrywide found at http://www.house.gov/apps/list/hearing/financialsvcs_dem/taylor_testimony_-_4.15.10.pdf.

Given the enormous size of the commitments reported by NCRC, the key questions are: (i) how many of these commitments were actually fulfilled by the banks that made them, (ii) where are these loans today, and (iii) how are these loans performing?

Currently, in light of the severely limited Commission investigation of this issue, there are only partial answers to these questions.

*Were the loans actually made?* The banks that made these commitments apparently came under pressure from community groups to fulfill them. In an interview by Brad Bondi of the Commission's staff, Josh Silver of the NCRC noted that community groups did follow up these commitments.

Bondi: Who follows up…to make sure that these banks honor their voluntary agreements or their unilateral commitments?

Silver: Actually part of some of these CRA agreements was meeting with the bank two or three times a year and actually going through, 'Here's what you've promised. Here's what you've loaned.' That would happen on a one-on-one basis with the banks and the community organizations.[156]

Nevertheless, when the Commission staff asked the four largest banks (Bank of America, Citibank, JPMorgan Chase and Wells Fargo) for data on whether the merger-related commitments were fulfilled and in what amount, most of the banks supplied only limited information. They contended that they did not have the information or that it was too difficult to get, and the information they supplied was sketchy at best.

In some cases, the information supplied to the Commission by the banks, in letters from their counsel, reflected fewer loans than they had claimed in press releases to have made in fulfillment of their commitments. The press release amounts were JPMorgan Chase (including WaMu, $835 billion), Citi ($274 billion), and Bank of America ($229 billion), totaled $1.3 trillion in CRA loans between 2001 and 2008, and had been presented to the Commission by Edward Pinto in the Triggers memo.[157] No Wells Fargo press releases could be found, but in response to questions from the Commission Wells provided a great deal of data in spread sheets that could not be interpreted or understood without further discussion with representatives of the bank. However, the Commission terminated the investigation of the merger-related CRA commitments in August 2010, before the necessary data could be gathered. For this reason, the Wells data could not be unpacked, interpreted in discussion with Wells officials, and analyzed.

After I protested the limited efforts of the Commission on this issue in October 2010, the Commission made a belated attempt to restart the investigation of the merger-related CRA commitments in November. However, only one bank had responded by the deadline for submission of this dissenting statement. As with the bank responses, additional work was required to understand the information received, and there was no time, and no Commission staff, to follow up.

As a result of the dilatory nature of the Commission's investigation, it was impossible to determine how many loans were actually made under their merger-related CRA commitments by the four banks and their predecessors. This in turn impeded any effort to find out where these loans are today and hence their delinquency rates. It appears that in many instances the Commission management constrained the staff in their investigation into CRA by limiting the number of document requests and interviews and by preventing the staff from following up with the institutions that failed to respond adequately to requests for data.

*Where are these mortgages today?* Where these loans are today must necessarily be a matter of speculation. Some of the banks told the FCIC staff that they do not distinguish between CRA loans and other loans, and so could not provide this information. Under the GSE Act, Fannie and Freddie had an affirmative obligation to help banks to meet their CRA obligations, and they undoubtedly served as a buyer for the loans made by the largest banks and their predecessors pursuant to

---

[156] Interview of Josh Silver of the National Community Reinvestment Coalition, June 16, 2010.

[157] Edward Pinto, Exhibit 2 to the Triggers memo, dated April 21, 2010, http://www.aei.org/docLib/Pinto-Sizing-Total-Federal-Contributions.pdf.

the commitments. In a press release in 2003, for example, Fannie reported that it had acquired $394 billion in CRA loans, about $201 billion of which occurred in 2002.[158] This amounted to approximately 50 percent of Fannie's AH acquisitions for that year.

In the Triggers memo, based on his research, Pinto estimated that Fannie and Freddie purchased about 50 percent of all CRA loans over the period from 2001 to 2007 and that, of the balance, about 10-15 percent were insured by FHA, 10-15 percent were sold to Wall Street, and the rest remain on the books of the banks that originated the loans.[159] Many of these loans are likely unsaleable in the secondary market because they were made at rates that did not compensate for risk or lacked mortgage insurance—again, the competition for these loans among the GSEs, FHA and the banks operating under CRA requirements inevitably raised their prices and thus underpriced their risk. To sell these loans, the banks holding them would have to take losses, which many are unwilling to do.

*What are the delinquency rates?* Under the Home Mortgage Disclosure Act HMDA), banks are required to provide data to the Fed from which the delinquency rates on loans that have high interest rates can be calculated. It was assumed that these were the loans that might bear watching as potentially predatory. When Fannie and Freddie, FHA, Countrywide and other subprime lenders and banks under CRA are all seeking the same loans—roughly speaking, loans to borrowers at or below the AMI—it is likely that these loans when actually made will bear concessionary interest rates so that their rate spread is not be reportable under HMDA. It's just supply and demand. Accordingly, the banks that made CRA loans pursuant to their commitments have no obligation to record and report their delinquency rates, and as noted above several of the large banks that made major commitments recorded by the NCRC told FCIC staff that they don't keep records about the performance of CRA loans apart from other mortgages.

However, in the past few years, Bank of America has been reporting the performance of CRA loans in its annual report to the SEC on form 10-K. For example, the bank's 10-K for 2009 contained the following statement: "At December 31, 2009, our CRA portfolio comprised six percent of the total residential mortgage balances, but comprised 17 percent of nonperforming residential mortgage loans. This portfolio also comprised 20 percent of residential net charge-offs during 2009. While approximately 32 percent of our residential mortgage portfolio carries risk mitigation protection, only a small portion of our CRA portfolio is covered by this protection."[160] This could be an approximation for the delinquency rate on the merger-related CRA loans that the four banks made in fulfilling their commitments, but without definitive information on the number of loans made and the banks' current holdings it is impossible to make this estimate with any confidence. In a letter from its counsel, another bank reported serious delinquency rates on the loans made pursuant to its merger-related commitments ranging from 5 percent to 50 percent, with the largest sample showing a 25 percent delinquency rate.

---

[158] "Fannie Mae Passes Halfway Point in $2 Trillion American Dream Commitment; Leads Market in Bringing Housing Boom to Underserved Families, Communities" http://findarticles.com/p/articles/mi_m0EIN/is_2003_March_18/ai_98885990/pg_3/?tag=content;col1.

[159] Triggers memo, p.47.

[160] Bank of America, 2009 10-K, p.57.

Further investigation of this issue is necessary, including on the role of the bank regulators, in order to determine what effect, if any, the merger-related commitments to make CRA loans might have had on the number of NTMs in the U.S. financial system before the financial crisis.

# IV. CONCLUSION

This dissenting statement argues that the U.S. government's housing policies were the major contributor to the financial crisis of 2008. These policies fostered the development of a massive housing bubble between 1997 and 2007 and the creation of 27 million subprime and Alt-A loans, many of which were ready to default as soon as the housing bubble began to deflate. The losses associated with these weak and high risk loans caused either the real or apparent weakness of the major financial institutions around the world that held these mortgages—or PMBS backed by these mortgages—as investments or as sources of liquidity. Deregulation, lack of regulation, predatory lending or the other factors that were cited in the report of the FCIC's majority were not determinative factors.

The policy implications of this conclusion are significant. If the crisis could have been prevented simply by eliminating or changing the government policies and programs that were primarily responsible for the financial crisis, then there was no need for the Dodd-Frank Wall Street Reform and Consumer Protection Act of 2010, adopted by Congress in July 2010 and often cited as one of the important achievements of the Obama administration and the 111[th] Congress.

The stringent regulation that the Dodd-Frank Act imposes on the U.S. economy will almost certainly have a major adverse effect on economic growth and job creation in the United States during the balance of this decade. If this was the price that had to be paid for preventing another financial crisis then perhaps it's one that will have to be borne. But if it was not necessary to prevent another crisis—and it would not have been necessary if the crisis was caused by actions of the government itself—then the Dodd-Frank Act seriously overreached.

Finally, if the principal cause of the financial crisis was ultimately the government's involvement in the housing finance system, housing finance policy in the future should be adjusted accordingly.

# APPENDIX 1

Hypothetical Losses in Two Scenarios (No feedback)
**Scenario 1 is what was known to market professional during the 2nd half of 2007; Scenario 2 is the actual condition of the mortgage market. Second mortgage/home equity loan losses are excluded.**
**Assumptions used:**
Number of mortgages= 53 million;
Total value of first mortgages=$9.155 trillion;
Losses on Prime=1.2%% (assumes 3% foreclosure rate & 40% severity);
Losses on Subprime/Alt-A=12% (assumes 30% foreclosure rate & 40% severity);
Average size of mortgage: $173,000

**Losses in Scenario 1**
Number of mortgages: 53 million
Prime=40 million
Subprime/Alt-A = 13 million (7.7. PMBS million + FHA/VA=5.2 million)
Aggregate Value:
Prime =$6.9 trillion ($173,000 X 40 million);
Subprime/Alt-A=$2.25 trillion ($173,000 X 13 million)
Losses on foreclosures: **$353 billion** ($6.9 trillion prime X 1.2%=$83 billion + $2.25 trillion subprime/Alt-A X 12%=$270 billion
**Overall loss percentage: 3.5%**

**Losses in Scenario 2**
Number of mortgages: 53 million
Prime: 27 million
Subprime/Alt-A:
Original subprime/Alt-A: 13 million
Other subprime/Alt-A: 13 million (10.5 F&F (excludes 1.25 million already counted in PMBS) + 2.5 million other loans not securitized (mostly held by the large banks))
Aggregate Value:
Prime= $4.7 trillion ($173,000 X 27 million);
Subprime/Alt-A = $4.5 trillion ($173,000 X 26 million)
Losses on foreclosures: **$596 billion** ($4.7 trillion X 1.2%=$56 billion + $4.5 trillion X 12%=$540 billion)
**Overall loss percentage: 6.5%, for an increase of 86%**

Note: No allowance for feedback effect—that is, fall in home prices as a result of larger number of foreclosures in Scenario 2. With feedback effect, losses would

be even larger in Scenario 2 because a larger number of foreclosures would drive down housing prices further and faster. This feedback effect will likely cause total first mortgage losses to approach $1 trillion or 10% of outstanding first mortgages.

# APPENDIX 2

Hypothetical Losses in Two Scenarios (with feedback)

**Scenario 1 is what was known to market professional during the 2nd half of 2007; Scenario 2 is the actual condition of the mortgage market. Second mortgage/home equity loan losses are excluded.**

**Assumptions used:**
Number of mortgages= 53 million;
Total value of first mortgages=$9.155 trillion;

**Scenario 1:**
Losses on prime=1.2%% (assumes 3% foreclosure rate & 40% severity);
Losses on self-denominated subprime & Alt-A=14% ((assumes 35% foreclosure rate & 40% severity);
Losses on FHA/VA=5.25% (assumes 15% foreclosure rate and 35% severity)

**Scenario 2:**
Losses on prime=1.6%% (assumes 3.5% foreclosure rate and 45% severity);
Losses on self-denominated subprime & Alt-A=25% (assumes 45% foreclosure rate & 55% severity);
Losses on FHA/VA & unknown subprime/Alt-A=15% (assumes 30% foreclosure rate & 50% severity)
Average size of mortgage:
Prime: $173,000 ($6.75 trillion/39 million)
  Subprime/Alt-A/FHA/VA: $182,000 ($2.4 trillion/13 million

**Losses in Scenario 1**
Number of mortgages: 53 million
Prime=40 million
Subprime/Alt-A=7.7 million PMBS
FHA, and VA=5.2 million
Aggregate Value:
Prime =$6.9 trillion ($173,000 X 39 million);
Subprime/Alt-A=$1.7 trillion ($220,000 X 7.7 million)
  FHA/VA= $700 billion ($130,000x5.2 million)
Total expected foreclosures: 4.7 million (3% X 39 million + 35% X 7.7 million + 15% X 5.2 million)
Losses on foreclosures: **$360 billion** ($6.9 trillion prime X 1.2%=$83 billion + 1.7 trillion subprime/Alt-A X 14%=$240 billion + $700 billion X 5.25%=37 billion)
**Overall loss percentage: 3.9%**

**Losses in Scenario 2**

Number of mortgages: 53 million

Prime: 27 million

Original subprime/Alt-A: 7.7 million

FHA/VA: 5.2 million

Other subprime/Alt-A: 13 million (10.5 F&F (excludes 1.25 million already counted in PMBS), 2.5 million other loans not securitized (mostly held by the large banks))

Aggregate Value:

Prime= $4.7 trillion ($173,000 X 27 million);

Original Subprime/Alt-A = $1.7 trillion ($220,000 X 7.7 million)

FHA/VA= $700 billion ($130,000x5.2 million)

Other subprime/Alt-A: $2 trillion ($154,000X13 million

Total expected foreclosures: 8.4 million (3.5% X 27 million=0.95 million, 45% X 7.7 million=3.5 million, 30% X 13 million=3.9 million)

Losses on foreclosures: **$890 billion** ($4.7 trillion X 1.6%=$60 billion + $1.7 trillion X 25%=$425 billion + $700 billion X 15% = $105 billion + $2 trillion X 15% = $300 billion)

**Overall loss percentage: 9.8%, for an increase of 150%**

# APPENDIX A: GLOSSARY

*Italicized terms within definitions are defined separately.*

**ABCP** see *asset-backed commercial paper*.

**ABS** see *asset-backed security*.

**ABX.HE** A series of *derivatives* indices constructed from the prices of 20 *credit default swaps* that each reference individual subprime *mortgage–backed securities*; akin to an index like the Dow Jones Industrial Average.

**adjustable-rate mortgage** A mortgage whose interest rate changes periodically over time.

**affordable housing goals** Goals originally set by the *Department of Housing and Urban Development* (now by the Federal Housing Finance Agency) for *Fannie Mae* and *Freddie Mac* to allocate a specified part of their mortgage business to serve low- and moderate-income borrowers.

**ARM** see *adjustable-rate mortgage*.

**ARS** see *auction rate securities*.

**asset-backed commercial paper** Short-term debt secured by assets.

**asset-backed security** Debt instrument secured by assets such as mortgages, credit card loans or auto loans.

**auction rate securities** Long-term bonds whose interest rate may be reset at regular short-term intervals by an auction process.

**bank holding company** Company that controls a bank.

**broker-dealer** A firm, often the subsidiary of an investment bank, that buys and sells securities for itself and others.

**capital** Assets minus liabilities; what a firm owns minus what it owes. Regulators often require financial firms to hold minimum levels of capital.

**Capital Purchase Program** *TARP* program providing financial assistance to 700-plus U.S. financial institutions through the purchase of senior preferred shares in the corporations on standardized terms.

**CDO** see *collateralized debt obligation*.

**CDO squared** CDO that holds other CDOs.

**CDS** see *credit default swap*.

**CFTC** see *Commodity Futures Trading Commission*.

**collateralized debt obligation** Type of security often composed of the riskier portions of *mortgage-backed securities*.

**commercial paper** Short-term unsecured corporate debt.

**Commercial Paper Funding Facility** Emergency program created by the *Federal Reserve* in 2008 to purchase three-month unsecured and *asset-backed commercial paper* from eligible companies.

**Commodity Futures Trading Commission** Independent federal agency that regulates trading in futures and options.

**Community Reinvestment Act** 1977 federal law encouraging *depository institutions* to make loans and provide services in the local communities in which they take deposits.

**Consolidated Supervised Entities program** A *Securities and Exchange Commission* program created in 2004 and terminated in 2008 that provided voluntary supervision for the five largest investment bank conglomerates.

**Counterparty** A party to a contract.

**CP** see *commercial paper.*

**CPP** see *Capital Purchase Program.*

**CRA** see *Community Reinvestment Act.*

**credit default swap** A type of credit *derivative* allowing a purchaser of the swap to transfer loan default risk to a seller of the swap. The seller agrees to pay the purchaser if a default event occurs. The purchaser does not need to own the loan covered by the swap.

**credit enhancement** Insurance or other protection that may be purchased for a loan or pool of loans to offset losses in the event of default.

**credit loss** Loss from delayed payments or defaults on loans.

**credit rating agency** Private company that evaluates the credit quality of securities and provides ratings on those securities; the largest are Fitch Ratings, Moody's Investors Service, and Standard & Poor's.

**credit risk** Risk to a lender that a borrower will fail to repay the loan.

**CSE** Consolidated Supervised Entity (see *Consolidated Supervised Entities program*).

**debt-to-income ratio** One measure of a borrower's ability to repay a loan, generally calculated by dividing the borrower's monthly debt payments by gross monthly income.

**delinquency rate** The number of loans for which borrowers fail to make timely loan payments divided by total loans.

**Department of Housing and Urban Development** Cabinet-level federal department responsible for housing policies and programs.

**Department of Justice** Cabinet-level federal department responsible for enforcement of laws and administration of justice, led by the attorney general.

**Department of Treasury** Treasury of the federal government; prints and mints all currency and coins, collects federal taxes, manages U.S. government debt instruments, supervises national banks and thrifts, and advises on domestic and international fiscal policy. Its mission includes protecting the integrity of the financial system.

**depository institution** Financial institution, such as a commercial bank, thrift (savings and loan), or credit union, that accepts deposits, including deposits insured by the *FDIC.*

**derivative** Financial contract whose price is determined (derived) from the value of an underlying asset, rate, index, or event.

**Fannie Mae** Nickname for the Federal National Mortgage Association (FNMA), a *government-sponsored enterprise* providing financing for the home mortgage market.

**FCIC** Financial Crisis Inquiry Commission.

**FDIC** see *Federal Deposit Insurance Corporation.*

**Federal Deposit Insurance Corporation** Independent federal agency charged primarily with insuring deposits at financial institutions, examining and supervising some of those institutions, and shutting down failing institutions.

**Federal Housing Administration** Part of the *Department of Housing and Urban Development* that provides insurance on mortgage loans made by FHA-approved lenders.

**Federal Housing Finance Agency** Independent federal regulator of *government-sponsored enterprises*; created by the *Housing and Economic Recovery Act* of 2008 as successor to the *Office of Federal Housing Enterprise Oversight* and the Federal Housing Finance Board.

**Federal Open Market Committee** Its members are the Board of Governors of the Federal Reserve

System and certain of the presidents of the Federal Reserve Banks; oversees market conditions and implements monetary policy through such means as setting interest rates.

**Federal Reserve Bank of New York** One of 12 regional Federal Reserve Banks, with responsibility for regulating bank holding companies in New York State and nearby areas.

**Federal Reserve** U.S. central banking system created in 1913 in response to financial panics, consisting of the Federal Reserve Board in Washington, DC, and 12 Federal Reserve Banks around the country; its mission is to implement monetary policy through such means as setting interest rates, supervising and regulating banking institutions, maintaining the stability of the financial system, and providing financial services to depository institutions.

**FHA** see *Federal Housing Administration.*

**FHFA** see *Federal Housing Finance Agency.*

**FICO score** A measure of a borrower's creditworthiness based on the borrower's credit data; developed by the Fair Isaac Corporation.

**Financial Crimes Enforcement Network** Treasury office that collects and analyzes information about financial transactions to combat money laundering, terroristfinancing, and other financial crimes.

**FinCEN** see *Financial Crimes Enforcement Network.*

**FOMC** see *Federal Open Market Committee.*

**foreclosure** Legal process whereby a mortgage lender gains ownership of the real property securing a defaulted mortgage.

**Freddie Mac** Nickname for the Federal Home Loan Mortgage Corporation (FHLMC), a *government-sponsored enterprise* providing financing for the home mortgage market.

**Ginnie Mae** Nickname for the Government National Mortgage Association (GNMA), a *government-sponsored enterprise*; guarantees pools of VA and FHA mortgages.

**Glass-Steagall Act** Banking Act of 1933 creating the *FDIC* to insure bank deposits; prohibited commercial banks from underwriting or dealing in most types of securities, barred banks from affiliating with securities firms, and introduced other banking reforms. In 1999, the *Gramm-Leach-Bliley Act* repealed the provisions of the Glass-Steagall Act that prohibited affiliations between banks and securities firms.

**government-sponsored enterprise** A private corporation, such as *Fannie Mae* and *Freddie Mac*, created by the federal government to pursue certain public policy goals designated in its charter.

**Gramm-Leach-Bliley Act** 1999 legislation that lifted certain remaining restrictions established by the *Glass-Steagall Act.*

**GSE** see *government-sponsored enterprise.*

**haircut** The difference between the value of an asset and the amount borrowed against it.

**hedge** In finance, a way to reduce exposure or risk by taking on a new financial contract.

**hedge fund** A privately offered investment vehicle exempted from most regulation and oversight; generally open only to high-net-worth investors.

**HOEPA** see *Home Ownership and Equity Protection Act.*

**Home Ownership and Equity Protection Act** 1994 federal law that gave the *Federal Reserve* new responsibility to address abusive and predatory mortgage lending practices.

**Housing and Economic Recovery Act** 2008 law including measures to reform and regulate the *GSEs*; created the *Federal Housing Finance Agency.*

**HUD** see *Department of Housing and Urban Development.*

**hybrid CDO** A *CDO* backed by collateral found in both cash CDOs and synthetic CDOs.

**illiquid assets** Assets that cannot be easily or quickly sold.

**interest-only loan** Loan that allows borrowers to pay interest without repaying principal until the end of the loan term.

**leverage** A measure of how much debt is used to purchase assets; for example, a leverage ratio of 5:1 means that $5 of assets were purchased with $4 of debt and $1 of *capital.*

**LIBOR** London Interbank Offered Rate, an interest rate at which banks are willing to lend to each other in the London interbank market.

**liquidity** Holding cash and/or assets that can be quickly and easily converted to cash.

**liquidity put** A contract allowing one party to compel the other to buy an asset under certain circumstances. It ensures that there will be a buyer for otherwise illiquid assets.

**loan-to-value ratio** Ratio of the amount of a mortgage to the value of the house, typically expressed as a percentage. "Combined" loan-to-value includes all debt secured by the house, including second mortgages.

**LTV ratio** see *loan-to-value ratio.*

**mark-to-market** The process by which the reported amount of an asset is adjusted to reflect the market value.

**monoline** Insurance company, such as AMBAC and MBIA, whose single line of business is to guarantee financial products.

**mortgage servicer** Company that acts as an agent for mortgage holders, collecting and distributing payments from borrowers and handling defaults, modifications, settlements, and foreclosure proceedings.

**mortgage underwriting** Process of evaluating the credit characteristics of a mortgage and borrower.

**mortgage-backed security** Debt instrument secured by a pool of mortgages, whether residential or commercial.

**NAV** see *net asset value.*

**negative amortization loan** Loan that allows a borrower to make monthly payments that do not fully cover the interest payment, with the unpaid interest added to the principal of the loan.

**net asset value** Value of an asset minus any associated costs; for financial assets, typically changes each trading day.

**net charge-off rate** Ratio of loan losses to total loans.

**non-agency mortgage-backed securities** *Mortgage-backed securities* sponsored by private companies other than a *government-sponsored enterprise* (such as *Fannie Mae* or *Freddie Mac*); also known as *private-label mortgage-backed securities.*

**notional amount** A measure of the outstanding amount of over-the-counter *derivatives* contracts, based on the amount of the underlying referenced assets.

**novation** A process by which counterparties may transfer *derivatives* positions.

**OCC** see *Office of the Comptroller of the Currency.*

**Office of Federal Housing Enterprise Oversight** Created in 1992 to oversee financial soundness of *Fannie Mae* and *Freddie Mac*; its responsibilities were assumed in 2008 by its successor, the *Federal Housing Finance Agency.*

**Office of the Comptroller of the Currency** Independent bureau within *Department of Treasury* that charters, regulates, and supervises all national banks and certain branches and agencies of foreign banks in the United States.

**Office of Thrift Supervision** Independent bureau within *Treasury* that regulates all federally chartered and many state-chartered savings and loans/thrift institutions and their holding companies.

**OFHEO** see *Office of Federal Housing Enterprise Oversight.*

**originate-to-distribute** When lenders make loans with the intention of selling them to other financial institutions or investors, as opposed to holding the loans through maturity.

**originate-to-hold** When lenders make loans with the intention of holding them through maturity, as opposed to selling them to other financial institutions or investors.

**origination** Process of making a loan, including underwriting, closing, and providing the funds.

**OTS** see *Office of Thrift Supervision.*

**par** Face value of a bond.

**payment-option adjustable-rate mortgage** (also called payment *ARM* or option *ARM*) Mortgages that allow borrowers to pick the amount of payment each month, possibly low enough to increase the *principal* balance.

**PDCF** see *Primary Dealer Credit Facility.*

**PLS** see *private-label mortgage-backed securities.*

**pooling** Combining and packaging a group of loans to be held by a single entity.

**Primary Dealer Credit Facility** Program established by the *Federal Reserve* in March 2008 that allowed eligible companies to borrow cash overnight to finance their securities.

**principal** Amount borrowed.

**private mortgage insurance** Insurance on the payment of a mortgage provided by a private firm at additional cost to the borrower to protect the lender.

**private-label mortgage-backed securities** see *non-agency mortgage-backed securities.*

**repurchase agreement (repo)** A method of secured lending where the borrower sells securities to the lender as collateral and agrees to repurchase them at a higher price within a short period, often within one day.

**SEC** see *Securities and Exchange Commission.*

**section 13(3)** Section of the Federal Reserve Act under which the *Federal Reserve* may make secured loans to nondepository institutions, such as investment banks, under "unusual and exigent" circumstances.

**Securities and Exchange Commission** Independent federal agency responsible for protecting investors by enforcing federal securities laws, including regulating stock and security options exchanges and other electronic securities markets, the issuance and sale of securities, *broker-dealers,* other securities professionals, and investment companies.

**securitization** Process of pooling debt assets such as mortgages, car loans, and credit card debt into a separate legal entity that then issues a new financial instrument or security for sale to investors.

**shadow banking** Financial institutions and activities that in some respects parallel banking activities but are subject to less regulation than commercial banks. Institutions include mutual funds, investment banks, and hedge funds.

**short sale** The sale of a home for less than the amount owed on the mortgage.

**short selling** To sell a borrowed security in the expectation of a decline in value.

**SIV** see *structured investment vehicle.*

**special purpose vehicle** Entity created to fulfill a narrow or temporary objective; typically holds a portfolio of assets such as *mortgage-backed securities* or other debt obligations; often used because of regulatory and bankruptcy advantages.

**SPV** see *special purpose vehicle.*

**structured investment vehicle** Leveraged *special purpose vehicle,* funded through medium-term notes and *asset-backed commercial paper,* that invested in highly rated securities.

**synthetic CDO** A *CDO* that holds *credit default swaps* that reference assets (rather than holding cash assets), allowing investors to make bets for or against those referenced assets.

**systemic risk** In financial terms, that which poses a threat to the financial system.

**systemic risk exception** Clause in the Federal Deposit Insurance Corporation Improvement Act (FDICIA) under which the *FDIC* may commit its funds to rescue a financial institution.

**TAF** see *Term Auction Facility.*

**TALF** see *Term Asset-Backed Securities Loan Facility.*

**TARP** see *Troubled Asset Relief Program.*

**Term Asset-Backed Securities Loan Facility** *Federal Reserve* program, supported by *TARP* funds, to aid securitization of asset-based loans such as auto loans, student loans, and small business loans.

**Term Auction Facility** Program in which the *Federal Reserve* made funds available to all *depository institutions* at once through a regular auction.

**Term Securities Lending Facility** Emergency program in which the *Federal Reserve* made up to $200 billion in Treasury securities available to banks or broker/dealers that traded directly with the Federal Reserve.

**tranche** From the French, meaning a slice; used to refer to the different types of mortgage-backed securities and CDO bonds that provide specified priorities and amounts of returns: "senior" tranches have the highest priority of returns and therefore the lowest risk/interest rate; mezzanine tranches have mid levels of risk/return; and "equity" (also known as "residual" or "first loss") tranches typically receive any remaining cash flows.

**Troubled Asset Relief Program** Government program to address the financial crisis, signed into law in October 2008 to purchase or insure up to $700 billion in assets and equity from financial and other institutions.

**TSLF** see *Term Securities Lending Facility*.

**undercapitalized** Condition in which a business does not have enough *capital* to meet its needs, or to meet its capital requirements if it is a regulated entity.

**Write-downs** Reducing the value of an asset as it is carried on a firm's balance sheet because the market value has fallen.

# APPENDIX B:
# LIST OF HEARINGS AND WITNESSES

**Public Meeting of the FCIC, Washington, DC, September 17, 2009**
Statements by commissioners

**Roundtable Discussion, Washington, DC, October 20, 2009**
Martin Baily, Senior Fellow in Economic Studies, Brookings Institution
Simon Johnson, Ronald A. Kurtz Professor of Entrepreneurship, Sloan School of Management, Massachusetts Institute of Technology
Hal S. Scott, Nomura Professor and Director of the Program on International Financial Systems, Harvard Law School
Joseph Stiglitz, Professor, Columbia Business School, Graduate School of Arts and Sciences (Department of Economics) and the School of International and Public Affairs
John B. Taylor, Mary and Robert Raymond Professor of Economics and the Bowen H. and Janice Arthur McCoy Senior Fellow at the Hoover Institution, Stanford University
Luigi Zingales, Robert C. McCormack Professor of Entrepreneurship and Finance and the David G. Booth Faculty Fellow, University of Chicago Booth School of Business

**Roundtable Discussion, Washington, DC, November 16, 2009**
David A. Moss, The John G. McLean Professor, Harvard Business School
Carmen M. Reinhart, Professor of Economics and Director of the Center for International Economics, University of Maryland

**Public Hearing, Washington, DC, Day 1, January 13, 2010**
*Session 1: Financial Institution Representatives*
Lloyd C. Blankfein, Chairman of the Board and Chief Executive Officer, Goldman Sachs Group, Inc.
James Dimon, Chairman of the Board and Chief Executive Officer, JPMorgan Chase & Co.
John J. Mack, Chairman of the Board, Morgan Stanley
Brian T. Moynihan, Chief Executive Officer and President, Bank of America Corporation

*Session 2: Financial Market Participants*
Michael Mayo, Managing Director and Financial Services Analyst, Calyon Securities (USA) Inc.
J. Kyle Bass, Managing Partner, Hayman Advisors, LP
Peter J. Solomon, Founder and Chairman, Peter J. Solomon Company

*Session 3: Financial Crisis Impacts on the Economy*

Mark Zandi, Chief Economist and Co-founder, Moody's Economy.com

Kenneth T. Rosen, Chair, Fisher Center for Real Estate and Urban Economics, University of California, Berkeley

Julia Gordon, Senior Policy Counsel, Center for Responsible Lending

C. R. "Rusty" Cloutier, President and Chief Executive Officer, MidSouth Bank, N.A., Past Chairman, Independent Community Bankers Association

### Public Hearing, Washington, DC, Day 2, January 14, 2010

*Session 1: Current Investigations into the Financial Crisis—Federal Officials*

Eric H. Holder Jr., Attorney General, U.S. Department of Justice

Lanny A. Breuer, Assistant Attorney General, Criminal Division, U.S. Department of Justice

Sheila C. Bair, Chairman, U.S. Federal Deposit Insurance Corporation

Mary L. Schapiro, Chairman, U.S. Securities and Exchange Commission

*Session 2: Current Investigations into the Financial Crisis—State and Local Officials*

Lisa Madigan, Attorney General, State of Illinois

John W. Suthers, Attorney General, State of Colorado

Denise Voigt Crawford, Commissioner, Texas Securities Board, and President, North American Securities Administrators Association, Inc.

Glenn Theobald, Chief Counsel, Miami-Dade County Police Department; Chairman, Mayor Carlos Alvarez Mortgage Fraud Task Force

### Forum to Explore the Causes of the Financial Crisis, American University Washington College of Law, Washington, DC, Day 1, February 26, 2010

*Session 1: Interconnectedness of Financial Institutions; "Too Big to Fail"*

Randall Kroszner, Norman R. Bobins Professor of Economics, University of Chicago

*Session 2: Macroeconomic Factors and U.S. Monetary Policy*

Pierre-Olivier Gourinchas, Associate Professor of Economics, University of California, Berkeley

*Session 3: Risk Taking and Leverage*

John Geanakoplos, James Tobin Professor of Economics, Yale University

*Session 4: Household Finances and Financial Literacy*

Annamaria Lusardi, Joel Z. and Susan Hyatt Professor of Economics, Dartmouth University; Research Associate at the National Bureau of Economic Research

### Forum to Explore the Causes of the Financial Crisis, American University Washington College of Law, Washington, DC, Day 2, February 27, 2010

*Session 5: Mortgage Lending Practices and Securitization*

Chris Mayer, Paul Milstein Professor of Real Estate, Columbia University; Visiting Scholar at the Federal Reserve Bank of New York and Research Associate at the National Bureau of Economic Research

*Session 6: Government-Sponsored Enterprises and Housing Policy*

Dwight Jaffee, Willis Booth Professor of Banking, Finance, and Real Estate; Co-chair, Fisher Center for Real Estate and Urban Economics, University of California, Berkeley

*Session 7: Derivatives and Other Complex Financial Instruments*

Markus Brunnermeier, Edwards S. Sanford Professor of Economics, Princeton University

*Session 8: Firm Structure and Risk Management*
Anil Kashyap, Edward Eagle Brown Professor of Economics and Finance and Richard N. Rosett Faculty Fellow, University of Chicago

*Session 9: Shadow Banking*
Gary Gorton, Professor of Finance, School of Management, Yale University

## Public Hearing on Subprime Lending and Securitization and Government-Sponsored Enterprises (GSEs), Rayburn House Office Building, Room 2123, Washington, DC, Day 1, April 7, 2010

*Session 1: The Federal Reserve*
Alan Greenspan, Former Chairman, Board of Governors of the Federal Reserve System

*Session 2: Subprime Origination and Securitization*
Richard Bitner, Managing Director of Housingwire.com; Author, *Confessions of a Subprime Lender: An Insider's Tale of Greed, Fraud, and Ignorance*
Richard Bowen, Former Senior Vice President and Business Chief Underwriter, CitiMortgage, Inc.
Patricia Lindsay, Former Vice President, Corporate Risk, New Century Financial Corporation
Susan Mills, Managing Director of Mortgage Finance, Citi Markets & Banking, Global Securitized Markets

*Session 3: Citigroup Subprime-Related Structured Products and Risk Management*
Murray C. Barnes, Former Managing Director, Independent Risk, Citigroup, Inc.
David C. Bushnell, Former Chief Risk Officer, Citigroup, Inc.
Nestor Dominguez, Former Co-head, Global Collateralized Debt Obligations, Citi Markets & Banking, Global Structured Credit Products
Thomas G. Maheras, Former Co-chief Executive Officer, Citi Markets & Banking

## Public Hearing on Subprime Lending and Securitization and Government-Sponsored Enterprises (GSEs), Rayburn House Office Building, Room 2123, Washington, DC, Day 2, April 8, 2010

*Session 1: Citigroup Senior Management*
Charles O. Prince, Former Chairman of the Board and Chief Executive Officer, Citigroup, Inc.
Robert Rubin, Former Chairman of the Executive Committee of the Board of Directors, Citigroup, Inc.

*Session 2: Office of the Comptroller of the Currency*
John C. Dugan, Comptroller, Office of the Comptroller of the Currency
John D. Hawke Jr., Former Comptroller, Office of the Comptroller of the Currency

## Public Hearing on Subprime Lending and Securitization and Government-Sponsored Enterprises (GSEs), Rayburn House Office building, Room 2123, Washington, DC, Day 3, April 9, 2010

*Session 1: Fannie Mae*
Robert J. Levin, Former Executive Vice President and Chief Business Officer, Fannie Mae
Daniel H. Mudd, Former President and Chief Executive Officer, Fannie Mae

*Session 2: Office of Federal Housing Enterprise Oversight*
Armando Falcon Jr., Former Director, Office of Federal Housing Enterprise Oversight
James Lockhart, Former Director, Office of Federal Housing Enterprise Oversight

### Public Hearing on the Shadow Banking System, Dirksen Senate Office Building, Room 538, Washington DC, Day 1, May 5, 2010

*Session 1: Investment Banks and the Shadow Banking System*

Paul Friedman, Former Senior Managing Director, Bear Stearns

Samuel Molinaro Jr., Former Chief Financial Officer and Chief Operating Officer, Bear Stearns

Warren Spector, Former President and Co-chief Operating Officer, Bear Stearns

*Session 2: Investment Banks and the Shadow Banking System*

James E. Cayne, Former Chairman and Chief Executive Officer, Bear Stearns

Alan D. Schwartz, Former Chief Executive Officer, Bear Stearns

*Session 3: SEC Regulation of Investment Banks*

Charles Christopher Cox, Former Chairman, U.S. Securities and Exchange Commission

William H. Donaldson, Former Chairman, U.S. Securities and Exchange Commission

H. David Kotz, Inspector General, U.S. Securities and Exchange Commission

Erik R. Sirri, Former Director Division of Trading & Markets, U.S. Securities and Exchange Commission

### Public Hearing on the Shadow Banking System, Dirksen Senate Office Building, Room 538, Washington DC, Day 2, May 6, 2010

*Session 1: Perspective on the Shadow Banking System*

Henry M. Paulson Jr., Former Secretary, U.S. Department of the Treasury

*Session 2: Perspective on the Shadow Banking System*

Timothy F. Geithner, Secretary, U.S. Department of the Treasury; Former President, Federal Reserve Bank of New York

*Session 3: Institutions Participating in the Shadow Banking System*

Michael A. Neal, Vice Chairman, General Electric; Chairman and Chief Executive Officer, GE Capital

Mark S. Barber, Vice President and Deputy Treasurer, GE Capital

Paul A. McCulley, Managing Director, PIMCO

Steven R. Meier, Chief Investment Officer, State Street

### Public Hearing on Credibility of Credit Ratings, the Investment Decisions Made Based on Those Ratings, and the Financial Crisis, The New School Arnhold Hall, Theresa Lang Community & Student Center, 55 West 13th Street, 2nd Floor, New York, NY, June 2, 2010

*Session 1: The Ratings Process*

Eric Kolchinsky, Former Team Managing Director, US Derivatives, Moody's Investors Service

Jay Siegel, Former Team Managing Director, Moody's Investors Service

Nicolas S. Weill, Group Managing Director, Moody's Investors Service

Gary Witt, Former Team Managing Director, US Derivatives, Moody's Investors Service

*Session 2: Credit Ratings and the Financial Crisis*

Warren E. Buffett, Chairman and Chief Executive Officer, Berkshire Hathaway

Raymond W. McDaniel, Chairman and Chief Executive Officer, Moody's Corporation

*Session 3: The Credit Rating Agency Business Model*

Brian M. Clarkson, Former President and Chief Operating Officer, Moody's Investors Service (written testimony only due to a medical emergency)

Mark Froeba, Former Senior Vice President, US Derivatives, Moody's Investors Service

Richard Michalek, Former Vice President/Senior Credit Officer, Moody's Investors Service

## Public Hearing on the Role of Derivatives in the Financial Crisis, Dirksen Senate Office Building, Room 538, Washington, DC, Day 1, June 30, 2010

*Session 1: Overview of Derivatives*

Michael Greenberger, Professor, University of Maryland School of Law

Steve Kohlhagen, Former Professor of International Finance, University of California, Berkeley, and former Wall Street derivatives executive

Albert "Pete" Kyle, Charles E. Smith Chair Professor of Finance, University of Maryland

Michael Masters, Chief Executive Officer, Masters Capital Management, LLC

*Session 2: American International Group, Inc. and Derivatives*

Joseph J. Cassano, Former Chief Executive Officer, American International Group, Inc. Financial Products

Robert E. Lewis, Senior Vice President and Chief Risk Officer, American International Group, Inc.

Martin J. Sullivan, Former Chief Executive Officer, American International Group, Inc.

*Session 3: Goldman Sachs Group, Inc. and Derivatives*

Craig Broderick, Managing Director, Head of Credit, Market, and Operational Risk, Goldman Sachs Group, Inc.

Gary D. Cohn, President and Chief Operating Officer, Goldman Sachs Group, Inc.

## Public Hearing on the Role of Derivatives in the Financial Crisis, Dirksen Senate Office Building, Room 538, Washington DC, Day 2, July 1, 2010

*Session 1: American International Group, Inc. and Goldman Sachs Group, Inc.*

Steven J. Bensinger, Former Executive Vice President and Chief Financial Officer, American International Group, Inc.

Andrew Forster, Former Senior Vice President and Chief Financial Officer, American International Group, Inc. Financial Services

Elias F. Habayeb, Former Senior Vice President and Chief Financial Officer, American International Group, Inc. Financial Services

David Lehman, Managing Director, Goldman Sachs Group, Inc

David Viniar, Executive Vice President and Chief Financial Officer, Goldman Sachs Group, Inc.

*Session 2: Derivatives: Supervisors and Regulators*

Eric R. Dinallo, Former Superintendant, New York State Insurance Department

Gary Gensler, Chairman, Commodity Futures Trading Commission

Clarence K. Lee, Former Managing Director for Complex and International Organizations, Office of Thrift Supervision

## Public Hearing on Too Big to Fail: Expectations and Impact of Extraordinary Government Intervention and the Role of Systemic Risk in the Financial Crisis, Dirksen Senate Office Building, Room 538, Washington DC, Day 1, September 1, 2010

*Session 1: Wachovia Corporation*

Scott G. Alvarez, General Counsel, Board of Governors of the Federal Reserve System

John H. Corston, Acting Deputy Director, Division of Supervision and Consumer Protection, U.S. Federal Deposit Insurance Corporation

Robert K. Steel, Former President and Chief Executive Officer, Wachovia Corporation

*Session 2: Lehman Brothers*

Thomas C. Baxter, Jr., General Counsel and Executive Vice President, Federal Reserve Bank of New York

Richard S. "Dick" Fuld Jr., Former Chairman and Chief Executive Officer, Lehman Brothers

Harvey R. Miller, Business Finance & Restructuring Partner, Weil, Gotshal & Manges, LLP

Barry L. Zubrow, Chief Risk Officer, JPMorgan Chase & Co.

## Public Hearing on Too Big to Fail: Expectations and Impact of Extraordinary Government Intervention and the Role of Systemic Risk in the Financial Crisis, Dirksen Senate Office Building, Room 538, Washington DC, Day 2, September 2, 2010

*Session 1: The Federal Reserve*

Ben S. Bernanke, Chairman, Board of Governors of the Federal Reserve System

*Session 2: The Federal Deposit Insurance Corporation*

Sheila C. Bair, Chairman, U.S. Federal Deposit Insurance Corporation

## Public Hearing on the Impact of the Financial Crisis—Greater Bakersfield, Kern County Board of Supervisors Chambers, 1115 Truxtun Avenue, Bakersfield, CA, September 7, 2010

*Session 1: Welcome*

Congressman Kevin McCarthy, California's 22nd District

Ray Watson, Kern County Supervisor, District 4

Irma Carson, Bakersfield City Councilwoman, Ward 1

*Session 2: Local Banking*

Arnold Cattani, Chairman, Mission Bank

Steve Renock, President and CEO, Kern Schools Federal Credit Union

D. Linn Wiley, Vice Chairman, CVB Financial Corporation and Citizens Business Bank

*Session 3: Residential and Community Real Estate*

Gregory D. Bynum, President, Gregory D. Bynum and Associates, Inc.

Warren Peterson, Warren Peterson Construction, Inc.

*Session 4: Local Housing Market*

Gary Crabtree, Principal Owner, Affiliated Appraisers

Lloyd Plank, Lloyd E. Plank Real Estate Consultants

*Session 5: Foreclosures and Loan Modifications*

Brenda Amble, Escrow Manager, Ticor Title

Laurie McCarty, Coldwell Banker Preferred

Jeannie McDermott, Small Business Owner

*Session 6: Forum for Public Comment*

James Stephen Urner

Marvin Dean

Marie Vasile

## Public Hearing on the Impact of the Financial Crisis—State of Nevada, University of Nevada, Las Vegas, Student Union Building, Las Vegas, NV, September 8, 2010

*Session 1: Economic Analysis of the Impact of the Financial Crisis on Nevada*

Jeremy Aguero, Principal, Applied Analysis

*Session 2: The Impact of the Financial Crisis on Businesses of Nevada*

Steve Hill, Founder, Silver State Materials Corporation; Immediate Past Chairman, Las Vegas Chamber of Commerce

William E. Martin, Vice Chairman and Chief Executive Officer, Service 1st Bank of Nevada

Wally Murray, President and Chief Executive Officer, Greater Nevada Credit Union

Philip G. Satre, Chairman, International Gaming Technology (IGT); Chairman, NV Energy, Inc.

*Session 3: The Impact of the Financial Crisis on Nevada Real Estate*

Daniel G. Bogden, United States Attorney, State of Nevada

Gail Burks, President and Chief Executive Officer, Nevada Fair Housing Center

Brian Gordon, Principal, Applied Analysis

Jay Jeffries, Former Southwest Regional Sales Manager, Fremont Investment & Loan

*Session 4: The Impact of the Financial Crisis on Nevada Public and Community Services*

Andrew Clinger, Director of the Department of Administration, Chief of the Budget Division, State of Nevada

Jeffrey Fontaine, Executive Director, Nevada Association of Counties

David Fraser, Executive Director, Nevada League of Cities

Dr. Heath Morrison, Superintendent, Washoe County School District

*Session 5: Forum for Public Comment*

**Public Hearing on the Impact of the Financial Crisis—Miami, Florida, Florida International University, Modesto A. Madique Campus, Miami, FL, September 21, 2010**

*Session 1: Overview of Mortgage Fraud*

William K. Black, Associate Professor of Economics and Law, University of Missouri–Kansas City

Ann Fulmer, Vice President of Business Relations, Interthinx; Co-founder, Georgia Real Estate Fraud Prevention and Awareness Coalition

Henry N. Pontell, Professor of Criminology, Law & Society and Sociology, University of California, Irvine

*Session 2: Uncovering Mortgage Fraud in Miami*

Dennis J. Black, President, D. J. Black & Company

Edward Gallagher, Executive Officer, Economic Crimes Bureau, Mortgage Fraud Task Force, Miami-Dade Police Department

Jack Rubin, Senior Vice President, JPMorgan Chase Bank

Ellen Wilcox, Special Agent, Florida Department of Law Enforcement

*Session 3: The Regulation, Oversight, and Prosecution of Mortgage Fraud in Miami*

J. Thomas Cardwell, Commissioner, Office of Financial Regulation, State of Florida

Wilfredo A. Ferrer, United States Attorney, Southern District of Florida

R. Scott Palmer, Special Counsel and Chief of the Mortgage Fraud Task Force, Office of the Attorney General, State of Florida

**Public Hearing on the Impact of the Financial Crisis—Sacramento, California Department of Education, Sacramento, CA, September 23, 2010**

*Session 1: Overview of the Sacramento Housing and Mortgage Markets and the Impact of the Financial Crisis on the Region*

Mark Fleming, Chief Economist, CoreLogic

*Session 2: Mortgage Origination, Mortgage Fraud and Predatory Lending in the Sacramento Region*

Karen J. Mann, President and Chief Appraiser, Mann and Associates Real Estate Appraisers & Consultants

Thomas C. Putnam, President, Putnam Housing Finance Consulting

Kevin Stein, Associate Director, California Reinvestment Coalition

Benjamin B. Wagner, United States Attorney, Eastern District of California

*Session 3: The Mortgage Securitization Chain: From Sacramento to Wall Street*

Vicki Beal, Senior Vice President, Transaction Management, Clayton Holdings, LLC

Kurt Eggert, Professor of Law, Chapman University School of Law

D. Keith Johnson, Former President and Chief Executive Officer, Washington Mutual's Long Beach Mortgage

*Session 4: The Impact of the Financial Crisis on Sacramento Neighborhoods and Families*

Pam Canada, Chief Executive Officer, NeighborWorks Home Ownership Center–Sacramento Region

Mona Tawatao, Regional Counsel, Legal Services of Northern California

Bruce Wagstaff, Agency Administrator, County of Sacramento Countywide Services Agency

Clarence Williams, President, California Capital Financial Development Corporation

Henry W. Wirz, President and Chief Executive Officer, SAFE Credit Union

*Public Testimony Presented*

Allen Carpenter

Lovie M. Hollis

Nia Lavulo

# NOTES

Unless otherwise specified, data come from the sources listed below.

Board of Governors of the Federal Reserve System, Flow of Funds Reports: Debt, international capital flows, and the size and activity of various financial sectors

Bureau of Economic Analysis: Economic output (GDP), spending, wages, and sector profit

Bureau of Labor Statistics: Labor market statistics

BlackBox Logic and Standard & Poor's: Data on loans underlying CMLTI 2006-NC2

CoreLogic: Home prices

Inside Mortgage Finance, 2009 Mortgage Market Statistical Annual: Data on origination of mortgages, issuance of mortgage-backed securities and values outstanding

Markit Group: ABX-HE index

Mortgage Bankers Association National Delinquency Survey: Mortgage delinquency and foreclosure rates

10-Ks, 10-Qs, and proxy statements filed with the Securities and Exchange Commission: Company-specific information

Many of the documents cited on the following pages, along with other materials, are available on www.fcic.gov.

## Chapter 1

1. Charles Prince, testimony before the FCIC, Hearing on Subprime Lending and Securitization and Government-Sponsored Enterprises (GSEs), day 2, session 1: Citigroup Senior Management, April 8, 2010, transcript, p. 10.

2. Warren Buffett, testimony before the FCIC, Hearing on the Credibility of Credit Ratings, the Investment Decisions Made Based on Those Ratings, and the Financial Crisis, session 2: Credit Ratings and the Financial Crisis, June 2, 2010, transcript, p. 208; Warren Buffett, interview by FCIC, May 26, 2010.

3. Lloyd Blankfein, testimony before the First Public Hearing of the FCIC, day 1, panel 1: Financial Institution Representatives, January 13, 2010, transcript, p. 36.

4. Ben S. Bernanke, closed-door session with FCIC, November 17, 2009; Ben S. Bernanke, testimony before the FCIC, Hearing on Too Big to Fail: Expectations and Impact of Extraordinary Government Intervention and the Role of Systemic Risk in the Financial Crisis, day 2, session 1: The Federal Reserve, September 2, 2010, transcript, p. 27.

5. Alan Greenspan, written testimony for the FCIC, Subprime Lending and Securitization and Government-Sponsored Enterprises (GSEs), day 1, session 1: The Federal Reserve, April 7, 2010, p. 9.

6. Richard C. Breeden, interview by FCIC, October 14, 2010.

7. Paul A. McCulley, testimony before the FCIC, Hearing on the Shadow Banking System, day 2, session 3: Institutions Participating in the Shadow Banking System, May 6, 2010, transcript, p. 249.

8. Arnold Cattani, testimony before the FCIC, Hearing on the Impact of the Financial Crisis—Greater Bakersfield, session 2: Local Banking, September 7, 2010, transcript pp. 25, 61.

9. William Martin, testimony before the FCIC, Hearing on the Impact of the Financial Crisis—State of Nevada, session 2: The Impact of the Financial Crisis on Businesses of Nevada, September 8, 2010, transcript, p. 76.

10. Inside Mortgage Finance, *The 2009 Mortgage Market Statistical Annual*, vol. 1, *The Primary Market* (: Inside Mortgage Finance, 2009), p. 4, "Mortgage Product by Origination."

11. Data provided to the FCIC by National Association of Realtors: national home price data from sales of existing homes, comparing second-quarter 1998 ($135,800) and second-quarter 2006 ($227,100), the national peak in prices.

12. Core-based statistical area house prices for Sacramento–Arden–Arcade–Roseville CA Metropolitan Statistical Area, CoreLogic data.

13. Data provided by CoreLogic, Home Price Index for Urban Areas. FCIC staff calculated house price growth from January 2001 to peak of each market. Prices increased at least 50% in 401 cities, at least 75% in 217 cities, at least 100% in 112 cities, at least 125% in 63 cities, and more than 150% in 16 cities.

14. Updated data provided by James Kennedy and Alan Greenspan, whose data originally appeared in "Sources and Uses of Equity Extracted from Homes," Finance and Economics Discussion Series, Federal Reserve Board, 2007-20 (March 2007).

15. "Mortgage Originations Rise in First Half of 2005; Demand for Interest Only, Option ARM and Alt-A Products Increases," Mortgage Bankers Association press release, October 25, 2005.

16. In 2007, the weekly wage of New York investment banker was $16,849; of the average privately employed worker, $841.

17. Federal Reserve Survey of Consumer Finances, tabulated by FCIC.

18. Angelo Mozilo, interview by FCIC, September 24, 2010.

19. Michael Mayo, testimony before the First Public Hearing of the FCIC, day 1, panel 2: Financial Market Participants, January 13, 2010, transcript, p. 114.

20. "Mortgage Originations Rise in First Half of 2005," MBA press release, October 27, 2005.

21. Yuliya Demyanyk and Yadav K. Gopalan, "Subprime ARMs: Popular Loans, Poor Performance," Federal Reserve Bank of St. Louis, *Bridges* (Spring 2007).

22. Ann Fulmer, vice president of Business Relations, Interthinx (session 1: Overview of Mortgage Fraud), and Ellen Wilcox, special agent, Florida Department of Law Enforcement (session 2: Uncovering Mortgage Fraud in Miami), testimony before the FCIC, Hearing on the Impact of the Financial Crisis—Miami, September 21, 2010.

23. Julia Gordon and Michael Calhoun, Center for Responsible Lending, interview by FCIC, September 16, 2010.

24. Faith Schwartz, at Consumer Advisory Council meeting, Thursday, March 30, 2006.

25. Federal Reserve Board, "Mean Value of Mortgages or Home-Equity Loans for Families with Holdings," in *SCF Chartbook,* June 15, 2009, tables updated to February 18, 2010.

26. Christopher Cruise, interview by FCIC, August 20, 2010.

27. Ibid.

28. Robert Kuttner, interview by FCIC, August 5, 2010.

29. Timothy Geithner, testimony before the FCIC, Hearing on the Shadow Banking System, day 2, session 2: Perspective on the Shadow Banking System, May 6, 2010, transcript, p. 146.

30. James Ryan, chief marketing officer at CitiFinancial and John Schachtel, executive vice president of CitiFinancial, interview by FCIC, February 3, 2010.

31. These points were made to the FCIC by consumer advocates: e.g., Kevin Stein, associate director, California Reinvestment Coalition, at the Hearing on the Impact of the Financial Crisis—Sacramento, session 2: Mortgage Origination, Mortgage Fraud and Predatory Lending in the Sacramento Region, September 23, 2010; Gail Burks, president and CEO, Nevada Fair Housing Center, at the Hearing on the Impact of the Financial Crisis—State of Nevada, session 3: The Impact of the Financial Crisis on Nevada Real Estate, September 8, 2010. See also Federal Reserve Consumer Advisory Council transcripts, March 25, 2004; June 24, 2004; October 28, 2004; March 17, 2005; October 27, 2005; June 22, 2006; October 26, 2006.

32. Bob Gnaizda, interview by FCIC, March 25, 2010.

33. James Rokakis, interview by FCIC, November 8, 2010.

34. Ibid.

35. Fed Governor Edward M. Gramlich, "Tackling Predatory Lending: Regulation and Education," remarks at Cleveland State University, Cleveland, Ohio, March 23, 2001.

36. Rokakis, interview.

37. John Taylor, chairman and chief executive officer, National Community Reinvestment Coalition, letter to Office of Thrift Supervision, July 3, 2000, provided to the FCIC.

38. Stein, testimony before the FCIC, transcript, pp. 73–74, 71.

39. U.S. Department of the Treasury and U.S Department of Housing and Urban Development, "Joint Report on Recommendations to Curb Predatory Home Mortgage Lending" (June 1, 2000).

40. Federal Reserve Board press release, December 12, 2001.

41. Sheila C. Bair, written testimony for the FCIF, First Public Hearing of the FCIC, day 2, panel 1: Current Investigations into the Financial Crisis—Federal Officials, January 14, 2010, p. 11.

42. Fed Governor Edward M. Gramlich, "Predatory Lending," remarks at the Housing Bureau for Seniors Conference, , January 18, 2002.

43. Sheila C. Bair, testimony before the FCIC, First Public Hearing of the FCIC, day 2, panel 1: Current Investigations into the Financial Crisis—Federal Officials, January 14, 2010, transcript, p. 97.

44. Sheila C. Bair, interview by FCIC, March 29, 2010.

45. *2009 Mortgage Market Statistical Annual*, 1:220, "Top B&C Lenders in 2000"; 1.223, "Top B&C Lenders in 2003."

46. Ibid., 1:237, "Subprime Origination by State in 2001"; and 1:235, "Subprime Originations by State in 2003."

47. Stein, testimony before the FCIC, September 23, 2010, transcript, p. 72.

48. Gail Burks, interview by FCIC, August 30, 2010.

49. Lisa Madigan, written testimony for the FCIC, First Public Hearing of the FCIC, day 1, panel 2: Current Investigations into the Financial Crisis—State and Local Officials, January 14, 2010, p. 4–5; "Home Mortgage Lender settled 'Predatory Lending' Charges," Federal Trade Commission press release, March 21, 2002.

50. *2009 Mortgage Market Statistical Annual*, 1:220, "Top 25 B&C Lenders in 2003."

51. Madigan, written testimony for the FCIC, January 14, 2010, pp. 4–5.

52. Ed Parker, interview by FCIC, May 26, 2010.

53. Prentiss Cox, interview by FCIC, October 15, 2010.

54. Ibid.

55. *2009 Mortgage Market Statistical Annual*, 1:45, 47, 49, 51.

56. Alphonso Jackson, interview by FCIC, October 6, 2010.

57. Cox, interview; Madigan, written testimony for the FCIC, January 14, 2010, p. 11.

58. Cox, interview. Madigan, testimony before the FCIC, January 14, 2010, transcript, pp. 121–122.

59. John D. Hawke Jr. and John C. Dugan, written statements for the FCIC, Hearing on Subprime Lending and Securitization and Government-Sponsored Enterprises (GSEs), day 2, session 2: Office of the Comptroller of the Currency, April 8, 2010, pp. 4–5 and pp. 4–8, respectively.

60. Madigan, written testimony for the FCIC, January 14, 2010, pp. 9, 10.

61. Cox, interview.

62. *2009 Mortgage Market Statistical Annual*, 1:4, "Mortgage Originations by Product." Nonprime = Alt-A and subprime combined.

63. Marc S. Savitt, interview by FCIC, November 17, 2010.

64. Rob Barry, Matthew Haggman, and Jack Dolan, "Ex-convicts active in mortgage fraud," *Miami Herald*, January 29, 2009.

65. J. Thomas Cardwell, written testimony for the FCIC, Hearing on the Impact of the Financial Crisis—Miami, session 3: The Regulation, Oversight, and Prosecution of Mortgage Fraud in Miami, September 21, 2010, p. 8.

66. Savitt, interview.

67. Gary Crabtree, written testimony for the FCIC, Hearing on the Impact of the Financial Crisis—Greater Bakersfield, session 4: Local Housing Market, September 7, 2010, p. 6.

68. Ibid.

69. Gary Crabtree, interview by FCIC, August 18, 2010. Crabtree, written testimony for the FCIC, September 7, 2010, pp. 6–7.

70. "FBI Warns of Mortgage Fraud 'Epidemic' from Terry Frieden," CNN news report, September 17, 2004.

71. Kirstin Downey, "FBI Vows to Crack Down on Mortgage Fraud; Hot Real Estate Market Drives Reports of 'Suspicious' Activity, Agency Says," Washington Post, February 15, 2005.

72. Financial Crimes Enforcement Network, Regulatory Policy and Programs Division, "Mortgage Loan Fraud: An Industry Assessment Based upon Suspicious Activity Report Analysis," November 2006. See also Financial Crimes Enforcement Network, "Annual Report: Fiscal Year 2008."

73. FinCEN response to FCIC interrogatories, October 14–15, 2010.

74. William K. Black, written testimony for the FCIC, Hearing on the Impact of the Financial Crisis—Miami, session 1: Overview of Mortgage Fraud, September 21, 2010, p. 8.

75. Alberto Gonzales, interview by FCIC, November 1, 2010; Michael Mukasey, interview by FCIC, October 20, 2010.

76. Federal Reserve Consumer Advisory Council Meeting, October 28, 2004, transcript, p. 44.

77. Ibid., p. 45.

78. Ruhi Maker, interview by FCIC, October 25, 2010.

79. Kirstin Downey, "Many Buyers Opt for Risky Mortgages," Washington Post, May 28, 2005.

80. "After the Fall: Soaring house prices have given a huge boost to the world economy. What happens when they drop?" The Economist, June 16, 2005.

81. Fed Chairman Alan Greenspan, "The Economic Outlook," prepared testimony before the Joint Economic Committee, 109th Cong., 1st sess., June 9, 2005.

82. Ibid.

83. Fed Chairman Ben S. Bernanke, "The Economic Outlook," prepared testimony before the Joint Economic Committee, U.S. Congress, 110th Cong., 1st sess., March 28, 2007.

84. Sheila Canavan, comments during of the Federal Reserve Consumer Advisory Council Meeting, October 27, 2005, transcript, p. 52.

85. David Leonhardt, "Be Warned: Mr. Bubble's Worried Again," New York Times, August 21, 2005.

86. Raghuram Rajan, interview by FCIC, November 22, 2010.

87. Ibid.

88. Ibid.

89. Raghuram G. Rajan, Fault Lines: How Hidden Fractures Still Threaten The World Economy (Princeton: Princeton University Press, 2010), p. 3.

90. Susan M. Wachter, interview by FCIC, October 6, 2010.

91. Mark Klipsch, quoted in "Blizzard Can't Stop ASF 2005 Conference," Asset Securitization Report, January 31, 2005.

92. Dennis J. Black, written testimony for the FCIC, Hearing on the Impact of the Financial Crisis—Miami, session 2: Uncovering Mortgage Fraud in Miami, September 21, 2010, p. 1; for the appraiser's petition, see http://appraiserspetition.com/.

93. Karen Mann, written testimony for the FCIC, Hearing on the Impact of the Financial Crisis—Sacramento, session 2: Mortgage Origination, Mortgage Fraud and Predatory Lending in the Sacramento Region, September 23, 2010.

94. 2009 Mortgage Market Statistical Annual, vol. 2, The Secondary Market, p. 13, "Non-Agency MBS Issuance by Type," and FCIC staff estimates based on analysis of Moody's SFDRS data.

95. Jamie Dimon, testimony before the FCIC, First Public Hearing of the FCIC, day 1, panel 1: Financial Institution Representatives, January 13, 2010, transcript, p. 78.

96. Madelyn Antoncic, interview by FCIC, July 14, 2010.

97. Anton R. Valukas, Report of Examiner, In re Lehman Brothers Holdings Inc., et al., Chapter 11 Case No. 08-13555 (JMP), (Bankr. S.D.N.Y.), March 11, 2010, 1:114, with n. 418.

98. Richard Bowen, interview by FCIC, February 27, 2010.

99. Richard Bowen, email to Robert Rubin, David Bushnell, Gary Crittenden, and Bonnie Howard, November 3, 2007.

100. Robert Rubin, testimony before the FCIC, Hearing on Subprime Lending and Securitization and Government-Sponsored Entities (GSEs), day 2, session 1: Citigroup Senior Management, April 8, 2010, transcript, p. 30.

101. Brad S. Karp, counsel for Citigroup, letter to FCIC, November 1, 2010, in response to FCIC request of September 21, 2010, for information regarding Richard Bowen's November 3, 2007, email, p. 2.

102. Bowen, interview.

103. J. Kyle Bass, testimony before the FCIC, First Public Hearing of the FCIC, day 1, panel 2: Financial Market Participants, January 13, 2010, transcript, pp. 143–44.

104. Herbert M. Sandler, "Comment on Joint ANPR for Proposed Revision to the Existing Risk-based Capital Rule," letter to Federal Reserve Board, Office of the Comptroller of the Currency, Federal Deposit Insurance Corporation, and Office of Thrift Supervision, January 18, 2006.

105. Lewis Ranieri, interview by FDIC, July 30, 2010.

106. Angelo Mozilo, email to Eric Sieracki, April 13, 2006, re: 1Q2006 Earnings.

107. Angelo Mozilo, email to David Sambol, April 17, 2006, subject: sub-prime seconds.

108. David Sambol, email to Angelo Mozilo, April 17, 2006, re: Sub-prime seconds (cc Kurland, McMurray, and Bartlett).

109. Angelo Mozilo, email to David Sambol, April 17, 2006, subject: re: Sub-prime seconds (cc Kurland, McMurray, and Bartlett).

110. Sabeth Siddique, interview by FCIC, September 9, 2010.

111. "Survey of Nontraditional Mortgages" (actual title redacted), confidential Federal Reserve document obtained by FCIC, produced November 1, 2005, pp. 2, 3.

112. Susan Bies, interview by FDIC, October 11, 2010.

113. John Dugan, testimony before the FCIC, Hearing on Subprime Lending and Securitization and Government-Sponsored Enterprises (GSEs), day 2, session 2: Office of the Comptroller of the Currency, April 8, 2010, transcript,

114. Sabeth Siddique, interviews by FCIC, September 9, 2010, and October 25, 2010.

115. Bies, interview.

116. Mortgage Insurance Companies of America, quoted in Kirstin Downey, "Insurers Want Action on Risky Mortgages; Firms Want More Loan Restrictions," *Washington Post*, August 19, 2006.

117. William A. Simpson, Mortgage Insurance Companies of America, "MICA Testimony on Non-Traditional Mortgages," before the Senate Subcommittee on Housing and Transportation and the Subcommittee on Economic Policy, 109th Cong., 2nd sess., September 20, 2006.

118. Siddique, interviews, October 25, 2010, and September 9, 2010.

119. Consumer Advisory Council Meeting, March 30, 2006, transcript.

120. Consumer Advisory Council Meeting, June 22, 2006, transcript.

121. Siddique, interview, October 25, 2010; Bies, interview.

122. There is no central clearinghouse to calculate structured finance assets. The FCIC's estimate is based on the amount of structured finance assets rated by Moody's along with unrated agency RMBS, along with an estimate for structured finance assets not rated by Moody's, using as sources Fannie Mae and Freddie Mac, Bloomberg, American CoreLogic Loan Performance, Fitch Ratings, Moody's, S&P, Thomson Reuters, and SIFMA.

123. Alan Greenspan, testimony before the FCIC, Hearing on Subprime Lending and Securitization and Government-Sponsored Enterprises (GSEs), day 1, session 1: The Federal Reserve, April 7, 2010, transcript, p. 29.

124. Mortgage Bankers Association, "National Delinquency Survey."

125. CoreLogic, Inc., August 26, 2010, news release, second quarter, 2010. Second-quarter figures were an improvement from 11.2 million residential properties (24%) in negative equity in the first quarter of 2010.

126. Mark Zandi, written testimony for the FCIC, First Public Hearing of the FCIC, day 1, panel 3: Financial Crisis Impacts on the Economy, January 13, 2010, pp. 14, 15.

127. Dean Baker, interview by FCIC, August 18, 2010.

128. Warren Peterson, testimony before the FCIC, Hearing on the Impact of the Financial Crisis—Greater Bakersfield, session 3: Residential and Community Real Estate, September 7, 2010, transcript, pp. 106–7, 119–20, 107–8; Warren Peterson, interview by FCIC, August 24, 2010.

## Chapter 2

1. Ben Bernanke, written testimony before the FCIC, Hearing on Too Big to Fail: Expectations and Impact of Extraordinary Government Intervention and the Role of Systemic Risk in the Financial Crisis, day 1, session 1, September 2, 2010, p. 2.

2. Alan Greenspan, "The Evolution of Banking in a Market Economy," remarks at the Annual Conference of the Association of Private Enterprise Education, Arlington, Virginia, April 12, 1997.

3. Charles Calomiris and Gary Gorton, "The Origins of Banking Panics: Models, Facts, and Bank Regulation," in Calomiris, *U.S. Bank Deregulation in Historical Perspective* (Cambridge: Cambridge University Press, 2000), pp. 98–100. Prior to the end of the Civil War, banks issued notes instead of holding deposits. Runs on that system occurred in 1814, 1819, 1837, 1839, 1857, and 1861 (ibid., pp. 98–99).

4. R. Alton Gilbert, "Requiem for Regulation Q: What It Did and Why It Passed Away," *Federal Reserve Bank of St. Louis Review* 68, no. 2 (February 1986): 23.

5. FCIC, "Preliminary Staff Report: Shadow Banking and the Financial Crisis," May 4, 2010, pp. 18–25.

6. Arthur E. Wilmarth Jr., "The Transformation of the U.S. Financial Services Industry, 1975–2000: Competition, Consolidation, and Increased Risks," *University of Illinois Law Review* (2002): 239–40.

7. Frederic S. Mishkin, "Asymmetric Information and Financial Crises: A Historical Perspective," in *Financial Markets and Financial Crises,* ed. R. Glenn Hubbard (Chicago: University of Chicago Press, 1991), p. 99; Wilmarth, "The Transformation of the U.S. Financial Services Industry, 1975–2000," p. 236.

8. Federal Reserve Board Flow of Funds Release, table L.208. Accessed December 29, 2010.

9. Kenneth Garbade, "The Evolution of Repo Contracting Conventions in the 1980s," *Federal Reserve Bank of New York Economic Policy Review* 12, no. 1 (May 2006): 32–33, 38–39 (available at http://papers.ssrn.com/sol3/papers.cfm?abstract_id=918498). To implement monetary policy, the Federal Reserve Bank of New York uses the repo market: it sets interest rates by borrowing Treasuries from and lending them to securities firms, many of which are units of commercial banks.

10. Alan Blinder, interview by FCIC, September 17, 2010.

11. Paul Volcker, interview by FCIC, October 11, 2010.

12. Fed Chairman Alan Greenspan, "International Financial Risk Management," remarks before the Council on Foreign Relations, November 19, 2002.

13. Richard C. Breeden, interview by FCIC, October 14, 2010.

14. Wilmarth, "The Transformation of the U.S. Financial Services Industry, 1975–2000," p. 241 and n. 102.

15. Thereafter, banks were only required to lend on collateral and set terms based upon what the market was offering. They also could not lend more than 10% of their capital to one subsidiary or more than 20% to all subsidiaries. Order Approving Applications to Engage in Limited Underwriting and Dealing in Certain Securities," *Federal Reserve Bulletin* 73, no. 6 (June 1987): 473–508; "Revenue Limit on Bank-Ineligible Activities of Subsidiaries of Bank Holding Companies Engaged in Underwriting and Dealing in Securities," *Federal Register* 61, no. 251 (Dec. 30, 1996), 68750–56.

16. Julie L. Williams and Mark P. Jacobsen, "The Business of Banking: Looking to the Future," *Business Lawyer* 50 (May 1995): 798.

17. Fed Chairman Alan Greenspan, prepared testimony before the House Committee on Banking and Financial Services, *H.R. 10, the Financial Services Competitiveness Act of 1997,* 105th Cong., 1st sess., May 22, 1997.

18. FCIC staff calculations.

19. FCIC staff calculations.

20. FCIC staff calculations using First American/CoreLogic, National HPI Single-Family Combined (SFC).

21. This data series is relatively new. Those series available before 2009 showed no year-over-year national house price decline. First American/CoreLogic, National HPI Single-Family Combined (SFC).

22. For a general overview of the banking and thrift crisis of the 1980s, see FDIC, *History of the Eighties: Lessons for the Future,* vol. 1, *An Examination of the Banking Crises of the 1980s and Early 1990s* (Washington, DC: Federal Deposit Insurance Corporation, 1997).

23. Specifically, between 1980 and 1994, 1,617 federally insured banks with $302.6 billion in assets and 1,295 savings and loans with $621 billion in assets either closed or received FDIC or FSLIC assistance. See Federal Deposit Insurance Corp., *Managing the Crisis: The FDIC and RTC Experience, 1980–1994* (Aug. 1998), pp. 4, 5.

24. William K. Black, Associate Professor of Economics and Law, University of Missouri–Kansas City, written testimony for the FCIC, Hearing on the Impact of the Financial Crisis, session 1: Overview of Mortgage Fraud, September 21, 2010, p. 4. And see Kitty Calavita, Henry N. Pontell, and Robert H. Tillman, *Big Money Crime: Fraud and Politics in the Savings and Loan Crisis* (Berkeley: University of California Press, 1997), p. 28.

25. FDIC, *History of the Eighties: Lessons for the Future,* 1:39.

26. U.S. Treasury Department, "Modernizing the Financial System: Recommendations for Safer, More Competitive Banks" (February 1991), p. 55.

27. Testimony of John LaWare, Governor, Federal Reserve Board, at Hearings before Subcommittee on Economic Stabilization of the Committee on Banking, Finance, and Urban Affairs on the "Economic Implications of the Too Big to Fail Policy," May 9, 1991, p. 11, http://fraser.stlouisfed.org/publications/tbtf/issue/3954/download/61094/housetbtf1991.pdf.

FDIC, *History of the Eighties: Lessons for the Future,* 1:251.

28. George G. Kaufman, "Too Big to Fail in U.S. Banking: Quo Vadis?" in *Too Big to Fail: Policies and Practices in Government Bailouts,* ed. Benton E. Gup (Westport, CT: Praeger, 2004), p. 163.

29. FCIC, "Preliminary Staff Report: Too-Big-to-Fail Financial Institutions," August 31, 2010, pp. 6–9.(Rep. McKinney is quoted from the transcript of the hearing before the House Committee on Banking, Housing, and Urban Affairs).

30. Ibid., pp. 10, 19.

## Chapter 3

1. Federal National Mortgage Association, *Federal National Mortgage Association, Background and History* (1975).

2. Department of Housing and Urban Development, *1986 Report to Congress on the Federal National Mortgage Association* (1987), p. 100.

3. See, e.g., Kenneth H. Bacon, "Privileged Position: Fannie Mae Expected to Escape Attempt at Tighter Regulation," *Wall Street Journal,* June 19, 1992, and Stephen Labaton, "Power of the Mortgage Twins: Fannie and Freddie Guard Autonomy," *New York Times,* November 12, 1991.

4. Armando Falcon Jr., written testimony for the FCIC, Hearing on Subprime Lending and Securitization and Government-Sponsored Enterprises (GSEs), day 3, session 2: Office of Federal Housing Enterprise Oversight, April 9, 2010, p. 2.

5. Wayne Passmore, "The GSE Implicit Subsidy and the Value of Government Ambiguity," Federal Reserve Board Staff Working Paper 2005–05. See also Congressional Budget Office, "Updated Estimates of the Subsidies to the Housing GSEs," April 8, 2004.

6. Federal Housing Finance Agency, *Report to Congress, 2009* (2010), pp. 141, 158.

7. Fannie Mae Charter Act of 1968, §309(h), codified at 12 U.S.C. §1723a(h). The 1992 Federal Housing Enterprises Financial Safety and Soundness Act repealed this provision and replaced it with more elaborate provisions. Currently, the GSEs typically define low- and moderate-income borrowers as those with income at or below median income for a given area.

8. Department of Housing and Urban Development, "Regulations Implementing the Authority of the Secretary of the Department of Housing and Urban Development over the conduct of the Secondary market Operations of the Federal National Mortgage Association (FNMA)," *Federal Register* 43, no. 158 (August 15, 1978): 36199–226.

9. President William J. Clinton, "Remarks on the National Homeownership Strategy," June 5, 1995.

10. President George W. Bush, "President's Remarks to the National Association of Home Builders," Greater Columbus Convention Center, Columbus, Ohio, October 2, 2004.

11. Andrew Cuomo, interview by FCIC, December 17, 2010.

12. Daniel Mudd, testimony before the FCIC, Hearing on Subprime Lending and Securitization and Government-Sponsored Enterprises (GSEs), day 3, session 1: Fannie Mae, April 9, 2010, transcript, pp. 18–19.

13. Richard Syron, interview by FCIC, August 31, 2010.

14. Senate Lobbying Disclosure Act Database (www.senate.gov/legislative/Public_Disclosure/ LDA_reports.htm); figures on employees and PACs compiled by the Center for Responsive Politics from Federal Elections Commission data.

15. Falcon, written testimony for the FCIC, April 9, 2010, p. 5.

16. James Lockhart, written testimony for the FCIC, Hearing on Subprime Lending and Securitization and Government-Sponsored Enterprises (GSEs), day 3, session 2: Office of Federal Housing Enterprise Oversight, pp. 4–8, 17 (quotation).

17. Senator Mel Martinez, interview by FCIC, September 28, 2010.

18. June E. O'Neill, remarks before the Conference on Appraising Fannie Mae and Freddie Mac, Washington, D.C., May 14, 1998, p. 8.

19. Federal Housing Finance Agency, *Report to Congress, 2008* (2009), tables 3, 4, 12, and 13.

20. Lawrence Lindsey, interview by FCIC, September 20, 2010.

21. Jim Callahan, interview by FCIC, October 18, 2010.

22. Securities Industry and Financial Markets Association (SIFMA), US ABS Outstanding.

23. Scott Patterson, interview by FCIC, August 12, 2010.

24. Gillian Tett, *Fool's Gold: How the Bold Dream of a Small Tribe at J. P. Morgan Was Corrupted by Wall Street Greed and Unleashed a Catastrophe* (New York: Free Press, 2009), pp. 32–33, 49, 70, 115.

25. Emmanuel Derman, interview by FCIC, May 12, 2010.

26. Volcker, interview.

27. Vincent Reinhart, interview by FCIC, September 10, 2010.

28. Lindsey, interview.

29. A futures contract is a bilateral contract in which one party, the long position, is compensated if the price or index or rate underlying the contract rises while the other party, the short position, is compensated if it goes down. An options contract grants the right but not the obligation to purchase or sell a commodity or financial instrument at a particular price in the future; the option holder derives a benefit if the price moves in his or her favor. In a swaps contract, the two parties exchange streams of payments based on different benchmarks.

30. Securities options are regulated by the SEC.

31. Commodity Futures Trading Commission, Exemption for Certain Swap Agreements, Final Rule, *Federal Registrar* 58 (January 22, 1993): 5587.

32. Brooksley Born, chairperson, Commodity Futures Trading Commission, "Concerning the Over-the-Counter Derivatives Market," prepared testimony before the House Committee on Banking and Financial Services, 105th Cong., 2nd sess., July 24, 1998.

33. GAO, "Financial Derivatives: Actions Needed to Protect the Financial System," GGD-94-133 (Report to Congressional Requesters), May 18, 1994.

34. Commodity Futures Trading Commission, "Division of Enforcement" (www.cftc.gov/anr/anrenf98.htm).

35. "Joint Statement by Treasury Secretary Robert E. Rubin, Federal Reserve Board Chairman Alan Greenspan, and Securities and Exchange Commission Chairman Arthur Levitt," Treasury Department press release, May 7, 1998.

36. Fed Chairman Alan Greenspan, "The Regulation of OTC Derivatives," prepared testimony before the House Committee on Banking and Financial Services, 105th Cong., 2nd sess., July 24, 1998.

37. GAO, "Long-Term Capital Management: Regulators Need to Focus Greater Attention on Systemic Risk," GAO/GGD-00-3 (Report to Congressional Requesters), October 1999, pp. 7, 18, 39–40. The notional amount of OTC derivatives contracts is a standard measure used in reporting the outstanding volume of such contracts. Its calculation is based on the value of the underlying instrument, commodity, index, or rate that the swap is based on. It therefore may be of limited use in measuring the potential exposure of the parties to the contracts. For example, an interest rate swap based on changes in interest rate on a $100 million loan would likely involve only a small percentage of the $100 million notional amount. On the other hand, price changes on an oil swap based on $100 million worth of oil could be even more than the notional amount, depending on the volatility in oil prices. For credit default swaps, which are discussed in more detail later in this volume, the notional amount is usually a close measure of the potential financial exposure of the issuer or seller of the swap.

38. Fed Chairman Alan Greenspan, "Private-sector Refinancing of the Large Hedge Fund, Long-Term Capital Management," prepared testimony before the House Committee on Banking and Financial Services, 105th Cong., 2nd sess., October 1, 1998.

39. Fed Chairman Alan Greenspan, "Financial Derivatives," remarks before the Futures Industry Association, Boca Raton, Florida, March 19, 1999.

40. "Over-the-Counter Derivatives Markets and the Commodity Exchange Act," report of the President's Working Group on Financial Markets, November 1999.

41. Gross market value is the current price at which the outstanding swaps contract can be sold or replaced on the market. As such, that amount reflects the current amount owing on a contract but does not reflect the possible future exposure on these generally long-term instruments.

42. Bank for International Settlements, data on semiannual OTC derivatives statistics.

43. Alan Greenspan, testimony before the FCIC, Hearing on Subprime Lending and Securitization and Government-Sponsored Entities (GSEs), day 1, session 1: The Federal Reserve, April 7, 2010, transcript, pp. 88–89.

44. Robert Rubin, testimony before the FCIC, FCIC Hearing on Subprime Lending and Securitization and Government-Sponsored Entities (GSEs), day 2, session 1: Citigroup Senior Management, April 8, 2010, transcript, pp. 108–10, 123–24.

45. Lawrence Summers, interview by FCIC, May 28, 2010.

46. Daniel K. Tarullo, *Banking on Basel: The Future of International Financial Regulation* (Washington, DC: Peterson Institute for International Economics, 2008), p. 58.

47. Final Rule—Amendment to Regulations H and Y," *Federal Reserve Bulletin* 75, no. 3 (March 1989), 164–66.

48. Tarullo, *Banking on Basel*, pp. 61–64.

49. For more on derivatives, see FCIC, "Preliminary Staff Report: Overview on Derivatives," June 29, 2010.

50. Warren Buffett, testimony before the FCIC, Hearing on the Credibility of Credit Ratings, the Investment Decisions Made Based on Those Ratings, and the Financial Crisis, session 2: Credit Ratings and the Financial Crisis, June 2, 2010, transcript, pp. 312, 326, 325.

51. Eric R. Dinallo, former superintendant, New York State Insurance Department, written testimony for the FCIC, Hearing on the Role of Derivatives in the Financial Crisis, session 2, Derivatives: Supervisors and Regulators, July 1, 2010, p. 7; Rochelle Katz, State of New York Insurance Department, letter to Bertil Lundqvist, Skadden, Arps, Slate, Meagher & Flom, LLP, June 16, 2000.

52. Data provided by AIG to the FCIC, CDS notional balances at year-end.

53. Bank for International Settlements, semiannual OTC derivatives statistics.

54. Dinallo testified that the market in CDS in September 2008 was estimated to be $62 trillion at a time when there was about $16 trillion of private-sector debt (written testimony for the FDIC, July 1, 2010, p. 9).

55. "AIGFP also participates as a dealer in a wide variety of financial derivatives transactions" (AIG, 2007 Form 10-K, p. 83). AIG's notional derivatives outstanding were $2.1 trillion at the end of 2007, including $1.2 trillion of interest rate swaps, $0.6 trillion of credit derivatives, $0.2 trillion of currency swaps, and $0.2 trillion of other derivatives (p. 163).

56. FCIC staff calculations using data from Office of the Comptroller of the Currency; call reports.

57. Data provided to the FCIC by Goldman Sachs.

## Chapter 4

1. 103 Public Law 103-328, September 29, 1994. Before the 1994 legislation, some states had voluntarily opened themselves up to out-of-state banks. FDIC, *History of the Eighties: Lessons for the Future*, vol. 1, *An Examination of the Banking Crises of the 1980s and Early 1990s* (Washington, DC: FDIC, 1997), p. 130.

2. These were the largest banks as of 2007. See FCIC, "Preliminary Staff Report: Too-Big-to-Fail Financial Institutions," August 31, 2010, p. 14.

3. Data from SNL Financial (www.snl.com/).

4. Public Law 104-208, sec. 2222, codified as 12 U.S.C. § 3311; law in effect as of January 3, 2007.

5. Arthur Levitt, interview by FCIC, October 1, 2010.

6. John D. Hawke and John Dugan, testimony before the FCIC, Hearing on Subprime Lending and Securitization and Government-Sponsored Enterprises (GSEs), day 2, session 2: Office of the Comptroller of the Currency, April 8, 2010, transcript, pp. 169, 175.

7. Fed Vice Chairman Roger W. Ferguson Jr., "The Future of Financial Services—Revisited," remarks at the Future of Financial Services Conference, University of Massachusetts, Boston, October 8, 2003.

8. Fed Chairman Alan Greenspan, "Government Regulation and Derivative Contracts," speech at the Financial Markets Conference of the Federal Reserve Bank of Atlanta, Coral Gables, Florida, February 21, 1997.

9. Richard Spillenkothen, "Notes on the performance of prudential supervision in the years preceding the financial crisis by a former director of banking supervision and regulation at the Federal Reserve Board (1991 to 2006)," May 31, 2010, p. 28.

10. See U.S. Department of the Treasury, *Modernizing the Financial System* (February 1991), pp. XIX-5, XIX-6, 67–69: "the existence of fewer agencies would concentrate regulatory power in the remaining ones, raising the danger of arbitrary or inflexible behavior. . . . Agency pluralism, on the other hand, may be useful, since it can bring to bear on general bank supervision the different perspectives and experiences of each regulator, and it subjects each one, where consultation and coordination are required, to the checks and balances of the others' opinion."

11. Fed Chairman Alan Greenspan, statement before the Senate Committee on Banking, Housing, and Urban Affairs, 103rd Cong., 2nd sess., March 2, 1994, reprinted in the *Federal Reserve Bulletin,* May 1, 1994, p. 382.

12. Securities Industry Association v. Board of Governors of the Federal Reserve System, 627 F.Supp. 695 (D.D.C. 1986); Kathleen Day, "Reinventing the Bank; With Depression-Era Law about to Be Rewritten, the Future Remains Unclear," *Washington Post,* October 31, 1999.

13. Edward Yingling, quoted in "The Making of a Law," *ABA Banking Journal,* December 1999.

14. The two-year exemption is contained in section 4(a)(2) of the Bank Holding Company Act. The Fed could have granted up to three one-year extensions of that exemption.

15. FCIC staff computations based on data from the Center for Responsive Politics. "Financial sector" here includes insurance companies, commercial banks, securities and investment firms, finance and credit companies, accountants, savings and loan institutions, credit unions, and mortgage bankers and brokers.

16. U.S. Department of the Treasury, *Modernizing the Financial System* (February 1991); Fed Chairman Alan Greenspan, "H.R. 10, the Financial Services Competitiveness Act of 1997," testimony before the House Committee on Banking and Financial Services, 105th Cong., 1st sess., May 22, 1997.

17. Katrina Brooker, "Citi's Creator, Alone with His Regrets," *New York Times,* January 2, 2010.

18. John Reed, interview by FCIC, March 24, 2010.

19. FDIC Institution Directory; SNL Financial.

20. Fed Governor Laurence H. Meyer, "The Implications of Financial Modernization Legislation for Bank Supervision," remarks at the Symposium on Financial Modernization Legislation, sponsored by Women in Housing and Finance, Washington, D.C., December 15, 1999.

21. Ben S. Bernanke, written testimony before the FCIC, Hearing on Too Big to Fail: Expectations and Impact of Extraordinary Government Intervention and the Role of Systemic Risk in the Financial Crisis, day 1, session 1: The Federal Reserve, September 2, 2010, p. 14.

22. Patricia A. McCoy et al., "Systemic Risk through Securitization: The Result of Deregulation and Regulatory Failure," *Connecticut Law Review* 41 (2009): 1345–47, 1353–55.

23. Fed Chairman Alan Greenspan, "Lessons from the Global Crises," remarks before the World Bank Group and the International Monetary Fund, Program of Seminars, Washington, DC, September 27, 1999.

24. David A. Marshall, "The Crisis of 1998 and the Role of the Central Bank," Federal Reserve Bank of Chicago, *Economic Perspectives* (1Q 2001): 2.

25. Commercial and industrial loans at all commercial banks, monthly, seasonally adjusted, from the Federal Reserve Board of Governors H.8 release; FCIC staff calculation of average change in loans outstanding over any two consecutive months in 1997 and 1998.

26. Franklin R. Edwards, "Hedge Funds and the Collapse of Long-Term Capital Management," *Journal of Economic Perspectives* 13 (1999): 198.

27. "Hedge Funds, Leverage, and the Lessons of Long-Term Capital Management," Report of the President's Working Group on Financial Markets, April 1999, p. 14.

28. Edwards, "Hedge Funds and the Collapse of Long-Term Capital Management," pp. 200, 197; and Bloomberg.

29. Ibid., pp. 197–205; Roger Lowenstein, *When Genius Failed: The Rise and Fall of Long-Term Capital Management* (New York: Random House, 2000), pp. 36–54, 77–84, 94–105, 123–30.

30. "Hedge Funds, Leverage, and the Lessons of Long-Term Capital Management," pp. 11–12.

31. William J. McDonough, president of the Federal Reserve Bank of New York, statement before the House Committee on Banking and Financial Services, 105th Cong., 2nd sess., October 1, 1998.

32. GAO, "Long-Term Capital Management: Regulators Need to Focus Greater Attention on Systemic Risk," GAO/GGD-00-3 (Report to Congressional Requesters), October 1999, p. 39.

33. "Hedge Funds, Leverage, and the Lessons of Long-Term Capital Management," pp. 13–14.

34. Lowenstein, *When Genius Failed,* pp. 205–18.

35. McDonough, statement before the House Committee on Banking and Financial Services, October 1, 1998.

36. Andrew F. Brimmer, "Distinguished Lecture on Economics in Government: Central Banking and Systemic Risks in Capital Markets," *Journal of Economic Perspectives,* no. 2 (Spring 1989) (lecture by a former Fed governor, analyzing the Fed's market interventions in 1970, 1980 and 1987, and concluding that the Fed had consciously assumed a "strategic role as the ultimate source of liquidity in the economy at large"); Kenneth Garbade, "The Evolution of Repo Contracting Conventions in the 1980s," Federal Reserve Bank of New York *Economic Policy Review* (May 2006): 33.

37. Harvey Miller, interview by FCIC, August 5, 2010.

38. Stanley O'Neal, interview by FCIC, September 16, 2010.

39. Fed Chairman Alan Greenspan, "Do efficient financial markets mitigate financial crises?" remarks before the 1999 Financial Markets Conference of the Federal Reserve Bank of Atlanta, October 19, 1999 (www.federalreserve.gov/boarddocs/speeches/1999/19991019.htm).

40. "Hedge Funds, Leverage, and the Lessons of Long-Term Capital Management," p. 16.

41. Ibid.

42. Ibid.

43. Philip Goldstein, et al. v. SEC, Opinion, Case No. 04-1434 (D.C. Cir. June 23, 2006).

44. *Time,* February 15, 1999; Bob Woodward, *Maestro: Greenspan's Fed and the American Boom* (New York: Simon & Schuster, 2000).

45. SIFMA (Securities Industry and Financial Markets Association), *Fact Book 2008,* pp. 9–10.

46. Board of Governors of the Federal Reserve System, *Federal Reserve Statistical Release Z.1: Flow of Funds Accounts of the United States,* 4th Qtr. 1996, p. 88 (Table L.213, line 18); 4th Qtr. 2001, p. 90 (Table L.213, line 20).

47. SEC Chairman William H. Donaldson, "Testimony Concerning Global Research Analyst Settlement," before the Senate Committee on Banking, Housing and Urban Affairs, 108th Cong., 1st sess., May 7, 2003.

48. SEC, "SEC Fact Sheet on Global Analyst Research Settlements," April 30, 2003; Financial Industry Regulatory Authority news release, "NASD Fines Piper Jaffray $2.4 Million for IPO Spinning," July 12, 2004.

49. Arthur E. Wilmarth Jr., "Conflicts of Interest and Corporate Governance Failures at Universal Banks During the Stock Market Boom of the 1990s: The Cases of Enron and WorldCom," George Washington University Public Law and Legal Theory Working Paper 234 (2007).

50. Fed Chairman Alan Greenspan, "International Financial Risk Management," remarks before the Council on Foreign Relations, Washington, DC, November 19, 2002.

51. Ferguson, "The Future of Financial Services—Revisited."

52. Spillenkothen, "Notes on the performance of prudential supervision in the years preceding the financial crisis," p. 28.

53. "First the Put; Then the Cut?" *Economist,* December 16, 2000, p. 81.

54. Fed Chairman Alan Greenspan, "Risk and Uncertainty in Monetary Policy," remarks at the Meetings of the American Economic Association, San Diego, California, January 3, 2004. See also Fed Governor Ben S. Bernanke, "Asset-Price 'Bubbles' and Monetary Policy," remarks before the N.Y. Chapter of the National Association of Business Economics, New York, October 15, 2002.

55. Fed Chairman Alan Greenspan, "Reflections on Central Banking," remarks at a symposium sponsored by the Federal Reserve Board of Kansas City, Jackson Hole, Wyoming, August 26, 2005.

56. Lawrence Lindsey, interview by FCIC, September 20, 2010.

57. The NYSE decided in 1970 to allow members to be publicly traded. See Andrew von Nordenflycht, "The Demise of the Professional Partnership? The Emergence and Diffusion of Publicly-Traded Professional Service Firms" (draft paper, Faculty of Business, Simon Fraser University, September 2006), pp. 20–21.

58. Peter Solomon, written testimony for the FCIC, First Public Hearing of FCIC, day 1, panel 2: Financial Market Participants, January 13, 2010, p. 2.

59. Brian R. Leach, interview by FCIC, March 4, 2010, p. 22.

60. Jian Cai, Kent Cherny, and Todd Milbourn, "Compensation and Risk Incentives in Banking and Finance," Federal Reserve Bank of Cleveland *Economic Commentary* (September 14, 2010).

61. Carola Frydman and Raven E. Saks, "Historical Trends in Executive Compensation, 1936–2005" (2007), p.3.

62. Cai, Cherny, and Milbourn, "Compensation and Risk Incentives in Banking and Finance."

63. Goldman Sachs, 2006 and 2009 10-K; Morgan Stanley, 2008 10-K; Merrill Lynch, 2005 and 2008 10-K.

64. "Gutfreund's Pay Is Cut," *New York Times,* December 23, 1987.

65. Merrill Lynch, "2007 Proxy Statement," p. 38.

66. Goldman Sachs, "Proxy Statement for 2008 Annual Meeting of Shareholders," March 7, 2008, p. 16: Blankfein received $600,000 base salary and a 2007 year-end bonus of $67.9 million.

67. Lehman Brothers, "Proxy Statement for Year-end 2007," p. 28; JP Morgan Chase, "2007 Proxy Statement," p. 16.

68. New York State Office of the State Comptroller, "New York City Securities Industry Bonus Pool," February 23, 2010. The bonus pool is for securities industry (NAICS 523) employees who work in New York City.

69. "Banks Set for Record Pay, Top Firms on Pace to Award $145 Billion for 2009, Up 18%, WSJ Study Finds," WSJ.com, January 14, 2010.

70. Sandy Weill, interview by FCIC, October 4, 2010.

71. Lord Adair Turner, interview by FCIC, November 30, 2010.

72. Ben S. Bernanke, testimony before the FCIC, Hearing on Too Big to Fail: Expectations and Impact of Extraordinary Government Intervention and the Role of Systemic Risk in the Financial Crisis, day 2, session 1: The Federal Reserve, September 2, 2010, transcript, p. 111.

73. Testimony of Armando Falcon Jr., former director Office of Federal Housing Enterprise Oversight, written testimony for the FCIC, Hearing on Subprime Lending and Securitization and Government-Sponsored Enterprises (GSEs), day 3, session 2: Office of Federal Housing Enterprise Oversight, April 9, 2010, pp. 8–10.

74. Sheila C. Bair, written testimony for the FCIC, First Public Hearing of the FCIC, day 2, panel 1: Current Investigations into the Financial Crisis—Federal Officials, January 14, 2010, p. 22.

75. Mary L. Schapiro, written testimony for the FCIC, First Public Hearing of the FCIC, day 2, panel 1: Current Investigations into the Financial Crisis—Federal Officials, January 14, 2010, p.18.

76. Bloomberg LLC, Financial Analysis Function, Public Filings for JPM, Citigroup, Bank of America, Goldman Sachs, and Lehman Brothers.

77. Fannie Mae, SEC filings 10-K and 10-Q; see the 2009 10-K, p. 70, Total Assets and Fannie Mae MBS held by Third Parties; Federal Housing Finance Agency, *Report to Congress, 2008* (2009), pp. 111, 128.

78. FCIC staff calculations.

79. SNL Financial Database and SEC public filings.

80. Calculated from proxy statements.

81. John Snow, interview by FCIC, October 7, 2010.

82. Ibid.

## Chapter 5

1. Gail Burks, written testimony for the FCIC, Hearing on the Impact of the Financial Crisis—State of Nevada, session 3: The Impact of the Financial Crisis on Nevada Real Estate, September 8, 2010, p. 3.

2. Tom C. Putnam, president, Putnam Housing Finance Consulting, written testimony for the FCIC, Hearing on the Impact of the Financial Crisis—Sacramento, session 2: Mortgage Origination, Mortgage Fraud and Predatory Lending in the Sacramento Region, September 23, 2010, pp. 3–4.

3. Board of Governors of the Federal Reserve System, *Federal Reserve Statistical Release Z.1: Flow of Funds Accounts of the United States,* release date, December 9, 2010, Table L.1: Credit Market Debt Outstanding, and Table L.126: Issuers of Asset-Backed Securities (ABS)

4. Jim Callahan, interview by FCIC, October 18, 2010.

5. Lewis Ranieri, former vice chairman of Salomon Brothers, interview by FCIC, July 30, 2010.

6. Federal Deposit Insurance Corporation, "Managing the Crisis: The FDIC and RTC Experience" (August 1998), pp. 29, 6–7, 407–8, 38.

7. Ibid., 417.

8. Ibid., pp. 9, 32, 36, 48

9. The figures throughout this discussion of CMLTI 2006-NC2 are FCIC staff calculations, based on analysis of loan-level data from Blackbox Inc. and Standard & Poor's; Moody's PDS database; Moody's CDO EMS database; and Citigroup, Fannie Mae Term Sheet, CMLTI 2006-NC2, September 7, 2006, pp. 1, 3. See also Brad S. Karp, counsel for Citigroup, letter to FCIC, November 4, 2010, p. 1, pp. 2–3. All ratings of its tranches are as given by Standard & Poor's.

10. Technically, this deal had two unrated tranches below the equity tranche, also held by Citigroup and the hedge fund.

11. Fed Chairman Ben S. Bernanke, "The Community Reinvestment Act: Its Evolution and New Challenges," speech at the Community Affairs Research Conference, Washington, D.C., March 30, 2007.

12. Ibid.

13. See Glenn Canner and Wayne Passmore, "The Community Reinvestment Act and the Profitability of Mortgage-Oriented Banks," Working Paper, Federal Reserve Board, March 3, 1997. Under the Community Reinvestment Act, low- and moderate-income borrowers have income that is at most 80% of area median income.

14. Fed Chairman Alan Greenspan, "Economic Development in Low- and Moderate-Income Communities," speech at Community Forum on Community Reinvestment and Access to Credit: California's Challenge, in Los Angeles, January 12, 1998.

15. John Dugan, interview by FCIC, March 12, 2010.

16. Lawrence B. Lindsey, interview by FCIC, September 20, 2010.

17. Souphala Chomsisengphet and Anthony Pennington-Cross, "The Evolution of the Subprime Mortgage Market," *Federal Reserve Bank of St. Louis Review* 88, no. 1 (January/February 2006): 40

18. Southern Pacific Funding Corp, Form 8-K, September 14, 1998

19. The top 10 list is as of 1996, according to FCIC staff calculations using data from the following sources: Inside Mortgage Finance, *The 2009 Mortgage Market Statistical Annual,* vol. 1, *The Primary Market* (Bethesda, Md.: Inside Mortgage Finance Publications, 2009), p. 214, "Top 25 B&C Lenders in 1996"; Thomas E. Foley, "Alternative Financial Ratios for the Effects of Securitization: Tools for Analysis," Moody's Investor Services, September 19, 1997, p. 5; and Moody's Investor Service, "Subprime Home Equity Industry Outlook—The Party's Over," Moody's Global Credit Research, October 1998.

20. "FDIC Announces Receivership of First National Bank of Keystone, Keystone, West Virginia," Federal Deposit Insurance Corporation and Office of the Comptroller of the Currency joint press release, September 1, 1999.

21. FCIC staff calculations using data from *Inside MBS & ABS.*

22. See Marc Savitt, interview by FCIC, November 17, 2010.

23. Henry Cisneros, interview by FCIC, October 13, 2010.

24. Glenn Loney, interview by FCIC, April 1, 2010.

25. Senate Committee on Banking, Housing, and Urban Affairs, *The Community Development, Credit Enhancement, and Regulatory Improvement Act of 1993,* 103rd Cong., 1st sess., October 28, 1993, S. Rep. 103–169, p. 18.

26. Ibid., p. 19.

27. 15 U.S.C. § 1639(h) 2006.

28. Loans were subject to HOEPA only if they hit the interest rate trigger or fee trigger: i.e., if the annual percentage rate for the loan was more than 10 percentage points above the yield on Treasury securities having a comparable maturity or if the total charges paid by the borrower at or before closing exceeded $400 or 8% of the loan amount, whichever was greater. See Senate Committee on Banking, Housing, and Urban Affairs, S. Rep. 103–169, p. 54.

29. Ibid., p. 24.

30. Board of Governors of the Federal Reserve System and Department of Housing and Urban Development, "Joint Report Concerning Reform to the Truth in Lending Act and the Real Estate Settlement Procedures Act" (July 1998), p. 56.

31. Griffith L. Garwood, director, Division of Consumer and Community Affairs, Board of Governors of the Federal Reserve System, "To the Officers and Managers in Charge of Consumer Affairs Examination and Consumer Complaint Programs," Consumer Affairs Letter CA 98–1, January 20, 1998

32. GAO, "Large Bank Mergers: Fair Lending Review Could Be Enhanced with Better Coordination," GAO/GGD-00–16 (Report to the Honorable Maxine Waters and the Honorable Bernard Sanders, House of Representatives), November 1999, p. 20.

33. Fed and HUD, "Joint Report," pp. I–XXVII.

34. Griffith L. Garwood, director, Division of Consumer and Community Affairs, Board of Governors of the Federal Reserve System, memorandum to the Committee on Consumer and Community Affairs, "Memorandum concerning the Board's Report to the Congress on the Truth in Lending and Real Estate Settlement Procedures Acts," April 8, 1998, p. 42.

35. Board of Governors of the Federal Reserve System, Federal Deposit Insurance Corporation, Office of the Comptroller of the Currency, and Office of Thrift Supervision, "Interagency Guidance on Subprime Lending" (March 1, 1999), p. 1

36. Ibid., pp. 1–7; quotation, p. 5.

37. U.S. Department of the Treasury and U.S. Department of Housing and Urban Development, "Curbing Predatory Home Lending" (June 1, 2000), pp. 13–14, 1–2, 81 (quotations, 2, 1–2).

38. Gail Burks, president and chief executive officer, Nevada Fair Housing Center, Inc., testimony before the FCIC, Hearing on the Impact of the Financial Crisis—State of Nevada, session 3: The Impact of the Financial Crisis on Nevada Real Estate, September 8, 2010, transcript, p. 242–43.See also Kevin Stein, associate director, California Reinvestment Coalition, written testimony for the FCIC, Hearing on the Impact of the Financial Crisis—Sacramento, session 2: Mortgage Origination, Mortgage Fraud and Predatory Lending in the Sacramento Region, September 23, 2010, pp. 8–9. See also his testimony at the same hearing, transcript, pp. 73–74. See Diane E. Thompson, of counsel, National Consumer Law Center, Inc., and Margot F. Saunders, of counsel, National Consumer Law Center, Inc., interview by FCIC, September 10, 2010.

39. Diane E. Thompson and Margot F. Saunders, both of counsel, National Consumer Law Center, interview by FCIC, September 10, 2010.

40. Gary Gensler, interview by FCIC, May 14, 2010.

41. Sheila Bair, testimony before the FCIC, First Public Hearing of the FCIC, day 2, panel 1: Current Investigations into the Financial Crisis—Federal Officials, January 14, 2010, transcript, p. 97.

42. Sheila Bair, interview by FCIC, March 29, 2010.

43. Sandra F. Braunstein, interview by FCIC, April 1, 2010, pp. 31–34.

44. Bair, interview.

45. Treasury and HUD, "Curbing Predatory Home Lending," p. 31.

## Chapter 6

1. Figures represented the compound average growth rate and FCIC staff calculations from CoreLogic National Home Price Index, Single-Family Combined (SCF); CoreLogic Loan Performance HPI August 2010.

2. Inside Mortgage Finance, *The 2009 Mortgage Market Statistical Annual*, vol. 1, *The Primary Market* (Bethesda, Md.: Inside Mortgage Finance, 2009), p. 4, "Mortgage Originations by Product."

3. Federal Reserve Board press release, May 27, 2004.

4. Fed Governor Ben S. Bernanke, "The Great Moderation," remarks at the meetings of the Eastern Economic Association, Washington, D.C., February 20, 2004. See also Olivier Blanchard and John Simon, "The Long and Large Decline in U.S. Output Volatility," *Brookings Papers on Economic Activity*, no. 1 (2001): 135–64.

5. Fed Governor Ben S. Bernanke, "Deflation: Making Sure 'It' Doesn't Happen Here," remarks before the National Economists Club, Washington, D.C., November 21, 2002.

6. FCIC staff calculations from Board of Governors of the Federal Reserve System, H.15 Selected Interest Rate release, 3-month AA Nonfinancial Commercial Paper Rate, WCPN3M (weekly, ending Friday); U.S. Department of Treasury, Daily Treasury Yield Curve Rates, 1990 to Present.

7. This example assumes that the homeowner is able to come up with a larger down payment to cover 20% of the higher-priced home. Here, the difference would be about $13,000.

8. Federal Housing Finance Agency, "Data on the Risk Characteristics and Performance of Single-Family Mortgages Originated from 2001 through 2008 and Financed in the Secondary Market" (September 13, 2010), Table 2a: Share of Single-Family Mortgages Originated from 2001 through 2008 and Acquired by the Enterprises or Finances with Private-Label MBS by Loan-to-Value Ratio and Borrower FICO Score at Origination, Adjustable-Rate Mortgages, p. 22. Prime borrowers are defined as those whose mortgages are financed by the government-sponsored enterprises.

9. Yuliya Demyanyk and Otto Van Hemert, "Understanding the Subprime Mortgage Crisis" (December 5, 2008), table 1: Loan Characteristics at Origination for Different Vintages, p. 7.

10. FCIC staff calculations from CoreLogic/First American, Home Price Index for Single-Family Combined State HPI data, last updated August 2010, and CoreLogic State Home Price Index, provided to the FCIC by CoreLogic. Staff calculations of all annual growth rates are compound annual growth rates from January to January.

11. U.S. Census Bureau, "Housing Vacancies and Homeownership, CPS/HVS," Table 14: Homeownership Rates for the US 1965 to Present.

12. Brian K. Bucks, Arthur B. Kennickell, and Kevin B. Moore, "Recent Changes in US Family Finances: Evidence from the 2001 and 2004 Survey of Consumer Finances," *Federal Reserve Bulletin* (2006): Tables 8A and 8B, pp. A20–A23, A8.

13. Congressional Budget Office, "Housing Wealth and Consumer Spending," Background Paper, January 2007, p. 15.

14. Mortgages may have been refinanced more than once in that year.

15. FCIC staff calculations with updated data provided by Alan Greenspan and James Kennedy, whose data originally appeared in "Sources and Uses of Equity Extracted from Homes," Finance and Economics Discussion Series, Federal Reserve Board, 2007-20 (March 2007).

16. CBO, "Housing Wealth and Consumer Spending," p. 2.

17. Fed Chairman Alan Greenspan, "The Economic Outlook," prepared testimony before the Joint Economic Committee, 107th Cong., 2nd sess., November 13, 2002.

18. Fed Chairman Alan Greenspan, "Federal Reserve Board's Semiannual Monetary Policy Report to the Congress," prepared testimony before the House Committee on Financial Services, 108th Cong., 2nd sess., February 12, 2004.

19. FCIC staff calculations from *2009 Mortgage Market Statistical Annual*, 1:4, "Mortgage Originations by Product" (total subprime volume); 2:13, "Non-Agency MBS Issuance by Type" (subprime PLS).

20. Ibid., 1:3, "Mortgage Origination Indicators"; 220, 227, "Mortgage Originations by Product."

21. Bart McDade, interview by FCIC, April 16, 2010.

22. Presentation to the Lehman Board of Directors, March 20, 2007. Lehman had also acquired three international lenders during this time period.

23. New Century, 1999 10-K, March 30, 2000, p. 2.

24. Final Report of Michael J. Missal, Bankruptcy Court Examiner, in RE: New Century TRS Holdings, Chapter 11, Case No. 07-10416 (KJC), (Bankr. D.Del.), February 29, 2008, p 42.

25. New Century, 2000 10-K, April 2, 2001, p. 15; New Century, 2003 10-K, March 15, 2004, p. 13. Rankings from *2009 Mortgage Market Statistical Annual*, 1:220, 223.

26. Aseem Mital and Angelo Mozilo, quoted in Erick Bergquist, "Under Scrutiny, Ameriquest Details Procedures," *American Banker* 170, no. 125 (June 30, 2005): 1. Volume and rankings from *2009 Mortgage Market Statistical Annual*, 1:220, 223.

27. Lewis Ranieri, interview by FCIC, July 30, 2010.

28. James M. Lacko and Janis K. Pappalardo, "The Effect of Mortgage Broker Compensation Disclosures on Consumers and Competition: A Controlled Experiment," Federal Trade Commission Bureau of Economics Staff Report (February 2004), p. 1.

29. Jay Jeffries, testimony before the FCIC, Hearing on the Impact of the Financial Crisis—State of Nevada, session 3: The Impact of the Financial Crisis on Nevada Real Estate, September 8, 2010, transcript, p. 177.

30. Brian Bucks and Karen Pence, "Do Borrowers Know Their Mortgage Terms?" *Journal of Urban Economics* 64 (2008): 223.

31. Michael Calhoun and Julia Gordon, interview by FCIC, September 16, 2010.

32. Annamaria Lusardi, "Americans' Financial Capability," report prepared for the FCIC, February 26, 2010, p. 3.

33. FCIC staff estimates based on analysis of Blackbox, S&P, and IP Recovery, provided by Antje Berndt, Burton Hollifield, and Patrik Sandas, in their paper, "The Role of Mortgage Brokers in the Subprime Crisis," April 2010.

34. William C. Apgar and Allen J. Fishbein, "The Changing Industrial Organization of Housing Finance and the Changing Role of Community-Based Organizations," working paper (Joint Center for Housing Studies, Harvard University, May 2004), p. 9.

35. Herb Sandler, interview by FCIC, September 22, 2010.

36. Wholesale Access, "Mortgage Brokers 2006" (August 2007), pp. 35, 37.

37. Jamie Dimon, testimony before the FCIC, First Public Hearing of the FCIC, panel 1: Financial Institution Representatives, January 13, 2010, transcript, p. 13.

38. October Research Corporation, executive summary of the *2007 National Appraisal Survey,* p. 4.

39. Dennis J. Black, written testimony for the FCIC, Hearing on the Impact of the Financial Crisis—Miami, session 2: Uncovering Mortgage Fraud in Miami, September 21, 2010, p. 8.

40. Karen J. Mann, written testimony for the FCIC, Hearing on the Impact of the Financial Crisis—Sacramento, session 2: Mortgage Origination, Mortgage Fraud and Predatory Lending in the Sacramento Region, September 23, 2010, p. 2.

41. Gary Crabtree, testimony before the FCIC, Hearing on the Impact of the Financial Crisis—Greater Bakersfield, session 4: Local Housing Market, September 7, 2010, transcript, p. 172.

42. Complaint, People of the State of New York v. First American Corporation and First American eAppraiseIT (N.Y. Sup. Ct. November 1, 2007), pp. 3, 7, 8.

43. Martin Eakes, quoted in Richard A. Oppel Jr. and Patrick McGeehan, "Along with a Lender, Is Citigroup Buying Trouble?" *New York Times,* October 22, 2000.

44. Pam Flaherty, quoted in Erick Bergquist, "Judging Citi, a Year Later: Subprime Reform 'on Track'; Critics Unsatisfied," *American Banker,* September 10, 2001.

45. "Citigroup Settles FTC Charges against the Associates Record-Setting $215 Million for Subprime Lending Victims," Federal Trade Commission press release, September 19, 2002.

46. Mark Olson, interview by FCIC, October 4, 2010.

47. Timothy O'Brien, "Fed Assess Citigroup Unit $70 Million in Loan Abuse," *The New York Times,* May 28, 2004.

48. Federal Reserve Board internal staff document, "The Problem of Predatory Lending," December 5, 2000, pp. 10–13.

49. Federal Reserve Board, Morning Session of Public Hearing on Home Equity Lending, July 27, 2000, opening remarks by Governor Gramlich, p. 9.

50. Scott Alvarez, interview by FCIC, March 23, 2010.

51. Alan Greenspan, written testimony for the FCIC, Hearing on Subprime Lending and Securitization and Government-Sponsored Enterprises (GSEs), day one, session 1: The Federal Reserve, April 7, 2010, p. 13.

52. Alan Greenspan, quoted in David Faber, *And Then the Roof Caved In: How Wall Street's Greed and Stupidity Brought Capitalism to Its Knees* (Hoboken, N.J.: Wiley, 2009), pp. 53–54.

53. "Truth in Lending," *Federal Register* 66, no. 245 (December 20, 2001): 65612 (quotation), 65608.

54. Robert B. Avery, Glenn B. Canner, and Robert E. Cook, "New Information Reported under HMDA and Its Application in Fair Lending Enforcement," *Federal Reserve Bulletin* 91 (Summer 2005): 372.

55. Alan Greenspan, interview by FCIC, March 31, 2010

56. Sheila Bair, testimony before the FCIC, Hearing on Too Big to Fail: Expectations and Impact of Extraordinary Government Intervention and the Role of Systemic Risk in the Financial Crisis, day 2, session 2: Federal Deposit Insurance Corporation, September 2, 2010, transcript, p. 191.

57. Dolores Smith and Glenn Loney, memorandum to Governor Edward Gramlich, "Compliance Inspections of Nonbank Subsidiaries of Bank Holding Companies," August 31, 2000.

58. GAO, "Consumer Protection: Federal and State Agencies Face Challenges in Combating Predatory Lending," GAO 04–280 (Report to the Chairman and Ranking Minority Member, Special Committee on Aging, U.S. Senate), January 2004, pp. 52–53.

59. Sandra Braunstein, interview by FCIC, April 1, 2010. Transcript pp. 32–33.

60. Greenspan, interview.

61. Ibid.

62. Edward M. Gramlich, "Booms and Busts: The Case of Subprime Mortgages," *Federal Reserve Bank of Kansas City Economic Review* (2007): 109.

63. Edward Gramlich, quoted in Greg Ip, "Did Greenspan Add to Subprime Woes? Gramlich Says Ex-Colleague Blocked Crackdown On Predatory Lenders Despite Growing Concerns," *Wall Street Journal*, June 9, 2007. See also Edmund L. Andrews, "Fed Shrugged as Subprime Crisis Spread," *New York Times*, December 18, 2007.

64. Patricia McCoy and Margot Saunders, quoted in Binyamin Appelbaum, "Fed Held Back as Evidence Mounted on Subprime Loan Abuses," *Washington Post*, September 27, 2009.

65. GAO, "Large Bank Mergers: Fair Lending Review Could be Enhanced with Better Coordination," GAO/GDD-00-16 (Report to the Honorable Maxine Waters and Honorable Bernard Sanders, House of Representatives), November 1999; GAO, "Consumer Protection: Federal and State Agencies Face Challenges in Combating Predatory Lending."

66. "Federal and State Agencies Announce Pilot Project to Improve Supervision of Subprime Mortgage Lenders," Joint press release (Fed Reserve Board, OTC, FTC, Conference of State Bank Supervisors, American Association of Residential Mortgage Regulators), July 17, 2007.

67. "Truth in Lending," pp. 44522–23. "Higher-priced mortgage loans" are defined in the 2008 regulations to include mortgage loans whose annual percentage rate exceeds the "average prime offer rates for a comparable transaction" (as published by the Fed) by at least 1.5% for first-lien loans or 3.5% for subordinate-lien loans.

68. Alvarez, interview.

69. Raphael W. Bostic, Kathleen C. Engel, Patricia A. McCoy, Anthony Pennington-Cross, and Susan M. Wachter, "State and Local Anti-Predatory Lending Laws: The Effect of Legal Enforcement Mechanisms," *Journal of Economics and Business* 60 (2008): 47–66.

70. "Lending and Investment," *Federal Register* 61, no. 190 (September 30, 1996): 50965.

71. Joseph A. Smith, "Mortgage Market Turmoil: Causes and Consequences," testimony before the Senate Committee on Banking, Housing, and Urban Affairs, 110th Cong., 1st sess., March 22, 2007, p. 33 (Exhibit B), using data from the Mortgage Asset Research Institute.

72. Lisa Madigan, written testimony for the FCIC, First Public Hearing of the FCIC, day 2, panel 2: Current Investigations into the Financial Crisis—State and Local Officials, January 14, 2010, p.12.

73. Commitments compiled at National Community Reinvestment Coalition, "CRA Commitments" (2007).

74. Josh Silver, NCRC, interview by FCIC, June 16, 2010.

75. Data references based on Reginald Brown, counsel for Bank of America, letter to FCIC, June 16, 2010, p. 2; Jessica Carey, counsel for JPMorgan Chase, letter to FCIC, December 16, 2010; Brad Karp, counsel for Citigroup, letter to FCIC, March 18, 2010, in response to FCIC request; Wells Fargo public commitments 1990–2010, data provided by Wells Fargo to the FCIC.

76. Karp, letter to FCIC, March 18, 2010, in response to FCIC request.

77. Carey, letter to FCIC, December 16, 2010, p. 9; Brad Karp, counsel for JP Morgan, letter to FCIC, May 26, 2010, p. 10.

78. FCIC calculation based on Federal Housing Finance Agency, "Data on the Risk Characteristics and Performance of Single-Family Mortgages Originated in 2001–2008 and Financed in the Secondary Market"(September 13, 2010), Table 1-C; this report covers all loans purchased or securitized by the GSEs or in private-label securitizations. Delinquency data provided by Wells Fargo covered 81% of loans.

79. "Orders Issued Under the Bank Holding Company Act," *Federal Reserve Bulletin* 75, no. 4 (April 1989): 304.

80. "Statement of the Federal Financial Supervisory Agencies Regarding the Community Reinvestment Act," *Federal Register* 54 (April 5, 1989): 13742. This remains the interagency policy. "Community Reinvestment Act: Interagency Questions and Answers Regarding Community Reinvestment; Notice," *Federal Register* 75 (March 11, 2010): 11666.

81. Glenn Loney, interview by FCIC, April 1, 2010.

82. "Community Reinvestment Act Regulations and Home Mortgage Disclosure; Final Rules," *Federal Register* 60, no. 86 (May 4, 1995): 22155–223.

83. Division of Consumer and Community Affairs, memorandum to Board of Governors, August 10, 1998.

84. Federal Reserve Board press release, "Order Approving the Merger of Bank Holding Companies," August 17, 1998, pp. 63–64.

85. Lloyd Brown, interview by FCIC, February 5, 2010.

86. Andrew Plepler, interview by FCIC, July 14, 2010.

87. Assuming 75% AAA tranche ($1.20), 10% AA tranche ($0.20), 8% A tranche ($0.30), 5% BBB tranche ($0.40), and 2% equity tranche ($2.00). See Goldman Sachs, "Effective Regulation: Part 1, Avoiding Another Meltdown," March 2009, p. 22.

88. David Jones, interview by FCIC, October 19, 2010. See David Jones, "Emerging Problems with the Basel Capital Accord: Regulatory Capital Arbitrage and Related Issues," *Journal of Banking and Finance* 24, nos. 1–2 (January 2000): 35–58.

89. Henry Paulson, testimony before the FCIC, Hearing on the Shadow Banking System, day 2, session 1: Perspective on the Shadow Banking System, May 6, 2010), transcript, p. 34.

90. Jones, interview.

## Chapter 7

1. For example, an Alt-A loan may have no or limited documentation of the borrower's income, may have a high loan-to-value ratio (LTV), or may be for an investor-owned property.

2. Inside Mortgage Finance, *The 2009 Mortgage Market Statistical Annual,* vol. 2, *The Secondary Market* (Bethesda, MD: Inside Mortgage Finance, 2009), p. 9, "Mortgage & Asset Securities Issuance" (showing Wall St. securitizing a third more than Fannie and Freddie); p. 13, "Non-Agency MBS Issuance by Type." FCIC staff calculations from 2004 to 2006 (for growth in private label MBS).

3. Charles O. Prince, interview by FCIC, March 17, 2010.

4. John Taylor, interview by FCIC, September 23, 2010.

5. William A. Fleckenstein and Frederick Sheeham, *Greenspan's Bubbles: The Age of Ignorance at the Federal Reserve* (New York: McGraw-Hill, 2008), p. 181.

6. Alan Greenspan, "The Fed Didn't Cause the Housing Bubble," *Wall Street Journal,* March 11, 2009. See also Ben Bernanke, "Monetary Policy and the Housing Bubble," speech at the Annual Meeting of the American Economic Association, Atlanta, Georgia, January 3, 2010.

7. Alan Greenspan, testimony before the Senate Committee on Banking, Housing, and Urban Affairs, 109th Cong., 1st sess., February 16, 2005.

8. Fed Chairman Ben S. Bernanke, "The Global Saving Glut and the U.S. Current Account Deficit," remarks at the Sandridge Lecture, Virginia Association of Economics, Richmond, Virginia, March 10, 2005.

9. Frederic Mishkin, interview by FCIC, October 1, 2010.

10. Pierre-Olivier Gourinchas, written testimony for the FCIC, Forum to Explore the Causes of the Financial Crisis, day 1, session 2: Macroeconomic Factors and U.S. Monetary Policy, February 26, 2010, pp. 25–26. .

11. Paul Krugman, interview by FCIC, October 6, 2010.

12. Ellen Schloemer, Wei Li, Keith Ernst, and Kathleen Keest, "Losing Ground: Foreclosures in the Subprime Market and Their Cost to Homeowners," Center for Responsible Lending, December 2006, p. 22.

13. *2009 Mortgage Market Statistical Annual*, vol. 1, *The Primary Market*, p. 4, "Mortgage Originations by Product."

14. Christopher Mayer, Karen Pence, and Shane M. Sherlund, "The Rise in Mortgage Defaults," *Journal of Economic Perspectives* 23, no. 1 (Winter 2009): Table 2, Attributes for Mortgages in Subprime and Alt-A Pools, p. 31.

15. *2009 Mortgage Market Statistical Annual*, 2:13, "Non-Agency MBS Issuance by Type."

16. *2009 Mortgage Market Statistical Annual*, 1:6, "Alternative Mortgage Originations"; previous data extrapolated in FCIC estimates from Golden West, Form 10-K for fiscal year 2005, and Federal Reserve, "Residential Mortgage Lenders Peer Group Survey: Analysis and Implications for First Lien Guidance," November 30, 2005.

17. Inside Mortgage Finance.

18. Countrywide, 2005 Form 10-K, p. 39; 2007 Form 10-K, p. 47 (showing the growth in Countrywide's originations).

19. Angelo Mozilo, email to Sambol and Kurland re: Sub-prime Seconds. See also Angelo Mozilo, email to Sambol, Bartlett, and Sieracki, re: "Reducing Risk, Reducing Cost," May 18, 2006; Angelo Mozilo, interview by FCIC. September 24, 2010.

20. David Sambol, interview by FCIC, September 27, 2010.

21. See Countrywide, Investor Conference Call, January 27, 2004, transcript, p. 5. See also Jody Shenn, "Countrywide Adding Staff to Boost Purchase Share," *American Banker*, January 28, 2004.

22. Patricia Lindsay, written testimony for the FCIC, hearing on Subprime Lending and Securitization and Government-Sponsored Enterprises (GSEs), day 1, sess. 2: Subprime Origination and Securitization, April 7, 2010, p. 3

23. Andrew Davidson, interview by FCIC, October 29, 2020.

24. Ibid.

25. David Berenbaum, testimony before Senate Committee on Banking, Subcommittee on Housing, Transportation and Community Development, 110th Cong., 1st sess., June 26, 2007.

26. Email and data attachment from former Golden West employee to FCIC, subject: "re: Golden West Estimated Volume of Adjustable Rate Mortgage Originations," December 6, 2010.

27. Herbert Sandler, interview by FCIC, September 22, 2010.

28. Washington Mutual, "Option ARM Focus Groups—Phase II," September 17, 2003; Washington Mutual, "Option ARM Focus Groups—Phase I," August 14, 2003, Exhibits 35 and 36 in Senate Permanent Subcommittee on Investigations, exhibits, *Wall Street and the Financial Crisis: The Role of High Risk Home Loans*, 111th Cong., 2nd sess., April 13, 2010 (hereafter cited as PSI Documents), PDF pp. 330–51, available at http://hsgac.senate.gov/public/_files/Financial_Crisis/041310Exhibits.pdf.

29. PSI Documents, Exhibits 35 and 36 pp. 330–51.

30. Ibid., pp. 330–51, 334.

31. Ibid., p. 345.

32. Ibid., p. 346.

33. Washington Mutual, "Option ARM Credit Risk," August 2006, PSI Document Exhibit 37, p. 366.

34. PSI Documents Exhibit 37, p. 366, showing average FICO score of 698; p. 356; comparing conforming and jumbo originations.

35. Ibid., p. 357.

36. Document listing Countrywide originations by quarter from 2003 to 2007, provided by Bank of America.

37. Countrywide October 2003 Loan Program Guide (depicting a maximum CLTV of 80 and minimum FICO of 680) and July 2004 Loan Program Guide (showing 90% 620 FICO).

38. Countrywide Loan Program Guide, dated March 7, 2005.

39. Federal Reserve, "Residential Mortgage Lenders Peer Group Survey: Analysis and Implications for First Lien Guidance," November 30, 2005, pp. 6, 8.

40. Angelo Mozilo, email to Carlos Garcia (cc: Stan Kurland), Subject: "Bank Assets," August 1, 2005.

41. Angelo Mozilo, email to Carlos Garcia (cc: Kurland), subject: "re: Fw: Bank Assets," August 2, 2005.

42. Countrywide, 2005 Form 10-K, p. 57; 2007 Form 10-K, p. F-45.

43. See Washington Mutual, 2006 Form 10-K, p. 53.

44. John Stumpf, interview by FCIC, September 23, 2010.

45. Countrywide, 2007 Form 10-K, p. F-45; 2005 Form 10-K, p. 57

46. Washington Mutual, 2007 Form 10-K, p. 57; 2005 Form 10-K, p. 55

47. Kevin Stein, testimony before the FCIC, Sacramento Hearing on the Impact of the Financial Crisis–San Francisco, day 1, session 2: Mortgage Origination, Mortgage Fraud and Predatory Lending in the Sacramento Region, September 23, 2010, transcript, p. 72.

48. Mona Tawatao, in ibid., p. 228.

49. Real Estate Lending Standards, *Federal Register* 57 (December 31, 1992): 62890.

50. Ibid.

51. Office of the Comptroller of the Currency, Board of Governors of the Federal Deposit Insurance Corporation, Office of Thrift Supervision, "Real Estate Lending Standards: Final Rule," SR 93–1, January 11, 1993.

52. Office of the Comptroller of the Currency, Board of Governors of the Federal Deposit Insurance Corporation, Office of Thrift Supervision, "Interagency Guidance on High LTV Residential Real Estate Lending," October 8, 1999.

53. Final Report of Michael J. Missal, Bankruptcy Court Examiner, In RE: New Century TRS Holdings, Chapter 11, Case No. 07-10416 (KJC), (Bankr. D.Del.), February 29, 2008, pp. 128, 149, 128.

54. Yuliya Demyanyk and Otto Van Hemert, "Understanding the Subprime Mortgage Crisis," *Review of Financial Studies,* May 2009.

55. Sandler, interview.

56. CoreLogic loan performance data for subprime and Alt-A loans, and CoreLogic total outstanding loans servicer data provided to the FCIC.

57. Christopher Mayer, Karen Pence, and Shane M. Sherlund, "The Rise in Mortgage Defaults," *Journal of Economic Perspectives* 23, no. 1 (Winter 2009): 32.

58. William Black, testimony for the FCIC, Miami Hearing on the Impact of the Financial Crisis, day 1, session 1: Overview of Mortgage Fraud, September 21, 2010, p. 27.

59. Richard Bowen, interview by FCIC, February 27, 2010.

60. Jamie Dimon, testimony before the FCIC, January 13, 2010, p. 60.

61. This particular deal would be described as an excess-spread over-collateralized-based credit enhancement structure; see Gary Gorton, "The Panic of 2007," paper presented at the Federal Reserve Bank of Kansas City's Jackson Hole Conference, August 2008, p. 23.

62. FCIC staff estimates based on analysis of data from BlackBox, S&P, and Bloomberg. The prospective loan pool for this deal originally contained 4,507 mortgages. Eight of these had been dropped from the pool by the time the bonds were issued. Therefore, these estimates may differ slightly from those reported in the deal prospectus because these estimates are based on a pool of 4,499 loans.

63. Ibid.

64. *Federal Register* 69 (January 7, 2004): 1904. The rules were issued in proposed form at *Federal Register* 68 (August 5, 2003): 46119.

65. See OTS Opinion re California Minimum Payment Statute, October 1, 2002, p. 6.

66. Comptroller of the Currency John Hawke, remarks before Women in Housing and Finance, Washington, D.C., February 12, 2002, attached to OCC News Release 2002-10, p. 2.

67. John Hawke, quoted in Jess Bravin and Paul Beckett, "Friendly Watchdog: Federal Regulator Often Helps Banks Fighting Consumers," *Wall Street Journal,* January 28, 2002.

68. Oren Bar-Gill and Elizabeth Warren, "Making Credit Safer," *University of Pennsylvania Law Review* 157 (2008): 182-83, 192-94.

69. See Watters v. Wachovia Bank NA, 550 U.S. 1 (2007).

70. John Dugan, testimony before the FCIC, Public Hearing on Subprime Lending and Securitization and Government-Sponsored Enterprises (GSEs), day 2, session 2: Office of the Comptroller of the Currency, April 8, 2010, transcript, p. 150.

71. Lisa Madigan, testimony before the FCIC, First Public Hearing of the FCIC, day 2, panel 2: Investigations into the Financial Crisis—State and Local Officials, January 14, 2010, transcript, p. 104.

72. John D. Hawke Jr., written testimony for the FCIC, Public Hearing on Subprime Lending and Securitization and Government-Sponsored Enterprises (GSEs), day 2, session 2: Office of the Comptroller of the Currency, April 8, 2010, p. 6.

73. Citigroup Warehouse Lines of Credit with Mortgage Originators, in Global Securitized Markets, 2000–2010 (revised), produced by Citigroup; staff calculations.

74. Charles O. Prince, interview by FCIC, March 17, 2010.

75. Moody's Special Report, "The ABCP Market in the Third Quarter of 1998," February 2, 1999.

76. Moody's 2007 Review and 2008 Outlook: US Asset-backed Commercial Paper, February 27, 2008.

77. Moody's ABCP Reviews of Park Granada and Park Sienna.

78. Moody's ABCP Program Review: Park Granada, July 16, 2007.

79. Letters from the American Securitization Forum (November 17, 2003) and State St. Bank (November 14, 2003) to the Office of Thrift Supervision.

80. Darryll Hendricks, interview by FCIC, August 6, 2010.

81. Citi August 29, 2006, Loan Sale.

82. Correspondence between Citi and New Century provided to FCIC. FCIC staff estimates from prospectus and Citigroup production dated November 4, 2010. Citi August 29, 2006, Loan Sale.

83. Fannie Mae Term Sheet.

84. For the more than 20 institutional investors around the world, see Citigroup letter to the FCIC re Senior Investors, October 14, 2010. The $582 million figure is based on FCIC staff estimates that, in turn, were based on analysis of Moody's PDS database.

85. See Brad S. Karp, counsel for Citigroup, letter to FCIC, about senior investors, October 14, 2010, p. 2. See also Eric S. Goldstein, counsel for JPMorgan Chase & Co., letter to FCIC, November 16, 2010.

86. Citigroup letter to the FCIC, November 4, 2010.

87. See, e.g., Simon Kennedy, "BNP Suspends Funds Amid Credit-Market Turmoil," August 9, 2007. (www.marketwatch.com/story/bnp-suspends-fund-valuations-amid-credit-market-turmoil).

88. See Brad S. Karp, letter to FCIC, about mezzanine investors, November 4, 2010, p. 1. The equity tranches were not offered for public sale but were retained by Citigroup.

89. FCIC staff estimates from prospectus and Citigroup production dated November 4, 2010.

90. Patricia Lindsay, interview by FCIC, March 24, 2010.

91. PSI Documents, Exhibit 59a: "Long Beach Mortgage Production, Incentive Plan 2004," and Exhibit 60a (quoting page 2 of WaMu Home Loans Product Strategy PowerPoint presentation).

92. John M. Quigley, "Compensation and Incentives in the Mortgage Business," Economists' Voices (The Berkeley Electronic Press, October 2008), p. 2.

93. Barclays Capital, Bear Stearns, BNP Paribas, Citigroup, Deutsche Bank, Goldman Sachs, HSBC, JPMorgan, Lehman Brothers, Morgan Stanley, and UBS.

94. Figures are average top-tier pay worldwide in mortgages and MBS sales and trading. See Options Group, "2005 Global Financial Market Overview & Compensation Report" (October 2005), pp. 42, 52; Options Group, "2006 Global Financial Market Overview & Compensation Report" (November 2006), pp. 59, 69; and Options Group, "2007 Global Financial Market Overview & Compensation Report" (November 2007), pp. 73, 82.

95. See Merrill Lynch, 2007 Proxy Statement, p. 46.

96. See FCIC staff analysis of Moody's Form 10-Ks for years 2005, 2006, and 2007.

97. See FCIC staff calculations based on Moody's Form 10-Ks for years 2003–07.

98. "Moody's Expands Moody's Mortgage Metrics to Include Subprime Residential Mortgages," September 6, 2006; FCIC staff estimate based on analysis of Moody's SFDRS and PDS databases.

99. The ratings from the three agencies measure slightly different credit risk characteristics. S&P and Fitch base their ratings on the probability that a borrower will default; Moody's bases its ratings on the *expected loss* to the investor. Despite such differences, investors and regulators tend to view the ratings as roughly equivalent. Ratings are divided into two categories: investment grade securities are rated BBB- to AAA, while securities rated below BBB- are considered speculative and are also referred to as junk (for S&P; similar levels for Moody's are Baa to triple-A).

100. Richard Cantor and Frank Packer, "The Credit Rating Industry," *FRBNY Quarterly Review* (Summer–Fall 1994): 6.

101. Andrew J. Donohue, director, Division of Investment Management, SEC, "Speech by SEC Staff: Opening Remarks before the Commission Open Meeting," Washington, DC, June 25, 2008. See also Lawrence J. White, "Markets: The Credit Rating Agencies," *Journal of Economic Perspectives* 24, no. 2 (Spring 2010): 214.

102. Lewis Ranieri, interview by FCIC, July 30, 2010.

103. Eric Kolchinsky, testimony before the FCIC, Hearing on the Credibility of Credit Ratings, the Investment Decisions Made Based on Those Ratings, and the Financial Crisis, session 1: The Ratings Process, June 2, 2010, transcript, pp. 19–20.

104. See 15 U.S.C. 78o-7(c)(2).

105. Jerome S. Fons, testimony before the House Committee on Oversight and Government Reform, 110th Cong., 2nd sess., October 22, 2008, p. 2.

106. Arnold Cattani, testimony before the FCIC, Hearing on the Impact of the Financial Crisis—Greater Bakersfield, session 2: Local Banking, transcript, p. 60.

107. Gary Witt, testimony before the FCIC, Hearing on the Credibility of Credit Ratings, the Investment Decisions Made Based on Those Ratings, and the Financial Crisis, session 1: The Ratings Process, June 2, 2010, transcript, p. 41.

108. Moody's Investors Service, "Introducing Moody's Mortgage Metrics: Subprime Just Became More Transparent," September 7, 2009.

109. David Teicher, Moody's Investors Service, interview by FCIC, May 4, 2010; "Moody's Mortgage Metrics: A Model Analysis of Residential Mortgage Pools," April 1, 2003.

110. Jay Siegel, interview by FCIC, May 26, 2010.

111. Teicher, interview.

112. Jay Siegel, testimony before the FCIC, Hearing on the Credibility of Credit Ratings, the Investment Decisions Made Based on Those Ratings, and the Financial Crisis, session 1: The Ratings Process, June 2, 2010, transcript, p. 29.

113. Roger Stein, interview by FCIC, May 26, 2010.

114. Moody's Investors Service, "Introducing Moody's Mortgage Metrics."

115. Stein, interview.

116. Jerome Fons, interview by FCIC, April 22, 2010.

117. Moody's Rating Committee Memorandum, August 29, 2006.

118. FCIC staff estimates based on analysis of Moody's PDS database.

119. Invoice from Moody's Investors Service to Susan Mills, Citigroup Global Markets Inc., October 12, 2006.

120. Standard & Poor's, Global New Issue Billing Form, Citigroup Mortgage Loan Trust 2006-NC2, September 28, 2006.

121. FCIC staff estimates based on analysis of Moody's SFDRS data as of April 2010.

122. Chris Cox, SEC chairman, prepared testimony before the Senate Banking Committee, 109th Cong., 2nd sess., June 15, 2006; "Freddie Mac, Four Former Executives Settle SEC Action Relating to Multi-Billion Dollar Accounting Fraud," SEC press release, September 27, 2007.

123. James Lockhart, director, FHFA, speech to American Securitization Forum in Las Vegas, New Mexico, February 9, 2009 (p. 2, slide 4 of presentation shows the chart).

124. OFHEO Special Examination Report, December 2003.

125. In 2006, OFHEO issued its final *Report of the Special Examination of Fannie Mae*. OFHEO said that management engaged in numerous acts of misconduct, involving well over a dozen different forms of accounting manipulation and violations of generally accepted accounting principles. As in the case of Freddie, OFHEO said Fannie's management sought to hit ambitious earnings-per-share targets that were linked to their own compensation.

126. Donald Bisenius, interview by FCIC, September 29, 2010.

127. *Mortgage Market Statistical Annual 2009.*

128. See Tables 5.1/5.2 in FHFA Conservatorship report for third-quarter 2010.

129. OFHEO Special Examination Report, September 2004, pp. 9–10.

130. Ibid., pp. 2, 10.

131. OFHEO, "2005 Report to Congress," June 15, 2005, p. 15.

132. Alan Greenspan, testimony before the FCIC, Hearing on Subprime Lending and Securitization and Government-Sponsored Enterprises (GSEs), day 1, session 1: The Federal Reserve, April 7, 2010, transcript, p. 13.

133. FHFA, "Mortgage Market Note: Goals of Fannie Mae and Freddie Mac in the Context of the Mortgage Market: 1996–2009," February 2010, p. 22; "FCIC calculations."

134. FHFA, *Report to Congress, 2008* (2009), pp. 116, 125.

135. BlackRock Solutions, "Fannie Mae's Strategy and Business Model, Supplementary Exhibits," December 2007.

136. Robert Levin, interview by FCIC, March 17, 2010.

137. Mark Winer, interview by FCIC, March 23, 2010.

138. John Weicher, former FHA commissioner, interview by FCIC, March 11, 2010.

139. Letter from Robert Levin to FCIC, June 17, 2010, p. 2.

## Chapter 8

1. Joe Donovan, Credit Suisse, quoted in Michael Gregory, "The 'What If's' in ABS CDOs," *Asset Securitization Report,* February 18, 2002.

2. FCIC staff calculations, using data from the U.S. Census, data in Moody's CDO PDS database, and data in Moody's CDO Enhanced Monitoring Service database. The FCIC selected CDOs with at least 10% of their collateral invested in mortgage-backed securities or with other characteristics that identified them as ABS CDOs.

3. Scott Eichel, quoted in Allison Pyburn, "CDO Machine? Managers, Mortgage Companies, Happy to Keep Fuel Coming," *Asset Securitization Report,* May 23, 2005.

4. Patrick Parkinson, interview by FCIC, March 30, 2010.

5. Jian Hu, "Assessing the Credit Risk of CDOs Backed by Structured Finance Securities: Rating Analysts' Challenges and Solutions," *Journal of Structured Finance* 13, no. 3 (2007): 46.

6. Wing Chau, interview by FCIC, November 11, 2010.

7. CDOs that bought relatively senior tranches of mortgage-backed securities were known as *high-grade;* those that bought the BBB-rated and other junior tranches were known as *mezzanine.*

8. Joe Donovan, quoted in Gregory, "The '"What If's' in ABS CDOs."

9. Laurie Goodman et al., *Subprime Mortgage Credit Derivatives* (Hoboken, NJ: John Wiley, 2008), p. 315.

10. Hu, "Assessing the Credit Risk of CDOs Backed by Structured Finance Securities," p. 47, Exhibit 5.

11. Issuance dropped in 2007 to $194 billion and virtually disappeared in 2008. FCIC staff estimates based on data provided by Moody's CDO Enhanced Monitoring System (EMS).

12. FCIC staff estimates based on analysis of Moody's CDO EMS database.

13. Nestor Dominguez, interview by FCIC, September 28, 2010.

14. Michael Lamont, interview by FCIC, September 21, 2010.

15. Chris Ricciardi, interview by FCIC, September 15, 2010.

16. Lamont, interview.

17. FCIC staff calculations using data in FCIC CDO manager and underwriter survey.

18. Mark Adelson, interview by FCIC, October 22, 2010.

19. FCIC staff calculations. Our estimate assumes an annual management fee of 0.10% of the total value of the deal—that is, the lowest normally earned in the industry—applied to the mortgage-focused multisector CDOs in the FCIC database. It does not include other income, such as interest on equity tranches retained by the managers. CDO managers responding to the FCIC survey reported management fees ranging from as low as 0.10% to as high as 0.40%.

20. "Summary of Key Fee Provisions for Cash CDOs as of January 2000–2010," prepared by Moody's for the FCIC.

21. FCIC Hedge Fund Survey. See FCIC website for details.

22. FCIC staff estimates based on Moody's CDO Enhanced Monitoring Service.

23. Bloomberg LLC, Financial Analyst Function; Bear Stearns Companies Inc., Form 10-K, for the fiscal year ended November 30, 2006, filed February 13, 2007, Exhibit 13.

24. The Options Group, "2005 Global Financial Market Overview & Compensation Report," October 2005, p. 16.

25. Moody's, Kleros Real Estate CDO III, Ltd., CDO EMS Data, last updated May 27, 2008.The following discussion of CMLTI 2006-NC2 relies on FCIC staff estimates based on analysis of Moody's CDO EMS database.

26. Ricciardi, interview.

27. For example, Kleros III tranches were in Buckingham CDO, Buckingham CDO II, and Buckingham CDO III, all deals underwritten by Barclays.

28. Adelson, interview.

29. Chau, interview.

30. James Grant, "Up the Capital Structure" (December 15, 2006), in *Mr. Market Miscalculates: The Bubble Years and Beyond* (Mount Jackson, VA: Axios Press, 2008), 186.

31. UBS Global CDO Group, Presentation on Product Series (POPS), January 2007.

32. Dan Sparks, interview by FCIC, June 15, 2010.

33. Dominguez, interview.

34. The ratio of the book value of assets to equity ranged from 2.5 to 28.3 times for all SIVs; the average was 13.6 times. Moody's Investors Service, "Moody's Special Report: Moody's Update on Structured Investment Vehicles," January 16, 2008, p. 13.

35. Mark Klipsch, quoted in Colleen Marie O'Connor, "Drought of CDO Collateral Tops Concerns," *Asset Securitization Report*, October 18, 2004.

36. Bear Stearns Asset Management, Collateral Manager Presentation; Ralph Cioffi, interview by FCIC, October 19, 2010; Bear Stearns High-Grade Structured Credit Strategies Master Fund, Ltd., financial statements for the year ended December 31, 2006 (total assets were $8,573,315,025); Bear Stearns High-Grade Structured Credit Strategies Enhanced Leverage Master Fund, Ltd., financial statements for the year ended December 31, 2006 (total assets were $9,403,235,402).

37. James Cayne, written testimony for the FCIC, Hearing on the Shadow Banking System, day 1, session 2: Investment Banks and the Shadow Banking System, May 5, 2010, p. 2; Warren Spector, interview by FCIC, March 30, 2010.

38. Cioffi, interview.

39. AIMA's Illustrative Questionnaire for Due Diligence of Bear Stearns High Grade Structured Credit Strategies Fund; Bank of America presentation to Merrill Lynch's Board of Directors, "Bear Steams Asset Management: What Went Wrong."

40. Bear Stearns High-Grade Structured Credit Strategies Master Fund, Ltd., financial statements for the year ended December 31, 2006; Financial Statements, Bear Stearns High-Grade Structured Credit Strategies Enhanced Leverage Master Fund, Ltd., financial statements for the year ended December 31, 2006; BSAM fund chart prepared by JP Morgan.

41. FCIC staff calculations using data from FCIC survey of hedge funds. The hedge funds responding to the survey had a total of $1.2 trillion in investments.

42. IMF, *Global Financial Stability Report*, April 2008, Table 1.2, page 23, "Typical 'Haircut' or Initial Margin."

43. Alan Schwartz, interview by FCIC, April 23, 2010.

44. Cioffi, interview.

45. Ibid.

46. Ibid.

47. Bear Stearns High-Grade Structured Credit Strategies, investor presentation, stating that "the fund is subject to conflicts of interest." Bear Stearns High-Grade Structured Credit Strategies Enhanced Leverage Fund, L.P., Preliminary Confidential Private Placement Memorandum, August 2006. Everquest Financial Ltd., Form S-1, p. 13.

48. Bear Stearns Asset Management Collateral Manager, presentation, stating that Klio I collateral includes 73% RMBS and ABS and 27% CDOs, Klio II collateral includes 74% RMBS and ABS and 26% CDOs, and Klio III collateral includes 74% RMBS and ABS and 26% CDOs; Cioffi, interview.

49. Everquest Financial Ltd., Form S-1, pp. 9, 3.

50. Bear Stearns Asset Management, Collateral Manager Presentation.

51. Cioffi and Tannin Compensation Table, produced by Paul, Weiss, Rifkind, Wharton & Garrison, LLP.

52. Matt Tannin, Bear Stearns, email to Bella Borg-Brenner, Stillwater Capital, March 16, 2007; Greg Quental, Bear Stearns, email to Andrew Donnellan, Bear Stearns, et al., June 6, 2007.

53. Charles Prince, interview by FCIC, March 17, 2010.

54. Regulators in Japan and the United Kingdom also came down on the company in 2004 and 2005. In September 2004, Japan's Financial Services Agency suspended Citibank's ability to operate branches in Japan because of the bank's participation in alleged illegal activity in that country, and in the following year the United Kingdom's Financial Services Authority fined Citigroup $25 million for engaging in a bond trading scheme labeled "Dr. Evil" by Citigroup bond traders. Financial Services Agency, Government of Japan, "Administrative Actions on Citibank, N.A. Japan Branch," September 17, 2004; Financial Services Authority, "Final Notice" to Citigroup Global Markets Limited, June 28, 2005 (www.fsa.gov.uk/pubs/final/cgml_28jun05.pdf); David Reilly, "Moving the Market: Citigroup to Take $25 Million Hit in 'Dr. Evil' Case," *Wall Street Journal,* June 29, 2005.

55. Prince, interview.

56. Robert Rubin, interview by FCIC, March 11, 2010.

57. Dominguez, interview by FCIC, March 2, 2010. The CDO desk earned revenues of $367 million in 2005. Paul, Weiss, Citigroup's counsel, letter to FCIC, March 31, 2010, in re the FCIC's second and third supplemental requests, "Response to Interrogatory No. 21."

58. Janice Warne, interview by FCIC, February 2, 2010; Paul, Weiss, Citigroup's counsel, letter to FCIC, March 1, 2010, "Response to Interrogatory No. 18."

59. Paul, Weiss, Citigroup's counsel, letter to FCIC, March 1, 2010, "Response to Interrogatory No. 18."

60. Moody's Investors Service, "CDOs with Short-Term Tranches: Moody's Approach to Rating Prime-1 CDO Notes," February 3, 2006, p. 11.

61. Citigroup Inc., Form 10-K, for the fiscal year ended December 31, 2007, filed February 22, 2008, p. 91.

62. Everquest Financial Ltd., Form S-1, May 9, 2007, p. 93.

63. Dominguez, interview, March 2, 2010.

64. Ibid.; Warne, interview.

65. Dominguez, interview, March 2, 2010.

66. Warne, interview.

67. GCIB Capital Markets Approval Committee, Coventree Capital, "Liquidity Put Option," draft as of December 13, 2002, p. 4.

68. Ron Frake, interview by FCIC, March 11, 2010.

69. "Formal Agreement" between the Comptroller of the Currency and Citibank, July 22, 2003.

70. Moody's Investors Service, "CDOs with Short-Term Tranches."

71. Ibid.; Bank of America Corporation, Form 10-Q for the quarterly period ended September 30, 2007, p. 19; Floyd Norris, "As Bank Profits Grew, Warning Signs Went Unheeded," *New York Times,* November 16, 2007.

72. Dominguez, interview, March 2, 2010.

73. Paul, Weiss, Citigroup's counsel, letter to FCIC, June 23, 2010, "Responses of Nestor Dominguez," p. 6.

74. OCC, "Subprime CDO Valuation and Oversight Review—Conclusion Memorandum," Memorandum from Michael Sullivan, RAD, and Ron Frake, NBE, to John Lyons, Examiner-in-Charge, Citibank, NA, January 17, 2008, p. 6,

75. Ibid.

76. Tobias Brushammar et al., memorandum to Nestor Dominguez et al., "Re: Liquidity Put Valuation," October 19, 2006, pp. 1, 3–4; "Liquidity Put Discussion," pt. 1, produced by Citi.

77. "Liquidity Put Discussion," produced by Citi.

78. Data provided by Moody's to the FCIC.

79. Gary Gorton, interview by FCIC, May 11, 2010.

80. AIG, 2008 10-K, p. 133. Assets are assigned a "risk weighting" or percentage that is then multiplied by 8% capital requirement to determine the amount of risk-based capital.

81. AIG, CDS notional balances at year-end 2000 through 2010 Q1, provided to the FCIC.

82. The total would reach $78 billion by 2007 (ibid.).

83. Gene Park, interview by FCIC, May 18, 2010.

84. Craig Broderick, testimony before the FCIC, Hearing on the Role of Derivatives in the Financial Crisis, day 1, session 3: Goldman Sachs Group, Inc. and Derivatives, June 30, 2010, transcript, pp. 289–90.

85. Moody's, "CDOs with Short-Term Tranches"; AIG, "Information Pertaining to the Multi-sector CDS Portfolio," provided to the FCIC.

86. Park, interview.

87. AIG, CDS notional balances at year-end, 2000 through 2010 Q1.

88. Alan Frost, interview by FCIC, May 11, 2010.

89. AIG Financial Products Corp. Deferred Compensation Plan, March 18, 2005, p. 2.

90. Joseph Cassano, email to All Users, re: 2007 Special Compensation Plan, December 17, 2007.

91. Joseph Cassano compensation history, provided by AIG to the FCIC.

92. AIG, Form 8-K, filed May 1, 2005.

93. "Fact Sheet on AIGFP," provided by Hank Greenberg, p. 4.

94. AIG, CDS notional balances at year-end.

95. Gene Park, email to Joseph Cassano, re: "CDO of ABS Approach Going Forward—Message to the Dealer Community," February 28, 2006.

96. Henry M. Paulson Jr., testimony before the FCIC, Hearing on the Shadow Banking System, day 2, session 1: Perspective on the Shadow Banking System, May 6, 2010, transcript, p. 22.

97. Henry M. Paulson Jr., written testimony for the FCIC, Hearing on the Shadow Banking System, day 2, session 1: Perspective on the Shadow Banking System, May 6, 2010, p. 2.

98. Goldman Sachs, 2005 and 2006 10-K (appendix 5a to Goldman's March 8, 2010, letter to the FCIC).

99. Appendix 5c to Goldman's March 8, 2010, letter to the FCIC.

100. Goldman's March 8, 2010, letter to the FCIC, p. 28 (subprime securities).

101. "Protection Bought by GS," spreadsheet provided by Goldman Sachs to the FCIC. Specifically, IKB purchased $30 million of Class A notes, $40 million of Class B notes, and $30 million of Class C notes on June 9, 2004. TCW purchased $50 million of Class A notes in January 2005, and Wachovia purchased $45 million of Class A notes in March 2005. See ibid., Exhibit 1.

102. FCIC staff calculations based on data provided by Goldman Sachs.

103. "Protection Bought by GS," spreadsheet.

104. FCIC calculations based on data provided by Goldman Sachs.

105. FCIC staff analysis based on data provided by Goldman Sachs.

106. Sparks, interview.

107. Of course, in theory the *net* impact on the financial system is not greater, because there is a winner for every loser in the derivatives market.

108. Sparks, interview.

109. From Goldman Sachs data provided to the FCIC in a handout titled "Amplification" and quoted at the FCIC's Hearing on the Role of Derivatives in the Financial Crisis, day 1, session 3: Goldman Sachs Group, Inc. and Derivatives, June 30, 2010.

110. FCIC staff analysis based on data provided by Goldman Sachs.

111. Lloyd Blankfein, chairman of the board and chief executive officer, Goldman Sachs Group, interview by FCIC, June 16, 2010; Sparks, interview.

112. Gary Cohn, testimony before the FCIC, Hearing on the Role of Derivatives in the Financial Crisis, day 1, session 3: Goldman Sachs Group, Inc. and Derivatives, June 30, 2010, transcript, p. 351.

113. Parkinson, interview.

114. Michael Greenberger, before the FCIC, Hearing on the Role of Derivatives in the Financial Crisis, day 1, session 1: Overview of Derivatives, June 30, 2010; oral testimony, transcript, p. 109; written testimony, p. 16.

115. Moody's Investors Service, "Summary of Key Provisions for Cash CDOs as of January 2000–2010."

116. Gary Witt, written testimony for the FCIC, Hearing on Credibility of Credit Ratings, the Investment Decisions Made Based on Those Ratings, and the Financial Crisis, day 1, session 1: The Ratings Process, June 2, 2010, pp. 12, 15.

117. Ibid., 12.

118. Gary Witt, testimony before the FCIC, Hearing on Credibility of Credit Ratings, the Investment Decisions Made Based on those Ratings, and the Financial Crisis, day 1, session 1: The Ratings Process, June 2, 2010, transcript, pp. 168, 436.

119. Moody's Investors Service, "Moody's Approach to Rating Multisector CDOs," September 15, 2000, p. 5.

120. Gary Witt, interview by FCIC, April 21, 2010.

121. Witt, written testimony for the FCIC, June 2, 2010, p. 17.

122. Gary Witt, follow-up interview by FCIC, May 13, 2010.

123. Witt, interview, April 21, 2010.

124. For example, Moody's assumed that borrowers with different credit ratings would not default at the same time. The agency split the securities into three subcategories based on the average FICO score of the underlying mortgages: prime (FICO greater than 700), midprime (FICO between 700 and 625), and subprime (FICO under 625). Creating three FICO-based subcategories rather than the traditional two (prime and subprime) resulted in lower correlation assumptions, because mortgage-backed securities in different subcategories were assumed to be less correlated. "Moody's Revisits Its Assumptions Regarding Structured Finance Default (and Asset) Correlations for CDOs," June 27, 2005, pp. 15, 5, 7, 9, 4; Gary Witt, interview by FCIC, May 6, 2010.

125. Hedi Katz, "U.S. Subprime RMBS in CDOs," Fitch Special Report, April 15, 2005, p. 3; Sten Bergman, "CDO Evaluator Applies Correlation and Monte Carlo Simulation to Determine Portfolio Quality," Standard & Poor's Global Credit Portal RatingsDirect, November 13, 2001, p. 8.

126. Ingo Fender and Janet Mitchell, "Structured Finance: Complexity, Risk and the Use of Ratings," BIS Quarterly Review (June 2005): 68 (www.bis.org/publ/qtrpdf/r_qt0506.pdf).

127. Based on an FCIC survey of 40 CDO managers and 11 underwriters about the process of creating and marketing CDOs.

128. Moody's Investors Service, "Structured Finance Rating Transitions: 1983–2006," January 2007, pp. 7, 64. Of structured finance securities originally rated triple-A between 1984 and 2006, 56% retained their original rating 5 years later, 5% were downgraded, and 39% were withdrawn.

129. Kyle Bass, testimony to the House Financial Services Committee, Subcommittee on Capital Markets, Insurance, and Government Sponsored Enterprises, Hearing on the Role of Credit Rating Agencies in the Structured Finance Market, 110th Cong., 1st sess., September 27, 2007, p. 11.

130. "Structured Finance Rating Transitions: 1983–2008," Moody's Credit Policy Special Comment, March 2009, p. 2.

131. Moody's Investors Service, "Announcement: Moody's Updates Its Key Assumptions for Rating Structured Finance CDOs," December 11, 2008.

132. Ben Bernanke, closed-door session with FCIC, November 17, 2009.

133. Ann Rutledge, email to FCIC, November 16, 2010. Ann Rutledge is a principal in R&R Consulting, a coauthor of Elements of Structured Finance (Oxford: Oxford University Press, 2010), and a former employee of Moody's Investor Service. She and co-principal Sylvain Raines first spoke to the FCIC on April 12, 2010.

134. From Moody's "Structured Finance: Special Report," the following page 1 headlines: "2004 U.S. CDO Review / 2005 Preview: Record Activity Levels Driven by Resecuritization CDOs and CLOs," February 1, 2005; "2005 U.S. CDO Review: Looking Ahead to 2006: Record Year Follows Record Year," February 6, 2006; "2008 U.S. CDO Outlook and 2007 Review: Issuance Down in 2007 Triggered by Subprime Mortgages Meltdown; Lower Overall Issuance Expected in 2008," March 3, 2008.

135. Moody's annual gross revenues for ABS CDO ratings was $11,730,234 in 2003, $22,210,695 in 2004, $40,332,909 in 2005, $91,285,905 in 2006, and $94,666,014 in 2007. Information provided by Moody's, May 3, 2010. See also Moody's Corporation 2006 10-K, p. 66 and Moody's Corporation, 2007 10-K.

136. Witt, testimony before the FCIC, June 2, 2010, transcript, p. 46.

137. Witt, written testimony for the FCIC, June 2, 2010, p. 11; Witt, interview, April 21, 2010.

138. Eric Kolchinsky, interview by FCIC, April 27, 2010.

139. Witt, interview, April 21, 2010.

140. FCIC staff estimates based on analysis of Moody's CDO EMS database.

141. Yuri Yoshizawa, interview by FCIC, May 17, 2010. The chart was labeled "Derivatives (America)."

142. Brian Clarkson, interview by FCIC, May 20, 2010.

143. Harvey Goldschmid, interview by FCIC, March 24, 2010; Annette Nazareth, interview by FCIC, April 1, 2010.

144. Office of Thrift Supervision, letter to the SEC, February 11, 2004.

145. Lehman Brothers, Inc., letter to the SEC, March 8, 2004; J.P. Morgan Chase & Co., letter to the SEC, February 12, 2004; Deutsche Bank A.G. and Deutsche Bank Secs., letter to the SEC, February 18, 2004.

146. Harvey Goldschmid, interview by FCIC, April 8, 2010.

147. Closed meeting of the Securities and Exchange Commission, April 28, 2004.

148. In 2005, the Division of Market Regulation became the Division of Trading and Markets. For the sake of simplicity, throughout this report it is referred to as the Division of Market Regulation.

149. Erik Sirri, interview by FCIC, April 1, 2010. Although there are more than 1,000 SEC examiners, collectively they regulate more than 5,000 broker-dealers (with more than 750,000 registered representatives) as well as other market participants.

150. Michael Macchiaroli, interview by FCIC, March 18, 2010.

151. The monitors met with senior business and risk managers at each CSE firm every month about general concerns and risks the firms were seeing. Written reports of these meetings were given to the director of market regulation every month. In addition, the CSE monitors met quarterly with the treasury and financial control functions of each CSE firm to discuss liquidity and funding issues.

152. Erik Sirri, written testimony for the FCIC, Hearing on the Shadow Banking System, day 1, session 3: SEC Regulation of Investment Banks, May 5, 2010.

153. Internal SEC memorandum, Re: "CSE Examination of Bear Stearns & Co. Inc.," November 4, 2005.

154. Securities and Exchange Commission, Office of Inspector General, "SEC's Oversight of Bear Stearns and Related Entities: The Consolidated Supervised Entity Program," Report No. 446-A, September 25, 2008, pp. 17–18.

155. Michael Macchiaroli, interview by FCIC, April 13, 2010.

156. Robert Seabolt, email to James Giles, Steven Spurry, and Matthew Eichner, October 1, 2007.

157. Matt Eichner, interview by FCIC, April 14, 2010; SEC, OIG, "SEC's Oversight of Bear Stearns and Related Entities: The Consolidated Supervised Entity Program," p. 109.

158. Goldschmid, interview.

159. GAO, "Financial Markets Regulation: Financial Crisis Highlights Need to Improve Oversight of Leverage at Financial Institutions," GAO-09-739 (Report to Congressional Committees), July 2009, pp. 38–42.

160. Erik Sirri, "Securities Markets and Regulatory Reform," remarks at the National Economists Club, Washington, D.C., April 9, 2009.

161. Harvey Goldschmid, interview, April 8, 2010.

162. "Chairman Cox Announces End of Consolidated Supervised Entities Program," SEC press release, September 26, 2008.

163. Mary Schapiro, testimony before the FCIC, First Public Hearing of the Financial Crisis Inquiry Commission, day 2, panel 1: Current Investigations into the Financial Crisis—Federal Officials, January 14, 2010, transcript, p. 39.

164. The Fed remained the supervisor of JP Morgan at the holding company level.

165. Mark Olson, interview by FCIC, October 4, 2010.

166. Federal Reserve System, "Financial Holding Company Project," January 25, 2008, p. 3.

## Chapter 9

1. Warren Peterson, written testimony for the FCIC, Hearing on the Impact of the Financial Crisis—Greater Bakersfield, session 3: Residential and Community Real Estate, September 7, 2010, pp. 1, 3.

2. Gary Crabtree, principal owner, Affiliated Appraisers, written testimony for the FCIC, Hearing on the Impact of the Financial Crisis—Greater Bakersfield, session 4: Local Housing Market, September 7, 2010, p. 2.

3. Lloyd Plank, Lloyd E. Plank Real Estate Consultants, written testimony for the FCIC, Hearing on the Impact of the Financial Crisis—Greater Bakersfield, session 4: Local Housing Market, September 7, 2010, p. 2.

4. CoreLogic Single Family Combined (SFC) Home Price Index, data accessed August 2010. FCIC calculation of change from January 1997 to April 2006, peak.

5. Professor Robert Shiller, Historical Housing data..

6. Final Report of Michael J. Missal, Bankruptcy Court Examiner, In RE: New Century TRS Holdings, Chapter 11, Case No. 07-10416 (KJC), (Bankr. D.Del), February 29, 2008, pp. 145, 138, 139–40 (hereafter Missal).

7. Ibid., p. 3.

8. Nomura Fixed Income Research, "Notes from Boca Raton: Coverage from Selected Sessions of ABS East 2005," September 20, 2005, pp. 5–7.

9. Alan Greenspan, "The Economic Outlook," testimony before the Joint Economic Committee, 109th Cong., 1st sess., June 9, 2005.

10. Christopher Mayer, written testimony for the FCIC, Forum to Explore the Causes of the Financial Crisis, day 2, session 5: Mortgage Lending Practices and Securitization, February 27, 2010, pp. 5–6.

11. Antonio Fatás, Prakash Kannan, Pau Rabanal, and Alasdair Scott, "Lessons for Monetary Policy from Asset Price Fluctuations Leaving the Board," International Monetary Fund, *World Economic Outlook* (Fall 2009), chapter 3.

12. James MacGee, "Why Didn't Canada's Housing Market Go Bust?" Federal Reserve Bank of Cleveland. *Economic Comment* (December 2, 2009).

13. Morris A. Davis, Andreas Lehnert, and Robert F. Martin, "The Rent-Price Ratio for the Aggregate Stock of Owner-Occupied Housing," Federal Reserve Board Working Paper, May 2005, p. 2.

14. Price data from CoreLogic CSBA Home Price Index, Single-Family Combined. Rent data is Bureau of Labor Statistics, metro-level Consumer Price Index (CPI-U), Owners' Equivalent Rent for Primary Residence; all index figures are adjusted so that Jan. 1997=1. Methods follow from Federal Reserve Bank of San Francisco Economic Letter, "House Prices and Fundamental Value," Number 2004–27, October 1, 2004.

15. National Association of Realtors Housing Affordability Index, accessed from Bloomberg as composite Index (HOMECOMP). The index began in 1986.

16. The index also assumes that the qualifying ratio of 25%, so that the monthly principal & interest payment could not exceed 25% of the median family monthly income. More about the methodology can be found at National Association of Realtors, Methodology for the Housing Affordability Index.

17. Ben Bernanke, letter to FCIC Chairman Phil Angelides, December 21, 2010, p. 2.

18. Kristopher S. Gerardi, Christopher L. Foote, and Paul S. Willen, "Reasonable People Did Disagree: Optimism and Pessimism about the U.S. Housing Market Before the Crash," Federal Reserve Bank of Boston Public Policy Discussion Paper No. 10-5, August 12, 2010.

19. Donald L. Kohn, "Monetary Policy and Asset Prices," speech delivered at "Monetary Policy: A Journey from Theory to Practice," a European Central Bank Colloquium held in honor of Otmar Issing, Frankfurt, Germany, March 16, 2006.

20. Richard A. Brown, "Rising Risks in Housing Markets," memorandum to the National Risk Committee of the Federal Deposit Insurance Corporation, March 21, 2005, pp. 1–2.

21. Board of Governors, memorandum from Josh Gallin and Andreas Lehnert to Vice Chairman [Roger] Ferguson, "Talking Points on House Prices," May 5, 2005, p. 3.

22. Missal, p. 40.

23. William Black, testimony before the FCIC, Hearing on the Impact of the Financial Crisis—Miami, Florida, session 1: Overview of Mortgage Fraud, September 21, 2010, transcript, p. 78; and email from William Black to FCIC, December 12, 2010.

24. Reply of Attorney General Lisa Madigan (Illinois) to the FCIC, April 27, 2010, p. 7.

25. Chris Swecker, Assistant Director Criminal Investigative Division Federal Bureau of Investigation, statement before the House Financial Services Subcommittee on Housing and Community Opportunity, 108th Cong., 2nd sess., October 7, 2004.

26. Florida Department of Law Enforcement, "Mortgage Fraud Assessment," November 2005.

27. Wilfredo Ferrer, testimony before the FCIC, Hearing on the Impact of the Financial Crisis—Miami, Florida, session 3: The Regulation, Oversight, and Prosecution of Mortgage Fraud in Miami, September 21, 2010, transcript, pp. 186–87.

28. Ann Fulmer, supplemental written testimony for the FCIC, Hearing on the Impact of the Financial Crisis—Miami, Florida, session 1: Overview of Mortgage Fraud, September 21, 2010, p. 2; Fulmer, testimony, transcript, pp. 80–81.

29. Ed Parker, interview by FCIC, May 25, 2010.

30. David Gussmann, interview by FCIC, March 30, 2010.

31. William H. Brewster, interview by FCIC, October 29, 2010.

32. Henry Pontell, written testimony for the FCIC, Hearing on the Impact of the Financial Crisis—Miami, Florida, session 1: Overview of Mortgage Fraud, September 21, 2010, p. 1.

33. Department of Justice, Office of the Inspector General, "The Internal Effects of the FBI's Reprioritization, September 2005," p. 1.

34. Chris Swecker, interview by FCIC, March 8, 2010.

35. Patrick Crowley, MortgageDaily.com, November 24, 2003.

36. Swecker, statement to the House Financial Services Subcommittee on Housing and Community Opportunity, October 7, 2004.

37. William Black, written testimony for the FCIC, September 21, 2010, p. 17.

38. Francisco San Pedro, interview by FCIC, September 20, 2010.

39. FinCEN report to the FCIC on Countrywide SAR activity, 1999–2009.

40. OCC, letter to Bank of America, June 5, 2007.

41. Darcy Parmer, interview by FCIC, June 1, 2010.

42. FinCEN, "Mortgage Loan Fraud: An Industry Assessment Based on SAR Analysis," November 2006, pp. 2, 6.

43. Swecker, statement before the House Financial Services Subcommittee on Housing and Community Opportunity, October 7, 2004.

44. Swecker, interview.

45. FinCEN, "Mortgage Loan Fraud Update: Suspicious Activity Report Filings from April–June 30, 2010," p. 21.

46. DOJ, letter from Assistant Attorney General Ronald Welch to the FCIC, April 28, 2010, pp. 1, 3, October 21, 2010, p. 2.

47. Robert Mueller, interview by FCIC, December 14, 2010.

48. Alberto Gonzales, interview by FCIC, November 1, 2010.

49. OFHEO, "2007 Performance and Accountability Report," pp. 13, 17.

50. Richard Spillenkothen, interview by FCIC, March 19, 2010.

51. Michael J. Mukasey, interview by FCIC, October 20, 2010.

52. DOJ response to FCIC request, April 16, 2010; see also DOJ response to FCIC request, April 28, 2010.

53. William Black, testimony before the FCIC, September 21, 2010, transcript, p. 38.

54. Swecker, interview.

55. Ellen Wilcox, special agent, Florida Department of Law Enforcement, testimony before the FCIC, Hearing on the Impact of the Financial Crisis—Miami, session 2: Uncovering Mortgage Fraud in Miami, September 21, 2010, transcript, p. 80; "Participant in $13 Million Mortgage Fraud Scheme Convicted by Polk County Jury," Office of Florida Attorney General Bill McCollum press release, August 28, 2008.

56. Tenth Judicial Circuit in and for Polk County, Florida, State of Florida vs. Scott Almeida, et al., OSWP No. 2005-0256-TPA; July 23, 2007, see paragraphs 2, 17, 18, 19, 28, and 32.

57. Wilcox, testimony before the FCIC, September 21, 2010, transcript, pp. 98–99.

58. Gary Gorton, "The Panic of 2007," paper presented at the Federal Reserve Bank of Kansas City, Jackson Hole Conference, "Maintaining Stability in a Changing Financial System," August 2008.

59. Adam B. Ashcraft and Til Schuermann, "Understanding the Securitization of Subprime Mortgage Credit," Federal Reserve Bank of New York Staff Report No. 318, March 2008, pp. 5–11.

60. Raymond McDaniel, quoted in the transcript of Moody's Managing Director's Town Hall Meeting, September 11, 2007.

61. Keith Johnson, former president and chief operating officer of Clayton Holdings, Inc., interview by FCIC, September 2, 2010.

62. Frank Filipps, interview by FCIC, August 9, 2010.

63. Vicki Beal, testimony before the FCIC, Hearing on the Impact of the Financial Crisis—Sacramento, session 3: The Mortgage Securitization Chain: From Sacramento to Wall Street, September 23, 2010, transcript, pp. 155, 155–56.

64. Beal, testimony before the FCIC, September 23, 2010, transcript, pp. 169, 157; see also Martha Coakley, Massachusetts Attorney General, comment letter to the Securities and Exchange Commission regarding proposed rule regarding asset-backed securities, Release No. 33-9117; 34-61858; File No. S7-08-10, August 2, 2010, p. 6.

65. Beal, testimony before the FCIC, September 23, 2010, transcript, pp. 169–70.

66. D. Keith Johnson, testimony before the FCIC, Hearing on the Impact of the Financial Crisis—Sacramento, session 3: The Mortgage Securitization Chain: From Sacramento to Wall Street, September 23, 2010, transcript, pp. 183–84.

67. Ibid., p. 211.

68. Beal, testimony before the FCIC, September 23, 2010, transcript, p. 172.

69. John J. Goggins, senior vice president and general counsel, Moody's, letter to FCIC regarding "September 27, 2010 Article Published in *The New York Times* Misconstruing Commission Testimony," September 30, 2010.

70. Johnson, testimony before the FCIC, September 23, 2010, transcript, p. 174.

71. Missal, p. 67.

72. Roger Ehrnman, interview by FCIC, September 2, 2010; Johnson, testimony before the FCIC, September 23, 2010, transcript, p. 178.

73. Tony Peterson, interview by FCIC, October 14, 2010.

74. Joseph Schwartz, vice president in charge of mortgage acquisition due diligence, Deutsche Bank, interview by FCIC, July 21, 2010; William Collins Buell VI, head of mortgage acquisition, JP Morgan, interview by FCIC, September 15, 2010.

75. Richard M. Bowen, written testimony for the FCIC, Hearing on Subprime Lending and Securitization and Government-Sponsored Enterprises (GSEs), day 1, session 2: Subprime Origination and Securitization, April 7, 2010, p. 2.

76. Richard M. Bowen, interview by FCIC, February 27, 2010; FCIC correspondence with Richard M. Bowen.

77. Inside Mortgage Finance, *The 2009 Mortgage Market Statistical Annual*, vol. 2, *The Secondary Market* (Bethesda, MD: Inside Mortgage Finance, 2009), p. 156; FCIC staff estimate based on analysis of Moody's CDO EMS database.

78. See, for example, James C. Treadway Jr., "An Overview of Rule 415 and Some Thoughts About the Future," remarks to the thirteenth annual meeting of the Securities Industry Association, Hot Springs, Virginia, October 8, 1983.

79. Shelley Parratt and Paula Dubberly, interview by the FCIC, October 1, 2010.

80. 17 C.F.R. Part 229.1111(a)(3), "Pool Assets," revised as of April 1, 2005.

81. See Part V of complaint filed by Cambridge Place Investment Management Inc., dated July 9, 2010, in Suffolk County (Massachusetts) Superior Court, Cambridge Place Investment Management, Inc., v. Morgan Stanley & Co., Inc., Case No. 10-27841, p. 71 (hereafter Cambridge Complaint), and Part V of complaint filed by Federal Home Loan Bank of Chicago, dated October 15, 2010, in Circuit Court of Cook County, Illinois (Chancery Division), Federal Home Loan Bank of Chicago v. Banc of America Funding Corp. et al., Case No. 10CH450B3, p. 173.

82. Cambridge Complaint, pp. 32–33, 61–63, 70–71, 75–76.

83. Bowen, interview.

84. D. Keith Johnson, former president and chief operating officer, Clayton Holdings, Inc., interview by FCIC, June 8, 2010.

85. A QIB was defined under Rule 144A to include "entities, acting for its own account or the accounts of other qualified institutional buyers, that in the aggregate owns and invests on a discretionary basis at least $100 million in securities of issuers that are not affiliated with the entity." See 17 C.F.R. 230.144A, "Private Resale of Securities to Institutions."

86. Dennis Voigt Crawford, testimony before the FCIC, First Public Hearing of the FCIC, day 2, session 2: Current Investigation into the Financial Crisis—State and Local Officials, January 14, 2010, p. 112.

87. Richard Breeden, interview by FCIC, October 14, 2010. See Public Law 104–290 (Oct. 11, 1996); Rule 144A contained provisions that ensured it did not expand to the securities markets in which retail investors did participate.

88. Federal Reserve Board, SR 9724, "Risk-Focused Framework for Supervision of Large Complex Institutions," October 27, 1997.

89. Alan Greenspan, "The Evolution of Bank Supervision," speech before the American Bankers Association, Phoenix, Arizona, October 11, 1999.

90. Eugene Ludwig, interview by FCIC, September 2, 2010.

91. Federal Reserve Bank of New York, "Report on Systemic Risk and Supervision," Draft of August 5, 2009, p. 2.

92. Rich Spillenkothen, "Notes on the performance of prudential supervision in the years preceding the financial crisis by a former director of banking supervision and regulation at the Federal Reserve Board (1991 to 2006)," May 31, 2010, 12.

93. Susan Bies, interview by FCIC, October 11, 2010.

94. Bernanke, letter to the FCIC, December 21, 2010.

95. John Snow, interview by FCIC, October 7, 2010.

96. Office of the Comptroller of the Currency, Board of Governors of the Federal Deposit Insurance Corporation, Office of Thrift Supervision, and National Credit Union Administration, "Credit Risk Management Guidance for Home Equity Lending," May 16, 2005.

97. *2009 Mortgage Market Statistical Annual*, 1:3; "Residential Mortgage Lenders Peer Group Survey: Analysis and Implications for Guidance," PowerPoint presentation, November 30, 2005, pp. 13, 3.

98. Sabeth Siddique, interview by the FCIC, September 9, 2010.

99. "Residential Mortgage Lenders Peer Group Survey: Analysis and Implications for Guidance," PowerPoint, November 30, 2005.

100. Bies, interview.

101. Office of the Comptroller of the Currency, Board of Governors of the Federal Deposit Insurance Corporation, Office of Thrift Supervision, and National Credit Union Administration, "Interagency Guidance on Nontraditional Mortgage Products," *Federal Register* 70 (December 29, 2005): 77,249, 72,252, 72,253.

102. Paul Smith, American Bankers Association, letter to the Federal Deposit Insurance Corporation, Board of Governors of the Federal Reserve System, Office of Thrift Supervision, and Office of the Comptroller of the Currency, March 29, 2006, p. 2.

103. Letter from American Financial Services Association to federal regulators 8, available at http://www.ots.treas.gov/_files/comments/d1e85ce1–07ab-4acf-8db5–8d1747afba0a.pdf.

104. Letters to the Office of Thrift Supervision from the American Bankers Association (March 29, 2006), p. 2; the American Financial Services Association (March 28, 2006), p. 8; and Indymac Bank (March 29, 2006), p. 4.

105. The Housing Policy Council of the Financial Services Roundtable, letter to the Office of Thrift Supervision, March 29, 2006, p. 6.

106. Siddique, interview.

107. Binyamin Appelbaum and Ellen Nakashima, "Banking Regulator Played Advocate Over Enforcer: Agency Let Lenders Grow Out of Control, Then Fail," *Washington Post*, November 23, 2008.

108. Bies, interview.

109. See, e.g. "Countrywide Seeks to Become Savings Bank; The Mortgage Lender Says It Is Planning to Apply to Convert Its Charter So It Will Be Regulated by One Federal Agency instead of Two," *Los Angeles Times*, November 11, 2006, based on *Bloomberg, Reuters.*

110. Kim Sherer, interview by FCIC, August 3 2003.

111. Countrywide, "Briefing Paper: Meeting with Office of Thrift Supervision, Thursday July 13, 2006."

112. Angelo Mozilo, email to John McMurray (cc Dave Sambol, Carlos Garcia), re: Pay Options, August 12, 2006; John McMurray, email to Angelo Mozilo (cc Kevin Bartlett, Carlos Garcia, Dave Sambol, re: Pay Options, August 13, 2006.

113. The cost of borrowing is reflected by credit spreads, the portion of interest rates that compensate investors for credit risk. Credit spreads are the interest rates that investors require above the so-called risk-free interest rate, usually measured in terms of Treasuries or interest rate swaps with similar characteristics.

114. Congressional Oversight Panel, "Commercial Real Estate Losses and the Risk to Financial Stability," February 10, 2010, pp. 58–60.

115. Loan Syndication Trading Association, "The US Loan Market Today," presentation.

116. Loan Syndication Trading Association, "Financial Reform and the Leveraged Loan Market," presentation.

117. Ibid., Loan Syndication Trading Association, "Challenges Facing CLOs ... and the Loan Market," presentation.

118. Ibid., p. 14. SEC, "Risk Management Reviews at Consolidated Supervised Entities," memorandum, April 26, 2007.

119. Michael Flaherty and Dena Aubin, "For Private Equity Market, All Eyes on First Data," *Reuters,* September 4, 2007.

120. SEC, "Risk Management Reviews of Consoldated Supervised Entities," memorandum, July 5, 2007.

121. Charles Prince, quoted in "Citigroup chief stays bullish on buyouts," *Financial Times,* July 9, 2007; testimony before the FCIC, Hearing on Subprime Lending and Securitization and Government-Sponsored Enterprises (GSEs), day 2, session 1: Citigroup Senior Management, April 8, 2010, transcript, pp. 49–50.

122. Roben Farzad, Matthew Goldstein, David Henry, and Christopher Palmeri, "Not So Smart," *BusinessWeek,* September 3, 2007.

123. Joseph Gyourko, "Understanding Commercial Real Estate: Just How Different from Housing Is It?" NBER Working Paper 14708, National Bureau of Economic Research, February 2009, pp. 23, 38.

124. CRE Finance Council, *Compendium of Statistics,* November 5, 2010, Exhibits 3, 2.

125. Joe Keohane, "Heartbreak Hotels," *Portfolio,* November 11, 2008.

126. "Hilton Debt Clogs Lenders' Balance Sheets," Commercial Mortgage Alert, February 20, 2009.

127. Tom Marano, interview by FCIC, April 19, 2010.

128. Jeff Mayer and Tom Marano, "Fixed Income Overview," Bear Stearns, March 29, 2007, p. 18.

129. Gyourko, "Understanding Commercial Real Estate: Just How Different from Housing Is It?" p. 1.

130. New York Federal Reserve Bank, "Maiden Lane LLC Holdings as of 9/30/2008."

131. Anton R. Valukas, Report of Examiner, *In re* Lehman Brothers Holdings Inc., et al., Chapter 11 Case No. 08-13555 (JMP), (Bankr. S.D.N.Y.), March 11, 2010, 2:356 (hereafter cited as Valukas).

132. Ibid., 2:356–58.

133. Madelyn Antoncic, "Lehman Brothers Risk Management," August 7, 2007, p. 5; and Antoncic, interview by FCIC, July 14, 2010.

134. Valukas, 1:43, 4; Antoncic, interview.

135. Valukas, 1:45–62, 79–80.

136. Jody Shenn, "Lehman Said to Return to Mortgage Market through Aurora Unit (Update 1)," *Bloomberg,* October 21, 2009.

137. SEC, "Risk Management Reviews of Consolidated Supervised Entities," memoranda, October 6, 2006; December 6, 2007; February 2, 2007; March 30, 2007; May 31, 2007; July 5, 2007; August 3, 2007; September 5, 2007; October 5, 2007.

138. Erik Sirri, interview by FCIC, April 1, 2010.

139. Valukas, 1:7; 18 nn. 63, 64; 3: 742, 815–22.

140. Valukas, 1:8, 20–21.

141. The People of the State of New York v. Ernst & Young LLP (N.Y. Sup. Ct. filed Dec. 21, 2010).

142. Ronald Marcus, interview by FCIC, July 23, 2010.

143. See Ronald S. Marcus, OTS, "Report of Examination Lehman Brothers Holdings Inc.," July 7, 2008, pp. 1–2.

144. David Sambol, interview by FCIC, September 27, 2010.

145. See Countrywide Financial Corporation, Form 10-K, March 1, 2007, p. 47. See also Fannie Mae, "Single-Family Conventional Acquisition Characteristics: Overall" (2007); Fannie Mae, "Single Family Conventional Acquisition Characteristics: Countrywide Financial Corporation" (2007); Countrywide, "Response to June 23 Request: 11 and 12: Summary."

146. "Single Family Guarantee Business: Facing Strategic Crossroads," June 27, 2005.

147. Ibid.

148. Daniel Mudd, interview by FCIC, March 26, 2010.

149. "Single Family Guarantee Business: Facing Strategic Crossroads."

150. "Single Family Guaranty Business Strategic Review Summary," PowerPoint presentation, July 19, 2005.

151. Citigroup, "Project Phineas: Presentation to the Board of Directors," executive summary, July 18 and 19, 2005.

152. "Single Family Conventional Acquisition Characteristics Overall," produced by Fannie Mae.

153. Tom Lund, interview by FCIC, March 4, 2010.

154. Christopher Dickerson to James B. Lockhart III, "Proposed Appointment of the Federal Housing Finance Agency as Conservator for the Federal National Mortgage Association," memorandum, September 6, 2008, p. 14

155. Fannie Mae, 3Q 2008 Form 10-Q, p. at 115; Fannie Mae, 2007 Form 10K, pp. 126–30.

156. By December 31, 2005, Freddie reported capital of $36.4 billion; $173 billion in loans to borrowers with FICO scores below 660; $80 billion in high LTV; and $93 billion in loans for non-owner-occupied homes. Federal Home Loan Mortgage Corporation, "Information Statement and Annual Report to Stockholders: For the fiscal year ended December 31, 2007," February 28, 2008, p. 74.

157. Richard Syron, interview by FCIC, August 31, 2010.

158. Anurag Saksena, interview by FCIC, June 22, 2010.

159. Donald Bisenius, interview by FCIC, September 29, 2010.

160. Saksena, interview.

161. "OFHEO, SEC Reach Settlement with Fannie Mae; Penalty Imposed," Office of Federal Housing Enterprise Oversight press release, May 23, 2006.

162. "Freddie Mac Voluntarily Adopts Temporary Limited Growth for Retained Portfolio," Federal Home Loan Mortgage Corporation press release, August 1, 2006.

163. OFHEO, Report of the Special Examination of Fannie Mae, May 2006.

164. OFHEO Report: "Fannie Mae Façade; Fannie Mae Criticized for Earnings Manipulation," Office of Federal Housing Enterprise Oversight press release, May 23, 2006.

165. James Lockhart, written testimony for the FCIC, Hearing on Subprime Lending and Securitization and Government-Sponsored Enterprises (GSEs), day 3, session 2: Office of Federal Housing Enterprise Oversight, April 9, 2010, p. 2.

166. Ibid., p. 1.

167. Robert J. Levin, Board of Director Presentation, PowerPoint presentation, January 2006.

168. Minutes of the February 21, 2006, meeting of the Board of Directors of Fannie Mae (approved on April 25, 2006).

169. Stephen B. Ashley, Chairman Fannie Mae, remarks prepared for delivery at the Senior Management Meeting, Cambridge, Maryland, June 27, 2006.

170. Fannie Mae, "Notes to Single Family Conventional Acquisition Report," August 3, 2007; See also Federal National Mortgage Association, Form 10-K, for the fiscal year ended December 31, 2006, filed August 16, 2007.

171. FCIC staff estimates based on data provided by Fannie Mae.

172. Federal National Mortgage Association, "Form DEF 14A," November 2, 2007, p. 42; Federal National Mortgage Association, Form 10-K, May 2, 2007, p. 202.

173. OFHEO, Report of the Special Examination for Fannie Mae, May 2006, p. 8.

174. Federal Home Loan Mortgage Corporation, Form 10-K, for the fiscal year ended December 31, 2005, filed June 28, 2006, pp. 3, 19. Federal Home Loan Mortgage Corporation, Form 10-K, for the fiscal year ended December 31, 2006, filed March 23, 2007, pp. 3, 22.

175. Federal Home Loan Mortgage Corporation, Proxy Statement and Notice of Annual Meeting of Stockholders (May 7, 2007), Summary Compensation Table, p. 52 (for 2006 figures). Federal Home Loan Mortgage Corporation, Proxy Statement and Notice of Annual Meeting of Stockholders (July 12, 2006), Summary Compensation Table, p. 37 (for 2005 figures).

176. Ibid.

177. OFHEO, Report of the Special Examination for Fannie Mae, May 2006, pp. 3, 9–10, 15.

178. Ibid., p 2.

179. Ibid.

180. Ibid., pp. 7–8.

181. Ibid.

182. Mark Winer, interview by FCIC, March 23, 2010.

183. Todd Hempstead, interview by FCIC, March 23, 2010.

184. Daniel Mudd, interview by FCIC, March 26, 2010.

185. Dickerson to Lockhart, Fannie Mae conservatorship memo, September 6, 2008, p. 14.

186. Minutes of a Meeting of the Fannie Mae Board of Directors, April 21, 2007.

187. Minutes of a Meeting of the Fannie Mae Board of Directors, May 21, 2007.

188. Federal National Mortgage Association, Form 10-K, for the fiscal year ended December 31, 2007, p. 24.

189. FCIC staff estimate based on data provided by Fannie Mae.

190. "Deepen Segments—Develop Breadth," Fannie Mae Strategic Plan, 2007–2011.

191. Enrico Dallavecchia, email to Daniel Mudd, "Budget 2008 and strategic investments," July 16, 2007.

192. Enrico Dallavecchia, email to Michael Williams, "RE:," July 16, 2007.

193. Daniel Mudd, email to Enrico Dallavecchia, "RE: Budget 2008 and strategic investments," July 17, 2007.

194. Enrico Dallavecchia, interview by FCIC, March 16, 2010.

195. Freddie Mac, "Freddie Mac's Business Strategy, Board of Directors Meeting," March 2–3, 2007, pp. 3–4.

196. Freddie Mac, "Freddie Mac's Business Strategy, Board of Directors Meeting," March 2–3, 2007, pp. 3–4, 70, 73.

197. OFHEO, 2006 Report of Examination for the Federal Home Loan Mortgage Corporation, pp. 8–9, 10–11.

198. Federal Housing Finance Agency, "Mortgage Market Note 10-2: The Housing Goals of Fannie Mae and Freddie Mac in the Context of the Mortgage," February 1, 2010.

199. "HUD Announces New Regulations to Provide $2.4 Trillion in Mortgages for Affordable Housing for 28.1 Million Families," Department of Housing and Urban Development, press release, October 31, 2000.

200. Mudd, interview.

201. Robert Levin, interview by FCIC, March 17, 2010.

202. "HUD Finalizes Rule on New Housing Goals for Fannie Mae and Freddie Mac," Department of Housing and Urban Development press release, November 1, 2004.

203. Mudd, testimony before the FCIC, Hearing on Subprime Lending and Securitization and Government-Sponsored Enterprises (GSEs), day 3, session: 1 Fannie Mae, April 9, 2010, transcript, pp. 63–64.

204. See FHFA, "Annual Report to Congress 2009," pp. 131, 148. The numbers are for mortgage assets + outstanding MBS guaranteed. Total assets + MBS are slightly greater.

205. OFHEO, "2008 Report to Congress," April 15, 2008.

206. Robert Levin, interview by FCIC, March 17, 2010; Robert Levin, testimony before the FCIC, Hearing on Subprime Lending and Securitization and Government-Sponsored Enterprises (GSEs), day 3, session 1: Fannie Mae, April 9, 2010, transcript, pp. 68–72.

207. Tom Lund, interview by FCIC, March 4, 2010.

208. Dallavecchia, interview.

209. Todd Hempstead, interview by FCIC, March 23, 2010.

210. Kenneth Bacon, interview by FCIC, March 5, 2010.

211. Stephen Ashley, interview by FCIC, March 31, 2010.

212. Levin, interview.

213. Mike Quinn, interview by FCIC, March 10, 2010.

214. Ashley, interview.

215. Armando Falcon, testimony before the FCIC, Hearing on Subprime Lending and Securitization and Government-Sponsored Enterprises (GSEs), day 3, session 2: Office of Federal Housing Enterprise Oversight, April 9, 2010, transcript, pp. 155–56, 192; .written testimony, p. 10.

216. Lockhart, written testimony for the FCIC, April 9, 2010, p. 6;; Lockhart, testimony before the FCIC, April 9, 2010, transcript, pp. 156–61.

217. James Lockhart, interview by FCIC, March 19, 2010.

218. Edward DeMarco, interview by FCIC, March 18, 2010; Maria Fernandez (with Alfred Pollard, Chris Dickerson, Jeffrey Spohn, and Jamie Newell), interview by FCIC, March 5, 2010.

219. Mike Price (with Janice Kuhl, Paul Manchester, Charlotte Reid, Alfred Pollard, and Kevin Sheehan), interview by FCIC, February 19, 2010.

220. Department of Housing and Urban Development, "HUD's Housing Goals for the Federal National Mortgage Association (Fannie Mae) and the Federal Home Loan Mortgage Corporation (Freddie Mac) for the Years 2005–2008 and Amendments to HUD's Regulation of Fannie Mae and Freddie Mac," *Federal Register* 69, no. 211 (2 Nov. 2004): 63629.

221. FHFA, "The Housing Goals of Fannie Mae and Freddie Mac in the Context of the Mortgage Market."

222. Daniel Mudd, letter to Brian Montgomery re affordable housing goals, December 21, 2007.

223. "Deepen Segments—Develop Breadth," Fannie Mae Strategic Plan.

224. Brian D. Montgomery, Federal Housing Commissioner, to Daniel Mudd, Fannie Mae, typed letter, April 24, 2008; Brian D. Montgomery, Federal Housing Commissioner, to Richard F. Syron, Fannie Mae, typed letter, April 24, 2008.

225. "Cost of Freddie Mac's Affordable Housing Mission," PowerPoint presentation, June 4, 2009, pp. 7–8, 10–11.

226. Freddie's net income was $4.8 billion in 2003, $2.6 billion in 2004, $2.1 billion in 2005, $2.3 billion in 2006, net loss of $3.1 billion in 2007, and net loss of $50.1 billion in 2008. Federal Home Loan Mortgage Corporation, Form 10-K, for the fiscal year ended December 31, 2009, filed February 24, 2010, Item 6, Selected Financial Data, p. 57 (for 2008 figure). Federal Home Loan Mortgage Corporation, "Information Statement and Annual Report to Stockholders: For the fiscal year ended December 31, 2007," February 28, 2008, Selected Financial Data and Other Operating Measures, p. 28 (for 2003–07 figures).

227. "Cost and Benefits of Mission Activities: Project Phineas," presentation, June 14, 2005.

228. March 13, 2007, Business Review Briefing; information confirmed by counsel to Fannie Mae on January 4, 2011.

229. "Fannie Mae's Housing Goals," Audit Team briefing, May 8, 2007.

230. "Fannie Mae Board of Directors Management Report," PowerPoint presentation, July 17, 2007.

231. "Cost of Freddie Mac's Affordable Housing Mission," PowerPoint presentation, June 4, 2009, pp. 7–8, 10–11.

## Chapter 10

1. Gary Gorton, interview by FCIC, May 11, 2010.

2. Lewis Ranieri, interview by FCIC, July 30, 2010.

3. Complaint, SEC v. Goldman Sachs & Co. and Fabrice Tourre (S.D.N.Y. April 16, 2010).

4. Office of the Comptroller of the Currency, Treasury; Office of Thrift Supervision, Treasury; Board of Governors of the Federal Reserve System; Federal Deposit Insurance Corporation; and Securities and Exchange Commission, "Interagency Statement on Sound Practices Concerning Elevated Risk Complex Structured Finance Activities" (Notice of final interagency statement), January 5, 2007.

5. Wing Chau, interview by FDIC, November 11, 2010.

6. FCIC, Survey of 40 CDO Managers, Schedule A and B (1st production served on 28 managers, 2nd production served on 12 managers).

7. Vertical Capital, email response to FCIC survey, October 29, 2010.

8. As two market observers would later write, "Starting in 2004, CDOs and CDO investors became the dominant class of agents pricing credit risk on sub-prime mortgage loans. . . . In the absence of restraints, lenders started originating unreasonably risky loans in late 2005 and continued to do so into 2007." Mark Adelson and David Jacob, "The Sub-prime Problem: Causes and Lessons," January 8, 2008, p. 1.

9. Scott Simon, quoted in Allison Pyburn, "CDO Investors Debate Morality of Spread Environment," *Asset Securitization Report*, May 9, 2005, p. 1.

10. Armand Pastine, quoted in ibid. According to the FCIC database, PIMCO did manage one more new CDO, Costa Bella CDO, which was issued in December 2006.

11. Source on downgrades: Bloomberg. Source on events on default: Moody's Investors Service, "Moody's downgrades ratings of Notes issued by Maxim High Grade CDO I, Ltd.," April 18, 2008, and "Moody's downgrades ratings of Notes issued by Maxim High Grade CDO II, Ltd.," April 18, 2008.

12. ACA Capital, 2006 10-K, p. 12.

13. "ISDA Publishes Template for Credit Default Swaps on Asset-Backed Securities with Pay As You Go Settlement," International Swaps and Derivatives Association press release, June 21, 2005 (www.isda.org/press/press062105.html). Under the terms of the pay-as-you-go swap, if the referenced mortgage-backed security does not receive the full interest and principal payments, the pay-as-you-go protection seller is required to pay the buyer the amount of the shortfall. For long investors—the protection provider under the swap—the advantage was the leverage embedded in the trade: they did not have to come up with the cash up front for the principal amount of the bond; they simply agreed to receive quarterly swap fees in return for accepting the risk of loss if the securities experienced a shortfall.

14. Laura Schwartz, interview by FCIC, May 10, 2010.

15. Laurie S. Goodman, Shumin Li, Douglas J. Lucas, Thomas A. Zimmerman, and Frank J. Fabozzi, *Subprime Mortgage Credit Derivatives* (Frank J. Fabozzi Series) (Hoboken, NJ: John Wiley, 2008), p. 176.

16. Greg Lippmann, interview by FCIC, May 20, 2010.

17. FCIC staff estimates based on analysis of Moody's CDO EMS database.

18. FCIC Hedge Fund Survey. From July through December 2006, several hedge funds with average assets under management of $4–$8 billion accumulated positions totaling more than $1.4 billion in mortgage-related CDO equity tranches and almost $3 billion of short positions in mortgage-related CDO mezzanine tranches. FCIC staff used a Moody's proprietary CDO database to estimate the total mortgage-related CDO equity tranche issuance. Please see FCIC website for more information about the hedge fund survey. Note: the FCIC did not survey hedge funds that fully liquidated or closed. These funds may have purchased substantial "long only" positions in mortgage-related securities.

19. FCIC Hedge Fund Survey. See FCIC website for details.

20. Rabobank's counsel, letter to Judge Fried of the Supreme Court of NY, May 11, 2010.

21. Norma Flow of Funds, information provided by Merrill Lynch.

22. Steven Ross, email to FCIC, December 21, 2010.

23. See letter from Rabobank's counsel, letter to Judge Fried, May 11, 2010; the letter was never filed with the court because the case was settled.

24. Document of Magnetar Investments in Norma, Attachment G-13 (showing Magnetar purchases of equity tranche in Norma); provided by Merrill Lynch.

25. Information provided by Merrill Lynch, December 22, 2010.

26. Complaint, SEC v. Goldman Sachs & Co. and Fabrice Tourre.

27. Ira Wagner, interview by FCIC, April 20, 2010.

28. Alan Roseman, interview by FCIC, May 17, 2010.

29. Schwartz, interview.

30. John Paulson, interview by FCIC, October 28, 2010.

31. "Goldman Sachs to Pay Record $550 Million to Settle SEC Charges Related to Subprime Mortgage CDO," SEC press release, July 15, 2010.

32. Jamie Mai and Ben Hockett, interview by FCIC, April 22, 2010.

33. Sihan Shu, interview by FCIC, September 27, 2010.

34. Steven Eisman, interview by FCIC, April 22, 2010.

35. James Grant, "Inside the Mortgage Machine," in *Mr. Market Miscalculates: The Bubble Years and Beyond* (Mount Jackson, VA: Axios, 2008), pp. 180–81, 182–83.

36. Eisman, interview.

37. Michael Burry, interview by FCIC, May 18, 2010.

38. Paulson, interview.

39. Burry, interview.

40. FCIC Hedge Fund Survey. See FCIC website for details.

41. John Geanakoplos, written testimony for the FCIC, Forum to Explore the Causes of the Financial Crisis, day 1, session 3: Risk Taking and Leverage, February 26, 2010, p. 16.

42. OCC, "Subprime CDO Valuation and Oversight Review—Conclusion Memorandum," memorandum from Michael Sullivan, RAD, and Ron Frake, NBE, to John Lyons, Examiner-in-Charge, Citibank, NA, January 17, 2008, p. 6; Paul, Weiss, Citigroup's counsel, letter to FCIC, June 23, 2010, "Responses of Nestor Dominguez."

43. Richard Bookstaber, interview by FCIC, May 11, 2010.

44. "RMBS and Citi-RMBS as a Percentage of Citi-CDO Portfolio Notionals," produced by Citi for the FCIC.

45. Federal Reserve Bank of New York, Federal Reserve Board, Office of the Comptroller of the Currency, Securities and Exchange Commission, U.K. Financial Services Authority, and Japan Financial Services Authority, "Notes on Senior Supervisors' Meetings with Firms," November 19, 2007, p. 3.

46. FCIC staff estimates, based on analysis of Moody's CDO EMS database.

47. Paul, Weiss, Citigroup's counsel, letter to FCIC, March 1, 2010, in re the FCIC's second supplemental request, "Response to Interrogatory no. 7"; Paul, Weiss, letter to FCIC, March 31, 2010, updated response to interrogatory no. 7, p. 5.

48. Nestor Dominguez, interview by FCIC, March 2, 2010; Paul, Weiss, letter of March 31, 2010, pp. 3–6.

49. Corporate Library Analyst Report for Citigroup Inc., April 16, 2007.

50. SEC staff (Sam Forstein, Tim McGarey, Mary Ann Gadziala, Kim Mavis, Bob Sollazo, Suzanne McGovern, and Chris Easter), interview by FCIC, February 9, 2010.

51. Comptroller of the Currency, memorandum, Examination of Citigroup Risk Management (CRM), January 13, 2005, p. 3.

52. Ronald Frake, Comptroller of the Currency, letter to Geoffrey Coley, Citibank, N.A., December 22, 2005.

53. Federal Reserve, "New York Operations Review, May 17–25, 2005," p. 4.

54. Federal Reserve Bank of New York Bank Supervision Group, "Operations Review Report," December 2009.

55. Federal Reserve Bank of New York, "Summary of Supervisory Activity and Findings, Citigroup Inc., January 1, 2005–December 31, 2005," April 10, 2006; Federal Reserve Bank of New York, "Summary of Supervisory Activity and Findings," Citigroup Inc., January 1, 2004–December 31, 2004," April 5, 2005.

56. Citigroup Inc., Form 8-K, April 3, 2006, Exhibit 99.1.

57. Federal Reserve Board, memo to Governor Susan Bies, February 17, 2006.

58. The board reversed a 15% reduction that had been implemented when the issues began and then added a 5% raise. Citigroup, 2006 Proxy Statement, p. 37.

59. Comptroller of the Currency, letter to Citigroup CEO Vikram Pandit (Supervisory Letter 2008-05), February 14, 2008; quotation, p. 2.

60. Federal Reserve Bank of New York, letter to Vikram Pandit and the Board of the Directors of Citigroup, April 15, 2008, pp. 6–7.

61. Timothy Geithner, testimony before the FCIC, Hearing on the Shadow Banking System, day 2, session 1: Perspective on the Shadow Banking System, May 6, 2010, transcript, p. 128.

62. Gene Park, interview by FCIC, May 18, 2010.

63. Andrew Forster, email to Gary Gorton, Alan Frost, et al., July 21, 2005.

64. Park, interview.

65. Gorton, interview.

66. Park, interview.

67. Gene Park, email to Joseph Cassano, February 28, 2006.

68. Park, interview.

69. Data supplied by AIG. The CDO—RFC CDO III Ltd.—was 93% subprime and 7% RMBS Home Equity, according to the AIG credit committee. A review by FCIC staff showed that the remaining 7% designated as RMBS Home Equity included subprime collateral.

70. AIG, "Residential Mortgage Presentation (Financial Figures are as of June 30, 2007)," August 9, 2007, p. 28.

71. Park, interview.

72. Joseph Cassano, interview by FCIC, June 25, 2010.

73. Park, interview.

74. Dow Kim, interview by FCIC, September 9, 2010.

75. Stanley O'Neal, interview by FCIC, September 16, 2010.

76. Kim, interview.

77. FCIC staff estimates based on analysis of Moody's CDO EMS database.

78. Complaint, Coöperatieve Centrale Raiffeisen=Boerenleenbank v. Merrill Lynch, No. 601832/09 (N.Y.S. June 12, 2009), paragraph 147.

79. Kim, interview.

80. FCIC analysis based on Moody's CDO EMS database.

81. Presentation to Merrill Lynch and Co. Board of Directors, "Leveraged Finance and Mortgage/CDO Review," October 21, 2007, p. 35.

82. Chau, interview.

83. FCIC staff analysis of Moody's CDO EMS database.

84. FCIC staff estimates based on Moody's CDO EMS database. Data supplied by Merrill Lynch. Relevant information not provided for Robeco High Grade CDO I.

85. FCIC staff analysis of Moody's CDO EMS database.

86. Data supplied by Merrill Lynch.

87. FCIC staff analysis of Moody's CDO EMS database. The total value of Baa tranches issued by CDOs in the FCIC database was $684 million in 2003 and $3.9 billion in 2007; Aa tranches, $1.4 billion in 2003 and $8.3 billion in 2007; A tranches, $522 million in 2003 and $4.3 billion in 2007.

88. FCIC staff telephone discussion with SEC staff, September 1, 2010.

89. FCIC staff analysis of Moody's CDO EMS database.

90. Chau, interview; for number of the CDOs he managed, FCIC staff analysis of Moody's Enhanced CDO Monitoring Database.

91. Super Senior Credit Transactions Principal Collateral Provisions, December 7, 2007, produced by AIG.

92. Presentation to the Merrill Lynch Board, "Leveraged Finance and Mortgage/CDO Review," p. 23; Jeff Kronthal, former head of Merrill Lynch's Global Credit, Real Estate and Structured Products, interview by FCIC, September 14, 2010.

93. Al Yoon, "Merrill's Own Subprime Warnings Unheeded," Reuters, October 30, 2007.

94. SEC, "Risk Management Reviews of Consolidated Supervised Entities," internal memo to Erik Sirri and others, February 2, 2007, p. 3.

95. Ibid., p. 1.

96. Yoon, "Merrill's Own Subprime Warnings Unheeded."

97. Kim, interview.

98. Senate Permanent Subcommittee on Investigations, *Fishtail, Bacchus, Sundance, and Slapshot: Four Enron Transactions Funded and Facilitated by U.S. Financial Institutions,* 107th Cong., 2nd sess., January 2, 2003, S-Prt 107–82, pp. 36, 37.

99. "Interagency Statement on Sound Practices" (Notice of final interagency statement), January 5, 2007 (see n. 4, above).

100. Office of the Comptroller of the Currency, Treasury; Office of Thrift Supervision, Treasury; Board of Governors of the Federal Reserve System; Federal Deposit Insurance Corporation; and Securities and Exchange Commission, "Interagency Statement on Sound Practices Concerning Complex Structured Finance Activities" (Notice of interagency statement with request for public comments),May 13, 2004.

101. Ibid., pp. 7–8.

102. John C. Dugan, Comptroller of the Currency, written testimony for the FCIC, Hearing on Sub-prime Lending and Securitization and Government-Sponsored Enterprises (GSEs), day 2, session 2: Office of the Comptroller of the Currency, April 8, 2010, Appendix E: OCC Supervision of Citibank, N.A., p. 10.

103. "Interagency Statement on Sound Practices" (Notice of final interagency statement), January 5, 2007, p. 6.

104. Basel Committee on Banking Supervision: Joint Forum, "Credit Risk Transfer," Bank for International Settlements, March 2005, pp. 3–4, 6–7, 5–10.

105. Ibid., p. 4.

106. Ibid.

107. Ibid., pp. 3–4.

108. SEC, Office of Compliance Inspections and Examinations, "Examination Report to Moody's Investor Services, Inc.," p. 4 (examination begun August 31, 2007).

109. Warren Buffett, testimony before the FCIC, Hearing on the Credibility of Credit Ratings, the Investment Decisions Made Based on Those Ratings, and the Financial Crisis, session 2: Credit Ratings and the Financial Crisis, June 2, 2010, transcript, p. 301.

110. Warren Buffett, interview by FCIC, May 26, 2010; Buffett, testimony before the FCIC, June 2, 2010, transcript, p. 302.

111. Eric Kolchinsky, written testimony for the FCIC, Hearing on the Credibility of Credit Ratings, the Investment Decisions Made Based on Those Ratings, and the Financial Crisis, session 1: The Ratings Process, June 2, 2010, p. 2.

112. Brian Clarkson, interview by FCIC, May 20, 2010.

113. Gary Witt, interview by FCIC, April 21, 2010. John Rutherford was the president and CEO of Moody's Corporation from the time of its spin-off from Dun & Bradstreet in 2000 until he retired from the firm in 2005.

114. Jerome Fons, interview by FCIC, April 22, 2010.

115. Raymond McDaniel, interview by FCIC, May 21, 2010.

116. Clarkson, interview.

117. Ibid.

118. McDaniel, interview.

119. Raymond McDaniel, testimony before the FCIC, Hearing on the Credibility of Credit Ratings, the Investment Decisions Made Based on Those Ratings, and the Financial Crisis, session 2: Credit Ratings and the Financial Crisis, June 2, 2010, transcript, pp. 203–4.

120. Scott McCleskey, interview by FCIC, April 16, 2010.

121. Clarkson, interview.

122. Witt, interview.

123. Mark Froeba, testimony before the FCIC, Hearing on the Credibility of Credit Ratings, the Investment Decisions Made Based on Those Ratings, and the Financial Crisis, session 3: The Credit Rating Agency Business Model, June 2, 2010, transcript, p. 347.

124. Clarkson, interview; McDaniel, interview.

125. Witt, interview; Gary Witt, testimony before the FCIC, Hearing on the Credibility of Credit Ratings, the Investment Decisions Made Based on those Ratings, and the Financial Crisis, Session 3: The Credit Rating Agency Business Model, June 2, 2010, transcript, p. 394.

126. Brian Clarkson, email to Ed Bankole, Pramila Gupta, Michael Kanef, Andrew Kriegler, Sam Pilcer, Andrew Silver, and Linda Stesney, subject: "June YTD AFG by analyst.xls," July 5, 2001.

127. William May, email to Gus Harris, subject: "RE: BES and PEs," January 12, 2006.

128. Yuri Yoshizawa, email to direct report managing directors, subject: "3Q Market Coverage-CDO," October 5, 2007.

129. Clarkson, interview.

130. McDaniel, interview.

131. Witt, testimony before the FCIC, June 2, 2010, transcript, pp. 456–57.

132. Moody's Investors Service: Managing Director's Town Hall Meeting, September 11, 2007, transcript, pp. 42, 51–52.

133. Witt, interview.

134. Andrew Kimball, internal email, October 21, 2007, attaching memorandum, "Credit policy issues at Moody's suggested by the subprime/liquidity crisis." The susceptibility of a ratings committee to external pressures was shown in the constant proportion debt obligation (CPDO) scandal in Europe.

135. Ibid., p. 3.

136. David Teicher, project manager at Moody's, interview by FCIC, May 4, 2010; Standard & Poor's, "Credit FAQ: The Basics of Credit Enhancement in Securitizations," RatingsDirect, June 24, 2008.

137. Richard Michalek, testimony before the FCIC, Hearing on the Credibility of Credit Ratings, the Investment Decisions Made Based on Those Ratings, and the Financial Crisis, session 3: The Credit Rating Agency Business Model, June 2, 2010, transcript, p. 361.

138. Witt, interview.

139. Clarkson, interview.

140. Fons, interview.

141. Kimball, memorandum, "Credit policy issues at Moody's," p. 1.

142. Eric Kolchinsky, testimony before the FCIC, Hearing on the Credibility of Credit Ratings, the Investment Decisions Made Based on Those Ratings, and the Financial Crisis, session 1: The Ratings Process, June 2, 2010, transcript, pp. 68–69.

143. E Kolchinsky, email to Y Fu and Y Yoshizawa, May 30, 2005.

144. Kolchinsky, testimony before the FCIC, June 2, 2010, transcript, pp. 68–69.

145. Eric Kolchinsky, interview by FCIC, April 14, 2010.

146. FCIC staff estimates, based on analysis of Moody's SFDRS database.

147. Riachra O'Driscoll, email to Yuri Yoshizawa, subject: "Magnolia 2006–5 Class Ds," April 27, 2006.

148. Kimball, memorandum, "Credit policy issues at Moody's," p. 2.

149. SEC, Office of Compliance Inspections and Examinations, "Examination Report for Moody's Investors Services, Inc.," p. 2.

## Chapter 11

1. William Dudley, interview by FCIC, October 15, 2010.

2. Inside Mortgage Finance, *The 2009 Mortgage Market Statistical Annual*, vol. 2, *The Secondary Market* (Bethesda, Md.: Inside Mortgage Finance, 2009), p. 13, "Non-Agency MBS Issuance by Type."

3. FCIC staff estimates based on Moody's CDO Enhanced Monitoring System (EMS) database.

4. *2009 Mortgage Market Statistical Annual*, 2:373, "Commercial MBS Issuance."

5. Ben S. Bernanke, chairman of the Federal Reserve, letter to Phil Angelides, chairman of the FCIC, December 21, 2010.

6. Mark Zandi, Celia Chen, and Brian Carey, "Housing at the Tipping Point," Moody's Economy.com, October 2006, pp. 6–7.

7. CoreLogic Home Price Index, Single-Family Combined (available at www.corelogic.com/Products/CoreLogic-HPI.aspx), FCIC staff calculations, January to January.

8. CoreLogic Census Bureau Statistical Area (CBSA) Home Price Index, FCIC staff calculations.

9. Data provided by Mark Fleming, chief economist for CoreLogic, in his written testimony for the FCIC, Hearing on the Impact of the Financial Crisis—Sacramento, session 1: Overview of the Sacramento Housing and Mortgage Markets and the Impact of the Financial Crisis on the Region, September 9, 2010, figures 4, 5.

10. Mark Fleming, testimony before the FCIC, Hearing on the Impact of the Financial Crisis—Sacramento, session 1: Overview of the Sacramento Housing and Mortgage Markets and the Impact of the Financial Crisis on the Region, September 23, 2010, transcript, p. 14.

11. Mortgage Bankers Association, National Delinquency Survey, data provided to the FCIC.

12. Ibid., with FCIC staff calculations.

13. FCIC staff analysis, "Analysis of housing data," July 7, 2010. The underlying data come from CoreLogic and Loan Processing Svcs. Tabulations were provided to the FCIC by staff at the Federal Reserve.

14. Subprime and Alt-A mortgages are defined as those included in subprime or Alt-A securitizations, respectively. GSE mortgages included mortgages purchased or guaranteed by Fannie Mae or Freddie Mac. FHA mortgages included mortgages insured by the FHA or VA.

15. FCIC staff analysis.

16. A recent analysis published by FHFA comes to very similar conclusions. See "Data on the Risk Characteristics and Performance of Single-Family Mortgages Originated from 2001 through 2008 and Financed in the Secondary Market," September 13, 2010.

17. FCIC staff analysis, "Analysis of housing data and comparison with Ed Pinto's analysis," August 9, 2010. In the sample data provided by the Federal Reserve, Fannie Mae and Freddie Mac mortgages with a FICO score below 660 had an average rate of serious delinquency of 6.2% in 2008. In public reports, the GSEs stated that the average serious delinquency rates for loans with FICO scores less than 660 in their guarantee books was 6.3%. Fannie Mae 2008 Credit Supplement, p. 5; Freddie Mac Fourth Quarter 2008 Financial Results Supplement, March 11, 2009, p. 15.

18. In the sample data provided by the Federal Reserve, Fannie Mae and Freddie Mac mortgages with LTVs above 90% had an average rate of serious delinquency of 5.7% in 2008. In public reports, the GSEs stated that the average serious delinquency rates for loans with LTVs above 90% in their guarantee books was 5.8%. Fannie Mae 2008 Credit Supplement, p. 5;

Freddie Mac Fourth Quarter 2008 Financial Results Supplement, March 11, 2009, p. 15.

19. Edward Pinto, "Memorandum: Sizing Total Federal Government and Federal Agency Contributions to Subprime and Alt-A Loans in U.S. First Mortgage Market as of 6.30.08," Exhibit 2 with corrections through October 11, 2010 (www.aei.org/docLib/PintoFCICTriggersMemo.pdf). The 26.7 million loans include 6.7 million loans in subprime securitizations and another 2.1 million loans in Alt-A securitizations, for a total of 8.8 million mortgages in subprime or Alt-A pools, which Pinto calls "self-denominated" subprime and Alt-A, respectively. To these, he adds another 8.8 million loans with FICO scores below 660, which he labels "subprime by characteristic." He also adds 6.3 million loans at the GSEs that are either interest-only loans, negative amortization loans, or loans with an LTV—including any second mortgage—greater than 90%, which he collectively refers to as "Alt-A by characteristic." The last additions include an estimated 1.4 million loans insured by the FHA and VA with an LTV greater than 90%—out of a total of roughly 5.5 million FHA and VA loans—and 1.3 million loans in bank portfolios that are inferred to have his defined "Alt-A characteristics."

20. Fannie Mae 2008 Credit Supplement, p. 5; Freddie Mac Fourth Quarter 2008 Financial Results Supplement, March 11, 2009.

21. Edward Pinto, "Yes, the CRA Is Toxic," City Journal, Autumn 2009.

22. Neil Bhutta and Glenn Canner, "Did the CRA Cause the Mortgage Market Meltdown?" Federal Reserve Board of Governors, March 2009. The authors use the Home Mortgage Disclosure Act data, which cover roughly 80% of the mortgage market in the United States—see Robert B. Avery, Kenneth P. Brevoort, and Glenn B. Canner, "Opportunities and Issues in Using HMDA Data," Journal of Real Estate Research 29, no. 4 (October 2007): 351–79.

23. Elizabeth Laderman and Carolina Reid, "Lending in low and moderate income neighborhoods in California: The Performance of CRA Lending During the Subprime Meltdown," November 26, 2008, working paper to be presented at the Federal Reserve System Conference on Housing and Mortgage Markets, Washington, DC, December 4, 2008.

24. FCIC, "Preliminary Staff Report: The Mortgage Crisis," April 7, 2010.

25. Bank of America response letter to FCIC, August 20, 2010.

26. John Reed, interview by FCIC, March 4, 2010.

27. Lewis Ranieri, interview by FCIC, July 30, 2010.

28. Nicolas Weill, interview by FCIC, May 11, 2010.

29. Ibid.

30. Nicolas Weill, email to Raymond McDaniel and Brian Clarkson, July 4, 2007.

31. Moody's Investors Service, "Early Defaults Rise in Mortgage Securitizations," Structured Finance: Special Report, January 18, 2007, pp. 1, 3.

32. Moody's Investors Service, "Moody's Downgrades Subprime First-lien RMBS-Global Credit Research Announcement," July 10, 2007.

33. Weill, interview.

34. FCIC staff estimates, based on analysis of Blackbox data.

35. Data on Bear Stearns provided by JP Morgan to the FCIC.

36. Moody's Investors Service, "Moody's Downgrades $33.4 billion of 2006 Subprime First-Lien RMBS and Affirms $280 billion Aaa's and Aa's," October 11, 2007; "October 11 Rating Actions Related to 2006 Subprime First-Lien RMBS," Structured Finance: Special Report, October 17, 2007, pp. 1–2.

37. FCIC staff estimates, based on analysis of Blackbox data.

38. FCIC staff estimates, based on analysis of Moody's SFDRS data as of April 2010.

39. Moody's Investors Service, "The Impact of Subprime Residential Mortgage-Backed Securities on Moody's-Rated Structured Finance CDOs: A Preliminary Review," Structured Finance: Special Comment, March 23, 2007, p. 2.

40. Yuri Yoshizawa, email to Noel Kirnon and Raymond McDaniel, cc Eric Kolchinsky, subject: "CSFB Pipeline information," March 28, 2007.

41. Moody's Investors Service, "First Quarter 2007 U.S. CDO Review: Climbing the Wall of Subprime Worry," Structured Finance: Special Report, May 31, 2007, p. 2.

42. Richard Michalek, testimony before the FCIC, Hearing on the Credibility of Credit Ratings, the Investment Decisions Made Based on Those Ratings, and the Financial Crisis, session 3: The Credit Rating Agency Business Model, June 2, 2010, transcript, pp. 448–49.

43. "2007 MCO Strategic Plan Overview," presentation by Ray McDaniel, July 2007.

44. Eric Kolchinsky—retaliation complaint, Chronology Prepared by Eric Kolchinsky.

45. FCIC staff estimates based on analysis of Moody's SFDRS; FCIC, "Preliminary Staff Report: Credit Ratings and the Financial Crisis," June 2, 2010.

46. Eric Kolchinsky, interview by FCIC, April 27, 2010. 4838–2303–6167 (checked–BLK ); Kolchinsky—retaliation complaint.

47. Eric Kolchinsky—retaliation complaint.

48. FCIC, "PSR: Credit Ratings and the Financial Crisis," pp. 30–33.

49. Bingham McCutchen, Fannie Mae counsel, letter to FCIC, September 21, 2010 (hereafter "Bingham Letter"); O'Melveny & Meyers LLP, Freddie Mac counsel, letter to FCIC, September 21, 2010 (hereafter "O'Melveny Letter").

50. Federal Housing Finance Agency, "Conservator's Report on the Enterprises' Financial Performance: Third Quarter 2010," tables 3.1 and 4.1.

51. Raymond Romano, interview by FCIC, September 14, 2010; Bingham Letter.

52. Bingham Letter.

53. Bingham Letter, Tab 3; Tab 1, "Repurchase Collections by Top Ten Sellers/Servicers."

54. O'Melveny letter.

55. "Bank of America announces fourth-quarter actions with respect to its home loans and insurance business," Bank of America press release, January 3, 2011.

56. Mortgage Insurance Companies of America, *2009–2010 Fact Book and Member Directory*, Exhibit 3: Primary Insurance Activity (Insurance in Force) p 17.

57. Documents produced for the FCIC by United Guaranty Residential Insurance, MGIC, Genworth, RMIC, Triad, PMI, and Radian.

58. FCIC staff calculations based on productions from Fannie and Freddie. Figures are for Alt-A, option ARM Alt-A, and subprime loans.

59. FHFA, "Conservator's Report: Third Quarter 2010." Accounting changes for impairments have resulted in offsetting gains of $8 billion.

60. "FHFA Issue Subpoenas for PLS Documents," Federal Housing Finance Agency news release, July 12, 2010.

61. Covington & Burling LLP, Freddie Mac counsel, letter to FCIC, October 19, 2010; see O'Melveny & Meyers LLP, letter to FCIC, dated October 19, 2010.

62. NERA Economic Consulting, "Credit Crisis Litigation Revisited: Litigating the Alphabet of Structured Products," Part VII of a NERA Insights Series, June 4, 2010, p. 1.

63. Defendants Wells Fargo Asset Securities Corp. and Wells Fargo Bank, N.A.'s Notice of Removal, Charles Schwab Corp. v. BNP Paribas Securities Corp, et al., No. cv-10-4030 (N.D. Cal. September 8, 2010).

64. Attorney General of Massachusetts, "Attorney General Martha Coakley and Goldman Sachs Reach Settlement Regarding Subprime Lending Issues," May 11, 2009; "Morgan Stanley to Pay $102 Million for Role in Massachusetts Subprime Mortgage Meltdown under Settlement with AG Coakley's Office," June 24, 2010.

65. Complaint, Cambridge Place v. Morgan Stanley et al., No. 10-2741 (Mass. Super. Ct. filed July 9, 2010), p. 28.

66. Sarah Johnson, "How Far Can Fair Value Go?" *CFO.com,* May 6, 2008.

67. Vikas Shilpiekandula and Olga Gorodetsky, "Who Owns Residential Credit Risk?" Lehman Brothers Fixed Income, U.S. Securitized Products Research, September 7, 2007.

68. Moody's Investor Service, "Default & Loss Rates of Structured Finance Securities: 1993–2009," Special Comment, September 24, 2010.

69. Ben Bernanke, closed-door session with the FCIC, November 17, 2009.

70. Vikas Shilpiekandula and Olga Gorodetsky, "Who Owns Residential Credit Risk?," September 7, 2007, p. 1. The Lehman analysts pegged ultimate subprime and Alt-A losses at $200 billion. Those forecasts were based, the analysts said, on a scenario in which house prices fell an average of 30% across the country. For the securitization figures, see Inside Mortgage Finance, *The 2009 Mortgage Market Statistical Annual,* vol. 2, *The Secondary Market.*

71. IMF, "Financial Stress and Deleveraging: Macro-Financial Implications and Policy," *Global Financial Stability Report,* October 2008, p. 78; IMF, "Containing Systemic Risks and Restoring Financial Soundness," *Global Financial Stability Report,* April 2008.

72. FCIC staff estimates, based on Moody's Investor Service, "Default & Loss Rates of Structured Finance Securities: 1993–2009," Special Comment, September 24, 2010, and analysis of Moody's Structured Finance Default Risk Service.

73. Ben Bernanke, testimony before the FCIC, Hearing on Too Big to Fail: Expectations and Impact of Extraordinary Government Intervention and the Role of Systemic Risk in the Financial Crisis, day 2, session 1: The Federal Reserve, September 2, 2010, transcript, p. 54.

## Chapter 12

1. FCIC staff calculations using data in worksheets Markit ABX.HE. 06-1 prices and ABX.HE. 06-2 prices, produced by Markit; Nomura Fixed Income Research, *CDO/CDS Update 12/18/06.* The figures refer to the BBB- index of the ABX.HE. 06-2.

2. Nomura Fixed Income Research, *CDO/CDS Update 12/18/06,* p. 2.

3. SEC, "Risk Management Reviews of Consolidated Supervised Entities," internal memo to Erik Sirri and others, January 4, 2007.

4. Jim Chanos, interview by FCIC, October 5, 2010.

5. SEC, "Risk Management Reviews of Consolidated Supervised Entities," memo, January 4, 2007.

6. Fed Chairman Ben S. Bernanke, "The Economic Outlook," testimony before the Joint Economic Committee, U.S. Congress, 110th Cong., 1st sess., March 28, 2007.

7. Henry Paulson, quoted in Julie Haviv, "Bernanke Allays Subprime Fears as Beazer Faces Probe," Reuters, March 28, 2007.

8. David Viniar, written testimony, *Wall Street and the Financial Crisis: The Role of Investment Banks,* Senate Permanent Subcommittee on Investigation, 111th Cong., 2nd sess., April 27, 2010, pp. 3–4.

9. Michael Dinias, email to David Viniar and Craig Broderick, December 13, 2006, Senate Permanent Subcommittee on Investigations, Exhibit 2.

10. Viniar, written testimony, Permanent Subcommittee on Investigation, pp. 3–4; Daniel Sparks, email to Tom Montag and Richard Ruzika, December 14, 2006, Senate Permanent Subcommittee on Investigations, Exhibit 3.

11. Kevin Gasvoda, email to Genevieve Nestor and others, December 14, 2006, Senate Permanent Subcommittee on Investigations, Exhibit 72.

12. David Viniar, email to Tom Montag, December 15, 2006, Senate Permanent Subcommittee on Investigations, Exhibit 3.

13. Stacy Bash-Polley, email to Michael Swenson and others, December 20, 2006, Senate Permanent Subcommittee on Investigations, Exhibit 151.

14. Tetsuya Ishikawa, email to Darryl Herrick, October 11, 2006, Senate Permanent Subcommittee on Investigations, Exhibit 170c; Geoffrey Williams, email to Ficc-Mtgcorr-desk, October 24, 2006, Senate Permanent Subcommittee on Investigations, Exhibit 170d.

15. Fabrice Tourre, email to Jonathan Egol and others, December 28, 2006, Senate Permanent Subcommittee on Investigations, Exhibit 61.

16. Daniel Sparks, email to Tom Montag, January 31, 2007, Senate Permanent Subcommittee on Investigations, Exhibit 91.

17. Fabrice Tourre, email to Marine Serres, January 23, 2007, Senate Permanent Subcommittee on Investigations, Exhibit 62.

18. Lloyd Blankfein, email to Tom Montag, February 11, 2007, Senate Permanent Subcommittee on Investigations, Exhibit 130.

19. FCIC calculations using data from "2004–2007 GS Synthetic CDOs," produced by Goldman Sachs.

20. Gretchen Morgenson and Louise Story, "Banks Bundled Bad Debt, Bet Against It and Won," *New York Times*, December 24, 2009.

21. Lloyd Blankfein, testimony before the FCIC, First Public Hearing of the FCIC, first day, panel 1: Financial Institution Representatives, January 13, 2010, transcript, pp. 26–27.

22. "Goldman Sachs Clarifies Various Media Reports of Aspect of FCIC Hearing," Goldman Sachs press release, January 14, 2010.

23. Gary Cohn, testimony before the FCIC, Hearing on the Role of Derivatives in the Financial Crisis, day 1, session 3: Goldman Sachs Group, Inc. and Derivatives, June 30, 2010, transcript, p. 267.

24. Michael Swenson, opening statement, *Hearing on Wall Street and the Financial Crisis: The Role of Investment Banks*, Senate Permanent Subcommittee on Investigations, pp. 2–3.

25. Complaint, Basis Yield Alpha Fund v. Goldman Sachs Group, Inc., et al. (S.D.N.Y. June 9, 2010), p. 29.

26. Blankfein, testimony before the FCIC, January 13, 2010, transcript, p. 140.

27. Craig Broderick, written testimony for the FCIC, Hearing on the Role of Derivatives in the Financial Crisis, day 1, session 3: Goldman Sachs Group, Inc. and Derivatives, June 30, 2010, p. 1.

28. Craig Broderick, email to Alan Rapfogel and others, May 11, 2007, Senate Permanent Subcommittee on Investigations, Exhibit 84.

29. High Grade Risk Analysis, April 27, 2007, p. 4; High Grade—Enhanced Leverage Q&/A, June 13, 2007, stating "the percentage of underlying collateral in our investment grade structures collateralized by 'sub-prime' mortgages is approximately 60. On the March 12, 2007, investor call, Matthew Tannin told investors that "most of the CDOs that we purchased are backed in some form by subprime" (Conference Call transcript, pp. 21–22).

30. Email from matt.tannin@gmail.com to matt.tannin@gmail.com, November 23, 2006.

31. Matthew Tannin, Bear Stearns, email to Chavanne Klaus, MEAG New York, March 7, 2007.

32. BSAM Conference Call, April 25, 2007, transcript, p. 5.

33. Matt Tannin, Bear Stearns, email to Klaus Chavanne, MEAG New York, March 7, 2007; Matthew Tannin, email to Steven Van Solkema, March 30, 2007; Complaint, SEC v. Cioffi, No. 08 Civ. 2457 (E.D.N.Y. June 19, 2008), p. 32.

34. Jim Crystal, Bear Stearns, email to Ralph Cioffi (and others), March 22, 2007; Ralph Cioffi, Bear Stearns, email to Ken Mak, Bear Stearns, March 23, 2007.

35. Warren Spector, testimony before the FCIC, Hearing on the Shadow Banking System, day 1, session 1: Investment Banks and the Shadow Banking System, May 5, 2010, transcript, pp. 83–84.

36. Information provided to FCIC by legal counsel to Bank of America, September 28, 2010.

37. Ibid.

38. Alan Schwartz, interview by FCIC, April 23, 2010. Notably, as one of only two tri-party repo clearing banks, JP Morgan had more information about BSAM's lending obligations than did most other market participants or regulators. As discussed in greater detail later in this chapter, this superior market knowledge later put JP Morgan in a position to step in and purchase Bear Stearns virtually overnight.

39. Email from Goldman to Bear, April 2, 2007.

40. Steven Van Solkema, Bear Stearns, internal email, Summary of CDO Analysis Using Credit Model, April 19, 2007.

41. Matt Tannin, Bear Stearns, email from Gmail account to Ralph Cioffi, Bear Stearns, at his Hotmail account, April 22, 2007.

42. BSAM Conference Call, April 25, 2007, transcript.

43. Iris Semic, email to Matthew Tannin et al., May 1, 2007.

44. Robert Ervin, email to Ralph Cioffi et al., May 1, 2007; email from Goldman (ficc-ops-cdopricing) to rervin@bear.com, May 1, 2007.

45. BSAM Pricing Committee minutes, June 5, 2007; Robert Ervin, email to Greg Quental et al., May 10, 2007, showing that losses for the High Grade fund would be 7.02% if BSAM used the prices Lehman's repo desk was using, rather than 11.45%—the loss without Lehman's marks.

46. Email from "BSAM Hedge Fund Product Management (Generic)," May 16, 2007, produced by JP Morgan.

47. BSAMFCIC-e0000013. An untitled chart produced by JPMorgan shows losses would have been over $50 million less; NAV estimate reconciliation chart, produced by JPMorgan, shows losses would have been almost $25 million less.

48. BSAM Pricing Committee minutes, June 4, 2007.

49. Ralph Cioffi, interview by FCIC, October 19, 2010.

50. Ralph Cioffi, email to John Geissinger, June 6, 2007.

51. Schwartz, interview.

52. Ibid.

53. Ibid.; CSE Program Memorandum to Erik Sirri and others through Matthew Eichner, July 5, 2007.

54. CSE Program Memorandum, July 5, 2007.

55. CSE Program Memorandum, July 5, 2007; Merrill Lynch analysis, "Bear Stearns Asset Mgm't: What Went Wrong"; Paul Friedman, interview by FCIC, April 28, 2010. While most of the Bear Stearns executives interviewed by FCIC staff did not recall the percentage discount at which the collateral seized by Merrill Lynch was auctioned, they did believe that it was significant (e.g., Robert Upton, interview by FCIC, April 13, 2010).

56. "While the High Grade fund was not in default/had not missed any margin calls, creditors were cutting off its liquidity by increasing haircuts or not rolling repo facilities." Bear Stearns Packet dated May 30, meeting held on June 20, produced by the Securities and Exchange Commission, p. 3; Upton, interview.

57. Warren Spector, email to Mary Kay Scucci, April 26, 2007.

58. Friedman, interview; Warren Spector, interview by FCIC, March 30, 2010; Sam Molinaro, interview by FCIC, April 9, 2010.

59. Thomas Marano, interview by FCIC, April 19, 2010; Spector, interview (on Marano's being sent to Marin).

60. Fed Chairman Ben S. Bernanke, letter to FCIC Chairman Phil Angelides, December 21, 2010.

61. James Cayne, interview by FCIC, April 21, 2010.

62. SEC, "Risk Management Reviews of Consolidated Supervised Entities," memo to Erik Sirri and others, August 3, 2007, p. 2; SEC, "Risk Management Reviews of Consolidated Supervised Entities," memo to Erik Sirri and others, July 5, 2007, p. 3, both produced by SEC.

63. Marano, interview.

64. Bill Jamison, internal email, June 21, 2007, produced by Federated.

65. JPMorgan, Directors Risk Policy Committee, "Worldwide Securities Services Risk Review," September 18, 2007; Michael Alix, interview by FCIC, April 8, 2010.

66. For the downgrades, see Moody's Investor Service, "Announcement: Moody's Downgrades Subprime First-Lien RMBS," July 10, 2007; Standard & Poor's, "S&PCorrect: 612 U.S. Subprime RMBS Classes Put on Watch Neg; Methodology Revisions Announced," July 10, 2007; Standard & Poor's, "Various U.S. First-Lien Subprime RMBS Classes Downgraded," July 12, 2007, p. 2; Glenn Costello, "U.S. Subprime Rating Surveillance Update," Fitch Ratings, July 2007.

67. FCIC, "Preliminary Staff Report: Credit Ratings and the Financial Crisis," June 2, 2010, p. 29.

68. Steven Eisman and Tom Warrack, Standard & Poor's Structured Finance, July 10, 2007, teleconference, transcript, p. 16.

69. Andrew Forster, telephone conversation, July 11, 2007, transcript, pp. 3–5.

70. Martin Sullivan, interview by FCIC, June 17, 2010; Steve Bensinger, interview by FCIC, June 16, 2010; Robert Lewis, interview by FCIC, June 15, 2010; Kevin McGinn, interview by FCIC, June 10, 2010; Andrew Forster, Elias Habayeb, and Steve Bensinger, testimony before the FCIC, Hearing on the Role of Derivatives in the Financial Crisis, day 2, session 1: American International Group, Inc. and Goldman Sachs Group, Inc., July 1, 2010, transcript, pp. 11, 61–62.

71. Clarence K. Lee, former managing director for Complex and International Organizations, Office of Thrift Supervision, testimony before the FCIC, Hearing on the Role of Derivatives in the Financial Crisis, day 2, session 2: Derivatives: Supervisors and Regulators, July 1, 2010, transcript, pp. 232–35.

72. Alan Frost, interview by FCIC, May 11, 2010.

73. Joseph Cassano, interview by FCIC, June 25, 2010.

74. "Information Pertaining to the Multi-Sector CDS Portfolio," produced by AIG, with FCIC staff calculations.

75. Andrew Davilman, email to Alan Frost, subject: "Sorry to bother you on"; Frost, email to Davilman, subject: "Re: Sorry to bother you on"; Davilman, email to Frost, subject: "Re: Sorry to bother you on"—all July 26, 2007.

76. Goldman Sachs International, Collateral Invoice to AIG Financial Products Corp., July 27, 2007, produced by Goldman Sachs.

77. AIG hedges, January 2006–December 2008, produced by Goldman Sachs.

78. Andrew Forster, interview by FCIC, June 23, 2010.

79. Daniel Sparks, interview by FCIC, May 11, 2010.

80. "Valuation & Pricing Related to Initial Collateral Calls on Transactions with AIG," produced by Goldman Sachs.

81. Jon Liebergall and Andrew Forster, telephone conversation, July 30, 2007, transcript, pp. 402–4.

82. David Viniar, written testimony for the FCIC, Hearing on the Role of Derivatives in the Financial Crisis, day 2, session 1: American International Group, Inc. and Goldman Sachs Group, Inc., July 1, 2010, p. 2.

83. Liebergall and Forster, telephone conversation, July 30, 2007, transcript, p. 407.

84. Tom Athan, email to Andrew Forster, August 1, 2007.

## Chapter 13

1. Henry Paulson, quoted in Kevin Carmichael and Peter Cook, "Paulson Says Subprime Rout Doesn't Threaten Economy," *Bloomberg*, July 26, 2007.

2. Moody's Investors Service, "Moody's ABCP Program Index: CP Outstanding as of 06/30/2007."

3. Moody's Investors Service, "Moody's Performance Overview: Rhineland Funding Capital Corporation," June 30, 2007.

4. As noted, in the United States, there was a minimal capital charge for liquidity puts equal to 10% of the base 8%, or 0.8%. Staff of Bundesanstalt fur Finanzdienstleistungsaufsicht (the Federal Financial Services Supervisory Authority, Germany's bank regulators), interview by FCIC, September 8, 2010. See also Office of the Comptroller of the Currency, "Interagency Guidance on the Eligibility of Asset-Backed Commercial Paper Liquidity Facilities and the Resulting Risk-Based Capital Treatment," August 4, 2005. For example, Citigroup would have held $200 million in capital against potential losses on the $25 billion in liquidity put exposure that it had accumulated on CDOs it had issued.

5. IKB, 2006/2007 Annual Report, June 28, 2007, p. 78.

6. Securities Fraud Complaint, Securities and Exchange Commission v. Goldman Sachs & Co. and Fabrice Tourre, no. 10-CV-3229 (S.D.N.Y. April 15, 2010), p. 6.

7. IKB staff, interview by FCIC, August 27, 2010; Securities and Exchange Commission (plaintiff) v. Goldman Sachs & Co. and Fabrice Tourre (defendants), Securities Fraud Complaint, 10-CV-3229, United States District Court, Southern District of New York, April 15, 2010, at 17, paragraph 58.

8. "Preliminary results for the first quarter (1 April-30 June 2007)," IKB press release, July 20, 2007.

9. IKB staff, interview; IKB, clarification of interview by FCIC, November 15, 2010; IKB, restated 2006/2007 Annual Report, p. 5.

10. Steven Meier, testimony before the FCIC, Hearing on the Shadow Banking System, day 2, session 3: Institutions Participating in the Shadow Banking System, May 6, 2010, transcript, p. 307.

11. Angelo Mozilo, testimony taken by the SEC in the matter of Countrywide Financial Corp., File No. LA-03370-A, November 9, 2007, pp. 150, 36–37.

12. Angelo Mozilo, email to Lyle Gramley, member of Board of Countrywide Financial Corporation (cc Michael Perry, chief executive officer, IndyMac Bank), August 1, 2007.

13. Eric Sieracki, quoted in Mark DeCambre, "Countrywide Defends Liquidity," *TheStreet.com*, August 2, 2007.

14. "Minutes of a Special Telephonic Meeting of the Board of Directors of Countrywide Financial Corporation," August 6, 2007, pp. 1, 2, 1.

15. Fed Chairman Ben Bernanke, letter to FCIC Chairman Phil Angelides, December 21, 2010.

16. Federal Reserve Staff, memo to Board of Governors of the Federal Reserve System, "Background on Countrywide Financial Corporation," August 14, 2007, pp. 1–2.

17. Ibid., pp. 12–13.

18. Countrywide Financial Corporation, Form 8-K, Exhibit 99.1, filed August 6, 2007. See also "Minutes of a Special Telephonic Meeting of the Boards of Directors of Countrywide Financial Corporation and Countrywide Bank, FSB," August 15, 2007.

19. Angelo Mozilo, interview by FCIC, September 24, 2010.

20. Kenneth Bruce, "Liquidity Is the Achilles Heel," Merrill Lynch Analyst Report, August 15, 2007, p. 4; Kenneth Bruce, "Attractive Upside, but Not without Risk," Merrill Lynch Analyst Report, August 13, 2007, p. 4.

21. Mozilo, interview; the article, by E. Scott Reckard and Annette Haddad, was titled "Credit Crunch Imperils Lender: Worries Grow about Countrywide's Ability to Borrow—and Even a Possible Bankruptcy."

22. Angelo Mozilo, quoted in "One on One with Angelo Mozilo, Chairman and CEO of Countrywide Financial," *Nightly Business Report*, PBS, August 23, 2007, transcript; and in "CEO Exclusive: Countrywide CEO, Pt. 1," *The Call*, CNBC, interview by Maria Bartiromo, August 23, 2007, transcript, p. 1.

23. Sebastian Boyd, "BNP Paribas Freezes Funds as Loan Losses Roil Markets," *Bloomberg*, August 9, 2007.

24. "BNP Paribas Investment Partners Temporally [*sic*] Suspends the Calculation of the Net Asset Value of the following funds: Parvest Dynamic ABS, BNP Paribas ABS EURIBOR and BNP Paribas ABS EONIA," BNP Paribas press release, August 9, 2007.

25. Paul A. McCulley, testimony before the FCIC, Hearing on the Shadow Banking System, day 2, session 3: Institutions Participating in the Shadow Banking System, May 6, 2010, pp. 237, 309.

26. Daniel M. Covitz, Nellie Liang, and Gustavo A. Suarez, "The Evolution of a Financial Crisis: Panic in the Asset-Backed Commercial Paper Market," August 24, 2009, p. 39.

27. Ibid., figure 1, panel B, p. 33.

28. "The Federal Reserve Is Providing Liquidity to Facilitate the Orderly Functioning of Financial Markets," Federal Reserve Board press release, August 10, 2007.

29. Federal Reserve Board, press release, August 17, 2007.

30. Henry Tabe, Moody's Investors Service, "SIVs: An Oasis of Calm in the Sub-prime Maelstrom: Structured Investment Vehicles," International Structured Finance: Special Report, July 20, 2007, p. 1.

31. Ibid.

32. Henry Tabe, interview by FCIC, October 4, 2010.

33. Moody's Investors Service, "From Illiquidity to Liquidity: The Path Toward Credit Market Normalization," Moody's International Policy Perspectives, September 5, 2007, p. 1.

34. Tabe, interview.

35. Moody's Investors Service, "Moody's Update on Structured Investment Vehicles," Moody's Special Report, January 16, 2008, p. 12.

36. Information provided to the FCIC by Deloitte LLP's counsel, August 2, 2010.

37. Moody's Rating Action, "Sigma Finance," September 30, 2008; Henry Tabe, *The Unravelling of Structured Investment Vehicles: How Liquidity Leaked through SIVs: Lessons in Risk Management and Regulatory Oversight* ([Chatham, Kent]: Thoth Capital, 2010), p. 60.

38. The SEC indicated it is aware of at least 44 money market funds that were supported by affiliates because of SIV investments. See Securities and Exchange Commission, "Money Fund Reform" (Proposed rule), June 20, 2009, p. 14 n. 38.

39. Christopher Condon and Rachel Layne, "GE Bond Fund Investors Cash Out After Losses from Subprime," *Bloomberg*, November 15, 2007.

40. The identity of the investor has never been publicly disclosed. See Shannon D. Harrington and Sree Vidya Bhaktavatsalam, "Bank of America to Liquidate $12 Billion Cash Fund," *Bloomberg*, December 10, 2007. See also Michael M. Grynbaum, "Mortgage Crisis Forces the Closing of a Fund," *New York Times*, December 11, 2007.

41. Rich Rokus, portfolio manager at Marshall Money Market Funds, interview by Crane Data, *Money Fund Intelligence*, June 2009; Crane Data, *Money Fund Intelligence*, January 2008.

42. Credit Suisse Institutional Money Market Fund, Inc., Notes to Financial Statements, December 31, 2008, Note 3, p. 30.

43. Florida Legislature, Office of Program Policy Analysis and Government Accountability, "The SBA [State Board of Administration] Is Correcting Problems Relating to Its Oversight of the Local Government Investment Pool," Research Memorandum, March 31, 2009, p. 2.

44. SBA report, "Update on Sub-Prime Mortgage Meltdown and State Board of Administration Investments," November 9, 2007, pp. 721–22.

## Chapter 14

1. Bloomberg Professional, Write downs and Credit Losses vs. Capital Raised (WDCI) function, data reported for second half of 2007. Write-downs are for losses to holdings in structured finance and mortgages.

2. Roy C. Smith, *Paper Fortune$: Modern Wall Street: Where It's Been and Where It's Going* (New York: St. Martin's 2009), p. 341.

3. Bloomberg Historical Prices Index December 31, 2007; CGS1U5; CBSC1U5; and CLEH1U5. Figures refer to credit default swaps on five-year senior debt.

4. Presentation to Merrill Lynch & Co. Board of Directors, "Leveraged Finance and Mortgage/CDO Review," October 21, 2007, p. 23.

5. Presentation to Merrill board, October 21, 2007, p. 23.

6. Dow Kim, interview by FCIC, September 10, 2010.

7. Presentation to Merrill Board of Directors, October 21, 2007, p. 23.

8. Ibid., pp. 23–24.

9. Presentation to Merrill Lynch Risk Oversight Committee, "Market Risk Management Update," September 26, 2007, p. 7.

10. Merrill Lynch, 1Q 2007 Earnings Call transcript, April 19, 2007, p. 3.

11. Merrill Lynch, 2Q 2007 Earnings Release, July 17, 2007, p. 1.

12. Merrill Lynch, 2Q 2007 Earnings Call transcript, July 17, 2007, pp. 8, 20.

13. Merrill Lynch Finance Committee Summary, July 22, 2007, p. 7.

14. Ibid.

15. Kim, interview.

16. Stanley O'Neal, interview by FCIC, September 16, 2010.

17. "ABS CDO Update" by Dale Lattanzio, July 2007, p. 10.

18. O'Neal, interview.

19. Merrill Lynch, 3Q 2007 Earnings Call transcript, October 24, 2007, pp. 7, 10.

20. SEC narrative chronology, Merrill Lynch specific, p. 1.

21. Nancy Moran and Rodney Yap, "O'Neal Ranks No. 5 on Payout List, Group Says: Table (Update1)," *Bloomberg*, November 2, 2007.

22. Kim interview; Merrill Lynch, 2007 Proxy Statement, April 27, 2007, p. 47.

23. Charles Prince, interview by FCIC, March 17, 2010; Robert Rubin, interview by FCIC, March 11, 2010.

24. Prince, interview.

25. Moody's Investors Service, "Structured Finance Rating Transitions: 1983–2006," Special Comment, January 2007.

26. Charles Prince, testimony before the FCIC, Hearing on Subprime Lending and Securitization and Government-Sponsored Enterprises (GSEs), day 2, session 1: Citigroup Senior Management, April 8, 2010, transcript, p. 11.

27. Prince, interview.

28. Tobias Brushammar, James Hua, Graham Jackson, and Subra Viswanathan, Citigroup memorandum to Nestor Dominguez, Janice Warne, Michael Raynes, and Jo-Anne Williams, subject: Liquidity Put Valuation, October 19, 2006.

29. Susan Mills, interview by FCIC, February 3, 2010; James Xanthos, interview by Financial Industry Regulatory Authority (FINRA), March 24, 2009.

30. Susan Mills, testimony before the FCIC, hearing on Subprime Lending and Securitization and Government-Sponsored Enterprises (GSEs), day 1, session 2: Subprime Origination and Securitization, April 7, 2010, transcript, pp. 186–87.

31. Mills, interview.

32. Murray Barnes, former managing director of Independent Risk, interview by FCIC, March 2, 2010.

33. Notes on Senior Supervisors' Meeting with Firms, meeting between Citigroup and Federal Reserve Bank of New York, Federal Reserve Board, Office of the Comptroller of the Currency, Securities and Exchange Commission, U.K. Financial Services Authority, and Japan FSA, November 19, 2007, p. 17.

34. Janice Warne, interview by FCIC, February 2, 2010; Nestor Dominguez, interview by FCIC, March 2, 2010.

35. Dominguez, interview.

36. Nestor Dominguez, testimony before the FCIC, Hearing on Subprime Lending and Securitization and Government-Sponsored Enterprises (GSEs), day 1, session 3: Citigroup Subprime-Related Structured Products and Risk Management, April 7, 2010, transcript, pp. 282–83.

37. Barnes, interview.

38. Ibid.

39. Notes on Senior Supervisors' Meeting with Firms, meeting with Citigroup, November 19, 2007, p. 6.

40. FCIC staff calculations.

41. Prince, testimony before the FCIC, April 8, 2010, transcript, p. 118; David Bushnell, interview by FCIC, April 1, 2010.

42. Bushnell, interview.

43. Ellen "Bebe" Duke, Citigroup Independent Risk, interview by FCIC, March 18, 2010.

44. Barnes, interview.

45. James Xanthos, interview by Financial Industry Regulatory Authority (FINRA), March 24, 2009.

46. Barnes, interview.

47. Prince, interview.

48. Robert Rubin, former chairman of the Executive Committee and adviser, interview by FCIC, March 11, 2010.

49. Thomas Maheras, former co-CEO of Citi Markets & Banking, interview by FCIC, March 10, 2010.

50. Prince, interview.

51. Citigroup, Presentation to the Securities and Exchange Commission Regarding Overall CDO Business and Subprime Exposure, June 2007, p. 11.

52. Paul, Weiss, Citigroup's counsel, response to FCIC Interrogatory #18, March 1, 2010.

53. Citigroup, 2Q 2007 Earnings Call Q&A transcript, July 20, 2007.

54. Complaint, Securities and Exchange Commission v. Citigroup Inc., 1:10-cv-01277 (D.D.C), July 29, 2010.

55. Federal Reserve Board of New York, letter to Vikram Pandit and the Board of the Directors of Citigroup, April 15, 2008, p. 11.

56. Dominguez, testimony before the FCIC, April 7, 2010, transcript, p. 281.

57. Maheras, interview, and testimony before the FCIC, Hearing on Subprime Lending and Securitization and Government-Sponsored Enterprises (GSEs), day 1, session 3: Citigroup Subprime-Related Structured Products and Risk Management, April 7, 2010, transcript, p. 269.

58. Bushnell, interview.

59. Prince, interview.

60. Complaint, Securities and Exchange Commission v. Citigroup Inc., p. 13.

61. Maheras, interview.

62. Prince, interview; Charles Prince, email to Robert Rubin, re, September 9, 2007, 9:43 A.M. (on Thomas Maheras and super seniors).

63. Robert Rubin, email to Charles Prince, September 9, 2007, 5:30 P.M.; Charles Prince, email to Robert Rubin, September 9, 2007, 5: 51 P.M.

64. Robert Rubin, interview by FCIC, March 11, 2010.

65. Prince, interview.

66. Ibid.

67. Citigroup, "Risk Management Review: An Update to the Corporate Audit and Risk Management Committee," October 15, 2007, p. 4.

68. Citigroup, Q3 2007 Earnings Call transcript, October 15, 2007.

69. Prince, interview.

70. Paul, Weiss, Citigroup's counsel, letter to FCIC in re the FCIC's second and third supplemental requests, March 31, 2010; Citigroup, 2008 Proxy Statement for fiscal year 2007, March 13, 2008, p. 74.

71. Federal Reserve Board of New York, letter to Vikram Pandit and the Board of Directors of Citigroup, April 15, 2008, p. 8.

72. FCIC staff calculations from Citigroup proxy statements (information for 2000–06) and information on 2007–09 provided by Paul, Weiss (on behalf of Citigroup), letter to FCIC, March 31, 2010, "Response to Interrogatory No. 7," pp. 3–6.

73. Robert Rubin, testimony before the FCIC, Hearing on Subprime Lending and Securitization and Government-Sponsored Enterprises (GSEs), day 2, session 1: Citigroup Senior Management, April 8, 2010, transcript, pp. 15–16.

74. John Reed, interview by FCIC, March 24, 2010.

75. AIG, Earnings Call credit supplement, August 9, 2007.

76. Joseph St. Denis, letter to House Committee on Oversight and Government Reform, U.S. House of Representatives, October 4, 2008, p. 4.

77. Joseph St. Denis, interview by FCIC, April 23, 2010.

78. Gene Park, interview by FCIC, May 18, 2010.

79. Jake Sun, interview by FCIC, June 21, 2010.

80. Alan Frost, interview by FCIC, May 11, 2010.

81. Pierre Micottis, interview by FCIC, June 24, 2010.

82. Park, interview.

83. PricewaterhouseCooper audit team, memo re 3Q07 review of AIG's super-senior CDS portfolio, November 7, 2007, p. 2.

84. Joseph Cassano, interview by FCIC, June 25, 2010.

85. Park, interview.

86. Goldman's submissions to the FCIC on its valuation and pricing related to collateral calls made to AIG are available on Goldman Sachs's website (http://www2.goldmansachs.com/our-firm/on-the -issues/responses-fcic.print.html).

87. Andrew Forster, telephone call to Jon Liebergall, July 30, 2007, transcript.

88. PricewaterhouseCooper, memo to AIGFP 2007 2Q review files, August 8, 2007.

89. Andrew Forster, email to Joseph Cassano and Pierre Micottis, November 9, 2007, enclosing marks from Merrill Lynch,

90. AIG, Earnings Call credit supplement, August 9, 2007, pp. 28, 14, 21, 22.

91. These estimates are based on Federal Reserve Bank of New York, "Maiden Lane III Quarterly Holdings Report," January 2010. This probably isn't a complete list of their positions, because not all CDO tranches are part of the Maiden Lane III portfolio. Of the 335 securities listed in that document, FCIC staff found data on 327 in Moody's CDO EMS database and Bloomberg. For those 327 securities, 313 suffered a downgrade and 206 became materially impaired (i.e., were downgraded to Ca/C). Of the 139 initially rated Aaa, 134 suffered downgrades and 55 became materially impaired.

92. Alan Frost, email to Andrew Forster, August 16, 2007.

93. Cassano, interview.

94. Frost, email to Forster, August 16, 2007.

95. Tom Athan, email to Andrew Forster, cc Adam Budnick, September 11, 2007.

96. Joseph Cassano, email to Elias Habayeb, November 11, 2007.

97. Minutes of the meeting of the AIG Audit Committee, November 6, 2007, p. 5.

98. Andrew Forster, email to Joseph Cassano, subject: GS Prices vs Others, November 18, 2007.

99. Goldman, submission to the FCIC, "Valuation & Pricing Related to Initial Collateral Calls on Transactions with AIG," pp. 2–3.

100. Based on staff analysis of data provided to the FCIC by the Depository Trust & Clearing Corporation and Markit. ABX includes all tranches of the ABX.HE 06-2. TABX is constructed based on the reference obligations for the 06-2 and 07-1 BBB and BBB- tranches of the ABX.

101. Cassano, interview.

102. Andrew Forster, email to Alan Frost, August 16, 2007.

103. Tim Ryan, PricewaterhouseCooper, interview by FCIC, June 1, 2010.

104. SEC staff briefing of FCIC staff, June 4, 2010.

105. Joseph Cassano, email to Andrew Forster, Pierre Micottis, James Bridgwater, and Peter Robinson, subject: Fw: SS CDS Valuation, October 8, 2007.

106. PricewaterhouseCooper, minutes of meeting at AIGFP, October 11, 2007. See also PwC audit team, memo re 3Q07 review of AIG's super-senior CDS portfolio, November 7, 2007, pp. 230–31.

107. AIG, 3Q 2007 Earnings Call transcript, November 7, 2007, pp. 5, 17.

108. PwC audit team memo, p. 6.

109. Goldman Sachs International, to AIG Financial Products Corp., "Amended Side Letter Agreement," November 23, 2007.

110. Joe Cassano, email to Bill Dooley, November 27, 2007, attaching memo from Andrew Forster, "Collateral Call Status."

111. Andrew Forster, "Collateral Call Status," memo prepared for Joe Cassano.

112. Joe Cassano, email to Bill Dooley, subject: Collateral Calls, November 27, 2007.

113. Joe Cassano, email to Bill Dooley, subject: GS call back, November 30, 2007.

114. Goldman Sachs International, Collateral Invoice to AIG Financial Products Corp., margin call, November 23, 2007.

115. PwC audit team, memo, November 7, 2007, p. 5.

116. PricewaterhouseCooper, notes of a meeting to discuss super-senior valuations and collateral disputes, November 29, 2007, p. 2, produced by PwC.

117. Andrew Forster, interview by FCIC, June 21, 2010.

118. Martin Sullivan, interview by FDIC, June 17, 2010.

119. PwC, notes of meeting of November 29, 2007, p. 2.

120. Ibid., p. 3.

121. Kevin McGinn, email to Paul Narayanan, November 20, 2007.

122. Sullivan, interview.

123. AIG Investor Conference Call, December 5, 2007, transcript, pp. 4–6, 25.

124. Joseph Cassano, email to Michael Sherwood and David Viniar, subject: CDO Valuations, January 16, 2008.

125. Andrew Davilman, interview by FCIC, June 18, 2010; David Lehman, interview by FCIC, June 23, 2010.

126. "AIG/Goldman Sachs Collateral Call Timeline," available on FCIC website at http://fcic.gov/hearings/pdfs/2010–0701-AIG-Goldman-supporting-docs.pdf.

127. PricewaterhouseCooper, memo to AIG workpaper files, February 24, 2008, pp. 2–3, 10.

128. PricewaterhouseCooper, notes on a February 6, 2008, meeting with AIG, February 13, 2008, p. 2.

129. Martin Sullivan, testimony before the FCIC, Hearing on the Role of Derivatives in the Financial Crisis, day 1, session 2: American International Group, Inc. and Derivatives, June 30, 2010, transcript, p. 233.

130. PricewaterhouseCooper, notes on the AIG Audit Committee meeting, February 7, 2008, p. 2.

131. Joseph Cassano, testimony before the FCIC, Hearing on the Role of Derivatives in the Financial Crisis. day 1, session 2: American International Group, Inc. and Derivatives, June 30, 2010, p. 233; Cassano, interview.

132. Office of Thrift Supervision, letter to AIG General Counsel and Board, March 7, 2008.

133. William Dudley, interview by FCIC, October 15, 2010.

134. Adam B. Ashcraft, Morten L. Bech, and W. Scott Frame, "The Federal Home Loan Bank System: The Lender of Next to Last Resort?" Federal Reserve Bank of New York Staff Reports, no. 357 (November 2008), p. 4.

135. Federal Reserve Board, "October 2007 Senior Loan Officer Opinion Survey on Bank Lending Practices," October 2007.

136. Frederic Mishkin, interview by FCIC, October 1, 2010.

137. Dudley, interview.

138. Ibid.

139. Ibid.

140. Standard & Poor's, "Detailed Results of Subprime Stress Test of Financial Guarantors," RatingsDirect, February 25, 2008.

141. Alan Roseman, interview by FCIC, May 17, 2010.

142. SEC, "Risk Management Reviews of Consolidated Supervised Entities," internal memo to Erik Sirri and others, November 6, 2007, p. 3.

143. Roseman, interview, May 17, 2010.

144. SEC, "Risk Management of Consolidated Supervised Entities," internal memo to Erik Sirri and others, January 2, 2008, p. 2.

145. Bill Lockyer, State of California 2008 Debt Affordability Report: Making the Municipal Bond Market Work for Taxpayers in Turbulent Times (October 1, 2008), p. 4.

146. John J. McConnell and Alessio Saretto, "Auction Failures and the Market for Auction Rate Securities" (The Krannert School of Management, Purdue University, April 2009), p. 10.

147. Erik R. Sirri, director of Trading and Markets, U.S. Securities and Exchange Commission, "Municipal Bound Turmoil: Impact on Cities, Towns and States," testimony before the House Financial Services Committee, 110th Cong., 2nd sess., March 12, 2008.

148. Georgetown University, "Annual Financial Report, 2008–2009," p. 5.

149. Jacqueline Doherty, "The Sad Story of Auction-Rate Securities, Barrons, May 26, 2008.

150. "SEC Finalizes ARS Settlements with Bank of America, RBC, and Deutsche Bank," SEC press release, June 3, 2009.

## Chapter 15

1. "Prime Asset," 2007 Upper HedgeWorld Prime Brokerage League Table, accessible at Gregory Zuckerman, "Hedge Funds, Once a Windfall, Contribute to Bear's Downfall," Wall Street Journal, March 17, 2008.

2. Jeff Mayer and Thomas Marano, "Fixed Income Overview," March 29, 2007, p. 8, produced by JP Morgan.

3. Inside Mortgage Finance, The 2009 Mortgage Market Statistical Annual, vol. 2, The Secondary Market (Bethesda, MD: Inside Mortgage Finance, 2009), pp. 18–25.

4. FCIC staff estimates, based on Moody's CDO EMS database. Different numbers are provided in Jeff Mayer and Thomas Marano, "Fixed Income Overview," March 29, 2007, p. 16.

5. Samuel Molinaro, interview by FCIC, April 9, 2010; Michael Alix, interview by FCIC, April 8, 2010.

6. SEC, "Risk Management Reviews of Consolidated Supervised Entities," memorandum to Robert Colby and others, May 8, 2006.

7. Robert Upton, interview by FCIC, April 13, 2010.

8. SEC, "Risk Management Reviews of Consolidated Supervised Entities," memorandum to Erik Sirri and others, March 1, 2007.

9. Ibid.

10. Bear Stearns, "Fitch Presentation," PowerPoint slides, August 2007.

11. Upton, interview.

12. Bear Stearns, Form 10-K for the year ended November 30, 2007, filed January 29, 2008, pp. 52, 22.

13. Upton, interview.

14. Ibid.

15. Standard & Poor's, Global Credit Portal RatingsDirect, "Research Update: Bear Stearns Cos. Inc. Outlook Revised to Negative; 'A+/A-1' Rating Affirmed," August 3, 2007.

16. Jimmy Cayne, interview by FCIC, April 21, 2010.

17. Matthew Eichner, interview by FCIC, April 14, 2010.

18. Wendy de Monchaux, interview by FCIC, April 27, 2010; Steven Meyer, interview by FCIC, April 22, 2010.

19. Mike Alix, interview by FCIC, April 8, 2010.

20. Eichner, interview.

21. Timeline Regarding Bear Stearns Companies Inc., April 3, 2008, produced by SEC.

22. SEC Office of Inspector General, Office of Audits, "SEC's Oversight of Bear Stearns and Related Entities: The Consolidated Supervised Entity Program," Report No. 446-A, September 25, 2008, pp. ix–x.

23. Michael Halloran, interview by FCIC.

24. Cayne, interview.

25. Samuel Molinaro, testimony before the FCIC, Hearing on the Shadow Banking System, day 1, session 1: Investment Banks and the Shadow Banking System, May 5, 2010, transcript, p. 43; Cayne, interview.

26. "Changes in Approved Commercial Paper List—10/01/2007–12/31/2007" and "Changes in Approved Commercial Paper List—1/01/2008–3/31/2008," produced by Federated Advised Funds.

27. Federal Reserve Bank of New York, "Tri-Party Repo Infrastructure Reform," white paper, May 17, 2010, p. 7.

28. Seth Carpenter, interview by FCIC, September 20, 2010.

29. Information provided by Federated to the FCIC.

30. Scott Goebel, Kevin Gaffney, and Norm Lind (Fidelity employees), interview by FCIC, February 25, 2010.

31. Steve Meier, executive vice president State Street Global Advisors, interview by FCIC, March 15, 2010.

32. Timeline Regarding the Bear Stearns Companies Inc., April 3, 2008, pp. 1–2, provided to the FCIC.

33. Alan Schwartz, interview by FCIC, April 23, 2010.

34. Lucian A. Bebchuk et al., "The Wages of Failure: Executive Compensation at Bear Stearns and Lehman 2000–2008," November 22, 2009, Table 2, p. 15; SNL Financial.

35. Thomas Marano, interview by FCIC, April 19, 2010.

36. Paul Friedman, quoted in William Cohan, House of Cards: A Tale of Hubris and Wretched Excess on Wall Street (New York: Doubleday, 2009), p. 71. Although Friedman acknowledged to the FCIC making the cited statements, and many others as well, he attributes them to anger and frustration over Bear Stearns's failure. Currently, Friedman is employed at Guggenheim Securities, Inc., where he works for Alan Schwartz, the former president of Bear Stearns. Paul Friedman, interview by FCIC, April 28, 2010.

37. The Corporate Library, "The Bear Stearns Companies Inc.: Governance Profile," June 20, 2008, p. 4.

38. Cayne, interview.

39. Molinaro, interview.

40. Cayne, interview; Schwartz (interview by FCIC) stated that bonuses for individual executives were discussed by the Compensation Committee, and the final recommendation for bonuses came from the CEO.

41. Alix, interview.

42. Bear Stearns, 2007 Performance Compensation Plan, p. I-1 (provided to the FCIC); Alix, interview. The salary cap had been raised from $200,000 to $250,000 in 2006 (Alix, interview; Cayne, interview).

43. Bebchuk et al., "The Wages of Failure," Table 1, p. 12; Table 2, p. 15; Table 4, p. 20. The budget authority for the SEC in 2008 was $906 million; in 2010, it was $1.026 billion.

44. In 2006, Alix received $3 million in total compensation, Cayne received more than $38.3 million in salary and bonus, and Schwartz received more than $35.7 million in salary and bonus. SNL Financial; interviews with Spector and Alix.

45. Marano, interview.

46. Tom Marano, email to Alan Schwartz and Richie Metrick, February 12, 2008.

47. Matthew Eichner, email to James Giles et al., January 30, 2008.

48. Lou Lebedin, interview by FCIC, April 23, 2010.

49. Timeline Regarding Bear Stearns Companies Inc., April 3, 2008, produced by SEC.

50. Upton, interview.

51. Minutes of Special Meeting of Bear Stearns Board of Directors, March 13, 2008.

52. Pat Lewis, Bear Stearns, email to Matthew Eichner, Steven Spurry, James Giles, and Kevin Silva, March 10, 2008.

53. Matthew Eichner, email to Brian Peters, March 11, 2008.

54. David Fettig, "The History of a Powerful Paragraph," Federal Reserve Bank of Minneapolis, June 2008.

55. James Embersit, email to Deborah Bailey, March 3, 2008.

56. In response to the FCIC's interrogatories, JP Morgan produced a list of all payments Bear Stearns made to or received from OTC derivatives counterparties from March 10, 2008, through March 14, 2008. The spreadsheet was created in September 2008 by Bear Stearns in response to a request by the SEC Division of Trading and Markets. The large volume of novations away from Bear Stearns during the week of March 10, 2008 and the previous week was confirmed by the New York Federal Reserve and International Swaps and Derivatives Association. (New York Federal Reserve personnel, interview by FCIC; ISDA personnel, interviews by FCIC, May 13 and 27, 2010).

57. Brian Peters, email to Matthew Eichner, March 11, 2008.

58. Stuart Smith, email to Bear Stearns, March 11, 2008; Marvin Woolard, email Stuart Smith et al., March 11, 2008; Kyle Bass, interview by FCIC, April 30, 2010.

59. Bass, interview.

60. Debby LaMoy, email to Faina Epshteyn, March 12, 2008; Faina Epshteyn, email to Debby LaMoy, March 12, 2008.

61. Marvin Woolard, email to Stuart Smith et al., March 12, 2008.

62. CNBC video, Schwartz and CNBC's David Faber, original air date March 12, 2008.

63. Yalman Onaran, "Bear Stearns Investor Lewis May Increase His Stake," Bloomberg News, March 11, 2008.

64. Matthew Eichner, email to Erik Sirri, Robert Colby, and Michael Macchiaroli, March 12, 2008.

65. Minutes of Special Meeting of Bear Stearns Board of Directors, March 13, 2008, pp. 1–2.

66. Upton, interview.

67. Matthew Eichner, email to Erik Sirri, Robert Colby, and Michael Macchiaroli, March 12, 2008.

68. Alan Schwartz, interview by FCIC; Matthew Eichner, email to Erik Sirri, Robert Colby, and Michael Macchiaroli, March 13, 2008.

69. Upton, interview.

70. Minutes of Special Meeting of Bear Stearns Board of Directors, March 13, 2008 ("[Schwartz] said there had been seventeen billion dollars in cash with a two billion eight hundred million dollar backstop, unsecured line. The Board was told that twelve to fifteen billion dollars had gone out of TBSCI in the last two days and that TBSCI had received a billion dollars in margin calls").

71. Upton, interview; Goebel, Gaffney, and Lind, interview; Steven Meier, interview by FCIC, March 15, 2010; Michael Macchiaroli, interview by FCIC, April 13, 2010.

72. Christopher Cox, written testimony for the FCIC, Hearing on the Shadow Banking System, day 1, session 3: SEC Regulation of Investment Banks, May 5, 2010, p. 6.

73. Timeline Regarding Bear Stearns Companies Inc., April 3, 2008, produced by SEC.

74. Jamie Dimon, interview by FCIC, October 20, 2010.

75. Alan Schwartz, testimony before the FCIC, Hearing on the Shadow Banking System, day 1, session 2: Investment Banks and the Shadow Banking System, May 5, 2010, transcript, p. 167; Schwartz, interview.

76. Schwartz., interview.

77. Ibid.; Molinaro, interview; Alix, interview.

78. John Chrin, interview by FCIC, April 28, 2010.

79. Dimon, interview by FCIC, October 20, 2010; minutes of Special Meeting of Bear Stearns Board of Directors, March 16, 2008.

80. Federal Reserve, "Report Pursuant to Section 129 of the Emergency Economic Stabilization Act of 2008: Loan to Facilitate the Acquisition of The Bear Stearns Companies, Inc. by JP Morgan & Co.," pp. 1, 4; Ernst & Young, "Project LLC: Summary of Findings and Observations Report," June 26, 2008, p. 10.

81. Contrary to what is stated in the board minutes (Special Meeting of Bear Stearns Board of Directors, March 16, 2008, p. 5), when FCIC staff interviewed Schwartz he said that the $2 a share price came from JP Morgan, not Paulson. Schwartz also told staff that because Bear did not receive "a lot of competing offers," it had to accept JP Morgan's offer of $2 a share.

82. Chrin, interview.

83. Alan Schwartz, testimony before the FCIC, Hearing on the Shadow Banking System, day 1, session 2: Investment Banks and the Shadow Banking System, May 5, 2010, transcript, p. 142.

84. Macchiaroli, interview.

85. Ben Bernanke, closed-door session with FCIC, November 17, 2009.

86. Ibid.

87. Timothy Geithner, president, Federal Reserve Bank of New York, "Actions by the New York Fed in Response to Liquidity Pressures in Financial Markets," prepared testimony before the Senate Committee on Banking, Housing, and Urban Affairs, 110th Cong., 2nd sess., April 3, 2008, p. 10.

88. Henry Paulson, testimony before the FCIC, Hearing on the Shadow Banking System, day 2, session 1: Perspective on the Shadow Banking System, May 6, 2010, transcript, pp. 68, 59, 78.

## Chapter 16

1. David Wong, interview by FCIC, October 15, 2010.

2. Josh Fineman and Yalman Onaran, "Lehman's Fuld Says 'Worst Is Behind Us' in Crisis (Update3)," Bloomberg, April 15, 2008.

3. Henry Paulson, testimony before the FCIC, Hearing on the Shadow Banking System, day 2, session 1: Perspective on the Shadow Banking System, May 6, 2010, transcript, p. 28.

4. Viral V. Acharya and T. Sabri Öncü, "The Dodd-Frank Wall Street Reform and Consumer Protection Act and a Little Known Corner of Wall Street: The Repo Market," *Regulating Wall Street,* July 16, 2010.

5. Sandie O'Connor, JP Morgan, interview by FCIC, March 4, 2010.

6. Jamie Dimon, interview by FCIC, October 20, 2010.

7. Adam Copeland, Antoine Martin, Michael Walker, "The Tri-Party Repo Market Before the 2010 Reforms," FRBNY Staff Report No. 477, November 2010, p. 24.

8. Steven Meier, testimony before the FCIC, Hearing on the Shadow Banking System, day 2, session 3: Institutions Participating in the Shadow Banking System, May 6, 2010, transcript, p. 276.

9. William Dudley, interview by FCIC, October 15, 2010.

10. Darryll Hendricks, interview by FCIC, August 6, 2010.

11. James Cayne, testimony before the FCIC, Hearing on the Shadow Banking System, day 1, session 2: Investment Banks and the Shadow Banking System, May 5, 2010, transcript, p. 168.

12. Seth Carpenter, interview by FCIC, September 20, 2010.

13. Federal Reserve, "Regulatory Reform: Primary Dealer Credit Facility (PCDF)," Usage of Federal Reserve Credit and Liquidity Facilities, data available at www.federalreserve.gov/newsevents/reform_pdcf.htm.

14. Anton R. Valukas, Report of Examiner, *In re* Lehman Brothers Holdings Inc., et al., Chapter 11 Case No. 08-13555 (JMP), (Bankr. S.D.N.Y.), March 11, 2010, 4:1396–98; quotation, 1396 (hereafter cited as Valukas; available at http://lehmanreport.jenner.com/).

15. William Dudley, email to Chairman, June 17, 2008.

16. Dimon, interview.

17. Ibid.

18. Hendricks, interview.

19. Lucinda Brickler, email to Patrick Parkinson, July 11, 2008; Lucinda Brickler et al., memorandum to Timothy Geithner, July 11, 2008.

20. The $200 billion figure is noted in Patrick Parkinson, email to Ben Bernanke et al., July 20, 2008.

21. Brickler et al., memorandum, p. 1.

22. Patrick Parkinson, email to Lucinda Brickler, July 11, 2008.

23. Patrick Parkinson, email to Ben Bernanke et al., July 20, 2008.

24. Ibid.

25. Based on chart in Federal Reserve Bank of New York, *Developing Metrics for the Four Largest Securities Firms,* August 2008, p. 5.

26. Ibid.

27. Tobias Adrian, Christopher Burke, and James McAndrews, "The Federal Reserve's Primary Dealer Credit Facility," Federal Reserve Bank of New York, *Current Issues in Economics and Finance* 15, no. 4 (August 2009): 2.

28. Erik Sirri, interview by FCIC, April 9, 2010, p. 3.

29. Fed Chair Ben Bernanke, "Lessons from the Failure of Lehman Brothers," testimony before the House Financial Services Committee, 111th Cong., 2nd sess., April 20, 2010, p. 1.

30. Valukas, 1:8 n. 30: Examiner's Interview of Timothy F. Geithner, Nov. 24, 2009, p. 4.

31. Valukas, 4:1486.

32. Sirri, interview.

33. William Brodows and Til Schuermann, Federal Reserve Bank of New York, "Primary Dealer Monitoring: Initial Assessment of CSEs," May 12, 2008, slides 9–10, 15–16.

34. Federal Reserve Bank of New York, "Primary Dealer Monitoring: Liquidity Stress Analysis," June 25, 2008, p. 3.

35. Ibid., p. 5.

36. Valukas, 4:1489.

37. Ibid., 4:1496, 1497.

38. Christopher Cox, statement before the House Financial Services Committee, 111th Cong., 2nd sess., April 20, 2010, p. 5.

39. Patrick Parkinson, email to Steven Shafran, August 8, 2008.

40. Counterparty Risk Management Policy Group, "Toward Greater Financial Stability: A Private Sector Perspective, The Report of the CRMPG II," July 27, 2005.

41. Federal Reserve Bank of New York, "Statement Regarding Meeting on Credit Derivatives," September 15, 2005; Federal Reserve Bank of New York, "New York Fed Welcomes New Industry Commitments on Credit Derivatives," March 13, 2006; Federal Reserve Bank of New York, "Third Industry Meeting Hosted by the Federal Reserve Bank of New York," September 27, 2006.

42. See Comptroller of the Currency, "OCC's Quarterly Report on Bank Trading and Derivatives Activities, First Quarter 2009," Table 1; the figures in the text are reached by subtracting exchange traded futures and options from total derivatives.

43. Chris Mewbourne, interview by FCIC, July 28, 2010.

44. This figure compares with a low in 2005, at the height of the mortgage boom, of $7 billion in problem assets. "Problem" institutions are those with financial, operational, or managerial weaknesses that threaten their continued financial viability; they are rated either a 4 or 5 under the Uniform Financial Institutions Rating System. FDIC reporting for insured institutions—i.e., the regulated banking and thrift industry overall. See *Quarterly Banking Profile: Fourth Quarter 2007= FDIC Quarterly* 2, no. 1 (December 31, 2007): 1, 4; *Quarterly Banking Profile: First Quarter 2008 = FDIC Quarterly* 2, no. 2 (March 31, 2008): 2, 4; *Quarterly Banking Profile: Second Quarter 2008 = FDIC Quarterly* 2, no. 3 (June 30, 2008): 1.

45. By 2009, the problem list would swell to 702 banks, with assets of $403 billion. *Quarterly Banking Profile: Fourth Quarter 2009 = FDIC Quarterly* 4, no. 1 (December 31, 2009): 4.

46. *Quarterly Banking Profile: First Quarter 2008,* p. 4.

47. Roger Cole, interview by FCIC, August 2, 2010.

48. FCIC interview with Michael Solomon and Fred Phillips-Patrick, September 20, 2010.

49. Federal Reserve Bank of New York, letter to Charles Prince, April 9, 2007.

50. Federal Reserve Bank of New York, Federal Reserve Board, Office of the Comptroller of the Currency, Securities and Exchange Commission, U.K. Financial Services Authority, and Japan Financial Services Authority, "Notes on Senior Supervisors' Meetings with Firms," November 19, 2007, p. 3.

51. Federal Reserve Board, "FRB New York 2009 Operations Review: Close Out Report," p. 3.

52. Timothy Geithner, testimony before the FCIC, Hearing on the Shadow Banking System, day 2, session 1: Perspective on the Shadow Banking System, May 6, 2010, transcript, p. 210.

53. Steve Manzari and Dianne Dobbeck, interview by FCIC, April 26, 2010.

54. Federal Reserve Board, "Wachovia Case Study," November 12 and 13, p. 20;

55. Angus McBryde, interview by FCIC, July 30, 2007.

56. Thompson received a severance package worth about $8.7 million in compensation and accelerated vesting of stock. In addition, he negotiated himself three years of office space and a personal assistant at Wachovia's expense. Thompson had previously received more than $21 million in salary and stock compensation in 2007 and more than $23 million in 2006; his total compensation from 2002 through 2008 exceeded $112 million.

57. Federal Reserve Bank of Richmond, letter to Wachovia, July 22, 2008, pp. 3–5.

58. Comptroller of the Currency, letter to Wachovia, August 4, 2008, with Report of Examination; letter, pp. 8, 3.

59. Ibid., pp. 3–6.

60. Ibid., letter, p. 2; Report of Examination, p. 18.

61. Ibid., Report of Examination, p. 12.

62. "Home Loans Discussion," materials prepared for WaMu Board of Directors meeting, April 18, 2006, p. 4; Senate Permanent Subcommittee on Investigations, *Wall Street and the Financial Crisis: The Role of High Risk Home Loans,* 111th Cong., 2nd sess., April 13, 2010, Exhibits, p. 83.

63. Senate Permanent Subcommittee on Investigations, *Wall Street and the Financial Crisis: Role of the Bank Regulators,* 111th Cong., 2nd sess., April 16, 2010, Exhibits, p. 6.

64. OTS Regional Director Darrel Dochow, letter to FDIC Regional Director Stan Ivie, July 22, 2008.

65. Offices of Inspector General, Department of the Treasury and Federal Deposit Insurance Corporation, "Evaluation of Federal Regulatory Oversight of Washington Mutual Bank," Report No. EVAL 10-002, April 2010, pp. 31, 12.

66. FDIC, Confidential Problem Bank Memorandum, September 8, 2008, p. 4.

67. Treasury and FDIC IGs, "Evaluation of Federal Regulatory Oversight of WaMu," p. 39.

68. Confidential OTS Memorandum to FDIC Regional Director, September 11, 2008; Treasury and FDIC IGs, "Evaluation of Federal Regulatory Oversight of WaMu," pp. 45–47.

69. Quoted in Damian Paletta, "FDIC Presses Bank Regulators to Use Warier Eye," *Wall Street Journal,* August 19, 2008.

70. Sheila Bair, interview by FCIC, August 18, 2010.

71. Treasury and FDIC IGs, "Evaluation of Federal Regulatory Oversight of WaMu," p. 3.

72. Comptroller of the Currency, *Large Bank Supervision: Comptroller's Handbook,* January 2010, p. 3.

73. Cole, interview.

74. Rich Spillenkothen, "Observations and Perspectives of the Director of Banking Supervision and Regulation at the Federal Reserve Board from 1991 to 2006 on the Performance of Prudential Supervision in the Years Preceding the Financial Crisis," paper prepared for the FCIC, May 21, 2010, p. 24.

75. Doug Roeder, interview by FCIC, August 4, 2010.

76. "Treasury Releases Blueprint for Stronger Regulatory Structure," Treasury Department press release, March 31, 2008.

## Chapter 17

1. Henry Paulson, interview by FCIC, April 2, 2010; Henry Paulson, *On The Brink: Inside the Race to Stop the Collapse of the Global Financial System* (New York: Business Plus, 2010), p. 57.

2. Paulson, interview.

3. James Lockhart, testimony before the FCIC, Hearing on Subprime Lending and Securitization and Government-Sponsored Enterprises (GSEs), day 3, session 2: Office of Federal Housing Enterprise Oversight, April 9, 2010, transcript, p. 163.

4. Daniel Mudd, letter to James Lockhart, August 1, 2007, p. 1.

5. Ibid., pp. 1, 5.

6. Daniel Mudd, letter to shareholders, in Fannie Mae, "2007 Annual Report," p. 3.

7. Thomas Lund, interview by FCIC, March 4, 2010.

8. Robert Levin, interview by FCIC, March 17, 2010.

9. James Lockhart, letter to Daniel Mudd, August 10, 2007, p. 1.

10. James Lockhart, letter to Senator Charles Schumer, August 10, 2007.

11. James Lockhart, written testimony for the FCIC, Hearing on Subprime Lending and Securitization and Government-Sponsored Enterprises (GSEs), day 3, session 2: Office of Federal Housing Enterprise Oversight, April 9, 2010, pp. 12, 2, 12.

12. Ibid., pp. 2, 4, 7.

13. Paulson, interview.

14. David Nason, Tony Ryan, and Jeremiah Norton, Treasury officials, interview by FCIC, March 12, 2010.

15. James Lockhart, quoted in Steven Sloan, "Setting an OFHEO Plan, But Wishing Otherwise," *American Banker*, December 21, 2007.

16. Fannie Mae, "Single-Family Book Characteristics Report," September 2008.

17. "OFHEO Provides Flexibility on Fannie Mae, Freddie Mac Mortgage Portfolios," OFHEO news release, September 19, 2007, p. 1.

18. Lockhart, written testimony for the FCIC, April 4, 2010, p. 13.

19. Ben Bernanke, quoted in Eric Dash, "Fannie Mae to Be Allowed to Expand Its Portfolio," *New York Times*, September 20, 2007.

20. Senator Charles E. Schumer, letter to OFHEO Director James B. Lockhart III, February 25, 2008; Schumer continued, "If you have decided that you will be keeping the capital surcharge in place . . . , I would like an explanation as to why you think upholding that restriction outweighs the importance of providing capital relief that could better position the GSEs to provide rescue products for borrowers stuck in unaffordable loans."

21. "Fannie Mae Reports 2007 Financial Results," Fannie Mae press release, February 17, 2008.

22. Daniel Mudd, interview by FCIC, March 26, 2010.

23. Robert Steel, email to Jeremiah Norton, February 28, 2008.

24. Michael Farrell, email to Robert Steel, March 6, 2008.

25. Emails between Robert K. Steel and Daniel Mudd, March 7, 2008.

26. Daniel Mudd, email to Robert Levin, March 7, 2008.

27. "Fannie Mae Insolvency and Its Consequences," p. 1; attachment to email from Jason Thomas to Robert Steel, March 8, 2008.

28. Robert Steel, email to David Nason, Tony Ryan, Jeremiah Norton, and Neel Kashkari, subject: "re: GSEs," March 16, 2008.

29. James Lockhart, interview by FCIC, March 19, 2010.

30. Paulson, interview.

31. James Lockhart, email to Daniel H. Mudd, Robert Steel, and Dick Syron, subject: "Re: announcement draft," March 17, 2008.

32. Ibid.

33. "OFHEO, Fannie Mae and Freddie Mac Announce Initiative to Increase Mortgage Market Liquidity," OFHEO news release, March 19, 2008.

34. Paulson, interview.

35. Joshua Rosner, "OFHEO Got Rolled," GrahamFisher Weekly Spew, March 19, 2008.

36. Donald Bisenius, interview by FCIC, September 29, 2010.

37. "Freddie Mac CEO Richard Syron Talks about the Stock Slide," *PBS Nightly Business Report*, Wednesday, August 6, 2008, transcript.

38. Lockhart, interview.

39. Daniel Mudd, letters to James Lockhart, August 1, 2008, and August 15, 2008.

40. Timothy P. Clark (senior adviser, Division of Banking and Supervision, Federal Reserve Board) and Scott Alvarez (general counsel, Federal Reserve Board), interview by FCIC, February 23, 2010.

41. "Board Grants Federal Reserve Bank of New York the Authority to Lend to Fannie Mae and Freddie Mac Should Such Lending Prove Necessary," Federal Reserve Board press release, July 13, 2008.

42. Alvarez, interview.

43. Treasury Secretary Henry Paulson, testimony on GSE initiatives, *Recent Developments in U.S. Financial Markets and the Regulatory Responses to Them*, Senate Committee on Banking, Housing, and Urban Affairs, 110th Cong., 2nd sess., July 15, 2008.

44. "Statement by Daniel H. Mudd, President and CEO," Fannie Mae press release, July 13, 2008.

45. Clark, interview

46. Mudd, interview.

47. Clark, interview.

48. Susan Eckert, Kevin Bailey, and other OCC staff, interview by FCIC, February 19, 2010.

49. Ibid.

50. Office of the Comptroller of the Currency, "Observations—Allowance Process and Methodology," August 2008 (last revised September 8, 2008), p. 3.

51. Paulson, interview.

52. Christopher H. Dickerson (FHFA Acting Deputy Director, Division of Enterprise Regulation), letter to Daniel H. Mudd (President and CEO of Fannie Mae), "Re: Notice of Proposed Capital Classification at June 30, 2008," August 22, 2008, pp. 1, 2; Christopher H. Dickerson (FHFA Acting Deputy Director, Division of Enterprise Regulation), letter to Richard F. Syron (President and CEO of Freddie Mac), "Re: Notice of Proposed Capital Classification at June 30, 2008," August 22, 2008.

53. "Draft—Mid-year Letter," pp. 11–13 (quotation, p. 13), attached to Christopher H. Dickerson, letter to Daniel H. Mudd, September 4, 2008.

54. Dickerson to Mudd, September 4, 2008; Christopher H. Dickerson, letter to Richard Syron, September 4, 2008, with "Draft Mid Year Letter" attached.

55. "Draft—Mid-year Letter" (Fannie), pp. 5–7.

56. Ibid., p. 5.

57. Ibid., p. 6.

58. Ibid., pp. 9–10.

59. "Draft Mid Year Letter" (Freddie), pp. 1, 1–2, 7.

60. Ibid., p. 8.

61. Mudd, interview.

62. Christopher H. Dickerson to James B. Lockhart III, memorandum, "Proposed Appointment of the Federal Housing Finance Agency as Conservator for the Federal Home Loan Mortgage Corporation," September 6, 2008 (hereafter Freddie conservatorship memorandum); Christopher H. Dickerson to James B. Lockhart III, memorandum, Proposed Appointment of the Federal Housing Finance Agency as Conservator for the Federal National Mortgage Association," September 6, 2008 (hereafter Fannie conservatorship memorandum).

63. Paulson, interview; Lockhart, interview; Paulson, *On the Brink*, p. 8.

64. Lockhart, testimony before the FCIC, April 9, 2010, transcript, p. 191.

65. Paulson, interview; Paulson, *On the Brink*, p. 10.

66. Paulson, *On the Brink*, p. 10.

67. Lund, interview.

68. Levin, interview.

69. Mudd, interview.

70. FHFA, Fannie conservatorship memorandum, pp. 2, 29.

71. FHFA, Freddie conservatorship memorandum, pp. 3, 29.

72. Syron, interview.

73. Daniel Mudd, testimony before the FCIC, Hearing on Subprime Lending and Securitization and Government-Sponsored Enterprises (GSEs), day 3," session 1: Fannie Mae, April 9, 2010, transcript, p. 38.

74. Paul Nash, FDIC, letter to FCIC, providing responses to follow-up questions to Sheila Bair's testimony during the September 2, 2010, hearing, p. 5.

75. Paulson, interview.

76. Neel Kashkari, interview by FCIC, November 2, 2010.

77. Tom Baxter, interview by FCIC, April 30, 2010; Kevin Warsh, interview by FCIC, October 28, 2010.

78. Warsh, interview.

79. Lockhart, testimony before the FCIC, April 9, 2010, transcript, p. 232.

80. Staff of the Federal Reserve System, Division of Banking Supervision and Regulation, memorandum to the Board of Governors, "Stress Scenarios on Bank Exposures to Government Sponsored Enterprise (GSE) Debt," January 24, 2005, p. 5.

81. Daniel Mudd, written testimony for the FCIC, Hearing on Subprime Lending and Securitization and Government-Sponsored Enterprises (GSEs), day 3, session 1: Fannie Mae, April 9, 2010, p. 3.

82. John Kerr, Scott Smith, Steve Corona (FHFA examination manager), and Alfred Pollard (FHFA general counsel), group interview by FCIC, March 12, 2010.

83. Lockhart, interview.

84. Edward DeMarco, interview by FCIC, March 18, 2010.

85. Mudd, interview.

86. Henry Cisneros, interview by FCIC, October 13, 2010.

87. Mudd, testimony before the FCIC, April 9, 2010, transcript, p. 104.

88. Robert Levin, testimony before the FCIC, Hearing on Subprime Lending and Securitization and Government-Sponsored Enterprises (GSEs), day 3, session 1: Fannie Mae, April 9, 2010, transcript, p. 104.

## Chapter 18

1. Joseph Sommer, counsel, Federal Reserve Bank of New York, email to Patrick M. Parkinson, deputy research director, Board of Governors of the Federal Reserve System, et al., "Re: another option we should present re triparty?" July 13, 2008.

2. James Dimon, interview by FCIC, October 20, 2010.

3. Barry Zubrow, testimony before the FCIC, Hearing on Too Big to Fail: Expectations and Impact of Extraordinary Government Intervention and the Role of Systemic Risk in the Financial Crisis, day 1, session 2: Lehman Brothers, September 1, 2010, p. 212.

4. Richard S. Fuld Jr., testimony before the FCIC, Hearing on Too Big to Fail: Expectations and Impact of Extraordinary Government Intervention and the Role of Systemic Risk in the Financial Crisis, day 1, session 2: Lehman Brothers, September 1, 2010, p. 148. See also Fuld's written testimony at same hearing, p. 6.

5. Ben Bernanke, testimony before the FCIC, Hearing on Too Big to Fail: Expectations and Impact of Extraordinary Government Intervention and the Role of Systemic Risk in the Financial Crisis, day 2, session 1: The Federal Reserve, September 2, 2010, transcript, pp. 26, 89.

6. Kenneth D. Lewis, interview by FCIC, October 22, 2010.

7. Bernanke, testimony before the FCIC, September 2, 2010, p. 22.

8. Bernanke told the examiner that the Federal Reserve, the SEC, and "markets in general" viewed Lehman as the next most vulnerable investment bank because of its funding model. Anton R. Valukas, Report of Examiner, *In re* Lehman Brothers Holdings Inc., et al., Debtors, Chapter 11 Case No. 08-13555 (JMP), (Bankr. S.D.N.Y.), March 11, 2010, 2:631 (hereafter cited as Valukas); see also 1:5 and n. 16, 2:609 and nn. 2133–34, 4:1417 and n. 5441, 4:1482 and n. 5728, 4:1494, and 5:1663 and n. 6269. Paulson, 2:632. Geithner told the examiner that following Bear Stearns's near collapse, he considered Lehman to be the "most exposed" investment bank, 2:631; see also 1:5 and n. 16, 2:609, 4:1417 and n. 5441, 4:1482 and n. 5728, 4:1491 and n. 5769, and 5:1663 and n. 6269. Cox reported that after Bear Stearns collapsed, Lehman was the SEC's "number one focus"; 1:5 and n. 16, and p. 1491 and n. 5769; see also 2:609, 631.

9. Timothy Geithner, quoted in Valukas, 1:8 and n. 30, 4:1496.

10. Donald L. Kohn, email to Bernanke, "Re: Lehman," June 13, 2008. Valukas, 2:615; 2:609 and n. 2134.

11. Harvey R. Miller, bankruptcy counsel for Lehman Brothers, interview by FCIC, August 5, 2010; Lehman board minutes, September 14, 2008, p. 34.

12. Erik R. Sirri, interview by FCIC, April 1, 2010.

13. Paolo R. Tonucci, interview by FCIC, August 6, 2010.

14. Specifically, Lehman drew $1.6 billion on March 18; $2.3 billion on March 19 and 20; $2.7 billion on March 24; $2.1 billion on March 25 and 26; and $2 billion on April 16. Lehman Brothers, "Presentation to the Federal Reserve: Update on Capital, Leverage & Liquidity," May 28, 2008, p. 15. See also Robert Azerad, vice president, Lehman Brothers, "2008 Q2—Liquidity Position (June 6, 2008)," p. 3. After its bankruptcy, Lehman drew $28 billion, $19.7 billion, and $20.4 billion, on September 15, 16, and 17, until Barclays replaced the Fed in providing financing. Valukas, 4:1399. See also David Weisbrod, senior vice president, Treasury and Securities Services–Risk Management, JPMorgan Chase & Co., email to James Dimon et al., "Re: TriParty Close," September 15, 2008.

15. Thomas A. Russo, former vice chairman and chief legal officer, Lehman Brothers, email to Richard S. Fuld Jr., forwarding article by John Brinsley (originally sent to Russo by Robert Steel), "Paulson Says Investment Banks Making Progress in Raising Funds," Bloomberg, June 13, 2008 (quoting Robert Steel), June 13, 2008.

16. Richard S. Fuld Jr., interview by FCIC, April 28, 2010.

17. Valukas, 2:713 and nn. 2764–65, 2:715 and n. 2774. See also Russo, email to Fuld, "Fw: Rumors of hedge fund putting together a group to have another run at Lehman," March 20, 2008 (forwarding discussions with SEC regarding short sellers).

18. Dan Chaudoin, Bruce Karpati, and Stephanie Shuler, Division of Enforcement, SEC, interview by FCIC, April 6, 2010; Mary L. Schapiro, chairman, SEC, written responses to written questions—specifically, response to question 13—from FCIC, asked after the hearing on January 14, 2010.

19. Jesse Eisinger, "The Debt Shuffle: Wall Street Cheered Lehman's Earnings, but There Are Questions about Its Balance Sheet," Portfolio.com, March 20, 2008.

20. David Einhorn, Greenlight Capital, "Private Profits and Socialized Risk," speech at Grant's Spring Investment Conference, April 8, 2008, p. 9. See also David Einhorn, "Accounting Ingenuity," speech at Ira W. Sohn Investment Research Conference, May 21, 2008, pp. 3–4.

21. Nell Minow, interview by FCIC, September 13, 2010.

22. Nell Minow, testimony before the House Committee on Oversight and Government Reform, Hearing on Lehman Brothers, 110th Cong., 2nd sess., October 6, 2008.

23. Kirsten J. Harlow, email to Timothy Geithner et al., "On-Site Primary Dealer Update: June 16," June 16, 2008.

24. William Dudley, email to Timothy Geithner, Donald Kohn, and others, June 17, 2008.

25. Kirsten J. Harlow, email to Kevin D. Coffey, examining officer, FRBNY, et al., "On-Site Primary Dealer Update: June 19," June 19, 2008.

26. Thomas Fontana, Citigroup, email to Christopher M. Foskett, Citigroup, et al., June 12, 2008.

27. Tim Clark, Federal Reserve, email to Kevin Coffey, Federal Reserve, et al., June 20, 2008.

28. Federal Reserve Bank of New York, "Primary Dealer Monitoring: Liquidity Stress Analysis," June 25, 2008.

29. Based on chart in Federal Reserve Bank of New York, "Developing Metrics for the Four Largest Securities Firms," August 2008, p. 9.

30. Federal Reserve Bank of New York, "Primary Dealer Monitoring: Liquidity Stress Analysis," June 25, 2008.

31. Karl Mocharko, assistant vice president and senior trader, Federated Investors, Inc., email to Gail Shanley, Federated Investors, Inc., et al., "Re: Federated SubCustodial Agreement—JPMC's comments," July 10, 2008; Charles Witek, Federated Investors, Inc., email to George V. Van Schaick, Lehman Brothers, et al., "FW: Federated SubCustodial Agreement—JPMC's comments," April 23, 2008. Despite the FRBNY's observation, Federated did not fully terminate its repo relationships with Lehman. In fact, as of September 12, Federated's repo exposure to Lehman was $2 billion, as reported in the Commission's Market Risk Survey of money market mutual funds.

32. Patrick M. Parkinson, email to David Marshall, et al., July 11, 2008; David Marshall, email to Patrick M. Parkinson, July 11, 2008.

33. Valukas, 4:1497–98 (quoting Timothy Geithner); see also Bart McDade, president and chief operating officer, Lehman Brothers, interview by FCIC, April 16, 2010.

34. William Dudley, email to Geithner et al., "Re: Lehman Good Bank/Bad Bank idea discussed last night," July 15, 2008.

35. Patrick M. Parkinson, email to Steven Shafran, Department of the Treasury, et al., "Fw: Gameplan and Status to Date," August 19, 2008.

36. Patrick M. Parkinson, email to Steven Shafran, August 11, 2008.

37. Patrick M. Parkinson, email to Arthur Angulo, Theodore Lubke, Til Schuermann, and William Brodows, August 15, 2010.

38. William Brodows, email to Patrick Parkinson, August 15, 2008.

39. Ibid.

40. Ibid.

41. Parkinson, email to Steven Shafran, August 19, 2008.

42. Ibid.

43. Steven Shafran, email to Patrick M. Parkinson, August 28, 2008.

44. Patrick M. Parkinson, email to Theodore Lubke, September 5, 2008.

45. Emil Cornejo, senior vice president, Department of the Treasury, Lehman Brothers, email to Janet Birney, senior vice president, Department of the Treasury, Lehman Brothers, et al., "JP Morgan Agenda forwarded for our review. FYI," September 3, 2008. See Lehman Briefing Memorandum, September 4, 2008; JP Morgan Agenda, September 4, 2008.

46. Meg McConnell, FRBNY, email to Arthur Angulo et al., "Meeting tomorrow at 9:00," September 8, 2008.

47. Ibid.

48. Patrick M. Parkinson, email to Steven Shafran, "Re: now I am on a conf call," September 9, 2008.

49. Henry M. Paulson Jr., *On the Brink: Inside the Race to Stop the Collapse of the Global Financial System* (New York: Business Plus, 2010), p. 178; Rita C. Proctor, assistant to the chairman, Board of Governors of the Federal Reserve, email to Donald L. Kohn et al., "This evening's conference call will take place at 5 P.M. instead of 6 P.M.," September 9, 2008.

50. Jim Wilkinson, email to Michele Davis, September 9, 2008.

51. Barry Zubrow, interview by FCIC, August 19, 2010.

52. Paul, Weiss, counsel to Steven Black, letter to FCIC, August 27, 2007, written responses to FCIC questions in email of August 26, 2007, p. 6.

53. John J. Hogan, JPMorgan Chase & Co., email to Steven D. Black, September 9, 2008, 7:07 P.M.; Steven Black, email to John Hogan, September 9, 2008, 8:24 P.M. See also Valukas, 4:1139, 1140 and n. 4204, and 1141.

54. Complaint, *In re* Lehman Brothers Holdings, Inc., et al., against JPMorgan Chase Bank, N.A., Chapter 11 Case No. 08-13555 (JMP) (Bankr. S.D.N.Y. May 26, 2010), pp. 14–15 (hereafter cited as Lehman Complaint).

55. Ibid.

56. Black responses, August 27, 2010, p. 6.

57. Matthew Rutherford, email to Tony Ryan, Department of the Treasury, et al., September 10, 2008.

58. Mark VanDerWeide, assistant general counsel, Board of Governors of the Federal Reserve System, email to Scott G. Alvarez, general counsel, Board of Governors of the Federal Reserve System, "lehman," September 10, 2008.

59. Patricia Mosser, email to William Dudley et al., "thoughts on Lehman," September 10, 2008.

60. See Michael Nelson, counsel and vice president, FRBNY, email to Christine Cumming, first vice president, FRBNY, et al., "revised Liquidation Consortium gameplan + questions," September 10, 2008, (attaching game plan),

61. See Patrick M. Parkinson, email to Donald Kohn et al., "Fw: revised Liquidation Consortium gameplan + questions," September 11, 2008 (attaching game plan).

62. Ibid.; Thomas Baxter, interview by FCIC, August 11, 2010.

63. Ken Lewis, interview by FCIC, October 22, 2010.

64. Susan McCabe, Goldman Sachs Group, Inc., email to William Dudley et al., "Hope you have the Radar screens on early this morning," September 11, 2008.

65. Rita C. Proctor, email to Bernanke, "Fw: Financial Markets Conference Call 9/11/08," September 11, 2008 (forwarding to Chairman Bernanke materials for the conference call).

66. Hayley Boesky, vice president, Markets Group, FRBNY, email to Meg McConnell et al., forwarding Louis Bacon, email to Hayley Boesky, "FW: Options for short-circuiting the market," September 11, 2008, 10:46 A.M.

67. Email chain between Jamie McAndrews, Tobias Adrian, Patrick Parkinson and Jeff Stehm, subject : "Fw : Default Management Group 9 Sep 2008.doc," September 11, 2008.

68. Hayley Boesky, email to Debby Perelmuter, senior vice president, FRBNY, et al., "Panic," September 11, 2008.

69. Jane Buyers-Russo, managing director, JP Morgan, email to Paolo R. Tonucci, "Fw: Letter to Lehman," Sept. 11, 2008, (attaching JPMorgan Chase & Co.'s September 11, 2008, Notice to Lehman Brothers Holdings Inc.).

70. Jane Buyers-Russo, email to Bryn Thomas, executive director, Broker Dealer Group, JPMorgan Chase & Co., et al., "Re: Lehman Brothers TriParty Collateral," September 12, 2008.

71. Paolo R. Tonucci, interview by FCIC, August 6, 2010.

72. See Valukas, 4:1158–65, 1162 and n. 4304.

73. Lehman Complaint, pp. 22–23, paragraphs 68, 71.

74. Barry Zubrow, written testimony for the FCIC, Hearing on Too Big to Fail: Expectations and Impact of Extraordinary Government Intervention and the Role of Systemic Risk in the Financial Crisis, day 1, session 2: Lehman Brothers, September 1, 2010, p. 7.

75. Richard S. Fuld, interview by FCIC, August 24, 2010.

76. Lehman Complaint, p. 23, paragraph 70.

77. Jim Wilkinson, email to Abby Aderman, Russell Reynolds Associates, "Re: Paulson Statement on Treasury and FHFA Action to Protect Financial Markets and Taxpayers," September 12, 2008.

78. Kevin M. Warsh, e-mail to J. Nellie Liang, senior associate director, Division of Research and Statistics, Board of Governors of the Federal Reserve System, September 12, 2008.

79. Valukas, 2:618.

80. Harvey R. Miller, interview by FCIC, August 5, 2010.

81. Tom Baxter, "Speaking notes: Financial Community Meeting," attached to email from Helen Ayala, NYFRB, to Steven Shafron, Treasure, September 12, 2008.

82. Thomas C. Baxter, interview by FCIC, August 11, 2010.

83. H. Rodgin Cohen, interview by FCIC, August 5, 2010.

84. Parkinson, email to Kohn et al., September 11, 2008.

85. Financial Services Authority of the United Kingdom, "Statement of the Financial Services Authority" before the Lehman bankruptcy examiner, pp. 4–5, paragraph 23.

86. Paulson, *On the Brink,* p. 193.

87. Patrick M. Parkinson, email to Lucinda Brickler, senior vice president, payments policy, FRBNY, "Re: triparty repo thoughts for this weekend," September 12, 2008.

88. Patrick M. Parkinson, interview by FCIC, August 24, 2010; see also Patrick M. Parkinson, email to Lucinda Brickler et al., "Re: another option we should present re triparty?" July 13, 2008.

89. John Thain, interview by FCIC, September 17, 2010.

90. Christopher Tsuboi, examiner, bank supervision/operational risk, FRBNY, email to Alejandro LaTorre, assistant vice president, Credit, Investment and Payment Risk Group, FRBNY, "memo re: Lehman's inter-company default scenario," September 13, 2008.

91. Scott Alvarez, email to Ben Bernanke et al., "Re: Fw: today at 7:00 p.m. w/Chairman Bernanke, Vice Chairman Kohn and Others," September 13, 2008.

92. Scott Alvarez, email to Mark VanDerWeide, "Re: tri-party," September 13, 2008.

93. Bart McDade, interview by FCIC, August 9, 2010.

94. Baxter, interview.

95. Paulson, *On the Brink,* p. 207.

96. Baxter, interview; Robert Diamond, interview by FCIC, November 15, 2010.

97. Paulson, *On the Brink,* pp. 212–13.

98. Financial Services Authority of the United Kingdom, "Statement of the Financial Services Authority" before the Lehman bankruptcy examiner, p. 9, paragraph 48.

99. Paulson, *On the Brink,* pp. 209–10. See also Baxter, interview.

100. Baxter, interview.

101. Jim Wilkinson, email to Jes Staley, September 14, 2008, 7:46 A.M.

102. Jim Wilkinson, email to Jes Staley, September 14, 2008, 9:00 A.M.

103. Paulson, *On the Brink,* p. 210.

104. Alistair Darling, quoted in United Kingdom Press Association, "Darling Vetoed Lehman Bros Takeover," *Belfast Telegraph,* October 9, 2010.

105. H. Rodgin Cohen, interview by FCIC, August 5, 2010.

106. Bart McDade, interview by FCIC, August 9, 2010.

107. Alex Kirk, interview by FCIC, August 16, 2010; McDade, interview, August 9, 2010.

108. Baxter, interview.

109. Thomas C. Baxter, letter to FCIC, October 15, 2010, attaching Exhibit 6, James P. Bergin, email to William Dudley et al., "Bankruptcy," September 14, 2008. See also Kirk, interview.

110. Ibid., attaching Exhibit 5, Lehman Brothers Holdings Inc., "Minutes of the Board of Directors, September 14, 2008," p. 2.

111. Ibid., attaching Exhibits 2 and 8.

112. On September 15, 2008, LBI borrowed $28 billion from PDCF against $31.7 billion of collateral; on September 16, 2008, LBI borrowed $19.7 billion against $23 billion of collateral; and on September 17, 2008, LBI borrowed $20.4 billion against $23.3 billion of collateral. See Valukas, 4:1399 and nn. 5374–75.

113. Kirk, interview.

114. Miller, interview.

115. Kirk, interview.

116. Miller, interview. In his interview, Kirk told FCIC staff that he thought there were more than 1 million derivatives contracts.

117. McDade, interview, August 9, 2010.

118. Baxter, interview.

119. Harvey R. Miller, written testimony for the FCIC, Hearing on Too Big to Fail: Expectations and Impact of Extraordinary Government Intervention and the Role of Systemic Risk in the Financial Crisis, day 1, session 2: Lehman Brothers, September 1, 2010, p. 8.

120. Miller, interview.

121. Ibid.

122. Ibid.

123. Ben S. Bernanke, closed-door session with FCIC, November 17, 2009.

124. Ibid.

125. Henry M. Paulson Jr., written testimony for the FCIC, Hearing on the Shadow Banking System, day 2, session 1: Perspective on the Shadow Banking System, May 6, 2010, p. 55.

126. Miller, written testimony for the FCIC, September 1, 2010, p. 14.

127. Ibid., p. 18.

128. Ibid., pp. 6, 12–13, 15, 11, 15.

129. Bernanke, testimony before the FCIC, September 2, 2010, transcript, p. 23.

130. Ben Bernanke, email to Kevin Warsh, member, Board of Governors of the Federal Reserve System, September 14, 2008.

131. Bernanke, testimony before the FCIC, September 2, 2010, p. 22.

132. Ibid., p. 24.

133. Ben Bernanke, "U.S. Financial Markets," testimony before the Senate Committee on Banking, Housing, and Urban Affairs, 110th Cong., 2nd sess., September 23, 2008.

134. 12 U.S.C. § 343, as added by act of July 21, 1932 (47 Stat. 715); and amended by acts of August 23, 1935 (49 Stat. 714), December 19, 1991 (105 Stat. 2386), and July 21, 2010 (124 Stat. 2113).

135. Scott G. Alvarez et al., memorandum, "Authority of the Federal Reserve to provide extensions of credit in connection with a commercial paper funding facility (CPFF)," March 9, 2009, p. 7.

136. Fuld, written testimony for the FCIC, September 1, 2010, pp. 7, 6, 3.

137. Bernanke, closed-door session with FCIC.

138. Ben S. Bernanke, chairman of the Federal Reserve, letter to Phil Angelides, chairman of the FCIC, December 21, 2010.

139. Thain, interview.

140. Ibid.

141. Ibid.

142. Dimon, interview.

143. Scott G. Alvarez, testimony before the FCIC, Hearing on Too Big to Fail: Expectations and Impact of Extraordinary Government Intervention and the Role of Systemic Risk in the Financial Crisis, day 1, session 1: Wachovia Corporation, September 1, 2010, transcript, p. 95. See also Baxter, letter to FCIC, October 15, 2010, p. 6.

## Chapter 19

1. Federal Reserve Bank of New York, notes about AIG meeting, September 12, 2008.

2. Ibid.

3. Ibid.

4. "AIG Commercial Paper Outstanding & Maturities—week of Sept 15th," September 16, 2008, produced by JPMorgan.

5. American International Group, Inc., Form 10-Q for the quarterly period ended June 30, 2008.

6. FRBNY, notes about AIG meeting.

7. Goldman Sachs International, Collateral Invoice (margin call) to AIG Financial Products Corp., July 27, 2007; data on collateral exposures and multisector CDOs supplied by AIG (see Timeline of Goldman Sachs/AIG collateral calls, pp. 50, 392, 404, available at the FCIC website at http://fcic.gov/hearings/pdfs/2010–0701-AIG-Goldman-supporting-docs.pdf); FRBNY, notes about AIG meeting.

8. Alejandro LaTorre, email to Christine Cumming, Timothy Geithner, William Dudley, et al., "Update on AIG," September 12, 2008.

9. FRBNY, notes about AIG meeting.

10. Mark Hutchings, interview by FCIC, June 22, 2010.

11. Eric Dinallo, testimony before the FCIC, Hearing on the Role of Derivatives in the Financial Crisis, day 2, session 2: Derivatives: Supervisors and Regulators, July 1, 2010, transcript, pp. 3,16.

12. Michael Moriarty, testimony before the Congressional Oversight Panel, Hearing on American International Group, 111th Cong., 2nd sess., May 26, 2010, p. 4.

13. Dinallo, testimony before the FCIC, July 1, 2010, pp. 16–17.

14. FRBNY, notes about AIG meeting.

15. Ibid.

16. "Systemic Impact of AIG Bankruptcy," attachment to FRBNY internal email from Alejandro LaTorre to Timothy Geithner, September 16, 2008.

17. FRBNY, internal memo about August 11, 2008, meeting with the AIG team of the Office of Thrift Supervision.

18. Ibid.

19. FRBNY, internal document about AIG, August 14, 2008.

20. Ibid.

21. Goldman Sachs, company update on AIG, August 18, 2008.

22. Ira Selig, email to Kevin Coffey, "Goldman Report on AIG," August 18, 2008.

23. FRBNY, internal document about AIG, September 2, 2008.

24. Ibid.

25. Ibid.; Goldman Sachs, company update on AIG, August 18, 2008.

26. FRBNY, notes about AIG meeting, September 12, 2008.

27. Ibid.

28. "AIG Commercial Paper Outstanding & Maturities—week of Sept 15th," September 16, 2008.

29. FRBNY, notes about AIG meeting, September 12, 2008.

30. Hayley Boesky, email to Bill Dudley et al., "AIG panic," September 12, 2008.

31. FRBNY, emails of September 12 and 13, 2008.

32. Thomas Baxter, interview by FCIC, April 30, 2010.

33. Robert Willumstad, interview by FCIC, November 15, 2010.

34. Patricia Mosser, email to Alejandro LaTorre et al., re: AIG/Board call, September 13, 2008, 12:54 P.M.

35. Patricia Mosser, email to Alejandro Latorre et al., September 13, 2008, 7:26 P.M.

36. FRBNY, internal memo about AIG, September 14, 2008.

37. Adam Ashcraft, email to Alejandro LaTorre et al., "AIG and the discount window," September 14, 2008.

38. Alejandro LaTorre, email to Adam Ashcraft et al., September 14, 2008.

39. Ibid.

40. J. C. Flowers, interview by FCIC, October 7, 2010.

41. Robert Willumstad, interview by FCIC, November 15, 2010.

42. Ibid.

43. Goldman Sachs International, Collateral Invoice to AIG Financial Products Group, September 15, 2008.

44. Data supplied by AIG (Tab 31 of the AIG/Goldman Sachs collateral call timeline).

45. Baxter, interview.

46. See Sarah Dahlgren, FRBNY, interview by FCIC, April 30, 2010.

47. Ibid.

48. Alexander J. Psomas, email to NY Bank Sup AIG Monitoring and Analysis, September 15, 2005.

49. Fed Chairman Ben Bernanke, letter to FCIC Chairman Phil Angelides, December 21, 2010.

50. Federal Reserve Board of Governors, press release, September 16, 2008.

51. Congressional Oversight Panel, "The AIG Rescue, Its Impact on Markets, and the Government's Exit Strategy," June 10, 2010, p. 98.

52. Ibid., executive summary, pp. 1, 8.

53. Treasury spokesman Andrew Williams, quoted in Hugh Son, "AIG's Rescue Had 'Poisonous' Effect, U.S. Panel Says (Update1)," *Bloomberg*, June 10, 2010.

54. Scott M. Polakoff, "American International Group's Impact on the Global Economy: Before, during, and after Federal Intervention," testimony before the. House Committee on Financial Services, Subcommittee on Capital Markets, Insurance, and Government Sponsored Enterprises, 111th Cong., 1st sess., March 18, 2009.

55. John Reich, interview by FCIC, May 4, 2010.

56. Michael E. Finn, prepared testimony before the Congressional Oversight Panel, May 26, 2010.

57. C. K. Lee, interview by FCIC, April 28, 2010. See also Memorandum of Understanding between Scott M. Albinson, managing director, OTS, and Danièle Nouy, secrétaire général de la Commission Bancaire, April 11, 2005.

58. OTS, Memo to Commission Bancaire regarding its supervisory role, January 2005.

59. Reich, interview.

60. Joseph Gonzalez, interview by FCIC, May 7, 2010.

61. Ibid.

62. OTS, Targeted Review of AIG Financial Products Corp., July 13, 2007.

63. AIG/Goldman Sachs collateral call timeline, p. 50.

64. Brad Waring, interview by FCIC, May 7, 2010.

65. Reich, interview.

66. Ibid.

## Chapter 20

1. John J. Mack, written testimony for the FCIC, First Public Hearing of the FCIC, day 1, panel 1: Financial Institution Representatives, January 13, 2010, p. 6.

2. Jamie Dimon, interview by FCIC, October 20, 2010.

3. Timothy Geithner, interview by FCIC, November 17, 2009.

4. Timothy Geithner, quoted by Robert Schmidt, "Geithner Slams Bonuses, Says Banks Would Have Failed (Update2)," *Bloomberg*, December 4, 2009.

5. Ben Bernanke, closed-door session with FCIC, November 17, 2009.

6. Specifically, the Fed broadened the PDCF to match the types of collateral that the two major clearing banks accepted in the tri-party repo system, including non-investment-grade securities and equities; previously, PDCF collateral had been limited to investment-grade debt securities. The Fed similarly broadened the TSLF to include all investment-grade debt securities; previously, TSLF collateral had been limited to Treasury securities, agency securities, and AAA-rated mortgage-backed and asset-backed securities. The Fed also increased both the frequency of TSLF auctions, to weekly instead of every two weeks, and their size. Federal Reserve Board press release, September 14, 2008.

7. On September 30, Goldman Sachs had a $15 billion balance in TSLF, and a $16.5 billion balance in PDCF. Federal Reserve Board, "Regulatory Reform: Usage of Federal Reserve Credit and Liquidity Facilities," PDCF.

8. Lehman initially asserted that there were around 930,000 derivative transactions at the time of bankruptcy. See Debtors' Motion for an Order pursuant to Sections 105 and 365 of the Bankruptcy Code to Establish Procedures for the Settlement or Assumption and Assignment of Prepetition Derivatives Contracts, Lehman Brothers Holdings Inc., et al, No. 08-13555 (Bankr. S.D.N.Y. Nov. 13, 2008), p. 4. See also Anton R. Valukas, Report of Examiner, *In re* Lehman Brothers Holdings Inc., et al., Chapter 11 Case No. 08-13555 (JMP), (Bankr. S.D.N.Y.), March 11, 2010, 2:573. By November 13, 2008, a special facility to unwind derivatives trades with Lehman had successfully terminated most of the 930,000 derivative contracts. Nevertheless, in January 2009, Lehman's counsel reported that 18,000 derivatives contracts had not been terminated. Moreover, there are massive unresolved claims relating to over-the-counter derivatives in the bankruptcy proceeding: as of May 2010, banks had filed more than $50 billion in claims for losses related to derivatives contracts with Lehman. See Debtors' Motion for an Order pursuant to

Sections 105 and 365 of the Bankruptcy Code to Establish Procedures for the Settlement or Assumption and Assignment of Prepetition Derivatives Contracts, Lehman Brothers Holdings Inc., et al., No. 08-13555 (Bankr. S.D.N.Y. Nov. 13, 2008) [Docket No. 1498], p. 4; Debtors' Motion for an Order Approving Consensual Assumption and Assignment of Prepetition Derivatives Contracts, Lehman Brothers Holdings Inc., et al., No. 08-13555 (Bankr. S.D.N.Y. Jan. 16, 2009) [Docket No.2561], p. 3.

9. Money market fund holdings of all types of taxable commercial paper decreased from $671 billion at the end of August 2008 to $505 billion at the end of September (data provided by ICI/Crane to the FCIC). BNY Mellon, in its role as tri-party clearing bank, reported that Treasury-backed repos rose from $195 billion (13%) to $466 billion (27%) of its tri-party business between March 31 and December 31, 2008 (data provided by BNY Mellon to the FCIC).

10. Harvey Miller, interview by FCIC, August 5, 2010.

11. The Reserve Fund, Semi-annual report to shareholders, March 2006.

12. Complaint, SEC v. Reserve Management Company Inc., Resrv Partners Inc., Bruce Bent Sr., Bruce Bent II, and The Reserve Primary Fund (S.D.N.Y. May 5, 2009), p. 12 (para. 35); "Fidelity, BlackRock, Dreyfus, Reserve Make Big Gains Past 12 Months," Crane Data News Archives, September 12, 2008.

13. The Reserve Primary Fund management, interview by FCIC, March 25, 2010.

14. SEC Complaint against Reserve Management Company Inc., pp. 2, 18 (paras. 3, 59), p. 30 (para. 101); The Reserve, "The Primary Fund: Plan of Liquidation and Distribution of Assets," December 3, 2008, p. 2.

15. SEC Complaint, pp. 26–33 (paras. 88–113); The Reserve, "The Primary Fund: Plan of Liquidation," p. 2.

16. SEC Complaint, p. 35 (para. 121). The SEC notes that the Primary Fund likely broke the buck prior to 11:00 A.M. on September 16 because of the redemption requests and the valuation of Lehman's debt; moreover, RMCI announced on November 26, 2008, that owing to an administrative error, its NAV should have been calculated as $0.99 between 11:00 A.M. and 4:00 P.M. on September 16 (pp. 34–33, paras. 119, 120).

17. Moody's Investors Service articles, "Sponsor Support Key to Money Market Funds," August 9, 2010, p. 4; "Moody's Proposes New Money Market Fund Rating Methodology and Symbols," September 7, 2010.

18. Patrick McCabe and Michael Palumbo, interview by FCIC, September 28, 2010.

19. Ibid.

20. Investment Company Institute, Historical Weekly Money Market Data. While nongovernment funds lost $434 billion during the period between September 10 and October 1, 2008, government funds—investing in Treasuries and GSE debt—increased by $357 billion during the same period.

21. McCabe and Palumbo, interview.

22. FCIC survey of money market mutual funds. Holdings for the five firms decreased from $58 billion to $29 billion from September 12, 2008, to September 19, 2008. See FCIC website for details.

23. Timothy Geithner, testimony before the FCIC, Hearing on the Shadow Banking System, day 2, session 2: Perspective on the Shadow Banking System, May 6, 2010, transcript, p. 135.

24. McCabe and Palumbo, interview.

25. "Treasury Announces Guaranty Program for Money Market Funds," Treasury Department press release, September 19, 2008. President George W. Bush approved the use of existing authorities by Secretary Henry M. Paulson Jr. to make available as necessary the assets of the Exchange Stabilization Fund (ESF) for up to $50 billion to guarantee payments to support money market mutual funds. The original objective of the ESF, established by the Gold Reserve Act of 1934, was to stabilize the value of the dollar in the depths of the Depression. It authorized the treasury secretary, with the approval of the president, to "deal in gold, foreign exchange, and other instruments of credit and securities" to promote international financial stability.

26. The program was called the Asset-Backed Commercial Paper Money Market Mutual Fund Liquidity Facility (AMLF).

27. Neel Kashkari, interview by FCIC, November 2, 2010.

28. John Mack, interview by FCIC, November 2, 2010.

29. New York Federal Reserve, internal email, October 22, 2008, p. 2.

30. David Wong, email to Fed and SEC officials, September 15, 2008.

31. Jonathan Stewart, FRBNY, internal email, September 17, 2008.

32. One year later, the Senior Supervisors Group—a cross-agency task force looking back on the causes of the financial crisis—would write, "Before the crisis [at the investment banks post-Lehman], many broker-dealers considered the prime brokerage business to be either a source of liquidity or a liquidity-neutral business. As a result, the magnitude and unprecedented severity of events in September–October 2008 were largely unanticipated." Senior Supervisors Group, "Risk Management Lessons from the Global Banking Crisis of 2008," October 21, 2009, p. 9.

33. Jonathan Wood, Whitebox Advisors, interview by FCIC, August 11, 2010.

34. The FCIC surveyed hedge funds that survived the crisis. Those in the three largest quartiles ranked by size received investor redemption requests averaging 20% of their assets in the fourth quarter of 2008 (the first available redemption date after the Lehman bankruptcy).

35. IFSL Research, "Hedge Funds 2009," April 2009.

36. David Wong, treasurer of Morgan Stanley, interview by FCIC, October 15, 2010.

37. Mack, interview.

38. Wong, interview.

39. Patrice Maher (Morgan Stanley), email to William Brodows (Federal Reserve BNY) et al., September 28, 2008, with data in an attachment. Hedge fund values are the Prime Brokerage Outflows (NY+International).

40. Wong, interview.

41. Matthew Eichner, internal email, September 16, 2008.

42. Angela Miknius, email to NY Bank Sup, September 18, 2008.

43. Amy G. White, internal NYFBR email, September 19, 2008.

44. Morgan Stanley, "Liquidity and Financing Activity: 08/28/08," "Liquidity and Financing Activity: 09/18/08," "Liquidity and Financing Activity: 10/03/08," reports to the New York Federal Reserve.

45. Morgan Stanley Corporate Treasury, "Meeting with Federal Reserve: September 20, 2008," attachment to Morgan Stanley email to NYFRB, September 20, 2008, including "Forward Forecast."

46. Morgan Stanley Corporate Treasury, "Liquidity Landscape: 09/12–09/18/2008," in attachment to Morgan Stanley email to NYFRB, September 20, 2008; Amy White, internal NYFRB emails, September 16 and 19, 2008.

47. Lloyd Blankfein, testimony before the FCIC, First Public Hearing of the FCIC, day 1, panel 1: Financial Institution Representatives, January 13, 2010, transcript, pp. 34–35.

48. Bernanke, closed-door session.

49. Thomas Baxter, interview by FCIC, April 30, 2010.

50. The switch to bank holding company status required a simple charter change. Both Morgan and Goldman already owned banks that they had chartered as industrial loan companies, a type of bank that is allowed to accept FDIC-insured deposits without having any Fed supervision over the bank's parent or other affiliated companies.

51. Federal Reserve, "Discount Window Payment System Risk: Getting Started," last updated November 17, 2009.

52. Mack, interview.

53. Mack, interview.

54. Wong, interview.

55. Amy G. White, internal FRBNY email, September 19, 2008.

56. It should be borne in mind that lack of regulation of this market rendered it extremely opaque. Shortcomings in transparency, lack of reporting requirements, and limited data collection by third parties make it difficult to document and describe the various market trading problems that emerged during the crisis.

57. Michael Masters, testimony before the FCIC, Hearing on the Role of Derivatives in the Financial Crisis, day 1, session 1: Overview of Derivatives, June 30, 2010, transcript, p. 26.

58. Depository Trust and Clearing Corporation data provided to the FCIC.

59. "The Global OTC Derivatives Market at End-June 1998," Bank of International Settlements press release, December 13, 1998; "OTC derivatives market activity in the second half of 2008," Bank of International Settlements press release, May 9, 2009, p. 7.

60. "Triennial and Regular OTC Derivatives Market Statistics," Bank of International Settlements press release, November 16, 2010, p. 7.

61. Moody's, "Moody's downgrades WaMu Ratings; outlook negative," September 11, 2008.

62. "OTS Fact Sheet on Washington Mutual Bank," OTS 08–046A, September 25, 2008, p. 3.

63. Jamie Dimon, interview by FCIC, October 20, 2010.

64. Sheila Bair, testimony before the FCIC, Hearing on Too Big to Fail: Expectations and Impact of Extraordinary Government Intervention and the Role of Systemic Risk in the Financial Crisis, day 2: session 2: Federal Deposit Insurance Corporation, September 2, 2010, exchange between Bair and Commissioner Douglas Holtz-Eakin, pp. 134, 149.

65. Scott Alvarez, testimony before the FCIC, Hearing on Too Big to Fail: Expectations and Impact of Extraordinary Government Intervention and the Role of Systemic Risk in the Financial Crisis, day 1, Session 1: Wachovia Corporation, September 1, 2010, transcript, p. 84.

66. Kashkari, interview.

67. Greg Feldberg, "Wachovia Case Study," presentation at LBO Supervision Conference, November 12–13, 2008, Atlanta, Georgia, p. 15. These rules, embodied in section 23A of the Federal Reserve Act, limit the support that a depository institution can provide to related companies in the same corporate structure; they are aimed at protecting FDIC-insured depositors from activities that occur outside of the bank itself. Exemptions have the effect of funding affiliate, nonbank assets within the federal safety net of insured deposits; they create liquidity for the parent company and/or key affiliates (and reduce bank liquidity) during times of market stress.

68. Robert Steel, interview by FCIC, August 18, 2010.

69. Scott Alvarez, written testimony for the FDIC, September 1, 2010, p. 4.

70. Robert Steel, written testimony before the FCIC, Hearing on Too Big to Fail: Expectations and Impact of Extraordinary Government Intervention and the Role of Systemic Risk in the Financial Crisis, day 1, session 1: Wachovia Corporation, September 1, 2010, p. 2.

71. David Wilson, interview by FCIC, August 4, 2010.

72. Sheila Bair, interview by FCIC, August 18, 2010.

73. Richard Westerkamp, Federal Reserve Bank of Richmond, interview by FCIC, August 13, 2010.

74. Wachovia was unable to roll $1.1 billion of asset-backed commercial paper that Friday; James Wigand and Herbert Held, memo to the FDIC Board of Directors, September 29, 2008, p. 2. On brokered certificates of deposit, see Westerkamp, interview.

75. John Corston, acting deputy director, Division of Supervision and Consumer Protection, FDIC, written testimony before the FCIC, Hearing on Too Big to Fail: Expectations and Impact of Extraordinary Government Intervention and the Role of Systemic Risk in the Financial Crisis, day 1, Session 1: Wachovia Corporation, September 1, 2010, p. 4.

76. Wilson, interview.

77. Rich Westerkamp, email to FCIC, November 2, 2010. Westerkamp said that the estimate of early redemption requests was based on a phone conversation with officials in Wachovia's treasury department, describing their conversations with investors; the figures were never verified.

78. Bair, interview.

79. Robert Steel, interview by FCIC, August 18, 2010.

80. Bair, interview; Steel, interview; FDIC staff, interview by FCIC re Wachovia, July 16, 2010.

81. Alvarez, written testimony for the FCIC, September 1, 2010, p. 5.

82. Steel, interview.

83. Ibid.

84. Wigand and Held, memo to the FDIC board, September 29, 2008, pp. 2, 4–5.

85. Federal Reserve staff, memo to the Board of Governors, subject: "Considerations Regarding Invoking the Systemic Risk Exception for Wachovia Bank, NA," September 28, 2008, p. 7.

86. John A. Beebe, Market Risk Team Leader, Federal Reserve Bank of Richmond, memo to Jennifer Burns, VP-LCBO, "Wachovia Large Funds Providers," September 27, 2008, pp. 1–2.

87. Federal Reserve staff, memo to the Board of Governors, subject: "Considerations Regarding Invoking the Systemic Risk Exception for Wachovia Bank, NA," September 28, 2008, p. 7.

88. Bair, interview; minutes of the telephonic meeting of Federal Deposit Insurance Corporation Board of Directors, September 29, 2008, p. 8.

89. Bair, interview.

90. FDIC memo to the FDIC Board of Directors, p. 8; Corston, written testimony for the FCIC, September 1, 2010, p. 10.

91. Specifically, under Wachovia's proposal, the FDIC would provide credit protection on $200 billion of loans, while Wachovia would absorb the first $25 billion in losses and the FDIC would potentially incur losses on the balance of the $200 billion. To offset that risk, Wachovia proposed that the FDIC receive $10 billion in preferred stock and warrants on common shares (FDIC memo to the FDIC Board of Directors, p. 8).

92. The FDIC board has five members: the comptroller of the currency, the director of OTS, and three other members appointed by the president. In *Too Big to Fail: The Inside Story of How Wall Street and Washington Fought to Save the Financial System from Crisis—and Themselves* (New York: Viking, 2009), Andrew Ross Sorkin (p. 497) wrote that before the September 29, 2008, FDIC board meeting, New York Federal Reserve Governor Geithner and other officials had a conference call with Bair (Paulson recused himself) during which Geithner urged Bair to help Citigroup acquire Wachovia by guaranteeing some of its potential losses. Geithner argued that allowing the FDIC to take over Wachovia would have the effect of wiping out shareholders and bond holders, which, he was convinced, would only spook the markets. He was still furious with Bair for the way she had abruptly taken over Washington Mutual, which had had a deleterious effect on investor confidence.

93. Federal Deposit Insurance Corporation Board of Directors meeting, September 29, 2008, transcript, pp. 21–22.

94. Minutes of telephonic meeting of the FDIC board, September 29, 2008, p. 8.

95. Ibid.; the $34.6 billion figure is as of September 30, 2008 (FDIC staff, memo to the Board of Directors, subject: "Third Quarter 2008 CFO Report to the Board," November 21, 2008, p. 1).

96. Minutes of telephonic meeting of the FDIC board, September 29, 2008, p. 8.

97. Bair, interview.

98. Steel, written testimony for the FCIC, September 1, 2010, p. 4. On the board's vote and the agreement in principle, see Steel, interview; see also Affidavit of Robert K. Steel, dated October 5, 2008, filed in Wachovia Corp. v. Citigroup, Inc., Case No. 08-cv-085093-SAS (S.D.N.Y.), pp. 3–4 and exhibit A.

99. Fed Chairman Ben Bernanke, letter to FCIC Chairman Phil Angelides, December 21, 2010.

100. Wachtell, Lipton, Rosen & Katz, on behalf of Wells, letter to Division of Corporation Finance, SEC, November 17, 2008, p. 3.

101. Richard Kovacevich, interview by FCIC, August 24, 2010.

102. Bair, interview.

103. Steel, interview.

104. Bair, interview. In his interview, Treasury's Kashkari told the FCIC that he disagreed. He felt that the highest priority was to transfer the risk of banks' troubled assets from the financial system to the government. Citigroup's FDIC-assisted acquisition would have removed potential losses on $270 billion of assets from the financial system by transferring those potential losses to the FDIC.

105. "Wells Fargo, Wachovia Agree to Merge: Creating Premier Coast-To-Coast Financial Services Franchise without Government Assistance," Wells Fargo press release, October 3, 2008.

106. Rich Delmar, Treasury Office of the Inspector General, interview by FCIC, August 25, 2010; Rich Delmar, memorandum for Inspector General Eric M. Thorson, "Inquiry Regarding IRS Notice 2008-83," September 3, 2009, pp. 3, 5, 11–12.

107. Richard Levy, interview by FCIC, August 19, 2010.

108. "Statement by Secretary Henry M. Paulson, Jr. on Comprehensive Approach to Market Developments," Treasury Department press release, September 19, 2008.

109. Senators Christopher J. Dodd and Richard C. Shelby, remarks before the Senate Committee on Banking, Housing, and Urban Affairs, *Turmoil in U.S. Credit Markets: Recent Actions Regarding Government-Sponsored Entities, Investment Banks, and Other Financial Institutions*, 110th Cong., 2nd sess., September 23, 2008, transcript, pp. 3, 6.

110. Secretary Henry Paulson, testimony before the Senate Banking Committee, *Turmoil in the U.S. Credit Markets*, transcript, p. 37.

111. Fed Chairman Ben Bernanke, "Economic Outlook," testimony before the Joint Economic Committee, 110th Cong., 2nd sess., September 24, 2008, transcript.

112. Fed Chairman Ben Bernanke, testimony before the House Financial Services Committee, *The Future of Financial Services: Exploring Solutions for the Market Crisis*, September 24, 2008, transcript, p. 48.

113. Mel Martinez, interview by FCIC, September 28, 2010.

114. The TARP legislation, drafted as the Emergency Economic Stabilization Act of 2008, was coupled in Public Law 110-343 with several other vote-attracting acts, including the Energy Improvement and Extension Act of 2008, the Tax Extenders and Alternative Minimum Tax Relief Act of 2008, the Paul Wellstone and Pete Domenici Mental Health Parity and Addiction Equity Act of 2008, and the Heartland and Hurricane Ike Disaster Relief Act of 2008. Congress originally said that the deposit insurance cap would revert to $100,000 at the beginning of 2010, but later extended the deadline through the end of 2013.

115. The quotation is part of the formal title of Public Law 110-343, of which the TARP legislation—officially named the Emergency Economic Stabilization Act of 2008—is a part.

116. "Board Announces Creation of the Commercial Paper Funding Facility (CPFF) to Help Provide Liquidity to Term Funding Markets," Federal Reserve Board press release, October 7, 2008. The CPFF complemented the Fed's other commercial paper program, the AMLF, which was created shortly after the Reserve Primary Fund broke the buck. While the AMLF targeted money market mutual funds, the CPFF aimed to create liquidity for qualified commercial paper issuers.

117. Federal Reserve Board, "Commercial Paper Funding Facility (CPFF)."

118. Ken Lewis from Bank of America, Robert Kelly from BNY Mellon, Vikram Pandit from Citigroup, Lloyd Blankfein from Goldman, Jamie Dimon from JP Morgan, John Thain from Merrill, John Mack from Morgan Stanley, Ronald Logue from State Street, and Richard Kovacevich from Wells.

119. Paulson, testimony before the FCIC, May 6, 2010, transcript, p. 70. Former assistant treasury secretary Phillip Swagel argued, "There is no authority in the United States to force a private institution to accept government capital" ("The Financial Crisis: An Inside View," Brookings Papers on Economic Activity, conference draft, Spring 2009, pp. 33–34).

120. Henry Paulson, *On The Brink: Inside the Race to Stop the Collapse of the Global Financial System* (New York: Business Plus, 2010), p. 365.

121. Dimon, interview.

122. The Temporary Liquidity Guarantee Program consisted of two programs, the Temporary Debt Guarantee Program (TDGP) and the Transaction Account Guarantee Program (TAGP). The TDGP at its highest point in May 2009 guaranteed $346 billion in outstanding senior debt; see "FDIC Announces Plan to Free Up Bank Liquidity," FDIC press release, October 14, 2008. The TAGP guaranteed $834 billion in deposits at the end of 2009.

123. "Factsheet on Capital Purchase Program," FinancialStability.gov, updated October 3, 2010.

124. "Remarks by Secretary Henry M. Paulson, Jr. on Financial Rescue Package and Economic Update," Treasury Department press release, November 12, 2008.

125. Paulson, testimony before the FCIC, May 6, 2010, transcript, p. 70.

126. U.S. Treasury Department Office of Financial Stability, "Troubled Asset Relief Program"; Transactions Report for Period Ending December 31, 2008: Capital Purchase Program;" "Factsheet on Capital Purchase Program."

127. U.S. Treasury Department Office of Financial Stability, "Troubled Asset Relief Program: Transactions Report for Period Ending October 15, 2010: Capital Purchase Program."

128. Office of the Special Inspector General for the Troubled Asset Relief Program, "Initial Report to the Congress," February 6, 2009, p. 6.

129. Congressional Oversight Panel, "September Oversight Report: Assessing the TARP on the Eve of Its Expiration," September 16, 2010, p. 27.

130. Office of Financial Stability, "Troubled Asset Relief Program: Two Year Retrospective," October 2010, pp. 15, 51; AIG, "What AIG Owes the U.S. Government," updated September 30, 2010.

131. Congressional Oversight Panel, "September Oversight Report," p. 27; Office of Financial Stability, "Troubled Asset Relief Program: Two Year Retrospective," p. 18; "Taxpayers Receive $10.5 Billion in Proceeds Today from Final Sale of Treasury Department Citigroup Common Stock," Treasury Department press release, December 10, 2010.

132. Office of the Special Inspector General for the Troubled Asset Relief Program, "Quarterly Report to Congress," October 26, 2010, table 2.1, p. 46 (obligation figures as of October 3, 2010, and expenditure figures as of September 30, 2010).

133. The money market funding is through the Asset-backed Commercial Paper Money Market Mutual Fund Liquidity Facility (AMLF); FCIC staff calculations.

134. Board of Governors of the Federal Reserve System, "Regulatory Reform: Agency Mortgage-backed Securities (MBS) Purchase Program."

135. The Fed had created the first Maiden Lane vehicle in March to take $29 billion in assets off the balance sheet of Bear Stearns, as described in chapter 15. See "AIG RMBS LLC Facility: Terms and Conditions," December 16, 2008; "AIG Discloses Counterparties to CDS, GIA and Securities Lending Transactions," AIG press release, March 15, 2009, Attachment D: Payments to AIG Securities Lending Counterparties.

136. Federal Reserve Bank of New York, "Maiden Lane III: Transaction Overview"; Federal Reserve and Treasury Department press release, November 10, 2008; "AIG CDO LLC Facility: Terms and Conditions," Federal Reserve Bank of New York press release, December 3, 2008; FRBNY, "Maiden Lane Transactions." $27.1 billion was paid to 16 counterparties and $2.5 billion was paid to AIGFP as an adjustment to reflect overcollateralization.

137. Office of the Special Inspector General for the Troubled Asset Relief Program, "Factors Affecting Efforts to Limit Payments to AIG Counterparties," SIGTARP-10-003, November 17, 2009, pp. 19–20.

138. Blankfein, testimony before the FCIC, January 13, 2010, transcript, pp. 90–93.

139. Data provided to Goldman Sachs to the FCIC.

140. David Viniar, testimony before the FCIC, Hearing on the Role of Derivatives in the Financial Crisis, day 2, session 1: American International Group, Inc. and Goldman Sachs Group, Inc., July 1, 2010, transcript, p. 148.

141. Goldman Sachs, email to FCIC, July 15, 2010.

142. Ibid.; and data provided by Goldman Sachs to the FCIC.

143. SIGTARP, "Factors Affecting Efforts to Limit Payments to AIG Counterparties," pp. 15–16, 18. The report said counterparties insisted on 100% coverage because (1) concessions "would mean giving away value and voluntarily taking a loss, in contravention of their fiduciary duty to their shareholders"; (2) they had a "reasonable expectation" that AIG would not default on further obligations, given the government assistance; (3) costs already incurred to protect against a possible AIG default "would be exacerbated if they were paid less than par value"; and (4) they were "contractually entitled" to receive the par value of the credit default swap contracts.

144. "In other words, the decision to acquire a controlling interest in one of the world's most complex and most troubled corporations was done with almost no independent consideration of the terms of the transaction or the impact that those terms might have on the future of AIG" (ibid., p. 28).

145. Ibid., summary, p. 1.

146. Congressional Oversight Panel, "June Oversight Report: The AIG Rescue, Its Impact on Markets, and the Government's Exit Strategy," June 10, 2010, pp. 10, 8.

147. Suzanne Kapner, "US Congressional Panel Attacks AIG Rescue," *Financial Times*, June 10, 2010.

148. Baxter, interview.

149. Sarah Dahlgren, interview by FCIC, April 30, 2008.

150. SIGTARP, "Factors Affecting Efforts to Limit Payments to AIG Counterparties," p. 29.

151. Timothy Geithner, quoted in Jody Shenn, Bob Ivry, and Alan Katz, "AIG 100-Cents Fed Deal Driven by France Belied by French Banks," *Bloomberg Businessweek*, January 20, 2010.

152. E.g., Baxter, interview; Jim Mahoney, Federal Reserve Bank of New York, interview by FCIC, April 30, 2010; Michael Alix, Federal Reserve Bank of New York, interview by FCIC, April 30, 2010.

153. Dahlgren, interview.

154. Baxter, interview.

155. GAO, "Federal Financial Assistance: Preliminary Observations on Assistance Provided AIG," GAO-09-4907 (Testimony: Before the Subcommittee on Capital Markets, Insurance, and Government Sponsored Enterprises, House Committee on Financial Services), March 18, 2009, p. 2; Federal Reserve press release, September 16, 2008.

156. AIG, "What AIG Owes the US Government," updated September 30, 2010.

157. Edward J. Kelly III, interview by FCIC, March 3, 2010.

158. Roger Cole, interview by FCIC, August 2, 2010.

159. Kelly, interview.

160. James R. Wigand and Herbert J. Held, memorandum to the FDIC Board of Directors, regarding recommendation for systemic risk determination for Citigroup, November 23, 2008, p. 5.

161. Kelly, interview.

162. Mark D. Richardson, email to John H. Corston, Jason C. Cave, et al., subject: "RE: CONFIDEN-TIAL—Citigroup—Deterioration of Stock Price and CDS Spreads," November 20, 2008; Mark D. Richardson, email, to John H. Corston, Jason C. Cave, et al., subject: "11-21-08 Citi Liquidity call notes," November 21, 2008.

163. Wigand and Held, November memo to the FDIC board regarding Citigroup, p. 5.

164. Bernanke, closed-door session.

165. Arthur J. Murton, email to John V. Thomas, Michael H. Krimminger, et al., subject: "RE: Proposed Conduit," November 22, 2008; Michael H. Krimminger, email to Arthur J. Murton, John V. Thomas, et al., subject: "RE: Proposed Conduit," November 22, 2008.

166. Vikram Pandit, testimony before the Congressional Oversight Panel, *Citigroup and the Troubled Asset Relief Program,* 111th Cong., 2nd sess., March 4, 2010, transcript, p. 79.

167. Kelly, interview.

168. GAO, "Federal Deposit Insurance Act: Regulators' Use of Systemic Risk Exception Raises Moral Hazard Concerns and Opportunities Exist to Clarify the Provision," GAO-10-100 (Report to Congressional Committees), April 2010, p. 2.

169. Wigand and Held, memo to the FDIC board regarding Citigroup, pp. 9, 10.

170. Department of the Treasury response to Congressional Oversight Panel, Questions for the Record, p. 3, *Citigroup and the Troubled Asset Relief Program,* March 4, 2010, p. 44.

"Joint Statement by Treasury, Federal Reserve, and the FDIC on Citigroup," joint press release, November 23, 2008.

171. "Joint Statement on Citigroup."

172. In total, Citigroup received almost $40 billion in capital benefits from the November 2008 government assistance. Half of the capital benefits were from Treasury's $20 billion TARP investment in Citigroup preferred stock; $16 billion of the capital benefits were derived from a change in the risk weighting of the ring-fenced assets. In addition, Citigroup issued Treasury and the FDIC $7 billion in preferred stock as payment for the guarantee on the ring fence; the result, after accounting for the insurance feature of the arrangement, was a $3.5 billion increase in capital for Citigroup.

173. Kelly, interview.

174. The warrants gave the government the right to buy 254 million shares at $10.61 a share; at the time, the stock was trading at $3.76 (Congressional Oversight Panel, "November Oversight Report: Guarantees and Contingent Payments in TARP and Related Programs," November 6, 2009, pp. 18–19).

175. FDIC Board of Directors meeting, closed session, November 23, 2008, transcript, p. 14.

176. Ibid., pp. 27–28.

177. Office of Financial Stability, "Troubled Asset Relief Program: Two Year Retrospective," October 2010, p. 30; "Taxpayers receive $10.5 billion in proceeds today from final sale of Treasury Department Citigroup common stock," Treasury Department press release, December 10, 2010.

178. "Merrill Lynch Reports Third Quarter 2008 Net Loss from Continuing Operations of $5.1 Billion," Merrill Lynch press release, October 16, 2008, p. 4; Merrill Lynch, 3Q 2008 Earnings Call transcript, October 16, 2008, p. 2.

179. Federal Reserve System, "Order Approving Bank of America Corporation Acquisition of a Savings Association and an Industrial Loan Company," November 26, 2008, pp. 7, 9. To approve such a proposal, the Bank Holding Company Act requires the Fed to determine that a transaction "can reasonably be expected to produce benefits to the public, such as greater convenience, increased competition, or gains in efficiency, that outweigh possible adverse effects, such as undue concentration of resources, decreased or unfair competition." 12 U.S.C. 1843(j)(2)(A).

180. Timothy J. Mayopoulous, former general counsel of Bank of America, written testimony before the House Oversight Committee, *Bank of America and Merrill Lynch: How Did a Private Deal Turn into a Federal Bailout? Part IV,* 111th Cong., 1st sess., November 17, 2009.

181. Ken Lewis, deposition *In Re: Executive Compensation Investigation: Bank of America–Merrill Lynch*, February 26, 2009, p. 9, available from House Committee on Oversight and Government Reform and the Subcommittee on Domestic Policy, *Bank of America and Merrill Lynch: How Did A Private Deal Turn into a Federal Bailout?* 111th Cong., 1st sess., June 11, 2009.

182. Bank of America, 4Q 2008 Earnings Call transcript, January 16, 2009, p. 16.

183. Ibid., pp. 3, 10, 16.

184. John Thain, interview by FCIC, September 17, 2009.

185. Complaint, SEC v. Bank of America (S.D.N.Y. Jan. 12, 2010); Final Consent Judgment As to Defendant Bank of America (S.D.N.Y. Feb. 4, 2010).

186. Ken Lewis, interview by FCIC, October 22, 2010.

187. Lewis, deposition *In Re: Executive Compensation Investigation: Bank of America—Merrill Lynch*, pp. 34, 38; Henry Paulson, written testimony before the House Committee on Oversight and Government Reform and the Subcommittee on Domestic Policy, *Bank of America and Merrill Lynch: How Did a Private Deal Turn into a Federal Bailout? Part III*, 111th Cong., 1st sess., July 16, 2009, p. 22.

188. Paulson, written testimony before the House Oversight Committee, July 16, 2009, p. 23 (quotation); Ben Bernanke, written testimony before the House Committee on Oversight and Government Reform and the Subcommittee on Domestic Policy, *Bank of America and Merrill Lynch: How Did a Private Deal Turn into a Federal Bailout? Part II*, 111th Cong., 1st sess., June 25, 2009, p. 18.

189. Lewis, interview.

190. Thain, interview

191. Paulson, written testimony before the House Oversight Committee, July 16, 2009, pp. 19, 25.

192. Chairman Ben Bernanke, email to General Counsel Scott Alvarez, "Re: Fw: BAC," December 23, 2008, available from House Oversight Committee, *Bank of America and Merrill Lynch: How Did a Private Deal Turn into a Federal Bailout? Part II*, June 25, 2009, p. 73; Representative Edolphus Towns, in ibid., p. 2.

193. Lewis, interview.

194. Minutes of a Special Meeting of Board of Directors of Bank of America Corporation, December 22, 2008, available in House Committee on Oversight and Government Reform, June 11, 2009, p. 183.

195. Minutes of a Special Meeting of the Bank of America board, December 30, 2008, available in ibid., p. 188.

196. Lewis, interview.

197. See Department of the Treasury, Office of Financial Stability, "Troubled Assets Relief Program: Transactions Report, for Period Ending November 16, 2010," November 18, 2010. In addition to drawing on these funds, it was also a "substantial user" of the Fed's various liquidity programs. The holding company and its subsidiaries had already borrowed $55 billion through the Term Auction Facility. It had also borrowed $15 billion under the Fed's Commercial Paper Funding Facility and $20 billion under the FDIC's debt guarantee program. And newly acquired Merrill Lynch had borrowed another $21 billion from the Fed's two Bear Stearns–era repo-support programs. Yet despite Bank of America's recourse to these programs, the regulators worried that it would experience liquidity problems if the fourth-quarter earnings were weak.

198. The amount of FDIC-guaranteed debt that can be issued by each eligible entity, or its cap, is based on the amount of senior unsecured debt outstanding as of September 30, 2008.

199. FRB and OCC staff, memorandum to Rick Cox, FDIC, subject: "Bank of America Corporation (BAC) Funding Vulnerabilities and Implications for Other Financial Market Participants," January 10, 2009, p. 2.

200. Sheila C. Bair, FDIC Chairman, written testimony before the House Committee on Oversight and Government Reform and the Subcommittee on Domestic Policy, *Bank of America and Merrill Lynch: How Did a Private Deal Turn into a Federal Bailout? Part V*, 110th Cong., 1st sess., December 11, 2009, p. 2.

201. FRB and OCC staff memo to Rick Cox, "Bank of America Corporation (BAC) Funding Vulnerabilities," pp. 2, 4; Mitchell Glassman, Sandra Thompson, Arthur Murton, and John Thomas, memorandum to the FDIC Board of Directors, subject: Bank of America, etc., January 15, 2009, pp. 8, 9.

202. Bair, written testimony before the House Oversight Committee, December 11, 2009, p. 3.

203. Glassman et al., memo to the FDIC board, January 15, 2009, p. 3. They agreed to this 25/75 split because 25% of the assets for the ring fence were from depository institutions and 75% were not. See closed meeting of the FDIC Board of Directors, January 15, 2009, transcript, p. 18.

204. Closed meeting of the FDIC board, January 15, 2009, transcript, p. 24. According to the FDIC staff, "Liquidity pressure may increase to critical levels following the announcement of fourth quarter 2008 operating results that are significantly worse than market expectations. Market reaction to BAC's operating results may have systemic consequences given the size of the institution and the volume of counterparty transactions involved. Without a systemic risk determination . . . significant market disruption may ensue as counterparties lose confidence in BAC's ability to fund ongoing operations. . . . [Economic developments] point to a clear relationship between the financial market turmoil of recent months and impaired economic performance that could be expected to worsen further if BAC and its insured subsidiaries were allowed to failed. Such an event would significantly undermine business and consumer confidence." Glassman et al., memo to the FDIC board, January 15, 2009, pp. 13–14.

## Chapter 21

1. Brian Moynihan, written testimony for the FCIC, First Public Hearing of the Financial Crisis Inquiry Commission, day 1, session 1: Financial Institution Representatives, January 13, 2010, p. 1.

2. Clarence Williams, written testimony for the FCIC, Hearing on the Impact of the Financial Crisis—Sacramento, session 4: Impact of the Financial Crisis on Sacramento Neighborhoods and Families, September 23, 2010, p. 8; and testimony before the FCIC, transcript, pp. 259–60.

3. Ed Lazear, interview by FCIC, November 10, 2010.

4. Jeannie McDermott, testimony before the FCIC, Hearing on the Impact of the Financial Crisis—Greater Bakersfield, session 6: Forum for Public Comment, September 7, 2010, transcript, pp. 211–13.

5. Marie Vasile, testimony before the FCIC, in ibid., transcript, pp. 244–51.

6. "National Delinquency Survey," Mortgage Bankers Association, Fourth Quarter 2007, March 2008, p. 4; Third Quarter 2010, November 2010, p. 4.

7. CoreLogic, "U.S. Housing and Mortgage Trends: August 2010," November 2010, p. 5.

8. Jeremy Aguero, principal analyst, Applied Analysis, written testimony for the FCIC, Hearing on the Impact of the Financial Crisis—State of Nevada, session 1: Economic Analysis of the Impact of the Financial Crisis on Nevada, September 8, 2010, p. 3.

9. Mauricio Soto, "How Is the Financial Crisis Affecting Retirement Savings?" Urban Institute, December 10, 2008, available at www.urban.org/url.cfm?ID=901206.

10. Steven K. Paulson, "Auditors Say Colorado Pension Plan Recovering," Associated Press, August 16, 2010.

11. Charles S. Johnson, "Montana Pension Funds Growing but Haven't Made Up Losses," *The Billings Gazette,* May 18, 2009.

12. The Conference Board news release, May 27, 2008.

13. The Conference Board news release, December 28, 2010.

14. Gregory D. Bynum, testimony before the FCIC, Hearing on the Impact of the Financial Crisis—Greater Bakersfield, session 3: Residential and Community Real Estate, September 7, 2010, transcript, p. 102.

15. Board of Governors of the Federal Reserve System, October 2010 Senior Loan Officer Opinion Survey on Bank Lending Practices, Net Percentage of Domestic Respondents Tightening Standards on Consumer Loans, Credit Cards, November 8, 2010.

16. American Bankruptcy Institute, "Annual Business and Non-business Filings by Year (1980–2009)."

17. Jeff Agosta, conference call with FCIC, February 25, 2010.

18. American Bankruptcy Institute, "Annual Business and Non-Business Filings by Year (1980–2009)."

19. Board of Governors of the Federal Reserve System, July 2007 Senior Loan Officer Opinion Survey on Bank Lending Practices, August 13, 2007, p. 13.

20. Liz Moyer, "Revolver at the Heads," *Forbes,* October 7, 2008. Gannett Corporation withdrew $1.2 billion, FairPoint Communications withdrew $200 million, and Duke Energy withdrew $1 billion.

21. Murillo Campello, John R. Graham, and Campbell R. Harvey, "The Real Effects of Financial Constraints: Evidence from a Financial Crisis," *Journal of Financial Economics* 97 (2010): 476.

22. Board of Governors of the Federal Reserve System, January 2009 Senior Loan Officer Opinion Survey, fourth-quarter 2008, p. 8.

23. Elizabeth Duke, governor, Federal Reserve Board, "Small Business Lending," testimony before the House Committee on Financial Services and Committee on Small Business, February 26, 2010, p. 1.

24. National Federation of Independent Businesses, "NFIB Small Business Economic Trends," December 2010, p. 12.

25. Ben Bernanke, "Restoring the Flow of Credit to Small Business," speaking at the Federal Reserve Meeting Series: "Addressing the Financing Needs of Small Businesses," Washington, DC, July 12, 2010.

26. C. R. "Rusty" Cloutier, past chairman, Independent Community Bankers of America, testimony before the FCIC, First Public Hearing of the FCIC, day 1, panel 3: Financial Crisis Impacts on the Economy, January 13, 2010, transcript, p. 194.

27. Federal Reserve Statistical Release, E.2 Survey of Terms of Business Lending, E.2 Chart Data: "Commercial and Industrial Loan Rates Spreads over Intended Federal Funds Rate, by Loan Size," spread for all sizes.

28. William J. Dennis Jr., "Small Business Credit in a Deep Recession," National Federation of Independent Businesses, February 2010, p. 18.

29. Jerry Jost, interview by FCIC, August 20, 2010.

30. Board of Governors of the Federal Reserve System, Senior Loan Officer Opinion Survey on Bank Lending Practices, April 2010.

31. Board of Governors of the Federal Reserve System, Senior Loan Officer Opinion Survey on Bank Lending Practices, July 2010.

32. Emily Maltby, "Small Biz Loan Failure Rate Hits 12%," CNN Money, February 25, 2009; "SBA Losses Climb 154% in 2008," Coleman Report (www.colemanpublishing.com/public/343.cfm).

33. Michael A. Neal, chairman and CEO, GE Capital, testimony before the FCIC, Hearing on the Shadow Banking System, day 2, session 3: Institutions Participating in the Shadow Banking System, May 6, 2010, transcript, p. 242.

34. GE, 2008 Annual Report, p. 38.

35. Mark S. Barber, testimony before the FCIC, Hearing on the Shadow Banking System, day 2, session 3: Institutions Participating in the Shadow Banking System, May 6, 2010, transcript, p. 263.

36. International Monetary Fund, International Financial Statistics database, World Exports.

37. International Monetary Fund, International Financial Statistics, World Tables: Exports, World Exports.

38. Jane Levere, "Office Deals, 19 Months Apart, Show Market's Move," New York Times, August 10, 2010.

39. National Association of Realtors, Commercial Real Estate Quarterly Market Survey, December 2010, pp. 4, 5.

40. Brian Gordon, principal, Applied Analysis, testimony before the FCIC, Hearing on the Impact of the Financial Crisis—State of Nevada, session 3: The Impact of the Financial Crisis on Nevada Real Estate, September 8, 2010, transcript, p. 155.

41. Anton Troianovski, "High Hopes as Builders Bet on Skyscrapers," Wall Street Journal, September 29, 2010.

42. Ibid.; Gregory Bynum, president, Gregory D. Bynum & Associates, Inc., testimony before the FCIC, Hearing on the Impact of the Financial Crisis—Greater Bakersfield, session 3: Residential and Community Real Estate, September 7, 2010, transcript, pp. 77–80, 77–78.

43. Federal Deposit Insurance Commission, "Failed Bank List," January 2, 2010.

44. February Oversight Report, "Commercial Real Estate Losses and the Risk to Financial Stability," Congressional Oversight Panel, February 10, 2010, pp. 2, 41, 45.

45. TreppWire, "CMBS Delinquency Rate Nears 9%, Up 21 BPs in August after Leveling in July, Rate Now 8.92%" Monthly Delinquency Report, September 2010, p. 1.

46. Allen Kenney, "CRE Mortgage Default Rate to Double by 2010," REIT.com, June 18, 2009. See also "Default Rates Reach 16-Year High," Globe St., February 24, 2010.

47. Ibid. Green Street Advisors, "Commercial Property Values Gain More Than 30% from '09 Lows," December 2, 2010, pp. 3, 1.

48. "Moody's/REAL Commercial Property Price Indices, December 2010," Moody's Investors Service Special Report, December 21, 2010; Moody's Investors Service, "US Commercial Real Estate Prices Rise 1.3% in October," December 20, 2010.

49. Congressional Oversight Panel, "Commercial Real Estate Losses," February Oversight Report, February 10, 2010, pp. 2–3.

50. Dr. Kenneth T. Rosen, chairman, Fisher Center for Real Estate and Economics, University of California at Berkeley, slides in testimony before the FCIC, First Public Hearing of the FCIC, day 1, panel 3: Financial Crisis Impacts on the Economy, January 13, 2010.

51. Elizabeth McNichol, Phil Oliff, and Nicholas Johnson, "States Continue to Feel Recession's Impact," Center on Budget and Policy Priorities, December 16, 2010.

52. Bruce Wagstaff, Sacramento Countywide Services Agency, testimony before the FCIC, Hearing on the Impact of the Financial Crisis—Sacramento, session 4: The Impact of the Financial Crisis on Sacramento Neighborhoods and Families, September 23, 2010, transcript, p. 234.

53. Sujit CanagaRetna, interview by FCIC, November 18, 2010.

54. McNichol, Oliff, and Johnson, "States Continue to Feel Recession's Impact."

55. "NCSL Fiscal Brief: Projected State Revenue Growth in FY 2011 and Beyond," National Conference of State Legislatures, September 29, 2010, p. 1.

56. Ibid.

57. State of California, Legislative Analyst's Office, "The 2011–12 Budget: California's Fiscal Outlook."

58. Kaiser Commission on Medicaid and the Uninsured, "Medicaid Enrollment: December 2009 Data Snapshot," September 2010, pp. 1, 3.

59. Kaiser Commission on Medicaid and the Uninsured, "Hoping for Economic Recovery, Preparing for Health Reform: A Look at Medicaid Spending, Coverage and Policy Trends," September 30, 2010, pp. 16, 25.

60. National League of Cities, "Recession's Effects Intensify in Cities," October 6, 2010.

61. Christopher W. Hoene and Michael A. Pagano, "City Fiscal Conditions in 2010," National League of Cities, October 2010, p. 3.

62. Ibid., pp. 7, 2.

63. Alan S. Blinder and Mark Zandi, "How the Great Recession Was Brought to an End," Moody's Analytics, July 27, 2010, p. 1.

64. Donald L. Kohn, vice chairman, Federal Reserve Board of Governors, "The Federal Reserve's Policy Actions during the Financial Crisis and Lessons for the Future," speech at Carleton University, Ottawa, Canada, May 13, 2010.

65. U.S. Department of the Treasury, Office of Financial Stability, "Troubled Asset Relief Program: Two Year Retrospective," October 2010, p. 8.

66. Congressional Budget Office, "Report on the Troubled Asset Relief Program," November 2010.

67. White House Office of Management and Budget, FY2011 Budget Historical Tables, Section 1, Table 1.1—Summary of Receipts, Outlays, and Surpluses or Deficits (-):1789–2015, Total Budget Deficit.

68. FDIC, "Failed Bank List."

69. "Quarterly Banking Profile: Third Quarter 2010," FDIC Quarterly 4, no. 4 (2010): 4.

70. FDIC, "Quarterly Banking Profile: First Quarter 2009," FDIC Quarterly 3, no. 2 (2009): 1, and "Quarterly Banking Profile: First Quarter 2010," FDIC Quarterly 4, no. 2 (2010); Board of Governors of the Federal Reserve System, Profit and Balance Sheet Developments at U.S. Commercial Banks in 2009.

71. FDIC, Statistics on Depository Institutions, Income and Expense, All Commercial Banks—Assets more than $1B—National, Standard Report #1 (reports issued on 3/31/2010 and 3/31/2009). Profit is logged as "Net income attributable to bank."

72. FDIC, Statistics on Depository Institutions, Income and Expense, All Commercial Banks—Assets less than $100M and Assets $100M to $1B; Standard Report #1 (reports issued on 3/31/2010 and 3/31/2009). Profit is logged as "Net income attributable to bank."

73. "Wall Street Bonuses Rose Sharply in 2009," New York State Comptroller Thomas P. DiNapoli press release, February 23, 2010.

74. N.Y. State Comptroller Thomas P. DiNapoli, "Economic Trends in New York State," October 2010.

## Chapter 22

1. FCIC calculations based on estimates from Hope Now and Moodys.com.

2. Mortgage Bankers Association National Delinquency Survey (the source for the rest of the delinquency and foreclosure rates in this chapter).

3. Julia Gordon, Center for Responsible Lending, "HAMP, Servicer Abuses, and Foreclosure Prevention Strategies," testimony before the Congressional Oversight Panel for the Troubled Asset Relief Program (TARP), COP Hearing on TARP Foreclosure Mitigation Programs, 111th Cong., 2nd sess., October 27, 2010, pp. 5, 30; CRL testimony based on Rod Dubitsky, Larry Yang, Stevan Stevanovic, and Thomas Suehr, "Foreclosure Update: Over 8 Million Foreclosures Expected," Credit Suisse (December 4, 2008), and Jan Hatzius and Michael A. Marschoun, "Home Prices and Credit Losses: Projections and Policy Options," Goldman Sachs Global Economics Paper (January 13, 2009), p. 16.

4. "RealtyTrac Year-End Report Shows Record 2.8 Million U.S. Properties with Foreclosure Filings in 2009—An Increase of 21 Percent from 2008 and 120 Percent from 2007," RealtyTrac, January 14, 2010.

5. "Delinquencies and Loans in Foreclosure Decrease, but Foreclosure Starts Rise in Latest MBA National Delinquency Survey," MBA press release, November 18, 2010.

6. Mark Fleming, chief economist, CoreLogic, testimony before the FCIC, Hearing on the Impact of the Financial Crisis—Sacramento, session 1: Overview of the Sacramento Housing and Mortgage Markets and the Impact of the Financial Crisis on the Region, September 23, 2010, transcript, p. 14.

7. FCIC staff estimates based on analysis of BlackBox data.

8. Laurie S. Goodman, senior managing director, Amherst Securities Group LP, written testimony before the House Financial Services Committee, *The Private Sector and Government Response to the Mortgage Foreclosure Crisis,*" 111th Cong., 1st sess., December 8, 2009, p. 3.

9. The index declined from 200.4 in April 2006 to 136.6 in March 2009, a decline of 31.8%.

10. "New CoreLogic Data Shows Third Consecutive Quarterly Decline in Negative Equity," CoreLogic Inc., December 13, 2010, p. 1; nationally, third-quarter figures were an improvement from 11.0 million residential properties—23%—in negative equity in the second quarter of 2010.

11. Jim Rokakis, treasurer of Cuyahoga County, Ohio, interview by FCIC, November 8, 2010.

12. Cuyahoga County experienced 13,943 foreclosure filings in 2006, 14,946 in 2007, 13,858 in 2008, and 14,171 in 2009. "Ohio County Foreclosure Filings (1995–2009): Cuyahoga County," Policy Matters Ohio.

13. Rokakis, interview.

14. The United States Conference of Mayors, "Impact of the Mortgage Foreclosure Crisis on Vacant and Abandoned Properties in Cities: A 77-City Survey," June 2010, pp. 3–4.

15. Guy Cecala, prepared testimony for the Congressional Oversight Panel for the Troubled Asset Relief Program (TARP), COP Hearing on TARP Foreclosure Mitigation Programs, 111th Cong., 2nd sess., October 27, 2010, p. 2.

16. John Taylor, interview by FCIC, October 27, 2010.

17. Congressional Oversight Panel, "December Oversight Report: A Review of Treasury's Foreclosure Prevention Programs," December 14, 2010, pp. 4, 7, 18.

18. HOPE NOW, "Industry Extrapolations and Metrics (October 2010)," December 6, 2010, p. 3.

19. New Jersey HomeKeeper Program, New Jersey Housing and Mortgage Financing Agency, approved September 23, 2010.

20. Kirsten Keefe, presentation to the meeting of the Federal Reserve System's Consumer Advisory Council, Washington, D.C., March 25, 2010, transcript, p. 34.

21. Diane E. Thompson, testimony to the Senate Committee on Banking, Housing, and Urban Affairs, *Problems in Mortgage Servicing from Modification to Foreclosure,* 111th Cong., 2nd sess., November 16, 2010, p. 3.

22. See, for example, National Consumer Law Center, "Why Servicers Foreclose When They Should Modify and Other Puzzles of Servicer Behavior," October 2009.

23. Joseph H. Evers, Office of the Comptroller of the Currency, deputy comptroller for large bank supervision, written testimony before the Congressional Oversight Panel for the Troubled Asset Relief Program (TARP), COP Hearing on TARP Foreclosure Mitigation Programs, 111th Cong., 2nd sess., October 27, 2010, pp. 7–10. The OCC reported that mortgage servicers have modified 1,239,896 loans since early 2008. By the end of the second quarter of 2010, more than 26% of the modifications were seriously delinquent; 9% were in the process of foreclosure; and 4% had completed foreclosure. The OCC examined modified loans that were 60 or more days delinquent that were modified during the second quarter of 2009, to determine when after loan modification that serious delinquency recurred. At 12 months after modification, 43% of loans were delinquent by two or more months; at nine months after modification, 41% were in arrears; at six months, 34%; and at three months after a loan change, nearly 19% were delinquent. The OCC noted that more recent modifications have performed better than earlier modifications.

24. Julia Gordon, senior policy counsel, Center for Responsible Lending, written testimony before the Congressional Oversight Panel for the Troubled Asset Relief Program (TARP), COP Hearing on TARP Foreclosure Mitigation Programs, 111th Cong., 2nd sess., October 27, 2010, p. 11.

25. David J. Grais, partner with Grais & Ellsworth LLP, interview by FCIC, November 2, 2010.

26. Calculation by Laurie Goodman, senior managing director, Amherst Securities. See PowerPoint presentation to the Grais and Ellsworth LLP conference "Robosigners and Other Servicing Failures: Protecting the Rights of RMBS Investors," October 27, 2010 (http://video.remotecounsel.com/mediasite/Viewer/?peid=12e6411377a744b9a9f2eefd1093871c1d).

27. Grais, interview.

28. Goodman testimony before the House Financial Services Committee, December 8, 2009.

29. See Deposition of Jeffrey Stephan, GMAC Mortgage LLC v. Ann M. Neu a/k/a Ann Michelle Perez, No. 50 2008 CA040805XXXX MB (Fla. Cir. Ct. Dec. 10, 2009), pp. 7, 10.

30. See, for example, Dwayne Ransom Davis and Melisa Davis v. Countrywide Home Loans, Inc.; Bank of America, N.A.; BAC GP LLC; and BAC Home Loans Servicing, LP, 1:10-cv-01303-JMS-DML (S.D. Ind. October 19, 2010).

31. Congressional Oversight Panel, "November Oversight Report: Examining the Consequences of Mortgage Irregularities for Financial Stability and Foreclosure Mitigation," November 16, 2010, p. 20.

32. See, e.g., Mortg. Elec. Registry Sys. v. Johnston, No. 420-6-09 Rdcv (Rutland Co. Vt. Super. Ct. Oct. 28, 2009), holding that MERS did not have standing to initiate foreclosure because the note and mortgage had been separated.

33. The Honorable F. Dana Winslow, written testimony before the House Committee on the Judiciary, *Foreclosed Justice: Causes and Effects of the Foreclosure Crisis*, 111th Cong., 2nd sess., December 2, 2010, pp. 2, 4.

34. Order, Objection to Claims of Citibank, N.A. 4-6-10, (Bankr. E.D. Cal. May 20, 2010), p. 3. The order cites *In re* Foreclosure Cases, 521 F. Supp. 2d 650 (S.D. Oh. 2007); *In re* Vargas, 396 B.R. 511, 520 (Bankr. C.D. Cal. 2008); Landmark Nat'l Bank v. Kesler, 216 P.3d 158 (Kan. 2009); LaSalle Bank v. Lamy, 824 N.Y.S.2d 769 (N.Y. Sup. Ct. 2006).

35. Winslow, written testimony before the House Committee on the Judiciary, pp. 2–3.

36. See John T. Kemp v. Countrywide Home Loans, Inc., Case No. 08-18700-JHW (D. N.J.), pp. 7–8.

37. Grais, interview.

38. Adam J. Levitin, associate professor of law, Georgetown University Law Center, testimony to Senate Committee on Banking, Housing, and Urban Affairs, *Problems in Mortgage Servicing from Modification to Foreclosure*, 111th Cong., 2nd sess., November 16, 2010, p. 20.

39. Congressional Oversight Panel, "November Oversight Report," pp. 5, 7.

40. Katherine Porter, professor of law, University of Iowa College of Law, written testimony before the Congressional Oversight Panel for the Troubled Asset Relief Program (TARP), COP Hearing on TARP Foreclosure Mitigation Programs, October 27, 2010, p. 8.

41. Levitin, written testimony before the Senate Committee on Banking, Housing, and Urban Affairs, p. 20.

42. Erika Poethig, written testimony for the House Subcommittee on Housing and Community Opportunity, *Impact of the Foreclosure Crisis on Public and Affordable Housing in the Twin Cities*, 111th Cong., 2nd sess., January 23, 2010, p. 5.

43. National Association for the Education of Homeless Children and Youth (NAEHCY) and First Focus, "A Critical Moment: Child and Youth Homelessness in Our Nation's Schools," July 2010, p. 2. In early 2010, NAEHCY and First Focus conducted a survey of 2,200 school districts. When they were asked the reasons for the increased enrollment of students experiencing homelessness, 62% cited the economic downturn, 40% attributed it to greater school and community awareness of homelessness, and 38% cited problems stemming from the foreclosure crisis.

44. Dr. Heath Morrison, testimony before the FCIC, Hearing on the Impact of the Financial Crisis—State of Nevada, session 4: The Impact of the Financial Crisis on Nevada Public and Community Services, September 8, 2010, transcript, pp. 261–64.

45. Gail Burks, testimony before the FCIC, Hearing on the Impact of the Financial Crisis—State of Nevada, session 3: The Impact of the Financial Crisis on Nevada Real Estate, September 8, 2010, transcript, pp. 230–31.

46. Karen Mann, president and chief appraiser, Mann and Associates Real Estate Appraisers & Consultants, written testimony for the FCIC, Hearing on the Impact of the Financial Crisis—Sacramento, session 2: Mortgage Origination, Mortgage Fraud and Predatory Lending in the Sacramento Region, September 23, 2010, p. 12; oral testimony, p. 66.

47. Dawn Hunt, homeowner in Cape Coral, FL, interview by FCIC, December 20, 2010.

48. Zip code 33991, default, foreclosures and REO, S&P Global Data Solutions RMBS database, July 2010.

49. Hunt, interview.

# INDEX

The index is available online at www.publicaffairsbooks.com/fcicindex.pdf